lonely planet

Spain

Damien Simonis
Neal Bedford
Susan Forsyth
John Noble
Miles Roddis
Andrea Schulte-Peevers

L ONELY PLANET PUBLICATIONS
M elbourne • Oakland • London • Paris

SPAIN

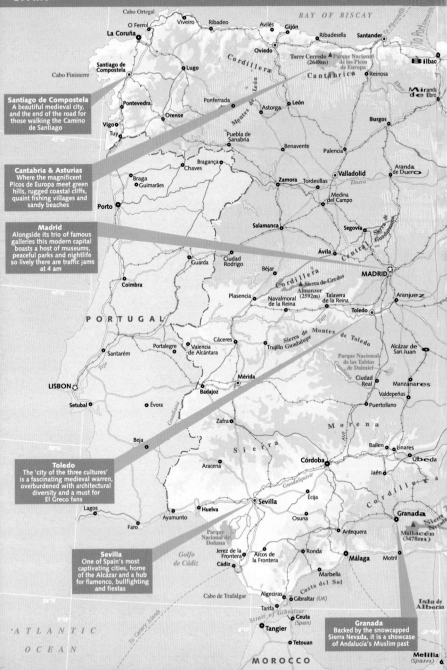

Santiago de Compostela
A beautiful medieval city, and the end of the road for those walking the Camino de Santiago

Cantabria & Asturias
Where the magnificent Picos de Europa meet green hills, rugged coastal cliffs, quaint fishing villages and sandy beaches

Madrid
Alongside its trio of famous galleries this modern capital boasts a host of museums, peaceful parks and nightlife so lively there are traffic jams at 4 am

Toledo
The 'city of the three cultures' is a fascinating medieval warren, overburdened with architectural diversity and a must for El Greco fans

Sevilla
One of Spain's most captivating cities, home of the Alcázar and a hub for flamenco, bullfighting and fiestas

Granada
Backed by the snowcapped Sierra Nevada, it is a showcase of Andalucía's Muslim past

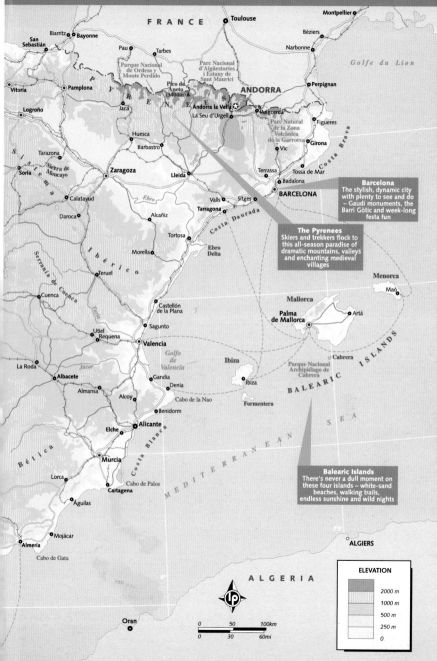

FRANCE

Montpellier

Toulouse

Béziers

Biarritz Bayonne

San
Sebastián

Narbonne

Golfe du Lion

Pau Tarbes

Parque Nacional
de Ordesa y
Monte Perdido

Parc Nacional
d'Aigüestortes
i Estany de
Sant Maurici

Perpignan

Vitoria

Pamplona

ANDORRA

P Y R E N E E S

Pico de
Aneto
(3404m)

Andorra la Vella

Logroño

Figueres

La Seu d'Urgell

Jaca

Puigcerdà

Huesca

Parc Natural
de la Zona
Volcànica
de la Garrotxa

Girona

Tarazona

Barbastro

Vic

Costa Brava

Soria

Sierra de
Moncayo

Zaragoza

Lleida

Terrassa

Tossa de Mar

Calatayud

Badalona

Sistema

Ebro

Valls

Sitges

BARCELONA

Daroca

Alcañiz

Tarragona

Barcelona
The stylish, dynamic city
with plenty to see and do
– Gaudí monuments, the
Barri Gòtic and week-long
festa fun

Ibérico

Tortosa

Costa Daurada

Morella

Ebro
Delta

Menorca

Teruel

Serranía
de
Cuenca

The Pyrenees
Skiers and trekkers flock to
this all-season paradise of
dramatic mountains, valleys
and enchanting medieval
villages

Maó

Cuenca

Castellón
de la Plana

Mallorca

Sagunto

Palma
de Mallorca

Artá

Utiel
Requena

Valencia

Golfo
de
Valencia

Ibiza

Cabrera

B A L E A R I C   I S L A N D S

La Roda

Albacete

Gandia

Denia

Parque Nacional
Archipiélago de
Cabrera

Almansa

Alcoy

Cabo de la Nao

Ibiza

Alicante

Benidorm

Formentera

Elche

M E D I T E R R A N E A N

S E A

Bética

Murcia

Costa Blanca

Lorca

Cabo de Palos

Balearic Islands
There's never a dull moment on
these four islands – white-sand
beaches, walking trails,
endless sunshine and wild nights

Cartagena

Águilas

Mojácar

Almería

Cabo de Gata

ALGIERS

A L G E R I A

Oran

ELEVATION

2000 m
1000 m
500 m
250 m
0

0   50   100km
0   30   60mi

Spain
3rd edition – March 2001
First published – May 1997

Published by
Lonely Planet Publications Pty Ltd ABN 36 005 607 983
90 Maribyrnong St, Footscray, Victoria 3011, Australia

Lonely Planet Offices
Australia Locked Bag 1, Footscray, Victoria 3011
USA 150 Linden St, Oakland, CA 94607
UK 10a Spring Place, London NW5 3BH
France 1 rue du Dahomey, 75011 Paris

Photographs
All of the images in this guide are available for licensing from
Lonely Planet Images.
email: lpi@lonelyplanet.com.au

Front cover photograph
Detail of Ayuntamiento (town hall) doors, Alicante (Damien Simonis)

ISBN 1 86450 192 8

Printed by The Bookmaker International Ltd
Printed in China

Although the authors
and Lonely Planet try
to make the informa-
tion as accurate as
possible, we accept
no responsibility for
any loss, injury or
inconvenience sus-
tained by anyone
using this book.

Contents – Text

Contents – Maps

MAP INDEX

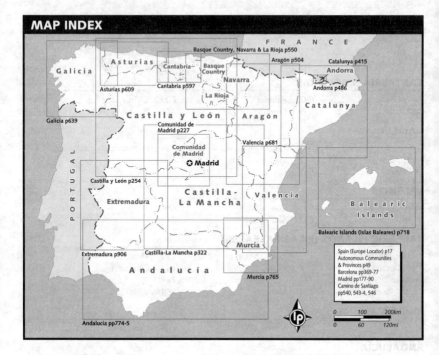

F R A N C E

Galicia

Asturias

Cantabria

Basque Country

Navarra

La Rioja

Aragón p504

Catalunya p415

Andorra

Andorra p486

Asturias p609

Cantabria p597

Basque Country, Navarra & La Rioja p550

Castilla y León

Aragón

Catalunya

Galicia p639

Comunidad de
Madrid p227

Comunidad
de Madrid

Valencia p681

Madrid

PORTUGAL

Castilla y León p254

Extremadura

Castilla-
La Mancha

Valencia

Balearic
Islands

Balearic Islands (Islas Baleares) p718

Extremadura p906

Castilla-La Mancha p322

Murcia

Andalucía

Murcia p765

Andalucía pp774-5

Spain (Europe Locator) p17
Autonomous Communities
& Provinces p49
Barcelona pp369-77
Madrid pp177-90
Camino de Santiago
pp540, 543-4, 546

0   100   200km
0   60   120mi

The Authors

Damien Simonis

With a degree in languages and several years' reporting and subediting on several newspapers (including the *Australian* and the *Age*), Sydney-born Damien left Australia in 1989. He has lived, worked and travelled extensively throughout Europe, the Middle East and North Africa. Since 1992, Lonely Planet has kept him busy in Jordan and Syria, Egypt and the Sudan, Morocco, North Africa, Italy (including guides on Venice, Florence and Tuscany) and the Canary Islands. In addition to this book, he has also written books on Madrid and Barcelona for Lonely Planet, and was last seen traipsing off to produce another Spanish title, *Catalunya*. He has also written and snapped for other publications in Australia, the UK and North America. When not on the road, Damien resides in splendid Stoke Newington, in deepest north London.

Neal Bedford

Born in Papakura, New Zealand, Neal gave up an exciting career in accounting after university to experience the mundane life of a traveller. With the urge to move, travel led him through a number of countries and jobs, ranging from au pair in Vienna, lifeguard in the USA, fruit picker in Israel and lettuce washer at rock concerts. Deciding to give his life some direction, he well and truly got his foot stuck in the door by landing the lucrative job of packing books in Lonely Planet's London office. One thing led to another and he managed to cross over to the mystic world of authoring. Neal currently resides in London, but the need to move will probably soon kick in and force him to try his luck somewhere else. This is his first book for Lonely Planet.

Susan Forsyth

Susan hails from Melbourne and survived a decade teaching in the Victorian state education system before activating long-postponed travel plans and heading off for a year as a volunteer lecturer in Sri Lanka. Here she met her future husband John Noble and narrowly escaped death at the feet of a charging elephant. Susan has since helped to update Lonely Planet's *Australia, Indonesia, Mexico, Sri Lanka* and *Travel With Children*, co-written two editions of *Andalucía* with John and three editions of *Spain* with a changing cast, and given birth to and nurtured two little *rubios* (blondies). She weathered five years in England's cold, wet but beautiful Ribble Valley before the family moved base to southern Spain a few years ago

John Noble

John comes from the Ribble Valley in northern England. After a Cambridge University degree he embarked on a newspaper career, but increasing interruptions for travel to various bits of the globe saw him eventually abandon Fleet Street for a Lonely Planet trail that has taken him to four continents via many LP books, from *Indonesia* and *Sri Lanka* to *Mexico, Andalucía* and *Walking in Spain*. John was a pioneer of Lonely Planet's coverage of the former Soviet Union, coordinating *USSR, Russia, Ukraine & Belarus*, co-authoring *Central Asia*, and writing *Baltic States* solo. For several years now he has been based in Spain, together with his wife and co-author Susan Forsyth and their children Jack and Isabella.

Miles Roddis

Having been lucky enough to live and work in Spain for three years in the late 1980s, Miles and his partner Ingrid bought a tatty old flat in the Barrio del Carmen, Valencia's oldest and most vibrant quarter. Now renovated, this shoe-box sized apartment is their principal home, the place to which they retreat to recover, unwind and write up.

Miles has contributed to Lonely Planet's *Africa on a Shoestring, West Africa, Read This First: Africa, Lonely Planet Unpacked, France, Western Europe, Europe on a Shoestring, Walking in Britain, Walking in France*, and – something that consumed five enormously satisfying months of his life – *Walking in Spain*.

Andrea Schulte-Peevers

Andrea is a Los Angeles-based writer, editor and translator who caught the travel bug from her mother, who had lugged her to all continents but Antarctica by the time her daughter turned 18. After finishing high school in Germany, Andrea decided the world was too big to stay in one place and moved first to London, then to Los Angeles. Armed with a degree from UCLA, she managed to turn her wanderlust into a professional career as a travel writer and may still chase penguins around the South Pole one of these days. Since joining the LP team in 1995 Andrea has authored or updated the guides to *Los Angeles, Berlin, Germany, California & Nevada* and *Baja California*.

FROM THE AUTHORS

Damien Simonis People all over the place have helped me out on this job in many different ways. On the home front, thanks to Steve Fallon and Carolyn O'Donnell for helping to keep the wheels turning at base in London, especially during and after the burglary episode.

Leonie Mugavin (Aus), Jenny Loy (USA) and Didier Buroc (France) helped out with some details in the Getting There & Away chapter.

In Madrid, David Ing was foolish enough to roll out the welcome mat on several occasions during my stays in Madrid – he went well beyond any known call of duty. Debbie, Gary and Alex Luhrman tried to do the same, but I thought I would spare them this time around!

As usual, a gaggle of friends and acquaintances in Madrid made my time not only productive, but also fun (well, as much as a busy work schedule allowed!). They include: Luis Aguilar-Pryde and Gabriela Contela, Javier Montero, Jean-Marc Simon, Luis Soldevila, Pablo García Tobin, Roberto Fortea, Eril Wiehahn, Nick McCafferty (he of the lists – keep up the good work!) and Dave Ross.

Up in Barcelona, I owe a great deal to Michael van Laake and Susan Kempster. In particular, Susan was singled out as the lucky recipient of repeated visits in which I made sure the couch was in good order. The rest of the gang at Carrer de Sant Pere més alt (Paloma, Ferran and Montse) always had the welcome mat out too. Silvia Folch gave me shelter in the early days of the project before scarpering off to India and a better life. Thanks also to other friends for good times had and those to come: Loreta, Rocio, Annabel Rodríguez and Nick Reddel, all of whom I saw far too infrequently owing to the business of work.

On the country estate in Solsona, Butterfly Mike et al helped provide an alternative perspective on things – not often enough!

Last but not least, thanks to John Noble, Susan Forsyth, Andrea Schulte-Peevers, Miles Roddis and Neal Bedford for their efforts on this edition. I owe a particular debt to John Noble, who as ever was on hand to help out with the seeming tidal wave of detail that goes into the introductory chapters of these tomes.

Neal Bedford First of all, big thanks to Damien Simonis and John Noble for their invaluable advice on Spain, and to Steve Fallon and Ryan Ver Berkmoes for setting me off on the right track. Thanks also to the staff of the tourist offices scattered around Extremadura and Castilla-La Mancha for their help and making my life a lot easier. For their company on the road, 'cheers' goes to Jutta, Olivier and Julia.

A special thanks goes to the whole London LP office for the support I received and allowing me a chance to try my hand as an author. In particular, Tim Ryder, Katrina Browning, Christine Stroyan, Paul Bloomfield, Marcel Gaston and Anna Sutton deserve a pint or three for their help, guidance and for putting up with my inane questions.

And most importantly, to the wonderful Christina, for listening, supporting, being there and believing in me.

John Noble & Susan Forsyth John Noble thanks everyone everywhere who helped in so many little ways. Special thanks are due to the hostal and hotel staff who took him in at ridiculous hours of the night and even sometimes fed him; José-Luis in Alquézar for laying bare the mysteries of river sports; Mariano Cruz, a hospitable mine of information on Granada province; the family back home for their tolerance while he wrote and wrote and checked proofs and maps and wrote yet more; and not least D864 FUV who, treated to four new tyres, responded with a faultless 4000km whirl through 23 of Spain's provinces, proving beyond doubt that Volkwagens definitely are the most reliable cars.

Susan Forsyth thanks her husband and *compañero* John for his patience and stamina; Rosemary and Sam for sharing their experience of the Camino de Santiago; Patricia Luce for a constant flow of tasty titbits; and the helpful staff of so many Andalucian and Galician tourist offices and town halls.

Miles Roddis Above all and everyone, thanks to Ingrid, who pushed me when shove was needed and who dragged me away when I needed to stand back. To Tamar, Oddette, Tristan and Damon for dedicated, indefatigable wee-small-hours research around Valencia's nightspots. To so many others too who chipped in their peseta's worth on Valencia after dark, especially Robert Dean and his students at the Escuela Oficial de Idiomas.

As always, I doff my *boina* to cheerful, patient tourist office staff throughout my patch. Very special thanks to Lourdes Sánchez in Valencia, zappy Antonio Crespo and Ana Montesinos in Alicante, Katia Gallego in Cartagena and Mª-Jesus Quiñanero in Lorca.

A backpack of thanks too to Tino Lopez of Televisat in Andorra la Vella for sorting out a computer glitch that saved me days of lost writing. And a much overdue thank you to Antonio de los Angeles and Elena who, book after book, have cheerfully responded to my unreasonable demands for photocopying maps just – but just – right.

Lastly, *muchísimas gracias* to Cris and Maria-Luisa for lending us a bolthole, to which I returned when a long day was over and from where I wrote – a place I wouldn't dream of telling the rest of the world about.

Andrea Schulte-Peevers Tourist officials throughout my area of coverage were generous in answering questions and patient in putting up with my rusty Spanish.

There are, however, a few people who stand out for going beyond the call of duty. Belén Cubo Allas was the perfect guide in Segovia and we'd like to thank Sofía Collazo López for getting us in touch. In Valladolid, special mention goes to Mónica Garcia Hernando for making us feel welcome and for her excellent English. In Soria, we'd like to thank Alberto Abad Pérez, Margarita and her parents for their unstinting hospitality and for making our stay in their province most memorable.

Heaps of thanks to Jasone Aretxabaleta of the Dirección General de Turismo del País Vasco for coming through on all fronts and for putting us in touch with great people to help us in researching this beautiful part of the country. In Bilbao, big fat kudos to Visi Urtiaga for being smart, funny and generous with tips and insight about her city. Diana Draper in San Sebastián deserves a big thank you for happily letting us in on the city's scenes and for sharing her favourite eating places. Warm thanks also to Jason Kykendall and Mar Martín Alonso for giving us a crash course in bar hopping around Salamanca – we had a great time. The biggest round of applause, though, belongs to my husband David Peevers for keeping me company – and sane – on the road. Thanks for your good humor and patience in checking out Castile's countless churches, castles and shower curtains.

Finally, a heartfelt *gracias* to coordinating author Damien Simonis, my fellow authors on this book and to all the folks at the LP office in Melbourne who worked on putting this edition into readers' hands.

This Book

Spain was first written by John Noble, Damien Simonis, Mark Armstrong, Susan Forsyth and Corinne Simcock. The second edition was researched and written by Damien (coordinating author), John, Susan, Tim Nollen and Fionn Davenport.

For this third edition, Damien (coordinating author) researched and wrote the Madrid, Comunidad de Madrid, Barcelona, Catalunya and Balearic Islands chapters and contributed to the introductory chapters. John and Susan updated the Andalucía, Aragón, Cantabria & Asturias and Galicia chapters, as well as contributing to the introductory chapters. Neal updated the Castilla-La Mancha and Extremadura chapters. Miles Roddis updated Andorra, Murcia and Valencia chapters, while Andrea updated the Castilla y León and Basque Country, Navarra & La Rioja chapters.

From the Publisher

This third edition was produced at Lonely Planet's Melbourne office and coordinated by Elizabeth Swan (editorial) and Yvonne Bischofberger (mapping and design). Assisting Elizabeth with editing and proofing was the great cast of Melanie Dankel, Janine Eberle, Russ Kerr, Kate Kiely, Fiona Meiers, Lara Morcombe, Shelley Muir, Anne Mulvaney, Darren O'Connell and Rebecca Turner. Yvonne was assisted in all things mapping by Cris Gibcus, Ann Jeffree, Gus Poó y Balbontín, Chris Thomas, Ray Thomson and Celia Wood, and assisted in layout by Csanád Csutoros and Celia. Yvonne produced the climate charts and Maria Vallianos designed the cover.

Thanks to Quentin Frayne for the Language chapter, Lisa Borg for Quark support, Matt King for his help with illustrations, and Lonely Planet Images, especially Barbara Dombrowski, for assisting with the photographs.

THANKS
Many thanks to the travellers who used the last edition and wrote to us with helpful hints, advice and interesting anecdotes. Your names appear in the back of this book.

Foreword

ABOUT LONELY PLANET GUIDEBOOKS

The story begins with a classic travel adventure: Tony and Maureen Wheeler's 1972 journey across Europe and Asia to Australia. Useful information about the overland trail did not exist at that time, so Tony and Maureen published the first Lonely Planet guidebook to meet a growing need.

From a kitchen table, then from a tiny office in Melbourne (Australia), Lonely Planet has become the largest independent travel publisher in the world, an international company with offices in Melbourne, Oakland (USA), London (UK) and Paris (France).

Today Lonely Planet guidebooks cover the globe. There is an ever-growing list of books and there's information in a variety of forms and media. Some things haven't changed. The main aim is still to help make it possible for adventurous travellers to get out there – to explore and better understand the world.

At Lonely Planet we believe travellers can make a positive contribution to the countries they visit – if they respect their host communities and spend their money wisely. Since 1986 a percentage of the income from each book has been donated to aid projects and human rights campaigns.

Updates Lonely Planet thoroughly updates each guidebook as often as possible. This usually means there are around two years between editions, although for more unusual or more stable destinations the gap can be longer. Check the imprint page (following the colour map at the beginning of the book) for publication dates.

Between editions up-to-date information is available in two free newsletters – the paper *Planet Talk* and email *Comet* (to subscribe, contact any Lonely Planet office) – and on our Web site at www.lonelyplanet.com. The *Upgrades* section of the Web site covers a number of important and volatile destinations and is regularly updated by Lonely Planet authors. *Scoop* covers news and current affairs relevant to travellers. And, lastly, the *Thorn Tree* bulletin board and *Postcards* section of the site carry unverified, but fascinating, reports from travellers.

Correspondence The process of creating new editions begins with the letters, postcards and emails received from travellers. This correspondence often includes suggestions, criticisms and comments about the current editions. Interesting excerpts are immediately passed on via newsletters and the Web site, and everything goes to our authors to be verified when they're researching on the road. We're keen to get more feedback from organisations or individuals who represent communities visited by travellers.

Lonely Planet gathers information for everyone who's curious about the planet – and especially for those who explore it first-hand. Through guidebooks, phrasebooks, activity guides, maps, literature, newsletters, image library, TV series and Web site we act as an information exchange for a worldwide community of travellers.

Research Authors aim to gather sufficient practical information to enable travellers to make informed choices and to make the mechanics of a journey run smoothly. They also research historical and cultural background to help enrich the travel experience and allow travellers to understand and respond appropriately to cultural and environmental issues.

Authors don't stay in every hotel because that would mean spending a couple of months in each medium-sized city and, no, they don't eat at every restaurant because that would mean stretching belts beyond capacity. They do visit hotels and restaurants to check standards and prices, but feedback based on readers' direct experiences can be very helpful.

Many of our authors work undercover, others aren't so secretive. None of them accept freebies in exchange for positive write-ups. And none of our guidebooks contain any advertising.

Production Authors submit their raw manuscripts and maps to offices in Australia, USA, UK or France. Editors and cartographers – all experienced travellers themselves – then begin the process of assembling the pieces. When the book finally hits the shops, some things are already out of date, we start getting feedback from readers and the process begins again …

WARNING & REQUEST

Things change – prices go up, schedules change, good places go bad and bad places go bankrupt – nothing stays the same. So, if you find things better or worse, recently opened or long since closed, please tell us and help make the next edition even more accurate and useful. We genuinely value all the feedback we receive. Julie Young coordinates a well travelled team that reads and acknowledges every letter, postcard and email and ensures that every morsel of information finds its way to the appropriate authors, editors and cartographers for verification.

Everyone who writes to us will find their name in the next edition of the appropriate guidebook. They will also receive the latest issue of *Planet Talk*, our quarterly printed newsletter, or *Comet*, our monthly email newsletter. Subscriptions to both newsletters are free. The very best contributions will be rewarded with a free guidebook.

Excerpts from your correspondence may appear in new editions of Lonely Planet guidebooks, the Lonely Planet Web site, *Planet Talk* or *Comet*, so please let us know if you *don't* want your letter published or your name acknowledged.

Send all correspondence to the Lonely Planet office closest to you:

Australia: Locked Bag 1, Footscray, Victoria 3011
USA: 150 Linden St, Oakland, CA 94607
UK: 10A Spring Place, London NW5 3BH
France: 1 rue du Dahomey, 75011 Paris

Or email us at: talk2us@lonelyplanet.com.au

For news, views and updates see our Web site: www.lonelyplanet.com

HOW TO USE A LONELY PLANET GUIDEBOOK

The best way to use a Lonely Planet guidebook is any way you choose. At Lonely Planet we believe the most memorable travel experiences are often those that are unexpected, and the finest discoveries are those that you make yourself. Guidebooks are not intended to be used as if they provide a detailed set of infallible instructions!

Contents All Lonely Planet guidebooks follow roughly the same format. The Facts about the Destination chapters or sections give background information ranging from history to weather. Facts for the Visitor gives practical information on issues like visas and health. Getting There & Away gives a brief starting point for researching travel to and from the destination. Getting Around gives an overview of the transport options when you arrive.

The peculiar demands of each destination determine how subsequent chapters are broken up, but some things remain constant. We always start with background, then proceed to sights, places to stay, places to eat, entertainment, getting there and away, and getting around information – in that order.

Heading Hierarchy Lonely Planet headings are used in a strict hierarchical structure that can be visualised as a set of Russian dolls. Each heading (and its following text) is encompassed by any preceding heading that is higher on the hierarchical ladder.

Entry Points We do not assume guidebooks will be read from beginning to end, but that people will dip into them. The traditional entry points are the list of contents and the index. In addition, however, some books have a complete list of maps and an index map illustrating map coverage.

There may also be a colour map that shows highlights. These highlights are dealt with in greater detail in the Facts for the Visitor chapter, along with planning questions and suggested itineraries. Each chapter covering a geographical region usually begins with a locator map and another list of highlights. Once you find something of interest in a list of highlights, turn to the index.

Maps Maps play a crucial role in Lonely Planet guidebooks and include a huge amount of information. A legend is printed on the back page. We seek to have complete consistency between maps and text, and to have every important place in the text captured on a map. Map key numbers usually start in the top left corner.

Although inclusion in a guidebook usually implies a recommendation we cannot list every good place. Exclusion does not necessarily imply criticism. In fact there are a number of reasons why we might exclude a place – sometimes it is simply inappropriate to encourage an influx of travellers.

Introduction

It has been said that Europe ends at the Pyrenees. While that has always been an ex-aggeration, any journey south of those mountains proves that, as an old tourism promotion campaign had it, Spain *is* different. With its plethora of colourful fiestas and indefatigable nightlife, its complete spectrum of scenery and its unique, well-preserved architectural and artistic heritage, Spain provides a variety of fun and fascina-tion that few countries can match.

Travel is easy, accommodation plentiful, the climate generally benign, the people re-laxed and fun-loving, the beaches long and sandy, and food and drink easy to come by and full of regional variation. More than 50 million foreigners a year visit Spain, yet you can also travel for days and hear no other tongue but Spanish. Once away from the holiday *costas,* you could only be in Spain. In the cities, narrow, twisting old streets suddenly open out to views of daring modern architecture, while spit-and-sawdust bars serving wine from the barrel rub shoul-ders with blaring, glaring discos. Travel out into the back country and you'll find, an hour or two from some of Europe's most stylish and sophisticated cities, villages where time has done its best to stand still since the Middle Ages.

Geographically, Spain's diversity is im-mense. In Andalucía, for example, you could ski in the Sierra Nevada and later the same day recline on a Mediterranean beach or traverse the deserts of Almería. There are endless tracts of wild and crinkled *sierra* to explore, as well as some spectacularly rugged stretches of coast between the

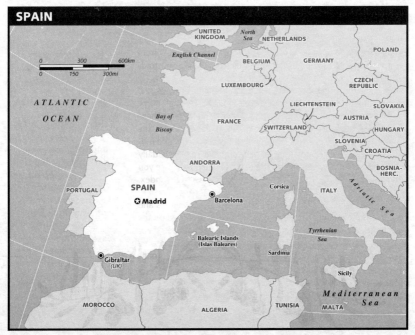

SPAIN

beaches – many of which are far less crowded and developed than you might imagine.

Culturally, the country is littered with superb old buildings, from Roman aqueducts and Islamic palaces to Gothic cathedrals. Almost every second village has a medieval castle. Spain has been the home of some of the world's great artists – El Greco, Goya, Dalí, Picasso – and has museums and galleries to match. The country vibrates with music of every kind.

The more you travel in Spain, the bigger it seems to get. It's surprising just how many Spains there are. Cool, damp, green Galicia is a world away from hot, dry Andalucía, home of flamenco and bullfighting. Fertile Catalunya in the north-east, with its separate language and independent spirit, seems a different nation from the Castilian heartland on the austere *meseta* at the centre of the Iberian Peninsula. Once you leave the beaten track, it can take as long to wind your way through a couple of remote valleys and over the sierra between them as it would to travel the highway or railway from Madrid to Barcelona. All you need to do is get out there and enjoy it!

Facts about Spain

HISTORY

The ancestors of today's Spaniards included Stone Age hunters from Africa; Phoenicians; Greeks, Romans, Visigoths and other European peoples; Berber tribes from Morocco; and Jews and Arabs from the Middle East. The ancestors of a good half of the people of the Americas today – and others dotted across the rest of the globe – were Spaniards. The key to this ebb and flow of peoples, cultures and empires is Spain's location: on both the Mediterranean Sea and the Atlantic Ocean, in Europe, yet a stone's throw from Africa, and as near to America as anywhere in the Old World. Such a pivotal position has entangled Spain in the affairs of half the world and half the world in Spain's.

In the Beginning

Caves throughout the country tell us plenty about Spain's earliest inhabitants. The most impressive, at Altamira near Santander, date from around 12,000 BC. Altamira's sophisticated, colourful paintings of bison, stag, boar and horses show confident brush strokes and realistic perspective – not primitive efforts.

Altamira was part of the Magdalenian hunting culture of southern France and northern Spain, a Palaeolithic (Old Stone Age) culture that lasted from around 20,000 BC to the end of the last Ice Age about 8000 BC. One of the many theories about the origins of the Basque people of northern Spain and south-western France is that they are descended from the Magdalenians.

But the story goes much further back. The oldest pieces of human bone in Europe have been found in Spain. Human bone fragments found in 1994 in the Sierra de Atapuerca near Burgos are widely accepted to be about 780,000 years old and probably come from ancestors of the later Neanderthals. Another piece of bone found near Orce, Granada province, in 1976 is reckoned to be from the skull of an infant ancestor of *Homo sapiens* eaten by a giant hyena over a million years ago. These finds suggest that humans reached Europe much earlier than was previously believed, and came directly from Africa, instead of via Asia as had been thought.

From the later Neanderthal era comes 'Gibraltar Woman', a skull from about 50,000 BC which was found in 1848. Current thinking is that the Neanderthals were displaced in about 40,000 BC, during the last Ice Age, by waves of migrants of African origin. The Cueva de Nerja in Andalucía is one of many Spanish sites of these Cro-Magnons, the first modern humans, who hunted mammoth, bison and reindeer. After the Ice Age, new peoples, probably from North Africa, arrived and their rock-shelter paintings of hunting and dancing survive on the east coast.

The Neolithic (New Stone Age) reached eastern Spain from Mesopotamia and Egypt about 6000 BC, bringing innovations such as the plough, crops, livestock raising, pottery, textiles and permanent villages. Between 3000 and 2000 BC arose the first metalworking culture, at Los Millares near Almería. The Los Millares people's ability to smelt and shape local copper deposits was a big breakthrough in agricultural and military terms. The same era saw the building of megalithic tombs (dolmens), made of large rocks, in many parts of the Iberian Peninsula's perimeter. The best examples are at Antequera in Andalucía.

The next big technological advance was bronze – an alloy of copper and tin, stronger than copper. About 1900 BC El Argar in Almería province became probably the first Bronze Age settlement on the Iberian Peninsula.

Iberians & Celts

Iberians is the general name given to the inhabitants of the Iberian Peninsula during the millennium or so before the Romans came. They mingled and mixed with other newcomers even before the Romans. From around 1000 to 500 BC, Celts (originally

Spanish History at a Glance

BC

c.12,000 Stone Age hunters at Altamira, near Santander, paint some of Europe's most sophisticated cave art.

c.3000–2000 Spain's first metalworking culture flourishes at the Copper Age site of Los Millares, near Almería.

c.1100 Phoenician traders start to found colonies at Cádiz and elsewhere in Andalucía.

c.1000–500 Celts settle north of the Río Ebro, bringing iron technology to the north.

c.800–600 The fabled Tartessos culture, influenced by Phoenician and Greek traders, flourishes in western Andalucía; later writers refer to it as a source of fabulous riches.

237 Carthage invades the Iberian Peninsula.

218 Rome defeats Carthage in the Second Punic War and begins a 600-year occupation of the Iberian Peninsula.

AD

3rd century Christianity reaches Spain.

3rd to 8th centuries Roman power wanes; a series of invasions of the Iberian Peninsula by Germanic tribes culminates in rule by the Christian Visigoths from the 6th century until 711.

711 Muslims invade the peninsula from North Africa, overrunning it within a few years, except for small areas in the Asturian mountains in the north.

c.722 Christians defeat Muslims at Covadonga, Asturias, the first success in the eight-centuries-long Christian Reconquista (Reconquest) of the peninsula.

756–1031 Córdoba dominates the Muslim areas of the peninsula, called Al-Andalus, reaching its political and cultural peak during the Caliphate period (929–1031); after 1008 the caliphate collapses into civil war and in 1031 splits into dozens of *taifas* (small kingdoms).

1085 Castile, a northern Christian kingdom, captures Toledo.

1091–1140s The Almoravids, a fanatical Muslim sect from North Africa, rule Al-Andalus.

1137 Aragón and Catalunya unite to form a powerful north-eastern Christian state, the Kingdom of Aragón.

1160–73 The Almohads, another North African Muslim sect, conquer Al-Andalus.

1195 The Almohads rout Castile's army at Alarcos, south of Toledo.

1212 The combined Christian armies of Castile, Aragón and Navarra rout the Almohads at Las Navas de Tolosa, Andalucía, opening the way for the last act of the Reconquista, the conquest of the south.

1248 Sevilla falls to Fernando III of Castile.

1248–1492 The Nasrid Emirate of Granada, comprising about half of Andalucía, survives as the last Muslim state on the peninsula.

1469 Isabel, heir to the Castilian throne, marries Fernando, heir to the Aragonese throne, uniting the peninsula's two most powerful Christian states.

1478 Isabel and Fernando, the Catholic Monarchs (Reyes Católicos), set up the Spanish Inquisition.

1492 (January) Isabel and Fernando capture Granada, the last Muslim possession on the peninsula.

from Central Europe) and other tribes from beyond the Pyrenees started to settle north of the Río Ebro. In contrast to the dark-featured Iberians, the Celts were fair, drank beer and ate lard. Celts and Iberians who merged on the *meseta* (the high table-land of central Spain) became the Celtiberians. Celts and Celtiberians typically lived in sizable hill fort towns called *castros*. The Celts introduced iron technology to the north about the same time the Phoenicians brought it to the south.

Spanish History at a Glance

1492 (April) Isabel and Fernando expel Jews who refuse Christian baptism.

1492 (October) Christopher Columbus, funded by the Catholic Monarchs, lands in the Bahamas, opening the way for Spanish conquest and colonisation in the Americas.

1500 Muslims revolt in Andalucía and are ordered to convert to Christianity or leave Spain.

1517–56 Reign of Carlos I, who also ruled the Low Countries and many other areas of Europe, involving Spain in wars that absorbed much of the new wealth from the Americas.

1556–98 Reign of Felipe II: Spain absorbs Portugal but loses Holland; the Spanish navy defeats the Ottoman Turks at Lepanto (1571) but its 1588 Armada is routed by the English; and Madrid is made national capital (1561).

17th century Spain enters economic decline and loses Portugal (1641).

1609–14 The *moriscos* (converted Muslims) are expelled from Spain

1805 Spanish sea power is ended when a Spanish-French fleet is defeated by Britain at Trafalgar.

1808–13 Spanish War of Independence (Peninsular War): Spanish guerrillas, with British and Portuguese support, drive out the French occupiers.

1813–25 Most of Spain's American colonies win independence.

late 1860s Anarchist ideas reach Spain and soon gain a wide following.

1873 First Republic: liberals declare Spain a federal republic of 17 states, resulting in chaos and restoration of the monarchy.

1898 Spanish-American War: Spain loses its last overseas possessions (Cuba, Puerto Rico, Guam and the Philippines).

1909 The 'Tragic Week' in Barcelona: a general strike turns into a frenzy of violence.

1917 A general strike is crushed by the army, anarchist and socialist movements grow and political violence escalates.

1923–30 Mild dictatorship of General Miguel Primo de Rivera.

1931–36 Second Republic: King Alfonso XIII goes into exile and, under successive left-wing, right-wing and left-wing governments, Spain polarises and political violence grows.

1936–39 Spanish Civil War: right-wing Nationalist rebels led by General Francisco Franco, helped by Nazi Germany and Fascist Italy, defeat left-wing Republican forces helped by the Soviet Union; about 350,000 Spaniards are killed.

1939–75 The Franco dictatorship: an estimated 100,000 are killed or die in prison as Nationalist repression continues after the civil war; economically, the late 1940s *años de hambre* (years of hunger) are followed by a boom in the 1960s.

1975 Franco dies and is succeeded by King Juan Carlos I.

1976–81 Juan Carlos' prime minister, Adolfo Suárez, engineers a return to democracy; Spain becomes a parliamentary monarchy with no official religion.

1982–96 Spain is governed by the centre-left Partido Socialista Obrero Español (PSOE) party led by Felipe González, which introduces a national health system, improves education and takes Spain into the then-EC (1986).

1996 The centre-right Partido Popular (PP) party, led by José María Aznar, takes power.

Phoenicians & Greeks

By about 1000 BC a flourishing culture had arisen in western Andalucía. The development of this and other societies in the south and east was influenced by Phoenician and, later, Greek traders, who exchanged oils, textiles, jewels and ivory for local metals. The Phoenicians, a Semitic people from present-day Lebanon, set up permanent trading colonies including Cádiz (which they called Gadir), Huelva (Onuba), Málaga (Malaca) and Almuñécar (Sex). Cádiz's supposed founding date of 1100 BC may make it the oldest city in Europe. Greek settlements, which began around 600 BC, tended to be farther north on the Mediterranean coast. The main one was Emporion (Empúries) in Catalunya (Cataluña).

These incomers brought the potter's wheel, writing, coinage, some musical instruments, the olive tree and vine, and domestic animals such as the donkey and hen. Around 700 BC iron replaced bronze as the most important metal in the lower Guadalquivir valley of western Andalucía. This Phoenician-influ-enced culture was very likely the fabled Tartessos, which later Greek, Roman and biblical writers mythologised as a place of unimaginable wealth. No one knows whether Tartessos was a city or a state. Some argue it was a trading settlement on the site of modern Huelva, while others believe it may lie beneath the marshes near the mouth of the Río Guadalquivir, and yet others equate it with the lost continent of Atlantis.

Carthaginians

From about the 6th century BC the Phoenicians and Greeks were pushed out of the western Mediterranean by Carthage, a former Phoenician colony in modern Tunisia. Cádiz became the Carthaginians' main Iberian settlement and there was a flourishing colony on Ibiza.

The Carthaginians came into conflict with the next rising Mediterranean power – Rome. After losing the First Punic War (264–241 BC), fought against Rome for control of Sicily, Carthage responded by invading the Iberian Peninsula under generals Hamilcar Barca, Hasdrubal and Hannibal. The first landing was in 237 BC.

The Second Punic War (218–201 BC) saw Hannibal march his elephants over the Alps towards Rome but also brought Roman legions to Spain to start another theatre of war. Hannibal was eventually forced to retreat, finally being routed in North Africa in 202 BC.

Romans

Though the Romans held sway on the peninsula for 600 years, it took them 200 years to subdue the fiercest of the local tribes.

The Basques in the north, though defeated, were never Romanised like the rest of Hispania, as the Romans called the peninsula. Legendary stands against the Romans included the eight-year revolt led by the shepherd-turned-guerrilla Virathius in the west and centre from around 150 BC and the siege of Numancia near Soria in 133 BC. Rome had to bring in its most illustrious generals to deal with these and other insubordinations.

By AD 50 most of the peninsula, particularly the south, had adopted the Roman way of life. This was the time of the Pax Romana, a long, prosperous period of stability. Hispania became urbanised and highly organised. The early Roman provinces were called Hispania Citerior and Hispania Ulterior, with their capitals at Carthago Nova (Cartagena) and Corduba (Córdoba). In the 1st century BC they were reorganised into Baetica (most of present-day Andalucía plus southern Extremadura and south-western Castilla-La Mancha), with its capital at Corduba; Lusitania (Portugal and northern Extremadura), with its capital at Augusta Emerita (Mérida), the greatest Roman city on the peninsula; and Tarraconensis (the rest), with its capital at Tarraco (Tarragona).

Rome gave the peninsula a road system, aqueducts, theatres, temples, amphitheatres, circuses, baths and the basis of its legal system and languages. The Roman era also brought many Jews, who settled throughout the Mediterranean part of the empire, and Christianity, which probably came with soldiers from North Africa and merchants in the 3rd century AD and first took root in Andalucía. Hispania gave Rome gold, silver, grain, wine, soldiers, emperors (Trajan, Hadrian and Theodosius) and some of the greatest Latin literature – that of Seneca, Martial, Quintilian and Lucan. Another notable export was *garum*, a spicy sauce derived from fish and used as a seasoning. The finest of Spain's Roman ruins are at Empúries, Itálica, Mérida, Tarragona and Segovia.

The Pax Romana started to crack when two Germanic tribes, the Franks and the Alemanni, swept across the Pyrenees in the late 3rd century AD, causing devastation. The end came when the Huns arrived in Eastern Europe from Asia a century later. Germanic peoples displaced by the Huns moved westwards, among them the Suevi and Vandals, who overran the Iberian Peninsula around AD 410.

Visigoths

Another Germanic people, the Visigoths, sacked Rome itself in AD 410. Within a few years, however, the Visigoths had become Roman allies, being granted lands in southern Gaul (France) and fighting on the emperor's behalf against other barbarian invaders on the Iberian Peninsula. But in the 6th century the Franks pushed the Visigoths out of Gaul. The Visigoths penetrated more deeply into the Iberian Peninsula and Toledo became their capital.

The rule of the roughly 200,000 long-haired Visigoths, who had a penchant for gaudy jewellery, over the several million more sophisticated Hispano-Romans was precarious and undermined by strife among their own nobility. The Hispano-Roman nobles still ran the fiscal system and their bishops were the senior figures in urban centres. Town life declined in quality under Visigothic rule.

The ties between the Visigoth monarchy and the Hispano-Romans were greatly strengthened in AD 587, when King Reccared converted to orthodox Christianity from the Visigoths' Arian version which denied that Christ was identical to God. But the Visi-goth kings still had to contend with regular revolts by nobles, bishops and others.

Culturally, the Visigoths tended to ape Roman ways. A few Visigothic churches can be seen today in northern Spain. One at Baños de Cerrato near Palencia, dating from 661, is probably the oldest church in the country.

The Muslim Conquest

By 700, with famine and disease in Toledo, strife among the aristocracy and chaos throughout the peninsula, the Visigothic kingdom was falling apart. This paved the way for the Muslim invasion of 711, which set Spain's destiny quite apart from that of the rest of Europe.

Following the death of Mohammed in 632, Arabs had spread through the Middle East and North Africa, taking Islam with them. If you believe the myth, they were ushered on to the Iberian Peninsula by the sexual adventures of the last Visigoth king, Roderick. Ballads and chronicles written long after the event relate how Roderick (to put it politely) seduced young Florinda, the daughter of Count Julian, the Visigotic governor of Ceuta in North Africa, and how her father sought revenge by approaching the Muslims with a plan to invade Spain. In dull fact Julian probably just wanted outside help in a struggle for the Visigothic throne.

In 711 Musa, the Arab governor of northwest Africa, ordered the governor of Tangier, Tariq ibn Ziyad, across the Strait of Gibraltar. Tariq landed at Gibraltar with around 10,000 men, mostly Berbers (indigenous North Africans). He had some of Roderick's Visigoth rivals as allies. Roderick's army was decimated, probably near the Río Guadalete in Andalucía, and he is thought to have drowned while fleeing the scene. Visigothic survivors fled north.

Within a few years the Muslims had conquered the rest of the Iberian Peninsula, except small areas in the Asturian mountains in the north. In many places they were welcomed by Jews and slaves, who had been badly treated under Visigothic rule. The Muslims pushed on over the Pyrenees, but were driven back by the Franks.

Muslim Spain

The Muslims (often referred to as Moors) were the dominant force on the peninsula for nearly four centuries, a potent force for 170 years after that and a lesser one for a further 250 years. Between wars and rebellions, Al-Andalus, the name given to Muslim territory on the peninsula, developed the most highly cultured society of medieval Europe.

Al-Andalus' frontiers were constantly shifting as the Christians strove to regain territory in the stuttering 800-year Reconquista (Reconquest). Up to the mid-11th century the frontier lay across the north of the peninsula, roughly from just south of Barcelona to northern Portugal, with a protrusion up to the central Pyrenees. Al-Andalus also suffered internal conflicts and at times Muslims and Christians even struck up alliances with each other in the course of quarrels with their own co-religionists.

Muslim political power and cultural developments centred initially on Córdoba (756–1031), then Sevilla (c.1040–1248) and lastly Granada (1248–1492). In these cities the Muslims built beautiful palaces, mosques and gardens, established bustling markets (zocos) and opened universities and public baths. They developed the Hispano-Roman agricultural base by improving irrigation and introducing new fruits and crops (oranges, lemons, peaches, sugar cane, rice and more).

Though military campaigns against the northern Christians could be bloodthirsty affairs, Al-Andalus' rulers allowed freedom of worship to Jews and Christians (mozárabes, or Mozarabs) under their rule. Jews mostly flourished, but Christians had to pay a special tax, so most either converted to Islam (to be known as muladíes, or muwallads) or left for the Christian north.

The Muslim settlers themselves were not a homogeneous group: beneath the Arab ruling class was a larger group of Berbers and tension between these two groups broke into Berber rebellion numerous times.

It seems as if the Arabs and Berber didn't bring many women with them; before long Muslim and local blood merged. This applied even at the highest levels of society for, as well as the acquisition of women for royal harems, there was frequent political intermarriage with the Christian royalty and aristocracy of the north.

The Cordoban Emirate & Caliphate Initially Al-Andalus was a province of the Emirate of Ifriqiya (North Africa), part of the Caliphate of Damascus which ruled the Muslim world. In 750 the Omayyad caliphal dynasty was overthrown by a rival clan, the Abbasids, who shifted the caliphate to Baghdad. But an Omayyad survivor managed to

establish himself in 756 in Córdoba as the independent emir of Al-Andalus, Abd ar-Rahman I. He began the construction of the Córdoba Mezquita (Mosque), one of the world's greatest Muslim monuments. Most of Al-Andalus was more or less unified under Cordoban rule for some fairly long periods. In 929 Abd ar-Rahman III bestowed on himself the title caliph, launching the Caliphate of Córdoba (929–1031), during which Al-Andalus reached its peak of power and lustre.

At this time Córdoba was the biggest and most dazzling city in Western Europe, thriving on a productive agriculture sector and the work of its skilled artisans. Astronomy, medicine, mathematics and botany flourished and one of the greatest Muslim libraries was established in the city. Abd ar-Rahman III's court was frequented by Jewish, Arab and Christian scholars.

Later in the 10th century the fearsome Cordoban general Al-Mansour (or Almanzor) terrorised the Christian north with 50-odd forays in 20 years. He destroyed the cathedral at Santiago de Compostela in north-western Spain in 997 and forced Christian slaves to carry its doors and bells to Córdoba, where they were incorporated into the great mosque. But after the death of Al-Mansour's son in 1008, rival claimants to the caliphate indulged in a devastating civil war. In 1031 the caliphate broke up into dozens of taifas (small kingdoms), with Sevilla, Granada, Toledo and Zaragoza among the most powerful.

Almoravids & Almohads Political unity was restored to Al-Andalus by the Almoravid invasion of 1091. The Almoravids, a fanatical Muslim sect of Saharan nomads who had conquered North Africa, were initially invited to the Iberian Peninsula to help the Sevilla taifa against the growing Christian threat from the north. Seventy years later another Berber sect, the Almohads, invaded the peninsula after overthrowing the Almoravids in Morocco. Both sects soundly defeated the Christian armies they encountered.

Under the Almoravids and the Almohads, religious intolerance sent Christian refugees fleeing north. But in time both mellowed in their adopted territory and Almohad rule saw a revival of the cultural achievements that the Almoravids had interrupted in Sevilla. In Córdoba the philosopher Averroës (1126–98) wrote commentaries on Aristotle, trying to reconcile science with religious faith, which had great influence on European Christian thought in the 13th and 14th centuries.

The Nasrid Emirate of Granada Almohad power eventually disintegrated in the face of internal disputes and Christian advances. After Sevilla fell to the Christians in 1248, Muslim territory on the Iberian Peninsula was reduced to the Emirate of Granada, comprising about half of modern Andalucía and ruled from the lush Alhambra palace by the Nasrid dynasty. Granada saw Muslim Spain's final cultural flowering, prospering with an influx of refugees from the Reconquista. It reached its peak in the 14th century under Yousouf I and Mohammed V, both of whom contributed to the splendours of the Alhambra.

Granada survived by playing off rival Spanish Christian states and Muslim Morocco against each other. Christian armies eventually started nibbling at its borders in the 15th century.

The Reconquista

The Christian reconquest of the peninsula began about 722 at Covadonga and ended with the fall of Granada in 1492. It was a stuttering affair, conducted by a tangled sequence of emerging, merging and demerging Christian states that were as often at war with each other as with the Muslims. But the Muslims were gradually pushed south as the northern kingdoms of Asturias, León, Navarra, Castile and Aragón developed and ultimately forged a sufficiently united front to oust Muslim rule from the peninsula.

Santiago Matamoros An essential ingredient in the Reconquista was the cult of Santiago (St James), one of the 12 apostles. In 813, the saint's supposed tomb was discovered in Galicia. The town of Santiago de Compostela grew around the church that was built on the spot, eventually to become the third most popular medieval Christian pilgrimage goal after Rome and Jerusalem. Visions of Santiago 'appeared' to Christian leaders before forays against the Muslims and he became the inspiration and special protector of soldiers in the Reconquista, earning the sobriquet 'Matamoros' (Moor-slayer). Today he is the patron saint of Spain.

The First 500 Years – the Rise of Castile Covadonga lies in the Picos de Europa in Asturias, where Visigothic nobles took refuge after the Muslim conquest.

The Muslim Legacy

The Muslims left a deep imprint on Spain – and not just in terms of the palaces, castles and mosques that rank among its greatest monuments today. For one thing, many Spaniards today are partly descended from the Muslims. For another, the narrow, labyrinthine street plan of many old villages and towns is of Muslim origin. Muslim crafts and architectural tastes, too, were adopted by Christians both inside and outside Al-Andalus, and many of their techniques and motifs remain in use in Spain even today. Flamenco song, though brought to its modern form by *gitanos* in post-Muslim times, has clear Islamic roots. The Spanish language is rich in words of Arabic origin – including *arroz* (rice), *alcalde* (mayor), *naranja* (orange) and *azúcar* (sugar). Many foods eaten in Spain today were introduced by the Muslims. Many churches are converted mosques. And so on.

It was also through Al-Andalus that much of the learning of ancient Greece was transmitted to Christian Europe. Arabs absorbed the Greek scientific and philosophical traditions in the eastern Mediterranean, and there were two meeting points in Europe between the Islamic and Christian worlds where this knowledge could find its way north – one was southern Italy, the other was Al-Andalus.

Christian versions of what happened there tell of a small band of fighters under their leader, Pelayo, crushing an enormous force of Muslims; Muslim accounts make it a rather less important skirmish. Whatever the facts of Covadonga, by 757 Christians occupied nearly a quarter of the peninsula. Progress thereafter was a lot slower.

The Asturian kingdom eventually moved its capital to León, which spearheaded the Reconquista until the Christians were set on the defensive by Al-Mansour in the 10th century. Castile, originally a small principality in the east of the kingdom of León, developed as the dominant Reconquista force. Taking its name from the castles built by its Christian conquerors, Castile grew from the 11th century as hardy adventurers set up towns in the no-man's-land of the Duero basin, spurred on by land grants in conquered territory and other rights and privileges *(fueros)*. It was the capture of Toledo by Alfonso VI of Castile in 1085 that led the Sevilla Muslims to call in the Almoravids.

Alfonso I of Aragón, on the southern flank of the Pyrenees, led the counterattack against the Almoravids, taking Zaragoza in 1118. After his death Aragón was united through royal marriage with Catalunya, creating a formidable new Christian power block (known to history as the Kingdom of Aragón although Catalunya was the stronger partner). Portugal emerged as an independent Christian kingdom in the 12th century.

Castile suffered a terrible defeat by the Almohads at Alarcos, south of Toledo, in 1195, but in 1212 the combined Christian armies of Castile, Aragón and Navarra routed a large Almohad force at Las Navas de Tolosa in Andalucía. This was the beginning of the end for Al-Andalus. León took the key towns of Extremadura in 1229 and 1230; Aragón took the Balearic Islands and Valencia in the 1230s; Fernando III 'El Santo' (Ferdinand the Saint) of Castile took Córdoba in 1236 and, in 1248, Sevilla (with help from the rival Muslim state of Granada); and Portugal expelled the Muslims in 1249. The sole surviving Muslim state on the peninsula was the Emirate of Granada.

The Lull (1250–1479) Fernando III's son, Alfonso X El Sabio (the Learned; 1252–84), proclaimed Castilian the official language of his realm. At Toledo he gathered around him scholars regardless of their religion, particularly Jews who knew Arabic and Latin. Muslims who stayed on in Christian territory were known as *mudéjares*. Many from western Andalucía were expelled to Granada or North Africa, after a 1264 rebellion in Jerez de la Frontera sparked by new taxes and rules requiring them to celebrate Christian feasts and live in ghettoes. Alfonso was plagued by further uprisings and plots, even from within his own family. This unrest continued in Castile until the 15th century, with the nobility repeatedly challenging the crown.

The late 13th and the 14th centuries were a time of cultural malaise in Castile, although architecture, the great art of the late Middle Ages, was an exception, reaching its heights in great cathedrals such as those at Toledo and León. This was also an era of growing intolerance towards the Jews and Genoese who were taking over Castilian commerce and finance, while the Castilians

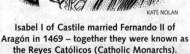

KATE NOLAN

Isabel I of Castile married Fernando II of Aragón in 1469 – together they were known as the Reyes Católicos (Catholic Monarchs).

were preoccupied with their low effort-high profit wool production. Jews were blamed for economic crises and even for the Black Death in the mid-14th century. Anti-Jewish feeling culminated in pogroms around the peninsula in the 1390s.

Aragón, meanwhile, looked outwards to the Mediterranean, taking Sardinia and Sicily, from where Catalan soldiers went off to fight the Ottoman Turks.

Both Castile and Aragón laboured under a series of ineffectual monarchs from the late 14th century until the time of Isabel and Fernando (Isabella and Ferdinand), whose marriage in Segovia Castle in 1469 would merge the two kingdoms. Isabel succeeded to the Castilian throne in 1474 and Fernando to Aragón's in 1479, both coming through civil wars to claim their inheritances. The joint rule of the Reyes Católicos (Catholic Monarchs), as they are known, dates from 1479.

The Fall of Granada After Emir Abu al-Hasan of Granada refused in 1476 to pay any more tribute to Castile, Isabel and Fernando launched the final crusade of the Reconquista in 1482, with an army largely funded by Jewish loans and the Catholic church.

By now the rulers of Granada had retreated to a pleasure-loving existence in the Alhambra and were riven by internal feuds. Matters degenerated into a confused civil war, of which the Christians took full advantage. Fernando and Isabel entered Granada, after a long siege, on 2 January 1492 – an appropriate start for what turned out to be the most momentous year in Spanish history.

The surrender terms were fairly generous to Boabdil, the last emir, who got the Alpujarras valleys south of Granada and 30,000 gold coins. The remaining Muslims were promised respect for their religion, culture and property, but this didn't last long.

The Catholic Monarchs

The pious Isabel and the Machiavellian Fernando were an unbeatable team. The war against Granada was just one of several steps they took to unify their realm. They checked the power of the Castilian nobility, granting Andalucian land to their supporters and excluding aristocrats from their administration. They also reformed a corrupt, immoral clergy. By the time Fernando died in 1516 (12 years after Isabel) all of Spain was under single rule for the first time since Visigothic days.

Jews & the Inquisition The urge for unity was not just territorial. The Catholic Monarchs revived the almost extinct Inquisition – originally founded in the 13th century to suppress heretics in France – to root out those who didn't practise Christianity as the Catholic church wished them to. The Spanish Inquisition focused most of all on *conversos,* Jews who had converted to Christianity, accusing many of continuing to practise Judaism in secret. Despite Fernando's part-Jewish background and Jewish loans for the Granada war, Jews were considered Muslim allies. The Inquisition was responsible for perhaps 12,000 deaths over 300 years, 2000 of them in the 1480s.

Under the influence of Grand Inquisitor Tomás de Torquemada, Isabel and Fernando in April 1492 ordered the expulsion from their territories of all Jews who refused Christian baptism. About 50,000 to 100,000 Jews converted, but some 200,000 – the first Sephardic Jews – left for other Mediterranean destinations. The bankrupt monarchy seized all unsold Jewish property. A talented middle class was decimated.

Persecution of the Muslims Cardinal Cisneros, Isabel's confessor and overseer of the Inquisition, tried to eradicate Muslim culture. Given the task of converting the Muslims of the former Granada emirate, he carried out forced mass baptisms, had Islamic books burnt and banned the Arabic language. This, combined with seizures of Muslim land, sparked a revolt in Andalucía in 1500. Afterwards, Muslims were ordered to convert to Christianity or leave. Most (around 300,000) underwent baptism and stayed, to be known as *moriscos* (converted Muslims), but their conversion was barely skin-deep and they never assimilated. The moriscos were finally expelled between 1609 and 1614.

Christopher Columbus In April 1492 the Catholic Monarchs granted Christopher Columbus (Cristóbal Colón to Spaniards) funds for his long-desired voyage across the Atlantic in search of a new trade route to the Orient. Isabel and Fernando were motivated by the need to fill empty coffers and the possibility of more Christian conversions.

Columbus set off from Palos de la Frontera (Andalucía) on 3 August with three small ships and 120 men. They stopped at the Canary Islands, then sailed west for 31 days, sighting no land. The rebellious crew gave Columbus two more days. But he landed on the island of Guanahaní (Bahamas), which he named San Salvador, found Cuba and Hispaniola and returned to a hero's welcome from the monarchs in Barcelona eight months after his departure.

Columbus made three more voyages, founding Santo Domingo on Hispaniola, finding Jamaica, Trinidad and other Caribbean islands, and reaching the mouth of the Orinoco and the coast of Central America. But he proved an unsuccessful administrator and was shipped home as a prisoner from his third voyage, though released on his return. He died poor, and apparently still believing he had reached Asia, in Valladolid in 1506.

After Isabel Fernando entangled Spain in European affairs by marrying his and Isabel's four children into the royal families of Portugal, Burgundy and England and the powerful Habsburg family of Central Europe. (The English connection failed when the youngest, Catalina, or Catherine of Aragón, was cast aside by Henry VIII.) The early death of two children left the third, Princess Juana, heir to the Castilian throne when Isabel died in 1504. Juana's husband, Felipe El Hermoso (Philip the Handsome), was heir to the Low Countries and to the Habsburg lands in Central Europe. But Juana, dubbed Juana la Loca (Joanna the Mad), was unfit to rule and, when Felipe died soon after, Fernando took over as regent of Castile until his own death in 1516. His annexation of Navarra in 1512 brought all of what's now Spain under one rule for the first time since Visigothic days.

The Habsburgs

Carlos I In 1517, 17-year-old Carlos I (Charles I), son of Juana la Loca and Felipe El Hermoso, came from Flanders to take up his Spanish inheritance. In 1519 Carlos also succeeded to the Habsburg lands in Austria and managed to win election as Holy Roman Emperor (as Charles V). Carlos now ruled all of Spain, the Low Countries, Austria, several Italian states and parts of France and Germany – more of Europe than anyone since the 9th century – plus the Spanish colonies in the Caribbean and Panama. To these he would add more of Central Europe and further big slices of the Americas.

Carlos spent only 16 years of his 40-year reign in Spain. At first the Spaniards did not care for a king who spoke no Castilian, nor for his appropriating their wealth. Castilian cities revolted in 1520–21 (Guerra de las Comunidades, or War of the Communities) but were crushed. Eventually the Spanish came round to him, at least for his strong stance against emerging Protestantism and his learning of Castilian. Under Carlos, Spain could have developed into an early industrial power, but he spent the bulk of the monarchy's new American wealth on an endless series of European conflicts. War weary, Carlos abdicated shortly before his death in 1556, dividing his territories between his son Felipe and his brother Fernando. Felipe got the lion's share, including Spain, the Low Countries and the American possessions.

The American Empire Carlos I's reign saw Spain conquer vast tracts of the American mainland. Ruthless but brilliant *conquistadors* such as Hernán Cortés (who subdued the Aztec empire with a small band of adventurers in 1519–21) and Francisco Pizarro (who did the same to the Inca empire in 1531–33) were, with their odd mix of brutality, bravery, gold lust and piety, the natural successors to the crusaders of the Reconquista.

By 1600, Spain controlled Florida, all the biggest Caribbean islands, nearly all of present-day Mexico and Central America and a strip of South America from present-day Venezuela to Argentina. The new colonies sent huge cargoes of silver, gold and other riches back to Spain, where the crown was entitled to one-fifth of the bullion (*quinto real*, or royal fifth). Sevilla enjoyed a mon-opoly on this trade and grew into one of Europe's richest cities by 1600.

Whether the Spanish empire was any more or less greedy and cruel than comparable enterprises is a topic of much pointless debate. The conquistadors sprang from one war culture and confronted others – which also indulged in practices such as slavery and mass human sacrifice. Many Spaniards considered the conquest to have as much a moral as an economic and political mission – that of winning new Christian souls. The clergy managed to spare the indigenous people some of the worst excesses of other colonists. At the instigation of the friar Bartolomé de Las Casas, Spain enacted laws that gave some protection to the indigenous people. Decimation of the native populations was at least as much a result of new diseases as of colonial oppression.

Felipe II Carlos I's son Felipe II (Philip II; 1556–98) presided over the zenith of Spanish power. His reign is a study in contradictions. He enlarged the overseas empire but lost wealthy Holland to a long drawn-out rebellion. His navy thrashed the Ottoman Turks, Spain's great Mediterranean rivals, at Lepanto (Greece) in 1571, but his Spanish Armada of 1588 was routed by England. He received greater flows of silver than ever from the Americas, but went bankrupt. He was a fanatical Catholic who spurred the Inquisition to new persecutions, yet readily allied Spain with Protestant England against Catholic France when it suited Spain's interests.

When Felipe claimed Portugal on its king's death in 1580, he not only united the Iberian Peninsula but also Europe's two great overseas empires. But there was no plan to absorb the new wealth. The Castilian gentry's disdain for commerce and industry allowed foreign merchants to dominate trade. Money that didn't find its way into foreign pockets or wasn't owed for European wars went towards building churches, palaces and monasteries. Spain, it

was said, had discovered the magic formula for turning silver into stone.

One of Felipe's most lasting decisions, made in 1561, was to turn the minor country town of Madrid into a new capital from which to mould his kingdom.

The Cultural Golden Age Mid-16th to late-17th century Spain was like a gigantic artisans' workshop, in which architecture, sculpture, painting and metalwork consumed around 5% of the nation's income. The age was immortalised on canvas by artists such as Velázquez, El Greco, Zurbarán, Murillo and Ribera, and in words by Miguel de Cervantes, the mystics Santa Teresa of Ávila and San Juan de la Cruz (St John of the Cross) and the prolific playwright Lope de Vega.

The 17th Century Under a trio of ineffectual kings, Spain saw its chickens come home to roost. Felipe III (Philip III; 1598–1621) preferred hunting to ruling and left government to the self-seeking Duke of Lerma. Felipe IV (Philip IV; 1621–65) concentrated on a long line of mistresses and handed over affairs of state to Count-Duke Olivares, who tried bravely but retired a broken man in 1643. Spain fought unsuccessful wars with France and Holland, lost Portugal and faced revolts in Sicily, Naples and Catalunya. Silver shipments from the Americas shrank disastrously. Carlos II (Charles II; 1665–1700), who liked picking strawberries, was unable to produce children, thus bequeathing the War of the Spanish Succession.

The gentry and the church, which was entitled to one-tenth of all production, led a comfortable existence, but for most Spaniards life was decidedly underprivileged.

The 18th Century
Under the new Bourbon dynasty, still in place today, the 18th century saw limited recovery from the decline of the 17th.

Felipe V Carlos II bequeathed his throne to his young relative Felipe V (Philip V; 1701–46), who also happened to be second in line to the French throne. The Austrian emperor Leopold, however, wanted to see his son Charles, a nephew of Carlos II, on the Spanish throne. The resulting War of the Spanish Succession (1702–13) was a contest for the balance of power in Europe. In the end Felipe V held on to Spain but renounced his right to the French throne. Spain lost several Italian states and its last possessions in the Low Countries to Austria, and Gibraltar and Menorca to Britain.

Felipe, with many French and Italian advisers, instituted reforms in economy and government, but land reform proved impossible. Two-thirds of the land was in the hands of the nobility and church and was underproductive, and large numbers of males, from nobles to vagrants, were unwilling to work.

This was Europe's age of the Enlightenment, but Spain's powerful church and Inquisition were at odds with the rationalism that trickled in from France.

Fernando VI & Carlos III Fernando VI (Ferdinand VI; 1746–59) replaced all foreign advisers with Spaniards, strengthened the navy and ended the Inquisition's dreaded *autos da fé* (elaborate execution ceremonies). The economy was on an upturn largely due to a revitalised Catalunya and the Basque shipbuilding industry. But agricultural Castile and Andalucía were left behind, unable to increase yields due to a lack of land reforms.

Carlos III (Charles III; 1759–88) was an enlightened despot. He expelled the backward-looking Jesuits, transformed Madrid, established a new road system out to the provinces and tried to improve agriculture. But food shortages fuelled unrest among the masses.

French Revolution & Spanish War of Independence (Peninsular War)

Carlos IV (Charles IV; 1788–1808) was dominated by his Italian wife, Maria Luisa of Parma; she hooked up with a handsome royal guard called Manuel Godoy, who became chief minister. This unholy trinity was ill suited to coping with the crisis presented by the French Revolution of 1789.

When Louis XVI of France (Carlos IV's cousin) was guillotined in 1793, Spain declared war on France. Two years later, with France's Reign of Terror spent, Godoy made peace, pledging military support for France against Britain. In 1805 a combined Spanish-French navy was beaten by the British fleet under Nelson off the Cabo de Trafalgar (between Cádiz and Gibraltar). This put an end to Spanish sea power and sealed Spain's colonial decline.

Two years later, Napoleon Bonaparte and Godoy agreed to divide Britain's ally Portugal between them. French forces poured into Spain, supposedly on the way to northern Portugal. By 1808 this had become a French occupation of Spain. The king, queen and Godoy fled to their Aranjuez palace outside Madrid, which angry mobs surrounded. Carlos abdicated in favour of his son Fernando. Napoleon then summoned the royal family and Godoy to Bayonne (France) and forced Fernando to abdicate in favour of Carlos, who was then made to abdicate again, this time in favour of Napoleon's brother Joseph Bonaparte (José I).

In Madrid crowds revolted and countrywide the Spanish populace took up arms in guerrilla fashion, reinforced by British and Portuguese forces led by the Duke of Wellington. By 1812, Napoleon's attention was diverted to his Russian campaign and the French withdrew in large numbers. They were finally expelled following their defeat at Vitoria in the Basque Country in 1813.

The 19th Century

Liberals vs Conservatives During the war, a national Cortes (parliament), meeting at Cádiz in 1812, had drawn up a new liberal constitution which incorporated many of the principles of the American and French prototypes. This upset the church and monarchy, setting the pattern for a contest lasting most of the 19th century between conservatives, who liked the status quo, and liberals, who wanted vaguely democratic reforms.

Fernando VII (Ferdinand VII; 1814–33) took the throne to popular acclaim but was little loved by the time he died. He revoked the Cádiz constitution, persecuted liberal opponents, re-established the Inquisition and invited the Jesuits back. In 1820 Colonel Rafael de Riego made the first of the 19th century's many *pronunciamientos* (pronouncements of military rebellion), in the name of liberalism. But French troops put Fernando back on the throne in 1823. Severe reprisals against the rebels and corrupt government drastically cut the king's popularity before his death.

Meanwhile the restless American colonies had taken advantage of Spain's problems to strike out on their own. By 1824 only Cuba and Puerto Rico remained Spanish.

First Carlist War Fernando's dithering over his successor resulted in the First Carlist War (1833–39), between supporters of his brother Don Carlos and his infant daughter Isabel. Don Carlos was supported by the church, other conservatives and regional rebels in the Basque Country, Navarra, Catalunya and Aragón – together known as the Carlists. The Isabel faction had the support of liberals and the army.

During the war violent anticlericalism emerged. Religious orders were closed and, in the Disentailment of 1836, church property and lands were seized and auctioned off by the government. As usual, only the wealthy benefited. The army emerged victorious.

Isabel II In 1843 Isabel, now all of 13, declared herself Queen Isabel II (Isabella II; 1843–68). One achievement of sorts during her inept reign was the creation of a rural police force, the Guardia Civil, mainly to protect the wealthy in the bandit-ridden countryside. There was an upturn in the economy, with progress in business, banking, mining and railways, plus some reforms in education, but the benefits accrued to few. Eventually radical liberals, and discontented soldiers led by General Juan Prim, overthrew Isabel in the Septembrina Revolution of 1868.

Second Carlist War & First Republic Spain still wanted a monarch and eventually Amadeo of Savoy, a son of the Italian king and known for his liberal sentiments, accepted the job in 1870. The aristocracy, who opposed Amadeo, split into two camps: one favouring Isabel II's teenage son Alfonso, the other backing Don Carlos' grandson Carlos. Thus began the three-way Second Carlist War (1872–76).

With the Carlists holding most of the north, Barcelona a law unto itself and anarchism making strides in Andalucía, Amadeo abandoned Spain in 1873. The liberal-dominated Cortes proclaimed Spain a federal republic of 17 states. But this First Republic, riven by internal divisions and unable to keep a grip on the regions, lasted only 11 months. In the end the army, no longer liberal, put Alfonso on the throne as Alfonso XII (1874–85), in a coalition with the church and landowners. The 1876 constitution, recognising both monarchy and parliament, produced a sequence of orderly changes of government *(turnos)* between supposed conservatives and liberals. Little actually separated them in policy, and electoral rigging was the norm.

Social Unrest

The 1890s brought economic growth, improved schools and rumblings among the industrial working class. In the humiliating Spanish-American War of 1898, Spain lost the last of its once vast overseas possessions – Cuba, Puerto Rico, the Philippines and Guam.

Alfonso XIII (1902–30) was initially sensitive to the liberal mood but became fed up with constitutional government and started interfering. There were 33 different governments during his reign. His friends were among the military, wealthy landowners and the rich, powerful church.

At the other end of the social scale, a powder keg was forming. Industry had brought both prosperity and squalid slums to cities which had attracted large-scale migration from the country, like Barcelona, Madrid and some Basque cities. In the country, the old problems of underproduction and land ownership by the few persisted. Many Spaniards left for Latin America. The working class increasingly gravitated towards Marxism and anarchism.

Anarchism The anarchist ideas of the Russian Mikhail Bakunin had reached Spain in the 1860s and gained support rapidly. Bakunin advocated replacing the state and church with a free society in which people would voluntarily cooperate with each other – a state of affairs to be prepared for by strikes, sabotage and revolts, and ultimately achieved by a spontaneous, angry revolution of the oppressed. In the 1890s and 1900s anarchists bombed Barcelona's Liceu opera house, assassinated two prime ministers and detonated a bomb at Alfonso XIII's wedding in 1906, which killed 24 people.

Anarchism appealed to the peasants of Andalucía, Aragón, Catalunya and the north-west, and to workers living in appalling conditions in Barcelona and other cities. In 1910, the anarchist unions were organised by the syndicalists (anarchist trade unionists) into the powerful Confederación Nacional del Trabajo (CNT; National Confederation of Work). The syndicalists saw organisation of labour as the way to an anarchist society, their main weapon being the general strike.

Socialism This movement grew more slowly than anarchism because of its strategy of steady change through parliamentary processes. The Unión General de Trabajadores (UGT; General Union of Workers), established in 1888, was moderate and disciplined. Its appeal was greatest in Madrid and Bilbao, where people were fearful of Catalan separatism. Its sharpest growth was between 1906 and 1910. Spanish socialists rejected Soviet-style communism.

Regionalism Parallel with the rise of the left was the growth of Basque and Catalan separatism. In Catalunya, this was led by big business interests. Basque nationalism emerged in the 1890s, largely due to the perceived threat to Basque identity from the many Castilians who had flocked to work in Basque industries.

Semana Trágica & General Strikes
After Berbers wiped out a contingent of Spanish troops in Morocco, part of which was a Spanish protectorate, in 1909 the government called up Catalan reserves to go to Morocco. The result was the so-called Semana Trágica (Tragic Week) in Barcelona, which began with a general strike and turned into a frenzy of violence. The government responded by executing many workers.

Spain stayed neutral during WWI and enjoyed an economic boom. When the king and the right refused widespread demands for parliamentary reforms in 1917, a general strike ensued but was crushed by the army. Anarchist and socialist numbers grew, inspired by the Russian Revolution, and political violence and general mayhem continued, especially in lawless Barcelona.

Primo de Rivera's Dictatorship
In 1921, 10,000 Spanish soldiers were killed by a small force of Berbers at Anual in Morocco. The finger of blame was pointed at King Alfonso, who had intervened to select the Spanish commander for the Moroccan campaign. But just as a report on the event was to be submitted to parliament in 1923, General Miguel Primo de Rivera, an eccentric Andalucian aristocrat, led an army rising in support of the king, then launched his own mild, six-year dictatorship.

Primo was a centralist who censored the press and upset intellectuals but gained the cooperation of the socialist UGT. Anarchists went underground. Primo founded industries, improved roads, made the trains run on time and built dams and power plants. But eventually, with an economic downturn following the Wall St crash and discontent in the army, Alfonso took the chance to return to dismiss him.

Second Republic (1931–36)
Alfonso had brought the monarchy into too much disrepute to last long himself. When a new republican movement scored sweeping victories in municipal elections in 1931, the king left for exile in Italy. The Second Republic that followed was a tumultuous period that polarised Spain and ended in civil war.

The Left in Charge (1931–33) La Niña Bonita (the Pretty Child), as the Second

Republic was called by its supporters, was welcomed by leftists and the poor masses, but conservatives were alarmed. Strife began within a month of the king's departure. In Navarra a new Carlist pretender, Don Jaime, called on anti-Republicans to rise up. There were church burnings and lootings, mostly initiated by anarchists but also by those in the pay of the right.

Elections during 1931 brought in a government composed of socialists, the so-called Radicals (actually more like centrists) and the Republican Action Party. The Cortes contained few workers and no one from the anarchist CNT, which continued with strikes and violence to bring on the revolution.

A new constitution in December 1931 gave women the vote, ended Catholicism's status as the official religion, disbanded the Jesuits, stopped government payment of priests' salaries, legalised divorce and banned clerical orders from teaching. The constitution gave autonomy-minded Catalunya its own parliament in return for support of the republic, but socialists and the right saw this as a threat to national unity. The constitution also promised land redistribution, which pleased the Andalucian landless, but failed to deliver much.

The Right in Charge (1933–36)
Anarchist disruption, an economic slump, alienation of big business, the votes of newly enfranchised women and disunity on the left all helped the right win the 1933 election. The new Catholic party Confederación Española de Derechas Autónomas (CEDA; Spanish Confederation of Autonomous Rights) won the most seats. Other new forces on the right included the fascist Falange, led by José Antonio Primo de Rivera, son of the 1920s dictator. The Falange practised blatant street violence. The left, including the emerging communists (who, unlike the socialists, supported the Russian Revolution), called increasingly for revolution.

By 1934 violence was spiralling out of control. The socialist UGT called for a general strike, Catalunya's president declared his province independent (albeit within a putative federal Spanish republic) and workers' committees took over the northern mining region of Asturias after attacking police and army posts. All these moves were quashed, but in Asturias it took a campaign of violent repression by the Spanish Foreign Legion (set up to fight Moroccan tribes in the 1920s), led by generals Francisco Franco and José Millán Astray. The events in Asturias firmly divided the country into left and right.

Popular Front Government & Army Uprising
In the February 1936 elections the Popular Front, a left-wing coalition with communists at the fore, narrowly defeated the right-wing National Front. Now the left feared a coup, the right a revolution. Suspect generals were moved out of the way (Franco to the Canary Islands).

Violence continued on both sides. Extremist groups grew (the anarchist CNT now had over a million members) and peasants were on the verge of revolution.

On 17 July 1936 the Spanish army garrison in Melilla in North Africa revolted against the government, followed the next day by some garrisons on the mainland. The leaders of the plot were five generals, among them Franco, who on 19 July flew from the Canary Islands to Morocco to lead his legionnaires. The civil war had begun.

The Civil War (1936–39)
The Spanish Civil War split communities, families and friends. Both sides committed atrocious massacres and reprisals, and employed death squads to eliminate members of opposing organisations, in the early weeks especially. The rebels, who called themselves Nationalists because they thought they were fighting for Spain, shot or hanged tens of thousands of supporters of the republic. Republicans did likewise to Franco sympathisers, including some 7000 priests, monks and nuns. Political affiliation often provided a convenient cover for settling old scores. In the whole war an estimated 350,000 Spaniards died.

Much of the military and the Guardia Civil went over to the Nationalists, whose campaign quickly took on overtones of a

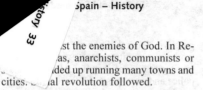

...st the enemies of God. In Re-
...as, anarchists, communists or
...ded up running many towns and
cities. ...ial revolution followed.

Nationalist Advance The basic battle
lines were drawn within a week of the rebellion in Morocco. Cities with military
garrisons that backed the rebels (most did)
and were strong enough to overcome any
opposition fell immediately into Nationalist
hands. North of Madrid, this meant everywhere except Catalunya, eastern Aragón,
the Basque coast, Cantabria and Asturias;
and in the south, western Andalucía and
Granada. Franco's force of legionnaires and
Moroccan mercenaries was airlifted from
Morocco to Sevilla by German warplanes in
August. Essential to the success of the revolt, they moved northwards through Extremadura towards Madrid, wiping out
fierce resistance in some cities. At Salamanca in October, Franco pulled all the Nationalists into line behind him, styling
himself as the Generalísimo (Supreme General). Before long he was to declare himself
head of state and adopt the title *caudillo,*
roughly equivalent to the German *Führer.*

Madrid, reinforced by the first battalions
of the International Brigades (armed foreign
idealists and adventurers organised by the
communists), repulsed Franco's first assault
in November then endured, under communist inspiration, over two years' siege.

Foreign Intervention In autumn 1936,
the International Brigades arrived to aid the
Republicans, but they never numbered
more than 20,000 and couldn't turn the tide
against the better armed and organised Nationalist forces.

Nazi Germany and Fascist Italy supported the Nationalists with weapons,
planes and men (75,000 from Italy, 17,000
from Germany), turning the war into a re-
hearsal for WWII. The Republicans had
some Soviet support – planes, tanks, artillery and advisers – but the rest of the international community refused to get
involved, although 25,000 or so French
fought on the Republican side. The war

came to be seen internationally as a struggle between fascism and communism, but it
was a more complex conflict than that –
and an essentially Spanish one, which
evolved from centuries-old tensions.

Republican Quarrels The Republican
government moved to Valencia in late 1936
to continue trying to preside over the diversity of political persuasions on the Republican side, from anarchists and communists
to moderate democrats and regional seces-
sionists. Barcelona was run for nearly a year
by anarchists and a Trotskyite militia called
the Partido Obrero de Unificación Marxista (POUM; Workers' Marxist Unification
Party). The Basques supported the Republic
because it promised them autonomy.

Italian and Nationalist troops took
Málaga in February 1937. In April German
planes bombed the Basque town of Gernika
(Guernica), causing terrible casualties; this
became the subject of Picasso's famous
pacifist painting. All the north coast fell in
the summer, giving the Nationalists control
of Basque industry. Republican counter-
attacks near Madrid and in Aragón failed.

Meanwhile tensions among the Republicans erupted into fierce street fighting in
Barcelona in May 1937, with the communists, who under Soviet influence were trying to unify the Republican war effort,
crushing the anarchists and Trotskyites. The
Republican government moved to Barcelona
in autumn 1937.

Nationalist Victory In early 1938 Franco
repulsed a Republican offensive at Teruel in
Aragón, then swept eastwards with 100,000
troops, 1000 planes and 150 tanks, isolating
Barcelona from Valencia. Italian bombers
from Mallorca started battering Barcelona.
In July the Republicans launched a last offensive as the Nationalists moved through
the Ebro valley. The bloody encounter, won
by the Nationalists, resulted in 20,000 dead.

The USSR withdrew from the war in
September 1938. In January 1939 the Nationalists took Barcelona unopposed. The
Republican government and hundreds of
thousands of supporters fled to France.

The Republicans still held Valencia and Madrid and had 500,000 people under arms, but internecine squabbling continued. In the end the Republican army simply evaporated. The Nationalists entered Madrid on 28 March 1939 and Franco declared the war over on 1 April.

Franco's Spain (1939–75)

War's Aftermath The Nationalist victors were merciless. Instead of reconciliation, more bloodletting ensued. Informing, private vendettas and executions were rife. An estimated 100,000 people were killed or died in prison after the war. The hundreds of thousands imprisoned included artists, intellectuals and teachers; others fled abroad, depriving Spain of a generation of scientists, artists, writers, educators and more.

Dictatorship Franco ruled absolutely. He was commander of the army and leader of both the government and the sole political party, the Movimiento Nacional (National Movement), a development of the Falange. The Cortes was merely a rubber stamp for decrees Franco chose to submit to it. Regional autonomy aspirations were not tolerated.

Franco hung on to power by never allowing any single powerful group – the church, the Movimiento, the army, monarchists or bankers – to dominate. The army provided many ministers and enjoyed a generous budget. Catholic orthodoxy was fully restored, with most secondary schools entrusted to the Jesuits, divorce made illegal and church weddings compulsory. The Movimiento was given control of press, propaganda and unions, with labour organised into 'vertical' unions covering entire sectors of the economy. Franco won some working-class support with carrots such as job security, paid holidays and social security, but there was no right to strike.

WWII & After WWII began a few months after the civil war ended. Franco kept Hitler at bay by promising an alliance but never committing himself to a date. Spanish communists and Republicans who had been in the French Resistance crossed the Pyrenees

General Francisco Franco was Spain's absolute ruler from 1939 to 1975.

to attack Franco's Spain but failed in September 1944; small guerrilla units continued a hopeless struggle in the north, Extremadura and Andalucía until the 1950s.

Franco's ambiguous stance during WWII won him no friends abroad. Spain was excluded from the United Nations and NATO and suffered a UN-sponsored trade boycott that helped turn the late 1940s into Spain's *años de hambre* (years of hunger). With the onset of the Cold War, Franco's anticommunism gained him some support. In 1953 he agreed to the USA's request for four bases in Spain in return for large sums in aid. In 1955 Spain was admitted to the UN.

Economic Miracle Spain was on the brink of insolvency by the late 1950s but the Stabilisation Plan of 1959, with its devaluation of the peseta and other deflationary measures, brought an economic upswing. The plan was engineered by a new breed of technocrats linked to the Catholic group Opus Dei (see the boxed text later in this chapter).

Spanish industry boomed. Thousands of young Spaniards went abroad to study and returned with a new attitude of teamwork. Modern machinery, techniques and marketing were introduced; transport was modernised; new dams provided irrigation and hydro power; and conservation and reforestation schemes reclaimed land from civil war blight and sheep grazing.

The recovery was funded in part by US aid and remittances from more than a million Spaniards working abroad, but above all by tourism, developed initially along Andalucía's Costa del Sol and Catalunya's Costa Brava. From 1960 to 1965, the annual number of tourists arriving in Spain jumped from four to 14 million.

Social Change A huge population shift from impoverished rural regions to the cities and tourist resorts took place. Many Andalucians went to Barcelona, with Sevilla, Valencia, Madrid and Bilbao also attracting people; elegant suburbs developed, as did shantytowns and, later, high-rise housing for the workers.

The Final Decade In 1964 Franco celebrated 25 years of peace, order and material progress. But the jails were still full of political prisoners and large garrisons were maintained outside every major city. Over the next decade, as the European economic boom faltered, labour strife grew and there were rumblings of discontent in the universities and even the army and church.

Regional problems resurfaced. The Basque nationalist terrorist group Euskadi Ta Askatasuna (ETA; Basques and Freedom), founded in 1959, gave cause for the declaration of six states of emergency between 1962 and 1975; heavy-handed police tactics won it support from Basque moderates.

Franco chose as his successor the Spanish-educated Prince Juan Carlos, grandson of Alfonso XIII (who had died in 1941). In 1969 Juan Carlos swore loyalty to Franco and the Movimiento Nacional.

Cautious reforms by Franco's last prime minister, Carlos Arias Navarro, produced violent reactions from right-wing extremists. By 1975 Spain seemed to be descending into chaos as Franco's health declined. Franco gave a final faltering speech, characteristically warning of a 'Judaeo-Masonic-Marxist conspiracy', in Madrid in October. On 20 November he died.

Transition to Democracy

Juan Carlos I & Adolfo Suárez Juan Carlos I, aged 37, took the throne two days later. The new king's links with Franco inspired little confidence in a Spain now clamouring for democracy. But Juan Carlos had kept his cards close to his chest and earned much of the credit for the successful transition to democracy that followed. He sacked prime minister Arias Navarro in July 1976, replacing him with Adolfo Suárez, a 43-year-old former Franco apparatchik with film-star looks. To general surprise, Suárez railroaded through the Francoist-filled Cortes a proposal for a new, two-chamber parliamentary system. Then in early 1977 political parties, trade unions and strikes were all legalised and the Movimiento Nacional was abolished.

New Constitution Suárez's centrist Unión del Centro Democrático (UCD; Union of the Democratic Centre) won nearly half the seats in the new Cortes in 1977. The left-of-centre Partido Socialista Obrero Español (PSOE; Spanish Socialist Worker Party), led by a charismatic young lawyer from Sevilla, Felipe González Márquez, came in second. In 1978 the Cortes passed a new constitution which made Spain a parliamentary monarchy with no official religion. In response to the regional autonomy fever that gripped Spain after the stiflingly centralist Franco era, the constitution also provided for a large measure of devolution. By 1983 this resulted in the country being divided into 17 'autonomous communities' with their own regional governments controlling a range of policy areas.

Social Liberation Personal and social life also enjoyed a rapid liberation after Franco. Contraceptives, homosexuality and divorce were legalised and during this era the *movida* (the late-night bar and *discoteca* scene that enables people almost anywhere in Spain to party till dawn or after) emerged. But Prime Minister Suárez faced mounting resistance from within his own party to further reforms in areas such as the police, army, education and legal system. In 1981 he resigned.

Attempted Coup During the investiture of Suárez's UCD successor, Leopoldo Calvo Sotelo, Lieutenant-Colonel Antonio Tejero Molina of the Guardia Civil marched with an armed detachment into the Cortes and held it captive for almost 24 hours. This attempted military putsch was snuffed out by the king, who made clear to any wavering generals that Tejero did not have his support. The nightmarish images of the wing-helmeted Tejero waving his pistol at cowering deputies proved to be the last spasm of Francoism's corpse.

The PSOE Years
In 1982 Spain made a final break with the past by voting the PSOE into power with a sizable overall majority. González was to be prime minister for 14 years.

Squeeze & Boom The PSOE's young, educated leadership came from the generation that had opened the cracks in the Franco regime in the late 1960s and early 70s. It legalised narcotics use in 1983 and abortion in 1985 (though in the face of major drug and alcoholism problems, public narcotics use was banned in 1992). The PSOE persuaded the unions to accept wage restraint and job losses to streamline industry. Unemployment rose from 16% to 22% by 1986. But in 1986 Spain joined the European Community (now the European Union, or EU), bringing on its second post-civil war boom, which lasted until 1991. Most Spaniards now had more money than ever before. The middle class grew ever bigger and Spain's traditionally stay-at-home women streamed into higher education and jobs.

The PSOE put a national health system in place by the early 1990s and made big improvements in state education, raising the university population to well over a million.

Slump & Scandal It was around halfway through the late 1980s boom that the good life began to go a bit sour. People observed that many of the glamorous new rich were making their money by property or share speculation, or plain corruption. Meanwhile, the government had failed to improve welfare provision for those left out of the fun.

In 1992 – five centuries after the country's pivotal year – Spain celebrated its return to the modern world in style with the Barcelona Olympics and the Expo 92 world fair in Sevilla. But the economy was now in slump (unemployment reached 22.5% the following year) and the PSOE was increasingly mired in scandals. Questions were asked about how it got hold of its substantial party funds. González's long-standing No 2, Alfonso Guerra, resigned as deputy prime minister in 1991 over an affair involving his wheeler-dealer brother's use of a government office.

It was a testament partly to González's personal appeal that the PSOE government survived the 1993 election. It lost its overall majority and had to rely on parliamentary support from the moderate Catalan nationalist party Convergència i Unió (CiU).

The slump bottomed out in 1993, but the scandals multiplied. Among the most bizarre was the case of Luis Roldán, the González-appointed head of the Guardia Civil from 1986 to 1993, who suddenly vanished in 1994 after being charged with embezzlement and bribery. He was arrested the following year in Bangkok and in 1997 went on trial in Spain for a raft of alleged crimes including taking over 352 million pesetas from secret slush funds set up to fight terrorism and organised crime. He was jailed for 28 years the following year.

Most damaging of all was the affair of the Grupos Antiterroristas de Liberación (GAL) death squads that had murdered 28 suspected ETA terrorists (several of whom were innocent) in France in the mid-1980s. A constant stream of GAL allegations and rumours contributed to the PSOE's electoral defeat in 1996. In 1998 a dozen senior police and PSOE men were jailed in connection with the affair, including José Barrionuevo, who had been González's interior minister in the mid-1980s.

PP Rule
The 1996 general election was won by the centre-right Partido Popular (PP; People's Party), led by José María Aznar, an Elton John fan and former tax inspector. The PP,

however, failed to get an overall majority and like the preceding PSOE government had to govern through a parliamentary alliance, this time with the CiU and other regional parties. One concession Aznar had to make was to allow Spain's 17 regional governments to spend 30% of the income tax raised in their regions (up from 15%), a move that pleased wealthy regions such as Catalunya but not the poorer ones.

Aznar cut public investment, sold off state enterprises and liberalised sectors such as telecommunications. In 1997 employers and unions signed a deal reforming Spain's employment contract and dismissal system: sackings were made easier but it was expected that more jobs would be created. By 1998 the economy was doing well and in 1999 Spain met the criteria for launching the new European currency, the euro.

At the time of the 2000 general election, Spain had the fastest growing economy in the EU. Since the PP came to power, unemployment had fallen from 23% to 15% – the highest in the EU. But these figures conceal the facts that an unusually high number of Spanish housewives claim the dole and that many who are officially jobless benefit from a big black economy and Spain's tradition of family support. The Aznar government had so far avoided damaging scandals, remained economically liberal and on church policy kept church traditionalists at a safe distance, disarming those who tarred the PP with the brush of being descended from a party originally formed by a former Franco minister.

The 2000 election was a triumph for Aznar and the PP, which gained the first-ever overall parliamentary majority for a centre-right party in democratic Spain. The PSOE had made an electoral alliance with the communist-led Izquierda Unida (IU; United Left) that excited few, and the PSOE's new leader, Joaquín Almunia, resigned immediately after the election. He was replaced by José Luis Rodríguez Zapatero, a 39-year-old lawyer from Castilla y León. Zapatero made a bright start in his new job by sweeping most previous PSOE high-ups, including Felipe González, out of the party hierarchy.

ETA The one field in which the PP has notably failed to make progress is the problem of the Basque terrorist organisation ETA. Thought to have been all but dismantled by the security forces in the early 1990s, the ETA returned in a big way in 1997 and 1998 with a chilling assassination campaign aimed largely at PP local councillors. Then in September 1998 it announced its first-ever cease-fire without a time limit. Some of ETA's latest killings have provoked particularly widespread outrage and prompted calls for talks and peace by nonviolent Basque nationalists. However, it's equally likely that ETA just wanted a breathing space in which to regroup after a series of recent arrests of its leading operatives and the jailing of the entire leadership of its political wing Herri Batasuna (HB).

The cease-fire did not, in any case, mean an end to street violence – fire bombs at the homes and businesses of opposition politicians, burnings of vehicles, bars, phone boxes and so on – in the Basque Country. The cease-fire ended in late 1999: vehicles carrying huge loads of explosives were intercepted en route to Madrid, and in 2000, assassinations started again, with an army officer, a PSOE politician and his bodyguard, and a journalist critical of ETA among the first victims. ETA has now murdered about 800 people in its three decades of existence.

What ETA wants is an independent, sovereign state, which covers the Basque Country, Navarra and the French Basque country. The nonviolent Basque independence parties, led by the Partido Nacionalista Vasco (PNV), have the same goal but do not use violence to attain it. Proindependence parties won 38% of the votes in the Basque Country at the general election in 2000, despite a boycott called by HB's electoral platform, Euskal Herritarok (Basque Citizens). The Aznar government refuses to talk to ETA unless it renounces violence.

GEOGRAPHY

Spain is probably Europe's most geographically diverse country, ranging from the near-deserts of eastern Andalucía to the green countryside and deep coastal inlets of Galicia, and from the sunbaked uplands of Castilla-La Mancha to the rugged, snow-capped Pyrenees. It covers 84% of the Iberian Peninsula and spreads over nearly 505,000 sq km, making it the biggest country in Western Europe after France.

Uplands

Spain is a mountainous country and with an average altitude of 650m it's the highest European country after Switzerland. In the past this rugged topography not only separated Spain's destiny from that of the rest of Europe, but also encouraged the rise of separate small states in both the Christian and Islamic parts of medieval Spain.

Meseta & Cordillera Central At the heart of Spain and occupying 40% of the country is the meseta – a tableland of boundless horizons, 400 to 1000m high. It covers most of Castilla y León, Castilla-La Mancha and Extremadura. Apart from a few major cities (including Madrid), the meseta is sparsely populated and much given over to grain-growing, although vineyards and long lines of olive trees stretch across the south, while Extremadura boasts extensive pastures.

Contrary to what Henry Higgins taught Eliza Dolittle, the meseta is not where most of Spain's rain falls, nor is it really a plain! Much of Castilla y León is rolling plains and hills, and the meseta is split in two by the Cordillera Central mountain chain, running from north-east of Madrid to the Portuguese border. Its two main ranges are the Sierra de Guadarrama north of Madrid and the Sierra de Gredos to the west, both of which reach above 2400m. South of the cordillera are the lower Montes de Toledo and Sierra de Guadalupe.

Mountains Around the Meseta On all sides except the west (where it slopes gradually down across Portugal), the meseta is bounded by mountain chains.

Across the north, close to the Bay of Biscay (Mar Cantábrico), is the damp Cordillera Cantábrica, straddling Castilla y León's borders with Cantabria and Asturias and rising above 2500m in the spectacular Picos de Europa. In the north-west the Montes de León and associated ranges cut off Galicia from the meseta.

The Sistema Ibérico runs down from wine-growing La Rioja to the olive orchards of southern Aragón, peaks at 2316m in the Sierra de Moncayo and varies from plateaus and high moorland to deep gorges and strangely eroded rock formations as in the Serranía de Cuenca.

The southern boundary of the meseta is the low, wooded Sierra Morena running across northern Andalucía.

Outlying Mountains Spain's highest mountains, however, lie on or towards its edges. The Pyrenees stretch 400km along the French border, from the Mediterranean Sea to the Bay of Biscay, and reach down into Catalunya, Aragón and Navarra, with the foothills extending west into the Basque Country. There are numerous 3000m peaks in Catalunya and Aragón, the highest being Aragón's Pico de Aneto (3408m).

Across southern and eastern Andalucía stretches the Cordillera Bética, a rumpled mass of ranges which includes mainland Spain's highest peak, Mulhacén (3478m), in the Sierra Nevada south-east of Granada. This system continues east into Murcia and southern Valencia, dips under the Mediterranean, then re-emerges as the Balearic islands of Ibiza and Mallorca. On Mallorca it rises to over 1400m in the Serra de Tramuntana. The other main Balearic island, Menorca, is a tip of the same underwater massif as Sardinia and Corsica.

Lowlands

Around and between all the mountains are five main, lower-lying areas.

Fertile Catalunya, in the north-east, is composed mainly of ranges of lower hills.

The Ebro basin, between the Sistema Ibérico to its south and the Cordillera Cantábrica and Pyrenees to its north, supports wine production in La Rioja, grain-growing in Navarra, and horticulture in eastern Aragón, although other parts of Aragón are near-desert.

Galicia in the north-west is hilly and green, with mixed farming; it's reminiscent of other Celtic lands such as Ireland and Brittany.

The coastal areas of Valencia and Murcia are dry plains transformed by irrigation into green *huertas* (market gardens and orchards). Similar areas farther south, around Almería in eastern Andalucía, are virtually desert.

The Guadalquivir basin, stretching across Andalucía between the Sierra Morena and Cordillera Bética, is a highly fertile zone where a wide range of produce, from grain to olives and citrus fruit, is grown.

Rivers

The major rivers are the Ebro, Duero, Tajo (Tagus), Guadiana and Guadalquivir, each draining a different basin between the mountains. These rivers, and many of their tributaries, are dammed here and there into long, snaking reservoirs to provide much of Spain's water and electricity.

The Ebro is the largest in volume, rising in the Cordillera Cantábrica and draining the southern side of the Pyrenees and the northern side of the Sistema Ibérico. It flows across north-eastern Castilla y León, La Rioja, Navarra and Aragón to enter the Mediterranean Sea in southern Catalunya.

The other major rivers empty into the Atlantic Ocean. The Duero flows west from the northern Sistema Ibérico and drains the northern half of the meseta, then continues across Portugal as the Douro.

The Tajo and the Guadiana rise in the southern Sistema Ibérico and flow across the southern half of the meseta, the Tajo draining the part north of the Montes de Toledo and the sluggish Guadiana draining the southern part. The Tajo continues west across Portugal to Lisbon as the Tejo, while the Guadiana turns south (its last stretch into the Golfo de Cádiz forms the Portuguese border).

The Guadalquivir flows from east to west across the middle of Andalucía.

Coasts

Spain's coasts are as varied as its interior.

Mediterranean Coast The long Mediterranean coast begins in the north with Catalunya's Costa Brava (Rugged Coast), pockmarked with rocky coves and inlets that have to some extent restricted the growth of concrete tourist resorts. The Costa Daurada, south of Barcelona, and the Costa del Azahar, north of Valencia, are flatter, with some long, sandy beaches and fairly mundane resorts (lively Sitges excepted). Sea temperatures on the *costas* (coasts) average 19°C or 20°C in June and October and a comfortable 22°C to 24°C from July to September.

South of Valencia, there are some attractive coves around Denia and Jávea, before the coast travels around Cabo La Nao to the infamous Costa Blanca, whose good, sandy beaches are disfigured by concrete package resorts such as Benidorm and Torrevieja. Alicante, like Málaga on the Costa del Sol, is a refreshingly Spanish city amid all this. Murcia's Mar Menor lagoon has warm waters, more good beaches and more high-rise development, but the hard-to-reach beaches on the Golfo de Mazarrón, west of Cartagena, are almost undeveloped. Sea temperatures on the Costa Blanca and the Murcian coast are mainland Spain's warmest: a degree or two higher than farther north.

Entering Andalucía, there's more resort development at Mojácar before you reach the rugged, beautiful 50km coast around Cabo de Gata, where mountains and near-desert come right down to beaches lapped by warm, turquoise waters. Several beaches here can only be reached by foot or boat. Immediately west of Almería is a narrow coastal plain covered by hideous plastic greenhouses. Beyond here the Costa del Sol stretches between Málaga and Gibraltar, where the package-tourism pressure cookers of Torremolinos, Fuengirola and Marbella form an almost continuously built-up strip 70km long. Surprisingly, Andalucian coastal waters are generally a couple of degrees cooler than Catalunya's.

Atlantic Coasts The Atlantic coasts have a wilder climate and colder seas than the Mediterranean.

The Costa de la Luz, much less developed than the Costa del Sol, stretches north-west from Tarifa, west of Gibraltar, to the Portuguese border. It has some fine, wide, dune-backed beaches, especially south of Cádiz and west of the Guadalquivir delta, which is an important water-bird and wildlife habitat.

Galicia's coast is Spain's most rugged, deeply indented with majestic estuaries called *rías,* dotted with appealing coves, beaches and fishing villages, and almost ignored by foreign package tourism. The Rías Bajas on the west-facing coast are the best known, but the Rías Altas on the north-facing coast are just as impressive in decent weather and include Spain's most awesome cliffs, at Cabo Ortegal and Serra de la Capelada.

All along the Bay of Biscay, the Cordillera Cantábrica comes almost down to the coast, providing a fine backdrop for resorts big and small (the biggest are Santander and San Sebastián), many of which have good beaches, and surfing centres such as Zarautz and Mundaka.

Balearic Islands The waters here are warmer than on the mainland, averaging 21°C in June and October and 25°C in August. The north coast of Mallorca is lined with high, wild cliffs and the hard-to-reach beaches on its coves are much quieter than those around Palma de Mallorca, on Mallorca's lower-lying east coast. Menorca is perhaps the islands' best-kept secret, and peppered with deserted coves and beaches awash in limpid, unspoiled waters. Ibiza and Formentera too are dotted by little beaches, but few with the stunning pristine beauty encountered in Menorca.

CLIMATE
The meseta and the Ebro basin have a continental climate: scorching in summer, cold in winter and dry. Madrid regularly freezes in December, January and February and temperatures climb above 30°C in July and August (locals describe it as: *nueve meses de invierno y tres de infierno* – nine months

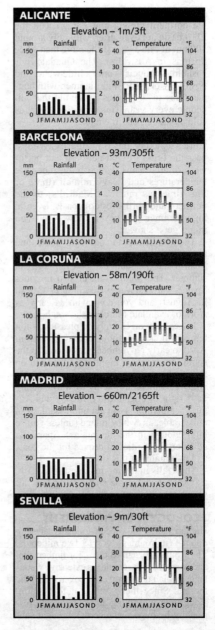

of winter and three of hell). Valladolid on the northern meseta and Zaragoza in the Ebro basin are even drier, with only around 300mm of rain a year (little more than Alice Springs in Australia). The Guadalquivir basin in Andalucía is only a little wetter and positively broils in high summer, with temperatures of 35°C-plus in Sevilla that kill people every year. This area doesn't get as cold as the meseta in winter.

The Pyrenees and the Cordillera Cantábrica backing the Bay of Biscay coast bear the brunt of cold northern and north-western airstreams, which bring moderate temperatures and heavy rainfall (three or four times as much as Madrid's) to the northern and north-western coasts. Even in high summer you never know when you might get a shower.

The Mediterranean coast as a whole, and the Balearic Islands, get a little more rain than Madrid and the south can be even hotter in summer. The Mediterranean also provides Spain's warmest waters (reaching 27°C or so in August) and you *can* swim as early as April or even late March in the south-east.

In general you can rely on pleasant or hot temperatures just about everywhere from April to early November (plus March in the south, but minus a month at either end on the northern and north-western coasts). In Andalucía there are plenty of warm, sunny days right through winter. In July and August, temperatures can get unpleasant, even unbearable, anywhere inland (unless you're high enough in the mountains). Spaniards abandon their cities in droves for the coast and mountains at this time.

Snowfalls in the mountains start as early as October and some snow cover lasts all year on the highest peaks.

ECOLOGY & ENVIRONMENT

Human hands have been radically altering Spain's environment for over two millennia. The Romans began to cut – for timber, fuel and weapons – the country's extensive woodlands, which until then even covered half the meseta. Since then, further deforestation, along with overtilling and overgrazing (especially by huge sheep herds), brought substantial topsoil erosion: most of the fertile 300-sq-km delta of the Río Ebro has been formed by eroded deposits in the past 600 years. Many animal species were drastically depleted by hunting. Urban and industrial growth, and in the 20th century the construction of hundreds of dams for hydroelectricity and irrigation, caused further change.

The resulting situation, judged by how well Spain's environment today can sustain human, animal and plant life, doesn't seem too bad. Despite uncertain rainfall and, in many areas, impoverished soils, the country supports a varied, often low-tech agriculture, although the irrigation and chemicals on which agriculture in part depends have brought problems. By European standards Spain is sparsely populated and most of its people live in towns and cities, which reduces their impact on the countryside. There's still lots of wilderness. Serious urban pollution is limited, since Spain is relatively lightly industrialised and urban authorities have taken appropriate action in many places. Protection given to many animal and bird species and some plant species has probably saved some, although it's probably too late for others.

Conservation

Environmental awareness took a huge leap forward in the post-Franco 1980s. The PSOE government made environmental pollution a crime and spurred a range of actions by regional governments, which now have responsibility for most environmental matters. In 1981 Spain had just 35 environmentally protected areas, covering 2200 sq km. Now there are over 400, covering more than 25,000 sq km (see Reserves & National Parks in the Flora & Fauna section later in this chapter).

Different regions give conservation different priorities: Andalucía has over 80 protected areas, while neighbouring Extremadura has just three. Nor are protected areas always well protected, often because their ecosystems extend beyond their own boundaries. Most notoriously, in 1998 the vital Doñana wetlands in Andalucía were damaged by a major spill of acids and heavy metals into a river that feeds them. Other wetlands, such as Catalunya's Ebro delta and Valencia's Albufera, have been damaged by pesticide pollution.

Of Spain's approximately 630 vertebrate species, 43 are considered in danger of extinction and a further 121 are rare or vulnerable. Loss of habitat is a major threat to many animal species. Of the 8000 plant species on the mainland and Balearic Islands, 82 are in danger of extinction and 585 rare or vulnerable. Plants are also threatened by ploughing, grazing, tourism and collection; some animals are threatened by illegal hunting.

See the Flora & Fauna section for more information on threats to animal and bird species, and Treatment of Animals in the Society & Conduct section for more on hunting.

Drought

Potentially Spain's worst environmental problem is drought. It struck in the 1950s and 60s, and again in the first half of the 1990s, despite huge investment in reservoirs (which number around 1300 and cover a higher proportion of Spain than of any other country in the world) and projects such as the Tajo-Segura water diversion system. This project can transfer 600 million cubic metres of water a year from the Tajo basin in central Spain to the heavily irrigated Valencia and Murcia regions on the Mediterranean coast. The 1990s drought damaged southern agriculture, brought water rationing for 10 million people, and even led to talk of water being shipped in by sea to keep tourism going on the Costa del Sol. However, the drought was broken by three wet winters from 1995 to 1998, which staved off disaster and filled up the reservoirs – for a while, at least.

Water is money in Spain and, when it's in short supply, local politicians often aren't keen to see it transferred out of their regions. In 1994 the government had to intervene to compel Castilla-La Mancha to transfer 55 million cubic metres to Murcia and Valencia. Plans for a 6000 billion peseta investment to ensure that all of Spain has adequate water supplies face similar political hurdles. The 'dry' regions are Andalucía, Castilla-La Mancha, Extremadura, Valencia, Murcia and parts of the Ebro basin in Aragón.

Other Problems

Although Spain's many dams and reservoirs provide irrigation and hydroelectricity (reducing the need for nuclear or dirtier forms of power) and conserve water, they inevitably destroy habitats.

Vegetables growing under huge areas of plastic in the south-east and plantations of thirsty eucalyptus trees (now going out of fashion) could destroy the natural vegetation of some areas.

Intensive agriculture and the spread of towns and cities (including tourist resorts) have lowered water tables in some areas, threatening vegetation and the quality of water supplies. Growing coastal urban areas add to the pollution of the seas, although sewage treatment facilities are being constantly improved. Spain gets creditable numbers of EU 'blue flags' for its beaches, indicating that they meet certain minimal standards of hygiene and facilities.

Industrial pollution is probably at its worst around Bilbao in Basque Country and the small, chemical-producing town of Avilés in Asturias.

FLORA & FAUNA
Flora

The variety of Spain's flora is astonishing, as anyone who witnesses the spectacular wildflower displays on roadsides and pastures in spring and early summer will testify. Mainland Spain and the Balearic Islands contain around 8000 of Europe's 9000 plant species, and 2000 of them are unique to the Iberian Peninsula (and North Africa). This abundance is largely due to the fact that the last Ice Age did not cover the entire peninsula, enabling plants killed off farther north to survive in Spain.

High-Altitude Plants Spain's many mountain areas claim much of the variety. The Pyrenees have about 150 unique species and even the much smaller Sierra Nevada in Andalucía has about 60. When the snows melt, the alpine and subalpine zones (above the tree line) bloom spectacularly with small rock-clinging plants and gentians, orchids, crocuses, narcissi and sundews. Particularly good orchid areas are the alpine meadows of the Picos de Europa (with 40 species) and the Serranía de Cuenca in the Sistema Ibérico.

Mountain Forests Higher mountain forests tend to be coniferous and are often commercial. The silver fir is common in the Pyrenees and Sistema Ibérico, while the Spanish fir is confined to a few small areas in western Andalucía. The Scots pine, with its flaking red bark, is common on the cooler northern mountains; the umbrella pine, with its large spreading top and edible kernel, is more common near coasts. Many pine forests are threatened by the pine processionary moth, whose hairy caterpillars devour pine needles. The caterpillars' large silvery nests are easy to spot in the trees; touching the caterpillars can provoke a nasty allergic reaction (see Cuts, Stings & Bites in the Health section of the Facts for the Visitor chapter). Deciduous forests – predominantly beech but also Pyrenean oak and other trees – are found mainly on the lower slopes of the damp northern mountains. Many orchids grow on forest floors.

Lowland Forests Mixed forests are dotted over the lowlands and meseta, and occasionally elsewhere. Many contain two useful evergreen oaks: the cork oak *(alcornoque),* whose thick bark is stripped every nine years for cork *(corcho),* and the holm or ilex oak *(encina),* whose acorns are gobbled up by pigs destined to become *jamón ibérico* (see the special section 'Eating & Drinking in Spain'). Where the tree cover is scattered, the resulting combined woodland-pastures are known as *dehesas.* These areas mostly occur in the south-western meseta and bloom with flowers in early summer. Mixed forests may also contain conifers for timber or eucalypts grown for wood pulp.

Scrub & Steppe Where there's no woodland and no agriculture, the land is often maquis scrub or steppe. Maquis occurs

where forests were felled and the land was then abandoned. Herbs such as lavender, rosemary and thyme are typical maquis plants, as are shrubs of the cistus family in the south and gorse, juniper, heather and the strawberry tree in the north. If the soil is acidic, there may also be broom. Orchids, gladioli and irises may flower beneath these shrubs, which are colourful in spring.

Steppe is produced by overgrazing or occurs naturally in hot, dry climates. Much of the Ebro valley and Castilla-La Mancha are steppe, as is the almost desert-like Cabo de Gata in Andalucía. These areas burst into colour after rain.

Fauna
Spain's wildlife is among Europe's most varied thanks to its wild terrain, which has allowed the survival of several species that have died out in many other countries, though some are now in perilously small numbers. Many of Spain's wild animals are nocturnal and you need to be both dedicated and lucky to track them down.

Mammals There are about 70 brown bears *(osos pardos)* in the Cordillera Cantábrica, and a few in the Pyrenees (mostly on the French side). Though hunting or killing these bears has been banned since 1973, their numbers have remained the same since the mid-1980s, despite conservation programs that cost 200 million pesetas in the 1990s. Bear experts complain of a low priority given to bear conservation by local administrations. The Pyrenean population is effectively extinct (although the French are attempting to boost numbers by importing bears from Slovenia) and its Cantabrian counterpart may be going that way too. In 1900 Spain had about 1000 brown bears: hunting and poisoning (accidental and deliberate) have been the main reasons for their decline.

Up to 2000 wolves *(lobos)* survive, mostly in the mountains of Galicia and north-western Castilla y León (the province of Zamora has the most wolves), though there are a few in the Sierra Morena in the provinces of Córdoba, Jaén and Ciudad Real. Though heavily protected, they're still regarded as an enemy by many local people. Farmers complain that they have to wait far too long for the compensation they are entitled to when their livestock is killed by wolves.

Things look better for the ibex *(cabra montés),* a stocky, high-mountain goat whose males have distinctive, long horns. It spends summer hopping agilely around high crags and descends to pastures in winter. Almost hunted to extinction by 1900, the ibex was protected by royal decree a few years later. There are now an estimated 70,000, the main populations being in the Sierra de Gredos and Andalucía.

The Iberian or pardel lynx *(lince ibérico),* unique to the Iberian Peninsula and smaller than the lynx of northern Europe, is considered the world's most endangered feline. Its numbers have been reduced to less than 600 in Spain and under 50 in Portugal by hunting and by a decline in the numbers of rabbits, its staple food. Now stringently protected, it lives in wild southern and western woodlands, including Parque Nacional de Doñana and Parque Natural Monfragüe.

Less uncommon beasts – though you'd still need to go looking for them – include the mainly nocturnal wild boar *(jabalí),* which likes thick woods, marshes and farmers' root crops; the red, roe and fallow deer *(ciervo, corzo, gamo)* found in forests and woodlands of all types; and the nocturnal genet *(gineta),* rather like a short-legged cat with a white coat spotted with black, and a long, striped tail, living in woodland and scrub in the south and north. The chamois *(rebeco, sarrio, isard* or *gamuza),* not unlike a smaller, shorter-horned ibex but actually a member of the antelope family, lives above and just within the tree line in the Pyrenees and the Cordillera Cantábrica, descending to pastures in winter. Other wild animals include the red squirrel *(ardilla)* in mountain forests; the mainly nocturnal Egyptian mongoose *(meloncillo)* in woods, scrub and marshes in the southern half of the country; the otter *(nutria);* the beech marten *(garduña)* in scattered deciduous forests and on rocky outcrops and cliffs; and the pine marten *(marta)* in some Pyrenees pine forests.

KATE NOLAN

The Iberian or pardel lynx is unique to Spain, where it is a fiercely protected species.

Birds of Prey Around 25 species of birds of prey, some of them summer visitors from Africa, breed in Spain. In the mountains or on the meseta you'll often see them circling or hovering. (Identifying them is a different matter! For some useful field guides, see Books in the Facts for the Visitor chapter.) Parque Natural Monfragüe and the Serranía de Cuenca are two places particularly noted for birds of prey.

The threatened lammergeier, with its majestic 2m-plus wingspan, is recovering slowly in the high Pyrenees (to 55 pairs in 1996) and is being reintroduced in its other Spanish habitat, the Sierra de Cazorla. Poisoned food and furtive hunting have been the bird's main threats. Its Spanish name, *quebrantahuesos* (bone-breaker), reflects its habit of smashing bones by dropping them on to rocks, so it can get at the marrow.

Spain's few hundred pairs of black vulture *(buitre negro),* Europe's biggest bird of prey, are probably the world's biggest population. Its strongholds are in the Sierra Pelada in western Andalucía, Parque Natural Monfragüe in Extremadura, the Montes de Toledo in Castilla-La Mancha and the Sierra de la Peña de Francia in Castilla y León.

Another emblematic bird is the Spanish imperial eagle *(águila imperial),* which was almost killed off by hunting and the decline in the rabbit population. Its white shoulders distinguish it from other imperial eagles. Around 130 pairs remain in such places as the Parque Nacional de Doñana, Parque Natural Monfragüe, the Pyrenees and Cantabria. Poisoned bait put out by farmers or hunters is its greatest enemy.

Other notable large birds of prey include the golden eagle *(águila real)*, griffon vulture *(buitre leonado)* and Egyptian vulture *(alimoche)*, all found in high mountain re-gions. Smaller birds of prey include the kestrel *(cernícalo)* and buzzard *(ratonero)*, which are both common, the sparrowhawk *(gavilán)*, various harriers *(aguiluchos)* and the acrobatic red kite *(milano real)* and black kite *(milano negro)*. Many of them are found around deciduous or lowland woods and forests. Black kites may be seen over open ground near marshes and rubbish dumps.

Flying High

Being the white stork's summer holiday destination can sometimes overwhelm a Spanish *pueblo*. Malpartida de Cáceres (population 2500) in Extremadura found itself virtually under siege in 1997: 534 storks came to stay that summer.

Look atop a church tower, tree or pylon in the centre, west or south-west of Spain and you'll probably spot one of the huge, ungainly nests in which the white stork *(Ciconia ciconia)*, known to Spaniards as a *cigüeña blanca*, makes its summer home. You may well hear them before you see them, thanks to their chicks' cacophonous clacking of their long bills to demand food from their parents. White storks don't chirp cheerfully like most feathery species as they lack sufficiently developed vocal cords.

Spain is the first leg in one of two migration routes for the stork from Africa. Crossing at the Strait of Gibraltar, flocks of as many as 3000 sweep northwards in January or February. These graceful beasts of the air rely heavily on thermals and updraughts to soar along their way – wing flapping is strictly for the (other) birds. As they pair off to breed, they abandon the crowd, build their impressive 60cm-high nests and hunker down to raise a family.

Many content themselves with a Spanish summer holiday, particularly in Andalucía, Extremadura and the two Castillas. But some don't even bother returning to Africa for the winter.

Back in the 1970s the species looked seriously threatened but the situation has since been reversed. One theory attributes this to one of humankind's less commendable products – refuse dumps. Storks feast on what people reject. It was estimated in 2000 that about 17,000 stork pairs reside in Spain – counting chicks, there could be as many as 80,000. Elsewhere in Europe their numbers are decreasing as their natural habitat is destroyed.

In Spain the main stork route and biggest concentration of nests lies across Extremadura. You'll be hard pressed *not* to see (and hear) them around Mérida, Cáceres, Trujillo, Plasencia and Jarandilla.

The white stork is one of 17 species of stork, related to herons, ibises and flamingos. It grows to about 1m, is white with black flight feathers and sports a dark red bill and red legs. The only other stork species in Europe is the less gregarious black stork *(Ciciona nigra)*, called the *cigüeña negra* in Spanish. The black stork too crosses from Africa at the Strait of Gibraltar, but tends to nest on cliff ledges and shy away from people – with good reason. Its population has dropped to as few as 200 pairs, as people have polluted watering and feeding places, but seems stable. Its stronghold is the western part of the southern meseta, especially Parque Natural Monfragüe.

KATE NOLAN

Water Birds Spain is a haven for numerous water birds, thanks to some large wetland areas. The most famous and important of the wetlands is the Guadalquivir delta in Andalucía, large sections of which are included in the Parque Nacional de Doñana and its buffer zones. Hundreds of thousands of birds winter here and many more call in during spring and autumn migrations. Other important coastal wetlands are the Albufera de Valencia, and the Ebro delta and Aiguamolls de l'Empordà in Catalunya.

Inland, thousands of ducks *(pato)* winter on the Tablas de Daimiel wetlands in Castilla-La Mancha, and, with cranes *(grulla)* too, at Laguna de Gallocanta, Spain's biggest natural lake (though it can virtually dry up in summer), 50km south of Calatayud in Aragón. Laguna de Fuente de Piedra near Antequera in Andalucía is Europe's main breeding site for the greater flamingo *(flamenco)*, with as many as 16,000 pairs rearing chicks in spring and summer. This beautiful pink bird can also be seen in many wetlands along the Mediterranean and southern Atlantic coasts, including in the Ebro delta and Parque Nacional de Doñana and on Cabo de Gata.

Other Birds Two species of rare large birds famous for their elaborate male courtship displays are the great bustard *(avutarda)*, which inhabits the plains of the meseta, and the capercaillie *(urogallo)*, a kind of giant black grouse, in the northern mountain woodlands. Spain has perhaps 8000 great bustards, more than the rest of Europe combined, though the bird is under pressure from the modernisation of agriculture. Weighing up to 14kg, the male in flight has been compared to a goose with eagle's wings.

Among the most colourful of Spain's many other birds are the golden oriole *(oropéndola)*, in orchards and deciduous woodlands in summer (the male has an unmistakable, bright-yellow body); the orange, black and white hoopoe *(abubilla)*, with its distinctive crest, which is common in open woodlands, on farmland and golf courses; and the gold, brown and turquoise bee-eater *(abejaruco)*, which nests in sandy banks in summer. All three are more common in the south. Various woodpeckers *(pitos or picos)* and owls *(búhos)* inhabit mountain woodlands.

Other Fauna Most of Europe's butterflies are found in Spain, including some unique to the Iberian Peninsula. There are also 20-odd bat species, four types of salamander, midwife toads, chameleons in Andalucía's Axarquía region, snakes and numerous lizards. Gibraltar is famous for its Barbary macaques, the only wild monkeys in Europe.

Twenty-seven species of marine mammals, including several each of whale and dolphin, live off Spain's shores. Cabo de Peñas, near Gijón on the Bay of Biscay, is a noted gathering ground. In the Mediterranean, some species are threatened by driftnet fishing (though this is not practised by Spanish fishing boats). Dolphin-spotting boat trips are a popular attraction at Gibraltar.

For information on Spain's few dangerous beasts, see Health in the Facts for the Visitor chapter.

National Parks & Reserves

Much of Spain's most spectacular and ecologically important country – about 40,000 sq km if you include national hunting reserves – is under some kind of official protection. Nearly all these areas are at least partly open to visitors, but degrees of conservation and access vary. For example, *Parques naturales* (natural parks), the most numerous category of protected area, may include villages with hotels, *hostales* (budget hotels) and camping grounds, or may limit access to a few walking trails with the nearest accommodation 10km away. A few reserves require special permits and others include sections with no public access. Fortunately, the most interesting usually have visitor centres with ample suggestions about how to spend your time. You'll find information on access, accommodation etc under specific destinations in this book.

National Parks The *Parques nacionales* are areas of exceptional importance for their fauna, flora, geomorphology or landscape and are the most strictly controlled protected areas. They are declared by the national parliament and administered by the national and regional governments. Mainland Spain and the Balearic Islands had, at the time of writing, eight national parks:

- Cabañeros in the Montes de Toledo, also in Castilla-La Mancha, with a high diversity of flora and fauna owing to unusual cultivation patterns in the past
- Parc Nacional d'Aigüestortes i Estany de Sant Maurici in the Catalan Pyrenees
- Parque Nacional Archipiélago de Cabrera, a group of rocky islets in the Balearic Islands
- Parque Nacional de Doñana in Andalucía's Guadalquivir delta, a vital haven for birds and mammals
- Parque Nacional de Ordesa y Monte Perdido, a spectacular section of the Aragón Pyrenees, with over 30 mammal species and a bird population that includes the lammergeier
- Parque Nacional de los Picos de Europa, a mountain refuge for endangered species straddling Asturias, Cantabria and Castilla y León
- Parque Nacional de las Tablas de Daimiel, a wetland area in Castilla-La Mancha
- Sierra Nevada in Andalucía, Spain's newest (1999) and biggest (862 sq km) national park, covering the upper parts of the highest mountain range on the mainland, with over 60 endemic plant species

The number of national parks is growing. The Islas Cíes off Galicia, an important seabird nesting ground, will probably be the next to be added to the list.

Other Protected Areas These are administered by Spain's 17 regional governments. There are hundreds of them, falling into at least 16 classifications and ranging in size from 100-sq-m rocks off the Balearics to the mountainous 2140-sq-km Parque Natural de Cazorla in Andalucía, famous for its abundant wildlife, 2300 plant species and beautiful mountain scenery.

Other important and interesting reserves include:

- Áreas Naturales de la Serra de Tramuntana, covering most of a spectacular mountain range on Mallorca
- Parc Natural Delta de l'Ebre in Catalunya, a wetland area vital for birds
- Parque Natural Monfragüe in Extremadura, with spectacular birds of prey
- Parque Natural Sierra de Grazalema in Andalucía, one of Spain's wettest and most beautiful mountain areas, with rich birdlife
- Parc Natural S'Albufera d'es Grau, a wetland area on Menorca, which was central to the whole island being declared a Unesco biosphere reserve in 1993

Reservas Nacionales de Caza Protected areas include some 15,000 sq km of National Hunting Reserves, which are usually well conserved for the sake of the wildlife that is to be hunted. Public access to these areas is usually pretty open (some hunting reserves include villages or towns) and you may well hike or drive across one without even knowing it. If you hear shots, though, be careful!

GOVERNMENT & POLITICS

Since 1978, three years after the death of Franco, Spain has been a constitutional monarchy. The king is commander of the armed forces, a role that proved decisive in the February 1981 coup attempt, when Juan Carlos I came down unequivocally against any move to impose a military government.

The Cortes Generales, or parliament, is bicameral, with the Congreso de los Diputados (lower house) and Senado (upper house). Both houses are elected through free, universal suffrage. From December 1982 until March 1996, the PSOE ruled modern Spain's destinies, guided by the seemingly invincible Felipe González. His fall in 1996 in an atmosphere of scandal and disillusion ushered in a shift to the right as José María Aznar's PP entered government. The shift, a little shaky at the outset, was confirmed by Aznar's overwhelming election victory in March 2000, in which he became Spain's first right-wing ruler with an absolute majority since Franco.

The most fundamental change in recent Spanish history has been the devolution of power from the central state to the 17 regions, known as *comunidades autónomas* (autonomous communities or regions), under the 1978 constitution. What began as a response to long-standing desires for greater self-rule by the obviously distinct communities of

Catalunya, the Basque Country and Galicia has become a generalised decentralisation from Madrid to all the regions.

The 17 autonomous regions are divided into provinces, most of which are named after their capital city (eg, Segovia is the capital of Segovia province). The provinces are divided into town and district administrative units, called *municipios*.

The physiognomy of the regions changed after Franco's demise. Castilla y León is made up of what were the separate regions of León (even today you can see graffiti in León calling for separation from Castilla) and Castilla la Vieja. The latter lost the coastal province of Cantabria, which became a separate region, and the province of Logroño, which in turn became the region of La Rioja. Castilla la Nueva absorbed Albacete province to its south-east from the region of Murcia and was renamed Castilla-La Mancha.

One result of the autonomous regions policy has been a massive duplication of bureaucracy, with each comunidad having its own parliament, while the central state also has separate representation in each comunidad.

Article 148 of the constitution lists areas of power eligible for transfer to the comunidades. These include transport, agriculture,

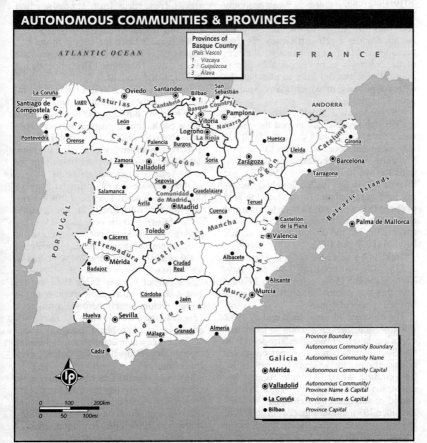

AUTONOMOUS COMMUNITIES & PROVINCES

Provinces of Basque Country (País Vasco)	
1	Vizcaya
2	Guipúzcoa
3	Álava

ATLANTIC OCEAN

FRANCE

ANDORRA

PORTUGAL

Balearic Islands

———	Province Boundary
———	Autonomous Community Boundary
Galicia	Autonomous Community Name
◉ **Mérida**	Autonomous Community Capital
◉ **Valladolid**	Autonomous Community/ Province Name & Capital
● <u>La Coruña</u>	Province Name & Capital
● Bilbao	Province Capital

0 100 200km
0 50 100mi

tourism, health policy and the environment. Negotiations on the transfer of powers continue even now, with Catalunya and the Basque Country particularly eager to attain as much elbowroom as possible. Taxation and spending are thorny issues. In late 2001 the state and regions are due to renegotiate the system of tax and spending distribution.

Talk is cheap and as long as the centrist Aznar has a stranglehold over Madrid, any moves towards greater devolution are about as likely as pigs taking flight.

ECONOMY

By the time the Spanish Civil War ended in 1939, the country's already weak economy had been devastated. Throughout WWII and into the early 1950s, the country laboured under a self-sufficiency program that appealed to the nationalist sensibilities of the country's more comfortably placed political elite but did little to alleviate the extreme poverty in which many Spanish people languished.

US economic aid from the early 1950s and a 1959 stabilisation plan helped the wheels turn a little faster. From the early 1960s an unprecedented boom was soon touted as a Francoist-inspired economic 'miracle'. Up until the world oil crisis in 1973–74, the miracle was in fact fuelled largely by growing foreign investment (Spain was the land of cheap labour *par excellence*), tourism and remittances from emigrant Spaniards; almost two million left the country to work abroad between 1959 and 1973.

Tourism has since the early 1960s played a key role in boosting the economy. Throughout the 1960s and into the 1970s it was the single most important pillar in Spain's spectacular growth.

The oil crisis hit Spain hard and by 1982 inflation and unemployment had reached crippling levels. The arrival in power of the Socialists ushered in a period of renewed, if more modest, growth with inflation coming down to single figures but unemployment remaining high. A new period of stagnation which began in 1989 has since 1994 shown signs of reversal but, in spite of Aznar's declaration that *España va bien* (Spain's going well), the country has serious problems to deal with.

Agriculture accounts for some 4.5% of Spain's GDP, well above the EU average. The most profitable farming is carried out along the Mediterranean coast and the Río Ebro. Intense plasticulture (hothouse agriculture using plastic) farming on the south coast, particularly around Almería and Huelva, contributes year-round high yields of everything from tomatoes to strawberries and cucumbers. Inland, farmers have to contend with extreme conditions in winter and summer, and persistent rainfall shortages and drought. The main products are wine, olives, citrus fruit, almonds, wheat and rice.

Fishing is another traditionally important sector. Spain's fleet, the largest in the EU, has to cast its nets far and wide to maintain its activities. The biggest fleets operate out of Galicia and Andalucía.

Some 35% of Spain's GDP comes from industry but, although Spain is among the top 10 industrialised nations in the world, much of the production is fuelled by sometimes fickle foreign investment (which in 1999 was up 10%). Aside from motor vehicles, other major products include steel (mostly in the north), textiles, chemicals and ships.

Of the services sector, tourism remains a huge component. In 1999 51.7 million visitors poured into Spain, bringing some US$25 billion into the economy. It was the third record-breaking year in a row and put Spain in second place behind France on a world ranking of the most popular tourist destinations.

Spain joined the then EC in 1986 and has always been an enthusiastic member of the European club, largely because it has been a net beneficiary of EU funds. The gravy train has brought problems though, and sectors hard-hit by new competition and quotas imposed from Brussels include wine, olives and fishing.

Signing up for the first wave of the single currency (the euro) has forced a tough austerity policy on the Spanish economy. Inflation was cranked back in the mid-1990s, although by 2000 it was running at 2.9%.

This is all well and good but the open sore of unemployment continues to plague Madrid. Official figures of *registered* unemployed were as low as 9.1% in early 2000 (the lowest since 1981). While it is true that the real figure has fallen steadily since 1994, it remains the EU's highest. Unemployment figures in Spain are a classic example of the fickleness of statistics, and an alternative measure indicates that by mid-2000 15% were unemployed (not bad if you consider that in 1993 it was up to around 22.5% by the same measure).

Of those with jobs, many struggle on part-time and temporary contract arrangements. And the average wage for full-time professionals is considerably lower than elsewhere in Western Europe, hovering at around 150,000 to 180,000 ptas a month. In 1999 Spain was the only EU country where salary growth was behind inflation.

Still, when all is said and done, Spain continues to enjoy a minor boom. Growth was high at 3.7% in 1999 and one sign of relative economic health is that in 1999 more cars were produced and sold in Spain than ever before.

POPULATION & PEOPLE

Spain has a total population of 39.8 million – less than four-fifths of a Spaniard for each of the more than 50 million visitors who flood into the country each year! Way back in 1594 it is estimated that the total population was about 8.2 million. By 1900 the figure had reached 18.6 million and in 1950, 28.4 million.

Spain never received any significant immigration from its empire, and its main ancestral peoples – Iberians, Basques, Celts, Romans, Jews, Visigoths, Franks, Arabs and Berbers – had all arrived by 1000 years ago. Although many Jews and Muslims were expelled in the 15th, 16th and 17th centuries, these peoples had already intermingled with the rest of the population.

As elsewhere in the West, the population is ageing. The average life expectancy since 1975 has risen by five years (up to 75 for men and 81 for women). In the same period the percentage of people over 65 has risen from 10% to 14.8%, while the number of those 15 and under has dropped from 27.5% to 18%.

The most striking thing about the Spanish population is its slow rate of growth. Along with that other great bastion of Catholicism and seemingly child-friendly society, Italy (and remember, the Pope doesn't view contraception kindly), Spain has the lowest birth rate in the world – the annual population increase is just 1.2%.

Statisticians have calculated that by 2050, the population will have dropped to 35.4 million (although this does not take into account the effects of increased immigration). More worrying is that some 30% are expected to be over 65, with just 14.8% aged 15 or under.

The Eurostat figures published in 1999 showed that, on average, Spaniards were the shortest people in Europe (along with the Portuguese) and among the slimmest.

Distribution

Spain is one of Europe's least densely populated countries, with about 77 people per square kilometre. Spaniards like to live together, in cities, towns or villages *(pueblos)*, a habit that probably goes back to past needs for defence and must have a lot to do with their gregarious nature. Only in the Basque lands are you likely to see much countryside dotted with single farmsteads and small fields. Elsewhere, farmers travel out from their pueblos to their fields in the morning and return at night.

The biggest cities are Madrid (with a population of 3.1 million), Barcelona (1.5 million), Valencia (739,000), Sevilla (701,000), Zaragoza (603,000) and Málaga (528,000). Greater Madrid and greater Barcelona each number about four million people and there are sizable conurbations around Bilbao, Valencia, Zaragoza and Sevilla. At the other end of the scale are Aragón, with only around 20 people per square kilometre outside its capital, Zaragoza, and the three meseta regions of Castilla-La Mancha (21 people per square kilometre, even including cities), Extremadura (25) and Castilla y León (27).

Regional Differences

The peoples with the strongest local identities – the Catalans, Basques and, to a lesser extent, the Galicians – owe a lot of their sense of difference to 19th-century cultural and political reawakenings and a reaction to decades of rigid centralist rule under Franco. These regions are on the fringes of the country, whose heartland is Castile. Some Basques and Catalans, and some Galicians, feel so strongly about their identity that they don't consider themselves Spaniards. All these peoples have their own languages and minority independence movements, the Basque terrorist organisation ETA being the most infamous.

Ethnic Minorities

Some consider Spain's *gitanos* (formerly called Gypsies but now known as the Roma) to be its only true ethnic minority, as interbreeding has made the rest of the population fairly homogeneous. Generally reckoned to be the originators – as well as the best performers – of flamenco, the gitanos are thought to have originated in India and reached Spain in the 15th century. As elsewhere, they have suffered discrimination. There are about 500,000 to 600,000 gitanos in Spain, more than half of them in Andalucía. Some still lead a wandering existence but most are settled. Barcelona, Granada, Madrid, Murcia and Sevilla all have sizable gitano communities.

Violent race riots in the Andalucian town of El Ejido in February 2000 underlined concerns surrounding the immigration debate in Spain. While economists predict that the ageing and shrinking population will make the increased import of foreign labour a necessity, others fear a stampede from across the Strait of Gibraltar.

Statistics on the foreign and migrant population in Spain seem fluid at best. According to figures of the Ministry of the Interior, there were 719,600 foreign residents from European countries living in Spain in 1998, including 74,000 Britons and 58,000 Germans. In addition, an estimated 390,000 other immigrants, principally from North Africa, South America and Asia, were legally on the books.

The number of migrants attempting to enter Spain from North Africa (legally or illegally) is growing. A special law was passed in early 2000 aimed at legalising an estimated 200,000 *clandestinos* in Spain. One study estimates that by 2025 some 20% of children in Spain will be of non-Spanish origin.

EDUCATION

Education is compulsory in Spain from the age of six to 16. About one-third of pupils attend Catholic schools, which are often subsidised by the state. Schooling in the state-run institutions is free.

Upon matriculation, students must also sit entrance exams for university. Students tend to study for six or so years, taking out qualifications such as the *diploma* after three years and the *licencia* after another two or three years' study. There are 47 public universities and polytechnics across Spain, as well as 15 private institutions. Some 1.6 million students are enrolled in tertiary institutions.

An estimated 96% of the population aged 15 and over is literate.

ARTS
Dance

Mention dance and Spain together and what traditionally springs to mind is flamenco and its associated forms (see Music later in this section). However, dance and ballet are alive and well too. Although contemporary dance pops up all around the country, Barcelona is its capital, with several shows to choose from almost any week of the year. Nacho Duato, head of and principal dancer of the Madrid-based Compañía Nacional de Baile since 1990, transformed it from a low-profile classical company into one of the world's most technically dazzling and accomplished contemporary dance groups. The Ballet Nacional de España, founded in 1978, mixes classical ballet with Spanish dance.

Here and there you'll find the occasional regional folk dance, such as Catalunya's *sardana* or the Málaga area's unique *verdiales* flag dances, done to exhilarating fiddle-and-percussion music.

Music

Spain pulsates with music. As if awakened from a long torpor, all the elements that make up the patchwork quilt of the country's musical geography seem to be gathering force. Flamenco, revived earlier this century but subsequently much ignored by most Spaniards, is undergoing a startling transformation. No longer the preserve of the initiated or dished up sloppily for tourists, it has become increasingly fashionable among locals as it has demonstrated greater innovation. The country's rock and pop scene, while not wildly successful beyond Spanish shores, is nonetheless busy and vibrant – and a good deal more so than in other European countries. Folk music peculiar to the many different regions of Spain is also blossoming and even on the classical front there are stirrings.

Classical & Opera

Of the great or once-great European nations, Spain has been noticeable in the realm of classical music by its absence. Rather, it has generally fallen to outsiders to pick up the country's vibrant rhythms and translate them into lasting homages. Who has not at least heard of *Carmen,* an opera whose leading lady epitomises all the fire, guile and flashing beauty of Andalucía and its women? Its composer, Frenchman Georges Bizet (1838–75), had been mesmerised by Moorish-influenced melodies of southern Spain in much the same way as Claude Debussy (1862–1918), whose penchant for the peninsula found expression in *Iberia.*

Another Frenchman, Emmanuel Chabrier (1841–94), immortalised his love for the country's sounds in *España,* while Maurice Ravel (1875–1937) whipped up his *Bolero* almost as an aside in 1927. Russians, too, have been swept away by the Hispanic. Mikhail Glinka (1804–57) arrived in Granada in 1845 and his resulting compositions inspired a new movement in Russian folk music. Nicolai Rimsky-Korsakov (1844–1908) popped into Spain on shore leave while in the Russian navy. At heart more composer than captain, he penned his delightful *Capriccio Espagnol.*

Spain itself was bereft of composers until the likes of Cádiz-born Manuel de Falla (1876–1946) and Enrique Granados (1867–1916) came onto the scene early in the 20th century. Granados and Isaac Albéniz (1860–1909) became great pianists and interpreters of their own compositions, such as the latter's *Iberia* cycle. The blind Joaquín Rodrigo (1901–99) was one of Spain's leading 20th century composers. In 1959, Miles Davis recorded a version of one of Rodrigo's celebrated pieces, *Concierto de Aranjuez* for guitar, which for some remains the greatest jazz rendering of any classical music work. It takes pride of place with other pieces inspired by Spanish themes on his *Sketches of Spain* album.

The best known of Spain's operatic performers is Plácido Domingo (1934–), followed closely by José Carreras (1946–). Joined by Italian tenor Luciano Pavarotti (1935–), they form the big three of contemporary male opera singers. One of the world's most outstanding sopranos is Catalunya's Montserrat Caballé (1933–). Teresa Berganza (1935–) is a well-known mezzo.

Classical Guitar

To many purists, the words 'classical' and 'guitar' cannot stand together. The guitar, they will explain, is not a noble instrument, but rather a popular expedient – folksy and highly enjoyable, but by no means elevated.

Be that as it may, a school of Spanish musicians has taken the humble guitar to dizzying heights of virtuosity and none more so than the great Andrés Segovia (1893–1987), born in Linares and steeped in the roots of flamenco and the passionate temperament of the south. He studied cello and piano, but his soul was in the guitar. Since it was hard to find a decent teacher of the instrument, he taught himself. He transcribed 150 works for other instruments into pieces for guitar and by the time he performed in Paris in 1924 he had established an international reputation for himself and the guitar.

Flamenco

This generic term covers a broad range of music and dance. It is rooted in the *cante hondo* (deep song) of the gitanos of

Andalucía and probably influenced by North African rhythms (or, indeed, music of Al-Andalus). The poet García Lorca and composer Manuel de Falla helped keep the genre alive with their grand competition in 1922, but by then it already had a well-established history. The gitanos had settled in Andalucía early in the 15th century, and by the end of the 18th century several centres of cante hondo (also known as *cante jondo*) had emerged, among them Cádiz, Jerez de la Frontera and the Triana area of Sevilla.

The guitar was invented in Andalucía: its origin lay in Arab lutes and about the 1790s a sixth string was added, probably by a Cádiz guitar-maker called Pagés. In the 1870s Antonio de Torres of Almería gave the instrument its modern shape and sonority.

The melancholy cante hondo is performed by a singer, who may be male *(cantaor)* or female *(cantaora),* to the accompaniment of a blood-rush of guitar from the *tocaor.* Although in its pure, traditional form this is sometimes a little hard for the uninitiated to deal with, it is difficult not to be moved by the very physical experience. The accompanying dance is performed by one or more *bailaores.* The *sevillana* (Andalucian folk dance) closely resembles, but should not be confused with, the bailaores' dance. Girls all over the country try to learn sevillanas at some time during their school careers.

It is impossible in this limited space to delve into the intricacies of the various orthodox schools of flamenco that have emerged over the past century (schools of Cádiz, Sevilla, Jerez, Córdoba and so on) or of the different kinds of song *(palos)* and music. They range from the most anguished *siguiriyas* and *soleás* to the more lively *bulerías, boleros, fandangos, alegrías* and *farrucas.* Suffice to say that there is more to it than meets the eye.

Although flamenco's home turf is in the south, many artists establish themselves in other major cities, especially Madrid, with its gitano *barrios* or districts and long-time flamenco bars. Indeed, in the 1950s musicians streamed in from the impoverished south to seek a better life in Madrid. One of the best-known dance studios in the country is the Academia Amor de Dios, south of the Lavapiés area.

Some of the greatest figures around the turn of the 19th century, to some the *Edad de Oro* (Golden Age) of flamenco, include the guitarist Ramón Montoya (1879–1949) and the singer Silverio Franconetti (1831–89). Manolo Caracol (1909–73) joined the great singer Lola Flores (1923–95) to introduce theatrical elements and even orchestral accompaniment, which injected new life into the genre but was not welcomed by purists.

Flamenco's real golden age may well be opening up before us. Never has it been so popular both in Spain and abroad, and never has there been such a degree of innovation. Strangely, among the most successful proponents of modern flamenco (or flamenco-style) music are the Gipsy Kings, who are from southern France, not Spain.

Paco de Lucía (1947–) is undoubtedly the best-known flamenco guitarist internationally. He has a virtuosity few would dare to claim they can match and is the personification of *duende,* that indefinable capacity to transmit the power of flamenco. Of the wealth of albums to choose from, the double album *Paco de Lucía Antología* is a good introduction to his work from 1967 to 1990. Paco de Lucía spends more time abroad than in Spain, but plenty of other good musicians fill the gap at home.

The list of fine flamenco guitarists is long, among them the Montoya family (some of whom are better known by the sobriquet of *los Habichuela*), especially Juan (1933–) and Pepe (1949–). Other artists to watch for include El Tomatito (1947–), Manolo Sanlúcar (1943–) and Moraíto Chico (1956–).

Paco de Lucía's friend El Camarón de la Isla (1950–92) was, until his death, the leading light of contemporary cante hondo; plenty of flamenco singers today try to emulate him. Another who has reached cult status is Enrique Morente (1942–), referred to by a Madrid paper as 'the last Bohemian'. Among other leading vocalists figure such greats as Carmen Linares (1951–), from the province of Jaén, and the Sevillano José Menese (1941–). Other top-notch singers include Remedios Amaya and Aurora Vargas

(1956–), Juan Peña Fernández (El Lebrijano; 1941–), Calixto Sánchez (1946–), Chano Lobato (1927–) and Vicente Soto (Sordera; 1927–). El Camarón's younger successors include Antonio Vargas (known as El Potito), Juan Cortés Duquende, Miguel Poveda (1973–). One of the rising female vocalists is Aurora (1972–).

Of Spain's flamenco dancers and choreographers, the greatest name this century is with little doubt Antonio Ruiz Soler (1921–96). Known to many simply as Antonio, he danced and choreographed an infinite variety of classical and inventive flamenco. He often combined classical, folkloric and flamenco dance and from 1981, as director of the Ballet Nacional de España, he took his creative genius around the world.

One of the all-time great bailaoras was the fiery Barcelona-born Carmen Amaya (1913–63). Leading contemporary figures include Joaquín Cortés (1969–) and Antonio Canales (1962–), who is more of a flamenco purist. Traditionalists dislike fashionable attempts to mix flamenco dance with ballet and other forms. One of the great traditional bailaores, Farruco (1936–97) was a wild gitano soul who argued that performers such as Cortés don't really dance flamenco. The only 'puro masculino' bailaor these days, Farruco used to say, was his teenage grandson Farruquito (1983–). And indeed 'little Farruco' is today on the verge of becoming a major star of flamenco dance.

Manuela Vargas (1941–), Antonio Gades (1936–), Cristina Hoyos (1946–), Miguel Peña Vargas (El Funi; 1939–) and Sara Baras (1971–) are other well-known dancers, some with their own successful companies.

If you want to give yourself a general introduction to the best of flamenco, try to see Carlos Saura's 1995 flick, *Flamenco*. A double-CD set of the music is also available.

Tourist-oriented flamenco shows, called *tablaos*, lack the genuine emotion of real flamenco, although a few are worth seeing if you have no alternative. The show-cum-vaudeville atmosphere will not be to everyone's taste.

For hints on where and when to catch good live flamenco in Spain, see Entertainment in

MICK WELDON

The passionate and fluid flamenco dance has its origins in Andalucía.

the Facts for the Visitor chapter. Some venues that stage regular flamenco are mentioned in city sections later in this book.

Nuevo Flamenco & Fusion Possibly the most exciting developments in flamenco have taken it to other musical shores. Two of the best-known groups that have experimented with flamenco-rock fusion since the 1980s are Ketama and Pata Negra, whose music is labelled by some as Gypsy rock. One of Ketama's best albums is *Canciones Hondas,* while Pata Negra's seventh, *Como Una Vara Verde,* is a good choice. A former member of Pata Negra, Raimundo Amador (1960–), has gone his own way and in 1996 made a CD with the American blues master BB King.

In the early 1990s, Radio Tarifa emerged with a mesmerising mix of flamenco, North African and medieval sounds. Its CD, *Rumba Argelina,* was a great hit. A more traditional flamenco performer, El Lebrijano (see earlier) has done some equally appealing combinations with classical Moroccan music. His CD *Encuentros,* recorded with the Andalusian Orchestra of Tangier, is a good sample.

The Cádiz-born Niña Pastori (1978–), who fronts an electric jazz-rock band, has taken flamenco away from the taverns with a fresh young sound. Her latest album is called *Cañailla*. 'Flamenco-billy' is the speciality of Mártires del Compás, a sextet whose rocky flamenco doesn't go down well with the purists. The group performs with almost too much gusto – the title of their latest CD alone, *Mordiende el Duende* (Biting the Duende) is enough to clue you in.

Perhaps most astonishing was Enrique Morente's 1996 collaboration with the Granada technopunks Lagartija Nick on *Omega,* an interpretation of Lorca's poetry collection, *Poeta en Nueva York* (Poet in New York), along with songs by the Lorca-influenced Leonard Cohen.

Further Information *Alma 100,* a free monthly flamenco magazine available free in tourist offices in Andalucía and flamenco venues in places such as Granada, Córdoba, Sevilla and Jerez, has long listings of up-coming flamenco performances, and ads for flamenco tuition. Another monthly mag is *El Olivo*. The Web site of the Centro Andaluz de Flamenco in Jerez de la Frontera (http://caf.cica.es) also includes a calendar of flamenco events and is an excellent place to start surfing the Internet for information on flamenco.

Pop & Rock In purely monetary terms, Julio Iglesias must be the country's most successful performer ever. Long a resident of the USA, he has for many years had millions swooning with his crooning in Spanish and various other languages. Mind you, in the past couple of years he has been increasingly upstaged by his equally smooth son Enrique. Apart from the Iglesias clan, the success of Spanish popular music abroad has been limited.

Kiko Veneno is one of the durables of Spanish rock. Catalan by birth but raised in Andalucía, his music is rooted in flamenco, but in no way detracts from his crisp rock sound. Although he's been around for quite a while, he has cut few albums, all of them good. Danza Invisible is another long-time

mainstream band from Málaga. One of the country's more popular groups at home and abroad is Mecano, two male musicians fronted by a powerful woman singer.

For something a little racier, Celtas Cortos has a sound reminiscent of the Pogues (some would say too much so and with less-inspired lyrics). If this sort of music appeals, a good choice of CD is *Cuéntame un Cuento*.

The Madrid quartet Dover is a popular indie band, competing with the Granada-based Los Planetas. The latter's third album, *Una Semana en el Motor de un Autobús,* came out in April 1998.

Gijón in Asturias seems to be something of a breeding ground for indie bands, among the more interesting of which is the quartet Manta Ray, whose latest album is *Esperanza*. Also worth keeping tabs on is the Asturian all-girl quintet, Nosoträsh.

Def Con Dos, Extremoduro, Ska-P, Reincidentes, Soziedad Alkohølika, Molotov and the Pleasure Fuckers are just a few other popular rock bands touring around the country. Members of Mojinos Escozíos, a Catalan-Sevilla group, describe themselves as 'fat, ugly and heavy (as in heavy metal) to the death'. Their lyrics prove that PC is not a concern – and they have been selling CDs like there's no tomorrow. Ruido Pegajoso is a little less extreme, successfully reinventing 1960s music.

For sheer decibel concentration, the group A Palo Seko is hard to beat. The Basque Country seems to have a particular predilection for heavy metal and generally angry-sounding bands. They keep popping up, as one reviewer put it, like *churros*. Eraso! is not a bad recent example.

Techno If techno is your thing, the Barcelonese trio Vanguard and compatriot An Der Beat are both riding high – more to be danced to than listened to. La Bongo is a popular hip-hop outfit. Titán is an underground group that has seen the light of day with a recording for Virgin; its music mixes elements of techno with rock.

In a more extreme vein is the loud and, for many, unbearable dance noise commonly known as *bakalao*. For this ear-splitting

Spanish contribution to the wonderful world of techno, Valencia seems to be something of a headquarters. A subcategory (for those capable of discerning a difference) is *mákina*.

Folk Although the odd group playing traditional folk music can be found across several regions, the best and most prolific source of folk is Galicia. The region's rich heritage is closely related to that of its Celtic cousins in Brittany and Ireland and has nothing at all in common with what might be considered quintessential 'Spanish' music such as flamenco. Emblematic of the music is the *gaita*, Galicia's version of the bagpipes. The most successful purveyor of Galicia's Celtic tradition is the highly polished group Milladoiro, which has cut many fine CDs.

Another group worth seeking out is Palla Mallada, from Santiago de Compostela, which does a mix of instrumental pieces, dances and traditional songs. Others include Na Lua, Berrogüetto, Chouteira and Luar Na Lubre. Santiago's Fía Na Roca combines traditional sounds with original compositions.

Among soloists, Uxía is an enchanting female vocalist, a gutsy version of Enya, who also seeks her inspiration in traditional *gallego* (Galician) folk music.

A highly versatile gallego performer of gaita and wind instruments is Carlos Núñez. He presents a slick show, involving violins, percussion, guitar and lute, and often invites a wide range of guest artists to play at his concerts, providing for a highly entertaining and eclectic mix of styles.

The Celtic tradition is also alive in Asturias and even Cantabria, but not to nearly the same extent as in Galicia. The most commercially successful folk music is that of bagpipe-rocker José Ángel Hevia from Asturias, whose album *Tierra de Nadie* has sold over a million copies. An interesting new band from Asturias is Tejedor, whose versions of local traditional songs are enjoyable. Mixing up its own compositions and folk tunes from Cantabria is the group Atlántica.

From the Basque Country, Oskorri is a fine electrical and acoustic band and one of the best folk-inspired groups to emerge from the region.

Cantautores Some of the great singer-songwriters of the movida are still in circulation. People such as Javier Krahe, who might loosely be compared with France's Georges Brassens or Germany's Wolf Biermann, still cover the late-night circuit in Madrid with their witty ballads of protest and mordant social commentary and are even experiencing something of a revival. For non-Spaniards they are the most challenging, for it is their lyrics that matter, not the music. The highly successful Pedro Guerra, from the Canary Islands, and Luis Pastor are younger members of this crowd.

Festivals For information on when and where to catch some of the more important music festivals, see Public Holidays & Special Events in the Facts for the Visitor chapter.

Literature
Medieval Works It is difficult to talk of a 'Spanish' literature much earlier than the 13th century, if you mean literature in Castilian. Before this, troubadours working in Vulgar Latin, Arabic and other tongues were doing the rounds of southern Europe and the great writers and thinkers in a Spain largely dominated by Muslims produced their treatises more often than not in Arabic or Hebrew.

Among the latter, the best known was the Muslim philosopher Averroës, or Ibn Rushd (1126–98), from Córdoba. His commentaries on Aristotle, trying to reconcile science with religious faith, had great influence on European Christian thought in the 13th and 14th centuries.

Alfonso X, king of Castilla and León (1252–84) and known as El Sabio (the Learned), did much to encourage the use of Castilian as a language of learning and literature, and wrote about diverse subjects.

Of all the works produced in Spanish in the Middle Ages, the *Poema de Mio Cid,* which has survived in a version penned in 1307 (although first written in 1140), is surely the best known. The epic tale of El Cid Campeador, or Rodrigo Díaz, whose exploits culminated in mastery over Valencia, bears little resemblance to the facts. Rather, it is concerned with telling a good story in which a towering figure overcomes all odds by his prowess and attains glory.

This was an age of didactic writing, of poetry and injunctions working at once on a literal, moral and allegorical level. Gonzalo de Berceo, who died in the late 1200s, composed some of the most elegant writing in this genre, culminating in his *Milagros de Nuestra Señora* (Miracles of Our Lady). Juan Ruiz, who wrote in the first half of the 14th century, was one of the period's finest poets and something of a humorist, often descending into the downright bawdy. His *Buen Amor* (1330) leads the reader along paths of good and evil, with a less constrained view of earthly peccadilloes than usually propounded in the edifying literature of the day.

The Golden Century The end of the Reconquista in 1492 and the glory days of the Catholic Monarchs imbued with optimism the writing of the first half of the 16th century. Garcilaso de la Vega (1501–36), steeped in Italian literary sensibilities and *au fait* with the likes of Ariosto and Bembo, left behind sonnets and eclogues of unparalleled beauty. His successor and perhaps the greatest of all Spanish poets was Luis de Góngora (1561–1627). Unconcerned by theories, morals or high-minded sentiments, Góngora manipulated words with a majesty that has largely defied attempts at critical 'explanation'; his verses are above all intended as a source of sensuous pleasure. With Góngora we are in the greatest period of Spanish letters – *El Siglo de Oro* (the Golden Century), which stretched roughly from the middle of the 16th century to the middle of the 17th.

This was equally the age of some of the country's greatest mystics. For San Juan de la Cruz, poetry, especially of a lightly erotic flavour, served as the best of imperfect tools to render the ecstasy of union between God and the soul. His works, such as *Noche Oscura* and *Llama de Amor Viva*, didn't appear until well after his death in 1591. His contemporary, Santa Teresa de Ávila (1515–82), headed down another road, capturing in evocative, if not always strictly correct, prose accounts of her spiritual explorations,

including *Camino de Perfección* and *Las Moradas o el Castillo Interior*.

Histories were gaining in popularity; the Jesuit Juan de Mariana (1535–1624) was a meticulous compiler.

The advent of the *comedia* in the early 17th century in Madrid produced some of the country's greatest playwrights. Lope de Vega (1562–1635), also an outstanding lyric poet, was perhaps the most prolific: more than 300 of the 800 plays and poems attributed to him remain. He explored the falseness of court life and roamed political subjects with his imaginary historical plays. Less playful and perhaps of greater substance is the work of Tirso de Molina (1581–1648), in whose *El Burlador de Sevilla* we meet the immortal character of Don Juan, a likable seducer who meets an unhappy end.

Yet another great name of the period is Pedro Calderón de la Barca (1600–81). The beauty of this grand master of the stage's works lies in his agile language and inventive techniques as a dramatist. The themes and story lines of his work were, however, comparatively run-of-the-mill. His more powerful pieces are *La Vida es Sueño* and *El Alcalde de Zalamea;* in both, Calderón upholds an idea of righteousness and justice irrespective of class and caste.

Also noteworthy is Francisco de Quevedo (1580–1645), an accomplished poet working in almost diametric opposition to Góngora. He is perhaps best known today for his prose – a sparkling virtuoso game of metaphor and wordplay, but often laden with a heavy dose of bitter and unforgiving social commentary. His *La Historia de la Vida del Buscón Llamado Don Pablos,* tracing the none-too-elevating life of an antihero, El Buscón, is laced with especial venom for the lower classes.

Cervantes & the Novel His life something of a jumbled obstacle course of trials, tribulations and peregrinations, Miguel de Cervantes Saavedra (1547–1616) had little success with his forays into theatre and verse. But today he is commonly thought of as the man who gave modern literature a new genre: the novel.

El Ingenioso Hidalgo Don Quijote de la Mancha started life as a short story, designed to make a quick peseta, but Cervantes found himself turning it into an epic tale by the time it appeared in 1605. The ruined *ancien régime* knight and his equally impoverished companion, Sancho Panza, embark on a trail through the foibles of his era – a journey whose timelessness and universality marked out the work for greatness. *Don Quijote* would a century later be a fundamental source of inspiration for the further development of the modern novel, particularly in France and Britain.

18th & 19th Centuries The 18th century was not exactly a halcyon period for Spanish letters. Its greatest figure was Juan Meléndez Valdés (1754–1817). His *Poesías* bring together his finest work, ranging from the humanistic and even a hint of the coming romanticism through to a more personal, sometimes erotic verse. Another outstanding figure of the times was the Benedictine monk Benito Jerónimo Feijóo (1676–1764), an enlightened essayist whose defence of rational thought and the diffusion of culture is summed up in the eight volume collection of his finest essays, *Teatro Crítico Universal.*

The age of the romantics touched Spain less than much of Europe. The country's greatest poetic exponent, José de Espronceda (1808–42), took his inspiration from Lord Byron. He reached the pinnacle of his often anguished work with *El Diablo Mundo*. Less tortured but with a fine sense of nuance was Gustavo Adolfo Becquer (1836–70). Galicia's Rosalía de Castro (1837–85) was another bright light of the age.

One novelist towers above the rest. Benito Pérez Galdós (1843–1920) is the closest Spain produced to a Dickens or a Balzac. His novels and short stories ranged from social critique to the simple depiction of society through the lives of its many players. His more mature works, such as *Fortunata y Jacinta,* display a bent towards naturalism and, in the early 20th century, even symbolism. Another harsh realist and an early feminist was Doña Emilia, Condesa de Pardo-Bazán. Her *Los Pazos de Ulloa* is a masterpiece.

From 1900 to Franco Miguel de Unamuno (1864–1936) was one of the leading figures of the so-called Generation of 98, a group of writers and artists working around and after 1898 (a bad year for Spain with the loss of its last colonies, Cuba and the Philippines, and an economic crisis at home). Unamuno's work is difficult, but among his most enjoyable prose is the *Tres Novelas Ejemplares,* imbued, like most of his novels and theatre, with a disquieting existentialism.

The greatest poet of the era was Antonio Machado. Steeped in symbolism, his poetry moves towards the metaphysical in his mature years, particularly in *Proverbios y Cantares. Nuevas Canciones* was written from 1917 to 1930. Machado's friend Juan Ramón Jiménez (1881–1958) won the 1956 Nobel literature prize for a poetic oeuvre *Platero y Yo,* a prose-poem telling of his childhood wanderings with his donkey.

The leading light in early 20th-century modernist poetry was the Nicaraguan Rubén Darío (1867–1916). Another experimental writer of note was Ramón María del Valle Inclán (1869–1936).

A little later came the brief flourishing of Andalucía's Federico García Lorca (1898–1936), whose verse and theatre leaned towards surrealism, leavened by a unique musicality and visual sensibility. His many offerings include *Canciones, Poema del Cante Jondo* and plays such as the powerful *Bodas de Sangre* (Blood Wedding). His career was cut short by Nationalist executioners in the early stages of the civil war. Associated with Lorca in the so-called Generation of 27 of Andalucian writers were the poets Rafael Alberti (1902–99), Vicente Aleixandre (1898–1984), the 1977 Nobel literature laureate, and Luis Cernuda (1902–63).

The Franco Years The censors of fascist Spain kept a lid, albeit one far from watertight, on literary development in Spain.

One of the few writers of quality who managed to work throughout the years of the dictatorship, and who continues to thrive, is the Galician Nobel prize-winning novelist Camilo José Cela (1916–). His most important novel, *La Familia de Pascual Duarte,* appeared in 1942 and marked a rebirth of the Spanish realist novel. His latest, *Madera de Boj,* takes the reader on an original and intriguing journey into Galicia, as told through the woes of shipwrecks and other mishaps along the Costa da Morte.

One of Spain's most important playwrights of the century was Antonio Buero Vallejo (1916–2000). He fought in the Republican army and spent seven years in prison from the end of the civil war. The 1950s and 1960s were his best years, in which his dramas were thinly veiled attacks against Franco's dictatorship. His first play, *Historia de una Escalera* (1949), was one of his best works.

Much work of worth was also produced by writers in exile, among them Francisco Ayala (1934–), Max Aub (1903–72), Juan Larrea (1895–1980) and Mercé Rodoreda (1909–83).

Contemporary Writing The death of Franco in 1975 signalled the end of the constraints placed on Spanish writers. Many of those now able to work in complete freedom were already active in exile during the Franco years and some chose to remain outside Spain. Juan Goytisolo (1931–) started off in the neorealist camp but his more recent works, such as *Señas de Identidad* and *Juan sin Tierra,* are decidedly more experimental.

A highly accessible writer is Barcelona-born José Luis Sampedro (1917–). He considers *Octubre, Octubre* to be his life testament. In his latest adventure, *El Amante Lesbiano,* he makes a frontal assault on what, for some, are social norms.

Jorge Semprún (1923–), who lost his home and family in the civil war, ended up in a Nazi concentration camp for his activities with the French Resistance in WWII. He writes mostly in French. His first novel, *Le Grand Voyage,* is one of his best.

Of course, younger authors are emerging all the time. One to note is Antonio Muñoz Molina (1956–), whose *El Invierno en Lisboa* (Winter in Lisbon) is a touching novel and won him considerable acclaim when it first appeared in 1987.

Galicia's Julián Ríos (1941–) won the *New York Times'* vote for the best book of the year with his 1998 *Amores Que Flotan.*

A particularly popular scribbler is former war reporter Arturo Pérez-Reverte (1951–), who for some years has done well at the till if not always with the critics. His latest effort, *La Carta Esférica,* has done well with the critics too. It is a treasure hunt that leads from the author's native Cartagena into the 18th century.

Rosa Montero (1951–) is a prominent journalist who has had considerable success with her novels, including *Te Trataré Como a una Reina* (I'll Treat You Like a Queen) and *La Hija del Caníbal* (The Cannibal's Daughter).

A promising new writer is Nuria Barrios (1962–), whose second book, *El Zoo Sentimental,* was published in 2000. In a series of stories, she uses animals as mirrors to reflect conflicting human sentiments.

Younger still is Marcos Giralt Torrente (1968–), whose first novel *París* won critical accolades. His second, *Nada Sucede Solo,* tells of a couple that leaves the rat race to do up a mill, only to have the wife's sister arrive and send things awry.

Surely one of the most disturbing, and disturbed, modern poets is Leopoldo María Panero (1948–), at the moment resident in a psychiatric home in the Canary Islands. Some of his most powerful verse is contained in *Poemas desde el Manicomio de Mondragón* (Poems from Mondragón Psychiatric Hospital).

Looking decidedly banal beside Panero is Francisco Brine (1932–), one of the country's leading poets. His work displays an unusually broad palette of style and subject matter, from the historical narrative through to an intense existentialism. The cream of his work is contained in *Obras Completas: 1960–97.*

Painting & Sculpture

The Beginnings Humans have been creating images in Spain for as long as 14,000 years, as the cave paintings in Altamira (Cantabria) attest.

Later, the Celtiberian tribes were producing some fine ceramics and statuary, perhaps influenced by the presence of Greeks, Carthaginians and ultimately Romans.

More strictly speaking, the origins of Spanish painting lie in the early Middle Ages. From this period some magnificent frescoes have been preserved. Although much-faded examples remain visible in some of the pre-Romanesque churches of Asturias, among the oldest and most invaluable surviving frescoes are those in the 11th-century Mozarabic Ermita de San Baudelio, near Berlanga de Duero (Castilla y León). In the same unique building is a rich serving of Romanesque frescoes from the following century. Some have been removed for display in the Prado in Madrid, the New York Met and Boston's Museum of Fine Arts.

The single most outstanding collection of 12th-century Romanesque frescoes can be seen in the Museu Nacional d'Art de Catalunya in Barcelona. It is a collection of pieces taken from churches and chapels across northern Catalunya and carefully preserved and presented in a unique display. The most outstanding frescoes of the same era still in situ are those of the Panteón Real of the Real Basílica de San Isidoro in León.

Catalan & Valencian Schools The producers of much of the painting from medieval Spain have remained anonymous, but a few leading lights managed to get some credit. Ferrer Bassá (c.1290–c.1348) is considered one of the country's first masters. Influenced by the Siennese school, his only surviving works are murals with a slight caricatural touch in Barcelona's Museu-Monestir de Pedralbes. He is considered the Spanish creator of the Italo-Gothic style.

The style soon displayed a more international flavour, best embodied in the work of Bernat Martorell (?–1452), a master of chiaroscuro. As the Flemish school gained influence, painters such as Jaume Huguet (1415–92) adopted the sombre realism, lightened with Hispanic splashes of gold, as can be seen from his *San Jorge* in the Museu Nacional d'Art de Catalunya.

Closely linked to Catalunya was the school of painters that emerged in neighbouring Valencia. Its major exponents included Lorenzo Zaragoza (1365–1402), Pere Nicolau (died 1410) and Andrés Marzal de Sax (died 1410), but Bartolomé Bermejo (died 1495) was the most interesting of the lot, incorporating Flemish influences and exploring the use of oil. Nothing better illustrates the Córdoba-born artist's gifts than the *Pietà* in Barcelona's cathedral museum.

Castile Local artists tended to be passed over in favour of foreigners in 15th-century Castilla. Their 'surnames' often give this away: Nicolás Florentino (from Florence; born Dello Delli, he did the *retablo*, or altarpiece, in the Catedral Vieja in Salamanca), Nicolás Francés (from France) and Juan de Flandes (from Flanders).

One local exception was Fernando Gallego (1445–1507), heavily influenced by Flanders' Rogier van der Weyden. Zamora's cathedral houses altarpieces by him; others can be seen in the Prado.

Also initially imbued with Hispano-Flemish thinking, Pedro Berruguete (1438–1504) is said to have done a stint in Urbino, Italy. Although there is no direct proof of this, his later work as court painter to Fernando and Isabel tends to support the claim. His son, Alonso (1488–1561), definitely enjoyed an extended stay in Urbino and, although a fine painter, is remembered for his sculpture. His alabaster *Resurrección* in Valencia's cathedral is a masterwork.

16th Century One of the most remarkable artists at work in Spain in the latter half of the 16th century was an 'adopted' Spaniard. Domenikos Theotokopoulos (1541–1614), known as El Greco (the Greek), was schooled in both Crete and Italy, but spent his productive working life in Toledo. His slender, exalted figures and, in the latter part of his career, a striking simplicity of colour and fluidity of movement are hallmarks that many tried to imitate but none emulated. One of his earlier works is also one of his greatest – *El Entierro del Conde de Orgaz* (The Burial of the Count of Orgaz) in Toledo's Iglesia de Santo Tomé.

El Greco and Spanish artists in general had a hard time raising interest in their material at the court of Felipe II, who above all preferred Titian and a series of lesser Italian Mannerists. Holding up the Spanish side to a certain extent was El Mudo (the Mute), Juan Navarrete (1526–79), who became one of Spain's first practitioners of 'tenebrism', a fashion that largely aped Caravaggio's chiaroscuro style.

The Golden Age As the 16th century gave way to the 17th, a remarkably fecund era in the history of Spanish painting dawned.

One of Navarrete's proteges was Francisco Ribalta (1565–1628). He ended up in Valencia, where he turned out mostly religious portraiture in which he deployed to great effect the tenebrist methods he had learned.

Across the Mediterranean in Italy, José (Jusepe) de Ribera (1591–1652) also came under the influence of Caravaggio. Many of his works found their way back to Spain and are now scattered about numerous art galleries. Ribera's mastery of light was bettered perhaps only by his contemporary Velázquez.

In Sevilla, meanwhile, another school gathered momentum under Francisco Pacheco (1564–1654). A true Renaissance man, he had an alumnus whom he set in the right direction. Not only did Diego Rodríguez de Silva Velázquez (1599–1660) marry Pacheco's daughter, but he also quickly rose to prominence after leaving his native Sevilla for Madrid. Within a year he was admitted to the magic circle of court painters, where he stayed for the rest of his life.

Velázquez stands in a class of his own. With him any trace of the idealised stiffness that characterised a by-now spiritless Mannerism fell by the wayside. Realism became a key and the majesty of his royal subjects springs from a capacity to capture the essence of the person – king or *infanta* – and the detail of their finery. And between commissions he'd take just as sympathetic a view of less fortunate members of the royal menagerie, such as court jesters and dwarfs.

His masterpieces include *Las Meninas* and *La Rendición de Breda* (The Surrender of Breda), both on view in the Prado, and a portrait of Pope Innocent X, which he carried out while in Rome in 1650.

A less exalted contemporary and close friend of Velázquez, Francisco de Zurbarán (1598–1664) moved *to* Sevilla as an official painter. Probably of Basque origin but born in Extremadura, he is best remembered for the startling clarity and light in his portraits of monks. He travelled a great deal and in Guadalupe a series of eight portraits can still be seen hanging where Zurbarán left them in the Hieronymite monastery. Zurbarán fell on hard times in the 1640s and was compelled by the plague to flee Sevilla. He died in poverty in Madrid.

Zurbarán has come to be seen as one of the masters of the Spanish canvas, but in his lifetime it was a younger and less inspired colleague who won all the prizes. Bartolomé Esteban Murillo (1618–82) took the safe road and turned out stock religious pieces and images of beggar boys and the like with technical polish but little verve.

Yet another solid artist of the same period and a student of Pacheco was Alonso Cano (1601–67), who spent his working life in Granada. Also a gifted sculptor and architect, he is sometimes referred to as the Michelangelo of Spain. Not a great deal of his work remains and his stormy life didn't help matters. He might well have joined the Velázquez gravy train in Madrid had he not been accused of his second wife's murder and been obliged to leave.

A parade of late baroque artists working over the course of the century have been loosely lumped together as the 'Madrid school'. A few names stand out: Antonio de Pereda (1608–78), the monk Fray Juan Rizi (1600–81), Juan Carreño de Miranda (1614–85) and Francisco Rizi (1614–85; the monk's younger brother). The last of them, and the most gifted, was Claudio Coello (1642–93). He specialised in the big picture, literally. Some of his enormous decorative canvases adorn El Escorial, among them his magnum opus, *La Sagrada Forma*.

(continued on page 75)

Spanish Architecture

Spain's place on the 'edge' of Europe and centuries of Muslim rule left an indelible imprint on the country's architectural heritage, setting it apart from the rest of Europe. Phoenicians, Carthaginians, Greeks, Romans and the Visigoths all left their mark. But they were overshadowed by the genius of the Arabs, who not only left behind extraordinary monuments, but also an artistic legacy that would continue to find expression long after the last Muslim kingdom had fallen to the Reconquista.

All the great European architectural movements – from Romanesque to Gothic, from baroque to neoclassicism – seeped into Spain, although usually later than elsewhere and often altered to suit local tastes. No other European country can boast the diversity of Spain. While the towering Gothic cathedrals of Burgos, León and Toledo were being raised to the greater glory of God in the first half of the 13th century, Granada became home to the Alhambra, one of the most remarkable visual delights the Muslim world has ever produced.

Across the whole country, countless magnificent churches and monasteries vie for your attention with castles and palaces of all shapes and sizes. The range, from startling feats of Roman engineering to the caprice of Antoni Gaudí, can seem overwhelming but is never tiresome.

Title Page: Palma de Mallorca's enormous cathedral (or La Seo) was completed in 1600, almost four centuries after construction began. The structure is predominately Gothic with traditional mudéjar touches.
(Photo: Damien Simonis)

Celtiberians & Greeks

The tribes that first inhabited the Iberian Peninsula, collectively known as Celtiberians, left behind a wealth of evidence of their existence. The most common living arrangement, called the *castro*, was a hamlet surrounded by stone walls and made up of circular stone houses. Several have been partly preserved in locations as disparate as La Guardia, on Galicia's southern coast, and Vinaceite, deep in Aragón. One of the best is near Coaña, in Asturias.

The Greeks and Carthaginians rarely made it far into the Spanish interior. Apart from some Carthaginian necropolises in Ibiza, a couple of spots in Andalucía and some Greek remains at Empúries (Catalunya), little is left to remind you of their presence.

Romans

The Roman legacy in Spain is not as great as in some other of the empire's former provinces. Spectacular exceptions include the aqueduct in Segovia (Castilla y León), the bridge at Alcántara (Extremadura) and the stout walls of Lugo (Galicia), while other charming Roman remnants include the bridge over the Río Esca at Burgui.

Vestiges of Roman towns can also still be seen. Among the more important are the ancient town of Augusta Emerita (in Mérida, Extremadura), ancient Tarraco (Tarragona, Catalunya), the amphitheatre and other ruins at Itálica (near Sevilla, Andalucía), and Sagunto (Valencia).

Below: The well-preserved amphitheatre Teatro Romano in Mérida (Extremadura) was built by the Romans around 15 BC.

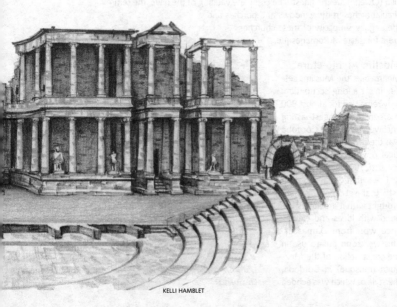

KELLI HAMBLET

SPANISH ARCHITECTURE

Modest remains have been imaginatively converted into underground museums in Barcelona and Zaragoza. Ancient Numancia, north of Soria (Castilla y León), is largely Roman, although it was preceded by a Celtiberian city that for a long time resisted imperial rule.

Visigoths

Filling the vacuum left by the departing Romans, the Visigoths employed a more humble but remarkably attractive style, which survives in a handful of small churches. The 7th-century Ermita de Santa María de Lara, at Quintanilla de las Viñas in Burgos province (Castilla y León), is one of the best. Fragments of this unique style can be seen in several cities across Spain, including Toledo.

Reputedly the oldest church in Spain is the 7th-century San Juan, in Baños de Cerrato, while the cathedral in nearby Palencia (Castilla y León) has Visigothic origins in the crypt. The horseshoe arch, later perfected by the Arabs, is characteristic of the Visigothic aesthetic.

Pre-Romanesque

When Spain was swamped by the Muslim invasion of 711, only the unruly northern strip of the country in what is today Asturias held out. During the 9th century, a unique building style emerged in this green corner of Spain cut off from the rest of Christian Europe. Of the 30-odd examples of pre-Romanesque architecture scattered about the Asturian countryside, the little Iglesia de Santa María del Naranco and Iglesia de San Miguel de Lillo (Oviedo) are the finest. The complete vaulting of the nave, the semicircular arches in the windows and porches and the angular simplicity of these churches are a foretaste of Romanesque.

Muslim Architecture

Meanwhile, the Muslims settled in for a long occupation: they remained for almost 800 years in their longest-lasting enclave, Granada. Córdoba was the centre of Muslim political power and culture for the first 300 years.

The Syrian Omayyad dynasty that set up shop here brought with it architects imbued with ideas and experience won from Damascus. This was soon put to use in the construction of the Mezquita (mosque) in Córdoba, the style of which was echoed

KELLI HAMBLET

Left: The Iglesia de Santa María del Naranco, near Oviedo (Asturias), is an evocative piece of pre-Romanesque architecture.

SPANISH ARCHITECTURE

Right: Inside Zaragoza's Aljafería palace, you'll find magnificent examples of Muslim architecture. (Aragón)

KELLI HAMBLET

across Muslim Spain. Horseshoe-shaped and lobed arches, the use of exquisite tiles in the decoration (mostly calligraphy and floral motifs), peaceful inner courtyards, complex stucco work, and stalactite ceiling adornments are all features easily recognisable and comparable with buildings raised in Damascus. Just outside Córdoba, the now ruined city of Medina Azahara was built in similar style.

Remnants of this Muslim legacy abound across Spain, although many grand examples have been lost. The most striking piece of Islamic architecture in northern Spain is the palace of the Aljafería in Zaragoza, a proud residence subsequently much altered by the Christians.

In the 12th century, the armies of Morocco's Almohad dynasty stormed across the by now hopelessly divided lands of Muslim Spain. To them we owe some of the marvels of Sevilla, in particular the square-based minaret known as the Giralda, which is even more beautiful than the minaret of the Koutoubia mosque in Marrakesh.

Muslim art reached new heights of elegance with the construction of the Alhambra palace in Granada. Built from the 13th to the 15th centuries, it is symptomatic of the direction taken by Islamic art at the time. Eschewing innovation, the Alhambra expresses a desire to refine already well-tried forms. In this it is an unqualified success and surely one of the Muslim world's most beautiful creations.

Around the same time, Pedro I decided to build himself a new palace in the *alcázar* (fortress) of what was by now Christian-controlled Sevilla. Granada's Mohammed V sent artisans to help out and the result is a jewel of Iberian Islamic architecture – built for a Christian monarch!

Mozarabic & Mudéjar

What sets much of Christian Spain's architecture apart from its counterparts elsewhere in Europe is the deep-seated influence exercised over it by Islamic styles.

Already in the 10th century, Christians practising in Muslim territory – known as *Mozárabes* (Mozarabs) – began to adopt elements of classic Islamic construction and export them to Christian-held territory. Although Mozarabic artisans contributed to many buildings, 'purely' Mozarabic structures are few and far between. Among the outstanding examples are the Iglesia de San Miguel de Escalada (east of León), the Ermita de San Baudelio (in Soria province) and the Iglesia de Nuestra Señora de Lebeña (on the eastern side of the Picos de Europa).

More important was the *mudéjar* influence, that of Muslims who remained behind in the lands of the Reconquista. Their skills were found to be priceless (but cheap) and throughout Spain their influence is evident.

One unmistakable mudéjar feature is the preponderance of brick: castles, churches and mansions all over the country were built of this material.

Another telltale feature is in the ceilings. Extravagantly decorated timber creations, often ornately carved, are a mark of the mudéjar hand. Several different types get constant mention. The term *armadura* refers to any of these wooden ceilings, especially when they have the appearance of being an inverted boat. *Artesonado* ceilings are characterised by interlaced beams leaving regular spaces (triangular, square or polygonal) for the insertion of decorative *artesas*.

The term *techumbre* (which can simply mean 'roof') applies more specifically to the most common of armaduras, where the skeleton of the ceiling (looked at from the end) looks like a series of 'A's.

In the Convento de Santa Clara in Salamanca, ramps have been installed, allowing close inspection of the original ceiling.

DAMIEN SIMONIS

DAMIEN SIMONIS

Far Left: A window of the Iglesia de San Miguel de Escalada, east of León, an outstanding mozarabic structure (Castilla y León)

Left: The mudéjar-styled entrance to the Casa de las Siente Chimeneas, one of Madrid's oldest buildings

Romanesque

As the Muslim tide was turned back and the Reconquista gathered momentum, the first great medieval European movement in design began to take hold in Spain, spreading from Italy and France. From about the 11th century, churches, monasteries, bridges, pilgrims' hospices and other buildings in the Romanesque style mushroomed in the north.

The first wave came in Catalunya, where Lombard artisans influenced by Byzantine building techniques soon covered the countryside with comparatively simple churches – the church of Sant Climent in Taüll is emblematic of this. Another outstanding example is the Monestir de Santa Maria in Ripoll; some 2000 Romanesque buildings survive in Catalunya. Soon more home-grown styles began to emerge across the rest of northern Spain.

Romanesque is easily identified by a few basic characteristics. The exteriors of most edifces bear little decoration and they tend to be simple, angular structures. In the case of churches in particular, the concession to curves comes with the semicylindrical apse – or, in many cases, triple apse. The single most striking element of decoration is the semicircular arch or arches that grace doorways, windows, cloisters and naves. The humble church of the Monasterio de Sigena, east of Zaragoza, has a doorway boasting 14 such arches, one encased in the other.

With all the baroque baubles, you could be excused for overlooking that the cathedral in Santiago de Compostela is itself a seminal work of Romanesque design, much imitated, for instance, in Orense and Tuy.

The Camino de Santiago is studded with Romanesque beauties. These include (from east to west) the Monasterio de Santo Domingo de Silos, the smaller cloister (Las Claustrillas) in the Monasterio de las Huelgas in Burgos and the restored Iglesia de San Martín in Frómista.

Right: The Iglesia de San Martín in Frómista (Castilla y León) is just one of the many Romanesque churches along the Camino de Santiago (see the special section later in this book).

KELLI HAMBLET

The Transition

During the 12th century, modifications in the Romanesque recipe became apparent. The pointed arch and ribbed vault of various kinds are clear precursors of the Gothic revolution to come.

The Monasterio de Santa María de la Oliva in Navarra was among the first to incorporate such features and other buildings followed. Cathedrals in Ávila (part-fortress; Castilla y León), Sigüenza (Castilla-La Mancha), Tarragona (Catalunya) and Tudela (Navarra) all display at least some transitional elements.

A peculiar side development affected south-western Castile. The cathedrals in Salamanca, Zamora and Toro all boast Byzantine lines, particularly in the cupola.

Gothic

In northern Europe, everyone marvelled at the towering new cathedrals made possible by the use of flying buttresses and other technical innovations.

The idea caught on later in Spain, but three of the most important Gothic cathedrals in the country, in Burgos, León and Toledo, went up in the 13th century. The former two owe much to French models, but the Spaniards soon introduced other elements. The huge decorative *retablos* (altarpieces) towering over the high altar were one such innovation. And although not an exclusively Spanish touch, the placing of the *coro* (choir stalls) in the centre of the nave became the rule rather than the exception in Spanish Gothic.

The main structural novelty in Spanish Gothic was star-vaulting (a method of weight distribution in the roof in which ribbed vaults project outwards from a series of centre points), while a clearly Hispanic touch is the cloister and gardens.

A problem with determining what style a monument belongs to is that often they belong to several. Many great buildings begun at the height of Romanesque glory were only completed long after Gothic had gained the upper hand. And although, for instance, the cathedral in Burgos was one of the first to go up, its magnificent spires were a result of German-inspired Late Gothic imagination. In many cases, these Gothic or Romanesque-Gothic buildings received a plateresque or baroque overlay at a later date. Sevilla's immense cathedral was completed in 1507 and betrays not a few Renaissance touches.

Mudéjar influences were also alive and well, most easily recognised in the giveaway penchant for working in brick rather than stone. Toledo is covered in buildings of a Gothic-mudéjar combination, while Aragón was blessed with a singular version of the theme. Zaragoza, Teruel, Tarazona and Calatayud all contain marvellous mudéjar works.

Finally, the so-called Isabelline style was a late addition to the cocktail. Taking some decorative cues from the more curvaceous traits of

KELLI HAMBLET

Islamic design, it was in some ways an indirect precursor to plateresque. Perhaps its ultimate expression is Toledo's San Juan de los Reyes, originally destined to be the final resting place of the Catholic Monarchs. Designed by French-born Juan Güas (1453–96), it is a medley of earlier Gothic and mudéjar elements, with a final decorative Isabelline flourish.

The 16th century saw a revival of pure Gothic, perhaps best exemplified in the new cathedral in Salamanca, although the Segovia cathedral was about the last, and possibly most pure, Gothic house of worship to be constructed in Spain.

Not only religious buildings flourished. Most of the innumerable castles scattered across the country went up in Gothic times. Many never saw action and were not intended to – a couple of the more extraordinary samples of mudéjar castle-building from this era are the Castillo de la Mota (Medina del Campo, Castilla y León) and the sumptuous castle at Coca, not far away.

Right: A masterpiece of Gothic grandeur, the cathedral in Burgos (Castilla y León) took three centuries to build.

Renaissance

The Renaissance in Spain can be roughly divided into three distinct styles. First was the Italian-influenced special flavour of plateresque. To visit Salamanca is to receive a concentrated dose of the most splendid work in the genre. The university facade especially is a virtuoso piece, featuring busts, medallions and swathes of complex floral design. Not far behind in intensity comes the facade of the Convento de San Esteban. Little of the work can be convincingly traced to any one hand and it appears that the principal exponent of plateresque, Alonso de Covarrubias (1488–1570), was busier in his home city of Toledo (the Alcázar and the Capilla de los Nuevos Reyes in the cathedral).

Next was the more purist Renaissance style that prevailed in Andalucía and had its maximum expression in the Palacio de Carlos V in Granada's Alhambra. Diego de Siloé (1495–1563) and his followers are regarded as masters. Siloé made his mark with Granada's cathedral; others followed him with such masterpieces as the Jaén cathedral and the Capilla de El Salvador in Úbeda (although this leans more to plateresque). The latter was designed by Andrés de Vandelvira (1509–75).

Juan de Herrera (1530–97) is the last and perhaps greatest figure of the Spanish Renaissance, but his work bears almost no resemblance to anything else of the period. His austere masterpiece is the palace-monastery complex of San Lorenzo de El Escorial (Comunidad de Madrid).

Baroque

The heady frills and spills of baroque can be seen all over Spain, but usually in the form of additions rather than complete buildings. Cádiz's baroque cathedral is an exception (although some neoclassical work was added). Three loose phases can be identified, starting with a sober baroque still heavily influenced by Herrera (see earlier), followed by a period of greater architectural exuberance (some would say, a sickening amount) and finally running into a mixture of baroque with the beginnings of neoclassicism.

The leading exponents of this often overblown approach to building and decoration were the Churriguera brothers. Alberto (1676–1750) designed Salamanca's Plaza Mayor, but he and brother José (1665–1735) are best known for their extraordinary retablos, or huge carved wooden backdrops for altars. Their memorable works feature twisting gilded columns, burdened with all manner of angels and saints.

Baroque reached new heights of opulence with the Sagrario in Granada's La Cartuja monastery and the Transparente in Toledo's cathedral. Sevilla is jammed with baroque gems. But baroque appears elsewhere too: the facade superimposed over the Romanesque original in the cathedral of Santiago de Compostela and the cathedral in Murcia are notable examples.

KELLI HAMBLET

Neoclassicism

In Spain as elsewhere, the pendulum swung away from the gaudy extremes of baroque as the 18th century closed. Tastes became more sober and the cleaner, restrained lines of neoclassicism came into fashion. In Spain, minor churches, bullrings and public buildings were built in this style, but little of greatness was achieved.

Modernisme

The end of the 19th century ushered in arguably one of the most imaginative periods in Spanish building. Catalunya was home to the *modernistas,* whose master was Antoni Gaudí (1852–1926). Although he exercised his fantasy outside Catalunya (in Astorga, León and Comillas), he and his peers left their most singular mark on Barcelona. Work continues even now (amid considerable controversy) on his most exciting project, the immense La Sagrada Família church. Other jewels in the Gaudí crown include the Casa Batlló and La Pedrera, not to mention Parc Güell.

Gaudí personifies, and in large measure transcends, a movement in architecture that brought a thunderclap of innovative greatness to an otherwise middle-ranking European city. But this startling wave of creativity subsided just as quickly – the bulk of the modernistas' work was done from the 1880s to about 1910. Right behind were two other architects, Lluís Domènech i Montaner (1850–1923) and Josep Puig i Cadafalch (1867–1957).

Above: The Palacio de Carlos V is a wonderful example of Renaissance architecture within the Alhambra in Granada (Andalucía).

Modernisme did not appear in isolation in Barcelona. To the British and French the style was called *Art Nouveau,* to the Italians it was *lo stile Liberty,* the Germans called it *Jugendstil* (Youth Style) and their Austrian confrères *Sezession* (Secession). Elsewhere in Spain though,

SPANISH ARCHITECTURE

it made very little impact. Madrid has only one seriously modernista building!

Modernista architects looked to the past for inspiration but at their most inventive flouted the rule books and created new and exciting cocktails. Many of the materials they used were traditional but their application was utterly innovative.

As many as 2000 buildings in Barcelona and throughout Catalunya display at least some modernista traces.

Modern

The main boulevards of Madrid are filled with portentous facades, which are owned by banks and ministries, from around the turn of the 20th century. Together they make an agreeable impression, without being of any notable architectural worth. Many fine private mansions have over several decades been lost to the bulldozer as banks, shopping conglomerates and big business have raised their inevitable skyscrapers. Some of these buildings are interesting, but few of them outstanding.

The single most eye-catching piece of modern architecture is with little doubt Frank Gehry's Museo Guggenheim in Bilbao.

MARTIN MOOS

Left: The extraordinary Teatre-Museu Dalí in Figueres (Catalunya), designed by Salvador Dalí, took 13 years to be converted from a burnt-out theatre to a museum. It now contains a great portion of the artist's work.

(continued from page 62)

18th Century The Bourbon kings had little interest in sponsoring Spanish talent, being obsessed, rather, with all things French and, to a lesser extent, Italian. Carlos III had Anton Raphael Mengs (1728–79) brought from Bohemia as court painter and he became the maker and breaker of rising artists. Aided by Zaragoza-born Francisco Bayeu (1734–95), he was a gifted if unexciting portraitist.

Goya Mengs could spot talent. He encouraged Francisco José de Goya y Lucientes (1746–1828), a provincial hick from Fuendetodos in Aragón, as a cartoonist in the Fábrica Real de Tapices in Madrid. Here began the long and varied career of Spain's only truly great artist of the 18th (and, indeed, even the 19th) century.

In 1776 he began designing for the tapestry factory and by 1799 was appointed Carlos IV's court painter. Illness in 1792 left him deaf. This perhaps influenced his style, which was increasingly unshackled by convention and often merciless.

Several distinct series and individual paintings mark the progress of his life and work. In the last years of the century he painted such enigmatic masterpieces as *La Maja Vestida* and *La Maja Desnuda*, identical portraits but for the lack of clothes in the latter. At about the same time he did the frescoes in Madrid's Ermita de San Antonio de la Florida and *Los Caprichos,* a biting ser-ies of 80 etchings lambasting the follies of court life and ignorant clergy.

The arrival of the French and war in 1808 profoundly affected his work. Unforgiving portrayals of the brutality of war are *El Dos de Mayo* and, more dramatically, *El Tres de Mayo.* The latter depicts the execution of Madrid rebels by French troops.

With the return of Fernando VII at the end of the war, Goya's position became more tenuous. After he retired to the Quinta del Sordo (Deaf Man's House), as he called his modest lodgings west of the Manzanares in Madrid, age and perhaps a bitterness prompted the creation of his most extra-ordinary paintings, the nightmarish *Pinturas Negras* (Black Paintings). Done on the walls of the house, they were later removed and now hang in the Prado. *Saturno Devorando a Su Hijo* (Saturn Devouring his Son) is emblematic of the hallucinatory horror of these works. He spent the last years of his life in voluntary exile in France, where he continued to paint until his death.

It is difficult to do justice to Goya's role in the evolution of European painting. An obvious precursor to many subsequent strands of modern art, he was an island of grandeur in a sea of mediocrity in Spain.

Late 19th Century Although no one of the stature of Goya can be cited, new trends were noticeable in the latter decades of the century. For the first time in centuries the focus shifted, briefly, back to Valencia. A trio from this region merit a mention: Ignacio Pinazo (1849–1916), Francisco Domingo (1842–1920) and Emilio Sala (1850–1910). Sala, who was clearly influenced by Degas, and Domingo lived and worked in Paris, but neither achieved great success. More successful in the long run was the Basque Ignacio Zuloaga (1870–1945).

Joaquín Sorolla (1863–1923), if anything, flew in the face of the French impressionists, preferring the blinding sunlight of the Valencian coast to the muted tones favoured in Paris. He is known for his cheerful, large-format images of beach life. His work can be studied at Madrid's Museo de Sorolla.

20th Century In a sense, the history of Spanish art turned full circle at the close of the 19th century, returning to Catalunya. Barcelona, a hothouse of social agitation and the home of Spanish modernism (see the special section 'Spanish Architecture'), was about the only environment in an otherwise depressed and sluggish Spain in which artists could hope to flourish. It was the perfect place for someone like Pablo Ruiz Picasso (1881–1973), born in Málaga, to come to flex his brushes.

Picasso is one of the monumental characters of Western European art. Having shown prodigious aptitude at an early age, he started visiting Paris in 1900. He had already absorbed lessons from his greatest forerunners – Goya, Velázquez and El Greco – and in Paris opened himself to the riches of Gauguin, Toulouse-Lautrec and Van Gogh.

Picasso was a turbulent character and gifted not only on canvas, but also as a sculptor, graphic designer and ceramicist. His work knew many abruptly changing periods. His Blue Period, until 1904, is characterised by rather sombre renditions of the lives of the down and out. The common denominator was the preponderance of blues on his palette. After his definitive move to Paris in 1904, he began the so-called Pink Period; the subjects became merrier and the colouring leaned towards light pinks and greys.

Picasso remained ever in search of new forms. *Les Demoiselles d'Avignon* (1907) broke with all forms of traditional representation, introducing a deformed perspective that would spill into cubism, of which he and Georges Braque (1882–1963) were the pioneers. Picasso's countryman, Madrid-born Juan Gris (1887–1927) was another leading cubist. Picasso experimented continually with different methods and by the mid-1920s was dabbling with surrealism. His best-known work is *Guernica,* a complex canvas portraying the horror of war and inspired by the German aerial bombing of the Basque town Gernika in 1937.

Picasso's output during and after WWII remained prolific and indeed he was cranking out paintings, sculptures, ceramics and etchings until the day he died.

Separated from Picasso by barely a generation, two other artists reinforced the Catalan contingent in the vanguard of first-class Spanish contributions to this century's art: Dalí and Miró. Although he started off dabbling in cubism, Salvador Dalí (1904–89) became more readily identified with the surrealists. This complex character's 'handpainted dream photographs', as he called them, are virtuoso executions brimming with fine detail and nightmare images dragged up from a feverish and Freud-fed imagination. Preoccupied with Picasso's fame, Dalí built himself a repu-

MICK WELDON

Pablo Picasso, a master of canvas and clay, was instrumental in changing the face of Western European art.

tation as an outrageous showman and self-promoter. The single best display of his works can be seen at the 'theatre-museum' he created in Figueres (Catalunya).

Slower to find his feet, Joan Miró (1893–1983) developed a joyous and almost childlike style that earned him the epithet 'the most surrealist of us all' from André Breton. His later period is his best known, characterised by the simple use of bright colours and forms.

Picasso, Dalí and Miró were a pretty hard act to follow and contemporary painters lack the greatness of this extraordinary trio. In the wake of the civil war, Fernando Zóbel (1924–84) collected his own works and those of his contemporaries in the 1950s 'Generación Abstracta' under one roof in a private museum in Cuenca. Gustavo Torner and Eusebio Sempere feature among those on display. Other names worth looking for are Antonio Saura (1930–), Manuel Millares (1926–72) and Antoni Tàpies (1923–).

The art of Madrid's Eduardo Arroyo (1937–) is steeped in the radical spirit that kept him in exile from Spain for 15 years from 1962.

Sevilla's Luis Gordillo (1934–) started his artistic career steeped in surrealism, from where he branched into pop art and photography. His later work in particular features serialisation of different version of the same image.

Other names worth looking out for if you are interested in what is happening in Spanish art today include: Óscar Seco, Álvaro Toledo, Francisco Leiro, Carlos Franco and Chelo Matesanz.

Cinema

While a handful of directors and actors keep the modern Spanish cinema industry ticking over, occasionally with some success beyond their own shores, the history of film in Spain has been a largely barren expanse with the occasional burst of brilliance.

Way back in 1897 a short film was made showing people at Zaragoza's basilica and later studios were set up in Barcelona.

Luis Buñuel The man now universally regarded as the greatest Spanish film maker emerged with the surrealist movement in the 1920s. Luis Buñuel, born in Calanda (Aragón) in 1900, only developed an interest in film after moving to Paris in 1926. By then he had already established himself in Spanish literary and art circles and for a long time was a close friend of Salvador Dalí.

Buñuel's first full attempt at film production, made when he was already under the sway of the surrealists, was *Un Chien Andalou* (1929), followed a year later by *L'Age d'Or*. Both were made with Dalí. They have lived on as classics, as has his next effort, a hard-hitting account of the desperation of rural life for which he returned to Spain. *Las Hurdes – Terre Sans Pain,* filmed in the hilly Las Hurdes region of Extremadura and the surrounding area, was banned in Spain and hence originally appeared in its French version. Buñuel remained in Spain, dubbing for Warner Brothers.

He did not really move back into filmmaking until winding up in Mexico in the mid-1940s, an exile from Francoist Spain. Mexico City then became his base, although he also continued to work in France.

Belle de Jour (1966), starring Catherine Deneuve, was a big success. Buñuel died in 1983 in Mexico City.

The Civil War & the Franco Years Meanwhile in Spain, censorship tended to stifle most creative impulses. During the civil war, the Republican side had beaten the Nationalists in the use of film as a propaganda tool, but this didn't prevent them from losing the war. Once Franco installed himself in power in 1939, a tight if not always consistent clamp was applied to the industry.

There were exceptions to the rule. Luis García Berlanga's (1921–) *Bienvenido Mr Marshall,* made in 1952, was a breath of Italian-style neorealism that managed to get through the net. The film observes the belated agreement on US aid to Spain under the Marshall Plan (in which the USA ignored its own disapproval of Franco in return for military bases) from a small Spanish village; about the only tangible result for the villagers is a rain of dust as Marshall's cavalcade of VIP cars charges through the town.

Juan Antonio Bardem (1922–), who wrote the script for *Bienvenido Mr Marshall,* followed in 1955 with *Muerte de un Ciclista* (Death of a Cyclist) and Berlanga chimed in again with *El Verdugo* (The Executioner) in 1964. Buñuel was invited to Spain at this time to produce a film. The result, *Viridiana,* was a biting film deemed worthy of a Palme d'Or at Cannes and was subsequently banned by Franco.

The next star to emerge was Carlos Saura (1932–), whose first film, *Los Golfos* (The Scoundrels), came out in 1959. He developed a more subversive style in the early 1970s, peaking with *Ana y los Lobos* (1973), in which the power of the church and army in Francoist Spanish society comes under attack. In the same year, Victor Erice's (1940–) *El Espíritu de la Colmena* (The Spirit of the Beehive) hit the screen; it is a quiet and beautifully crafted picture in which one of the cinema's outcast figures, Frankenstein's monster, becomes real for a beekeeper's little daughter.

Cinema after Franco The late 1970s and the 1980s breathed new life into Spanish cinema, with a few directors producing work appreciated not only in Spain, but also abroad. Pedro Almodóvar (1949–) is Spain's best-known cinema export, having won many fans with such quirkily comic looks at modern Spain as *Mujeres al Borde de un Ataque de Nervios* (Women on the Verge of a Nervous Breakdown; 1988) and *Atame* (Tie Me Up, Tie Me Down; 1989). Darker sentiments are explored in productions such as *Matador* (1985), where the blood lust of the *corrida* (bullfight) and the lust of the bed are closely tied together.

Vicente Aranda (1926–) has been less prolific than Almodóvar, but found acclaim with *Amantes* (1991), set in 1950s Madrid and based on the real story of a doomed love triangle. Three years later he hit the screens again with the steamy *La Pasión Turca* (The Turkish Passion). In 1992, Fernando Trueba (1955–) brought out *Belle Epoque,* which examines the melancholy underside to bliss through the story of four sisters' pursuit of a young chap. It won an Oscar.

Almodóvar in particular has moved away from the deadening burden of Franco and the civil war years (although even he falls occasionally into the trap) and other directors are following suit. That said, British director

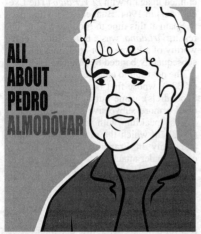

ALL
ABOUT
PEDRO
ALMODÓVAR

MICK WELDON

Ken Loach tried his hand in 1995 at the war theme. The UK-Spanish production that resulted is probably one of the most successful treatments of the subject on film to date – *Tierra y Libertad* (Land and Freedom).

Spanish cinema continues to demonstrate considerable creative vigour. Almodóvar swept the 2000 Goyas (Spain's version of the Oscars) with his *Todo Sobre Mi Madre* (All About My Mother; 1999). He then went on to get the Oscar for the best non-English-language movie – only the third time a Spanish director has managed the feat. The movie is a masterpiece of quirky commentary that ties together the lives of the most improbable collection of women (including a couple of transsexuals).

Solas (1999), the debut film by Andalucía's Benito Zambrano (1965–), takes a moving look at the vicissitudes of a mother and daughter living the oppressive anachronism of deep Spain in a country that has, at least in appearance, made giant strides towards modernity.

Ventura Pons (1945–) is a veteran of Catalan theatre and film-making. His *Morir (o No)* (2000) follows seven stories that end in someone's death and then dovetails them into one tale in which none of the characters dies.

Daniel Calparsoro (1968–) has tended to see the dark side in his flicks. His fourth and latest, *Asfalto,* looks at some less savoury aspects of life in the mean streets of Madrid, although he insists the message is positive. His other films have been equally violent and somewhat uneven, but there is promise. Another relatively new face in Spanish cinema is Miguel Albaladejo (1967–). His films ooze originality and his latest, *Ataque Verbal,* is a comedy made up of seven short stories, each involving two characters.

Theatre

Thanks mainly to a big theatre development program by the PSOE governments of the 1980s and 90s, most cities have a theatre. Productions range from old classics to modern comedy or avant-garde fare, with a fair swag of foreign drama in translation. Madrid and Barcelona are the epicentres, with Barcelona having an edge when it comes to avant-garde productions. Straight theatre is unlikely to appeal, however, if your understanding of Spanish – or, in Barcelona, Catalan – is less than fluent.

SOCIETY & CONDUCT

Spaniards can be economical with etiquette and thank-yous but this does not signify unfriendliness. One way in which you may notice people expressing their fellow feeling is the general *'Buenos días'* they often utter to all and sundry when they enter a small shop or bar and the *'Adiós'* when they leave. Spaniards don't expect foreigners to speak much Spanish – although you need some words to get by outside tourist centres and of course it helps a lot if you *can* communicate in Spanish.

Most Spaniards don't really show much interest in communicating more than superficially with transient visitors. Invitations to Spanish homes are rare enough to be a mark of true friendship.

But they are famous for being gregarious and the family is of paramount importance, with children adored and always a good talking point. At the same time they're an individualistic, proud people.

Day, Night & Time

The Spanish attitude to time *is* more relaxed than in most Western cultures. But things that need a fixed time – trains, buses, cinemas, football matches – get one and it's generally stuck to. Things that need to get done, get done. Waiters may not always be in a hurry, but they come before too long.

What's different is the daily timetable. The Spanish *tarde* (afternoon) doesn't really start until 4 pm or so and goes on until 9 pm or later. Shops and offices close from around 2 to 5 pm, then mostly open again until around 8 pm. In hot summer months people stay outside late, enjoying the coolness. At fiestas don't be surprised to see merry-go-rounds packed with children at 3 am. And of course Friday and Saturday nights, all year round, barely begin until midnight for those doing the rounds of bars and discos.

What's in an Apellido?

You may soon notice that there's something not quite straightforward about Spaniards' names. María García and Pedro Blanco present no problem, but what to make of Almudena López López, Francisco Sánchez G or Isabel de Colón Villalobos?

Spaniards typically have three names: a given name *(nombre)* and two surnames *(apellidos)*. The first of the surnames is the person's father's first surname. The second surname is the mother's first surname. So Isabel, the daughter of Antonio Romero Cervantes and Alicia Ruiz Álvarez, is Isabel Romero Ruiz.

In practice many people don't bother with their second surname or occasionally just shorten it to an initial – so our Isabel is simply Isabel Romero or maybe Isabel Romero R. But if the first surname is a particularly common one (García, Fernández, López, González and Rodríguez are the most common), a person is more likely to keep the second one in use too – and may even, when a short version of their name is wanted, use only the second surname. A famous case of this is the writer Federico García Lorca, who is known as either García Lorca or just Lorca, but never as García.

Women don't change their names when they marry, but may tack one of their husband's surnames (preceded by *de*) on to their own name. So if Isabel Romero were to marry Pedro Colón, she could call herself Isabel Romero de Colón!

Siesta Contrary to popular opinion, most Spaniards do not have a sleep in the afternoon. The siesta is generally devoted to a long, leisurely lunch and lingering conversation. But then again, if you've stayed out until 6 am...

Treatment of Animals

There is little doubting the cruelty of bullfighting, Spain's national blood sport, and the subject can generate animated debate. For aficionados it is an art, a virtuoso display of courage that generally ends in the honourable death of the bull – a better fate than the abattoir they will tell you. Its opponents are simply sickened by it. You can contact the following organisations for information and suggested action:

People for the Ethical Treatment of Animals (PETA)
UK: (☎ 020-7388 4922, fax 7388 4925) PO Box 3169, London NW1 2JF
USA: (☎ 757-622 PETA, fax 622 1078) 501 Front St, Norfolk, VA 23510
World Society for the Protection of Animals (WSPA)
Canada: (☎ 416-369 0044, fax 369 0147) 44 Victoria St, Suite 1310, Toronto, Ontario M5C 1Y2
UK: (☎ 020-7793 0540, fax 7793 0208, ⓔ wspahq@gn.apc.org) 2 Langley Lane, London SW8 1TJ
USA: (☎ 617-522 7000, fax 522 7077, ⓔ wspa@world.std.com) PO Box 190 Boston, MA 02130

For more information about bullfighting, see the special section on the subject following the Facts for the Visitor chapter.

RELIGION
Roman Catholicism
It's impossible not to notice the importance of the Roman Catholic church in Spain. So many of the country's great occasions are religious fiestas; so many of its most magnificent buildings are cathedrals or churches, lavishly adorned and lovingly tended by the faithful. The great majority of Spaniards have church baptisms, weddings and funerals. According to surveys, around 85% of them say they are Catholics.

All this is hardly surprising in a country whose very existence is the result of a series of medieval anti-Muslim crusades and which gave the world the Jesuits to fight the Protestant Reformation in the 16th century. Under Franco the church and state were so closely tied that the Vatican allowed the government to appoint Spanish bishops, while the government paid priests' salaries and granted the church numerous other privileges, including lots of money. The government still subsidises the church heavily and nearly one-third of Spanish children go to state-subsidised Catholic schools, even though Spain has had no official religion since 1978. Only about 40% of Spaniards now go to church once a month or more, and the numbers of priests, monks and nuns are all falling.

Spain has a long-standing anticlerical tradition too, originating in the 19th century when the church became identified with conservative opposition to political change. Liberal and left-wing movements were frequently accompanied by church-burnings and killings of priests, monks and nuns. This reached a bloody crescendo in the civil war, in which some 7000 were killed.

But so deeply is Catholicism ingrained in Spanish life that men who hardly ever go to church vie for membership of the brotherhoods that carry holy images around the streets in Easter processions, while thousands of less than pious folk take part in giant pilgrimages to holy sites and other religion-based fiestas. The early 20th-century philosopher Miguel Unamuno's quip, 'Here in Spain we are all Catholics, even the atheists', still holds a lot of truth.

Other Faiths
Protestantism was eradicated by the Inquisition in the 16th century before it could even get a toehold. Today there are up to 350,000 Protestants in Spain, many of them in Catalunya. The Jehovah's Witnesses are one of the leading Protestant churches.

Muslims and Jews played enormous roles in medieval Spain but were stamped on at the end of that period (see the History section earlier). Spain counts as many as 400,000 Muslims, most of them immigrants from Africa, although there are perhaps 1000 Spanish-born converts, many of whom live in Granada.

The Jewish community numbers about 15,000, many of them from Morocco. Franco allowed Jewish refugees to enter Spain in WWII and in 1982 Sephardic Jews (Jews of Spanish and North African origin) were officially invited to return to Spain, 490 years after their expulsion by the Catholic Monarchs.

Opus Dei

The Catholic secular organisation Opus Dei (Work of God) doesn't have quite the power in post-Franco Spain that it did during the dictatorship, but it remains influential in areas such as the media, education and business. José María Aznar, prime minister since 1996, is a practising Catholic and the higher echelons of his Partido Popular (PP) party include many who are at least close to Opus Dei, but Aznar has kept his distance from church traditionalists.

Founded in 1928 by an Aragonese, Josemaría Escrivá (1902–75), Opus Dei has members in some 80 countries around the world. Its stated mission is to promote among Christians a life consistent with Christian faith and to contribute to the evangelisation of every sphere of society. It stresses the sanctification of work, which means working with maximum competence in accordance with the law and ethics; trying to serve fellow citizens and contribute to the progress of society; and seeking union with God through work.

Escrivá noticed that economic progress tended to turn people away from Catholicism. He attempted to reverse this by inspiring Catholics with a new ethic of work and self-reliance, concentrating Opus Dei's work in areas such as higher education, in a successful effort to gain support among the influential.

The organisation sees itself as nonpolitical, but it is religiously conservative. It places a strong emphasis on confession and members are encouraged to attain holiness through prayer, the sacraments and mortification. It received a burst of unwelcome publicity in 2000 when an exhibition at Valladolid university, advocating the use of condoms as protection against AIDS, was destroyed by a group of youths following a protest about the exhibition by Opus Dei members of the university's academic staff. One of them, José Luis Martínez López Muñiz – who had been an adviser to Aznar earlier in his career – wrote that the exhibition made the university's law faculty resemble a centre of youth corruption and even a brothel.

Opus Dei's philosophy lends itself to conservative economic policies. Members and supporters were at the forefront of Spain's 1960s economic takeoff under Franco (though other members, Opus Dei says, were expelled from Spain because of their opposition to Franco). The fellowship is the subject of all sorts of conspiracy theories among people at the other end of the political spectrum.

Opus Dei, which has its headquarters in Rome, found early favour with Pope John Paul II, who in 1982 established it as a 'personal prelature' (a kind of nonterritorial church jurisdiction, in contrast to territorial jurisdictions such as dioceses). In 1992 Escrivá was beatified (a step towards canonisation) in unusually rapid time.

Opus Dei runs eight universities and 250 schools around the world. It's also said to control a significant number of TV networks, newspapers, press agencies and publishing houses. For more on Opus Dei, see the Torreciudad section in the Aragón chapter.

LANGUAGE

Spanish, or Castilian *(castellano)*, as it is often and more precisely called, is spoken throughout Spain, but there are also three widely spoken regional languages: Catalan (*català;* another Romance language, with close ties to French) is spoken in Catalunya, the Balearic Islands and Valencia; Galician (*galego;* similar enough to Portuguese to be regarded by some as a dialect) is spoken in Galicia; and Basque (*euskara;* of obscure, non-Latin origin) is spoken in the Basque Country and Navarra.

For pronunciation details and useful phrases, see the Language chapter at the back of this book. The glossary, also at the back, contains some common words in Castilian, Basque, Catalan and Galician Spanish. It is followed by the food glossary – a handy menu decoder.

Facts for the Visitor

SUGGESTED ITINERARIES

Where you should go depends on what you like doing. Every part of Spain has its own compelling reasons to be visited. Nor does it matter much in which order you take your chosen destinations: Spain is easy enough to travel around for you to make up your itinerary as you go.

The basic choice is between a wide-ranging tour that takes you to as many varied parts of the country as you can manage or a narrower focus on a smaller number of places to explore in greater depth. Following are a few highlights to help you start planning. Also check the Public Holidays & Special Events and Activities sections of this chapter for further ideas on places and events you might like to work into your timetable.

Cities & Towns

Madrid and Barcelona are obviously the most vibrant cities, with the most to see and do. They're a strong contrast but both are essential experiences if you want a feel for the country.

Sevilla, with its exciting southern atmosphere, isn't far behind the 'big two' for excitement and also introduces you to the distinctive region of Andalucía. Other cities and towns with a particularly strong pull include Santiago de Compostela and Pontevedra in Galicia; San Sebastián in the Basque Country; Segovia, Ávila, Salamanca, León, Toledo and Cuenca in the old Castilian heartland; Trujillo in Extremadura; Valencia on the Mediterranean coast; and Granada and Ronda in Andalucía.

Coasts

The Costa Brava in Catalunya is rugged enough not to be been completely overwhelmed by tourist development and still secretes many pretty coves, villages and beaches. The Balearic Islands (Islas Baleares) have many fine, isolated little beaches, especially on Menorca, while Mallorca's cliff-strewn northern coast is one of the

most spectacular in the country. Cabo de Gata in eastern Andalucía is lined with excellent, isolated and, by Spanish standards, underpopulated beaches, backed by some fine, rugged coastal scenery. The Costa de la Luz on Andalucía's Atlantic coast has more good beaches and is relatively underdeveloped; Tarifa at its southern end is one of Europe's top windsurfing centres.

In Galicia, the Rías Bajas and Rías Altas are two series of majestic estuaries not unlike the Norwegian fjords, dotted with good beaches, fishing villages and low-key resorts. Spain's most awesome coastal scenery is here too. On the Bay of Biscay coast are the country's best surf beaches and, at San Sebastián, probably its most beautiful city beach.

Countryside & Wilderness

The Pyrenees, especially in Catalunya and Aragón, are strung with imposing peaks and lovely valleys. Two of the best areas to head for are the national parks: Aigüestortes i Estany de Sant Maurici in Catalunya and Ordesa y Monte Perdido in Aragón.

In the north-west, the Picos de Europa range, which straddles Cantabria, Asturias and Castilla y León, is justly famous for its wild and beautiful mountain scenery. Galicia is Spain's greenest area – rolling countryside abutting a dramatic coast.

In the central west, the Sierra de Gredos and its western offshoots, such as the Sierra de Peña de Francia, contain further impressive ranges and charming, remote valleys, such as those of La Vera, Jerte and Ambroz in northern Extremadura. There's yet more impressive mountainous terrain in the Serranía de Cuenca area on the border of Castilla-La Mancha and Aragón, and in Mallorca's Serra de Tramuntana.

In Andalucía, the mountains around Ronda, the Alpujarras valleys south of the Sierra Nevada and the *sierras* (mountain range) of Cazorla and Segura, east of Baeza, stand out for their beauty, while the semi-desert scenery east of Almería is weird enough to have been used as the setting for dozens of western movies.

PLANNING
When to Go

Spain can be enjoyable any time of year. The *ideal* months to visit are May, June and September (plus April and October in the south). At these times you can rely on good to excellent weather, yet avoid the sometimes extreme heat – and the main crush of Spanish and foreign tourists – of July and August, when temperatures can climb to 45°C in inland Andalucía and Madrid is unbearable and almost deserted.

But there's decent weather in some parts of Spain virtually year round. Winter along the southern and south-eastern Mediterranean coasts is mild, while in the height of summer you can retreat to the north-west, to beaches or high mountains anywhere to escape excessive heat.

The best festivals are mostly concentrated between Semana Santa (the week leading up to Easter Sunday) and September-October. For more details, see Public Holidays & Special Events in this chapter.

If you plan to pursue some specific activity, you may need to choose your time carefully. See Activities later in this chapter and destination sections in the regional chapters.

Maps

Small-Scale Maps Some of the best maps for travellers are published by Michelin, which produces the 1:1,000,000 *Spain Portugal* map and six 1:400,000 regional maps covering the whole country. These are all pretty accurate, even down to the state of minor country roads, frequently updated and detailed yet easy to read. They're widely available in Spain if you don't manage to pick them up before you go. Also good are the GeoCenter maps published by Germany's RV Verlag.

Probably the best physical map of Spain is *Península Ibérica, Baleares y Canarias* published by the Centro Nacional de Información Geográfica (CNIG), the publication arm of the Instituto Geográfico Nacional (IGN). Ask for it in good bookshops or map shops.

The Best & The Worst

It's tough picking just 10 of the best things about Spain. Here are our personal favourites:

Top Ten
1 Sevilla (except in July and August)
2 The rías of Galicia
3 Valencia's mid-March Las Fallas festival
4 The Picos de Europa
5 Museo Guggenheim in Bilbao
6 Parc Nacional d'Aigüestortes i Estany de Sant Maurici
7 Cabo de Gata
8 Madrid nightlife
9 Granada
10 Beaches, bars and clubs of the Balearic Islands

Thinking of things we don't like about Spain is a lot harder, but we'd be quite happy never to experience any of the following again:

Bottom Ten
1 The Costa del Sol
2 Albacete
3 Benidorm
4 Spanish bureaucracy (don't tangle with it!)
5 Reinosa, Cantabria
6 Spanish motorbike noise
7 *Callos* (tripe – a popular food item)
8 The 'Costa Plástica' – vast areas around Almería covered in plastic sheeting for forced vegetable cultivation
9 Heavy industry around Bilbao
10 Beachwear on the Costa Blanca

Large-Scale Maps There are two organisations that publish detailed close-up maps of small parts of Spain. The CNIG covers most of the country in 1:25,000 (1cm to 250m) sheets, most of which are recent. The CNIG and the Servicio Geográfico del Ejército (SGE; Army Geographic Service) each publish a 1:50,000 series; the SGE's tend to be much more up to date. The CNIG also has a *Mapa Guía* series of maps of national and natural parks, mostly at 1:50,000 or 1:100,000 and published in the 1990s.

Many of the CNIG maps bear the IGN's name instead.

Also useful for hiking and exploring some areas are the Editorial Alpina's *Guía Cartográfica* and *Guía Excursionista y Turística* series. The series combines information booklets in Spanish (or sometimes Catalan) with detailed maps at scales ranging from 1:25,000 to 1:50,000. They're worth their price (around 675 ptas), although the maps have their inaccuracies. The Institut Cartogràfic de Catalunya does good 1:50,000 maps for each of the 41 *comarcas* (districts) of Catalunya, but there's no equivalent for other parts of Spain.

The CNIG has sales offices in most of Spain's provincial capitals. Its head office (☎ 91 597 95 14, fax 91 553 29 13), Calle General Ibáñez de Íbero 3, 28003 Madrid, will send you a free catalogue of its maps, which you can then order by fax or mail. The 1:25,000 and 1:50,000 maps are 500 ptas each plus postage (tell them which maps you want and they'll tell you the total cost and how to pay). Visit its Web site at www.cnig.ign.es.

The SGE's one map shop in mainland Spain (☎ 91 711 50 43, fax 91 711 14 00) is at Calle de Darío Gazapo 8 (Cuartel Alfonso X), 28024 Madrid; it's open from 9 am to 1.30 pm weekdays. Once you've established which maps you want, you can place an order by fax or mail. The SGE will then send you a bill which you have to prepay by bank transfer within Spain or by cheque in pesetas from outside Spain. Once SGE has received your money, it will send you the maps. The 1:50,000 maps are 303 ptas each. CNIG or SGE maps bought from other shops often cost more than the above prices, owing to delivery costs, mark-up and so on.

Editorial Alpina publications and CNIG and SGE maps are often available in town bookshops near walking and trekking areas. But to make sure you get them visit a specialist map or travel bookshop such as La Tienda Verde in Madrid, or Altaïr or Quera in Barcelona. Some map specialists in other countries, such as Stanfords, 12-14 Long Acre, London WC2E 9LP, also have a good ranges of Spain maps.

City Maps For finding your way around cities, the free maps handed out by tourist offices are often adequate. If you want something more comprehensive, most cities are covered by one or another of the Spanish series such as Telstar, Alpina and Everest, which have street indexes; they're available in bookshops. Check their publication dates as some are rather out of date. For a sturdy and helpful map of Barcelona, see Lonely Planet's *Barcelona city map*. Michelin does good maps of Madrid and Barcelona.

Road Atlases See the Car & Motorcycle section in the Getting Around chapter.

What to Bring

Bring as little as possible. Everything you bring, you have to carry. You can buy just about anything you need in Spain, in any case.

Luggage If you'll be doing any walking with your luggage, even just from stations to hotels and back, a backpack is the only sensible answer. One with straps and openings that can be zipped inside a flap is more secure. If you'll be using taxis, or your own car, you might as well take whatever luggage is easiest to open and shut, unpack and pack. Either way, a small day pack is also useful.

Inscribing your name and address on the inside of your luggage, as well as labelling it on the outside, increases your chances of getting it back if it's lost or stolen. Packing things in plastic bags inside your backpack/suitcase is a good way of keeping them organised and, if it rains, dry.

Clothes & Shoes In high summer you may not need more than one layer of clothing, even at 4 am. At cooler times, layers of thin clothing, which trap warm air and can be peeled off if necessary, are better than a single thick layer. For the kind of temperatures and rainfall you can expect, see Climate in the Facts about Spain chapter. It's a good idea to pack some good clothes (something other than jeans and T-shirts) for visits to clubs and top-end restaurants – they don't have to be too formal, though.

You need a pair of strong shoes, even strong trainers, no matter what type of trip you're making. You'll probably also appreciate having a lighter pair sometimes. And if you plan on going to smart clubs or restaurants, you'll need something other than trainers. If you can combine these requirements into two pairs or even one, you'll save space in your luggage!

Useful Items Apart from any special personal needs, or things you might require for particular kinds of trips (camping gear, hiking boots, surfboard etc), consider the following:

- an under-the-clothes money belt or shoulder wallet, useful for protecting your money and documents in cities
- a towel and soap, often lacking in cheap accommodation
- sunscreen lotion, which can be more expensive in Spain than elsewhere
- a small Spanish dictionary and/or phrasebook
- books, which can be expensive and hard to find outside main cities and tourist resorts
- photocopies of your important documents, kept separate from the originals
- a Swiss army knife
- minimal unbreakable cooking, eating and drinking gear if you plan to prepare your own food and drinks
- a medical kit (see Health later in this chapter)
- a padlock or two to secure your luggage to racks and to lock hostel lockers
- a sleeping sheet to save on sheet rental costs if you're using youth hostels (a sleeping bag is unlikely to be useful unless you're camping)
- an adapter plug for electrical appliances
- a torch (flashlight)
- an alarm clock
- sunglasses
- binoculars, if you plan to do any wildlife spotting

RESPONSIBLE TOURISM

Travelling responsibly in Spain boils down to the same as travelling responsibly anywhere, including in your home country: don't scrawl graffiti on ancient monuments, don't pick the flowers in national parks, don't start fires, don't leave litter, and so on.

Spaniards are on the whole gregarious, tolerant people with several decades of experience in coping with the odd ways of foreign visitors and, short of blatantly insulting someone, it's not easy to give offence or cause cultural trauma. Disrespectful behaviour in churches – including excessively casual dress – will not go down well, though.

TOURIST OFFICES
Local Tourist Offices

All cities and many smaller towns have an *oficina de turismo* or *oficina de información turística*. In provincial capitals you'll sometimes find more than one tourist office – one specialising in information on the city alone, the other carrying mostly provincial or regional information. There seems, however, to be no set rule on this division of labour. National and natural parks also often have visitor centres offering useful information. Their opening hours and quality of information vary widely.

There is a nationwide tourist information line in several languages, which might come in handy if you are calling from elsewhere in Spain. For basic information in Spanish, English and French, call ☎ 901-30 06 00 from 9 am to 6 pm daily.

Tourist Offices Abroad

You can get information from the Spanish national tourist offices in 19 countries, including:

Belgium (☎ 02-280 19 26, ℮ bruselas@
tourspain.es) Avenue des Arts 21, B-1040
Brussels
Canada (☎ 416-961 3131, ℮ toronto@
tourspain.es) 2 Bloor St W, 34th floor, Toronto
M4W 3E2
Denmark (☎ 33 15 11 65, ℮ copenhague@
tourspain.es) NY Ostergade 34, 1, DK-1101
Copenhagen
France (☎ 01 45 03 82 57, ℮ paris@
tourspain.es) 43 Rue Decamps, 75784 Paris,
Cedex 16
Germany (☎ 030-882 60 36, ℮ berlin@
tourspain.es) Kurfürstendamm 180, D-10707
Berlin. Branches in Düsseldorf, Frankfurt-am-
Main and Munich.
Italy (☎ 06-678 31 06, ℮ roma@tourspain.es)
Via del Mortaro 19, interno 5, 00187 Rome
Japan (☎ 03-3432 6141, ℮ tokio@tourspain.es)
Daini Toranomon Denki Bldg 4f, 3-1-10
Toranomon, Minato-ku, Tokyo 106

Netherlands (☎ 070-346 59 00, 🄴 lahaya@
 tourspain.es) Laan Van Meerdervoort 8a, 2517
 The Hague
Portugal (☎ 01-357 19 92, 🄴 lisboa@
 tourspain.es) Avenida Sidónio Pais 28 3° Dto,
 1050 Lisbon
UK (☎ 020-7486 8077, brochure request ☎ 0891
 669920 at 50p a minute, 🄴 londres@
 tourspain.es) 22-23 Manchester Square,
 London W1M 5AP
USA (☎ 212-265 8822, 🄴 oetny@tourspain.es)
 666 Fifth Ave, 35th floor, New York, NY 10103.
 Branches in Chicago, Los Angeles and Miami.

VISAS & DOCUMENTS
Passport

Citizens of the 15 European Union (EU)
member states and Switzerland can travel to
Spain with their national identity card
alone. If such countries do not issue ID
cards – as in the UK – travellers must carry
a full valid passport (UK visitor passports
are not acceptable). All other nationalities
must have a full valid passport.

Check that your passport's expiry date is at
least some months away, otherwise you may
not be granted a visa, should you need one.

By law you are supposed to have your
passport or ID card with you at all times in
Spain. It doesn't happen often, but it could
be embarrassing if you are asked by the police to produce a document and you don't
have it with you. You will usually need one
of these documents for police registration
when you take a hotel room.

Visas

Spain is one of 15 countries that has signed
the Schengen Convention, an agreement
whereby all EU member countries (except
the UK and Ireland) plus Iceland and Norway agreed to abolish checks at internal
borders by the end of 2000. The other EU
countries are Austria, Belgium, Denmark,
Finland, France, Germany, Greece (from
2001), Italy, Luxembourg, the Netherlands,
Portugal and Sweden. Legal residents of
one Schengen country do not require a visa
for another Schengen country. In addition,
nationals of many other countries, including
the UK, Canada, Ireland, Japan, New
Zealand and Switzerland, do not require

visas for tourist visits of up to 90 days to
any Schengen country.

Various other nationals not covered by the
Schengen exemption can also spend up to 90
days in Spain without a visa. These include
citizens of Australia, Israel and the USA.
However, all non-EU nationals entering
Spain for any reason other than tourism (such
as study or work) should contact a Spanish
consulate as they may need a specific visa. If
you are a citizen of a country not mentioned
in this section, you should check with a Spanish consulate whether you need a visa.

The standard tourist visa issued by Spanish consulates is the Schengen visa, valid
for up to 90 days. A Schengen visa issued
by one Schengen country is generally valid
for travel in all other Schengen countries.
However, individual Schengen countries
may impose additional restrictions on certain nationalities. It is therefore worth
checking visa regulations with the consulate
of each Schengen country you plan to visit.

You must apply for the visa in your country of residence. If you are going to visit
more than one Schengen country, you are
supposed to apply for the visa at a consulate
of your main destination country, or, if you
have no main destination, then the first
country you intend to visit. It's worth ap-
plying early for your visa, especially in the
busy summer months.

Those needing a visa must apply *in person* at the consulate. Postal applications are
not accepted. In the UK you will be required to produce a UK residence permit,
proof of sufficient funds, an itinerary, return
tickets and a letter of recommendation. Finally, the visa does *not* guarantee entry.

You can apply for no more than two visas
in any 12-month period and you cannot
renew them once inside Spain. Options include 30-day and 90-day single-entry visas
(in London these cost UK£17.75 and
UK£21.30 respectively), 90-day multiple-
entry visas (UK£24.85), and various transit
visas. Schengen visas are free for spouses
and children of EU nationals.

Since passports are often not stamped on
entry (unless you arrive by air from outside
the Schengen area), the 90-day rule can

generally be interpreted flexibly, since no one can prove how long you have been in the country.

If your passport has been stamped and you wish to stay longer, you can try leaving the country for a non-Schengen country, such as Morocco or the UK, and then re-entering.

You *could* avoid the visa if you are willing to gamble. Travelling from the UK by boat or train there is a chance that your passport will not be checked on entering France or Belgium. From there you could travel overland with some hope (but no certainty) of not having your passport checked. Travelling by air, however, you have no chance. Take this seriously, as travellers have been bundled on to planes back to the country they flew from.

Coming from Morocco, you are unlikely to get into Spain's North African enclaves of Ceuta or Melilla without a Spanish visa (if you are supposed to have one), and passports are generally checked again when you head on to the peninsula. You may well be able to board a boat from Tangier (Morocco) to Algeciras and certainly to Gibraltar but, again, passports are generally closely checked by the Spaniards at Algeciras and you could be sent back to Morocco. If you go via Gibraltar, you may just sneak across at La Línea without having your passport checked – but you can't bank on it.

Visa Extensions & Residence Schengen visas cannot be extended. Nationals of EU countries, Norway and Iceland can virtually (if not technically) enter and leave Spain at will. Those wanting to stay in Spain longer than 90 days are supposed to apply during their first month for a *tarjeta de residencia* (resident's card). This is a lengthy bureaucratic procedure: if you intend to subject yourself to it, consult a Spanish consulate before you go to Spain as you will need to take certain documents with you.

People of other nationalities who want to stay in Spain longer than 90 days are also supposed to get a resident's card, and for them it's a truly nightmarish process, starting with a residence visa issued by a Spanish consulate in your country of residence. Start the process light years in advance.

Non-EU spouses of EU citizens resident in Spain can apply for residency too. The process is lengthy and those needing to travel in and out of the country in the meantime could ask for an *exención de visado* – a visa exemption. In most cases, the spouse is obliged to make the formal application in their country of residence, which is a real pain.

Travel Insurance

A travel insurance policy to cover theft, loss of luggage or tickets, medical problems and perhaps cancellation or delays in your travel arrangements is a good idea (for more on medical insurance, see Health later in this chapter).

A wide variety of policies is available and your travel agent will be able to make recommendations. The international student travel policies handled by STA Travel or other student travel organisations are usually good. Check the small print:

- Some policies exclude 'dangerous activities', which can include scuba diving, motorcycling, even trekking.
- Some policies may impose a surcharge for expensive photo equipment and the like.
- Check whether the policy covers ambulances or an emergency flight home.
- Policies often require you to pay up front for medical expenses, then to claim from the insurance company afterwards, showing receipts, but you might prefer to find a policy which involves the insurance company paying the doctor or hospital direct.

Buy travel insurance as early as possible. If you buy it in the week before you leave home, you may find, for example, that you are not covered for delays to your trip caused by industrial action.

Paying for your ticket with a credit card often provides limited travel accident insurance and you may be able to reclaim payment if the operator doesn't deliver. Ask your credit card company what it will cover.

Insurance papers, and the international medical aid numbers that generally accompany them, are valuable documents, so treat them like air tickets and passports. Keep the details (photocopies or handwritten) in a separate part of your luggage.

Driving Licence & Permits

For information on driving licences, International Driving Permits and vehicle papers and insurance, see under Car & Motorcycle in the Getting There & Away chapter.

Hostel Cards

A valid HI (Hostelling International) card or youth hostel card from your home country is required at most HI youth hostels in Spain. If you don't already have one, you can get an HI card, valid until 31 December of the year you buy it in, at most HI hostels in Spain. You pay in instalments of 300 ptas for each night you spend in a hostel, up to 1800 ptas. (People legally resident in Spain for at least a year can get a Spanish hostel card for 1000 ptas). The cards are also available from the TIVE youth travel organisation, which has offices in many of Spain's regional and some provincial capitals (see Useful Organisations later in this chapter).

Student, Teacher & Youth Cards

These cards can get you worthwhile discounts on travel and reduced prices at some museums, sights and entertainment venues.

The International Student Identity Card (ISIC), for full-time students (700 ptas in Spain), and the International Teacher Identity Card (ITIC), for full-time teachers and professors (1000 ptas in Spain), are issued by over 5000 organisations worldwide, mostly student travel-related and often selling student tickets. In Spain both cards are available from TIVE offices. They include:

Australia

STA Travel
Melbourne: (☎ 03-9349 2411) 222 Faraday St, Carlton, Victoria 3053
Sydney: (☎ 02-9360 1822) 9 Oxford St, Paddington, NSW 2021

Canada

Travel Cuts (☎ 416-979 2406) 187 College St, Toronto
Voyages Campus (☎ 514-398 0647) Université McGill, 3480 rue McTavish, Montreal

UK

STA Travel (☎ 020-7361 6145) 86 Old Brompton Rd, SW7 3LH

Usit Campus (☎ 0870 240 1010) 52 Grosvenor Gardens, London SW1W 0AG

USA

Council Travel
Los Angeles: (☎ 310-208 3551) 10904 Lindbrook Dve, CA 90024
New York: (☎ 212-822 2700) 205 East 42nd St, NY 10017
San Francisco: (☎ 415-421 3473) 530 Bush St, CA 94108

Anyone under 26 can get a GO25 card or a Euro<26 card. Both these give similar discounts to the ISIC and are issued by most of the same organisations. The Euro<26 has a variety of names, including the Under 26 Card in England and Wales and the Carnet Joven Europeo in Spain. For information you can contact Under 26 (☎ 020-7730 7285), 52 Grosvenor Gardens, London SW1W 0AG, UK. In Spain, the Euro<26 is issued by various youth organisations, including TIVE (see Hostel Cards earlier in this section), at branches of the USIT Unlimited (☎ 902-25 25 75) youth travel agencies or at the Centro Regional de Información y Documentación Juvenil (CRIDJ; ☎ 91 580 42 42) in Madrid at Gran Vía 10, which is open from 9 am to 2 pm and 5 to 8 pm weekdays. You don't have to be Spanish to get the card in Spain, which costs 1000 ptas.

As an example of the sort of discounts you can expect in Spain, the better things on offer for Euro<26 card holders include 20% or 25% off most 2nd-class train fares, 10% or 20% off many Trasmediterránea ferries and some bus fares, good discounts at some museums and discounts of up to 20% at some youth hostels.

Copies

Keep photocopies of the data pages of your passport and other identity cards, and even your birth certificate if you can manage it. This will help speed up the replacement process if the originals go missing. If your passport is stolen or lost, notify the police, get a statement and then contact your embassy or consulate as soon as possible.

Other worthwhile things to photocopy include air tickets, travel insurance documents with emergency numbers, credit cards (and phone numbers to contact in case of card loss), driving licence and vehicle documentation. Keep all of this, and a list of your travellers cheque numbers, separate from the originals. Leave extra copies with someone reliable at home.

EMBASSIES & CONSULATES
Your Own Embassy

It's important to realise what your own embassy – the embassy of the country of which you are a citizen – can and can't do to help you if you get into trouble. Generally speaking, it won't be much help in emergencies if the trouble you're in is remotely your own fault. Remember that you are bound by the laws of the country you are in. Your embassy will not be sympathetic if you end up in jail after committing a crime locally, even if such actions are legal in your own country.

In genuine emergencies you might get some assistance, but only if other channels have been exhausted. For example, if you need to get home urgently, a free ticket home is exceedingly unlikely – the embassy would expect you to have insurance. If you have all your money and documents stolen, it might assist with getting a new passport, but a loan for onward travel is out of the question.

Some embassies used to keep letters for travellers or have a small reading room with home newspapers, but these days the mail-holding service has usually been stopped and even newspapers tend to be out of date.

Spanish Embassies & Consulates

Spanish embassies and consulates can be found in:

Andorra
Embassy: (☎ 82 00 13) Carrer Prat de la Creu 34, Andorra la Vella
Australia
Embassy: (☎ 02-6273 3555, e embespau@ mail.mae.es) 15 Arkana St, Yarralumla, Canberra, ACT 2600
Consulates: Brisbane (☎ 07-3221 8571), Melbourne (☎ 03-9347 1966), Perth (☎ 08-9322 4522) and Sydney (☎ 02-9261 2433)

Canada
Embassy: (☎ 613-747 2252, e spain@ DocuWeb.ca) 74 Stanley Ave, Ottawa, Ontario K1M 1P4
Consulates: Montreal (☎ 514-935 5235) and Toronto (☎ 416-977 1661)
France
Embassy: (☎ 01 44 43 18 00, e ambespfr@ mail.mae.es) 22, avenue Marceau, 75008 Paris, Cedex 08
Germany
Embassy: (☎ 030-261 60 81, e embesde@ mail.mae.es) Lichtensteinallee 1, 10787 Berlin
Consulates: Düsseldorf (☎ 0211-43 90 80), Frankfurt-am-Main (☎ 069-959 16 60) and Munich (☎ 089-98 50 27)
Ireland
Embassy: (☎ 01-269 1640) 17A Merlyn Park, Balls Bridge, Dublin 4
Japan
Embassy: (☎ 03-3583 8533, e embesjpj@ mail.mae.es) 1-3-29 Roppongi, Minato-ku, Tokyo 106
Morocco
Embassy: (☎ 07-26 80 00, e embesjpj@ mail.mae.es) 3 Zankat Madnine, Rabat
Consulates: Casablanca (☎ 02-22 07 52), Rabat (☎ 07-70 41 47) and Tangier (☎ 09-93 70 00)
Netherlands
Embassy: (☎ 070-364 38 14, e embespnl@ mail.mae.es) Lange Voorhout 50, 2514 EG The Hague
New Zealand
See Australia
Portugal
Embassy: (☎ 01-347 2381, e embesppt@ mail.mae.es) Rua do Salitre 1, 1250 Lisbon
UK
Embassy: (☎ 020-7235 5555, e espemblon@ espemblon.freeserve.co.uk) 39 Chesham Place, London SW1X 8SB
Consulates: Edinburgh (☎ 0131-220 18 43); London (☎ 020-7589 8989) 20 Draycott Place, SW3 2RZ; and Manchester (☎ 0161-236 1233)
USA
Embassy: (☎ 202-452 0100) 2375 Pennsylvania Ave NW, Washington, DC 20037
Consulates: Boston (☎ 617-536 2506), Chicago (☎ 312-782 4588), Houston (☎ 713-783 6200), Los Angeles (☎ 213-938 0158), Miami (☎ 305-446 5511), New Orleans (☎ 504-525 4951), New York (☎ 212-355 4080) and San Francisco (☎ 415-922 2995)

Embassies & Consulates in Spain

The main embassies are in Madrid. Some countries also maintain consulates in major cities, particularly in Barcelona (see that chapter). Embassies and consulates in Madrid (Madrid map references are listed – see that chapter) include:

Australia
Embassy: (Map 5; ☎ 91 441 93 00) Plaza del Descubridor Diego de Ordás 3-2, Edificio Santa Engrácia 120

Canada
Embassy: (Map 3; ☎ 91 431 45 56) Calle de Núñez de Balboa 35

France
Embassy: (Map 3; ☎ 91 310 11 12) Calle del Marqués Ensenada 10

Germany
Embassy: (Map 3; ☎ 91 557 90 00) Calle de Fortuny 8

Ireland
Embassy: (Map 3; ☎ 91 436 40 95) Paseo de la Castellana 46

Morocco
Embassy: (Map 5; ☎ 91 563 79 28) Calle de Serrano 179
Consulate: (Map 5; ☎ 91 561 21 45) Calle de Leizaran 31

Netherlands
Embassy: (Map 5; ☎ 91 350 32 36) Avenida del Comandante Franco 32

New Zealand
Embassy: (Map 2; ☎ 91 523 02 26, 91 531 09 97) Plaza de la Lealtad 2

Portugal
Embassy: (Map 3; ☎ 91 561 47 23) Calle de Castelló 128
Consulate: (Map 3; ☎ 91 577 35 38) Calle Lagasca 88

Tunisia
Embassy: (Map 4; ☎ 91 447 35 16) Plaza de Alonso Martínez 3

UK
Embassy: (Map 3; ☎ 91 308 06 18) Calle de Fernando el Santo 16
Consulate: (Map 3; ☎ 91 308 53 00) Calle del Marqués Ensenada 16

USA
Embassy: (Map 3; ☎ 91 577 40 00) Calle de Serrano 75

CUSTOMS

Duty-free allowances for travellers entering Spain from outside the EU include 2L of still table wine; 1L of spirits or 2L of fortified wine, sparkling wine or other liqueurs; 60mL of perfume; and 200 cigarettes or 50 cigars or 250g of tobacco. Duty-free allowances for travel between EU countries were abolished in 1999. For duty-paid items taken from one EU country into another, allowances include 90L of wine, 10L of spirits, 110L of beer and 800 cigarettes.

MONEY

You can get by easily enough with a single credit or debit card enabling you to withdraw cash from ATMs, but it's sound thinking also to take some travellers cheques and a second card (if you have one). The combination gives you a fallback if you lose a card or for some reason are unable to use it.

Currency

Spain's currency for everyday transactions until early 2002 is the peseta (pta). This comes in coins of one, five, 10, 25, 50, 100, 200 and 500 ptas, and notes of 1000, 2000, 5000 and 10,000 ptas. A 5 ptas coin is known as a *duro,* and it's fairly common for small sums to be quoted in duros: *dos duros* for 10 ptas, *cinco duros* for 25 ptas, *veinte duros* for 100 ptas.

The euro (€), the new currency that Spain shares with Austria, Belgium, Finland, France, Germany, Greece, Ireland, Italy, Luxembourg, the Netherlands and Portugal, has been in use since 1999 for some noncash transactions such as bank transfers. The euro will also become the currency of cash transactions in all 12 countries in early 2002. As that time approaches, more and more prices and receipts will be denominated in both currencies, to prepare people for the change.

Euro coins and notes will appear on 1 January 2002 and then there will be a two-month transition period, in which pesetas and euros will circulate side by side and pesetas can be exchanged for euros free of charge at banks. After 28 February 2002, the euro will be the sole currency of Spain and the 11 other 'euro zone' countries.

The euro is divided into 100 cents (or *céntimos* in Spain). Coin denominations will be one, two, five, 10, 20 and 50 cents, €1 and €2. The notes will be €5, €10, €20, €50,

€100, €200 and €500. All euro coins of each denomination will be identical on the side showing their value, but there will be 12 different obverses, each representing one of the 12 euro zone countries. All euro notes of each denomination will be identical on both sides. *All* euro coins and notes will be legal tender throughout the euro zone.

Exchange Rates

The values of euro zone currencies against the euro (and therefore against each other) were fixed permanently in 1999. Exchange rates between euro zone and non-euro zone currencies are variable.

country	unit		peseta		euro
Australia	A$1	=	106 ptas	=	€0.63
Canada	C$1	=	122 ptas	=	€0.73
euro	€1	=	166 ptas	=	-
France	10FF	=	253 ptas	=	€1.52
Germany	DM1	=	85 ptas	=	€0.51
Japan	¥100	=	164 ptas	=	€0.99
Morocco	Dr10	=	170 ptas	=	€1.02
New Zealand	NZ$1	=	82 ptas	=	€0.50
Portugal	100$00	=	83 ptas	=	€0.50
Spain	100 ptas =		-	=	€0.60
UK	UK£1	=	271 ptas	=	€1.63
USA	US$1	=	180 ptas	=	€1.08

Exchanging Money

You can change cash or travellers cheques in currencies of the developed world without problems (except, sometimes, queues) at virtually any bank or exchange office. Many banks have ATMs. Spain's international airports usually have bank branches and exchange offices, and seaports and road crossings into Spain will have at least one or the other close by. If coming from Morocco, get rid of any dirham before you leave.

Banks tend to offer the best exchange rates and are very common in cities; even small villages often have one. Banks mostly open from about 8.30 am to 2 pm weekdays and 9 am to 1 pm Saturday. Some don't open on Saturday in summer.

Exchange offices – usually indicated by the word *cambio* (exchange) – exist mainly in tourist resorts and other places that attract high numbers of foreigners. Generally, they offer longer opening hours and quicker service than banks, but worse exchange rates. In some exchange offices, the more money you change, the better the exchange rate you'll get.

Wherever you change, it's well worth asking about commissions first, and confirming that exchange rates are as posted (posted rates may not have been updated since yesterday, or last week). Every bank seems to have a different commission structure: commissions may be different for travellers cheques and cash, and may depend on how many cheques, or how much in total, you're cashing. A typical commission is 3%, with a minimum of 300 to 500 ptas, but there are places with a minimum of 1000 ptas and sometimes 2000 ptas. Places that advertise 'no commission' usually offer poor exchange rates to start with. An exception is Spain's national bank, Banco de España, which changes banknotes (only) of euro-zone currencies at the full interbank rate free of commission, up to a maximum of the equivalent of €2000 (about 332,000 ptas) per person per day. This service is available at 23 branches in Spain, including at Calle Alcalá 50, Madrid; Plaça de Catalunya 17-18, Barcelona; and Plaza de San Francisco 7, Sevilla.

Travellers Cheques These protect your money because they can be replaced if they are lost or stolen. In Spain they can be cashed at the many banks and exchange offices and usually attract a higher exchange rate than cash. You usually can't use them like money to make purchases. American Express and Thomas Cook are widely accepted brands with efficient replacement policies. For American Express travellers cheque refunds you can call ☎ 900-99 44 26 from anywhere in Spain.

It doesn't really matter whether your cheques are denominated in pesetas (or, from 2002, euros) or in the currency of the country you buy them in. Get most of your cheques in fairly large denominations (the equivalent of 10,000 ptas or €100 or more) to save on any per-cheque commission charges.

It's vital to keep your initial receipt, and a record of your cheque numbers and the ones you have used, separate from the cheques themselves.

Take along your passport when you cash travellers cheques.

ATMs & Credit Cards Credit cards (such as Visa) can be more widely used than debit cards (such as Maestro or Cirrus) because they can generally be used for over-the-counter cash advances at bank branches as well as for direct purchases and withdrawing cash from ATMs. They may also give you access to more money per day. The exchange rate used for credit card currency exchanges is usually more in your favour than for cash exchanges. However some debit cards such as those in the Cirrus and Maestro networks enable you to access money in personal bank accounts from Spain without any cash-advance fee.

You can ask your card issuer before leaving home about rates and charges. It's also advisable to ask how widely you can use your card, how to report a lost card, whether your personal identification number (PIN) will be acceptable (some European ATMs don't accept PINs of more than four digits), and to know your withdrawal/spending limits.

Payment by card is accepted by many Spanish businesses, including restaurants, cafes and accommodation (especially from the mid-range price up), petrol stations, and Renfe, the national rail network, for long-distance trains. Among the most widely accepted cards in Spain are Visa, Master Card, EuroCard, Eurocheque, American Express, Cirrus, Maestro, Plus, Diners Club and JCB.

A very high proportion of Spanish banks, even in small towns and some villages, have an ATM *(cajero automático)* that will dispense pesetas at any time if you have the right piece of plastic to slot into it. This will save you having to queue at the bank counter.

American Express cards are among the easiest to replace if lost – you can call ☎ 902-37 56 37 or ☎ 91 572 03 03 (in Madrid) at any time. Always report a lost card straight away: for Visa cards call ☎ 900-97 44 45,

for MasterCard/ EuroCard ☎ 900-97 12 31 and for Diners Club ☎ 91 547 40 00.

International Transfers To have money transferred from another country, you need to organise someone to send it to you, through a bank there or a money-transfer service such as Western Union (www.westernunion.com) or MoneyGram (www.moneygram.com), and a bank (or transfer-service agent) in Spain at which to collect it. If there's money in your bank account at home, you may be able to instruct the bank yourself.

For information on Western Union services in Spain, call the toll-free number ☎ 900-63 36 33; for MoneyGram call ☎ 901-20 10 10. Both have agents in many cities and towns in Spain and around the world.

To set up a transfer through a bank, either get advice from the bank at home on a suitable pick-up bank in Spain, or check with a Spanish bank about how to organise it. You'll need to let the sender have the name, address and city of the Spanish bank branch, and any contact or code numbers required.

A bank-to-bank telegraphic transfer typically costs around US$20 to US$30 and can take a week. Western Union and MoneyGram are quicker (in both cases the money can supposedly be handed over to the recipient within 10 to 15 minutes of being sent), but a bit more expensive. Their charges are on sliding scales: to transfer US$400 from the US to Spain costs the sender around US$30 to US$40 and the recipient nothing. It's also possible to have money sent quickly by American Express.

Security

Your money, in whatever form, is at risk unless you look after it carefully, especially when you're in tourist resorts and major cities. Carry only a limited amount of cash and keep the bulk in more easily replaceable forms such as travellers cheques or plastic. If your accommodation has a safe, use it. If you have to leave money in your room, divide it into several stashes and hide them in different places.

For carrying money on the street, the safest thing is a moneybelt or wallet that you can keep under your clothes. An external moneybelt is only safe if it can't be sliced off by a quick knife cut. Watch out for people who touch you or seem to be getting unnecessarily close, in any situation.

Costs

If you are extremely frugal, it's just about possible to scrape by on 3000 ptas a day by staying in the cheapest possible accommodation, avoiding restaurants except for an inexpensive set lunch, minimising your visits to museums and bars and generally not moving around too much.

A more comfortable economy budget would be 6000 ptas a day. This could allow you 1500 to 2000 ptas for accommodation; 300 ptas for breakfast (coffee and a pastry); 1000 to 1500 ptas for lunch or dinner; 600 to 800 ptas for another, lighter meal; 250 ptas for public transport; 500 to 1000 ptas for entry fees to a museum, sights or entertainment; and a bit over for a drink or two and intercity travel. Places such as Madrid, Barcelona, Sevilla and San Sebastián will place a greater strain on your moneybelt.

If you've got 20,000 to 25,000 ptas a day you can stay in excellent accommodation, rent a car and eat some of the best food Spain has to offer.

Ways to Save Two people can travel more cheaply (per person) than one by sharing rooms. You'll also save by avoiding the peak tourist seasons, when most room prices go up: these vary from place to place, depending on local festivals and climate, but run from about July to mid-September in most places. A student or youth card, or a document such as a passport proving you're over 60, brings worthwhile savings on some travel costs and entry to some museums and sights (see Visas & Documents earlier in this chapter). A few museums and sights are cheaper for EU passport holders.

More information on accommodation, food and travel costs can be found under Accommodation in this chapter, in the special section 'Eating & Drinking in Spain' and in the Getting Around chapter.

Tipping & Bargaining

The law requires restaurant menu prices to include the service charge, and tipping is a matter of personal choice – most people leave some small change if they're satisfied: 5% would normally be adequate and 10% generous. Most people leave a couple of coins at the bar or on cafe tables. Porters will generally be happy with 200 ptas and most won't turn their noses up at 100 ptas. Taxi drivers don't have to be tipped but a little rounding up won't go amiss.

The only places in Spain where you might bargain are markets – though even there most things have fixed prices – and, occasionally, cheap hotels, particularly if you're staying for a few days.

Taxes & Refunds

In Spain, value-added tax (VAT) is known as IVA (pronounced 'ee-ba'; *impuesto sobre el valor añadido*). On accommodation and meals, it's 7% and is usually included in quoted prices. On retail goods and car hire, IVA is 16%. To ask 'Is IVA included?', say *'¿Está incluido el IVA?'*.

Visitors are entitled to a refund of the 16% IVA on purchases costing more than 15,000 ptas from any shop if they are taking the goods out of the EU within three months. Ask the shop for an invoice showing the price and IVA paid for each item and identifying the vendor and purchaser. Then present the invoice to the customs booth for IVA refunds when you leave Spain. The officer will stamp the invoice, which you hand in at a bank in the airport or port for the reimbursement.

POST & COMMUNICATIONS
Postal Rates

Rates for a postcard or letter weighing up to 20g are 70 ptas from Spain to other European countries, 115 ptas to North America and 185 ptas to Australia, New Zealand or eastern Asia. Three A4 sheets in an air-mail envelope weigh between 15g and 20g. An aerogram to anywhere in the world costs 85 ptas.

Certificado (registered mail) costs an extra 175 ptas for international mail. *Urgente* service, which means your mail may arrive two or three days quicker, costs around an extra 270 ptas for international mail. You can send mail both certificado and urgente.

A day or two quicker than urgente service is Postal Exprés, also called Express Mail Service (EMS), which is available at most post offices. Packages weighing between 250g and 500g, for example, cost 3500 ptas

to other European countries and 5000 ptas to North America – a lot more expensive than regular mail but significantly cheaper than courier services.

Sending Mail

Stamps are sold at most *estancos* (tobacconist shops with 'Tabacos' in yellow letters on a maroon background), as well as at all post offices *(oficinas de correos,* or *correos)*. Cities have quite a lot of post

Getting Addressed

You might think that if you have the address of a hotel, office or cafe, you should have little trouble locating it. But if the Pensión España should turn out to be at C/ Madrid 2°D Int, not far from Gta Atocha and just around the corner from P° del Prado, you could be forgiven for being a little confused. Here's a key to common abbreviations used in addresses:

Almd	Alameda		P° or Po	Paseo
Av or Avda	Avenida		Pje	Pasaje
C/	Calle		Pl, Pza or Pª	Plaza
Cllj	Callejón		Pllo	Pasillo
Cno	Camino		Pte	Puente
Cril	Carril		Rda	Ronda
Ctra or Ca	Carretera		s/n	sin número (without number)
Gta	Glorieta (major roundabout)		Urb	Urbanización

The following are used where there are several flats, hostales, offices etc in a building. They're often used in conjunction, eg, 2°C or 3°I Int:

2°	2nd floor
3°	3rd floor
4°	4th floor
C	centro (middle)
D or dcha	derecha (right-hand side)
I or izq	izquierda (left-hand side)
Int	interior (a flat or office too far inside a building to look on to any street – the opposite is Ext, exterior)

MICK WELDON

If someone's address is Apartado de Correos 206 (which might be shortened to Apdo Correos 206 or even just Apdo 206), don't bother going looking for it at all. An *apartado de correos* is a post-office box.

Note also that the word 'de' is often omitted: Calle de Madrid (literally 'Street of Madrid') may be truncated to C/ Madrid. In fact it's not uncommon for streets to be referred to by their names alone: Calle de Alfonso Rodríguez will just as likely be referred to as Alfonso Rodríguez.

offices and most villages have one too. Main post offices in cities and towns usually open from about 8.30 am to 8.30 pm weekdays and 9 am to 1.30 pm Saturday. Village offices may have shorter hours. Estancos usually open during normal shop hours.

It's quite safe and reliable to post mail in the yellow street postboxes (*buzones*) as well as at post offices. Delivery times are erratic but ordinary mail to other Western European countries normally arrives within a week, to North America within 10 days and to Australia or New Zealand within two weeks.

Receiving Mail

Delivery times are similar to those for outbound mail. Poste restante mail can be addressed to you at poste restante (or better, *lista de correos*, the Spanish name for it) at any place in Spain that has a post office. It will be delivered to the place's main post office unless another is specified in the address. Take your passport when you pick up mail. It helps if people writing to you capitalise or underline your surname and include the postcode in the address. A typical lista de correos address looks like this, with the name of the province following that of the town:

Mark PETERS
Lista de Correos
36200 Vigo
Pontevedra
Spain

For some quirks of address abbreviations, see the boxed text 'Getting Addressed'. Travellers with an American Express card or travellers cheques can use the free client mail-holding service at American Express offices in Spain. You can get a list of these from American Express. Take your passport when you pick up mail.

Telephone

Spain is well provided with street pay phones, which are blue and easy to use for both international and domestic calls. They accept coins and/or slot-in Spanish phonecards (*tarjetas telefónicas*), which come in 1000 and 2000 ptas denominations and, like

postage stamps, are sold at post offices and estancos.

Coin pay phones inside bars and cafes – often green – normally have cost scales a little higher than street pay phones. Phones in hotel rooms can be a good deal more expensive: managements set their own rates, so it's worth asking the costs before using one.

Costs Calls made from pay phones using coins or a slot-in card cost about 35% more than calls from private lines. The table shows approximate costs of three-minute, pay-phone calls:

call to	cost (ptas)
Number starting with 900	free
Local area	25
Number starting with 901	35
Same province	65
Number starting with 902	75
Other province	110
Other EU country	230
Spanish mobile phone	
(any number starting with 6)	230
North America	280
Australia	820

All these calls except those to mobile phones are cheaper between 8 pm and 8 am (6 pm to 8 am for local calls), and all day Saturday and Sunday. Calls to mobile phones are cheaper from 10 pm to 8 am weekdays, 2 pm to midnight Saturday and all day Sunday. The discounts are around 50% for provincial and interprovincial calls

Code Conduct

All Spanish addresses have a five-digit postcode, and using it may help your mail arrive a bit quicker. Villages, towns and small cities have one postcode for the whole place (eg, 29400 for Ronda in Andalucía). But 79 of Spain's biggest cities each encompass several different postcodes. The postcodes given in this book for these larger places are those to be used on mail addressed to the lista de correos at the main post office.

and calls to mobile phones, and around 10% for local and international calls.

A variety of discount cards are available which can significantly cut call costs, especially for international calls – see under Phonecards and eKno later in this section.

Domestic Dialling Spain has no telephone area codes. All numbers have nine digits and you just dial that nine-digit number, wherever in the country you are calling from.

Dial ☎ 1009 to speak to a domestic operator, including for a domestic reverse-charge (collect) call *(una llamada por cobro revertido)*. For directory inquiries dial ☎ 1003; calls cost about 60 ptas.

The Spanish Yellow Pages (or Páginas Amarillas) are now on the Internet at www.paginas-amarillas.es. For emergency numbers, see Emergencies later in this chapter.

International Dialling To make an international call from Spain, dial the international access code (☎ 00), then the country code, area code and then the number you want. For international collect calls, dial ☎ 900 99 00, followed by a code for the country you're calling: ☎ 61 for Australia, ☎ 44 for the UK, ☎ 64 for New Zealand, ☎ 15 for Canada and for the USA, ☎ 11 (AT&T) or ☎ 14 (MCI). Codes for other countries – usually the normal country code – are often posted up in pay phones. You'll get straight through to an operator in the country you're calling. The same numbers can be used with direct-dial calling cards.

If for some reason the above doesn't work, in most places you can get an English-speaking Spanish international operator on ☎ 1008.

For international directory inquiries, dial ☎ 025 and be ready to pay about 150 ptas.

Calling Spain from Abroad Spain's country code is ☎ 34. Follow this with the full nine-digit number you are calling.

Mobile Phones Mobile phone *(teléfono móvil)* use has mushroomed in Spain. Spain uses GSM 900/1800, compatible with the rest of Europe and Australia but not with the North American GSM 1900 or the totally different system in Japan (though some North Americans have GSM 1900/ 900 phones that do work in Spain). If you have a GSM phone, check with your service provider about using it in Spain, and beware of calls being re-routed internationally (very expensive for a 'local' call). Most Spanish towns of medium size or bigger have mobile-phone shops. MoviStar, found on almost any city's main street, sells phones for around 10,000 ptas, including 4000 ptas of calls. Some shops offer the phone itself for virtually nothing – you just pay for the call time that it comes credited with (maybe 5000 or 10,000 ptas).

Phonecards You'll notice a wide range of local and international discount phonecards on sale in Spain's main travellers' centres such as Barcelona, Madrid and Sevilla. Most cards are not meant to be slotted into the phone; they operate through special access that you dial to initiate your call. If you're thinking of buying one, look closely into call costs (including any taxes payable, such as IVA) and exactly where you can use the card from.

eKno Communication Service Lonely Planet's eKno global communication service provides low-cost international calls – for local calls you're usually better off with a local phonecard. eKno also offers free messaging services, email, travel information and an online travel vault, where you can securely store all your important documents. You can join online at www.ekno.lonelyplanet.com, where you will find the local-access numbers for the 24-hour customer-service centre. Once you have joined, always check the eKno Web site for the latest access numbers for each country and updates on new features.

Fax
Most main post offices have a fax service: sending one page costs about 350 ptas within Spain, 1115 ptas to elsewhere in Europe and 2100 to 2500 ptas to other countries.

However, you'll often find cheaper rates at shops or offices with 'Fax' signs.

Email & Internet Access

An easy way of accessing email and Internet while you're on the road is using cybercafes and other public access points. You'll find these in many Spanish cities and towns, especially those with universities. Some are mentioned in city and town sections of this guide; visit www.netcafeguide.com for more.

To keep in touch via email, charges for an hour online range between 200 and 600 ptas. It's easiest to use Web-based email, which you can access anywhere in the world from any Internet-connected computer. Some accounts are free, such as eKno (www.ekno.lonelyplanet.com), Yahoo! Mail (www.yahoo.com) or Hotmail (www.hotmail.com).

If you plan to carry your notebook or palmtop computer with you, remember that the power supply voltage in Spain may vary from that of your home country, risking damage to your equipment. A universal AC adaptor for your appliance will enable you to plug it in anywhere without frying the innards. You'll also need a plug adaptor for Spain – often it's easiest to buy these before you leave home. Your PC-card modem may or may not work outside your home country – and you won't know for sure until you try. The safest option is to buy a reputable 'global' modem before you leave home, or a local PC-card modem if you're spending an extended time in Spain. The telephone sockets in Spain may be different from those at home, so ensure that you have at least a US RJ-11 telephone adaptor that works with your modem. You can almost always find an adaptor that will convert from RJ-11 to the local variety. For more information on travelling with a portable computer, check out www.teleadapt.com or www.warrior.com.

Major Internet service providers (ISPs) such as AOL (www.aol.com), CompuServe (www.compuserve.com) and AT&T Business Internet Services (www.attbusiness.net) have dial-in nodes throughout Europe, including main Spanish cities. It's best to download a list of the dial-in numbers before you leave home.

INTERNET RESOURCES

The World Wide Web is a rich resource for travellers. You can research your trip, hunt down bargain fares, book hotels, check on weather conditions or chat with locals and other travellers about the best places to visit (or avoid!).

Start your Web explorations at the Lonely Planet Web site (www.lonelyplanet.com). Here you'll find succinct summaries on travelling to Spain, postcards from other travellers and the Thorn Tree bulletin board, where you can ask questions before you go or dispense advice when you get back. You can also find travel news and updates to many of our most popular guidebooks. The subWWWay section links you to the most useful travel resources elsewhere on the Web. Lonely Planet's Spain page is at www.lonelyplanet.com/dest/eur/spa.htm.

The following are a few of the huge number of useful Web sites for visitors to Spain:

All About Spain A varied site with information on everything from fiestas to hotels as well as a Yellow Pages guide to tour operators around the world that do trips in Spain.
www.red2000.com

Cities.Com Search for Madrid, Barcelona and other major cities on this site and it takes you to a list of other potentially interesting sites, some of which appear in this list.
www.cities.com

Ciudad Hoy One of the better listings sites (in Spanish) for many Spanish cities. Search for Madrid, for example, and you are transferred to Madridhoy.net, a comprehensive site with broad listings, general news, links to the White and Yellow Pages sites and more.
www.ciudadhoy.com

Excite Travel Excite's travel Web pages, with a farefinder, bookings information and links to metro maps, restaurant tips and the like.
http://city.net/countries/spain/madrid

Geoplaneta Route and holiday planner for Spain.
www.geoplaneta.com

Internet Café Guide At this site you can get a list of Internet cafes in Spain. It's not as up-to-date as you might expect, but it's a start.
www.netcafeguide.com

Página del Quijote If you have more than a passing interest in Cervantes' famed character, then this is the place to satiate your curiosity on all things quixotic.
www.donquijote.com

Renfe Timetables, tickets and special offers on Spain's national rail network.
www.renfe.es

Turespaña This is the Spanish tourist office's official site, with lots of general information about the country and some interesting links.
www.tourspain.es

TuSpain This site is aimed more at foreign residents and leans towards information in the south of the country. You can pick up tips on language schools and how to go about buying a house in Spain if you like the place that much!
http://tuspain.com

For a couple of hints on access to the Internet in Spain, see Email & Internet Access earlier in this chapter.

BOOKS

Most books are published in different editions by different publishers in different countries. As a result, a book might be a hardcover rarity in one country and readily available in paperback in another. Fortunately, bookshops and libraries search by title or author, so they are best placed to advise you on the availability of the listed recommendations.

Spain has inspired a deep fascination among foreign writers for two centuries. There's a huge wealth of literature in English on the country – and obviously plenty in Spanish too.

In London there are several good bookshops devoted to the business of travel. For guidebooks and maps, Stanfords (☎ 020-7836 2121), 12-14 Long Acre WC2E 9LP, is acknowledged as one of the better first ports of call. A well-stocked source of travel literature is Daunts Books for Travellers (☎ 020-7224 2295), 83 Marylebone High Street W1M 4AL.

For books in Spanish, one of the best options is Grant & Cutler (☎ 020-7734 2012), 55-57 Great Marlborough St, London W1V 2AY.

Books on Spain (☎ 020-8898 7789, fax 88 98 8812, e keithharris@books-on-spain .com), PO Box 207, Twickenham TW2 5BQ, UK, can send you mail-order catalogues of hundreds of old and new titles on Spain. Visit its Web site at www.books-on-spain.com.

In Australia, the Travel Bookshop (☎ 02-9261 8200), 3/175 Liverpool Street, Sydney, is worth a browse. In the USA, try Book Passage (☎ 415-927 0960), 51 Tamal Vista Blvd, Corte Madera, California, and the Complete Traveler Bookstore (☎ 212-685 9007), 199 Madison Ave, New York. In France, L'Astrolabe rive gauche (☎ 01 46 33 80 06), 14 rue Serpente, Paris, is recommended.

Lonely Planet

If trekking or walking is on your agenda, you'll find a wealth of route descriptions for all the main areas and lots of practical and informative background in Lonely Planet's *Walking in Spain*. Lonely Planet also publishes companion guides on *Andalucía, Canary Islands, Barcelona* and *Madrid*.

World Food Spain by Richard Sterling is a trip into Spain's culinary soul, from tapas to *postres* and the *menú del día* to the *carta de vinos*, with a comprehensive culinary dictionary. The *Spanish phrasebook* will enable you to fill some of the gaps between *¡hola!* and *adiós*.

For people travelling on from Spain, other Lonely Planet travel guides include *France, Portugal* and *Morocco*.

Guidebooks

Of the many guides in Spanish to different parts of Spain, those published by El País/Aguilar stand out for their concise, intelligent and honest coverage and handy format. There are around 60 guides in various series, covering provinces, cities, routes such as the Camino de Santiago, tapas bars in various cities, and one-offs such as the excellent *Pequeños Hoteles con Encanto* (Small Hotels with Charm), *Alojamientos en Monasterios* (Lodgings in Monasteries) and *Pequeños Pueblos con Encanto* (Small Villages with Charm). For walking guides, see Activities later in this chapter. Other guides include:

Blue Guide Spain This isn't a bad companion if you want lots of detail about the country's architecture and art in a historical context.

Yachtsman's Guide to Spain and Portugal Yachties might want the bilingual guide, updated annually and available in Spain in specialist bookshops, yacht clubs and El Corte Inglés.

Travel – 19th Century Classics

The Bible in Spain by George Borrow. This book provides an English clergyman's view of the 19th-century Spain in which he tried to spread the Protestant word. It's an amusing read both for the man himself and for his experiences.

A Handbook for Travellers in Spain by Richard Ford. This book, written in 1845, set standards that few guidebook writers have matched since. It remains a classic, not only for telling us how things were in places we see now, but also for its irascible English author, who is by turns witty, prejudiced, highly informative and downright rude.

Tales of the Alhambra by Washington Irving. The author was an American who took up residence in Granada's Alhambra palace when it was in an abandoned state in the early 19th century. This title, written in 1832, weaves a series of still-enchanting stories around the folk with whom he shared his life and was largely responsible for the romantic image of Al-Andalus – and, by extension, of Spain – which persists to this day.

Travel – 20th Century

As I Walked Out One Midsummer Morning by Laurie Lee (1969). Lee walked off from his Gloucestershire home in 1934, aged 19. He arrived by boat at Vigo, then walked the length of Spain, playing his fiddle for a living. The book is a delightful account of his adventures that also records the sights, smells and contrasting moods of turbulent pre-civil war Spain. *A Moment of War* (1991) describes Lee's bizarre experiences in the International Brigades during the civil war. In the third of his Spanish 'trilogy', *A Rose for Winter,* Lee tells of his return to Andalucía 15 years later.

Between Hopes and Memories: A Spanish Journey by Michael Jacobs. An amusing and personal reflection on Spain.

Cities of Spain by David Gilmour. A recent work, which focuses on culture and history.

A Literary Companion – Spain by Jimmy Burns. An entertaining tour of the country as seen through the eyes of the great and good of letters down through the years.

Our Lady of the Sewers by Paul Richardson. Very entertaining story, if at times a trifle hard to believe, in which the author goes in search of the strange but true.

Roads to Santiago by Cees Nooteboom. A quirky travel journal, full of whimsy and detour.

South from Granada by Gerald Brenan. In the 1920s Brenan settled in a remote village south of Granada, aiming to educate himself unimpeded by his British mores and traditions. This book, written in 1957, is his absorbing account of local life and visits from members of the Bloomsbury set with whom he was associated. In 1949 Brenan returned to explore Franco's Spain, an experience recounted in *The Face of Spain* (1950).

Spanish Journeys by Adam Hopkins. This book is cast in a similar vein as Gilmour's *Cities of Spain* (see earlier).

Spanish Pilgrimage – A Canter to St James by Robin Hanbury-Tenison. This recounts travels along the Camino de Santiago, as does Bettina Selby's *Pilgrim's Road.* He had a penchant for white horses; she did it by bike.

History & Politics

A History of Spain, edited by John Lynch. If you are looking for a detailed and somewhat academic exploration of Spanish history, the series covers the subject in more than a dozen separate volumes by various authors.

Imperial Spain, 1469-1716 by JH Elliot. Probably the best single book covering the country's golden age and its immediate aftermath.

Moorish Spain by Richard Fletcher. One of the best histories of Spain's fascinating Islamic era.

Spain: the Root and the Flower by John A Crow. This is an American Hispanophile's insightful, scholarly, but rarely dry, ramble through history and culture from early times to the 1980s.

The Spanish Labyrinth by Gerald Brenan. Written in 1943, this is an in-depth but readable unravelling of the tangle of political and social movements in the half-century or so before the civil war. Brenan had high praise for Jan Morris' slim volume, *Spain,* a minor masterpiece of synthesis.

The Story of Spain by Mark Williams. For a colourful but thorough and not over-long survey of Spanish history, this book is hard to beat.

A Traveller's History of Spain by Juan Lalaguna. A concise and worthwhile account of Spanish history.

Civil War & Franco Era

The Assassination of Federico García Lorca by Ian Gibson. This book, by the noted Lorca scholar (and now Spanish citizen), chillingly pieces together the murky story of one of the war's more infamous atrocities, the murder near Granada of the poet and playwright Lorca. The book also gives background on Lorca and the war.

Blood of Spain by Ronald Fraser. A fascinating collection of eyewitness accounts of the war.

Franco by Paul Preston. A big biography of one of history's little dictators.

Homage to Catalonia by George Orwell. This is the story of his involvement in the civil war, moving from the euphoria of the early days in Barcelona to disillusionment with the disastrous infighting on the Republican side.

The Spanish Civil War by Hugh Thomas. The civil war is said to be the second-most written-about conflict in history (after WWII) and has spawned some wonderful books over the years. Thomas' book is probably the classic account of the civil war in any language. It's long and dense with detail, yet readable, even-handed and humane.

The Spanish Tragedy by Raymond Carr. This succinct title is another well-written and respected account of the civil war.

Regions

Andalucía and Catalunya, two strongly contrasting regions at opposite ends of the country, seem to have inspired foreigners more than any other part of Spain.

Andalucia by Michael Jacobs. Runs comprehensively through all the important cultural and historical aspects of Andalucía, from Muslim architecture to Lorca and the Sevillan golden age to flamenco.

Andalucía: A Portrait of Southern Spain by Nicholas Luard (1984). This book evokes life in the hinterland behind Tarifa and Algeciras in the 1960s and 70s, when foreign residents were still quite a rarity there.

Barcelona by Robert Hughes (1992). Going into more depth than Colm Tóibín's book (see later), it approaches the city's past and art with mordant wit and a keen eye.

Driving Over Lemons by Chris Stewart (1999). The big hit of recent English-language writing about Spain, this is the entertaining tale of drummer-cum-writer-cum-sheep shearer Chris Stewart's small farm in Las Alpujarras, and the quirky characters and situations he encounters.

Homage to Barcelona by Colm Tóibín (1990). An excellent personal introduction to the city's modern life and artistic and political history; Tóibín is an Irish journalist who lived there.

Inside Andalusia by David Baird. Written in 1993, this is an always interesting collection of portraits of people and places in this region.

The Pueblo by Ronald Fraser. A revealing insight into Spanish attitudes to the changes of the past decades (notably tourism) by looking at the fate of the village of Mijas on the Costa del Sol.

The Sierras of the South by Alastair Boyd. A vivid story of life around Ronda in the Andalucian hill

country in the 1950s and 60s. Boyd also penned *The Essence of Catalonia*.

Un Hiver À Majorque (A Winter in Mallorca) by George Sand. An account of an 1830s sojourn in an abandoned monastery on the island with her lover, the composer Chopin, and her two children. There was little love lost between the locals and the French writer.

Voices of the Old Sea by Norman Lewis. A semi-fictional work set on the Costa Brava that probes similar issues as *The Pueblo* (see earlier).

Hemingway

Death in the Afternoon by Ernest Hemingway. This is his well-known book on bullfighting.

For Whom the Bell Tolls by Ernest Hemingway. Probably the most-read of all English-language books set in Spain, this terse tale of the civil war, written in 1941, is full of Spanish atmosphere and all the emotions unleashed in the war. Its plot keeps you hanging on until the last sentence.

Fiesta by Ernest Hemingway. This book made the Sanfermines bull-running festival at Pamplona world famous; it's also published under the title *The Sun Also Rises*.

Society, Culture & Arts

The Arts in Spain by John Moffitt. Part of the handy Thames & Hudson series on artistic movements, this book ranges from cave paintings to the 20th century.

Fire in the Blood by Ian Gibson. A personal and controversial introduction to modern Spain, which is based on a British TV series. Gibson has written weighty biographies of Lorca and Salvador Dalí.

In Search of the Firedance by James Woodall. A hard-to-beat introduction to flamenco.

Moorish Culture in Spain by Titus Burckhardt. A classic book on the unique architecture and culture of Islamic Spain.

The New Spaniards by John Hooper. Another excellent book on modern Spain, written by former *Guardian* Madrid correspondent, whose writings range comprehensively from the arts through politics and bullfighting to sex.

Romanesque Art by Meyer Schapiro. This interesting book, another one of the Thames & Hudson series, covers this pre-Gothic architectural and artistic era.

Food & Wine

There are dozens of books on Spanish cookery. Three of the best are *The Foods and Wines of Spain* by Penelope Casas, *Cooking in Spain* by Janet Mendel and the slimmer

Spain on a Plate by María-José Sevilla. All have good background on the country's widely varied regional cuisines as well as recipes. You could also try:

To the Heart of Spain by Ann & Larry Walker. Hard to categorise, this is a mix of cookbook, wine survey and travel diary.

Flora & Fauna
Collins Field Guide to the Birds of Britain and Europe by Roger Peterson, Guy Mountfort & PAD Hollom.
Collins Pocket Guide Birds of Britain and Europe by H Heinzel, RSR Fitter & J Parslow.
Flowers of South-West Europe, A Field Guide by Oleg Polunin & BE Smythies. The single best guide to flowers and shrubs in Spain.
Spain's Wildlife by Eric Robins. Covers the country's most interesting animals and birds – and their prospects for survival – in an informative way, spiced with plenty of personal experience and some good photos.
Where to Watch Birds in Southern Spain by Ernest Garcia & Andrew Paterson. Serious birdwatchers in Andalucía and Extremadura will find this book invaluable.
Wildlife Travelling Companion Spain by John Measures. A good traveller's guide, focusing on 150 of the best sites for viewing flora and fauna, with details of how to reach them and what you can hope to see.

FILM
It's strange but true that the films of how the American West was won were often shot in Spain; some 100 westerns were filmed in the desertscape around Almería in Andalucía. Not only that, but such classics as *A Fistful of Dollars* and *The Good, The Bad And The Ugly* were actually directed by an Italian, Sergio Leone.

If the oddity of that doesn't impress, Hong Kong's martial arts king has also been in Spain. Jackie Chan appeared in *Wheels on Meals,* directed by Samon Hung in 1984 and set in Barcelona. It is a classic of kung-fu slapstick.

Otherwise, Spain has not been high among foreign directors' choice of stage or even subject.

Several directors have done versions of Bizet's *Carmen,* including Cecil B de Mille's production in 1915 and a 1984 film starring Plácido Domingo.

Alain Resnais's *La Guerre est Finie* (1966), starring Yves Montand and based on a script by Jorge Semprún, recounted three days in the life of a Spaniard in exile who is caught up in an anti-Franco plot.

A classic is Henry King's *The Sun Also Rises* (1943), starring Tyrone Power and Ava Gardner. It is based on Hemingway's tale of the lost generation of American expats in Paris and Spain. Hemingway's *For Whom The Bell Tolls* was also filmed in 1943 and starred Gary Cooper.

Jodie Foster starred with Ellen Barkin and Isabella Rossellini in Mary Lambert's *Siesta* in 1987. This was Foster's last film before making it big and it was a bit of a flop. Claire (Foster) wakes up blood-soaked at the end of a airport runway in Spain and doesn't know what's going on. She roams Spanish streets penniless as she tries to get a grip.

Whit Stillman's *Barcelona* (1994) follows the loves and trials of two American cousins in post-Franco Barcelona.

Interesting but hardly a hit was *Surviving Picasso* (1996), which was directed by James Ivory and featured Anthony Hopkins as Picasso.

Gérard Depardieu starred in *1492: Conquest of Paradise* (1992), a powerful film version of Columbus' discovery of the Americas in the service of Spain's Catholic Monarchs.

For a discussion of Spanish cinema, see Cinema in the Arts section of the Facts about Spain chapter.

NEWSPAPERS & MAGAZINES
Spanish Press
Spain has a thriving and free press. Daily newspapers sell around four or five million copies between them, working out at one for every eight to 10 people (a similar figure to Italy), compared to one for every 2½ people in the UK. The sales figures in part reflect the Spanish habit of sharing newspapers; it's actually reckoned that about one-third of Spaniards read papers regularly.

For some reason Spaniards have never taken to the idea of what's generously called a 'popular' press. There is no equivalent of the *Sun* or the *New York Daily News* here. However, one of the best-selling dailies is *Marca,* which is devoted exclusively to sport.

The major daily newspapers are the liberal *El País,* the conservative *ABC,* and *El Mundo,* which specialises in breaking political scandals. For solid reporting of national and international events, *El País* is hard to beat.

There's also a welter of regional dailies, some of the best being Barcelona's *La Vanguardia* and *El Periódico* (both in Spanish, although the latter also does a Catalan edition) and *Avui* (in Catalan) and Andalucía's *Sur* and *El Correo.* The Basque Country has two papers produced partly in the Basque language: *Deia* and ETA's mouthpiece, *Egin.*

A new Internet 'newspaper' started up in 2000; you'll find it at www.estrelladigital.es.

Foreign-Language Press

Coastal areas with large expat populations have a few predominantly English-language publications. Some of them are best for wrapping your fish and chips in, but in Andalucía the free weekly *Sur in English* reviews local news quite thoroughly and has good small ads, while *Lookout* is a glossy monthly magazine with some interesting features.

International press such as the *International Herald Tribune, Time* and *Newsweek,* and newspapers from Western European countries, reach major cities and tourist areas on the day of publication; elsewhere they're a bit harder to find and a day or two late.

RADIO

There are several hundred radio stations around the country, mainly on FM, and they run the gamut from a lot of loud babble interspersed with silly noises to nonstop good music. Many are independent but some are run by town councils. The state network, Radio Nacional de España (RNE), has four stations. RNE 1, with general interest and current affairs programs, and RNE 5, with sport and entertainment, are on AM (medium wave); RNE 2, with classical music, and RNE 3 (or 'Radio d'Espop'), with admirably

varied pop and rock music, are on FM (VHF). The most popular is commercial pop and rock station 40 Principales, on FM. Frequencies vary from place to place: *El País* publishes local wavelength guides in its *Cartelera* what's-on section.

Some of the expat-populated *costas* have the odd foreign-language station, such as the English-language Onda Cero International (101.6 MHz FM) on the Costa del Sol. These stations' programming is mostly middle-of-the-road, though they often carry BBC World Service news (on the hour), with better reception than the BBC itself.

You can pick up BBC World Service broadcasts on a variety of frequencies. Broadcasts are directed at Western Europe on, among others, 648, 9410 and 12,095 kHz (short wave). Voice of America can be found on various short-wave frequencies, including on 9700, 9760 and 15,205 kHz depending on the time of day. The BBC and VOA broadcast around the clock, but the quality of reception varies considerably and you may have to do a lot of dial twiddling, especially from midnight to 5 am.

TV

Spaniards are Europe's greatest TV watchers after the British, but do some of their watching in bars and cafes, which makes it more of a social activity.

Most TVs receive between five and seven channels. Two come from the state-run Televisión Española (TVE1 and La 2) and three are independent (Antena 3, Tele 5 and Canal Plus). In some areas one or two stations are run by regional governments, such as Madrid's Telemadrid, Catalunya's TV-3 and Canal 33, Galicia's TVG, the Basque Country's ETB-1 and ETB-2, Valencia's Canal 9 and Andalucía's Canal Sur. Apart from news (of which there's a respectable amount), TV programming consists largely of game and talk shows, sport, *telenovelas* (soap operas) and English-language films dubbed into Spanish.

Canal Plus is a pay channel, however nonsubscribers can get most programs except films (the channel's speciality), for which you need a decoder.

Satellite TV is popular too – mainly in private homes, although some bars, cafes and top-end hotels have it too. Foreign channels you may come across include BBC World (mainly news and travel), BBC Prime (other BBC programs), CNN, Eurosport, Sky News, Sky Sports, Sky Sports 2, Sky Movies and the German SAT 1.

PHOTOGRAPHY

Most main brands of film are widely available, and processing is fast and generally efficient. A roll of print film (36 exposures, ISO 100) costs around 700 ptas and can be processed in a day or less for around 1700 ptas. There are often better deals if you have two or three rolls developed together. The equivalent in slide *(diapositiva)* film is around 800 ptas plus 800 ptas for processing.

There is a new Lonely Planet photography manual, *Travel Photography: A Guide to Taking Better Pictures,* written by internationally renowned travel photographer, Richard I'Anson. It's full colour throughout and designed to take on the road.

TIME

Mainland Spain and the Balearic Islands have the same time as most of the rest of Western Europe: GMT/UTC plus one hour during winter and GMT/UTC plus two hours during the daylight-saving period, which runs from the last Sunday in March to the last Sunday in October. The UK, Ireland, Portugal and the Canary Islands, a part of Spain out in the Atlantic Ocean, are one hour behind mainland Spain.

Spanish time is normally USA Eastern Time plus six hours, and USA Pacific Time plus nine hours. But the USA tends to start daylight saving a week or two later than Spain, so you must add one hour to the time differences in the intervening period.

Morocco is on GMT/UTC all year round. From the last Sunday in March to the last Sunday in October, subtract two hours from Spanish time to get Moroccan time; the rest of the year, subtract one hour.

In the Australian winter (Spanish summer), subtract eight hours from Australian Eastern Standard Time to get Spanish time;

in the Australian summer subtract 10 hours. The difference is nine hours for a few weeks in March.

ELECTRICITY

Electric current in Spain is 220V, 50 Hz, as in the rest of continental Europe, but a few places are still on 125V or 110V (sockets are often labelled where this is the case). The voltage may even vary in the same building. Don't plug 220V (or British 240V) appliances into 125V or 110V sockets unless they have a transformer. North American 60 Hz appliances with electric motors (ie, some CD and tape players) may perform poorly.

Plugs have two round pins, again like the rest of continental Europe.

WEIGHTS & MEASURES

The metric system is used. You'll find metric conversion charts at the back of this guide. Like other continental Europeans, the Spanish indicate decimals with commas and thousands with points.

LAUNDRY

Self-service laundrettes are uncommon. Small laundries *(lavanderías)* are fairly common; staff will usually wash, dry and fold a load for 1000 to 1200 ptas. Some youth hostels and a few budget *hostales* have washing machines for guests' use.

TOILETS

Public toilets are not common, but it's OK to wander into many bars and cafes to use their toilet even if you're not a customer. It's worth carrying some toilet paper with you as many toilets lack it. If there's a bin beside the toilet, put paper etc in it – it's there because the local drains couldn't cope otherwise.

HEALTH

Most travellers experience no health problems in Spain.

Predeparture Planning

Immunisations It is recommended you seek medical advice at least six weeks before travel. You should have a tetanus-diphtheria booster, if necessary, and you might consider vaccination against hepatitis A and/or B – the latter if you might have sexual contact with the local population, stay longer than six months in southern Europe or be exposed through medical treatment. Hepatitis B vaccination is now widespread for infants and for children aged 11 or 12 who did not complete the series as infants.

Health Insurance Visitors from other EU countries and Norway, Iceland and Liechtenstein are entitled to free Spanish national health emergency medical care on provision of an E111 form, which you must get in your home country before you go to Spain. Ask your health service how to get the form. In the UK it's issued free by post offices: just supply your name, address, date of birth and National Insurance number. If you go for treatment in Spain, you will be asked for a photocopy of the E111, so you might as well get a couple when you get the form.

With an E111, you'll probably still have to pay at least some of the cost of medicines bought from pharmacies, even if a doctor has prescribed them (unless you're a pensioner), and perhaps for a few tests and procedures.

An E111 is no good for private consultations or treatment in Spain, which includes virtually all dentists and some of the better clinics and surgeries, or for emergency flights home. If you want to avoid paying for these, you'll need to take out medical travel insurance. For more information, see Travel Insurance in the Visas & Documents section earlier in this chapter.

Many US health insurance policies stay in effect, at least for a limited period, if you travel abroad. Most non-European national health plans (including Australia's Medicare) don't, so you must take out special medical insurance.

Other Preparations Make sure you're healthy before you start travelling. If you are going on a long trip make sure your teeth are OK. If you wear glasses take a spare pair and your prescription.

If you require a particular medication take an adequate supply, as it may not be available locally. Take part of the packaging showing the generic name, rather than the brand, which will make getting replacements easier. It's a good idea to have a legible prescription or letter from your doctor to show that you use the medication legally.

Basic Rules

Food If a place to eat looks clean and well run and the vendor also looks clean and healthy, then the food is probably safe. In general, places that are packed with travellers or locals will be fine, while empty restaurants are questionable.

Make sure your diet is well balanced. If your diet is poor or limited in variety, if you're travelling hard and fast and therefore missing meals or if you simply lose your appetite, you can soon start to lose weight and place your health at risk.

Water Domestic, hotel and restaurant tap water is safe to drink in most places in Spain. In places with water shortages you might want to check if the water's OK: lowering of water tables might introduce some undesirable ingredients into the supply. If you're in any doubt you can ask '¿Es potable el agua (de grifo)?' ('Is the (tap) water drinkable?'). Water from public spouts and fountains is not reliable unless it has a sign saying 'Agua Potable'. Don't drink where it says 'Agua No Potable'.

Natural water, unless it's straight from an unpolluted spring or running off snow or ice without interference from people or animals, is not safe to drink unpurified.

Safe bottled water is available everywhere, generally for 40 to 75 ptas for a 1.5L bottle in shops and supermarkets.

The simplest way of purifying water is to boil it thoroughly. Vigorous boiling should be satisfactory; at high altitude, however, water boils at a lower temperature, so germs are less likely to be killed. Boil it for longer at high altitude. If you can't boil water it should be treated chemically. Chlorine tablets will kill many pathogens, but not some parasites such as giardia and amoebic cysts. Iodine is more effective in purifying water and is available in tablet form.

Medical Kit Check List

Following is a list of items you should consider including in your medical kit – consult your pharmacist for brands available in your country.

- Aspirin or paracetamol (acetaminophen in the USA) – for pain or fever
- Antihistamine – for allergies, eg, hay fever; to ease the itch from insect bites or stings; and to prevent motion sickness
- Cold and flu tablets, throat lozenges and nasal decongestant
- Multivitamins – consider for long trips, when dietary vitamin intake may be inadequate
- Antibiotics – consider including these if you're travelling well off the beaten track; see your doctor, as they must be prescribed, and carry the prescription with you
- Loperamide or diphenoxylate – 'blockers' for diarrhoea
- Prochlorperazine or metaclopramide – for nausea and vomiting
- Rehydration mixture – to prevent dehydration, which may occur, eg, during bouts of diarrhoea; this is particularly important when travelling with children
- Insect repellent, sunscreen, lip balm and eye drops
- Calamine lotion, sting relief spray or aloe vera – to ease irritation from sunburn and insect bites or stings
- Antifungal cream or powder – for fungal skin infections and thrush
- Antiseptic (such as povidone-iodine) – for cuts and grazes
- Bandages, Band-Aids (plasters) and other wound dressings
- Water purification tablets or iodine
- Scissors, tweezers and a thermometer – note that mercury thermometers are prohibited by airlines

Medical Problems & Treatment

For serious medical problems and emergencies, the Spanish public health service provides care to rival that of any country in the world. Seeing a doctor about something more mundane can be less than enchanting, because of queues and obscure appointment systems, though you should get decent attention in the end. The expense of going to a private clinic or surgery often saves time and frustration: you'll typically pay 3000 to 6000 ptas for a consultation (not counting medicines). All dental practices are private, in any case.

If you want to see a doctor quickly, or need emergency dental treatment, you could go along to the *urgencias* (emergency) section of the nearest hospital. Many towns also have a *centro de salud* (health centre) with an urgencias section.

Take along as much documentation as you can muster when you deal with medical services – passport, E111 with photocopies, insurance papers. Tourist offices, the police and your accommodation can tell you where to find medical help or call an ambulance. You could also contact your country's nearest consulate in Spain for advice. Many major hospitals and emergency medical services are mentioned and/or shown on maps in this book's city sections – for some telephone numbers, see also the Emergencies section later in this chapter.

Pharmacies *(farmacias)* can help with many ailments. A system of duty pharmacies *(farmacias de guardia)* ensures that each town or each district of a city has a pharmacy open all the time. When a pharmacy is closed, it posts the name of the nearest open one on the door.

Environmental Hazards

Altitude Sickness At altitudes over 2500m, less oxygen reaches the muscles and brain, requiring the heart and lungs to work harder. Symptoms of Acute Mountain Sickness (AMS) usually develop during the first 24 hours at altitude but may be delayed by up to three weeks. Mild symptoms include headaches, lethargy, dizziness, difficulty sleeping and loss of appetite. Severe symptoms include breathlessness, a dry, irritative cough (which may progress to the production of pink, frothy sputum), severe headache, lack of coordination and balance, confusion, irrational behaviour, vomiting, drowsiness and unconsciousness. There is no hard-and-fast rule on what is too high: AMS has been fatal at 3000m, although 3500 to 4500m is the usual range. The only mountains higher than 3000m in mainland Spain are in the Pyrenees and Andalucía's Sierra Nevada. None of these exceeds 3500m.

Treat mild symptoms by resting at the same altitude until recovery, usually a day or two. Paracetamol or aspirin can be taken for headaches. If symptoms persist or become worse, *immediate descent is necessary*; even 500m can help.

Heat Exhaustion Dehydration and salt deficiency can cause heat exhaustion. Take time to acclimatise to high temperatures, drink sufficient liquids and don't do anything too physically demanding.

Salt deficiency is characterised by fatigue, lethargy, headaches, giddiness and muscle cramps; salt tablets may help, but adding extra salt to your food is better.

Heatstroke This serious, occasionally fatal, condition can occur if the body's heat-regulating mechanism breaks down and the body temperature rises to dangerous levels. Long, continuous periods of exposure to high temperatures and insufficient fluids can leave you vulnerable to heatstroke.

The symptoms are feeling unwell, not sweating very much (or at all) and a high body temperature (39 to 41°C, 102 to 106°F).

Everyday Health

Normal body temperature is up to 37°C or 98.6°F; more than 2°C (4°F) higher indicates a high fever. The normal adult pulse rate is 60 to 100 per minute (children 80 to 100, babies 100 to 140). As a general rule the pulse increases about 20 beats per minute for each 1°C (2°F) rise in fever.

Respiration (breathing) rate is also an indicator of illness. Between 12 and 20 breaths per minute is normal for adults and older children (up to 30 for younger children, 40 for babies). People with a high fever or serious respiratory illness breathe more quickly than normal.

Where sweating has ceased, the skin becomes flushed and red. Severe, throbbing headaches and a lack of coordination will occur, and the sufferer may be confused or aggressive. Eventually the victim will become delirious or convulse. Hospitalisation is essential, but meanwhile get victims out of the sun, remove their clothing, cover them with a wet sheet or towel and then fan continually. Give fluids if they are conscious.

Hypothermia Too much cold can be just as dangerous as too much heat. Though unlikely in Spain, it could occur in the mountains in winter.

Hypothermia occurs when the body loses heat faster than it can produce it and the body's core temperature falls. It's surprisingly easy to progress from very cold to dangerously cold through a combination of wind, wet clothing, fatigue and hunger. It is best to dress in layers: silk, wool and some of the new artificial fibres are good insulating materials. A hat is important. A strong, waterproof outer layer (and a 'space' blanket for emergencies) are essential. Carry basic supplies, including food containing simple sugars to generate heat quickly and fluids to drink.

Symptoms of hypothermia are exhaustion, numb skin (particularly toes and fingers), shivering, slurred speech, irrational or violent behaviour, lethargy, stumbling, dizzy spells, muscle cramps and violent bursts of energy. Irrationality may take the form of sufferers claiming they are warm and trying to take off their clothes.

To treat mild hypothermia, first get the person out of the wind and/or rain, and replace wet clothes with dry, warm ones. Give them hot liquids – not alcohol – and some high-kilojoule, easily digestible food. Do not rub victims; instead allow them to slowly warm themselves. The early recognition and treatment of mild hypothermia is the only way to prevent severe hypothermia, a critical condition.

Prickly Heat This itchy rash, caused by excessive perspiration trapped under the skin, usually strikes people who have just arrived in a hot climate. Keeping cool, bathing often, drying the skin and using a mild talcum or prickly heat powder, or resorting to air-conditioning, may help.

Sunburn You can get sunburnt surprisingly quickly, even through cloud. Use sunscreen, a hat and barrier cream for your nose and lips. Calamine lotion or a commercial after-sun preparation are good for mild sunburn. Protect your eyes with good quality sunglasses, particularly if you'll be near water, sand or snow.

Infectious Diseases

Diarrhoea Simple things like a change of water, food or climate can all cause a mild bout of diarrhoea, but a few rushed toilet trips with no other symptoms are not indicative of a major problem.

Dehydration is the main danger with any diarrhoea, particularly in children or the elderly, as it can occur quite quickly. Under all circumstances *fluid replacement* (at least equal to the volume being lost) is the most important thing to remember. Weak black tea with a little sugar, soda water, or soft drinks allowed to go flat and diluted 50% with clean water are all good.

The most likely cause of severe diarrhoea in travellers is bacterial diarrhoea. Another cause of persistent diarrhoea is **giardiasis**, which is caused by a common parasite, *Giardia lamblia*. Symptoms include stomach cramps, nausea, a bloated stomach, watery, foul-smelling diarrhoea and frequent gas. Giardiasis can appear several weeks after you have been exposed to the parasite. The symptoms may disappear for a few days and then return; this can go on for several weeks. Seek medical advice if you think you have giardiasis.

Fungal Infections These occur more commonly in hot weather and are usually found on the scalp, between the toes (athlete's foot) or fingers, in the groin and on the body (ringworm). You get ringworm (which is a fungal infection, not a worm) from infected animals or other people. Moisture encourages these infections.

To prevent fungal infections wear loose, comfortable clothes, avoid artificial fibres, wash frequently and dry carefully. If you get an infection, wash the area at least daily with a disinfectant or medicated soap and water, and rinse and dry well. Apply an anti-fungal cream or powder such as tolnaftate. Try to expose the area to air or sunlight as much as possible and wash all towels and underwear in hot water, change them often and let them dry in the sun.

Hepatitis Hepatitis is a general term for inflammation of the liver. Its symptoms are fever, chills, headache, fatigue, feelings of weakness and aches and pains, followed by loss of appetite, nausea, vomiting, abdominal pain, dark urine, light-coloured faeces, jaundiced (yellow) skin and yellowing of the whites of the eyes. People who have had hepatitis should avoid alcohol for some time after the illness, as the liver needs time to recover.

Hepatitis A is transmitted by contaminated food and drinking water. You should seek medical advice, but there is not much you can do apart from resting, drinking lots of fluids, eating lightly and avoiding fatty foods. **Hepatitis E** is transmitted in the same way as hepatitis A; it can be particularly serious in pregnant women.

There are almost 300 million chronic carriers of **hepatitis B** in the world and Spanish children are routinely vaccinated against it. Hepatitis B can lead to long-term problems such as irreparable liver damage or even liver cancer. It is spread through contact with infected blood, blood products or body fluids, for example through sexual contact, unsterilised needles and blood transfusions, or contact with blood via small breaks in the skin. Other risk situations include having a shave, a tattoo or body piercing with contaminated equipment. The disease can lead to long-term problems such as chronic liver damage, liver cancer or a long-term carrier state. **Hepatitis C** is spread in the same way as hepatitis B and can also lead to long-term complications.

There are vaccines against hepatitis A and B, but there are no vaccines against the other types of hepatitis. Avoiding risk situations is an important preventative measure.

HIV/AIDS Infection with the human immunodeficiency virus (HIV) may lead to acquired immune deficiency syndrome (AIDS), which is a fatal disease. Any exposure to blood, blood products or body fluids may put the individual at risk. The disease is often transmitted through sexual contact or dirty needles – vaccinations, acupuncture, tattooing and body piercing can be potentially as dangerous as intravenous drug use. HIV/AIDS can also be spread through infected blood transfusions.

If you do need an injection, ask to see the syringe unwrapped in front of you, or take a needle and syringe pack with you. Fear of HIV infection should never preclude treatment for serious medical conditions.

A few years ago Spain had the highest AIDS rate in Europe, the major reason being intravenous drug use. But the number of new cases (9.3 per 100,000 inhabitants in 1998) is now half of what it was in the mid-1990s.

HIV and AIDS are *VIH* and *sida*, respectively, in Spanish. The Fundación Anti-Sida España has a free information line (☎ 900-11 10 00) and a Web site at www.fase.es. Two gay organisations able to provide AIDS information are Coordinadora Gai-Lesbiana in Barcelona (☎ 93 298 00 29), with a Web site at www.pangea.org/org/cgl, and Cogam in Madrid (☎ 91 532 45 17); its Web site is at www.ctv.es/USERS/cogam.

Sexually Transmitted Diseases HIV/AIDS and hepatitis B can be transmitted through sexual contact – see the relevant sections earlier for more details. Other STDs include gonorrhoea, herpes and syphilis; sores, blisters or rashes around the genitals and discharges or pain when urinating are common symptoms. In some STDs, such as wart virus or chlamydia, symptoms may be less marked or not observed at all, especially in women. Chlamydia infection can cause infertility in men and women before any symptoms have been noticed. Syphilis symptoms eventually disappear completely but the disease

continues and can cause severe problems in later years. While abstinence from sexual contact is the only 100% effective STD prevention, using condoms (*condones* or *preservativos* in Spanish) is also effective. The different sexually transmitted diseases each require specific antibiotics.

Insect-Borne Diseases

Leishmaniasis This is a group of parasitic diseases transmitted by sandflies, which are found in many parts of the Mediterranean area. The strain found in Spain, mainly in country areas near the Mediterranean coasts, is a form of visceral leishmaniasis called leishmania infantum. Visceral leishmaniasis is characterised by irregular bouts of fever, substantial weight loss, anaemia and swelling of the spleen and liver. It can be fatal for children under five and people with immune system deficiencies, such as AIDS sufferers. Avoiding sandfly bites is the best precaution: cover up and apply repellent. Sandflies are most active at dawn and dusk. The bites are usually painless but itchy. If you suspect leishmaniasis, seek medical advice as laboratory testing is required for diagnosis and treatment.

Cuts, Bites & Stings

Cuts & Scratches Wash well and treat any cut with an antiseptic such as povidone-iodine. Where possible avoid bandages and Band-Aids, which can keep wounds wet.

Insects, Scorpions & Centipedes Bee and wasp stings are usually painful rather than dangerous. But people who are allergic to them may have severe breathing difficulties and require urgent medical care. Calamine lotion or a sting-relief spray will give relief and ice packs will reduce the pain and swelling.

Scorpion stings are notoriously painful but Spanish scorpions are not considered fatal. Scorpions often shelter in shoes or clothing.

Some Spanish centipedes (*ciempiés* or *escolopendras)* have a very nasty, but not fatal, sting. Steer clear of those composed of clearly defined segments, which may be marked by, for instance, alternate black and yellow stripes.

Also beware of the hairy, reddish-brown caterpillars *(procesionarias)* of the pine processionary moth, which live in easily discernible silvery nests in pine trees in many parts of Spain, and have a habit of walking around in long lines (hence the name). Touching the caterpillars' hairs sets off a severely irritating allergic skin reaction. It's even more harmful to animals, which get gangrene of the tongue if not treated straight away.

Mosquito and other insect bites can be a nuisance – in the Pyrenees, for instance – but none of the mosquitoes in Spain carry malaria. You can avoid bites by covering your skin and using an insect repellent.

Jellyfish Jellyfish *(medusas),* with their stinging tentacles, generally occur in large numbers or hardly at all. Heeding local advice is the best way of avoiding them. Dousing in vinegar will deactivate any jellyfish stingers that have not 'fired'. Calamine lotion, antihistamines and analgesics may reduce the reaction and relieve the pain.

Ticks Check for ticks all over your body if you have been walking through a potentially tick-infested area, such as long grass or woodlands in spring or summer, as ticks can cause skin infections and other more serious diseases. If a tick is found attached, press down around its head with tweezers, grab the head and gently pull upwards. Avoid pulling the rear of the body as this may squeeze the tick's gut contents through the attached mouth parts into the skin, increasing the risk of infection and disease. Smearing chemicals on the tick will not make it let go and is not recommended.

Snakes The only venomous snake that is even relatively common in Spain is Lataste's viper *(víbora hocicuda* or *víbora de Lataste)*. This is a smallish, triangular-headed creature, rarely more than 50cm long, and is coloured grey with a zigzag pattern. It lives in dry, rocky areas, away from humans. Its bite can be fatal and needs

to be treated as soon as possible with a serum kept by state clinics in major towns. Also to be avoided is the Montpellier snake *(culebra bastarda),* which is blue with a white underside and prominent ridges over the eyes. It lives mainly in scrub and sandy areas but keeps a low profile and is unlikely to be a threat unless trodden on.

To minimise your chances of being bitten by snakes, always wear boots, socks and long trousers when walking where they may be present. Don't put your hands into holes and crevices, and be careful when collecting firewood.

Snake bites do not cause instantaneous death and antivenins are usually available. Immediately wrap the bitten limb tightly, as you would for a sprained ankle, and then attach a splint to immobilise it. Keep the victim still and seek medical help, if possible with the dead snake for identification. Don't attempt to catch the snake if there is a possibility of being bitten again. Tourniquets and sucking out the poison are now comprehensively discredited procedures.

Women's Health

Gynaecological Problems Antibiotic use, synthetic underwear, sweating and contraceptive pills can lead to fungal vaginal infections in hot climates. These infections are characterised by a rash, itch and discharge and can be treated with a vinegar or lemon-juice douche, or with yoghurt. Nystatin, miconazole or clotrimazole pessaries or vaginal cream are the usual treatment. Good personal hygiene and wearing loose-fitting clothes and cotton underwear may help prevent these infections.

Sexually transmitted diseases (see the earlier section) are a major cause of vaginal problems. Symptoms include a smelly discharge, painful intercourse and sometimes a burning sensation when urinating. Medical attention should be sought and male sexual partners must also be treated. Besides abstinence, the best preventative is to practise safer sex using condoms.

Pregnancy Most miscarriages happen during the first three months of pregnancy.

Miscarriage is not uncommon and can occasionally lead to severe bleeding. The last three months should also be spent within reasonable distance of good medical care. A baby born as early as 24 weeks stands a chance of survival, but only in a good modern hospital. Pregnant women should avoid all unnecessary medication but vaccinations should still be had when needed. Additional care should be taken to prevent illness, and particular attention should be paid to diet and nutrition. Alcohol and nicotine, for example, should be avoided.

WOMEN TRAVELLERS

Women travellers should be ready to ignore stares, catcalls and unnecessary comments, though harassment is much less frequent than you might expect. Men under about 35, who have grown up in the post-Franco era, conform less to old-fashioned sexual stereotypes, though you might notice that sexual stereotyping becomes more pronounced as you move from north to south in Spain, and from city to country.

You still need to exercise common sense about where you go on your own. So think twice about going by yourself to isolated stretches of beach, lonely country areas or down empty city streets at night. You are generally safer where there are crowds. It's highly inadvisable for a woman to hitch alone – and not a great idea even for two women together.

Topless bathing and skimpy clothes are in fashion in many coastal resorts, but people tend to dress more modestly elsewhere.

Spain's women's liberation movement, after the amazingly constrictive Franco era (when wives could not legally take a job or even go on a long journey without their husband's permission), took the form less of radical feminism than of sexual permissiveness. Women flooded into the workforce and higher education. Some of the causes – and leaders – of the 1970s women's movement were taken up by the Partido Socialista Obrero Español (PSOE; or Spanish Socialist Worker Party) governments of the 1980s and the movement fizzled out as a major independent force. Today it's stronger in the

north than in the south. Many women who go out to work still run the household and take most of the responsibility for the children. One consequence is that they're having fewer children: Spain has the world's lowest birth rate (1.06 children per fertile woman).

Organisations

There are women's bookshops in Madrid, Barcelona (see those chapters) and a few other cities that are also useful sources of information on women's organisations and activities. Many women's organisations are listed (though not usually in English) at www.secociti.org/mujer/mujer.htm.

For information on rape crisis centres, see the Emergencies section later in this chapter.

GAY & LESBIAN TRAVELLERS

Gay and lesbian sex are legal in Spain and the age of consent is 16 years, the same as for heterosexuals. In 1996 the conservative Partido Popular (PP) government put the brakes on a law intended to establish the legal rights of de facto gay couples. The regional governments of Catalunya and Aragón have both approved such laws, and in mid-2000 the government of Navarra opened the way for the adoption of children by homosexual couples.

The gay male scene is more developed than the lesbian one. Lesbians and gay men generally keep a fairly low profile, but can be more open in the cities. Madrid, Barcelona, Sitges, Torremolinos and Ibiza have particularly lively scenes. Sitges is a major destination on the international gay party circuit; gays take a leading role in the wild *carnaval* there in February-March. As well, there are gay parades, marches and events in several cities on and around the last Saturday in June, when Madrid's gay and lesbian pride march takes place.

You'll find gay and lesbian bars, discos, bookshops and information or social centres listed in some city sections of this book.

The Madrid-based *Entiendes*, a gay magazine, is on sale at some newsstands for 500 ptas and has a quarterly English edition. International gay and lesbian guides worth tracking down are the *Spartacus Guide for Gay Men,* published by Bruno Gmünder Verlag, Mail Order, PO Box 61 01 04, D-10921 Berlin; and *Places for Women,* published by Ferrari Publications in Phoenix, Arizona, in the USA. The Spartacus list also includes the comprehensive *Spartacus National Edition España,* in English and German.

Organisations

A good source of information on gay places and organisations throughout Spain is the Coordinadora Gai-Lesbiana (☎ 93 298 00 29, fax 93 298 06 18), Carrer de Finlandia 45, 08014 Barcelona. Its Web site is at www.pangea.org/org/cgl. In Madrid, the equivalent is Cogam (☎/fax 91 532 45 17), Calle del Fuencarral 37, 28004. Both can provide information on help groups, AIDS, places to go, bars and just about anything else you might want to know. Another useful organisation is Fundación Triángulo (☎/fax 91 593 05 40), Calle de Eloy Gonzalo 25, Madrid, which has the latest news on gay rights and issues in Spain. Its trilingual Web site is at www.redestb.es/triangulo/.

DISABLED TRAVELLERS

Some Spanish tourist offices in other countries can provide a basic information sheet with some useful addresses for disabled travellers and give details of accessible accommodation in specific places.

You'll find some accessible accommodation in main centres but it may not be in the budget category. Some 25 Spanish youth hostels are classed as suitable for wheelchair users. Unfortunately, many hotels that claim to be accessible retain problem features.

Organisations

The UK-based Royal Association for Disability & Rehabilitation (Radasr) publishes a useful guide called *European Holidays & Travel Abroad: A Guide for Disabled People,* which provides a good overview of facilities available to disabled travellers throughout Europe. Contact Radar (☎ 020-7250 3222), Unit 12, City Forum, 250 City Rd, London EC1V 8AS. Visit its Web site at www.radar.org.uk.

Another organisation in the UK worth calling is Holiday Care (☎ 01293-774535), 2nd floor, Imperial Buildings, Victoria Rd, Horley, Surrey RH6 7PZ. It produces an information pack on Spain for disabled people and other travellers with special needs. Tips range from hotels with disabled access and places where you can hire equipment through to tour operators dealing with the disabled. Visit the Web site at www.freespace.virgin.net/hol.care.

Cruz Roja Española, the Spanish Red Cross (☎ 91 533 45 31), Calle de Federico Rubino y Gali 3, 28003 Madrid, may be able to help with travel arrangements. Instituto Nacional de Servicios Sociales (Inserso; ☎ 91 347 88 88), Calle de Ginzo de Limia 58, 28029 Madrid, is the Spanish government department for the disabled, with branches in all 50 provinces.

ONCE (☎ 91 577 37 56), Calle de José Ortega y Gasset 18, 28001 Madrid (Map 3), is the Spanish association for the blind. Its Web site is at www.once.es.

Federación ECOM (☎ 93 451 55 50), Gran Via de les Corts Catalanes 562, 08011 Barcelona, is a large voluntary organisation that has a lot of information for the disabled, including on travel, covering Barcelona and Catalunya.

SENIOR TRAVELLERS

There are reduced prices for people over 60, 63 or 65 (depending on the place) at some museums and attractions and occasionally on transport (see the Getting There & Away and Getting Around chapters). Some of the luxurious *paradores* (state-owned hotels; see Accommodation later in this chapter) offer discounts for people over 60. You should also seek information in your own country on travel packages and discounts for senior travellers, through senior citizens' organisations and travel agents.

TRAVEL WITH CHILDREN

Spaniards as a rule are very friendly to children. Any child whose hair is less than jet black will get called *rubia* (blonde) if she's a girl or *rubio* if he's a boy. Accompanied children are welcome at all kinds of accommodation, and in virtually every cafe, bar and restaurant, where outside tables often allow kids a bit of space and freedom while the grown-ups sit and eat or drink. Spanish children stay up late and at fiestas it's common to see even tiny ones toddling the streets at 2 or 3 am. Visiting kids like this idea too – but can't cope with it quite so readily.

Most young children don't like moving around too much but are happier if they can settle into places and make new friends. It's easier on parents too if you don't have to pack up and move on every day or two. Children are also likely to need extra time to acclimatise and extra care to avoid sunburn. Be prepared for minor health problems brought on by change of diet or water or disrupted sleeping patterns.

Spanish street life and bustle, and the novelty of being in new places, provide some distraction for kids but most of them will probably get bored unless some of the time is devoted to their favoured activities. Apart from the obvious attractions of beaches, playgrounds are fairly plentiful and in many places you can find excellent special attractions such as amusement parks (eg, Catalunya's Port Aventura and Sevilla's Isla Mágica), aquaparks, boat and train rides, child-friendly museums, zoos, aquariums – and let's not forget Mini Hollywood and other western movie sets in the Almería desert. Bring some of the children's own toys, books etc and let them have time to get on with some of the activities they are used to back at home.

Most children are fascinated by the ubiquitous street-corner *kioscos* selling sweets or *gusanitos* (corn puffs) for a few pesetas. The magnetism of these places often overcomes a child's inhibitions enough for them to carry out their own first Spanish transactions.

Nappies, creams, lotions, baby foods etc are as easily available in Spain as in any other European country, but if there's some particular brand you swear by it's best to bring it with you.

Children benefit from cut-price or free entry at many sights and museums. Those under four travel free on Spanish trains and those aged four to 11 normally pay 60% of the adult fare.

Lonely Planet's *Travel with Children* has lots of practical advice and first-hand stories from Lonely Planet authors and others.

USEFUL ORGANISATIONS

The Instituto Cervantes, with branches in over 30 cities around the world, exists to promote the Spanish language and the cultures of Spain and other Spanish-speaking countries. It's mainly involved in Spanish teaching, and library and information services. The library at the London branch (☎ 020-7235 0353), 102 Eaton Square, London SW1 W9AN, has a wide range of reference books, literature, books on history and the arts, periodicals, over 1000 videos including feature films, language-teaching material, electronic databases and music CDs. In New York, the institute (☎ 212-689 4232) is at 122 East 42nd St, Suite 807, New York, NY 10168. You can find further addresses on the institute's Web site at www.cervantes.es.

TIVE, the Spanish youth and student travel organisation, is good for reduced-price youth and student travel tickets. It also issues various useful documents such as HI youth hostel cards and ISIC cards (see Visas & Documents earlier in this chapter). The administration of TIVE is now run at regional level. The Madrid office (☎ 91 543 74 12, fax 91 544 00 62) is at Calle de Fernando El Católico 88 (Madrid Map 2).

DANGERS & ANNOYANCES

Spain is generally a pretty safe country. The main thing you have to be wary of is petty theft (which may of course not seem so petty to you if your passport, cash, travellers cheques, credit card and camera all go missing). But with a few simple precautions you can minimise the risk and any worries.

For some specific hints about looking after your luggage and money and on safety for women, see the What to Bring, Money and Women Travellers sections, respectively, earlier in this chapter.

Before you leave home, inscribe your name, address and telephone number *inside* your luggage and take photocopies of the important pages of your passport, travel tickets and other important documents. Keep the copies separate from the originals and ideally leave one set of copies at home. These steps will make things easier if you do suffer a loss or theft.

Travel insurance against theft and loss is another good idea; see the Health section in this chapter.

Theft & Loss

Theft is mostly a risk in tourist resorts, big cities and when you first arrive in the country or at a new city and may be off your guard. Barcelona, Madrid and Sevilla have the worst reputations for theft and, occasionally, muggings.

The main things to guard against are pickpockets, bag snatchers and theft from cars. Carry any valuables under your clothes if possible – not in a back pocket, a day pack or anything that could be snatched away easily – and keep your eyes open for people who get unnecessarily close to you on the streets and in public transport. Don't leave baggage unattended and avoid crushes. Also be cautious with people who come up to offer or ask you something (such as the time or directions) or start talking to you for no obviously good reason. These could be attempts to distract you and make you an easier victim.

Always remove the radio and cassette player from your car and never leave any belongings visible when you leave the car. Better still, don't leave anything in an unattended car (which is often harder than it sounds).

Anything left lying on the beach can disappear in a flash when your back is turned. Avoid dingy, empty city alleys and backstreets, or anywhere that just doesn't feel 100% safe, at night.

You can also help yourself by not leaving anything valuable lying around your room, above all in any hostel-type place. Use a safe if one is available.

If anything valuable does go missing, you'll need to report it to the police and get a copy of the report if you want to make an insurance claim. Occasionally, this might even help you get it back. If your passport

has gone, contact your embassy or consulate for help in issuing a replacement. Many countries have consulates in a few cities around Spain (such as Barcelona, Valencia, Alicante, Málaga and Sevilla) and your embassy can tell you where the nearest one is. Embassies and consulates can also give help of various kinds in other emergencies, but as a rule cannot advance you money to get home.

EMERGENCIES

A single emergency telephone number for ambulance, police or fire (☎ 112) is in use throughout Spain, although it appears it may not yet be fully operational all over the country.

Otherwise, you can call ☎ 061 for an ambulance in many places. Other medical emergency numbers and the locations of many hospitals and clinics are given in this book's city and town sections. For more on Spanish medical facilities and health problems, see the Health section earlier in this chapter. If you're seriously ill or injured, someone should let your embassy or consulate know.

In many places the fire brigade *(bomberos)* is on ☎ 080 or ☎ 085, but in others it's on some completely different number.

The Asociación de Asistencia a Mujeres Violadas (Association for Assistance to Raped Women; ☎ 91 574 01 10), Calle de O'Donnell 42, Madrid, offers advice and help to rape victims and can refer you to similar centres in other cities, though only limited English may be spoken. The phone line is open from 10 am to 2 pm and 4 to 7 pm weekdays; there's a recorded message in Spanish at other times.

On the subject of assault, the nationwide Comisión de Investigación de Malos Tratos a Mujeres (Commission of Investigation into the Abuse of Women) has a free 24-hour national emergency line for victims of physical abuse: call ☎ 900-10 00 09.

Terrorism

Throughout the mid-1990s the Basque terrorist organisation ETA has maintained its campaign of terror, striking as far away from

La Policía – Who's Who

Spanish police are, on the whole, more of a help than a threat to the average law-abiding traveller. Most are certainly friendly enough to be approached for directions on the street. Highway police can be hard on locals but tend to steer clear of foreign vehicles unless they stop to give help (but see the Getting There & Away chapter for information on documents and equipment you should carry in your vehicle). Unpleasant events such as random drug searches do occur, but not with great frequency.

There are three main types of *policía*: the Policía Nacional, the Policía Local (also known as Policía Municipal) and the Guardia Civil (the words policía and guardia refer to the forces, but also stand for each individual member).

Guardia Civil

The main responsibilities of the green-uniformed members of the Guardia Civil are roads, the countryside, villages, prisons, international borders and some environmental protection. These are the guys who used to wear those alarming winged helmets, which were phased out in the 1980s but still resurface on some ceremonial occasions.

The Guardia Civil was set up in the 19th century to quell banditry but soon came to be regarded as a politically repressive force that clamped down on any challenge to established privilege. Although its image has softened since responsibility for it has been switched from the defence ministry to the interior ministry, it's still a military body in some ways: most officers have attended military academy and members qualify for military decorations.

Policía Nacional

This force covers cities and bigger towns and is the main crime-fighting body because most crime happens on its patch. Those who wear uniforms are in blue. There is also a large contingent in plain clothes, some of whom form special squads dealing with drugs, terrorism and the like. Most of them will be found in large bunker-like police stations called *comisarías,* shuffling masses of paper dealing with things such as issuing passports, DNIs *(documentos nacionales de identidad,* or national identity cards) and residence cards for foreigners who like Spain enough to opt for long-term entanglement with its bureaucracy.

Policía Local

The Policía Local (sometimes known as the Policía Municipal) are controlled by city and town councils and deal mainly with minor matters such as parking, traffic and bylaws. They wear blue-and-white uniforms. In Catalunya the equivalent force is called the Guàrdia Urbana. Spain has no real equivalent of 'bobby on the beat' street-patrol police.

Regional Police

Finally, four of Spain's 17 autonomous communities have their own police forces in addition to the above three: Catalunya (where it's called the Mossos d'Esquadra), the Basque Country (the Ertzaintza), Valencia and Galicia.

Contacting the Police

If you need to go to the police, any of them will do, but you may find the Policía Local are the most helpful.

Anywhere in Spain you can call ☎ 091 for the Policía Nacional or ☎ 092 for the Policía Local. Guardia Civil numbers vary from place to place, although often you can reach them on ☎ 062. Some further police numbers and locations of main stations are given in city and town sections of this book.

its home territory as Sevilla. In 1999 it broke a cease-fire with a series of car-bomb assassinations in Madrid and the Basque Country. Its main targets seem to be political figures.

Annoyances

Spain is a mellow place and there ain't much to get annoyed about. That said, you should expect a few attempts to short-change you and you've got to be prepared for more noise than you're probably used to! While a certain amount of noise and crowds can make anybody feel more alive, it can be hard to understand why young Spanish males deliberately tinker with their motorbike exhausts to make the blessed things even noisier than they need to be. There's some sort of legislation about silencers but no one dreams of enforcing it.

LEGAL MATTERS

If you're arrested you will be allotted the free services of a duty solicitor *(abogado de oficio)*, who may speak only Spanish. You're also entitled to make a phone call. If you use this to contact your embassy or consulate, the staff will probably be able to do no more than refer you to a lawyer who speaks your language. If you end up in court, the authorities are obliged to provide a translator.

Drugs

Spain's liberal drug laws were severely tightened in 1992. The only legal drug is cannabis and it's only legal in amounts for personal use, which means very small amounts.

Public consumption of any drug is apparently illegal, yet there are still some bars where people smoke joints openly. Other bars will ask you to step outside if you light up. The only sure moral of these stories is to be very discreet if you do use cannabis. There is a reasonable degree of tolerance when it comes to people having a smoke in their own home, but it would be unwise in hotel rooms or guesthouses and could be risky in even the coolest of public places.

Travellers entering Spain from Morocco should be prepared for intensive drug searches, especially if they have a vehicle.

BUSINESS HOURS

Generally, Spaniards work Monday to Friday from about 9 am to 2 pm and then again from 4.30 or 5 pm for another three hours. Shops and travel agencies are usually open these hours on Saturday too, though some may skip the evening session. Big supermarkets and department stores, such as the nationwide El Corte Inglés chain, often stay open from about 9 am to 9 pm Monday to Saturday. A few shops in tourist resorts open on Sunday in the summer. Many government offices don't bother opening in the afternoon, any day of the year.

Museums all have their own opening hours: major ones tend to open for something like normal Spanish business hours (with or without the afternoon break), but often have their weekly closing day on Monday.

For bank and post office hours, respectively, see the Money and Post & Communications sections earlier in this chapter.

PUBLIC HOLIDAYS & SPECIAL EVENTS

Public Holidays

There are at least 14 official holidays a year – some observed nationwide, some locally.

When a holiday falls close to a weekend, Spaniards like to make a *puente* (bridge), meaning they take the intervening day off too. On the odd occasion when some holidays fall close, they make an *acueducto* (aqueduct)!

National holidays are:

Año Nuevo (New Year's Day)   1 January
Viernes Santo (Good Friday)   March/April
Fiesta del Trabajo (Labour Day)   1 May
La Asunción (Feast of the Assumption)
       15 August
Fiesta Nacional de España (National Day)
       12 October
**La Inmaculada Concepción (Feast of the
   Immaculate Conception)**   8 December
Navidad (Christmas)   25 December

Regional governments set five holidays and local councils two more. Common dates include:

Epifanía (Epiphany) or **Día de los Reyes Magos (Three Kings' Day)** 6 January – On this day children receive presents; it's observed everywhere.

Día de San José (St Joseph's Day) 19 March

Jueves Santo (Maundy Thursday) March/April – The day before Good Friday, this holiday is observed everywhere except Catalunya and Valencia.

Corpus Christi June – This is the Thursday after the eighth Sunday after Easter Sunday; it's observed widely.

Día de San Juan Bautista (Feast of St John the Baptist) 24 June – This is King Juan Carlos' saint's day and is observed widely.

Día de Santiago Apóstol (Feast of St James the Apostle) 25 July – As Spain's patron saint's day, this holiday is observed widely.

Día de la Constitución (Constitution Day) 6 December

Holiday Times

The two main periods when Spaniards go on holiday are Semana Santa (the week leading up to Easter Sunday) and during August. At these times accommodation in resorts can be scarce and transport heavily booked, but other cities are often half-empty.

Special Events

Spaniards indulge in their love of colour, noise, crowds, dressing up and partying at innumerable local fiestas and *ferias* (fairs); even small villages will have at least one, probably several, in the year, all with their own unique twists. Many fiestas are religion-based but are celebrated with a party spirit. Main local festivals are noted in city and town sections of this book and tourist offices can supply more detailed information. A few of the most outstanding include:

January

Festividad de San Sebastián Everyone in San Sebastián dresses up and goes berserk (20 January).

February/March

Carnaval Several days of fancy-dress parades and merrymaking in many places, usually ending on the Tuesday 47 days before Easter Sunday (wildest in Cádiz and Sitges, also good in Ciudad Rodrigo)

March

Las Fallas Several days of all-night dancing and drinking, first-class fireworks and processions; in Valencia, but also celebrated in Gandía and Benidorm (15–19 March).

March/April

Semana Santa (Holy Week) Parades of holy images and huge crowds, notably in Sevilla, but also big in Málaga, Córdoba, Toledo, Ávila, Valladolid and Zamora (the week leading up to Easter Sunday).

April

Moros y Cristianos Colourful parades and 'battles' between Christian and Muslim 'arm-ies' in Alcoy, near Alicante, make this one of the best of several similar events in the Valencia and Alicante provinces through the year (22–24 April).

Feria de Abril A week-long party in Sevilla after the religious fervour of Semana Santa (late April).

Romería de la Virgen de la Cabeza Hundreds of thousands of people make a mass pilgrimage to the Santuario de la Virgen de la Cabeza near Andújar, Jaén province (last Sunday in April).

May

Feria del Caballo (Horse Fair) Colourful equestrian and other festivities in Andalucía's horse capital, Jerez de la Frontera (early May).

Concurso de Patios Cordobeses Scores of beautiful private courtyards are open to the public for two weeks in Córdoba (early to mid-May).

Fiestas de San Isidro Madrid's major fiesta, with bullfights, parades, concerts and more (third week of May).

May/June

Romería del Rocío Festive pilgrimage by up to one million people to the shrine of the Virgin at the Andalucian village of El Rocío (focused on Pentecost weekend, the seventh after Easter).

Corpus Christi Religious processions and celebrations in Toledo and other cities (on or shortly before the ninth Sunday after Easter Sunday).

June

Hogueras de San Juan Midsummer bonfires and fireworks, notably along the south-eastern and southern coasts (around 24 June)

July

Fiesta de San Fermín/Sanfermines Festival with the famous Running of the Bulls in Pamplona, an activity also pursued in dozens of other cities and towns through the summer (6–14 July)

Día de la Virgen del Carmen On or near this day of the patron of fisherfolk, her image is carried into the sea or paraded on it amid a flotilla of small boats at most coastal towns (16 July).

Día de Santiago (Feast of St James) The national saint's day, spectacularly celebrated in

Santiago de Compostela, site of his tomb (25 July).

August

Semana Grande or **Aste Nagusia** A week of general celebration, heavy drinking and hangovers on the north coast (dates vary from place to place).

La Tomatina Wild tomato-throwing festival in Buñol, Valencia (last Wednesday in August).

September

Festes de la Mercè A week-long party in Barcelona (around 24 September).

Arts Festivals Spain's calendar abounds in arts festivals (any excuse for a party!). These festivals will enliven visits to their host cities: Mérida's Festival de Teatro of drama and dance from late June to August; Barcelona's concurrent Grec festival of music, dance and theatre; Córdoba's two-week Festival Internacional de Guitarra, starting in late June; San Sebastián's International Jazz Festival in July; Santander's mainly musical Festival Internacional in July and August; Sevilla's Bienal de Flamenco in the September of even-numbered years; and the November Festival Internacional de Jazz de Barcelona, which also includes blues.

Rock, Pop & Dance Festivals Music festivals are growing in number and popularity with the young crowd. Summer is busy with festivals. The Doctor Music Festival (also affectionately known as *las vacas* – literally 'the cows' – perhaps because organisers tend to choose pastoral settings) is the country's biggest musical event. It usually takes place in July and for years was held in the Catalan Pyrenees. In 2000 it switched to Asturias.

Madrid's big one is Festimad, an early-May orgy of varied music in bars, halls and on open-air stages. It was cancelled in 2000 because organisers feared that it was becoming too commercial. They plan to stage it again in 2001. A world music version is Womad, which is usually staged in Cáceres in May-June.

The Benicasim Festival north of Valencia is a long-weekend indie get-together in early August. Attending the whole three days costs 15,000 ptas, which includes a spot in the camping ground.

There are many other smaller-scale festivals in summer, some just one night long. You'll see plenty of posters telling you about them. Outside the summer season, Andalucía holds the weekend-long Espárrago Rock Festival in late March or April, highlighting Spanish and foreign alternative rock. In 2000 it was due to take place in Jerez de la Frontera and promised to be a killer concert, featuring artists such as The Cranberries, Skunk Anansie, Lou Reed and Dover. It was, sadly, washed out.

Just down the road in Málaga, the annual World Dance Festival sees the port area turned into a massive dance venue for one Saturday night in May, with more than 100,000 people enjoying live international dance music.

The biggest crowds get together for modern dance gatherings with DJs (*pinchadiscos*) and bands pumping out techno, house, eurobeat, euroenergy and their relatives for a night or two. Barcelona's Festival Sonar, held in June, is the main annual event of this kind.

For any of these festivals expect to pay a minimum of 10,000 ptas to get in.

ACTIVITIES

Spanish tourist offices can provide detailed information on possibilities for many activities from walking, skiing, mountaineering or windsurfing to horse riding, bird-watching, golf or wine tours. If you fancy going in a guided group, see the Organised Tours section of the Getting There & Away chapter for a few pointers. Spanish tourist offices can also usually tell you about tour companies running a vast range of activity holidays.

Cycling

Mountain biking is popular among both Spaniards and foreigners. There are kilometre upon kilometre of good and bad tracks and roads for biking in many areas, including Andalucía and Catalunya. Tourist offices often have information on routes. A good general source for mountain bikers who can read Spanish is *100 Rutas en Bicicleta de Montaña* by Juanjo Pedales (Espasa Calpe, 1995). Some tourist offices in Andalucía sell a booklet called *Bicicleta,* sometimes also available in English. It contains 120 suggested mountain-bike routes in Andalucía and costs 600 ptas. The Spanish for mountain bike is *bici todo terreno* (BTT).

For information on cycle touring in Spain, see under Bicycle in the Getting Around chapter.

Finding bikes of any kind to rent is a hit-or-miss affair regarding both availability and price, which can vary enormously. Catalunya is fairly well provided with rental outlets for both mountain bikes and touring bikes, but elsewhere you should bring your own if you're dead set on the idea.

Skiing
Spain is not the first country that leaps to mind when talk turns to Europe's ski centres, but its profile was significantly lifted by the world skiing championships in the Sierra Nevada near Granada in 1996. Andorra is much better known and has several good, well-established resorts.

The skiing facilities and conditions in Spain are surprisingly good and the costs are low, although in general the snow is not quite up to the standards of the Alps or even the French side of the Pyrenees. The season normally runs from December to April, with the best snow in February, but snow cover can be unpredictable, even in the higher altitude resorts.

Spain's main ski resorts are in the Pyrenees and include La Molina and Baquiera-Beret in Catalunya; Candanchú, Formigal and Cerler in Aragón; and five resorts in Andorra. The other major resort is in the Sierra Nevada, outside Granada in the south. Minor ski fields (with unreliable snowfall) cater to locals in the Sierra de Guadarrama, north of Madrid; the Cordillera Cantábrica; and even La Rioja and southern Aragón.

Ski package holidays from other countries are a novelty to Spain (but not to Andorra). Travel agencies in Spanish cities offer affordable packages for one day or longer. If you prefer to organise it yourself on the spot, a day's ski pass *(forfait)* at the better resorts in Spain and Andorra costs up to 4600 ptas a day (depending on the resort and season) or up to 19,800 ptas for five days; equipment rental can cost anything from 1700 ptas up to 2500 ptas a day. It is cheapest to rent directly at the resorts. Ski school costs anything up to 4000 ptas an hour for individual tuition or around 15,000 ptas for five days of group lessons.

You can find a range of accommodation, from mid-priced hostales upwards, in or near most resorts.

The high season – when the slopes are the most crowded and prices for lift passes, ski school and accommodation are at their peak – generally means the Christmas and New Year holiday period, February, Semana Santa and weekends almost all season long. At these times, the slopes are the most empty from 9 to 11 am and 1 to 3 pm while the Spanish skiers take breakfast and lunch.

Spanish and Andorran pistes are all graded green *(verde)* for beginners, blue *(azul)* for easy, red *(rojo)* for intermediate and black *(negro)* for difficult, although there's some variation in criteria between resorts.

The good resorts for cross-country skiing include Candanchú (Aragón), Baqueira-Beret (Catalunya) and several in Andorra. Snowboarding is growing fast in popularity at many ski resorts.

Spanish tourist offices in other countries and tourist offices in Spanish and Andorran cities and towns near the ski resorts usually have fairly detailed information on skiing.

Walking & Trekking
With its large tracts of wilderness, Spain offers limitless opportunities for short and long walks. Some wonderful areas are easily accessible and can be enjoyed on day or half-day walks, as well as by committed trekkers.

Trekking Trekking is popular among Spaniards as well as foreigners. Outstanding mountain areas are the Pyrenees in Aragón and Catalunya, the Picos de Europa straddling Cantabria, Asturias and León provinces, the Sierra de Gredos west of Madrid, the Sierra Nevada and Alpujarras valleys in Andalucía and the Serra de Tramuntana on Mallorca.

GRs, PRs & Other Paths Spain, particularly the north, has a large network of long-distance paths, called *senderos de Gran Recorrido* (GRs), which were developed by the Fédération Française de la Randonneé Pédestre (FFRP). Wherever possible these cross-country routes, some several hundred kilometres long, avoid roads and tracks used by vehicles. Not all, however, are marked or maintained for their full length – or even for much of their length in some cases.

Among the longest of the GRs are:

• the well-marked, well-established and spectacular GR-11 or Senda Pirenáica, which runs the length of the Spanish Pyrenees from Cap de Creus on the coast of Catalunya to Hondarribia (Fuenterrabía) on the Bay of Biscay in the Basque Country
• the GR-10 from Puçol on the coast of Valencia to La Alberca, just 70km from the Portuguese border (though the stretch across Ávila province doesn't yet exist)
• the GR-7 from Andorra all the way south to Murcia and Andalucía, which for most of its route forms part of the so-called E4 Mediterranean Arc, a path from Greece to Algeciras via Bulgaria, Romania, Hungary, Austria, Germany, Switzerland and France; it's nearly all open, except for sections in Bulgaria, Romania and Andalucía

Spain's most famous long walk is the Camino de Santiago (part of which forms the GR-65). This ancient pilgrimage route, in use since 11th century, can be started at various places in France. It then crosses the Pyrenees at Roncesvalles and runs across Navarra, La Rioja, Castilla y León and Galicia to the cathedral in Santiago de Compostela, shrine of Spain's patron saint Santiago (St James). For information on this walk, see the special section 'Camino de Santiago'.

Of course most people don't walk the full length of these long-distance paths. Most are quite easily accessible by road (and often public transport) at many points and it's perfectly feasible to join them for just a few hours' amble if you're not committed to more serious walking.

Spain also has many *senderos de Pequeño Recorrido* (PRs), shorter footpaths suitable for day or weekend walks. Like GRs, these vary widely in the quality of trails and markings. There are also lots of good paths that haven't become either GRs or PRs.

National parks, natural parks and other protected areas (see Flora & Fauna in the Facts about Spain chapter) may restrict visitors to limited zones and routes, but often have well-marked walks through some of their most interesting areas, with interpretive information available.

Simply walking country roads and paths between villages and towns, instead of taking the bus, can be highly enjoyable and a great way to meet the locals.

Not all of Spain's coasts are covered with concrete hotels and there are some good coastal walks in places such as Galicia, the Costa Brava and Andalucía's Cabo de Gata.

Seasons The best seasons for walking and trekking vary from region to region. In the Pyrenees, late June to early September is best; in Andalucía, mid-April to mid-June and September to mid-October are the most pleasant, but the high Sierra Nevada is only really accessible from mid-July to September; and in the Picos de Europa, May, June and September are good. The weather in high mountains is never predictable at any time, however.

Further Information Tourist offices can often help with walking and trekking information. There are many mountain walking and climbing clubs in Spain that can give information on routes, refuges and equipment shops, including the Federación Madrileña de Montañismo (☎ 91 448 50 56) in Madrid. Other clubs are mentioned in regional chapters in this book.

Walking guides to Spain are available in English, French and other languages, as well as in Spanish. Lonely Planet's *Walking in Spain* covers routes in all the main trekking areas and has plenty of advice on equipment, preparation, seasons, accommodation etc.

A good companion on the Camino de Santiago route is *The Way of St James – The Pilgrimage Route to Santiago de Compostela* by Dr Elias Valiña Sampedra, a book with detailed colour maps. Mountain guides worth tracking down include *Walks & Climbs in the Pyrenees* by Kev Reynolds, and *Walks & Climbs – Picos de Europa* by Robin Walker. In Spanish, the Colección El Búho Viajero series of hiking and walking books published by Libros Penthalon covers many regions of Spain in detail. Detailed Spanish walking guides are generally called *topoguías*. It's best to get them before you head off; try specialist bookshops in your own country or bookshops such as Altaïr or Quera in Barcelona or La Tienda Verde in Madrid.

For information on maps for walkers, see the Planning section earlier in this chapter. References to some appropriate maps for specific areas are made in regional chapters of this book.

Surfing
The Basque Country has some good waves at San Sebastián, Zarautz, which stages a round of the world championship each September, and Mundaka, with its legendary left, among others. Santander in Cantabria also attracts surfers in force and there are other good spots in Cantabria and Asturias. You'll find boards (and wet suits) available in most surf spots if you're not carrying your own.

Windsurfing
Tarifa, Spain's southernmost point, is a windsurfer's heaven, with strong breezes all year round, a big windsurfing scene and long, uncrowded beaches. In Galicia, Praia de Lariño on the Ría de Muros and La Lanzada beach on the Ría de Pontevedra can be good.

Rafting, Canoeing & Hydrospeed
The turbulent Noguera Pallaresa in northwestern Catalunya is Spain's top white-water river, with a string of grade III and IV drops. Rafting, canoeing and hydrospeed (water-tobogganing) are at their best here in May and June. Numerous local companies offer outings. The Río Sella in Asturias also

has some good white water and more than 1000 canoeists from around the world take part in the 22km Descenso del Sella race, from Arriondas in the Picos de Europa to Ribadesella on the coast, on the first weekend in August.

Diving & Snorkelling
Some of the rockier parts of the Mediterranean coast are good – notably the Illes Medes off L'Estartit, Catalunya, but also San Sebastián, Cadaqués, Isla de Tabarca, Cabo de Gata and Almuñécar. Snorkelling and diving trips and diving gear rental are available at all of these places.

COURSES
A spot of study in Spain is a great way not only to learn something but also to meet people – Spaniards as well as other travellers – and get more of an inside angle on local life than the average visitor.

Language
Branches of the Instituto Cervantes (see Useful Organisations earlier in this chapter) can send you long lists of places offering Spanish-language courses in Spain. Some Spanish embassies and consulates can also provide information on courses.

Universities, which exist in most sizable cities, offer some of the best-value language courses; those at Salamanca, Santiago de Compostela and Santander have good reputations. Sevilla, Granada, Madrid and Barcelona are also popular places to study Spanish. Private language schools as well as universities cater for a wide range of levels (from beginners up), course lengths, times of year, intensity and special requirements. Many courses have a cultural component as well as pure language. University courses often last a term, although some are as short as two weeks or as long as a year. Private colleges can be more flexible. One with a good reputation is ¿Don Quijote?, with branches in Salamanca, Barcelona and Granada. There's further information on some courses in the city sections of this book.

Costs vary widely. A typical four-week course at a university, with 20 one-hour classes a week, will be around 40,000 or 50,000 ptas. Many places offer accommodation with families, in student lodgings or in flats if you want it. Accommodation offers generally range from around 30,000 ptas a month with no meals to about 60,000 ptas for full board.

It's also worth asking whether your course will lead to any formal certificate of competence. The Diploma de Español como Lengua Extranjera (DELE) is recognised by Spain's Ministry of Education and Science.

Other Courses

You can take courses in lots of other subjects too. Some places offering language courses also offer courses in other aspects of Spanish culture. The Instituto Cervantes and Spanish tourist offices are good places to start asking about possibilities.

WORK

With the EU's highest unemployment rate, Spain doesn't exactly have a labour shortage. Unlike in France, there's no casual work for foreigners in fruit picking or harvests. But there are a few ways of earning your keep (or almost) while you're here.

Nationals of EU countries, Norway and Iceland may work in Spain without a visa, but for stays of more than three months they are supposed to apply within the first month for a *tarjeta de residencia* (residence card); for information on this laborious process, see Visas & Documents earlier in this chapter. Virtually everyone else is supposed to get, from a Spanish consulate in their country of residence, a work permit and, if they plan to stay more than 90 days, a residence visa. These procedures are well-nigh impossible unless you have a job contract lined up before you begin them; in any case you should start the processes a long time before you aim to go to Spain. That said, quite a few people do work, discreetly, without bothering to tangle with the bureaucracy.

Language Teaching

This type of work is an obvious option, for which language-teaching qualifications are a big help. There are lots of language schools in all the big cities, and often one or two in smaller towns. They're listed under 'Academias de Idiomas' in the Yellow Pages. Getting a job in one is harder if you're not an EU citizen. Some schools do employ people without work papers, usually at lower than normal rates. Giving private lessons is another worthwhile avenue, but is unlikely to bring you a living wage straight away.

Sources of information on possible teaching work – school or private – include foreign cultural centres (the British Council, Alliance Française etc), foreign-language bookshops, universities and language schools. Many have notice boards where you may find work opportunities or can advertise your own services.

Tourist Resorts

Summer work on the Mediterranean coasts is another possibility, especially if you get there early in the season and are prepared to stay awhile. Many bars, restaurants and other businesses are run by foreigners. Check any local press in foreign languages, such as the Costa del Sol's *Sur In English,* which has some ads for waiters, nannies, chefs, babysitters and cleaners, as well as 'closers', 'liners' and others wanted to hawk time-share properties to foreign holiday-makers.

Busking

A few travellers earn a crust (but not much more) busking in the main tourist cities.

Yacht Crewing

It is possible to stumble upon work as crew on yachts and cruisers. The best ports to look include (in descending order) Palma de Mallorca, Gibraltar and Puerto Banús.

In summer the voyages tend to be restricted to the Mediterranean, but from about November to January quite a few boats head for the Caribbean. Such work is usually unpaid.

ACCOMMODATION

There's generally no need to book ahead for a room in the low or medium seasons (see the boxed text 'Seasonal Variations' for what these terms mean), but when things get busier it's advisable – and in peak periods it can be essential – to make a reservation if you want to avoid a wearisome search for a room. At most places a phone call earlier the same day is all that's needed, giving your approximate time of arrival. If you end up running late, a second phone call saying you're still on your way will avoid the room being given to someone else. Many hotels will help you book ahead to a hotel in your next destination. It's also possible to make room reservations by mail and in many cases fax and email, but getting written confirmation is not always so easy. Two Web sites with online hotel booking facilities are InterHotel (http://interhotel.com/spain/es) and Madein-spain (www.madeinspain.net).

Virtually all accommodation prices are subject to IVA (value-added tax), at a rate of 7%. This is often included in the quoted price at cheaper places, but less often at more expensive ones. To check, ask: '¿Está incluido el IVA?' ('Is IVA included?').

Room prices given in this book include IVA unless stated otherwise. But many establishments, especially in the budget category, will forget about IVA if you don't require a receipt.

Camping

Spain has something like 1000 officially graded camping grounds (campings). Some are well located in woodland or near beaches or rivers, but others are stuck away on the unattractive edges of towns and cities. Very few are near city centres, and camping isn't particularly convenient if you're relying on public transport.

Camping grounds are officially rated as 1st class (1ª C), 2nd class (2ª C) or 3rd class (3ª C). There are also a few grounds that are not officially graded, usually equivalent to 3rd class. The facilities generally range from

Seasonal Variations

Prices at any type of accommodation may vary with the season. Many places have separate price structures for the high season (temporada alta), mid-season (temporada media) or low season (temporada baja), all usually displayed on a notice in the reception or close by. Although these notices look official and the prices on them have been registered, hoteliers are not bound by them. They are free to charge less, which they quite often do, or more, which happens fairly rarely.

What the high season is depends on where you are, but in most places it's summer – which can mean a period as short as mid-July to the end of August or as long as Easter to October. The Christmas-New Year period and Semana Santa are also high, or at least mid, season in some places. Local festivals that attract lots of visitors often count as high season too.

Differences between low-season and high-season prices vary widely around the country. They tend to be biggest – typically 30% or 50% – in coastal resorts and other places that attract a lot of tourism in summer. But even in these places you may still find some accommodation that keeps virtually the same prices year round. Occasionally there are bigger differences. Some hotels and hostales in Sevilla, for instance, charge three times as much during Semana Santa and the city's Feria de Abril festivities as they do in winter. On the coast some hotels seem to create a kind of 'super' high season within high season, usually lasting from mid-July to mid-August. This can express itself either in extra-high prices or in obligatory half- or full-board arrangements.

Major seasonal price variations are noted in Places to Stay sections throughout this book.

Many establishments, especially the cheaper ones, also vary prices according to demand. You may also be able to obtain a discount if you stay for more than a couple of nights.

Another problem that often comes with the high season is a shortage of single rooms. Many hotels and pensiones in fact have few single rooms in any case, but normally let out doubles at reduced rates. In the high season when demand for rooms is high, singles or reduced-rate doubles can become as rare as hen's teeth.

reasonable to very good, though any ground can be crowded and noisy at busy times (especially July and August). Even a 3rd-class camping ground is likely to have hot showers, electrical hook-ups and a cafeteria. The best ones have heated swimming pools, supermarkets, restaurants, travel agencies, a laundry service, children's playgrounds and tennis courts. Sizes range from a capacity of under 100 people to over 5000.

Camping grounds usually charge per person, per tent and per vehicle – anywhere between 250 and 800 ptas for each, though 500 ptas is typical. Children usually pay a bit less than adults. Many sites are open all year, though quite a few close from around October to Easter.

The annual *Guía Oficial de Campings,* available in bookshops for about 800 ptas, lists most of the country's camping grounds and their facilities and prices. Tourist offices can always direct you to the nearest camping ground.

You sometimes come across a *zona de acampada* or *área de acampada,* a country camping ground with minimal facilities (maybe just tap water and/or a couple of barbecues), no supervision and no charge. If it's in an environmentally protected area, you may need to obtain permission from the local environmental authority to camp here.

With certain exceptions – such as many beaches and environmentally protected areas and a few municipalities that ban it – it is legal to camp outside camping grounds (though not within 1km of official ones!). Signs usually indicate where wild camping is not allowed. If in doubt you can always check with tourist offices. You'll need permission to camp on private land.

Note that Camping Gaz is the only common brand of camping gas available; screw-on canisters are near-impossible to find.

Hostels

Spain's 200 or so youth hostels (*albergues juveniles,* not be confused with hostales, or budget hotels) are often the cheapest places for lone travellers, but two people can usually get a double room elsewhere for a similar price. Some hostels are only moderate value, lacking in privacy, often heavily booked by school groups, and with night-time curfews and no cooking facilities (though if there is nowhere to cook there is usually a cafeteria). Others, however, are conveniently located, open 24 hours and composed mainly of double rooms or small dorms, often with private bath. An increasing number have rooms adapted for the disabled. Some even occupy fine historic buildings. Hostels can be good places for meeting people.

Most Spanish youth hostels are members of the Red Española de Albergues Juveniles (REAJ, or Spanish Youth Hostel Network), the Spanish representative of Hostelling International (HI), also called the International Youth Hostel Federation (IYHF). REAJ's head office (☎ 91 347 77 00, fax 91 401 81 60) is at Calle de José Ortega y Gasset 71, 28006 Madrid.

Most Spanish hostels are also members of the youth hostels association of their region (Andalucía, Catalunya, Valencia etc). Each region usually sets its own price structure and has a central booking service where you can make reservations for most of its hostels. Central booking services include:

Andalucía (☎ 902-51 00 00, fax 95 503 58 48,
  @ reservas@inturjoven.junta-andalucia.es)
  Calle del Miño 24, Los Remedios, 41011
  Sevilla
Catalunya (☎ 93 483 83 63, fax 93 483 83 50)
  Carrer de Rocafort 116-122, 08015 Barcelona
Valencia (☎ 96 386 92 52, fax 96 386 99 51)
  Calle de l'Hospital 11, 46001 Valencia

HI's annual Europe hostels directory contains details of all REAJ hostels; the REAJ also publishes an annual list. Some of the autonomous regions publish their own hostel guides, too. Further information about REAJ, regional associations and their hostels is available in English, French and Spanish on the Web site at www.mtas.es/injuve/intercambios/albergues/reaj.html.

Just a few youth hostels are run by other organisations or as private concerns, in which case they probably won't appear in regional guides – although they may still be REAJ members and appear in REAJ and HI directories!

Prices often depend on the season and vary between 500 and 1400 ptas for under 26s and between 600 and 1900 ptas for 26-and-overs. In some hostels the price includes breakfast. Many hostels require you to rent sheets (around 300 ptas for your stay) if you don't have your own or a sleeping bag.

Most hostels require you to have an HI card or a membership card from your home country's youth hostel association; others don't require a card (even though they may be HI hostels) but may charge more if you don't have one. Obtaining an HI card in Spain is easy (see Visas & Documents earlier in this chapter).

Hostales, Hospedajes, Pensiones, Hotels & Paradores

Officially, hotels are places with one to five stars, *hostales* have one to three stars and *pensiones* have one or two stars. These are the categories used by the annual *Guía Oficial de Hoteles* (sold in bookshops for 1300 ptas), which lists many of these places in Spain (but not one-star pensiones), with approximate prices.

In practice, accommodation places use all sorts of overlapping names to describe themselves, especially at the budget end of the market. In broad terms, the cheapest are usually places just advertising *camas* (beds), *fondas* (traditionally a basic eatery and inn combined, though one of these functions is now often missing) and *casas de huéspedes* or *hospedajes* (guesthouses).

A pensión (basically a small private hotel) is usually a small step up. You'll often be sharing bathrooms in any of these and are likely to pay from 1250/2500 to 3000/4000 ptas for a single/double room. The rooms will be bare and basic, and they may be small and lack a window, but most of them are clean. Most discomfort is likely to come from lumpy, sagging or sloping beds or failure of hot-water supplies. Some cheap establishments forget to provide towels, soap or enough blankets, or to replenish the toilet paper. Don't hesitate to ask for these necessities.

Next up the scale are hostales (budget hotels), which are essentially not much different from pensiones, except that some are considerably more comfortable and more rooms tend to have their own bathrooms. Hostales may have more lounge space too. Hostal prices range from pensión levels up to 8000 or 9000 ptas for a double in the best ones. Some hostales are bright, modern and pleasant places to stay; others are less so. An increasing number are upgrading and modernising their rooms into cosy, comfortable accommodation all with TV and private bath or shower – nice for those who can afford the higher prices that result, but the trend also reduces the amount of budget accommodation available.

Establishments calling themselves hotels range from simple places, where a double room could cost 4000 ptas, to wildly luxurious, five-star resort hotels where you could pay 60,000 ptas or more. Even in the cheapest, all rooms are likely to have an attached bathroom. Some of Spain's most charming places to stay are small or medium-sized hotels occupying characterful old city buildings or rambling country properties with pleasant gardens and pools. These often have economical or mid-range prices from around 5000 to 10,000 ptas a double.

The label *residencia* tacked on to a hostal or hotel name means it has no restaurant.

In a special category are the paradores, officially *paradores de turismo,* a chain of 85 high-class hotels around the country. Many are in converted castles, palaces, mansions, monasteries or convents. These can be wonderful places to stay. Room-only prices start at 9200/11,500 ptas plus IVA for singles/doubles in low season and you're looking at about 14,000/17,500 ptas plus IVA for most paradores in high season. Special offers can make paradores more affordable for some people: the over-60s can get 35% off room and breakfast prices at many paradors for much of the year (especially from October to June) and some paradores offer B&B for two people for less than 12,000 ptas in winter. You can find out the current offers via the parador Web site (www.parador.es) or by contacting the paradores' central reservation service, the Central de Reservas (☎ 91 516 66 66, fax 91 516 66 57, ⓔ info@parador.es), Calle Requena 3, 28013 Madrid.

Many places to stay have a range of rooms at different prices. At the budget end, prices will vary according to whether the room has a washbasin *(lavabo)*, shower *(ducha)* or full bathroom *(baño completo)*, which includes toilet, bath and basin. At the top end you may pay more for a room on the outside *(exterior)* of the building or with a balcony *(balcón)* and will often have the option of a suite. Many places have rooms for three, four or more people where the per-person cost is much lower than in a single or double – good news for families.

Checkout time at most establishments is nearly always noon.

Casas Rurales

Spaniards' burgeoning interest in their own countryside and environment has brought a boom in recent years in rural tourism, with many small new places to stay there. These *casas rurales* are usually comfortably renovated village houses or farmhouses, with just a handful of rooms. Some have meals available, while at some you'll have to self-cater. Two people usually pay from 3000 to 8000 ptas or so. Tourist offices can usually provide leaflets listing casas rurales and other country accommodation in their areas.

Refugios

Refugios are mountain shelters for walkers and climbers and are quite liberally scattered around most of the popular mountain areas except in Andalucía, which has only a handful. They're mostly run by mountaineering and walking organisations. Accommodation – normally bunks squeezed into a dorm – is usually on a first-come, first-served basis, though for some refugios you can book ahead. In busy seasons (July and August in most areas) they can fill up quickly and you should try to book or arrive by mid-afternoon to be sure of a place. Prices per person range from nothing to 1300 ptas or so a night. Many refugios have a bar and meals available as well as a cooking area (but not cooking equipment). Blankets are usually provided but you'll have to bring any further bedding yourself.

Apartments & Villas

In many places, there are self-catering apartments you can rent for as little as one night. Villas and houses are most widely available on the main holiday coasts and in popular country areas (see Casas Rurales earlier). A simple one-bedroom apartment for two or three people might cost as little as 3000 ptas a night, though more often you'll be looking at 5000 ptas or more, and prices can jump further in peak seasons. Apartments are most worth considering if you plan to stay several days or more, in which case there will usually be discounts from the daily rate.

Tourist offices can supply lists of places for rent, and in Britain the *Sunday Times* carries a lot of private ads for such places. British-based house and villa agencies (don't expect low prices) include:

Individual Travellers Spain (☎ 01798 869485)
  Web site: www.indiv-travellers.com
Magic of Spain (☎ 020-8748 4220)
  Web site: www.magictravelgroup.co.uk
Secret Spain (☎ 01527-578900)
Simply Spain (☎ 020-8541 2222)
  Web site: www.simply-travel.com

Monasteries

A rather offbeat possibility is staying in a monastery. In spite of the expropriations of the 19th century and a sometimes rough run in the 20th, plenty of monastic orders have survived across the country. Vocations are generally not what they once were, however, and many monasteries now offer rooms to outsiders – often fairly austere monks' or nuns' cells. Generally, they are single sex arrangements and the idea in some is to seek a refuge from the outside world and indulge in a little quiet contemplation. A few of these places have been listed in this guide.

FOOD & DRINK

For detailed information on food and drink, see the special section 'Eating & Drinking in Spain' later in this book.

SHOPPING

You can find some very attractive and reasonably priced handicrafts if you look in the right places. In some crafts there's wide regional variation and many products tend not to be found far from where they are made. Apart from craft shops, which abound in the producing areas, you may pick up crafts at weekly or daily markets in villages or towns and even in department stores. There are some excellent flea markets (mercadillos) and car boot sales (rastros) around the country – good for bargains (see under Shopping in the city sections of this book). The single most likely place you'll find any particular item in most cities is the nationwide department store El Corte Inglés.

Pottery

There are many attractive regional varieties of pottery. Products are cheap: crockery, jugs, plant pots, window boxes and tiles are likely to cost a fraction of the price of similar products at home. Islamic influence on design and colour is evident in much of the country. Attractive and original techniques include the use of metallic glazes and *cuerda seca* (dry cord) in which lines of manganese or fat are used to separate areas of different colour. Toledo, Sevilla, Granada and Úbeda are centres of cuerda seca production.

The dominant colours of Granada ceramics are white splashed with green and blue, often with a pomegranate as the centrepiece of the pattern. In Córdoba the product is finer, with black, green and blue borders on white. Talavera de la Reina near Toledo produces Italian-influenced pottery in blue and green. Brighter colours are used in some other parts of the country. Manises in Valencia province, whose pottery tradition is of 14th-century Morisco origin, uses yellow, olive green and blue. There are plenty of speciality pottery shops in Valencia city. Teruel in Aragón employs deep green and purple, with *mudéjar* decoration. Some excellent, more individual pieces are made in Níjar in eastern Andalucía.

Textiles & Clothes

Inexpensive, colourful rugs, blankets and hangings are made all over the country, with Andalucía and Galicia probably the most noted regions. Items known as *jarapas* feature weft (lengthways) threads made of different types of cloth. Other textiles include lace tablecloths and pillowcases (especially from Galicia), and embroidery. Places particularly known for their embroidery include Segovia, La Alberca (Salamanca), Carbajales (Zamora), and Lagartera, Oropesa and Talavera (Toledo).

Ibiza city is something of a magnet for fashion victims and a good place to buy clothes, with items of most conceivable fads, fashions and revivals available. Barcelona and the Costa Brava resort of Cadaqués have interesting boutiques too.

Leather

Though prices of Spanish leather goods aren't as low as they used to be, you can still get good deals on leather jackets, bags, wallets, belts, shoes and boots in many places, especially Andalucía. Exquisite riding boots can be purchased in 'horsy' places such as Jerez de la Frontera and El Rocío. Tooled leather products such as embossed, polychromed poufs make a good not-too-bulky present: you can simply roll up the leather and insert the filling back at home. Córdoba, Granada, Salamanca, Cáceres and Ubrique (Cádiz) are all leather-tooling centres.

Other Crafts

Damascene weapons (made of steel encrusted with gold, silver or copper) are still produced in Toledo. There's some pleasing woodwork available, such as Granada's marquetry boxes, tables and chess sets, some of which are inlaid with bone or mother-of-pearl. Baskets and furniture made from plant fibres are made throughout Spain but are most evident near the coasts. L'Ollería (Valencia) is a centre of wicker, straw and esparto grass products. Esparto goods are inexpensive and durable; Ibiza is another centre of their production. Esparto-soled and rope-soled shoes are made on Ibiza and Mallorca.

Gold and silver jewellery abound, and Santiago de Compostela in Galicia is probably the world centre of jewellery made from the shiny black mineral jet, often in ornate silver settings.

Glass-blowers still operate in Palma de Mallorca and a few other places on Mallorca.

ENTERTAINMENT

The innumerable fiestas that spatter the Spanish calendar provide heaps of colourful spectacle and, more often than not, a celebratory atmosphere. And simply sitting over a coffee or a glass of wine at a plaza cafe and watching Spanish life go on around you is often entertainment enough in itself.

Local papers often carry fairly thorough entertainment listings and Madrid, Barcelona and one or two other cities have their own what's-on magazines (see the relevant chapters for details). Some national papers such as *El País* have regional sections giving pretty good local listings. Tourist offices can always tell you about major events, and sometimes have publications listing what's on.

Bars, Clubs & Discos

Spain has some of the best nightlife in Europe; wild and *very* late nights, especially on Friday and Saturday, are an integral part of the Spanish experience. Even some small cities have very lively scenes. Most young Spaniards don't think about going out until midnight or so, though you can begin a tour of tapas bars at 8 or 9 pm. Bars, which come in all shapes, sizes and themes, are the main attractions until around 2 or 3 am. Some play great music, which will get you hopping before you move on, if you can afford it, to a *discoteca* or electronic-music *sala* until 5 or 6 am – or later! (Some house *salas* don't open until that sort of hour.) Discos can be expensive and some won't let you in wearing jeans or trainers, but they aren't to be missed if you can manage to splurge.

Rock, Pop, Folk & Jazz

Spain's home-grown rock and pop scene is large and lively (see Music in the Facts about Spain chapter). The biggest cities usually offer a good and varied choice of bands, often including foreign visitors, several nights of the week. Elsewhere, gigs are mainly on weekends. Venues range from bars to clubs to theatres, stadiums and bullrings. The summer spawns hosts of festivals: some are devoted exclusively to music but Spaniards love music and almost any festival will incorporate it (see Public Holidays

& Special Events earlier in this chapter). Local folk music traditions are strongest in the north-west (especially Galicia) and jazz has its following countrywide, with dedicated venues in some cities.

Flamenco

Flamenco song, dance and music has enjoyed an upsurge in popularity in recent years, partly thanks to a wave of mainly young artists who mix it with rock, jazz, blues, rap and other idioms in what can be termed 'flamenco fusion'. Many bars and clubs – especially in flamenco's homeland, Andalucía, but also in Madrid, Barcelona, Extremadura and Murcia – stage regular flamenco nights, where you just pay for your drinks (and sometimes a small Entry charge). Big-name artists also perform in theatres. Tourist offices tend to direct you towards *tablaos,* regular shows for a tourist audience with high-ish prices. Some of these are tacky and very routine; others are not bad. In summer, Andalucian cities, towns and villages stage dozens of flamenco festivals. These are typically long-drawn-out and open-air affairs, maybe not getting going until midnight and lasting until dawn, with copious quantities of alcohol being drunk.

Flamenco fans band together in clubs called *peñas,* which stage live performance nights; most peñas will admit genuinely interested visitors and the atmosphere can be most intimate and informal.

Classical Music, Dance & Theatre

For the culturally inclined, there are lots of performances, and often festivals, around the country (see Public Holidays & Special Events earlier in this chapter). Theatre is nearly all in Spanish, of course. For some background on the Spanish arts scene, see Arts in the Facts about Spain chapter.

Cinema

Cinemas abound and films are inexpensive. Foreign movies are usually dubbed into Spanish but in the biggest cities a few cinemas show films in their original languages with Spanish subtitles – look for the letters 'v.o.' *(versión original)* or 'v.o.s.' *(versión original subtitulada)* in listings.

SPECTATOR SPORTS
Football

Fútbol (soccer) at least equals bullfighting as Spain's national sport. Around 300,000 fans attend the games in the Primera División (First Division) every weekend from September to May, with millions more following the games on TV. Spain suffers from little football hooliganism but Spaniards still take their favoured teams' fortunes very seriously.

Almost any game in the Primera División is worth attending for the Spanish crowd experience even if you're not a huge fan of the game itself. Those involving the big two clubs, Real Madrid and Barcelona, have an extra passion to them. These two have large followings throughout the country and something approaching a monopoly on the silverware: between them they have carried off the league title in all but 14 seasons since 1950. Real Madrid, thanks largely to Franco's support in the 1950s, has won Europe's major club competition, the European Cup (now the Champions League), a record eight times. Real's and Barcelona's players and coaches are national celebrities – and their directors have very high expectations: when Real won their seventh European Cup in 1998 they promptly sacked their coach, Jupp Heynckes, because they had only finished fourth in the league.

Other leading clubs include Valencia, Athletic Bilbao, Deportivo La Coruña (league champions for the first time in 2000 after several near-misses), Real Zaragoza, Celta Vigo (renowned for attractive, attacking football), Espanyol (of Barcelona), Málaga, Real Sociedad of San Sebastián and – though these last two were relegated from the First Division in 2000 – Atlético Madrid and Real Betis (of Sevilla). The promotion and relegation system allows a few lesser teams their hour of glory among the big boys. Some recent seasons have witnessed the odd spectacle of Barcelona and Real Madrid entertaining CF Extremadura from the town of Almendralejo, whose entire population wouldn't even half-fill the big clubs' stadiums.

League games are mostly played on Saturday and Sunday, and you can pay at the gate (from about 2000 ptas) for all but the biggest matches (for which tickets have to be bought in advance). Games in the Copa del Rey (Spain's equivalent of the FA Cup) and matches in European competitions are held midweek at night. Watch the press (including the sports paper *Marca*) for details of upcoming fixtures.

Other Sports

Champions such as Arantxa Sánchez Vicario, Conchita Martínez, Carlos Moya and Alex Corretja (tennis), Miguel Induráin (cycling) and Severiano Ballesteros, José-María Olazábal and Miguel-Ángel Jiménez (golf) have all inspired popularity in their sports. All play a few times a year in their home country, though Spain stages none of the really big annual international events in their sports. But golf's Ryder Cup, between Europe and the USA, took place at Valderrama, Andalucía, in 1997 – the first time it had been held in Europe outside the UK.

Bike-mad Spain stages up to three grands prix of the annual world motorcycle championship. The one at Jerez de la Frontera in May is probably the country's biggest sporting event, with around 150,000 spectators annually. Others take place at Jarama, near Madrid, and the Montmeló circuit 20km north of Barcelona. The Spanish Formula One motor-racing grand prix is held at Montmeló, usually in May. Spain's version of the Tour de France cycling race is the three-week Vuelta a España, usually held in September.

The Bullfight

PLAZA DE TOROS

AÑO 1929

DESPACHO DE ...ETES

The low-lying sun floods the arena with heavy summer light from the west. There is a buzz as places fill. Families jostle for space with older, beret-bearing enthusiasts, their faces creased with years of farm toil, and bright young things sporting sky-blue sunglasses. Some clutch plastic cups of beer, others swig red wine from animal-hide *botas*.

All but those who have paid for the comfort of real seats in the shade *(sombra)* have brought some kind of cushion: bare concrete or wooden slats can pall after a while on unprotected behinds.

Many have chosen to huddle on the cheap benches facing the unforgiving midsummer sun *(sol)*. At one end of the ring, high up in the top rows, a brass band strikes up a stirring *paso doble,* while on the opposite side the president of the fight and his adjutants await the arrival of the *toros* (bulls).

The *corrida* (bullfight) is a spectacle with a long history. It is not, as some suggest, simply a ghoulish alternative to the slaughterhouse (itself no pretty sight). Aficionados say the bull is better off dying at the hands of a *matador* (killer) than in the *matadero* (abattoir). The corrida is about many things – death, bravery, performance. No doubt, the fight is bloody and cruel. To witness it is not necessarily to understand it, but might give an insight into some of the thought and tradition behind it. Many Spaniards loathe the bullfight, but there is no doubting its overall popularity. If on a bar-room TV there is football on one channel and a corrida on another, the chances are high that football fever will cede to the fascination of the fiesta.

Contests of strength, skill and bravery between man and beast are no recent phenomenon. The ancient Etruscans liked a good bullfight, and the Romans caught on. Of course things got a little kinky under the Romans and half the time there was no fight at all, merely the merciless butchery of Christians and other criminal fodder.

La lidia, as the art of bullfighting is also known, really took off in an organised fashion in Spain in the mid-18th century. In the 1830s, Pedro Romero, the greatest *torero* (bullfighter) of the time, was at the age of 77 appointed director of Escuela de Tauromaquia de Sevilla, the country's first bullfighters' college. It was around this time too that breeders succeeded in creating the first reliable breeds of *toro bravo* (fighting bull).

El Matador & La Cuadrilla

Traditionally, young men have aspired to the ring in the hope of fame and fortune, much as boxers have done. Most attain neither one nor the other. Only champion matadors make good money and some make a loss. For the matador must rent or buy his outfit and equipment, pay for the right to fight a bull and also pay his *cuadrilla* (team).

If you see a major fight, you will notice this team is made up of quite a few people. Firstly there are several *peones*, junior bullfighters under the orders of the main torero, who is the matador. The peones come

Title page: The Plaza de Toros Monumental de Las Ventas in Madrid is the world's largest bullring.
(Photographer: Juliet Coombe)

out to distract the bull with great capes, manoeuvre him into the desired position and so on.

Then come the horseback-mounted *picadores*. Charged by the bull, which tries to eviscerate the horse, the picador shoves his lance into the withers of the bull – an activity that weakens and angers the bull. Animal-lovers may take small consolation from the fact that since the 19th century the horses at least have been protected by heavy padding.

The peones then return to the scene to measure their courage against the (hopefully) charging bull. The picador is shortly followed by the *banderilleros*. At a given moment during the fight, one or two banderilleros will race towards the bull and attempt to plunge a pair of colourfully decorated *banderillas* (short prods with harpoon-style ends) into the bull, again aiming for the withers. This has the effect of spurring the animal into action – the matador will then seek to use this to execute more fancy manoeuvres.

Then there is the matador himself. His dress could be that of a flamenco dancer. At its simplest, in country fiestas, it is generally a straightforward combination of black trousers or tights, white shirt and black vest. At its most extravagant, the *traje de luces* (suit of lights) can be an extraordinary display of bright, spangly colour – the name is apt.

All the toreros, with the occasional exception of the matadors, wear the black *montera* (the Mickey Mouse ears hat). The torero's standard

Right: A mounted *picador* teases the bull with lances, weakening the animal and testing its bravery.

VITO VAMPATELLA

weapons are the *estoque* or *espada* (sword) and the heavy silk and percale *capa* (cape). You will notice, however, that the matador, and the matador alone, employs a different cape with the sword – a smaller piece of cloth held with a bar of wood called the *muleta* and used for a number of different passes.

La Corrida

To summarise all that takes place on the day of a corrida is no easy task. In many cases, corridas are held over several days, or even weeks, and the whole fiesta is known as the *feria*. The bulls are transported from their farms to a location near the ring, often days in advance. In Madrid, they are kept at an Andalucian-style ranch in the Casa de Campo known as Batán.

MICK WELDON

In some towns, the bulls are brought to another point in town from where they are let loose on the morning of the corrida to charge to the ring. The *encierro*, as it is known, in Pamplona was made famous by Ernest Hemingway, but scores of towns across the country celebrate it. Barriers are set up along a route to the ring, and some people feel inclined to run with the bulls (see the boxed text 'The Running of the Bulls' in the Basque Country, Navarra & La Rioja chapter). It's a dangerous business and people get hurt, sometimes mortally.

When the bulls arrive, the cuadrillas, president and breeders get together to look over the animals and draw lots to see who is going to fight which one. It depends a little on how many breeders are represented, how many matadors and teams there are and so on. The selected bulls are later huddled into darkened corrals, where they await their moment.

The bullfight generally begins at 6 pm, hence the title of Hemingway's manual on the subject, *Death in the Afternoon*. As a rule, six toros and three matadors are on the day's card. If any bulls are considered not up to scratch, they are booed off (at this point the president will display a green handkerchief) and replacements brought on. Each fight takes about 10 to 15 minutes.

When the fateful moment comes, the corral is opened, light gushes in and the bull charges out, sensing a chance to escape. You wonder if it feels disappointment as it barrels out into the ring to be confronted by the peones, darting about and flashing their rose-and-yellow coloured capes at the heaving beast. The matador then appears and executes his *faenas* (moves) with the bull. To go into the complexities of what constitutes a fine faena would require a book.

Suffice to say, the more closely and calmly the torero works with the bull, pivoting and dancing before the bull's horns, the greater will be the crowd's approbation. After a little of this, the matador strides off

Above: Bred for conflict the *toro bravo*, or fighting bull, is treated like a king until the final, fatal day.

and leaves the stage first to the picadores, then the banderilleros, before returning for another session. At various moments during the fight, the brass band will hit some stirring notes, adding to the air of grand spectacle. The moves must be carried out in certain parts of the ring, which is divided into three parts: the *medios* (centre); *tercios* (an intermediate, chalked-off ring); and *tablas* (the outer ring).

When the bull seems tired out and unlikely to give a lot more, the matador chooses his moment for the kill. Placing himself head-on, he aims to sink the sword cleanly into the animal's neck *(estocada)* for an instant kill. It's easier said than done.

A good performance followed by a clean kill will have the crowd on its feet waving handkerchiefs in the air in clear appeal to the president to award the matador an *oreja* (ear) of the animal. The president usually waits to assess the crowd's enthusiasm before flopping a white handkerchief onto his balcony. If the fight was exceptional, the matador might *cortar dos orejas* – cut two ears off. On rare occasions the matador may be awarded the tail as well. What he does with them when he gets home is anyone's guess.

The sad carcass is meanwhile dragged out by a team of dray-horses and the sand raked about in preparation for the next bull. The meat ends up in the butcher shop.

When & Where

Corridas are mainly a spring and summer activity, but it is occasionally possible to see them at other times. The season begins more or less officially in the first week of February with the fiestas of Valdemorillo and Ajalvir, near Madrid, to mark the feast day of San Blas. Virtually all encierros and corridas are organised as part of a town's fiesta or other.

In the Comunidad de Madrid, for instance, there are any number of local fiestas and the encierros can be a wild and unpredictable affair. In many towns the plaza mayor serves as a makeshift bullring. Often, the small-town fights are amateurish affairs known as *capeas*.

Above: Love it or hate it, the bullfight's confrontation with death, as well as its elements of bravery and performance, make it extremely popular in Spain.

The most prestigious feria in the world is that held in Madrid over four weeks from mid-May as part of the Fiesta de San Isidro.

Bullfighting magazines such as the weekly *6 Toros 6* carry full details of who's fighting, where and when. When fights are coming up locally, gaudy posters advertise the fact and give ticket information. In addition to the top corridas, which attract 'name' matadors and big crowds, there are plenty of lesser ones in cities, towns and villages. These are often *novilleras*, in which immature bulls *(novillos)* are fought by junior matadors *(novilleros)*. In small places the plaza mayor may serve as a makeshift bullring.

If you're interested in knowing more about bullfighting, a good place to start is the Web site Toros Links (www.sol.com/list/toros.htm).

The Matadors

If you are spoiling for a fight, look out for the big names. They are no guarantee you'll see a high-quality corrida, as that depends in no small measure on the animals themselves, but it is a good sign. The last true star of the fiesta, Luis Miguel Dominguín, a hero of the 1940s and 50s, died in 1996. Another maestro was Rafael Ortega (1921–97). Their present-day successors count among their number some fine performers, but perhaps none of their stature.

Names to look for include: Jesulín de Ubrique, a true macho whose attitudes to women don't go down well with everyone; Enrique Ponce, a serious class act; Joselito (José Miguel Arroyo); Rivera Ordóñez; Julián 'El Juli' López, a recently-arrived teenage sensation; Curro Romero, born in the 1920s and still fighting; José Tomás; and Manuel 'El Cordobés' Díaz, one of the biggest names, although for some, his style borders on mocking the animal and is considered unnecessarily cruel. He is not the only one to go by the name El Cordobés. One of the older hands to use it is Manuel Benítez, who, at 63 years of age, decided to get back into the ring again in 2000 just for the fun of it!

Ethics of the Fight

Is the bullfight 'right'? Passions are frequently inflamed by the subject. Many people feel ill at the sight of the kill, although this is a merciful relief and surely no worse than being lined up for the production-line

Above: The Plaza de Toros in Málaga (Andalucía)

Women's Touch

It's a man's world. You may wonder why, but to some women the idea of dancing with bulls appeals as much as it does to some men. Problem is, the men involved in the same activity generally take a dim view of such feminine intrusions.

Until she decided to leave the ring in 1999, one woman had managed to challenge the macho norms and rose to brief stardom as the only woman ever to take full honours as a matador in Madrid. **Cristina Sánchez** not only faced the danger of the bulls, but also had to take on the full brunt of often poorly disguised establishment scorn. In the end, she faltered and bowed out. For women, the fight has always been as intense outside the ring as in.

Nicolasa Escamilla, 'La Pajuelera', was the first woman to take on the bulls seriously, back in the late 18th century. Goya was so impressed that he left behind a sketch of her in combat in Zaragoza. **Martina García**, born in 1814, was fighting until the age of 66. As often as she killed her toros she found herself being flipped by them. Towards the end of the century, Sevilla's **Dolores Sánchez**, 'La Fragosa', became one of the first toreras to don the *traje de luces* (suit of lights) and abandon the skirt. Machismo and the fight go hand in hand; the former caught up with the handful of active toreras in 1908, when a law was promulgated forbidding women to fight bulls, considering it 'improper and contrary to civilised manners and all delicate sentiment'.

Only in 1974 did **Ángela Hernández** succeed in having the law repealed, but this did little to change attitudes. **Maribel Atiénzar** began her career in 1977 and found she could only appear if she renounced the right to take on mature bulls as a fully recognised matador. In the language of the bullring, she was unable to *tomar la alternativa*. In this ritual the senior matador acknowledges a junior's capacity as a matador and hands him the sword and cape. With this, a torero's right to fight as a full matador (and hence be paid considerably more) is recognised everywhere in Spain but Madrid – the mecca of the corrida, which has its own qualifying hurdle. Maribel 'took the alternative' in Mexico, an achievement not recognised at all in Spain.

Cristina Sánchez, born in 1972, took the alternative in Madrid's Las Ventas – the ultimate achievement for any bullfighter – in mid-1996 and confirmed it in 1998. No woman had ever managed anything like it before.

kill in an abattoir. The preceding 10 or so minutes of torture are cruel. The animal is frightened and in pain. Let there be no doubt about that. Aficionados will say, however, that these bulls have been bred for conflict and that their lives before this fateful day are better than those of other farm animals. Toros bravos are treated like kings. To other western cultures – and to many Spaniards too – the bullfight is 'uncivilised', yet there is something about this direct confrontation with death that invites reflection. As an integral part of Spanish culture, it deserves to be experienced; there is nothing to say that anyone should also *like* it.

Beyond Spain

La lidia is not merely a Spanish preoccupation. It is a regular, if lower-profile, part of the calendar of events in southern France and Portugal also.

The Portuguese specialise in horseback toreros, known in Spanish as *rejoneadores*. *Corridas de rejones*, still occasionally seen in Spain, once served as a kind of cavalry training. On the ground, it has been illegal to kill bulls in the ring in Portugal since 1928; picadores are also out-lawed. Instead of the matador, a team of *forcados* wrestle the bull (whose horns are blunted) to the ground. The *estocada* is simulated with a banderilla and the bull later slaughtered in an abattoir. In some towns close to the Spanish frontier the Portuguese stage corridas *a la española* regardless, and a government ruling in 2000 (which imposes fines on their organisers but no longer consider the matador culpable) looked like paving the way to legalisation of 'complete' corridas.

The bullfight has a big following in Latin America, particularly in Mexico, although Spaniards consider the quality there to be inferior.

VITO VAMPATELLA

Right: A wounded bull eyes the confident *torero*

Getting There & Away

Spain is one of Europe's top holiday destinations and is well linked to other European countries by air, rail and road. Regular car ferries and hydrofoils run to Morocco and there are ferry links to the UK, Italy and the Canary Islands.

As competition in the air grows, flying is increasingly the cheapest and fastest option from other European countries. Never assume you will save money by travelling overland.

Some good direct flights are available from North America. Those coming from Australasia have fewer choices and should watch out for deals that include free internal European flights (see the Australia section under Air in this chapter).

Travel Insurance

See the Visas & Documents and Health sections in the Facts for the Visitor chapter for hints on travel insurance, something you should always consider.

AIR
Airports & Airlines

The main gateway to Spain is Madrid's Barajas airport, although many European direct flights serve other centres, particularly Barcelona, Málaga and Palma de Mallorca. Occasional flights, mostly charters, also fly direct to a range of other Spanish cities from centres such as Paris and London.

Iberia flies to 19 Spanish cities (many via Madrid) from around the world but is generally the expensive way to go.

The high season for travel to Spain is July and August, as well as Easter and Christmas.

Buying Tickets

The plane ticket may be the single most expensive item in your budget, so check around the travel agencies. Start early: some of the cheapest tickets have to be bought months in advance and popular flights sell out quickly. For much of the year it is possible to dig up good deals from Europe.

Look at the ads in newspapers and magazines (including the Spanish press in your home country) and watch for special offers. Then phone around travel agencies (airlines generally do not supply the cheapest tickets). Find out the fare, the route, the duration of the journey and any restrictions (see the boxed text 'Air Travel Glossary'), then decide which is best for you.

If travelling from the UK or USA you will find some of the cheapest flights are advertised by obscure bucket shops whose names haven't reached the telephone directory. They sell tickets at discounts of up to 50%. Airlines may deny it, but many release tickets to selected bucket shops – it's better to sell tickets at a huge discount than not at all. Many such firms are honest but there are a few rogues who will take your money and disappear. If you feel suspicious, leave a deposit of 20% or so and pay the balance when you get the ticket. If they insist on cash in advance, go somewhere else. Once you have the ticket, ring the airline to confirm you are booked on the flight.

You could pay a little more and opt for the safety of a better known travel agency. Firms such as STA Travel, with offices worldwide, Council Travel in the USA or Travel Cuts in Canada are not going to disappear overnight and leave you clutching a receipt for a nonexistent ticket, and they do offer good prices to most destinations.

The days when some travel agencies would routinely fleece travellers by running off with their money are, happily, almost over. Paying by credit card generally offers protection, as most card issuers provide refunds if you can prove you didn't get what you paid for. Similar protection can be obtained by buying a ticket from a bonded agency, such as one covered by the Air Transport Operators License (ATOL) scheme in the UK.

Passengers are increasingly booking travel over the Internet. Major travel agencies and many airlines have Web sites that allow you

Air Travel Glossary

Cancellation Penalties If you have to cancel or change a discounted ticket, there are often heavy penalties involved; insurance can sometimes be taken out against these penalties. Some airlines impose penalties on regular tickets as well, particularly against 'no-show' passengers.

Courier Fares Businesses often need to send urgent documents or freight securely and quickly. Courier companies hire people to accompany the package through customs and, in return, offer a discount ticket which is sometimes a phenomenal bargain. However, you may have to surrender all your baggage allowance and take only carry-on luggage.

Full Fares Airlines traditionally offer 1st class (coded F), business class (coded J) and economy class (coded Y) tickets. These days there are so many promotional and discounted fares available that few passengers pay full economy fare.

Lost Tickets If you lose your airline ticket an airline will usually treat it like a travellers cheque and, after inquiries, issue you with another one. Legally, however, an airline is entitled to treat it like cash and if you lose it then it's gone forever. Take good care of your tickets.

Onward Tickets An entry requirement for many countries is that you have a ticket out of the country. If you're unsure of your next move, the easiest solution is to buy the cheapest onward ticket to a neighbouring country or a ticket from a reliable airline which can later be refunded if you do not use it.

Open-Jaw Tickets These are return tickets where you fly out to one place but return from another. If available, this can save you backtracking to your arrival point.

Overbooking Since every flight has some passengers who fail to show up, airlines often book more passengers than they have seats. Usually excess passengers make up for the no-shows, but occasionally somebody gets 'bumped' onto the next available flight. Guess who it is most likely to be? The passengers who check in late.

Promotional Fares These are officially discounted fares, available from travel agencies or direct from the airline.

Reconfirmation If you don't reconfirm your flight at least 72 hours prior to departure, the airline may delete your name from the passenger list. Ring to find out if your airline requires reconfirmation.

Restrictions Discounted tickets often have various restrictions on them – such as needing to be paid for in advance and incurring a penalty to be altered. Others are restrictions on the minimum and maximum period you must be away.

Round-the-World Tickets RTW tickets give you a limited period (usually a year) in which to circumnavigate the globe. You can go anywhere the carrying airlines go, as long as you don't backtrack. The number of stopovers or total number of separate flights is decided before you set off and they usually cost a bit more than a basic return flight.

Transferred Tickets Airline tickets cannot be transferred from one person to another. Travellers sometimes try to sell the return half of their ticket, but officials can ask you to prove that you are the person named on the ticket. On an international flight tickets are compared with passports.

Travel Periods Ticket prices vary with the time of year. There is a low (off-peak) season and a high (peak) season, and often a low-shoulder season and a high-shoulder season as well. Usually the fare depends on your outward flight – if you depart in the high season and return in the low season, you pay the high-season fare.

to book and pay for travel online. Several of these Web sites appear throughout this chapter.

Use the fares quoted in this book as a guide only. Quoted fares do not necessarily constitute a recommendation for the carrier.

Travellers with Specific Needs

If you have special needs – you have a broken leg, are vegetarian, travelling in a wheelchair, taking the baby, terrified of flying – tell the airline so they can make arrangements. Remind them when you reconfirm and again when you check in. It may be worth ringing airlines before booking a flight to find out how they can handle your needs.

Airports and airlines can be surprisingly helpful, but they need warning. Most international airports provide escorts from check-in to plane where needed and there should be ramps, lifts and accessible toilets and phones. Aircraft toilets, however, could be a problem; travellers should discuss this with the airline and, if necessary, with their doctor.

Guide dogs for the blind often have to travel in a pressurised baggage compartment with other animals; smaller guide dogs may be admitted to the cabin. Guide dogs, like other animals, are subject to quarantine laws (six months in isolation etc) when entering or returning to countries free of rabies, such as Australia.

Deaf travellers can ask for airport and in-flight announcements to be written down.

Children under two travel for 10% of the price (or free, on some airlines), as long as they don't occupy a seat. They don't get a baggage allowance. 'Skycots' should be provided if requested in advance. They take a child weighing up to 10kg. Children aged between two and 12 can usually occupy a seat for one-half to two-thirds of the full fare and get a baggage allowance. Pushchairs can often be taken as hand luggage.

Departure Tax

Airport taxes are factored into ticket prices, but fares are generally quoted without the taxes. They can range from about 3200 ptas up to 10,700 ptas, depending on the destination. Passport formalities are minimal.

The UK & Ireland

London is one of the best centres in the world for discounted air tickets.

The weekend editions of national newspapers sometimes have information on cheap fares. In London also try the *Evening Standard*, the listings magazine *Time Out* and *TNT*, a free weekly magazine ostensibly for antipodeans. As in North America, travellers are increasingly turning to the Internet to search for fares and book flights.

One of the more reliable travel agencies is STA Travel (☎ 020-7361 6145 for European flights). STA Travel has branches in London, as well as on many university campuses and in Bristol, Cambridge, Leeds, Manchester and Oxford. Its Web site at www.statravel.co.uk is worth a look.

Trailfinders (☎ 020-7937 5400 for European flights) is a similar agency to STA Travel. Its short-haul booking centre is at 215 Kensington High St and the Web site is at www.trailfinders.com.

Usit Campus (☎ 0870 240 1010), 52 Grosvenor Gardens, London SW1W 0AG, is in the same league. There are several branches around London and beyond. Its Web site is at www.usitcampus.co.uk.

Other popular travel agencies include Flightbookers (☎ 020-7757 2000), 177–178 Tottenham Court Rd, and Bridge the World (☎ 020-7734 7447), 4 Regent Place, London W1. Visit their Web sites are at www.ebookers.co.uk and www.b-t-w.co.uk, respectively.

The two flag airlines linking the UK and Spain are British Airways (☎ 0345 222111), 156 Regent St, London W1R 5TA, and Spain's Iberia (☎ 020-7830 0011 in London, ☎ 0990 341341 rest of UK), Venture House, 27-29 Glasshouse St, London W1R 6JU. Visit their Web sites for more information: www.british-airways.com and www.iberia.com, respectively. Of the two, BA is more likely to have special deals. But BA's standard open-return ticket to Madrid costs UK£480 (plus taxes). You would have to be unlucky or feeling generous to pay that kind of money.

Spain's Air Europa (☎ 0870 240 15 01 in the UK, ☎ 902-40 15 01 in Spain) has a flight daily except Saturday to London from Madrid and occasionally offers good prices. Comparable UK airlines flying to Spain include Monarch (☎ 0870 040 5040) and British Midland (☎ 0870 607 0555).

Think about where in Spain you want to end up. If you're not tied to a particular region, you may find more competitive fares to places such as Málaga or Alicante than to Madrid or Barcelona. Competitive fares with scheduled airlines range from about UK£150 to UK£230 depending on airline, fare conditions, time of year and destination.

Budget, ticketless airlines have since the late 1990s revolutionised air travel to Spain from the UK. Alongside charters and other cut-price options, these airlines frequently offer air tickets that beat trains or buses on cost. You buy flights direct with the airline, not through travel agencies. A return fare is really made up of two one-way flights, and the price of each leg will depend on various factors (eg, the season, how far in advance you book, special offers). This fare structure also makes it easy to organise open-jaw tickets (ie, you pay a one-way fare to one destination and leave from another). What the budget airlines all have in common is that fares rise as tickets sell, so the earlier you get in the less you're likely to spend.

EasyJet (☎ 0870 600 00 00 in the UK, ☎ 902-29 99 92 in Spain) has services from London's Luton airport and Liverpool to Madrid, Barcelona, Málaga and Palma de Mallorca for as little as UK£49 one way. In slow periods (such as weekdays in winter), one-way prices have been known to drop as low as UK£19! To these prices you need to add departure taxes (in this case UK£10). Once fares approach the UK£99 mark (one way) it is time to look elsewhere. You can book tickets on its Web site at www.easyjet.com.

Providing direct competition is the BA-run Go (☎ 0845-605 4321 in the UK, ☎ 901-333500 in Spain), which flies to the same destinations as easyJet, along with Alicante, Bilbao and Ibiza. Departures are from London Stansted (a 40-minute train ride from Liverpool Street train station). A variety of fares are possible. If you comply with certain restrictions (easily done if you are planning to spend a week or more in Spain) you are looking at around UK£50 to UK£60 one way plus taxes to, say, Madrid. You can book online at www.go-fly.com.

A newcomer on the budget airline scene is KLM uk's Buzz (☎ 0870 240 7070). It operates a summer service (and Saturday only) from London's Stansted airport to Jerez de la Frontera, in south-western Andalucía. Fares start at UK£100. Check its Web site at www.buzzaway.com.

Virgin Express (☎ 0207 744 0004) also flies to Spain although you have to travel via Brussels. Visit its Web site at www.virgin-express.com.

Spanish Travel Services (STS; ☎ 020-7387 5337), 138 Eversholt St, London NW1 1BL, uses scheduled airlines and charter flights. If you're having no luck with the budget airlines it may be worth trying this company. To Madrid or Barcelona it offers return flights with BA, Iberia and Air Eur-opa for as little as UK£140 to UK£160, including taxes. In low season the fares can go as low as UK£90, including taxes.

The arrival of the cheapie airlines has somewhat sidelined charter flights, but if you're getting no joy with STS consider the charter-flight option. The Charter Flight Centre (☎ 020-7565 6755), 15 Gillingham St, London SW1 V1HN, sometimes has reasonable deals.

The most fruitful destination/exit point for charters is Málaga. If you are flying out of Málaga in winter, return flights can cost less than 20,000 ptas. One-way bargains of 6500 ptas are possible.

In southern Spain, watch the local English-language rags for cheap flights. Otherwise, check around the budget travel agencies.

If you're coming from Ireland, compare what is available direct and from London; getting to London first may save you money. CityJet (☎ 01 844 5566) has direct flights from Dublin to Málaga.

Fly-Drive Packages including flights and prebooked hire cars can be attractive, especially in the high season, when local car rental prices will always exceed (often double) those of prebooked cars. Travel agencies and tour operators can make arrangements.

Passes Lufthansa (in conjunction with other airlines) offers flight coupons in a system called YES. You buy up to 10 coupons – each worth UK£59 (plus taxes) and valid for a one-way flight within 20 European countries, including Spain. For UK£236 you could fly London-Madrid-Milan-Berlin-London. The offer is for under-26s or students under 31 and coupons are valid for six months. Alitalia has a similar deal called Europa Pass.

Continental Europe

Air travel between Spain and other places in continental Europe is worth considering if you are pushed for time. Short hops can be expensive, but for longer journeys you can often find airfares that beat overland alternatives on cost.

France The student travel agency OTU Voyages (☎ 01 40 29 12 12) has a central Paris office at 39 ave Georges Bernanos and another 42 offices around the country. Visit its Web site at www.otu.fr.

Usit-Voyages (☎ 01 42 44 14 00) is a safe bet for reasonable student and cut-price travel. It has four offices in Paris, including 85 Blvd St Michel, and other branches around the country. STA Travel's Paris agent is Voyages Wasteels (☎ 01 43 25 58 35) at 11 rue Dupuytren; its Web site is at www.voyages.wasteels.fr.

It is possible to find charter or discounted return flights from Paris to places such as Madrid, Barcelona and Málaga for around 1000FF to 1600FF. Regular flights on Iberia to either Madrid or Barcelona can cost under 2000FF. It is also possible to fly direct to Sevilla, Valencia and Palma de Mallorca from Paris and some provincial centres.

Air Littoral (☎ 0803-834 834) operates flights from Madrid and Barcelona to Nice, with onward connections all over France and on to Italy. Regional Airlines (☎ 0803-005 200) operates flights from Bordeaux to Barcelona, Madrid and Bilbao. Neither of

these airlines is cheap, as they're aimed more at local business people.

From Spain you can find return fares for as low as 23,000 ptas in low season, but in the high season you are looking at around 35,000 ptas from, say, Madrid to Paris.

Germany In Berlin you could try STA Travel (☎ 030-311 09 50) at Goethestrasse 73. There are also offices in Frankfurt am Main, including Bockenheimer Landstrasse 133 (☎ 069-70 30 35), and in 16 other cities across the country. For more information, check STA's Web site at www.statravel.de.

High-season return flights from Frankfurt to Madrid range from DM394 with Lan Chile to DM568 with Sabena. Taxes range from DM39 to DM53.50.

Italy One place to look for cheap fares is Centro Turistico Studentesco (CTS), with branches countrywide. In Rome it is at Via Genova 16 (☎ 06-4 67 91).

Virgin Express (☎ 800-097097 in Italy, ☎ 93 226 66 71 in Barcelona, ☎ 91 662 52 61 in Madrid) has one flight a day from Rome to Barcelona and another to Madrid. Virgin Express is another ticketless airline of the kind described under The UK & Ireland section earlier. One-way fares can range from the promotional sum of L119,000 to the rather more onerous L256,000 for a flexible fare which allows date changes.

Netherlands & Belgium Amsterdam is a popular departure point. The student travel agency NBBS (☎ 020-624 09 89), Rokin 66, offers reliable and reasonably low fares. Compare its prices with the bucket shops along Rokin before deciding. NBBS has branches throughout the city and in Brussels, Belgium. Also try its Web site at www.nbbs.nl.

Brussels is the main hub for Virgin Express (☎ 02-752 05 05). Up to seven flights a day connect Brussels with Barcelona and Madrid. To Barcelona, fares in summer range from about f3800 to f5200 each way; to Madrid it's more like f3300 to f4700.

Portugal Only those in a tearing hurry will consider flying between Madrid and Lisbon.

Low-season flights can cost 27,000 ptas return (including taxes) but in summer the fares are likely to exceed 30,000 ptas. In Lisbon, Tagus (☎ 311 30 37), Rua Camilo Castelo Branco 20, is a travel agency worth a try; it has other branches all over the city.

Canary Islands

Las Islas Canarias are so far away that mainlanders can't resist jokes about the islanders being Africans. Few visitors to mainland Spain combine their trip with another to the Canary Islands. There is certainly no financial incentive to do so, as charter flights to the Canaries from other European capitals often cost less than from mainland Spain.

From Madrid and other centres, Iberia, Spanair, Air Europa and charters fly to Santa Cruz de Tenerife, Las Palmas de Gran Canaria and, less frequently, Lanzarote and Fuerteventura. A return charter fare or special offer with the regular airlines can be as low as 18,900 ptas. A more standard fare would be around 28,000 to 35,000 ptas.

Morocco

There is little in the way of cheap flights to North Africa. Among the cheaper tickets available from Madrid at the time of writing was one for 49,800 ptas return to Casablanca flying Royal Air Maroc (RAM), with a maximum stay of two weeks; from Madrid to Marrakesh the fare was 55,600 ptas. Occasionally, you stumble across better deals. A return flight from Casablanca to Madrid with RAM was Dr2975; from Tangier was Dr2364.

You have more, and often cheaper, options from southern Spain. Morocco's Regional Air Lines flies direct from Gibraltar to Casablanca (UK£104 return) on most days, and daily from Málaga to Casablanca and Tangier.

The Spanish airline Binter Mediterráneo flies from Málaga, Almería and Granada to Melilla, the Spanish enclave on the Moroccan coast, with return fares starting at 13,000 to 16,050 ptas (depending on the departure airport). From Melilla, you can cross the frontier to Nador, from where you can fan across Morocco by bus. Binter Mediterráneo

has two return flights a week from Granada and Málaga to Marrakesh for around 30,000 ptas, or Dr2960 going the other way.

The USA

The North Atlantic is the world's busiest long-haul air corridor and the range of flight options is bewildering. Several airlines fly 'direct' (many flights involve a stop elsewhere in Europe en route) to Spain, landing in Madrid and Barcelona. These include Iberia, British Airways and KLM. If your trip will not be confined to Spain, ask your travel agent if cheaper flights are available to other European cities.

The *New York Times*, *LA Times*, *Chicago Tribune* and *San Francisco Examiner* produce weekly travel sections loaded with travel agency ads. The magazine *Travel Unlimited*, PO Box 1058, Allston, Mass 02134, publishes details of cheap airfares.

Standard fares can be expensive. Discount and rock-bottom options from the USA include charter flights, stand-by and courier flights. One agency that can come up with good, cheap flights is Discount Tickets (☎ 212-391-2313) in New York.

Reliable travel agencies include STA Travel (☎ 800-781-4040) and Council Travel (☎ 800-2COUNCIL). Check out their Web sites at www.sta-travel.com and www.counciltravel.com and both have offices in major cities:

Council Travel
(☎ 310-208-3551) 931 Westwood Blvd, Los Angeles, CA 90024
(☎ 212-254-2525) 254 Greene St, New York, NY 10003
(☎ 415-421-3473) 530 Bush St, San Francisco, CA 94108

STA Travel
(☎ 310-824-1574) 920 Westwood Blvd, Los Angeles, CA 90024
(☎ 212-627-3111) 10 Downing St (corner of 6th Ave and Bleeker St), New York, NY 10014
(☎ 415-391-8407) 51 Grant Ave, San Francisco, CA 94108

Stand-by fares are often sold at 60% of the normal price for one-way tickets. Airhitch (☎ 212-864-2000, or ☎ 800-326-2009 toll free), 2641 Broadway, 3rd floor, #100, New York, NY 10025, is a specialist. You'll need to give a general idea of where and when you need to go; a few days before your departure you will be presented with a choice of two or three flights. A one-way fare from the USA to Europe costs from US$159 (east coast) to US$239 (west coast) plus taxes.

Airhitch has other offices in the USA, including one in Los Angeles (☎ 310-726-5000, or ☎ 1-888-AIRHITCH). In Europe it operates a central office in France (☎ 01 47 00 16 30) at 5 rue de Crussol, 75001, Paris. Seasonal offices (which means they can be shut from November to April) operate in Amsterdam, Berlin, Prague and Rome. Contact its Madrid representative on ☎ 91 366 79 27 or try the Web site at www.airhitch.org.

Iberia (☎ 1-800-772-4642 toll free) flies nonstop between Madrid and New York, but often you can get better deals with other airlines if you are prepared to fly via other European cities.

Fares with scheduled flights on regular airlines in low season (November to mid-December) can be great value. BA has flights from New York to Madrid (change in London) from around US$499 return. In high season (June to August) Iberia has flights for about US$763. Fares between airlines fluctuate greatly and you should always shop around. Pick the wrong airline and you could easily shell out US$1200 return in August. From the west coast (say Los Angeles), fares are inevitably higher, although occasionally you will stumble across amazing deals. BA had a low-season return ticket for US$654, while in high season several airlines hovered around the US$1130 mark.

Spain's Air Europa (☎ 718-244-7055, or ☎ 888-2EUROPA in the USA) occasionally offers good flight deals between Madrid and New York.

Courier flights involve you accompanying a parcel to its destination. A New York–Madrid return fare on a courier flight can cost under US$300 in low season (more from the west coast). You may have to be a US resident and apply for an interview first. Most flights depart from New York.

Now Voyager (☎ 212-431-1616), Suite 307, 74 Varrick St, New York, NY 10013, is a courier flight specialist. You pay an annual membership fee (around US$50), which entitles you to as many courier flights as you like. The Denver-based Air Courier Association (☎ 303-278-8810) also does this kind of thing.

Increasingly, travellers are turning to the Internet to look for flight deals and book tickets. Most airlines and many travel agencies now operate interactive Web sites allowing you to do this.

An alternative worth considering are Europe by Air coupons (☎ 888-387-2479). You purchase a minimum of three US$90 coupons before leaving from North America. Each coupon is valid for a one-way flight within the combined system of 10 participating regional airlines in Europe (exclusive of local taxes, which you will be charged when you make the flight). The coupons are valid for 120 days from the day you make your first flight. A few words of caution – using one of these coupons for a one-way flight won't always be better value than local alternatives, so check out the latter before committing yourself to any given flight. Europe by Air's Web site is at www.eurair.com.

If you can't find a good deal, consider a cheap transatlantic hop to London and stalk the bucket shops there.

At the time of writing, no airline leaving *from* Madrid could claim to offer unbeatable value. Low-season return flights can cost around 55,000 ptas to the east coast (eg, New York or Washington); to the west coast you are looking at more like 75,000 ptas. In high season, about the best you could hope for to the east coast is 85,000 ptas return.

Canada

Scan the travel agency ads in the *Globe & Mail*, *Toronto Star* and *Vancouver Sun*.

Canada's main student travel organisation is Travel Cuts (known as Voyages Campus in Québec). The two main offices are in Toronto (☎ 416-977-0441), 74 Gerrard St East, and Montréal (☎ 514-398-0647), Université McGill, 3480 rue McTavish. Its Web site is at www.travelcuts.com.

Iberia has direct flights from Montreal to Madrid three times weekly. Other major European airlines offer competitive fares to most Spanish destinations via other European capitals. Typical low season fares hover around the C$620 mark. In high season they can inflate to as much as C$1400, although BA and Iberia had a good deal at C$621 at the time of writing. Flights from Vancouver cost around C$250 more in low season and around C$1000 in high season.

For courier flights originating in Canada, contact FB on Board Courier Services (☎ 514-631-2077 in Toronto).

Australia

STA Travel (Australia-wide fast fares on ☎ 1300 360 960) and Flight Centre (☎ 1300 362 665 or ☎ 131 600) are major dealers in cheap airfares, although heavily discounted fares can often be found at your local travel agent Visit their Web sites at www.statravel .com.au and www.flightcentre.com.au, respectively.

The Saturday editions of the Melbourne *Age* and the *Sydney Morning Herald* have many advertisements offering cheap fares to Europe.

As a rule there are no direct flights from Australia to Spain. You will have to fly to Europe via Asia and change flights (and possibly airlines).

Low season return fares to Madrid or Barcelona are from around A$1370 to A$1590 on airlines including Olympic Airways, Thai International and Lauda Air.

On some flights between Australia and European cities such as London, Paris and Frankfurt, a return ticket between your destination and a European capital is thrown in for free. Madrid and Barcelona can be choices in these deals. Such flights cost around A$1790 to A$2300 in low season.

For courier flights, try Jupiter (☎ 02-9317 2113), 3/55 Kent Rd, Mascot, Sydney 2020.

New Zealand

As with Australia, STA Travel and Flight Centre are popular travel agencies. The cheapest fares to Europe are generally routed through the USA, although in the case of Spain you may get a deal via Latin America. An RTW ticket may be cheaper than a normal return. Otherwise, you can fly from Auckland to pick up a connecting flight in Melbourne or Sydney. Low season return fares to Europe start from around NZ$2015 with Thai International and Air New Zealand.

Useful addresses include:

Flight Centre (☎ 09-309 6171) Auckland Flight Centre, Shop 3A, National Bank Towers, 205-225 Queen St, Auckland www.flightcentre.com.au
STA Travel (☎ 0800 800 272) Canterbury University, Ilam Rd, Christchurch www.statravel.com.au
Usit Beyond (formerly Campus Travel; ☎ 09-379 4224) 18 Shortland St, Auckland www.usitbeyond.co.nz

Asia

Although most Asian countries are now offering fairly competitive fare deals, Bangkok, Hong Kong and Singapore are still the best places to shop around for discount tickets. Return fares from Bangkok to Spain are from 33,000B to 43,700B (US$878 to US$1,150), and from Hong Kong expect to pay from HK$9800 to HK$10,460 (US$1259 to US$1344).

STA Travel has branches in Bangkok, Hong Kong, Kuala Lumpur, Singapore and Tokyo.

LAND

If you are travelling by bus, train or car to Spain, check whether you require visas to the countries you intend to pass through. Although the following information on bus and rail passes concentrates on availability in the UK, most passes can be acquired throughout Europe.

Bus Passes

Eurolines offers a Eurolines Pass. A low-season pass valid for 30/60 days costs UK£175/219 (UK£139/175 for under-26s and senior citizens over 60) and allows unlimited travel between 21 European countries. The only Spanish cities included are Barcelona and Madrid. Fares increase to

UK£245/283 (UK£195/227) between mid-June and mid-September. The pass is available at Eurolines offices across Europe or you can book on ☎ 0870 5143 219. For more information on fares, visit the Eurolines Web site at www.eurolines.com/europass.

Busabout, a UK-based hop-on, hop-off bus service, is aimed at younger travellers. You buy a pass valid for up to seven months travel as often as you like between cities in Western Europe. Buses following a set route stop every two days at the hop-off points, which in Spain include Barcelona, Zaragoza, San Sebastián, Madrid, Toledo, Valencia, Granada, Málaga, La Línea, Tarifa, Sevilla and Salamanca.

The type of passes available range from 15 days (UK£155) through to seven months – the whole summer season of the service (UK£659). The prices are discounted for those with an international student card. These passes only really pay off if you plan to do a lot of long-haul travel. They also oblige you to stick to a certain route and certain destinations. Beyond the network you'll have to use local alternatives (which is no great trauma), so travellers wanting full flexibility would want to think twice. On top of the pass price a London link costs an extra UK£30, or UK£15 if you get a pass of one month or more.

You can buy Busabout tickets direct from the company (☎ 020-7950 1661) or from suppliers such as Usit Campus and STA Travel. Its Web site is at www.busabout.com.

Train Passes

Eurail Pass This pass is for non-European residents, which means you are not entitled to one if your passport shows you have been in Europe continuously for six months or more (in which case consider the better value InterRail card). These cards are expensive, so look at the options before committing yourself.

People over 26 pay for a 1st-class pass (Eurailpass) and those under 26 for a 2nd-class pass (Eurail Youthpass). Plan to spend a lot of time on trains – you'll need to cover more than 2400km within two weeks to get value for money. The cards are good for travel in 17 European countries, but forget it if you intend to travel mainly in Spain.

Standard passes are valid for 15 or 21 days, or for one, two or three months. These cost US$554/718/890/1260/1558, respectively. Children aged between four and 11 pay half price for a 1st-class pass. The Eurail Youthpass version comes in at US$388/499/623/882/1089. Treat your pass like gold, as it is virtually impossible to obtain replacements or refunds in the event of loss or theft.

Eurail also offers Flexipasses, with which the traveller is entitled to 10 or 15 days' train travel over a two-month period. These cost respectively US$458/599 (in 2nd class) for those under 26 and US$654/862 (in 1st class) for over-26s.

Eurail Saverpass is for two to five people travelling together and is available for 15 or 21 days or one, two or three months. The price per person is US$470/610/756/1072/1324, respectively. The Eurail Saver Flexipass entitles you to 10 or 15 days of train travel over a two-month period and costs US$556/732 (children pay half price).

The EurailDrive Pass gives the bearer four days of unlimited 1st-class train travel combined with two days of car rental. There are various permutations on this and prices start at US$385 per person, based on two people travelling together (bear in mind that supplements are payable on high speed trains such as France's TGV and Spain's AVE). If you fail to obtain this pass at home, you can purchase it at the Rail Europe Travel Centre (☎ 0870 584 8848) at 179 Piccadilly, London, W1V 0BA.

Europass This is another train pass for people not resident in Europe. It provides between five and 15 days of unlimited travel within a two-month period in five 'core' countries (ie, France, Spain, Germany, Switzerland and Italy).

As with Eurail passes, travellers who are over 26 pay for a 1st-class pass, while under-26s can get a cheaper Europass Youth for travel in 2nd class. The passes can be obtained at the same outlets as Eurail passes. The basic five-country pass costs US$728

(US$513 for the youth version) for the 15-day option.

Freedom Pass You can also get Freedom passes (known as Euro-Domino outside the UK) for any one of 28 European countries, valid for from three to eight days travel over a month. For Spain, a 1st-class, eight-day pass costs UK£196. Second class is UK£159 and a youth version (for under-26s) is UK£122. This is a more attractive option than Eurail if you intend to spend a decent amount of time exploring Spain but again, you would need to be on trains a lot to get full value from the pass. You are better off with an InterRail card if you can get one. For more information, check out the Web site at www.raileurope.co.uk.

InterRail Pass If you are a resident in any European country in the InterRail network, or can demonstrate that you have been in Europe for six months or more, think about an InterRail pass. The InterRail map of Europe is divided into zones, one of which is composed of Spain, Portugal and Morocco.

The ticket is designed for under-26s but there is a more expensive version for older folk, the InterRail 26+. Twenty-two days of unlimited 2nd-class travel in one zone costs UK£129/179, respectively. Better value is the one-month ticket in two zones for UK£169/235 (which from the UK would get you across France too). A three-zone pass for one month costs UK£195/269. If you think you can stand careering around virtually all of Europe, you could go for the one-month all-in UK£219/309 ticket.

Bear in mind that you must pay full fare on the Eurostar from London and the supplement on certain high-speed trains such as Spain's AVE and France's TGV.

Cardholders get discounts on travel in the country of residence where they purchase the ticket, as well as on a variety of other services such as ferry travel.

In the UK you can buy InterRail passes at the Rail Europe Travel Centre (see Eurail Passes earlier), some mainline train stations and selected travel agencies (such as Usit Campus).

Spanish Rail Passes For information on passes available inside Spain, see the Getting Around chapter.

Discount Tickets
If you're under 26 you can get Voyages Wasteels or Billet International de Jeunesse (BIJ) tickets for international train travel. They amount to the same thing and, from London at any rate, represent a surprisingly small saving.

Always ask about discounts. As a rule, toddlers under four travel for free, while kids aged four to 11 travel for half the adult fare. Senior travellers can get a Rail Europe Senior card (valid for only a year for trips that cross at least one border). You pay UK£5 for the card, but you must already have a Senior Citizens Rail Card (UK£18), available to anyone who can prove they are over 60 (you are not required to be a UK resident). The pass entitles you to roughly 30% off standard fares. Groups often qualify for discounts too.

For information about train discounts within Spain, see the Getting Around chapter.

The UK
Bus If you plan to head straight into Spain from the UK, travelling by bus is the cheapest option. Eurolines (☎ 0870 5143 219), 52 Grosvenor Gardens, Victoria, London SW1, which is a few blocks away from the bus terminal itself, runs buses to Barcelona on Saturday, Monday (leaving at 11 am; connection to Alicante) and Wednesday (10 pm). The trip takes 24 to 26 hours. The one-way and return fares are, respectively, UK£79 and UK£111 (UK£70 and UK£101 for under-26s and senior citizens).

A bus goes from London to Madrid via San Sebastián on Monday and Friday at 9.30 pm, arriving 28 hours later. One-way and return fares are UK£84 and UK£129 (UK£75 and UK£116 for under-26s and seniors). The one-way trip from Madrid back to London costs 15,900 ptas.

Buses run from London to farther destinations in Spain, including the Costa del Sol, Santander, Santiago de Compostela and Sevilla. The single biggest disadvantage of the bus is that you can't get off along the way. Fares drop in the low season.

Under-26s pay 10% less on most bus services, as do seniors over 60 (over 50 on some National Express channel crossing services). Children up to age 12 generally pay half price.

Train Your choices from London are limited by the options in Paris, where you must change trains (for more details, see under France in this section).

If you optimise your choice of departure from London to keep waiting times for connections to a minimum, the trip by train to either Barcelona or Madrid is comparable with the bus for journey times. Obviously there are plenty of possibilities for the Paris leg via ferry and Seacat services (or with Eurostar).

Trains run from Charing Cross or Victoria stations to Paris (via ferry or Seacat from Dover to Calais or Folkestone to Boulogne); Eurostar leaves from Waterloo. You arrive at the Gare du Nord, and must get to the Gare d'Austerlitz (take the RER B to St Michel and change there for the RER C to Austerlitz), Gare Montparnasse (Metro 4) or Gare de Lyon (RER B to Châtelet and then RER A for Gare de Lyon). See also under France later in this section.

The one-way/return fares to Barcelona and Madrid are UK£90/143 and UK£104/174 (more if you take the Eurostar); tickets are valid for two months. Under-26s can get Wasteels or Billet International de Jeunesse (BIJ) tickets for UK£68/121 and UK£80/143, respectively. These prices can rise in high season. If you intend to get the overnight sleeper from Paris, factor in another UK£10 for the couchette.

For information on all international train travel (including Eurostar services), call European Rail (☎ 020-7387 0444) or go the Wasteels office opposite platform 2 at Victoria station. You can also get information on Eurostar and train passes from the Rail Europe Travel Centre (☎ 0870 584 8848) at 179 Piccadilly, London, W1V 0BA. For Eurostar services, you can also make inquiries and buy tickets at Waterloo station, from where the trains depart as well as other large mainline stations. Its Web site is at www .eurostar.co.uk.

Car & Motorcycle For details of sending your car by ferry direct to Spain or France from the UK, see the Sea section later in this chapter. Another option is Eurotunnel, the Channel Tunnel car train connecting Folkestone with Calais. It runs around the clock, with up to four crossings (35 minutes) an hour in high season. You pay for the vehicle only and fares vary according to the time of day and season. Low-season economy return tickets cost UK£219 or UK£119 for motorcycles; high-season fares can cost as much as UK£180 each way. You can book in advance by phone (☎ 0870 535 3535) or online (www.eurotunnel.com), but the service is designed to let you just roll up.

An interesting Web site loaded with advice for people planning to drive around Europe is www.ideamerge.com/motoeuropa. If you want help with route planning, try out www.euroshell.com.

Paperwork & Preparations Proof of ownership of a private vehicle should always be carried (Vehicle Registration Document for UK-registered cars) when driving through Europe. All EU member states' driving licences (pink or pink and green) are recognised (although you are supposed to get a Spanish licence if you stay for more than a year – many foreign residents ignore this requirement). The old-style UK green licence is not accepted.

Other foreign licences are supposed to be accompanied by an International Driving Permit (although in practice, for renting cars or dealing with traffic police, your national licence will suffice). The International Driving Permit is available from automobile clubs in your country and is valid for 12 months.

Third-party motor insurance is a minimum requirement and it is compulsory to have a Green Card, an internationally recognised proof of insurance, which can be obtained from your insurer. Also ask your insurer for a European accident statement form, which can simplify matters in the event of an accident. Never sign statements you can't read or understand: insist on a translation and sign that only if it's acceptable.

A European breakdown assistance policy such as the AA Five Star Service or RAC Eurocover Motoring Assistance is a good investment. In Spain, get help from the Real Automovil Club de España (RACE; see under Car & Motorcycle in the Getting Around chapter).

Every vehicle travelling across an international border should display a nationality plate of its country of registration. Two warning triangles (to be used in the event of a breakdown) are compulsory in Spain. Recommended accessories are a first-aid kit, a spare bulb kit and a fire extinguisher. If the car is from the UK or Ireland, remember to have the headlights adjusted for driving in continental Europe.

In the UK, get more information from the RAC (☎ 0870 572 2722) or the AA (☎ 0870 550 0600).

Rental Many people opt to get to Spain by other means, then rent a car once they arrive. Prebooking a car through a multinational agency – such as Hertz, Avis, Budget Car or Europe's largest rental agency, Europcar – before leaving home will enable you to find the best deals. Prebooked and prepaid rates are generally cheaper and it may be worth your while looking into fly-drive combinations and other programs. You simply pick up the vehicle on arrival and return it to a nominated point at the end of the rental period. Ask your travel agent for information or contact one of the major car rental agencies.

Holiday Autos (☎ 0990 300400) sometimes has good rates for Europe, for which you need to prebook; its main office is in the UK. Another possibility is Car Rental Direct (☎ 020-7625 7166); its Web site is at www.car-rental-direct.com.

Another option, if you don't know when you want to rent, is to call home from Spain and reserve through an agency there. This way you get the benefits of booking from home.

No matter where you rent, make sure you understand what is included in the price (unlimited kilometres, tax, insurance, collision damage waiver etc) and what your liabilities are. The minimum rental age in Spain is 21 years. A credit card is usually required.

For more details of rental rates and options within Spain, see under Car & Motorcycle in the Getting Around chapter.

Purchase Only residents may legally purchase vehicles in Spain (see under Car & Motorcycle in the Getting Around chapter).

Otherwise, the UK is probably the best place to buy a vehicle for travelling around Europe, as second-hand prices are good. But bear in mind that you will be getting a left-hand drive car (ie, steering wheel on the right). If you want a right-hand drive car and can afford to buy a new one, prices are relatively low in Belgium, the Netherlands and Luxembourg.

Camper Van A popular way of touring Europe is for three or four people to band together and buy a camper van to drive around. London is the usual embarkation point. Look at the ads in London's free *TNT* magazine. Private vendors gather daily at the Van Market on Market Rd, London N7 (near Caledonian Road tube station).

Motorcycle Spain, like the rest of Europe, is ideal for motorcycle touring, with every possible kind of terrain from mountain back roads to coastal highways. Motorcycles are easier to squeeze around city traffic and park and you will never need to book ahead to get a bike onto a ferry.

Anyone considering joining a motorcycle tour from the UK might want to join the International Motorcyclists Tour Club (UK£19 per annum plus UK£3 joining fee). The club has 400 members and, in addition to holidays in Europe, runs social weekends. The present secretary, James Clegg, can be contacted on ☎ 01484-66 48 68.

France

Bus Enatcar and ALSA, among the bus companies representing Eurolines in Spain, have buses between various Spanish cities (including Barcelona, Madrid, Málaga, Oviedo and Santiago de Compostela) and Paris, with other destinations en route.

Eurolines has offices in several French cities; in Paris the main office is at the bus station (☎ 01 49 72 51 51), 28 Ave du Générale de Gaulle. It has another more central office (☎ 01 43 54 11 99) at rue St Jacques 55, off Blvd St Michel. The one-way fare from Madrid is 12,900 ptas.

Local bus services cross the Franco-Spanish frontier at several locations. Details appear in the appropriate regional and city chapters.

Train About the only truly direct trains to Madrid and Barcelona are the *trenhotels*, expensive sleeping-car trains. The Barcelona service leaves from Paris at 8.47 pm daily and arrives between 8.53 and 9 am (stopping at Dijon, Figueres and Girona). The standard one-way fare is 757FF.

The Madrid equivalent (stopping at Poitiers, Vitoria, Burgos and Valladolid) leaves from Paris at 7.37 pm and arrives at Madrid Chamartín at 8.58 am. The one-way fare is 809FF.

Otherwise, the cheapest and most convenient option to Barcelona is the 9.47 pm from Paris Austerlitz, changing at Latour-de-Carol and arriving at Barcelona's Estació Sants at 11.27 am. A reclining seat costs 492FF one way or 562FF in a 2nd-class couchette. There is an alternative train with a change at Portbou (on the coast).

For Madrid, the most convenient bet if you don't want to take the sleeper train is the 11.14 pm from Paris Austerlitz via Irún. A 2nd-class seat costs 627FF while a 2nd-class couchette is 715FF one way. First-class couchettes cost considerably more – the difference is four people to a compartment rather than six. Under-26s get a 25% reduction. Note also that fares rise in July and August.

There are several other possibilities. Two or three TGV trains leave from Paris Montparnasse for Irún, where you change to a normal train for the onward trip to Madrid. Up to three TGVs also put you on the road to Barcelona (leaving from Paris' Gare de Lyon), with a change of train at Montpellier or Narbonne. Prices and timetables vary, so check the latest details.

Leaving from Spain, the frequency of trains is similar. The trenhotel departs from Barcelona's Estació Sants at 8.05 pm and arrives in Paris at 8.14 am. From Madrid, the trenhotel leaves at 7 pm and arrives at 8.29 am. From Barcelona the cheapest bed costs 25,900 ptas, or you can get a couchette for 16,900 ptas. From Madrid, you pay 30,400 ptas and 17,800 ptas, respectively.

A direct Talgo service also connects Montpellier with Barcelona (245FF or 6400 ptas in 2nd class, 4½ hours) and Valencia. A couple of other slower services (with a change of train at Portbou) also make this run. All these trains stop in Perpignan.

Car & Motorcycle For general information on taking your vehicle across Europe, see the UK section earlier in this chapter. The main crossings from France into Spain are the highways to Barcelona and San Sebastián at either end of the Pyrenees.

Portugal
Bus From Madrid, three Eurolines buses a week go to Lisbon (around 5850 ptas one way, seven hours) via Salamanca, departing from Estación Sur de Autobuses at 11 pm and arriving at Avenida de Casal Ribeiro at 7 am. AutoRes (☎ 91 551 72 00, ☎ 902-19 29 39 for bookings) also has a daily bus to Lisbon from its station on Calle de Fernández Shaw in Madrid (5795 ptas). A weekly service connects Lisbon with Barcelona.

Other services to the Portuguese capital run from Málaga (via Sevilla and Cádiz), Benidorm (via Alicante and Badajoz) and La Coruña (via Santiago de Compostela and Tuý). There are also services to Oporto from Madrid and to the Algarve from Sevilla. Local buses cross the border from towns such as Huelva (Andalucía), Badajoz (Extremadura) and Verín (Galicia).

Train A daily train runs between Madrid and Lisbon. It leaves from Madrid's Chamartín station at 10.45 pm and arrives in Lisbon at 8.40 am. Going the other way the train leaves at 9.56 pm and arrives at 8.35 am. The one-way fare is 6585 ptas if you choose to sit. Otherwise, the cheapest couchette solution costs 9240 ptas. Another train operates between Vigo in Galicia and Oporto, running via Tuy.

Car & Motorcycle Main roads run into central Portugal from Salamanca, Badajoz and Cáceres, while the highway from Sevilla via Huelva takes you to the Algarve. In the north there are plenty of minor approach roads from Galicia, but the main highway runs via Tuy across the Río Miño and down the Portuguese coast.

Andorra

Bus Regular buses connect Andorra with Barcelona and other destinations in Spain (including Madrid) and France (for details see the Andorra chapter). Passport checks for visas are not always made on this route – but don't bank on it.

Other European Destinations

Bus Eurolines and other companies operate buses from Madrid, Barcelona and other major cities across France and into Germany (Frankfurt am Main ☎ 01805-25 02 54, Hamburg, Munich and Düsseldorf), the Benelux countries, Italy (Madrid to Rome costs 19,300 ptas), Switzerland and on to Eastern European destinations such as Prague (19,875 ptas from Madrid).

Train Direct trains link Barcelona with Geneva, Zürich, Turin and Milan at least three times a week. Reaching other destinations in Europe beyond these will require a change in these cities or in Paris.

Morocco

An ambitious plan to unite Spain and Morocco by tunnel could become a reality some time this century. Until then, you'll have to adopt a more conventional approach. Buses from several Spanish cities converge on Algeciras to make the ferry crossing to Tangier and head into Morocco. The trip to Tangier from Madrid can cost as little as 8300 ptas. For details on Spain-Morocco ferries, see under Sea in this chapter.

SEA
The UK
Portsmouth-Bilbao Throughout the year P&O European Ferries (☎ 0870 242 4999 in the UK) operates a ferry from Portsmouth

to Bilbao. As a rule there are two sails a week and the voyage time is about 35 hours from the UK and 30 hours the other way. There are only two boats in January. The company's Web site is at www.poef.com. For more details, see Getting There & Away in the Bilbao section of the Basque Country, Navarra & La Rioja chapter.

Plymouth/Portsmouth-Santander Brittany Ferries (☎ 0870 536 0360 in the UK) at Milbay Docks in Plymouth, operates a twice-weekly car-ferry service to Santander from mid-March to mid-November (24 hours). Just one other trip occurs in December, departing from Portsmouth (30 to 33 hours). Check out the Web site at www .brittanyferries.co.uk. For more details, see Getting There & Away in the Santander section in the Cantabria & Asturias chapter.

Via France You can transport your car by ferry to France. P&O Stena Line (☎ 0870 600 0600 in the UK) has frequent car ferries from Dover to Calais (1¼ hours). A typical advance-purchase return fare for a car and two passengers is UK£184. It is cheaper to travel before 7 am and after 8 pm. Check its Web site at www.posl.com.

For the Eurotunnel car-train service through the Channel Tunnel, see under The UK in the Land section earlier in this chapter.

With your foot flat on the floor through France, you may save a little time over the direct Spain ferries. Whether or not it is cheaper depends on the French tollways you take, how much juice your vehicle burns and mechanical problems en route.

Italy

After a 15-year absence, the so-called *canguro* shipping run between Barcelona and Genoa was relaunched in September 1998. It is operated by Grimaldi and operates three times a week (for details see the Barcelona chapter).

Canary Islands
A Trasmediterránea (☎ 902-45 46 45) car ferry leaves from Cádiz for Santa Cruz de Tenerife and Las Palmas de Gran Canaria

every Tuesday at 7 pm. It's a long and bumpy ride, arriving at Las Palmas on Thursday at 9 am and 2 pm in Santa Cruz de Tenerife. The boat back to Spain leaves from Santa Cruz at 9 am on Saturday, calling in at Las Palmas (departing at 2.30 pm) and Arrecife (Lanzarote; departing at 10.30 pm) on the way. Unless you especially like ocean voyages or have to transport a car, you are better off flying.

One-way fares (including meals) range from 29,660 to 59,990 ptas per person, depending on the type of cabin. To transport a standard car costs 24,695 ptas one way. For more information, check its Web site at www.trasmediterranea.es.

Morocco

Trasmediterránea (☎ 902-45 46 45) and Euro-Ferrys (☎ 956 65 11 78) and some Moroccan companies operate at least 20 daily roll-on, roll-off car ferries and hydrofoils between Algeciras and Tangier. Many more operate in summer to handle the hordes of Moroccan residents in Europe returning home on holiday. The ferry takes about 2½ hours; the hydrofoil manages it in an hour.

At least 40 ferries and hydrofoils cross from Algeciras to the Spanish enclave of Ceuta, from where you can easily travel overland into Morocco. Travel times are 1½ hours and 40 minutes, respectively.

The superfast Buquebús (car and passenger) service (☎ 902-41 42 42) connects Algeciras with Ceuta in just 30 to 35 minutes. It also runs a service from Málaga to Ceuta in 1½ hours.

Two daily ferries also cross to Tangier from Tarifa and Cádiz (see those sections for details).

Five or six days a week, and three times daily from mid-June to late August, a Trasmediterránea ferry leaves from Almería for Melilla, Spain's enclave in north-eastern Morocco. The trip takes up to eight hours. A similar service runs to Melilla from Málaga. Ferri Maroc (☎ 950 27 48 00) and Limadet (☎ 950 27 12 80) both sail between Almería and Nador, the Moroccan town neighbouring Melilla, with similar frequency and prices to the Trasmediterránea service.

You could also go to Morocco via Gibraltar, using one of the twice-weekly car ferries.

For more details and fares, see Getting There & Away in the Algeciras, Almería, Gibraltar, Málaga and Tarifa sections.

Warning Anyone driving from Morocco to Spain should be prepared for rigorous searches both in the enclaves of Ceuta and Melilla, and on disembarking on the mainland.

Algeria

Romeu y Compañía (☎ 96 514 15 09) runs car and passenger ferries from Alicante to Oran in Algeria. In summer, ferries run at least once or twice a week, but in low season the frequency drops to twice a month. Algeria is not an advisable destination while decapitation continues to be a common form of greeting from the country's more violent minority. If you're still interested, see the Alicante section of the Valencia chapter for more details.

ORGANISED TOURS

A lot of companies offer tours to Spain, generally concentrating on a couple of regions for a week or two. Spanish tourist offices can provide a list of tour operators. What follows is a brief guide only to the kinds of options available.

The UK

Short Breaks & Holidays Brittany Ferries (see the earlier Sea section) is one of several companies that offers brief trips in northern Spain, lasting from two to seven days. Such holidays can cost from UK£120 for two nights to UK£350 for five nights, which includes the ferry crossing and good accommodation.

Cresta Holidays (☎ 0870 333 3303), Tabley Court, Victoria St, Altrincham, Cheshire WA14 1EZ, offers a range of city tours, fly-drive trips and other holidays to Spain. Another Spain specialist is The Individual Travellers Spain (☎ 0870 773 773 in the UK only, ☎ 01798-869 485 for all other callers, ℮ holidays@indiv-travellers.com), Manor Court Yard, Bignor, Pulborough RH20 1QD.

Walking Holidays Explore Worldwide (☎ 01252-76 00 00), 1 Frederick St, Aldershot, Hants GU11 1LQ, can take you trekking in the Picos de Europa in northern Spain or the Sierra Nevada near Granada, or trekking and sightseeing in Andalucía. The company has offices worldwide or you can inspect its Web site at www.explore.co.uk.

Headwater (☎ 01606-81 33 33), 146 London Rd, Northwich, Cheshire CW9 5HH, organises week-long walking holidays. Its Web site is at www.headwater.com.

Cycling Holidays Bolero International Holidays organises cycling holidays through France to the Costa Brava from UK£184 to UK£304. The company can be contacted through European Bike Express (☎ 01642-25 1 4 40), 31 Baker St, Middlesbrough, Cleveland TS1 2LF.

Discover Adventure (☎ 01722-74 11 23, @ info@discoveradventure.com), 5 Netherhampton Cottage, Netherhampton Rd, Netherhampton, Salisbury SP2 8PX, offers one-week mountain-bike tours in Andalucía (Sierra Nevada, Alpujarras and Sierra de Cazorla) for UK£650 per person; it also organises walking trips in the same area.

Language Tours Caledonia Languages Abroad (☎ 0131-621 7721, fax 0131-621 7723), The Clockhouse, Bonnington Mill, 72 Newhaven Rd, Edinburgh EH6 5QG, organises trips to southern Spain with language study and activities components. Its Web site is at www.caledonianlanguages .co.uk.

Self-Catering Several operators offer packages in villas, cottages and apartments for those who want to run their own show from a comfortable location. The Individual Travellers Spain (see contact details earlier in this section) has plenty of accommodation on offer.

The USA

A plethora of operators run tours from the USA. Spanish Heritage Tours (☎ 800-221-2250), 47 Queens Blvd, Forest Hills, NY 11375, is a reputable mainstream operator that can organise a broad array of tours.

Escapade Vacations (☎ 800-942 2114), 630 Third Ave, New York, NY 10017, offers a range of tours, from coach trips staying in paradores, to more flexible 'plan-it-yourself' packages.

Alta Tours (☎ 800-338 4191), 870 Market St, Suite 784, San Francisco CA 94102, organises anything from posh corporate trips to customised itineraries for student groups. It also has a standard palette of tours ranging from one to two weeks across various parts of the country and into Portugal.

Saranjan Tours (☎ 800-858 9594, 12865), PO Box 292, Kirkland WA 98033, does everything from city breaks to walking trips in Andalucía and the Pyrenees.

Australia

You can organise tours of Spain through the following operators:

Ibertours Travel (☎ 03-9670 8388) 1st floor, 84 William St, Melbourne, Victoria 3000
Web site: www.ibertours.com.au
Spanish Tourism Promotions (☎ 03-9650 7377, @ sales@spanishtravels.com.au) Level 1, 178 Collins St, Melbourne, Victoria 3000
Ya'lla Tours (☎ 03-9523 1988) 661 Glenhuntly Rd, Caulfield, Victoria 3162
Web site: www.yallatours.com.au

WARNING

The information in this chapter is vulnerable to change: prices for international travel are volatile, routes are introduced and cancelled, schedules change, special deals come and go and visa requirements are amended. Before you part with your cash, you should get as much information as you can. This chapter is no substitute for your own research.

Getting Around

AIR

Several airlines link the major cities of Spain, but as a rule air travel within Spain is costly. The most frequent connections are between Madrid and Barcelona. Generally you are better off with buses and trains. Flights to farther-flung corners such as the Balearic Islands are more useful.

Main airports are at Barcelona, Madrid, Málaga, Palma de Mallorca (Balearic Islands) and Santiago de Compostela.

Iberia and its subsidiaries, Iberia Regional-Air Nostrum (a franchisee established in 1994 and based in Valencia) and Binter Mediterráneo, have an extensive network covering all Spain. Call ☎ 902-40 05 00 for information. For information on Canary Islands flights, see the Getting There & Away chapter.

These airlines operate four basic types of ticket, although all sorts of offers and other permutations mean that you can often do better than the published fares. These main ticket types are listed in order from cheapest to dearest (the cheaper ones are not available on all routes):

Estrella The cheapest – buy the ticket at least two days ahead; return between four and 14 days later (return tickets only).

Supermini Buy ticket at least four days ahead; spend one Saturday night in destination (return tickets only). Valid for three months.

Reducida Buy ticket at least three days ahead; spend at least one night in destination (return tickets only). Valid for three months.

Flexible No restrictions, refundable (one-way or return).

A standard one-way fare from Madrid to Barcelona ranges from 12,150 to 16,200 ptas. Be sure to ask about discounts and special rates. You get 25% off flights leaving after 11 pm (admittedly there are few of these). People under 22 or over 63 get up to 25% off *return* flights and are sometimes entitled to further reductions for night flights and on minifares.

Competing with Iberia and its subsidiaries are Spanair (☎ 902-13 14 15) and Air Europa (☎ 902-40 15 01). These airlines used to be considerably cheaper, but the gap has closed in recent years.

Air Europa is the bigger of the two, with regular flights connecting Madrid, Barcelona and the Canary Islands, plus flights to internal destinations (such as Alicante, Asturias, Bilbao, Málaga, Palma de Mallorca, Salamanca, Sevilla, Valladolid, Vitoria and Zaragoza). Three to eight Air Europa flights connect Madrid with Barcelona daily (four on weekends). The cheapest one-way *turista* (economy) fare is 10,400 ptas. The return fare ranges from 12,000 to about 30,000 ptas.

With Iberia, the best standard return fare from the capital to Palma de Mallorca is 29,050 ptas, to Santiago de Compostela 29,000 ptas and to Málaga is 28,900 ptas. In low season (winter) you can be looking at fares to these destinations for as low as 14,500 ptas.

One-way fares are more (sometimes much more) than half the tourist-class return fare. Tickets can easily be booked with nationwide travel agencies such as Halcón Viajes. For youth fares, inquire at offices of TIVE (see Useful Organisations in the Facts for the Visitor chapter) in major cities around Spain.

BUS

A plethora of companies provide bus links, from local routes between villages to fast intercity connections. It is often cheaper to travel by bus than by train, particularly on long-haul runs.

Local services can get you just about anywhere, but most buses connecting villages and provincial towns are not geared to tourist needs. Even frequent weekday services can drop off to a trickle on weekends. Often just one bus runs daily between smaller places during the week and none operate on Sunday. It's usually unnecessary to make reservations; just arrive early enough to get a seat.

On many regular runs (say, from Madrid to Toledo) the ticket you buy is for the next bus due to leave and *cannot* be used on a later bus. Advance purchase in such cases is generally not possible.

For longer trips (such as Madrid-Sevilla, or to the *costas*), and certainly in peak season, buy your ticket in advance. The main bus stations, such as the Estación Sur de Autobuses in Madrid, can be a stifling sea of queues during major holidays.

In most larger towns and cities, buses leave from a single bus station *(estación de autobuses)*.

In smaller places, buses tend to operate from a set street or plaza, often unmarked. Locals will know where to go. Usually a specific bar sells tickets and has timetable information.

People under 26 should ask about discounts on long-distance trips. Occasionally a return ticket is cheaper than two singles.

Some sample one-way fares between cities include:

from	to	travel time (hours)	fare (ptas)
Barcelona	Sevilla	16	9135
	Zaragoza	3½	1655
Madrid	Alicante	5¼	2995
	Barcelona	7 to 8	3400
	Burgos	2¾	1950
	Córdoba	4½	1600
	Granada	5	1960
	Lisbon (Portugal)	7	5850
	Málaga	6	2650
	Oviedo	4¾	3825
	San Sebastián	5¾ to 6½	3800
	Santander	5¾	3300
	Santiago de Compostela	9	5135
	Sevilla	6	2745
Sevilla	Granada	2¾	2700

TRAIN

Generally, the mainline trains with the national rail network, Renfe (Red Nacional de los Ferrocarriles Españoles), are reliable if not always superfast. Indeed, Renfe claims a 95% to 99.7% punctuality rate for the trains running on its more than 12,000km of track.

It's always worth checking the relative merits of the bus. Trains tend to be more agreeable for long trips, but more expensive. Express buses between major cities are often faster, with more frequent departures, than the train. For information (in Spanish), call Renfe (☎ 902-24 02 02) or have a look at its Web site at www.renfe.es.

Types of Train

A host of different trains coast the wide-gauge lines of the Spanish network. The difference is usually in the speed of the journey, the number of stops made and, as a consequence, the price. A saving of a couple of hours on a faster train can mean a big hike in the fare.

For short hops, bigger cities have a local network known as *cercanías*. From Madrid, for instance, cercanías trains cover the entire Comunidad de Madrid region.

Most long-distance *(largo recorrido)* trains have 1st and 2nd class. The cheapest and slowest of these are *regionales*, which are generally all-stops services between provinces within one region (although a few travel between regions). If your train is a *regional exprés* it will make fewer stops.

The Tren Regional Diesel (TRD) is a new train that has been put into service to speed up regional travel, particularly in Andalucía.

All trains that do journeys of more than 400km are denominated *Grandes Líneas* services – really just a fancy way of saying long distance. Among these are *diurnos* and *estrellas*, the standard inter-regional trains. The latter is the night-time version of the former.

Faster, more comfortable and expensive are the Talgos (Tren Articulado Ligero Goicoechea Oriol). They make only major stops and have such extras as TVs in the carriages. The Talgo Pendular is a sleeker, faster version of the same thing, which picks up speed by leaning into curves.

Some Talgos and other modern trains are used for limited-stop trips between major cities. These services are known as InterCity (and when they're really good, as InterCity Plus!).

A classier derivative is the Talgo 200, a Talgo Pendular using the standard-gauge, high-speed Tren de Alta Velocidad Española (AVE) line between Madrid and Sevilla, on part of the journey to such southern destinations as Málaga, Cádiz and Algeciras. The trip from Madrid to Cádiz takes five hours and to Málaga is a little shorter.

The most expensive way to travel is to take the high-speed AVE train along the Madrid-Sevilla line (another line between Madrid and Barcelona is slowly being laid, and it will eventually link up with the French TGV).

There are a couple of other one-off classy services, such as the Barcelona-Valencia-Alicante Euromed trains. This is basically an AVE train running on normal Spanish track – it still manages to crank up to 220km/h. In late 1999 a stylish new train known as Arco entered service between Portbou and Alicante (via Barcelona and Valencia). It is marginally slower and cheaper than the Euromed. Another one is the Alaris service between Madrid and Castelló (via Albacete and Valencia).

Autoexpreso and Motoexpreso wagons are sometimes attached to long-distance services for the transport, respectively, of cars and motorbikes.

A *trenhotel* is an expensive sleeping-car train. There can be up to three classes on these trains: *turista* (for those sitting or in a couchette), *preferente* (sleeping car) and *gran clase* (sleeping in sheer bloody luxury).

Couchettes & Sleepers

Couchettes are known as *literas* in Spain and are fold-out bunk beds (generally in compartments of six berths). Their standard price, in addition to your ticket, is 1500 ptas. The discounts listed later in this section are also applied to literas.

If you want a sleeper, you have half a dozen choices, ranging from shared cabins to luxury singles. Prices vary according to your choice and the distance you travel.

Timetables & Reservations

Train timetables are posted at most stations. *Llegadas* (arrivals) tend to be listed on white posters and *salidas* (departures) on yellow ones. Often separate information on specific lines is also posted or you can ask at the *taquillas* (ticket windows). Timetables for cercanías are generally posted separately, and in some cases (eg, at Madrid's Atocha station) the same goes for all regional services. Atocha presumably is served by so many trains that it has become impractical to post a comprehensive timetable. This makes getting a global picture of your options rather tricky.

Leaflets with timetables for specific lines are generally available free of charge at stations, but Renfe does not sell a comprehensive rail guide.

On most trains you will never need to book in advance, but if you want to be sure of a place, it may nevertheless be wise to do so. Bookings can be made at stations and Renfe offices and through many travel agencies. There is usually no booking fee applicable unless you have the ticket(s) mailed to you. Also, people with Eurail or InterRail passes will be charged between 500 and 1500 ptas to reserve a seat, depending on the service.

You can make bookings for trains online at www.renfe.es.

Passes

Apart from the international passes described in the Getting There & Away chapter, several passes are available in Spain.

With the Euro<26, GO25 or ISIC student card you can get reductions on rail tickets (see Costs & Discounts later in this section), or you can buy an ExploreRail card. This allows the holder unlimited travel on 2nd-class trains across Spain, except the AVE and Euromed. You can also upgrade to 1st class by paying the difference. It is valid for seven, 15 or 30 days, and costs 19,000/23,000/30,000 ptas, respectively – a bargain for anyone contemplating serious rail travel in Spain. You can include cercanías trains by paying 22,000/28,000/37,000 ptas, respectively. It's sold by authorised travel agencies, including Usit Unlimited (☎ 902 32 52 75); its Web site is at www.unlimited.es.

The Tarjeta Dorada is a senior citizens' pass issued by Renfe for 500 ptas. The kind of rail discounts available are outlined later.

You must be over 60 and a resident in Spain. The card entitles you to a 25% discount on rail fares Friday to Sunday and up to 40% off during the week.

Renfe also issues a Tarjeta Turística, also known as a Spain Flexipass. It is for non-European residents and is valid for three to 10 days' travel in a two-month period on all Spanish trains. In 2nd class, a three/10-day pass costs US$155/365. A 1500 ptas supplement has to be paid in *turista* class on AVE and Talgo 200 trains but there's a 20% discount on Algeciras-Tangier ferries. The Flexipass is sold by travel agencies outside Europe and at a few main stations and Renfe offices in Spain.

Costs & Discounts

The variety of possible fares is even more astounding than the number of train types. All fares quoted should be considered a rough sample of basic 2nd-class fares on the diurnos and estrellas (the cheapest fares).

Cercanías have one fare (unless you get a season pass for a particular line). On regionales and some of the faster long-distance trains (diurnos and InterCitys) you have the easy choice of 2nd- or 1st-class seats (a regional exprés will generally cost a little more as you are paying for the privilege of arriving more quickly). The evening trains (estrellas) offer 1st- and 2nd-class seats, couchettes and in some cases *camas* (sleeping compartments) – see Couchettes & Sleepers earlier in this section. The ordinary Talgos are a faster and more comfortable version of the other long-distance services.

If you buy a return ticket you can get a 20% discount (25% if the return is on the same day). Children under four travel free, while those aged four to 11 get 40% off. Reductions are possible for holders of some youth passes, such as the Euro<26 card (also known as Carnet Joven in Spain), which allows a 20% discount.

On some major lines you can purchase multiple-trip Bonocity passes. These are four-journey passes (ie, two each way) valid for six months and *transferable,* offering a slight reduction over normal single fares.

An example is the Madrid-Zaragoza, which costs 8200 ptas. There are several other types of commuter pass along these lines.

Some typical one-way 2nd-class fares on diurno/estrella or regional trains (remember often there will be dearer and faster options) include:

from	to	travel time (hours)	fare (ptas)
Madrid	Barcelona	6½ to 9½	5100
	Granada	6 to 9½	3600
	León	4¼ to 5¼	3400
	Málaga	5 to 6¾	5000
	Salamanca	3¼	2100
	Santander	9	4100
	San Sebastián	6½ to 8¾	4600
	Valencia	5 to 5½	3000
	Zaragoza	3 to 3½	3000
Barcelona	Granada	12½	6400
	Pamplona	6½ to 10	4400
	San Sebastián	8¼ to 10	4600
	Zaragoza	3½ to 4½	2900
León	San Sebastián	5	3600
Bilbao	Zaragoza	4¾ to 5½	3100

Talgo 200 With the Talgo 200 (which operates from Madrid to Málaga, Cádiz and Algeciras) the story becomes more complex. There are two classes: *turista* and the more luxurious *preferente;* and two fare types for each class: *valle* and *llano.* The latter is the more expensive during busier times. The cheapest one-way fare from Madrid to Málaga is 6900 ptas. Finally, you need to see if any discounts apply. There is a discount of 20% for getting a return ticket and 25% if the return is on the same day. Holders of the Euro<26 and Tarjeta Dorada passes get a 25% discount Monday to Thursday; this rises to 30% for one-way trips and 40% for return tickets.

You can use the various recognised international rail passes, such as Eurail, Europass, Euro-Domino etc (for more information see the Getting There & Away chapter), on Talgo 200 trains. You pay a 1500 ptas supplement in turista class and 3500 ptas in preferente (if you have a 1st-class pass).

Finally, a multiple commuter ticket, the Abono 10, entitles you to 10 one-way trips between Madrid and Málaga (80,000 ptas in preferente; 55,000 ptas in turista) within a three-month period.

AVE The AVE is complicated further by the existence of a third, ultraluxury class *(club)* – to which the two fare bands also apply. The Madrid-Sevilla trip can be done in as little as 2¼ hours with no stops. The same discounts apply on return trips as for the Talgo 200, while holders of the Euro<26 card or Tarjeta Dorada pass get a fixed 25% off.

You have the right to request a full refund on your AVE ticket if you arrive at your destination more than five minutes' late. The cheapest one-way fare to Sevilla from Madrid is 8400 ptas.

Other Services The Barcelona-Valencia Euromed service also offers preferente and turista options, as do the new Arco and Alaris services.

Fines
If you board a train without a ticket, you are to some degree at the mercy of the inspector. You may simply be obliged to buy a full one-way ticket for your journey, but you could just as easily be told to cough up double. If you are in real trouble you will be forced off the train and be made liable to a fine of up to 85,000 ptas!

Other Railways
There are several other railway lines that operate, mostly in northern Spain. The Ferrocarriles de Vía Estrecha (FEVE) company runs trains on narrow-gauge track from O Ferrol in Galicia to Gijón and Oviedo in Asturias, and from there to Bilbao in the Basque Country via Santander in Cantabria.

The Eusko Trenbideak (ET/FV) line in the Basque Country complements Renfe services with lines serving northern towns and linking Bilbao, San Sebastián, Irún and Hendaye (France).

International rail passes *cannot* be used for free travel or discounts on any of these railway lines.

CAR & MOTORCYCLE
If bringing your own car, remember to have your insurance and other papers in order (see the Getting There & Away chapter).

Road Rules
In built-up areas the speed limit is 50km/h, which rises to 100km/h on major roads and up to 120km/h on *autovías* and *autopistas* (toll-free and tolled dual-lane highways, respectively). Cars towing caravans are restricted to a maximum speed of 80km/h. The minimum driving age is 18.

Motorcyclists must use headlights at all times and wear a crash helmet if riding a bike of 125cc or more. The minimum age for riding bikes and scooters of 80cc and over is 16 and for those 50cc and under is 14. A licence is required.

Spanish truck drivers often have the courtesy to turn on their right indicator to show that the way ahead of them is clear for overtaking (and the left one if it is not and you are attempting this manoeuvre).

Vehicles already in roundabouts have right of way.

The blood-alcohol limit is 0.05% (0.03% for drivers with less than two years' experience and professional drivers) and breath-testing is carried out on occasion. If fitted, rear seat belts must be worn. Fines for many traffic offences, including driving under the influence of alcohol, range from 50,000 to 100,000 ptas.

Nonresident foreigners can be fined up to 50,000 ptas on the spot – the minor compensation is that they get 20% off normal fines if they settle immediately. You can contest the fine in writing (and in English) within 10 days, but don't hold your breath for a favourable result.

Road Atlases
Several road atlases are available, including the *Mapa Oficial de Carreteras,* put out by the Ministry of Public Works, Transport & Environment for 2300 ptas. One of the best atlases on the market, and available in and outside Spain, is the *Michelin Motoring Atlas – Spain & Portugal.* In Spain it's called *Michelin Atlas de Carreteras y*

Turístico – España Portugal and costs 2590 ptas. It is for the most part faithfully accurate.

Both atlases include maps of all the main towns and cities. You can find them at most decent bookshops and some petrol stations in Spain.

Road Assistance

The Real Automóvil Club de España's head office (RACE; ☎ 900-20 00 93) is at Calle de José Abascal 10 in Madrid. For its 24-hour, countrywide emergency breakdown assistance you can try calling ☎ 91 593 33 33 in Madrid or ☎ 900-11 22 22 elsewhere around the country. As a rule, however, these numbers are for RACE members. Your own national motoring organisation, which like the RAC and AA may have a mutual agreement with the RACE, will generally provide you with a special emergency assistance number for use when in Spain.

City Driving & Parking

Driving in the bigger Spanish centres can be a nerve-racking experience at the start. Road rules and traffic lights are generally respected, but the pace and jostling take a little getting used to. The quietest time to drive in the cities is between about 2 and 5 pm, when most Spaniards are either eating or snoozing.

Parking can be difficult. Where possible, avoid leaving luggage and valuables in unattended vehicles. If you must leave luggage in vehicles, you should probably use paid car parks (around 200 ptas per hour). Most bigger cities operate a restricted parking system and, although many locals ignore the fines, you risk your car being towed away if you double-park or leave your vehicle in a designated no-parking zone. Recovering the vehicle can cost from 10,000 to 16,000 ptas.

Los Toros de Osborne

As you roam the highways of Spain, every now and then the silhouette of a truly gigantic black bull looms on the horizon ahead, looking your way. When you get closer to the creature, you realise it's only two-dimensional, made of metal and held up by scaffolding. But what's it for?

It's not a silent homage to bullfighting erected by the local folk, nor a sign that you're entering a notable bull-breeding area. It's a sherry and brandy advert for the Osborne company of El Puerto de Santa María, Andalucía. At the last count there were 93 *toros de Osborne*, each weighing 50 tonnes, standing beside roads all over the country. And over the years, they have raised almost as much dust as a champion fighting bull trying to stay alive on a hot Sunday afternoon.

Why doesn't Osborne put its name on the bulls if it wants to advertise, you might ask? From 1957, when the first bull was erected on the Madrid-Burgos road, until 1988, it did. Then a new law banned advertising hoardings beside main roads, to prevent drivers being distracted. Osborne left the bulls standing but removed its name, which seemed to pacify the authorities – until 1994, when word got around that the law was going to be enforced strictly, meaning no more bulls. This provoked an enormous furore, with intellectuals writing to the newspapers about the national heritage, the government of Andalucía declaring the 21 bulls in Andalucía protected monuments, and Osborne taking the fight to the courts. In 1997 Spain's supreme court decided that the bulls had transcended their original advertising purpose and were now part of the Spanish landscape.

DAMIEN SIMONIS

Tollways

Spain, fortunately, is not yet 'blessed' with too many autopistas (tollways), most of which are located in the north. Keep in mind if you are driving into Spain from France that the A-7 from the French border to Barcelona via Girona (Gerona), which continues south to Murcia, and the A-8 from Irún to Bilbao are both autopistas – and expensive. Some stretches along the autopista are toll-free.

You can pay tolls with cash or with many credit/debit cards, which you swipe in machines at the tollgate. The tolls are fairly hefty although in general they are coming down as part of a plan to align Spanish tolls with the European average. For example, Bilbao to Zaragoza costs 6780 ptas and the French border to Alicante is 7015 ptas.

Other autopistas include: the A-1 from Burgos to Miranda de Ebro (1125 ptas); the A-2, which connects the A-7 with Zaragoza (2425 ptas); the A-4 from Sevilla to Cádiz (1035 ptas); the A-6, a stretch of motorway along the Madrid route to La Coruña that starts at Villalba and cuts out in Adanero (1055 ptas); the A-9 that links La Coruña to Santiago de Compostela (580 ptas); the A-15 from Pamplona to Tudela (975 ptas); the A-19 from Barcelona to Palafolls (480 ptas); the A-66 from Oviedo to León (1420 ptas); and the A-8 from Bilbao to the French border (2100 ptas).

In some cases, autopistas can easily be avoided in favour of virtually parallel, and sometimes more scenic, highways. If you are intent on slipping them, keep an eye open for the magic word: *peaje* (toll). The downside is that these alternative roads are sometimes clogged with traffic.

Petrol

Gasolina in Spain is pricey, but generally cheaper than in its major EU neighbours (including France, Germany, Italy and the UK). About 30 companies, including several

Road Distances (Km)

	Alicante	Badajoz	Barcelona	Bilbao	Córdoba	Granada	La Coruña	León	Madrid	Málaga	Oviedo	Pamplona	San Sebastián	Sevilla	Toledo	Valencia	Valladolid	Zaragoza
Alicante	---																	
Badajoz	696	---																
Barcelona	515	1022	---															
Bilbao	817	649	620	---														
Córdoba	525	272	908	795	---													
Granada	353	438	868	829	166	---												
La Coruña	1031	772	1118	644	995	1043	---											
León	755	496	784	359	733	761	334	---										
Madrid	422	401	621	395	400	434	609	333	---									
Málaga	482	436	997	939	187	129	1153	877	544	---								
Oviedo	873	614	902	304	851	885	340	118	451	995	---							
Pamplona	673	755	437	159	807	841	738	404	407	951	463	---						
San Sebastián	766	768	529	119	869	903	763	433	469	13	423	92	---					
Sevilla	609	217	1046	933	138	256	947	671	538	219	789	945	1007	---				
Toledo	411	368	692	466	320	397	675	392	71	507	510	478	540	458	---			
Valencia	166	716	349	633	545	519	961	685	352	648	803	501	594	697	372	---		
Valladolid	615	414	663	280	578	627	455	134	193	737	252	325	354	589	258	545	---	
Zaragoza	498	726	296	324	725	759	833	488	325	869	604	175	268	863	396	326	367	---

foreign operators, run petrol stations in Spain, but the two biggest are the home-grown Repsol and Cepsa.

Prices vary (up to 4 ptas/L) between service stations (*gasolineras*) and fluctuate with oil tariffs and tax policy. Super (due to be phased out by January 2002 in accordance with EU policy) costs 149.9 ptas/L and diesel (or *gasóleo*) 113.9 ptas/L. Lead-free (*sin plomo;* 95 octane) costs 139.9 ptas/L and a 98 octane variant (also lead free) that goes by various names, up to 153.9 ptas/L.

Petrol is about 10% cheaper in Gibraltar than in Spain and 15% cheaper in Andorra. It's also cheap in Spain's tax-free enclaves of Ceuta and Melilla in North Africa.

You can pay with major credit cards at many service stations.

Rental

All major international car-rental companies are represented throughout Spain and there are some local operators too. Automatic cars are quite uncommon.

Car rental is generally expensive, and it is worth organising prebooked car rental before arriving in Spain, for example, as part of a fly-drive deal (see the UK section under Land in the Getting There & Away chapter).

If you do rent a car after arriving in Spain, shop around. You need to be at least 21 years' old and have held a driving licence for a minimum of two years. It is easier, and obligatory with some companies, to pay with a credit card.

Standard rates with the bigger firms can hover around 8000 to 9000 ptas per day for a small car, with unlimited kilometres. This can come down to around 5200 ptas per day if you rent for a week. On top of this you need to calculate 1900 ptas per day in collision damage waiver, as well as 950 ptas per day in theft and third-party insurance. Add a further 16% IVA and you have the total daily cost.

Local firms such as Julià Car are generally cheaper than the big international names. From these, a typical small car like a Ford Ka or Fiat Punto, with minimum compulsory insurance, should cost around 2800 ptas per day plus 25 ptas per kilo-metre, plus IVA. For unlimited kilo-metres, the cost is around 18,000 ptas for three days or 35,000 ptas a week, plus IVA. You pay collision damage waiver and third-party insurance on top, which can come to around 1500 ptas per day.

In the coastal areas most frequented by foreign tourists – basically, that means at Málaga airport, the Costa del Sol, Nerja and the Almería resorts – you can usually pick up a small car from a local car-rental agency for 16,000 to 20,000 ptas a week all inclusive, depending on the season. Car rental in the Balearic Islands is also markedly cheaper than on the mainland.

Renting motorcycles and mopeds on the mainland is expensive and outlets are few and far between. In the Balearic Islands it's a different story, where a small motor scooter can cost as little as 1300 ptas per day.

Warning Several travellers have reported theft from their cars when parked at roadside restaurants and the like. Rental cars and cars with foreign number plates are targeted. When you do call in at highway rest stops, try to park close to the buildings and leave nothing of value in view.

Purchase

Only people legally resident in Spain may buy vehicles there. One way around this is to have a friend who is a resident put the ownership papers in their name.

Car-hunters need a reasonable knowledge of Spanish to get through paperwork and understand dealers' patter. Trawling around showrooms or looking through classifieds can turn up second-hand Seats (eg, Ibiza) and Renaults (4 or 5) in good condition starting at around 300,000 ptas. The annual cost of third-party insurance, with theft and fire cover and national breakdown assistance, comes in at between 40,000 and 50,000 ptas.

Vehicles of five years and older must be submitted for a roadworthy check, known as Inspección Técnica de Vehículos (ITV). If the vehicle passes, you get a sticker for two years. Ensure that this check has been done when buying: the test costs about 4000 ptas.

You can get your hands on second-hand 50cc *motos* (scooters) for anything from 40,000 to 100,000 ptas.

BICYCLE

Bicycle rental is not too common in Spain, although it is more so in the case of mountain bikes *(bici todo terreno)* and in some of the more popular regions such as Andalucía. If you plan to bring your own bike, check with the airline about any hidden costs. It will usually have to be disassembled and packed for the journey.

You should travel light on a bike tour, but bring tools and some spare parts, including a puncture repair kit and a spare inner tube. Panniers are essential to balance your possessions on either side of the bike frame. A bike helmet is a good idea, as are a solid bike lock and chain to prevent theft.

One organisation that can help you plan your bike tour is the Cyclists' Touring Club (CTC; ☎ 01483-417217), Cotterell House, 69 Meadrow, Godalming, Surrey GU7 3HS, UK. It can supply information to members on cycling conditions, itineraries and cheap insurance. A yearly membership costs UK£25 or UK£15 for people aged under 26.

If you get tired of pedalling it is often possible to take your bike on the train. You have to be travelling overnight in a sleeper or couchette to have the (dismantled) bike accepted as normal luggage. Otherwise, it can only be sent separately as a parcel. Some regional trains have space for bicycles, others don't, so ask before buying tickets. Bikes are permitted on most cercanías trains. It's often possible to take your bike on a bus – usually you'll just be asked to remove the front wheel.

The European Bike Express is a bus service that enables cyclists to travel with their machines. It runs in summer (April to October) from north-eastern England to Spain, with pick-up/drop-off points en route. The one-way/return fare is UK£99/169 (UK£159 return for CTC members); for information call ☎ 01642-251440 in England. For one or two hints on mountain biking in Spain, see under Activities in the Facts for the Visitor chapter.

Books

If you read Spanish, you may find some of the locally produced cycling guides of use. There are many to choose from.

Libros Penthalon publishes a series of cycling and walking books on many areas called the *Colección El Búho Viajero*. The books generally come with maps and route planning tips that shouldn't require too deep a knowledge of the language.

HITCHING

Hitching is never entirely safe and we don't recommend it. Travellers who decide to hitch should understand that they are taking a small but potentially serious risk. You'll also need plenty of patience and common sense. Women should avoid hitching alone, and even men should consider the safer alternative of hitching in pairs.

Hitching is illegal on autopistas and autovías, and difficult on major highways. You can try to pick up lifts before the toll-booths on autopistas. Otherwise, you need to choose a spot where cars can safely stop before highway slipways, or use minor roads. The going can be slow on the latter, as the traffic is often light. On the plus side, vehicles can stop easily and their drivers may be more inclined to do so than those screaming up and down the fast lanes. Overall, Spain is *not* a hitchhiker's paradise. Veterans of the road have particular trouble in the south, where drivers seem most suspicious.

BOAT

Ferries and hydrofoils link the mainland ('La Península' to Spaniards) with the Balearic Islands and with Spain's North African enclaves of Ceuta and Melilla. For details, see the Sea section in the Getting There & Away chapter and the appropriate Getting There & Away sections throughout this book.

LOCAL TRANSPORT

In most Spanish cities you will not need to use the local public transport much, as accommodation, attractions and mainline bus and train stations are generally within fairly comfortable walking distance. Where this is not the case, local buses connect bus and train stations with city centres.

Bus

The bus networks in larger cities can be complicated and, with some exceptions, are probably best avoided. In Madrid and Barcelona the underground rail systems are an easier option and in most other cities you can cover most of the ground on foot.

Metro

Known as *el metro*, Madrid's and Barcelona's extensive underground rail networks make getting around easy if your feet are protesting. Bilbao also has a metro system.

Taxi

By European standards, taxis are fairly cheap. Flag fall and fares vary between cities, and

you pay extra for luggage and airport pick-up. For more details, see the relevant city Getting Around sections throughout this book.

ORGANISED TOURS

If you want to travel around Spain in an organised tour, arrange it through travel agencies in your own country (see the Getting There & Away chapter).

Guided coach tours can be organised in Spain. Pullmantur (Madrid Map 4), which operates through local travel agencies, offers organised tours ranging from two days in Toledo (from Madrid) to 12-day trips through Andalucía and Morocco or 14-day journeys through Andalucía, Portugal and Galicia.

Guided tours of the major cities are an option but, with a few exceptions, not especially good value.

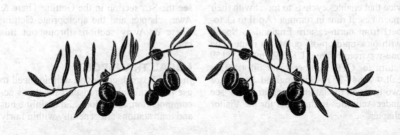

Madrid

postcode 20080 • pop 3.1 million

There is little point in portraying Madrid as something it is not. It is not one of Europe's awe-inspiringly beautiful cities. It is not even particularly old and much of what may have constituted its historical legacy has over the centuries been all too quickly sacrificed to make way for the new. Madrid is a modern city, a product largely of the 19th and 20th centuries, and the expanses of its outer dormitory suburbs and peripheral high-rise apartment jungles are an oppressive introduction for anyone driving in for the first time.

Seen from the air, this city of more than three million (the surrounding region, known as Comunidad de Madrid, counts a further two million) appears to rise out of nothing upon an unforgivingly dry plateau. Madrid may lack the historical richness and sophistication of Rome or Paris and, moving closer to home, the physical beauty of Barcelona, but it oozes a life and character that, given the opportunity to work its magic (it doesn't take long), cannot leave you indifferent.

Leaving aside the art galleries, the splendour of the Plaza Mayor and Palacio Real, and the elegance of the Parque del Buen Retiro, the essence of Madrid is in the life pulsing through its streets. In no other European capital will you find the city centre so thronged so late into the night as here, especially on weekends. Everyone seems to stay out late, as though some unwritten law forbade sleeping before dawn. In this sense it is a city more to be lived than seen. This can work out fine, as Madrid also happens to make an ideal base for plenty of day trips. Toledo, Segovia, El Escorial, Ávila, Aranjuez and the Sierra de Guadarrama – just to name a few – are all within easy striking distance.

HISTORY

Few historians place much credence in claims that a Roman settlement called Mantua (not to be confused with the Italian version) once stood on the banks of the Río

Highlights

- *Churros y chocolate* at Chocolatería San Ginés after a night (and early morning) out in the bars of Santa Ana & Huertas
- Bargain-hunting in El Rastro flea market
- A Sunday morning stroll in the Parque del Buen Retiro
- Sipping summertime *cañas* and enjoying the magnificent views to the Sierra de Guadarrama at Las Vistillas
- The big three art galleries: the Prado, the Reina Sofía and the Thyssen-Bornemisza
- A chicken-and-cider lunch at Casa Mingo
- Relaxing over a coffee and paper on Plaza Mayor

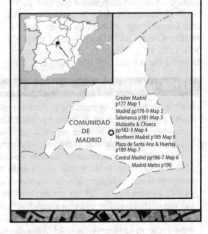

Greater Madrid p177 Map 1
Madrid pp178-9 Map 2
Salamanca p181 Map 3
COMUNIDAD DE MADRID Malasaña & Chueca pp182-3 Map 4
Northern Madrid p185 Map 5
Plaza de Santa Ana & Huertas p189 Map 7
Central Madrid pp186-7 Map 6
Madrid Metro p190

Manzanares. The first concrete references to Madrid emerge around the 10th century. Then it was the Muslim centre of Magerit, ceded to Alfonso VI in 1085. Surrounded by cities of far greater importance, such as Toledo, Segovia and Valladolid, Madrid was little more than a fortified village when Felipe II decided in 1561 to make it the permanent capital of the Spanish empire. The monarch conceived the city, then dominated by a stout *alcázar,* or Muslim-era fortress, as the future administrative centre, the hub from which the spokes of power would reach out to the farthest corners of the empire. He was driven by another consideration. Toledo was a more obvious choice for the capital, but its role as seat of the Church in Spain was incentive enough for Spain's temporal ruler to seek less claustrophobic lodgings.

Valladolid briefly assumed the role of capital in 1601, but the aberration lasted only five years. Madrid attracted not only civil servants: writers such as Cervantes, Lope de Vega and Calderón all lived and worked here through the 17th century.

The arrival of Carlos III in the 18th century was good news for noses (he himself was blessed with an impressive honker). He not only cleaned up the city (it had a reputation for being among the filthiest in Europe), but also completed the new Palacio Real, inaugurated the botanical gardens and carried out numerous other public works. Known as 'Madrid's best mayor', he was an enlightened ruler who did much to foster the intellectual life of the city. But

he ran into trouble when his unpopular Italian minister, Squillace, declared long capes illegal in an attempt to reduce crime. Squillace argued that, since the street cleaning had been improved, the capes were no longer necessary for keeping muck off other garments. The *madrileños* would have none of it and after long riots the measure was repealed.

Calamity befell Madrid with invasion by Napoleon. On 2 May 1808, a motley band of madrileños rose up in vain against the occupation, which lasted, with some interruptions, until May 1813.

As Joseph Bonaparte marched out, Fernando VII waltzed back in, marking the restoration of the Bourbon family to the throne. But the country's problems were far from over. The turbulence of the Carlist wars followed and political uncertainty remained the rule well into the 20th century. In 1931 the Second Republic was proclaimed in Madrid. Franco's troops first attempted, and failed, to take Madrid in 1936. The subsequent siege and slow, grinding advance of his Nationalist forces lasted until the civil war ended in 1939.

Pablo Iglesias & the Birth of Spanish Socialism

Madrid, for hundreds of years the political nerve centre of Spain and its one-time empire, has produced surprisingly few of its leading political figures. Kings and queens were almost always from somewhere else and, in more recent times, Franco came from Galicia, while the long-running Socialist prime minister until 1996, Felipe González, is from Andalucía.

The founder of González' party, however, was a local boy. Well, almost. Born in Franco's home town of O Ferrol in 1850, Pablo Iglesias was brought to Madrid in his infancy and there he remained. A printer by trade, he began trade-union activities at the age of 20. One year later he got a workers' paper, *La Emancipación*, off the ground. With the rise of Marxist ideas across Europe, in 1879 Iglesias was elected president of a new association that constituted Spain's first clandestine workers' party.

Two years later, the Partido Socialista Obrero Español (PSOE; Spanish Socialist Workers' Party) went public. Its advances were rapid. Within seven years it had branches across the country and Iglesias was running its mouthpiece, *El Socialista*. The Unión General de Trabajadores (UGT; General Workers' Union) was organised thereafter, with strong PSOE influence. By the turn of the century, Socialist MPs were winning seats in local government.

Iglesias himself was elected several times to the Cortes, or national parliament, from 1910 to 1916. By then ailing and increasingly shy of the limelight, Iglesias had become a working-class myth. Even in the wake of the general strike called in 1917 by the UGT, which was suppressed without any ceremony, Iglesias was left in peace. He remained president of the PSOE and UGT, albeit in a largely honorary fashion, until his death in 1925.

ORIENTATION

One of the most striking aspects of Madrid's layout is the absence of water. The pathetic dribble that constitutes the Río Manzanares doesn't flow through the city centre like the Thames, Seine or Tiber. Indeed, it barely flows at all and most visitors to Madrid leave blissfully unaware of the Manzanares' existence.

Madrid is also surprisingly compact. The main north-south artery, Paseo de la Castellana (which becomes Paseo de los Recoletos and Paseo del Prado at its southern end), lies in a shallow depression and connects the city's two main train stations, Chamartín and Atocha.

The area around the southern portion of this promenade captures the interest of out-of-towners. The core of the city's oldest quarters is squeezed in between Paseo del Prado in the east and the Palacio Real to the west. Roughly halfway between them is the Puerta del Sol, once a city gate but long since the point from which distances to all corners of the country are measured.

The majestic Plaza Mayor lies a short stroll west of the Puerta del Sol, surrounded by a warren of captivating back streets. South-east of Sol, the old *barrios* are a happening, dynamic mix of seemingly endless restaurants, bars and cafes.

The tangle of lanes spills southward into the equally fascinating working-class barrio of Lavapiés. In the heat of the long summer nights, families jostle with revellers for space in the streets in a voluble but good-natured competition to fill the air with an energy rarely wasted on sleep – except in the hot, languid afternoons of the siesta. Moving westward to the area around Calle de Toledo you enter a slightly more polished version of Lavapiés, La Latina. On the way northwards to the Palacio Real it in turn feeds into one of the oldest parts of the city, once known as the *morería*, or Moorish quarter, where the bulk of the town's Muslim populace lived after Madrid was taken by the Christians in 1085.

Madrid's great art galleries – the must-sees on everyone's list – are clustered about the Paseo del Prado. Not far from the gallery of the same name spreads out one of the city's green lungs, the elegant Parque del Buen Retiro ('El Retiro' for short). Once the preserve of royals and dandies, it now throws open its gates to all those in search of respite from the city's hectic atmosphere.

The densest concentrations of accommodation can be found in a couple of zones. The area around the Puerta del Sol and Plaza de Santa Ana is saturated with little *pensiones* and *hostales*. Similarly blessed are the barrios of Malasaña and Chueca, immediately north of Gran Vía.

Maps

The free maps at tourist offices are sufficient, but better ones are available for sale. The Michelin Madrid Map N 1042, which comes with a complete street directory and costs 880 ptas, is one of the best fold-out maps of the city.

If you want something more comprehensive, you have several choices. *Madrid,* published by Vía XXI Ediciones, costs 2950 ptas and is a good colour product with street index. Less complete but adequate for most people is the *Gui'a Urbana de Madrid* published by GeoPlaneta; it costs 1700 ptas.

A handy map that will fit into your back pocket is Neguri Editorial's *Plano y Guía de Madrid* (2200 ptas).

INFORMATION
Tourist Offices

The main tourist office (Oficina de Turismo; Map 6; ☎ 91 429 49 51) is at Calle del Duque de Medinaceli 2. It's open 9 am to 7 pm weekdays and 9 am to 1 pm Saturday. The office at Chamartín train station (Map 5; ☎ 91 315 99 76) is open 8 am to 8 pm weekdays and 8 am to 1 pm Saturday. The one at the Aeropuerto de Barajas (Barajas airport; ☎ 91 305 86 56) is on the ground floor in Terminal T1 and is open at the same hours.

Another tourist office (Map 6; ☎ 91 364 18 76), Ronda de Toledo 1, is in the Centro Comercial de la Puerta de Toledo. It's open 9 am to 7 pm weekdays and 9.30 am to 1.30 pm Saturday.

The Patronato Municipal de Turismo (Map 6; ☎ 91 588 29 06), Plaza Mayor 3, specialises in the city. It is open 10 am to 8 pm weekdays; 10 am to 2 pm and 3 to 8 pm Saturday and 10 am to 3 pm Sunday.

The city's general information line (dealing with everything from public transport to shows) is on ☎ 010. It operates 8.30 am to 9.30 pm weekdays. You can also try the Comunidad de Madrid's regional info line on ☎ 012.

Foreign Consulates

For foreign embassies and consulates in Madrid, see Embassies & Consulates in the Facts for the Visitor chapter.

Money

There is no shortage of banks across central Madrid; most have ATMs that accept a wide range of plastic. When changing cash or cheques, always ask about commission. This can vary from bank to bank, but not greatly.

Exchange booths abound. Don't be fooled by all the 'No Commission' signs: the exchange rates are often inferior to official bank rates. Some of these places act as agents for Western Union and MoneyGram. For more on how these work, see Money in the Facts for the Visitor chapter. MoneyGram has a booth on Plaza de España (Map 4), as well as at Atocha and Chamartín train stations (Maps 2 and 5, respectively).

American Express (Map 6; 24 hours 91 527 03 03, ☎ 900-99 44 26 for replacing lost travellers cheques) is at Plaza de las Cortes 2. It's open 9 am to 5.30 pm weekdays and 9 am to noon Saturday.

Post

The main post office (correos; Map 2) is in the ornate Palacio de Comunicaciones on Plaza de la Cibeles. Lista de correos (poste restante) is at windows 78–80. Take your passport with you. To send big parcels, head for Puerta N on the southern side of the post office on Calle de Montalban – they even offer a reasonably priced packing service. The office is open 8 am to 9.30 pm weekdays and 8.30 am to 2 pm Saturday.

The post office also has a public fax service, as do many shops and offices around the city; look for the 'Fax' signs.

Telephone

The main Telefónica office (locutorio; Map 4) at Gran Vía 30 is open 9.30 am to midnight daily. It has telephone cabins, telex services and phone directories for the whole country.

Private phone companies specialising in cut-rate overseas calls are beginning to appear in Madrid. One is Sol Telecom (Map 7), Puerta del Sol 6. It is open 8 am to 11 pm daily and claims to undercut Telefónica by up to 60%. Another is the VIC locutorio at Calle de los Reyes (Map 4; one of several branches), just off Plaza de España.

Email & Internet Access

It's taken a while, but Madrid seems to have discovered the Internet and embraced the cybercafe idea. Cafes and other outlets where you can get online have begun to sprout all over the place. Prices can vary quite dramatically, so shop around.

Aroba52 (Map 4; ☎ 91 758 13 90) Calle de los Reyes. This is one of a number of dirt cheap places around Plaza de España. It charges 300 ptas per hour on computers connected by ISDN line. Or you can buy 10 hours for 2500 ptas (to use when you want).

Cervecería El Alamo (Map 4) Calle del Alamo 7. Here you pay 300 ptas per hour. It's open until midnight (closed Sunday).

Connection Room (Map 2; ☎ 91 399 34 39) Calle de Cea Bermúdez 66. It's open 8 am to midnight daily. One hour online costs 700 ptas.

La Casa de Internet (Map 2; ☎ 91 446 55 41) Calle de Luchana 20. You pay 900 ptas per hour online (students 700 ptas). They also do international phone calls via Internet and will even sell you a computer if they can. It's open 10 am (4 pm on weekends) to midnight daily.

Nevada 2000 (Map 4; ☎ 91 531 15 13) Calle de los Reyes 7. This is a gaming parlour where you can go online for 300 ptas per hour.

Open Nautas (Map 4; ☎ 91 444 00 69) Calle de San Hermenegildo 4. This place is open seven days from 10 am (noon on weekends) to midnight. Going online costs 700 ptas per hour.

Xnet Café (Map 4; ☎ 91 594 09 99) Calle de San Bernardo 81. They have an original approach here. You buy a drink for 500 ptas and the staff will let you sit down for 45 minutes' Net time.

WWW2.Call.Home (Map 6; ☎ 91 354 01 04) Plaza Puerta de Moros 2. You can make cheap phone calls, send and receive faxes, muck around on Photoshop and so on. Oh, and you can go online for 500 ptas per hour. It's open daily until 11 pm (from 10 am weekdays, 11 am Saturday and noon Sunday).

Travel Agencies

Madrid is not the ideal place for bargain-basement flights. That said, it is possible to get reasonable deals to major destinations and in some cases – such as London – steals.

One agency with a reputation for getting the best available deals is Viajes Zeppelin (Map 4; ☎ 91 542 51 54), Plaza de Santo Domingo 2. Zeppelin also has offices at Calle de la Infanta Mercedes 62 (Map 5; ☎ 91 571 82 58) and Calle de la Hermosilla 92 (Map 2; ☎ 91 431 40 36).

One of the country's biggest agencies is Halcón. It is reliable and has 68 offices spread right across Madrid. Its national reservation number is ☎ 902-30 06 00.

Students and young people can try looking around several other agencies. Juventus Viajes (Map 4; ☎ 91 319 41 35), Calle de Fernando VI 9; and Cadimar Viajes (Map 4; ☎ 91 542 59 05), on the corner of Calle de San Leonardo de Dios and Plaza de España, are both worth a look.

Usit Unlimited (Map 4; ☎ 902-25 25 75) at Plaza de Callao 3 is a specialised youth and student travel agency.

Also if you are a student or are under 26, visit the youth travel office of TIVE (Map 2; ☎ 91 543 74 12) at Calle de Fernando El Católico 88. It's open 9 am to 1 pm weekdays.

Student & Youth Information

You can get information on youth and student affairs, youth cards for travel discounts and HI cards at the Centro Regional de Información y Documentación Juvenil (CRIDJ; Map 4; ☎ 91 580 42 42) at Gran Vía 10. It's open 9 am to 2 pm and 5 to 8 pm weekdays.

Gay & Lesbian Information

The Colectivo de Gais y Lesbianas de Madrid (Cogam; Map 4; ☎/fax 91 532 45 17) has an information office and social centre (Urania's Café) at Calle de Fuencarral 37. Its info line (☎ 91 523 00 70) is open 5 to 9 pm daily.

Fundación Triángulo (☎/fax 91 593 05 40), Calle de Eloy Gonzalo 25, is another source of information on gay issues.

Nexus (☎ 91 522 16 86) can help with AIDS counselling. For more information on AIDS, see Health in the Facts for the Visitor chapter.

The *Mapa Gaya de Madrid* lists gay bars, discos, saunas and other places of specific gay and lesbian interest in the city. You can pick up a copy in the Berkana bookshop (Map 4; ☎ 91 532 13 93) at Calle de Gravina 11, in Chueca.

Madrid's gay & lesbian pride march is held on the last Saturday in June.

Books, Periodicals & Bookshops

The whimsical reader might search out *Madrid – A Travellers' Companion,* edited by Hugh Thomas (author of *The Spanish Civil War*). Everyone from the Duke of Wellington to Hemingway has something to say in this delightful stroll through the city's life and history.

If you read Spanish, a comprehensive and limpid survey of the city's history is *Madrid – Historia de una Capital* by Santos Juliá, David Ringrose and Cristina Segura. Less of a tome is *Historia Breve de Madrid* by Fidel Revilla, Ramón Hidalgo and Rosalía Ramos.

The free monthly English-language *In Madrid* has local listings, articles on Madrid and other useful information. You can pick it up at various bars (especially Irish pubs and the like), restaurants and shops all over town as well as at several consulates, schools (such as International House) and occasionally at the tourist offices. Otherwise, call on ☎ 91 364 16 97 to find out where you can get it. Another handy publication is *The Broadsheet.*

La Casa del Libro (Map 4), Gran Vía 29-31, has a broad selection of books on all subjects and a respectable section with books in English, French and other languages.

For English-language books, try Librería Booksellers (Map 2), Calle de José Abascal 48. For French books, try Librería Henri Avellan (Map 2), Calle del Duque de Sesto 5.

Librería de Mujeres (Map 6), Calle de San Cristóbal 17, is a women's bookshop and well-known feminist meeting place.

On Cuesta de Claudio Moyano, along the southern edge of the botanical gardens, a row of 30-odd bookstalls bursts with a cornucopia of second-hand books, mostly in Spanish.

About the best shop in Madrid for trekking and walking literature and maps is La Tienda Verde (Map 5), Calle de Maudes 38. The owners have another shop at No 23 dedicated more to general travel and ecology.

Libraries

One of the most venerable old libraries in Madrid is in the Ateneo de Madrid (Map 7), Calle del Prado 21. It is worth poking your head in here just to admire the study rooms of another age and the hall lined with portraits of important personages – also of another age.

Otherwise, look for public libraries under Bibliotecas Públicas in the Páginas Amarillas (Yellow Pages). You could also try the various cultural centres or subject libraries at the Universidad Complutense.

Film & Photography

You can have film developed all over the city. Photo Express (Map 4) at Gran Vía 84, right on Plaza de España, is reliable.

A reputable place for camera repairs is Playmon (Map 2; ☎ 91 573 57 25), Calle de Jorge Juan 133.

For second-hand camera equipment of all sorts, head for Fotocasión (Map 6; ☎ 91 467 64 91), Calle de Carlos Arniches 22, near El Rastro.

Cultural Centres

If you're yearning for a whiff of home, you might consider wandering into one of the foreign cultural centres. They all have libraries and organise film nights and other activities.

France
  Institut Français (Map 3; ☎ 91 308 49 50)
  Calle del Marqués de la Ensenada 12
  Alliance Française (Map 3; ☎ 91 435 15 32)
  Calle de Velázquez 94

Germany
  Goethe Institut (Map 3; ☎ 91 391 39 44)
  Calle de Zurbarán 21
Italy
  Istituto Italiano di Cultura (Map 6; ☎ 91 547 52 04) Calle Mayor 86
UK
  British Council (Map 2; ☎ 91 337 35 00)
  Paseo del General Martínez Campos 31
USA
  Washington Irving Center (Map 3; ☎ 91 564 55 15) Paseo de la Castellana 52

Laundry

Well-placed coin-operated laundrettes in central Madrid include: Lavandería Alba (Map 4) on Calle del Barco 26; Lavomatique (Map 7) on Calle de Cervantes, open 9 am to 8 pm weekdays and 10 am to 2 pm Saturday (400 ptas to wash a load and 100 ptas to dry); Lavandería España (Map 7) on Calle del Infante.

Lost & Found

The Negociado de Objetos Perdidos (Map 2; ☎ 91 588 43 46), Plaza de Legazpi 7, is open 9 am to 2 pm. If you leave something in a taxi you need to call ☎ 91 588 43 44.

Medical Services

If you have medical problems pop into the nearest Insalud clinic – often marked 'Centro de Salud'. Make sure you have all your insurance details with you (including your E111 if you are an EU citizen). A handy clinic in the city centre is at Calle de las Navas de Tolosa 10 (Map 5).

If you don't have medical insurance or an E111, your best bet is to head to the Hospital General Gregorio Marañón (Map 2; ☎ 91 586 80 00), Calle del Doctor Esquerdo. In emergencies they will treat you regardless.

You can also get help at the Anglo-American Medical Unit (Map 2; ☎ 91 435 18 23), Calle del Conde de Aranda 1. Staff speak Spanish and English and the unit is open 9 am to 8 pm weekdays.

One 24-hour pharmacy is the Farmacia del Globo (Map 7; ☎ 91 369 20 00), Plaza de Antón Martín 46. Another is the Real Farmacia de la Reina Madre (Map 6; ☎ 91 548 00 14) at Calle Mayor 15.

Emergency

For an ambulance, call the Cruz Roja on
☎ 91 522 22 22 or ☎ 91 335 45 45; Insalud
on ☎ 061 or the general emergency number
☎ 112.

Apart from hospital casualty departments
(see Medical Services earlier), there are five
first-aid stations *(urgencias)* scattered
around Madrid to help with medical emergencies (open 24 hours). The handiest is
Centro (☎ 91 521 00 25), Calle de las Navas
de Tolosa 10 (see Medical Services earlier);
another such centre (open 8 am to 9 pm) is
Tetuán (Map 5; ☎ 91 588 66 69), Calle de
Bravo Murillo 357.

Dangers & Annoyances

Pickpockets are rife in the more touristy
parts of Madrid and on some metro lines,
and of course foreigners are the prime targets. The Lavapiés area can also be prob-
lematic. The usual precautions are required
(see Dangers & Annoyances in the Facts
for the Visitor chapter).

Parts of the Parque del Oeste are given
over to prostitution by night and not ideal
for a late-evening stroll. Paseo de Camoens
y Valero and Paseo de Ruperto Chapi are
where most of the tricks are done. The Casa
de Campo is also swarming with ladies of
the night, pimps and junkies. The area
around Calle de la Luna, near Gran Vía, is
similar.

WALKING TOUR

What follows aims to suggest a general
route through 'essential Madrid'. If you
plan to spend time in any of the monuments
and museums, or prefer simply meandering
at will and stopping in at the many enticing
bars and cafes, you will need several days
to do justice to such a circuit.

Unless you want to head for the big art
galleries first, the most fitting place to begin
exploring the city is the **Puerta del Sol**, the
official centre of Madrid.

Walk up Calle de Preciados and take the
second street on the left, which will bring
you out on to Plaza de las Descalzas. Look
at the **baroque doorway** in the Caja de
Madrid building – it was built for King

Felipe V in 1733 and faces the **Convento
de las Descalzas Reales**.

Moving south down Calle de San Martín
you come to the **Iglesia de San Ginés**, a
baroque church that stands on the site of
one of Madrid's oldest places of Christian
worship. Behind it is the wonderful **Chocolatería de San Ginés**, generally open 7 to 10
pm and 1 to 7 am.

Continue down to and cross Calle Mayor
and then walk onto Madrid's grandest
square, **Plaza Mayor**. After a coffee on the
square, head west along Calle Mayor until
you come to the historic **Plaza de la Villa**,
with Madrid's 17th-century *ayuntamiento*
(town hall). On the same square stand the
16th-century **Casa de Cisneros** and the
Gothic-*mudéjar* **Torre de los Lujanes**, one
of the city's oldest buildings, dating from
the Middle Ages.

Take the street down the left side of the
Casa de Cisneros, cross the road at the end,
go down the stairs and follow the cobbled
Calle del Cordón out onto Calle de Segovia.
Almost directly in front of you is the mudé-
jar tower of the **Iglesia de San Pedro el
Viejo**. Proceeding down Costanilla de San
Pedro you reach the **Iglesia de San Andrés**.

From here you cross Plaza de la Puerta de
Moros and head south-west to the **Basílica
de San Francisco el Grande**, or you can
head east past the market along Plaza de la
Cebada – once a popular spot for public
executions – to arrive at the Sunday flea
market of **El Rastro**. Otherwise, head west
into the tangle of lanes that forms what was
once the **morería** (Islamic quarter) and
emerge back on Calle de Bailén and the
wonderful **terrazas** (terraces) of Las Vistillas
– great for drinking in the views.

Follow the viaduct north to the **Catedral
de Nuestra Señora de la Almudena**, the
Palacio Real (Royal Palace) and Plaza de
Oriente, with its statues, fountains and
hedge mazes. The eastern side of the plaza
is closed off by the **Teatro Real**.

At its northern end, Calle de Bailén runs
into **Plaza de España**. Nearby, you could
visit the **Museo de Cerralbo**, the **Templo de
Debod** and, close to the Río Manzanares,
the **Ermita de San Antonio de Florida**,

which contains a masterpiece by Goya. If you were to continue north from the square, you would pass through the barrio de Argüelles, with some pleasant summer terrazas, and on towards the main centre of Madrid's Universidad Complutense.

The eastern flank of Plaza de España marks the beginning of **Gran Vía**. This Haussmannesque boulevard was slammed through the tumbledown slums north of Sol in the 1910s and 1920s.

At the eastern end of Gran Vía, note the superb dome of the **Metropolis** building. Continue east along Calle de Alcalá until you reach **Plaza de la Cibeles**, Madrid's favourite roundabout.

Head north (left) up the tree-lined promenade of Paseo de los Recoletos. On the left you'll pass some of the city's best-known cafes, including Gran Café de Gijón, Café-Restaurante El Espejo and El Gran Pabellón del Espejo. On your right is the enormous **Biblioteca Nacional** (National Library) and, a little farther on, a statue of Columbus in Plaza de Colón.

From here walk around the back of the National Library, where the **Museo Arqueológico Nacional** is housed. Southwards along Calle de Serrano (which is the backbone of Madrid's most chic shopping district) is Plaza de la Independencia, in the middle of which stands the **Puerta de Alcalá**.

Turn right, then left at Plaza de la Cibeles to head south down Paseo del Prado, an extension of the city's main tree-lined boulevard, and you'll soon reach the art gallery with which it shares its name. On the other side of the boulevard, the **Museo Thyssen-Bornemisza** is, along with the **Prado**, a must.

The area around and north of the Prado is laced with museums, while stretching out behind it to the east are the wonderful gardens of the **Parque del Buen Retiro**. Immediately south of the Prado is the **Real Jardín Botánico**. Looking onto the manic multilane roundabout that is Plaza del Emperador Carlos V are the city's main train station, **Atocha**, and the third in Madrid's big league of art galleries, the **Centro de Arte Reina Sofía**.

Head a few blocks north along Paseo del Prado again and west up Calle de las Huertas

(through the tiny Plaza de Platería Martínez). The 17th-century **Convento de las Trinitarias** (closed to the public), which backs onto this street, is where Cervantes lies buried. Turn right up Costanilla de las Trinitarias and continue along Calle de San Agustín until you come to Calle de Cervantes, then turn left. On your right you will pass the **Casa de Lope de Vega** at No 11.

A left turn at the end of Calle de Cervantes into Calle de León will bring you back onto Calle de las Huertas, which, you may have already noticed, is one of Madrid's happening streets. Anywhere along here or up on Plaza de Santa Ana will make a great place to take a load off at the end of this gruelling tour! For specific tips, consult the Entertainment section of this chapter. From Plaza de Santa Ana it's a brief stroll back to our starting point, the Puerta del Sol.

MUSEO DEL PRADO (MAP 2)

Built towards the end of the 18th century in the Prado (Meadow) de los Jerónimos, the Palacio de Villanueva was originally conceived as a house of science, incorporating a natural history museum and laboratories. Events overtook the noble enterprise and during the Napoleonic occupation the building was converted ignominiously into cavalry barracks. Under Fernando VII an art gallery finally opened then in 1819. Of the more than 7000 works in the Prado collection, fewer than half are on view at any given time.

Plans are afoot to expand the gallery by building a new section in the cloisters of the Iglesia de San Jerónimo El Real; this will be linked to the main building. Some of the collection may also end up in the Museo del Ejército, which appears destined to be transferred to Toledo.

One of the beauties of the collection is the generous coverage given to certain masters. Strings of rooms are devoted to the works of three of Spain's greatest – Velázquez, Goya and El Greco. These elements of the Prado's offerings are the cream, but there is plenty of good stuff by a range of Flemish and Italian painters, as well as artists of other nationalities. The Prado demands more than one visit.

Velázquez

Of this 17th-century master's works, *Las Meninas* is what most people come to see, and rightly so. Executed in 1656, it is more properly known as *La Familia de Felipe IV*. It depicts Velázquez himself on the left and, in the centre, the Infanta Margarita. There is more to it than that, though: the artist in fact portrays himself painting the king and queen, whose images appear, according to some experts, in mirrors behind Velázquez. His mastery of light and colour are never more apparent than here. It takes pride of place in Room 12, the focal point of the Velázquez collection on the 1st floor.

The bulk of Velázquez's works are in Rooms 12, 14, 15, 15A and 16. Among some of his outstanding portraits are *La Infanta Doña Margarita de Austria* (who stars in *Las Meninas*- and *Baltasar Carlos a Caballo*. *Cristo Crucificado* manages to convey the agony of the Crucifixion with great dignity. *La Rendición de Breda* (The Surrender of Breda) is another classic.

El Greco

Domenikos Theotokopoulos, Velázquez's senior by 58 years, is represented on the ground floor, in rooms 60A, 61A and 62A. The long, slender figures characteristic of this singular Cretan artist, who lived and worked in Toledo, are hard to mistake. Particularly striking are *La Crucifixión* and *San Andrés y San Francisco,* finished towards the end of the 16th century.

Goya

Francisco José de Goya y Lucientes is the most extensively represented of the Spanish masters in the Prado. Late to reach the heights of his grandeur, Goya, more than anyone, captured the extremes of hope and misery his country experienced before, during and after the Napoleonic invasion. In Room 89, on the 2nd floor, hang what are probably his best-known and most intriguing oils, *La Maja Vestida* and *La Maja Desnuda*. These portraits of an unknown woman (who may have been Goya's lover, the Duquesa de Alba), are identical save for the lack of clothing in the latter.

The horrors of war had a profound effect on Goya's view of the world. *El Dos de Mayo* and, still more dramatically, *El Tres de Mayo,* bring to life the 1808 anti-French revolt and subsequent execution of insurgents in Madrid. They're in Room 39.

The whole south wing of the 2nd floor is devoted to Goya and includes many of his preparatory paintings for tapestries, religious paintings and drawings. On the 1st floor, Rooms 32 and 34 to 39 contain more of his work, including his *Pinturas Negras* (Black Paintings). Among the most disturbing of these works is *Saturno Devorando a Su Hijo* (Saturn Devouring His Son).

Other Spanish Artists

In the shadow of these greats comes a small contingent of important artists and a gaggle of minor ones. Of the former there are substantial collections of work by Bartolomé Esteban Murillo, José de Ribera (they dominate Rooms 25 to 29 on the 1st floor), Francisco de Zurbarán (Room 18A, 1st floor) and Alonso Cano (Room 17A).

Flemish Artists

The 17th-century works are the backbone of the collection and, while for most visitors the Spanish contribution is paramount, there is a wealth of Flemish art.

The pick of the work of Hieronymus Bosch (c.1450–1516) lives in Room 56A on the ground floor. While *The Garden of Earthly Delights* is no doubt the star attraction of this fantastical painter's collection, all reward inspection. The closer you look, the harder it is to escape the feeling that he must have been doing some extraordinary drugs.

Peter Paul Rubens (1577–1640) gets a big run here. His works are concentrated mainly in Rooms 9 and 11 on the first floor).

Italian Artists

The Italians haven't been left out either. They occupy Rooms 49, 56B, 60, 61, 61B, 62, 62B, 63, 63B and 75, on the ground floor. Included are Sandro Botticelli (1445–1510), Andrea Mantegna (1431–1506), Raphael (1483– 1520), Tintoretto (1518–94) and, especially, Titian (Tiziano Vecelli; 1487– 1576).

Elsewhere (in Rooms 4 to 6 on the first floor) there are some works by Tiepolo (1692–1770) and Caravaggio (1571–1610).

Dutch & German Artists

Apart from a Rembrandt (Holland) and a few samples of Dürer and Carlos III's court painter, Anton Rafael Mengs (1728–79), there is not much to speak of from the Protestant strongholds of Germany and independent Holland.

French Artists

A small collection of paintings from Spain's eternal enemy, France, huddles together in Rooms 2 to 4 on the first floor. Artists include Nicolas Poussin (1594–1665), Jean-Antoine Watteau (1684–1721) and Louis Michel Van Loo (1707–71).

Casón del Buen Retiro (Map 2)

A short walk east of the Prado, the one-time ballroom of the now nonexistent Palacio del Buen Retiro is home to a selection of lesser-known 19th-century works. Artists include Joaquín Sorolla, Aureliano de Beruete and Vicente López. The latter's portrait of Goya hangs here. The facility was closed at the time of writing for major refurbishment as part of the grand plans for the Prado.

Entry

The Prado is open 9 am to 7 pm Tuesday to Saturday. On Sunday and holidays it closes at 2 pm. You can enter the Prado by either the northern Puerta de Goya or the southern Puerta de Murillo. The latter leads you into the ground floor, while you can access the ground and first floors from the former.

One ticket covers the Prado and Casón del Buen Retiro (500 ptas, students half-price). Entry is free on Sunday and Saturday afternoon (from 2.30 to 7 pm), as well as on selected national holidays. It is also free anytime for those under 18 and over 65. For other possible tickets, see the boxed text 'Museum & Gallery Entry' in this chapter.

Guides & Information

There is little free printed information. The hand-out map guides you to the main schools and major artists. Otherwise, attractive little booklets in several languages can be extracted from machines placed in a couple of the rooms. You'll find one on Goya in the rooms devoted to Goya on the second floor. Another on Bosch and Flemish painting is available in the room dedicated to Bosch. They cost 200 ptas.

MUSEO THYSSEN-BORNEMISZA (MAP 6)

This is one of the most wide-ranging private collections of mostly European art in the world. It has been accumulated over two generations by the Thyssen-Bornemiszas, a family of German-Hungarian magnates. Spain managed to acquire the prestigious collection when it offered to overhaul the neoclassical Palacio de Villahermosa specifically to house most of it. Almost 800 works have hung here since 1992, with a further 80 at the Monestir de Pedralbes (Barcelona). The museum is at Paseo del Prado 8. Plans are afoot to expand the permanent collection by another 300 to 400 works.

The exhibition is spread out over three floors, starting from the top (second) floor, where you begin with 13th- and 14th-century religious art, and work your way downstairs to the avant-garde and pop art on the ground floor.

Second Floor

The first three rooms are dedicated to medieval art, with a series of remarkable triptychs and paintings (predominantly Italian and Flemish) to get the ball rolling. They include some by Duccio di Buoninsegna (c.1255–1318), who led the Sienese school into a gentle break from Byzantine forms in the late 13th and early 14th centuries.

Room 5 contains, among others, some works by Italy's Piero della Francesca (1410–92) and a *Henry VIII* by Holbein the Younger (1497–1543). Room 6 (the long Galería Villahermosa) hosts among others a sampling of Italian masters such as Raphael, Lorenzo Lotto (c.1480–1556) and Tintoretto (1518–94).

In Room 7 are some exemplary works by the brothers Gentile (1429–1507) and

Museum & Gallery Entry

You can take advantage of several options to reduce the cost of entry to Madrid's museums and galleries. In the case of the three big art galleries – the Prado (standard entry charge 500 ptas), Centro de Arte Reina Sofía (500 ptas) and Museo Thyssen-Bornemisza (700 ptas), you can get a Paseo del Arte ticket for 1275 ptas for all three, valid year round.

Better still for one-off visitors, entry to the first two is free on Saturday afternoon (from 2.30 pm) and Sunday. People under 18 or over 65 get into the Prado free any time. Students and seniors over 65 pay 400 ptas for the Thyssen-Bornemisza, and children under 12 get in free.

A year's ticket for unlimited visits to either the Prado or the Reina Sofía costs 4000 ptas. A yearly ticket to both and a series of nine other museums throughout the country is 6000 ptas.

Many other galleries, museums and other sights have free entry at least one day a week. In a few cases this is restricted to EU citizens, but others may be able to sneak through too. Saturday afternoon, Sunday and Wednesday are the most common free times.

Most, but not all, museums and monuments close on Monday. Just about everything is closed on Sunday afternoon. In July and August some close parts of their displays for want of staff, most of whom take annual leave around this time. A few minor museums even close entirely through August.

Giovanni Bellini (1430–1516), who together with their father, Jacopo (1400–70), launched the Venetian Renaissance in painting. Rooms 8, 9 and 10 are given over to German and Dutch 16th-century masters. Among them are a few works by Cranach (1472–1553).

Room 11 is dedicated to El Greco (with four pieces) and Venetian contemporaries Tintoretto, Titian and Jacopo Bassano (1517–92).

Caravaggio and José de Ribera (Lo Spagnoletto), who was much influenced by the former, dominate the next room. Look out for the fine views of Venice by Canaletto (1697–1768), accompanied by some of the best works of Francesco Guardi (1712–93), in Room 17. Rubens leads the way in the last rooms on this floor, which are devoted to 17th-century Dutch and Flemish masters.

First Floor

The Dutch theme continues on the next floor, with interiors and landscapes. They are followed by Room 27, which is devoted to a still-life series; and in Room 28 you'll find a Gainsborough (1727–88) – one of the few British works in the collection. Next comes a representative look at North American art of the 19th century, including pieces by John Singer Sargent (1856–1925) and James Whistler (1834–1903).

All the great impressionist and postimpressionist names get a mention in Rooms 32 and 33, with works by Pissarro, Renoir, Degas, Monet, Manet, Toulouse-Lautrec, Cézanne, Gauguin and Van Gogh. The rest of the floor is dedicated to various movements in expressionist painting. In Room 35 you'll find canvases by Egon Schiele, Henri Matisse, Edvard Munch and Oskar Kokoschka.

Ground Floor

Here you move into the 20th century, from cubism through to pop art. In Room 41, you'll see a nice mix of Picasso, Juan Gris and Georges Braque. More Picasso beyond cubism follows in Room 45, accompanied by works of Marc Chagall, Max Ernst, Vasily Kandinsky and Joan Miró. In Room 46 the leap is made back across the Atlantic, with Jackson Pollock and Willem de Kooning (a Dutchman who moved to the USA in 1926) the stars. Lucien Freud (Sigmund's grandson and Berlin-born), David Hockney and Roy Lichtenstein all get a mention in Rooms 47 and 48.

Entry

The gallery is open 10 am to 7 pm Tuesday to Sunday. Entry is 700 ptas, students and seniors (over 65) 400 ptas, and children aged 12 and under get in free. Separate temporary exhibitions generally cost more, generally 500 ptas (students and seniors 300 ptas).

CENTRO DE ARTE REINA SOFÍA (MAP 6)

Adapted from the remains of an 18th-century hospital, the Centro de Arte Reina Sofía, Calle de Santa Isabel 52, is home to the best Madrid has to offer in modern art, principally spanning the beginning of the 20th century into the 1980s.

Organisation of the permanent collections on show has been greatly improved and expanded over the past couple of years. The permanent collection is on the first floor (Rooms 1 to 17) and top floor (Rooms 18 to 45). The ground floor houses a cafe, an excellent art bookshop and temporary exhibition space. There is also exhibition space on the 2nd floor.

For most visitors the big lure is Picasso's *Guernica*. Don't just rush straight for it, though, as there's plenty of other good material.

The first three rooms take you from Catalan modernisme and other turn-of-the-century work through to the 1920s. Room 4 is dedicated to Juan Gris' cubism and Room 5 to the bronze sculptures of Pablo Gargallo.

Guernica fully dominates the long hall that is Room 6, surrounded by a plethora of preparatory sketches. Already associated with the Republicans when the civil war broke out in 1936, Picasso was commissioned by Madrid to do the painting for the Paris Exposition Universelle in 1937. Picasso incorporated features of others of his works into this, an eloquent condemnation of the horrors of war – more precisely, of the German bombing of Gernika (Guernica), in the Basque Country, in April of the same year. It has been surrounded by controversy from the beginning and was at the time viewed by many as a work more of propaganda than of art. The 3.5m by 7.8m painting subsequently migrated to the USA and only returned to Spain in 1981, to languish in the Casón del Buen Retiro until its transfer to the Reina Sofía. Calls to have it moved to the Basque Country continue unabated.

Joan Miró takes up a parallel corridor (Room 7) to the Picasso collection. Some 20 canvases by Dalí hang in Room 10, including a portrait of the film maker Luis Buñuel (1924) and the surrealist extravaganza *El Gran Masturbador* (1929). The remaining rooms on the 1st floor are given over to a broad range of mostly Spanish artists up until the 1940s.

The top-floor collection takes up the baton and continues until the 1980s. Among notable names are Antoni Tàpies, Eduardo Arroyo, Eduardo Chillida, Fernando Zóbel and Eusebio Sempere. A sprinkling of non-Spaniards (usually no more than one item apiece) can also be seen, including a Kandinsky (Room 9), Francis Bacon and Henry Moore (both Room 24).

Entry

The gallery is open 10 am to 9 pm Monday to Saturday (except Tuesday, when it is closed) and 10 am to 2.30 pm Sunday (500 ptas; students half-price). Entry is free for pensioners, and for everyone else on Saturday from 2.30 pm and all Sunday.

HABSBURG MADRID

Spain under Carlos I and Felipe II reached the apogee of imperial greatness, its possessions spreading from Vienna to the Low Countries, from Sevilla to the Americas. Felipe's immediate Habsburg successors were largely responsible for expressing that glory in the centre of Madrid.

Puerta del Sol (Map 7)

Once the site of a city gate, the Puerta del Sol is Madrid's most central point. On the southern side a small plaque marks 'Km 0', from where distances along the country's highways are measured.

The semicircular junction owes its present appearance in part to the Bourbon king Carlos III, whose statue (the nose is unmistakable) stands proudly in the middle. Just to the north of Carlos, the statue of a bear nuzzling a *madroño* (strawberry tree, so-called because its fruit looks something like a strawberry) is not only the city's symbol but also a favourite meeting place for locals, as is the clock tower on the southern side. On New Year's Eve, people thronging the square wait impatiently for the clock to strike 12, and at each gong swallow a grape.

Plaza Mayor (Map 6)

The heart of imperial Madrid beats in the 17th-century Plaza Mayor, a stroll west of Puerta del Sol. Designed in 1619 and built in Herrerian style, of which the slate spires are the most obvious expression, it was long a popular stage for royal festivities and *autos de fe*.

On a sunny day the plaza's cafes do a roaring trade, with some 500 busy tables groaning under the weight of the rather expensive drinks. In the middle stands an equestrian statue of Felipe III, who ordered construction of the square. The colourful frescoes on the **Real Casa de la Panadería**, so-called for the royal bakery built here at the same time as the square in 1619 (although the present building was done in 1673 after a fire), were painted in 1992.

JANE SMITH
Madrid's coat of arms features a brown bear hugging a *madroño* tree.

South of the square, Calle de Toledo is no longer the main road to Madrid's one-time competitor for the title of national capital. It's an interesting boulevard though and you might want to have a quick look at the **Basílica de San Isidro**, long the city's principal church until Nuestra Señora de la Almudena was completed. The Instituto de San Isidro next door once went by the name of Colegio Imperial, where, from the 16th century, many of the country's leading figures were schooled.

Iglesia de San Ginés (Map 6)

Between Calle Mayor and Calle del Arenal, north of Plaza Mayor, San Ginés is one of Madrid's oldest churches: it's been here in one form or another since at least the 14th century. It houses some fine paintings, including an El Greco, but is only open for services.

Plaza de la Villa (Map 6)

Back on Calle Mayor and heading west, you pass the central market in Plaza de San Miguel before entering Plaza de la Villa.

The 17th-century **ayuntamiento** on the western side of the square is a typical Habsburg edifice in the Madrid baroque style and with Herrerian slate-tile spires. Tending more to the Gothic on the opposite side of the square is the **Casa de los Lujanes**, whose brickwork tower is said to have been 'home' to the imprisoned French monarch François I after his capture in the Battle of Pavia. The **Casa de Cisneros**, built in 1537 by the cardinal's nephew, is plateresque in inspiration. A block south is the 18th-century baroque remake of the **Iglesia del Sacramento**. Along Calle Mayor as you approach Calle de Bailén looms the Renaissance **Palacio del Duque de Uceda**, identifiable by the soldiers milling around outside, as it is now used as a military headquarters, the Capitanía General.

Convento de las Descalzas Reales (Map 4)

Halfway between Calle del Arenal and Plaza del Callao, the grim walls of this one-time palace serve as a mighty buttress to protect the otherworldly interior from the modern-day chaos outside.

Doña Juana, daughter of Carlos I and mother of Portugal's ill-fated Dom Sebastian, commandeered the palace for conversion into a convent in the 16th century. She was followed by the Descalzas Reales (Barefooted Royals), a group of illustrious women who became Franciscan nuns. A maximum of 33 nuns can live here, perhaps because Christ is said to have been 33 when he died. The 26 nuns in residence still live according to the rules of the closed order.

The compulsory guided tour (in Spanish) takes you up a gaudily frescoed grand stairway to the upper level of the cloister. The vault was painted by Claudio Coello and at the top of the stairs is a portrait of Felipe II and family members on the royal balcony.

You then pass several of the convent's 33 chapels. The first contains a remarkable

El Dos de Mayo

In early 1808, the French army marched into Madrid amid much confusion in the wake of the voluntary and cowardly abdication of Carlos IV and Fernando VII. General Tomás de Morla, who had armed the citizenry to help defend the city, soon found he could not control his unruly forces, which were quickly overwhelmed by Napoleon's troopers. Morla's decision to surrender probably saved the city from the wholesale destruction promised by the French emperor in the event of continued resistance.

But the madrileños were not to be so easily pacified. In the last days of April, men began to converge on Madrid from the neighbouring countryside. Pamphlets exhorting the populace to revolt were circulated and tension grew. On the morning of 2 May, the blood-letting began, with isolated troops coming under attack from armed townspeople, starting around the Palacio Real and what is now Plaza del Dos de Mayo.

The French commander, Murat, soon had units camped outside the city move in. The 'mob', as he saw it, was concentrated at various points throughout the city but those in the centre, at the Puerta del Sol, have gone down in history as a symbol of Spanish patriotism. Murat sent in Polish infantry and Mameluke cavalry – a fearsome unit brought to Europe from Egypt for precisely this kind of occasion.

The motley band of madrileños gathered at the Puerta del Sol fought with whatever came to hand – rifles, knives, bricks. As the Mamelukes charged into the crowds, sabres cutting into the rebels, local women joined in the fight, stabbing at the Mamelukes' horses and bombarding them with household items from the houses above. As the imperial forces gained the upper hand, the rebels were pushed into Calle Mayor, where some commandeered houses to subject the troops to a bloody crossfire.

All was in vain. By the end of the day the streets, here and elsewhere in the city, had been cleared. Some of the rebels were rounded up to be shot the next day, and road blocks around the city cut off all chance of escape.

Goya immortalised the events of this day and the shootings of the following day in his grim paintings, *El Dos de Mayo* and *El Tres de Mayo*, which now hang in the Prado. And *el dos de Mayo* (2 May) went into the annals of Spanish history as the quintessence of the country's patriotic fervour. It also marked the beginning of the Guerra de la Independencia (War of Independence) which to the British, who ultimately tipped the balance and forced Napoleon out of Spain five years later, came to be known simply as the Peninsular War.

carved figure of a dead Christ recumbent. This is paraded annually in a moving Good Friday procession. At the end of the passage you are led into the antechoir and then the choir stalls themselves, where Doña Juana is buried and a *Virgen la Dolorosa* by Pedro de la Mena is seated in one of the 33 oak stalls.

The convent is open 10.30 am to 12.45 pm and again (except Friday) 4 to 5.30 pm Tuesday to Saturday, and 11 am to 1.45 pm Sunday and holidays. Entry is 700 ptas, or 300 ptas for students and EU pensioners. All EU citizens can get in free on Wednesday.

Convento de la Encarnación (Map 4)

You could also drop into this less well-known monastery. Founded by Empress Margarita de Austria, it is still inhabited by nuns of the Augustine order (Agustinas Recoletas). Inside the monastery, you'll find a copious art collection, mostly dating from the 17th century, and a host of gold and silver reliquaries. The most famous of these contains the blood of San Pantaleón, which purportedly liquefies every year on 28 June.

On Plaza de la Encarnación, just north of the Teatro Real, the monastery is open at the same hours as the Convento de las Descalzas Reales. Entry costs 475 ptas, or 275 ptas for students and EU pensioners. All EU citizens are admitted free on Wednesday.

(continued on page 193)

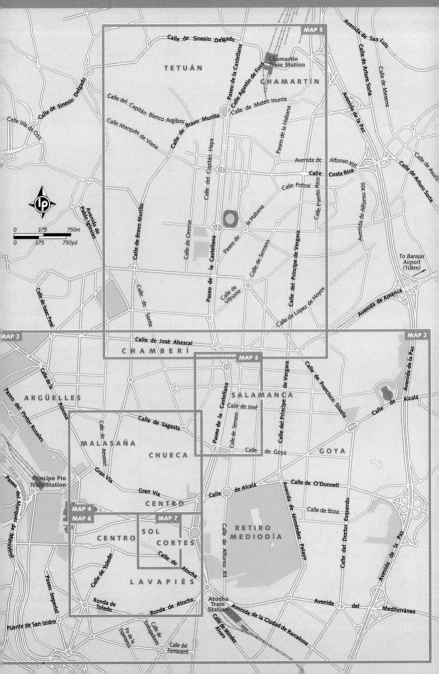

MAP 2 - MADRID

MAP 2 - MADRID

The Metropolis building marks one end of Gran Vía

DAMIEN SIMONIS

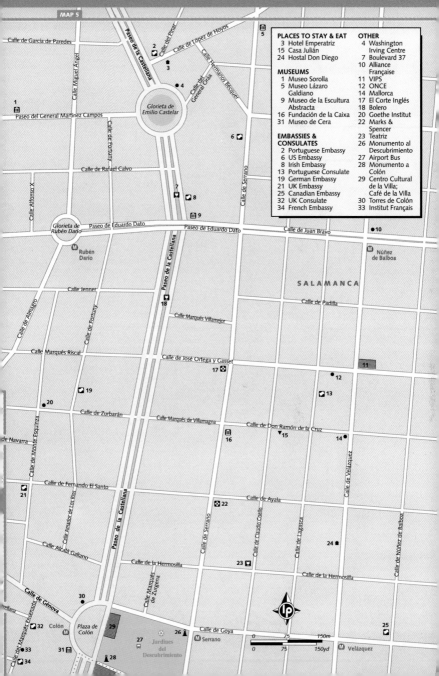

MAP 5

PLACES TO STAY & EAT
3 Hotel Emperatriz
15 Casa Julián
24 Hostal Don Diego

MUSEUMS
1 Museo Sorolla
5 Museo Lázaro Galdiano
9 Museo de la Escultura Abstracta
16 Fundación de la Caixa
31 Museo de Cera

EMBASSIES & CONSULATES
2 Portuguese Embassy
6 US Embassy
8 Irish Embassy
13 Portuguese Consulate
19 German Embassy
21 UK Embassy
25 Canadian Embassy
32 UK Consulate
34 French Embassy

OTHER
4 Washington Irving Centre
7 Boulevard 37
10 Alliance Française
11 VIPS
12 ONCE
14 Mallorca
17 El Corte Inglés
18 Bolero
20 Goethe Institut
22 Marks & Spencer
23 Teatriz
26 Monumento al Descubrimiento
27 Airport Bus
28 Monumento a Colón
29 Centro Cultural de la Villa; Café de la Villa
30 Torres de Colón
33 Institut Français

Calle de García de Paredes

Calle Miguel Ángel

Paseo de la Castellana

Calle del Pinar

Calle de López de Hoyos

Calle de Hermanos Bécquer

Calle del General Oráa

Glorieta de Emilio Castelar

Paseo del General Martínez Campos

Calle de Fortuny

Calle Alfonso X

Calle de Rafael Calvo

Calle de Serrano

Glorieta de Rubén Darío

Paseo de Eduardo Dato

Paseo de Eduardo Dato

Calle de Juan Bravo

Rubén Darío

Núñez de Balboa

Calle Jenner

Paseo de la Castellana

SALAMANCA

Calle de Padilla

Calle de Almagro

Calle de Fortuny

Calle Marqués Villamejor

Calle Marqués Riscal

Calle de José Ortega y Gasset

de Navarra

Calle de Monte Esquinza

Calle de Zurbarán

Calle Marqués de Villamagna

Calle de Don Ramón de la Cruz

Calle de Velázquez

Calle de Fernando El Santo

Calle de Amador de los Ríos

Paseo de la Castellana

Calle de Ayala

Calle de Serrano

Calle de Claudio Coello

Calle de Lagasca

Calle de Núñez de Balboa

Calle Alcalá Galiano

Calle de la Hermosilla

Calle de Génova

Calle del Marqués de Zurgena

Calle de la Hermosilla

rellana

Colón

Plaza de Colón

Jardines del Descubrimiento

Calle de Goya

Serrano

Velázquez

0   75   150m
0   75   150yd

MAP 4 - MALASAÑA & CHUECA

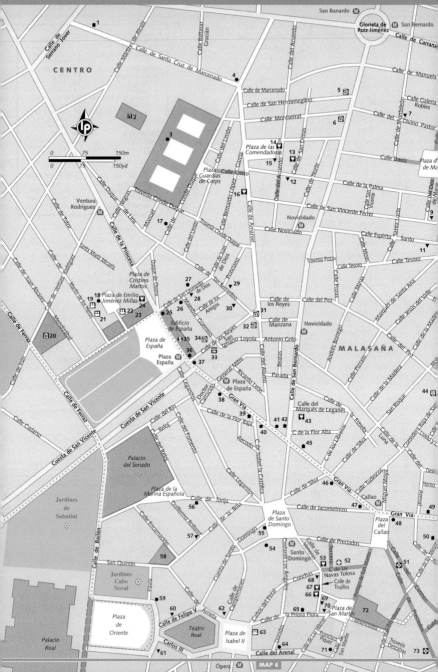

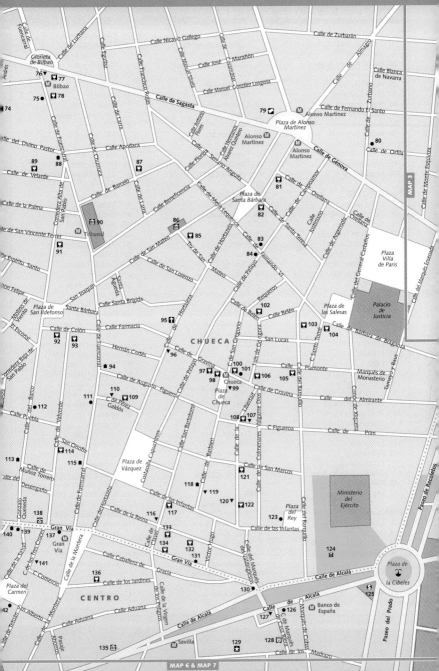

Calle de Fuencarral
Calle de Luchana
Calle Fernflor
Calle de Nicasio Gallego
Calle Manuel Silvela
Calle José · Marañón
Calle de Zurbarán
Calle de Almagro
Calle Blanca de Navarra
Andés
Glorieta de Bilbao
76 ▼
77
Calle de Francisco Rojas
Calle Manuel González Longoria
Calle de Fernando el Santo
Bilbao
75 ●
78
Calle de Sagasta
79
Alonso Martinez
80
74
Calle de Lira
Calle Antonio Flores
Calle Hermosilla Álvarez Quintero
Plaza de Alonso Martinez
Alonso Martinez
Calle de Monte Esquinza
MAP 3
Calle del Divino Pastor
Calle de Fuencarral
Calle de Apodaca
Calle de Churruca
Calle de Barceló
87
Alonso Martinez
Alonso Martinez
Calle de Génova
Calle de Orfila
MAP 3
89
88
Calle de Velarde
81
Calle de Campoamor
Calle de Orellana
Calle de Orellana
Calle de la Palma
Serrano Anguita
Plaza de Santa Bárbara
82
Calle de Santa Teresa
Calle de Argensola
Calle del General Castaños
Plaza Villa de Paris
Calle de San Vincente Ferrer
90
Tribunal
86
85
Calle de Mejía Lequerica
Calle de Hortaleza
83
84
Fernando· VI
Calle del Marqués Ensenada
Calle de San Mateo
Tv de San
Mateo
91
Calle de San Lorenzo
Calle de Pelayo
Requena
102
Plaza de las Salesas
Palacio de Justicia
Espíritu Santo
Plaza de San Ildefonso
San Joaquín
Santa Águeda
Santa Brígida
Santa Bárbara
Calle de Belén
Calle Belén
103
Calle de Bárbara de Braganza
104
Felipe
Molino de Viento
95
Calle de Hortaleza
CHUECA
San Lucas
El Escorial
Calle de Colón
Calle Farmacia
Piamonte
92
93
Hernán Cortés
96
Gravina
100
101
105
Marqués de Monasterio
Corredera Baja de San Pablo
Calle de Fuencarral
94
Calle de Augusto · Figueroa
97
98
Chueca
99
Calle de Gravina
106
Calle del Barquillo
Calle del Almirante
Calle del Barco
111
110
109
Calle de Pérez Galdós
107
108
C. Figueroa
Calle de Prim
112
Calle de Valverde
San Onofre
Calle de Pelayo
Calle de Barbieri
Calle de San Marcos
121
Plaza de Vázquez
Plaza del Rey
Ministerio del Ejército
Paseo de Recoletos
113
Muñoz Torrero
Calle de
115
Calle de San Bartolomé
118
119
Calle de las Infantas
120
122
123
Desengaño
alle del
Costanilla Capuchinos
Calle de la Reina
116
117
124
Gonzalo Quesada
138
Gran Via
Calle de Fuencarral
Calle de la Montera
133
134
132
131
Victor Hugo
Calle del Marqués de Valdeiglesias
Calle de las Infantas
Plaza de la Cibeles
140
139
137
Gran Via
141
C. Comercio
Caballero de
Gracia
Gran Via
125
Plaza del Carmen
136
Calle de los Jardines
130
Calle de Alcalá
42
San Alberto
Calle Aduana
Calle Aduana
CENTRO
Calle de Alcalá
Calle de la Virgen de los Peligros
Alcalá
126
Banco de España
127
C. de Marqués de Cubas
128
Sevilla
129
Madrazo

MAP 6 & MAP 7

MAP 4 - MALASAÑA & CHUECA

PLACES TO STAY
1 Albergue Santa Cruz de Marcenado
39 Hostal Alcázar Regis
42 Hostal Besaya
45 Hostal Lamalonga
49 Hotel California
50 Hotel Regente
65 Hostal Paz
88 Hostal Sil
94 Hostal Medieval
113 Hotel Laris
115 Hostal Ginebra
118 Hotel Mónaco
140 Hotel Arosa

PLACES TO EAT
7 Café Isadora
9 Pizzeria Mastropiero
10 Café Manuela
11 Tetería de la Abuela
12 La Dama Duende
15 Taquería de Birrä
28 Restaurante Veracruz
29 Restaurante Bali
30 Adrish
57 Taberna La Bola
60 Taberna del Alabardero
61 Café de Oriente
62 Restaurante La Paella Real
68 Casa Parrondo
69 El Locro
70 Fado
76 Café Comercial
96 Café La Sastrería
99 La Gastrotéca de Stephane y Arturo
107 Restaurante Momo
110 Restaurante Dame Noire
116 Undata
119 La Carreta
120 Restaurante Extremadura
127 Círculo de Bellas Artes
141 Restaurante Integral Artemisa

BARS & CLUBS
8 Café Magerit
13 Siroco
14 Café Moderno
16 Midnight
24 Arena
43 Morocco
53 Ales
66 Strong
67 El Templo del Gato (California Music Bar)
74 Café del Foro
77 Vinos
78 Corripio
81 Cervecería de Santa Bárbara
82 Cervecería Bulevar
85 Vaiven
87 Pachá
89 La Vía Lactea
91 Triskel
92 Bodega de la Ardosa
93 The Quiet Man
97 Acuarela Café
98 Truco
100 Sierra Ángel
102 Café Belén
103 Big Bamboo
104 Finnegan's
105 Kingston's
106 Rimmel
108 Truck
109 Cruising
114 Ya'sta!
117 Rick's
121 Bar La Carmencita
122 Libertad 8
132 Cock Bar
133 Del Diego Bar
134 Museo Chicote
136 El Sol

SHOPS
18 VIPS
38 VIPS
46 VIPS
51 FNAC Store
64 7-Eleven
71 Madrid Rock
73 El Corte Inglés
75 VIPS
101 Berkana Bookshop
137 Madrid Rock
139 La Casa del Libro

OTHER
2 Palacio de Liria
3 Antiguo Cuartel del Conde Duque
4 Moto Alquiler
5 Open Nautas
6 Xnet Café
17 RoomMadrid
19 Alphaville Cinema
20 Museo de Cerralbo
21 Renoir Cinema
22 Princesa Cinema
23 Torre de Madrid; Air France; Sabena; Virgin Express
25 Cadimar Viajes
26 Hertz
27 Europcar
31 Nevada 2000
32 Cervecería El Alamo
33 Telephones (VIC locutorio)
34 Aroba52
35 MoneyGram
36 Photo Express
37 National/Atesa rentacar
40 KLM
41 Avis
44 Teatro Lara
47 Carrión Building
48 USIT Unlimited
52 Centro de Salud
54 Viajes Zeppelin
55 Localidades La Alicantina
56 Café de Chinitas (Flamenco)
58 Convento de la Encarnación
59 Pullmantur
63 Real Cinema
72 Convento de las Descalzas Reales
79 Tunisian Embassy
80 International House
83 Juventus Viajes
84 Sociedad General de Autores y Editores
86 Museo Romántico
90 Museo Municipal
95 Iglesia de San Antón
111 Cogam & Urania's Café
112 Lavandería Alba
123 Casa de las Siete Chimeneas
124 Palacio Buenavista
125 Banco de España
126 Renfe Booking Office
128 Teatro de Bellas Artes
129 Main Police Station
130 Edificio Metropolis Building
131 CRIDJ
135 Real Academia de Bellas Artes de San Fernando
138 Telephones
142 Localidades Galicia

CHAMARTÍN

Chamartín
Train Station

Avenida de Pío XII

To Inerso
(500m)

inesio

Delgado

Calle de Burgos

To Lufthansa
Airlines
(100m)

Ventilla

Plaza de Castilla

Plaza Duque

Calle Caldos de la
División Azul

Plaza de
Castilla

Duque de
Pastrana

TETUAN

Plaza de Castilla

Calle de Pinos Alta

Calle Agustín de Foxá

Paseo de la Castellana

Calle de Mauricio Legendre

Calle Manuel Ferrero

Calle de la Hiedra

Calle de Mateo Inurria

To El Bosque (1km)

Avda del Comandante
Franco

Calle de Mateo Inurria

Calle Denoso

Calle Abedul

Pío XII

Bravo Murillo

Calle José Gastón
Tobeñas

Calle Francisco Suárez

Calle de Jerez

Valdeacederas

Calle del Limonero

Calle de la Infanta Mercedes

Calle Apolonio Morales

Paseo de la Habana

Calle de Macarena

Estrecho

Tetuán

Calle Rosario del Pino

Calle de Francisco Gervás

Calle Haya

Calle de Capitán

Calle Félix Boix

Calle Fray Bernardino
Sahagún

Avenida de Alfonso XIII

Calle de Sor

Angela de la Cruz

Plaza de
Cuzco

Calle Doctor Fleming

Calle de Juan Ramón Jiménez

Calle de Padre Damián

Avenida de Alberto Alcocer

Plaza de la
República
Dominicana

Calle Costa Rica

Calle de Orense

Calle Cuzco

Calle del General Yagüe

Paseo de la Castellana

Calle Potosí

Plaza de la
República
del Ecuador

C de Uruguay

Calle del Príncipe de Vergara

Calle de Zurita

Avenida del Brasil

Paseo de la Habana

Calle de Serrano

Calle del Puerto

Calle Juan de Ollas

Calle Infanta Mercedes

Estadio
Santiago
Bernabéu

Plaza de
Sagrados
Corazones

Avenida de Concha Espina

Avenida de Ramón y Cajal

Calle de Teruel

Avenida General Perón

Calle del Darro

Plaza de
Lima

Calle del Séere

Calle de Mercedes

Calle de Pradillo

Alvarado

Calle de Comandante Zorita

Calle del General Moscardó

Calle de Orense

Santiago
Bernabéu

Paseo de la Habana

Calle del Alga

Calle del Sil

Calle de Pradillo

Calle de Hernani

Calle Luis Muriel

Calle de Serrano

C de Leizarán

Calle de Raimundo

Calle de los Artistas

Fernández Villaverde

Nuevos
Ministerios

Calle del Tambre

C de Guadiana

Doctor Arce

Calle de Maudes

Potosí

Plaza del Poeta
Manuel del Palacio

Calle de Joaquín Costa

Avenida
República
Argentina

Calle del Príncipe de Vergara

Gómez Ortega

Calle de Alenza

Calle Alonso Cano

Calle de Modesto Lafuente

Calle Carbonero y Sol

Calle de Velázquez

Calle de Rodríguez Marín

Calle del General Zabala

Calle de Chinchilla

Cruz del
Rayo

Calle de Santa

Calle de Cristóbal Bordíu

Calle de Vitruvio

Calle de Serrano

Calle Particular

Calle de Francisco

Calle Gabriel Lobo

Calle de Recaredo

Ríos Rosas

Ergueta

Calle de Ríos Rosas

Plaza San Juan
de la Cruz

Calle de Oquendo

Calle de López de Hoyos

Avenida de
Cartagena

Plaza del
Descubridor
Diego de Ordás

Calle de Espronceda

Calle de María de Molina

Av de América

Calle de José Abascal

CHAMBERÍ

Calle de María de Molina

Avenida de América

C de
Pedro de Valdivia

MAP 2   MAP 2

Centro de Salud
Netherlands Embassy
Instalación Deportiva
Municipal Chamartín
China Crown; Viajes
Zeppelin
Irish Rover
Moroccan Embassy
Moroccan Consulate
Thai Airways International
Auditorio Nacional de
Música
Museo de la Ciudad
American Airlines
Renoir Cinema
La Tienda Verde
Continental-Auto
Bus Station
La Tienda Verde
Australian Embassy
Iberia
Aerolíneas Argentinas

MAP 6 - CENTRAL MADRID

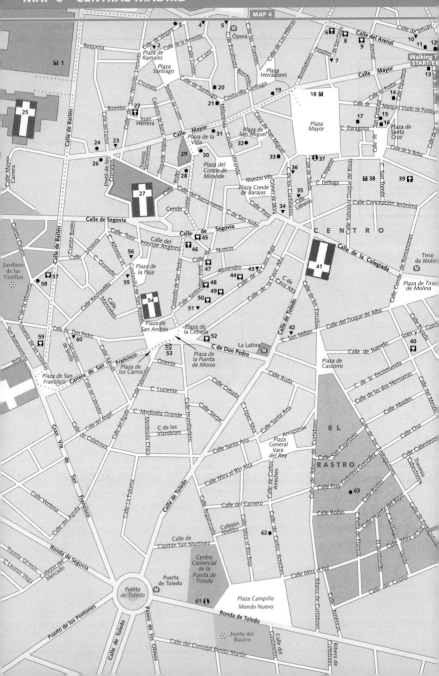

MAP 4

Walking T
START/E

CENTRO

EL
RASTRO

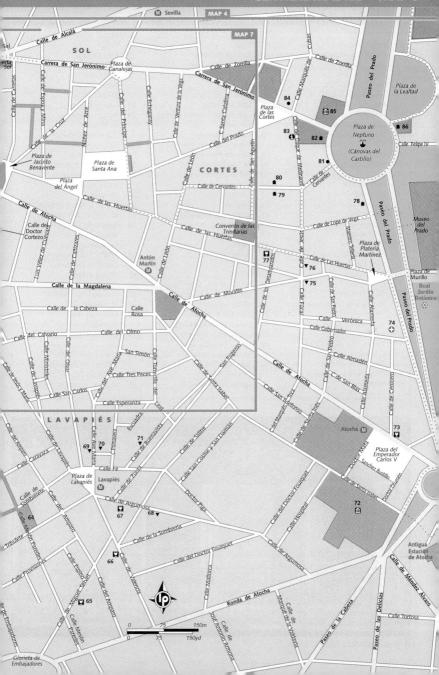

CENTRAL MADRID - MAP 6

PLACES TO STAY
11	Hotel Moderno
12	Hostal Cosmopolitan
13	Hostal Riesco
14	Hostal Madrid
16	Hostal Santa Cruz;
	Hostal Cruz Sol
17	Hostal Montalvo
20	Hostal Mairu
21	Hostal Pinariega
33	Hostal La Macarena
78	Hostal Sudamericano;
	Hostal La Coruña
79	Hostal Gonzalo
80	Hostal Dulcinea
82	Hotel Palace
86	Hotel Ritz

PLACES TO EAT
2	Café de los Austrias
4	Café Vergara
5	Café del Real
7	Chocolatería de San Ginés
10	Casa Labra
23	Casa Ciríaco
34	Casa Paco
35	Casa Antonio
36	Restaurante Sobrino de Botín
42	Oliveros
43	Restaurante Julián de Tolosa
51	Casa Pepa
55	Restaurante Gure Etxea
56	El Estragón
60	Taquería de Birrä II
68	El Granero de Lavapiés
69	Babilonya

70	Nuevo Café Barbieri
71	Elqui
75	La Vaca Verónica
76	Maceira

BARS & CLUBS
8	Teatro Joy Eslava
9	Palacio Gaviria
40	Taberna de Antonio Sánchez
44	La Chata
45	Café del Nuncio
47	Taberna de Cien Vinos
48	Taberna Almendro 13
49	La Soleá
50	Taberna Tempranillo
52	El Viajero
57	Bar Ventorrillo
59	Travesía
65	La Mancha de Madrid
66	El Boquerón
67	Eucalipto
73	Kapital
77	El Hecho

CHURCHES
6	Iglesia de San Ginés
22	Iglesia de San Nicolás
	de los Servitas
25	Catedral de Nuestra
	Señora de la Almudena
27	Iglesia del Sacramento
39	Iglesia de Santa Cruz
41	Basilica de San Isidro
46	Iglesia de San
	Pedro El Viejo
54	Iglesia de San Andrés

OTHER
1	Palacio Real
3	Real Musical
15	Librería de Mujeres
18	Real Casa de la
	Panadería
19	Madrid Rock
24	Istituto Italiano di Cultura
26	Palacio del Duque
	de Uceda
	(Capitanía General)
28	Casa de Cisneros
29	Ayuntamiento
30	Casa de los Lujanes
31	Real Farmacia de la
	Reina Madre
32	Mercado
37	Tourist Office (Patronato
	Municipal de Turismo)
38	Palacio de Santa Cruz;
	Ministerio de Asuntos
	Exteriores
53	WWW2.Call.Home
58	Corral de la Morería
61	Tourist Office
62	Fotocasión
63	El Rastro Flea Market
64	La Corrala
72	Centro de Arte
	Reina Sofía
74	Centro de Salud
81	VIPS
83	Main Tourist Office
	(Oficina de Turismo)
84	American Express
85	Museo Thyssen-Bornemisza

JULIET COOMBE

A fresco on Plaza Mayor, Madrid

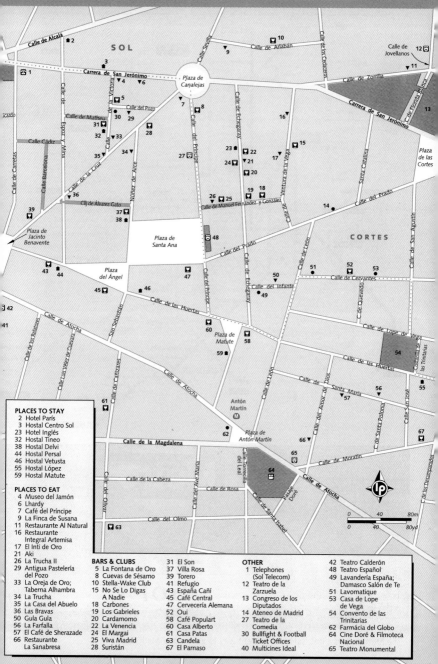

PLACES TO STAY
2 Hotel París
3 Hostal Centro Sol
23 Hotel Inglés
32 Hostal Tineo
38 Hostal Delvi
44 Hostal Persal
46 Hostal Vetusta
55 Hostal López
59 Hostal Matute

PLACES TO EAT
4 Museo del Jamón
6 Lhardy
7 Café del Príncipe
9 La Finca de Susana
11 Restaurante Al Natural
16 Restaurante
    Integral Artemisa
17 El Inti de Oro
21 Aki
26 La Trucha II
29 Antigua Pastelería
    del Pozo
33 La Oreja de Oro;
    Taberna Alhambra
34 La Trucha
35 La Casa del Abuelo
36 Las Bravas
50 Gula Gula
54 La Farfalla
57 El Café de Sherazade
60 Restaurante
    La Sanabresa

BARS & CLUBS
5 La Fontana de Oro
8 Cuevas de Sésamo
10 Stella-Wake Club
15 No Se Lo Digas
    A Nadie
18 Carbones
19 Los Gabrieles
20 Cardamomo
22 La Venencia
24 El Margai
25 Viva Madrid
28 Suristán
31 El Son
37 Villa Rosa
39 Torero
41 Refugio
43 España Cañí
45 Café Central
47 Cervecería Alemana
52 Oui
58 Café Populart
60 Casa Alberto
61 Casa Patas
63 Candela
67 El Parnaso

OTHER
1 Telephones
   (Sol Telecom)
12 Teatro de la
   Zarzuela
13 Congreso de los
   Diputados
14 Ateneo de Madrid
27 Teatro de la
   Comedia
30 Bullfight & Football
   Ticket Offices
40 Multicines Ideal

42 Teatro Calderón
48 Teatro Español
49 Lavandería España;
   Damasco Salón de Te
51 Lavomatique
53 Casa de Lope
   de Vega
54 Convento de las
   Trinitarias
62 Farmácia del Globo
64 Cine Doré & Filmoteca
   Nacional
65 Teatro Monumental

MADRID METRO

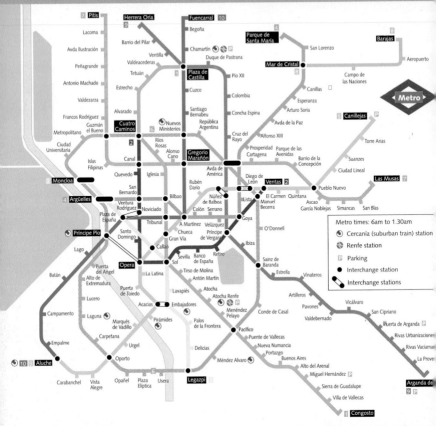

7 Pitis
Herrera Oria
Fuencarral 10
Lacoma
Begoña
Avda Ilustración
Parque de
Santa María
Barajas
Barrio del Pilar
San Lorenzo
Avda Ilustración
Ventilla
Chamartín ⓒ ❷ ₽
Peñagrande
Aeropuerto
Valdeacederas
Duque de Pastrana
Plaza de
Castilla
Mar de Cristal
Tetuán
Antonio Machado
Estrecho
Pío XII
Campo de
las Naciones
Valdezarza
Cuzco
Canillas
Alvarado
Santiago
Bernabeu
Colombia
Esperanza
Francos Rodríguez
Nuevos
Ministerios
Arturo Soria
Canillejas
Guzmán
el Bueno
Cuatro
Caminos
República Argentina
Concha Espina
Avda de la Paz
Metropolitano
Ciudad
Universitaria
2
Ríos
Rosas
Cruz del
Rayo
Alfonso XIII
Torre Arias
Canal
Alonso
Cano
Prosperidad
Parque de las
Avenidas
Monncloa
Islas
Filipinas
Gregorio
Marañón
Cartagena
Suanzes
Las Musas 7
Quevedo
Iglesia
Avda de
América
Barrio de la
Concepción
Ciudad Lineal
Argüelles
San
Bernardo
Rubén
Darío
Diego de
León
Ventas 2
Pueblo Nuevo
Ventura
Rodríguez
Bilbao
Núñez
de Balboa
Lista
El Carmen Quintana
Moncloa
Noviciado
Colón Serrano
Manuel
Becerra
Ascao
García Noblejas Simancas San Blas
Plaza de
España
Tribunal
A. Martínez Velázquez
Goya
Príncipe Pío ⓒ
Santo
Domingo
Chueca
Gran Vía
Príncipe
de Vergara
O'Donnell
Lago
Callao
Sevilla Banco
de España Retiro
Ibiza
Batán
Puerta
del Ángel
Opera
La Latina
Sol
Tirso de Molina
Sainz de
Baranda
Alto de
Extremadura
Puerta
de Toledo
Antón Martín
Estrella
Vinateros
Lucero
Lavapiés
Atocha
Atocha Renfe
ⓒ ❷ ₽
Artilleros
Pavones
Vicálvaro
Campamento
Laguna ⓒ
Acacias Embajadores
Menéndez
Pelayo
Conde de Casal
Valdebernardo
San Cipriano
Puerta de Arganda ₽
Laguna ⓒ
Marqués
de Vadillo
Pirámides
Palos
de la Frontera
Pacífico
Rivas Urbanizaciones
Empalme
Carpetana
Urgel
Delicias
Puente de Vallecas
Nueva Numancia
Portazgo
Buenos Aires
Rivas Vaciamad
La Prove
10 ₽ Aluche
Oporto
Usera
Méndez Álvaro ⓒ
Alto del Arenal
Miguel Hernández ₽
Arganda de
9 ₽
Carabanchel
Vista
Alegre
Opañel
Plaza
Elíptica
Legazpi
Sierra de Guadalupe
Villa de Vallecas
1 Congosto

Metro times: 6am to 1.30am
ⓒ Cercanía (suburban train) station
❷ Renfe station
₽ Parking
● Interchange station
⬤ Interchange stations

◄ Metro ►

Sol

The Metro offers a fast, safe and efficient way to get around Madrid.

ELLIOT DANIEL

Parts of Madrid's Gran Vía are flanked by old, elegant buildings.

The ornate Palacio de Comunicaciones on Plaza de la Cibeles

Parque del Buen Retiro, Madrid

Torres Puerta Europa, Madrid

Huerta de los Frailes, San Lorenzo de El Escorial, (Com. de Madrid)

MARTIN MOOS

Cafe-goers enjoying the sun on Plaza Mayor, Madrid

ELLIOT DANIEL

Livin' la vida loca, Sol district

ELLIOT DANIEL

Shoe-shining, Plaza Mayor

JULIET COOMBE

Dancing on Plaza Mayor

JULIET COOMBE

Posters of concerts and cds double as wallpaper along a Madrid street

(continued from page 176)

PALACIO REAL & AROUND
Palacio Real (Map 6)

When the Alcázar, the oft-altered forerunner of the Palacio Real, burned down in 1734, few mourned its demise. Felipe V took the opportunity to indulge in a little architectural magnificence, planning to build a palace that would dwarf all its European counterparts. He drafted in the Italian architect Filippo Juvara (1678–1736). On his death, another Italian, Giovan Battista Sacchetti (?–1764) finished the job.

The result, which Felipe did not live to see completed, is the Palacio Real, an Italianate baroque colossus with some 2800 rooms – of which you are allowed to visit around 50. Carlos III was the first monarch to move in, but the present king is only rarely in residence. It is occasionally closed for state ceremonies of pomp and circumstance.

The **Farmacia Real** is the first set of rooms you strike after buying your tickets at the southern end of the patio known as the Plaza de Armas (or Plaza de la Armería). The pharmacy is an endless parade of medicine jars and stills for mixing royal concoctions. Westwards across the plaza is the **Armería Real** (Royal Armoury), a shiny collection of weapons and armour, mostly dating from the 16th and 17th centuries. The full suits of armour, such as those of Felipe III, are among the most striking items on show.

Access to the apartments is at the northern end of Plaza de Armas. The main stairway is a grand statement of imperial power leading first to the Halberdiers' rooms and eventually to the Salón del Trono (Throne Room). The latter is sumptuous to the point of making you giddy, its crimson velvet wall coverings complemented by a Tiepolo ceiling. Shortly after, you'll encounter the Salón de Gasparini, with its exquisite stucco ceiling and walls resplendent with embroidered silks. The Sala de Porcelana is a heady flourish, with myriad pieces from the one-time Retiro porcelain factory screwed into the walls. The themes change as you progress, with the grand Comedor de Gala (Gala Dining Room) marking a distinct break.

The palace is open 9.30 am to 6 pm Monday to Saturday (to 5 pm, October to April), and 9 am to 2.30 pm Sunday and holidays (to 2 pm, October to April). It closes on days when official receptions are held.

Entry costs 900 ptas (1000 ptas if you join a guided tour), or 400 ptas for students and EU pensioners. All EU citizens get in free on Wednesday (bring your passport).

Jardines de Sabatini (Map 4)

Several entrances allow access to this somewhat neglected, French-inspired garden on the northern flank of the Palacio Real.

Campo del Moro (Map 2)

Much more inspired are the wonderful gardens of the Campo del Moro (Moor's Field), so-called because an Almoravid army drew up here beneath the walls of Madrid in 1110 in the hope of retaking the town for the Muslims.

The only entrance to the English-style gardens is on the western side, from Paseo de la Virgen del Puerto. Inside the grounds is the Museo de los Carruajes, in which royal carriages could be seen until it was closed for restoration.

The gardens are open 10 am (9 am Sundays and holidays) to 8 pm.

Plaza de Oriente (Map 4)

Eastwards across Calle de Bailén from the palace is the majestic Plaza de Oriente, once partly occupied by dependencies of the Alcázar and given its present form under French occupation in the early 1800s. The square is dominated by an equestrian statue of Felipe IV and littered with 20 statues of mostly ancient monarchs, many of which had been destined to adorn the Palacio Real until it was found they were too heavy.

Backing on to the eastern side of the square is the city's premier, and unhappiest, opera house, the **Teatro Real**. Started in 1818, it was several decades in the making and has since been burned down, blown up in the civil war and shut several times for restoration. It finally reopened in October 1997 after nine years of restoration that cost a staggering 21 million pesetas.

Catedral de Nuestra Señora de la Almudena (Map 6)

South of the Palacio Real, this stark and cavernous church, Madrid's neogothic cathedral, was completed in mid-1992 after more than 110 years of construction. Until it was finished the Basílica de San Isidro on Calle de Toledo had functioned as the city's leading church. The cathedral is open 10 am to 2 pm and 6 to 8 pm.

Muralla Árabe (Map 2)

Behind the cathedral apse and down Cuesta de la Vega is a short stretch of the so-called Arab Wall, the city wall built by Madrid's early medieval Muslim rulers. Some of it dates as far back as the 9th century, when the initial Muslim fort was raised. In summer, the city council organises open-air theatre and music performances here.

Iglesia de San Nicolás de los Servitas (Map 6)

Considered the oldest surviving church in Madrid, Iglesia de San Nicolás de los Servitas may well have been built on the site of Muslim Magerit's second mosque – if indeed such a mosque existed. Apart from the restored 12th-century mudéjar bell tower, the present church dates to the 15th century.

LA LATINA
Viaduct & Calle de Segovia (Map 6)

A viaduct was first raised in the late 19th century but the present version dates to the 1940s. It is also a popular spot for suicides – or at least it was until they put up the plastic barriers in the late 1990s.

While you're here, head down to Calle de Segovia and cross to the southern side. Just east of the viaduct on a characterless apartment block (No 21) wall is one of the oldest coats-of-arms of the city. The site once belonged to Madrid's ayuntamiento.

Calle de Segovia itself runs west between parks to a nine-arched bridge, the **Puente de Segovia**, which Juan de Herrera built in 1584.

Climb up the southern side from Calle de Segovia and you reach Calle de la Morería. The area from here south to the Basílica de

San Francisco el Grande and south-east to the Iglesia de San Andrés was the heart of the **morería**, or Moorish quarter. Strain the imagination a little and the maze of winding and hilly lanes even now retains a whiff of the North African medina. This is where the Muslim population of Magerit concentrated in the wake of the 11th-century Christian takeover of the town.

Across Calle de Bailén, the terrazas of Las Vistillas offer one of the best vantage points in Madrid for a drink (see Entertainment later in this chapter), with views to the Sierra de Guadarrama. During the civil war Las Vistillas was heavily bombarded by Nationalist troops from the Casa de Campo, who in turn were shelled from a Republican bunker here.

Basílica de San Francisco El Grande (Map 2)

Completed under the guidance of Francesco Sabatini, the baroque basilica has some outstanding features, including frescoed cupolas and chapel ceilings by Francisco Bayeu.

Built on the site where legend claims St Francis of Assisi built a chapel in 1217, it is one of the biggest churches in the city and has a curious ground plan.

The church is open 11 am to 1 pm and 4 to 7 pm Tuesday to Saturday. Entrance is supposedly by guided visit at 100 ptas per person, although at the time of writing there seemed precious little to stop you just wandering in and taking a look around.

Iglesia de San Andrés & Around (Map 6)

This proud church was largely gutted during the civil war. Work still continues to this day on restoration. Like a good many of Madrid's churches, it looks its best when lit up at night as a backdrop for the local cafe life. This was long the resting place of the remains of Madrid's patron saint, San Isidro Labrador, until they were moved to the Basílica de San Isidro.

Iglesia de San Pedro El Viejo (Map 6)

The outstanding feature of this church is its clearly mudéjar bell tower. Along with the fine brick bell tower of the Iglesia de San Nicolás de los Servitas, a little way to the north, it is one of the few surviving testaments to the industriousness of mudéjar builders.

LAVAPIÉS (MAP 6)

With the exception of La Corrala, an intriguing traditional tenement block built around a central courtyard, which functions now as a makeshift stage for (mainly summertime) theatre, there are no specific sights in this lively quarter. La Corrala is at Calle de Mesón de Paredes 65, opposite the ruins of a church.

The real attraction of Lavapiés is the gritty feel of one of the city's last true *barrios* (districts). Thought to be where the bulk of the city's Jewish population once lived (the existence centuries ago of at least one synagogue in the area is documented), it now hosts an interesting mix of working class *gatos*, Roma and predominantly North African immigrants.

PLAZA DE ESPAÑA & AROUND

A curiously unprepossessing square given its grand title, Plaza de España is flanked to the east by the Edificio de España, reminiscent of some of the bigger efforts of Soviet monumentalism but somehow not unpleasing to the eye, and to the north by the rather ugly Torre de Madrid. Taking centre stage in the square itself is a statue of Cervantes. At the writer's feet is a bronze of his most famous characters, Don Quijote and Sancho Panza.

Museo de Cerralbo (Map 4)

You could walk past this noble mansion and barely notice it among the bustle in the tight, narrow streets just west of Plaza de España. Inside is a haven of 19th-century opulence. The 17th Marqués de Cerralbo – politician, poet and archaeologist – was also an inveterate collector. You can see the results of his efforts in what were once his Madrid lodgings, at Calle de Ventura Rodríguez 17.

The upper floor boasts a gala dining hall and a grand ballroom. The mansion is jammed with the fruits of the collector's eclectic meanderings – from religious paintings to

Oriental pieces to clocks and suits of armour. Occasionally there's a gem, such as El Greco's *Éxtasis de San Francisco*.

The museum is open 9.30 am to 2.30 pm Tuesday to Saturday, and 10 am to 2 pm Sunday. It is closed on Monday and public holidays. Entry costs 400 ptas (students 200 ptas). It's free on Wednesday and Sunday.

Templo de Debod (Map 2)

Looking out of place in the Jardines del Paseo del Pintor Rosales, this 4th-century BC Egyptian temple was saved from the rising waters of Lake Nasser, formed by the Aswan High Dam, and sent block by block to Spain in 1970.

The temple is open 10 am to 2 pm and 6 to 8 pm (9.45 am to 1.45 pm and 4.15 to 6.15 pm from 1 October to 31 March) Tuesday to Friday, and 10 am to 2 pm weekends. Entry costs 300 ptas, or half for pensioners or anyone under 18. Entry is free for everyone on Wednesday and Sunday.

Ermita de San Antonio de la Florida (Map 2)

Among the finest works produced by Goya are in this small hermitage, also known as the Panteón de Goya, about a 10-minute walk north from the Campo del Moro. Here you'll find two small chapels. In the southern one the ceiling and dome are covered in frescoes by the master (restored in 1993). Those on the dome depict the miracle of St Anthony, who is calling on a young man to rise from the grave and absolve his father, unjustly accused of his murder. Around them swarms a typical Madrid crowd. Usually in this kind of scene the angels and cherubs appear in the cupola, above all the terrestrial activity, but Goya places the human above the divine.

The painter is buried in front of the altar. His remains were transferred in 1919 from France, where he died in self-imposed exile.

The chapel is open 10 am to 2 pm and 4 to 8 pm Tuesday to Friday and 10 am to 2 pm weekends (and in the hot summer months of July and August). Entry is 300 ptas, or half for pensioners and children under 14. Entry is free for everyone on Wednesday and Sunday.

Across the train tracks on Calle de Francisco is the **Cementerio de la Florida**, where 43 rebels executed by Napoleon's troops lie buried; they were killed on the nearby Montaña del Príncipe Pío in the pre-dawn of 3 May 1808 after the Dos de Mayo rising. The event was immortalised by Goya and a plaque was placed here in 1981. The forlorn cemetery, established in 1796, is generally closed.

Antiguo Cuartel del Conde Duque & Palacio de Liria (Map 4)

Over Calle de la Princesa, on the western edge of the Malasaña district (see Malasaña & Chueca later in this chapter), is the grand barracks known as the Antiguo Cuartel del Conde Duque. This has a day job housing government archives and as an occasional art exposition centre and now and then does a night gig as a music venue.

Virtually next door, the 18th-century Palacio de Liria, rebuilt after a fire in 1936 and surrounded by an enviably green oasis, retains an impressive collection of art, period furniture and *objets d'art*. To organise a visit, send a formal request with your personal details to Palacio de Liria, Atención Don Miguel, Calle de la Princesa 20, 28008 Madrid. The waiting list is long and most mortals content themselves with staring through the gates into the grounds.

Gran Vía (Map 4)

Gran Vía arches off eastwards from Plaza de España. It is a chokingly busy boulevard with more energy than elegance, although it gains some of the latter in the approach to Calle de Alcalá.

From luxury hotels to cheap hostales, pinball parlours and dark old cinemas to jewellery stores and high fashion, from fast food and sex shops to banks, Gran Vía has it all. It's a good place to take the city's pulse. Behind the grand facades lie some of the tackier scenes of madrileño life.

The street was pushed through here in the first decades of the 20th century, sweeping away entire neighbourhoods. In the following years, grand if often bland buildings were raised along much of its length.

Among the more interesting ones is the **Edificio Metropolis** (finished in 1910), which marks the beginning of Gran Vía.

MALASAÑA & CHUECA

Just north of Gran Vía is one of Madrid's sleazier red-light zones, populated by an interesting, if not entirely savoury, collection of pimps, junkies and wasted-looking hookers. This warren of long, narrow streets intersected by even squeezier lanes is known officially as the Barrio de Universidad, but more generally as Malasaña. For the purposes of this guide, that definition extends some blocks west across Calle de San Bernardo into the area bounded by Gran Vía, Calle de la Princesa and Calle de Alberto Aguilera. Chueca is a small area around the square and metro stop of the same name.

Long one of Madrid's slummiest areas, the heart of Malasaña retains a sense of decay, but mostly in a delightful sort of way. Away from the seedy red-light zone around Calle de la Luna, it is for the most part a lively haven of restaurants, bars and other drinking dens.

Museo Municipal (Map 4)

The main attraction here is the restored baroque entrance, originally raised in 1721 by Pedro de Ribera. Until its conversion into a museum in 1929, the building had served as a hospice.

Inside the museum, you are taken on an interesting but hardly masterful tour through the history of Madrid. On the ground floor, Madrid de los Austrias (in other words Habsburg Madrid) is brought to life, up to a point, through paintings and models.

The theme continues on the floor above, where the various rooms take you from Bourbon Madrid through to the final years of the 19th century. Of interest are a couple of Goyas and possibly more than anything else a huge model of Madrid done in 1830 by a military engineer called León Gil de Palacios (1778–1849).

The museum is at Calle de Fuencarral 78, and is open 9.30 am to 8 pm (to 2.30 pm only in July and August) Tuesday to Friday and 10 am to 2 pm weekends. It's closed on Monday and public holidays. Entry is 300 ptas and half-price for pensioners and under 18s. It's free for everyone on Wednesday and Sunday.

Museo Romántico (Map 4)

The late-18th-century building in which this curious little museum is housed was rented back in 1920 by the Marqués de la Vega-Inclán to house the tourism body he himself had founded, the Comisaría Regia de Turismo. In 1924, Vega-Inclán turned the building into the Museo Romántico, a minor treasure trove of mostly 19th-century paintings, furniture, porcelain and other bits and bobs from a bygone age.

The museum is at Calle de San Mateo 13, just east of the Museo Municipal. It is open 9 am to 2.45 pm Tuesday to Saturday, and 10 am to 1.15 pm Sunday. It is closed Monday, holidays and all August; entry is 400 ptas, students half-price. Pensioners get in free, as does everyone else on Sunday.

Sociedad General de Autores y Editores (Map 4)

A couple of blocks east of the Museo Romántico on Calle de Pelayo, this joyously self-indulgent ode to Modernisme looks akin to a huge ice-cream cake half-melted by the summer sun. It is virtually one of a kind in Madrid, although a couple of other much more modest examples of the genre are scattered about.

PLAZA DE COLÓN TO THE PRADO

The modern Plaza de Colón, with the almost surreal Edificio de Colón on its western side, is at first glance a rather uninspired affair. Its physical aspect, although softened by the fountains of the Centro Cultural de la Villa, is certainly nothing to write home about. The statue of Colón (Columbus) seems neglected and the **Monumento al Descubrimiento** (Monument to the Discovery – of America, that is), for all its cleverness, does not leave a lasting impression. It was cobbled together in the 1970s.

Biblioteca Nacional & Museo del Libro (Map 2)

Perhaps one of the most outstanding of the many grand edifices erected in the 19th century on the avenues of Madrid, the Biblioteca Nacional was commissioned by Isabel II in 1865 and completed in 1892.

Some of the library's collections have been imaginatively arranged among displays recounting the history of writing and the storage of knowledge. The Museo del Libro, opened in 1995, is a worthwhile stop for any bibliophile yearning to see a variety of Arabic texts, illuminated manuscripts, centuries-old books of the Torah and still more. If your Spanish is up to it, the displays come to life with interactive video commentaries.

The museum is usually open 10 am to 9 pm Tuesday to Saturday, and 10 am to 2 pm Sunday. Entry is free. The museum was due to remain closed until late 2000 because of renovation work in the library.

Museo Arqueológico Nacional (Map 2)

Out the back of the same building, at Calle de Serrano 13, the portentous entrance to this museum of archaeology may seem just a little too heavy for your liking. Inside you will find a delightfully varied collection spanning everything from prehistory to the Iberian tribes, imperial Rome, Visigothic Spain, the Muslim conquest and specimens of Romanesque, Gothic and mudéjar handiwork. There is a lot in here and those passing through Madrid more than once while touring Spain could well benefit from a second visit.

The basement contains displays on prehistoric man, the Neolithic age and on to the Iron Age. Modest collections from ancient Egypt, Etruscan civilisation in Italy, classical Greece and southern Italy under imperial Rome can also be seen. There are also some Spanish specialities: ancient civilisation in the Balearic and Canary Islands.

The ground floor is the most interesting. Sculpted figures such as the *Dama de Ibiza* and *Dama de Elche* reveal a flourishing artistic tradition implanted among the Iberian tribes – and no doubt influenced by contact with Greek, Phoenician and Carthaginian civilisation. The latter bust continues to attract controversy over its authenticity a century after it was found near the Valencian town.

The arrival of imperial Rome brought predictable changes. Some of the mosaics here are splendid. The display on Visigothic Spain, and especially material from Toledo, marks a clear break, but only previous experience with Muslim Spain (eg, the great cities of Andalucía) or other Muslim countries can prepare you for the wonders of Muslim art. The arches taken from Zaragoza's Aljafería are a centrepiece.

The influences of pure Islamic precepts persist in the later mudéjar style of re-Christianised Spain, which stands in remarkable contrast with Romanesque and later Gothic developments – all of which can be easily appreciated by soaking up the best of this eclectic collection.

Outside, stairs lead down to a partial copy of the prehistoric cave paintings of Altamira (Cantabria), which will be as close to the paintings as many people get.

The museum is open 9.30 am to 8.30 pm Tuesday to Saturday and 9.30 am to 2 pm Sunday. It's closed on Monday and national holidays. Entry is 500 ptas, except on Sunday and from 2.30 pm Saturday, when it's free. Pensioners always get in free.

Museo de Cera (Map 3)

This is a rather pathetic version of a wax museum. Still, 450 characters have been captured in the sticky stuff – you'll need a good dose of imagination to recognise some of them. In addition, you can board the Tren del Terror (500 ptas) or the Simulador (400 ptas) – the latter shakes you up a bit as though you were inside a washing machine. Another side show is the Multivisión animated 'experience' (200 ptas). All a bit dire really, although it might amuse pesky small people.

It is open 10 am to 2.30 pm and 4.30 to 8.30 pm weekdays, and 10 am to 8.30 pm weekends and holidays. Entry is 1500 ptas to the lot or 1000 ptas to the wax museum alone (600 ptas for children aged 10 and under). You can pay separately for any one of the other attractions.

Plaza de la Cibeles (Map 2)

The fountain of the Cybele is one of Madrid's most beautiful. Since it was erected in 1780 by Ventura Rodríguez, this assessment has remained much the same.

The goddess Cybele had Atalanta and Hippomenes, recently paired off thanks to the intervention of Aphrodite, converted into lions and shackled to her chariot for having profaned her temple. They had been put up to this by Aphrodite, irritated by the apparent ingratitude of the newlyweds for her good work.

The building you are least likely to miss on the square is the sickly-sweet **Palacio de Comunicaciones** – newcomers find it hard to accept that this is only the central post office. Diametrically opposite this is the **Palacio Buenavista**, which now belongs to the army. A block behind it to the west on the tiny Plaza del Rey is the **Casa de las Siete Chimeneas**, a 16th-century mansion that received its name because of the seven chimneys it still boasts. Nowadays, it is home to the Ministry of Culture.

Museo Naval (Map 2)

A block south, seafaring folk may well find this museum interesting. It is jammed with models, Maps, arms and the like. Of greatest historical interest is Juan de la Cosa's parchment map of the known world, put together in 1500. Its accuracy on Europe is quite astounding, and it is supposedly the first map to show the Americas.

The museum is open 10.30 am to 1.30 pm Tuesday to Sunday; entry is free.

Museo de Artes Decorativos (Map 2)

At Calle de Montalbán 12, this museum is full of sumptuous period furniture, ceramics, carpets, tapestries and the like spanning the 15th to the late 19th centuries. It is actually quite a bit more interesting than it sounds. Spread over five floors, you are presented with an enormous variety of objects.

It is open 9.30 am to 3 pm Tuesday to Friday and 10 am to 2 pm weekends and holidays; 400 ptas, students half-price. Pensioners get in free, as does everyone else on Sunday.

Museo del Ejército (Map 2)

In 1803 the chief minister, Manuel Godoy, ordered the establishment of an army museum in one of the few remaining parts of the one-time Palacio del Buen Retiro. Filled with weapons, flags, uniforms and other remnants of Spanish military glory, the museum is housed in what was the Salón de Reinos del Buen Retiro, at Calle de Méndez Núñez 1.

An interesting room with portraits of Franco is devoted to the Nationalist campaign in the civil war, while the Sala Árabe (decorated in Alhambra-style) contains various curios, including the sword of Boabdil, the last Muslim ruler of Granada. He signed the instrument of surrender to the Catholic monarchs that marked the end of the Reconquista in 1492.

Just what the immediate future holds in store for the museum is not entirely clear. The plan is to shift it to the Alcázar in Toledo and so make room for the expansion of the Prado gallery around 2005.

For the time being, the museum is open 10 am to 2 pm Tuesday to Sunday and entry costs 100 ptas (students half-price). Pensioners get in free, as does everyone else on Saturday.

Iglesia de San Jerónimo el Real (Map 2)

The church was the nucleus of one of the most powerful monastic groups in Madrid. The Isabelline style inside is actually a 19th-century remake that took its cues from San Juan de los Reyes in Toledo.

Next door, what remains of the 17th-century cloisters looks set to disappear as it becomes part of the extension of the Prado. The plan caused some uproar and neighbours' balconies sport placards demanding the cloister (or what's left of it) be saved.

Plaza de Neptuno (Map 6)

Officially known as Plaza de Cánovas del Castillo, the next roundabout south of Cibeles is commanded by an 18th-century sculpture of the sea god, by Juan Pascual de Mena. It is a haughty focal point, flanked

not only by the Museo Thyssen-Bornemisza and the Prado, but also by the city's famous competitors in the hotel business, the Ritz and the Palace.

A block east of the roundabout on Calle de Felipe IV is the custodian of the Spanish language, the **Real Academia Española de la Lengua** (Map 2).

Parque del Buen Retiro (Map 2)

After a heavy round of the art galleries, a stroll in Madrid's loveliest public gardens might be the best way to end the day. The gardens are at their busiest on weekends, when street performers appear.

Once the preserve of kings, queens and their intimates, the park is now open to all. You can hire boats to paddle about on the artificial lake *(estanque)*, watched over by the massive structure of Alfonso XII's mausoleum.

Weekend buskers and tarot readers ply their trade around the same lake, while art and photo exhibitions take place at one of a couple of places, especially the **Palacio de Exposiciones**. Puppet shows for the kids are a summertime feature (look for Tiritilandia, or Puppet Land).

The **Palacio de Cristal**, a charming metal and glass structure, was built in 1887 as a winter garden for exotic flowers. It is also the scene of occasional exhibitions.

At the southern end of the park near the rose gardens (or La Rosaleda), a statue of **El Ángel Caído** (the Fallen Angel, ie, Lucifer) brings a slightly sinister note to the place. The south-western end of the park is a popular cruising haunt for young gay men.

Real Jardín Botánico (Map 2)

Ask most madrileños about the city's botanical gardens and they won't know what you are talking about. All the worse for them, as the Real Jardín Botánico is a refuge more beautiful than El Retiro, although not nearly as extensive. Created in 1755 on the banks of the Río Manzanares, they were moved here in 1781 by Carlos III.

The gardens are open 10 am daily and close at anything from 6 to 9 pm, depending on the time of year. Entry is 250 ptas.

MADRID

Antigua Estación de Atocha (Map 2)

The old train station at Atocha has become something of a botanical sight in itself. From here the high-speed AVE leaves for Sevilla and the interior of the old terminal has been converted into a tropical garden – certainly a pleasant, if slightly sweaty, departure or arrival point. Virtually across the road is the Centro de Arte Reina Sofía (see earlier in this chapter).

JANE SMITH

Real Fábrica de Tapices (Map 2)

Founded in the 18th century to provide the royal family and other bigwigs with tapestries befitting their grandeur, this workshop is still producing works today. If you like tapestries and carpets of a high quality and price, a visit is well worth your while. With some luck you will get to see how they are made, and have been made over the centuries. The factory, at Calle de Fuenterrabía 2, is open 10 am to 2 pm weekdays (except holidays). Entry is 300 ptas.

THE PRADO TO SOL

The main reason for heading into the area known to locals as Huertas, roughly contained in the triangle west of Paseo del Prado and between Calle de Atocha and Carrera de San Jerónimo, is to eat and drink. It is a smaller, brighter and perhaps more touristy version of Malasaña.

Mention has already been made, in the Walking Tour section earlier, of Cervantes' burial place and the **Casa de Lope de Vega** (Map 7). The latter, at Calle de Cervantes 11, is open 9.30 am to 2 pm Tuesday to Friday and 10 am to noon Saturday (200 ptas). The playwright lived here for 25 years until his death in 1635 and the place is filled with memorabilia related to his life and times.

Where Carrera de San Jerónimo runs into Plaza de las Cortes stands the **Congreso de los Diputados** (Map 7). Originally a Renaissance building stood here, but it was completely revamped in 1843 and given a facade with a neoclassical portal. Next door the modern extension tacked on to it seems a rather odd afterthought.

Real Academia de Bellas Artes de San Fernando (Map 4)

If you need another art injection, try this somewhat fusty old institution at Calle de Alcalá 13. Fernando VI founded it in the 18th century as a centre to train promising artists. Little seems to have changed since then.

The first floor, mainly devoted to a mix of 16th- to 19th-century paintings, is the most noteworthy. You can see works by José de Ribera, Zurbarán, El Greco, Bravo Murillo and Goya, which include a couple of self-portraits, portraits of King Fernando VII and the infamous minister Manuel Godoy and a take on bullfighting. Upstairs you can also see some drawings by Picasso.

The museum is open 9 am to 7 pm Tuesday to Friday and until 2.30 pm the rest of the week. Entry costs 400 ptas. Pensioners get in free, as does everyone on weekends. Since the paintings' captions give poor explanations, you may find it worthwhile investing 100 ptas in a small booklet (it comes in several languages).

SALAMANCA & AROUND

Madrid's most chichi quarter, the Salamanca area to the north-east of the city centre, is lined with elegant apartments and smart department stores. Apart from shopping, you can take in a little culture.

Puerta de Alcalá

The gate was begun under the supervision of Francesco Sabatini at Plaza de la Cibeles to celebrate the arrival of Carlos III in Madrid in 1769. Completed in 1778, it was later moved to its present spot on Plaza de la Independencia.

Museo Sorolla (Map 3)

If you liked Sorolla's paintings in the Casón del Buen Retiro, don't miss this museum. In the artist's former residence, it contains the most comprehensive collection of his work in Spain, mostly the sunny Valencian beach scenes for which he is best known. It's set amid cool gardens at Paseo del General Martínez Campos 37.

The museum is open 10 am to 3 pm Monday to Saturday and 10 am to 2 pm Sunday and holidays; entry is 400 ptas, students half-price. Pensioners pay nothing, nor does anyone else on Sunday.

Museo Lázaro Galdiano (Map 3)

A surprisingly rich former private collection awaits you in this museum at Calle de Serrano 122. Aside from some fine works by artists such as Van Eyck, Bosch, Zurbarán, Ribera, Goya, Gainsborough, Constable and others, this is a rather oddball assembly of all sorts of collectibles. The ceilings were all painted according to their room's function. The exception is Room 14, where the artist created a collage from some of Goya's more famous works, including *La Maja* and the frescoes of the Ermita de San Antonio de la Florida, in honour of the genius.

It's open 10 am to 2 pm Tuesday to Sunday; 500 ptas, students half-price. Entry is free on Saturday. The museum is also open for evening visits from 7 to 11 pm, July to September.

Museo de la Escultura Abstracta (Map 3)

This interesting open-air collection of 17 abstracts includes works by Eduardo Chillida, Joan Miró, Eusebio Sempere and Alberto Sánchez. The sculptures are under the overpass where Paseo de Eduardo Dato crosses Paseo de la Castellana. All but one are on the eastern side of Paseo de la Castellana.

OUTSIDE THE CENTRE
Museums

Madrid seems to have more museums and art galleries than the Costa del Sol has highrise apartments. The following are a sample.

Museo de América (Map 2)

For centuries, Spanish vessels plied the Atlantic between the mother country and the newly won colonies in Latin America. Most carried gold one way and adventurers the other, but the odd curio from the indigenous cultures found its way back.

The two levels of the museum show off a representative display of ceramics, statuary, jewellery and instruments of hunting, fishing and war, along with some of the paraphernalia of the colonisers. The Colombian gold collection, dating as far back as the 2nd century AD, and a couple of shrunken heads are eye-catching. Temporary exhibitions with Latin American themes are regularly held too.

The museum is at Avenida de los Reyes Católicos 6, and is open 10 am to 3 pm Tuesday to Saturday and until 2.30 pm Sunday and holidays; entry is 500 ptas, students half-price, and free on Sunday.

Faro de Madrid (Map 2)

The odd tower (or lighthouse) just in front of the Museo de América is designed not to control air traffic, but to transport visitors up for panoramic views of Madrid. There is no cafe up here, so be warned. The observatory is open 10 am to 1.45 pm and 5 to 6.45 pm (and as late as 8.45 pm in high summer) Tuesday to Sunday; the ride in the lift (elevator) costs 200 ptas.

Museo de la Ciudad (Map 5)

Described perfectly by one traveller as 'a must for the infrastructure buff', this rather dry technical museum traces the growth and spread of Madrid, with abundant information on municipal services and the like. Established in 1992, it's at Calle del Príncipe de Vergara 140 and is open 10 am to 2 pm and 4 to 7 pm Tuesday to Friday. On weekends it's open for the morning session only. Entry is free.

Museo de la Moneda (Map 2)

If you like coins, this is the place for you: the national mint. Collections in the slightly dingy museum range from ancient Greek to the present day. The museum is at Calle del Doctor Esquerdo 36, and is open 10 am to 2.30 pm and 5 to 7.30 pm Tuesday to Friday and 10 am to 2.30 pm weekends and holidays. Entry is free.

Art Galleries

The city is sprinkled with small private galleries and a couple of important foundations where you can check out the latest trends in contemporary work. There are many exhibition spaces, so the best advice is to keep an eye on newspapers and gig guides such as the *Guía del Ocio*.

Among the most important is the **Fundación Juan March** (Map 2), Calle de Castelló 77. The foundation has its own collection and is responsible for organising some of the better temporary exhibits each year. The **Fundación La Caixa** (Map 3), at Calle de Serrano 60, is another busy bee, putting on regular contemporary art exhibits.

Parque del Oeste (Map 2)

Spread out between the university and Moncloa metro station, this is a tranquil and, in parts, quite beautiful park for a wander or shady laze in the heat of the day.

By night it undergoes a transformation, as the city's transsexual prostitute population and their clients come out to play. Part of the beat is reserved for female streetwalkers too. Most of the activity takes place in cars, which become remarkably numerous as the night wears on. The area is not the ideal choice for a late-evening family stroll.

Casa de Campo (Map 2)

This huge and rather unkempt semiwilderness stretching west of the Río Manzanares undergoes similar metamorphoses. It was in regal hands until 1931, when the recently proclaimed republic threw open its 1200 hectares to the people.

By day, cyclists and walkers eager for something resembling nature, but with no time or desire to leave Madrid, clog the byways and low roads that criss-cross the park. There are also tennis courts and Madrid's most central swimming pool (see Swimming in this chapter), and an amusement park for the kids (see Entertainment in this chapter).

Madrid's **zoo**, also in the park, contains some 3000 animals and a respectable aquarium. It is open 10.30 am to sunset on weekdays. The best part is the dolphin section and the **aquarium** (1655 ptas).

Finally, the none-too-exciting **teleférico** (cable car) from Paseo del Pintor Rosales (on the corner of Calle del Marqués de Urquijo) starts at a high point in the middle of the park. It starts operating at 11 am (noon October to March) and continues until 10 pm; it runs daily from 1 April to the last weekend of September, weekends and holidays only through the rest of the year (365 ptas one way, 520 ptas return).

At night it becomes a rather different place, filling with prostitutes, pimps, junkies and their pals.

SWIMMING

There are outdoor municipal pools in several locations around the city, open from June to September. During the rest of the year several municipal indoor pools, such as the Instalación Deportiva Municipal Charmartín (Map 5) at Plaza de Perú, open their doors. There are also various private pools. For information on pools and other municipal sporting installations around town, call the Oficina de Información Deportiva (☎ 91 540 39 39).

About the handiest location is the Instituto Municipal de Deportes in the Casa de Campo (Map 2). From June to September it is open 10 am to 8 pm daily. During the rest of the year, the indoor pool is open 11 am to 6 pm weekdays. Entry costs 520 ptas or you can buy a *bono,* good for 20 visits, for 7800 ptas.

LANGUAGE COURSES

The Universidad Complutense offers a range of language and culture courses throughout the year. Contact the Secretaría de los Cursos para Extranjeros (☎ 91 394 53 25, fax 91 394 52 98), Facultad de Filología (Edificio A), Universidad Complutense, Ciudad Universitaria, 28040 Madrid.

You could also sign up at the overworked and chaotic Escuela Oficial de Idiomas (Map 5; ☎ 91 533 00 88, 91 554 99 77), Calle de Jesús Maestro s/n. It offers courses in Spanish for foreigners (Español para Extranjeros) at most levels.

Many of the language schools aimed at teaching locals English and other foreign tongues also run courses in Spanish for foreign visitors.

WORK

About the most common source of work for foreigners in Madrid is teaching their native language. You can start your job search at the cultural centre of your country, but there is a sea of language schools around Madrid.

For English-speakers, the top choices are the British Council (see Cultural Centres in this chapter) and International House (Map 4; ☎ 91 310 13 14), Calle de Zurbano 8.

ORGANISED TOURS
Central Circuit

You can pick up a special Madrid Vision bus around the centre of Madrid 10 times a day (five daily from November to March). A full return trip costs 1700 ptas and you can board the bus at any of 14 clearly marked stops. Taped commentaries in eight languages, including English, are available, and the bus stops at several major monuments such as the Prado and near Plaza Mayor. If you buy the 2200 ptas ticket, you can use the buses all day to get around (2900 ptas buys you the same right for two days running). You can get more information at tourist offices or in most travel agencies.

Similar is Sol Open Tours (☎ 902-30 39 03). Buses follow a circuit, calling at 15 stops en route, every half-hour or so 10 am to 6.30 pm. You buy a ticket for 1600 ptas and can hop on and off at will. A couple of other similar bus-tour companies doing much the same thing appeared in the course of 2000.

Frankly, you're better off investing in 10-trip Metrobus tickets and getting around by yourself.

Descubre Madrid

The Patronato Municipal de Turismo has chosen more than 120 itineraries around the capital. Tours are free and are conducted in Spanish. You can pick up calendars detailing when and where the walks are held at any branch of the Caja de Madrid bank, which co-sponsors the Descubre Madrid program.

Paseos por el Madrid de los Austrias

The Patronato Municipal de Turismo organises Saturday morning walks around the centre of old Madrid (500 ptas). They start at 10 am (English) and noon (Spanish). Meet outside the Patronato office (Map 6) at Plaza Mayor 3 half an hour before.

SPECIAL EVENTS
Fiestas de San Isidro

Madrid's single greatest *fiesta* celebrates the city's patron saint, San Isidro, starting on 15 May. It kicks off with the *pregón,* a speech delivered by the mayor and goes on for a week. There are free music performances around the city and the country's most prestigious *feria,* or bullfight season, at the huge Plaza de Toros Monumental de las Ventas (Map 2) – the feria lasts for a month. Compulsive aficionados of bullfighting may want to take a peek at the Museo Taurino out the back of the bullring; it's usually open 9.30 am to 2.30 pm weekdays.

Other Fiestas

The Malasaña district, which can be busy enough at any time, has its biggest party on 2 May, which follows a national holiday on 1 May (Labour Day). For obvious reasons, the celebrations centre on Plaza del Dos de Mayo.

The Fiesta de San Juan is held in the Parque del Buen Retiro over the seven days leading up to 24 June.

The few locals who haven't left town in the second week of August will be celebrating the consecutive festivals of San Cayetano (Lavapiés), San Lorenzo (La Latina) and La Paloma (around Calle de Calatrava in La Latina). In the last week of September the Fiesta de Otoño (Autumn Festival) is held in Chamartín; this is about the only time you'd be tempted to hang around here and *not* get a train out.

September is a big month for local fiestas in several barrios of Madrid and towns around the capital.

Halfway through September, the Partido Comunista de España (Spanish Communist Party) holds its yearly fund-raiser in the Casa de Campo. The Fiesta del PCE lasts a weekend and is a mixed bag of regional food pavilions, rock concerts and political soapboxing.

Dyed in the Wool

Especially around the Fiesta de San Isidro, the *chulapos* and *manolas* of Madrid come out of the woodwork. The gents dress in their traditional short jackets and berets and the women in *mantones de Manila*, and put their best feet forward in a lively *chotis*.

What is all this? The mantón de Manila is an embroidered silk shawl, which few people now wear, except during fiestas. The chotis is a traditional working-class dance not unlike a polka. One of the most common versions involves a quick three-step to the left, the same to the right, and is topped off with a brisk twirl. Only a small portion of the really *castizo* ('pedigree') madrileños bother with this any more, but those who do so do it with a certain pride.

The chulapo – or dyed-in-the-wool, born-and-bred madrileño – is now more commonly known as a *chulo*. Now this is a word to beware of. It generally implies a degree of bravado and even arrogance of character, although in the eyes of madrileños this is no bad thing. But to many people the word bears quite negative qualities – brash, showy. The word can also mean 'pimp', so you'd want to be sure of your company and context before bandying it around too much. The fast-talking, hard-living, Madrid version of James Dean is also typecast as a *macarra*, which at its worst also means a spiv.

These breezy types, especially the kind you'd come across in the inner working-class barrios such as Lavapiés, were also once generally referred to as *manolos* (Manolo is a common first name). So it stands to reason that their girls should be known as manolas! To complete the picture, full-blooded madrileños are also known to the rest of Spain as *gatos* (cats) – a nice image to reflect their city savvy.

PLACES TO STAY

Madrid is crawling with pensiones, hostales and hotels, so there should rarely be trouble finding a place to stay. However, since 1998 Madrid's hoteliers have been enjoying a boom, which means that at peak holiday periods (eg, Christmas and Easter) you should try to book ahead. Many of the budget places will not, however, accept reservations – they want to see your face and the colour of your money first hand. This also means that, sooner or later, you should always be able to come up with something!

Prices quoted below should be seen as a guide only. Proprietors often modify them at whim and have their own scale according to the size of individual rooms, length of intended stay etc.

PLACES TO STAY – BUDGET
Camping

The camping ground within easiest striking distance is *Camping Osuna* (☎ *91 741 05 10), on Avenida de Logroño near the airport. Take metro No 5 to Canillejas (the end of the line), from where it's about 500m away. It charges 660 ptas per person, car and tent.

Another option is *Camping Madrid* (☎ *91 302 28 35), on the N-I highway north of town. Take the Alcobendas bus from Plaza de Castilla, from where it's a fairly short ride. It costs 600 ptas per person, car and tent.

Youth Hostels

There are two HI youth hostels in Madrid. *Albergue Richard Schirrman* (☎ *91 463 56 99)* is in the Casa de Campo (metro: El Lago; bus No 33 from Plaza Ópera). B&B in a room of four costs 1200/1700 ptas for those under/over 26.

Albergue Santa Cruz de Marcenado (Map 4; ☎ 91 547 45 32, Calle de Santa Cruz de Marcenado 28) has rooms for four, six and eight people. B&B costs 1200/1700 ptas for those under/over 26.

An HI membership card is necessary for both hostels. You can obtain one at the hostels or in central Madrid at the youth travel office of TIVE or at the Centro Regional de Información y Documentación Juvenil (see under Documents in the Facts for the Visitor chapter).

Hostales & Hotels

Around Sol If you don't mind the traffic, *Hostal Cosmopolitan (Map 6; ☎ 91 522 66 51, 3rd floor, Puerta del Sol 9)* has basic singles/doubles with washbasin costing just 1800/3300 ptas.

A much more attractive deal is the characterful *Hostal Riesco (Map 6; ☎ 91 522 26 92, fax 91 532 90 88, Calle del Correo 2)*, which has comfortable rooms looking right onto Puerta del Sol. Rooms with bathroom cost 4000/5800 ptas.

Hostal Tineo (Map 7; ☎ 91 521 49 43, Calle de la Victoria 6) charges 3500/5500 ptas for rooms with washbasin only and up to 5000/6500 ptas for rooms with bathroom.

Busting the low-budget bank a little is *Hostal Madrid (Map 6; ☎ 91 522 00 60, fax 91 532 35 10,* e *hsmadrid@teleline.es, Calle de Esparteros 6)*. It has good, clean secure rooms with TV, air-con and heating, phone and even a safe in each room; you pay 6000/9000 ptas.

Hostal Centro Sol (Map 7; ☎ 91 522 15 82, fax 91 522 57 78, Carrera de San Jerónimo 5) is a funny place with long corridors, but the smallish rooms (on the 2nd and 4th floors) are secure and in top order with their own bath, TV, phone, heating and air-con, and minibar. The rooms are good value at 6000/7500/9500 ptas for singles/doubles/triples.

Around Plaza Mayor The following are all on Map 6. South-west of Puerta del Sol towards Plaza Mayor, *Hostal Santa Cruz (☎/fax 91 522 24 41, Plaza de Santa Cruz 6)* is in a prime location. Rooms with their own bath cost from 3600/5200 ptas, and two of the rooms look out over the square. A better option still in the same building is the revamped *Hostal Cruz Sol (☎ 91 532 71 97)*. Rooms start from 3700/5700 ptas and have a bath, TV and air-con.

Closer to Plaza de Mayor is another good deal, *Hostal Montalvo (☎ 91 365 59 10, Calle de Zaragoza 6)*, where you can expect to pay up to 6500 ptas for a double with bath, TV, phone and air-con. It takes approximately two minutes to be seated on Plaza Mayor for your morning coffee.

The pick of the crop around Plaza Mayor is *Hostal La Macarena (☎ 91 365 92 21, fax 91 366 61 11, Cava de San Miguel 8)*. It's the only place to stay on the square's western side and is in a fine, well-manicured building. Rooms are kept immaculately clean and are

secure, and all have bathroom, TV and air-con/heating. Singles/doubles/triples cost 6500/8500/10,500 ptas and are worth every peseta.

Plaza de Santa Ana, Huertas & Atocha
Atocha train station is close to the city centre, so it is worth making the effort to walk up Calle de Atocha towards Plaza de Santa Ana if you arrive here. All the places listed below are marked on Map 7, unless otherwise stated.

Roughly halfway between the station and Santa Ana, *Hostal López (☎/fax 91 429 43 49, Calle de las Huertas 54)* is a good choice. Singles/doubles start at 3600/4500 ptas without own bath or 4200/5200 ptas with. It's on a quiet part of an otherwise lively street.

Hostal Gonzalo (Map 6; ☎ 91 429 27 14, Calle de Cervantes 34) is in sparkling nick. Rooms with shower and TV are 5000/6200 ptas. You can get a few hundred pesetas off if you stay at least three days.

Better than either is *Hostal Dulcinea (Map 6; ☎ 91 429 93 09, fax 91 369 25 69,* e *donato@teleline.es, Calle de Cervantes 19)*, across the road from Hotel Gonzalo. It has very clean rooms and is often full. You pay 5500/6000 ptas. If you are alone you will usually get a double to yourself. The owners have some apartments in the same street.

Hostal Persal (☎ 91 369 46 43, fax 91 369 19 52, Plaza del Ángel 12) is another place that is edging out of budgeteers' range. Comfortable rooms with bath, TV and phone cost 5800/8700 ptas, including breakfast.

Hostal Matute (☎ 91 429 55 85, fax 91 429 55 85, Plaza de Matute 11) has spacious if somewhat musty rooms for 3500/5000 ptas with shower and loo. These mainly look on to the street and can be noisy. Others, at 4500/6000 ptas, look on to an internal patio (nothing special in itself), are quiet and have bathrooms.

Hostal Vetusta (☎ 91 429 64 04, Calle de las Huertas 3) has admittedly small, but cute, rooms with their own shower starting at 3000/4500 ptas. A couple of rooms out the back look on to Plaza de Santa Ana.

MADRID

Hostal Delvi (☎ 91 522 59 98, 3rd floor, Plaza de Santa Ana 15) is a friendly enough place with OK rooms, some having glimpses of the square. The singles are tiny. You'll pay from 2000/2500 for rooms without bath or 4000 ptas for a double with.

Around Ópera The tiny *Hostal Paz (Map 4; ☎ 91 547 30 47, Calle de la Priora Flora 4)* looks horrible from the outside, but the cheap singles/doubles inside are reasonable value, if a little cramped, at 2600/4000 ptas. All rooms have TV and air-con/heating, but except for a couple of doubles with their own shower, bathrooms are shared.

Quietly tucked away is *Hostal Mairu (Map 6; ☎ 91 547 30 88, Calle del Espejo 2)*, a simple place with rooms for 2600/4200 ptas. Doubles with their own bath will cost you 4400 ptas.

Nearby, *Hostal Pinariega (Map 6; ☎/fax 91 548 08 19, Calle de Santiago 1)* is a sunnier alternative, which offers rooms from 3500/4800 ptas, with shower and washbasin. If you want a bathroom, you pay 4000/5800 ptas.

Paseo del Prado & Retiro If you want to be a stone's throw from the Prado, you have a couple of choices on the grand boulevard. *Hostal Sudamericano (Map 6; ☎ 91 429 25 64)* at No 12 is not bad, with singles/doubles starting at 3800/5000 ptas. Rooms are simple and bathrooms are in the corridor. There are a few tiny singles that cost 2600 ptas. In the same building, *Hostal La Coruña (Map 6; ☎ 91 429 25 43)* has similar rooms with TV for 3000/5000 ptas.

Gran Vía, Malasaña & Chueca Gran Vía is laden with accommodation, but it's a noisy area. The following can be found on Map 4.

Hostal Lamalonga (☎ 91 547 26 31, Gran Vía 56) is a reliable place, offering singles/doubles with bath from 4500/6500 ptas. *Hostal Alcázar Regis (☎ 91 547 93 17, fax 91 559 07 85, Gran Vía 61)* is not a bad choice at the cheaper end of the scale along this heaving boulevard. Rooms cost 4000/6000 ptas.

The stylish *Hostal Besaya (☎ 91 541 32 07, Calle de San Bernardo 13)* has good rooms costing up to 5900/8000 ptas with bath. It's a little overpriced.

Calle de Fuencarral is choked with hostales and pensiones, especially at the Gran Vía end. *Hostal Ginebra (☎ 91 532 10 35, Calle de Fuencarral 17)* is a reliable choice not far from Gran Vía. All rooms have TV and phone; singles with washbasin start at 3200 ptas, while rooms with bathroom cost 4200/5000 ptas.

Hostal Medieval (☎ 91 522 25 49, Calle de Fuencarral 46) has spacious and bright rooms with shower for 3000/4500 ptas. Doubles with bathroom cost 5500 ptas. *Hostal Sil (☎ 91 448 89 72, fax 91 447 48 29, Calle de Fuencarral 95)* charges 5500/7500 ptas for good rooms with bath, TV, phone and air-con/heating.

Hotel Laris (☎ 91 521 46 80, fax 91 521 46 85, Calle del Barco 3) is nudging mid-range but has decent rooms with all the extras for 5800/8700 ptas.

PLACES TO STAY – MID-RANGE
Around Sol
For a hint of faded elegance, the *Hotel Inglés (Map 7; ☎ 91 429 65 51, fax 91 420 24 23, Calle de Echegaray 8)* is OK at 8500/12,000 ptas plus IVA for singles/doubles. You get the feeling everything could do with some freshening up but the hotel has some curious rooms that seem almost like small apartments.

Hotel Moderno (Map 6; ☎ 91 531 09 00, fax 91 531 35 50, ℮ info@hotel-moderno .com, Calle del Arenal 2), just off Puerta del Sol, has comfortable enough rooms for 10,400/13,000 ptas plus IVA, but you are really paying for the position more than anything else.

Hotel París (Map 7; ☎ 91 521 64 96, fax 91 531 01 88, Calle de Alcalá 2) is an old stalwart around here and reasonable value. Rooms with the usual extras are 9000/12,000 ptas (plus IVA), including breakfast.

Gran Vía, Malasaña & Chueca
The following are all on Map 4. *Hotel Regente (☎ 91 521 29 41, fax 91 532 30 14,*

e info@hotelregente.com, Calle de los Mesoneros Romanos 9) has decent mid-range rooms with bath, TV, air-con and phone for 6500/10,000 ptas plus IVA.

Hotel California (☎ 91 522 47 03, fax 91 531 61 01, Gran Vía 38) is a smart choice, with attractive rooms going for 8525/10,900 ptas plus IVA.

Hotel Mónaco (☎ 91 522 46 30, fax 91 521 16 01, Calle de Barbieri 5) is one of the rare, truly quirky places, in the most likeable sense of the expression, in Madrid. Just wandering into the foyer is a trip. Rooms are olde worlde camp (try for room 123, with mirror above the bed!) and cost 7490/10,700 ptas.

Salamanca, Goya & Beyond

Those wanting to mix in the smarter parts of town could try **Hostal Don Diego** (Map 3; ☎ 91 435 07 60, fax 91 431 42 63, Calle de Velázquez 45) for size. It has comfortable singles/doubles with bath, TV, minibar and phone for 7600/10,500 ptas plus IVA.

PLACES TO STAY – TOP END

Note firstly that stated prices can often be negotiated down, especially on slow weekends, in August or if you are travelling in groups. Savings can nudge 50% in some places when your luck is in. When booking ahead, always look into this.

There is no shortage of bland, four- and five-star hotels (with all the mod cons) scattered across Madrid, particularly along the main drags such as Paseo de la Castellana. An attractive alternative to these and just off the Castellana is **Hotel Emperatriz** (Map 3; ☎ 91 563 80 88, fax 91 563 98 04, *e* emperatriz@mad.servicom.es, Calle de López de Hoyos 4). Its tranquil singles/doubles generally cost 23,000/28,000 ptas plus IVA.

One of the better addresses in Madrid and an excellent choice in terms of price is **Hotel Arosa** (Map 4; ☎ 91 532 16 00, fax 91 531 31 27, *e* arosa@hotelarosa.com, Calle de la Salud 21), just off Gran Vía. It has charming rooms and comes highly recommended. Rooms start at 14,295/22,295 ptas plus IVA.

Heading to the top of the league is one of Madrid's old classics, **Hotel Palace** (Map 6;

☎ 91 360 80 00, fax 91 360 81 00, *e* palace1@mol.es, Plaza de las Cortes 7). Elegant suites come in at 56,000/63,000 ptas plus IVA in high season. Not far away is its old rival, **Hotel Ritz** (Map 6; ☎ 91 521 28 57, fax 91 532 87 76, Plaza de la Lealtad 5). At 49,000/64,000 ptas plus IVA, this is Madrid's priciest location.

LONG-TERM ACCOMMODATION

For longer stays in Madrid, you can usually make a deal in the pensiones and smaller hostales to include meals, laundry and so on.

For flatshares and rental, check the notice boards at cultural institutes, university campuses and the Escuela Oficial de Idiomas (see Language Courses earlier in this chapter), as well as in the *Segundamano* magazine. Another possible source is RoomMadrid (Map 4; ☎ 91 548 03 35) at Calle del Conde Duque 7. You fill in a form and are matched with potential flatshares. It charges 15,000 ptas for the service.

Finding a room in shared flats is not too difficult, but look around, as you can be offered some pretty dismal mouse holes for big money. Indeed, since early 1999 rents have been soaring in Madrid after a year in which house prices rose enormously. With luck and persistence you can find good-quality rooms in central locations for around 40,000 ptas a month. Your bills will include electricity *(luz)*, water, gas (most older places still use bottled butane gas, which sells for around 1000 ptas per orange *bombona*), phone and *comunidad* (a fixed bimonthly charge for building maintenance, sometimes included in the rent).

PLACES TO EAT

Madrid is riddled with restaurants, snack bars and fast-food outlets, so rumbling tummies need not suffer long. Madrid is also one of the few Spanish cities to have a fair sprinkling of non-Spanish options.

Because the line dividing bar and restaurant is often blurred, some of the places included in the Entertainment section under Pubs & Bars also serve food. They have been listed as bars because the food can be regarded as an adjunct to the drink.

MADRID

PLACES TO EAT – BUDGET

One traveller's budget restaurant may be another's splurge, so these categories are a little arbitrary. Those hoping to satisfy their hunger for around 1000 to 1500 ptas could try the following places (in a few cases you can opt to spend a little more – say up to around 2000 ptas – and broaden your range of choices).

Around Sol & Plaza Mayor

Plaza Mayor and the immediate area offer plenty of possibilities, but a good number are tourist traps, serving up average food at not-so-average prices. They huddle together especially along Calle de la Cava de San Miguel and Calle de los Cuchilleros.

A wonderful old tapas bar is *Casa Labra* (Map 6; Calle de Tetuán 11), which has been going in much the same style since 1860. Locals pile in here after a day's work or shopping, but more than a hundred years ago Pablo Iglesias and pals founded the Spanish socialist party while sipping on wine here.

If you feel like snuggling into a northern Spanish environment, head for *Casa Parrondo* (Map 4; ☎ 91 522 62 34, Calle de Trujillos 9). This Asturian cider tavern and restaurant offers hearty tapas (lots of chorizo and cheese) and well prepared food. The lunchtime *menú del día* (daily set meal) is good value at 1400 ptas. It's closed on Sunday evening.

La Latina

Oliveros (Map 6; Calle de San Millán 4) opened up in early 2000 after being shut for more than 10 years. The Oliveros family has done everything to maintain the style and atmosphere of the place their family took over in 1921 (it had been serving up food since 1857). Locals in particular seem pleased with the 1750 ptas set meal.

Plaza de Santa Ana, Huertas & Atocha

Aside from the bars, the area around Plaza de Santa Ana is busy with eating options. In and around Calle de la Cruz, Calle de Espoz y Mina and Calle de la Victoria is a cluster of restaurants and bars, many specialising in seafood with a more or less legitimate *gallego* (Galician) touch. All the following are on Map 7 unless otherwise indicated.

At *Maceira* (Map 6; Calle de Jesús 7) you can splash your *pulpo a la gallega* (Galician- style octopus) down with a crisp white Ribeiro. It's closed at lunchtime on Monday.

In *La Casa del Abuelo* (Calle de la Victoria 14), on a back street south-east of Puerta del Sol, you can sip a *chato* (small glass) of the heavy, sweet El Abuelo red wine, made in Toledo province, while munching on heavenly prawns, grilled or with garlic. Across the road are two other good tapas options: at No 4 is *La Oreja de Oro* and, next door, the recently spiffed-up, Andalucian-style *Taberna Alhambra* (☎ 91 521 07 08, Calle de la Victoria 9). After these, duck around the corner to *Las Bravas* on Callejón de Álvarez Gato for a *caña* and the best *patatas bravas* (spicy fried potatoes) in town. The antics of the bar staff are enough to merit a pit stop, and the distorting mirrors are a minor Madrid landmark.

La Trucha (☎ 91 532 08 90, Calle de Núñez de Arce 6) is one of Madrid's great bars for tapas. It closes on Sunday and Monday. It's just off Plaza de Santa Ana, and there's another (☎ 91 429 58 33, Calle de Manuel Fernández y González 3) nearby. You can eat your fill at the bar or sit down in the restaurant.

Something of an institution is the *Museo del Jamón* (☎ 91 521 03 46, Carrera de San Jerónimo 6). Walk in here or one of several branches around town and you'll understand the name. Huge clumps of every conceivable type of ham dangle all over the place. You can eat plates and plates of ham – the Spaniards' single most favoured source of nutrition.

Cheaper still and good is *Restaurante La Sanabresa* (☎ 91 429 03 38, Calle del Amor de Dios 12), where you can get a *menú* for just 900 ptas.

La Finca de Susana (☎ 91 369 35 57, Calle de Arlabán 4) is a great new spot in Madrid. Soft lighting and a veritable jungle of greenery create a soothing atmosphere for a meal that doesn't have to cost more than about 2000 ptas. Try the salads, grilled vegetables and variations on the carpaccio theme.

Vegetarian The *Restaurante Al Natural* (☎ 91 369 47 09, Calle de Zorrilla 11) is a good vegetarian place and also has a nonvegetarian menu. It's closed on Sunday evening.

Elqui (Map 6; ☎ 91 468 04 62, Calle de Buenavista 18) is a handy self-service vegetarian buffet-style place. It's open daily but only for lunch on Monday (until 4 pm) and for dinner (a la carte) on Friday and Saturday evening.

International Cuisine The *El Inti de Oro* (☎ 91 429 67 03, Calle de Ventura de la Vega 12) is a quality Peruvian joint. Try the melt-in-your-mouth *merluza con salsa de camarones* – hake done in a light prawn sauce and served with rice. Wash it down with imported Peruvian beer (Cristal). For a full meal expect to shell out around 3500 ptas per head.

The Middle Eastern and North African eateries and *salones de té* (teahouses) popping up around Lavapiés are fun. They are often simple, with tasty Arab food and, often on weekends, some belly dancing. *Babilonya (Map 6; Calle del Ave María)*, just opposite the Nuevo Café Barbieri off Plaza de Lavapiés, is a perfect example.

Early Morning A funny little place is *La Farfalla (☎ 91 369 46 91, Calle de Santa María 17)*. It does an odd mix of salads, vegetarian, pseudo-Italian and other dishes. The big news is it does this until 4 am! Expect to pay about 2000 ptas per head for a full meal with wine and coffee.

Gran Vía, Malasaña & Chueca

Plunge into the labyrinth of narrow streets and alleyways north of Gran Vía to satisfy your taste buds. The following are all on Map 4.

For a cheap pizza and beer outdoors, *Restaurante Sandos (Plaza del Dos de Mayo 8)* is fine. It also offers a decent *menú* for 850 ptas. Better still is the crowded *Pizzeria Mastropiero (Calle de San Vicente*

Ferrer 34) on the corner of Calle del Dos de Mayo, a justifiably popular Argentine-run joint where you can get pizza by the slice. They also do a *tarta de chocolate con dulce de leche* (chocolate tart with a thick caramel sauce) to die for.

Río Manzanares Area

Head down past the Príncipe Pío train station towards the Río Manzanares and turn northwards. Here you'll find *Casa Mingo (Map 2; ☎ 91 547 79 18, Paseo de la Florida 34)*, a great old place for chicken and cider. A full roast chicken, salad and bottle of cider – plenty for two – will cost less than 2000 ptas. They've been pouring cider here since 1888.

Around Plaza de España

Restaurante Veracruz (Map 4; ☎ 91 247 11 50, Calle de San Leonardo de Dios 5) has a *menú* (including a bottle of wine) for 950 ptas. The menu is topped off by wonderful home-made desserts. Manuel García López has been welcoming locals here since 1961. He takes a break each Sunday.

Salamanca, Goya & Beyond

A great lunch stop just north of El Retiro is *Alfredo's Barbacoa (Map 2; ☎ 91 576 62 71, Calle de Lagasca 5)*. On the menu are lightly spiced spare ribs for 1035 ptas and some good steaks. You can eat in or takeaway. It's closed on Sunday evening and Monday.

For midday tapas, the *Taberna de Daniela (Map 2; ☎ 91 575 23 29, Calle del General Pardiñas 21)* is one of the best-known places in the snootier Goya barrio. The tile decor is great, but service can be patchy and you're probably better off at the bar.

Self-Catering

The *mercado* (Map 6) on Plaza de San Miguel, just off Plaza Mayor, is the main fresh produce market. Self-caterers can also try *Marks & Spencer's food department* (Map 3) for foodstuffs generally unavailable in Spanish shops. The food departments in *El Corte Inglés* stores are also good.

PLACES TO EAT – MID-RANGE

Opening your purse wider will improve your options greatly. At the places listed below you can expect to pay anything from 2000 to 3500 ptas for a full meal with all the trimmings.

Around Sol & Plaza Mayor

Casa Paco (Map 6; ☎ 91 366 31 66, Plaza de la Puerta Cerrada 11) is a classic spot to enjoy madrileño cooking at reasonable prices. They specialise in steaks but not on Sundays, when they sleep instead. More of an institution is *Casa Ciríaco (Map 6; ☎ 91 548 06 20, Calle Mayor 84)*, a bar and restaurant with loads of character. It was founded in 1917 in a building previously popular with would-be assassins: one threw a bomb from a balcony at Alfonso XIII as he passed by with his queen, Victoria Eugenia, on their wedding day in 1906. The attack failed, but 24 people died. On the subject of eating, mains cost anything from 1000 to 2700 ptas. It's closed Wednesday.

If it's paella your heart desires, the best advice is to head for Valencia. Failing that, you could try the *Restaurante La Paella Real (Map 4; ☎ 91 542 09 42, Calle de Arrieta 2)*. This place does a whole range of rice-based dishes from 1840 to 2425 ptas per head. It's not cheap, but halfway decent paella never is in Madrid. It's shut on Sunday evening.

International Cuisine A fine Argentinian restaurant is *El Locro (Map 4; ☎ 91 522 43 82, Calle de Trujillos 2)*, whose speciality, predictably enough, is succulent slabs of grilled meat. It closes on Wednesday. Mains cost up to around 2300 ptas, but the lunch *menú* comes in at 1200 ptas. Friday and Saturday nights they throw in some tango music.

Fado (Map 4; ☎ 91 532 21 02, Plaza de San Martín 2) is a good Portuguese restaurant and something of a Madrid stalwart. Come for the seafood dishes in particular. It's closed on Monday.

La Latina

Restaurante Julián de Tolosa (Map 6; ☎ 91 365 82 10, Calle de la Cava Baja 8) has a pleasingly simple brick-and-timber decor

and a limited menu. If you feel like a *chuletón* (huge chop), it will cost from 2500 ptas per head. It's closed on Sunday.

A few doors down, *Casa Pepa (Map 6; ☎ 91 366 72 12, Calle de la Cava Baja 38)* is an altogether different style of place, with low lighting and a hushed feel. It's been getting quite a few accolades. The mains of fish or meat cost around 2500 ptas.

Vegetarian The *El Estragón (Map 6; ☎ 91 365 89 82, Plaza de la Paja 10)* is a delightfully atmospheric restaurant that has become something of a hit in Madrid. You should be able to get away with spending 2500 ptas for a full meal.

Plaza de Santa Ana, Huertas & Atocha

La Vaca Verónica (Map 6; ☎ 91 429 78 27, Calle de Moratín 38) is a refreshing locale offering Mediterranean cuisine with a little fantasy. Expect to pay about 2000 ptas per meal. It's closed Saturday lunchtime and Sunday.

At the rather camp *Gula Gula (Map 7; ☎ 91 420 29 19, Calle del Infante 5)* the thing to do is dig into its amazing salad buffet for 2000 ptas. It's closed on Monday.

Vegetarian The *Restaurante Integral Artemisa (Map 7; ☎ 91 429 50 92, Calle de Ventura de la Vega 4)* is excellent. A full meal will cost around 2000 ptas and there is another branch (Map 4; ☎ 91 521 87 21) off Gran Vía at Calle de las Tres Cruces 4.

International Cuisine A cheerful Japanese spot is *Aki (☎ 91 420 10 49, Calle de Echegaray 9)*. You can sit at the bar and nibble at sushi and a wide variety of other specialities. The sushi special mix for 3000 ptas is quite enough for a main meal.

Lavapiés

Vegetarian You can pick up some good vegetarian food and a couple of nonvegetarian dishes at *El Granero de Lavapiés (Map 6; ☎ 91 467 76 11, Calle de Argumosa 10)*. Expect to pay around 2000 ptas for a meal. It's open daily for lunch but only Friday and Saturday for dinner.

Gran Vía, Malasaña & Chueca

Everything in this section is on Map 4 unless otherwise indicated.

For excellent *extremeño* food, make for *Restaurante Extremadura* (☎ 91 531 89 58, Calle de la Libertad 13). A meal with wine can come to around 3000 ptas per person. It's shut on Sunday night and Monday. There is a more modern and less enticing branch at No 31, which is closed on Tuesday night and Wednesday.

Restaurante Momo (☎ 91 532 71 62, Calle de Augusto Figueroa 41) has an above-average set evening menu for 1500 ptas, including wine. The cuisine tends to be inventive, steering well clear of standard Spanish stuff.

Undata (☎ 91 523 33 63, Calle de Clavel 5) is a cool place to dine if the minimalist, shiny chrome deal is your thing. It offers up what could be described as international Mediterranean cuisine, a bit of a pastiche. Prices are moderate. It's closed Sunday lunchtime and Monday evening.

International Cuisine For mouth-watering steak tartare and other French temptations, head for *Restaurante Dame Noire* (☎ 91 531 04 76, Calle de Pérez Galdós 3). It's open for dinner only Tuesday to Sunday.

Good Mexican food and excellent margaritas can be had at the *Taquería de Birrä* (☎ 91 522 80 49, Plaza de las Comendadoras 2), which has a lovely summertime terraza. Otherwise, head for its other branch (Map 6; ☎ 91 366 45 39, Calle de Don Pedro 11), just off Calle de Bailén near the Palacio Real.

Not only can you eat good meaty Argentine food at *La Carreta* (☎ 91 532 70 42, Calle de Barbieri 10), but you can do so until about 4 am on weekends.

Around Plaza de España

La Dama Duende (Map 4; ☎ 91 532 54 41, Calle de la Palma 63) is a tastefully simple little eatery with a touch of class. Try the *pez espada con salsa de puerros* (swordfish in leek sauce) and be sure to follow with one of the delicious desserts. You will probably pay around 3000 ptas per head.

International Cuisine *Adrish* (Map 4; ☎ 91 542 94 98, Calle de San Bernardino 1) offers about Madrid's best attempt at Indian food and does pretty convincing dishes, so expect to pay at least 2500 ptas per head.

Restaurante Bali (Map 4; ☎ 91 541 91 22, Calle de San Bernardino 6) is Madrid's only Indonesian restaurant. The authentic cooking is a welcome alternative to Iberian fare. A good meal should come in at 5000 ptas or less for two. It's closed on Sunday night and Monday lunchtime.

Salamanca, Goya & Beyond

Casa Julián (Map 3; ☎ 91 431 35 35, Calle de Don Ramón de la Cruz 10) specialises in grilled meats and, for this part of town, is a no-nonsense and atmospheric place. Grilled flesh of various red varieties is around 1500 ptas per person. It closes on Sunday evenings.

Restaurante El Pescador (Map 2; ☎ 91 402 12 90, Calle de José Ortega y Gasset 75) is a seafood specialist that's been around forever. It's closed on Sunday.

International Cuisine All of the best Chinese restaurants (and none match those you may be used to in your respective China towns, from London to Sydney) seem to be scattered about the north of the city. One of them is *China Crown* (Map 5; ☎ 91 572 14 64, Calle de la Infanta Mercedes 62). Expect to pay about 2000 ptas. It also does an acceptable dim-sum.

PLACES TO EAT – TOP END

Eating at the restaurants listed below will see your wallet lightened by sums from about 4000 ptas up.

Around Sol & Plaza Mayor

At *Restaurante Sobrino de Botín* (Map 6; ☎ 91 366 42 17, Calle de los Cuchilleros 17) the *menú* costs 4050 ptas. The restaurant is popular with those who can afford it and featured in Pérez Galdós' novel *Fortunata y Jacinta*.

Taberna del Alabardero (Map 4; ☎ 91 547 25 77, Calle de Felipe V 6) is fine for a splurge – expect little change per person from 6000 ptas. Or just try a few tapas at the bar.

MADRID

La Latina

Restaurante Gure-Etxea (Map 6; ☎ 91 365 61 49, Plaza de la Paja 12) is a fine Basque eatery and typically expensive. The *menú de degustación*, which allows you to sample a range of excellent Basque dishes, costs 3650 ptas per head.

Plaza de Santa Ana, Huertas & Atocha

Lhardy (Map 7; ☎ 91 521 33 85, Carrera de San Jerónimo 8) has been serving up gourmet tapas since 1839. It is closed on Sunday and holidays.

International Cuisine A good restaurant with a French leaning is *La Gastroteca de Stéphane y Arturo (Map 4; ☎ 91 532 25 64, Plaza de Chueca 8)*. Expect to part with at least 4000 ptas. It's closed Saturday lunchtime, all day Sunday and public holidays.

Around Plaza de España

Taberna La Bola (Map 4; ☎ 91 547 69 30, Calle de la Bola 5) has been stirring up a storm with its traditional *cocido a la madrileña* (Madrid-style stew) since 1880. The atmosphere reflects the years, making this a worthwhile once-off in spite of the prices. It's closed on Sunday evening.

CAFES & TEAHOUSES

There is no shortage of places to get a drink in Madrid – some areas are wall-to-wall bars. The neat Anglo-Saxon division between cafes (for coffee or tea and scones) and pubs or bars (for getting plastered) is a feature absent from the madrileño approach to drinking in society. Nevertheless, some bars are fairly evidently *not* intended for a leisurely *café con leche* and a read of the paper; these are dealt with under Entertainment. Others clearly do lean this way and what follow are some suggestions for these quieter pursuits.

Around Plaza Mayor

Café del Real (Map 6; ☎ 91 547 21 24), on Plaza de Isabel II, is an atmospheric place with a touch of elegance. It gets busy at night but also makes a pleasant spot for breakfast; head for the low-ceilinged upstairs section.

Up Calle de Vergara to Plaza de Ramales is a series of fine cafes. *Café Vergara (Map 6; ☎ 91 559 11 72, Calle de Vergara 1)* is good, and the rather stiff *Café de los Austrias (Map 6; ☎ 91 435 78 65, Plaza de Ramales 1)* seems as imperial as its name suggests.

Café de Oriente (Map 4; ☎ 91 541 39 74, Plaza de Oriente 2) feels like a set out of Mitteleuropa – it's well worth stopping by. If you are feeling peckish, it serves some very expensive food.

From Colón to the Prado

Just near Plaza de Colón, *Café-Restaurante El Espejo (Map 2; ☎ 91 308 23 47, Paseo de los Recoletos 31)* doubles as one of Madrid's most elegant cafes. You could also sit in the turn-of-the-century style *Pabellón del Espejo* outside. Despite appearances, it was only opened in 1990. Both are a little expensive and the latter also forms the nucleus of one of Madrid's more expensive summer *terrazas*.

Just down the road is the equally graceful *Gran Café de Gijón (Map 2; ☎ 91 521 54 25, Paseo de los Recoletos 21)*, which has been serving coffee and meals since 1888.

Another wonderful old place with chandeliers and an atmosphere belonging to another era is the cafe at the *Círculo de Bellas Artes (Map 4; ☎ 91 531 85 03, Calle de Alcalá 42)*. You have to buy a temporary club membership (100 ptas) to drink in here, but it's worth it.

Malasaña

Café Comercial (☎ 91 521 56 55, Glorieta de Bilbao 7) is an old Madrid cafe with a good whiff of its *castizo* past. The odd foreigner stops in, but it's just far enough off the usual tourist trail to be reasonably genuine. It and all the following are on Map 4.

Café Manuela (☎ 91 531 70 37, Calle de San Vicente Ferrer 29) lies on that borderline between cafe and bar. It is a young, hip place with a vaguely alternative flavour. *Café Isadora (☎ 91 445 71 54, Calle de Divino Pastor 14)* is great for chatting away the early evening over a coffee or cocktail.

An enchanting teahouse with a hint of the 1960s is *Tetería de la Abuela (Calle de*

Espíritu Santo 19). Along with the great range of teas, you can indulge in scrummy crepes.

For a somewhat camp but pleasant ambience, and a great cup of coffee and cheesecake, try *Café La Sastrería (☎ 91 532 07 71, Calle de Hortaleza 74)*. In keeping with the tailor theme, the black-clad waiters wear measuring tapes for ties.

Huertas & Lavapiés

Calle de las Huertas has a string of cafes and bars to choose from. On Plaza de Canalejas, you'll strike a fine, old madrileño bar, *Café del Príncipe* (Map 7). It does good food if you're peckish and the people-watching is an attraction in itself.

A wonderful old place, once the haunt of the artistic and hopefully artistic, *Nuevo Café Barbieri (Map 6; ☎ 91 527 36 58, Calle del Ave María 45)* provides newspapers to browse through while you sip your *cortado*.

If you'd prefer tea, there are several *teterías* (teahouses) in the Granada fashion dotted about the place. *Damasco Salón de Te* (Map 7) on Calle del Infante and *El Café de Sherazade (Map 7; Calle de Santa María 18)* are equally good.

PASTRY SHOPS

Central Madrid is riddled with pastry shops. A particularly good one is *Antigua Pastelería del Pozo (Map 7; ☎ 91 522 38 94, Calle del Pozo 8)*, near the Puerta del Sol. In operation since 1830 (and for 20 years before that as a bread bakery), it is the city's oldest dealer in tooth-rotting items.

ENTERTAINMENT

What Madrid may lack in grand sights, it makes up for in the life of its bars and clubs, its cinemas, theatres and cafes. Madrileños take their enjoyment seriously and there is every opportunity to join them.

The busiest time of year on Madrid's calendar – from theatre to rock concerts – runs from late September to early December in the Fiesta de Otoño (see Special Events earlier in this chapter).

You'll want to get some tips. *El País* has a daily listings section *(cartelera)* which is good for cinema and theatre. Original-language films and where they are shown are clearly indicated (look for movies in *versión original,* or *v.o. subtitulada)*. Also listed are museums, galleries, music venues and the like. *El Mundo* publishes a weekly magazine liftout, *Metropoli,* on Friday. Rival newspaper *ABC* brings out *Guía de Madrid* on the same day. The latter is better organised and strong on cinema and where to eat.

The weekly entertainment bible is, however, the *Guía del Ocio,* available at newsstands for 125 ptas.

You can generally get tickets for plays, concerts and other performances at the theatre concerned, but there are centralised ticketing offices too. Quite a few lottery ticket booths also sell tickets for theatre, football and bullfights. Try the Localidades La Alicantina (Map 4) on Plaza de Santo Domingo or Localidades Galicia (Map 4; ☎ 91 531 27 32) on Plaza del Carmen 1.

For many bands and popular music acts you can often get tickets at the Madrid Rock record store, at Calle Mayor 38 (Map 6), Gran Vía 25 and Calle de San Martín 3 (both Map 4). You can pay for tickets in cash only. The FNAC store (Map 4) on Calle de Preciados also sells tickets to major concerts in and beyond Madrid. Telephone booking is also possible. The Caixa de Catalunya operates the Tel-Entrada system, which covers many shows of all kinds. You call ☎ 902-38 33 33, pay for tickets by credit card and pick them up at the theatre before the show starts.

Pubs & Bars

Things have calmed down a little since the heyday of the *movida* in the years after Franco's death, but Madrid can still easily boast a breadth and depth of nightlife without compare anywhere else in Europe. Where else will you see bumper-to-bumper traffic at four in the morning? What follows is little more than a taste.

Plaza de Santa Ana, Huertas & Atocha

Plaza de Santa Ana is lined with interesting bars although clearly they have been discovered by locals and out-of-towners alike. Thursday night is best, as on Friday and

Saturday the place is full to bursting. All the following are on Map 7.

Cervecería Alemana (Plaza de Santa Ana 6) is a century-old meeting place and a traditional haunt of bullfighters.

La Fontana de Oro (Calle de la Victoria 2) is a reasonable 'Irish-style' pub with rather a longer history than most. Before occupation of the city by Napoleon's troops early in the last century, it was a hotbed of political dissent, as wine and antigovernment talk flowed freely.

Although it gets hellishly crowded on weekends, you should at least poke your head into *Viva Madrid (Calle de Manuel Fernández y González 7)*. The tiles and heavy timber ceilings make a distinctive setting for drinks earlier in the evening. Equally beautiful, but even more cheekily expensive, is *Los Gabrieles (Calle de Echegaray 17)*, just a few steps away. If tiles are your thing, another good choice is *España Cañí (Plaza del Ángel 14)*, west off Plaza de Santa Ana. The staff do a nice sangria.

To step into a space/time warp, slip into *La Venencia (Calle de Echegaray 7)* for a sherry. This place is the real thing: it looks as though nothing has been done to clean it in many a long year. Ill-lit and woody, it is the perfect place to sample one of six varieties of sherry – from the almost sweet *amontillado* to the rather biting *fino*.

Across the road, *El Margai (Calle de Echegaray 10)* is a classy little bar with a long drinks menu – and the drinks are *very* good. All Madrid seems to be raving about its cocktails.

At *Cardamomo (Calle de Echegaray 15)* there's flamenco and related music, although nothing live. Virtually around the corner, *Carbones*, on Calle de Manuel Fernández y González, is busy, open until about 4 am and features a good selection of mainstream music on the jukebox.

Cuevas de Sésamo (Calle del Príncipe 7) is a wonderful old cellar bar that specialises in sangria. The walls are plastered with meaningful aphorisms and the air is heavy with smoke – just the way bars used to be.

Casa Alberto (Calle de las Huertas 18) was founded in 1827 in a building where Cervantes did a spot of writing. It's a fine old place for vermouth on tap; you can also get a meal. It's closed Sunday night and Monday.

Café Populart (Calle de las Huertas 22) often has music, generally jazz or Celtic. For more jazz with your drinks, *Café Central (Plaza del Ángel 10)* is another good choice.

Just beyond the hubbub of Huertas is *El Parnaso (Calle de Moratín 25)*, a quirky but engaging spot. The area around the bar is jammed with an odd assortment of decorative paraphernalia, while out the back you get the feeling you're sitting in an ancient tramcar.

El Hecho (Calle de las Huertas 56) is a cosy little cocktail bar generally open until 3 am. It does great daiquiris and *mojitos* (a delicious and popular Cuban rum-based concoction), for which they have quite a name around town.

Around Sol & Plaza Mayor The *Casa Antonio (Map 6; Calle de Latrones 10)* is a wonderful old Madrid watering hole with loads of character and vermouth on tap.

El Templo del Gato (Map 4; Calle de Trujillos 7) is a Madrid classic. The music has a west coast tendency (which explains the alternative name, *California Music Bar)* and the atmosphere is of a gutsy rock bar. It closes around 4 am.

La Latina Calle de la Cava Baja in particular is full of taverns and eating houses. The places listed here are on Map 6 unless otherwise mentioned. *La Chata (Calle de la Cava Baja 24)* has a spectacular tiled frontage and is nice for a quick caña or two. Don't spend all your time here though. *Taberna Tempranillo (Calle de la Cava Baja 38)* has plenty of character and an endless selection of Spanish wines that you'll be encouraged to sample. You can get a beer anywhere, so take a look at the wine list here instead.

Taberna Almendro 13 (Calle del Almendro 13) has become a popular watering hole with locals. You can also get a bite to eat. Loiter about upstairs or head underground for seating. *Taberna Cien Vinos (Calle del Nuncio 17)* is a pleasant little locale to sit back in and wrap your taste buds around wines from around the country.

Just by the summertime terrazas of the Jardines de las Vistillas (see Terrazas later in this chapter) is a handful of intriguing places. The gaudily coloured *Travesía (Travesía de las Vistillas 8)* attracts a diverse crowd with its cocktails and South American music.

Café del Nuncio (Calle del Nuncio 12) straggles down a stairway passage to Calle de Segovia. You can drink on one of the several cosy levels inside or, better still in summer, tipple outdoors.

Lavapiés This district is one of the last worker-gitano quarters in central Madrid. While the bars are often *cutre* (basic, spit-and-sawdust style), they brim with a raw energy. All these spots are on Map 6.

Taberna de Antonio Sánchez (Calle de Mesón de Paredes 13) is an old-time drinking place with a slightly conspiratorial air; it serves beer, wine and snacks, and that's about it.

An excellent place for cañas and seafood *pinchos* (snacks) is *El Boquerón (Calle de Valencia 14)*, which has a rough-around-the-edges feel and is popular with people in the area. Around the corner you can hang out in *La Mancha de Madrid*, on Calle de Miguel Servet, which attracts a colourful array of local tipplers earlier in the evening.

Just around the corner from the Teatro Olimpia is *Eucalipto (Calle de Argumosa 4)*, something of a local hub and a great place for daiquiris.

Gran Vía, Malasaña & Chueca Along with the Santa Ana and Huertas area, the web of streets and lanes stretching northwards off Gran Vía is Madrid's other great party paradise, with more bars, pubs, dance places and general drinking potential than you can shake a stick at. All these places are on Map 4.

If you really want to get basic, the place marked *Vinos (Calle de Sagasta 2)* is for you; it serves wine and various cheeses. Around the corner you can get an Asturian cider and an *empanada* (pie) for 185 ptas at *Corripio (Calle de Fuencarral 102)*.

Cervecería de Santa Bárbara (Plaza de Santa Bárbara 8) is a classic old Madrid drinking house and is generally packed early in the night. It is a good place to kick off a night in Malasaña.

Cervecería Bulevar (Calle de Santa Teresa 2) is another fun and busy meeting place nearby. Even on a Saturday night it's possible to reach the bar. It's open until 2 am (4 am on Friday and Saturday).

Big Bamboo (Calle de Barquillo 42) is a smoky little joint where punters sway to the reggae rhythms until at least 6 am. You pay 500 ptas (which includes a beer) to get in, which ain't bad at all. Another nearby reggae place currying favour at the moment is *Kingston's (Calle de Barquillo 29)*.

Café Belén (Calle de Belén 5) is a good spot to retire for a quiet romantic cocktail. The music is low key and eclectic and the punters are intent on enjoying each other's company rather than being raucous and rowdy.

Bodega de la Ardosa (Calle de Colón 13) is a wonderful, dimly lit bar where you can sip on a vermouth drawn from the barrel. If it really must be a Guinness, step around the corner to *The Quiet Man (Calle de Valverde 44)*.

On the Irish theme, *Finnegan's (Plaza de las Salesas 9)* has become an obligatory stop for aficionados of the dark fluids. Calle de San Vicente Ferrer has a fair quota of bars, and on the corner of Corradera Alta de San Pablo is *Triskel (Calle de San Vicente Ferrer 3)*, yet another jolly Irish joint.

La Vía Láctea (Calle de Velarde 18) is a bright, thumping sort of place with a young, *macarra* crowd. It is an old classic from the days of the movida that has somehow managed to survive.

In *Café del Foro (Calle de San Andrés 38)* the decor of traditional Madrid shopfronts surrounds an intimate stage where you can often hear good live music.

For one of the best mojitos in the area, pop into the *Café Magerit (Calle del Divino Pastor 21)*.

Plaza del Dos de Mayo can seem like a scene from a young alcoholic *Ben-Hur*, with madrileños careering around in all directions clutching large cups and bottles of various beverages.

Up on Plaza de las Comendadoras, the lightly Art Deco *Café Moderno* is a cosy place in winter, especially if you're there on a Thursday night for the belly dancing!

The Chueca area (see also Gay & Lesbian Venues later in this chapter) is not exclusively gay. Everyone can enjoy this pleasingly seedy district. Watch out for the wonderful, gloomy old vermouth bar, *Sierra Ángel (Calle de Gravina 11),* overlooking Plaza de Chueca.

Heading towards Gran Vía, *Libertad 8 (Calle de la Libertad 8)* was a favoured haunt of the Left around the time of Franco's demise. It still gets an animated crowd to see singer-songwriters perform, or sit in on the odd poetry reading. Another pleasant place with tiled walls and a cosy feel is *Bar La Carmencita (Calle de la Libertad 16).*

The simply decorated *Del Diego Bar (Calle de la Reina 12)* does great cocktails for around 900 ptas. The music and atmosphere are good and it fills up pretty quickly.

Museo Chicote (Gran Vía 12) is an Art Deco special (founded in 1931) and long the haunt of Madrid's chic and well connected. Hemingway and other swells used to hang out here and in the 1940s and 50s it was *the* place to be seen. The decor reflects the era but the music often jars. Drinks are average and pricey – you are paying for the tradition rather than the quality. The bar used to be directly connected with *Cock Bar (Calle de la Reina 16),* which once served as a discreet salon for a higher class of prostitution. The ladies in question have gone, but this popular bar retains plenty of atmosphere – even if the name is a little startling.

Salamanca, Goya & Beyond The *Teatriz (Map 3; Calle de la Hermosilla 15)* is a chichi hang-out with a difference. The former Teatro Beatriz, decorated by French designer Philippe Starck, has an eerily lit bar right on the stage. Drinks are for heavily lined wallets only, as is the food. It sounds like odd advice, but check out the toilets.

Moving north, Avenida del Brasil (Map 5) hosts half a dozen bars that keep a faithful crowd more than occupied until around 6 am. The best is the immense and immensely popular *Irish Rover* at No 7.

Live Music

Bands don't usually appear on stage before 10 pm and often wait until midnight. You can dance at some of these venues.

Rock Concerts Several venues are used for major concerts, whether Spanish groups or international acts. A common one is the *Plaza de Toros Monumental de Ventas* (see Bullfighting later in this chapter). Others include the *Antiguo Cuartel del Conde Duque* (Map 4) and the *Teatro Monumental* (Map 7). A smaller venue but one that regularly features name acts from Spain and abroad is *La Riviera (Map 2; ☎ 91 435 85 08, Paseo de la Virgen del Puerto s/n),* near the Puente de Segovia.

Sala Caracol (Map 2; ☎ 91 528 69 77, Calle de Bernardino Obregón 18) is another long-standing venue for Spanish and foreign acts.

Jazz One of Madrid's better known jazz haunts is *Clamores Jazz Club (Map 2; ☎ 91 445 79 38, Calle de Alburquerque 14).* It is generally open all week. Usually there is no cover charge, and the place gets quite a good selection of acts. You can also catch the occasional jazz performance at *Café Central* and *Café Populart* (both on Map 7; see Pubs & Bars earlier in this chapter).

Latin The *Galileo Galilei (Map 2; ☎ 91 534 75 57, Calle de Galileo 100)* attracts a good mix of Hispanic dance groups and vocalists.

A good place to indulge in salsas, merengues and other Latin grooves is *Vaiven (Map 4; ☎ 91 319 28 18, Travesía de San Mateo 1).* There is no cover charge, but a beer costs about 600 ptas.

El Son (Map 7; Calle de la Victoria 6) rocks away daily from 7 pm to the wee hours. Often it has music playing live from Cuba, and midweek you can get in some saucy salsa lessons with the island's teachers.

Flamenco There are several *tablaos* (flamenco performance spots) in central Madrid, but most are designed for the tourist crowd. They generally feature dinner and flamenco shows of indifferent quality, much avoided by locals. They all feature in entertainment guides. The best of this poor lot appears to be *Café de Chinitas (Map 4; ☎ 91 559 51 35, Calle de Torija 7)*. You will almost certainly need to book ahead. Another is *Corral de la Morería (Map 6; ☎ 91 365 84 46, Calle de la Morería 17)*.

To get a feel for the more genuine article, you have several options. You can try the handful of *peñas flamencas* (flamenco clubs), or bars where flamenco music is often played, although not necessarily live.

For some, *La Soleá (Map 6; ☎ 91 365 52 64, Calle de la Cava Baja 34)* is the last real flamenco bar in Madrid, where aficionados enjoy performers who know it all. At *Candela (Map 7; ☎ 91 467 33 82, Calle del Olmo 3)* the *gitanos* (Roma people, formerly known as Gypsies) practise their music and dance out the back (and you probably won't be allowed to watch), but the bar is charged with an Andalucian flamenco atmosphere. Occasionally you'll get lucky and witness impromptu jam sessions.

Casa Patas (Map 7; ☎ 91 369 04 96, Calle de Cañizares 10) is a little more organised and plays host to recognised masters of flamenco guitar, song and dance.

Teatro Lara (Map 4; ☎ 91 521 05 52, Calle de la Corredera Baja de San Pablo 15) also sometimes puts on flamenco shows.

Other The *Suristán (Map 7; ☎ 91 532 39 09, Calle de la Cruz 7)* gets in a wide variety of acts, from Cuban to African. Music usually kicks off at 11.30 pm and there is sometimes a cover charge of up to 1000 ptas (including a drink).

Clubs & Discos

On weekends in particular, it is quite possible to continue the 'night' well into the day. While most places tend to start edging punters out around dawn, a 9 or 10 am finish is the norm in a few clubs, which in Spain still tend to be called *discotecas*.

Gran Vía, Malasaña & Chueca All the following are on Map 4. *Morocco (Calle del Marqués de Leganés 7)* is still a popular stop on the Madrid dance circuit, although some say it has passed its peak. It usually swings into gear from about 1 am.

Ya'sta! (Calle de Valverde 10) is another place that doesn't swing into action until the early morning. It has a reputation as a meat market, but is a lot of good sweaty dance fun.

Pachá (Calle de Barceló 11) is an old favourite that seems to come and go. It is open until 5 am and entry can cost up to 2000 ptas (including your first drink).

Around Plaza de España All of the following are on Map 4. *Arena (Calle de la Princesa 1)* offers music for all tastes – funky, house, techno and acid jazz – until 6.30 am from Wednesday to Sunday.

Midnight (Calle de Amaniel 13) is one of the few clubs to steer clear of house, but the punters still manage to have fun. It's open until the wee hours from Thursday to Saturday.

Siroco (Calle de San Dimas 3) gets in new DJs every week to pump out sounds ranging from hip hop to Spanish pop. It's open until 6 am from Thursday to Saturday.

Plaza de Santa Ana, Sol & Latina The *Villa Rosa (Map 7; Plaza de Santa Ana 15)* is as remarkable for its decor as anything else, but from about 1 am is a mellow place for a drink and some shaking of stuff on the small dance floor. The tile decoration outside (pictures of Sevilla, Granada and Córdoba) and within, as well as the vaguely *artesonado*-style ceiling, make it a unique spot.

On Calle de la Cruz are a couple of dance spaces. You may well have to queue if you have no passes or fliers for them. *Torero (Map 7; Calle de la Cruz 26)* has two floors, featuring Spanish music upstairs and international tunes downstairs.

Oui (Map 7; Calle de Cervantes 7) puts on all sorts of music through the week in a build-up to a diet of hip hop, techno and drum 'n' bass on the weekend.

No Se Lo Digas A Nadie (Map 7; Calle de Ventura de la Vega 7) is a popular dance spot open until at least 3 am. The real hardcore night owls can later make their way to **Stella-Wake Club** *(Map 7; Calle de Arlabán 7)*, open until about 10 am on weekends. Friday and Saturday nights typically heave with house.

El Sol *(Map 4; Calle de los Jardines 3)* is another 'in' location with tireless madrileños. You pay 1200 to get in, which includes a drink.

El Viajero *(Map 6; Plaza de la Cebada 11)* is good for acid jazz, trip hop and funk.

Palacio Gaviria *(Map 6; Calle del Arenal 9)* is indeed palatial. It's divided into a series of old-style salons to meet most middle-of-the-road tastes, from waltzes to mainstream disco blah, with a couple of small corners scattered about for a quiet drink or a snog. The place gets going at about 2 am and entry can cost up to 2000 ptas. A beer is 900 ptas and a mixed drink is 1500 ptas.

Just next door is one of Madrid's premier nightspots, **Teatro Joy Eslava** *(Map 6; ☎ 91 366 37 33 for reservations, Calle del Arenal 11)*, which started life as a comedy theatre in 1871. It is now deadly serious dance fun and entry is 2000 ptas on weekends.

Kapital *(Map 6; Calle de Atocha 125)* boasts seven floors of heaving bods from Thursday to Saturday, starting at midnight and closing at dawn. Expect queues and an entry charge of up to 2000 ptas.

Gay & Lesbian Venues

Most of Madrid's gay and lesbian life is played out around the Chueca area. This is the area to go not only for night time distraction but also for hotels catering to gays, gay shops, saunas and associations. A heavy concentration of the city's gay population actually lives in the neighbourhood too. Except where specified, all these places are on Map 4.

Bars The *Acuarela Café (Calle de Gravina 10)* is a quiet place for an intimate drink in a gay arty atmosphere. Right next door on the corner with the square is *Truco*, one of the city's few predominantly lesbian bars, although plenty of straights seem to end up here too.

Rimmel *(Calle de Luis de Góngora 4)* and **Cruising** *(Calle de Pérez Galdós 5)* are among the more popular gay haunts. The latter has a dark room and puts on occasional shows.

Clubs & Discos At *Truck (Calle de la Libertad 28)* you can get down to popular hits from the 60s onwards – a lively, fun place.

Rick's *(Calle de Clavel 8)* is a heaving bar that fills to bursting most nights. They throw the doors open at 11 pm and stay up until the wee hours.

Ales *(Calle de Veneras 2)* is a classic of the gay night circuit, open 1.30 am to dawn. Entry costs from 500 to 1500 ptas depending on the night and whether there is some kind of show – usually of the drag persuasion.

Strong *(Calle de Trujillo 7)* is a fairly intense gay guys disco with a particularly active dark room. It's open every night from midnight to dawn and entry costs 1000 ptas.

Refugio *(Map 7; Calle del Doctor Cortezo 1)* is a popular gay dance club open from midnight to dawn. It's relaxed and a few straights manage to find their way in too. You pay 1000 ptas to get in, which includes a drink.

Terrazas

Many of the places listed earlier have terrazas – tables set up on the footpath or plaza – most of which spring up like mushrooms in the summer. The season is from about April to October and the bars that run them pay for a specific extra licence to operate.

Probably the best located one is *Bar Ventorrillo* (Map 6) on Corral de la Morería, just by the Jardines de las Vistillas. This is a wonderful spot to relax and drink in the views of the Sierra de Guadarrama, especially around sunset. During the Fiestas de San Isidro (see Special Events earlier in this chapter) bands play in the gardens.

Some of the terrazas, such as those that emerge along Paseo de la Castellana and Paseo de los Recoletos, are something of a haunt for *la gente guapa* (the beautiful people) – those who want to be seen spending serious money for their libations. A perfect case in point is *Bolero (Map 3; Paseo de la*

Castellana 33), where a modest beer costs 600 ptas. *Boulevard 37 (Map 3; Paseo de la Castellana 37)* is largely the domain of better-off university students. For a more staid beginning to the evening, *El Espejo (Map 2; Paseo de los Recoletos 31)* is hard to beat for elegance (see also Places to Eat earlier in this chapter).

Less pretentious and considerably more pleasant are the terrazas that go up in Argüelles – more specifically, on Paseo del Pintor Rosales. With parkland on one side and considerably less traffic than on Paseo de la Castellana, these places also exercise a little more control over their prices. *Terraza España* (Map 2) is one of several.

Madrid's squares make perfect locations for outdoor drinking. Several of the bars on Plaza de Santa Ana operate terrazas, as does *Café de Oriente (Map 4; Plaza de Oriente)*; see Places to Eat earlier in this chapter. Bars spread summertime liquid satisfaction across such squares as Plaza del Dos de Mayo and Plaza de las Comendadoras, both in the Malasaña area (Map 4), as well as Plaza del Conde Barajas (just south off Plaza Mayor) and around Plaza de los Carros.

Classical Music & Opera

At the city's grandest stage, the *Teatro Real (Map 4; ☎ 91 516 06 06, bookings through the Caja de Madrid bank on ☎ 902-48 84 88)*, tickets for the opera or ballet can range from 1000 ptas for a spot so far away you need a telescope to around 20,000 ptas.

The *Auditorio Nacional de Música (Map 5; ☎ 91 337 01 40, Calle del Príncipe de Vergara 146)* is the main venue for classical music. On a smaller scale, the *Fundación Juan March (Map 2; ☎ 91 435 42 40, Calle de Castelló 77)* holds regular Sunday concerts.

If you can't get into the Teatro Real, the *Teatro Calderón (Map 7; ☎ 91 369 14 34, Calle de Atocha 18)* plays second fiddle for opera. The *Teatro de la Zarzuela (Map 7; ☎ 91 524 54 00, Calle de Jovellanos 4)* is the place for that very Spanish genre of classical dance and music, the *zarzuela*. The theatre was built in 1856 in vague imitation of Milan's La Scala.

For other musical and operatic performances, the Centro Cultural de la Villa (see Theatre later in this section) and the *Teatro Monumental (Map 7; ☎ 91 429 81 19, Calle de Atocha 65)* are the main venues to look out for.

Cinemas

A standard cinema ticket costs around 850 ptas, but many cinemas have at least one day set aside as the *día del espectador* (viewer's day) for cut-price tickets (usually about 200 ptas off).

One of the best concentrations of cinemas for original-language films is on and around Calle de Martín de los Heros and Calle de la Princesa (Map 4). The *Renoir* and *Princesa (both ☎ 91 541 41 00)*, and *Alphaville (☎ 91 559 38 36)* cinema complexes around here all screen such movies.

The *Cine Doré (Map 7; ☎ 91 549 60 11, Calle de Santa Isabel 3)*, which houses the Filmoteca Nacional, is a wonderful old cinema that shows classics past and present, all in the original language. It has a cheap restaurant attached. If you're in Madrid for any length of time, consider getting a *bono*, which gives you cut-price tickets.

You can also see subtitled movies at *Multicines Ideal (Map 7; ☎ 91 369 25 18, Calle del Doctor Cortezo 6)*, the *Renoir (Map 5; ☎ 91 541 41 00, Calle de Raimundo Fernández Villaverde 10)* or *Real Cinema (Map 4; ☎ 91 547 45 77)* on Plaza de Isabel II.

The huge-screen *Cine Imax (☎ 91 467 48 00)* is in the Parque Enrique Tierno Galván at Camino de Meneses s/n, south of Atocha train station. For this 3D-cinema experience you pay between 900 and 1400 ptas, depending on what's showing.

Theatre

Autumn is a busy season for theatre after the torpor of summer. Although the theatre, music and dance scene is not as diverse or of as high a quality as in some other European capitals, there is plenty happening and a plethora of venues large and small, of which the following are a representative selection.

The beautiful old *Teatro de la Comedia (Map 7; ☎ 91 521 49 31, Calle del Príncipe 14)*

MADRID

is home to the Compañía Nacional de Teatro Clásico and often stages gems of classic Spanish and European theatre. The *Teatro de Bellas Artes (Map 4; ☎ 91 532 44 38, Calle del Marqués de Casa Riera 2)* also leans towards the classics.

The *Teatro Español (Map 7; ☎ 91 429 62 97, Calle del Príncipe 25)* is another venue where you can see mainstream drama. A theatre has stood on this spot since 1583, when it was known as the Corral del Príncipe. It later became known as the Teatro del Príncipe and in 1849 was renamed the Teatro Español.

At the *Centro Cultural de la Villa (☎ 91 575 60 80)*, under the waterfall at Plaza de Colón, you can see anything from classical music concerts to comic theatre, opera and quality flamenco.

Amusement Parks

Travellers with kids on the leash can let them loose at the *Parque de Atracciones*, full of rides, shows and all the usual diversions you would expect of such a Luna Park. (In 2000 it opened up with several new rides and shows.) The park is in the Casa de Campo area west of the city centre (metro: Batán). It is open daily except some Mondays from May to mid-September. Opening times vary considerably (usually from noon until midnight or later, but generally from 6 pm in late July and August). In winter it tends to open on weekends and holidays only, from noon to 7 pm. The cheapest ticket (600 ptas) allows you entry alone. An unlimited all-rides stamp on your hand costs 2675 ptas for adults and 1500 ptas for children up to the age of seven. Single-ride tickets are also available.

SPECTATOR SPORTS
Football

Even if soccer (as it is known to some) doesn't interest you, a good match in Spain provides an insight into an essential aspect of Spanish leisure.

Real Madrid Football Club is one of Europe's best teams and has a fine stadium, the *Estadio Santiago Bernabéu (Map 5; ☎ 91 398 43 00)*, which has a capacity of 85,000.

Games are quite an occasion as long as the opposition is good enough to fire up the home team and the crowd. Check the daily press for upcoming games.

Tickets generally cost from 2500 to 9000 ptas. They can be bought on the day or in advance at the stadium or from ticket offices (more expensive) at Calle de la Victoria, near Puerta del Sol. You can also try Localidades La Alicantina and Localidades Galicia (see the introduction to this chapter). Another option is to book them over the phone through the Servi-Caixa (☎ 902-33 22 11).

The city's other main club (rapidly heading for second division as we write), Atlético de Madrid, is based at the *Estadio Vicente Calderón (Map 2; ☎ 91 366 47 07)*, south-west of the centre at Calle de la Virgen del Puerto (metro: Pirámides). Tickets cost the same and are available at the stadium or the same advance purchase locations mentioned above.

A local derby, or better still a match between Real Madrid and archrivals Barcelona, is a guarantee that sparks will fly – although getting tickets can be difficult for these matches.

JANE SMITH

Spaniards love *fútbol* – and it's worth checking out a match while in Madrid.

Bullfighting

In spite of the Hemingway-inspired fame of the Pamplona fiesta, connoisseurs would rather get a front seat in Madrid's *Plaza de Toros Monumental de Las Ventas (Map 2; ☎ 91 356 22 00, Calle de Alcalá 237)* for a good fight. The ring is the biggest in the bullfighting world. The best fiesta begins in mid-May, marking the holiday for Madrid's patron saint, San Isidro Labrador (see Special Events earlier in this chapter), and lasts well into June. It is the most important bullfight season in the world, making or breaking *toreros* (bullfighters) and bull breeders alike. Otherwise, *corridas* (bullfights) are organised regularly on weekends over the summer.

You can also see corridas at the *Plaza de Toros Vista Alegre* (which was completely renovated in 2000), near the metro station of the same name.

For more information on the season at Las Ventas, and lots of background material too, visit the Las Ventas Web site at www.las-ventas.com.

Tickets *(entradas)* start at 525 ptas for standing room in the sun *(sol)* and a long way from the action. They can rise to about 17,000 ptas for front row seats in the shade *(sombra)*. Cheaper seats in the shade can come in at anything from 3000 to 7000 ptas, depending on where the seat is in the ring.

You can purchase tickets at the rings, from the ticket offices on Calle de la Victoria (Map 7) or other places selling theatre tickets and the like (see Tickets under Entertainment earlier in this chapter). Note that the ticket offices add 20%. It is wise to buy tickets in advance, although you may be able to get basic seating in the sun on the day. Scalpers also operate outside the rings and ticket offices. During the San Isidro feria booking is mandatory. Ringside seats in the shade have been known to go for as much as two million pesetas!

For more detailed information on bullfighting, see the special section 'The Bullfight' earlier in this book.

SHOPPING

On Sunday morning, the Embajadores area of Madrid seems to contain half the city's population as all and sundry converge on El Rastro, the flea market. Starting from Plaza de Cascorro, its main axes are Calle de Ribeira de Curtidores and Calle de los Embajadores. A good deal of what's on sale is rubbish, but the atmosphere alone is worth the effort, and you can find interesting items. There are a good many junk and antique stores sprinkled about too.

Those looking to do some shopping in a more chichi environment should head for Calle de Serrano (Map 3), the city's premier shopping street, in Salamanca. Of interest to those hanging around Madrid for the long haul is Marks & Spencer, whose food department carries all sorts of goodies otherwise unavailable in Madrid. Also well worth exploring is the area around Calle del Almirante, just east of Plaza de Chueca, considered the city's best alternative fashion showcase.

Leather goods and shoes are one of the best buys in the city. You'll find several good stores along Calle de Serrano.

Madrid's, and indeed Spain's, best-known department store chain is El Corte Inglés. There's one located just off the Puerta del Sol on Calle de Preciados (Map 4). A couple of others are marked on the Maps 2 and 3.

For specialist purchases, you need to look elsewhere. Hunt around along Calle Mayor (Map 6), especially towards its western end, for guitars and other instruments. Calle del Prado (Map 7) is a good place for a higher class of furniture and other antique items.

There are plenty of kitsch souvenirs of Madrid sold around Plaza Mayor and Sol, along Gran Vía or around the Prado. A popular item is a bullfighting poster with your name inscribed as lead torero.

If you're looking for gifts of quality Spanish wines and foodstuffs, there are several shops in the Salamanca area. Mallorca (Map 3) at Calle de Velázquez 59 is a good one.

CDs and cassettes are not especially cheap in Spain but, if you're looking for local music difficult to find at home, try the music sections of El Corte Inglés or FNAC, on Calle de Preciados. Madrid Rock (for addresses, see Tickets under Entertainment) probably has the broadest general music selection and most competitive prices.

For the late-night munchies and other emergencies, there is a sprinkling of stores across central Madrid. VIPS is the most widespread, and there are 7-Elevens too (some have been marked on the maps).

If you want a more comprehensive guide to shopping in Madrid, ask the tourist office for its *Guía de Compras* booklet.

GETTING THERE & AWAY
Air
Regular and charter flights from all over the world arrive at Madrid's Aeropuerto de Barajas (☎ 91 393 60 00, flight information ☎ 902-35 35 70), 13km north-east of the city. You can also get flight information online (for all Spanish airports) at www.aena.es.

The airport building is divided into three terminals (T1, T2 and T3). A new terminal building is due to be built by the end of 2003. The arrivals halls are on the ground floor and departures are upstairs. Check-in *(facturación)* is mostly done on the upstairs level.

Two left-luggage offices *(consignas)* operate at the airport, one in the T1 terminal (near the bus stop and taxi stand) and the other in T2 (near the metro entrance).

You'll find several banks with ATMs, a post office, tourist information, hotel booking stand, and general information office throughout the airport. The metro, buses and taxis link the airport with the centre of Madrid.

Internal flights are not particularly good value unless you are in a burning hurry. Nor is Madrid exactly the budget airfare capital of Europe. That said, bargain flights to popular destinations such as London, New York and the Canary Islands can be found.

For hints on good travel agencies, see Information earlier. For more information on flights and airfares, see the Air sections in the Getting There & Away and Getting Around chapters.

Most airlines have representatives at the airport, as well as in Madrid itself. They include:

Aerolíneas Argentinas (Map 4; ☎ 91 590 20 60) Calle de María de Molina 40
Air France (Map 4; ☎ 91 330 04 12, bookings ☎ 901-11 22 66) Torre de Madrid, Plaza de España 18

American Airlines (Map 5; ☎ 91 453 14 00) Calle de Orense 4
British Airways (☎ 91 387 43 00 or 902-11 13 33) Calle de Pinar 7
Iberia (Map 5; ☎ 91 587 75 36, bookings ☎ 902-40 05 00) Calle de Velázquez 130
KLM (Map 4; ☎ 91 305 43 47) Gran Vía 59
Lufthansa Airlines (Map 5; ☎ 902-22 01 01) Calle del Cardenal Marcelo Spinola 2
Regional Airlines (Map 2; ☎ 91 401 21 36) Calle del General Pardiñas 62
Sabena (Map 4; ☎ 91 540 18 51) Torre de Madrid, Plaza de España 18
SAS (Map 4; ☎ 91 454 66 00) Edificio de España, Gran Vía 86
Thai Airways International (Map 5; ☎ 91 782 05 21) Calle del Príncipe de Vergara 185
Virgin Express (Map 4; ☎ 91 541 14 94) Torre de Madrid, Plaza de España 18

Bus
There are as many as eight bus stations *(estaciónes de autobuses)* dotted about Madrid with companies servicing different parts of the country. The tourist offices can provide detailed information on where you need to go for your destination.

The Estación Sur de Autobuses (metro: Méndez Álvaro) on Calle de Méndez Álvaro, is the city's principal bus station just south of the M-30 ring road. It serves most destinations to the south and many in other parts of the country. Most bus companies have a ticket office here, even if their buses depart from elsewhere. You can get information on ☎ 91 468 42 00.

The station is big and operates a left-luggage office, which is open 6.30 am to midnight. From this station is direct access to the No 6 metro line and *cercanías* (suburban trains) to Atocha and Chamartín train stations.

Quite a few companies operate out of other stations around the city. Of these some useful ones include:

AutoRes (Map 2; ☎ 91 551 72 00, bookings ☎ 902-19 29 39) Calle de Fernández Shaw 1. It operates buses to Extremadura, western Castilla y León (eg, Tordesillas, Salamanca and Zamora) and Valencia via eastern Castilla-La Mancha, for instance Cuenca.
Continental-Auto (Map 5; ☎ 91 533 04 00, bookings ☎ 902-33 04 00) Calle de Alenza 20.

This company runs buses north to Burgos, Logroño, Navarra, the Basque Country, Santander and Soria. It also runs buses to Toledo from the Estación Sur and to Alcalá de Henares and Guadalajara from the Intercambiador de Avenida de América (Map 2), an underground bus station. Note that the station at Calle de Alenza is due to close some time in 2000. The bus routes operating from there will be transferred to the Intercambiador de Avenida de América.

Herranz (☎ 91 890 41 00) Its buses to San Lorenzo de El Escorial leave from the Intercambiador de Autobuses, a bus station below ground level at the Moncloa metro station (Map 2). The buses leave from platform 3.

La Sepulvedana (Map 2; ☎ 91 530 48 00) Paseo de la Florida 11. It operates buses to La Granja de San Ildefonso, Navacerrada and San Rafael (near Cercedilla). Buses for Talavera de la Reina also depart from here.

La Veloz (Map 2; ☎ 91 409 76 02) Avenida del Mediterráneo 49. It has regular buses to Chinchón.

Some sample one-way fares from Madrid include (in some cases competing companies offer different prices – always check):

destination	travel time (hours)	fare (ptas)
Alicante	5¼	2995
Barcelona	7 to 8	3400
Córdoba	4½	1600
Granada	5	1960
Málaga	6	2625
Oviedo	4¾	3825
San Sebastián	5¾ to 6½	3800
Santiago de Compostela	9	5135
Sevilla	6	2745

Train

Madrid is served by two main train stations. The bigger of the two is Atocha (Map 2), at the southern end of the city centre. Trains from here fan out right across the country. Chamartín train station (Map 5) lies in the north of the city.

The bulk of trains for the rest of Spain depart from Atocha, especially those going south. International services arrive at and leave from Chamartín. Several services for northern destinations depart from Chamartín.

Some services to Granada, Algecíras and so forth start in Chamartín, and don't even necessarily stop at Atocha on the way through. When buying a ticket, be sure that you find out which station the train leaves from. Of the two, Atocha is handier for the centre of town, hotels and so on.

International services to France and Portugal start at Chamartín and do *not* pass through Atocha.

The main Renfe booking office (Map 4; ☎ 91 328 90 20), Calle de Alcalá 44, is open 9.30 am to 8 pm weekdays.

For more details and sample fares, see under Train in the Getting Around chapter earlier in this book.

Car & Motorcycle

Madrid is surrounded by two ring-road systems – the innermost M-30 and newer M-40 (eventually a third, the M-50, will form the outer ring). Madrid, like Paris, is a hub from which spokes head out in all directions; these can be clogged at rush hour (around 8 to 10 am, 2 pm, 4 to 5 pm and 8 to 9 pm). Sunday night, especially on the highways from the south, can also be bad. If you intend to hitch, get well out of town first.

Rental The big-name car-rental agencies have offices all over Madrid. Avis, Budget, Europcar, Hertz and Atesa/EuroDollar have booths at the airport. Some addresses include:

Avis (Map 4; ☎ 902-13 55 31 or 91 547 20 48) Gran Vía 60
Budget (☎ 902-20 12 12 or 91 577 63 63) Aeropuerto de Barajas
Europcar (Map 4; ☎ 91 541 88 92) Calle de San Leonardo 8
Euro Rental (Map 2; ☎ 91 356 65 78) Avenida de los Toreros 12
Hertz (Map 4; ☎ 91 542 58 03, reservations ☎ 902-40 24 05) Edificio de España, Plaza de España
Juliá Car (☎ 91 779 18 60) Puerto de Used 20 (call this number or book through travel agencies where you see the Juliá Car sign)
National/Atesa (Map 4; ☎ 902-10 01 01 or 91 542 50 15) Gran Vía 80

You can rent motorbikes from Moto Alquiler (Map 4; ☎ 91 542 06 57), Calle del Conde

Duque 13, but it's a pricey business. Something like a Yamaha 650 will cost you 16,000 ptas per day plus tax, with a refundable deposit of 175,000 ptas on your credit card. If you just take the bike for a day, rental time is from 8 am to 8 pm. For a scooter (eg, 50cc Honda Sky), rates start at 4500 ptas plus 16% IVA per day. The refundable deposit is 50,000 ptas.

Bicycle

Karacol Sport (Map 2; ☎ 91 539 96 33), Calle de Tortosa 8, rents out mountain bikes. The best offer is a weekend (from Friday to Monday) for 4000 ptas. There's a refundable deposit of 5000 ptas and you need to leave an original document (passport, driving licence or the like).

GETTING AROUND

Madrid is well served by a decent underground rail system (metro) and an extensive bus service. In addition, you can get from the north to the south of the city quickly by using cercanías between the Atocha and Chamartín train stations. Taxis are also a viable option.

To/From the Airport

Metro This is the easiest way into town. From the airport you get line 8 to Mar de Cristal, where you change to line 4 to head into the city. Depending on where you want to end up, you may well have to change again. The line will eventually run to Nuevos Ministerios.

The entrance to the metro at the airport is from the upper level of T2 terminal. It should not take much more than 30 minutes to reach the middle of town (eg, Colón station).

Bus The airport bus arrives at and departs from an underground terminal in Plaza de Colón (Map 3). When heading out to the airport, you could opt to pick it up at a stop next to the Avenida de América metro station, which helps you dodge most of the city traffic. Generally, the metro is easier. If for whatever reason you want to catch the bus, the fare is 385 ptas and buses leave every 12 to 15 minutes. Allow about 30 minutes in average traffic conditions.

Taxi A taxi to/from the centre will cost you about 2000 ptas, depending on traffic and how much luggage you have. To the Chamartín train station you might pay about 1500 ptas, or 1900 ptas to Atocha. There are taxi ranks outside all three terminals.

Those in a real hurry can use the Aero-CITY service (☎ 91 571 96 96), Calle de Orense 69. It will take you 'door-to-door' from central Madrid to the airport and vice versa. Depending on how many passengers book this minibus, the fare can range from 600 to 1500 ptas per person. It operates 24 hours.

Bus

An extensive bus system operates throughout Madrid and outlying suburbs. Unless you buy season passes, you can get tickets on the bus or at most tobacconists (estancos). A single ride costs 135 ptas, or a Metrobus ticket of 10 rides is 705 ptas; the latter entitles you to use buses and the metro, and you can share tickets.

Monthly or season passes (abonos) only make sense if you are staying for the long term and using local transport frequently. You need to get an ID card (carnet) from metro stations or tobacconists. Take a passport-sized photo and your passport or public transport photocard. A monthly ticket for central Madrid (Zona A) costs 4620 ptas and is valid for unlimited travel on bus, metro and cercanías.

Twenty night bus lines (búhos) operate from midnight to 6 am. They run from Puerta del Sol and Plaza de la Cibeles.

Information booths can be found at Puerta del Sol, Plaza de Callao and Plaza de la Cibeles. Or call ☎ 91 406 88 10.

Metro

The metro (☎ 91 552 59 09 for information) is a fast, efficient and safe way to navigate Madrid and generally easier than coming to grips with bus routes. It operates from about 6.30 am to 1.30 am (2.30 am on Friday and Saturday nights) and you can buy tickets from booths or machines. Fares are the same as for buses. This book contains a colour map of the entire metro system.

Cercanías

The short-range regional trains go as far afield as El Escorial, Alcalá de Henares, Aranjuez and other points in the Comunidad de Madrid. They are also handy for making a quick north-south hop between Atocha and Chamartín mainline train stations (with stops at Nuevos Ministerios and in front of the Biblioteca Nacional on Paseo de los Recoletos only). A direct link between Chamartín, Atocha and Príncipe Pío stations, the so-called Pasillo Verde (Green Corridor), is also useful. Metro tickets are no good on these lines, even if travelling between Atocha and Chamartín. A cercanías ticket between these stations costs 140 ptas.

Car & Motorcycle

As Latin cities go, Madrid is not the most hair-raising to drive in, although there is a fair amount of horn-honking, sloppy lane recognition, nippy manoeuvring, and general madness to get used to. Avoid peak hours, when the whole city heaves with the masses struggling to and from work. From about 2 to 4 pm the streets are dead. Once in the city, search for a car park or, if you are not fazed by the likelihood of getting a fine, the nearest likely looking parking space. Driving from sight to sight within Madrid is pointless.

Most of central Madrid is governed by the Operación de Regulación de Aparcamiento (ORA) parking system. This means, apart from designated loading zones, no-parking areas and the like, all parking positions that appear legitimate are only so for people with yearly permits, or coupons obtainable from tobacconists. That said, many locals don't bother with the coupons and you can get away with quite a lot. However, if you park in a designated no-parking area, you risk being towed. Double parking is also risky in this way if you intend to wander far from your vehicle. Should your car disappear, call the Grúa Municipal (city towing service) on ☎ 91 345 00 50. Getting it back costs 16,000 ptas.

If you wish to play it safe, there are plenty of parking stations across the city, starting at about 200 ptas an hour and a little less for each subsequent hour.

For details on vehicle rental, see the Getting There & Away section earlier and the Getting Around chapter.

Taxi

By European standards, taxis are inexpensive and well regulated. You can pick up a cab at ranks throughout town or simply flag one down. Flag fall is 190 ptas and you should make sure the driver turns the meter on. You pay 90 ptas per kilometre (120 ptas between 10 pm and 6 am). The fare from Barajas airport to Plaza de Colón should be around 2000 ptas, while the trip from Chamartín train station to the same square will be no more than 1000 ptas. There are several supplementary charges, usually posted up inside the taxi. They include 400 ptas for going to the airport, 150 ptas for running to rail or bus stations, 150 ptas between 11 pm and 6 am and also on public holidays, as well as 50 ptas for each piece of luggage.

You can call a taxi on ☎ 91 445 90 08, ☎ 91 547 82 00, ☎ 91 547 85 00, ☎ 91 371 21 31 or ☎ 91 371 37 11.

Warning

If you have a rental car in Madrid, take extra care. Groups of delinquents are known to zero in on them occasionally, puncturing a tyre and then robbing the driver when they act to change it. This is reportedly a particular problem on the road from the airport to the centre of town.

Comunidad de Madrid

Covering about 8000 sq km, the region around Madrid is home to two million people. Sealed off to the north and west by the Sierra de Guadarrama, it can be considered part of what was once known as Castilla la Nueva (New Castile).

The capital continues to spread into the Comunidad, converting villages into drab suburbs or simply creating new ones. Through that growing urban sprawl radiate highways to the rest of the country, passing a handful of interesting places within easy one-day striking distance.

To the south lie Aranjuez and Chinchón. The former is the site of one of the royal palaces Madrid's rulers created for themselves; Chinchón is a charming village centred on a classic old Castilian plaza.

Heading east towards Guadalajara, the old university town of Alcalá de Henares is a quick train ride away. A slower journey by train (but fast enough by car on the road to Ávila) is the royal residence of El Escorial. It lies in the Sierra de Guadarrama, the low mountain range that marks the length of the Comunidad's border with Castilla y León. Farther north there is plenty of scope for walking – and in winter, with luck, a bit of low-grade skiing.

Highlights

- Spending a day at the splendid El Escorial
- A long lunch of suckling pig at Mesón Cuevas del Vino in Chinchón
- A ride on the Tren de la Fresa (Strawberry Train) to Aranjuez
- Walks – or even a little skiing – in the Sierra de Guadarrama

Monasterio de San Lorenzo de El Escorial p228

✪ MADRID

SAN LORENZO DE EL ESCORIAL & AROUND

postcode 28200 • pop 10,995 • elev 1032m

Sheltering against a protective wall of the Sierra, the majestic palace-monastery complex of San Lorenzo de El Escorial serves today for ordinary *madrileños* as a focal point for escape from the pressure-cooker of the capital, just as it did for kings and sycophants of old. At just over 1000m above sea level, and protected from the worst of the winter's icy northern winds, the site enjoys an exceptionally healthy climate.

Kings and princes have a habit of promising extravagant offerings to God, the angels, saints and anyone else who'll listen, in return for help in defeating their foes. Felipe II was no exception before the Battle of St Quentin against the French on St Lawrence's day, 10 August 1557. Felipe's victory was decisive, and in thanks he ordered the construction in the saint's name of the San Lorenzo complex, above the hamlet of El Escorial. A huge monastery, royal palace and mausoleum for Felipe's parents, Carlos I and Isabel, were raised under the watchful eye of the architect Juan de Herrera. The austere style reflects Felipe's own severe outlook. To the academics, El Escorial is a key to understanding developments in Spanish architecture over the subsequent two centuries.

The palace-monastery became an important intellectual centre, with a burgeoning

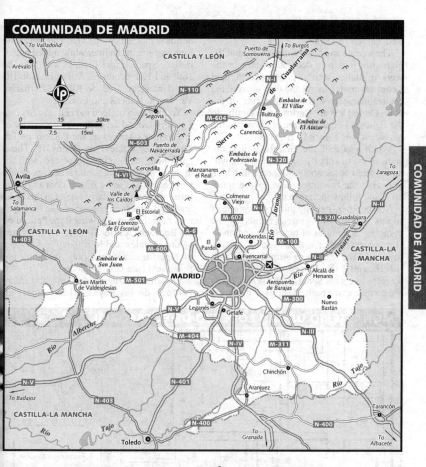

COMUNIDAD DE MADRID

library and art collection and even a laboratory where scientists could dabble in alchemy. Felipe II died in El Escorial on 13 September 1598. Various additions were made to the complex in the following centuries. In 1854 the monks belonging to the Hieronymite order, who had occupied the monastery from the beginning, were obliged to leave, to be replaced 30 years later by Augustinians.

The tourist office (☎ 91 890 15 54), at Calle de Floridablanca 10, is open 10 am to 2 pm and 3 to 5 pm weekdays (mornings only on Saturday).

The Monastery

The main entrance lies on the western side. Above the gateway a statue of St Lawrence stands watch, holding a symbolic gridiron, the instrument of his martyrdom (he was roasted alive on one). Indeed, the shape of the monastery complex recalls the same object. You enter the **Patio de los Reyes**, which houses the statues of the six kings of Judah. Directly ahead lies the sombre **basílica**. As you enter, look up to the unusual flat vaulting below the choir stalls before the main body of the church. Once inside, turn left to view Benvenuto Cellini's white Carrara marble statue of Christ crucified, carved in 1576.

The marble and bronze reredos behind the high altar is rich in decoration, largely the work of Italian artists. Leone and Pompei Leoni are among them, and they also did the bronze statue groups on either side of the altar. On the left are Carlos I and family; to the right are Felipe II, three of his wives and his eldest son, Prince Don Carlos.

When you exit the church, follow the signs to the ticket office *(taquilla)*. You will have little choice about the order in which you visit the monastery and palace quarters; just follow the arrows.

You begin by passing through a couple of rooms in the north-eastern corner of the complex. A handful of tapestries and an El Greco hang here. You then head downstairs to inspect the **Museo de Arquitectura** and, subsequently, the **Museo de Pintura**. The former covers (in Spanish) the story of how the complex was built. A series of dioramas and models lend some insight into the building methods of the age. The Museo de Pintura contains an interesting mixed bag of Italian, Spanish and Flemish art from the 16th and 17th centuries. Artists include Titian, Tintoretto, José de Ribera, Zurbarán, Van Dyck, Rubens and Coxcie.

You are then obliged to head upstairs into a gallery around the eastern protuberance of the complex known as the **Palacio de los Austrias** or Palacio de Felipe II. These apartments are richly decorated with all manner of paintings, maps and exquisite woodcarvings (some of the doorways and furniture are particularly fine). On this same level and directly above the Museo de Arquitectura in the northern wing is the **Palacio de los Borbones**. Carlos III renovated this part of the complex and in it today is a display of tapestries. You can only see it by appointment (see later for details).

From here you descend to the 17th-century **Panteón de los Reyes**, where almost all

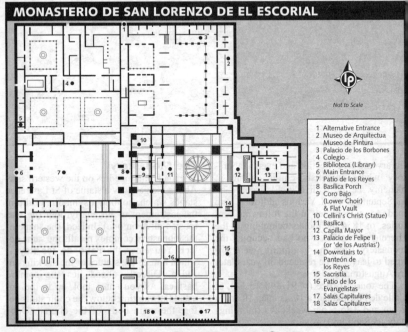

MONASTERIO DE SAN LORENZO DE EL ESCORIAL

Not to Scale

1 Alternative Entrance
2 Museo de Arquitectua
  Museo de Pintura
3 Palacio de los Borbones
4 Colegio
5 Biblioteca (Library)
6 Main Entrance
7 Patio de los Reyes
8 Basilica Porch
9 Coro Bajo
  (Lower Choir)
  & Flat Vault
10 Cellini's Christ (Statue)
11 Basilica
12 Capilla Mayor
13 Palacio de Felipe II
   (or 'de los Austrias')
14 Downstairs to
   Panteón de
   los Reyes
15 Sacristía
16 Patio de los
   Evangelistas
17 Salas Capitulares
18 Salas Capitulares

Spain's monarchs since Carlos I lie interred with their spouses. The royal corpses lie in gilded marble coffins of subdued baroque magnificence.

Backtracking, you find yourself in the **Panteón de los Infantes**, whose nine vaults were built in the 19th century. Here lie buried *infantes* (the second-born of monarchs), princes and childless queens. Don Juan de Austria (Don John of Austria), victor over the Turks at the Battle of Lepanto, lies beneath a memorial in the fifth vault. Maria Teresa de Austria is buried in the third vault. Most intriguing – tasteless even? – is the carousel-style mausoleum for princes who died as toddlers.

Stairs lead up from the Patio de los Evangelistas to the **salas capitulares** (chapter houses) in the south-eastern corner of the monastery. Their vaulted ceilings are decorated with frescoes in the so-called Pompeian style and with a free-wheeling element of trompe l'oeil. These bright, airy rooms contain a minor treasure chest of works by El Greco, Titian, Tintoretto, José de Ribera Hieronymus Bosch (known as 'El Bosco' to the Spaniards).

When you emerge, return to the entrance before the Patio de los Reyes. Here you can enter the **biblioteca**, once one of Europe's finest libraries and still a haven for 40,000 precious books.

Grounds & Annexes

The sober looking buildings that face the entrance to the monastery complex are known as the Casas de Infantes and Casa de la Reina, while those along Paseo de la Florida were known as the Casa de Oficios. In general they were used to house visiting dignitaries.

Your ticket gives you access to the **Huerta de los Frailes**, the orderly gardens just south of the monastery. In the **Jardín del Príncipe** that leads down to the town of El Escorial (and the train station) is the **Casita del Príncipe**, built under Carlos III for his heir.

Following Paseo de Carlos III (the road to Ávila) out of town, you pass on the left the entrance to La Herrería, in the grounds of which stands La Silla de Felipe – a seat, carved of stone, from which Felipe observed

construction of his monastery. Farther on is the **Casita de Arriba** (or Casita del Infante), another 18th-century neoclassical gem from the hands of Juan de Villanueva, who was responsible for the Casita del Príncipe. The present king, Juan Carlos I, lived here for a couple of years in the early 1960s.

Opening Times & Tickets

San Lorenzo is open 10 am to 6 pm (to 5 pm, October to March) Tuesday to Sunday. Only the basilica is free. Entry is 900 ptas (students 400 ptas). For an extra 100 ptas you can tag along for a guided tour of the *panteones* and the Palacio de los Austrias. It is possible to join a guided tour of the Palacio de los Borbones on Friday and Saturday. To do so, you must book at least a day in advance by calling ☎ 91 890 59 03. It costs 550 ptas per person.

The Casita de Arriba and its gardens are open 10 am to 7 pm in Easter week and August (375 ptas). At the time of writing, the Casita del Príncipe was closed for repairs.

Everything is closed on Monday. Entry on Wednesday is free for EU citizens.

You have the option of buying an all-inclusive ticket including all the elements of El Escorial and the Valle de los Caídos (see later) for 1500 ptas.

Valle de los Caídos

Spain's ambivalent attitude to 40 years of Francoism is best demonstrated in this oversized memorial to 'the Fallen'. An optimist might imagine the site was dedicated to all Spain's civil war dead; a browse inside quickly dispels such thinking. Built by prison labour – leftists and other opposition undesirables – it is a crude piece of monumentalism in the awful architectural taste of the great dictators. This concrete colossus is the most flagrant reminder of the country's dictatorial past, but travellers along the highways and byways of Spain will soon notice it is not the only one. That so many street names, plaques and other reminders of Franco *(el caudillo)* remain in place continues to be a source of controversy.

The turn-off and ticket booth is 9km north of El Escorial. It's another 6km drive to the shrine – you are not supposed to stop en route. There is something spooky about the subterranean basilica and little, artistically, to recommend it. By the altar lies Franco himself. Also buried here is 'José Antonio'. Before the civil war, the dashing José Antonio Primo de Rivera, son of the 1920s dictator Miguel Primo de Rivera, led the Falange, the party that later formed the fascist political component of Franco's Nationalist movement. Executed in Alicante by the Republicans in late 1936, he became a martyr figure for the Nationalists.

You can also drive up to the base of the enormous cross above the basilica, or catch a cable car (funicular). The views are splendid.

The site is open 9.30 am to 7 pm (10 am to 6 pm from 1 October to 31 March) daily except Monday (700 ptas). The funicular operates four times a day and the return trip costs 375 ptas. About the only way there, if you don't have a vehicle, is to get the daily Herranz bus from El Escorial.

Places to Stay & Eat
There is no need to stay in El Escorial, although it's a pleasant enough overnight stop.

You'll find a couple of youth hostels within about 1km of San Lorenzo, *Albergue El Escorial* (☎ 91 890 59 24, Calle de la Residencia 14) and *Albergue Santa María Buen Aire* (☎ 91 890 36 40), at Finca la Herrería. The latter also offers camping. B&B in dorms costs 1200 ptas for HI members under 26 and 1700 ptas for older folk. Six kilometres away from El Escorial is the enormous *Caravaning El Escorial* (☎ 91 890 24 12), where you pay 680 ptas per person, car and tent. It gets crowded with madrileños on weekends.

Otherwise, the cheapest place to stay is *Hostal Vasco* (☎ 91 890 16 19, Plaza de Santiago 11), which has comfy doubles for 4900 ptas.

A few places line Calle de Juan de Toledo, the road to El Valle de los Caídos. The best value is *Hostal Cristina* (☎ 91 890 19 61) at No 6, which charges about 5500/7000 ptas for singles/doubles.

Calle de Floridablanca is flanked by a trio of expensive upper mid-range places, and the top establishment is *Hotel Victoria*

Palace (☎ 91 890 15 11, fax 91 890 12 48, Calle de Juan de Toledo 4). Doubles cost up to 18,600 ptas (plus IVA) in high season.

Restaurante Los Pescaitos (☎ 91 890 77 20, Calle de Joaquín Costa 8) is an ample locale boasting some sea shanty decoration in questionable taste, but the seafood is good and appreciated by locals. The financially challenged can get a decent set lunch for 1100 ptas.

Getting There & Away
Bus The Herranz bus company (☎ 91 890 41 00) runs buses every 20 minutes from 7 am to 10.45 pm (18 services on weekends) from the Intercambiador de Autobuses at the Moncloa metro station in Madrid to San Lorenzo de El Escorial (one hour, 405 ptas one way). The same company (office on Calle de la Reina Victoria 3) runs a bus to El Valle de los Caídos at 3.15 pm from El Escorial, returning at 5.30 pm. The all-inclusive price of the return trip and entry costs 970 ptas.

Train Up to 26 sluggish *cercanías* (suburban trains; line C-8a) serve El Escorial from Atocha train station (via Chamartín) in Madrid (one hour and 10 minutes, 430 ptas). Seven of these go on to Ávila. The station is in the town of El Escorial itself, quite a hike from San Lorenzo and its hamlet. You can walk (about 2km uphill) or catch a local bus linking the two.

Car & Motorcycle From Madrid take the A-6 and follow the exits. From El Escorial, the M-505 winds across the low western ranges of the Sierra de Guadarrama to Ávila – a pretty drive with wonderful views back across San Lorenzo de Escorial shortly before you top the rise.

SOUTH OF MADRID
Aranjuez
postcode 28039 • pop 38,680

A refreshing patch of green in sun-drenched central Spain, Aranjuez continues to play its centuries-old role as a haven from the capital, 48km to the north. The difference is that it's no longer a royal playground – the privilege has been extended to all and sundry. The area is an important breeding ground for butterflies – so important that engineers had to skirt around it when they built the N-IV *autovía* (toll-free road)!

Information The tourist office (☎ 91 891 04 27), Plaza de San Antonio 9, is open 10 am to 2 pm and 4 to 6 pm weekdays.

Palacio Real When Felipe II built his summer palace here on the lush banks of the Río Tajo in the 16th century, there had already been a country residence on the site for 200 years. What was in Felipe's day a modest 20-room affair, later destroyed by fire, was to become under his successors the 18th-century excess that stands today. With more than 300 rooms and inspired by Versailles (an ever-popular model with European monarchs), it is filled with a cornucopia of ornamentation. Of all the rulers who spent time here, Carlos III and Isabel II left the greatest mark.

Carlos III had a new portrait done of himself every year (one hangs in an apartment here) but, unwilling to waste time posing for each painting, he had court painters copy the first one each year! He took a keener interest in interior decorating. The Sala de Porcelana (Porcelain Room) is extravagant, its walls covered in hand-crafted porcelain figures (more than vaguely reminiscent of a similar chamber in Madrid's Palacio Real). It took two years to complete the decoration. The Sala Fumadora is almost as remarkable – a florid imitation of an Alhambra interior, with Arabic inscriptions in stucco and an intricate stalactite ceiling carved in wood.

After touring the palace, a stroll in the gardens makes for a relaxing antidote. The English elms that predominate are a reminder that the gardens are more than just a happy accident. The **Jardín de la Isla**, right by the palace and forming a tranquil island in a bend in the Tajo, is nice, but the more extensive **Jardín del Príncipe** along the Chinchón road is more appealing.

Within its shady perimeter you'll find two other man-made attractions. The **Casa de Marinos** contains royal pleasure boats from days gone by. Farther away, towards Chinchón, is the **Casa del Labrador**, a tasteless royal jewellery box crammed to the rafters with gold, silver, silk and some second-rate art. Built for Carlos IV in 1805, it is the final Versailles touch, an attempt to emulate the Petit Trianon.

The garden itself is a minor miracle, a mix of local and exotic plant species that have rubbed along nicely since Spanish botanists and explorers started bringing back seeds from all over the world in the 19th century. The town council has laid out some walking and bike trails through the grounds.

Entry The Palacio Real is open 10 am to 6.30 pm Tuesday to Sunday (an hour less from October to April). Entry costs 700 ptas, but is free for EU citizens on Wednesday. Entry to the Casa del Labrador costs 700 ptas (you must book ahead on ☎ 91 891 03 05) and the Casa de Marinos costs 350 ptas. The gardens (the palace ticket covers all the gardens) are open from 10 am until sunset all year round.

Places to Stay & Eat There is little temptation to stay in Aranjuez but you have six hotels and a camping ground to choose from. *Camping Soto del Castillo* (☎ 91 891 13 95) lies between the N-IV and the Río Tajo and is open from March to October.

The cheapest of the hotels is *Hostal Rusiñol* (☎ 91 891 01 55, Calle de San Antonio 76), a couple of blocks from the tourist office. It has singles/doubles for 1950/3300 ptas and doubles with bathroom for 5400 ptas.

On the food front, many restaurants are cheekily expensive. One of the best deals in town is *Casa de Comidas Gobernación* (☎ 91 891 65 76, Calle de Gobernación 2), just off the central arcaded Plaza de San Antonio. This place is popular and offers a lunch *menú del día* (daily set meal) of 1100 ptas. *La Rana Verde* (☎ 91 891 13 25, Calle de la Reina 1), on the banks of the Tajo, is the town's best-known restaurant but rather tired. Still you may want to shell out 3000 ptas for frogs' legs and the riverside location.

COMUNIDAD DE MADRID

Getting There & Away Frequent cercanías (line C-3) connect with Madrid's Atocha station (45 minutes, 430 ptas), and occasional trains go to Toledo. The Automnibus Urbanos bus company (☎ 91 530 46 06) has 10 (Sunday) to 31 daily services from Estación Sur de Autobuses in Madrid. The trip takes an hour and costs 405 ptas.

A delightful option from April to October is the Tren de la Fresa (Strawberry Train). This day excursion sees you seated aboard a restored steam train with attendants in period dress serving up free – you guessed it – strawberries. The 3250 ptas (2000 ptas for children under 12) price tag includes the return trip from Atocha station, a bus transfer to the centre of Aranjuez and entry to monuments. Information and timetables are available at Atocha; call ☎ 902-22 88 22. The train runs on what was the first railway line from Madrid and the original Tren de la Fresa earned its nickname because people from Aranjuez used it to take strawberries up to Madrid for sale. Disappointment can set in when the steam engine has to be replaced by a boring old diesel locomotive.

Chinchón
postcode 28370 • pop 3856
Home of a well-known brew of *anís,* the aniseed-based heart-starter favoured by not a few Spaniards, Chinchón is an agreeable settlement 50km south-east of Madrid. The focal point is the *plaza mayor,* ringed by centuries-old two and three-tiered balconies, most of which now accommodate dining madrileños. The plaza also doubles as a bullring. Just north of the plaza lies the 16th-century Iglesia de la Asunción, containing an *Asunción* attributed to Goya. A few steps south of the square on Calle del Generalísimo is a former 18th century Augustinian monastery. It now serves as a *parador* (☎ 91 894 08 36). A couple of kilometres south of the centre you can see castle ruins. The fortress was raised at the end of the 16th century but was left in its present state by the depredations of the War of the Spanish Succession and by Napoleon's troops in 1808.

Several distilleries produce the Chinchón anís on the eastern edge of town. If you want to buy a bottle, head for the Alcoholera de Chinchón on Plaza Mayor.

Places To Stay & Eat The *Hostal Chinchón (☎ 91 893 53 98, Calle de José Antonio 12),* just off Plaza Mayor, is a pleasant place with an internal patio. Single/double rooms with bath and TV will set you back 4280/6420 ptas.

You can scout around the several restaurants right on Plaza Mayor, or head away from the centre. A special but pricey option is *Mesón Cuevas del Vino (☎ 91 894 02 06, Calle de Benito Hortelano 13).* This cavernous bodega, lined with huge wine barrels and popular with weekenders from Madrid, serves great Castilian food, but you won't get away for less than 3000 ptas per person. It's closed on Tuesday.

Getting There & Away Buses of the La Veloz company (☎ 91 409 76 02) run regularly (55 minutes, 405 ptas) between Chinchón and Madrid, at Avenida del Mediterráneo 49. There are four buses per day (two on Saturday, none on Sunday) to and from Aranjuez, at Calle del Almibar, near the Plaza de Toros; the fare is 125 ptas.

ALCALÁ DE HENARES
postcode 28801 • pop 163,700
A little way north of the Roman town of Complutum (of which nothing remains) and 35km east of Madrid on the N-II to Zaragoza, Alcalá de Henares entered a period of greatness when Cardinal Cisneros founded a university here in 1486. Now centred on a much-restored Renaissance building in the centre of what is virtually a satellite of Madrid, the university was long one of the country's main seats of learning. In 1836, however, Alcalá was dealt a blow with the transfer of the Universidad Complutense to the capital. The rot was only arrested with the reopening of the university in 1977. The town is also dear to the hearts of Spaniards as the birthplace of the country's literary figurehead, Miguel de Cervantes Saavedra.

Information

A tourist office (☎ 91 889 26 94) is just off Plaza de Cervantes, the town's main square, at Callejón de Santa María s/n. It is open 10 am to 2 pm and 4 to 6.30 pm daily (5 to 7.30 pm from June to September).

Universidad

You can wander through parts of the universidad any time. Various faculty buildings, dating mostly to the 17th century, are scattered about the centre of town and you can wander around them from 9 am to 9 pm on weekdays.

The core of the university is the Colegio Mayor de San Ildefonso. You can wander through here too, but to see inside the buildings you need to join a guided tour. The ornate entrance of the Colegio Mayor, facing Plaza de San Diego, is in the plateresque style. Of particular interest inside (and only accessible on the guided visit) are the Paraninfo (the auditorium where the nation's most prestigious literary prize, the Premio Cervantes, is presented), with a fine *mudéjar* ceiling, and the Capilla de San Ildefonso. The latter contains the tomb of Cardinal Cisneros.

The guided tours take place five times daily between 11.30 am and 5.30 pm weekdays. On weekends and holidays there are 10 visits between 11 am and 7 pm. The visits cost 350 ptas.

Museo Casa Natal de Miguel de Cervantes

It is thought Cervantes was born at Calle de la Imagen 2, on the corner of Calle Mayor. Here the locals have recreated his place and filled it with period furniture and bits and pieces relating to his life. It's open 10.15 am to 1.30 pm and 4 to 6.30 pm Tuesday to Sunday.

Around Town

Other sights worth seeking out include the early 17th-century Cistercian Monasterio de San Bernardo, which is open for infrequent but daily guided tours only (350 ptas); the Capilla del Oidor, with some Gothic-mudéjar decoration and a recon-struction of the font in which Cervantes was baptised.

Places to Stay & Eat

There is no need to stay here, but *Pensión Levante* (☎ 91 888 07 51, Calle de Juan Guerra 5) is the cheapest place in town with basic singles/doubles for 2000/3500 ptas. If you want something classier and closer to the centre, *Hotel El Bedel* (☎ 91 889 37 00, Plaza de San Diego 6) has beautifully maintained rooms for 8300/13,500 ptas plus IVA.

Hostería del Estudiante (☎ 91 888 03 30, Calle de los Colegios 3) is an expensive but charming restaurant backing onto the Paraninfo in the main university building. You will probably pay around 5000 ptas for fine Castilian cooking in this Renaissance building.

Getting There & Away

The easiest way to get to Alcalá is by one of the frequent cercanías trains shuttling between Madrid (Chamartín station) and Guadalajara. The fare is 350 ptas and it takes 33 minutes.

SOUTH OF ALCALÁ

Those with cars might be tempted by a quick excursion to **Nuevo Baztán**, 21km south of Alcalá. In the early 18th century, José Benito Churriguera was instructed to lay out a village and design its main buildings in an early Spanish attempt at town planning. It's virtually a ghost town now, and Churriguera's church and neighbouring palace are in poor shape.

Empresa Argabus (☎ 91 433 91 49) runs buses (No 261) to/from Calle del Conde de Casal in Madrid (three per day on weekdays, two on Saturday and one on Sunday). The same company also has a daily bus to Alcalá de Henares at 7 am and from Alcalá (Calle de Luis Vives) at 3.15 pm.

SIERRA DE GUADARRAMA

The hills of the Sierra de Guadarrama form a getaway for madrileños but are little frequented by foreigners. Longer-term visitors to the capital may care to explore it,

COMUNIDAD DE MADRID

popping into the odd *pueblo* (village) and doing a little walking to relieve the big-city stress.

Colmenar Viejo
postcode 28770 • pop 29,682
There's little to see in this town, virtually a satellite of Madrid. But if you are in Madrid in the first days of February, get up here to witness the colourful Vaquilla, a fiesta with pagan origins dating back to the 13th century. A highly ornamental 'heifer' is made to be pranced about the town before being 'slaughtered' by *toreros* (bullfighters) dressed in Andalucian style. Buses run frequently from Plaza de Castilla in Madrid; the fare costs 295 ptas.

Manzanares El Real
postcode 28410 • pop 3363
Not far from Colmenar Viejo, before the granite mountain backdrop of La Pedriza, lies the charming 15th-century Castillo de los Mendoza in the town of Manzanares El Real. The castle is open 10 am to 2 pm and 4 to 6 pm Tuesday to Sunday (10 am to 5 pm in winter); entry is 300 ptas.

Several trails lead into the nearby Pedriza park, one of which brings you to freshwater pools. Rock climbers have a wealth of options, with 1500 climbing routes in the park. For advice, try the Federación Madrileña de Montaña (☎ 91 593 80 74) at Calle de Apodaca 16, in Madrid. Also check out the park's visitors centre.

Hostal El Tranco (☎ 91 853 00 63, Calle del Tranco 4) has good singles/doubles for 5800/8000 ptas. When times are slow they may halve these rates.

Bus No 724 runs to Manzanares from Plaza de Castilla in Madrid. It costs 310 ptas.

Cercedilla
postcode 28470 • pop 5328 • elev 1188m
The mountain town of Cercedilla and the area surrounding it are popular with walkers and mountain bikers. Several trails are marked out through the Sierra, the main one known as the Cuerda Larga or Cuerda Castellana. This is a forest track that takes in 55 peaks between the Puerto de Somosierra

in the north and Puerto de la Cruz Verde in the south-west. It would take days to complete, but shorter walks include day excursions up the Valle de la Fuenfría and a climb up Monte de Siete Picos.

Mountain bikers can take their bikes up on the local train to Puerto de los Cotos (a lovely ride in itself), scoot across to the Bola del Mundo (in good winters the top end of Guadarrama's best ski piste) and pedal downhill to Cercedilla.

You can get information at the Centro de Información Valle de la Fuenfría (☎ 91 852 22 13), which is a couple of kilometres from Cercedilla train station.

Group walks, mountain-bike rides or rock-climbing trips can be organised through the Puerto de Navacerrada ski-lift and sports operator, Deporte y Montaña (☎ 91 594 30 34, fax 91 594 21 34), Calle de Sagasta 13 in Madrid. Or visit its Web site at www.puertonavacerrada.com.

Accommodation is scarce in this area.

Northern Guadarrama
If you want to avoid the crowds around Cercedilla, try for quieter walking farther north. One possibility is a 10km plateau trail that connects Canencia with Garganta de los Montes (Valle de Lozoya). You're looking at about three hours walking each way. You could stay at *Hostal Colorines (☎ 91 868 74 71, Calle Real 110)* in Canencia. It has singles/doubles for 3000/5000 ptas. Continental Auto has buses from Plaza de Castilla in Madrid to Canencia (695 ptas).

Skiing in the Guadarrama
Skiing 60km from Madrid? When the snow falls you can shoot down the pistes of Navacerrada (☎ 91 852 14 35), Cotos (☎ 91 852 08 57) and Valdesqui (☎ 91 852 04 16), just on the border with Segovia province. Snowless years are common and the available pistes not extensive, but it's a popular business with madrileños on the weekend, when the area should be avoided. Navacerrada is the main centre and there are 13km of mostly easy – and frustratingly short – runs. Overall, the best runs are at Valdesqui. A daily ski-lift pass costs 3700 ptas.

You're not likely to want to stay, especially as the place isn't fully equipped as a resort.

You can reach Navacerrada by train from Cercedilla (up to nine per day; 26 minutes) or bus from Madrid (station at Paseo de la Florida 11). During winter a special train service, known as the Tren de la Nieve, operates from Cercedilla to the pistes of Navacerrada and Cotos (from where it's a 20-minute walk on to Valdesqui). If you're driving, note that available parking is generally full by 9 am on weekends with good snow.

NORTH OF MADRID
Palacio Real de El Pardo

Just north of Madrid is the nearest of several regal escape hatches. This one ended up as Franco's favoured residence, although the present building served Felipe II in the same fashion as far back as 1558. Of the art displayed inside, the several hundred tapestries stand out, particularly those based on cartoons by Goya.

About 500m from the palace is the **Casita del Príncipe**, an elaborate 'cottage' built for Carlos IV in 1786, while he was still heir apparent. At the time of writing, it was closed for restoration.

The palace is open 10.30 am to 6 pm (to 5 pm, October to April) Monday to Saturday and 9.30 am (10 am, October to April) to 1.40 pm Sunday and holidays. Entry is 700 ptas (students 300 ptas).

An outing to El Pardo could be neatly combined with a lunch stop. You'll find plenty of busy restaurants around Plaza del Caudillo (just to remind you of the great man).

The palace and grounds are on the Carretera de El Pardo, about 15km north-west of central Madrid. Bus No 601 (155 ptas) leaves every 15 minutes from a stop on Plaza de la Moncloa (metro: Moncloa) in Madrid.

Alcobendas
postcode 28100 • pop 86,146

At Alcobendas, 17km north of Madrid along the N-I to Burgos, the only thing of interest is the Cosmocaixa interactive science museum (☎ 91 484 52 00) in the Parque de Andalucía. There is a permanent exhibition, *Ciencias del Mundo,* with all sort of interactive gismos allowing kids (and grown-ups) to push buttons, pull levers and generally get a glimpse of what makes our world work. A digital planetarium and other specialised sections are occasionally complemented with temporary exhibitions on specific themes. It's open 10 am to 10 pm daily (500 ptas).

Bus Nos 151, 153, 154 and 157 assure a frequent service to Alcobendas from Madrid's Plaza de Castilla. The ticket will cost you 185 ptas.

Buitrago & the Valle de Lozoya

About 15km short of the Puerto de Somosierra rise the picturesque walls of Buitrago, surrounded by a pretty reservoir. The Iglesia de Santa María del Castillo was built in 1321, but largely destroyed in 1936. Now restored, it displays mudéjar and Romanesque elements. There is also a modest castle, and you can walk along part of the walls (ask for the keys at the Museo de Picasso, opposite the Iglesia de Santa

COMUNIDAD DE MADRID

Who Do You Think You're Kidding, Mr Marshall?

In the unassuming village of Guadalix de la Sierra, 7km west of the Burgos highway and 50km north of central Madrid, are set some of the most memorable scenes of the 1952 classic movie *Bienvenido Mr Marshall*, directed by Luis García Berlanga. Guadalix starred as the archetypal Spanish pueblo with the name Villar del Río and whitewashed in the Andalucian manner. The townspeople gathered on the great day to greet progress and the Americans, who simply drove straight through town without stopping. A *caña* in Bar La Central on Plaza Mayor is worthwhile: the walls sport photos from the days when the filming was done. The square looked rather different then – half-real and half-movie set.

María). The museum itself contains auto-graphed bits and pieces given by the artist to his barber, who lived here. It's open 11 am to 1.30 pm and 4 to 6 pm daily except Tuesday; entry is free.

If you happen to be around in the run-up to Christmas, you may catch the Belén Viviente. In most Spanish towns it is trad-itional to set up a Nativity scene in the main square, the town hall and so on. In some they do it life-size. Since the late 1980s the villagers have gotten together each year to play out Biblical scenes throughout the town – in 1999 more than 400 villagers took part.

You could stay, if need be, at *Hostal Madrid París* (☎ 91 868 11 26, Avenida de Madrid 23), which has singles/doubles for as little as 1500/3000 ptas midweek. Prices rise and availability diminishes on week-ends. *Cervecería Plaza* offers a range of seafood.

Eating & Drinking in Spain

Dunking churros in a big mug of chocolate, eating a leisurely paella lunch, snacking on tapas during a bar crawl or savouring a hearty Rioja or Priorato red wine – it's not hard to see why eating and drinking is a national pastime in Spain. And it's an easy lifestyle for travellers to adopt, whatever your budget. Lonely Planet's *World Food Spain* by Richard Sterling is an entertaining and informative companion if you would like to enrich your eating and drinking experiences.

For a Spanish food glossary, see the Language chapter at the back of this book.

FOOD

Spanish cooking is typically Mediterranean in its liberal use of olive oil (of which Spain produces one-third of the world's supply), garlic, onions, tomatoes and peppers. It reflects Roman, Arabic, Jewish, New World and (in the north) French influences, but the Arabic contribution is what sets it apart in Europe. Spices such as saffron and cumin, honeyed sweets and pastries, and the use of fruits and almonds with savoury dishes are all legacies of the Muslim era.

Traditional Spanish food is simple fare based on fresh ingredients with a hint of herbs and spices. But imported foodstuffs, convenience foods, exposure to other cuisines and the hectic pace of modern life are rapidly changing the old habits. In all but the most rustic of kitchens, gas cookers have replaced open fires, electric blenders the mortar and pestle, and fridges and freezers have rendered salting and pickling much less important.

JANE SMITH

Many typically Spanish dishes and foods are eaten countrywide, though often prepared differently in different regions. These include:

bacalao – salted dried cod, soaked to regain moisture before cooking
charcutería or *chacinas* – cured pork products, including many forms of *embutido* (sausage), many eaten cold
chuletas and *solomillo* – chops/cutlets and sirloin, respectively, which are two of the most common cuts of pork, beef or lamb
flan – a caramel custard dessert
garbanzos – chickpeas
gazpacho – a cold, thick, blended soup of tomatoes, peppers, onion, garlic, breadcrumbs, lemon and oil
habas – broad beans
jamón – ham
mariscos and *pescado* – seafood and fish in innumerable varieties
paella and other rice dishes
pinchitos morunos – Moroccan-style kebabs, usually made with pork
sopa de ajo – garlic soup
tortilla española – potato omelette, often served cold

Title page: Happy with the finished product at cooking school.
(Photo: Oliver Strewe)

Above: Spain is the world's largest producer and consumer of olive oil.

The *cocido* (stew), a one-pot feast of beans and vegetables, plus meat and sausage if available, was traditionally the mainstay of the Spanish diet, though it's less common today. A cocido can be divided to make up a three-course meal, with the broth eaten first followed by the vegetables and lastly the meat.

Seafood and meat are eaten almost everywhere. Seafood is fantastic on all coasts, particularly the Atlantic, and is cooked in 1001 ways, but doesn't particularly cheap.

Paella

Spain's most famous dish – served throughout the country in various guises – takes its name from the wide, shallow, two-handled metal pan in which it's cooked and served. Outside restaurants, it appears mainly on Sunday and holidays. Paella is best cooked on a wood fire out of doors – what better way to feed a crowd?

Paella evolved from the rice dishes that emerged in medieval times in the Valencia area. Rice came to Spain in the 8th century with the Muslims. With their expulsion in the 17th century, rice cultivation in Spain declined and then was banned because the wetlands necessary to its growth were associated with malaria. In the late 19th century, the prohibition was lifted and lands on the Ebro delta in Catalunya and in the marshlands of the Guadalquivir in Andalucía were given over to rice cultivation.

Into the paella pan went seasonal vegetables, wetland wildlife (frogs, ducks, snails, eels and partridges), seafood and saffron, if available. A tasty flavour results from the simmering rice absorbing all the juices. Tourism increased the popularity of this attractive, bright-yellow dish, with titbits of chicken (substituted for wild duck) and seafood often being added.

JANE SMITH

A Valencian paella contains green beans, white butter beans, snails, chicken and pork bites, but no seafood. In Sevilla and Cádiz, big prawns and sometimes crayfish are added while some other ingredients are omitted. On the Costa del Sol, green peas, clams, mussels and prawns garnished with red peppers and slices of lemon are a popular combination. Saffron is expensive so today food colouring or *pimentón* (paprika) is more commonly used.

Spaniards nearly always eat paella at lunchtime because it's considered too heavy for the evening meal, which is lighter than lunch. Many restaurants will only serve paella to a minimum of two people, to make the effort of preparing it worthwhile. Some require you to order it in advance, as the ingredients need to be super fresh.

Above: Tomatoes are a common ingredient of Spanish cooking, and the featured fruit at the tomato-throwing festival in Buñol (see the Valencia chapter).

Regional Specialities

Many of Spain's regions, especially Catalunya (Cataluña) and the Basque Country, are extremely proud of their food, and regional cuisines have flourished. Basque and Catalan food preparation is generally more elaborate than elsewhere and results in arguably the best food in Spain.

Paella

The following recipe, provided by Lorraine Smart from Cómpeta, Málaga, serves three or four people and requires a pan about 30cm in diameter. The meat, fish, seafood and vegetable content can vary. The essential ingredients are olive oil, rice, stock, and saffron or its substitute.

Ingredients

olive oil
1 onion, chopped
3 cloves garlic, chopped
1 red pepper, chopped
1 large tomato, chopped
approx 500g rabbit or chicken, cut roughly
125g cubed pork
1 chorizo sausage (or salami), sliced
100g peas
150g peeled prawns
250g mussels
250g clams
650ml chicken or seafood stock
250g short-grain white rice

JANE SMITH

¼ teaspoon saffron threads (or paprika or food colouring)
salt and pepper to taste
For the garnish: lemon wedges dipped in chopped parsley, three or four unshelled medium-sized prawns (or one king prawn) per person.

Method

Several hours before cooking, put the unshelled prawns, mussels and clams in cold water with a handful of porridge oats. This flushes out the shellfish.

Fry the onions, garlic and red pepper in olive oil until soft. Add the tomatoes and simmer for five minutes. Take the mixture out of the pan and put it to one side. Now, in more olive oil, fry the rabbit/chicken and pork until they're half-cooked. Add the onion-tomato mix, chorizo slices, stock, rice and saffron. The paella now needs to cook slowly with the lid on for 20 minutes. Stir as little as possible. (Meanwhile, the shellfish need to be cooked quickly in boiling water. Take them out as soon as they open and discard any that do not open. Keep the mussel shells for garnish.) After 10 minutes, add the peeled prawns and peas to the paella.

Five minutes' later, add the cooked shellfish. Five minutes' more and the 20 minutes are up. Your paella is ready to garnish and serve! To garnish, you can arrange the mussel shells around the edge of the pan and the unshelled prawns overlapping in the centre. Serve with lemon wedges.

OLIVER STREWE

OLIVER STREWE

OLIVER STREWE

ANDERS BLOMQVIST

Top: Painted tiles with a chocolate theme, Mérida (Andalucía) – whether nibbled or sipped, chocolate is a much-loved treat in Spain.

Middle Left: Cured sausage and red wine outside the *Bodega de Sarria*, Puente de la Reina (Navarra)

Middle Right: Mushrooms are becoming a more common ingredient of Spanish cooking; here they're for sale at Barcelona's La Boqueria market.

Bottom: Locals and tourists lunching *al fresco*, by a decorative stone wall in Gaudí's Parc Güell, Barcelona

OLIVER STREWE

OLIVER STREWE

DAVID PEEVERS

Top: Chefs in the kitchen of the popular *Los Carcoles* restaurant in Barcelona.

Middle: A Basque-style *pintxo* (snack) – *¡qué delicioso!*

Bottom: *Mesón de José María*, a firm favourite of Segovia's restaurant scene

The North Catalan cuisine has strong French and Italian influences and sauces are often served with meat and fish. Pasta is also common, as are unusual combinations such as meat with seafood and poultry with fruit. The Basques are really serious about eating: there are whole cooking societies (traditionally for men only) devoted to fine food. Basque cuisine, like Catalan, incorporates ingredients from the mountains and the sea and gives importance to sauces.

In Cantabria and Asturias, the food reflects the cool, damp climate, with stews, apples, chestnuts, freshwater fish, seafood and cured meats predominating. Galicia is famous for its octopus, oysters, scallops, fish soups and stews, and *empanadas* (pies). Lamb, game birds and freshwater fish are common fare in Navarra and Aragón. Islamic-influenced sweets such as *mazapán* (marzipan) are also typical of Aragón.

The Centre High and bleak, Castilla y León is the *zona de los asados*, the region of roasts – pork, lamb and game. Castilla-La Mancha has similar fare, with game and wheat dishes common. Extremadura has two contrasting cuisines: simple peasant foods and rich cooking harking back to the region's medieval monasteries.

The East In Valencia and Murcia, rice dishes, seafood, eels and abundant high-quality fruit and vegetables make for a tasty cuisine. Murcia is known for its sweet pepper salads, whole baked fish and snails.

Andalucía This large southern region's food reflects its geographical diversity. In the sierras, hams are cured (see the boxed text 'Jamón, Jamón') and game dishes abound. On the coasts, the abundant seafood ends up in soups, is fried or, in the case of sardines, is grilled on spits over driftwood fires. Pinchitos morunos and gazpacho are true Andalucian foods. The fruit and vegetables are delicious and fresh, for the growing season here lasts all year.

Balearic Islands Mallorca has strong links with Catalunya and similar French and Italian culinary influences. Numerous invaders – Greeks, Romans, Arabs, Barbary pirates and modern-day tourists – have also left their mark. Pork and seafood take first place. Menorca was ruled by Britain for 80 years and so gin, puddings, jams, stuffed turkey and even macaroni cheese have become a part of the local fare. Ibiza's traditional cuisine has vanished.

Right:
Seafood platter

JANE SMITH

Jamón, Jamón

Appetising is not the word that may leap to mind when you first set eyes on a dozen or so pigs' back legs dangling from the ceiling of a Spanish bar. But to most Spaniards there's no more mouthwatering prospect than a few thin, succulent slices of this cured *jamón* (ham). If you try it, you'll probably see why. You can eat two or three slices as a tapa, have it in a bocadillo for 300 to 400 ptas or get a ración for 600 to 1000 ptas.

All Spanish cured hams are known as *jamón serrano* ('mountain-cured ham', though nowadays the climatic conditions of the mountains are reproduced in sheds and cellars at any altitude). The best is jamón ibérico, also called *pata negra* (black leg), from the black Iberian breed of pig, believed to be descended from the wild boar. And the best of the best is *jamón ibérico de bellota,* from Iberian pigs fattened in the wild on the autumn acorn *(bellota)* crop. A glass of fino sherry is the traditional accompaniment to jamón ibérico.

Murcia, Galicia, Teruel in Aragón and Piornal in Extremadura all produce noted jamón serrano, while Guijuelo in Salamanca province has a fair ibérico. But the best jamones of all are considered to be from Montánchez in Extremadura, Trevélez in the Alpujarras south of Granada and, above all, Jabugo in north-western Andalucía, from free-range pigs from the Sierra Morena oak forests. The best Jabugo hams are graded from one to five jotas (Js); and cinco jotas (JJJJJ) hams are said to come from pigs that have eaten only acorns.

The curing process basically involves leaving the leg of the slaughtered pig in sea salt for a few days, then removing the salt (this process may be done twice) before hanging it up to mature – for between a few months to over two years, depending on the ham. Great attention has to be paid to the temperature (gradually increasing) and humidity (not too dry) during the drying process. Curing 'seals' the hams, which is why they're not covered with swarms of flies when you see them hanging in bars.

Traditionally, hams were cured in cellars at home by the pig-owning family, but the process is now becoming more and more industrialised. Some families still hold *matanza* (slaughtering) gatherings around 11 November; after the pigs have indulged in the autumn acorn harvest.

One kilogram of jamón serrano in a shop is likely to be about 2000 ptas. Ibérico can be double that.

Ordinary uncured cold ham, by the way, is called *jamón York;* you'll find it as dull as ditchwater after tasting serrano or ibérico.

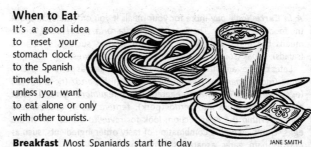

JANE SMITH

When to Eat

It's a good idea to reset your stomach clock to the Spanish timetable, unless you want to eat alone or only with other tourists.

Breakfast Most Spaniards start the day with a *desayuno* (light breakfast), perhaps coffee with a *tostada* (toasted roll or slice of bread) or *bollo* (pastry; *pasta* in Catalunya). You can put an infinite variety of things in or on your tostada, from *aceite de oliva* (olive oil), *tomate frotado* (crushed tomato) or *manteca* (pork lard) to a slab of *tortilla* (omelette), a slice of *lomo a la plancha* (grilled pork loin) or plain old *mantequilla y mermelada* (butter and jam).

Churros con chocolate – long, deep-fried doughnuts to dip in thick hot chocolate – are a delicious, calorie-laden start to the day, and are unique to Spain. They're also popular after drinking expeditions; Madrid, for instance, has several late-night *chocolaterías* (shops that sell chocolate).

A *tortilla* (omelette) is a good option for a more substantial breakfast, though Spaniards usually eat eggs at other times of the day. *Huevos fritos* are fried eggs and *huevos revueltos* are scrambled. *Huevos pasados por agua* are lightly boiled eggs; request *huevos cocidos* if you want them hard-boiled.

Lunch Lunch is Spain's main meal of the day; it's eaten between about 1.30 and 4 pm and known as *comida* or *almuerzo*. It can consist of several courses including a soup and/or salad, followed by meat or fish with vegetables or a rice dish or bean stew, then a light dessert.

Menú del Día Most restaurants offer a *menú del día* (daily set menu; often shortened to *menú*) – the budget traveller's best friend – for around 800 to 1500 ptas. You normally get a starter, a main course, *postre* (dessert), bread and wine. Often there's a choice of two or three dishes for each course. The *menú* is normally posted up outside, and if it makes no mention of drinks, dessert, bread, coffee or 'IVA incluido', expect the cost of the meal to increase.

Platos Combinados The *plato combinado* is a near relative of the *menú*. It literally translates as 'combined plate' and may consist of a steak and egg with chips and salad, or fried squid with potato salad. Insipid photos of what's available can be off-putting, but more often than not platos combinados are fine. They're usually available in the evening too.

Above: *Churros con chocolate* for breakfast – almost too good to be true!

A la Carte You'll pay more for your meals if you order a la carte but the food will be better. The Spanish menu (*la carta*, not *el menú*, which means the menú del día) begins with starters such as *ensaladas* (salads), *sopas* (soups) and *entremeses* (hors d'oeuvres).

Later courses are often listed under headings such as *pollo* (chicken), *carne* (meat), *mariscos* (seafood), *pescado* (fish), *arroz* (rice), *huevos* (eggs), *verduras/hortalizas* (vegetables) and *legumbres* (pulses). Meat may be subdivided into *cerdo* (pork), *ternera* (beef) and *cordero* (lamb). Within the eggs section, look for *revuelto* dishes, which are eggs scrambled with a combination of tasty other ingredients, such as prawns, ham, garlic, asparagus, mushrooms...

Desserts have a low profile: *helados* (ice cream), fruit and flan are often the only choices. There may be *arroz con leche* (cold rice pudding) or *tocino del cielo* (heavenly bacon), a caramel custard with a vaguely bacon-like appearance.

Dinner The *cena* (evening meal) for Spaniards tends to be lighter than lunch and may be eaten as late as 10 or 11 pm. But lots of people still go out for a bigger dinner in restaurants, though before about 9 pm you're unlikely to see anyone but foreigners doing this. Others get through the evening on tapas.

In-Between Times It's common (and a great idea!) to go to a bar or cafe for a *merienda* (snack) around 11 am and/or 7 pm. A great snack is a *bocadillo*, a white-bread roll filled with cheese, ham, salad, grilled pork or 1001 other possibilities... Try not to leave Spain without sampling a *bocadillo de tortilla española* or *de jamón serrano*, a roll filled with potato omelette or cured ham.

Then there are tapas...

Where to Eat

Cafes & Bars Spanish life revolves around cafes and bars. The latter come in various guises, including *bodegas* (old-style wine bars), *cervecerías* (beer bars), *tascas* (bars that specialise in tapas), *tabernas* (taverns) and let's not forget *pubs*. Tapas are available in many of these places, while some serve more substantial fare too. You'll often save 10% to 20% if you eat at the bar rather than at a table, particularly if the tables are in a smart attached dining room or on the *terraza* (ie, outside).

Restaurants Throughout Spain you'll find plenty of *restaurantes* serving good simple food at affordable prices, often featuring regional specialities. There are also some ordinary to woeful places, particularly in tourist haunts, and plenty of classy upmarket eateries too.

A *mesón* is a simple eatery with home-style cooking, usually attached to a bar, while a *comedor* is usually a dining room at a bar or hostal – with food that is likely to be functional and inexpensive. A *venta* is typically a family-run establishment, probably once an inn, off

Tapas

These saucer-sized mini-snacks are part of the Spanish way of life and come in infinite variety. You can make a meal of tapas, go on to a meal afterwards or – a great Spanish pastime – tour a few bars with a couple of friends sampling their tapas. The art of tapas-hopping, it's often said, is to have just one tapa and one drink in each bar. Tapas don't usually, despite what you may have heard, add up to a true substitute for a full meal, but for the odd evening they do very nicely.

The Spanish word *tapa* translates as 'lid'. Today's snacks supposedly originated in Andalucía's sherry area in the 18th or 19th century when bar owners placed a piece of bread on top of a drink to deter flies; this developed into the custom of putting a titbit, such as olives or a piece of sausage, on a lid to cover the drink – something salty to encourage drinking. Today, tapas have become a cuisine of their own and each region and city has its specialities. They're still sometimes free, though this custom has all but disappeared in many areas. A typical tapa costs between 100 and 200 ptas (check before you order as some of these snacks are a lot dearer).

Some typical tapas include olives, slices of cured meats or cheese, potato salad, diced salad, potato omelette, bite-sized portions of fried fish, *albóndigas* (meat or fish balls), chickpeas with spinach, *solomillo* (slices of grilled steak) or *lomo* (pork loin), *pinchitos* (mini-kebabs), rabbit stew, *callos* (tripe), *gambas* (prawns) and *boquerones* (anchovies) marinated in vinegar or *rebozados* (fried in batter). But the variety of combinations and concoctions is endless.

Bars often display a range of tapas on the counter or chalk a list on a board. There may be a printed tapas menu. Otherwise, it seems, you're expected to know what's available and the situation can be rather confusing. A place that appears not to have tapas may actually specialise in them! Failing all else, you just have to ask what tapas there are, then try to recognise a few words in the long stream of verbiage that you're likely to be answered with.

A *ración* is a meal-sized serving of these snacks, suitable for two or more people; a *media-ración* is half a ración. One person can make a meal out of two media-raciones. When ordering, make it clear if it's a tapa you're after, not a media ración or ración, or you'll end up paying three or five times what you planned. A *tabla* is a board loaded with a selection of tapas – typically hams, sausages, cheeses – like a ración, it's good for a group of people to share.

San Sebastián and Sevilla, at opposite ends of the country, are two of the best cities for tapas-hopping, with amazing numbers of bars serving an amazing variety of tasty titbits. In the Basque Country and Asturias, tapas are often called *pintxos*.

the beaten track; the food can be delectable and cheap. A *marisquería* or *merendero* is a seafood restaurant. A *chiringuito* is a small open-air bar or kiosk, or sometimes a more substantial beachside restaurant.

Spanish law requires restaurant menu prices to include a service charge. Any tip beyond that is a matter of personal choice.

Self-Catering

Spain's *mercados* (food markets) are fun. Buy a selection of fruits, vegetables, cold meat or sausage, olives, nuts and cheese, pick up some bread from a bakery, stop in at a supermarket for a bottle of wine and head for the nearest picturesque spot. This can make a pleasant change from sitting in restaurants and you can put together a cheap, filling meal.

JANE SMITH

Only some youth hostels and just a few *pensiones* and *hostales* have facilities for cooking.

Cheese

Except in the north, Spain's climate and terrain are unsuitable for dairy cattle. Oil and lard, rather than butter, are used in cooking and butter is rarely spread on bread. That said, Spain does produce at least 36 varieties of *queso* (cheese). Most are fairly strong and some of the best are made from goat's or ewe's milk.

Spanish supermarkets stock a selection of local cheeses, many cheeses from other parts of Europe and also Spanish copies of cheeses such as Brie and Camembert. Spanish cheese is generally pricey, around 1500 ptas a kilogram, while you can buy Edam or Gouda for as little as 1000 ptas a kilogram. Spanish cheeses you might like to sample include:

Burgos – made from ewe's milk, this comes in a rindless round and is particularly delicious with honey, nuts and fruit.
Cabrales – strong Asturian cow's, goat's and sheep's-milk cheese matured in caves; it's encased in leaves and the inside is blue and creamy.
Manchego – the most famous of Spanish cheeses, it is traditionally made from ewe's milk, but now often with other milk, and cured in oil. It can be soft, fresh and mild or hard, crumbly and strong. The rind is brown/black, the inside is pale yellow.
Pasiego – made from cow's milk near Santander, this cheese has a firm, white and creamy inside.
Roncal – a hard cheese with tiny holes inside and made in Navarra's Roncal valley from ewe's milk, sometimes combined with cow's milk; the rind is brown.

For more information on cheese, see the boxed text 'Say Cheese' in the Cantabria & Asturias chapter.

Above: Spain grows 262 varieties of olive, many of which are grown in the big olive-producing region of Andalucía.

Vegetarian Food

Outside the big cities and university towns, eating in Spain can be difficult if you're a vegetarian and a real headache if you're a vegan. Vegetarian restaurants are often only open for lunch or may be tucked away in a far corner of town; they also tend to come and go depending on demand. Some restaurants in tourist or student areas cater for vegetarians in the *menú del día,* but you can't count on it. Ethnic restaurants (including Chinese and Italian, both of which are pretty common) usually offer vegetarians some scope.

The good news is that Spanish fruits and vegetables are wonderfully fresh all year round, so salads in any restaurant or cafe are a good bet. Red pepper salads such as *pipirrana* are common. To be on the safe side when you order, you should specify *'Soy vegetariano/a, no me gusta carne/jamón/pollo/atún/huevos'* ('I'm vegetarian, I don't like meat/ham/chicken/tuna/eggs'). Or simply say *'Sin...'* ('Without...').

More generally, you can ask *'¿Qué hay sin carne, jamón, pollo, marisco o pescado?'* ('What is there without meat, ham, chicken, seafood or fish?'). Check the vegetables section of the menu but remember that even dishes listed here won't necessarily come without meat unless you specify. *Alcachofas* (artichokes) and *espárragos* (asparagus) often appear on menus; they may be lightly cooked and served with mayonnaise, or tossed in oil and garlic. *Berenjenas* (aubergines) are often sliced thinly, dipped in batter and quickly fried – good as a side dish or a tapa. A full serve is usually plenty for two people.

A good vegetarian dish is *pisto,* similar to ratatouille, a fry-up of zucchinis (courgettes), green peppers, onions and potatoes. *Menestra* is another vegetarian dish – of artichokes, chard, peas and green beans. *Garbanzos con espinacas* (chickpeas with spinach) is a filling and tasty stew. *Setas* (wild mushrooms) often turn up on menus; usually they're cooked in olive oil and garlic, but are better in a sauce *(salsa).* *Escalivada* is a Catalan cold dish of aubergines, peppers and onions in an oil-and-garlic sauce. *Pimientos rellenos* (stuffed peppers) generally contain meat or prawns. Tofu and *seitán,* a miso-like vegetable protein, usually only crop up in vegetarian restaurants.

If you eat eggs, tortillas or *huevos revueltos* (scrambled eggs) are good stand-bys; you can order them with asparagus, artichokes or other vegetables. A *cocido* (stew), though it may include plenty of beans, will more often than not include bits of meat or contain meat stock. The same goes for soups, although gazpacho is a safe bet. Occasionally a meat and fish-free *empanada* (pie) will turn up. And a *bocadillo vegetal* (salad sandwich) is filling – but again, you have to ensure that it doesn't contain meat or other undesirables

If you get fed up, your best bet is to cater for yourself.

Table Talk

Here are a few basic words that can come in handy whatever kind of meal you're eating:

English	Spanish
bill (check)	*cuenta*
bottle	*botella*
bread	*pan*
breakfast	*desayuno*
change	*cambio*
cold	*frío/a*
cup	*taza*
dining room	*comedor*
dinner	*cena*
food, meal	*comida*
fork	*tenedor*
glass	*vaso* or *copa*
hot (temperature)	*caliente*
hot (spicy, piquant)	*picante*
ice	*hielo*
kitchen	*cocina*
knife	*cuchillo*
lunch	*almuerzo* or *comida*
menu	*carta*
plate	*plato*
spoon	*cuchara*
sweet	*dulce*
table	*mesa*
vegetarian	*vegetariano/a*
waiter/waitress	*camarero/a*
water	*agua*

JANE SMITH

Above: *'¡Camarera! Una botella de cerveza fría, un vaso y una carta, por favor.'* (see list to the left for translation tips)

DRINKS

Nonalcoholic Drinks

Coffee Coffee in Spain is strong. Addicts should specify how they want their fix. A *café con leche* is about 50% coffee, 50% hot milk; foreigners are often served a large cup or glass *(grande* or *doble)* unless they specify *'pequeño'*. Say *'en vaso'* if you want it in a glass, *'sombra'* if you want lots of milk. A *café solo* is a short black; *café cortado* is a short black with a little milk.

Tea Spaniards by and large prefer coffee, but a wave of *teterías* (Islamic-style teahouses) is gradually gaining strength, especially in Andalucía. These places serve all manner of teas, including *infusiones* (herbal concoctions) in an ambience of soft cushions and floaty music. You're usually looking at 200 ptas or more per drink. The British manner of drinking tea is as little comprehended in Spain as in most other places outside Britain. Regular black tea is called *té negro:* it usually comes as a teabag in a small cup of not-exactly-boiling water. Ask for milk to be separate *(leche aparte)* – otherwise you'll end up with your teabag floating in lukewarm milky water. Most places also have *té de manzanilla* (camomile) or *de menta* (mint tea).

Chocolate Spaniards brought chocolate back from Mexico and adopted it enthusiastically. As a drink, it's served thick; sometimes it even appears among desserts on menus. Generally it's a breakfast drink taken with churros (see Breakfast earlier in this special section).

Soft Drinks *Zumo de naranja* (orange juice) is the main freshly squeezed juice available, but expensive at around 250 ptas a glass. Boxed juices come in all varieties in shops and are good and cheap.

Refrescos (cool drinks) include the usual international brands of soft drinks, local brands such as Kas and expensive *granizado* (iced fruit crush). Clear, cold water from a public fountain or tap is a Spanish favourite, but check that it's potable. For tap water in restaurants, ask for *agua de grifo*. *Agua mineral* (bottled water) comes in innumerable brands, either *con gas* (fizzy) or *sin gas* (still). A 1.5L bottle of still water costs between 40 and 75 ptas in a supermarket.

A *batido* is a flavoured milk drink or milk shake.

Horchata (*orxata* in Catalan), made from the juice of *chufa* (tiger nuts), sugar and water, tastes like soya milk with a hint of cinnamon. You'll come across it both fresh and bottled: Chufi is a delicious brand.

Alcoholic Drinks

Wine Spain is a wine-drinking country and so *vino* (wine) accompanies many a meal or tapa. Spanish wine is strong because of the sunny climate. It can be *blanco* (white), *tinto* (red) or *rosado* (rosé). Wine is generally cheap though there is no shortage of expensive wines. A 500 ptas bottle of wine from a supermarket or wine merchant will be better than average. The same money in a restaurant will get you an average drop. Cheap *vino de mesa* (table wine) sells for less than 200 ptas a litre in shops.

You can order wine by the *copa* (glass) in bars and restaurants: the *vino de la casa* (house wine) may come from a barrel or jug at 125 ptas, sometimes less, a glass.

Spain regulates its wine fairly carefully so you can judge something of its quality from the label. The letters DOC stand for *denominación de origen calificada* and refer to wine areas that have maintained consistent high quality over a very long period. Rioja is the only DOC at present, though Jerez may join it. DO, *denominación de origen,* is one step down from DOC. There are 50-odd DO areas around Spain. A DOC or DO label tells you that the wine has been produced

Regional Wine Specialities

Wine is made everywhere in Spain, with La Rioja, Catalunya, Castilla-La Mancha and the Jerez de la Frontera area in Andalucía producing the country's best (Jerez's speciality is sherry). With wine production thriving and experimentation rife, competition is fierce and new wines are constantly entering the scene.

For ordinary drinking, some of the cheaper reds from La Rioja or Valdepeñas (Castilla-La Mancha) are generally OK, as are *cavas* (sparkling champagne-like wines from Catalunya) and Catalunya's still whites, such as Penedès. Rosé is cheap; those from Navarra, Rueda (Castilla y León) and Utiel-Requena (Valencia) are good.

The best wines of **Galicia** include white Albariños from the Rías Baixas and red or white Ribeiros. In the **Basque Country**, a sharp, white wine known as *txacoli* is popular. In **Aragón** the Somontano area near Huesca is into high-tech wine production and comes up with some good whites. **Catalunya's** best wines are reds from Priorato, and cava and fruity whites from Penedès.

The **Rioja** DOC region includes areas of Navarra and the Basque Country bordering its heartland in La Rioja. The region is best known for its reds – the current trend is towards production of mature wines rather than those for the cheaper end of the market. **Navarra** is an upcoming wine producer with lots of experimentation happening.

In **Castilla y León**, the Ribera del Duero region produces excellent reds that rival those of Rioja, while the Rueda area was famous for its whites until challenged by developments in Galicia. Now rosé is fast overtaking whites in Rueda. Toro, near Salamanca, produces some powerful reds.

Extensive **Castilla-La Mancha** produces half of all Spanish wine. It has a reputation for a cheap and (if you're lucky) cheerful drop, but new wines are changing the picture. The La Mancha and Valdepeñas DOs offer the best ranges of budget-priced wines in the country.

The **Valencia** and **Murcia** regions have traditionally produced bulk wine and, more recently, concentrated grape juice for export. However, there are some good-value wines being produced in the Utiel-Requena area of Valencia (whites and rosés), and in the Murcian areas Jumilla (reds) and Yecla (reds, whites and rosés). **Extremadura** mainly produces wine for local consumption, grape juice or distilled liquor.

Wine production in Spain began in **Andalucía** when the Phoenicians founded Cádiz around 1100 BC and introduced vine cultivation. The region is famous for sherry, a fortified wine produced by a special ageing process, mostly in the Jerez de la Frontera area (see the boxed text 'Sherry' in the Andalucía chapter). Málaga dessert wines made from the muscatel grape have been fashionable and, though their popularity has declined, they are served from the barrel in some of the city's bars.

JANE SMITH

to certain supervised standards by
serious wine-growers – though each
DOC and DO covers a wide range of
wines of varying quality (usually indicated by the price)

Other categories of wine, in descending order, are: *denominación
de origen provisional* (DOP); *vino de la tierra; vino comarcal;* and *vino
de mesa*.

Vino joven is wine made for immediate drinking, while *vino de
crianza* has to be stored for certain minimum periods: a red needs
two full calendar years with a minimum of six months in oak; and a
white or rosé needs one calendar year. *Reserva* wines require three
years storage for reds and two years for whites and rosés. *Gran
reserva* wines are particularly good vintages that must have spent at
least two calendar years in storage and three in the bottle. They're
mostly reds.

Above: Sherry *(jerez)* does all its ageing in wooden barrels; unlike wine, sherry will not improve in the bottle.

Beer A common way to order a *cerveza* (beer) is to ask for a *caña*, which is a small draught beer. *Corto* and, in the Basque Country, *zurrito* are other names for this. A larger beer (about 300ml) is called a *tubo* (which comes in a straight glass) or in Catalunya a *jarra*, which has a handle. All these words apply to draught beer; if you just ask for a *cerveza* you may well get bottled beer, which can be more expensive. A small bottle of beer is called a *botellín* or a *quinto;* a bigger one (330mL) is a *tercio* or a *mediana*. Estrella de Galicia is the best beer we have found in Spain. San Miguel, Cruzcampo and Victoria are other decent brands.

A *clara* is a beer with a dash of lemonade.

Other Drinks *Sangría* is a wine and fruit punch sometimes laced with brandy. It's refreshing going down but can leave you with a sore head! You'll see jugs of it on tables in restaurants but it also comes ready-mixed in bottles in shops at around 300 ptas for 1.5L. *Tinto de verano* is a mix of wine and Casera, a brand of lemonade. *Sidra* (cider) is produced and largely consumed in Asturias and the Basque Country.

Coñac (Spanish brandy) is popular and cheap. In bars, you'll notice some locals starting the day with a coffee and a brandy, or a glass of *anís* (aniseed liqueur). Popular brandies include Centenario, Magno, 103 and Soberano. Spanish-produced spirits are generally much cheaper than imports. Larios gin made in Málaga is an example.

Spain produces a huge range of *licores* (liqueurs). *Aguardiente* is a colourless grape-based liqueur. *Pacharán* is a red liqueur made with aniseed and sloes, the fruit of the blackthorn.

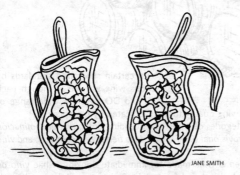

JANE SMITH

Left: Jugs of chille *sangría*, a very drinkabl concoction of wine, fru and spices

Castilla y León

Roughly taking in the territories of the former kingdom of León and Castilla la Vieja (Old Castile), this vast region offers a string of more or less important cities dotted across often desolate plains. Among the 'musts' are Salamanca, León, Segovia, Ávila and Burgos.

As if to confirm the adage that the exception proves the rule, however, fringe areas provide enormous contrast to the monotony of 'deep Castilla'. The Leonese side of the Picos de Europa mountains (see the Cantabria & Asturias chapter), the Sierra de la Peña de Francia (near Extremadura), the Sierra de Gredos (bordering Castilla-La Mancha) and the Sanabria area (just short of Galicia) are some of the more obvious such exceptions. Searing summer heat and bitter winter cold further characterise the tendency to extremes in this old heartland of Spain.

As with most of central Spain, centuries of poverty have left their mark on the area's cuisine. The nippy winter climate and local peasant produce have favoured the development of a variety of meat dishes, and Spaniards readily recognise the region as the best to hunt out roast everything, with *cochinillo* (suckling pig) a particular speciality, above all in Segovia. *Cordero asado* (roast lamb) and *cabrito* (kid) are also reliable favourites.

Castilla y León is also a major wine producer, with growing areas straddling the Río Duero. Major centres are Toro, which makes easy-to-drink, light reds, while Rueda specialises in whites. The best crop comes from Ribera del Duero, known for its complex red wines.

For this guide, the region has been roughly divided into four zones, with some of the routes described radiating away from a theoretical starting point of Madrid.

The South-West

Starting from Madrid and passing through El Escorial, an obvious route suggests itself across the most southerly tract of

Castilla y León, taking in the towns of Ávila, Salamanca and Ciudad Rodrigo, from where the road continues west into Portugal. Along the way, you could detour to the Sierra de Gredos for some mountain walks and the timeless villages of the Sierra de la Peña de Francia, 40km east of Ciudad Rodrigo.

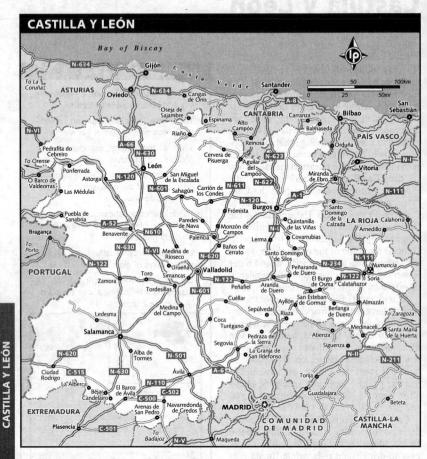

CASTILLA Y LEÓN

ÁVILA

postcode 05080 • pop 38,200 • elev 1130m

Huddled behind hefty walls, Ávila is one of the chilliest cities in Spain, infamous for its long, bitter winters. Nevertheless, it is a remarkable sight for visitors at any time of year, especially in summer. Although Ávila is not as lively as Segovia or as captivating as Toledo, the town still makes a suitable day trip from Madrid or, better yet, an overnight destination.

History

According to myth, one of Hercules' sons founded Ávila. The more prosaic truth,

however, gives the honour to obscure Iberian tribes who were soon assimilated into Celtic society and later largely Romanised and Christianised. For almost 300 years, Ávila changed hands regularly between Muslims and Christians, until the fall of Toledo to Alfonso VI in 1085.

In the following centuries, 'Ávila of the Knights' became an important commercial centre. Its well-established noble class was not averse to a skirmish in the wars with the Muslims or, later, in the imperial escapades in Flanders and South America. The edict issued in 1492 expelling all Jews from Spain

– followed a century later by moves to get rid of the *moriscos* (christianised Muslims) – robbed the city of much of its lifeblood. Meanwhile, Fray Tomás de Torquemada was busy at the end of the 15th century organising the most brutal phase of the Spanish Inquisition. He ended his days in Ávila.

Decades later, Santa Teresa began her mystical journey and the unwelcome campaign to reform the Carmelites in Ávila. By the time Teresa died in 1582, the city's heyday was over and it has only recently begun to shake off the deep slumber of neglect that ensued.

Orientation

The old centre is enclosed by a rough quadrangle of robust walls at the western end of town, with the cathedral butting into the walls at their eastern extremity. The Renfe train station is about a 10-minute walk northeast of the cathedral, while the bus station (*estación de autobuses*) is a little closer, just off Avenida de Madrid. Several *hostales* (budget hotels) cluster around the cathedral, and a few others are near the train station.

The tourist office, post office and banks are all near the cathedral.

Information

Tourist Offices The helpful tourist office (☎ 920 21 13 87, fax 920 25 37 17), Plaza de la Catedral 4, is open 9 am to 2 pm and 5 to 7 pm weekdays, and 10 am to 2 pm and 5 to 8 pm weekends. In summer, there's also a tourist information kiosk (☎ 920 35 71 26) outside Puerta de San Vicente.

Money Several banks on Calle de los Reyes Católicos and Calle de General Franco near the cathedral exchange money and also have ATMs.

Post & Communications The main post office (*correos*) is located just north of the cathedral. Internet access and fax services are offered by Antel at Calle Estrada 12.

Medical Services & Emergency The Policía Nacional (☎ 920 25 10 10) has its headquarters at Paseo San Roque 34. The Hospital Provincial (☎ 920 35 72 00) is at Calle de Jesús de Gran Poder 42. For an ambulance, call the Cruz Roja on ☎ 920 22 22 22.

Catedral

Ávila's cathedral is not just a house of worship but also an ingenious fortress: its stout granite apse forms the central bulwark in the eastern wall of the town, the most open to attack and hence the most heavily fortified.

Around the western side, the main facade conceals the Romanesque origins of what is essentially the earliest Gothic church in Spain. It also betrays some unhappy 18th-century meddling in the main portal. Inside, the red and white limestone employed in the columns stands out.

You can catch a partial peek of the interior for free, but in order to proceed to the inner sanctum – plus the cloister, sacristy and small museum – you'll have to produce 250 ptas. Highlights of the latter are a painting by El Greco and a splendid silver monstrance by Juan de Arfe. Worth inspecting in the church itself are the Renaissance-era carved walnut choir stalls and a dazzling altar painting begun by Pedro de Berruguete showing the life of Jesus in 24 scenes. In an alabaster tomb behind the main altar lies buried the 15th-century bishop and intellectual Don Alonso de Madrigal, called El Tostado (the Toasted One) for his dark-skinned complexion. Cathedral hours are seasonal but doors should be open from at least 10 am to 1 pm and 3.30 to 5 pm, closed Sunday morning.

Basílica de San Vicente

Lying outside the great fortified gate of the same name, this Romanesque basilica is striking in its subdued elegance. A series of largely Gothic modifications in sober granite contrasts with the warm sandstone of the Romanesque original. Work started in the 11th century, supposedly on the site where three martyrs – Vicente and his sisters – were slaughtered by the Romans in the early 4th century. Their canopied sepulchre is a nice piece of Romanesque work. The church is open 10 am to 1.30 pm and 4 to

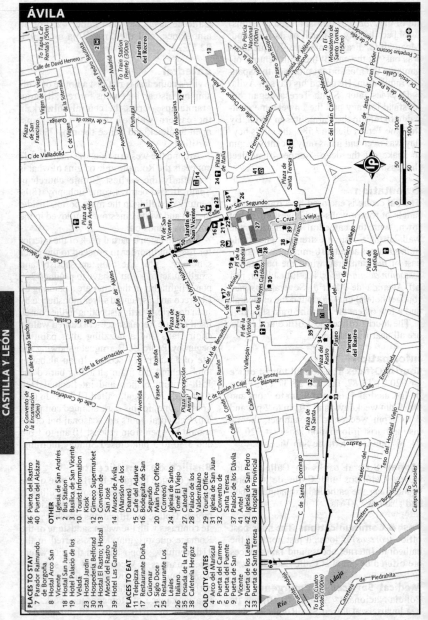

ÁVILA

PLACES TO STAY
7 Parador Raimundo
   de Borgoña
8 Hostal Arco San
   Vicente
18 Hostal San Juan
19 Hotel Palacio de los
   Velada
23 Hostal Jardín
30 Hospedería Belforad
34 Hostal El Rastro; Hostal
   San José
35 Mesón del Rastro
39 Hotel Las Cancelas

PLACES TO EAT
11 Telepizza
17 Restaurante Doña
   Guiomar
21 Siglo Doce
25 Restaurante Los
   Leales
26 Italiano
35 Posada de la Fruta
38 Cafetería Hergoz

OTHER
1 Iglesia de San Andrés
2 Bus Station
3 Basílica de San Vicente
10 Tourist Information
   Kiosk
12 Gimeco Supermarket
13 Convento de
   San José
14 Museo de Ávila
   (Mansión de los
   Deanes)
15 Café del Adarve
16 Bodeguita de San
   Segundo
20 Main Post Office
   (Correos)
24 Palacio de los
   Valderrábano
27 Catedral
28 Palacio de los
   Valderrábano
29 Tourist Office
32 Convento de
   Santa Teresa
37 Palacio de los Dávila
41 Antel
42 Iglesia de los Leales
43 Hospital Provincial

OLD CITY GATES
4 Arco del Mariscal
5 Puerta del Carmen
6 Puerta del Puente
9 Puerta de San
   Vicente
22 Puerta de los Leales
33 Puerta de Santa Teresa
36 Puerta del Rastro
40 Puerta del Alcázar

euro currency converter   100pta = €0.60

6.30 pm daily, though this may vary slightly (200 ptas). The Jardín de San Vicente across the road was once a Roman cemetery.

El Monasterio de Santo Tomás

Commissioned by the Catholic Monarchs, Fernando and Isabel, and completed in 1492, this complex is an exquisite example of the Isabelline style of architecture. Three interconnected cloisters lead up to the church that contains the alabaster tomb of Don Juan, the monarchs' only son who died at age 19. It is backed by an altarpiece by Pedro de Berruguete depicting scenes from the life of St Thomas Aquinas. The magnificent choir stalls, in Flemish-Gothic style, are accessible from the upper level of the third cloister, the Claustro de los Reyes, so-called because Fernando and Isabel often attended mass here. It is thought that the inquisitor Torquemada is buried in the sacristy.

The monastery, about 500m south-east of the cathedral, is usually open 10 am to 1 pm and 4 to 8 pm daily (100 ptas). It also harbours the **Museo de Arte Oriental**, which keeps shorter hours (closed Monday); entry is 200 ptas.

In Santa Teresa's Footsteps

Santa Teresa, has left her mark all over the city. This even includes the numerous pastry shops hawking the local speciality, *yemas,* a scrummy, sticky business made of egg yolk and sugar she allegedly invented. All sites described below are open daily, but hours vary throughout the year. Pick up the most current schedule at the tourist office, which is free.

The **Convento de Santa Teresa**, built over the saint's birthplace in 1636, is the epicentre of the cult around Teresa. The room where she was born is now a chapel smothered in gold and lorded over by a baroque altar featuring a statue of the saint. The souvenir shop next door gives access to a small room crammed with Teresa relics, including a sole of one of her shoes and her ring finger (complete with ring), which supposedly spent the Franco years by the *generalísimo's* bedside. Entry here and to the convent is free. There's also a

small museum dedicated to the saint, accessible from Calle Aizpuru (300 ptas).

Nearby, the **Iglesia de San Juan** contains the baptismal font in which Teresa was baptised (free). A five-minute walk east of the cathedral is the **Convento de San José**, the first convent Teresa founded (1562). Its clandestine construction was executed with the help of her sister, brother-in-law and the bishop of Ávila; the saint herself is said to have helped build the chapel. For more Teresa memorabilia, visit the small museum (150 ptas).

North of the city walls, the **Convento de la Encarnación** is where Santa Teresa fully took on the monastic life and lived for 27 years, launching her reform movement. A Renaissance complex modified in the 18th century, this convent contains further mementos of her life as well as a replica of her cell; entry is 150 ptas.

Santa Teresa de Ávila

Teresa de Cepeda y Ahumada – a Catholic mystic and reformer – was born in Ávila on March 28, 1515 as one of 10 children of a merchant family. Raised by Augustinian nuns after her mother's death, she joined the Carmelite Order at age 20. Shortly thereafter, Teresa nearly succumbed to a mysterious illness that paralysed her legs for three years. In her early years as a nun, she was plagued by self-doubt and struggled with her spiritual development. But after experiencing various visions and mystical experiences, her true vocation began to crystallise: she would reform the Carmelites.

With the help of many supporters Teresa founded convents of the Carmelitas Descalzas (Shoeless Carmelites) all over Spain. She also co-opted San Juan de la Cruz (St John of the Cross) to begin a similar reform in the masculine order, a task that earned him several stints of incarceration by the mainstream Carmelites. Santa Teresa's writings were first published in 1588 and proved enormously popular, perhaps partly for their earthy style. She died in 1582 in Alba de Tormes, where she is buried. She was canonised by Pope Gregory XV in 1622.

CASTILLA Y LEÓN

City Walls

With its eight monumental gates and 88 towers, Ávila's *muralla* (city wall) is one of the world's best preserved medieval defensive perimeters. Raised between the 11th and 12th centuries on the remains of earlier efforts by the Muslims and Romans, the wall has been much restored and modified with various Gothic and Renaissance touches. The most impressive gates, the Puerta de San Vicente and Puerta del Alcázar, are flanked by towers more than 20m high and stand on either side of the cathedral's apse, the central defensive point of the eastern wall. You can walk atop a short portion of the wall and enjoy the fabulous view. Access is from the Puerta de Alcázar from 10 am to 8 pm daily (shorter in low season); 200 ptas.

Churches & Mansions

Ávila is besprinkled with interesting churches. The Romanesque **Iglesia de Santo Tomé El Viejo** on Plaza de Italia has been impressively restored to house mostly Roman artefacts, including a splendid floor mosaic. It's an annex of the **Museo de Ávila** housed in the adjacent Mansión de los Deanes. Both are open 10 am to 2 pm and 4.30 to 7.30 pm, closed Sunday afternoon and Monday, longer hours in summer (200 ptas for both, weekends are free).

Built a little later is the **Iglesia de San Pedro** on Plaza de Santa Teresa, which has a nice rose window. North of the old city, the 12th-century **Iglesia de San Andrés**, a pure example of the Romanesque, is Ávila's oldest church. Note the masterfully carved capitals inside. Churches are usually open from about 10 am to 2 pm and 4 to 7 pm daily.

The city also has its fair share of noble mansions, some of which now serve as top-end hotels. The **Palacio de los Velada** and **Palacio de los Valderrábano**, on Plaza de la Catedral, fall into this category. The **Palacio de los Dávila** once belonged to one of the city's most illustrious noble families.

Los Cuatro Postes

Just north-west of the city on the road to Salamanca, this spot not only affords fine views of Ávila's walls, but also marks the place where Santa Teresa and her brother were caught by their uncle as they tried to run away from home. They were hoping to achieve martyrdom at the hands of the Moorish infidels.

Special Events

Ávila's principal festival (15 October) honours, not surprisingly, Santa Teresa. The early-morning Good Friday procession is equally noteworthy. Easter in general is marked by a stream of solemn marches and other events beginning on Holy Thursday.

Places to Stay – Budget

Camping The nearest camping ground is **Camping Sonsoles** (☎ 920 25 63 36), 2km south of town on the N-403 to Toledo. It is open from June to September. Rates are 400 ptas each per person, car and tent.

Hostales One of the cheapest places, **Hostal Jardín** (☎ 920 21 10 74, Calle de San Segundo 38) has fairly scruffy singles/doubles with washbasin for 3000/4000 ptas and a few with bath for 4000/5500 ptas. A better choice is **Hostal San Juan** (☎ 920 25 14 75, Calle de los Comuneros de Castilla 3) where rooms with phone, TV, shower and toilet cost 3800/7000 ptas. Better still is **Hostal El Rastro** (☎ 920 21 12 18, fax 920 25 16 26, Plaza del Rastro 1). Full of character and with a good restaurant, it offers rooms from 3880/5560 ptas.

Places to Stay – Mid-Range

Ávila's lodging scene has been enriched by two new modern and charming boutique hotels, both offering airy and comfortable rooms and friendly, English-speaking staff. **Hospedería Belforad** (☎ 920 35 23 21, Calle de los Reyes Católicos 22) is built on the site of a synagogue and charges 6000/8900 ptas for rooms with bath. At the equally charming **Hostal Arco San Vicente** (☎ 920 22 24 98, fax 920 22 95 32, Calle de López Núñez) rates are 5300/8000 ptas. If they're full, try **Hotel Las Cancelas** (☎ 920 21 22 49, fax 920 21 22 50, Calle de la Cruz Vieja 6) whose traditionally furnished, perfectly adequate rooms cost 5000/8000 ptas.

Places to Stay – Top End

Parador Raimundo de Borgoña (☎ *920 21 13 40, fax 920 25 11 73, Marques de Canales y Chozas 2)* is one of those exceptional hotels that dazzle with class, not glitz. Occupying a 16th-century palace, it has rooms sheathed in warm colour schemes and elegant public areas. Some rooms have views of the town wall. Rates peak at 13,500/17,500 ptas.

A top-ranked alternative is *Hotel Palacio de los Velada* (☎ *920 25 51 00, fax 920 25 49 00)* on Plaza de la Catedral, which boasts great architecture and rooms for 16,000/19,000.

Places to Eat

For a cheap, decent pizza, you could do worse than *Telepizza* (☎ *920 25 50 01, Avenida de Portugal 2)*. *Restaurante Los Leales* (☎ *920 21 13 29, Plaza de Italia 4)* has a choice of set lunches from 1000 ptas and is a favourite local stand-by.

Cafeteria Hergoz (Calle de General Franco 3) is a pastry shop with an attached dining area serving good-value *platos combinados,* burgers and *bocadillos*. *Italiano* (☎ *920 25 25 90, Calle de San Segundo 30)* offers salads, pizza and pasta for under 1000 ptas, as does *Siglo Doce* (☎ *920 25 28 85),* just inside Puerta de los Leales.

A good moderately priced choice is *Hostal Mesón del Rastro* (☎ *21 12 18, Plaza del Rastro 1)*. The 1700-ptas *menú del día* (daily set meal) is served both for lunch and dinner (a rarity) and is great value. The *comedor* (dining room), with its dark wood beams and wrought-iron work, exudes Castilian charm.

Pleasant *Posada de la Fruta* (☎ *920 22 09 84, Plaza de Pedro Dávila 8)* is really two restaurants in one. Simple, informal meals can be had at the cafeteria/bar with seating in a high-ceilinged light court. Behind is the traditional comedor where the *menú* costs 1850 ptas and a la carte dishes start at 1000 ptas. *Restaurante Doña Guiomar* (☎ *920 25 37 09, Calle de Tomás Luis de Victoria 3)* has a touch of class but is a bit on the pricey side, with a menu for 3000 ptas.

For stocking up on fruit, cheese, soft drinks and the like, *Gimeco (Calle Eduardo Marquina 18)* is the most central supermarket.

Entertainment

Ávila is not exactly the most happening town in Spain, but to soak up a youthful vibe, drop in at the hip *Cafe del Adarve (Calle de San Segundo 50)*. Abstract canvasses, metal sculptures and an ancient well form part of the decor, but in summer seats on the enclosed courtyard are the most coveted. Slightly older folks may feel more comfortable at the *Bodeguita de San Segundo* across the street, a wine and tapas bar that's often standing-room only.

Otherwise, Plaza de la Victoria and Plaza de Santa Teresa are the places to look for bars, tapas and front-row people-watching seats. Later in the evening, you'll find some *marcha* (action) along Calle de Vallespín and west to the Puerta del Puente.

Getting There & Away

Bus Buses are OK for nearby and out-of-the-way destinations, but main cities are more easily reached by train. Buses to Madrid leave up to eight times on weekdays, down to three on weekends (1½ hours, 930 ptas), while Salamanca is served four times on weekdays (1½ hours, 700 ptas) and Segovia up to seven times (one hour, 550 ptas). Destinations in the Sierra de Gredos include Navarredonda de Gredos and Arenas de San Pedro, though service is usually restricted to one bus, weekdays only.

Train Up to 30 trains daily run to Madrid (1½ hours, 865 ptas) and a handful head to Salamanca (same price and duration). Other Castilian cities with direct service include Burgos, Valladolid and León.

Car & Motorcycle From Madrid, you need to get onto the N-VI. Follow this or the parallel A-6 *autopista* (tollway) to Villacastín, then head west on the N-110. From Ávila, the N-501 heads north to Salamanca and the N-110 east will take you to Segovia. For the Sierra de Gredos, catch the N-502.

If you're headed to the Sierra de Gredos, you should consider renting a car since public transport ranges from impractical to nonexistent. There's a Hertz office (☎ *920 35 30 60)*, but the local agency Tapia (☎ *920 22*

CASTILLA Y LEÓN

22 33), Calle de Segovia 24, usually has better prices and conditions.

Getting Around
Local bus No 1 runs past the Renfe train station to Plaza de la Catedral.

SIERRA DE GREDOS
Taking over where the Sierra de Guadarrama outside Madrid trails off, the Sierra de Gredos is a mighty mountain chain dividing the two Castiles – in modern terms, Castilla y León and Castilla-La Mancha to its south. The highest peak is the Almanzor (2592m); it is orbited by slightly smaller mountains which together form the Circo de Gredos.

The occasional castle or sanctuary may warrant attention, but the main attraction here is the scenery. Walking is good to excellent, and activities such as mountain biking and rock climbing are becoming more popular. Spring and autumn are the best times for outdoor activity; summers can be stifling, while in winter the trails are often smothered in snow.

Unless you're travelling under your own steam, getting around the area is difficult. There are bus services from Ávila

Toros de Guisando

A curiosity just inside Castilla y León's boundary with the Comunidad de Madrid are the so-called Toros de Guisando (Bulls of Guisando; not to be confused with the hamlet of Guisando in the Sierra de Gredos). Four weather-beaten stone animals, lined up behind a hedge, are said to have stood there since pre-Roman times. One theory claims they marked a border between Celtiberian tribes. At this spot, or perhaps in what remains of a monastery halfway up the hill west of the road, Isabel (as in Fernando and Isabel, the Catholic Monarchs) was supposedly sworn in as heir to the Castilian throne in 1468.

The taurine foursome stands along the C-501, about 5km west of the junction with the N-403, the main highway between Ávila and Toledo. The nearest town is San Martín de Valdeiglesias.

and Madrid, but they are sporadic, slow and often limited to weekdays. You might want to consider renting a car to avoid frustration.

There are three main routes through the Sierra: The C-502 travels north-south paralleling an old Roman road (still visible in parts) through a steep valley. Cutting across the northern foothills, the C-500 affords scenic views of the mountains while passing through several hamlets. Following the southern flank of the mountain chain, the C-501 offers a pretty drive from Arenas towards Candeleda and on into Extremadura's La Vera valley.

Arenas de San Pedro & Around
postcode 05400 • pop 6400
Arenas de San Pedro, the southern Sierra's hub, is a popular summer escape for sun-stunned Castilians and *madrileños*. Sights worth a quick look in the town centre are the stout 15th-century **Castillo de la Triste Condesa**, the sober 14th-century Gothic parish church and the **Roman bridge**. A 10-minute walk north of here is the neoclassical **Palacio del Infante Don Luis de Borbón** – a gilded cage for Carlos III's imprisoned brother.

Far more attractive, and providing access to walking trails, are El Hornillo, El Arenal and Guisando, a trio of villages at a distance of 6km, 9km and 5km from Arenas, respectively. All three are served by bus – once a day and on weekdays only.

One popular walking trail leads from El Arenal to Puerto de la Cabrilla. Gaining some 1000m over a distance of 4.5km, it makes for a rather strenuous work-out. Budget about five to seven hours round-trip. The tourist information centre (☎ 920 37 50 01) at Plaza de la Nueva España 1 in Arenas has more walking suggestions and maps, as does the tourist office in Ávila.

Places to Stay & Eat In Arenas, *Hostal El Castillo* (☎ 920 37 00 91, Carretera de Candeleda 2) has small, spartan but clean singles/doubles for 2500/3000 ptas (those with bath are 1000 ptas more). Nearby, *Hostería Los Galayos* (☎ 920 37 13 79, Plaza de Condestable Dávalos 2) offers solid if unexciting food and has rooms with TV, phone and bath for 4000/7000 ptas. Both are near the castle in the town centre.

In El Arenal, *Hostal Isabel* (☎ *920 37 51 48)*, on Calle de las Angustias, is the only game in town offering comfortable rooms (doubles only) for 3500 ptas with washbasin or 3800 ptas with shower and loo. Guisando has two *hostales* and a large *camping ground* (☎ *920 37 40 21)*.

Getting There & Away At least four buses run daily to Arenas de San Pedro from Madrid and there's one weekday service from Ávila.

The Northern Flank of the Sierra de Gredos

Veering off the C-502 near Puerta de Picos, the C-500 connects a series of nondescript, but scenically located, hamlets. From Hoyos del Espino a small road, the AV-931, leads into the Sierras, dead-ending after 12km at La Plataforma. This is the jumping-off point for one of the most popular and scenic walks, leading to the **Laguna Grande**, a glassy mountain lake in the shadow of the Pico de Almanzor.

The easy to moderate walk along a well-defined trail takes about 2½ hours each way. Next to the lake is a *refugio* (shelter), which is often full, and good camping. From here it's possible to climb to the top of the Almanzor (difficult) in about two hours or to continue for two hours west to the Circo de Cinco Lagunas (easy to moderate). From there you could either backtrack or descend via the Garganta del Pinar towards the town of Navalperral de Tormes, a strenuous endeavour that can take as much as five hours.

Places to Stay Most villages along the C-500 offer accommodation. A fine camping ground is *Camping Gredos* (☎ *920 20 75 85)* on the access road to the Plataforma. *Albergue Juvenil* (☎ *920 34 80 05)* in Navarredonda de Gredos has its own Olympic-size swimming pool and charges 1000/1450 ptas for juniors/seniors. More comfort and the same views are available at the

nearby *Parador de Gredos* (☎ *920 34 80 48, fax 920 34 82 05)*, albeit at a much steeper rate – singles/doubles start at 9200/11,500 ptas. Hoyos de Espina has eight places to stay, including *Hostal La Maja* (☎ *920 34 90 65, Calle La Majada 2)*, where rooms with bath cost 2500/5000 ptas.

Sierra de Béjar

The C-500 continues west to **El Barco de Ávila**, which has a pretty setting on the Río Tormes and is lorded over by a proud if ruinous castle. Past here, the road enters the province of Salamanca and the Sierra de Béjar, the continuation of the Sierra de Gredos. After about 30km it reaches the town of Béjar, whose partly walled old quarters line up at the western end of a high ridge. Among worthwhile sights is the eye-catching 16th-century **Palacio Ducal**, just west of Plaza Mayor, now serving as a college.

Candelario The most scenic village in this region, tiny Candelario is about a 5km detour from Béjar. Rubbing against a steep mountain face, this charming enclave is a popular summer resort and a great base for outdoor activities. It features typical mountain architecture of stone and wood houses clustered closely together to protect against the harsh winter climate. A special feature are the little streams that parallel many of the cobbled lanes and the ornate *batipuertas*, wooden half-doors in front of the regular entrance doors.

If you want to spend the night, the cheapest bet is *Pensión Casa Gabriel* (☎ *923 41 31 76, Calle de Humilladero 2)*, where rooms with washbasin cost 3500/5000 ptas. It's open from July to December only. A step up is *Hostal El Pasaje* (☎ *923 41 32 10, Calle Las Eras)*, which has doubles with shower and toilet for 5500 ptas. There's also a *camping ground* (☎ *923 41 32 04)* about 400m from the town. For dinner, try *Meson La Romana* (☎ *923 41 32 72, Calle de Núñez Losada)*, which does reasonably priced meats cooked on an open woodfire grill.

Getting There & Away Béjar is served by buses from Salamanca and various other destinations, including Madrid and Plasencia. Drivers could follow the C-515 to La Alberca in the Sierra de Francia and on to Ciudad Rodrigo. For details on these destinations, see the Salamanca section.

SALAMANCA
postcode 37080 • pop 160,500

If any major Castilian city can be said to jump with action, it is Salamanca. With its eclectic and quirky collection of bars, cafes and restaurants catering for an enormous student population, this compact and ancient city should be considered a must on any Castilian itinerary. The beauty of its historical university and churches are without equal in Spain, which is partly what draws throngs of young people from around the world here to study Spanish – and to party. Salamanca has been designated as a Cultural Capital of Europe in 2002 and has been busy sprucing itself up in preparation for the year-long celebration.

History

In 220 BC, Celtiberian Salamanca was besieged by Hannibal. Later, under Roman rule, it was an important staging post on the Via Lata (Ruta de la Plata, or Silver Route) from the mines in northern Spain to the south. After the Muslim invasion of Spain, it changed hands repeatedly.

Possibly the greatest turning point in the city's history was the founding of the university in 1218. It became the equal of Oxford and Bologna, and by the end of the 15th century was the focal point of some of the richest artistic activity in the country, in part due to the generous patronage of Queen Isabel of Castile. In few other places will you witness the virtuosity in plateresque and Renaissance work on hand in Salamanca.

The city followed the rest of Castile into decline in the 17th century, aggravated by the Napoleonic invasion in the early 19th century. The Industrial Revolution helped turn things around, and by the time Spanish literary hero Miguel de Unamuno became rector at the university in 1900, Salamanca had essentially recovered.

Orientation

The old centre is compact and easily walked. It lies north of the Río Tormes and at its heart lies Spain's grandest *plaza mayor* (main plaza). A fair range of accommodation can be found between Plaza Mayor and the river, an area that encompasses most of the university buildings. The train and bus stations are about equidistant from the centre, the former to the north-east and the latter to the north-west. If the 20 or so minutes walk from either doesn't appeal, buses connect both to the centre and taxis are cheap.

Information

Tourist Offices The Oficina Municipal de Turismo (☎ 923 21 83 42) at Plaza Mayor 14 concentrates on the city and is open 9 am to 2 pm and 4.30 to 6.30 pm daily. For the remainder of the province, as well as basic city information, go to the tourist office (☎ 923 26 85 71, fax 923 26 24 92) in the Casa de las Conchas, Calle de la Compañía 2. It's open 10 am to 2 pm and 5 to 8 pm, closed Saturday afternoon and Sunday. In summer, offices also open at the train and bus stations.

Money There is no shortage of banks around the centre. American Express is represented by Viajes Salamanca (☎ 923 26 77 31), at Plaza Mayor 11.

Post & Communications You'll find the main post office at Gran Vía 25 and a *locutorio* (telephone office) on Plaza Mayor. The latter is open 9.30 am to 11.30 pm daily. Places offering Internet access include Campus Cibermático on the ground floor of Plaza Mayor 10, and Abaco on Calle Zamora across from O'Neill's Irish pub. Rates vary a bit but should be around 150/250/450 per 15/30/60 minutes.

Laundry There's a coin-operated laundry at Pasaje Azafranal 18, near Plaza de España.

Medical Services & Emergency Two clinics close to the centre are Hospital Clínico Universitario (☎ 923 29 11 00), Paseo de San

SALAMANCA

PLACES TO STAY
6 Hotel Gran Vía
15 Pensión Robles
19 Le Petit Hotel
20 Hotel El Toboso
23 Hostal Orly
25 Pensión Los
 Ángeles; Campus
 Cibermático
30 Gran Hotel
33 Hostal Plaza Mayor
40 Pensión Las Vegas
41 Hostal Tormes
42 Pensión Lisboa
44 Hostal La Perla
 Salamantina
49 Hostal Laguna
60 Albergue Juvenil
66 Pensión Feli
67 Hostal Peña de
 Francia

PLACES TO EAT
2 Café Unamuno
22 Restaurante El Clavel
29 Mesón Cervantes
32 MusicArte Café
35 Crêperie Cordon Bleu
37 El Bardo
39 El Patio Chico
46 El Grillo Azul
53 Café El Ave

OTHER
1 Hospital Santísima
 Trinidad
3 Teatro de la Caja
4 Posada de las Almas
5 Laundromat
7 Main Post Office (Correos)
8 Policía Nacional
9 Captain Haddock
10 Morgana

11 Convento de las
 Úrsulas; Camelot Disco
12 Colegio de Arzobispo
 Fonseca
13 Palacio de Monterrey
14 La Regenta
16 Abaco
17 O'Neill's
18 Museo Taurino
21 Tío Vivo
24 Telephones (Locutorio)
26 Viajes Salamanca
 (American Express)
27 Oficina Municipal de
 Turismo
28 Mercado Central
31 Iglesia de San Martín
34 Cum Laude
36 Café El Corrillo
38 Casa de las Conchas;
 Tourist Office

43 Taberna La Rayuela
45 Potemkin
47 Submarine
48 El Gran Café Moderno
50 Torre del Clavero
51 The Irish Rover
52 Real Clericía de San
 Marcos
54 Museo de Salamanca
55 Museo de la Universidad
56 Patio de las Escuelas
 Menores
57 Universidad Civil
58 Convento de las Dueñas
59 Convento de Las Claras
61 Convento de San Esteban
62 Catedral Nueva
63 Catedral Vieja
65 Casa Lis
66 Huerta de Calixto
 y Melibea

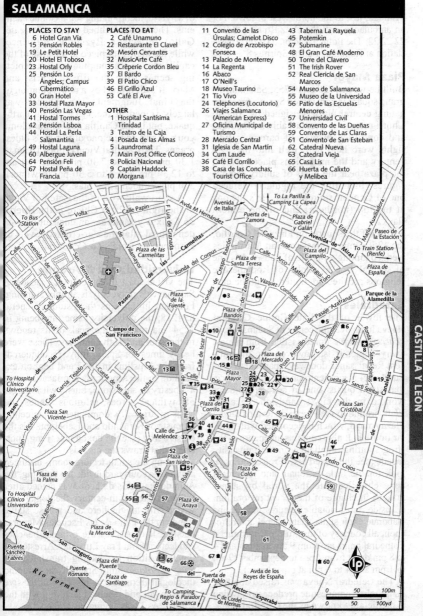

CASTILLA Y LEÓN

euro currency converter €1 = 166pta

Vicente 58–182, and Hospital Santísima Trinidad, just to the north-west of town. For an ambulance, call the Cruz Roja on ☎ 923 22 22 22. The Policía Nacional (☎ 092) has a station at Ronda de Sancti-Spiritus 8.

Plaza Mayor
Built between 1729 and 1755, Salamanca's grand square is considered Spain's most engaging central plaza. Designed by Alberto Churriguera, it is a remarkably harmonious and controlled display of baroque. Bullfights were held here well into the 19th century and the medallions placed around the plaza bear the busts of sundry famous figures, including the regularly defaced one of Generalísimo Franco. He's the one at the top (northern) end of the eastern flank.

Just off the square, on Plaza del Corrillo, the 12th-century **Iglesia de San Martín** lies wedged among a huddle of houses. It's one of several nice examples of Romanesque religious architecture dotted about the city.

Catedrales
The tower of the Late Gothic **Catedral Nueva** lords over the centre of Salamanca, its *churrigueresque* dome visible from almost every angle. It is, however, the magnificent Renaissance doorways, particularly the Puerta del Nacimiento on the western face, that stand out as one of several miracles worked in the city's sandstone facades. Walk around to the Puerta de Ramos facing Plaza Anaya, which is decorated with similar flourish. It also contains an encore to the 'frog spotting' challenge on the university facade (see the boxed text 'Frog Spotting'): look for the little astronaut and ice-cream cone chiselled into the portal by stonemasons in charge of the recent restoration.

Inside, most notable features include the elaborate choir stalls, main chapel and retrochoir, all courtesy of the prolific Churriguera. Cathedral hours are from 9 am to 2 pm and 4 to 8 pm daily from April to September (9 am to 1 pm and 4 to 6 pm at other times).

The Catedral Nueva was raised abutting its largely Romanesque predecessor, which is predictably known as the **Catedral Vieja**.

Begun as early as 1120, this church is a bit of a hybrid, incorporating some Gothic elements. The unusual ribbed cupola (Torre del Gallo) reflects a Byzantine influence, while the main altarpiece in the apse of the capilla mayor is a sumptuous work depicting scenes from the life of Christ and Mary. It's all topped by a representation of the Final Judgment. The cloister was largely ruined in the 1755 Lisbon earthquake, but in the Capilla de San Bartolomé you can still admire one of Europe's oldest organs. The Catedral Vieja is open 10 am to 1.30 pm and 4 to 7.30 pm daily (10 am to 12.30 pm and 4 to 5.30 pm in winter); 300 ptas, students 200 ptas.

A short walk west of the Catedral Vieja, to the right of Patio Chico, is the **Huerta de Calixto y Melibea**, an enchanting garden named after the star-crossed lovers of Fernando de Roja's *La Celestina*.

Universidad Civil & Around
The visual feast of the entrance facade to Salamanca's university is simply stunning. Founded initially as the Estudio General in 1218, the university came into being in 1254 and reached the peak of its renown in the 15th and 16th centuries. These were heady times for Spain, fully 'reconquered' from the Muslims in 1492 and bent on expansion in the Americas. The facade, more a tapestry in sandstone, bursts with images of mythical heroes, religious scenes and coats of arms. It's dominated in the centre by busts of Fernando and Isabel, but it's the elusive frog (see the boxed text 'Frog Spotting') that draws the crowds.

Among the small lecture rooms arranged around the courtyard inside the building, the **Aula de Fray Luis de León** was named after the celebrated 16th-century theologian and writer who taught here and whose statue stands in the Patio de las Escuelas Menoras outside. It conserves the original benches and lectern from Fray Luis' day. Arrested by the Inquisition for having translated the *Song of Solomon* into Spanish, the sardonic theologian returned to his class after five years in jail and resumed lecturing with the words, 'As I was saying yesterday...'

Upstairs, the university library boasts fine Late Gothic features and a beautiful *techumbre* (carved wooden ceiling). Some 2800 ancient manuscripts lie in the custody of what is one of the oldest university libraries in Europe. The university can be visited from 9.30 am to 1.30 pm and 4 to 7 pm Monday to Saturday and 10 am to 1 pm Sunday and holidays (300 ptas, students half-price; includes entrance to the Museo de la Universidad – see the following section).

Patio de las Escuelas Menores Head out of the university and walk over to the south-western corner of the little square, off which opens the cloister of the Escuelas Menores. Among the arches lies the **Museo de la Universidad**, where you can see an impressive ceiling fresco of the zodiac along with a fairly standard collection of clerical robes and art. It has the same opening hours as the university. Check out the Sala de Exposiciones, where you can admire two techumbres – one clearly *mudéjar* and the other with Renaissance Italian influences.

Museo de Salamanca This modest gallery is housed in the former residence of Queen Isabel's doctor and is as interesting for its architecture as for the paintings and sculptures within. Notable are the little patio and the techumbre ceiling in Sala 1. It is open 9.45 am to 1.45 pm and 4.45 to 10.45 pm Tuesday to Friday, and 10.15 am to 1.15 pm and 4.45 to 7.45 pm weekends, closed Sunday afternoon (200 ptas, students half-price).

Casa de las Conchas One of Salamanca's most endearing buildings was named for the scallop shells clinging to its facade. Its owner, Dr Rodrigo Maldonado de Talavera, was a doctor at the court of Isabel and a member of the Order of Santiago, whose symbol is the shell. It now houses the public library, entered via a charming bi-level courtyard, and the tourist office.

Real Clerícía de San Marcos Across the street is the Universidad Pontificia, whose main attraction is the colossal baroque

Frog Spotting

A compulsory task facing all visitors to the Universidad Civil in Salamanca is to search out the frog sculpted on to the facade. Once pointed out, it is easily enough seen, but you can expend considerable time in vain searching otherwise. So why bother?

Well, they say that those who detect it without help can be assured of good luck and even marriage (if you consider that good luck) within a year. Some hopeful students see a guaranteed examinations victory in it. If you believe all this, stop reading now. If you do want help, look at the busts of Fernando and Isabel. From there, swing your gaze to the largest column on the extreme right of the facade. Slightly above the level of the busts are sculpted a series of skulls, atop the leftmost of which sits our little amphibious friend (or what's left of his eroded self).

MICK WELDON

church. It's only open in the half-hour before Mass; times are posted by the entrance.

Convento de San Esteban & Around

Standing proud in the south-eastern corner of the old city, the facade of this monastery's church is in effect a huge altar in stone, with the stoning of San Esteban (St Stephen) its central motif. Inside, the centrepiece is also a retablo – this time an ornate masterpiece by José Churriguera. Through the Gothic-Renaissance cloister you can climb upstairs to the church's choir stalls. The monastery is open 9 am to 1 pm and 4 to 6 pm daily. Entry to the cloister costs 200 ptas.

Convento de las Dueñas Easily the most beautiful cloister in the city is the irregular, pentagonal one gracing this convent of Dominican nuns, who still make and sell a range of traditional pastries. It's open 10.30 am to 1 pm and 4.30 to 5.30 pm daily (200 ptas).

Torre del Clavero If you walk north a couple of blocks along Gran Vía, you will notice this defensive tower a block away to your left. It's a 15th-century octagonal fortress on a square base adorned with smaller cylindrical towers. You can then turn right for the Convento de Las Claras.

Convento de Las Claras This convent started life as a Romanesque building but has been rebuilt on several occasions. You can climb up some stairs to inspect at close quarters the 14th- and 15th-century *mudéjar artesonado* ceilings, hidden from view for almost three centuries by a lower ceiling. You can only visit this part of the convent with a guide and will get more out of it if you understand Spanish. It's open 9.30 am to 1.40 pm and 4 to 6.40 pm weekdays and 9 am to 2.40 pm weekends (200 ptas).

Colegio del Arzobispo Fonseca & Around
A short stroll west of Plaza Mayor brings you to another series of Salamantine monuments. Also known as the Colegio de los Irlandeses (Irish College), this one was built in the 16th century in a sober plateresque style. Of particular note are the main entrance and harmoniously proportioned courtyard. You can visit the college from 10 am to 2 pm and 4 to 6 pm daily. The antique clock collection is open 4 to 6 pm Tuesday to Friday and 11 am to 2 pm weekends and holidays (100 ptas).

Convento de las Úrsulas Nearby, this Late Gothic nunnery was founded by Archbishop Alonso de Fonseca in 1516 and now contains his magnificent marble tomb, sculpted by Diego de Siloé. The nunnery is open 11 am to 1 pm and 4.30 to 6 pm daily (100 ptas). The nuns actually rent out part of the space to a nightclub called Camelot (see Entertainment later in this section).

Palacio de Monterrey A 16th-century holiday home of the Duques de Alba, the palace is a seminal piece of Spanish Renaissance architecture. The dukes pop in every now and then, and visitors are not permitted inside.

Other Museums
Casa Lis Fans of Art Nouveau and Art Deco will probably get a kick out of the gallery devoted to both in this *modernista* house on Calle de Gibraltar, built in 1905. It is open 11 am to 2 pm and 5 to 9 pm Tuesday to Friday (4 to 7 pm in winter) and 10 am to 9 pm weekends and holidays (11 am to 8 pm in winter); 300 ptas, students 200 ptas.

Museo Taurino Salamanca province is bull-breeding territory; indeed it is one of the more important sources of *toros bravos* (fighting bulls) for the country. Those interested can learn a little more at this museum, just north of Plaza Mayor. It is open 6 to 9 pm Tuesday to Sunday (noon to 2 pm on weekends also); 200 ptas.

Places to Stay – Budget
Camping & Hostels There are four camping grounds near Salamanca, of which the following are the closest two to town. *Camping Regio* (☎ 923 13 88 88), 4km out of Salamanca on the N-501 to Madrid, is open all year and charges 450 ptas each per tent, person, car and electricity. *Camping La Capea* (☎ 923 25 10 66), on the N-630 also about 4km out of town, is slightly cheaper but only open from 1 April to 30 September.

Book ahead for Salamanca's central HI *Albergue Juvenil* (☎ 923 26 91 41, fax 923 21 42 27, e esterra@mmteam.disbumad.es, Calle Escoto 13-15). It's open year round and charges 1750 ptas per bunk, including bed linen and breakfast.

CASTILLA Y LEÓN

Hostales & Pensiones It is hard to beat a room in one of the little places on Plaza Mayor, provided you can snag one overlooking the square. *Pensión Los Ángeles (☎ 923 21 81 66)* at No 10 has rather basic singles/doubles with washbasin for 1900/2900 ptas and a few doubles with shower for 4500 ptas. *Pensión Robles (☎ 923 21 31 97)* at No 20 has perfectly adequate rooms with shower and toilet for 2200/3500 ptas.

Calle de Meléndez has a few places. *Pensión Lisboa (☎ 923 21 43 33)* at No 1 is good value, offering rooms with bath for 3400/3800 ptas; there are also a few cheaper ones with shared facilities. Hugely popular, and usually full, is the tiny *Pensión Las Vegas (☎ 923 21 87 49)* at No 13, where clean rooms with shared facilities cost 2000/3500 ptas.

Hostal La Perla Salamantina (☎/fax 923 21 76 56, Calle de Sánchez Barbero 7) charges 2500/4900 ptas for bright and clean rooms with bath, or 2100/3500 ptas with washbasin only. A good choice, if others are filling up, is *Hostal Peña de Francia (☎ 923 21 66 87, Calle de San Pablo 96)*, which charges 2700/3700 ptas for rooms with bath and 2100/3200 ptas for those without.

Hostal Tormes (☎/fax 923 21 96 83, fax 923 21 19 83, Rúa Mayor 20) is OK if a touch drab. The most expensive rooms go for 3500/4800 ptas, with bath. Down the road from the main university building is *Pensión Feli (☎ 923 21 60 10, Calle de los Libreros 58)*, which has cheerful rooms for 2400/3400 ptas without bath.

Places to Stay – Mid-Range
All rooms in this category have private bath, unless noted. *Hostal Laguna (☎/fax 923 21 87 06, fax 923 21 87 06, Calle del Consuelo 19)* has doubles only for 3500 ptas without and 5000 ptas with bath. For more comfort, try *Le Petit Hotel (☎ 923 26 55 67, Ronda de Sancti-Spíritus 39)* whose small but tidy rooms with phone and TV cost 4000/6500 ptas.

Hostal Orly (☎ 923 21 61 25, Calle del Pozo Amarillo 5-7) offers reasonable if unexciting rooms with such assets as TV and phone for 4000/6000 ptas; rates skyrocket

to 10,000 ptas on certain holidays. A much better deal is *Hotel El Toboso (☎/fax 923 27 14 62, fax 923 27 14 64, Calle del Clavel 7)*. The attractive timber and tile reception is no front, and the rooms are worth the 4700/6800 ptas charged.

Just off the main square is *Hostal Plaza Mayor (☎ 923 26 20 20, fax 923 21 75 48, Plaza del Corrillo 20)*, a stylish and clean establishment offering rooms with all mod cons for 4500/7500 ptas. Also a good choice in this category is *Hotel Gran Vía (☎ 923 21 54 01, fax 923 21 09 54, Calle de Rosa 4)*, which charges 5000/7000 ptas.

Places to Stay – Top End
For the best city panorama, book into *Parador de Salamanca (☎ 923 19 20 82, fax 923 19 20 87, Calle Teso de la Feria 2)*, which holds court over the city from its own hilltop perch south of the river. Stylish and generously sized rooms offer all the amenities you'd expect from a luxury hotel. Exercise fiends will enjoy the outdoor swimming pool and tennis courts. Rooms start at 11,600/14,500 ptas, leaping to 13,200/16,500 ptas in high season.

An even pricier in-town alternative is the slightly stuffy *Gran Hotel (☎ 923 21 35 00, fax 923 21 35 01, Plaza del Poeta Iglesias 5)*, which charges 17,000/22,000 ptas.

Places to Eat
Good places for breakfast are *Café Unamuno (Calle de Zamora 55)*, which serves filling fare from 375 ptas, and *Crêperie Cordon Bleu (Doctrinos 8)*, where you can get stuffed crepes and coffee from 150 ptas.

For lunch, good choices are *Café El Ave (☎ 923 26 45 11, Calle de los Libreros 24)*, a smoky affair serving platos combinados for around 700 ptas and a *menú* for 1100 ptas. A better bet is *El Bardo (☎ 923 21 90 89, Calle de la Compañía 8)* nearby, which bustles with students and does decent *paella* for 1100 ptas.

At night-time, people squeeze into the rustic *La Parrilla (Calle Van Dick 55)*, a tiny stand-up bar north of the old centre. Sandwiches with woodfire-grilled pork cutlets or ribs go for a bargain 170 ptas, drink included! *El Patio Chico (☎ 923 26 86 16,*

CASTILLA Y LEÓN

Calle de Meléndez 13) is a lively place for beers and filling tapas for around 400 ptas a throw; the *menú* is 1500 ptas.

For a break from meaty fare, head to *El Grillo Azul (☎ 923 21 92 33, Calle Grillo 1),* which serves salads and organic rice and pasta dishes for under 1000 ptas. It's closed Sunday night and Monday.

Right on Plaza Mayor, near the tourist office, *Mesón Cervantes,* with attractive upstairs dining, offers good-quality lunches from 2000 ptas. For another walk on the expensive side, try *Restaurante El Clavel (☎ 923 21 61 75, Calle del Clavel 6).* Expect to pay from 4000 ptas for a full meal.

Entertainment

The bimonthly *En Salamanca* booklet contains information on bars, cultural events, theatre and the like.

Cafes & Bars Salamanca, with its myriad bars, is the perfect after-dark playground. Nightlife here starts very late – even during the week – with many bars not filling until midnight or even later and the partying continuing until the wee hours.

If you don't mind paying 250 ptas for your coffee, it's hard to beat sipping your way through the morning at a cafe on Plaza Mayor. A few steps outside the grand square, *MusicArte Café (Plaza del Corrillo 22)* is a hip hang-out for coffee, cake and sandwiches at much better prices.

A suitable destination for a quiet drink and talk is *Captain Haddock,* a romantic, candle-lit haunt with a muted nautical theme. It's in a courtyard off Calle Consejo. Nearby, *La Regenta (Espoz y Mina 19-20)* recreates a pre-industrial coffeehouse ambience with heavy curtains, antique furniture and pillar candles.

Taberna La Rayuela (Rúa Mayor 19), pleasantly low-lit and intimate, is popular early in the evening. *Café El Corrillo (Calle de Meléndez 8)* is great for a beer and live jazz. A drink in *Tío Vivo (Calle del Clavel 3)* is a must, if only to experience the whimsical decor pairing carousel horses with early movie projectors and other odd-ball antiquities.

Salamanca's two Irish pubs both enjoy a loyal following. *O'Neill's (Calle de Zamora 14)* is the classic, but *The Irish Rover* on Calle Rúa Antigua, near the Casa de las Conchas, wins fans with its Victorian theatre-style decor. The food's good and cheap at both.

Another good area to look for marcha lies just east of the Mercado Central – Calle de San Justo, Calle de Varillas and Calle del Consuelo in particular are loaded with bars. A Salamanca classic on nearby Gran Vía is *El Gran Café Moderno* at No 75, which is made to look like an early 20th-century Parisian street.

Clubs & Discos Many of Salamanca's cafe-bars morph into dance clubs after midnight; there's usually no cover charge. Places to try include the endearing *Posada de las Almas* on Plaza de San Boal, a fantasy world inhabited by life-sized papier-mâché figures and doll houses. It attracts a mixed crowd (both in terms of gay/straight and Spanish/foreign). The same is true of *Submarine* in Calle San Justo, just off Gran Vía, which looks just like its namesake and gets almost as claustrophobic on busy nights.

Camelot is a lively disco in a space that's actually part of the Convento de las Úrsulas on Calle de la Compañía, though the decor is incongruously industrial. It's popular among foreign students. *Cum Laude (Calle del Prior 7)* is a rambling space that apes the elegance of a *palacio* (palace) and plays mostly dance music.

Other candidates include *Morgana* on the corner of Cuesta del Carmen and Calle de Iscar Peira, and *Potemkin* on Calle del Consuelo, which has live music.

Theatre The *Teatro de la Caja (Plaza de Santa Teresa)* is a frequent scene for concerts and performances of all sorts.

Getting There & Away

Bus The bus station is north-west of the town centre on Avenida de Filiberto Villalobos. AutoRes has frequent services to Madrid (3¾ hours, 1750 ptas; express 2½ hours, 2250 ptas). About eight buses serve Valladolid (1½ hours, 940 ptas).

Plenty of buses go to Alba de Tormes (180 ptas) and there is at least one daily, except Sunday, to La Alberca (365 ptas). Regular buses run to Zamora (595 ptas), Ávila (700 ptas) and Ciudad Rodrigo (735 ptas), and there are services also to Béjar, Ledesma and throughout the province.

The ALSA company runs buses as far afield as Galicia, Asturias, Cantabria and Cádiz.

Train Four trains leave daily for Madrid's Chamartín station (2½ hours, 2130 ptas) via Ávila (1¾ hours, 865 ptas). There's also frequent service to Valladolid (1¾ hours, 865 ptas). The Lisbon train leaves at 4.41 am.

Car & Motorcycle The N-501 leads southeast to Madrid via Ávila, while the N-630 heads north to Zamora. Heading for Portugal, take the N-620 west via Ciudad Rodrigo. Its eastern continuation goes to Valladolid and Burgos. For the Sierra de la Peña de Francia, take the C-512 south-west.

Getting Around
Bus No 4 runs past the bus station and around the old town perimeter to Gran Vía. From the train station, the best bet is bus No 1, which heads into the centre along Calle de Azafranal. Going the other way, it can be picked up at the Mercado Central.

AROUND SALAMANCA
Ledesma & Embalse de Almendra
Following the Río Tormes north-west, you reach the small town of **Ledesma**, a grey, partly walled settlement. A medieval bridge still spans the river, and there are a few churches of minor interest, including the Gothic Iglesia de Santa María la Mayor on Plaza Mayor. You can also see remains of the castle of the Duques de Alburquerque.

A couple of buses serve the town each day from Salamanca, and if you get stuck there are a couple of pensiones. If you have transport, you might want to keep trailing the river, which feeds the **Embalse de Almendra**, a huge reservoir not far short of the Portuguese border.

Alba de Tormes
postcode 37800 • pop 4340
The resting place of Santa Teresa de Ávila, Alba de Tormes is a mildly interesting and easily accomplished half-day excursion from Salamanca. Apart from the stout and highly visible **Torreón** – the only surviving section of the former castle of the Duques de Alba – people come to visit the remains of Santa Teresa, buried in the Convento de las Carmelitas she founded in 1570. There are plenty of buses from Salamanca.

CIUDAD RODRIGO
postcode 37500 • pop 14,890
About 80km south of Salamanca and less than 30km from the Portuguese border, Ciudad Rodrigo is a sleepy but attractive walled town and a pleasant final stop on the way out of Spain. From the time the Romans left after several centuries of occupation, little is known of the city until Count Rodrigo González arrived in the 12th century to refound the settlement as Civitas Roderici. It has always been something of a frontline city with Portugal, but never did Ciudad Rodrigo suffer as much as under siege during the Peninsular War against Napoleon. The city fell in 1811, but a year later Wellington turned the tide and dislodged the French.

Information
The tourist office (☎ 923 46 05 61), Plaza de las Amayuelas 5, is open 9 am to 2 pm and 5 to 7 pm weekdays and 10 am to 2 pm and 5 to 8 pm weekends. The post office is at Calle de Dámaso Ledesma 12.

Things to See
The **catedral**, the construction of which was begun in 1165, is without doubt the city's outstanding sight. The Puerta de las Cadenas, giving onto Plaza de San Salvador, with its Gothic reliefs of Old Testament figures, is impressive. More striking, though, is the elegant Pórtico del Perdón. Inside, the *pièce de résistance* is the dizzyingly detailed carved oak choir stalls. Entry to the cloister/museum is 200 ptas (free on Wednesday afternoon).

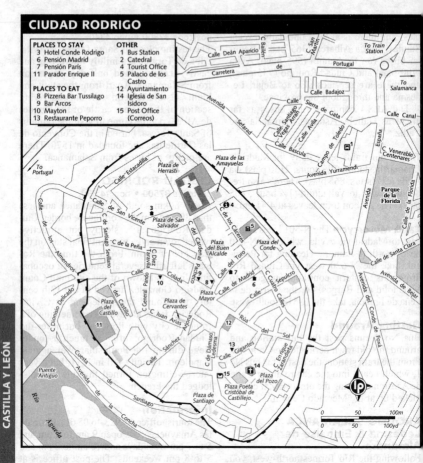

CIUDAD RODRIGO

PLACES TO STAY
3   Hotel Conde Rodrigo
6   Pensión Madrid
7   Pensión París
11 Parador Enrique II

PLACES TO EAT
8   Pizzeria Bar Tussilago
9   Bar Arcos
10 Mayton
13 Restaurante Peporro

OTHER
1   Bus Station
2   Catedral
4   Tourist Office
5   Palacio de los
    Castro
12 Ayuntamiento
14 Iglesia de San
    Isidoro
15 Post Office
    (Correos)

CASTILLA Y LEÓN

The town is liberally strewn with interesting palaces, mansions and churches.
Among the latter is the **Iglesia de San
Isidoro**, with Romanesque-mudéjar elements. Pay a visit to the **correos** to admire the
artesonado ceilings. The first-floor gallery
of the **ayuntamiento** (town hall) is a good
spot to photograph the plaza mayor. The
16th-century **Palacio de los Castro**, on
Plaza del Conde, boasts one of the town's
most engaging platteresque facades. You
can climb up onto the city walls and follow
their length of about 2.2km around the
town.

Special Events
Carnaval in February is a unique time to be
in Ciudad Rodrigo. Apart from the outlandish
fancy dress and festivities, you can witness
(or join in) a colourful *encierro* (running of
the bulls) and *capeas* (amateur bullfights).
It is one of the earliest events in the Spanish bullfighting calendar.

Places to Stay & Eat
There is a pair of adequate pensiones in
the heart of the old town. ***Pensión Madrid***
(☎ 923 46 24 67, Calle de Madrid 20) has
doubles with washbasin for 3000 ptas

Pensión París (☎ *923 48 23 49, Calle del Toro 10)* offers no-frills singles/doubles for 2000/3500 ptas.

For a minor splurge, book into the venerable *Hotel Conde Rodrigo* (☎/fax *923 46 14 08, Plaza de San Salvador 9),* where traditionally furnished rooms go for 6300/7300 ptas. For sheer luxury in a crenellated castle, head for the newly spiffed up *Parador Enrique II* (☎ *923 46 01 50, fax 923 46 04 04),* on Plaza del Castillo. Its rooms will set you back 12,000/15,000 ptas, with slight discounts in the low seasons.

For a tasty set lunch, head to *Restaurante Peporro* (☎ *923 46 24 40, Calle de los Gigantes 5). Pizzeria Bar Tussilago* (☎ *923 48 22 26, Calle Julian Sanchez 7)* does pizza and salads for under 700 ptas. *Bar Arcos* on the Plaza Mayor is good for a coffee or platos combinados. For a more formal ambience, try *Mayton* (☎ *923 46 07 20, Calle Colada 9),* where set lunches are 1450 ptas and mains cost 800 to 2500 ptas.

Getting There & Away

Up to 11 buses run to Salamanca daily (735 ptas). There are no direct buses into the Sierra de Francia – you need to return to Salamanca. A daily train to Lisbon passes through at 5.46 am.

SIERRA DE FRANCIA

A northern extension of Extremadura's Las Hurdes, this compact mountain range encloses a sprinkling of villages seemingly caught in a time warp, protected by the cool of this craggy, grey-green oasis. It's hard to imagine that until not very long ago this was one of the most godforsaken parts of Spain.

Ridden with malaria until the early 20th century, things hadn't improved much in 1932 when Luís Buñuel came to film the locals' 'lifestyle' for *Las Hurdes – Terre Sans Pain* (Land without Bread), the first part of which was shot here. When King Alfonso XIII visited in June 1922, the only milk available for his coffee was human! Touched by this abject misery, he was supposedly responsible for the introduction of the area's first cows (malaria hadn't been greatly conducive to raising them before).

Today the area is famous for its quaint villages and also popular for walking, biking and trout fishing. The village of La Alberca, about 75km south of Salamanca, makes a good base for exploration.

La Alberca

postcode 37624 ● pop 1050 ● elev 1416m

The most heavily visited mountain village in the Sierra de Francia, historic La Alberca is a harmonious huddle of narrow alleys flanked by higgledy-piggledy houses built of heavy stone, wood beams and plaster. Tourism has arrived with a vengeance, and things can get uncomfortably claustrophobic on summer weekends. Numerous stores sell handicrafts – some good, some kitsch – and local products like *jamón* (smoked ham) and *turrón* (nougat). Cosy bars and restaurants cluster on Plaza Mayor.

Camping Al-Bereka (☎ *923 41 51 95),* about 2km outside of town on the road to Salamanca, is open from March to October and charges 500 ptas per person, 475 per tent and 400 per car. La Alberca has 10 hotel options, the cheapest of which is *Pensión Hernandez* (☎ *923 41 50 39, Calle de Tablado 3),* where bare-bone singles/doubles cost 2000/4000 ptas. Those with slightly deeper pockets are better off at the comfortable *Hostal La Alberca* (☎ *923 41 52 37),* on Plaza del Padre Arsenio, with modern rooms for 3500/5000 ptas, including bath.

If you have a vehicle, or time and a hitching thumb, the surrounding villages are even more authentically caught up in the past. **Mogarraz**, to the east, and **Miranda del Castañar**, farther east again, are among the more intriguing. The latter has another camping ground, *El Burro Blanco* (☎ *923 16 11 00).*

Valle de las Batuecas

The drive south into Extremadura through this dreamy valley is spectacular. Just outside of La Alberca, a sweeping panorama of cascading lower mountain ranges the colour of green velvet opens up before you. The road corkscrews down into the valley, requiring you to negotiate some pretty hairy hairpin curves. It passes through

CASTILLA Y LEÓN

beautiful landscape that has been praised by poets, including Unamuno, and which is especially nice in spring when purple heather blankets the hillsides, and wildflowers are in bloom. A Castilian idiom even describes someone lost in thought as 'being in Batuecas.'

About 10km down is a small Carmelite monastery (open to visitors), past which rushes a babbling brook that you can follow on foot up into the surrounding hills. About a two-hour walk brings you to some caves with rock carvings. It rains a lot here, so be warned – a sudden downpour could make your descent to the monastery difficult to say the least.

Peña de Francia
Head north from La Alberca along the C-512 and you soon strike the turn-off to the highest peak in the area, the Peña de Francia (1732m), topped by a monastery. From here glorious views extend east to the Sierra de Gredos, south into Extremadura and west to Portugal.

The Central Plateau

With Valladolid, the regional capital, in its geographical heart, the central plateau of Castilla y León is dotted with towns and cities of varying interest. The landscape is characterised by great sweeps of barren rural plains, wrinkled by often less-than-breathtaking sierras, although there are exceptions to the rule: the approaches to Galicia around the Lago de Sanabria and some of the hill country around Segovia provide a welcome contrast. What follows is an arbitrarily traced route supposing a starting point in Segovia, just across from the Comunidad de Madrid.

To make the most of what there is to see, especially if time is limited, a vehicle to chew up distance is a handy asset. That said, it is feasible to follow much of this or a similar route with public transport. Where this gets tricky is with the smaller villages, which are often served by only one bus daily and not at all on weekends.

SEGOVIA
postcode 40080 • pop 54,750 • elev 1002m
To some, the ridge-top city of Segovia resembles a warship ploughing through the sea of Castile, the base of its prow formed by the confluence of the Río Eresma and Río Clamores. The town is loaded with monuments, and those contemplating visiting on a day trip from Madrid will have a full program. In 1975, Unesco made Segovia a World Heritage City, and the lofty city walls and Roman aqueduct protect the old centre from any incursion by the characterless modern urban tangle below it to the south-east. The trio of key sights are the aqueduct, cathedral and Alcázar, but there's also a slew of others worth investigation for the less time-conscious.

History
The Celtic settlement of Segobriga was occupied by the Romans in 80 BC and rose to some importance in the imperial network. As Christian Spain recovered from the initial shock of the Muslim attack, Segovia became something of a frontline city until the invaders were definitively evicted in 1085. The Muslims left behind a flourishing wool and textile industry, which only began to decline in the mid-16th century. A favourite residence of Castile's roaming royalty, the city backed Isabel and saw her proclaimed queen in the Iglesia de San Miguel in 1474.

In 1520, the rebellious Comuneros found unequivocal support in Segovia, led by Juan Bravo (see the boxed text 'Juan Bravo & the Comuneros' later in this chapter). From then on it was all downhill for the town until the 1960s, when tourism and some light industry helped it pull itself up by the bootstraps.

Orientation
The old town of Segovia is strung out along a ridge, rising in the east and peaking in the fanciful towers of the Alcázar to the west. If you arrive by train, bus No 2 will take you to Plaza Mayor, site of the cathedral, tourist office and plenty of hotels, restaurants and bars. From the bus station, it's about a 10-minute

Native ibex roam free in the Sierra de Gredos (Castilla y León).

Streets in Cuenca (Castilla-La Mancha)

Palace in Penaranda de Duera (Castilla y León)

View of sunkissed Toledo from the Puente de San Martín (Castilla-La Mancha)

Fortified Alcázar in Segovia (Castilla y León)

Chatting in Ciudad Rodrigo (Castilla y León)

The windmills of Castilla-La Mancha

Celebrating Holy Week in Ávila (Castilla y León)

walk north. Drivers will reach the same square by following the 'Centro Ciudad' signs. The main road connecting Plaza Mayor and the aqueduct is a pedestrian thoroughfare that changes name several times along the way; locals know it simply as Calle Real.

Information
Tourist Offices The municipal tourist office (☎ 921 46 03 34, fax 921 46 03 30), Plaza Mayor 10, is open 9 am to 2 pm and 5 to 7 pm weekdays, and 10 am to 2 pm and 5 to 8 pm weekends. A second branch (☎ 921 46 29 06) by the aqueduct is open 10 am to 8 pm daily.

Money Banks abound along Calle de Juan Bravo near Plaza Mayor and on Avenida de Fernández Ladreda near the aqueduct.

Post & Communications The main post office is at Plaza de los Huertos 5. Also here is the Telefónica office *(locutorio)*, open 10 am to 2 pm and 5 to 10 pm daily. To check email, head to Kitius (☎ 610 77 55 05), Avenida Fernández Ladreda 28, which charges an exorbitant 300/500/900 ptas per 15/30/60 minutes.

Medical Services & Emergency The Policía Nacional are at ☎ 091, with a station at Paseo Ezequiel González, on the corner of Carretera de Ávila. For an ambulance, call the Cruz Roja on ☎ 921 44 02 02 or ☎ 061. The Hospital General (☎ 921 41 91 00) is about 1.5km south-west of the aqueduct on the Ávila highway.

Acueducto & Around
The 728m granite block bridge you see today, made up of 163 arches, is the most extraordinary element of the engineering effort that went into the once 16km-long Roman aqueduct raised here in the 1st century AD. It measures up to 29m high, and not a drop of mortar was used to hold the thing together. A recent billion-peseta restoration has left everyone hoping that it will withstand another 2000 years without succumbing to the ravages of time, pollution and erosion.

While at this end of town, you could inspect a few churches. **Iglesia de San Millán**, off Avenida de Fernández Ladreda, is a worn example of the Romanesque typical of Segovia, with porticoes and a mudéjar bell tower. A couple of other late Romanesque churches around here are the **Iglesia de San Justo** and the **Iglesia de San Clemente**.

To the Catedral
From the Plaza de Azoguejo beside the aqueduct, Calle Real climbs into the innards of Segovia. About a quarter of the way up to Plaza Mayor, you strike the **Casa de los Picos**, a Renaissance mansion named for the diamond-shaped bosses that cover its facade. It's home to a school of applied arts and usually hosts free exhibits.

A little farther on you reach **Plaza de San Martín**, one of the most captivating little squares in Segovia. It is presided over by a statue of Juan Bravo and the 14th-century **Torreón de Lozoya** with free exhibitions. The *pièce de résistance* is, however, the Romanesque **Iglesia de San Martín**, with the Segovian touch of mudéjar tower and arched gallery. The interior boasts a Flemish Gothic chapel. The former *cárcel* (prison) next door now houses the public library.

The shady **Plaza Mayor** is the nerve centre of old Segovia, lined by an eclectic assortment of buildings, arcades and cafes. The **Iglesia de San Miguel**, where Isabel was proclaimed Queen of Castile, recedes humbly into the background before the splendour of the cathedral across the square.

Catedral
Completed in 1577, 50 years after its Romanesque predecessor had burned to the ground in the revolt of the Comuneros, the cathedral is a last, powerful expression of Gothic architecture in Spain. The austere interior is anchored by an imposing choir and enlivened by 20-odd chapels. Of these, the Capilla del Cristo del Consuelo houses a magnificent Romanesque doorway preserved from the original church. Through here you can get to the Gothic cloister and a museum featuring predominantly religious

CASTILLA Y LEÓN

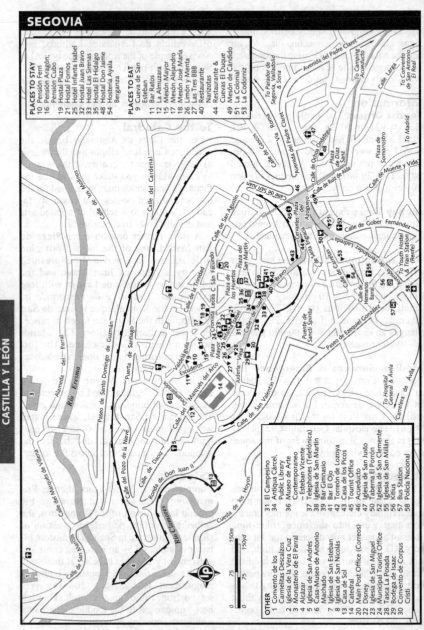

SEGOVIA

PLACES TO STAY
10 Pensión Ferri
16 Pensión Aragón;
    Pensión Cubo
19 Hostal Plaza
21 Hostal Fornos
25 Hotel Infanta Isabel
32 Hostal Juan Bravo
33 Hotel Las Sirenas
35 Hostal El Hidalgo
48 Hostal Don Jaime
54 Hostería Ayala
    Berganza

PLACES TO EAT
9   Cueva de San
    Esteban
11 Bar Ratos
12 La Almuzara
15 Mesón Mayor
17 Mesón Alejandro
18 Mesón José María
26 Limón y Menta
27 Las Tres BBB
40 Restaurante
    Narizotas
44 Restaurante &
    Cuevas El Duque
49 Mesón de Cándido
51 La Colonial
53 La Codorniz

OTHER
1   Convento de los
    Carmelitas Descalzos
2   Iglesia la Vera Cruz
3   Monasterio de El Parral
4   Alcázar
5   Iglesia de San Andrés
6   Casa-Museo de Antonio
    Machado
7   Iglesia de San Esteban
8   Iglesia de San Nicolás
13 Casa de Sol
14 Catedral
20 Main Post Office (Correos)
22 Disney
23 Iglesia de San Miguel
24 Municipal Tourist Office
28 Tasca La Posada
29 Bodega de Isaac
30 Convento de Corpus
    Cristi
31 El Campesino
34 Antigua Cárcel,
    Public Library
36 Museo de Arte
    Contemporaneo
    – Esteban Vicente
37 Telephones (Telefónica)
38 Iglesia de San Martín
39 Bar Gimnasio
41 Bar El Ojo
42 Torreón de Lozoya
43 Casa de los Picos
45 Tourist Office
46 Acueducto
47 Iglesia de San Justo
50 Taberna El Porrón
52 Iglesia de San Clemente
55 Iglesia de San Millán
56 Kitius
57 Bus Station
58 Policía Nacional

art. The cathedral and museum are open 9 am to 7 pm daily (9.30 am to 6 pm in autumn and winter); 300 ptas to the museum. At the time of research, an entry charge to the cathedral itself was being considered.

To the Alcázar

The direct route to the Alcázar from Plaza Mayor is via Calle Marqués del Arco. About halfway along you pass yet another Romanesque church, the **Iglesia de San Andrés**. Before getting this far, you could turn right down Calle de los Desemparados for the **Casa-Museo de Antonio Machado** at No 5. Machado, one of Spain's pre-eminent 20th-century poets, lived in this house from 1919 to 1932 and it still contains his furnishings and personal effects. It's open from Friday to Sunday only (free). A few paces farther down the road rises the six-level tower of the 13th-century Romanesque **Iglesia de San Esteban**, which has a baroque interior.

Turning left off Calle Marqúes del Arco via Calle Judería Nueva will take you down to Calle del Socorro and the **Casa de Sol** at No 11. This former abattoir usually houses the Museo de Segovia but is under renovation until at least mid-2002.

Alcázar

Rapunzel towers, turrets topped with slate witch's hats and a moat deep enough to drown Godzilla (well, almost) are just a few of the Alcázar's more distinctive features. Its fairytale design inspired Walt Disney's vision of Sleeping Beauty's castle in Disneyland – or so Segovia's wily town propagandists would have us believe. Fortified since Roman days, the site takes its name from the Arabic *al-qasr* (castle) and was rebuilt and expanded in the 13th and 14th centuries, but the whole lot burned down in 1862. What you see today is an evocative over-the-top reconstruction of the original.

Highlights include the **Sala de las Piñas**, whose ceiling drips with a crop of 392 pineapple-shaped 'stalactites', and the **Sala de Reyes** (Kings' Room) featuring a three-dimensional frieze of 52 sculptures of Spanish kings who fought during the Reconquista. Before you leave, climb the Torre de Juan II for magnificent views. The Alcázar hours are from 10 am to 7 pm daily (6 pm in autumn and winter); 400 ptas.

Churches & Convents

Another rich smorgasbord of religious buildings stretches across the luxuriant valley of the Río Eresma to the north of the city – a pleasant area for a wander in the shadow of the walls, and a favourite with local picnickers.

The most interesting of Segovia's churches – and the best-preserved of its kind in Europe – is the twelve-sided **Iglesia de la Vera Cruz**. Built in the 13th century by the Knights Templar on the pattern of the church of the Holy Sepulchre in Jerusalem, it long housed what is said to be a piece of the *Vera Cruz* (True Cross), now in the nearby village church of Zamarramala (on view only at Easter). The curious two-storey chamber in the circular nave is where the knights stood vigil over the holy relic. The church is open 10.30 am to 1.30 pm and 3.30 to 7 pm Tuesday to Sunday (to 6 pm in autumn and winter, closed November); 200 ptas. For fantastic views of the town and the Sierra de Guadarrama, walk uphill behind the church for approximately 1km.

Just west of Vera Cruz, San Juan de la Cruz is buried in the **Convento de los Carmelitas Descalzos**. A bit farther east, **Monasterio de El Parral** is open 10 am to 12.30 pm and 4 to 6.30 pm Monday to Saturday (10 to 11.30 am Sunday); free. Ring the bell to get in and be shown part of the cloister and church, the latter a proud Flamboyant Gothic structure, even if the facade was never finished. The monks chant a Gregorian Mass daily at 1 pm (noon on Sunday).

About 1.3km south-west of the aqueduct, just off Avenida de Padre Claret, the **Convento de San Antonio El Real** is also worth a look. Once the summer residence of Enrique IV, it includes a Gothic-mudéjar church with a splendid ceiling. In summer, the convent is open 10 am to 2 pm and 4.30 to 7.30 pm Tuesday to Saturday; otherwise

CASTILLA Y LEÓN

Juan Bravo & the Comuneros

When Carlos I ascended the throne in 1516 – uniting under his sceptre Spain and Austria – many Castilian noble families did not exactly roll out the welcome mat. And indeed, the newcomer's absolutist ways soon proved bad news for local overlords, as non-Spaniards moved into key positions of power. When Carlos I left for the Netherlands in May 1520, he confirmed a growing fear that Spanish interests would be subordinated to the needs of the Holy Roman Empire. In response, the core Castilian cities – including Segovia, Toledo, Salamanca, León and Burgos – rose up in revolt. Thus began the Guerra de las Comunidades (War of the Communities).

In Segovia, Juan Bravo emerged as one of the main leaders of the movement which, in July of 1520, assumed the powers of state for itself. Although often depicted as a popular uprising, it was more about maintaining local privilege in the face of central, absolute and, to top it all, foreign control.

Segovia was soon under siege, but although co-Comunero Juan de Padilla, marching from Toledo, was unable to help, Bravo managed to keep the Royalists out. The Royalists then decided to sack Medina del Campo instead, an act of aggression that only helped push the undecided into the rebel Comunero camp. By September, the Comuneros had gained the backing of the queen, Juana la Loca (the Crazy), and the Royalists were in deep trouble. They pulled out all stops, declaring that they would prohibit the outflow of Spanish cash and halt the nomination of non-Spaniards to positions of power.

At the same time, though, the rebel camp was coming asunder, with the moderates beginning to back-pedal. In the following months the Comuneros won several indecisive battles, but the Royalists eventually gained the upper hand after taking Tordesillas (where Queen Juana la Loca was confined). Finally, Padilla was defeated at the Battle of Villalar on 23 April 1521. He, Juan Bravo and other leaders were promptly rounded up and executed. Toledo, under Padilla's wife María Pacheco, held out for a while, but soon had to throw in the towel as well. Absolute imperial rule had arrived in Spain.

hours are 4 to 6 pm Monday to Saturday (300 ptas).

Museo de Arte Contemporaneo – Esteban Vicente
In a perfect marriage of space and function, this new museum of contemporary art occupies a 15th-century palace of Enrique IV, complete with Renaissance chapel and múdejar coffered ceiling. A donation of 148 abstract paintings and sculptures by Segovian-born artist, Esteban Vicente, forms the core of the exhibit, which is supplemented by high-calibre temporary shows. Vicente, a near-centenarian still living in New York, is a representative of the New School of Expressionism (others include de Kooning and Rothko). His works are characterised by a highly emotional component as he strives for harmony and balance between form and colour. The museum, just north of Plaza San Martín, is open 11 am to 2 pm and 4 to 7 pm, closed Sunday afternoon and Monday (400 ptas, students half-price).

Special Events
Segovians let their hair down for the Fiestas de San Juan y San Pedro, celebrated on 24–29 June with parades, concerts and bullfights. Fiesta San Frutos on 25 October celebrates the town's patron saint.

Places to Stay – Budget
Camping & Hostels *Camping Acueducto* (☎ *921 42 50 00, Carretera L-601*) is about 2km south-east of town. It is open from April to September and charges 500 ptas each per person, tent and car. From the train station, take bus No 2 to the aqueduct, then No 3, destination Carmen/Segovia Nueva.

The HI *Albergue de la Juventud Emperador Teodosio* (☎ *921 44 11 11*) on Avenida del Conde de Sepúlveda, is only open in July and August. It's a fair way out of town (although handy for the train station) and charges 900/1300 ptas juniors/seniors.

Hostales & Pensiones If you don't mind zero-frills rooms, you could stay at any of these bargain-basement lodgings, all near the cathedral. *Pensión Aragón (☎ 921 46 09 14, Plaza Mayor 4)*, on the first floor, charges 1600 ptas for its four single rooms. Upstairs, *Pensión Cubo (☎ 921 46 09 17)* is even cheaper at 1300 ptas. The going rate at *Pensión Ferri (☎ 921 46 09 57, Calle de Escuderos 10)*, around the corner, is 1600/2500 ptas for singles/doubles.

If you can afford a little more, your best bet is *Hostal Juan Bravo (☎ 921 46 34 13, Calle de Juan Bravo 12)*. Central and with friendly proprietors, it offers rooms with bath for 4700 ptas and a couple of bathless doubles for 3800 ptas. A few steps off Plaza Mayor, *Hostal Plaza (☎ 921 46 03 03, fax 921 46 03 05, Calle del Cronista Lecea 11)* has 26 rooms of various sizes and comfort. Your basic shared-bath version costs 3100/4500 ptas, others with bath cost 5000/ 5800 ptas.

Beyond the old town, but close to the aqueduct, is the spick-and-span *Hostal Don Jaime (☎ 921 44 47 87, Calle de Ochoa Ondategui 8)*. Doubles with bath and TV cost 5600 ptas; singles (shared facilities only) are 3200 ptas.

Places to Stay – Mid-Range

Rates below are for rooms with private facilities. In the centre, *Hostal El Hidalgo (☎ 921 46 35 29, Calle de José Canalejas 3-5)* has solid but unspectacular rooms for 4500/ 5975 ptas. *Hotel Las Sirenas (☎ 921 46 26 63, fax 921 46 26 57, Calle de Juan Bravo 30)* offers more comforts, including TV and phone, for 6500/9000 ptas. Nicest of the bunch is the new *Hostal Fornos (☎/fax 921 46 01 98, Calle Infanta Isabel 13)*, whose delightful, rather spacious rooms display more than a touch of style, but are a bit on the pricey side for 6000/8000 ptas. Top of the tree, *Hotel Infanta Isabel (☎ 921 46 13 00, fax 921 46 22 17, Calle de Isabel la Católica 1)* has all the comforts you require at 8000/12,700 ptas.

Places to Stay – Top End

For deep-pocketed travellers, the new *Hostería Ayala Berganza (☎ 921 46 04 48, fax 921 46 23 77, ℮ hosteriaayaber@futurnet.es,*

Calle de Carretas 5) should be a top choice. Rooms inside this charmingly restored 15th-century palace ooze sophistication and old world charm – albeit for a whopping 14,500 to 20,000 ptas.

An alternative is *Parador de Segovia (☎ 921 44 37 37, fax 921 43 73 62)*, on Carretera de Valladolid, a modern bastion of civilisation presiding over the town from its hilltop perch about a five-minute drive away from the centre. Views of the historical town are particularly stunning at night. Rates are 14,000/18,500 ptas.

Places to Eat

Segovians have a culinary love affair with the pig. Just about every restaurant proudly boasts its *horno de asar* (roasts) and they say that 'pork has 40 flavours – all of them good'. The main speciality is *cochinillo asado* (roast suckling pig), but *judiones de la granja* (a lima bean dish with pork chunks) also figures big on menus. The local dessert is a rich, sweet concoction drenched in *ponche*, a popular Spanish spirit, and hence known as *ponche segoviano*.

Restaurants A widely respected Segovian favourite is *Mesón José María (☎ 921 46 11 11, Calle del Cronista Lecea 11)*. An atmosphere of conviviality reigns in the well-ventilated, rustic bar where wine from the dedicated proprietor's own estate flows in abundance. This is also a good spot for breakfast. The formal dining room has friendly service and serves inspired versions of traditional favourites and is also one of the best places for cochinillo (2300 ptas).

Tasca La Posada (☎ 921 46 21 71, Calle de la Judería Vieja 5) is best for tapas and *raciones* (meal-sized serves of tapas) but also does set lunches, including a judiones de la granja/cochinillo combo for 2500 ptas. Also good and reasonable for tapas is *Mesón Mayor (☎ 921 46 09 15, Plaza Mayor 3)*.

Great atmosphere and set lunches for around 1000 ptas give *Cueva de San Esteban (☎ 921 46 09 82, Calle de Valdeláguila 15)* the edge, although its a la carte menu is a bit on the pricey side. There's also an entrance

CASTILLA Y LEÓN

off Calle de los Escuderos. *Mesón Alejandro* (☎ *921 46 00 09, Plaza Potro 5)* is similar.

At *Restaurante Narizotas* (☎ *921 46 26 79, Plaza de Medina del Campo 1)* you can eat well for about 2500 ptas and there's pleasant outdoor seating in summer. Near the bus station, *La Codorniz* (☎ *921 46 38 97, Calle de Hermanos Barral 1)* has a rambling menu with prices that won't break the bank.

Women-owned *La Almuzara* (☎ *921 46 06 22, Marqués del Arco 3)* is the place to go if you're feeling 'pigged out', so to speak. The menu features lots of vegetarian dishes, pastas and salads and the ambience is warm and artsy. It's closed Monday and Tuesday lunchtime.

For a special occasion, visit *Duque* (☎ *46 24 87, Calle de Cervantes 12),* Segovia's oldest dining establishment (since 1895). For a full meal you'll be lucky to get much change from 4500 ptas. For less formality, try it's *cueva* (cellar), in the same building but entered at Calle de Santa Engracia 10. This is a snug place for a drink, and you can have anything on the restaurant menu as well. In the same price bracket and another old Segovian favourite is *Mesón de Cándido* (☎ *921 42 81 03, Plaza del Azoguejo 5).*

Cafes The *Las Tres BBB* (☎ *921 46 21 26, Plaza Mayor 13)* stands for *bueno, bonito y barato* (good, attractive and cheap) and serves dishes that meet just those criteria. *Bar Ratos* (☎ *921 46 04 38),* on Calle de los Escuderos, is a simple eatery specialising in big bocadillos (350 to 800 ptas).

Near the aqueduct, *La Colonial (Avenida Fernández Ladreda 19)* is a dynamic coffeehouse with an unusual decor blending art nouveau stained glass with 'negro' sculptures. For a mouthwatering array of pastries, including some of the best ponche segoviano around, head to *Limón y Menta* (☎ *921 44 40 02, Calle Infanta Isabel 2).* It also does bocadillos and there's a little cafe at the back.

Entertainment

Locals quite appropriately call Calle de la Infanta Isabel 'Calle de los Bares' (Street of the Bars). This is *the* destination for serious drinking, cheap eating and merriment all around. *Disney* at No 5 and *El Campesino* at No 12 are two popular watering holes. Bars and discos also cluster at the Plaza end of Calle de los Escuderos.

In fine weather, Plaza Mayor is the obvious place for hanging out and people-watching, but a quieter alternative is Plaza de San Martín where *Bar Gimnasio* and *Bar El Ojo* are the gathering spots of choice.

You'll also find decent watering holes on Calle de la Judería Vieja. *Tasca La Posada* (see Places to Eat) can get quite lively, and closet-sized *Bodega de Isaac (Puerta del Sol 1)* is often packed with flamenco aficionados. *Taberna El Porrón (Calle del Carmen 11),* near the aqueduct, is a funky drinking place with a student-age clientele.

Getting There & Away

Bus The bus station is just off Paseo de Ezequiel González, near Avenida de Fernández Ladreda. La Sepulvedana serves Madrid up to 30 times daily (1½ hours, 825 ptas), Linecar goes to Coca (one hour, 395 ptas), Cuéllar (one hour, 450 ptas), Valladolid (2¾ hours, 860 ptas) and Salamanca (three hours, 1270 ptas). There's also occasional service to Ávila. Many services do not operate on Sundays.

Train Trains for Madrid leave at two-hour intervals up to nine times daily (1¾ hours, 790 ptas). All other destinations are served by bus.

Car & Motorcycle Of the two main roads down to the N-VI, which links Madrid and Galicia, the N-603 is the prettier. The alternative N-110 cuts south-west across to Ávila and north-east to the main Madrid-Burgos highway. The CL-601 travels via La Granja and is the main access road to the Sierra de Guadarrama.

Getting Around

Bus No 2 connects the train station with the aqueduct and Plaza Mayor. Otherwise, walking is the best way to get about.

AROUND SEGOVIA
La Granja de San Ildefonso
It is not hard to see why the Bourbon king Felipe V chose this site, in the western foothills of the Sierra de Guadarrama 12km east of Segovia, to create his version of Versailles, the palace of his French grandfather Louis XIV, the Sun King. In 1720 French architects and gardeners, with some Italian help, began laying out the elaborate gardens. El Real Sitio de la Granja de San Ildefonso remained a favourite summer residence with Spanish royalty for the next couple of centuies.

La Granja's centrepiece is the garden's 28 fountains. Some of them are switched on at 5.30 pm on Wednesday, Saturday and Sunday starting Easter Week (subject to change). The gardens are open 10 am to 9 pm daily and entry is free except when the fountains are on (325 ptas).

The 300-room **Palacio Real**, restored after a fire in 1918, is impressive but perhaps the lesser of La Granja's jewels. You can visit about half of the rooms, including its Museo de Tapices (Tapestry Museum). The palace is open 10 am to 6 pm daily from June 1 to September 30. Otherwise, hours are 10 am to 1.30 pm and 3 to 5 pm ,10 am to 2 pm Sunday (700 ptas, students 300 ptas, free on Wednesdays for EU passport holders).

The village around the palace caters mostly to tourists and has several bars, restaurants and hotels around Plaza de los Dolores, the central square. Buses to La Granja depart regularly from Segovia's main bus station (20 minutes, 105 ptas).

A CASTLE TRAIL
Pedraza de la Sierra
postcode 40172 • pop 464 • elev 1073m
This captivating, walled village about 37km north-east of Segovia is more an open-air museum than a living community. Quite dead during the week, its considerable number of restaurants and bars come to life with the arrival of weekend swarms from Madrid and Segovia.

At the far end stands the lonely **Castillo de Pedraza**, open 11 am to 2 pm and 5 to 8 pm Wednesday to Sunday (less in winter);

500 ptas. At the opposite end of town, by the only town gate, is the 14th-century prison, open on weekends only. Bus services to Pedraza are sporadic at best.

Turégano
About 30km north of Segovia, Turégano is dominated by a unique 15th-century castle-church complex built by the then Archbishop of Segovia, Juan Arias Dávila, who decided to make a personal fortress of the town. The castle walls are built around the facade of the Iglesia de San Miguel.

Coca
A typically dusty, inward-looking Castilian village, Coca is presided over by a stunning all-brick **castle** *(castillo)* that is a virtuoso piece of Gothic-mudéjar architecture. It was built in 1453 by the powerful Fonseca family and is surrounded by a deep moat. The beautiful exterior was once matched by an equally breathtaking Renaissance interior, which was nearly stripped of its ornamentation in the 19th century. Guided visits run from 10.30 am to 1 pm and 4.30 to 6 pm weekdays, and 11 am to 1 pm and 4 to 6 pm weekends and holidays (to 7 pm in summer); 300 ptas.

The town is just over 50km north-west of Segovia and about 60km south of Valladolid. Up to five buses run daily to Coca from Segovia's main bus station (one hour, 395 ptas).

Cuéllar
Located 60km north of Segovia on the CL-601 to Valladolid, Cuéllar is yet another time-worn Castilian settlement, dominated by a massive 15th-century castle-cum-palace. Guided tours are offered weekends only from noon to 2 pm and 4 to 8 pm (300 ptas). Up to 13 buses with daily departures make the one-hour trip from Segovia (650 ptas). Six buses run daily from Valladolid to Cuéllar.

VALLADOLID
postcode 47080 • pop 333,200
Once the de facto capital of imperial Spain and a flourishing centre of the Spanish

Renaissance, Valladolid is now a modern giant with lively and down-to-earth character. Not beautiful in a conventional travel brochure way, the city has enough first-rate monuments and museums to give anyone a generous sightseeing fill. And thanks to a large student population its many spirited bars and restaurants are rarely devoid of customers. If you can, make it an overnight stop; early birds could stretch a point and make a day trip of it from Madrid.

History

Little more than a hamlet in the early Middle Ages, Valladolid had become a major centre of commerce, education and art by the time Fernando de Aragón and Isabel of Castile discreetly contracted matrimony here in 1469. As Spain's greatest-ever ruling duo, they carried Valladolid to the height of its splendour. Its university was one of the most dynamic on the peninsula and things only got better under Carlos I, who based the Consejo Real here and so made Valladolid the seat of imperial government. In 1420, Isabel's confessor and merciless Inquisitor General Fray Tomás de Torquemada was born here (see the boxed text 'Torquemada & the Inquisition'), while in 1506, a sad and unrewarded Christopher Columbus ended his days in the city.

Ironically, the seeds of Valladolid's decline were sown here too, with the birth of Felipe II in 1527. Thirty-three years later he chose to make Madrid the capital, to the displeasure not only of Valladolid but also of several other contenders for the honour (including Toledo).

Valladolid lingered in relative obscurity until the mid-19th century and the arrival of the Industrial Revolution. Today it is a major manufacturing and trade centre and also the administrative capital of the Autonomía de Castilla y León.

Orientation

The centre of Valladolid lies east of the Río Pisuerga. At its southern edge are the train station and the nearby bus station. From here it's about a 2.5km walk to the Museo Nacional de Escultura, as far north as

you're likely to want to go. The tourist office is on Calle de Santiago, Valladolid's main shopping street. Spread out between the museum and tourist office are the other sights, as well as hotels, restaurants and banks.

Information

The tourist office (☎ 983 34 40 13), Calle de Santiago 19, is open 9 am to 2 pm and 5 to 7 pm daily. There are plenty of banks with ATMs around here as well. The main post office is on Plaza de la Rinconada. For Internet access, go to Bocattanet at Calle María de Molina 16. It's open 11 am to 2 pm and 5 to 10.30 pm Monday to Saturday and 6.30 to 11 pm Saturday; an hour of surfing costs 500 ptas. The most central Policía Nacional is at Calle de Felipe II. Next door is the Hospital de la Cruz Roja Española (☎ 983 22 22 22).

Museo Nacional de Escultura

Spain's premier showcase of polychrome wood sculpture is housed in the former Colegio de San Gregorio (1496), a flamboyant example of the Isabelline Gothic style. The dizzying facade is especially intricate and spills over with statues, heraldic symbols and floral motifs. Exhibition rooms orbit a splendid two-story galleried courtyard. Alonso de Berruguete, Juan de Juní and Gregorio Fernández are the star artists shown here.

The chronologically presented exhibit kicks off with several rooms showcasing fragments from Berruguete's main commission, the high altar for Valladolid's Iglesia de San Benito. The enormously expressive quality of this artist is easily recognisable here. Other works to look out for are Juní's *El Entierro de Christo* in Room XV upstairs and *El Belén Napolitano,* a room-sized creche with hundreds of figurines in Room XXX. Back downstairs is a small wing dedicated to Fernández, whose melodramatic intensity is especially well reflected in his painfully lifelike sculpture of a dead Christ.

Museum hours are 10 am to 2 pm and 4 to 6 pm, closed Sunday afternoon and

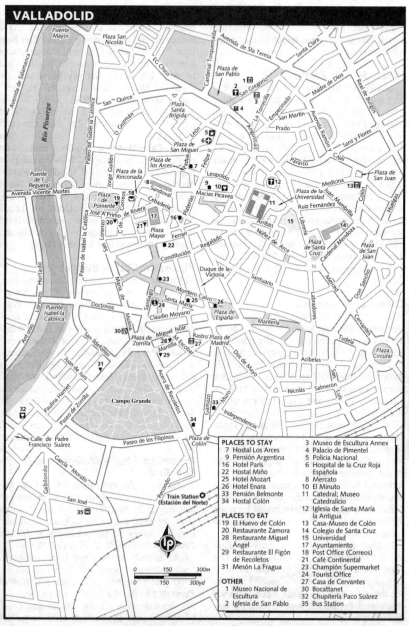

VALLADOLID

PLACES TO STAY
7 Hostal Los Arces
9 Pensión Argentina
16 Hotel París
22 Hostal Miño
25 Hotel Mozart
26 Hotel Enara
33 Pensión Belmonte
34 Hostal Colón

PLACES TO EAT
19 El Huevo de Colón
20 Restaurante Zamora
28 Restaurante Miguel Ángel
29 Restaurante El Figón de Recoletos
31 Mesón La Fragua

OTHER
1 Museo Nacional de Escultura
2 Iglesia de San Pablo
3 Museo de Escultura Annex
4 Palacio de Pimentel
5 Policia Nacional
6 Hospital de la Cruz Roja Española
8 Mercato
10 El Minuto
11 Catedral; Museo Catedralicio
12 Iglesia de Santa María la Antigua
13 Casa-Museo de Colón
14 Colegio de Santa Cruz
15 Universidad
17 Ayuntamiento
18 Post Office (Correos)
21 Café Continental
23 Champión Supermarket
24 Tourist Office
27 Casa de Cervantes
30 Bocattanet
32 Chupitería Paco Suárez
35 Bus Station

0 150 300m
0 150 300yd

Monday (400 ptas, free on weekends). Tickets are also good for the museum annex across the road, which houses temporary exhibitions.

Plaza de San Pablo
Virtually next to the museum, this square is dominated by the **Iglesia de San Pablo**, whose main facade is another masterpiece of Isabelline Gothic with every square inch finely worked, carved and twisted to produce a unique fabric in stone. Also fronting the square is the **Palacio de Pimentel** where, on 12 July 1527, Felipe II was born. It is now home to the Diputación Provincial. A fantastic tiled mural in the entrance hall shows scenes from the life of the king. Even more impressive are the dazzling artesonado ceilings in the Salón de Plenos and the Sala de Comisiones, but to see these, you must first call ☎ 983 42 71 00. The building is open daily, and entry is free.

Catedral & Around
Valladolid's cathedral was begun by Juan de Herrera in 1582 under orders of Felipe II, but never completed and is really quite disappointing. Of note is the altarpiece by Juní and a processional monstrance by Juan de Arfe in the **Museo Catedralicio**. The latter is open 10 am to 1.30 pm and 4.30 to 7 pm Tuesday to Friday and 10 am to 2 pm weekends (350 ptas).

More interesting is the **Iglesia de Santa María la Antigua**, a 14th-century Gothic church with an elegant Romanesque tower (open before and after services only). The grand baroque facade to the east of the cathedral belongs to the main building of the **universidad** and is the work of Narciso Tomé. On Plaza de la Universidad between the two stands a statue of Cervantes, who spent a few years here.

Farther east again is the early Renaissance **Colegio de Santa Cruz** (1487). The main portal is an early example of plateresque, and you should wander inside to see the patio and also sneak a peek into the chapel with Fernández' superrealistic *Christo de la Luz* sculpture.

Casas de Cervantes & Columbus
After an unfortunate incident in which Cervantes found himself doing a short stint behind bars in Valladolid, police documents were left behind that made it possible to identify his house, happily preserved at Calle del Rastro 7 behind a quiet little garden. You can visit from 9.30 am to 3.30 pm Tuesday to Saturday and 10 am to 3 pm Sunday (400 ptas, students 200 ptas, free on Sunday).

The **Casa-Museo de Colón** is actually a replica of the house in which the ultimately hapless Genoese explorer lived and ended his days in 1506. Now a museum, it contains a motley collection of indigenous American art (Aztec, Incan and Mayan) and a few documents and other mementos. It is open 10 am to 2 pm and 5 to 7 pm, closed Sunday afternoon and Monday (free).

Places to Stay – Budget
Valladolid is riddled with places to stay that won't rob your bank account. Cheapest of the bunch is the threadbare *Pensión Belmonte* (☎ *983 30 01 79, Calle Gamazo 27*), near the train station, where singles/doubles cost 1900/3200 ptas. More central options include *Pensión Argentina* (☎ *983 39 00 81, Calle de Macias Picavea 7*) right on a lively bar street; *Hostal Los Arces* (☎ *983 35 38 53, Calle de San Antonio de Padua 2*) and *Hostal Miño* (☎ *983 35 36 61, Plaza Mayor 9*). All have rooms with washbasin for about 2000/3000 ptas and a few with shower and toilet for 500 or 1000 ptas more.

Places to Stay – Mid-Range & Top End
A step up is *Hostal Colón* (☎ *983 30 40 44, Acera de Recoletos 12*), with rooms starting at 2500/4100 ptas; doubles with bath are 5100 ptas. One of the best value for the money in this category is *Hotel Enara* (☎ *983 30 03 11, Plaza de España 5*) whose slightly tattered but large and perfectly adequate rooms with bath cost 5000/7000 ptas. Another good choice is *Hotel París* (☎ *983 37 06 25, Calle de la Especería 2*). Rooms with all the trimmings cost 6000/8000 ptas. If you need a full range of

CASTILLA Y LEÓN

amenities, check into **Hotel Mozart** (*☎ 983 29 77 77, fax 983 29 21 90, Calle Menéndez Pelayo 7*) where luxury is taken very seriously at a price tag of 10,500/15,000 ptas.

Places to Eat

Tapas bar-hopping is a favourite pastime in Valladolid. Good areas to explore are along Calle de Paraíso near the university and the streets just west of Plaza Mayor. A good place here is the funkily decorated **El Huevo de Colón** (*Calle de Correos 11*). The speciality are plates of freshly cooked *gambas* (prawns), but salads and even burgers figure on the menu as well. Almost everything is well under 1000 ptas.

For more substantial meals, you could try **Restaurante Zamora** (*☎ 983 33 00 71*), which does a *menú* for 1870 ptas and several fairly healthy dishes such as garlic chicken (800 ptas) and salads (450 to 850 ptas).

One of the best places for classic Castilian fare is **Restaurante El Figón de Recoletos** (*☎ 983 39 60 43, Acera de Recoletos 3*), which is one of the town's top restaurants. Prices, sadly, reflect this – you'll get little change from 5000 ptas. Another traditional place, with wainscoted walls and nautical decor, is the nearby **Restaurante Miguel Ángel** (*☎ 983 39 85 04, Calle de Mantilla 1*). Slightly cheaper is **Mesón La Fragua** (*☎ 983 33 71 02, Paseo de Zorrilla 10*) with mains coming in at around 1500 to 2000 ptas.

For self-caterers, there's a well-stocked **Champión** supermarket, with integrated deli takeaway food counter, on Calle de Santiago at Montero Clavo. It's open 9.15 am to 9.15 pm daily except Sunday. The *mercato* (public market) at Calle Francisco Zarandona is also a good source of fresh produce.

Entertainment

Central Valladolid brims with welcoming bars and cafes and you'll quickly find a personal favourite. Calle de Paraíso (see Places to Eat) attracts a mid-twenties and up crowd, while Calle de Padre Francisco Suárez is the strip of choice of the 'just-past-teenage' set. **Chupitería Paco Suárez** at No 2 is a favourite watering hole here.

Near the cathedral, an excellent and popular cafe-bar is **El Minuto** (*Calle de Macias Picavea 15*), which is also flanked by several other prospects for late-night drinking. Plaza Mayor is perfect for people-watching. Here, on the corner of Calle de Jesús, you'll find the hip **Café Continental**, which also features occasional live music.

Getting There & Away

Bus Alsa Grupo makes the trip to Madrid at least hourly between 6.30 am to 9.30 pm (2¼ hours, 1580 ptas), while La Regional goes hourly to Palencia (410 ptas). Also served several times daily are Tordesillas (435 ptas), Medina del Campo (415 ptas) and Zamora (810 ptas), as well as other Castilian capitals and larger cities throughout Spain.

Train Valladolid is a major train hub and it's easy to travel just about anywhere in Spain from here. Up to 20 trains daily go to Madrid (three hours, 1930 ptas), and about 11 run to León (two hours, 1450 ptas) and 14 to Burgos (1½ hours, 1090 ptas). There are also frequent services to Salamanca (1¾ hours, 865 ptas,) and four trains to Bilbao (3½ hours, 2800 ptas). Medina del Campo is served throughout the day (35 minutes, 330 ptas).

Car & Motorcycle The N-620 motorway passes Valladolid en route from Burgos to Tordesillas, where it picks up with the N-VI between Madrid and La Coruña. The N-601 heads north-west to León and south to hit the N-VI and A-6 west of Segovia.

Getting Around

Local bus Nos 2 and 10 pass the train and bus stations on their way to Plaza de España, while No 19 terminates in Plaza de Zorrilla.

AROUND VALLADOLID
Medina de Rioseco & Around
postcode 47800 • pop 5000

Like other towns in Valladolid province, Medina de Rioseco grew wealthy in the 14th century by being a major trading centre. Today it is but a shadow of its medieval grandeur but a couple of worthwhile sights remain. The **Iglesia de Santa María de**

CASTILLA Y LEÓN

Torquemada & the Inquisition

There is hardly a more notorious body in the history of the Catholic Church than the Spanish Inquisition, and its most infamous member was undoubtedly Fray Tomás de Torquemada (1420–98).

Dostoevsky immortalised him as the articulate Grand Inquisitor who puts Jesus himself on trial in *Crime and Punishment*, and Monty Python created a memorable parody of the religious zealot in their Flying Circus.

Torquemada may have been articulate, but he was no comedian: in the 15 years he was Inquisitor General of the Castilian Inquisition he ran some 100,000 trials and sent about 2000 people to burn at the stake.

Born in Valladolid of well-placed Jewish *conversos* (converts to Christianity), Torquemada was deeply affected by the Spanish cult of *sangre limpia* (pure blood), the racist doctrine that inevitably accompanied the 800-year struggle to rid Spain of non-Christian peoples. Since Spain had the largest Jewish population in medieval Europe and conversion and intermarriage were commonplace, few could claim to have sangre limpia. The Spanish nobility in particular were nevertheless obsessed with the concept, and many – including Torquemada himself – went to extremes to disguise their lineage.

He joined the Dominicans, and the ruthless administration of the affairs of the Inquisition were undoubtedly the result of his efforts. Fray Tomás first came to the attention of Fernando and Isabel in 1479, when the middle-aged monk was appointed the queen's personal confessor.

Four years later he was nominated by Pope Sixtus IV to head the Castilian Inquisition, and he immediately took to his duties with relish. He devised a series of guidelines for rooting out conversos and other heretics, including his favourite targets, the *marranos*, Jews who only pretended to convert but continued to practice Judaism in private. If someone wore fancy clothes on a Saturday, they were Jews. If a home was cleaned on a Friday night and candles lit earlier than usual, the household was Jewish. If someone ate unleavened bread and began their meal with celery and lettuce during Holy Week, they were Jews. If they said prayers facing a wall and bowed back and forth while doing so, they were Jews.

ERROL HUNT

Mediavilla is a grandiose Isabelline Gothic work with three star-vaulted naves and the famous **Capilla de los Benavente** anchored by an eye-popping altarpiece by Juan de Juní. Down the hill, the portals of the light-flooded **Iglesia de Santiago** allow for a survey in architectural styles: the northern is Gothic, the main one neoclassical and the southern one plateresque.

Pensión Domingo (☎ 983 70 00 30, Plaza de Santo Domingo 3) has no-frills singles/doubles for just 1000/2000 ptas. For more comfort, try *Hostal Duque de Osuna (☎ 983 70 01 79, Avenida de Castilviejo 16),* in the modern part of town, where rooms with bath go for 3000/ 5000 ptas.

Restaurante Pasos (☎ 983 70 10 02, Calle de Lázaro Alonso 4) has loads of atmosphere and a *menú* for 1800 ptas. *The*

Irish River, another example of the Irish pub invasion, is just opposite. At least two buses connecting Valladolid, 45km to the south-east, and León call in here.

Urueña

For an off-the-beaten-track diversion, head 20km south-west from Medina de Rioseco down the C-519 and take the turn-off south-east for Urueña (signposted). This minuscule backwater is still almost entirely surrounded by powerful and well-preserved walls. There's a walkway along the upper part, allowing you to stare out from the stout defences across the endless patchwork plains of the Tierra de Campos and wonder at glories past. Urueña is equally accessible from Tordesillas and Toro on the road to Zamora – by car, that is.

Torquemada & the Inquisition

If convicted, the lightest punishment dished out by Torquemada and his cronies was the confiscation of the victim's property, a convenient fund-raiser for the war of Reconquista against the Muslims. The condemned were then paraded through town wearing the *sambenito*, a yellow shirt emblazoned with crosses that was short enough to expose their genitals. They were marched to the doors of the local church, where they were then flogged. And that was the fate of the lucky ones.

If you were unlucky, you underwent unimaginable tortures (see the Santillana del Mar section in the Cantabria & Asturias chapter) before going through an *auto de fé*, a public burning at the stake. Those that recanted and kissed the cross were garrotted before the fire was set, while those that recanted only were burnt quickly with dry wood. If you stayed firm and didn't recant, the wood used for the fire was green and slow-burning, prolonging your misery.

Torquemada's career reached its apogee (or nadir) in 1490, when he presided over the La Guardia show trial, where eight Jews and conversos were accused of crucifying a Christian child and participating in the so-called 'blood libel', where Jews were supposed to sacrifice a Christian child to appease a vengeful God (a common – and unfounded – fear among medieval Catholics).

Although no victim was ever identified and no body ever discovered, the hapless innocents were condemned to death and duly executed. Seizing on the mass publicity around the trial, Torquemada pushed the Catholic Monarchs to issue an edict expelling all Jews from Spain. Two prominent Jews sought to halt the madness and offered Fernando and Isabel 30,000 ducats to let them stay.

Strapped for cash, they were tempted to accept but Torquemada convinced them otherwise, saying 'Judas sold his Master for thirty ducats. You would sell Him for thirty thousand...Take him and sell Him, but do not let it be said that I have had any share in this transaction'. Two years later, on March 31, 1492, Fernando and Isabel issued their Edict of Expulsion, and all Jews were forced to leave within two months on pain of death. Torquemada had accomplished his goal.

The following year, he retired to the monastery of Santo Tomás·in Avilá, from where he continued to administer the affairs of the Inquisition. In his final years he became obsessed with the fear that he might be poisoned, and refused to eat anything without having a unicorn's horn nearby as an antidote. Nobody got to him, however, and he died in his sleep in 1498.

CASTILLA Y LEÓN

Medina del Campo
postcode 47400 • pop 20,165
A mostly morose stop 45km south-west of Valladolid, Medina del Campo does have one or two redeeming features. Most impressive is the dignified mudéjar **Castillo de la Mota**, once a residence of the Catholic Monarchs and later a state prison. It's open 11 am to 2 pm and 4 to 7 pm, closed Sunday afternoon and Monday (free), but there isn't much to see inside.

In town, make for the huge rambling Plaza Mayor de la Hispanidad (Plaza de España). Queen Isabel died in the **Palacio Real**, an unassuming edifice on the western side of the square.

You won't have any problems finding somewhere to stay and there are plenty of restaurants, especially near Plaza Mayor.

Calle de Ángel Molina is loaded with bars. Buses run from various points around the town, but for most destinations you're better off with trains. More than 20 daily run to Madrid and there is regular service to Salamanca, Valladolid and Ávila.

Olmedo
postcode 47410 • pop 3560
If you're a fan of múdejar architecture, but without the time to travel all over Castilla y León, you could instead visit the **Parque Temático del Mudéjar** in this provincial town about 45km south of Valladolid. Integrated into a landscape of lakes, rivers and gardens are replicas of a dozen mudéjar monuments, mostly churches but also the mighty Castillo de Coca. The park, which also contains the tourist office, sprawls at the north-eastern

edge of town and is open 10 am to 2 pm and 4 to 8 pm daily except Monday; 500 ptas.

Olmedo itself is worth a stroll. Main sights include the Romanesque **Iglesia de San Miguel** and the Gothic **Iglesia de Santa María del Castillo**. At least two buses daily connect Valladolid with Olmedo.

PALENCIA
postcode 34080 • pop 77,900

Not generally on the beaten tourist track, tranquil Palencia is not without appeal and is certainly deserving of a stopover. Its main attraction is an immense Gothic cathedral whose sober exterior belies the extraordinary riches awaiting within. It's this contrast that has earned it the nickname of 'La Bella Desconocida' (The Unknown Beauty). There's a slew of other churches, as well as several museums, to round off your visit.

Known to the Romans as Pallantia and later as an important Visigothic centre, Palencia was repeatedly destroyed in the early centuries AD. It was King Sancho el Mayor de Navarra who laid the groundwork for its medieval ascendancy when he restored the town in 1035. Palencia reached its zenith when King Alfonso VIII founded Spain's first university here in 1208. Decline set in rapidly after the 15th century and to this day it has retained a small-town character.

Orientation & Information

The bus and train stations are adjacent just north of the town centre. From nearby Plaza de León, Calle Mayor forms the main north-south axis, part of it is pedestrianised. Several hotels lie near or just off it, as do most of banks, bars and restaurants.

The tourist office (☎ 979 74 00 68, fax 979 70 08 22), Calle Mayor 105, is open 10 am to 2 pm and 4 to 9 pm weekdays; it has slightly different hours on weekends. The post office is on Plaza de León. You'll find a Telefónica office on the corner of Calle del Patio de Castaño and Calle de Menéndez Pelayo. The Hospital Provincial (☎ 979 72 82 00) is just west of the cathedral on Calle de los Pastores.

Catedral

Of the cathedral's otherwise nondescript exterior, the ornate **Puerta del Obispo** (Bishop's Door) is the most striking element. But you really need to get inside to appreciate this treasure-trove of art. Pause a moment to take in the dimensions: at 130m long, 56m wide and 30m high it is one of the most massive of the Castilian cathedrals.

One of the most stunning chapels is the **Capilla El Sagrario** whose ceiling-high altarpiece tells the story of Christ in dozens of exquisitely carved and painted panels. High up on a ledge is the sarcophagus of Queen Doña Urraca. The stone screen behind the choir stalls, or *trascoro,* is a masterpiece of bas-relief attributed to Gil de Siloé and is considered the most beautiful retrochoir in Spain. Nearby is the oak pulpit with delicate carvings of the Evangelists by Juan de Ortiz, allegedly made from a single tree.

From the retrochoir, a plateresque stairwell leads down to the crypt, actually a remnant of the original Visigothic church and a later Romanesque replacement. The crypt is known as the Cueva de San Antolín because King Wamba supposedly had the French martyr's remains moved here from Narbonne.

The tour also takes in the **Museo Catedralicio** where you'll see some fine Flemish tapestries and a *San Sebastián* by El Greco. A whimsical highlight is a trick painting by German 16th-century artist Lucas Cranach the Elder. Looking at it straight on, it seems to be a surreal dreamscape predating Dalí by some 400 years. Only when viewed from the side is the true image revealed – a portrait of Emperor Carlos V.

The cathedral's hours are 9.30 am to 1.30 pm and 4 to 6.30 pm, closed Sunday afternoon. Entry is free but many of the more interesting sights may only be seen on a guided 45-minute tour (300 ptas); check with the nuns in the sacristy. On the tour, the guide lights up various corners of the cathedral and also takes you to the freshly restored cloister.

Things to See

Of the 10 so other churches around town, it's worth seeking out the **Iglesia de San Pablo**,

CASTILLA Y LEÓN

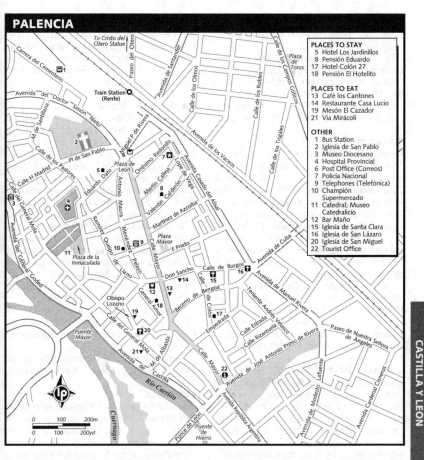

PALENCIA

PLACES TO STAY
5 Hotel Los Jardinillos
8 Pensión Eduardo
17 Hotel Colón 27
18 Pensión El Hotelito

PLACES TO EAT
13 Café los Cantones
14 Restaurante Casa Lucio
19 Mesón El Cazador
21 Via Mirácoli

OTHER
1 Bus Station
2 Iglesia de San Pablo
3 Museo Diocesano
4 Hospital Provincial
6 Post Office (Correos)
7 Policía Nacional
9 Telephones (Telefónica)
10 Champión Supermercado
11 Catedral; Museo Catedralicio
12 Bar Maño
15 Iglesia de Santa Clara
16 Iglesia de San Lázaro
20 Iglesia de San Miguel
22 Tourist Office

To Cristo del Otero Statue

Train Station (Renfe)

Plaza de Toros

0   100   200m
0   100   200yd

CASTILLA Y LEÓN

in the convent of the same name near the bus station, and the **Iglesia de San Miguel**. The former bears a Renaissance facade and in its main chapel you can see an enormous plateresque altarpiece. San Miguel stands out for its tall Gothic tower and, according to the legend, El Cid was betrothed to his Doña Jimena here. If you've got the time, you could also swing by the **Iglesia de San Lázaro** and the **Iglesia de Santa Clara**.

Of note too is the **Museo Diocesano** within the 18th-century Palacio Episcopal on Calle de General Mola. Its 10 rooms showcase art from the Middle Ages through

the Renaissance. Pride of place goes to works by Pedro Berruguete and an altarpiece starring the Virgin attributed to Diego de Siloé.

Just outside town, the 20m-high **Cristo del Otero** statue was erected in 1930 and dominates, Rio-style, the surrounding plains.

Places to Stay

Pensión Eduardo (☎ 979 74 29 48, Calle de Valentín Calderón 5) has comfortably sized, spanking clean singles/doubles costing 2000/3000 ptas. Better still is *Pensión El Hotelito* (☎ 979 74 69 13, Calle del General

Amor 5). The nicer doubles with bath cost 4280 ptas, while those with washbasin go for 2140/3745 ptas.

For a little more class, try *Hotel Los Jardinillos* (☎ 979 75 00 22, *Calle de Eduardo Dato 2)*, which charges 4300/6400 ptas, or *Hotel Colón 27* (☎ 979 74 07 00, *fax 979 74 07 20, Calle Colón 27)*, where rooms with bath, TV and phone cost 4000/ 6300 ptas.

Places to Eat
Mesón El Cazador (☎ 979 75 09 12, *Calle del Obispo Lozano 7)* is a cosy little restaurant with a *menú* for 1500 ptas. *Restaurante Casa Lucio* (☎ 979 74 81 90, *Calle de Don Sancho 2)* is a more elegant alternative, with a varied menu and main courses starting at 1200 ptas. *Vía Mirácoli* (☎ 979 75 20 50)*, on Calle del General Mola, is a cosy and upmarket Italian restaurant with a *menú* for 1875 ptas. There are also several restaurants on Plaza Mayor.

For drinks and tapas, *Café Los Cantones* (*Calle Mayor 43)* is a pleasant spot. *Bar Maño* (*Calle del General Franco 5)* is an atmospheric old place. Self-caterers will find a huge selection at the *Champión* supermarket on Calle de Menéndez Pelayo.

Getting There & Away
Buses regularly serve Valladolid and other main cities in adjacent provinces, as well as Madrid seven times daily (3¼ hours, 1925 ptas). Other destinations include Aguilar de Campóo, Frómista, Sahagún and Paredes de Nava, but these towns are more adequately served by train departing Palencia several times daily.

Roads fan out in all directions. The N-620 leads south-west to Valladolid and Salamanca and north-east to Burgos. The N-611 travel north to Santander via Frómista and Aguilar de Campóo, while the N-610 heads west to pick up the N-601 from Valladolid to León.

AROUND PALENCIA
Baños de Cerrato
A couple of kilometres west of the belching industrial rail junction of Venta de Baños lies Spain's oldest church, the 7th-century

Basílica de San Juan, in Baños de Cerrato. Built by the Visigoths and modified many times since, it has a pleasing simplicity. Get a train from Palencia to Venta de Baños, then walk. It's open 10.30 am to 1.30 pm daily except Monday.

Paredes de Nava
The eminent 16th-century sculptor Alonso Berruguete was born in Paredes in 1488. His father Pedro was himself an artist of some distinction, having worked in Ávila and Toledo and studied in Urbino, Italy. Paredes counts no fewer than four major churches, mostly in great disrepair. The exception is the eclectic **Iglesia de Santa Eulalia**, built in the 13th century and continually fiddled with for the following 300 years. Its museum contains some important artworks, including several pieces by the Berruguetes senior and junior. Official opening hours are 10 am to 1 pm Saturday and 5 to 7 pm Sunday. On other days, you should get in by calling ahead on ☎ 979 83 04 69.

There are a couple of places to stay, including *Pensión Sofía* (☎ 979 83 07 74, *Calle de Santa María 3)*, with simple rooms for 3200 ptas.

Several trains and a couple of buses run daily to Palencia, about 25km south-east.

Frómista
The exceptional Romanesque **Iglesia de San Martín** (1066) is the main reason for calling in here. The harmoniously proportioned church was faithfully restored in the early 20th century. A veritable menagerie of human and zoomorphic figures decorates its facade, while the capitals inside are richly decorated as well. You can enter from 10 am to 2 pm and 4.30 to 8 pm daily (3.30 to 6.30 pm in winter); free.

For places to stay, see the special section 'Camino de Santiago'. There are two buses daily from Palencia and another from Burgos. The Palencia-Santander train line also passes through Frómista. On the way up you'll notice a couple of castles, one at Fuentes de Valdepero (9km out of Palencia) and the other at Monzón de Campos (4km farther on).

From Frómista you can veer off westwards and follow the Camino de Santiago, or pursue the N-611 farther north into Cantabria via Aguilar de Campóo (see the following Montaña Palentina section).

MONTAÑA PALENTINA
The hills straddling the northern fringe of the province of Palencia are collectively known as the Montaña Palentina and are an attractive and little-visited foretaste of the Cordillera Cantábrica that divides Castile from Spain's northern Atlantic regions.

Aguilar de Campóo
The squat form of Aguilar de Campóo's medieval **castle** stands watch over this quiet town, the historic heartland of Spanish biscuit (cookie) production. Set a few kilometres east of a big dam and about 15km short of the regional boundary with Cantabria, the town makes a pleasant base for exploring the region, which is dotted with Romanesque churches and cool hilly countryside.

Tourist, post and telephone offices are all on or just off the elongated Plaza de España, which is capped at its eastern end by the majestic **Colegiata de San Miguel**, a 14th-century Gothic church with a fine Romanesque entrance and small museum of religious art. Both are open daily from May to September, weekdays only at other times.

Downhill from the castle is the graceful Romanesque **Ermita de Santa Cecilia** (usually closed). Just outside town on the road to Cervera de Pisuerga is the restored **Monasterio de Santa María la Real** of Romanesque origin. Its 13th-century Gothic cloister with delicate capitals is a masterpiece.

You'll find plenty of accommodation, including a few places right on Plaza de España. *Hostal Siglo XX* (☎ 979 12 29 00) at No 11 has perfectly good singles/doubles from 2000/3500 ptas. The square is swarming with *cafes* and *bars* and a couple of *restaurants*. There's also a *parador* (luxury hotel) in town, should you feel inclined towards a splurge.

Regular trains and a few buses link Aguilar de Campóo with Palencia, and at least one bus daily goes to Burgos and Santander.

Romanesque Circuit
The area around Aguilar is studded with little villages and churches of interest. One circuit for those with their own transport takes you south along the N-611 towards Palencia. At **Olleros de Pisuerga** is a little church carved into rock while, farther south on a back road, the Benedictine **Monasterio de Santa María de Mave** has an interesting 13th-century Romanesque church. The prize in this area lies to the south-west, along the P-222 – the **Monasterio de San Andrés de Arroyo** is an outstanding Romanesque gem, especially its cloister (one side of which was later restyled in a mixture of plateresque and Gothic).

The C-627 highway heading to **Cervera de Pisuerga** is lined with still more little churches dating from as far back as the 12th century. Cervera de Pisuerga itself is dominated by an imposing Late Gothic church, the **Iglesia de Santa María del Castillo**. There are several places to stay, including the homey *Hostal Galeria* (☎ 979 87 02 34, Plaza Mayor 16), with singles/doubles going for 3000/5000 ptas. Or try the warmly furnished *Casa Goyetes* (☎ 979 87 05 68, El Valle 4), which charges 4000/5800 ptas.

From Cervera you could complete the circle and return to Aguilar. Alternatively, a narrow mountain road winds west along the so-called *ruta de los pantanos* (dams route), describing an arc to Guardo, just short of the provincial frontier with León. The N-621 north from Cervera is a lovely road into Cantabria and to the southern face of the Picos de Europa (see the Cantabria & Asturias chapter).

THE ROAD TO ZAMORA
Castilla is at its least flattering around Valladolid, and the road to Zamora is no exception. But while you won't want to hang around for the parched, featureless countryside, there are several worthwhile stops en route.

Tordesillas
postcode 47100 • pop 7725
Commanding a rise on the northern flank of the Río Duero, this originally Roman town became part of the front line between the

CASTILLA Y LEÓN

Christians and Muslims after the latter had been thrown back from the north in the 9th century.

There is a tourist office in Las Casas del Tratado, near the Iglesia de San Antolín. It's open 10.30 am to 2 pm and 5 to 8 pm Wednesday to Saturday and 10 am to 2 pm Sunday and holidays.

Real Monasterio de Santa Clara Much of the history of Tordesillas has been dominated by this mudéjar-style convent, still home to 14 Franciscan nuns living in almost total isolation from the outside world. What started in 1340 as a palace for Alfonso XI later became a residence for the mistress of Pedro I who, in his testament, charged his daughter Beatriz with turning it into a convent. In 1494, the signing of the Treaty of Tordesillas took place here (see the boxed text 'The Treaty of Tordesillas' in this chapter).

It was home to the mad queen Juana la Loca after her husband, Felipe I died in 1506; she stayed until her own death in 1555 and in fact was buried here for 19 years before her body was transferred to Granada (as she had wished). Juana was shunted aside after her husband's death, although she officially remained queen and negotiated with the Comuneros during their

The Treaty of Tordesillas

In 1494, only two years after Columbus' 'discovery' of America, Spain's Catholic Monarchs sat down with Portugal at the negotiating table in Tordesillas to hammer out a treaty regulating who got what in the New World. The Spanish-born Borgia pope, Alexander VI, had earlier simply pronounced that everything west of the Azores Islands belonged to Spain, something Lisbon considered slightly lopsided. The Tordesillas deal pushed the limiting line 370 leagues (a little less than 1800km) farther west, giving Portugal Brazil. Later on, Spain and Portugal began to recognise that more than one demarcation line for America, or at least the southern half of it, was required, and they thrashed it all out again in the Treaty of Zaragoza in 1529.

uprising (see the boxed text 'Juan Bravo & the Comuneros' in the Segovia section).

The guided tour takes in some remarkable rooms, including a wonderful mudéjar patio left over from the palace, and the church, whose stunning ceiling, or techumbre, is a masterpiece of woodwork. The convent is open 10 am to 1 pm and 3.30 to 6.30 pm Tuesday to Saturday, and 10.30 am to 1.30 pm and 3.30 to 5.30 pm Sunday and holidays. Hours are slightly shorter from October to March. Entry is 475 ptas, students 275 ptas, free on Wednesday to EU passport holders. A separate guided tour of the Arab baths is 250 ptas (closed Wednesday).

Around Town The deconsecrated Gothic **Iglesia de San Antolín** houses a religious art museum, open 10.30 am to 2 pm and 4 to 7 pm daily except Monday (250 ptas). The heart of town is formed by the pretty, porticoed Plaza Mayor, whose deep yellow paintwork contrasts with dark brown woodwork and black *rejas* (grilles).

Places to Stay & Eat All of Tordesillas' hotels, many of which are expensive, are on or near the highways to Madrid, Valladolid and Salamanca. One characterless but quiet, clean place is *Hostal Bastida (☎ 983 77 08 42, Avenida de Valladolid 42)*. You can get singles/doubles with bath for 3000/5000 ptas per person and it's handy for buses. Nearby at No 26, *Hotel Los Toreros (☎ 983 77 19 00)* has comfier rooms with TV and bath for 5500/7500 ptas.

There are a few affordable eateries on Plaza Mayor, including *Don Pancho (☎ 983 77 01 74)* at No 9, although *Mesón Antolín (☎ 983 79 67 71, Calle San Antolín 8)* is supposed to be better.

Getting There & Away Buses for Valladolid (435 ptas) and Zamora leave regularly from Avenida de Valladolid, near Calle de Santa María.

Toro
postcode 49800 • pop 9250
The drama of Toro's position north of the Río Duero, about equidistant (35km) between

Tordesillas and Zamora, only becomes clear when you get into the centre of this topsy-turvy place. Coming from Zamora, the wandering English writer Laurie Lee was quite unprepared for the 'ancient, eroded, red-walled town spread along the top of a huge flat boulder', which, to his surprise, 'half-ruined though it certainly was – was... buzzing with life'. His account, from *As I Walked Out One Midsummer Morning,* still holds true today.

Having seen the whole historical parade – Celts, Romans, Visigoths, Muslims et al – Toro reached the height of its glory between the 13th and 16th centuries. Fernando and Isabel cemented their primacy in Christian Spain at the Battle of Toro in 1476. Today it's at the heart of a well-known red wine region. The tourist office (☎ 980 69 18 62) is in the ayuntamiento on Plaza de España.

Things to See Toro is studded with Romanesque churches, the most prominent of which is **Colegiata Santa María La Mayor.** It boasts a fine Romanesque doorway in the northern facade and the even more magnificent Romanesque-Gothic Pórtico de la Majestad. Treasures inside include the famous 15th-century painting called *Virgen de la Mosca* (Virgin of the Fly). See if you can spot the fly on the virgin's robe. Church hours are 10 am to 1 pm and 5 to 8 pm daily (less in winter, open for services only in January and February).

From behind the cathedral you have a superb view south across the fields to the Romanesque bridge over the Duero. The nearby 10th-century Alcázar conserves its walls and seven towers.

South-west of town, the **Monasterio Sancti Spiritus** features a fine Renaissance cloister and the striking alabaster tomb of Beatriz de Portugal, wife of Juan I. It is open daily except Monday and has a small museum too (250 ptas).

Places to Stay & Eat Toro has half a dozen places to stay accommodating all budgets. Cheapest of the bunch is the bare-bones *Pensión Castilla* (☎ 980 69 03 81, Plaza de España 19), which has singles/doubles for 1500/2500 ptas. For a bit more comfort, try **Hostal Doña Elvira** (☎ 980 69 00 62, Calle de Antonio Miguelez 47), which rents out rooms with washbasin for 2100/3000 ptas and also has a few doubles with private facilities for 4600 ptas. All rooms have TV.

Plaza de España and surrounds bustles with plenty of little places to eat. **Casa Lorenzo** (☎ 980 69 11 53, Gonzales Oliveros 21) comes recommended for its hearty Zamoran dishes.

Getting There & Away Forget the train – the station is 2km downhill and few trains stop here anyway. Regular buses to Zamora and Valladolid leave from near the junction of Avenida de Carlos Pinilla and Calle de la Corredera, while Madrid buses leave from the edge of town at Calle de Santa Catalina de Roncesvalles. There are two direct services to Salamanca on weekdays.

ZAMORA
postcode 49080 • pop 66,017
Another strategic fortress town on the northern bank of the Río Duero, Zamora is far enough away from other major Castilian cities not to figure highly on travellers' itineraries. It's a subdued place, its religious character reflected in a dozen or so medieval churches to which the town owes its nickname 'Romanesque Museum.' All stand in the old town *(casco antiguo)* in the western half of the city, which is becoming increasingly quiet as residents move east into the modern suburbs.

History
Roman Ocelum Durii was a significant way station along the Ruta de la Plata (Silver Route) from Astorga to southern Spain. The Romans were replaced by the Visigoths, who in turn collapsed before the Muslims who laid waste to Zamora twice. It was not until the 11th century that the Christians began serious reconstruction. By the 12th and 13th centuries, when a fever of church-building formed the architectural core of what you see today, Zamora had reached its zenith as a commercial centre.

CASTILLA Y LEÓN

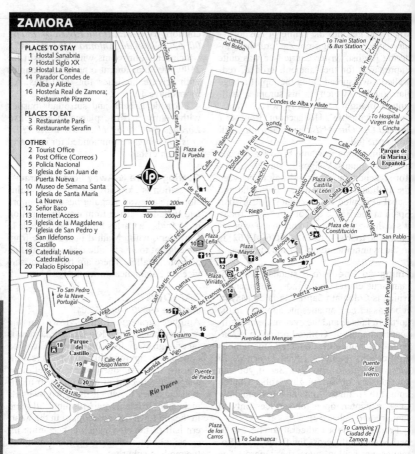

ZAMORA

PLACES TO STAY
1 Hostal Sanabria
7 Hostal Siglo XX
9 Hostal La Reina
14 Parador Condes de
    Alba y Aliste
16 Hostería Real de Zamora;
    Restaurante Pizarro

PLACES TO EAT
3 Restaurante Paris
6 Restaurante Serafin

OTHER
2 Tourist Office
4 Post Office (Correos)
5 Policía Nacional
8 Iglesia de San Juan de
   Puerta Nueva
10 Museo de Semana Santa
11 Iglesia de Santa María
    La Nueva
12 Señor Baco
13 Internet Access
15 Iglesia de la Magdalena
17 Iglesia de San Pedro y
    San Ildefonso
18 Castillo
19 Catedral; Museo
    Catedralicio
20 Palacio Episcopal

Orientation

The bus and train stations are a good half-hour walk roughly north-east of the town centre, from where it's another 15 minutes south-west to the cathedral and the heart of the old town. Accommodation is spread out roughly between Plaza Mayor and Calle Alfonso IX, which marks the eastern boundary of the city centre.

Information

The tourist office (☎ 980 53 18 45, fax 980 53 18 45), Calle de Santa Clara 20, is open 9 am to 2 pm and 5 to 7 pm weekdays and 10 am to 2 pm and 5 to 8 pm weekends. The post office is at Calle de Santa Clara 15. There are plenty of banks on and around Plaza de Castilla y León. Internet access is available in the cafe on the western side of Plaza Viriato. In an emergency, dial ☎ 091 or the Policía Nacional (☎ 980 53 04 62) at Calle San Atilano 3. The Hospital Virgen de la Concha (☎ 980 54 82 00) is at Avenida Requejo, about 1km east of the old centre.

Catedral

Crowning medieval Zamora's highest point, the largely Romanesque cathedral features a square tower, a Byzantine-style dome orbited by little turrets, and notable portals, especially the ornate southern **Puerta del Obispo**. Inside, the early Renaissance **choir stalls** are a masterpiece; carvings depicts clerics, animals and – if you look closely – even a naughty encounter between a monk and a nun. The cathedral is open 10 am to 1 pm and 5 to 8 pm daily from March to mid-October. Closed in January and February, it's otherwise open from Friday to Sunday only.

Adjacent to the main entrance is the **Museo Catedralicio**, whose star attraction is a collection of Flemish tapestries, the oldest of which, depicting the Trojan War, dates to the 15th century. The museum's hours are 11 am to 2 pm and 5 to 8 pm (4 to 6 pm in winter), closed Monday (300 ptas).

For a look at what's left of the city wall and its **castle**, head to the little park just west of the cathedral.

Churches

Zamora churches are of Romanesque origin but all have been subjected to other style influences. Among those retaining some of their Romanesque charm are the **Iglesia de San Pedro y San Ildefonso** (with Gothic touches), **Iglesia de la Magdalena** (the southern doorway is considered the city's finest) and **Iglesia de San Juan de Puerta Nueva**. **Iglesia de Santa María La Nueva**, near the Museo de Semana Santa, is actually a medieval replica of a 7th-century church destroyed by fire in 1158. Zamora's churches are open 10 am to 1 pm and 5 to 8 pm from March to October. In winter, they're open Friday to Sunday only.

Museo de Semana Santa

Zamora is famous for its elaborate celebrations of Semana Santa (Easter Week). The city has devoted an entire museum to the carved and painted *pasos* (statues depicting the Passion of Christ) which are hauled around town during the colourful processions. It's open 10 am to 2 pm and 5 to 8 pm (4 to 7 pm in winter), closed Sunday afternoon (300 ptas).

Places to Stay

Camping Cuidad de Zamora (☎ 629 85 42 13, ℮ collantes@redestb.es) is a new camping ground on the C-605, about 2.5km south of town. Charges are 550 ptas per person, 400 ptas per tent and 575 ptas per car (less during low season).

One of Zamora's best bargains is *Hostal Sanabria (☎ 980 52 66 72)* on Plaza de la Puebla, which charges 2000/3000 ptas for simple singles/doubles with washbasin. *Hostal Siglo XX (☎ 980 53 29 08, Plaza del Seminario 1)* is in a pleasant, quiet spot and has simple rooms with washbasin for 3000/4000 ptas.

More attractive is *Hostal La Reina (☎ 980 53 39 39, Calle de la Reina 1),* which charges 3650 ptas for doubles with bath and also has a few singles with washbasin only for 2000 ptas. *Hostería Real de Zamora (☎ 980 53 45 45, fax 980 53 45 22, Cuesta de Pizarro 7)* is in a 16th-century structure and offers sophistication and style with a price tag of 6975/8900 ptas for rooms with TV and phone.

The pick of the crop is *Parador Condes de Alba y Aliste (☎ 980 51 44 97, fax 980 53 00 63, Plaza Viriato 5),* in a sumptuous 15th-century palace, where previous 'guests' have included Isabel and Fernando. Historic features, such as a Renaissance cloister and carved staircases, perfectly complement the mod cons, friendly staff and outdoor swimming pool. Princely rooms crest at 14,800/18,500 ptas.

Places to Eat

Several simple eateries orbit Plaza Mayor. For a solid meal, *Restaurante Paris (☎ 980 51 43 25, Avenida Pórtugal 14)* and *Restaurante Serafin (☎ 980 53 14 22, Plaza Maestro Haedo 10)* are good, mid- to upper-priced restaurants serving *cocina zamorana* (Zamoran cuisine). For cuisine with delightful Basque accents, splurge on a meal at *Restaurante Pizarro (☎ 980 53 45 45)* in the same building as the Hostería Real de Zamora.

Entertainment

Plaza Mayor's cafes and bars are suitable for people-watching. For late-night drinking,

CASTILLA Y LEÓN

Calle de los Herreros, just south of the square, is jammed with gritty pubs and bars. For a bit more class, search out *Señor Baco*, a cafe-bar on Calle Corral Pintado.

Getting There & Away

Bus The bus station is a good 30-minute walk from the centre and there are no local buses. Still, bus is generally the best way to get to Zamora. Regular services link it with Salamanca (595 ptas), León (965 ptas), Astorga (1100 ptas) and Madrid (1290 ptas) via Toro (185 ptas).

Train The train station is just downhill from the bus station. There are up to four trains daily to Madrid (3¼ hours, 4300 ptas), all of them stopping in Ávila (1½ hours, 3000 ptas). Three trains head for Galicia (Vigo, Pontevedra and La Coruña). There's also direct service to regional destinations such as Toro, Puebla de Sanabria and Medina del Campo.

Car & Motorcycle For routes out of Zamora, see the Around Zamora section.

AROUND ZAMORA
San Pedro de la Nave

This 7th-century church, about 20km north-west of Zamora, is a rare and outstanding example of Visigothic church architecture, which blended Celtic, Germanic and Byzantine elements. Of special note are the intricately sculptured capitals, a stylistic touch not common until the 12th century. The church was moved a few kilometres to its present site in El Campillo during the construction of the Esla reservoir in 1930.

North to León

The N-630 heads directly north from Zamora to León. There is little to hold you up on the way, but in **Benavente**, 65km north, a parador has been built around the impressive Torre del Caracol, a squat 15th-century castle tower. About 30km before, just south of the village of Granja de Moreruela, lie the ramshackle ruins of a 12th-century **monastery** in a perfect state of bucolic abandon, 4km down a track west of the highway.

From Benavente you could skew west along the N-525 for Puebla de Sanabria and on to Galicia (see under To Galicia later in this section), or keep bearing north for León or north-west towards Astorga where you can pick up the Camino de Santiago (for details, see the special section 'Camino de Santiago' later in this book).

To Portugal

Even if Portugal is not on your itinerary, if you have a vehicle it is worth heading west on the N-122 to the northern Portuguese town of **Bragança**, whose old quarter is lorded over by an immaculately preserved fortress, now home to a military museum. About 60km outside of Zamora, you'll also pass picturesque **Alcañices** with its traditional architecture.

To Galicia

An alternative route to Galicia runs north-west from Zamora between the Sierra de la Culebra and Sierra de la Cabrera. Leave the town on the N-630 north, then pick up the N-631 at the Embalse de Ricobayo, which eventually merges with the N-525. Heading west on this road takes you through the **Lago de Sanabria Nature Park**, a popular outdoor recreation area. The heart of the region is the little town of **Puebla de Sanabria**, whose captivating web of medieval alleyways unfolds around the 15th-century castle. You can enter the castle at will and wander around the walls.

Camping is possible from April to mid-September at *Isla de Puebla* (☎ 980 56 79 54). Hotels include *Hostal Galicia* (☎ 980 62 01 06, Calle de las Ánimas 22), which has no-frills singles for 1850 ptas, while the nearby *Hotel Victoria* (☎ 980 62 00 12, Calle del Arrabal 29) has doubles with bath for 6000 ptas. *Cervecería Veti*, just off Plaza Mayor, has cheap tapas and wine.

Buses from Zamora and Benavente serve La Puebla on weekdays. By car you can follow the N-525 west from La Puebla over the Portilla de la Canda on the way to Verín in Galicia. From there you could swing northwards to Orense or push on for the Rías Bajas on the Atlantic.

The North-West

Once the centre of Christian Spain, León now stands like a sentinel at the rim of the great Castilian heartland. The city, with its magnificent cathedral and cosmopolitan feel, certainly gets the lion's share of visitors, but the countryside is full of interesting diversions as well. To the west lies Astorga, capital of La Maragatería, whose people are still successfully clinging to century-old traditions. Still closer to Galicia is the El Bierzo valley, with Ponferrada as its anchor, and the otherworldly landscape of Las Médulas.

The last major city on the Camino de Santiago before it climbs west into the sierras that separate Castile from Galicia, León is also the final staging post on the road north towards the Cordillera Cantábrica and Asturias. And even the Picos de Europa mountains spill over here into Castilla y León's most northerly reaches. Even before you cross into Galicia, Asturias or Cantabria, you can feel the coming changes in climate, landscape, language and people.

LEÓN

Postcode 24080 • pop 147,300

For a couple of centuries, León was the flourishing capital of the expanding Christian kingdom of Asturias and León, and the city retains a powerful hold over its visitors. In possession of the two jewels of Spanish Romanesque and Gothic creativity, the city is also liberally sprinkled with less exalted reminders of its glory days. Its bustling city centre is in itself a successful marriage of medieval inheritance and thoughtful modern town planning.

History

In AD 70 a Roman legion made camp at a place where later the city of León would rise. The imperial troops were based here to control the gold mines of Las Médulas, farther west. A residual settlement muddled along until the Asturian King Ordoño II decided to move his capital here from Oviedo

in the 10th century. Later sacked by Al-Mansour, León was nevertheless maintained by Alfonso V as the capital of his growing kingdom, a role it continued to play until the union with Castile in 1230. It was in this period that the city reached its zenith. Centuries of decline followed, but mining brought León back to life in the 19th century.

Not only in this respect, the city has more in common with its Asturian neighbours across the Cordillera to the north than with its Castilian sister cities to the south and east. During the Second Republic, León's workers joined their Asturian comrades in the bloody, and ultimately futile, October Revolt of 1934.

Orientation

The train and bus stations lie on the western bank of the Río Bernesga, while the heart of the city is concentrated on the eastern side. Cross the river at the bridge nearest the train station and head east along Avenida de Ordoño II. From the river to the cathedral it's about 1km, with Plaza de Santo Domingo marking the halfway point. There are plenty of banks, hotels and pensiones on or off this axis, with many restaurants and bars near the cathedral.

Note that Calle de Generalísimo Franco has been renamed Calle de Ancha, and the former Avenida de José Antonio and its continuation, Avenida del General Sanjurjo, is now the Gran Vía de San Marcos.

Information

Tourist Offices The tourist office (☎ 987 23 70 82, fax 987 27 33 91), opposite the cathedral, is open 9 am to 2 pm and 5 to 7 pm weekdays and 10 am to 2 pm and 5 to 8 pm weekends.

Money Banks with ATMs and exchange services are scattered throughout the city centre, though they seem to concentrate along Avenida de Ordoño II.

Post & Communications The main post office is on Avenida de la Independencia, just off Plaza de San Francisco. There's a

CASTILLA Y LEÓN

telephone locutorio with Internet access at Calle de la Rúa 8. It's open 9.30 am to 2.30 pm and 4.30 to 11 pm weekdays and 10 am to 2 pm and 5 to 9.30 pm Saturday; an hour of surfing costs 450 ptas.

Travel Agencies TIVE (☎ 987 20 09 51), Calle del Arquitecto Torbado 4, can help with student travel information and low-priced tickets. It's only open 9 am to 2 pm weekdays.

Medical Services & Emergency In emergencies, call the police on ☎ 091; the Policía Nacional is on Calle de Villa de Benavente. The Hospital Nuestra Señora de la Regla (☎ 987 23 69 00) is north of the cathedral. For an ambulance call either ☎ 987 24 24 24 or ☎ 987 22 22 22.

Walking Tour
Starting from the busy traffic circus of the Plaza de Santo Domingo and heading east to the Plaza de San Marcelo, you'll see the Renaissance-era palace that now houses the **ayuntamiento**. A few paces farther east along the latter plaza stands Antoni Gaudí's contribution to León's skyline, the rather subdued neo-Gothic **Casa de Botines** (1893).

Next up, as you enter Calle de Ancha is another Renaissance block, the **Palacio de los Guzmanes** (1560), whose best features are the facade and patio. Another few hundred metres brings you to the **catedral**, from where you could venture north-west to the equally unmissable **Real Basílica de San Isidoro**. A 15-minute walk west leads to the **Hostal San Marcos**, or you can backtrack from the basilica to Calle de Ancha along Gran Vía San Marcos. This serves as a jumping-off point for the medieval heart of León.

It's fun just to wander the warren of crooked lanes, but worth making a conscious effort to see is the 17th-century **Plaza Mayor**. Sealed off on three sides by shady porticoes, its bars and cafes come alive at night. It's usually also home to a lively Saturday market, although this had been temporarily moved to beside the cathedral due to construction.

Another captivating square is **Plaza de Santa María del Camino**, a broad, uneven cobblestone expanse whose most outstanding features are the Romanesque **Iglesia de Santa María del Mercado** and an extremely photogenic old house and bar.

Catedral
León's 13th-century cathedral, with its soaring towers and flying buttresses, is the Mt Everest of Castilian houses of worship. It is also the city's spiritual heart and main tourist draw. Whether spotlit by night or bathed in the glorious northern sunshine, what is one of Spain's greatest masterpieces of Gothic fancy exudes an almost luminous quality.

Approaching from the west, your eyes will be captivated by an extraordinary facade with a radiant rose window, three richly sculptured doorways and two muscular towers. Even greater splendour, though, awaits past the main entrance, lorded over by the scene of the Last Supper. A riot of stained-glass windows, French in inspiration and mostly executed from the 13th to the 16th centuries, will make you feel like you've entered the inside of a kaleidoscope There seems to be more glass than brick – 128 windows with a surface of 1800 sq metres in all – but mere numbers cannot convey the ethereal quality of light permeating this cathedral.

Other treasures include a silver urn by Enrique de Arfe containing the remains of San Froilán, León's patron saint (on the altar). Also note the magnificent choir stalls, and the rich chapels in the ambulatory behind the altar, especially the one containing the tomb of Ordoño II.

The florid cloister, with its 15th-century frescoes, gives way to **Museo Catedralicio-Diocesano**, with a high-quality collection distributed over 13 rooms. Works by Juni and Gaspar Becerra, as well as a precious assemblage of early Romanesque carved statues of the Virgin Mary, rank among the numerous highlights.

The cathedral is open 8.30 am to 1.30 pm and 4 to 7 pm daily (to 8 pm in summer); free. Museum and cloister must be visited on a tour (in Spanish) during which the guides open and close each room as they go. These are offered from 9.30 am to 1.30 pm and 4 to 7 pm (to 6.30 pm Saturday, closed Sunday) from July to September. Hours are slightly shorter the rest of the year. The cost is 500 ptas for the full tour (1¼ hours) or 300 ptas for the short tour (30 minutes, but only covering the more boring bits). Entry to the cloister only is 100 ptas.

Real Basílica de San Isidoro

A step back further in history, San Isidoro is as seminal a work of Romanesque as the cathedral is a gem of Gothic. Fernando I and Doña Sancha founded the church in 1063 to house the remains not just of the saint, but also of themselves and 21 other early Leonese and Castilian kings and queens, as well as assorted minor royalty. Napoleon's troops sacked San Isidoro in the early 19th century, leaving behind them only a handful of sarcophagi.

These still rest with quiet dignity in the so-called **Panteón Real** beneath a canopy of some of the finest Romanesque frescoes in all of Spain, if not Europe. Motif after colourful motif drenches the vaults and arches of this extraordinary hall, held aloft by marble columns with intricately carved capitals. Biblical scenes dominate and include the Annunciation, King Herod's slaughter of the innocent infants, the Last Supper and a striking representation of Christ Pantocrator. The agricultural calendar on one of the arches adds a worldy dimension.

The pantheon once formed the portico of the original church, now a small museum where you can admire the shrine of San Isidoro, a mummified finger of the saint and treasures such as an agate chalice and polychrome wood Madonnas. A library houses a priceless collection of manuscripts.

The main basilica is a hotchpotch of styles, but the two main portals are again pure Romanesque. Of particular note is the **Puerta del Perdón** (on the right), which has been attributed to Maestro Mateo, the genius of the cathedral at Santiago de Compostela.

The church (free) remains open night and day by historical royal edict, but seeing the

Panteón and museum entails joining a 30-minute guided tour (in Spanish only; 400 ptas) usually given from 10 am and 1.30 pm and 4 to 6.30 pm, closed Sunday afternoon; times vary slightly with the seasons.

Hostal de San Marcos

More than 100m long and festooned with an awe-inspiring facade, the Convent of San Marcos has more the appearance of a palace than the pilgrim's hospital it was at its founding in 1173. The platersque exterior, sectioned off by slender columns and decorated with delicate medallions and friezes, dates to 1513, by which time the edifice had become a monastery of the Knights of Santiago.

Much of the former convent is now a supremely elegant parador. As you enter, take a peek into the former chapterhouse with its splendid artesonado ceiling immediately to your right. Continue on – with confidence – to gain free access to the exquisite cloister with ancient tombstones and sculpture. The cloister is technically part of the **Museo de León**, accessible through the church on the eastern end of the structure. It is given over mostly to archaeology and open 10 am to 2 pm and 5 to 8.30 pm (4.30 to 8 pm from October to April), closed Monday and Sunday afternoon (200 ptas).

Special Events

Although not known for the splendour of its fiestas, León does stir for Semana Santa and, more so, from 21 to 30 June for the Fiestas de San Juan y San Pedro.

Places to Stay – Budget

Camping The nearest camping ground is *Ciudad de León* (☎ 987 68 02 33, fax 987 21 47 98), about 3km south on the N-601 (exit Golpejar). It's open from June to mid-September and charges 475 ptas per person, plus 525 ptas each per tent and car.

Hostales & Pensiones If you don't mind no-frills accommodation with shared facilities, León offers its share of budget-friendly options. Cheapest of the bunch are

CASTILLA Y LEÓN

Pensión Roma (☎ 987 22 46 63, Avenida de Roma 4), which charges just 900/1500 ptas for singles/doubles, and **Pensión Santa Cruz** (☎ 987 25 98 94, Calle Santa Cruz 8), where rooms cost 1200/2100 ptas. The latter charges 150 ptas for showers. The charm quotient in either is basically zero.

A step up is **Pensión Berta** (☎ 987 25 70 39, Plaza Mayor 8), whose friendly owners rent out rickety but clean doubles for 3000 ptas; the location is unbeatable. **Hospedaje Suárez** (☎ 987 25 42 88, Calle de Ancha 7) offers the same standard and prices, while **Hostal Bayón** (☎ 987 23 14 46, Calle del Alcázar de Toledo 6) clocks in at 3600 ptas for rooms with washbasin.

Places to Stay – Mid-Range & Top End

Hotel Reina (☎ 987 20 52 12, Calle de Puerta de la Reina 2) has a wide range of rooms. Those with washbasin cost 1870/3365 ptas, while others with full bath are good value at 4000/5000 ptas. **Hostal Orejas** (☎/fax 987 25 29 09, Calle de Villafranca 8), with 49 rooms, is one of the larger establishments. Rooms with satellite TV, phone, minibar and bathroom cost 5500/6500 ptas, while those with washbasin go for 4000/5000 ptas.

One of the best-value places in town is **Hostal Londres** (☎ 987 22 22 74, Avenida de Roma 1), which has charming rooms and owners. The seven doubles with TV and bath range from 4500 to 6000 ptas, depending on the season. A good place, but perhaps a tad pricey, is **Hostal Padre de Isla II** (☎ 987 80 97, Avenida Padre de Isla 8), with quiet, largish doubles for 8500 ptas.

Jumping up in the price department is **Hotel París** (☎ 987 23 86 00, fax 987 27 15 72, Calle de Ancha 18), which has mod-con filled rooms for 7000/10,000 ptas. **Hostal de San Marcos** (☎ 987 23 73 00, fax 987 23 34 58, Plaza de San Marcos 7) has rooms fit for royalty at 19,000 to 21,500 ptas.

Places to Eat

The lifeblood of León's eating and drinking activity flows most thickly through the aptly dubbed Barrio Húmedo (Wet Quarter), a heavy concentration of bars and restaurants packed into the crowded tangle of lanes south off Calle de Ancha. Its epicentre is Plaza de San Martín, a particularly pleasant car-free square with lots of outdoor tables in fine weather. There's plenty of tapas bars and informal eateries here, but for more substantial fare visit **El Tizón** (☎ 987 25 60 49) at No 1; the abundant set lunch costs 1600 ptas.

Just south of the plaza is **Restaurante Belmán** (☎ 987 21 37 00, Calle de Misericordia 15), a small and uncluttered locale that has a selection of set lunches for under 1000 ptas and mains from 1100 to 1800 ptas.

Off to the east is one of the city's best pizzerias, the rustic **Pizzeria La Competencia** (☎ 987 84 94 77), wedged into tight Calle Mulhacín. Its deliciously crispy, generously topped pies go down particularly well with a bottle of house wine for just 400 ptas. The salads are a winner as well.

Restaurante Honoré (Calle de los Serradores 4) has a good-value set lunch for 950 ptas, while **Café Carmela** (Calle de Caño Badillo 7) has an inviting and relaxed atmosphere for enjoying snacks and coffee. **Mesón Leonés del Racimo de Oro** (☎ 987 25 75 75), on the same street at No 2, is a long-established restaurant favoured by an older crowd. Set lunches cost about 1200 ptas and mains range from 1500 to 2300 ptas.

In a similar price league, **La Bodega Regia** (☎ 987 21 31 73, Calle del General Mola 9) is a good spot for outdoor eating in summer. **Restaurante La Posada** (☎ 987 25 82 66, Calle de la Rúa 33) is another popular restaurant serving regional specialities.

Casa Palomo (☎ 987 25 60 18, Calle de la Escalerilla 8) is a quality establishment, with a menú for 1300 ptas. Next door is the **Restaurante & Sidrería Vivaldi** (☎ 987 26 07 60, Calle Platerías 4), which is one of the few places in León where you can get Asturian cider.

For self-caterers, **Alimerika** (Avenida Roma 2) is a well-stocked supermarket with a bakery and cheese, sausage and produce counters. Cheese lovers will want to make a stop at **Don Queso** (Calle Azabachería 20), which stocks every imaginable variety.

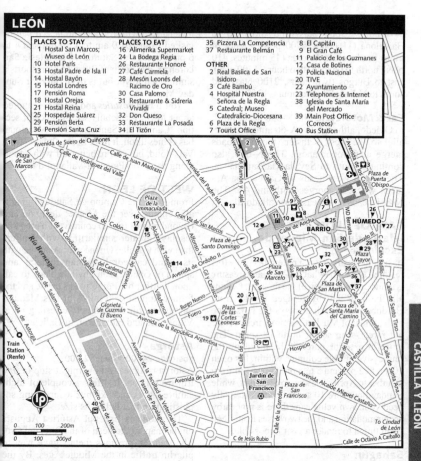

LEÓN

PLACES TO STAY
1 Hostal San Marcos; Museo de León
10 Hotel París
13 Hostal Padre de Isla II
14 Hostal Bayón
15 Hostal Londres
17 Pensión Roma
18 Hostal Orejas
21 Hostal Reina
25 Hospedaje Suárez
29 Pensión Berta
36 Pensión Santa Cruz

PLACES TO EAT
16 Alimerika Supermarket
24 La Bodega Regia
26 Restaurante Honoré
27 Café Carmela
28 Mesón Leonés del Racimo de Oro
30 Casa Palomo
31 Restaurante & Sidrería Vivaldi
32 Don Queso
33 Restaurante La Posada
34 El Tizón
35 Pizzera La Competencia
37 Restaurante Belmán

OTHER
2 Real Basílica de San Isidoro
3 Café Bambú
4 Hospital Nuestra Señora de la Regla
5 Catedral; Museo Catedralicio-Diocesana
6 Plaza de la Regla
7 Tourist Office
8 El Capitán
9 El Gran Café
11 Palacio de los Guzmanes
12 Casa de Botines
19 Policía Nacional
20 TIVE
22 Ayuntamiento
23 Telephones & Internet
38 Iglesia de Santa María del Mercado
39 Main Post Office (Correos)
40 Bus Station

Entertainment

Away from the traditional Barrio Húmedo area, a series of streets heading north of Calle de Ancha is lined with bars to suit most tastes.

El Gran Café on Calle de Cervantes is a classy and popular spot for a drink, but there are plenty of other possibilities along this street and on Calle de Fernando Regueral and Calle del Sacramento.

On Calle de Ancha itself is the hip *El Capitán* (☎ 987 26 27 72) at No 8, with red velvet curtains, candlelight and mirrors which give it a bit of a boudoir ambience.

Check out the curios from around the world beneath the glass bar top.

Café Bambú, behind the cathedral on Avenida de los Cubos, is a sedate vantage point for gazing on the floodlit apse of the cathedral.

Getting There & Away

Bus ALSA has up to a dozen buses to Madrid daily (3½ hours, 2665 ptas). Frequent buses also run to Astorga (30 minutes, 405 ptas,), Oviedo (1¾ hours, 1015 ptas) and Valladolid (two hours, 1070 ptas). There's also service to Bilbao, Burgos and San Sebastián.

euro currency converter €1 = 166pta

CASTILLA Y LEÓN

Train Up to 10 trains daily leave for Madrid (4¼ hours, 3600 ptas) and three go to Barcelona (11 hours, 5700 ptas). Plenty of trains head west to Astorga (45 minutes, 410 ptas), north to Oviedo (two hours, 1700 ptas), east to Burgos (two hours, 2100 ptas) and south to Valladolid (two hours, 1265 ptas).

Car & Motorcycle The N-630 heads north to Oviedo, although the A-66 autopista parallel to the west is faster (the two roads merge at Campomanes). The N-630 also continues south to Sevilla via Salamanca. The N-120 west heads to Galicia via Astorga where it merges with the A6. The N-601 heads south-east for Valladolid.

EAST OF LEÓN
Iglesia de San Miguel de Escalada
In simplicity often lies a potent beauty – this restored and somewhat out-of-place treasure is a fine demonstration of the thought. Originally built in 930 by refugee monks from Córdoba, the church displays the horseshoe arch typical of Muslim-inspired architecture but rarely seen so far north in Spain. The graceful exterior porch is balanced by the impressive marble columns within. It's open 10 am to 2 pm and 5 to 8 pm (4 to 6 pm from October to April) Tuesday to Saturday, while Sunday hours are 10 am to 3 pm. You really need your own vehicle, as there is no nearby accommodation and the two buses from León seem timed to render a visit impossible.

Sahagún
An unremarkable place today, Sahagún was once home to one of Spain's more powerful abbeys, in charge of some 90 monasteries. This concentration of power angered locals so much that they took to sacking the place towards the end of the Middle Ages. Today the abbey is a crumbling ruin, its more important remnants kept in a small museum by Benedictine nuns. More often than not the place is closed and there's not a nun to be seen.

Next to the former abbey is the **Iglesia de San Tiros** (1123), an important stop on the Camino de Santiago. It's of pure Roman-esque design and sports a múdejar bell tower laced with rounded arches. It can be visited from 10.30 am to 1.30 pm and 4 to 6 pm Tuesday to Saturday. The **Iglesia San Lorenzo**, just north of Plaza Mayor, sports a similar bell tower but is open only for Sunday Mass.

You'll find *hostales* and *eateries* scattered about town; for details see the special section 'Camino de Santiago'. The occasional bus comes through from León, and one from Valladolid, but you're better off with a train along the León-Palencia-Valladolid line.

WEST OF LEÓN
From León the Camino de Santiago gradually climbs over the Montes de León and beyond into El Bierzo country – an area that displays greater similarities with Galicia than with Castilla. On the way, Astorga, with its grand cathedral, Roman remains and splash of Gaudí, is an obvious place to call upon. Farther on, Ponferrada's castle and the former Roman gold mines of Las Médulas are also worth detours before resting up in Villafranca and moving on to Galicia.

Astorga
postcode 24700 • pop 12,500
Astorga is a pleasant overnight stop or day trip from León. It offers a couple of high-calibre sights and exhibits a surprising sophistication that belies its size.

The Romans first put Astúrica Augusta on the map, at the head of the Ruta del Oro. The trade in precious metals gave way to pilgrim traffic in the Middle Ages. By the 15th century, Astorga had become wealthy and important, which inspired the construction of the cathedral. The 3rd-century walls were also rebuilt then, but the town had to wait for the 19th century to acquire its perhaps most distinctive feature – the neo-Gothic Palacio Episcopal.

Astorga is the capital of a district known as the Maragatería. Many claim the Maragatos, who with their mule trains dedicated themselves almost exclusively to the carrying trade, were descendants of the first Berbers to enter Spain in the Muslim armies of the 8th century. Other theories argue that

CASTILLA Y LEÓN

Celtic and Phoenician tribes were their longtime ancestors, but the mystery of their origin remains essentially unsolved.

Orientation & Information Astorga's old centre is compact and easily navigated. The cathedral and Palacio Episcopal huddle together in the north-western corner of the old town, with the tourist office (☎ 987 61 82 22, fax 987 60 30 65) opposite the latter. It's open 10 am to 2 pm and 4 to 8 pm daily from May to October; otherwise, hours are 10.30 am to 1.30 pm and 4 to 7 pm, closed weekend afternoons.

Catedral The most striking element of Astorga's cathedral is its plateresque southern facade, made from caramel-coloured sandstone and dripping in sculptural detail. Work, begun in 1471 on the site of its Romanesque predecessor, proceeded in stop-start fashion over three centuries, resulting in a predictable mix of styles. On the inside,

the cathedral is mainly Gothic, with the 16th-century altarpiece by Gaspar Becerra monopolising the visitor's gaze. The attached **Museo de la Catedral** features the usual religious art, documents and artefacts. Both are open 10 am to 2 pm and 4 to 8 pm daily (11 am to 2 pm and 3.30 to 6.30 pm in winter); 250 ptas.

Palacio Episcopal Fairytale turrets, frilly facades and surprising details – the playful Palacio Episcopal integrates all the stylistic hallmarks of its Catalan architect, Antoni Gaudí. Built for the local bishop from the end of the 19th century, it now houses the **Museo de los Caminos**, with a moderately interesting assemblage of Roman artefacts and coins, medieval sculpture, Gothic tombs and items related to the Camino de Santiago. Tickets for 400 ptas are also good for the Museo Catedralicio; both have the same opening hours, although the Palace is closed Sunday, except in August.

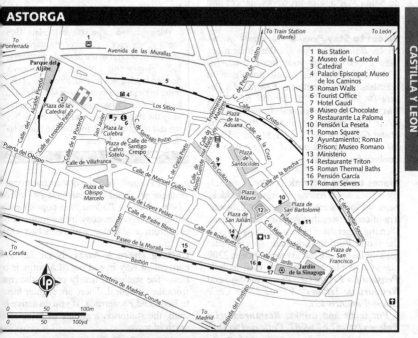

ASTORGA

To Ponferrada
To Train Station (Renfe)
To León

Avenida de las Murallas

Parque del Aljibe

Los Sitios

Plaza de la Catedral

Calle del Alcalde Pineda
Calle del Leopoldo Parci
Calle de la Portería
San Javier
Plaza la Culebra
Calle de Santiago Postas
Calle de Santiago Crespo
Plaza de Santiago Calvo Sotelo
Puerta del Obispo
Calle de Villafranca
Calle de Manuel Gullón
Calle de Gracia Prieto
Plaza de Obispo Marcelo
Calle de López Peláez
Carmen
Calle de Padre Blanco
Paseo de la Muralla
Bastión
Carretera de Madrid-Coruña

C de Pedro de Castro
C de Santiago
Calle de Alonso Castrillo José Mª Goy
Pío Gullón

Plaza de la Aduana
Calle de la Cruz
Calle de la Brecha
Plaza de San Bartolomé
Plaza de Santocildes
Calle de Matías Rodríguez
Plaza Mayor
Plaza de San Julián
Calle de Rodríguez Cela
Plaza de San Francisco
Calle del Jardín
Jardín de la Sinagoga

To La Coruña
To Madrid

Enfermeras Mártires
Calle Cristo
Calle de Santiago
Padres Redentoristas
C del Perpetuo Socorro

0   50   100m
0   50   100yd

1 Bus Station
2 Museo de la Catedral
3 Catedral
4 Palacio Episcopal; Museo de los Caminos
5 Roman Walls
6 Tourist Office
7 Hotel Gaudí
8 Museo del Chocolate
9 Restaurante La Paloma
10 Pensión La Peseta
11 Roman Square
12 Ayuntamiento; Roman Prison; Museo Romano
13 Ministerio
14 Restaurante Triton
15 Roman Thermal Baths
16 Pensión García
17 Roman Sewers

Museo del Chocolate Chocolate ruled Astorga's local economy in the 18th and 19th centuries, a rarely known fact commemorated by this small private collection. Looking at quirky old machinery, colourful advertising and lithographs offers a nice break from Castile's religious art circuit. The museum, at Calle de José María Goy 5, is open noon to 2 pm and 5 to 8 pm, closed Sunday afternoon and Monday (free but donation welcomed).

Ruta Romana Astorga has a respectable number of Roman ruins which can be seen on guided tours organised by the tourist office (in Spanish only) from Easter to October daily at noon and at 5 pm (200 ptas). Highlights include the town walls, thermal baths, sewers and the *ergástula* (prison). An extra 100 ptas buys entry to the **Museo Romano**.

Special Events During the last week of August, Astorga celebrates the Festividad de Santa Marta with fireworks, dances and bullfights.

Places to Stay *Pensión García (☎ 987 61 60 46, Bajada Postigo 3)* offers little more than a bed to put your head down for 2700/4200 ptas per single/double with washbasin. Much better is *Pensión La Peseta (☎ 987 61 72 75, fax 987 61 53 00, Plaza de San Bartolomé 3)* but it costs 5700/7500 ptas. The pick of the crop is *Hotel Gaudí (☎ 987 61 56 54, fax 987 61 50 40, Calle de Eduardo de Castro 6),* with doubles for 9500 ptas.

Places to Eat & Drink The local speciality is the *cocido maragata,* a stew of chickpeas, various meats, potatoes and cabbage. Tradition dictates that you first eat the meat, then the vegetables before finishing up with the broth. Portions are huge, so one order usually feeds two; the average price is 2200 ptas. Good places to try this dish include *Pensión La Peseta* (see Places to Stay) and *Restaurante Triton (☎ 987 61 87 49, Calle Gabriel Franco 12).*

For tapas and drinks, *Restaurante La Paloma (☎ 987 61 68 63, Calle de Pío Gul-*

The First Chocolatiers

Conquistador Hernán Cortés, they say, first sipped a bitter chocolate drink in the palace of Moctezuma back in the 16th century. It wasn't long before the odd new beverage became popular in Europe, but when it did, it was an exclusive drink affordable only to the nobility and the wealthy.

When the first loads landed in Spain's Galician ports, several wily Maragatos – there to pick up the cargo for distribution around the country – quickly recognised the cocoa beans' business potential and dropped a bunch in their own capital – Astorga. The townsfolk soon churned out chocolate in commercial quantities, establishing Astorga as one of the country's main centres of chocolate making by the early 17th century.

The process used in Astorga was much the same as it had been in Mexico. The cocoa beans were toasted over a wood fire, hand-peeled and the grains ground over a small fire together with sugar and often cinnamon. The liquid mixture was then poured into wooden or zinc moulds and left to cool – simple.

Things started to go sour in the late 19th century, however, as greater mechanisation and competition sent the price of chocolate in Spain plummeting. Cheaper, foreign brands flooded the Spanish market, forcing local factories to close. The industry was virtually dead by the 1950s. Today, only a handful of people keep the tradition alive, and you can still buy the real *chocolate de Astorga* in the town's little Museo del Chocolate.

lón 16) is good. To hang out with Astorga' younger set, head to *Ministerio (☎ 987 6 31 88, Calle La Bañeza 9),* a popular cafe pub that derives its cosy living room ambi ence from an abundance of framed art work

Getting There & Away By far the mos convenient way in and out of Astorga is by bus – the station is nearly across the roa from the cathedral. There are regular buse to León and Ponferrada. If you do arrive by train, the station is a couple of kilometre north of town.

Around Astorga

Whatever you make of the stories surrounding the Maragatos, the 5km detour west to **Castrillo de los Polvazares** is a pleasant diversion. The 17th-century hamlet is built of a vivid ferrous stone, its blazing orange colour made all the more striking by the brilliant green paint job on the doors and window frames. In late July the place livens up with the Fiestas de la Magdalena. If you'd like to stay, there are a couple of *hostales* and several *restaurants* to choose from.

Ponferrada

Named after an iron bridge *(pons ferrata)* built in 1092, Ponferrada, about 60km west of Astorga, is not among the region's more enticing towns. The arrival of the steel industry in the early 20th century and the resultant urban sprawl have left behind little of interest for the visitor, save its castle and what remains of the old centre. Stay in the town only if you have no other choice. The tourist office (☎ 987 42 42 36), Calle de Gil y Carrasco 4, lies in the shadow of the castle walls.

Castillo Templario The castle is an unmistakable landmark, its ancient walls rising high over the Río Sil below. Take the old bridge from the town centre over the river and head right for the castle and Plaza de la Virgen de la Encina. The entrance is round the other side, near the more modern bridge to the west. The Knights Templar raised this fortress-monastery in the 13th century and it is still an imposing edifice which, unfortunately, can only be seen on guided tours given daily at 11 am, and 1, 4.30 and 7.30 pm (200 ptas).

Churches Top billing among Ponferrada's handful of churches goes to the Gothic-Renaissance **Basílica de la Virgen de la Encina**, up the hill past the tourist office on the square of the same name. It contains accomplished reredos from the school of Gregorio Fernández. Also worth a look is the baroque **Iglesia de San Andrés** at the foot of the castle entrance.

Places to Stay & Eat If you must, finding accommodation should be no problem. Near the train station is *Hostal Roma* (☎ 987 41 19 08, Avenida Ferrocarril 16), where beds in singles/doubles with washbasin cost 1300 ptas per person. Also fairly central and a step up in comfort is the largish *Hostal Santa Cruz* (☎/fax 987 42 83 51, Calle Marcelo Macías 4), which rents rooms with bath for a reasonable 4300/4500 ptas.

Another comfortable option fairly close to the old centre is *Hostal San Miguel* (☎ 987 41 10 47, Calle de Luciana Fernández 2), which has doubles only, with TV and phone, for 5500 ptas.

Mesón Mosteiro (☎ 987 42 68 05, Calle del Reloj 10) does cheap set meals. *Mesón El Quijote* (☎ 987 42 88 90, Calle de Gregoria Campillo 3) in the new town is also OK, and there is a pair of cheap places on Calle Matachana, an alley a couple of blocks farther away from the river, including *Riaño* (☎ 987 41 11 76) at No 6.

Getting There & Away The bus station is awkwardly located at the northern end of town (take local bus No 3 for the centre). Regular buses run through Ponferrada between Villafranca del Bierzo and León (via Astorga). ALSA has up to 10 daily buses to Madrid (five hours, 3105 ptas). Heading west, there are buses to most main Galician cities, with eight to Lugo (1¾ hours, 1055 ptas) and seven to Santiago de Compostela (4½ hours, 2415 ptas).

The train station is on the western side of the centre. Nine trains daily run to León (two hours, 945 ptas) via Astorga (one hour, 515 ptas), and four or five go eastwards into Galicia. Madrid and Barcelona are served twice daily.

Las Médulas

A unique excursion takes you to the ancient Roman gold mines at Las Médulas, about 20km south-west of Ponferrada, once the main source of gold of the entire Roman empire. An army of slaves honeycombed the area with canals and tunnels (some more than 40km long!) through which they pumped water to break up the rock and free from it the precious metal. The result is a singularly unnatural natural phenomenon. The final tally allegedly came to some 3 million kilograms.

Exploring the area is best done under your own steam. To get to the heart of the former quarries, drive beyond Las Médulas village (4km south of Carucedo and the N-536 highway). Several trails weave away among chestnut patches and bizarre sunset-coloured formations left behind by the miners.

The East

BURGOS
postcode 09080 •pop 161,500

One of the most heavily visited cities in Castilla y León, Burgos is home to what many consider to be Spain's greatest Gothic cathedral. Beneath its majestic spires lies buried the local boy and legendary hero El Cid (see the boxed text 'El Cid – Myth & Man' in this chapter).

Like so many Castilian towns, Burgos started life as a strategic fortress – in 884, most historians believe – facing off both the Muslims and the rival kingdom of Navarra. It was orbited by several villages – or *burgos* – which eventually melted together to form the basis of a new city. Centuries later, Burgos thrived as a way station on the Camino de Santiago pilgrim route and as a trading centre between the interior and the northern ports.

Until well into the 17th century, the city's wealth came in from wool exports, mostly through Bilbao, which in turn sold Burgos much needed iron. Franco made Burgos his 'capital' during the civil war, and the industrial development he encouraged here in the 1950s and 60s brought a degree of prosperity.

One note about the climate: temperatures here are so extreme that locals joke that Burgos has 'nine months of winter and three months of hell.' And even the touristic slogan is a pun: 'Burgos – No te deja frío', which translates as 'Burgos – It won't leave you cold'!

Orientation

The heart of old Burgos, dominated by th cathedral, is wedged between the Río Ar lanzón and the hill to the north-west tha still bears remnants of the town's old castle South of the river, in the newer half of towr you'll find the bus and train stations.

Information

Tourist Offices The main regional touris office (☎ 947 20 31 25, fax 947 27 65 29) Plaza Alonso Martínez 7, has good infor mation on the city and entire province o Burgos. It is open 10 am to 2 pm and 5 to pm weekdays and 10 am to 2 pm Saturday The municipal tourist office (☎/fax 947 2 87 10), inside the Teatro Principal on Pase del Espolón, is open 10 am to 2 pm and 5 t 8 pm, closed Sunday afternoon.

Money There are banks all over centra Burgos. Citibank has a branch on Plaza de Rey Fernando, near the cathedral.

Post & Communications The main pos office is on Plaza del Conde de Castro You'll find a telephone locutorio with goo international rates on Plaza de Alons Martínez 3. It's open 10 am to 2 pm and to 10.30 pm daily. For Internet access, th Ciber-Café (☎ 947 20 27 22) at Calle de l Puebla 21 is a hip place but charges a rathe steep 500 ptas for the first 30 minutes, the 300 ptas for each subsequent half-hour.

Medical Services & Emergency Th Policía Nacional (☎ 947 22 04 66) is a Avenida de Castilla y León 3, but in emer gencies you can also call ☎ 091. The Hos pital General Yagüe (☎ 947 28 18 00) is a Avenida del Cid Campeador 96.

Old Quarter

Burgos' pleasant old quarter is accessed vi two main bridges across the Río Arlanzór One is the historic Puente de San Pablo, be yond which looms a romanticised **statue o El Cid**, looking as if he was about to set o in hot pursuit of some recalcitrant Mus lims. About 300m to the west is the Puent de Santa María, which culminates in th magnificent **Arco de Santa María**, once part of the 14th-century walls and now home to temporary exhibitions. Also worth a look are the delicate artesonado ceiling on the first floor and a 17th-century pharmacy. It is open 11 am to 2 pm and 5 to 9 pm, closed Sunday afternoon and Monday (free). Between the two bridges is the **Paseo de Espolón**, a lovely park for strolling or a picnic.

Catedral

It is difficult to imagine that on the site of this Gothic giant there once stood a modest Romanesque church. Work on its replacement began in 1221, and within 40 years the bulk of it was finished, a dizzying masterpiece in the French Gothic style. The twin towers, which went up in the 15th century, each represent 84m of richly decorated fantasy. Probably the most impressive of the portals is the **Puerta del Sarmental**, on the southern flank, although the honour could also go to the **Puerta de la Coronería**, on the northern side, which shows Christ surrounded by the Evangelists.

Of the chapels inside, the **Capilla del Condestable**, on the eastern end of the ambulatory behind the main altar, is a remarkable late 15th-century production. Bridging Gothic and plateresque styles, it also contains the tombs of the Constable of Castile and his wife. The sculptures at this end of the church behind the high altar are a highlight, as is the **Escalera Dorada** (Gilded Stairway, 1520) on the northern side, the handiwork of Diego de Siloé.

Beneath the star-vaulted central dome lies the **tomb of El Cid**, while the most intriguing chapel is probably the first on the right, called **Capilla del Santísimo Cristo**. It harbours a much revered 13th-century crucifix made from buffalo hide (known as the Cristo de Burgos). Also worth a look is the peaceful cloister.

At the time of writing, great swathes of the cathedral were off limits because of restoration, which may well continue for a few more years. It is open 9.30 am to 1 pm and 4 to 7 pm daily. Entry to the cloister and adjoining **Museo Catedralicio** is 400 ptas.

Churches

Of the half-dozen or so other churches dotted about the city, a couple stand out.

Iglesia de San Esteban, a powerful Gothic structure of the 14th century, houses the **Museo del Retablo** with its collection of mainly 16th- and 17th-century altarpieces. In summer, it's open 10.30 am to 2 pm and 4.30 to 7 pm, closed Sunday afternoon and Monday. In winter, you'll find doors unlocked on weekends only.

The other is **Iglesia de San Nicolás**, most noteworthy for its humungous carved stone altar by Francisco de Colonia with scenes from the life of St Nicolas. It's open weekends and all day Monday year round. From July to September, weekday hours are 9 am to 2 pm and 4 to 8 pm; the rest of the year it's only open 6.30 to 7.30 pm.

Monasterio de las Huelgas

After the cathedral, this monastery is second in importance among Burgos' sights. About a 30-minute walk west of the city centre on the southern bank, it was once among the most prominent monasteries in all Spain. Founded in 1187 by Eleanor of Aquitaine, daughter of Henry II of England and wife of Alfonso VIII of Castile, it's still home to 35 Cistercian nuns today.

A small section of the church is the only part accessible without a guided tour (in Spanish only), which you should join if you want to fully appreciate this place's treasures. The three main naves of the church are walled off and are a veritable royal pantheon, containing the tombs of numerous kings and queens, including those of Eleanor and Alfonso. Also here is a spectacular gilded Renaissance altar topped by a larger-than-life Jesus figure being taken off the cross.

The highlight, though, is the **Museo de Ricas Telas**, reached via a lovely Romanesque cloister known as Las Claustrillas. It contains robes and garments once worn by the very royals interred in the aforementioned tombs. These were opened in 1942 and the clothes removed for conservation purposes.

Guided tours depart from 10.30 am to 1.15 pm and 3.30 to 5.45 pm daily, except

BURGOS

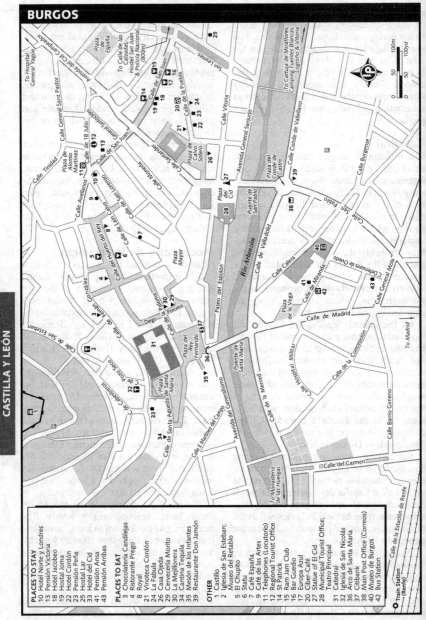

PLACES TO STAY
10 Hotel Norte y Londres
13 Pensión Victoria
18 Hotel Jacobeo
19 Hostal Joma
22 Hotel Cordón
23 Pensión Peña
25 Hostal Lar
33 Hotel del Cid
41 Pensión Ansa
43 Pensión Arribas

PLACES TO EAT
3 Chocolatería Candilejas
8 Ristorante Prego
9 Royal
21 Vinoteca Cordón
24 La Fabula
26 Casa Ojeda
29 Cervecería Morito
30 La Mejillonera
34 Cantina Tequila
35 Mesón de los Infantes
39 Restaurante Don Jamón

OTHER
1 Castillo
2 Iglesia de San Esteban;
   Museo del Retablo
5 El Chupito
6 Statu
7 Café España
11 Café de las Artes
   Telephones (Locutorio)
12 Regional Tourist Office
15 St Patrick
16 Ram Jam Club
17 Bar Guedio
20 Europa Azul
27 Ciber-Café
28 Statue of El Cid
   Municipal Tourist Office;
   Teatro Principal
31 Catedral
32 Iglesia de San Nicolás
36 Arco de Santa María
37 Citibank
38 Main Post Office (Correos)
40 Museo de Burgos
42 Bus Station

Sunday afternoon and Monday (shorter hours in winter); 700 ptas, students 300 ptas, free on Wednesday for EU passport holders.

Women who fancy a stint with the Cistercian nuns in the Monasterio de las Huelgas can stay for up to eight days, paying a voluntary contribution. For more information, call ☎ 947 20 16 30 or fax 947 27 36 86.

About 750m west of the convent is the **Hospital del Rey**, once a hospice for pilgrims on the Camino de Santiago and now the law faculty. Of interest is the plateresque Puerta del Romero.

Cartuja de Miraflores

You can only visit the church of this strict Carthusian monastery, located in peaceful woodlands 4km east of the city centre. But it is worth the effort for a trio of 15th-century masterworks by Gil de Siloé, the most dazzling of which is without doubt the ornate star-shaped alabaster tomb of Juan II and Isabel of Portugal, the parents of Isabel la Católica. Gil de Siloé also carved the tomb of her brother, the Infante Alfonso, and helped with the giant retablo that forms a worthy backdrop to the royal mausoleum. In a side chapel is an incredibly lifelike statue of the orden's founder, San Bruno, who hailed from Cologne.

The church is open 10.15 am to 3 pm and 4 to 6 pm Monday to Saturday. On Sunday and holidays it is open 11.20 am to 12.30 pm, 1 to 3 pm and 4 to 6 pm (free). It's worth investing 50 ptas in a detailed English-language pamphlet. The walk to the monastery takes about one hour and leads along the Río Arlanzón through the lush Parque de la Quinta and is particularly pleasant.

Museo de Burgos

The archaeological section of the museum, housed in the Casa de Miranda, contains some fine Gothic tombs and other artefacts covering a wide period. In the Casa de Ángulo is a fine arts collection, including some modern pieces. The museum is open 10 am to 2 pm and 4 to 7.30 pm Tuesday to Friday, 10 am to 2 pm and 4.45 to 8.15 pm Saturday, and 10 am to 2 pm Sunday (200 ptas, free for students daily and for everyone on weekends).

Special Events

Burgos' big fiestas take place in the last days of June and the first two weeks of July to celebrate the Festividad de San Pedro y San Pablo (Feast of Sts Peter and Paul). There are bullfights, pilgrimages and much merry-making, particularly on the first Sunday of July, the Día de las Peñas. Another big event is the Festividad de San Lesmes, for the city's patron saint, on 30 January.

Places to Stay – Budget

Camping & Hostels The nearest camping ground, *Camping Fuentes Blancas (☎/fax 947 48 60 16)*, is about 4km from the centre on the road to the Cartuja de Miraflores. It's open April to September and served by hourly bus No 26. Charges are 540 ptas each per person and car, plus 475 ptas for a small tent.

Hostales & Pensiones Beg, borrow and/or steal to secure a bed at *Pensión Peña (☎ 947 20 62 23, Calle de la Puebla 18)*. Impeccable, completely refurbished singles/doubles sport delightful touches such as handpainted washbasins and cost a mere 1700/2900 ptas.

Also in the old centre is *Pensión Victoria (☎ 947 20 15 42, Calle de San Juan 3)*, which comes reader-recommended and has OK rooms with washbasin for 2800/4000 ptas. *Hostal Joma (☎ 947 20 33 50, Calle de San Juan 26)* is basic but in the heart of the action. Rooms go for 1750/3100 ptas.

If you're strapped for cash and don't mind being a bit away from the centre, a couple of places near the bus station might do just fine. Virtually around the corner from the terminal is the decidedly no-frills *Pensión Arribas (☎ 947 26 62 92, Calle de los Defensores de Oviedo 6)*, with simple rooms (doubles only) for 3000 ptas. For slightly more comfort head to the homey *Pensión Ansa (☎ 947 20 47 67, Calle de Miranda 9)*, opposite the bus station, which has nicer rooms at 3000/4200 ptas, but some of the singles are tiny.

Places to Stay – Mid-Range

An excellent choice in this category is *Hostal San Juan (☎/fax 947 20 51 34,*

Calle de Bernabe Perez Ortiz 1), whose quirky Trotsky-lookalike proprietor rents out pleasant, recently overhauled, rooms with TV, shower and toilet for 6000 ptas, single or double occupancy. Rates go down to 3000/4500 ptas from October to June.

Another good bet is **Hostal Lar** (☎/fax 947 20 96 55, Calle de Cardenal Benlloch 1), which charges 4000/6100 ptas for rooms with private facilities.

Heading up the scale is the stylish and fairly new **Hotel Jacobeo** (☎ 947 26 01 02, fax 947 26 01 00, ☻ jacobeo@cidmultimedia .es, Calle de San Juan 24). Considering the wide range of amenities offered, it's actually quite good value at 6600/9000 ptas (less in the low season).

If they're full, you could try the nearby 50-room **Hotel Norte y Londres** (☎ 947 26 41 25, fax 947 27 73 75, Plaza de Alonso Martínez 10) in a rather charming old build-ing near the tourist office. Comfy rooms with bath, TV and phone cost 5500/9800 ptas.

Places to Stay – Top End
If you can spare a little more dough, you can make an enormous leap in quality by stay-ing at **Hotel Cordón** (☎ 947 26 50 00, fax 947 20 02 69, Calle de la Puebla 6), where fine rooms cost 8000/14,000 ptas. Or book yourself into what many consider the city's best establishment, **Hotel del Cid** (☎ 947 20 87 15, fax 947 26 94 60, Plaza de Santa María 8), which charges 9600/16,000 ptas.

Places to Eat
A good place for tapas and a beer is **Restaur-ante Don Jamón** (☎ 947 27 28 72), on Plaza del Conde de Castro. **Cervecería Mo-rito**, on Calle de la Sombrerería, is very popular with locals for its cheap drinks, bud-get-friendly platos combinados and good

El Cid – Myth & Man

In Spanish history, the name of El Cid is often associated with bravery, unswerving loyalty and superhuman strength. It is a romantic, idealised image, based less on historical accounts than on a 12th-century epic poem in which the anonymous author extols the virtues and ex-ploits of this legendary soldier. Reality, though, presents a much different picture.

El Cid (from the Arabic sidi for 'chief' or 'lord') was born Rodrígo Diaz in Vivar, a hamlet about 10km north of Burgos, in 1043. After the death of Ferdinand I, he – ill-advisedly, as it turned out – became involved in the power struggle among the king's five heirs, which ended in his banishment from Castile in 1076. He then embarked on a career as a sol-dier of fortune, offering his services to this ruler and that, not caring whether they were Christian or Muslim but growing more powerful and wealthy with each exploit.

Eventually though, upon hearing that the Moors had expelled all the Christians from Valencia, El Cid decided to recapture the city and to become its ruler. This he accomplished in 1094 after a devastating siege. After this final adventure, the man also known as El Campeador (the Champion), decided it was time to retire. He spent the remainder of his days in Valencia where he died in 1099. His remains were returned to Burgos where he lies buried, along with his wife, Jimena, in the cathedral.

MARTIN HARRIS

patatas bravas (fried potatoes with spicy tomato sauce). Mollusc fans will want to stop in at the nearby *La Mejillonera (Calle de la Paloma 33)*, a stand-up place where mussel snacks can be had for 300 ptas per plate.

Leaning a little more to the tourist trade, but solid nonetheless, is *Mesón de los Infantes (☎ 947 20 59 82)*, in a courtyard behind the Arco de Santa María, where set lunches go for 1600 ptas and a three-course dinner will set you back about 4000 ptas. For a break from the Castilian diet, dig into Mexican-style burritos or tacos at *Cantina Tequila (☎ 947 20 92 98, Calle de Santa Agueda 10)*. If you choose carefully, you'll lighten your wallet by just 1200 ptas or less here.

Deep pockets aren't required either at the cafeteria-style *Royal (Plaza de Huerto del Rey 23)*, which serves a wide range of platos combinados, salads and sandwiches. On the same square at No 4 is *Ristorante Prego (Calle del Huerto del Rey 4)*, which does scrummy pizzas at a pricey 1700 ptas each, while pasta dishes start at 1000 ptas.

For a splurge, try *Casa Ojeda (☎ 947 20 90 52, Calle de la Victoria 5)*, a Burgos classic all sheathed in dark wood and specialising in plate-bending meat dishes cooked in a clay oven. The upstairs dining room is popular with the expense account crowd, but you can save money by eating in the equally cosy downstairs bar area where platos combinados clock in at 1400 ptas.

Calle de la Puebla has a couple of restaurants with a more contemporary flair. The brightly pigmented *La Fabula (☎ 947 26 30 92)* at No 18 does nouveau Castilian cuisine with slimmed down rice and fish dishes mostly around the 2000 ptas mark. At No 3 is *Vinoteca Cordón (☎ 947 27 72 79)* whose impressive wine selection complements the gourmet food. The set lunch costs 2200 ptas.

For dessert, head for *Chocolatería Candilejas (Calle de Fernán González 36)*, which serves killer cakes, churros and milk shakes *(batidos)*, all homemade. It's open daily after 6 pm.

Entertainment

Cafes Burgos has a few pleasant little cafes to hang around in, one of the better ones being *Café España (Calle de Lain Calvo 12)*. You might also like to pop in at *Café de las Artes* a few doors down at No 31 which has a magazine rack, occasional live music and, as its name implies, has an artsy vibe.

Bars & Clubs If you want a night on the tiles, ease into it in the bars along Calle de San Juan. Popular haunts along this drag include *Ram Jam Club* at No 29, *Bar Guedio* at No 30 and *Europa Azul* at No 34. Or for a Guinness try *St Patrick* at No 23.

From here the marcha migrates to the area around Calle del Huerto del Rey, locally known as Las Llanas. Here you'll find several fairly noisy music bars to suit most tastes, including *Statu* and *El Chupito*.

There are few decent clubs in Burgos, but the last stage of the pub-crawl scene is the Bernardos area, around Calle de las Calzadas, where you'll find more than your fill of alcohol and loud music.

Getting There & Away

Bus The bus station is at Calle de Miranda 3. Continental-Auto runs up to 12 buses daily to Madrid, more on Fridays (1950 ptas). The same company also services Vitoria (920 ptas) and San Sebastián (1800 ptas). Buses also run to Bilbao, Pamplona, Logroño and Valladolid, as well as most towns in Burgos province.

Train Burgos is connected with Madrid up to nine times daily (four hours, 3060 ptas) and with Bilbao up to six times daily (three hours, 2000 ptas). Several trains serve León (two hours, 2100 ptas) and Salamanca (3½ hours, 2500 ptas). There are also connections to Galicia, Barcelona and other Spanish cities.

Car & Motorcycle For Madrid, take the N-1 directly south. The N-234 branches off south-east to Soria and on to Zaragoza and ultimately Barcelona. The N-623 north leads to Santander, while the A-1 autopista goes most of the way to Vitoria and hooks up with the A-68 autopista to Bilbao.

CASTILLA Y LEÓN

AROUND BURGOS
Quintanilla de las Viñas

If you take the Soria road (N-234) out of Burgos, a worthwhile stop some 35km out is the 7th-century **Ermita de Santa María de Lara**. This modest Visigothic hermitage preserves some fine bas-reliefs around its external walls, which are among the better examples of religious art from this era to survive in Spain. It is supposedly open 9.30 am to 2 pm and 4 to 7 pm (9 am to 4 pm in winter) Wednesday to Sunday, but you may have to track down the guardian in the village itself.

Covarrubias

This pretty hamlet struggles to digest the tourist influx in summer and on weekends. Spread along the banks of the Río Arlanza, it is made up of a cluster of attractive arcaded half-timbered houses fronting a network of little squares. More solid is the squat 10th-century **Torreón de Doña Urraca**, towering over the remains of Covarrubias' medieval walls.

A little farther along the river, the Late Gothic **Colegiata de San Cosme y Damián** rises up. It has nice cloisters and contains the stone tomb of Fernán González, the 10th-century founder of Castile. It's open 10.30 am to 2 pm and 4 to 7 pm, closed Monday (250 ptas).

Covarrubias is a charming spot to stay. *Casa Galín (☎/fax 947 40 65 52, Plaza de Doña Urraca 4)* has comfortable doubles with bathroom for 4000 ptas. Singles/doubles with washbasin go for 2000/3500 ptas. For a bit more money, you can stay at the historic *casa rural* **Los Castros** *(☎ 947 40 63 68, Calle de los Castros 10),* whose five doubles at 6000 ptas (breakfast included) are a veritable steal. Another good bet is the charming new *Hotel Rey Chindasvinto (☎ 947 40 65 60, Plaza del Rey Chindasvinto 5),* which offers a full range of amenities for 5000/9000 ptas – not bad for a three-star hotel.

Three buses travel from Burgos to Covarrubias on weekdays, and one on Saturday. The C-110 leads west to Lerma and east to hook up with the Burgos-Soria highway (N-234).

Santo Domingo de Silos

This is the monastery whose monks made the pop charts in the mid-90s, in Britain and elsewhere, with recordings of Gregorian chants. It appears probable that, as long ago as the 7th century, the Visigoths had a religious centre here. But it's not until the arrival of Santo Domingo (St Dominic) in 1040 that a surer light penetrates the swirling mists of our Dark Age ignorance. He began construction of the Benedictine abbey, still inhabited by 26 monks today (after a period of disuse in the wake of the great confiscation of church property in the 19th century).

The jewel is the cloister, a treasure chest of some of the most remarkable and imaginative Romanesque art in all Spain. As you proceed around the courtyard, take a closer look at the sculpted capitals depicting everything from lions to Harpies, intermingled with occasional floral and geometrical motifs betraying the never distant influence of Islamic art in Spain. More important still are the pieces executed on the corner pillars, representing episodes from the life of Christ.

The galleries are covered by mudéjar artesonado ceilings from the 14th century. In the north-eastern corner sits a 13th-century image of the Virgin Mary carved in stone, and nearby is the original burial spot of Santo Domingo.

Much of the monastery is off limits to visitors, but the guide you will compulsorily have at your side will also show you inside the 17th-century *botica*, or pharmacy. The museum contains the predictable collection of religious artworks, Flemish tapestries and the odd medieval sarcophagus. The 18th-century church is considerably less interesting.

Church doors are open 6 am to 2 pm and 4 to 9.30 pm daily. The cloister and pharmacy may be visited from 10 am to 1 pm and 4.30 to 6 pm daily, closed Sunday morning. Guided tours are 250 ptas, free on Monday.

If you'd like to hear the monks chant, come to the church at 6, 7.30 or 9 am (noon on Sunday) or at 1.45, 7 or 9.40 pm; free. Hours may vary slightly throughout the year.

Men can rent a heated room here for 3000 ptas with meals included, but it's a

CASTILLA Y LEÓN

popular thing to do and you'll need to book well ahead. Call the Padre Hospedero between 11 am and 1 pm on ☎ 947 38 07 68 or ☎ 947 39 00 68. You can stay for a period of three to 10 days.

Otherwise, there's a handful of lodging options. The cheapest is **Hostal Cruces** (☎ 947 39 00 64, Plaza Mayor 2), offering decent singles/doubles with bath for 3000/5000 ptas. There are two other dearer hotels on the same square. **Hotel Arco de San Juan** (☎/fax 947 39 00 74, Pradera de San Juan 1) is nearby and has good rooms with bathroom and phone for 4000/6500 ptas.

Autobuses Arceredillo runs two buses from Burgos to Santo Domingo de Silos on weekdays and one on Saturday.

Desfiladero de Yecla
A couple of kilometres down the back road (BU-911) to Caleruega from Santo Domingo, the spectacular Desfiladero de Yecla, a magnificent gorge, opens up. It is easily visited thanks to the installation of a walkway. There is a small office in Santo Domingo de Silos, nearly opposite Hostal Cruces, where you can get information on the gorge.

ROUTES NORTH OF BURGOS
Most people heading north from Burgos just belt up the highway until they reach Cantabria, the Picos de Europa mountains or the Basque Country. Although at least one bus daily serves most towns from Burgos on weekdays, getting around these parts is laborious without your own transport.

Valle de Sedano & North
The N-623 highway carves a pretty trail from Burgos, particularly between the mountain passes of Portillo de Fresno and Puerto de Carrales. About 15km north of the Portillo de Fresno, a side road takes you through a series of intriguing villages in the Valle de Sedano. The town of the same name has a fine 17th-century church, but more interesting is the little Romanesque one above Moradillo de Sedano; the sculpted main doorway is outstanding.

Plenty of villages flank the highway on the way north, but **Orbaneja del Castillo** is

the area's best-kept secret. Take the turn-off for Escalada and follow the bumpy road until you reach the waterfall. Park where you can and climb up beside the waterfall to the village, completely hidden from below. A dramatic backdrop of strange rock walls lends this charming spot a uniquely enchanting air.

SOUTH TO THE RÍO DUERO
The road south from Burgos to Madrid crosses some particularly bleak Castilian country. Still, there are some worthwhile places to check out. At Aranda de Duero you could convert your north-south flight into a riverside excursion from east to west along the Río Duero, the third-longest and second-biggest river in the Iberian Peninsula.

Lerma
An ancient settlement, Lerma hit the big time in the early 17th century when Grand Duke Don Francisco de Rojas y Sandoval, minister under Felipe II from 1598 to 1618, launched an ambitious project to create another El Escorial. He clearly failed, but the cobbled streets of the old town retain a degree of charm today.

Pass through the **Arco de la Cárcel** (Prison Gate) off the main road to Burgos to climb up the long Calle del General Mola to the massive Plaza Mayor. This is fronted by the oversized **Palacio Ducal**, symbol of the duke's megalomania and notable for its courtyards. To the right of the square is the Dominican nuns' **Convento de San Blas**. A short distance north-west of Plaza Mayor, at the opposite end from the palace, opens up a pretty passageway and viewpoint over the Río Arlanza, whose arches connect with the 17th-century **Convento de Santa Teresa** on Plaza de Santa Clara, which is also home to the tourist office.

Pensión Martín (☎ 947 17 00 28, Calle del General Mola 23) rents beds for 1500 ptas in singles, doubles and triples. For more comfort, **Hostal Docar** (☎ 947 17 10 73, Calle de Santa Teresa de Jesús 18) charges 3900/5800 ptas for singles/doubles with bathroom. For more charm, try the casa rural **El Zaguan** (☎ 947 17 21 65, Calle de

CASTILLA Y LEÓN

Barquillo 6), which is in an 18th-century home with stone walls and beamed ceilings. Rooms (doubles only) with bath and TV cost 6000 ptas.

The traditional *Mesón del Duque* (☎ 947 17 21 22, *Calle de Audiencia 2*), just off Plaza Mayor, is not a bad choice of restaurant.

There are regular buses from Burgos, and some buses coming north from Aranda de Duero or Madrid also stop here, as do trains running between Madrid and Burgos.

Aranda de Duero

The main attraction in this crossroads town is the main portal of the Late Gothic **Iglesia de Santa María**. This remarkably rich sculptural flourish was executed in the 15th and 16th centuries and incorporates scenes ranging from the Three Kings at Bethlehem to the death of Christ. The nearby earlier Gothic **Iglesia de San Juan** is also worth a look.

There's precious little to keep you here overnight, but you will have a few options. Closest to the old part of town is *Pensión Sole* (☎ 947 50 06 07, *Puerta Nueva 16*), with singles only going for 3500 ptas without bath or 4000 ptas with. An alternative is *Hostal Rosales* (☎ 947 50 21 90, *Calle de Rosales 5*), which charges 1700/2600 ptas for singles/doubles with washbasin and 3400 ptas for doubles with shower and toilet.

For classic Castilian cooking – roast lamb – several reasonable *restaurants* compete for trade on and around Plaza del Arco Isilla. Look for the 'Asador' signs.

Buses connect Aranda with Madrid and most major cities in Castilla y León and some beyond. Several trains stop here as well. Aranda is right on the N-I for Burgos or Madrid, or you can branch off east or west on the N-122 to follow the Río Duero.

Peñaranda de Duero

About 20km east of Aranda on the C-111, the village of Peñaranda de Duero exudes considerably greater charm. A Celtic fortress village in origin, most of its surviving riches are grouped around the Plaza Mayor. The **Palacio Condes de Miranda** is a grand Renaissance palace with a fine plateresque entrance, double-arched patio and beautiful

ceilings in various styles. Free guided tours operate up to eight times daily except Monday. The 16th-century **Iglesia de Santa Ana** is also impressive in that it integrates columns and busts found at the Roman settlement of Clunia into an otherwise baroque design. For superb views of the village and surrounding country, take a walk up to the medieval castle ruins.

Hotel Señorío de Vélez (☎ 947 55 22 01, *fax 947 55 22 02, Plaza de los Duques de Alba 1*), right in the heart of town, has its own restaurant and charges 4000/6500 ptas for singles/doubles. There are four *casas rurales* in the area as well.

If you are driving around and have time to kill, there are modest Roman ruins at **Clunia**, about 15km north-east, and an interesting monastery at **Vid**, just 7km south on the N-122 between Aranda and Soria.

Sepúlveda
postcode 40300 • pop 1400 • elev 1009m

With its houses staggered along a ridge carved out by the gorge of the Río Duratón, Sepúlveda is one of many weekend escape hatches for stifled madrileños. The town, known under the Romans as Septempublicam, lies about 50km south of Aranda de Duero, west of the N-I and belongs to the province of Segovia.

The warm ochre tones of Sepúlveda's public buildings, fronting the central Plaza de España, are an enviable setting for a hot Sunday roast; the town is considered one of the best in Spain for roast lamb. The ayuntamiento houses a tourist office and backs onto what remains of the old castle. High above it all rises impassively the 11th-century **Iglesia del Salvador**, considered the prototype of this variant of Castilian Romanesque, marked by the single arched portico. It is open on the third Sunday of every month.

Hostal Postigo (☎ 921 54 01 72, *Calle del Conde Sepúlveda 22*), just off Plaza de España, charges 5000/6000 ptas for singles/doubles with your own facilities. If it's full, try *Hostal Hernanz* (☎ 921 54 03 78, *Calle del Conde Sepúlveda 4*), which asks 4000/6000 ptas for comfortable rooms with a good range of amenities. Both places have

CASTILLA Y LEÓN

restaurants attached, but there's several more around Plaza de España, including *Restaurante Filka* (☎ 921 54 00 87) at No 2. Here, as in the others, a huge dish with a quarter of a lamb (more than enough for two people), well roasted in a wood-fired oven will cost about 4500 ptas.

At least two buses link Sepúlveda daily with Madrid, while Segovia is served once daily except Sunday.

Parque Natural del Hoz del Duratón

A good chunk of land north-west of Sepúlveda has been constituted as a natural park. The centrepiece is the Hoz del Duratón (Duratón gorge), in particular where it widens out behind the dam just south of Burgomillodo. A dirt track leads 5km west from the hamlet of Villaseca to the **Ermita de San Frutos**. In ruins now, the hermitage was founded in the 7th century by San Frutos and his brother and sister, San Valentín and Santa Engracia. They lie buried in a tiny chapel nearby. This is a magic place, overlooking one of the many serpentine bends in the gorge with squadrons of buzzards and eagles soaring above. Weekends can get claustrophobic, as a surprising number of people crowd in, pretty much wrecking the atmosphere. Some people take kayaks up to Burgomillodo to launch themselves down the waters of the canyon.

Duratón

About 6km east of Sepúlveda, just outside the village of Duratón, the **Iglesia de Nuestra Señora de la Anunciación** is a fine example of Romanesque church-building in rural Castile.

Castilnovo

Some 12km south of Sepúlveda, this rather cute little castle has more the air of a private conceit by some moneyed eccentric. Originally built in the 14th century and largely mudéjar, it has undergone a lot of alterations and is currently owned by the Associación Cultural Hispano-Mexicana, which also maintains a museum. Visits are by prior

arrangement only (☎ 921 53 11 33) and cost 500 ptas per person.

WEST ALONG THE RÍO DUERO
Peñafiel
postcode 47300 • pop 5050

At the heart of the Ribera del Duero wine region, Peñafiel is home to the new state-of-the-art **Museo Provincial del Vino**, cleverly ensconced within the walls of the mighty **Castillo de Peñafiel**. If you read Spanish, you will probably enjoy learning about the ins-and-outs of wine growing, production and history through interactive displays, dioramas, backlit panels and computer terminals.

Not requiring any language skills, a visit to the castle itself is perhaps even more memorable. Riding high above the medieval Castilian stronghold of Peñafiel, it must be about the longest and narrowest castle in Spain. Its crenellated walls and towers stretch over 200m and were raised and modified over 400 years from the 11th century onward. The sight of it in the distance alone is worth the effort of getting here.

Both the castle and museum are open 11.30 am to 2.30 pm and 4.30 to 8.30 pm daily except Monday (slightly shorter hours from October to Easter). Entry is 600 ptas or 250 ptas for the castle only. Wine tastings are an additional 1000 ptas.

There's a handful of lodging options, including the central *Hostal Chicopa* (☎ 983 88 07 82, Plaza de España 2), with basic but OK rooms for 2500/3200 ptas. Just off the square is the small, pedestrianised town centre, and on Calle de José Antonio Girón de Velasco you'll find several *bars* and *Restaurante El Bodegón* (☎ 983 88 07 43) at No 16, where you can dig into a moderately priced meal.

Four or five buses a day run to Valladolid, about 60km west of here.

EAST ALONG THE RÍO DUERO
From Aranda, you can follow the Río Duero east towards Almazán, or take the N-122 direct for Soria, Castilla y León's easternmost provincial capital. Both routes are dotted with curious little *pueblos* (villages) and plenty of worthwhile detours. Apart from

CASTILLA Y LEÓN

what is mentioned below, it is worth heading off on your own tangent down the rural byways. Some of the hamlets you encounter in this area really give the impression that time has stood still for centuries.

San Esteban de Gormaz

This dusty little town contains a couple of little Romanesque gems hidden away in its centre, the 11th-century churches of San Miguel and Del Rivero. Both sport the porticoed side galleries that characterise the Romanesque style of the Segovia and Burgos areas, and indeed San Miguel is thought by some to have served as a model for other churches. There are three places to stay here if you need to.

El Burgo de Osma
postcode 42300 • pop 5000

Some 12km east of San Esteban de Gormaz and veering away from the Duero, this town is a real surprise packet. Once important enough to host its own university, El Burgo de Osma is an elegant if somewhat rundown little old town, dominated by a quite remarkable cathedral. Nearby lies the partly excavated Celtiberian castro of Uxama, the area's first settlement.

Begun in the 12th century as an essentially Romanesque building, the **catedral** was continued in a Gothic key and finally topped with a weighty baroque tower. It's filled with art treasures, including the 16th-century main altarpiece (a collaboration by Juan de Juní and Juan Picardo). The jewel in the crown is the so-called Beato de Osma, a precious 11th-century codex (manuscript) that can be seen in the Capilla Mayor. Also of note is the light-flooded, circular Capilla de Palafox, a rare example of the neoclassical style in this region. The Museo Catedralicio is just off the Late Gothic cloister and contains a worthwhile exhibit of religious artefacts. They can be seen on guided tours offered from 10 am to 1 pm and 5 to 7 pm, closed Monday in winter (350 ptas). Entry to the cathedral itself is free.

From Plaza de San Pedro, where the cathedral stands, Calle Mayor, its portico borne by an uneven phalanx of stone and wooden pillars, leads into Plaza Mayor. This is fronted by the 18th-century ayuntamiento and the more sumptuous Hospital de San Agustín, now a contemporary art gallery; entry is free.

Outside the main approach to the town is the 16th-century Renaissance former university. If you exit El Burgo from near Plaza de San Pedro, take a left for the village of Osma and high up on a hill you'll see the ruins of the Castillo de Osma.

Of the handful of places to stay, the cheapest is *Casa Agapito* (☎ 975 34 02 12, Calle de la Universidad 1), which charges 2000/3000 ptas for singles/doubles with washbasin; doubles with shower and toilet are 4000 ptas. On the same street at No 33 is *Hostal La Perdiz* (☎ 975 34 03 09), where greater comfort in rooms with TV, phone and bath costs 5500/9000 ptas.

The discerning traveller with dosh will go for *Hotel Il Virrey* (☎ 975 34 13 11, fax 975 34 08 55, Calle Mayor 2-4), where charming rooms with all mod-cons go for 7000/11,000 ptas. Rates soar on weekends in February and March when Spaniards from as far afield as Madrid flock here to 'pig out', as it were. After the ritual slaughter of a pig in the morning, diners indulge in an all-you-can eat foodathon later that day. At 5000 ptas per head it's not the cheapest feed you'll ever have, but the experience is quite unique. Other restaurant choices are rather limited. A fairly new entry is *Asador El Burgo* (☎ 975 34 04 89, Calle Mayor 71), which does the usual meaty Castilian fare with aplomb and at reasonable prices.

Buses link El Burgo with Soria and places as far afield as Valladolid. Minor roads lead south to Berlanga de Duero and north to the Cañón del Río Lobos.

Cañón del Río Lobos

Some 15km north of El Burgo de Osma, the Parque Natural del Río Lobos not only presents some rather bizarre rockscapes, but is home to vultures and various other birds of prey. Just outside the park is an information centre, and about 4km in from the road, along the tiny river, stands the Romanesque

CASTILLA Y LEÓN

Ermita de San Bartolomé. You can walk deeper into the park but free camping is forbidden.

If you want to stay in the area, the best choice is El Burgo de Osma. *Camping Cañón del Río Lobos* (☎ 975 36 35 65), near Ucero, is open from June to the end of August.

Gormaz

Some 14km south of El Burgo, on the Río Duero, is the virtual ghost town of Gormaz. The great castle with 21 towers was built by the Muslims in the 10th century and altered in the 13th. Its ruins still convey enormous dignity and the views alone justify the effort of getting here. The nearest place to stay is in nearby Quintanas de Gormaz where you'll find the pleasant *Casa Grande de Gormaz* (☎ 975 34 09 82) on Camino de las Fuentes. This grand old house has 11 singles/doubles, most of which cost 6000/8500 ptas, though some doubles clock in at 10,000 ptas. For sustenance, you've got a couple of reasonably priced *restaurants* to choose from.

Berlanga de Duero

About 15km east of Gormaz, Berlanga is lorded over by a powerful but ruinous castle. Down below, the **Colegiata de Santa María del Mercado** is a fine Late Gothic church, with the star-shaped vaulting inside perhaps its most pleasing aspect. It's usually closed; ask in town for María Jesus if you want to take a peek inside. The area around the pretty Plaza Mayor, with the occasional Renaissance house, is equally charming. Outside the old town centre on a desolate open plot is the Picota – to which petty criminals were tied in the good old days.

Hotel Fray Tomás (☎ 975 34 30 33, fax 975 34 31 69, Calle Real 16) has comfortable singles/doubles with bath, which are perhaps a tad overpriced at 4000/7000 ptas. A more reasonable alternative is *Posada Los Leones* (☎ 975 34 32 75), a casa rural on Calle de los Leones, with attached restaurant, which charges 4000/7000 ptas.

Beyond Berlanga de Duero

About 8km south-east of the town stands the **Ermita de San Baudelio**. The simple exterior belies a remarkable 11th-century Mozarabic interior – a real gem. A great pillar in the centre of the only nave opens up at the top like a palm tree to create horseshoe arches. Until recently, the hermitage's walls were decorated with Mozarabic and 12th-century Romanesque frescoes, but these have now been moved to the Prado in Madrid. It is open 10 am to 2 pm Wednesday to Sunday all year. Afternoon hours (Wednesday to Saturday only) vary by season but are usually from 4 to 7 pm. Another 17km south, **Rello** still retains much of its medieval defensive walls.

To Madrid

For those wanting to maintain a vaguely southerly trajectory from this part of Castilla y León, the N-110 winds south-west from San Esteban de Gormaz to join up with the N-I highway between Madrid and Burgos just short of the Puerto de Somosierra mountain pass. Along the way, stop in at Ayllón and Riaza.

Ayllón This village lies about 50km south-west of El Burgo de Osma and bathes in the same orange glow that characterises El Burgo's townscape. You enter by a medieval archway and immediately are confronted on the right by the ornate facade of a late-15th-century noble family's mansion in Isabelline style. The uneven, porticoed Plaza Mayor is capped at one end by the Romanesque Iglesia de San Miguel, and nearby stands the Renaissance-era Iglesia de Santa María la Mayor. Turn right behind this and follow the narrow street for about half a kilometre and you will come to the extensive remains of another Romanesque church, now oddly incorporated into a rambling private residence. There are two *hostales* should you get stuck.

Riaza About 20km south of Ayllón, Riaza's main claim to fame is its charming old circular Plaza Mayor. The sandy arena in the centre is still used for bullfights. If you want to stay, about the cheapest place is *Hostal Las Robles* (☎ 921 55 00 54) where singles/doubles cost 1500/2200 ptas. Bull fans might like to eat at the *Restaurante Matimore* on

CASTILLA Y LEÓN

Plaza Mayor. It is a mini-museum of bull-fight posters, and the walls also support four rather large stuffed bulls' heads.

Six kilometres away is the local ski resort of **La Pinilla**. It's nothing superb, but if there have been good falls and you happen to have your skis handy...

SORIA
postcode 42080 • pop 32,400 • elev 1055m
As far as provincial capitals go, Soria is rather diminutive. But what it lacks in size, it makes up for in substance with its laid-back old centre and a sprinkling of stunning monuments sure to impress not only architecture and art history buffs. Its setting on the Río Duero has also inspired several poets, most notably Antonio Machado. Calm and laid-back in the daytime, Soria has a surprisingly lively nightlife.

History
Although possibly populated before Roman times, Soria only appears in the history books with the arrival of the Muslims. Until the crowns of Castile and Aragón were united at the end of the 15th century, Soria was a hive of commercial and political activity, straddling the frontier territory between Old Castile, Aragón and Navarra. With the decline of the wool trade after the 16th century, however, it lost importance and, along with the expulsion of the Jews, much of its business drive.

Information
The tourist office (☎/fax 975 21 20 52), on Plaza de Ramón y Cajal, is open 9 am to 2 pm and 5 to 7 pm weekdays and 10 am to 2 pm and 5 to 8 pm weekends, less in winter. There are several banks near the tourist office. The main post office is on Paseo del Espolón and a small telephone locutorio is on Calle de la Aduana Vieja. The most central hospital is the Hospital General (☎ 975 22 10 00) at Paseo de Santa Barbara; in a medical emergency call the Cruz Roja on ☎ 975 22 22 22.

Casco Viejo & Around
The narrow streets of Soria's old town (*casco viejo*) have some character and are worth a stroll. Plaza Mayor, the heart of the quarter, is fronted by the attractive Renaissance-era **ayuntamiento** and the **Iglesia de Santa María la Mayor** with its Romanesque facade. Overlooking the centre a block north is the majestic ochre **Palacio de los Condes Gomara**. Dating from the late 16th century, it is with little doubt Soria's most impressive piece of secular architecture.

Farther north again, on Calle de Santo Tomé, is Soria's most beautiful church, the Romanesque **Iglesia de Santo Domingo** whose exquisitely sculptured portal is truly eye-popping, especially at sunset when its reddish stone seems to be aglow.

Among other worthwhile churches is the **Iglesia de San Juan de Rabanera**, built in the 12th century and restored early in the present one. Hints of Gothic and even Byzantine art gleam through the mainly Romanesque hue of this building.

Heading east towards the Río Duero you pass the **Concatedral de San Pedro** with a 12th-century cloister at its most charming feature. Its delicate arches are divided by slender double pillars topped with beautiful capitals adorned with floral, human and animal motifs. Also of note is the plateresque main facade.

Museo Numantino
Prehistory buffs with a passable knowledge of Spanish should enjoy this well-organised museum dedicated to finds from ancient sites across the province of Soria, especially Numancia (see Around Soria later in this chapter). The exhibit starts out with bones of mammoths found south of Soria in what might have been a hunting ground swamp. It continues with ceramics, tools, jewellery and other objects, accompanied by detailed explanations of the historical developments in various major Celtiberian and Roman settlements. The museum's hours are 10 am to 2 pm and 5 to 9 pm daily in summer (otherwise to 7.30 pm), closed Monday (200 ptas).

Beside the Río Duero
The most striking of Soria's sights is the 12th-century **Monasterio de San Juan de Duero**. What most catches the eye are the

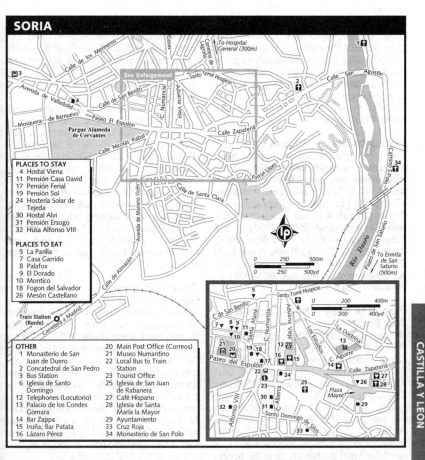

SORIA

PLACES TO STAY
4 Hostal Viena
11 Pensión Casa David
17 Pensión Ferial
19 Pensión Sol
24 Hostería Solar de Tejeda
30 Hostal Alvi
31 Pensión Ersogo
32 Husa Alfonso VIII

PLACES TO EAT
5 La Parilla
7 Casa Garrido
8 Palafox
9 El Dorado
10 Montico
18 Fogon del Salvador
26 Mesón Castellano

OTHER
1 Monasterio de San Juan de Duero
2 Concatedral de San Pedro
3 Bus Station
6 Iglesia de Santo Domingo
12 Telephones (Locutorio)
13 Palacio de los Condes Gomara
14 Bar Zappa
15 Iruña; Bar Patata
16 Lázaro Pérez
20 Main Post Office (Correos)
21 Museo Numantino
22 Local Bus to Train Station
23 Tourist Office
25 Iglesia de San Juan de Rabanera
27 Café Hispano
28 Iglesia de Santa María la Mayor
29 Ayuntamiento
33 Cruz Roja
34 Monasterio de San Polo

CASTILLA Y LEÓN

exposed, gracefully interlaced arches of its partly ruined cloister, which artfully blends mudéjar and Romanesque influences. The capitals inside the church are worth a closer look for their intense iconography. The monastery is open 10 am to 2 pm and 5 to 9 pm in summer (to 6 or 7 pm otherwise), closed Monday and Sunday afternoon (100 ptas, free on weekends).

A lovely walk south for a couple of kilometres takes you first past the 13th-century church of the former Knights Templar **Monasterio de San Polo** to the fascinating, baroque **Ermita de San Saturio**. This octago-nal structure squats right over the cave where Soria's patron saint spent much of his life. He's typically depicted from his waist up, leading locals to joke that, without a lower body, being a saint could not have been so hard. It's open 10 am to 2 pm and 4.30 to 9 pm (to 6.30 pm from October to April); free.

Special Events

Since the 13th century, the 12 *barrios* (districts) of Soria have celebrated with some fervour the Fiestas de San Juan y de la Madre de Dios in the second half of June. The main events occur on Jueves (Thursday) La Saca, when each of the barrios presents a bull to be fought the next day. The day following the fight some of the meat is auctioned, after which dancing and general carousing go on into the wee hours of Sunday. Hangovers and all, the *cuadrillas* or 'teams' representing the 12 barrios parade in all their finery and stage folk dances and the like. If you can find a room, this is the time to be in Soria.

Places to Stay – Budget

The following places are all in central Soria and rent out virtually indistinguishable no-frills rooms with shared facilities: *Pensión Sol (☎ 975 22 72 02, Calle Ferial 8)* charges 1750/3400 ptas for singles/doubles; at *Pensión Ferial (☎ 975 22 12 44, Plaza Salvador 6)* the going rate is 1800/3000 ptas; and *Pensión Ersogo (☎ 975 21 35 08, Calle de Alberca 4)* asks 2200/3200 ptas. A step up is *Pensión Casa David (☎ 975 22 00 33, Calle del Campo 6)*, which charges 2000/4000 ptas for rooms with a washbasin.

Places to Stay – Mid-Range & Top End

Despite its austere facade, *Hostal Viena (☎ 975 22 21 09, Calle de García Solier 5)* comes with some recommendations. Rooms have TV, phone and air-con and cost 2250/4000 ptas with washbasin or 5500 ptas for doubles with bath.

If you can afford a little more, check in at the brand-new *Hostería Solar de Tejeda (☎/fax 975 23 00 54, e solardetejeda@ wanadoo.es, Calle de Claustrilla 1)*, a charming boutique hotel right in the pedestrian zone. Rooms have whimsical decor and many amenities and cost 7500/8500 ptas (1000 ptas less outside out of summer). Less charm but also good value is offered by the business-style *Husa Alfonso VIII (☎ 975 22 62 11, Calle Alfonso VIII 10)*, with nicely appointed, large rooms going for 5500/9700 ptas.

Places to Eat

Soria has a surprisingly interesting culinary scene, which is anchored by two establishments with institution status. *Mesón Castellano (☎ 975 21 30 45, Plaza Mayor 2)*, with beamed ceilings and dangling flanks of ham, makes some of the best tapas in town. Full meals in its comedor are in the 4000 to 5000 ptas range. Similar is *Fogon del Salvador (☎ 975 23 01 94, Plaza El Salvador 1)*, owned by a bullfight aficionado, which is evident in the decor.

For places that are easier on the wallet, go to Calle Vicente Tutor, popularly known as El Tubo Ancho (the Narrow Pipe). *Palafox (☎ 975 22 00 76)* at No 2 and *El Dorado (☎ 975 22 02 72)* next door make substantial bocadillos, while *Montico* across the street gets creative with mussel-based snacks. *Casa Garrido (☎ 22 20 68)* at No 8 is a cosy spot, all dark wood and solid, meaty Castilian cooking with set lunches for 1500 ptas. Nearby is *La Parilla (☎ 975 21 41 52, Calle Tejera 20)*, whose open kitchen produces solid if unspectacular fare; the *menú* is 1200 ptas.

Entertainment

Soria's lively nightlife centres largely on two areas of which Plaza San Clemente is perfect for kicking off the marcha. Of the handful or so bars around here, *Iruña (☎ 975 22 68 31)* at No 2 and *Bar Patata (☎ 975 21 30 36)* at No 1 have the best range of tapas. The spit-and-sawdust crowd should look in at *Lázaro Pérez (Calle del Collado 52)*, although it's a bit male-dominated. Move on to Calle Zapatería where a good place for a drink is exotic *Bar Zappa* at No 38. *Café Hispano*, nearby on Plaza San Gil, is open from 3 pm and is a comfortable place to hang out.

Getting There & Away

The bus station is about a 20-minute walk north of the centre on the road to Valladolid. There's regular service to Logroño (805 ptas), Burgos (1275 ptas), Zaragoza (1100 ptas), Valladolid (1420 ptas), Madrid (1645 ptas) and Barcelona (3835 ptas). Provincial towns such as Medinaceli, Almazán and Peñafiel are served as well.

The train station is south-west of the centre (local buses connect with Plaza de Ramón y Cajal) but direct connections are limited. Five trains a day leave for Madrid (three hours, 1825 ptas) via Almazán (330 ptas).

If you're driving, take the N-111 north for Logroño; for Madrid, the same road connects with the N-II south of Soria. The N-122 goes west to Burgo de Osma. Going east, it merges with the A-68 to Zaragoza.

AROUND SORIA
Numancia
The mainly Roman ruins left today at Numancia, 8km north of Soria, suggest little of the long history of this city. Inhabited as early as the Bronze Age, Numancia would much later prove one of the most resistant cities to Roman rule. Several attempts by the Romans to take control of it were frustrated until finally Scipio, who had crushed Carthage, managed to starve the city into submission in 134 BC.

Under Roman rule, Numancia was an important stop on the road from Caesaraugustus (Zaragoza) to Asturica (Astorga). Ceramics unearthed here have revealed an advanced artistic tradition among not only the Romanised inhabitants of the city, but also their Celtiberian forebears. The site is open 10 am to 2 pm and 5 to 9 pm daily from June to August (4 to 7 pm in April, May, September and October, and 3.30 to 6 pm from November to March), closed Sunday afternoon and Monday (300 ptas).

Sierra de Urbión
Some of the most surprisingly green and unspoilt country in Castilla y León lies to the north-west of Soria. The Sierra de Urbión stretches north into La Rioja and is a popular weekend excursion destination with the people of Soria. The focal point is the **Laguna Negra**, 18km north of the pretty village of Vinuesa. The glacial lake lies still like a mirror at the base of brooding rock walls. The road is not in great shape, but the objective is well worth the battering to your shock absorbers (there are no buses). It's possible to walk to the Laguna de Urbión in La Rioja, or to the summit of the Pico de Urbión, above the village of Duruelo de la Sierra, and then on to a series of other tiny glacial lakes.

Vinuesa, a good base for the area, has two hostales. *Hostal Urbión* (☎ 975 37 84

94) has singles/doubles for 2500/3500 ptas (or doubles with bath for 4000 ptas) and a popular, if somewhat pricey, restaurant. Alternatively, you could try for a room at *Casa del Cura* (☎ 975 27 04 64) on Calle de la Estación in **Herreros**, a hamlet just off the N-234 highway to the south-east of Vinuesa. The nearest camping ground to the Laguna is *Camping El Cobijo* (☎ 975 37 83 31). It's open from March to mid-October.

Calatañazor
postcode 42193 • pop 71 • elev 1071
This dusty, but oddly romantic, village, about 30km west of Soria, is certainly an original place to stop. As you round a tight bend in the road, the grave stone walls and odd modest turret of this one-time Muslim fort (the name comes from the Arabic *Qala'at an-Nassur,* literally 'the vulture's citadel') present a timeless face. Believe it or not, scenes from the movie *Doctor Zhivago* were shot here. Climb the crooked, cobbled lanes through the town gate, and you step back hundreds of years into a medieval village. Simply wander through this little maze, lined by ochre stone and adobe houses topped with red tile roofs and conical chimneys typical of the area.

There are three tiny museums, a church and splendid views from the ruined fortress over a vast field called **Valle de la Sangre** (Valley of Blood). This was the setting of an epic 1002 battle that left Muslim ruler Almanzor defeated; he later died in nearby Medinaceli.

If you want to stay, there are several casas rurales, including the delightful *El Palomar* (☎ 975 18 32 84) with attached restaurant. Rates range from 5000 to 7000 ptas.

SOUTH OF SORIA
Almazán
postcode 42200 • pop 5960
Three of this small town's massive gates remain to testify to a past more illustrious than the present in this quiet backwater. It frequently changed hands between the Muslims and Christians, and for a short three months was chosen by Fernando and Isabel as their residence.

CASTILLA Y LEÓN

On Plaza Mayor, the Romanesque **Iglesia de San Miguel** sports an octagonal cupola-cum-bell tower that shows mudéjar influences. Inside is a bas-relief depicting the killing of Thomas à Beckett at the hands of British King Henry II. It was commissioned by Henry's daughter, Eleanor of Aquitaine, the wife of Alfonso VII, as a gesture of penance on behalf of her father. The official church hours are 11 am to 2 pm and 5 to 7 pm, closed Monday (shorter hours in winter).

The prettiest facade of the Gothic-Renaissance **Palacio de los Hurtado de Mendoza** also looks out over Plaza Mayor. Inside is a nice patio and artesonado ceiling.

If you want to stay, *Hostal El Arco (☎ 975 31 02 28, Calle de San Andrés 5-7)* is situated by one of the three city gates and has singles with washbasin for 1900 ptas and doubles with shower and toilet for 4000 ptas. *Restaurante Puerto Rico (☎ 975 30 00 73, Calle de los Caballeros 10)* is a good cheap restaurant in the old town.

There are frequent bus and train connections with Soria, 35km north.

Medinaceli
postcode 42240 • pop 900 • elev 1270m
Entering Medinaceli along a slip road just north of the N-II motorway, you find a modern one-horse town. The old Medinaceli is actually draped along a high, windswept ridge 3km to the north. Its most incongruously placed landmark is a 2nd-century AD **triumphal arch**, which is all that remains of the Roman settlement. Little is left to remind you of Medinaceli's Muslim occupiers either. The quiet streets are redolent more of the noble families that lived here after the town fell to the Reconquista in 1124. The most notable religious building is the Gothic **Colegiata de Santa María**. There's a tourist office (☎ 989 73 41 76) on Plaza Mayor.

Accommodation here is fairly cheap. *Hostal Medinaceli (☎ 975 32 61 02, Calle*

del Portillo 1) has singles/doubles with bath for 3000/4500 ptas and the newer *Hostería El Mirador (☎ 975 32 62 64),* on Campo de San Nicolas, offers rooms for 4000/5000 ptas. You'll find several more *hostales* in the new town.

Regular buses to Soria (585 ptas) and the occasional one to Madrid leave from outside the ayuntamiento in the new town. Three trains daily call in to Medinaceli on the Madrid-Zaragoza line. There is no transport between the old and new towns – it's quite a hike.

Santa María de la Huerta
This dusty, insignificant village off the N-II and just short of the Aragonese frontier, contains a jewel in the form of a Cistercian monastery founded in 1162. Monks lived here until the monastery was expropriated in 1835. The order was allowed to return in 1930 and 18 Cistercians are now in residence. Before entering the monastery, note the church's impressive 12th-century facade with its attractive rose window.

Inside the monastery, you pass through two cloisters, the second of which is by far the more beautiful. Known as the **Claustro de los Caballeros**, it is Spanish Gothic in style, although the medallions on the 2nd floor bearing coats of arms and assorted illustrious busts, such as that of Christopher Columbus, are a successful plateresque touch. Off this cloister is the *refectorio,* or dining hall. Built in the 13th century, it is remarkable, especially for the absence of columns to support the vault. The monastery is open 9 am to 1 pm and 3 to 7 pm, closed Sunday afternoon (300 ptas).

The only place to stay is the basic *Pensión Santa María (☎ 975 32 72 18)* at the turn-off to the monastery. It has singles/doubles for 1600/3000 ptas.

A couple of buses connect the village with Almazán and Soria.

Castilla-La Mancha

The autonomous community of Castilla-La Mancha is a post-Franco creation with Toledo as its capital. It covers roughly what was known as Castilla la Nueva (New Castile), the territory south from Toledo that was added to the Corona de Castilla (Castilian Crown) as the Reconquista progressed through the Middle Ages. The boundaries of the region's five provinces are those drawn up in 1833, when La Mancha – the harsh, dry southern plateau that served as a front-line buffer zone against the last of Spain's Muslim rulers after the Battle of Las Navas de Tolosa in 1212 – ceased to exist as an administrative unit. Embodied by its literary hero Don Quijote, La Mancha (which comes from an Arabic expression meaning 'dry, waterless land') has nevertheless remained very much alive in the Spanish imagination.

With the exception of Toledo, little of this region is seen by the millions of foreigners who pour into Spain each year. The empty expanses alone are quite unique in Western Europe, reminiscent of some of the more monotonous stretches of rural Australia or south-western USA. Many people end up crossing Castilla-La Mancha from Madrid or Toledo en route to somewhere else. Those with limited time are probably right to skip the bulk of this dispiriting, hot land of treeless plains and glum, bald hills. A closer look, however, reveals a wide smattering of pretty villages, medieval castles and, on occasion, some surprisingly varied and fertile landscape. The absence of busloads of camera-clicking tour groups presents an opportunity to see some of Spain as it really is. Given the distances involved, however, having your own vehicle is a significant asset.

The cuisine of Castilla-La Mancha, like that of much of Spain, is firmly based in peasant tradition. In and around Toledo, where *la caza* (hunting) has long been a big contributor to the local table, venison and partridge figure largely. The plains are hot but not unproductive.

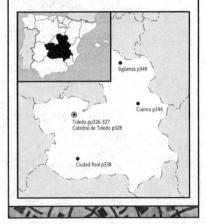

Sigüenza p349

Cuenca p344

Toledo pp326-327
Catedral de Toledo p328

Ciudad Real p338

The strong *queso manchego* (La Manchan goat and/or sheep cheese) is sold everywhere and appreciated by gourmets. Among the odder manchego dishes is *migas,* basically fried breadcrumbs mixed with garlic and other ingredients. They are better than they sound.

Traditionally, La Mancha has been given over to intense wine production. Next to olive groves, the grapevine is one of the most common agricultural sights across the country. Quality always came second to quantity, but with EU quotas forcing drastic cutbacks, growers are now concentrating

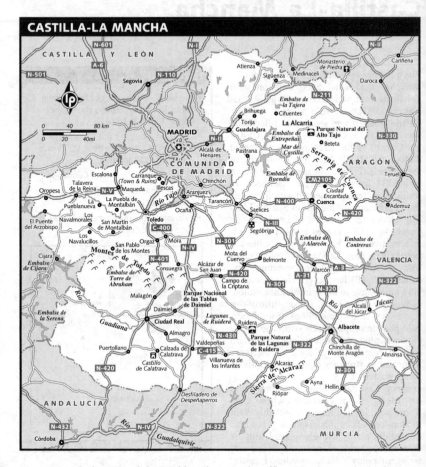

CASTILLA-LA MANCHA

more on producing a good drop. Although not Spain's greatest wines, the products from the La Mancha and Valdepeñas areas are DO (Denominación de Origen, literally 'Denomination of Origin') wines.

The regional tourist board puts out a series of pamphlets laying out theme-oriented driving routes in Castilla-La Mancha. These in-depth tours describe every last village, castle, ruin, and scenic overlook in the region, while a companion set of city guides contains information on festivals, arts and cuisine as well. They are available in English and worth picking up at any

tourist office. It's also worth checking out the region's Web site at www.jccm.es for a taster before you go.

Toledo

postcode 45080 • pop 66,989
They still call it La Ciudad Imperial – and for a while Toledo indeed looked set to become the heart of a united Spain. The Iberian Peninsula's Rome and something of an army town, this remarkable medieval city bristles with monumental splendour.

By the time El Greco arrived here from Italy in 1577, Toledo's chances of becoming the permanent capital had all but evaporated. Sixteen years earlier, Felipe II had moved the court to the relatively undistinguished location of Madrid, a site that, unlike the claustrophobic Toledo, lent itself to rapid expansion in all directions as might befit a great empire. Toledo's city elders were slow to realise that, partly owing to an earlier revolt against Carlos I, they had missed the boat, and until the end of the century the city continued to enjoy one of its greatest moments of economic and artistic development. When the penny finally dropped, artists, nobles, courtesans and sycophants left in droves, leaving Toledo to sink slowly into provincial disrepair.

Like a creaky museum, spruced up but not without problems, *la ciudad de la tres culturas* (the city of the three cultures) has survived as a unique centre where Romans and Visigoths once ruled, and for a time Jews, Muslims and Christians – and all those who converted from one religion to another – lived in comparative harmony. The artistic legacy is a complex cross-breeding of European and Oriental values that can be seen elsewhere in Spain, but rarely with the intensity found here.

The seat of the head of the Catholic church in Spain for most of its Christian history, Toledo exerts a strange and sometimes dark fascination over those who stay around long enough to get over the initial monument shock and summer crowds. To see the city in the gloomy depths of winter, shrouded in fog and even more introverted than usual, is in some ways to get a truer measure of its character.

Toledo's twisting lanes and blind alleys, decorated internal patios hidden by grim facades and its sheer architectural diversity make it worthy of more attention than most visitors give it. Travellers who have passed through Damascus, Cairo or Fés will recognise the labyrinth of the *medina,* but in none of those cities will they also be confronted by the Gothic grandeur of a cathedral or the grim composure of Toledo's oft-remodelled Alcázar.

The sad part of Toledo's story is taking place almost unnoticed. People are abandoning the old city for the characterless but comfortable new suburbs sprawled out beneath it, leaving behind only public servants, students and the rent-protected elderly. If this continues, the shops and businesses will also decline, leaving only a motley collection of souvenir stalls and eateries to satisfy summer tourist crowds. The old city appears destined to become an empty open-air museum – a place without a soul.

History

Its strategic position made ancient Toletum an important way station in the days of Rome's domination of the Iberian Peninsula. In the 6th century, long after Rome had ceased to have any influence on the affairs of Hispania, the Visigothic King Atanagild moved the site of his capital from Sevilla to Toletum. At once, the city also became the religious heart of the Visigothic kingdom, with no less than 18 councils held here to deal with problems such as the conversion of the Visigoths to Catholicism, the faith of the majority of the subjugated Hispano-Roman populace. But Toledo also became the scene of endless feuds between Visigothic nobles which so weakened their state that when the Muslims crossed the Strait of Gibraltar in 711 they had little problem in taking Toledo on their lightning-fast march north.

Toledo was the main city of central Muslim Spain. After the collapse of the caliphate in Córdoba in 1031 it became the capital of a vast and independent Arab *taifa* (small kingdom). For the following 50 years the city was unrivalled as a centre of learning and arts in Spain, and for a brief time its power ranged across all modern Castilla-La Mancha, to Valencia and to Córdoba itself.

Alfonso VI marched into Toledo in 1085, a significant victory on the long and weary road of the Reconquista. Shortly thereafter, the Vatican recognised Toledo as seat of the church in Spain. In the following centuries the city was also one of the most important of several temporary residences of the Castilian monarchy. Since the Archbishop of Toledo was a vocal proponent of the Reconquista

CASTILLA-LA MANCHA

and the monarchs' right-hand man at this time, Toledo's position as a flourishing power base was assured. Christians, Jews and Muslims managed to get along tolerably well for a period, but by 1492, when Granada fell to the Catholic Monarchs, the situation had changed. Shortly afterwards Spain's Muslims and Jews were compelled to convert to Christianity or flee.

Carlos I looked set to make Toledo his permanent capital in the 16th century, in spite of the revolt against him that began in the city and degenerated into the so-called Guerra de las Comunidades (see the boxed text 'Juan Bravo and the Comuneros' in the Castilla y León chapter for more on this civil conflict). His successor, Felipe II, dashed any such ideas with his definitive move to Madrid, and Toledo began to recede into the background.

In the early months of the 1936–39 civil war, Nationalist troops (and some civilians) were kept under siege in the Alcázar, but were eventually relieved by a force from the south in a move that some claim cost Franco a quick victory. By diverting his units to Toledo, he missed an opportunity to get to Madrid before the arrival of the International Brigades – one of those 'what if?' scenarios that so intrigue historians. In 1986 Unesco declared the city a monument of world interest to humanity.

Orientation

Toledo is built upon a hill around which the Río Tajo (Tagus) flows on three sides; modern suburbs spread beyond the river and walls of the old town.

The main bus station (estación de autobuses) lies just to the north-east of the old town (casco antiguo), and the train station a little farther east across the Tajo. Both are connected by local bus to the centre.

Whether you arrive on foot or by local bus, you're bound to turn up sooner or later at Plaza de Zocodover (known as Zocodover or Zoco to the locals), the main square of the old town. Most hotels and a good number of bars and restaurants are spattered around the nearby labyrinth of medieval alleyways – which can be quite confusing on arrival.

Information

Tourist Offices The main tourist office (☎ 925 22 08 43, fax 925 25 26 48) is just outside Toledo's northern main gate, the Puerta Nueva de Bisagra, though it has little to offer. It is open 9 am to 6 pm weekdays, 9 am to 7 pm Saturday and 9 am to 3 pm Sunday. A smaller, more helpful information office can be found in the *ayuntamiento* (town hall); it's open 10.30 am to 2.30 pm and 4.30 to 7 pm (mornings only on Monday). The Delegación Provincial de Educación y Cultura, Plaza de Zocodover 7, can give you a full list of youth hostels and university residences throughout Castilla-La Mancha. It is open 9 am to 2 pm weekdays.

Money There is no shortage of banks and ATMs in central Toledo. The Caja Rural, Plaza de Zocodover 14, has an ATM and automatic cash-changing machine.

Post & Communications The main post office *(correos)* is at Calle de la Plata 1. It is open 8.30 am to 8.30 pm weekdays and 9.30 am to 2 pm Saturday. Your best bet for Internet access is Discad Multimedia at Miguel de Cervantes 17, east of Plaza de Zocodover towards the river. Cafetería Scorpions, at Calle del Pintor Matías Moreno 10, also has Internet access.

Internet Resources The Web site at www.diputoledo.es provides information on the city and the province of Toledo.

Books Apart from the usual tourist books, Spanish readers wanting a quality guide and account of the city should consider *Rutas de Toledo* (4000 ptas), published by Electa and available all over town.

Medical Services & Emergency There is a Policía Nacional *comisaría* (police station) in the old city on Plaza de la Ropería. For an ambulance or urgent medical help, the Cruz Roja (Red Cross) can be contacted on ☎ 925 22 22 22. You'll find a Centro de Salud (health centre; ☎ 925 21 50 54) at Calle de la Sillería 2. Duty night pharmacies

CASTILLA-LA MANCHA

change daily on a rotational basis; the week's *farmacias de guardia* are posted up in most pharmacies.

Things to See

Take time to wander and soak up some of the most distinctive architectural combinations in Spain. The Arab influence on all you see is a singular expression of Spain's mixed heritage, one that also passes through the Gothic of the cathedral and the more restrained monumentalism of the work of architects Juan de Herrera and Alonso Covarrubias.

In summer, many of Toledo's attractions tend to open for about an hour longer than the times cited. Some offer discounts for students and over 65s (usually half-price) and are free on Saturday afternoon and Sunday.

Zocodover From 1465 until the 1960s, Zocodover was the scene of El Martes, the city's Tuesday market and successor to the Arab *souq ad-dawab* (livestock market) from which the square derives its name. The market is now held downhill from the Museo de Santa Cruz, but Zocodover remains the old town's focal point. Apart from the market, it was here that *toledanos* for centuries enjoyed their bullfights or crowded to witness *autos de fe* (public burnings at the stake) carried out by the Inquisition. You can see the house of the 16th-century Inquisitor Alfonso Castellón (with the Doric doorway) on nearby Plaza de Agustín, just up from Pensión Segovia.

Juan de Herrera, who built El Escorial, wanted to convert the square into a grand Castilian *plaza mayor* (main plaza) in the late 16th century, but he was blocked by church interests. The eastern facade is all he managed to erect along the line of the former Arab city wall, punctuated by the gate now known as the Arco de la Sangre. The southern flank dates from the 17th century.

Toledo's forbidding facades often hide sumptuous houses, so it's worth keeping your eyes open for unexpected glimpses of internal courtyards. Calle de la Sillería has a couple of nice examples. Look for No 6 and No 3; the former's patio is adorned with an elegant fountain, while the latter is considered one of the most beautiful houses in Toledo.

Alcázar Just south off Zocodover, at the highest point in the city, looms Toledo's most recognisable edifice, the Alcázar. It is possible the Romans fortified it first. Abd ar-Rahman III raised a fortress *(al-qasr)* here in the 10th century and it was altered after the Christians retook the town in the following century. Covarrubias and Herrera rebuilt it as a royal residence for Carlos I, but the court moved to Madrid and it became a white elephant, eventually winding up as the Academia de la Infantería (now on the opposite bank of the Tajo).

The Alcázar was largely destroyed during the Republican siege of Franco's forces in 1936, but Franco had it rebuilt and turned into a military museum. It is a fascinating memorial to the siege and, by extension, the fascist dictator – an eloquent expression of Spain's ambiguous approach to its past. You can visit the shot-up room where Colonel (later General) Moscardó refused to surrender despite threats by the 'reds' to kill his captured son, whom he told by phone to 'get ready to die' (he was shot some time later). Moscardó's words can be heard on crackling tape in half a dozen languages. And in case anyone feels left out, the words hang framed on the walls in just about every tongue imaginable from Ukrainian to Korean.

The museum is open 10 am to 2.30 pm, closed Monday (200 ptas).

Museo de Santa Cruz Just outside what were once the Arab city walls along Zocodover, this museum on Calle de Cervantes started life as a hospital in the early 16th century. Apart from several El Grecos (look for the *Asunción de la Virgen),* the museum contains a mixed bag of largely religious objects, including 15th-century tapestries, furnishings, war standards from the Battle of Lepanto in 1571, medieval documents and other odds and ends. Built in a mix of Gothic and Spanish Renaissance styles on a Greek-cross floor plan, the former hospital is flanked by a pleasant cloister. It is open 10 am to 6.30 pm (to 2 pm Sunday), sometimes closing at lunchtime; entry is 200 ptas.

CASTILLA-LA MANCHA

TOLEDO

PLACES TO STAY
3 Pensión Santa Úrsula
7 Pensión Amalí
8 Circo Romano
12 Castillo de San Servando
   & Youth Hostel
15 Pensión Virgen
   de la Estrella
17 Hostal del Cardenal
20 Pensión Segovia
21 Pensión Castilla
22 Hostal Las Armas
27 Hotel Imperio
35 Hotel Maravilla
48 Pensión Nuncio Viejo
56 Hostal Nuevo Labrador
57 Pensión Lumbreras
58 Hotel Carlos V
78 La Belviseña
80 Hotel Santa Isabel
82 Pensión Santa Úrsula
84 Hotel Pintor El Greco
90 Hotel El Diamantista

PLACES TO EAT
19 Restaurante Hierbabuena
24 La Abadía
26 Jacaranda Bar
34 Naca Naca
39 El Patio
41 El Armiño
44 Cafetería Scorpions
49 Restaurante Alex
50 Restaurante Aurelio
52 Ludeña
63 Bar La Ria
69 Osiris Bar
74 El Torreón
76 Restaurante Aurelio

81 El Tropezón
83 El Delfín
85 Palacio de Fuensalida

OTHER
1 La Barra
2 El Pasito
4 Plaza de Toros
5 María Cristina Cinema
6 Hospital de Tavera
7 Circo Romano
9 Tourist Office
10 Bus Station
11 Hospital Provincial
13 Open-Air Cinema
14 Discos
16 Iglesia de Santiago
   del Arrabal
18 Mezquita de Cristo de la Luz

23 Tbeo
25 Camelot
28 Centro de Salud
29 Sildavia
30 Museo de Santa Cruz
31 Discad Multimedia
32 Delegación Provincial de
   Educación y Cultura
33 Bus Station
36 Caja Rural
37 Policía Nacional
38 Main Post Office (Correos)
40 Cervecería 1700
42 Monasterio de Santo
   Domingo El Antiguo
43 Iglesia de Santa Leocadia
45 Iglesia de San Román &
   Museo de los Concilios
   y Cultura Visigótica

46 Las 3 Culturas
47 Plaza Padre Juan
   de Mariana
51 Mezquita de las
   Tornerías
53 Plaza de la Magdalena
54 Taxi Rank
55 Alcázar
59 Teatro Rojas
60 Supermercado
61 Catedral
62 Cervecería Lupulo
64 Museo de Arte
   Contemporáneo
65 Antigüedades
66 Iglesia de San Juan
   de los Reyes
67 Museo de Victorio
   Macho

68 Sinagoga de Santa
   María La Blanca
70 Iglesia de Santo Tomé
71 El Café de Garcilaso
72 Museo de Taller
   del Moro
73 Convento Santa Úrsula
75 Ayuntamiento &
   Tourist Information
77 El Último
79 Iglesia de San Lucas
86 Casa y Museo de
   El Greco
87 Sinagoga del Tránsito
   y Museo Sefardí
88 La Venta del Alma
89 Arab Baths
91 Ferry
92 Kiosko Base

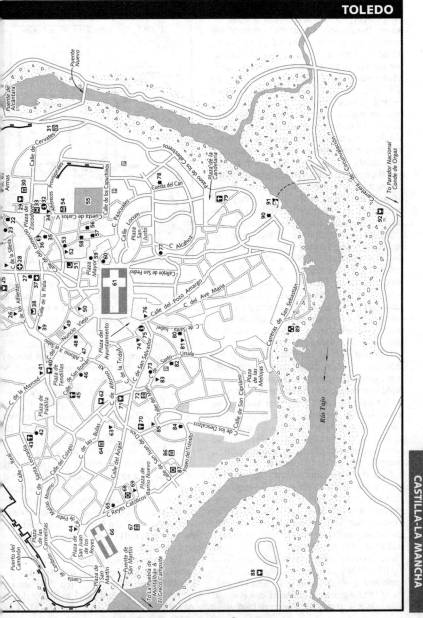

CASTILLA-LA MANCHA

Catedral From the earliest days of the Visigothic occupation of the ancient Roman Toletum, the modern site of the cathedral has been the centre of worship in the city. In 646, Toledo's archbishop was first recognised as the primate of the Catholic Church in Spain. Three centuries of Muslim rule saw the Visigoths' basilica converted into Toledo's central mosque. Alfonso VI promised, in the instruments of surrender signed by Christians and Muslims in 1085, that the mosque would be preserved as a place of worship for Toledo's considerable Muslim population. Predictably enough, the promise was broken and the mosque destroyed to make way for a cathedral. The construction of a new house of worship began in the 13th century and proceeded slowly over the following centuries. Essentially a Gothic structure, the cathedral nevertheless is a hotchpotch of styles reflecting the mixed history of the city. *Mudéjar* elements are plain to see in the interior decoration and the Spanish Renaissance makes itself felt in various chapels that line the church naves. Behind the main altar lies a masterpiece of *churrigueresque* baroque, the Transparente. A lavish 18th-century embellishment, it also serves to remedy the lack of light in the cathedral.

Entering through the **Puerta Llana** at the side, you are immediately in the cathedral's main nave. The centre is dominated by the highly unusual **coro** (choir stalls), a feast of sculpture and carved wooden stalls. The lower tier was carved in the 15th century in Late Gothic style and depicts the conquest of Granada, while the upper Renaissance level features images of saints and apostles, many by Alonso de Berruguete.

Opposite is the **Capilla Mayor**, too small to accommodate the choir stalls as originally planned, but an extraordinary work of art dating back to 1498. This altar serves in part as a mausoleum for Cardinal Mendoza (prelate and adviser to Fernando and Isabel) and several kings. The masterpiece is the *retablo* in Flemish Gothic style, depicting scenes from the life of Christ and culminating with a *Calvario* and an *Asunción de la Virgen*. The oldest of the magnificent stained glass is in the rose window above the Puerta del Reloj.

CATEDRAL DE TOLEDO

1 Puerta del Mollete
2 Claustro
3 Puerta del Reloj
4 Sacristía
5 Sala Capitular
6 Puerta de los Leones
7 Puerta Llana
8 Coro
9 Capilla Mayor
10 Capilla de la Torre

All the chapels and rooms off the main church body are worth visiting. Among the 'don't misses' are the **Capilla de la Torre**, in the north-western corner, and the **sacristía**. The latter contains what amounts to a small gallery of El Greco (see the boxed text 'El Greco in Toledo'), while the former houses what must be one of the most extraordinary monstrances in existence, the Custodia de Arfe, by the celebrated 16th-century goldsmith Enrique de Arfe. With 18kg of pure gold and 183kg of silver, this 16th-century conceit bristles with some 260 statuettes. Its big day is the feast of Corpus Christi (see Special Events in the Facts for the Visitor chapter), when it is paraded around the streets of Toledo on a special vehicle that prevents it tipping over in spite of the medieval streets.

The **sala capitular** (chapter house) boasts a remarkable 500-year-old *artesonado* ceiling in the so-called Cisneros style and Renaissance murals depicting the life of Christ and the Virgin Mary.

The cathedral's cool and pretty cloister is entered through the **Puerta del Mollete** facing the square under the Arco del Palacio, which links the cathedral to the Palacio Arzobispal (Archbishop's Palace). For

El Greco in Toledo

DAMIEN SIMONIS

El Greco, as the subject, not the creator of art

After a long apprenticeship in Crete, where he was born in 1541, Domenikos Theotokopoulos moved to Venice in 1567 to be schooled as a Renaissance artist. He learned to extract the maximum effect from few colours, concentrating the observer's interest in the faces of his portraits and leaving the rest in relative obscurity, a characteristic that remained one of his hallmarks. From 1572 he learned from the mannerists of Rome and the work left behind by Michelangelo.

He came to Toledo in 1577 hoping to get a job decorating El Escorial. Things didn't quite work out, and Felipe II rejected him as a court artist. In Toledo, itself recently knocked back as permanent seat of the royal court, the man who came to be known simply as El Greco felt sufficiently at home to hang around, painting in a style different from anything local artists were producing. He even managed to cultivate a healthy clientele and command good prices. His rather high opinion of himself and his work, however, did not endear him to all and sundry. He had to do without the patronage of the cathedral administrators, the first of many clients to haul him to court for his obscenely high fees.

El Greco liked the high life, and with things going well in the last decade of the 16th century, he took rooms in a mansion on the Paseo del Tránsito, where he often hired musicians to accompany his meals. As Toledo's fortunes declined, so did El Greco's personal finances, and although the works of his final years are among his best, he often found himself unable to pay the rent. He died in 1614, leaving his works scattered about the city, where many have remained to this day.

---

centuries the city's destitute would line up at this entrance for daily bread distribution.

The cathedral is open 10.30 am to 6 pm Monday to Saturday and 4 to 6 pm Sunday. Tickets (700 ptas; no student discount) can be bought at the souvenir shop across the street from the main (side) entrance.

El Greco Trail Hordes of tourists pile down Toledo's narrow streets searching out the paintings of El Greco. The first stop is the **Iglesia de Santo Tomé** on Plaza del Conde, which contains his masterpiece, *El Entierro del Conde de Orgaz* (The Burial of the Count of Orgaz). When the count, a 14th-century benefactor of the church, was buried in 1322, Sts Augustine and Stephen supposedly descended from heaven to attend the funeral. El Greco's work depicts the miracle and features some of his chums in the lower, terrestrial part of the painting.

The church is open 10 am to 5.45 pm daily; entry is 200 ptas.

Afterwards you can follow the tourist stream past rows of souvenir shops to **Casa y Museo de El Greco** on Calle de Samuel Leví. This was set up as a museum by a noble chap, Don Benigno de Vega-Inclán, in 1910, but it is unlikely that El Greco actually ever lived here. Inside you will find *Vista y Plano de Toledo* and about 20 of the Cretan's minor works. The museum also has a small collection of minor works from the 17th-century Toledo, Madrid and Sevilla schools. It's open 10 am to 2 pm and 4 to 6 pm, closed Sunday evening and Monday (200 ptas).

If you want to develop your own El Greco trail, other places in Toledo where you can see his works include the Museo de Santa Cruz, the sacristía of the cathedral, the Monasterio de Santo Domingo El Antiguo and the Hospital de Tavera.

CASTILLA-LA MANCHA

Jewish Quarter Toledo still considers itself the 'city of the three cultures'. Near El Greco's supposed house is what was once the *judería,* or Jewish quarter. 'Once' because, as a huge plaque in the cathedral proudly proclaims, the bulk of Toledo's Jews, like those elsewhere in Spain, were expelled in 1492. In prior centuries, Toledo's Jews worshipped in 11 synagogues.

Of the two synagogues that survive, **Sinagoga del Tránsito** on Calle de los Reyes Católicos is the most interesting. Built in 1355 by special permission of Pedro I (construction of synagogues was by then prohibited in Christian Spain), its main prayer hall has been expertly restored. The mudéjar decoration is particularly striking. Academics are still puzzling over the full meaning of the Hebrew inscriptions that line the walls, but less attention seems to have been paid to those in Arabic in the ceiling. From 1492 until 1877 it was variously used as a priory, hermitage and military barracks. As the modern **Museo Sefardí** it now houses affords insights into the history of Jewish culture in Spain. The complex is open 10 am to 1.45 pm and 4 to 5.45 pm, closed Sunday afternoon and Monday (400 ptas).

A short way north along Calle de los Reyes Católicos, **Sinagoga de Santa María La Blanca** is characterised by the horseshoe arches that delineate the five naves – classic Almohad architecture. Opening times are 10 am to 1.45 pm and 3.30 to 6.45 pm daily (200 ptas).

San Juan de los Reyes A little farther north lies one of the city's most visible sights. The Franciscan monastery and church was founded by Fernando and Isabel to demonstrate the power of the crown over the nobles and the supremacy of the Catholic faith in Spain – for how else could you interpret the decision to erect such an edifice in the heart of the Jewish quarter? The rulers had planned to be buried here but, when they took Granada in 1492, they opted for the brilliance of the southern city's Muslim palace.

Begun by the Breton architect Juan Güas in 1477, San Juan de los Reyes was finished only in 1606. Throughout the church and two-storey cloister the coat of arms of Fernando and Isabel (or in other words of united Spain) dominates, and the chains of Christian prisoners liberated in Granada hang from the walls. The prevalent late Flemish Gothic style is tarted up with lavish Isabelline ornament and counterbalanced by unmistakable mudéjar decoration, especially in the cloister, where typical geometric and vegetal designs stand out. The church and cloister are open 10 am to 1.45 pm and 3.30 to 6.45 pm daily (200 ptas).

Muslim Toledo Although many of Toledo's great buildings betray the influence of its medieval Muslim conquerors, little that is specifically Muslim remains.

On the northern slopes of town you'll find the **Mezquita de Cristo de la Luz**, a modest mosque built at the turn of the 1st millennium which suffered the usual fate of being converted to a church – as the religious frescoes make clear. The narrow, steep Calle del Cristo de la Luz continues past the mosque and its charming gardens, and under a gate the Muslims knew as Bab al-Mardum (also the original name of the mosque). Here, the city wall marked the boundary between the Muslim medina proper and Ar-Rabal, the 'outer suburbs'. Entry to the mosque is free, but only when the guardian is around (forget it from about 1 to 4 pm). If you can't see the guardian, try calling at No 11.

The remnants of another modest mosque, **Mezquita de las Tornerías**, now house an arts and crafts display.

Museums Around the corner from Iglesia de Santo Tomé and the adjoining 15th-century Palacio de los Condes de Fuensalida is the 14th-century **Taller del Moro** on Calle del Taller del Moro. Formerly part of a noble family's residence, it now houses a modest museum with a small collection of mudéjar decorative items, ceramics, wood architraves and stucco work. It is open 10 am to 2 pm and 4 to 6.30 pm, closed all day Monday and Sunday afternoon (100 ptas).

The **Museo de Arte Contemporáneo**, housed in the restored 16th-century mudéjar Casa de las Cadenas is home to a modest collection of Spanish modern art, including a couple of pieces by Joan Miró and some early 20th-century Toledo landscapes by Aureliano de Beruete. Opening hours and entry are as for the Taller del Moro.

The Iglesia de San Román, an impressive hybrid of mudéjar and Renaissance styles, houses the **Museo de los Concilios y Cultura Visigótica**. The documents, jewellery and other items housed here are perhaps less interesting than the building itself, located up Calle de San Román from Plaza del Padre Juan de Mariana. Opening hours and entry are as above.

Farther north, below Plaza de Padilla, **Monasterio de Santo Domingo El Antiguo** is one of the oldest convents in Toledo, dating from the 11th century. It houses some of El Greco's early commissions (most are copies) and an eclectic display of religious artefacts. It's open 11 am to 1.30 pm and 4 to 7 pm, closed Sunday morning (150 ptas).

Outside the city walls on the road to Madrid, the one-time **Hospital de Tavera**, built in 1541, contains an interesting art collection, including some of El Greco's last works. It is open 10.30 am to 1.30 pm and 3.30 to 6 pm daily (500 ptas).

The new kid on the block is the **Museo de Victorio Macho**, opposite Sinagoga de Santa María La Blanca. Originally the house and workshop of sculptor Victorio Macho, it now houses many of his works, a hall for temporary exhibitions and an auditorium screening a film on the history of Toledo (in English if need be). His *La Madre* piece is so lifelike it's disturbing. The museum is open 10 am to 7 pm Monday to Saturday and 10 am to 3 pm Sunday (500 ptas).

Around the City Walls Large portions of the old city walls remain intact, and for many people the first sight of old Toledo is the hefty turrets of the 16th-century **Puerta Nueva de Bisagra**, emblazoned with Carlos I's coat of arms and as imposing now as they must have appeared to visitors approaching from Madrid down the Camino Real de Castilla.

Just outside the Puerta Nueva de Bisagra is a shaded park with outdoor cafes. Down the hill to the west is another park in which fragments of the former **Circo Romano**, or Roman Circus remain. There's not a lot to look at, but you can see the elliptical outline.

You can follow the walls around to the west until you reach the solid **Puerta del Cambrón** (Buckthorn Gate), also known as Puerta de los Judíos (Jews' Gate) for its proximity to the judería. A short walk from here past Iglesia de San Juan de los Reyes brings you down to one of the two remaining medieval bridges in Toledo – the **Puente de San Martín**, several times rebuilt and altered since its initial construction in the 14th century.

From here a path continues on along the river, a nice shady walk in the summer heat. At the southern tip of the old town, you'll find (if you poke around) the remnants of what were once **Arab baths** and cloth-dyeing tubs. The site is not marked – follow the path off the Carreras de San Sebastián road westward from near Hotel El Diamantista.

Outside the City For more fresh air and some of the best views of the city, head over the Puente de Alcántara to the southern bank of the Río Tajo. Alternatively, you can get the tiny cable-ferry (if it's running) from near Hotel El Diamantista, in the southern end of the old town, and walk up the opposite bank. Scattered about this hinterland are many *cigarrales,* country estates of wealthy toledanos.

Bitter Tears & Peaceful Strolls

Most day-trippers to Toledo follow a well-defined and restricted route through the city, and it is quite easy to flee the crowds by diving off into less explored barrios. The medieval labyrinth that spreads south of the cathedral and the Alcázar was, and to an extent remains, a largely working-class district, and reading the various explanatory plaques in the streets (unfortunately, in Spanish only) adds flavour to an otherwise uncluttered stroll. The waters of the Pozo Amargo (Bitter Well), in the centre of this area, are said to have gone bad after a young Jewish woman's Christian lover was murdered by her father, for in her grief she spent much of the remainder of her life crying tears of bitterness into the well.

CASTILLA-LA MANCHA

Swimming

Midsummer in Toledo is scorching, and several pools open in the hot months. The best is the Piscina Municipal on the roundabout at the northern end of Avenida de la Reconquista (take bus No 1 from Zocodover or walk).

Special Events

The feast of Corpus Christi falls on the Thursday of the ninth week after Easter and is by far the most extraordinary event on Toledo's religious calendar. Several days of festivities culminate in a procession in which the massive Custodia de Arfe (see Catedral earlier in this section) is paraded around the city. It is preceded on the Thursday by hundreds of people marching in traditional dress in the name of countless religious fraternities (cofradías) and other groups, as well as the army (the troops always get a big hand in this traditionally military town).

Easter is also marked by several days of solemn processions by masked members of cofradías. In the key days of Holy Week some of these processions take place around midnight.

The Feast of the Assumption is on 15 August. On this day of the Sagrario de la Virgen, you can drink of the cathedral's well water. The water is held by many to have miraculous qualities; the queues for a swig from an earthenware botijo (jar with spout and handle) can be equally astonishing.

Places to Stay

Camping & Youth Hostel There are two convenient camping grounds, the closest of which is *Circo Romano* (☎ 925 22 04 42, Avenida de Carlos III 19). Better but more awkward for those without their own vehicle, is *El Greco* (☎/fax 925 22 00 90, e elgreco@retemail.es). It's a couple of kilometres south-west of town, on the road to La Puebla de Montalbán, and has good views of Toledo from the pool. Both charge 620/630/560 ptas per person/tent/car.

The HI *youth hostel* (☎ 925 22 45 54) is beautifully located in the Castillo de San Servando, a castle that started life as a Visigothic monastery and later belonged to the Knights Templar. B&B costs 1200 ptas (under-26) or 1400 ptas per person. A membership card is necessary.

Hostales, Pensiones & Hotels – Old City
The fair range of accommodation is offset by the number of people looking for a bed, especially from about Easter to September, so arrive early. Lower-end places generally skimp on heating in winter and have only communal showers. Some of the mid-range and top-end hotels have discount rooms in January and February.

Toledo's cheapest place lies in the maze of alleys directly south of the Alcázar, an area little visited by tourists, which retains the air of the medieval working-class quarter it once was. *La Belviseña* (☎ 925 22 00 67, Cuesta del Can 5) is a basic affair with singles/doubles for 1500/2500 ptas. *Pensión Virgen de la Estrella* (☎ 925 25 31 34, Calle Real del Arrabal 18), just inside the Puerta Nueva de Bisagra, is in the same class and has rooms for 1500/3000 ptas.

Farther into the tangle of the old town is *Pensión Segovia* (☎ 925 21 11 24, Calle de Recoletos 2). It's a pleasant place with simple rooms for 2200/3000 ptas. Literally around the corner is the cheerful *Pensión Castilla* (☎ 925 25 63 18) with tiny rooms at 2200/3900 ptas, some with bath. Virtually on Zocodover, *Hostal Las Armas* (☎ 925 22 16 68, Calle de las Armas 7) is several hundred years old and retains a run-down flavour. Rooms cost 2200/3400 ptas.

Near the Alcázar, *Pensión Lumbreras* (☎ 925 22 15 71, Calle de Juan Labrador 9) has reasonable singles/doubles/triples around a pleasant courtyard for 1700/3200/4500 ptas, and the family-run *Hostal Nuevo Labrador*, (☎ 925 22 26 20) has rooms for 3500/6000 ptas plus IVA. *Pensión Nuncio Viejo* (☎ 925 22 81 78, Calle del Nuncio Viejo 19), on the other side of the cathedral, is pretty but its doubles are unexceptional at 3900 ptas, or 4400 ptas with own bathroom.

Moving up the scale, *Pensión Santa Úrsula* (☎ 925 22 34 26, Calle de Santa Úrsula 14) has decent doubles with bathroom for 6000 ptas. The friendly *Hotel Santa*

CASTILLA-LA MANCHA

sabel (☎/fax 925 25 31 36, e santa-isabel@ *trrakis.es, Calle de Santa Isabel 24*) is good value at 3925/6075 ptas plus IVA, with parking on the premises.

Hotel Maravilla (☎ 925 22 83 17, fax 925 22 81 55, Plaza de Barrio Rey 5) is in a quiet spot off Zocodover. Rooms with bath cost 4000/6500 ptas. Nearby is the pleasant *Hotel Imperio* (☎ 925 22 76 50, e himperio@teleline.es, Calle de las Cadenas 7) charging 4280/6200 ptas. The gracious *Hotel El Diamantista* (☎ 925 25 14 27, Plaza de Retama 5), down on the river and away from the hustle and bustle, charges 6420/8025 ptas.

Set in a beautiful garden just down from Puerta Nueva de Bisagra is *Hostal del Cardenal* (☎ 925 22 49 00, fax 925 22 29 91, e cardenal@macom.es, Paseo de Recaredo 24). Rooms are good value at 7800/12,600 ptas plus IVA, less in low season. Pricier is *Hotel Pintor El Greco* (☎ 925 21 42 50, fax 925 21 58 19, e elgreco@estanciases.es, Calle de Alamillos del Tránsito 13), where rooms cost 11,760/14,700 ptas plus IVA. *Hotel Carlos V* (☎ 925 22 21 00, fax 925 22 21 05, e info@carlosV.com, Calle de Trastámara 1) has rooms for 10,600/15,525 ptas plus IVA.

Hostales, Pensiones & Hotels – Outside the Old City If all else fails, there is a cluster of places near Plaza de Toros, a five-minute walk north along Carretera de Madrid from Puerta Nueva de Bisagra. The most amenable of these is probably the homely *Pensión Amalí* (☎ 925 22 70 18, Calle de Alonso Berruguete 1) with doubles at 4600 ptas.

On the southern bank of the Tajo and boasting magic views of the city is Toledo's premier establishment, *Parador Nacional Conde de Orgaz* (☎ 925 22 18 50, fax 22 51 66, e toledo@parador.es). Rooms cost 18,500 plus IVA. Without a car it's awkward to reach, although bus No 7 from Zocodover goes close.

Places to Eat

The cuisine of Toledo and indeed the whole region is based on simple peasant fare. Partridge, cooked in a variety of fashions, is probably the premier dish and particularly representative of Toledo. *Carcamusa*, a meat dish, is also typical, as is *cuchifritos*, a kind of potpourri of lamb, tomato and egg cooked in white wine with saffron.

Restaurants Toledo is predictably full of restaurants, many serving up average food for not-so-average prices.

For excellent *bocadillos* – great after a round of the bars – it is hard to beat *Ñaca Ñaca* on Zocodover. If you just want to pick at a pâté and cheese platter over a beer, try *Jacaranda Bar* (*Callejón de los Dos Codos 1*). It's a chilled out place where you can eat the equivalent of a full meal for about 1200 ptas. *Ludeña* (*Plaza de la Magdalena 13*) is an excellent little place for a full meal (set lunch for 1500 ptas) or simply a beer and tapas.

Among the cheap lunch spots, the friendly *El Delfín*, opposite the Museo de Taller del Moro, has a *menú del día* (daily set meal) for 950 ptas. For 50 ptas more, *El Tropezon* next to Hotel Santa Isabel offers fine fare that even the priests think is good. For outdoor dining, the *Osiris Bar* on the shady Plaza de Barrio Nuevo is a good pit stop, with set lunches from 1300 ptas. Other outdoor options include the slightly pricier *Restaurante Alex* on Plaza del Amador de los Ríos, or *El Patio* (*Plaza de Vicente 4*), which sits in a lovely courtyard.

Palacio de Fuensalida (*Plaza del Conde 2*), in the palace of the same name and near Iglesia de Santo Tomé, serves *paella* under vaulted ceilings. For slow service but good food (including a selection of pizzas), the family-run *El Armiño* (*Calle de las Tendillas 8*) is solid.

La Abadía (*Plaza de San Nicolás 3*), as well as being a popular bar, offers excellent downstairs dining with typical Toledan dishes such as *perdiz estofada* (stewed partridge). The top *menú* is rather pricey at 3450 ptas.

For Toledo's best seafood, *Bar La Ría* (*Callejón de los Bodegones 6*) is hard to beat. Allegedly run by Galicians, it has a wide menu – problem is, it's popular and tiny. A good meal will cost at least 2000

CASTILLA-LA MANCHA

ptas per person. Have a shot at the *maris-cada,* a cold and hot seafood platter.

Among the best known of Toledo's more expensive restaurants is *Restaurante Aurelio (Calle de la Sinagoga 1).* You will eat very well for about 5000 ptas per person. There is an extension across the road at No 6 and the proprietors have another restaurant at Plaza del Ayuntamiento 4. Better still is *Restaurante Hierbabuena (Callejón de San José 17).* The food is expensive but imaginatively classy – a considerable step up from the usual traditional fare.

Cafes The cafes on Zocodover are pleasant for a morning coffee or lunchtime beer, but the prices reflect the predominantly tourist clientele – that is, you pay double the usual.

Near the cathedral, *El Torreón (Plaza del Consistorio 3)* is a nice stop for coffee or lunch.

Cafetería Scorpions (Calle del Pintor Matias Moreno 10) is a trendier place to while away a Sunday afternoon. It has board games, a pool table and Internet access.

Just outside Toledo is a charming old roadside hostelry – *La Venta del Alma (Carretera de Piedrabuena 25).* Cross the Puente de San Martín and turn left up the hill – it's a couple of hundred metres up on your left.

For splendid views of the city, head out of town. Where the Carretera de Circunvalación (the ring road on the southern bank of the Tajo) forks for the parador, there is a small roadside drink stop, the *Kiosko Base.* Or you could enjoy more sweeping views and more expensive drinks from the *parador* itself. Farther up again, *Hotel Doménico* has a beer terrace with views – about the only place you'll get a breeze in the stifling midsummer months.

Self-Catering There is a *supermercado* on Plaza Mayor inside the Mercado Municipal building for your own supplies and an occasional *produce market* on the Plaza itself.

Entertainment
Bars & Discos Toledo isn't known for outstanding nightlife, but there are enough watering holes and noisy discos bursting with the city's young student population to keep you happy for a couple of days.

Start on a sedate note at *1700,* a pleasant *cervecería* (beer bar) on Plaza de las Tendillas. A couple of places serve a variety of Spanish and foreign beers – a decent one is *Lupulo,* just off Calle de Alfonso XII. Another is *La Abadía,* but more for the affluent crowd. In the streets around here particularly Calle de los Alfileritos and Calle de la Sillería, are many of the old city's busier, student-oriented bars. *Tbeo,* hidden away on Calle de la Sillería, caters for the more alternative crowd and *Camelot (Calle del Cristo de la Luz 10)* is a standard late-night watering hole.

At *Sildavia (Calle de Santa Fe 12)* go downstairs and ask for your favourite cocktail in a *porrón,* the glass version of a wine pouch – stained shirts are inevitable. If jazz and blues is required, head for *El Ultimo* on Plaza del Colegio de Infantes.

For more old-fashioned dancing and a decidedly more refined atmosphere, *El Café de Garcilaso (Calle de Rojas 5)* is a unique spot that doesn't get moving until quite late.

In the new part of the city there is a throng of late-night bars spilling onto the pavement around Plaza de Cuba and Calle Honduras. *El Pasito* and *La Barra* are the most popular, but the latter serves the best tapas.

Most of the young people finish the night in one of the discos down by the Miradero (a terrace overlooking the northern end of town), on the road from Zocodover to Puerta Nueva de Bisagra.

Theatre & Cinema *Teatro Rojas* (☎ 925 22 39 70) on Plaza Mayor often has an interesting program of theatre and dance, sometimes with prestigious Spanish and foreign companies. Tuesday nights are reserved for film cycles, often foreign pictures in the original language. Check for weekend kids' matinees. Otherwise, there is the *María Cristina cinema complex (Calle del Marqués de Mendigorría 10),* opposite Plaza de Toros. In summer, an open-air cinema functions at the Miradero.

Spectator Sports

Bullfighting aficionados can occasionally indulge their whims at the Plaza de Toros (built in 1866) on the road to Madrid. Quality bullfights *(corridas)* are more the exception than the rule.

Shopping

For centuries, Toledo was renowned for the excellence of its swords. Few people need such weapons these days, but toledanos keep forging them, along with all sorts of other metalwork. Sword sheaths, lighters and other objects bearing damascene *(damasquinado)* decoration (a fine encrustation of gold and/or silver in Arab artistic tradition) can make decent souvenirs. Another Arab bequest is the art of ceramics, which the whole region churns out in all imaginable forms. Toledo is bursting with stores selling this stuff, so shop around.

Among all the souvenir shops it is possible to find a few places of a more original bent and higher quality. The Antigüedades shop at Calle de los Reyes Católicos 8, near the Sinagoga de Santa María La Blanca, has good antiques – among them a lot of Jewish religious items – and attractive lithographs. For hand-painted copies of mainly medieval art on solid wood bases, peek into Las 3 Culturas, Calle de San Román 3.

Toledo is also famed for its marzipan *(mazapán),* which city merchants flog to all and sundry. There is good and bad. The Santo Tomé brand is reputable. You could also try El Convento, made by Dominican nuns at the Monasterio de Jesús y María. Take bus No 4 from Zocodover along Avenida de Europa to Buenavista. At the second roundabout, turn right up the hill, and the new monastery is to your left after another roundabout. When you enter you'll see a kind of antique rotating dumb waiter. The nuns don't want to see or be seen, so hit the buzzer and tell them what you want, then put your money in the dumb waiter and they rotate the marzipan out. Convento Santa Ursula (open 10.30 am to 6 pm), round the corner from Museo de Taller del Moro, is another place to buy handmade marzipan.

Getting There & Away

For most major destinations, you will need to backtrack to Madrid.

Bus Galiano Continental buses run every half-hour between Madrid (Estación Sur) and Toledo's bus station (☎ 925 22 36 41) from about 6 am to 10 pm daily (8.30 am to 11.30 pm Sunday and holidays). Direct buses (one hour, 585 ptas) run roughly every hour; the remainder call at all *pueblos* (villages). Other companies run to most surrounding towns and villages, such as Orgaz, Alcázar de San Juan and La Puebla de Montalbán. The AISA bus company has a service to Cuenca at 5.30 pm, to Albacete at 3 pm and Ciudad Real at 3.30 pm weekdays.

Train Built in 1920 in the neomudéjar style, Toledo's train station (☎ 925 22 30 99) is a pretty introduction to the city. There are no longer any *cercanías* (suburban trains) operating to Madrid's Atocha station, but regular train services still ply the route.

Car & Motorcycle The N-401 connects Toledo with Madrid. Heading south, you can take the same road to Ciudad Real, from where it becomes the N-420 to Córdoba. If you want the N-IV Autovía de Andalucía, the main motorway running south from Madrid to Córdoba and Sevilla, take the N-400 for Aranjuez. The N-403 heads northwest for Ávila and continues as the N-501 for Salamanca.

Getting Around

You won't want wheels to explore the nooks and crannies of Toledo's old town, but buses circulate through it and connect with outlying suburbs. Handy buses run between Zocodover and the train station (Nos 5 and 6) or the bus station (No 5).

There is a taxi rank just up from Zocodover in the shadow of the Alcázar, and another at the bus station. Or you can call one on ☎ 925 25 50 50.

Parking is possible, but not easy. Car parks charge around 190 ptas per hour.

CASTILLA-LA MANCHA

AROUND TOLEDO
Carranque
Since its discovery in 1983, archaeologists have been excavating what they believe to be the foundations of a late 4th-century Roman basilica, which would make it the oldest in Spain. The remains of a 12th-century monastery with some valuable mosaics are also undergoing excavation and study. At the time of writing, no official date was obtainable as to when the site would be open to the public. Check with the tourist office in Toledo. Carranque is just off the N-401 highway some 35km north of Toledo.

Castles
Castilla-La Mancha is littered with castles in varying states of upkeep. Some are readily accessible by public transport, while others are near impossible to get to without your own wheels. The following is a selection of castles within striking distance of Toledo.

Orgaz About 40km south of Toledo on the N-401 to Ciudad Real, this cheery village boasts a modest 15th-century **castle** *(castillo)*. It's in good nick but only open every second Wednesday from April to November. According to a rather enigmatic plaque, El Cid's wife, Doña Jimena, 'played here'. The leafy Plaza Mayor is flanked by attractive buildings with heavy wood-beam arcades and an 18th-century church built by Alberto Churriguera. Buses run fairly regularly from Toledo.

If you have a vehicle, a more interesting way of reaching Orgaz is via the C-400 road. About 20km out of Toledo, the ruined Arab castle of **Almonacid de Toledo** rises up directly in front of you. Some legends suggest El Cid lived here, but the lonely ruins have long been abandoned. A few kilometres farther down the road is another, smaller castle, in the centre of the village of **Mascaraque**.

Castillo de Montalbán Standing majestically over the Río Torcón valley some 30km south-west of Toledo, this hulking ruin is believed to have been erected by 12th-century Knights Templar. Its isolated setting leaves much to the imagination. Officially, it's open

from May to January only, but there's little to stop you wandering around at any time. Unfortunately, you'll need a vehicle to get here. Take the C-401 from Toledo to the C-403 junction and turn right towards La Pueblo de Montalbán. Ten kilometres up you'll see signs pointing to the castle.

Escalona This town sports a castle ruin of Arab origin, prettily located on the banks of the Río Alberche. If you're mobile it's worth stopping for and is located 52km north-west of Toledo on the N-403.

The West

TALAVERA DE LA REINA
postcode 45600 • pop 70,922
Scene of a key battle between Wellington and the French in 1809, and overrun by the Muslim Almoravid dynasty seven centuries earlier, Talavera betrays little evidence of its long and varied history. Though the town was the birthplace of Fernando de Rojas whose *Celestina* (published in 1499) is judged by some as Europe's first great novel, the only evidence of artistic activity of any sort today lies in the ubiquitous ceramics for which the town has long been justly famed. A fine example of their use is the facade of the **Teatro Victoria**, just off Plaza del Padre Juan de Mariana. Within the old city walls is the **Museo Ruiz de Luna** which houses a good collection of ceramic plates, jugs and even an impressive tiled altar, much of which dates from the 16th and 17th centuries. The museum is in a beautifully restored convent at Calle de San Agustín el Viejo s/n, and is open from 10 am to 2 pm and 4 to 6.30 pm, closed Sunday afternoon and Monday (100 ptas). To make your own purchases, follow the road leading north to the N-V motorway, which is lined with ceramics factories and shops. The tourist office (☎ 925 82 63 22) can be found on Ronda del Cañello, east of the old city walls, open 10 am to 7 pm Monday to Saturday and 11 am to 2.30 pm Sunday.

There is no particular reason to stay, but you'll find a few *hostales* (budget hotels around if you need them. *Hostal Edan* (☎ 925 80 69 89, Paseo de Extremadura 24) has doubles for 4800 ptas.

The bus station is in the town centre. Regular buses between Madrid and Badajoz stop here and 10 go to Toledo daily (735 ptas, 90km east). You can also reach Mérida, Cáceres, Plasencia and Trujillo. Talavera is on the Madrid-Lisbon train line, not one of Spain's fastest.

AROUND TALAVERA DE LA REINA
More pleasant than Talavera is the village of **Oropesa**, 34km west along the N-V. Its 14th-century **castle** (open 10 am to 2 pm and 4 to 8 pm daily except Monday; 200 ptas) looks north across the plains to the Sierra de Gredos and also hosts a *parador* (☎ 925 43 00 00), which has comfortable doubles for 15,000 ptas plus IVA.

Another 13km south, **El Puente del Arzobispo** is another well-known ceramics centre. There are plenty of places where you can inspect the town's wares. The bridge after which the town is named was built in the 14th century.

MONTES DE TOLEDO
Beginning as the low foothills that lie south of Toledo astride the road to Ciudad Real, the Montes de Toledo rise westwards towards Extremadura. Exploring the Montes takes you into the heart of some of the most sparsely populated country of Spain's interior. You can't get much farther away from the tourist routes, but you could make a slow trip through the mountains on the way from Toledo to Guadalupe (or vice-versa). Most towns are served by the occasional bus – often no more than one a day on weekdays – from Toledo.

If you have a vehicle, the most straightforward route is the C-401, which skirts the northern slopes of the Montes. Eleven kilometres short of Navahermosa, a trail leads south to **Embalse de Torcón**, a popular lakeshore picnic spot.

Beyond Navahermosa you have several options for branching south. Some of the more heavily wooded areas offer unexpect-edly charming vistas, and apart from the odd tiny pueblo, you will hardly see a soul. One longish route that gives a taste of the area would see you dropping south off the C-401 at Los Navalmorales. Take the TO-752 towards Los Navalucillos, a few kilometres after which is a peaceful *bar* right on the banks of the lively little Río Pusa. From here, you keep heading south past run-down little villages until you hit a T-junction. Turning right (west) you wind 35km to the northern reaches of the huge **Embalse de Cijara**, part of a chain of reservoirs fed by the Río Guadiana. After the tiny village of Cijara, swing north towards **Puerto Rey**, a mountain pass from where you can branch off west along a back road to the C-401 and the last curvy stretch towards Guadalupe (see the Extremadura chapter).

Yet another alternative is to head for the **San Pablo de los Montes** area. You can take the TO-781 via Argés south of Toledo, and onward via Las Ventas with Peña Aguilera (which is renowned for its venison). San Pablo de los Montes is an average hill town, but a 10km drive farther south and over the mountaintop brings you to **Baños de Robledillo**, with thermal springs.

Balnearios Baños de Robledillo (☎ 925 41 53 00) has beds for 1500 ptas per person, doubles with en suite bathroom for 2300 ptas, and a *restaurant*. For 900 ptas you can soak in the curative waters. Call ahead to make sure it is open.

The South

CIUDAD REAL
postcode 13003 • pop 59,392
Just 110km down the road from the Imperial City of Toledo lies its royal counterpart, Ciudad Real. Founded by Castilian King Alfonso X in 1255 to check the power of the Knights of Calatrava, who were based in nearby Almagro, Ciudad Real quickly became an important provincial capital, although only finally eclipsing Almagro in the 18th century. Remnants of the old city are few, but there's enough to warrant a brief visit.

CASTILLA-LA MANCHA

Information

The Oficina de Información Turística (☎ 926 21 29 25), Avenida de Alarcos 21, is open 10 am to 2 pm and 4 to 7 pm Monday to Saturday, closed Sunday afternoons. It has a reasonable stock of information on the province. The main post office is on Plaza de la Constitución.

Things to See

Coming from the north, you enter Ciudad Real by the **Puerta de Toledo**, a 14th-century defensive gate built in mudéjar style by Alfonso XI.

Inside the largely modern city there are a number of museums, with the pick of the crop the **Museo Provincial**, Calle del Prado 4, which offers a reasonable display of archaeological finds dating from Palaeolithic times, along with a collection of artworks, mostly provincial, covering the past four centuries. It's open 10 am to 2 pm daily except Monday, and 5 to 8 pm Tuesday to Saturday; free.

Of the few churches to be seen, the most striking is the 14th-century Gothic **Iglesia de San Pedro**.

Places to Stay & Eat

Accommodation is unexceptional, so try not to be caught in Ciudad Real. Just outside the southern end of the city centre is *Pensión Escudero (☎ 926 25 23 09, Calle de Galicia 48),* with basic rooms starting at 2200/3600 ptas with shared bathroom. Bus No 5 from the train station runs past it. If you've got a lot more cash to spare, the four-star *Hotel Santa Cecilia (☎ 926 22 85 45, Calle de Tinte 3)* will set you back 13,500 ptas plus IVA.

For all your food and drinking requirements, head for Avenida del Torreón del Alcázar and the parallel Calle de los Hidalgos. The former is lined with cafes and restaurants, such as *El Torreón* at No 7, which specialises in game from the region, and *El Barco* at No 11, more of a bar with a sailing theme (in this part of the country?) and decent seafood. In Calle de los Hidalgos you can snack well on tapas while imbibing *cañas* in the string of bars. Otherwise, the *Restaurante Villa Real (Calle de las Postas 12)* has a *menú* for 1500 ptas.

CIUDAD REAL

PLACES TO STAY & EAT
6 Restaurante Villa Real
10 El Torreón
11 El Barco
12 Hotel Santa Cecilia

OTHER
1 Puerta de Toledo
2 Main Post Office (Correos)
3 Museo Provincial
4 Plaza Mayor
5 Ayuntamiento
6 Oficina de Información Turística
8 Plaza del Pilar
9 Iglesia de San Pedro
13 Bus Station
14 Parque de Gasset

Getting There & Away

Bus The bus station is south of the town centre, off Ronda de Ciruela. There's a bus to Toledo at 8 am, another to Córdoba at 11 am and six per day to Madrid. Most surrounding towns can be reached by bus.

Train The bulk of trains linking Madrid with Andalucía, including the high-speed AVE to Sevilla, call in at Ciudad Real (☎ 926 22 02 02; the station is east of the town centre). Trains also head east to Albacete, Valencia and Alicante, as well as to Badajoz in Extremadura. Local bus Nos 5 and 2 run to the station from Plaza del Pilar in the centre.

CIUDAD REAL PROVINCE

Almagro

postcode 13270 • pop 8436

It may have come second in the struggle for local supremacy with Ciudad Real, but Almagro has retained a charm long lost in its competitor. De facto medieval capital of what

CASTILLA-LA MANCHA

even today is still known as the Campo de Calatrava, Almagro underwent a unique face-lift in the 16th century after the arrival of several German families, including the Fuggers of Augsburg, bankers to Spain's Carlos I. It is largely to them and their successors that Almagro's porticoed **Plaza Mayor** owes its present distinctive appearance.

At No 18 you'll find **El Corral de Comedias**, a 17th-century theatre still often used, especially for the annual Festival Internacional de Teatro Clásico in July. It is open 10 am to 2 pm and 4 to 7 pm Tuesday to Friday (shorter hours on the weekend); buy tickets (400 ptas) at the small Museo del Teatro (same hours) across the square. A smattering of churches, convents and public buildings around the town make Almagro a pleasant spot for a little exploration. The Oficina de Turismo de Almagro (☎ 926 86 07 17) is two streets south of Plaza Mayor at Calle de Bernardas 2.

Almagro is preferable to Ciudad Real for an overnight stop. *Hospedería Convento de la Asunción de Calatrava (☎ 926 88 20 87, Calle de Ejido de Calatrava s/n)* is good value with singles/doubles starting at 3000/4000 ptas. Nearby, *Hotel Don Diego (☎ 926 86 12 87, fax 926 86 05 74, Calle de Bolaños 1)* charges 5350/8560 ptas (more in the high season). If you're desperate, there's also a spattering of *hotels* on the road to Bolaños de Calatrava.

If you want to do it in a little more style, the *parador (☎ 926 86 01 00),* in a former convent on Ronda de San Francisco, has rooms for 14,000/17,500 ptas plus IVA.

There are several cafes and bars on Plaza Mayor; the *Restaurante Airén* at No 41 has tables on the square.

Two trains daily go to Madrid and up to four to Ciudad Real and Jaén. You can also get to Alicante and Barcelona, both in the morning. Buses run from near Hotel Don Diego to Ciudad Real, but there are none on Sunday.

Castillo de Calatrava

About 30km south of Almagro, the brooding walls of the castle-and-monastery complex of Calatrava La Nueva (signposted as

The Battle of Alarcos

On 19 July 1195, the greatest of all the Almohad rulers, Yacoub Al-Mansour (the Victorious), drew his forces up near the settlement of Alarcos, about 5km south-west of Ciudad Real, to face the Castilian army of Alfonso VIII. Unwilling to wait for the arrival of reinforcements marching from the north, Alfonso decided to unleash his cavalry at the Muslim forces, recently arrived from Morocco to restore Muslim control over Spain. Alfonso's horsemen crushed Al-Mansour's vanguard but quickly found themselves surrounded. A promising start thus turned into a rout.

According to the Almohad chronicler Ibn Idari: 'Allah granted us victory and the defeated Christians turned their backs and abandoned their swords. The tyrant's camp was sacked and swept as in a harvest with the Christians' deaths – said to be around 30,000...Alfonso, the enemy of God, escaped to Toledo...'. Some say only 300 soldiers survived the disaster.

A Christian observer saw Alfonso's role a little differently: 'The noble king advanced and, plunging in amongst the enemy, felled with manliness many Moors...but as his men realised that Spain was in imminent danger, pulled him from the battle. He later arrived in Toledo with a few soldiers, aggrieved by the great misfortune.'

Al-Mansour never really capitalised on his victory, and 17 years later it was made irrelevant by the crushing Christian victory in the Battle of Las Navas de Tolosa. Today, there is little to see at the battleground except a chapel dedicated to Our Lady of Alarcos.

Castillo de Calatrava) command magnificent views across the sierra of the same name. Once a forward base of the medieval order of knights that long controlled this frontier area of La Mancha during the Reconquista, the complex (free) is open 10 am to 2 pm and 4 to 7 pm Tuesday to Sunday. Even if closed it merits a visit for the site and view alone. From Calzada de Calatrava, it's 7km south along the CR-504 and is accessible only with your own vehicle.

CASTILLA-LA MANCHA

Parque Nacional de Las Tablas de Daimiel

You get used to a steady diet of olive-studded red plains and forbidding plateaus while traversing much of southern Castilla-La Mancha, but a couple of exceptions prove the rule.

The reedy lakes of Las Tablas, 11km north of Daimiel, are no great inspiration, but an early morning stroll here in spring or autumn can be profitable for the birdwatcher. The park's information centre is open from 8 am to dusk daily. There is no public transport to the park, and years of near drought have taken their toll. Fortunately, heavy rains in late 1995 and a subsequent deal to transfer water from the Río Tajo arrested the slow but steady decline.

Parque Natural de las Lagunas de Ruidera

A more unexpectedly green patch in the middle of parched Castilla-La Mancha is the Parque Natural de las Lagunas de Ruidera. Surrounding a series of small lakes, with the odd waterfall and diverse bird life, it is a favoured summer retreat for hot and bothered Castilians. There is an HI youth hostel on the Laguna Colgada, the *Albergue Juvenil Alonso Quijano* (☎ 967 21 50 12), charging 1450 ptas if you're under 26, 3050 ptas otherwise, and meals are available (membership card required). Among several other options farther around the lakes is *Hostal El Molino* (☎ 926 69 90 73), which has doubles for 3000 ptas or 3500 ptas with own bath. There are a few camping grounds too. The tourist office (open from Wednesday to Sunday) in the town of Ruidera has local maps.

You really need wheels to get into and around the park. The town of Ruidera and the lakes are about halfway between Ciudad Real and Albacete on the N-430 highway, and buses connect with Albacete.

Valdepeñas

The people of Castilla-La Mancha usually drink their own local wines but make an exception for the fruit of the Valdepeñas area's vines, which finds its way around not only the region, but the whole country. For those weary of long, dusty drives between the odd castle and provincial towns, a spot of wine tasting in one of this town's several *bodegas* (cellars) might be just the ticket. The best are north of town on the road to Madrid. If that's not your scene, don't bother stopping in this surprisingly large and uninviting place.

Villanueva de los Infantes
postcode 13320 • pop 5792

About 30km east of Valdepeñas along the C-415 road to Alcaraz (see the Sierra de Alcaraz section later in this chapter) lies Villanueva de los Infantes, the fruit of a repopulation campaign in La Mancha as the Muslims fell back into Andalucía after the Battle of Las Navas de Tolosa in 1212. Like Almagro, the town's **Plaza Mayor** offers its most pleasing aspect, although the deep ochre-coloured buildings and heavy wooden balconies are altogether in a different style. On the square stands the **Iglesia de San Andrés**, with two doors and a pulpit in plateresque style. The 16th-century poet Francisco Gómez Quevedo y Villegas was buried here. Also like Almagro, Villanueva is studded with old nobles' houses and rewards a bit of a wander and even an overnight stay. There's an extremely helpful tourist office on Plaza Mayor (☎ 926 36 13 21). Four streets south of Plaza Mayor is the lovely former convent *Hospedería El Buscón Queveda* (☎/fax 926 36 17 88, @ buscon@paralelo40.org, Calle Frailes 1), with singles/doubles a bargain for 5550/8900 plus IVA. Quevedo spent his last days here, and his room is set up as though he was about to return. Buses head west to Ciudad Real.

SOUTH-EAST TO ALBACETE

The highways leading south-east from Madrid to Albacete and on into Valencia take you through arguably some of the most depressing examples of Spanish countryside. The shrivelled, treeless expanses of La Mancha soon weary all but the most enthusiastic lovers of scorched earth. If you're heading to the Valencian *costas* from Madrid, about all you can do is scream down the road as fast as your wheels will carry you. Offerings along the way are sparse, but there are a few potential stops to break the journey.

Windmills & More Castles

Consuegra Following the C-400 out of Toledo (see Around Toledo earlier in this chapter) the first stop of interest beyond Mora is Consuegra, set in classic La Mancha country. The tumbledown village huddles below a hill topped by a 13th-century **castle** that once belonged to the Knights of Malta. A number of rooms have been reconstructed, along with a wonderful tower, giving a good indication of how the Knights would have lived. The castle is open 9.15 am to 1.45 pm and 3.45 to 5.45 pm daily (300 ptas). Fans of Don Quijote will be delighted to know that a dozen restored windmills, the best in the area, flank the castle. The site is well chosen – it gets quite blowy. There's a helpful tourist office (☎ 925 47 57 31) in the Bolero mill (they all have names), open 9 am to 2 pm and 4.30 to 7 pm daily (from 10.30 am weekends), April to October, where you can explore the workings of the mill. You can see at least one in action during the annual Fiesta de la Rosa del Azafrán, held on the last weekend of October.

The best option to kip down is *Hotel Las Provincias* (☎ 925 48 03 00), out on the Toledo–Alcázar de San Juan highway. Singles/doubles cost 3500/7000 ptas. If you haven't got wheels to get away on, there are up to eight daily buses between Consuegra and Toledo (three on weekends) and up to three to Madrid.

Campo de la Criptana & Around

Don Quijote thought he might do battle here, mistaking for enemies the windmills that are the only interesting feature in this otherwise dispiriting place. The Infotur tourist office (☎ 926 56 22 31), in the Poyatos mill, is open 10 am to 2 pm and 4 to 7 pm (5 to 8 pm in summer), closed all day Monday and Sunday afternoon. If you *have* to stay, there are a few small hotels in town, including *Hostal Sancho* (☎ 926 56 00 12) on Plaza Mayor, with doubles for 3200 ptas.

The odd train and regional bus calls in, but options are greater from Alcázar de San Juan, 7km west of Campo de la Criptana (about seven buses daily run between the two). In fact, if you're travelling around this area without your own wheels, you could wind up in Alcázar, a major train junction. Apart from the 18th-century Iglesia de Santa María (it is thought Cervantes was baptised here) in the square of the same name, and the nearby Torreón (Tower) de Don Juan de Austria, there is nothing to draw you to Alcázar but its transport options. If you get stuck here overnight, *Hostal Aldonza* (☎ 926 54 15 540), right near the train station, has decent rooms for 4000/6000 ptas. Trains leave for destinations throughout the country, including Albacete, Barcelona, Cádiz, Ciudad Real, Madrid, Málaga and Sevilla. Occasional buses serve Belmonte, Cuenca and Toledo.

The windmill-obsessed can see still more at **Mota del Cuervo**, 29km north-east of Campo de la Criptana, at the junction with the N-301.

Belmonte About 25km north-east of Mota del Cuervo is one of the better preserved Castilian castles. Set on a low knoll above the village of the same name, the 15th-century **Castillo de Belmonte**, with its six round towers, was for a while home to France's Empress Eugénie after her husband Napoleon III lost the French throne in 1871. It's open 10 am to 1 pm and 4.30 pm to sunset daily (300 ptas); there's not an awful lot to see inside. Also worth a visit, if you can find the curate, is Iglesia Colegial de San Bartolomé, or **Colegiata**, with an impressive retablo. If you need to stay, *La Muralla* (☎ 967 17 10 45) is clean and cheap at 4000 ptas per double, or *Palacio Buenavista Hospedería* (☎ 967 18 75 80), near the church, is lovely and charges 8500 ptas plus IVA.

ALBACETE

postcode 02003 • pop 143,799

Named after its location (*al-basit*, in Arabic, refers to the plains), this dull provincial city expanded rapidly after malarial swamps were drained in the 19th century – too late to create anything of great interest. At best, it may serve as a transport junction for people wandering about this part of the country.

If you do get stuck between connections, wander towards the centre and down Paseo de la Libertad, which soon becomes Calle de

Tilting at Life

Time and again as you march across the glum stretches of La Mancha you are reminded by roadside plaques and signs that you are in the territory of Don Quijote. The potty and idealistic *manchego* knight, or rather his creator, Miguel de Cervantes, could not have chosen a more challenging territory for his character's search for a new individualism, unfettered by the rigidity of 16th-century Spanish society.

But Cervantes, however well he may have known La Mancha, sensibly spent most of his years elsewhere, painting his life on a much vaster canvas than he allows his hapless but tenacious hero. A brief look at Cervantes' CV reveals an equally tenacious and perhaps even more accident-filled existence. Having passed his younger years between Valladolid, Salamanca, Madrid and Sevilla, the 19-year-old writer and soon-to-be adventurer fled to Italy in 1568 to escape a prison sentence for assault. Three years later he was wounded at the Battle of Lepanto. In 1573 he participated in the seizure of Tunis, and in 1575 he hopped on a galley for Spain from Naples. It seems natural that Cervantes, ever in trouble, should have been on board the boat that was separated from the convoy and taken by corsairs. Sold as a slave in Algiers, he only managed to escape, after four failed attempts, in 1580. After trying unsuccessfully to get passage to America, he married and almost settled down in Sevilla. Vexation was never far from Cervantes' door, however, and in 1602 he ended up in chains for his involvement in a bank's collapse. He did time again a few years later under an unproved charge of murder, and subsequently moved to Madrid, where in the years until his death in 1616 he wrote the bulk of his work, of which *El Ingenioso Hidalgo Don Quijote de la Mancha* was the jewel in his literary crown.

Tesifonte Gallego. A few streets down and off to the right you'll find the **catedral**, appealing enough with its four Ionic columns. Otherwise, you could kill an hour or two in the leafy Parque de Abelardo Sánchez, farther down Calle de Tesifonte Gallego, and the **Museo Provincial** (200 ptas) therein.

The tourist office (☎ 967 58 05 22), at Calle del Tinte 2, is open 10 am to 2 pm and 4.30 to 6.30 pm weekdays, 10 am to 6 pm Saturday, and until 3 pm Sunday. There's an Internet cafe at Calle Mayor 59, sharing the photo shop Yahvé 2, east of the tourist office.

There is a ton of accommodation in all categories if you end up needing to stay here. *La Feria* (☎ 967 21 00 77, San Sebastian 6), about five minutes' walk west of Plaza Mayor, has doubles for 3000 ptas.

The bus station, next to the train station, is at the north-eastern end of town. Enatcar buses serve Madrid, Barcelona, Alicante, Valencia and Sevilla. There's a bus to Toledo at 5.30 am and to Cuenca at 6 am and 3 pm (nothing to either on Sunday). Buses run to most places in the province, including Chinchilla de Monte Aragón, Alcaraz and other villages in the Sierra, Ruidera and Almansa.

Trains serve Alicante, Ciudad Real, Madrid, Toledo and Valencia.

AROUND ALBACETE

There are several interesting little places scattered around Albacete, and at its more distant margins the scenery changes quite unexpectedly for the better.

Two local castles that Albacete's tourist office pushes hard are located just off the N-430 motorway towards Valencia. First is the restored fortress in **Chinchilla de Monte Aragón**, a whitewashed village with a pretty square, served by bus from Albacete. About 60km farther on, a square-turreted **castle** built by the Muslims stands high above the town of **Almansa**.

CASTILLA-LA MANCHA

Río Júcar

Cutting a deep, tree-filled gorge to the north-east of Albacete, the Río Júcar makes for a pleasant back-road drive. About halfway along the east-west route, **Alcalá del Júcar** is impossible to miss – its 15th-century castle tower is an unmistakable landmark. The village houses are piled crazily one above the other up the steep bank of the Júcar; the foot of the town is a wonderful place to admire this while having a drink or even a swim in the pool. The tourist office is located at the foot of the town as well.

There is a *camping ground* and a few cheap *pensiones*. The comfortable *Hostal El Júcar* (☎ *967 47 30 55, Calle Balán 1*) has singles/doubles for 2800/5000 ptas, and there is a *restaurant* attached.

Sierra de Alcaraz

Stretching across the southern strip of Albacete province, the cool, green peaks of the Sierra de Alcaraz are laced with small, intensively farmed plots, dotted with villages and are a great escape from the dusty plains around Albacete. The Río Mundo begins its life as a waterfall near Riópar, and **Alcaraz** is itself an attractive little town with a pretty plaza mayor. You can follow a circuit through or past Alcaraz, Vianos, Riópar, Ayna, and Bogarra. Donkey-mounted shepherds still watch over their small flocks of sheep in the remoter corners of this low mountain territory. The odd bus gets to some of these towns, but you'd be better off with a vehicle – and good hiking boots. There are a few *hostales* in the area, including Alcaraz and Vianos.

The North-East

CUENCA

postcode 16002 • pop 43,733

Castilla-La Mancha's most interesting town after Toledo offers relief from the parched countryside typical of most of the region. Spreading north and east of the city, the Serranía de Cuenca is a heavily wooded and fertile zone of low mountains and green fields. With a vehicle you could explore the city and the local region in two or three days.

History

Although it was probably inhabited before Roman times, nothing much is known of Cuenca until the period of Muslim occupation. Fortified by one Ismail bin Dilnun early in the 11th century, the city became a flourishing textile centre. The Christians took their time about conquering the place, and it fell only in 1177 to Alfonso VIII. The city continued to prosper in the following centuries, but the malaise that crippled much of the interior of Spain from the 16th century led to a decline from which Cuenca only began to recover during the 20th century.

Orientation

Cuenca is relatively small, its old centre a narrow rise high up at the northern end of the city between the river gorges of the Júcar and Huécar. The train and bus stations are virtually opposite each other near the centre of the new town, and a 10-minute walk from the foot of the old town. It's a long climb to Plaza Mayor, the main square in the old town.

Information

Tourist Office The Infotur office (☎ 969 23 21 19), Calle de Alfonso VIII 2, just before the arches of Plaza Mayor, is very helpful. It's open 9.30 am to 2 pm and 4 to 6 pm daily.

Money There are plenty of banks in the new town, especially around Calle de la Carretería.

Post & Communications The main post office is on the corner of Calle del Parque de San Julián and Calle del Dr Fleming, and the main Telefónica office is at Paseo de San Antonio s/n. La Repro (e franquicias@larepro.com), near the train and bus stations, doubles as an Internet cafe and photocopying shop.

Internet Resources Cuenca's official Web site at www.cuenca.org is a good place to start planning your visit.

Medical Services & Emergency If you need the police in a hurry, call ☎ 091. In a medical emergency, call ☎ 969 23 01 31 for

CASTILLA-LA MANCHA

CUENCA

PLACES TO STAY
1 Pensión La Tabanqueta
4 Hotel Leonora de Aquitania
5 Parador
6 Posada de San José
27 Pensión Tintes
28 Posada de San Julián
31 Hostal Avenida
33 Pensión Central
34 Hotel Figón de Pedro
35 Pensión Marin

PLACES TO EAT
8 Restaurante San Nicolás
12 Bar La Tinaja
14 Mesón Casas Colgadas

OTHER
2 Castillo Walls
3 Iglesia de San Pedro
7 Bar Dulcinea
9 Plaza San Nicolás
10 Iglesia de San Miguel
11 Catedral
13 Museo Diocesano
15 Casas Colgadas & Museo de Arte Abstracto Español
16 Museo de Cuenca
17 Ayuntamiento
18 Infotur Tourist Office
19 Museo de Las Ciencias
20 Torre de Mangana
21 Iglesia de la Santa Cruz
22 Teatro Auditorio
23 Iglesia de San Felipe
24 Iglesia Plaza de El Salvador
25 Discos
26 Main Post Office (Correos)
29 Supermercado
30 La Caixa Bank
32 Deutsche Bank
36 Local Bus Nos 1 and 2 to Plaza Mayor
37 La Repro
38 Discos & Pubs
39 Bus Station
40 Plaza de Toros

the Cruz Roja. Hospital de la Virgen (☎ 969 22 42 11) is off Avenida de la Cruz Roja at the north-western edge of the new town.

Catedral
Everyone seems to agree that the western facade of this Gothic cathedral is an unfortunately tasteless aberration. The initial errors were committed in the 1600s and compounded by restoration early in the 20th century. Built on the site of a mosque, the nave dates back as far as the early 13th century, although other elements such as the apse were constructed in the mid-15th century. The modern stained glass windows add cheery colour to an otherwise drab interior. There is a small **Museo de la Catedral** inside, open 11 am to 2 pm and 4 to 6 pm (worth the 200 ptas), but the cathedral itself tends to open earlier in the morning.

Casas Colgadas
Possibly the most striking element of the medieval city is these so-called 'hanging houses', some of which jut out precariously over the steep defile of the Huécar. This is economical use of restricted living space! A couple of much-restored examples,

characterised by layers of wooden balconies, now contain a posh restaurant and an art museum (see Museums following).

Museums

All the museums are closed on Sunday afternoon and Monday. Depending on your taste in art, the star of the Cuenca line-up may be the **Museo de Arte Abstracto Español**. The setting, one of the casas colgadas, sports a fine artesonado-coffered ceiling, and the artists represented include Chillida, Millares, Sempere and Zobel. Initially a private initiative of Fernando Zobel to unite works by fellow artists of the 1950s Generación Abstracta, it now includes works up to the present day. The museum is open 11 am to 2 pm and 4 to 6 pm (to 8 pm Saturday); entry is 500 ptas.

Virtually opposite each other on Calle del Obispo Valero are the **Museo de Cuenca** (at No 12) and the **Museo Diocesano**. The former has a reasonable archaeological collection from the Cuenca area, ranging from prehistory through the Romanisation of this part of classical Hispania and on up to the 12th century. Of the religious art and artefacts in the latter, the 14th-century Byzantine diptych is the jewel in the crown. How such a piece ended up in Cuenca, no one seems to know. The Museo de Cuenca is open 10 am to 2 pm and 4 to 6 pm, while the Museo Diocesano opens an hour later in the morning and two hours longer on Saturday (200 ptas each).

South of Plaza Mayor in a former convent, the **Museo de Las Ciencias** (Science Museum) is a surprising find in Cuenca. Displays range from a time machine (prepare for the annoying jolts), to the development of the human species and a study of the resources of Castilla-La Mancha. There are plenty of interactive gadgets to keep all ages happy. The museum is open 10 am to 2 pm and 4 to 7 pm daily, closed Sunday afternoons (free).

Muslim Cuenca

Down the hill from the old town along Calle de Alfonso VIII, you'll notice the **Torre de Mangana** off to the west, all that remains of a fortress built by Cuenca's Muslim rulers.

Places to Stay

Camping There are several camping grounds around Cuenca. *Caravaning Cuenca* (☎ 969 23 16 56) is 8km out of town on the road towards the Ciudad Encantada.

Pensiones & Hotels – Old Town At the very top of the old town, *Pensión Real* (☎ 949 22 99 77, Calle Larga 41) offers fine views of Cuenca and charges 3500 ptas for doubles. Bus No 2 from the stations stops here. Opposite Iglesia de San Pedro is the clean and simple *Pensión La Tabanqueta* (☎ 969 21 12 90, Calle de Trabuco 13) charging 2000 ptas per person. Ask for a room with views of the Júcar gorge.

Just beyond the cathedral, *Posada de San José* (☎ 969 21 13 00, Ronda de Julián Romero 4) is a lovely 16th-century residence with doubles for 9100 ptas plus IVA. The only other possibility is *Hotel Leonora de Aquitania* (☎ 969 23 10 00, Calle de San Pedro 60), a classy place but with less character than the others. Singles/doubles cost 9950/14,500 ptas plus IVA.

Pensiones & Hotels – New Town The new part of Cuenca is littered with places to stay. *Pensión Tintes* (☎ 969 21 23 98, Calle de los Tintes 7) has basic rooms for about 1500 ptas per person in summer. It is just outside the old town, as is *Posada de San Julián* (☎ 969 21 17 04, Calle de las Torres 1), a cavernous old place with doubles for 3000 ptas (4000 ptas with bathroom).

A spartan-like place is *Pensión Central* (☎ 969 21 15 11, Calle del Doctor Chirino 9), with rooms for 1500/2600 ptas. The friendly *Pensión Marín* (☎ 969 22 19 78, Calle de Ramón y Cajal 53) is a short walk from the train station, with rooms for 1300/2400 ptas.

Hostal Avenida (☎ 969 21 43 43, Calle de la Carretería 25) has basic singles for 2500 ptas and doubles with bath for 3500 ptas (more in summer). A decent budget to mid-range place is *Hotel Figón de Pedro* (☎ 969 22 45 11, Calle de Cervantes 13), with rooms for 4000/6000 ptas plus IVA.

Parador The top of the tree is the *parador* (☎ 969 23 23 20) in the converted

Dominican Convento de San Pablo on the southern bank of the Río Huécar. Rooms cost 14,000/17,500 ptas plus IVA. A footbridge connects the parador with the old town across the Huécar gorge.

Places to Eat

Restaurants There are several restaurants scattered around Plaza Mayor in the heart of the old town – easily the nicest part of town to eat in. The city's star is the rather expensive *Mesón Casas Colgadas (Calle de los Canónigos 3)* next to the Museo de Arte Abstracto Español. It is a wonderful location, but you won't get away for much less than 3000 ptas. Another decent establishment for solid manchego food is *Restaurante San Nicolás (Calle de San Pedro 15)*, with mains ranging between 2000 and 3000 ptas. If you're not fussed about eating in the old town, your choices expand down the hill. *Pensión Tintes* (see Places to Stay) has a pleasant dining room with a *menú* for 1500 ptas.

Cafes The cafes on Plaza Mayor are perfect for a relaxing drink and people-watching. *Bar La Tinaja (Calle del Obispo Valero 4)* and *Bar Dulcinea (Calle de San Pedro 10)* are both pleasant, popular places for a drink.

Entertainment

You can join the young set that crowds together along Calle de San Miguel for loads of noisy evening *copas* (drinks). There are a couple of bars here, but many of the locals just bring their own.

If you're looking for a bit more excitement later on in the evening, you'll find some discos across the road from the train station, and a few others on Calle del Doctor Galindez.

Shopping

You might want to pick up a special bottle of the local firewater, Resoli, made in the shape of the Casas Colgadas – an unusual souvenir idea.

Getting There & Away

Bus Up to nine buses daily (two express) with AutoRes serve Madrid (2½ hours, 1325 ptas or 1650 ptas for the express). Other com-

panies run buses to Valencia (1500 ptas, up to three a day) and Albacete (up to three a day), and one to Barcelona (nine hours, 4385 ptas) via Teruel. This last one leaves at 9.30 am. There is one bus daily to Toledo (5.30 am), Alicante (11.30 am), Beteta (2.30 pm) and Belmonte (3 pm Monday to Saturday).

Train Cuenca lies on a train line connecting Madrid to Valencia. Five trains a day go to Madrid (Atocha). They take 2½ hours and a 2nd-class ticket costs 1405 ptas. Four go to Valencia (3¼ hours, 1545 ptas).

Car & Motorcycle From Madrid, the quickest route to Cuenca is the N-III, turning east onto the N-400 at Tarancón.

Getting Around

Local bus Nos 1 and 2 for Plaza Mayor leave from near the train station.

SERRANÍA DE CUENCA

The rivers Júcar and Huécar flow through Cuenca from the high hinterland to the north-east of the city known as the Serranía de Cuenca. If you have transport (there are no buses), the area is worth a day of exploration.

From Cuenca, take the CM-2105 (formerly CU-921) about 30km to the so-called **Ciudad Encantada**, or Enchanted City. Extremely popular with locals, this series of rocks eroded into some quite fantastical shapes have been lent equally outlandish names by human observers. Still, it is possible to see a boat on its keel, a dog and a Roman bridge if you let your imagination carry you away. The site is open 10 am to 7 pm daily (300 ptas). There is a *hostal* opposite the entrance with a restaurant and bar.

You could head back to the CM-2105 and proceed east. The country is pleasant, dotted by a couple of sleepy villages and the clear blue lake of the **Embalse de la Toba**. About 6km on from Huélamo, a turn-off to the right leads across the Montes Universales to Albarracín (see the Aragón chapter) – a perfect place to end the day's drive and stay overnight.

Alternatively, the CM-2105 swings north to the **Nacimiento del Río Cuervo**, a pretty enough spot with a couple of small waterfalls where the Río Cuervo rises. From here you could loop around towards **Beteta** and the gorge of the same name, or cross the provincial frontier into Guadalajara to make for the pleasant if unspectacular **Parque Natural del Alto Tajo**. To the west lies La Alcarria (see the Guadalajara section following).

AROUND CUENCA
Alarcón
One hundred kilometres or so south of Cuenca is the triangle-based Muslim castle at Alarcón, which has been converted into a *parador* (☎ 969 33 03 15), with rooms for 19,000 ptas plus IVA.

Segóbriga
These impressive Roman-era ruins may date as far back as the 5th century BC. Visigoths then added their own touches to what had become a small but wealthy trade centre. The best-preserved structures are a Roman theatre and amphitheatre. Other remains include the outlines of a Visigothic basilica and a section of the aqueduct, which helped keep the city green in what is otherwise quite a barren desert. The small **Museo de Segóbriga** is located on the site (closed Monday). It seems you can explore the ruins at any time.

The site is near Saelices, 2km south of the N-III motorway between Madrid and Albacete. From Cuenca, drive west 55km on the N-400, then turn south on the C-202.

GUADALAJARA
postcode 19001 • pop 67,108
Founded as Roman Arriaca and today a small provincial capital, Guadalajara (from the Arabic *wad al-hijaara,* or 'stony river') was in its medieval Muslim heyday the principal city of a large swathe of northern Spain under the green banner of Islam. At that stage, Madrid was no more than a military observation point. In 1085, however, the Castilian king Alfonso VI finally took Guadalajara as the Reconquista moved ponderously south. Under the Mendoza family, the city experienced its most prosperous era from the 14th to the 17th centuries, but from then on it was repeatedly sacked during the War of the Spanish Succession, the Napoleonic occupation and the Spanish Civil War.

Little remains of the city's glory days, but the much-restored **Palacio de los Duques del Infantado**, where the Mendoza family held court, is worth visiting. Its striking facade is a fine example of Gothic-mudéjar work. The heavily ornamental patio is equally admirable. The local art museum is here too. The palace is open 10 am to 2 pm and 4 to 7 pm Tuesday to Saturday, and Sunday morning; entry is free.

The tourist office (☎/fax 949 21 16 26) is at Plaza de los Caídos 6, opposite the palacio. It's open 10 am to 2 pm and 4 to 7.30 pm daily (morning only on Sunday).

Guadalajara is a simple day trip from Madrid, but you can stay if need be. A cheap, no-frills possibility is *Hostal Venecia* (☎ 949 21 13 52, Calle del Doctor Benito Hernando 12), where rooms cost 1700/3500 ptas. *Restaurante Miguel Ángel* on Calle de Alfonso López de Haro, just off Calle Mayor, has a pleasant atmosphere, and offers *menús* at 2500 ptas.

The bus station is on Calle del Dos de Mayo, a short walk from the palacio. About 20 daily buses connect Guadalajara with Madrid (Avenida de América) and charge 480 ptas one way. Buses from Madrid stop here en route to Zaragoza (four a day), Soria (at least one a day) and Teruel (one a day). Sigüenza, Pastrana and Brihuega get two connections daily on weekdays, one on Saturday and none on Sunday.

The train station is 2km out of town. Regular *cercanías* go to Madrid (Atocha and Chamartín) from about 5 am to 11.30 pm. Up to eight regional trains go to Sigüenza, beyond which occasional trains go on to Soria and Zaragoza.

LA ALCARRIA & AROUND
Mar de Castilla
The N-320 south-east from Guadalajara (it soon becomes the C-200) takes you towards the so-called Mar de Castilla, a collection of lakes formed by dams built in the late 1950s, in an area known as La Alcarria. Hardly a touristic goal of the first order, but it was immortalised in an enchantingly simple account

CASTILLA-LA MANCHA

of a walking trip made there in 1946 by Camilo José Cela, *Viaje a La Alcarria*.

Pastrana
postcode 19100 • pop 1209

Of the many pueblos Cela called in at, Pastrana is the most worthwhile for a brief stop. Forty-two kilometres south of Guadalajara along the C-200, it is a tranquil medieval town. The area closest to the main road, Albaicín, was once populated mainly by *moriscos,* converts from Islam to Christianity. Passing through here you arrive at **Plaza de la Hora**, an airy and somewhat uncared-for square fronted by the impressive and equally unloved **Palacio Ducal**, where the one-eyed Princess of Eboli, Ana Mendoza de la Cerda, was confined in 1581 for a love affair with the Spanish King Felipe II's secretary. She died here 10 years later. The tourist office (☎ 949 37 06 72, ⓔ turismo@ pastrana.org) is on Plaza del Dean, just off the main road.

Walk from the square along the main street and you soon reach the massive, gloomy **Iglesia de Nuestra Señora de la Asunción.** Inside is a small museum containing jewels and other personal effects of the Princess of Eboli. There are also some interesting 15th-century Portuguese tapestries. Entry is 300 ptas, if the person with the keys is around.

You can stay and eat at *Hostal Moratín* (☎ 949 37 06 28), a decent place on Calle de Moratín, just in from the main highway. Doubles with bath cost 4000 ptas. *Hospedería Real de Pastrana* (☎/fax 949 37 10 60), in the Canvento del Carmen on the outskirts of town, is sumptuous, and has singles/ doubles for 5550/8900 ptas.

A bus leaves early in the morning for Madrid, and two a day (on weekdays) go to Guadalajara.

Around Pastrana

Some 20km north-east of Pastrana is the area's main reservoir, the **Embalse de Entrepeñas**, where you can swim. From there you can push north on the C-204 to **Cifuentes**, with its 14th-century castle, and on to the N-II, which you take for a few kilometres before it branches off north again for Sigüenza.

There are other alternatives. From Guadalajara you could follow the motorway north-east and turn off at **Torija**, which has a rather impressive castle that contains a small museum dedicated to *Viaje a La Alcarria* (free; closed weekends). Take the C-201 for La Alcarria's second town after Pastrana, **Brihuega**, a leafy village that preserves stretches of its medieval walls. The drive east along the Río Tajuña is one of the more pleasant in this part of Castilla-La Mancha. The road forms a T-junction with the N-204, from where you can head north for Sigüenza or south to the great lake of the Embalse de Entrepeñas (see earlier in this section).

Yet another option from La Alcarria is to head east from the lake towards **Parque Natural del Alto Tajo**, which also makes for some unexpectedly pretty drives. Combined with the Serranía de Cuenca (see under Cuenca earlier in this chapter) farther south and east, the area is a popular weekend escape hatch for *madrileños* fleeing their hectic city lives.

SIGÜENZA
postcode 19250 • pop 4880 • elev 1005m

This tranquil medieval town, built on a low hill cradled by the Río Henares and a slender tributary, disguises a less peaceful past. Fighting here during the civil war was heavy and it was a long while before most, but not all, of the scars of the conflict could be removed.

Originally a Celtiberian settlement, Segontia became an important Roman and, later, Visigothic military outpost. The 8th-century arrival of the Muslims put the town in the frontline provinces facing the Christians. Sigüenza stayed in Muslim hands for considerably longer than towns farther south-west such as Guadalajara and Toledo (which fell in 1085), resisting until the 1120s. It was occupied by the Aragonese and later ceded to the Castilians, who turned Sigüenza and its hinterland into a vast church property. The bishops remained complete masters, material and spiritual, of the town and land until the end of the 18th century. About this time things began to go downhill, as Sigüenza found itself repeatedly in the way of advancing armies, from the War of the Spanish Succession until the civil war.

Information

The Infotur tourist office (☎ 949 34 70 07, ℮ siguenza@siguenza.com), in the Ermita del Humilladero, is open 10 am to 2 pm and 4.30 to 7 pm weekdays and 9 am to 2.30 pm and 4.30 to 7 pm weekends. Check out its helpful Web site at www.siguenza.com. There are several banks (some with ATMs) where you can change money on and near Calle del Cardenal Mendoza. The post office is on Calle de la Villa Viciosa and is open only until 2.30 pm on weekdays (1 pm on Saturday). In a medical emergency, call the Cruz Roja on ☎ 949 39 15 03.

Catedral

The heart of the old town is made up of the combination of the cobbled Plaza Mayor and Plaza del Obispo Don Bernardo. Rising up on their northern flank is the city's centre-piece, the completely oversized cathedral. It was begun as a Romanesque structure in 1130, and work continued for four centuries as the church was expanded and adorned. The largely Gothic result is laced with elements of other styles, from Renaissance through plateresque to mudéjar. The church was heavily damaged during the civil war and subsequently restored.

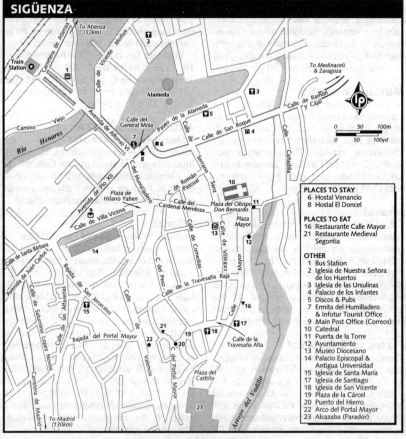

SIGÜENZA

PLACES TO STAY
6 Hostal Venancio
8 Hostal El Doncel

PLACES TO EAT
16 Restaurante Calle Mayor
21 Restaurante Medieval Segontia

OTHER
1 Bus Station
2 Iglesia de Nuestra Señora de los Huertos
3 Iglesia de las Ursulinas
4 Palacio de los Infantes
5 Discos & Pubs
7 Ermita del Humilladero & Infotur Tourist Office
9 Main Post Office (Correos)
10 Catedral
11 Puerta de la Torre
12 Ayuntamiento
13 Museo Diocesano
14 Palacio Episcopal & Antigua Universidad
15 Iglesia de Santa María
17 Iglesia de Santiago
18 Iglesia de San Vicente
19 Plaza de la Cárcel
20 Puerto del Hierro
22 Arco del Portal Mayor
23 Alcazaba (Parador)

CASTILLA-LA MANCHA

You can wander about the dark nave for free, or for 300 ptas you can be guided around the church's chapels, sacristy and neglected Gothic cloister. First up you'll probably be shown the **capilla mayor**, a chapel containing the reclining marble statue of El Doncel (Don Martín Vázquez de Arce), who died fighting the Muslims in the final stages of the Reconquista. Of particular beauty is the **Sacristía de las Cabezas**, whose ceiling is covered with hundreds of heads sculpted by Covarrubias. His intention was to represent all humanity, and his characters, Christian and Muslim, range from knights to knaves. The **Capilla del Espíritu Santo** boasts a doorway combining plateresque, mudéjar and Gothic styles. Inside is a remarkable dome and an *Anunciación* by El Greco. The cathedral is open 9 am to 1.30 pm and 4.30 to 8 pm daily, and 11 am to noon and 4.30 to 5.30 pm Sunday.

Museo Diocesano

Across the square from the cathedral, this museum has a fairly extensive collection of religious art from Sigüenza and the surrounding area, including a series of mainly 15th-century retablos. The museum is open noon to 2 pm and 4 to 7 pm Tuesday to Friday, and 11 am to 2 pm and 5 to 7 pm weekends (300 ptas).

Alcazaba

Calle Mayor heads south up the hill from the cathedral to what was once the archbishops' castle, originally built by the Muslims and still known as the Alcazaba. There has probably been some kind of fort here since pre-Roman times, but what you see today is the much-restored residence erected by the archbishops. It now functions as a parador (see Places to Stay & Eat following).

Places to Stay & Eat

There's a handful of accommodation possibilities in Sigüenza. *Hostal Venancio (☎ 949 39 03 47, Calle de San Roque 1)* has adequate singles/doubles without bathroom for 2000/3800 ptas. *Hostal El Doncel (☎ 949 39 00 01, ⓔ hostaldoncel@futurnet.es)*, across the road, has rooms with shower, TV

and phone starting at 5400/5800 ptas plus IVA, and a restaurant attached. A real treat, the *parador (☎ 949 39 01 00)* in the Alcazaba has doubles for 15,000 ptas plus IVA.

Restaurante Medieval Segontia (Calle del Portal Mayor 2) serves solid meals, including a *menú* for 1200 ptas, while the more expensive *Restaurante Calle Mayor (Calle Mayor 21)* offers fine dining for around 2500 ptas.

Getting There & Away

Buses mostly serve towns around Sigüenza, and are far from frequent. They stop on Avenida de Alfonso VI, near the train station. From Madrid (Atocha and Chamartín) there are up to 13 regional trains, the quickest taking about 1½ hours. Some go on to Zaragoza and Soria (and vice versa).

Sigüenza lies north of the N-II highway. The main exits are the C-204 coming from the west and the C-114 from the east. The C-114 then heads north towards Almazán or Soria in Castilla y León.

AROUND SIGÜENZA
Palazuelos & Carabias

About 10km north of Sigüenza, the sleepy little villages of Palazuelos and Carabias retain neglected remnants of their more distant past, the former with walls and a castle and the latter with a Romanesque church.

Atienza

postcode 19270 • pop 494 • elev 1169m

Those travelling between Sigüenza and Almazán or Soria to the north should consider a trip to Atienza, 32km north-west of Sigüenza. A charming walled medieval village dominated by the inevitable castle ruins, Atienza is jammed with half a dozen largely Romanesque churches. There's a small museum in the Iglesia de San Gil and another in the Iglesia de San Bartolomé east of the town centre (200 ptas). If you come by bus you'll have to stay, and *Fonda Molinero (☎ 949 39 90 17, Calle de Héctor Vázquez 11)*, with beds for 1500 ptas is an adequate option. A couple of buses leave early in the morning for Guadalajara, Madrid and Sigüenza.

Barcelona

postcode 08080 • pop 1.5 million

Some say Barcelona is the most southern city of northern Europe. It has earned this description not only through its nearness to France, but also by its industrious (and industrial) character, densely packed urban centre and obeisance to cool and chic – not exactly the fiesta-and-siesta image of more southerly Spanish regions.

In fact, Barcelona shares the good and bad of the south *and* north. It's probably Spain's most cosmopolitan and stylish city, and certainly one of its richest. But it has its hard side: wealth and poverty face each other daily on its streets.

Barcelona is the capital of a region, Catalunya (Cataluña in Castilian), that has its own language, distinct character and turbulent history. In many ways it thinks of itself as a separate country. This gives the city a rather self-absorbed aspect that sits oddly with the openness you'd expect of a major Mediterranean port.

Set on a plain rising gently from the sea to a range of wooded hills, Barcelona enjoys fine vistas, lovely and unusual parks and a fascinating medieval core dotted with pearls of Gothic construction. Beyond this core is perhaps some of the world's most bizarre architecture: surreal modernist spectacles capped by Antoni Gaudí's La Sagrada Família church.

Barcelona has great nightlife, superb restaurants and top-class museums. It's been breaking ground in art, architecture and style for at least a century, from the early 20th-century *modernista* architects led by Gaudí, to the adventurous redevelopments on the waterfront and Montjuïc hill brought to life by the 1992 Olympics; and from Pablo Picasso and Joan Miró, whose spirits haunt the city, to the weird postmodern concoctions of contemporary artists and nightclub designers.

HISTORY

Barcelona has a history that for long periods was distinct from the rest of Spain; this is

Highlights

- Rambling along La Rambla, Spain's most famous street
- Barri Gòtic, a classic medieval quarter
- Museu Picasso, Spain's best collection of this major modern artist's work
- La Sagrada Família, Spain's most original 'work-in-progress'
- Montjuïc, the hill of parks, museums and stadiums that hosted the 1992 Olympics
- A first-class Catalan meal at the city's finer restaurants
- Quaffing an absinthe or two in *Bar Marsella*
- Sipping *cava* (Catalan champagne) at *El Xampanyet*
- Dancing at stylish *Otto Zutz*
- Following the *modernista* trail of architecture

FRANCE

CATALUNYA

BARCELONA
Barcelona Metro p369
Barcelona pp370-1 Map 1
L'Eixample & Gràcia pp372-3 Map 2
Central Barcelona pp374-5 Map 3
Ciutat Vella pp376-7 Map 4

largely responsible for its independent-mindedness today.

Early Barcelona

Barcelona was probably founded by the Carthaginians in about 230 BC, taking the surname of Hamilcar Barca, Hannibal's father. Roman Barcelona covered an area within today's Barri Gòtic and was overshadowed by Tarraco (Tarragona), 90km to the south-west. Under the Visigoths, and then under the Muslims who took it in AD 713, Barcelona remained a modest place.

The Counts of Barcelona

Frankish armies pushed the Muslims back from present-day France and set up a buffer zone along the south of the Pyrenees known as the Frankish March, which included Barcelona. Indeed the Catalan language's closest relative is said to be the *langue d'oc,* the old tongue of southern France.

As the Frankish empire fractured in the 9th century, one Guifré el Pilós (Wilfrid the Hairy – so named because he had hair where most people don't) gained control of several of the march's counties. In 878 he founded the house of the Counts of Barcelona, which by the late 10th century ruled, from Barcelona, an independent principality covering most of modern Catalunya except the south, plus Roussillon (part of modern-day France). This was the only Christian state on the Iberian Peninsula not to fall under the sway of Sancho III of Navarra in the early 11th century.

Catalunya, and especially Barcelona, grew rich on pickings from the collapse of the Muslim caliphate of Córdoba in the 11th century. Count Ramon Berenguer I was able to buy the counties of Carcassonne and Béziers, north of Roussillon, with Muslim gold bounty. Under Ramon Berenguer III (1082–1131) Catalunya launched its own fleet and sea trade developed. This was also the era of great Catalan Romanesque art.

The Golden Age

In 1137 Ramon Berenguer IV was betrothed to Petronilla, heiress of Catalunya's western neighbour Aragón, creating a joint state and setting the scene for Catalunya's golden age. He took southern Catalunya from the Muslims in the 1140s and his successors styled themselves as the Monarchs of Aragón.

Meanwhile, Castile was laying sole claim to the reconquest of Muslim territory in the south – a claim recognised by Aragón's Alfonso II in 1179. Suffering reverses in France too, Catalunya turned to the Mediterranean. Jaume I (1213–76) took the Balearic Islands and Valencia from the Muslims in the 1230s.

Jaume I's son Pere II conquered Sicily in 1282. Then followed a spectacular expansion of Catalunya's Mediterranean trade-based empire, albeit hampered at home by divisions in the ruling family, the odd war with Castile and trouble with the aristocracy in Aragón. Malta (1283), Athens (1310), Corsica (1323), Sardinia (1324) and Naples (1423), as well as several ports in North Africa, all fell, for varying periods, under Catalan dominance.

Decline & Castilian Domination

Like many empires, Catalunya's came to exhaust its homeland. Sea wars with Genoa, resistance in Sardinia, the rise of the Ottoman Empire and the loss of the gold trade all drained the coffers. The Black Death and famines killed about half of Catalunya's population in the 14th century.

After Martí I, the last of Guifré el Pilós' dynasty, died heirless in 1410, control shifted away from Catalan hands. Fernando succeeded to the Aragonese throne in 1479 and married Queen Isabel of Castile, uniting Spain's two most powerful monarchies. Catalunya effectively became part of the Castilian state.

Disaffection led to revolts, the last during the War of the Spanish Succession (1702–13), in which Catalunya sided with Britain and Austria against Felipe V, the French Bourbon contender for the Spanish throne. But Catalunya ended up fighting alone and Barcelona fell in 1714 after a 14-month siege. Felipe V abolished the Generalitat (parliament), built a huge fort, the Ciutadella, to watch over Barcelona and banned the writing and teaching of Catalan.

Economic Growth & the Renaixença

The late 18th and 19th centuries finally brought new economic development. From 1778 Catalunya was permitted to trade with America, boosting shipping and launching an industrial revolution – Spain's first – based on American cotton. Wine, cork and iron industries also developed. So did working-class poverty, overcrowding, disease and unrest. To ease the crush, Barcelona's medieval walls were demolished in 1854 and in 1869 work began on l'Eixample, an extension of the city beyond Plaça de Catalunya, which was then its limit. The flourishing bourgeoisie paid for lavish, ostentatious buildings, many of them in the unique, Art Nouveau-influenced modernista style, whose leading exponent was Antoni Gaudí.

Modernisme was the most visible aspect of the Catalan Renaixença (Renaissance), a movement for the revival of Catalan language and culture in the late 19th century. By the turn of the century Barcelona was also Spain's hotbed of avant-garde art, with close links to Paris.

Mayhem

The decades around the turn of the 20th century were ones of wild mayhem in Barcelona, which became a swirling vortex of anarchists, Republicans, bourgeois regionalists, gangsters, police terrorists, political gunmen called *pistoleros* and meddling by Madrid.

Anarchists were reckoned to be behind the Semana Trágica (Tragic Week) in 1909 when, following a military call-up for a Spanish campaign in Morocco, mobs wrecked 70 religious buildings and workers were shot on the streets.

In the post-WWI slump, unionism took hold, led by the anarchist Confederación Nacional del Trabajo (CNT), which embraced as much as 80% of the city's workers. During a wave of strikes in 1919–20, employers hired assassins to eliminate union leaders.

Catalan Nationalism Rampant

Within days of the formation of Spain's Second Republic in 1931, Catalan nationalists led by Francesc Macià and Lluís Companys proclaimed Catalunya a republic within an imaginary 'Iberian Federation'. Madrid pressured them into accepting a unitary Spanish state, but Catalunya got a new regional government, with the old title of Generalitat.

After the leftist Popular Front won the February 1936 Spanish general election, Catalunya gained, for a brief time, genuine autonomy.

The Civil War

For nearly a year after Franco's rising began, Barcelona was run by revolutionary anarchists and the Partido Obrero de Unificación Marxista (POUM; Workers' Marxist Unification Party) Trotskyist militia, with Companys president only in name. In 1937 the Catalan communist party (PSUC) took control and disarmed the anarchists and POUM. Barcelona fell to the Nationalists on 25 January 1939.

The Franco Era

Franco banned public use of Catalan and by the 1950s opposition had turned to peaceful mass protests and strikes. In 1960 an audience at the city's Palau de la Música Catalana sang a banned Catalan anthem in front of Franco. The ringleaders included a young Catholic banker, Jordi Pujol, who spent two years in jail as a result, and was to become Catalunya's president in the post-Franco era.

The big social change under Franco was the flood of immigrants from poorer parts of Spain, chiefly Andalucía, attracted by economic growth in Catalunya. Some 750,000 people came to Barcelona in the 1950s and 60s, and almost as many to the rest of Catalunya. Many lived in appalling conditions.

After Franco

The 1978 Spanish constitution bowed to Catalan nationalism by creating the autonomous community of Catalunya, with Barcelona as its capital. The Generalitat, its parliament, has wide powers over matters like agriculture, education, health, industry, tourism and trade.

Jordi Pujol's moderate nationalist Convergència i Unió (CiU) coalition has controlled the Generalitat since the first elections in 1980. Barcelona itself has favoured the Partit Socialista de Catalunya (PSC), aligned with the national Partido Socialista Obrero Español (PSOE).

Modern-Day Catalanism

Catalunya is engaged in an ongoing struggle for more autonomy within Spain, but full independence is a dream dreamt only by a few. The pro-independence party Esquerra Republicana de Catalunya (ERC; Republican Left of Cataluña) has won only 8% to 10% of the vote in recent elections. ERC is avowedly nonviolent and there's no Catalan equivalent of the Basque ETA terrorist movement. But there's still a deep antipathy among many Catalans towards the Spanish state and its influence over Catalunya.

Catalans remain strongly aware of their region's historic rivalry with Castilla and are infused with the sense that Catalunya enjoyed its golden ages when it was independent or under minimal Castilian influence. They like to think of themselves as more civilised and worldly than other Spaniards. These notions have probably been reinforced since the 1940s by the arrival of around two million people from poorer parts of Spain, chiefly Andalucía, seeking work. The rest of Spain looks on Catalans (whom they sometimes disparagingly refer to as *polacos,* or Poles) as somewhere between irritatingly quirky and provocatively arrogant.

The cliche is that Catalans are harder-working, more sober and more commercially minded than other Spaniards. They certainly seem to be less addicted to noise, colour and flamboyance – compare the sedate Catalan national dance, the *sardana,* with Andalucian flamenco – although Catalan *festes* (fiestas) can still be riotous.

Because of immigration from other parts of Spain, today probably less than half the almost four million people in Barcelona and its satellite towns speak Catalan, although the figure is around two-thirds in Catalunya as a whole and nearly everyone claims to understand it.

Everyone in Barcelona *does* speak Spanish; French is fairly widely understood and English less so. Although you'll find all street names, and many signs and menus, in Catalan, you'll have no greater language difficulty here than anywhere else in Spain. If you know some Spanish and/or French, you can make sense of much written Catalan (see the Language chapter at the back of the book for some useful words and phrases, and the boxed text 'Catalan Cuisine' in the Catalunya chapter for help with Catalan menus).

The 1992 Olympics spurred a burst of public works, bringing new life to areas such as Montjuïc, where the major events were held, and the once-shabby waterfront, now strung with promenades, beaches, marinas, restaurants, leisure facilities and new housing. The Olympics also focused world attention on Barcelona's prosperity and cultural, entertainment and tourist attractions, making the city something of a household name. The city hasn't looked back.

ORIENTATION

Barcelona's coastline runs roughly from north-east to south-west, and many streets are parallel or perpendicular to it.

La Rambla & Plaça de Catalunya

The focal axis is La Rambla, a 1.25km boulevard running north-west and slightly uphill from Port Vell (Old Harbour) to Plaça de Catalunya. The latter marks the boundary between the old centre, the Ciutat Vella, and the more recent parts farther inland.

Montjuïc & Tibidabo

Two good landmarks for orientation are the hills of Montjuïc and Tibidabo. Montjuïc, the lower of the two, begins about 700m south-west of the bottom (south-eastern end) of La Rambla. Tibidabo, with its landmark TV tower and golden Christ statue, is 6km north-west of the top (north-western end) of La Rambla. It's the high point of the range of wooded hills forming the backdrop to the city.

Ciutat Vella

The Ciutat Vella (Old City), a warren of narrow streets, centuries-old buildings and a lot of budget and mid-range accommodation, spreads either side of La Rambla. Its heart is the lower half of the section east of La Rambla, called the Barri Gòtic (Gothic Quarter). West of La Rambla is El Raval, whose lower half is the seedy Barri Xinès (Chinese Quarter, a strange expression meaning red-light zone).

The Ciutat Vella continues north-east of the Barri Gòtic, across Via Laietana, to the area called La Ribera, east of which lies the pretty Parc de la Ciutadella.

Waterfront

Port Vell has an excellent modern aquarium and two marinas. At its north-eastern end is La Barceloneta, the old sailors' quarter, from where beaches and a pedestrian promenade stretch 1km north-east to the Port Olímpic, a harbour built for the Olympics and now surrounded by lively bars and restaurants.

L'Eixample

Plaça de Catalunya at the top of La Rambla marks the beginning of l'Eixample (el Ensanche in Spanish, meaning 'the Enlargement'), the grid of straight streets into which Barcelona grew in the 19th century. This is where you'll find most of Barcelona's modernista architecture, including La Sagrada Família.

Gràcia

Beyond l'Eixample you're in the suburbs, some of which have plenty of character as they began life as villages outside the city. Gràcia, beyond the wide Avinguda Diagonal on the northern edge of central l'Eixample, is a net of narrow streets and small squares with a varied population and can be a lively place to spend a Friday or Saturday night. Just north of Gràcia is Gaudí's Parc Güell.

Main Transport Terminals

The airport is 14km south-west of the centre at El Prat de Llobregat. The main train station is Estació Sants (Map 1), located 2.5km west of La Rambla, on the western fringe of l'Eixample.

The main bus station, Estació del Nord (Map 1), is 1.5km north-east of La Rambla.

Maps

Tourist offices hand out free city and transport maps that are OK, but Lonely Planet's *Barcelona city map* is better. If you can't find it, try the Michelin No 40 *Barcelona* map (950 ptas). You can buy it with a comprehensive street index (Michelin No 41), bringing the price to 1200 ptas. Plenty of stalls on La Rambla sell maps, but prices vary considerably.

INFORMATION
Tourist Offices

The Oficina d'Informació de Turisme de Barcelona (Map 3; ☎ 906-30 12 82 from within the country, ☎ 93 304 34 21 from abroad) at Plaça de Catalunya 17-S (underground) concentrates on city information, and staff can also book accommodation. It's open 9 am to 9 pm daily.

In the *ajuntament* (town hall; Map 4) on Plaça de Sant Jaume there is another information office with similar hours.

The regional tourist office (Map 2; ☎ 93 238 40 00) is in the Palau Robert, Passeig de Gràcia 107. It is open 10 am to 7 pm Monday to Saturday, and 10 am to 2.30 pm Sunday. It has a host of material, audiovisual stuff, a bookshop and a branch of Turisme Juvenil de Catalunya (where you can get Euro<26 cards).

Turisme de Barcelona in Estació Sants (Map 1) covers Barcelona only. It's open 8 am to 8 pm daily (October to May it closes at 2 pm weekends and holidays).

There's also a tourist office (☎ 93 478 05 65) in the airport's EU arrivals hall, open 9.30 am to 8 pm Monday to Saturday, and 9.30 am to 3 pm Sunday (about a half-hour later in summer). It has information on all Catalunya. The office (☎ 93 478 47 04) at the international arrivals hall is open the same hours.

Another useful office for information on events (and tickets) is the Palau de la Virreina arts information office (Map 4) at La Rambla de Sant Josep 99.

You can find out about accommodation on ☎ 93 304 32 32 or at www.deinfo.es/barcelona-on-line.

A couple of general information lines worth bearing in mind are ☎ 010 and ☎ 012.

The first is for Barcelona and the latter for all Catalunya (run by the Generalitat). You sometimes strike English-speakers although for the most part operators are Catalan/Castilian bilingual. They can often answer quite obscure questions.

Foreign Consulates

Most of the consulates in Barcelona are open 9 or 10 am to 1 or 2 pm weekdays. Some have been marked on the maps. See also the Embassies & Consulates section in the Facts for the Visitor chapter.

Money

Barcelona abounds with banks, many with ATMs, including several around Plaça de Catalunya and more on La Rambla and on Plaça de Sant Jaume in the Barri Gòtic.

The exchange offices that you see along La Rambla and elsewhere are open for longer hours than banks but generally offer poorer rates.

American Express (Map 2; ☎ 93 415 23 71, ☎ 93 217 00 70) at Passeig de Gràcia 101 (the entrance is on Carrer del Rosselló) has a machine giving cash on AmEx cards. The office is open 9.30 am to 6 pm weekdays and 10 am to noon Saturday. There is another branch at La Rambla dels Caputxins 74 (Map 4), which is open 9 am to midnight daily from April to September; the rest of the year 9 am to 8.30 pm weekdays and 10 am to 7 pm Saturday (closed for lunch 2 to 3 pm).

Post & Communications

The main post office (*correos;* Map 4; ☎ 902-19 71 97) is on Plaça d'Antoni López, opposite the north-eastern end of Port Vell. It's open for stamp sales, poste restante (window Nos 7 and 8) and information 8 am to 9.30 pm Monday to Saturday.

The post office also has a public fax service, as do many shops and offices around the city.

Another useful post office is at Carrer d'Aragó 282 (Map 2), just off Passeig de Gràcia, which is open 8.30 am to 8.30 pm weekdays, and 9.30 am to 1 pm Saturday. Other district offices tend to open 8 am to 2 pm weekdays only.

American Express (see Money earlier) holds mail if you have AmEx cards and travellers cheque.

There are telephone and fax offices at Estació Sants (open 8.30 am to 9.30 pm daily except Sunday) and Estació del Nord.

Email & Internet Access Dozens of places, ranging from cafes to computer stores, offer Internet access. It is a fast changing scene and prices are tending to fall rapidly. Some options include:

Café Insòlit (Map 3; ☎ 93 225 81 78, ☻ bar .internet@insolit.es), in the waterfront Maremàgnum shopping complex. It's open until midnight most nights, except Friday and Saturday, when it goes to 5 am. Going online costs 1000 ptas an hour.

Cybermundo (Map 5; ☎ 93 317 71 42) Carrer de Bergara 3. It's open 9 am to 1 am daily. You pay as little as 200 ptas an hour (before 5 pm).

El Café de Internet (Map 2; ☎ 93 302 11 54, ☻ cafe@cafeinternet.es) Gran Via de les Corts Catalanes 656. You càn go online for 600 ptas a half-hour, or 800 ptas an hour for students.

Travel Agencies

Usit Unlimited (Map 3; ☎ 93 412 01 04), at Ronda de la Universitat 16, sells youth and student air, train and bus tickets. It has a branch in the Turisme Juvenil de Catalunya office (Map 1) at Carrer de Rocafort 116-122.

Viajes Wasteels at Catalunya metro station (Map 3) has similar youth and student fares.

Halcón Viatges is a reliable chain of travel agencies that sometimes has good deals. Its branch at Carrer de Pau Claris 108 (Map 2) is one of 28 around town. Its national phone reservation number is ☎ 902-30 06 00.

Bookshops

Many newsstands, especially on La Rambla, carry a wide range of foreign newspapers. Here's a selection of Barcelona's many good bookshops:

La Rambla

Llibreria & Informaciò Cultural de la Generalitat de Catalunya (Map 4; ☎ 93 302 64 62) Rambla dels Estudis 118. A good first stop for books and pamphlets on all things Catalan, although a lot of it is highly specialised and technical.

Llibreria de la Virreina (Map 4; ☎ 93 301 77 75) Palau de la Virreina, La Rambla de Sant Josep 99. An assortment of art/architecture and art history books, many with at least some relevance to Barcelona.

Barri Gòtic & El Raval

Antinous (Map 4; ☎ 93 301 90 70) Carrer Josep Anselm Clavé 6. Good gay bookshop-cum-cafe.

Documenta (Map 4; ☎ 93 317 25 27) Carrer del Cardenal Casañas 4. Stocks novels in English and French; also sells maps.

Próleg (Map 4; ☎ 93 319 24 25) Carrer de la Dagueria 13. Women's bookshop.

L'Eixample

Altaïr (Map 2; ☎ 93 454 29 66) Carrer de Balmes 71. Great travel bookshop with maps, guides and travel literature.

Come In (Map 2; ☎ 93 453 12 04) Carrer de Provença 203. Specialist in English-teaching books; also has plenty of novels and books on Spain, in both English and French.

Laie (Map 2; ☎ 93 518 17 39) Carrer de Pau Claris 85. Novels and books on architecture, art and film in English, French, Spanish and Catalan.

Librería Francesa (Map 2; ☎ 93 215 14 17) Passeig de Gràcia 91. Lots of novels and guidebooks in French.

Llibreria Bosch (Map 3; ☎ 93 317 53 08) Ronda de la Universitat 11. This is another of the city's stalwarts.

The English Bookshop (Map 1; ☎ 93 425 44 66) Carrer d'Entença 63. A good range of literature, teaching material and children's books.

Gràcia

Bookstore (Map 1; ☎ 93 237 95 19) Carrer de la Granja 13. Second-hand English-language books.

For some recommended books on Barcelona, see the Books section in the Facts for the Visitor chapter.

Cultural Centres

There are English-language libraries at the British Council (Map 1; ☎ 93 241 99 77) at Carrer d'Amigó 83, as well as the Institute for North American Studies (Map 2; ☎ 93 200 24 67), Via Augusta 123. Institut Français de Barcelona (Map 2; ☎ 93 209 59 11) at Carrer de Moià 8 puts on films, concerts and exhibitions.

Gay & Lesbian Information

Casal Lambda (Map 4; ☎ 93 412 72 72) at Carrer Ample 5 in the Barri Gòtic is a gay and lesbian social, cultural and information centre. Coordinadora Gai-Lesbiana (Map 1; ☎ 93 298 00 29, fax 93 298 06 18, e cogailes@ pangea.org), Carrer de Finlàndia 45, is the city's main coordinating body for gay and lesbian groups. Some of the latter, such as Grup de Lesbianes Feministes, are to be found at Ca la Dona (Map 2; ☎ 93 412 71 61), Carrer de Casp 38. There is a free gay helpline (which is also the number for Stop Sida, the AIDS helpline) on ☎ 900-60 16 01.

Photography

There are plenty of places to have films developed. Panorama Foto, which has seven branches around town, including one at Passeig de Gràcia 2 (Map 3), will develop most photos, including slides, in an hour.

Laundry

Self-service laundries are a rarity indeed. One is Lavomatic (Map 4), Carrer del Consolat de Mar 43–45. A 7kg load costs 575 ptas and drying costs 105 ptas for five minutes.

Wash'N Dry (Map 2), on the corner of Carrer de Torrent de l'Olla and Carrer Ros de Olano in Gràcia, charges 700 ptas for an 8kg load and 100 ptas for six minutes' drying time. It is open 7 am to 10 pm.

Lost Property

The city's main lost-and-found *(objetos perdidos)* office can be contacted on ☎ 93 402 31 61. If you leave anything in a taxi, you can call ☎ 93 223 40 12 to see if it's been handed in. If you leave anything in the metro, try the Centre d'Atenció al Client (Map 3; ☎ 93 318 70 74) at the Universitat stop.

Medical Services

Hospitals with emergency service include Hospital de la Creu Roja (Map 1; ☎ 93 300 20 20), Carrer del Dos de Maig 301, and Hospital de la Santa Creu i de Sant Pau (Map 1; ☎ 93 291 90 00), Carrer de Sant Antoni Maria Claret 167.

For an ambulance, call ☎ 061, ☎ 93 329 97 01 or ☎ 93 300 20 20; for emergency dental help, contact ☎ 93 277 47 47.

There's a 24-hour pharmacy at Carrer d'Aribau 62 (Map 3) and another at Passeig de Gràcia 26. A third, Farmàcia Saltó (☎ 93 339 63 32), is somewhat out of the centre at Avinguda de Madrid 222. Otherwise, for information on on-duty chemists call ☎ 010.

Emergency

The general EU standard emergency number is ☎ 112. You can reach all emergency services on this number and occasionally even get multilingual operators.

Barcelona abounds with different kinds of police. The Guàrdia Urbana (City Police; Map 4; ☎ 092) has a station at La Rambla 43, opposite Plaça Reial. If you need to report theft or loss of passport and other belongings, head to the Comisaría of the Policía Nacional (Map 3; ☎ 091), Carrer Nou de la Rambla 80. There's usually an English-speaker on duty.

Dangers & Annoyances

The Barri Xinès, the lower end of La Rambla and the area around Plaça Reial, although much cleaned up in recent years, remain dodgy – watch your wallets.

LA RAMBLA (MAP 4)

Head to Spain's most famous street for a first taste of Barcelona's atmosphere. Flanked by narrow traffic lanes, the middle of La Rambla is a broad, pedestrian boulevard, lined with cafes and restaurants and crowded every day beyond midnight with a cross-section of Barcelona's permanent and transient population.

La Rambla gets its name from a seasonal stream (*raml* in Arabic) that once ran here. It was outside the city walls until the 14th century and built up with monastic buildings and palaces in the 16th to 18th centuries. Unofficially it's divided into five sections with their own names.

Rambla de Canaletes

A block off to the east of this first stretch at the northern end of La Rambla along Carrer

de la Canuda is Plaça de la Vila de Madrid, with a sunken garden where some **Roman tombs** have been exposed.

Rambla dels Estudis

This second stretch of La Rambla, from below Carrer de Santa Anna to Carrer de la Portaferrissa, is also called Rambla dels Ocells (Birds) because of its twittering **bird market**.

Rambla de Sant Josep

This section from Carrer de la Portaferrissa to Plaça Boqueria is lined with **flower stalls**, which give it the alternative name Rambla de les Flors. The **Palau de la Virreina**, La Rambla de Sant Josep 99, is a grand 18th-century rococo mansion housing an arts-entertainment information and ticket office run by the ajuntament.

The next building down is La Rambla's most colourful: the **Mercat de la Boqueria**, a bustling covered food market. Plaça Boqueria, where four side streets meet just north of Liceu metro station, is your chance to walk all over a Miró – the colourful **Mosaïc de Miró** in the pavement, with one tile signed by the artist.

Barcelona seems to take pride in being a pleasure centre and in the **Museu de l'Eròtica**, at No 96, you can observe how people have been enjoying themselves since ancient times – lots of Karma Sutra and porn flicks from the 1920s. The centre is open 10 am to midnight daily (975 ptas).

Rambla dels Caputxins

Also called Rambla del Centre, this stretch runs from Plaça Boqueria to Carrer dels Escudellers. On the western side is the **Gran Teatre del Liceu**, Barcelona's famous 19th-century opera house reopened in 1999 five years after its destruction in a fire.

On the eastern side of Rambla dels Caputxins, farther south, is the entrance to the Plaça Reial (see the Barri Gòtic section later in this chapter). Just below this point, La Rambla becomes seedier, with a few strip clubs and peep shows reflecting this section's former status as Barcelona's chief red-light area.

Rambla de Santa Mònica

The final stretch of La Rambla widens out to approach the Columbus monument overlooking Port Vell. On the eastern side, at the end of narrow Passatge de la Banca, is the **Museu de Cera** (Wax Museum), which has tableaux of a *gitano* (gypsy) cave, a bullring medical room and a hall of horror as well as wax figures of Cleopatra, Franco etc – not bad as wax museums go. It's open 10 am to 1.30 pm and 4 to 7.30 pm weekdays, and 11 am to 2 pm and 4.30 to 8.30 pm weekends and holidays (1100 ptas).

Monument a Colom (Map 3)

The bottom of La Rambla, and the harbour beyond it, are supervised by the tall Columbus monument, built in the 1880s. You can ascend by lift (250 ptas) from 9 am to 8.30 pm daily (June to September). It's open 10 am to 7.30 pm (with a break from 2 to 3.30 pm weekdays) in April and May, while closing time is 6.30 pm the rest of the year.

Museu Marítim (Map 3)

West of the Monument a Colom on Avinguda de les Drassanes stand the **Reials Drassanes** (Royal Shipyards), a rare work of nonreligious Gothic architecture. They now house the Museu Marítim, which together with its setting, forms a fascinating tribute to the seaborne contacts that have shaped Barcelona's history.

The shipyards, first built in the 13th century, gained their present form (a series of long bays divided by stone arches) a century later. Extensions in the 17th century

---

Barcelona Museums

Every Barcelona museum has its own concoction of opening days and hours, sometimes with seasonal variations. Many have a range of prices too, with students and seniors often paying half-price and under-16s getting in for free. Some are free to everyone on the first Sunday of the month and/or half-price on nonholiday Wednesdays. Where only one price is given in this chapter, that's the normal full adult price.

---

made them big enough to accommodate the building of 30 galleys. In their shipbuilding days (up to the 18th century) the sea came right up to them.

Inside is an impressive array of boats, models, maps, paintings and more, with sections devoted to ships' figureheads, Columbus and Magellan, and 16th-century galleys (the full-scale replica of Don Juan of Austria's royal galley from the Battle of Lepanto is a highlight).

The museum is open 10 am to 7 pm daily (800 ptas, students and seniors 600 ptas). Entry is free from 3 pm on the first Saturday of the month.

BARRI GÒTIC (MAP 4)

Barcelona's 'Gothic quarter', east of La Rambla, is a classic medieval warren of narrow, winding streets, quaint little plazas and wonderful structures from the city's golden age. It also has most of the city's best budget accommodation and plenty of good bars, cafes and restaurants. Few of its great buildings date from after the early 15th century.

The Barri Gòtic stretches from La Rambla in the west to Via Laietana in the east and roughly from Carrer de la Portaferrissa in the north to Carrer de la Mercè in the south. Carrer de Ferran and Carrer de Jaume I, cutting across the middle, form a kind of halfway line: these streets and those to their north tend to be peppered with chic little shops, while those to their south become darker and, below Carrer de Ferran, seedier.

Plaça de Sant Jaume

This square at the eastern end of Carrer de Ferran has been Barcelona's political hub on and off since the 15th century. Facing each other across it are the Palau de la Generalitat (the seat of Catalunya's government) on the northern side and the ajuntament on the southern side. Both have fine Gothic interiors, which the general public can only enter at limited times.

The **Palau de la Generalitat**, founded in the early 15th-century, is open only on 23 April, the Dia de Sant Jordi (St George, Catalunya's patron saint), when it's decked out with roses and also very crowded, and

24 September (Festes de la Mercè). At any time, however, you can admire the original Gothic main entrance on Carrer del Bisbe Irurita.

Outside, the only feature of the **ajuntament** now worthy of note is the disused Gothic entrance on Carrer de la Ciutat. From 10 am to 2 pm on Saturday and Sunday, you can tour the inside to visit, above all, the Saló de Cent, a fine arched hall created in the 14th century (but since remodelled) for the medieval city council, the Consell de Cent.

Catedral & Around

You can reach Barcelona's cathedral, its most magnificent Gothic structure, by following Carrer del Bisbe Irurita north-west from Plaça de Sant Jaume. The narrow old streets around the cathedral are traffic-free but dotted with buskers.

At the northern end of Carrer del Bisbe Irurita, poke your head into the courtyards of the 16th-century **Casa de l'Ardiaca** (Archdeacon's House) and the 13th-century **Palau de Bispat** (Bishop's Palace). On the outside of both buildings at the very end of Carrer del Bisbe Irurita you can make out the bottom parts of the rounded **Roman towers** that guarded a Roman gate here. The lower part of the Casa de l'Ardiaca's north-western wall was part of the **Roman walls**.

The best view of the cathedral is from Plaça de la Seu beneath its main **north-western facade**. Unlike most of the building, which dates from between 1298 and 1460, this facade was not created until the 1870s, although it is closely based on a 1408 design. It is unusual in that it reflects northern European Gothic styles rather than the sparer, Catalan version.

The interior of the cathedral is a broad, soaring space divided into a central nave and two aisles by lines of elegant, thin pillars. The cathedral was one of the few churches in Barcelona spared by the anarchists in the civil war, so its ornamentation, never over-lavish, is intact.

In the first chapel on the right from the north-western entrance, the main Crucifixion figure above the altar is the **Sant Crist de Lepant**, said to have been carried on the prow of the Spanish flagship at the battle of Lepanto. Farther along this same wall, past the south-west transept, are the wooden **coffins** of Count Ramon Berenguer I and Almodis, his wife, the founders of the 11th-century Romanesque predecessor of the present cathedral.

The **crypt** beneath the main altar contains the tomb of Santa Eulàlia, one of Barcelona's patron saints and a good Christian lass of the 4th century, who suffered terrible tortures and death at the hands of the pagan Romans.

You can visit the cathedral's **roof** and tower by an *ascensor* (lift), which rises every half-hour from 10.30 am to 12.30 pm and 4.30 to 6.30 pm daily except Sunday, from the Capella de les Animes del Purgatori near the north-east transept. Tickets cost 200 ptas.

From the south-west transept, exit to the lovely **claustre** (cloister), with its trees, fountains and flock of geese (there have been geese here for centuries). One of the cloister chapels commemorates 930 priests, monks and nuns martyred in the civil war. The interior of the cathedral is open 8.30 am to 1.30 pm and 4 to 7.30 pm (5 to 7.30 pm Saturday and Sunday).

Opposite the south-eastern end of the cathedral, narrow Carrer del Paradis leads back down towards Plaça de Sant Jaume. Inside No 10 are four columns of Barcelona's main **Temple Romà d'Augustí** (Roman Temple of Augustus), built for emperor worship in the 1st century AD. You can visit (free) from 10 am to 2 pm and 4 to 8 pm Monday to Saturday, 10 am to 2 pm Sunday (take the official times with a pinch of salt – if the door's open, wander in).

Plaça del Rei & Around

Just a stone's throw east of the cathedral, Plaça del Rei is the former courtyard of the Palau Reial Major, the palace of the counts of Barcelona and monarchs of Aragón.

Museu d'Història de la Ciutat Most of the tall, centuries-old buildings surrounding Plaça del Rei are now open to visitors as the City History Museum. This is one of

Barcelona's most fascinating museums, combining large sections of the palace with a subterranean walk through Roman and Visigothic Barcelona.

The entrance to the museum is through the **Casa Padellàs** on Carrer del Veguer just south of Plaça del Rei. Casa Padellàs, built for a 15th-century noble family, has a courtyard typical of Barcelona's Gothic mansions, with an outdoor staircase up to the 1st floor. Today the staircase leads to a restored Roman tower and a section of Roman wall. Below ground is a remarkable walk through excavated **Roman and Visigothic Barcelona** – complete with sections of a Roman street, Roman baths, remains of a Visigothic basilica and a Visigothic baptismal pool. The route extends underneath the cathedral, where there are traces of the earlier Romanesque structure. You emerge from this part of the museum at a hall and ticket office set up on the northern side of the Plaça del Rei. To

your right is the Saló del Tinell and to the left ahead of you is the Capella Reial de Santa Àgata.

A fan-shaped stairway in the northern corner of Plaça del Rei leads up to the Saló del Tinell, on the left, and the Capella Reial de Santa Àgata on the right. The **Saló del Tinell** was the royal palace's throne hall, a masterpiece of strong, unfussy Catalan Gothic, built in the mid-14th century with wide, rounded arches holding up a wooden roof. The **Capella Reial de Santa Àgata**, also from the 14th century, whose spindly bell tower rises from the north-eastern side of Plaça del Rei, was the palace's chapel. It's plain inside except for its 15th-century altarpiece, painted wood roof and relatively recent stained glass.

Head into Plaça del Rei down the fan-shaped stairs and bear left to the entrance to the multi-tiered *Mirador del Rei Martí* (Lookout Tower of King Martin), built in 1555. It is part of the museum and leads you

The martyrdom of Santa Eulàlia, as depicted in a sculpture in Barcelona's cathedral

to the gallery above the square. You can also climb to the top of the tower, which dominates Plaça del Rei and affords excellent views over the city.

The history museum is open 10 am to 2 pm and 4 to 8 pm Tuesday to Saturday, and 10 am to 2 pm Sunday (500 ptas, free on the first Saturday of the month from 4 to 8 pm). You can pay an extra 200 ptas to watch a 3-D video that traces, in entertaining fashion, the history of the city, before you commence your visit proper.

Palau del Lloctinent The south-western side of Plaça del Rei is taken up by the Palau del Lloctinent (Viceroy's Palace), built in the 1550s as the residence of the Spanish viceroy of Catalunya.

Museu Frederic Marès A short distance down Carrer dels Comtes is the Museu Frederic Marès, in another part of the Palau Reial Major. Marès was a rich 20th-century Catalan sculptor, traveller and obsessive collector. He specialised in medieval Spanish sculpture, huge quantities of which are displayed on the ground and 1st floors, including some lovely coloured wood sculptures of the Crucifixion and the Virgin. The top two floors, known as Museu Sentimental, hold a mind-boggling array of other Marès knick-knacks, from toy soldiers and cribs to scissors and tarot cards. The museum is open from 10 am daily except Monday (to 2 pm Sunday and holidays, 5 pm Tuesday and Thursday and 7 pm on the remaining days). Entry costs 400 ptas but is free on the first Sunday of the month.

Roman Walls

From Plaça del Rei it's worth a little detour to see the two best surviving stretches of Barcelona's Roman walls. One is on the south-western side of Plaça de Ramon Berenguer Gran, with the Capella Reial de Santa Àgata atop them. The other is a little farther south, by the northern end of Carrer del Sotstinent Navarro. They date from the 3rd and 4th centuries, when the Romans rebuilt their walls after the first attacks by Germanic tribes from the north.

Plaça de Sant Josep Oriol & Around

This small plaza not far off La Rambla is the prettiest in the Barri Gòtic. Its bars and cafes attract buskers and artists and make it a lively place to hang out for a while. It's surrounded by some of the Barri Gòtic's quaintest little streets, many of them dotted with other appealing cafes, restaurants and shops. The plaza is dominated by the **Església de Santa Maria del Pi**, a Gothic church built from the 14th to 16th centuries, open 8.30 am to 1 pm and 4.30 to 9 pm daily (9 am to 2 pm and 5 to 9 pm Sunday and holidays). The beautiful rose window above its entrance on Plaça del Pi is claimed to be the world's biggest. The inside of the church was gutted by fire in 1936 and most of the stained glass is modern. The third chapel on the left is dedicated to Sant Josep Oriol, with a map showing spots in the church where he is said to have worked numerous miracles.

The area between Carrer dels Banys Nous and Plaça de Sant Jaume is known as the Call and was Barcelona's **Jewish quarter** – and centre of learning – from at least the 11th century until anti-Semitism saw the Jews expelled from it in 1424.

Plaça Reial & Around

Just south of Carrer de Ferran, near its La Rambla end, is Plaça Reial, an elegant shady square surrounded by eateries, bars, nightspots and budget accommodation. The plaza's 19th-century neoclassical architecture looks as if it would be at home in some Parisian quarter, but before its 1980s cleanup this area had a fearsome reputation for poverty, crime and drugs. Indeed the whole area between Carrer d'Avinyò and La Rambla was once a red-light zone and a notorious den of lowlife.

The plaza still has a restless atmosphere, with respectable tourists, ragged buskers and down-and-outs coming face to face. Don't be put off, but watch your bags and pockets. The lampposts by the central fountain are Gaudí's first known works.

This southern half of the Barri Gòtic is imbued with the memory of Picasso, who lived as a teenager with his family on Carrer de la

Mercè, had his first studio on Carrer de la Plata and was a regular visitor to a brothel at Carrer d'Avinyò 27, which may have inspired his 1907 painting *Les Demoiselles d'Avignon*.

EL RAVAL

West of La Rambla, the Ciutat Vella spreads to Ronda de Sant Antoni, Ronda de Sant Pau and Avinguda del Paral.lel, which together trace the line of Barcelona's 14th-century walls. Known as El Raval, the area contains one of the city's most dispiriting slums, the seedy red-light zone and drug-abusers' haunt of the Barri Xinès. Take care in this area.

Museu d'Art Contemporàni & Around (Map 3)

More upbeat is the Plaça dels Àngels in the north of El Raval. Here the vast, white Museu d'Art Contemporàni de Barcelona (MACBA) opened in 1995. Artists frequently on show include Antoni Tàpies, Joan Brossa, Paul Klee, Alexander Calder and Miquel Barceló. It's open 11 am to 7.30 pm weekdays except Tuesday, 10 am to 8 pm Saturday, and 10 am to 3 pm Sunday and holidays (775 ptas or 350 ptas on nonholiday Wednesdays).

On Carrer de Montalegre behind the museum is the **Centre de Cultura Contempòrania de Barcelona** (Map 3), a complex of auditoriums and exhibition and conference halls created in the early 1990s from an 18th-century hospice. The big courtyard, with a vast glass wall on one side, is spectacular. Exhibitions are held here regularly.

Antic Hospital de la Santa Creu (Map 4)

Two blocks south of Plaça dels Àngels is an architectural masterpiece from another age. Founded in the early 15th century as the city's main hospital, the Antic Hospital de la Santa Creu today houses the Biblioteca de Catalunya (Catalunya's national library) and the Institut d'Estudis Catalans. Take a look inside the library to admire some fine Catalan Gothic construction.

Palau Güell (Map 4)

A few steps off La Rambla at Carrer Nou de la Rambla 3-5, the Palau Güell is the only

Ruta del Modernisme

Modernisme enthusiasts should consider picking up a Ruta del Modernisme ticket at the Casa Amatller. The 600 ptas (students and seniors 400 ptas) ticket is valid for 30 days and is astoundingly good value. It entitles you to half-price entry to the following sights: Palau Güell, Palau de la Música, La Pedrera, La Sagrada Família, Fundació Tàpies, Museu Gaudí (in Parc Güell), Museu de la Música, Museu de Zoologia and Museu Nacional d'Art Modern. Of the buildings comprising the Manzana de la Discordia (Map 2), all in private hands, you can enter the foyer of Casa Amatller to pick up this ticket, but that's it. For more information call ☎ 93 488 01 39. Casa Amatller is open 10 am to 7 pm daily (to 2 pm Sunday).

Gaudí house completely open to the public in Barcelona and one of the few modernista buildings in the Ciutat Vella. Gaudí built it in the late 1880s for his most important patron, the industrialist Eusebi Güell, as a guest wing and social annexe to Güell's main mansion on La Rambla. The Palau Güell lacks some of Gaudí's later playfulness but is still a characteristic riot of styles – Art Nouveau, Gothic, Islamic – and materials. After the civil war it was in police hands and political prisoners were tortured in its basement.

Features to look out for include the carved wooden ceilings and fireplace, the stonework, the use of mirrors, stained glass and wrought iron, and the main hall with its dome reaching right up to the roof. There's little colour until you come out on the roof with its spectacularly tiled and fantastically shaped chimney pots. The Palau Güell is open 10 am to 1.30 pm and 4 to 6.30 pm daily except Sunday (400 ptas, students 200 ptas), and tours usually start on the hour.

Picasso, who hated Gaudí's work, began his Blue Period in 1902 in a studio across the street at Carrer Nou de la Rambla 6.

LA RIBERA (MAP 4)

La Ribera is the area of the Ciutat Vella north-east of the Barri Gòtic, from which it's divided by noisy Via Laietana, riven through

BARCELONA

the city in 1907. La Ribera has intriguing, narrow streets, some major sights and good bars and restaurants, and lacks the seedy character of some parts of the Barri Gòtic.

Palau de la Música Catalana

This concert hall (Map 3) at Carrer de Sant Pere més alt 11 is one of the high points of modernista architecture. It's not exactly a symphony, more a series of crescendos in tile, brick, sculptured stone and stained glass. Built between 1905 and 1908 by Lluís Domènech i Montaner for the Orfeó Català musical society, with the help of some of the best Catalan artisans of the time, it was conceived as a temple for the Catalan Renaixença.

You can see some of its splendours – such as the main facade with its mosaics, floral capitals and sculpture cluster representing Catalan popular music – from the outside and glimpse lovely tiled pillars inside the ticket office entrance on Carrer de Sant Francesc de Paula. But best is the richly colourful auditorium upstairs, with its ceiling of blue and gold stained glass and, above a bust of Beethoven, a towering sculpture of Wagner's Valkyries (Wagner was No 1 in the Renaixença charts).

To see this, you need to attend a concert or join a guided tour. These tours, which take 50 minutes, take place daily every half-hour from 10 am to 3.30 pm. You can buy tickets from Les Muses del Palau shop at Carrer de Sant Pere més alt 1 up to a week in advance. They cost 700 ptas. For information call ☎ 93 268 10 00. You can get in for half-price with a Ruta del Modernisme ticket (see the boxed text earlier).

Museu Picasso

Barcelona's most visited museum, the Museu Picasso, occupies three of the many fine medieval stone mansions on narrow Carrer de Montcada. The street was cut through the southern part of La Ribera in the 12th century as an approach to the port, then farther east than it is today. The mansions belonged to nobles and merchants who grew rich off Mediterranean trade.

The Museu Picasso, at No 15-19, is at its best with the artist's Barcelona periods. It

shows clearly how the young Picasso learned to handle a whole spectrum of subjects, styles and treatments before developing his own forms of expression.

On the 1st floor are ceramics and 1890s paintings from Barcelona, Madrid and Málaga. The 2nd floor starts with work of 1900–4 from Barcelona and Paris, with more impressionist-influenced paintings such as *Waiting* and Blue Period canvases such as *The Defenceless*. There's also the haunting *Portrait of Senyora Canals* (1905) from the following Pink Period.

Among the later works, all done in Cannes in 1957, are a complex technical series *(Las Meninas)*. These consist, for the most part, of studies on Diego Velázquez's masterpiece of the same name (which hangs in the Prado in Madrid), but also include eight appealing treatments of *Pichones* (Pigeons).

The museum is open 10 am to 8 pm Tuesday to Saturday and holidays, and 10 am to 3 pm Sunday (725 ptas, free on the first Sunday of each month). There are additional charges for special exhibitions.

Museu Tèxtil i d'Indumentària

The Textile and Costume Museum is in the 14th-century Palau dels Marquesos de Llió at Carrer de Montcada 12. Its 4000 items range from 4th-century Coptic textiles to 20th-century local embroidery. The highlight is the big collection of clothing from the 16th century to the 1930s. It's open 10 am to 8 pm Tuesday to Saturday and 10 am to 3 pm Sunday and holidays. Entry is 400 ptas, or 700 ptas if you combine it with the Museu Barbier-Mueller d'Art Precolombí next door. Both museums are free on the first Saturday of each month.

Museu Barbier-Mueller d'Art Precolombí

Occupying the Palau Nadal at 14 Carrer de Montcada, this museum holds one of the most prestigious collections of pre-Colombian art in the world. The artefacts from South American 'primitive' cultures come from the collections of the Swiss businessman Josef Mueller (who died in 1977) and his son-in-law Jean-Paul Barbier, who directs the Musée Barbier-Mueller in Geneva. It is open 10 am to 8 pm Tuesday to Saturday, and 10 am to 3 pm Sunday and holidays (500 ptas, or 700 ptas combined with the Museu Tèxtil i d'Indumentària).

Along Carrer de Montcada

Several other mansions on the street are now commercial art galleries where you're welcome to browse (they often stage exhibitions). The biggest is **Galeria Maeght** at No 25 in the 16th-century Palau dels Cervelló.

Barcelona has dozens of other art galleries, by the way; you'll find listings in *Guía del Ocio* (see Entertainment later in this chapter).

Església de Santa Maria del Mar

Carrer de Montcada opens at its south-eastern end into **Passeig del Born**, a plaza where jousting tournaments took place in the Middle Ages and which was Barcelona's main square from the 13th to 18th centuries. At the south-western end of Passeig del Born stands one of Barcelona's finest Gothic churches, Santa Maria del Mar. Built in the 14th century, Santa Maria was lacking in superfluous decoration even before anarchists gutted it in 1909 and 1936. This only serves to highlight its fine proportions, purity of line and sense of space. There's a beautifully slim arcade in the apse and some lovely 15th- to 18th-century stained glass. The church is open 9 am to 1.30 pm and 4.30 to 8 pm daily.

PARC DE LA CIUTADELLA (MAP 3)

East of La Ribera and north of La Barceloneta, Parc de la Ciutadella is perfect if you just need a bit of space and greenery, but also has some more specific attractions.

After the War of the Spanish Succession, Felipe V built a huge fort (La Ciutadella) to keep watch over Barcelona. It became a much loathed symbol of everything Catalans hated about Madrid and was later used as a political prison. Only in 1869 did the government allow its demolition. The site was turned into a park and used as the main site for the Universal Exhibition of 1888. It's open 8 am to 8 pm daily (to 9 pm, April to September). Arc de Triomf and Barceloneta, both about 500m away, are the nearest metro stations.

The single most impressive object in the park is the monumental **Cascada** near the Passeig de les Pujades entrance, created in 1875–81 by Josep Fontsère, with the help of the young Gaudí. It's a dramatic combination of classical statuary, rugged rocks, greenery and thundering water.

South-east of here, in the fort's former arsenal, are the **Museu Nacional d'Art Modern de Catalunya** and the **Parlament de Catalunya**, where the Generalitat meets. The art gallery, despite its title, is devoted to Catalan art from the mid-19th century to the 1920s, the era of modernisme and its classicist antithesis, Noucentism (literally '19th-centuryism'). Look for works by the two leading lights of modernista art, Ramon Casas and Santiago Rusiñol, especially Casas' drawings of the habitués of Els Quatre Gats restaurant and Rusiñol's landscapes. The museum is open 10 am to 7 pm Tuesday to Saturday, and 10 am to 2.30 pm Sunday and holidays (500 ptas). A Ruta del Modernisme ticket gets you in for half-price (see the boxed text earlier).

The southern end of the park is occupied by the large **Parc Zoològic** (zoo), which is best known for its albino gorilla called Copito de Nieve (Snowflake), who was orphaned by poachers in Africa in the 1960s. It's open 10 am to 7.30 pm daily (to 5 pm in winter). Entry is 1550 ptas.

Along the Passeig de Picasso side of the park are several buildings constructed for, or just before, the Universal Exhibition. These include two arboretums, the specialised Museu de Geologia and the **Museu de Zoologia** or Castell dels Tres Dragons, open 10 am to 2 pm Tuesday to Sunday, and until 6.30 pm Thursday (400 ptas). The contents of this museum are less interesting than the building itself, by Lluís Domènech i Montaner, who put medieval castle trimmings on a pioneering steel frame.

North-west of the park along Passeig de Lluís Companys is the imposing modernista **Arc de Triomf** (Map 1), with unusual, almost Islamic-style brickwork.

PORT VELL (MAP 3)

Barcelona's old port at the bottom of La Rambla, once such an eyesore that it caused public protests, has been transformed since the 1980s into an attractive and people-friendly environment with some excellent leisure developments.

For a view of the harbour from the water, you can take a **golondrina** (excursion boat; ☎ 93 442 31 06) from Moll de les Drassanes in front of the Monument a Colom. A 35-minute trip to the breakwater *(rompeolas)* and lighthouse *(faro)* on the seaward side of the harbour is 500 ptas; a one-hour, 20-minute trip to Port Olímpic is 1300 ptas (900 ptas for under-19s). This latter trip is on a glass-bottom catamaran. The number of departures depends largely on season and demand. Breakwater trips normally go at least hourly in the daytime, Port Olímpic trips at least three times daily. North-east from the golondrina quay stretches the palm-lined promenade **Moll de la Fusta**.

At the centre of the redeveloped harbour is the **Moll d'Espanya**, a former wharf linked to Moll de la Fusta by a wave-shaped footbridge, **Rambla de Mar**, which rotates to let boats enter the marina behind it. At the end of Moll d'Espanya is the glossy Maremàgnum shopping and eating complex, but the major attraction is **L'Aquàrium** (☎ 93 221 74 74) behind it – an ultramodern aquarium that opened in 1995. It's claimed to be Europe's biggest aquarium and to have the world's best Mediterranean collection. One of the highlight is the 80m-long shark tunnel. Entry is a steep 1450 ptas (four- to 12-year-olds and seniors 950 ptas). It's open 9.30 am to 9 pm (to 11 pm in July and August). Beyond L'Aquàrium is the Imax Port Vell big-screen cinema.

The **cable car** *(telefèric* or *funicular aereo)* strung across the harbour to Montjuïc provides another view of the city. You can get tickets at Miramar (Montjuïc; Map 1) and the Torre de Sant Sebastià (in La Barceloneta; Map 1). Access to the Torre de Jaume I, halfway along, was suspended at the time of writing. A return

ticket from Miramar to Sant Sebastià will cost 1200 ptas, or 1000 ptas one way. The cable car operates 10.30 am to 7 pm daily (to 5.30 pm in winter).

LA BARCELONETA & PORT OLÍMPIC (MAPS 1 & 3)

It used to be said that Barcelona had 'turned its back on the sea', but an ambitious Olympics-inspired redevelopment program has returned a long stretch of coast north-east of Port Vell to life.

La Barceloneta is an old sailors' quarter now mostly composed of dreary five- and six-storey apartment blocks. It's known for its seafood restaurants, although some of the most characteristic ones were knocked down in the redevelopment. In the Palau de Mar building facing the harbour is the **Museu d'Història de Catalunya** (History of Catalunya Museum; Map 3). It's an almost Disneyesque sort of place, incorporating lots of technological wizardry, with audio-visuals and interactive information points galore. Nearly all the labelling is in Catalan, but you can request a returnable explanatory booklet in several languages, including English. Covering the region's prehistory and history to 1980, the museum has re-creations including a Roman house and a civil war air-raid shelter. The museum is open 10 am to 7 pm Tuesday to Thursday (to 8 pm Friday and Saturday), and 10 am to 2.30 pm Sunday and holidays (500 ptas).

Barcelona's fishing fleet ties up along the Moll del Rellotge, south of the museum. On La Barceloneta's seaward side are the first of Barcelona's **beaches**, now cleaned up and popular on summer weekends. **Passeig Marítim** (Map 1), a 1.25km promenade from La Barceloneta to Port Olímpic (through an area formerly full of railway sidings and warehouses) is pleasant.

Port Olímpic (Map 1) was built for the Olympic sailing events and is now surrounded by bars and restaurants. An eye-catcher on the approach from La Barceloneta is the giant copper *Peix* (Fish) sculpture by Frank Gehry, one of a series of modern sculptures dotted around this part of town. The area behind Port Olímpic –

dominated by Barcelona's two tallest sky-scrapers, the luxury Hotel Arts Barcelona and the Torre Mapfre office block – is the Vila Olímpica, the living quarters for the Olympic participants, now mostly sold off as expensive apartments. To the north-east are more beaches.

L'EIXAMPLE (MAP 2)

L'Eixample (the Enlargement), stretching 1km to 1.5km north, east and west of Plaça de Catalunya, was Barcelona's 19th-century answer to overcrowding in the medieval city.

Work on l'Eixample began in 1869, following a design by the architect Ildefons Cerdà, who specified a grid of wide streets with plazas formed by their cut-off corners. Cerdà also planned numerous green spaces but these didn't survive the intense demand for l'Eixample real estate.

L'Eixample has been inhabited from the start by the city's middle classes, many of whom still think it's the best thing about Barcelona. Along its grid of straight streets are the majority of the city's most expensive shops and hotels, plus a range of eateries and several nightspots. The main sightseeing objective is modernista architecture, the best of which – apart from La Sagrada Família – is clustered on or near l'Eixample's main avenue, Passeig de Gràcia.

Manzana de la Discordia

The so-called 'Apple (read Block) of Discord' on the western side of Passeig de Gràcia, between Carrer del Consell de Cent and Carrer d'Aragó, gets its name from three houses remodelled in a highly contrasting manner between 1898 and 1906 by three of the leading modernista architects.

At No 35, on the corner of Carrer del Consell de Cent, is **Casa Lleo Morera**, Lluís Domènech i Montaner's contribution, with Art Nouveau carving outside and a bright, tiled lobby in which floral motifs predominate. You can no longer visit the 1st floor, giddy with swirling sculptures, rich mosaics and whimsical decoration.

At No 41, **Casa Amatller** by Josep Puig i Cadafalch, combines Gothic window frames

with a stepped gable borrowed (deliberately) from urban architecture of the Netherlands. The pillared entrance hall and the staircase lit by stained glass are like the inside of some romantic castle. You can wander around the ground floor and pick up a Ruta del Modernisme ticket here.

Next door at No 43 is **Casa Batlló**, one of Barcelona's gems. Of course it's by Gaudí. The facade, sprinkled with bits of blue, mauve and green tile and studded with wave-shaped window frames and balconies, rises to an uneven blue tiled roof with a solitary tower. The roof represents Sant Jordi (St George) and the dragon, and if you stare long enough at the building, it seems almost to be a living being. You might fluke your way into the foyer (but not beyond) if the main entrance is open.

While in this area you may want to pop into the **Museu del Parfum** (Map 2), Passeig de Gràcia 39 in the Regia store. It contains everything from ancient scent receptacles to classic Eau de Cologne bottles. It's open 10 am to 8.30 pm weekdays, 10.30 am to 2 pm and 5 to 8.30 pm Saturday.

Fundació Antoni Tàpies

Around the corner from the Manzana de la Discordia, at Carrer d'Aragó 255, this is both a pioneering modernista building of the early 1880s and the major collection of a leading 20th-century Catalan artist. The building, designed by Domènech i Montaner, combines a brick-covered iron frame with Islamic-inspired decoration. Antoni

---

Manzana de la Discordia

Despite the Catalanisation of most Barcelona names in recent decades, the Manzana de la Discordia has kept its Spanish name to preserve a pun on *manzana*, which means both 'city block' and 'apple'. According to Greek myth, the original Apple of Discord was tossed on to Mt Olympus by Eris (Discord) with orders that it be given to the most beautiful goddess, sparking jealousies that helped start the Trojan War. The pun won't transfer into Catalan, in which block is *illa* and apple is *poma*.

The Modernistas

Most visitors to Barcelona will have heard of Antoni Gaudí (gow-**dee**), whose La Sagrada Família church is one of the city's major drawcards. But Gaudí (1852–1926) was just one, albeit the most spectacular, of a generation of inventive architects who left their mark on Barcelona between 1880 and 1910. These were the *modernistas*, or Catalan modernists.

Modernisme is usually described as a version of Art Nouveau, from which it certainly derived its taste for sinuous, flowing lines and decorative artisanry. Art Nouveau also inspired modernisme's adventurous combinations of materials such as tile, glass, brick, and iron and steel (which provide the unseen frames of many buildings). But Barcelona's modernistas used an astonishing variety of other styles too: Gothic and Islamic, Renaissance and Romanesque, and Byzantine. Some of their buildings look like fairy-tale castles. They were trying to create a specifically Catalan architecture, often looking back to Catalunya's medieval golden age for inspiration.

It's significant that the two other leading modernista architects, the tongue-twisting Lluís Domènech i Montaner (1850–1923) and Josep Puig i Cadafalch (1867–1957), were also prominent in the Catalan nationalist political movement. Gaudí too was a Catalan nationalist, although he turned increasingly to spiritual concerns as he grew older.

L'Eixample, where most of Barcelona's new building was happening at the time, is home to many of the modernista creations. Others in the city include Gaudí's Palau Güell and Parc Güell; Domènech i Montaner's Palau de la Música Catalana, Castell dels Tres Dragons and Hotel España restaurant; and Puig i Cadafalch's Els Quatre Gats. There are many, many more.

Nor was modernisme confined to architecture: you can explore its painting and drawing side at the Museu Nacional d'Art Modern de Catalunya.

Tàpies, whose experimental art has often carried political messages (he opposed Francoism in the 1960s and 70s) launched the *fundació* in 1984 to promote contemporary art, donating a large collection of his own work. Plans are afoot to broaden the collection.

The Fundació is open 10 am to 8 pm Tuesday to Sunday; entry is 700 ptas, students 350 ptas.

La Pedrera

Back on Passeig de Gràcia, at No 92, is another Gaudí masterpiece, built between 1905 and 1910 as a combined apartment and office block. Formally called the Casa Milà after the businessman who commissioned it, it's better known as La Pedrera (The Quarry) because of its uneven grey stone facade, which ripples around the corner of Carrer de Provença. The wave effect is emphasised by elaborate wrought-iron balconies.

The Fundació Caixa Catalunya office (☎ 93 484 59 95) has opened the place up to visitors, organising it as the Espai Gaudí

(Gaudí Space) and guiding visitors through the building and up onto the roof, with its giant chimneypots looking like multicoloured medieval knights. One floor below the roof, where you can appreciate Gaudí's taste for McDonald's M-style arches, is a modest museum dedicated to his work. You can see models and videos dealing with each of his buildings.

Downstairs on the next floor you can inspect an apartment (El Pis de la Pedrera). It is fascinating to wander around this elegantly furnished home, done up in the style a well-to-do family might have enjoyed at the turn of the last century.

La Pedrera is open 10 am to 8 pm daily. Guided visits take place at 6 pm (11 am weekends and holidays). You can elect to pay 600 ptas just to see the Espai Gaudí and the roof terrace *or* the apartment. It is worth paying the full 1000 ptas to see both if you have failed to purchase a Ruta del Modernisme ticket.

(continued on page 381)

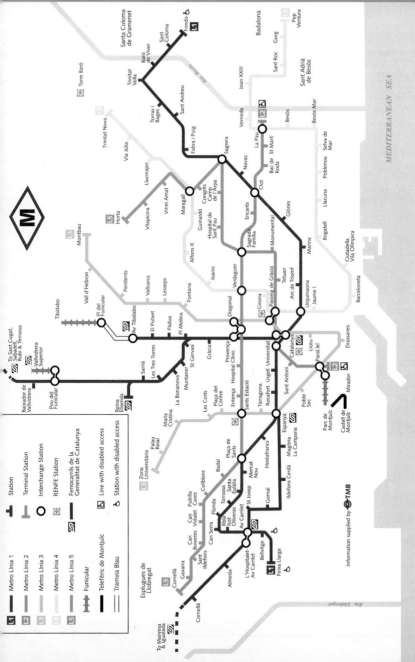

Barcelona Metro map. Legend:

- Metro Línia 1
- Metro Línia 2
- Metro Línia 3
- Metro Línia 4
- Metro Línia 5
- Funicular
- Telefèric de Montjuïc
- Tramvia Blau

- Station
- Terminal Station
- Interchange Station
- RENFE Station
- Ferrocarrils de la Generalitat de Catalunya
- Line with disabled access
- Station with disabled access

Information supplied by TMB

MAP 1 - BARCELONA

PLACES TO STAY
3 Alberg Mare de Déu
  de Montserrat
10 Alberg Studio
20 Alberg Pere Tarrès
62 Hotel Arts Barcelona
66 Hostal de Joves

PLACES TO EAT
2 Mirablau Terrazza
6 Sannin
14 La Taverna del Cel Ros

BARS & CLUBS
1 Mirablau
5 KGB

8 La Cova del Drac
16 The Music Box
38 Torres de Ávila
74 Savannah

OTHER
4 Casa Museu Gaudí
7 Bookstore
9 British Council
11 US Consulate
12 Museu-Monestir de
  Pedralbes
13 Palau Reial de Pedralbes
  (Museu de Ceràmica &
  Museu de les Arts
  Decoratives)

14 Japanese Consulate
15 Giorgio Armani
17 Gianni Versace
18 FNAC
19 L'Illa del Diagonal
21 Ronicar Rentacar
22 Netherlands Consulate
23 El Corte Inglés
24 Australian Consulate
25 Swiss & Irish Consulates
26 Cinema Renoir-Les Corts
27 Camp Nou
28 Museu del Futbol
  Club Barcelona
29 Coordinadora Gai-Lesbiana
30 Farmacia Salto

OTHER (CONTINUED)
31 Estació d'Autobusos de Sants
32 Aerobús Stop
33 Dona i Ocell Sculpture
34 Turisme Juvenil de Catalunya,
   Xarxa d'Albergs de Catalunya
   & Usit Unlimited
35 Punt d'Informació Juvenil
36 Xampany
37 The English Bookshop
39 Poble Espanyol
40 Tennis Municipal Pompeia

OTHER (CONTINUED)
41 Piscines Bernat Picornell
42 Palau Sant Jordi
43 Galería Olímpica
44 Palau Nacional (Museu
   Nacional d'Art de Catalunya)
45 Museu Etnològic
46 Teatre Mercat de les Flors
47 Museu d'Arqueologia
48 Teatre Grec
49 Fundació Joan Miró
50 Estació Parc Montjuïc
   (Funicular & Telefèric)
51 Terminus Bus Nos 50 & 61
52 Castell (Telefèric)
53 Museu Militar
54 Estació Mirador (Telefèric)
55 Telefèric (Funicular Aereo) to
   Torre de Jaume I & Torre de
   San Sebastià (La Barceloneta)
56 Ferry Terminal &
   Trasmediterránea
57 Barcelona-Genoa Ferry Dock
58 Torre de Jaume I
59 World Trade Center
60 Torre de Sant Sebastià
61 Peix Sculpture
62 Torre Mapfre
63 Cinema Icària-Yelmo
67 Palau de Justicia
68 Arc de Triomf
69 Estació del Nord
70 L'Auditori
71 Teatre Nacional de Catalunya
72 Plaça de Braus Monumental
73 Els Encants Flea Market
75 Hospital de la Creu Roja
76 Hospital de la Santa
   Creu i Sant Pau

MAP 2 - L' EIXAMPLE & GRÀCIA

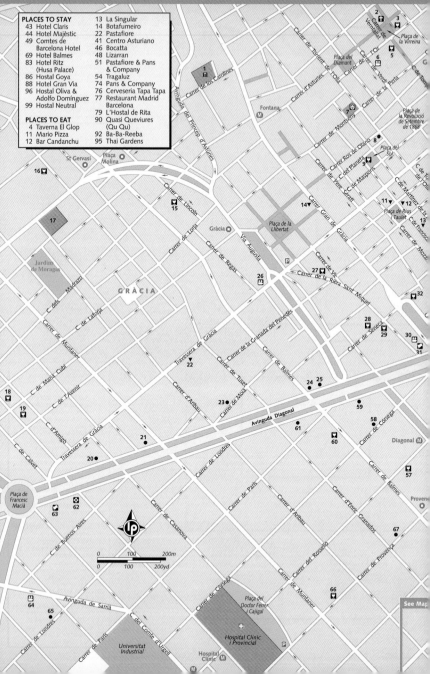

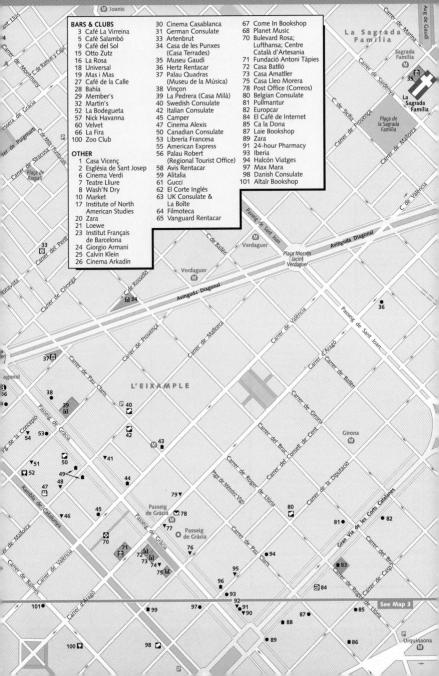

BARS & CLUBS
- 3 Café La Virreina
- 5 Café Salambó
- 9 Café del Sol
- 15 Otto Zutz
- 16 La Rosa
- 19 Mas i Mas
- 27 Café de la Calle
- 28 Bahía
- 29 Member's
- 32 Martin's
- 52 La Bodegueta
- 57 Nick Havanna
- 60 Velvet
- 66 La Fira
- 100 Zoo Club

OTHER
- 1 Casa Vicenç
- 2 Església de Sant Josep
- 6 Cinema Verdi
- 7 Teatre Lliure
- 8 Wash'N Dry
- 10 Market
- 17 Institute of North American Studies
- 20 Zara
- 21 Loewe
- 23 Institut Français de Barcelona
- 24 Giorgio Armani
- 25 Calvin Klein
- 26 Cinema Arkadín

- 30 Cinema Casablanca
- 31 German Consulate
- 33 Artenbrut
- 34 Casa de les Punxes (Casa Terrades)
- 35 Museu Gaudí
- 36 Hertz Rentacar
- 37 Palau Quadras (Museu de la Música)
- 38 Vinçon
- 39 La Pedrera (Casa Milà)
- 40 Swedish Consulate
- 42 Italian Consulate
- 45 Camper
- 47 Cinema Alexis
- 50 Canadian Consulate
- 53 Librería Francesa
- 55 American Express
- 56 Palau Robert (Regional Tourist Office)
- 58 Avis Rentacar
- 59 Alitalia
- 61 Gucci
- 62 El Corte Inglés
- 63 UK Consulate & La Boîte
- 64 Filmoteca
- 65 Vanguard Rentacar

- 67 Come In Bookshop
- 68 Planet Music
- 70 Bulevard Rosa; Lufthansa; Centre Català d'Artesania
- 71 Fundació Antoni Tàpies
- 72 Casa Batlló
- 73 Casa Amatller
- 75 Casa Lleo Morera
- 78 Post Office (Correos)
- 80 Belgian Consulate
- 81 Pullmantur
- 82 Europcar
- 84 El Café de Internet
- 85 Ca la Dona
- 87 Laie Bookshop
- 89 Zara
- 91 24-hour Pharmacy
- 93 Iberia
- 94 Halcón Viatges
- 97 Max Mara
- 98 Danish Consulate
- 101 Altaïr Bookshop

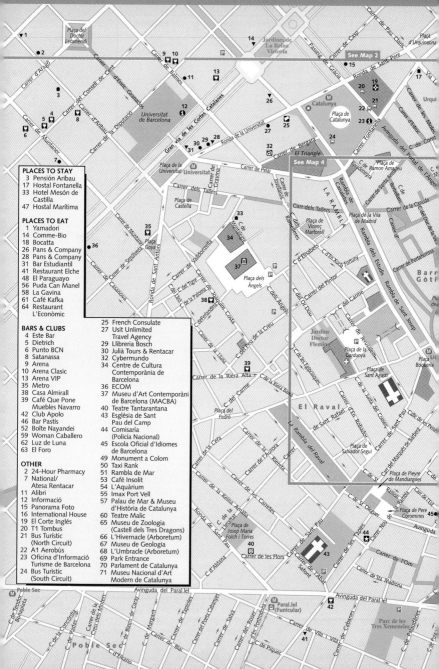

MAP 3 - CENTRAL BARCELONA

PLACES TO STAY
3 Pensión Aribau
17 Hostal Fontanella
33 Hotel Mesón de Castilla
47 Hostal Marítima

PLACES TO EAT
1 Yamadori
14 Comme-Bio
18 Bocatta
26 Pans & Company
28 Pans & Company
31 Bar Estudiantil
41 Restaurant Elche
56 El Paraguayo
56 Puda Can Manel
58 La Gavina
61 Café Kafka
64 Restaurant L'Econòmic

BARS & CLUBS
4 Este Bar
5 Dietrich
6 Punto BCN
8 Satanassa
9 Arena
10 Arena Clasic
13 Arena VIP
35 Metro
37 Casa Almirall
39 Café Que Pone Muebles Navarro
42 Club Apolo
46 Bar Pastís
52 Boîte Nayandei
59 Woman Caballero
62 Luz de Luna
63 El Foro

OTHER
2 24-Hour Pharmacy
7 National/ Atesa Rentacar
11 Alibri
15 Informació
15 Panorama Foto
16 International House
19 El Corte Inglés
20 T1 Tombus
21 Bus Turístic (North Circuit)
22 A1 Aerobús
23 Oficina d'Informació Turisme de Barcelona
24 Bus Turístic (South Circuit)

25 French Consulate
27 Usit Unlimited Travel Agency
29 Llibreria Bosch
30 Julià Tours & Rentacar
32 Cybermundo
34 Centre de Cultura Contemporània de Barcelona
36 ECOM
37 Museu d'Art Contemporàni de Barcelona (MACBA)
40 Teatre Tantarantana
45 Església de Sant Pau del Camp
44 Comisaria (Policía Nacional)
45 Escola Oficial d'Idiomes de Barcelona
49 Monument a Colom
50 Taxi Rank
51 Rambla de Mar
53 Café Insolit
54 L'Aquàrium
55 Imax Port Vell
57 Palau de Mar & Museu d'Història de Catalunya
60 Teatre Malic
65 Museu de Zoologia (Castell dels Tres Dragons)
66 L'Hivernacle (Arboretum)
67 Museu de Geologia
68 L'Umbracle (Arboretum)
69 Park Entrance
70 Parlament de Catalunya
71 Museu Nacional d'Art Modern de Catalunya

Cascada

Parc de la Ciutadella

71

70

Jrquinaona

Trafalgar

16

Plaça de Sant Pere

Plaça del Comerç

Passeig de Lluís Companys

Passeig de Joaquim Renart

65

66

67

68

69

Parc Zoòlogic Acurama

Passeig de Picasso

Palau de la Música Catalana

64

Plaça de Sant Agustí Vell

Plaça de Pons i Clerch

63

62

61

60

Mercat de Santa Caterina (Closed)

Mercat Del Born

Plaça Antoni Maura

La Ribera

Plta d'En Marcus

Plaça Comercial

Plaça de la Seu

Plaça de R Berenguer El Gran

Plaça del Rei

Jaume I

Plaça de l'Àngel

Jaume I

Plaça de Santa Maria del Mar

59

Estació de França

Passeig de Circumval·lació

Ronda del Litoral

Plaça de Sant Jaume

Plaça de Sant Miquel

Plaça del Palau

Barceloneta

Carrer del Doctor Aiguader

Balboa

Plaça de Pau Vila

La Barceloneta

Plaça de George Orwell

Plaça d'Antoni López

Plaça de la Font

Plaça Reial

58

57

Plaça de la Barceloneta

Plaça del Poeta Bosca

Plaça de la Merçè

Plaça del Duc de Medinaceli

Mirador del Port Vell

Marina

56

46

Museu de Cera

48

47

Museu Maritim

49

50

53

51

52

Plaça del Portal de la Pau

Plaça del Ictinia

55

54

Maremàgnum

Port de Barcelona

Port Vell

Moll dels Pescadors

0   100   200m
0   100   200yd

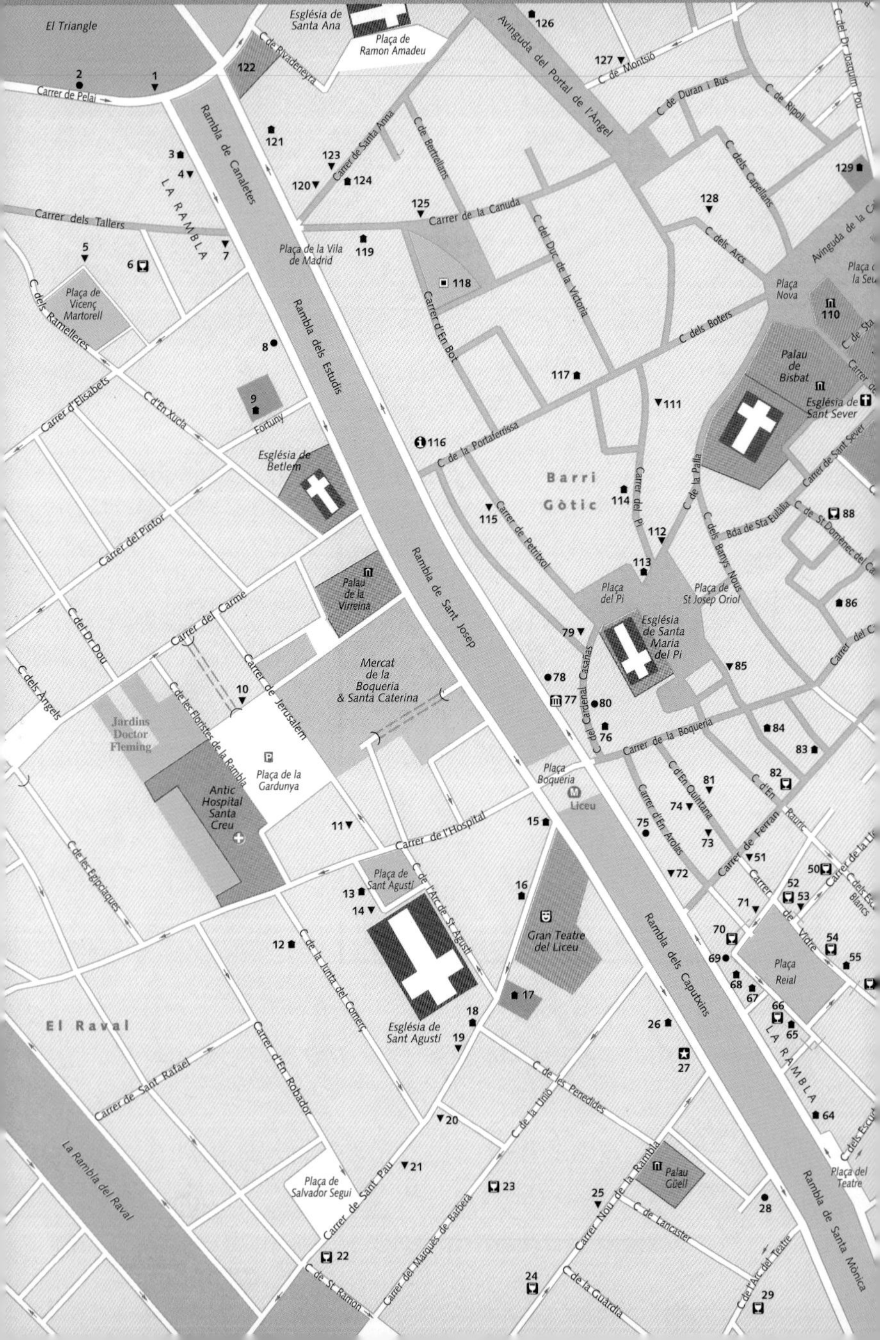

MAP 4 - CIUTAT VELLA

El Triangle

Plaça de Ramon Amadeu

Església de Santa Ana

2

1

122

Carrer de Pelai

Rambla de Canaletes

LA RAMBLA

121

3

4

123

Carrer de Santa Anna

120

124

125

119

Plaça de la Vila de Madrid

Carrer de la Canuda

126

Avinguda del Portal de l'Àngel

127

C. de Montsió

C. de Duran i Bas

C. de Ripoll

129

128

C. dels Arcs

C. dels Capellans

Carrer dels Tallers

5

6

7

Plaça de Vicenç Martorell

C. dels Ramelleres

C. d'Elisabets

C. d'en Xuclà

Rambla dels Estudis

8

9

Fortuny

Església de Betlem

Carrer del Pintor

Carrer del Carme

Palau de la Virreina

Carrer de Sant Josep

Mercat de la Boqueria & Santa Caterina

Carrer del Dr Dou

C. dels Àngels

Carrer de Jerusalem

10

Jardins Doctor Fleming

Carrer de les Portes de l'Àngel

Antic Hospital Santa Creu

Plaça de la Gardunya

P

11

Carrer de l'Hospital

Plaça de Sant Agustí

13

14

12

C. de la Junta del Comerç

C. de l'Arc de St. Agustí

Església de Sant Agustí

18

19

El Raval

Carrer de Sant Rafael

Carrer d'en Robador

20

21

Plaça de Salvador Seguí

22

Carrer de Sant Pau

La Rambla del Raval

C. de St. Ramon

C. del Marquès de Barberà

23

Carrer de la Canuda

118

117

116

C. de la Portaferrissa

115

C. de Petritxol

Barri Gòtic

114

112

113

111

C. dels Boters

Plaça Nova

Palau de Bisbat

Església de Sant Sever

110

C. de la Palla

Bda. de Sta Eulàlia

C. de Sta Eulàlia

C. de St. Domènec del

88

86

84

83

82

Plaça del Pi

Plaça de St Josep Oriol

Església de Santa Maria del Pi

79

78

77

76

80

85

Carrer de la Boqueria

C. d'en Quintana

81

74

73

75

C. d'en Aroles

72

71

70

69

68

67

66

65

64

Plaça Boqueria

Liceu

Rambla dels Caputxins

15

16

17

Gran Teatre del Liceu

26

27

Plaça Reial

52

53

50

51

54

55

C. del Vidre

C. d'en Rauric

Carrer de Ferran

C. de la Lleona

C. dels Escudellers

25

24

C. de la Unió de les Penedides

C. de Lancaster

Palau Güell

28

29

Plaça del Teatre

Rambla de Santa Mònica

LA RAMBLA

MAP 4 - CIUTAT VELLA

PLACES TO STAY
3   Pensión Noya
9   Le Meridien
12 Hotel Jovertat
13 Hotel San Agustín
15 Hostal Mare Nostrum
16 Hostal Residencia Òpera
17 Hotel España &
    Fonda Espanya
18 Hotel Peninsular
26 Hotel Oriente
30 Hostal El Cantón
41 Alberg Juvenil Palau
42 Casa Huéspedes Mari-Luz
44 Hostal Levante
46 Pensión Alamar
55 Hotel Roma Reial
63 Hotel Barcelona House
64 Hotel Cuatro Naciones
65 Youth Hostel Kabul
67 Pensió Colom 3
68 Pensión Villanueva
76 Hostal Paris
83 Pensión Fernando
84 Albergue Arco
86 Hotel Call
99 Hotel Suizo
113 Hotel Jardi
114 Hostal Galerias Maldà;
    Cinema Maldà
117 Hostal-Residencia
    Rembrandt
119 Hostal Campi
121 Hotel Continental
124 Hotel Nouvel
126 Hostal Lausanne
129 Hotel Colón
135 Pensión Lourdes

PLACES TO EAT
1   Café Zurich
4   Pastafiore
5   Bar Kasparo
7   Pans & Company
10 Ra
11 El Convent
14 Rita Blue
19 Restaurant Els Tres Bots
20 Restaurante Pollo Rico
21 Kashmir Restaurant Tandoori
25 Salsitas
35 Bar Celta
36 Tasca El Corral
37 Sidrería La Socarrena
43 La Cereria
45 La Verónica
47 Felafel & Kebab Takeaway
51 Pans & Company

53 El Taxidermista
58 Wagamama
59 Buen Bocado
60 Los Caracoles
62 La Fonda Escudellers
71 Les Quinze Nits
72 Cafè de l'Òpera
73 Les Quatre Barres
74 Sushi-ya
79 Irati
81 Can Culleretes
85 Mesón Jesús
87 Salterio
92 Bocatta
95 Santa Clara
98 Il Caffè di Roma
100 La Colmena
101 Bon Mercat
111 Croissanterie del Pi
112 Xocolateria La Xicra
115 Granja La Pallaresa
120 Bocatta
123 Self-Naturista
125 The Bagel Shop
127 Els Quatre Gats
128 Pans & Company
130 Comme-Bio
131 Lluna Plena
132 Restaurante Bunga Raya
136 Senyor Parellada
138 La Flauta Mágica
139 L'Ou Com Balla
143 Centre Cultural
    Euskal Etxea
147 Gades
149 Cal Pep
154 Restaurant Set Portes

BARS & CLUBS
6   L'Ovella Negra
22 Bar Marsella
23 The Quiet Man
24 London Bar
29 Moog
31 Antinous
38 Bar Center Point
40 Harlem Jazz Club
48 Shanghai
49 Al Limón Negro
50 Bar Malpaso
52 Sidecar
54 Karma
56 Thiossan
57 Zoo
61 Dot
66 Jamboree
70 Glaciar
82 Schilling

88 B.O.2
93 Paradise Bar
137 El Nus
140 El Xampanyet
144 Miramelindo
145 El Copetín
146 Borneo
148 Mudanzas
152 La Vinya del Senyor

MUSEUMS & GALLERIES
77 Museu de l'Eròtica
102 Casa Padellàs (Museu
    d'Història de la Ciutat)
107 Museu Frederic Marès
108 Museu Diocesà; Casa de la
    Pia Almoina
133 Museu Picasso
134 Museu Tèxtil i d'Indumentària
    & Museu Barbier-Mueller
    d'Art Precolombí
142 Galeria Maeght

OTHER
2   FNAC
8   Champion Supermarket
27 Guàrdia Urbana
28 Tablao Cordobés
32 Casal Lambda
33 Universitat Pompeu Fabra
34 Església de la Mercè
39 Main Post Office (Correus)
69 Barcelona Pipa Club
75 American Express
78 24-Hour Pharmacy
80 Documenta Bookshop
89 Palau de la Generalitat
90 Ajuntament
91 Centre d'Informació Turisme
    de Barcelona
94 Temple Romà d'Augustí
96 Església de Sants
    Just i Pastor
97 Próleg Bookshop
103 Capella Reial de Santa Àgata
104 Saló del Tinell
105 Mirador del Rei Martí
106 Palau del Lloctinent
109 Capella de Santa Llúcia
110 Casa de l'Ardiaca
116 Llibreria & Informaciò Cultural
    de la Generalitat de Catalunya
118 Roman Tombs
122 Marks & Spencer
141 Palau de Dalmases & Bar
150 Un Menys
151 Església de Santa Maria del Mar
153 Lavomatic

Yachts moored in Barcelona's harbour, which is lined with cafes and restaurants

Striking stained glass windows and statues of La Sagrada Familia

Passeig de Colom, Barcelona

A monument in Barcelona's Plaça de la Sardana celebrating the traditional dance of the *sardana*

Tiled chimney pots of Gaudi's Palau Güell

Chickens roasting in a Barri Gòtic restaurant

A busker 'chatting' on Barcelona's La Rambla

Sculpted rooftop of the Gaudí-designed La Pedrera

A papier mâché dragon at a Barcelona *fiesta*

(continued from page 368)

Palau Quadras & Casa de les Punxes

Within a few blocks north and east of La Pedrera are two of Puig i Cadafalch's major buildings. The nearer is the Palau del Baró de Quadras at Avinguda Diagonal 373, created between 1902 and 1904 with detailed neogothic carvings on the facade and fine stained glass. It houses the Museu de la Música, with a collection of international instruments from the 16th century to the present. It's open 10 am to 2 pm Tuesday to Sunday. From late September to late June it opens until 8 pm on Wednesday. Entry is 400 ptas.

The Casa Terrades is on the other side of Avinguda Diagonal, 1½ blocks east at No 420. This apartment block of 1903–5, like a castle in a fairy tale, is better known as the Casa de les Punxes (House of the Spikes) because of its pointed turrets.

La Sagrada Família

If you have time for one only sightseeing outing in Barcelona, this should probably be it. La Sagrada Família inspires awe by its sheer verticality and, in the true manner of the great medieval cathedrals it emulates, it's still not even half-built, after more than 100 years. If it's ever finished, the topmost tower will be more than half as high again as those standing today.

The Temple Expiatori de la Sagrada Família (Expiatory Temple of the Holy Family) was the project to which Gaudí dedicated his life. It stands in the east of l'Eixample and is open to visitors daily from 9 am. From April to the end of August it closes at 8 pm; in March, September and October at 7 pm; from November to February at 6 pm. The entry charge of 800 ptas for everybody (the money goes towards the building program) includes a good museum in the crypt.

The entrance is by the south-western facade fronting Carrer de Sardenya and Plaça de la Sagrada Família. Inside is a bookstall where you should invest 500 ptas in the *Official Guide* if you want a detailed account of the church's sculpture and symbolism. To get your bearings, you need to realise that this facade, and the opposite one facing Plaça de Gaudí, each with four skyscraping towers, are at the *sides* of the church. The main facade, as yet unbuilt, will be at the south-eastern end, on Carrer de Mallorca. The 170m central tower will be above the crossing, halfway between the two existing facades.

Nativity Facade This, the north-eastern facade, is the building's artistic pinnacle, mostly done under Gaudí's personal supervision and much of it with his own hands. You can climb high up inside some of the four towers by a combination of lifts (when they're working) and narrow spiral staircases, a vertiginous experience. The towers are destined to hold tubular bells capable of playing complex music at great volume. Their upper parts are decorated with mosaics spelling out *'Sanctus, Sanctus, Sanctus, Hosanna in Excelsis, Amen, Alleluia'*. When asked why he lavished so much care on the tops of the spires, which no one would see from close up, Gaudí answered: 'The angels will see them'.

Beneath the towers is a tall, three-part portal on the theme of Christ's birth and childhood. It seems to lean outward as you stand beneath looking up. Gaudí used real people and animals as models for many of the sculptures.

The three sections of the portal represent, from left to right, Hope, Charity and Faith. Among the forest of sculpture on the Charity portal, you can make out, low down, the manger surrounded by an ox, an ass, the shepherds and kings, with angel musicians above. Directly above the blue stained-glass window is the Archangel Gabriel's Annunciation to Mary. At the top is a green cypress tree, a symbolic refuge in a storm for the white doves of peace dotted over it.

Lower sculptures on the Hope portal show the Flight into Egypt and the Massacre of the Innocents, with Jesus and Joseph in their carpenters' workshop just above. Sculpture on the Faith portal includes, in the centre of the lower group, the child Jesus explaining the Scriptures to the temple priests.

Gaudí & La Sagrada Família

The idea for La Sagrada Família came from Josep Maria Bocabella, a rich publisher who was worried about the growth of revolutionary ideas in Barcelona and set up a religious society dedicated to Sant Josep, patron saint of workers and the family. Construction of the society's church (it's not a cathedral) began in 1882 under Francesc de Villar, who planned a relatively conventional neogothic structure. Villar fell out with Bocabella and was replaced, in 1884, by the 31-year-old Antoni Gaudí.

Gaudí, born into an artisan family in Reus, southern Catalunya, and trained as a metalsmith, was already a successful modernista architect. Up to 1910 he worked on other projects in Barcelona and elsewhere as well as La Sagrada Família. After that he devoted himself entirely to La Sagrada Família, attending to every detail and becoming increasingly single-minded, spiritual, ascetic and unkempt. When he was run over by a tram on Gran Via de les Corts Catalanes in 1926, he had been living in a workshop at La Sagrada Família. His clothes were held together by pins and at first no one recognised him. He died in hospital three days later.

As he worked on La Sagrada Família, Gaudí evolved steadily grander and more original ideas for it. He stuck to the basic Gothic cross-shaped ground plan with an apse, but eventually devised a temple 95m long and 60m wide, able to seat 13,000 people and with a central tower 170m high and 17 others of 100m or more. With his characteristic dislike for straight lines (there were none in nature, he said), Gaudí gave his towers swelling outlines inspired by the weird peaks of the holy mountain Montserrat outside Barcelona, and encrusted them with a tangle of sculpture that seems an outgrowth of the stone.

At Gaudí's death only the crypt, the apse walls, one portal and one tower had been finished. Three more towers were added by 1930 – completing the north-eastern (Nativity) facade – but in 1936 anarchists burned and smashed everything they could in La Sagrada

Família, including the workshops, models and plans. Work restarted in the 1950s using restored models and photographs of drawings, with only limited guidance on how Gaudí had thought of solving the huge technical problems of the building. Today the south-western (Passion) facade, with four more towers, isn't very far off completion, and the nave, started in 1978, is coming along nicely.

Constant controversy has dogged the building program. There are those who say the quality of the new work and its materials – concrete instead of stone for the new towers – are inferior to the earlier parts; others who say that in the absence of detailed plans, the shell should have been left as a kind of monument to Gaudí; and yet others who simply oppose the spending of large amounts of money on a new church (although the funding is all private). The chief architect, Jordi Bonet, and his supporters, aside from their desire to see Gaudí's mighty vision made real, argue that their task is a sacred one – it's not just any old building, but a church intended, as its 'Temple Expiatori' title indicates, to atone for sin and appeal for God's mercy on Catalunya. The way things are going, it might be finished by 2020 – a truly medieval construction timetable.

MICK WELDON

Interior The semicircular apse wall at the north-western end of the church was the first part to be finished (in 1894). From the altar steps you can look down the nave at work in progress, with the walls and columns near completion and the roofs begun. The main Glory Facade on the south-eastern end will, like the north-eastern and south-western facades, be crowned by four towers – the total of 12 representing the 12 apostles. Further decoration will make the whole building a microcosmic symbol of the Christian church, with Christ represented by the massive 170m central tower above the transept and the five remaining planned towers symbolising the Virgin Mary and the four evangelists.

Passion Facade This south-western facade, on the theme of Christ's last days and death, has been constructed since the 1950s with, like the Nativity Facade, four needling towers and a large, sculpture-bedecked portal. The sculptor, Josep Subirachs, has not attempted to imitate Gaudí's work but has produced strong images of his own. The sculptures, on three levels, are in an S-shaped sequence starting with the Last Supper at bottom left and ending with Christ's burial at top right.

Museu Gaudí With the same opening hours as the church, the museum includes interesting material on Gaudí's life and other work, as well as models, photos and other material on La Sagrada Família. You can see a good example of his plumb line models, which showed him the stresses and strains he could get away with in construction.

GRÀCIA (MAP 2)
Gràcia is the area north of the middle of l'Eixample. Once a separate village, then in the 19th century an industrial *barrio* (district) famous for its republican and liberal ideas, it became fashionable among radical and bohemian types in the 1960s and 70s. Although now more sedate and gentrified, it retains much of its style of 20 years ago, with a mixed-class population. Gràcia's interest lies in the atmosphere of its narrow

streets, small plazas and the bars and restaurants lining them. An evening or night-time wander is the best way to savour these. Diagonal and Fontana are the nearest metro stations to central Gràcia.

The liveliest plazas are **Plaça del Sol**, **Plaça de Rius i Taulet** with its clock tower, and **Plaça de la Virreina** with the 17th-century Església de Sant Josep. Three blocks northeast of Plaça de Rius i Taulet there's a big covered **market**. West of Gràcia's main street, Carrer Gran de Gràcia, there's an early Gaudí house, the turreted, vaguely *mudéjar* (decorative Muslim style of architecture) **Casa Vicenç** at Carrer de les Carolines 22.

MONTJUÏC (MAP 1)
Montjuïc, the hill overlooking the city centre from the south-west, is home to some of Barcelona's best museums and leisure attractions, some fine parks and the main group of 1992 Olympics sites. It's well worth a day or two of your time.

The name Montjuïc (Jewish Mountain) indicates there was once a Jewish settlement here. Before Montjuïc began to be turned into parks in the 1890s, its woodlands had long provided food-growing and breathing space for the people of the cramped Ciutat Vella. Montjuïc also has a darker history: its castle was used by the Madrid government to bombard the city after political disturbances in 1842 and as a political prison right up to the Franco era. The first main burst of building on Montjuïc came in the 1920s, when it was chosen as the stage for Barcelona's 1929 World Exhibition. The Estadi Olímpic, the Poble Espanyol and some museums all date from this time. Montjuïc got a face-lift and more new buildings for the 1992 Olympics.

Abundant roads and paths, with occasional escalators, plus buses and even a chairlift allow you to visit Montjuïc's sights in any order you choose. The five main attractions – the Poble Espanyol, the Museu Nacional d'Art de Catalunya, the Estadi Olímpic, the Fundació Joan Miró and the views from the castle – would make for a full day's sightseeing.

Getting There & Away

You *could* walk from Ciutat Vella (the foot of La Rambla is 700m from the east end of Montjuïc). Local bus Nos 50 and 61 make their way up here from Plaça d'Espanya and other parts of town. The Bus Turístic (see Getting Around later) also makes several stops on Montjuïc. Or you could hop on one of those silly little road trains, which leave from the same spot as the bus and create havoc for normal traffic trying to get up the same hill!

Another way of saving your legs is the funicular railway from the Paral.lel metro station to Estació Parc Montjuïc. This goes from 11 am to 10 pm daily from mid-June to mid-September; 10.45 am to 8 pm during the Christmas and Easter holiday periods; and 10.45 am to 8 pm Saturday, Sunday and holidays only during the rest of the year. Tickets cost 250/375 ptas one way/return.

From Estació Parc Montjuïc, the Telefèric de Montjuïc chairlift will carry you yet higher, to an upper entrance of the now closed Parc d'Atraccions (Mirador stop) and then the castle (Castell stop). This operates 11.30 am to 9.30 pm daily, mid-June to the end of September; 11 am to 2.45 pm and 4 to 7.30 pm in October and the Christmas and Easter holiday periods; 11 am to 2.45 pm and 4 to 7.30 pm Saturday, Sunday and holidays only during the rest of the year. Tickets cost 475/675 ptas one way/return.

Another option is the cable car or *funicular aereo,* which runs between Miramar and Sant Sebastià (La Barceloneta). For details, see Port Vell earlier in this chapter.

Around Plaça d'Espanya

The approach to Montjuïc from Plaça d'Espanya gives you the full benefit of the landscaping on the hill's northern side and allows Montjuïc to unfold for you from the bottom up. On Plaça d'Espanya's northern side is the big **Plaça de Braus Les Arenes** bullring, built in 1900 but no longer used for bullfights. The Beatles played here in 1966. Behind the bullring is the **Parc Joan Miró**, created in the 1980s, and worth a quick detour mainly for Miró's giant, highly phallic sculpture *Dona i Ocell* (Woman and Bird) in the north-western corner.

Fountains & Museu Nacional d'Art de Catalunya

Avinguda de la Reina Maria Cristina, lined with modern exhibition and congress halls, leads from Plaça d'Espanya towards Montjuïc. On the hill ahead of you is the Palau Nacional de Montjuïc and stretching up a series of terraces below it are Montjuïc's fountains, starting with the biggest, **La Font Màgica**. These come most alive with a lights-and-music show on summer evenings. The regular show lasts about 15 minutes and takes place every half hour from 9.30 to 11.30 pm Thursday to Sunday, from June to September. During the rest of the year it runs from 7 to 9 pm Friday and Saturday.

The Palau Nacional, built in the 1920s for displays in the World Exhibition, houses the **Museu Nacional d'Art de Catalunya**. The museum's Romanesque section consists mainly of 11th- and 12th-century murals, woodcarvings and altar frontals (painted, low-relief wooden panels that were forerunners of the elaborate *retablos* adorning later churches). These works, gathered from decaying country churches in northern Catalunya early in the 20th century, constitute probably Europe's greatest collection of Romanesque art. The museum's other main section is devoted to Gothic art, but is less interesting.

The first thing you see as you enter the Romanesque section is a remake of the apse of the church of Sant Pere de la Seu d'Urgell, dominated by a beautiful fresco from the early 12th century. In this first hall (Àmbit I) there are coins from the early days of the Comtes de Barcelona, capitals from columns used in Muslim monuments and some finely decorated altar frontals.

In Àmbit III, the frescoes from the church of Sant Pere d'Àger stand out (item No 31). The depiction of Christ on wood from the church of Sant Martí de Tost (No 47 in Àmbit IV) is in a near-perfect state of preservation. One of the star attractions is the fresco of Mary and the Christ Child from the apse of the church of Santa Maria de Taüll (No 102 in Àmbit VII).

The museum is open 10 am to 7 pm Tuesday to Saturday (to 9 pm Thursday), 10 am to 2.30 pm Sunday and holidays (800 ptas, free on the first Thursday of the month).

Poble Espanyol

This 'Spanish Village' in the north-west of Montjuïc, 10 minutes' walk from Plaça d'Espanya or the Museu Nacional d'Art, is both a tacky tourist trap and an intriguing scrapbook of Spanish architecture. Built for the Spanish crafts section of the 1929 exhibition, it's composed of plazas and streets lined with surprisingly good copies of typical buildings from all the country's regions.

You enter from Avinguda del Marquès de Comillas, beneath a towered medieval gate from Ávila. Inside, to the right, is an information office with free maps. Straight ahead from the gates is a *plaza mayor,* or town square, surrounded with mainly Castilian and Aragonese buildings. Elsewhere you'll find an Andalucian barrio, a Basque street, Galician and Catalan quarters and even, at the eastern end, a Dominican monastery. The buildings house dozens of mid-range to expensive restaurants, cafes, bars, craft shops and workshops, and a few souvenir shops.

The Poble Espanyol is open from 9 am daily (to 8 pm Monday, to 2 am Tuesday to Thursday, to 4 am Friday and Saturday, and until midnight on Sunday). Entry is 975 ptas (1200 ptas combined with Galería Olímpica – see later). Students and children aged seven to 14 pay 550 ptas. After 9 pm on days other than Friday and Saturday, it's free. At night, the restaurants, bars and discos become a lively corner of Barcelona nightlife. If you want more information or a guided tour, call ☎ 93 325 78 66.

Museu Etnològic & Museu d'Arqueologia

Down the hill east of the Museu Nacional d'Art, these museums are worth a visit if their subjects interest you, although neither is very excitingly presented and most explanatory material is in Catalan.

The Museu Etnològic on Passeig de Santa Madrona has extensive displays covering a range of cultures from other continents and puts on some interesting temporary exhibitions. It's open 10 am to 3 pm (to 7 pm Tuesday and Thursday, except in summer), daily but Monday. Entry is 400 ptas (free on the first Sunday of the month).

The Museu d'Arqueologia, at the corner of Passeig de Santa Madrona and Passeig de l'Exposició, covers Catalunya and related cultures elsewhere in Spain. Items range from copies of pre-Neanderthal skulls to lovely Carthaginian necklaces and jewel-studded Visigothic crosses. There's good material on the Balearic Islands (Rooms X to XIV) and Empúries, or Emporion, the classical city on the Costa Brava (Rooms XV and XVI). It's open 9.30 am to 7 pm Tuesday to Saturday, and 10 am to 2.30 pm Sunday (400 ptas).

Anella Olímpica

The 'Olympic Ring' is the group of sports installations where the main events of the 1992 Olympics were held, on the ridge above the Museu Nacional d'Art. Westernmost is the **Institut Nacional d'Educació Física de Catalunya** (INEFC), a kind of sports university, designed by the best-known contemporary Catalan architect, Ricardo Bofill. Past a circular arena, the Plaça d'Europa, with the Torre Calatrava telephone tower behind it, is the **Piscines Bernat Picornell** building, where the swimming and diving events were held; it's now open to the public (see the Swimming section later in this chapter).

Next comes a pleasant little park, the Jardí d'Aclimatació, followed by the **Estadi Olímpic**, the main stadium of the games. It's open 10 am to 6 pm daily (free); enter at the northern end. If you saw some of the Olympics on TV, the 65,000-capacity stadium may seem surprisingly small. So may the Olympic flame-holder rising at the northern end, into which a long-range archer spectacularly deposited a flaming arrow in the opening ceremony. The stadium was opened in 1929 but completely restored for 1992. At the southern end of the stadium (enter from the outside) is the **Galería Olímpica**, which has an exhibition, including videos, on the 1992 games. It is open 10 am to 1 pm and 4 to 6 pm weekdays (to 8 pm in summer) and 10 am to 2 pm on holidays (400 ptas).

West of the stadium is the **Palau Sant Jordi**, a 17,000-capacity indoor sports, concert and exhibition hall opened in 1990 and designed by the Japanese architect Arata Isozaki.

Cementiri del Sud-Ouest

On the hill south of the Anella Olímpica you can see the top of a huge cemetery, the Cementiri del Sud-Ouest or Cementiri Nou, which extends right down the southern side of the hill. Opened in 1883, it's an odd combination of elaborate architect-designed tombs for rich families and small niches for the rest. It contains the graves of numerous Catalan artists and politicians.

Fundació Joan Miró

Barcelona's gallery for the greatest Catalan artist of the 20th century, Joan Miró, is 400m north of and downhill from Estadi Olímpic.

Miró gave 379 paintings, sculptures and textile works, and almost 5000 drawings, to the collection, but only a selection of these is displayed at any one time. The displays tend to concentrate on Miró's more settled last 20 years, but there are some important exceptions. The ground-floor Sala Joan Prats shows the younger Miró moving away, under surrealist influence, from his *relative* realism, then starting to work towards his own recognisable style. This section also includes the 1939–44 Barcelona Series of tortured lithographs, Miró's comment on the Spanish Civil War.

The Sala Pilar Juncosa, upstairs, also displays works from the 1930s and 40s. Another interesting section is devoted to the 'Miró Papers', which include many preparatory drawings and sketches, some on bits of newspaper or cigarette packets. 'A Joan

---

Joan Miró

Joan Miró was born and grew up in the Barri Gòtic and lived a third of his life in Barcelona. A shy man, he practised and studied art from childhood but had no natural ability for life-like drawing, being more attracted to art lacking perspective. He was deeply drawn to the Catalan countryside and coast, and divided his time from 1919 to the early 1930s between winters in Paris and summers at his family's farmhouse at Mont-roig on the southern Catalan coast. In Paris he mixed with Picasso, Hemingway, Joyce & co and made his own mark, after several years of struggle, with an exhibition in 1925. In the early 1930s he went through an artistic crisis, temporarily rejecting painting in favour of collage and other techniques.

By the 1940s Miró's characteristic style had emerged: arrangements of lines and symbolic figures in primary colours, with shapes reduced to their essence. Among his most important images are women, birds (the link between earth and the heavens), stars (the unattainable heavenly world, source of imagination) and a sort of net entrapping all these levels of the cosmos. In the 1960s and 70s Miró devoted more time to sculpture and textiles. From 1956 he lived on Mallorca, home of his wife Pilar Juncosa.

An anti-Francoist, Miró had a stormy relationship with Barcelona after the civil war, but in the early 1970s he set up the Fundació Joan Miró to display his own work and promote avant-garde art. He was supported in the project by two close Barcelona friends, the art patron and hat-shop owner Joan Prats, to whom Miró had given many paintings in exchange for hats, and the architect Josep Lluís Sert. Sert designed the building, which is notable for its abundant natural light.

MICK WELDON

Miró' is a collection of work by other contemporary artists, donated in tribute to Miró.

The Fundació has a contemporary art library open to the public, a good specialist art bookshop and a cafe. It also stages exhibitions and recitals of contemporary art and music. The gallery is open 10 am to 7 pm (an hour longer in the summer months) Tuesday to Saturday (to 9.30 pm Thursday) and 10 am to 2.30 pm Sunday and holidays; entry is 800 ptas.

Castell de Montjuïc & Around

The south-east of Montjuïc is dominated by the Castell (castle). Near the bottom of the ruined remains of what was the Parc d'Atraccions (amusement park) are the Estació Parc Montjuïc telefèric/funicular station and the ornamental **Jardins de Mossèn Jacint Verdaguer**. The one-time amusement park is destined to become part of a larger botanical garden.

From the **Jardins del Mirador** opposite the Mirador telefèric station there are fine views over the port of Barcelona.

The Castell de Montjuïc dates in its present form from the late 17th and 18th centuries. For most of its existence it has been used to watch over the city and as a political prison and killing ground. Anarchists were executed here around the turn of the 20th century, fascists during the civil war and Republicans after it – most notoriously Lluís Companys in 1940. The army finally handed it over to the city in 1960. The castle is surrounded by a network of ditches and walls, and today houses the **Museu Militar** with a section on Catalan military history, plus old weapons, uniforms, maps, castle models and so on (open 9.30 am to 7.30 pm daily except Monday). Entry to the museum is 200 ptas. Best of all are the excellent views from the castle area of the port and city below.

Towards the foot of this part of Montjuïc, above the thundering traffic of the main road to Tarragona, the **Jardins de Mossèn Costa i Llobera** have a good collection of tropical and desert plants; they are open 10 am to sunset.

PARC GÜELL (MAP 1)

North of Gràcia and about 4km from Plaça de Catalunya, Parc Güell is where Gaudí turned his hand to landscape gardening. It's a strange, enchanting place where his passion for natural forms really took flight, to the point where the artificial almost seems more natural than the natural.

Parc Güell originated in 1900 when Count Eusebi Güell bought a tree-covered hillside (then outside Barcelona) and hired Gaudí to create a miniature garden city of houses for the wealthy, in landscaped grounds. The project was a commercial flop and was abandoned in 1914, but not before Gaudí had created 3km of roads and walks, steps and a plaza in his inimitable manner, plus the two gatehouses. In 1922 the city bought the estate for use as a public park.

The park is open from 9 am daily: to 9 pm, June to September; to 8 pm, April, May and October; to 7 pm, March and November; to 6 pm in other months (entry is free). It's extremely popular, and its quaint nooks and crannies are irresistible to photographers, who on busy days have trouble keeping out of each other's pictures.

The steps up from the entrance, guarded by a mosaic dragon/lizard, lead to the **Sala Hipóstila**, a forest of 84 stone columns (some of them leaning), intended as a market. To the left from here curves a gallery whose twisted stonework columns and roof give the effect of a cloister beneath tree roots – a motif repeated in several places in the park. On top of the Sala Hipóstila is a broad open space whose centrepiece is the **Banc de Trenadís**, a tiled bench curving sinuously around its perimeter.

The spired house to the right is the **Casa Museu Gaudí**, where Gaudí lived for most of his last 20 years (1906–26). It contains furniture by him and other memorabilia. It's open 10 am to 8 pm daily from May to September; to 7 pm in March, April and October; and to 6 pm the rest of the year. As a rule it's open only 10 am to 2 pm Sunday and may close between 2 and 4 pm in low season (300 ptas).

Much of the park is still wooded but full of pathways. The best views are from the cross-topped **Turo del Calvari** in the south-western corner.

Getting There & Away

The simplest way to Parc Güell is to take the metro to Lesseps, then walk for 10 to 15 minutes: follow the signs north-east along Travessera de Dalt then left up Carrer de Larrard, which brings you almost to the park's two Hansel and Gretel-style gate-houses on Carrer d'Olot.

TIBIDABO (MAP 1)

Tibidabo (542m) is the highest hill in the wooded range that forms the backdrop to Barcelona. It's a good place for some fresh air (it's often a few degrees cooler than in the city) and, if the air's clear, views over the city and inland as far as Montserrat. Tibidabo gets its name from the devil who, trying to tempt Christ, took him to a high place and said: *'Haec omnia tibi dabo si cadens adoraberis me'* ('All this I will give you if you will fall down and worship me').

Getting There & Away

First, get an FGC train to Avinguda del Tibidabo from Catalunya station on Plaça de Catalunya, a 10-minute ride for 150 ptas. Outside Avinguda del Tibidabo station, hop on the *tramvia blau,* Barcelona's last surviving tram, which runs up between fancy turn-of-the-20th-century mansions to Plaça del Doctor Andreu (275/400 ptas one way/ return). The tram runs daily in summer, and on Saturday, Sunday and holidays the rest of the year, every 15 or 30 minutes from 9 am to 9.30 pm. On other days a bus (150 ptas) serves the route at similar times. From Plaça del Doctor Andreu, the Tibidabo funicular railway climbs through the woods to Plaça de Tibidabo at the top of the hill (300 ptas, 400 ptas return), every 15 to 30 minutes from 7.15 am to 9.45 pm daily. If you're feeling active, you can walk up or down through the woods instead. The funicular only operates when the Parc d'Atraccions is open.

The cheaper alternative is bus No T2, the 'Tibibús', from Plaça de Catalunya to Plaça de Tibidabo (230 ptas). This runs on Saturday, Sunday and holidays year-round, every

30 minutes from 10.30 am. From late June to early September it runs weekdays too, every hour from 10.30 am. The last bus down leaves from Tibidabo 30 minutes after the Parc d'Atraccions closes.

Temple del Sagrat Cor

The Church of the Sacred Heart, looming above the top funicular station, is meant to be Barcelona's answer to Paris' Sacré Coeur. It's certainly equally visible and even more vilified by aesthetes. It's actually two churches, one on top of the other. The top one is surmounted by a giant Christ and has a lift to the roof (100 ptas). Visiting times are 8 am to 7 pm daily.

Parc d'Atraccions

The reason most Barcelonins come up to Tibidabo is for some thrills (but hopefully no spills) in this fun fair (☎ 93 211 79 42), close to the top funicular station. Entry is 700 ptas plus extra for each ride, or 2400 ptas with access to all rides – including seven minutes in the Hotel Krueger, a house of horrors inhabited by actors playing out their Dracula, Hannibal Lecter and other fantasies. The fun fair's opening times change with the season, so check with a tourist office: in summer it's usually open daily from noon until late at night; in winter it may open on Saturday, Sunday and holidays only, from about noon to 7 pm. A cloud is hanging over the ageing fun park, and at the time of writing it was unclear if it would open beyond October 2000.

Torre de Collserola

The 288m Torre de Collserola telecommunications tower (☎ 93 406 93 54 for information) was built in 1990–92. The external glass lift to the visitors observation area, 115m up, is as hair-raising as anything at the Parc d'Atraccions. From the top they say you can see for 70km on a clear day. It's open 11 am to 2.30 pm and 3.30 to 6 pm Wednesday to Friday and 11 am to 6 pm weekends and holidays; these hours may be extended to 8 pm in summer. It's closed in January. To get there take the same transport as for Tibidabo. The ride up costs 500 ptas.

CAMP NOU (MAP 1)

Hard on the heels of the Museu Picasso as one of Barcelona's most visited museums, comes the Museu del Futbol Club Barcelona at the club's giant Camp Nou stadium, 3.5km west of Plaça de Catalunya. Barça, as it's known, is one of Europe's top football (soccer) clubs, having carried off the Spanish championship a couple of dozen times and the European Cup more than once. Barça has also been described as Catalunya's unarmed army: the club was banned for a while in the 1920s because the Spanish government feared its potential for focusing Catalan nationalism and today its annual matches with Real Madrid act as a modern safety valve for the age-old rivalry between Catalunya and Castilla. The many world greats who have worn Barça's blue and red stripes include Johann Cruyff and Diego Maradona.

Camp Nou, built in the 1950s and enlarged for the 1982 World Cup, is one of the world's biggest stadiums, holding 120,000 people, and the club has a world record membership of 110,000. Soccer fans who can't get to a game (see Entertainment earlier) should find the museum, on the Carrer d'Aristides Maillol side of the stadium, worthwhile. The best bits are the photo section, the goal videos and the visit to seats high up overlooking the pitch.

The museum is open 10 am to 6.30 pm Monday to Saturday (Tuesday to Saturday from October to March) and 10 am to 2 pm Sunday and holidays (500 ptas).

PEDRALBES (MAP 1)

Pedralbes is a wealthy residential area situated north of Camp Nou, with some worthwhile attractions.

Palau Reial

Right by Palau Reial metro station, across Avinguda Diagonal from the main campus of the Universitat de Barcelona, is the entrance to the Jardins del Palau Reial, a verdant park open daily. In the park is the Palau Reial de Pedralbes, an early 20th-century building that has served as a residence for Gaudí's patron Eusebi Güell, King Alfonso

XIII, the president of Catalunya and General Franco. Today it houses the Museu de Ceràmica, with a good collection of Spanish ceramics from the 13th to 19th centuries, including work by Picasso and Miró, and the Museu de les Arts Decoratives. Both museums are open 10 am to 6 pm Tuesday to Saturday (to 3 pm Sunday); entry is 700 ptas for both.

Museu-Monestir de Pedralbes

This peaceful old convent, now a museum of monastic life also housing part of the Thyssen-Bornemisza art collection, stands at the top of Avinguda de Pedralbes. The easiest way here is to get the suburban FGC train to Reina Elisenda (the end of the line) from Catalunya station and then either walk (about 10 minutes) or pick up one of the buses running along Passeig de la Reina Elisenda de Montcada (such as Nos 22, 64 and 75).

The convent, founded in 1326, still houses a community of nuns who inhabit separate closed quarters. The museum entrance is on Plaça del Monestir, a divinely quiet corner of Barcelona; opening hours are 10 am to 2 pm Tuesday to Sunday (700 ptas; 400 ptas only for either the monastery or the Thyssen-Bornemisza collection).

The architectural highlight is the large, elegant, three-storey cloister, a jewel of Catalan Gothic built in the early 14th century.

The Col.lecció Thyssen-Bornemisza (entry from the ground floor), quartered in the (painstakingly restored) one-time dormitories of the nuns and the Saló Principal, is part of a wide-ranging art collection acquired by Spain in 1993. Most of it went to the Museo Thyssen-Bornemisza in Madrid; what's here is mainly religious work by European masters, including Canaletto, Titian, Tintoretto, Rubens, Zurbarán and Velázquez.

SWIMMING

The Olympic pool on Montjuïc (Map 1), the Piscines Bernat Picornell (☎ 93 423 40 41), is open to the public from 7 am to midnight weekdays, until 9 pm Saturday and 7.30 am to 4.30 pm Sunday (1200 ptas, which includes use of the good gym). Access to the outdoor pool alone costs 650 ptas in summer only. It's open 10 am to 6 pm Monday to Saturday (9 am to 9 pm in summer) and 10 am to 2.30 pm Sunday (9 am to 8 pm in summer).

LANGUAGE COURSES

Some of the best-value Spanish-language courses are offered by the Universitat de Barcelona, which runs intensive courses (40 hours tuition over periods ranging from two weeks to one month; 45,000 ptas) all year. Longer Spanish courses, and courses in Catalan, are also available. For more information you can ask at the university's Informació office (Map 3) at Gran Via de les Corts Catalanes 585. It's open 9 am to 2 pm weekdays. Otherwise, try (for Spanish) its Instituto de Estudios Hispánicos (☎ 93 403 55 19, fax 93 403 54 33) or (for Catalan) its Servei de Llengua Catalana (☎ 93 403 54 77, fax 93 403 54 84), both in the same building as the Informació office.

The university-run Escola Oficial d'Idiomes de Barcelona (Map 3; ☎ 93 324 93 30, fax 93 934 93 51) at Avinguda de les Drassanes s/n is another place offering economical 80-hour summer Spanish courses, as well as longer part-time courses in Spanish and Catalan. Across Catalunya there are more than 220 schools where you can learn Catalan. Pick up a list at the Llibreria & Informaciò Cultural de la Generalitat de Catalunya (Map 4; ☎ 93 302 64 62), Rambla dels Estudis 118.

International House (Map 3; ☎ 93 268 45 11, fax 93 268 02 39, ℮ ihbarcelona@bcn.ihes.com) is at Carrer de Trafalgar 14. Intensive courses start at around 50,000 ptas per week. Staff can organise accommodation with families or in *pensiones*.

Ads for courses and private tuition are posted at the university, Come In bookshop at Carrer de Provença 203, and the British Council.

ORGANISED TOURS
Bicycle Tours

Un Menys bicycle shop (Map 4; ☎ 93 268 21 05), Carrer de la Espartería 3, organises bicycle tours around the old centre of town, La Barceloneta and Port Olímpic. Day-time tours take place on Saturday and Sunday, starting at the shop at 10 am and finishing at 12.30 pm. The 2500 ptas cost includes a stop for a drink in Port Vell. The night version is on Tuesday and Saturday, starting at 8.30 pm and finishing at midnight. The 6000 ptas price tag includes a drink stop and a meal along the Barceloneta waterfront. If you have a large group, it will do these tours on other days of the week too.

Other Tours

The Bus Turístic (see the Getting Around section later in this chapter) is better value than conventional tours for getting around the sights, but if you want a guided trip, try Julià Tours (Map 3; ☎ 93 317 64 54), Ronda de la Universitat 5, and Pullmantur (Map 2; ☎ 93 318 02 41), Carrer del Bruc 645. Both companies do daily city tours by coach, plus out-of-town trips to Montserrat, Vilafranca del Penedès, the Costa Brava and Andorra. Their city tours are about 4750 ptas for a half-day, 10,500 ptas a full day.

A walking tour of the Ciutat Vella on Saturday and Sunday mornings departs from the Oficina d'Informació de Turisme de Barcelona on Plaça de Catalunya (English at 10 am; Spanish and Catalan at noon). The price is 1000 ptas.

For other guide services and tailor-made tour options, get in touch with the Barcelona Guide Bureau (☎ 93 310 77 78, fax 93 268 22 11).

SPECIAL EVENTS

Barcelona's main festivals include:

April

Dia de Sant Jordi The day of Catalunya's patron saint and also the Day of the Book: men give women a rose, women give men a book, publishers launch new titles; La Rambla and Plaça de Sant Jaume (where the Generalitat building is open to the public) are filled with book and flower stalls on this day, 23 April.

June

Dia de Sant Joan Midsummer celebrations with bonfires, even in the squares of l'Eixample, and fireworks (a big display on Montjuïc) mark the evening preceding this holiday (24 June).
Dia per l'Alliberament Lesbià i Gai The gay and lesbian festival and parade held on 28 June.

June–August
Grec Arts Festival Music, dance, theatre at many locations, from late June to August.

August
Festa Major de Gràcia Big local festival held in Gràcia, with decorated streets, dancing, music etc (around 15 August).

September
La Diada Catalunya's national day, marking the fall of Barcelona in 1714, and a holiday in Barcelona (11 September).

Festes de la Mercè The city's major festival; several days of merrymaking including concerts, dancing, a swimming race across the harbour, *castellers* (human castle-builders), a fireworks display synchronised with the Montjuïc fountains, dances of giants on the Saturday and *correfocs,* a parade of firework-spitting dragons and devils from all over Catalunya, on the Sunday. It's held around 24 September.

October/November
Festival Internacional de Jazz de Barcelona Jazz and blues around the city, held in late October to late November.

PLACES TO STAY – BUDGET
Camping
The nearest camping ground is the big *Cala Gogó (☎/fax 93 379 46 00, Carretera de la Platja s/n),* 9km south-west of the centre at, El Prat de Llobregat, near the airport. It's open from mid-March to mid-October and charges 3400 ptas for a site, car and two adults. You can get there by bus No 65 from Plaça d'Espanya, or by Renfe train from Plaça de Catalunya to El Prat, then a 'Prat Platja' bus.

There are some better (but still vast) sites a few kilometres farther out, to the south-west on the coastal C-246 road, the Autovía de Castelldefels. All are reachable by bus No L95 from the corner of Ronda de la Universitat and Rambla de Catalunya. They include (with prices for a car, a tent and two adults):

El Toro Bravo (☎ 93 637 34 62) Carretera C-246, Km 11, Viladecans – open all year, it's a tad shabby (3400 ptas)

Filipinas (☎ 93 658 28 95) Carretera C-246, Km 12, Viladecans – open all year, this is one of the best value-for-money places (3400 ptas)

La Ballena Alegre (☎/fax 93 658 05 04) Carretera C-246, Km 12.4, Viladecans – open April to end of September, and also good (4300 ptas)

Eleven kilometres north-east of the city, *Camping Masnou (☎ 93 555 15 03, Camí Fabra 33, El Masnou)* is open all year. It's 200m from El Masnou train station (reached by suburban *rodalies/cercanías* trains from Catalunya station on Plaça de Catalunya) and charges 2740 ptas for a car, tent and two adults.

All are inconvenient if you want late nights in Barcelona, because the only way back late at night is by taxi.

Youth & Backpacker Hostels
Barcelona has four HI hostels and several non-HI hostels. All require you to rent sheets (150 to 350 ptas) if you don't have any, and some lock their gates in the early hours so aren't suitable if you plan to party on late. Except at the Kabul, which doesn't take bookings, it's advisable to call ahead in summer. Most have washing machines.

The non-HI *Youth Hostel Kabul (Map 4; ☎ 93 318 51 90, fax 93 301 40 34, Plaça Reial 17)* is in the Barri Gòtic. It's a rough-and-ready place but does have, as its leaflets say, a 'great party atmosphere' and no curfew. The price is 2000 ptas, plus 1000 ptas key deposit. Safes are available for valuables. There's room for 130 people in bare bunk rooms holding up to 10 each.

The biggest and most comfortable hostel is the 183-place *Alberg Mare de Déu de Montserrat (Map 1; ☎ 93 210 51 51, fax 93 210 07 98, Passeig Mare de Déu del Coll 41-51).* It's 4km north of the centre, a 10-minute walk from Vallcarca metro or a 20-minute ride from Plaça de Catalunya on bus No 28, which stops almost outside the gate. The main building is a former private mansion with a mudéjar-style lobby. Most rooms sleep six. A hostel card is needed: if you're under 25 or have an ISIC card, B&B is 1900 ptas; otherwise it's 2500 ptas. The hostel is in HI's International Booking Network (IBN). You can also book through the central booking service of Catalunya's official youth hostels organisation, the Xarxa d'Albergs de Joventut (☎ 93 483 83 63, fax 93 483 83 50). (Note: the other Barcelona hostels, even the HI ones, are not in the Xarxa.)

Alberg Juvenil Palau (Map 4; ☎ 93 412 50 80, Carrer del Palau 6) in the Barri Gòtic has a friendly atmosphere and just 40 places in separate-sex bunk rooms. The cost is 1600 ptas, including breakfast.

Hostal de Joves (Map 1; ☎ 93 300 31 04, Passeig de Pujades 29) faces the northern end of Parc de la Ciutadella, a few minutes' walk from the Arc de Triomf metro station. It has 68 bunk places in small, rather grim dorms. The price is 1500 ptas, including breakfast.

Another handy but spartan place, off Carrer de la Boqueria, is *Albergue Arco (Map 4; ☎ 93 301 31 93, Carrer de l'Arc de Santa Eulàlia 1)*. It is open 24 hours a day and a bed in a separate-sex dorm costs 1400 ptas.

Alberg Pere Tarrès (Map 1; ☎ 93 410 23 09, fax 93 419 62 68, Carrer del Numància 149), 1km north of Estació Sants, has 92 places in dorms of four to eight bunks. B&B costs from 1500 to 2000 ptas, depending on age and whether you have a hostel card. The gates are shut from 11 am to 3 pm and 11 pm to 8.30 am (they're opened briefly to let guests in at 2 am).

The small and distant *Alberg Studio (Map 1; ☎ 93 205 09 61, fax 93 205 09 00, Carrer de la Duquessa d'Orleans 58)*, off Passeig de la Reina Elisenda de Montcada, 4km north-west of Plaça de Catalunya, is open only from 1 July to 30 September, and has 50 places. It stays open 24 hours and charges 1700 ptas. FGC trains run to the nearby Reina Elisenda station from Catalunya station.

Hostales, Pensiones & Hotels

Barcelona is flavour of the decade, so competition for rooms can be fairly intense. Many of the places below are often full, so you may want to let your fingers do the walking.

Bathrooms are often in the corridor and shared at these places. Prices sometimes fall a little in the low season or if you stay for a week or more.

La Rambla Pensión Noya (Map 4; ☎ 93 301 48 31, Rambla de Canaletes 133), at the top of La Rambla, above Restaurante Nuria, has 15 smallish but clean rooms (shower and toilet in the corridor) at 3000/6000 ptas for singles/doubles in high season. Front rooms overlooking La Rambla can be noisy.

Down near the bottom of La Rambla at No 4, time seems to have passed by *Hostal Marítima (Map 3; ☎ 93 302 31 52)*, once a backpackers' stalwart. Still the rooms are adequate and clean, and the price hasn't changed in years – 2000 ptas per person. The entrance is on Passatge de la Banca leading to the Museu de Cera.

Barri Gòtic This central, atmospheric area has many of the better budget places. A few of those listed below are not strictly speaking in the Barri Gòtic, but within a couple of minutes' walk of it.

Hostal Lausanne (Map 4; ☎ 93 302 11 39, Avinguda del Portal de l'Àngel 24) is a good spot, with security and helpful staff. Popularity has made prices sneak up, but on balance this remains a great place to stay. Clean doubles without bath cost 5500 ptas. Getting a single seems impossible.

An excellent deal is *Hostal Campi (Map 4; ☎ 93 301 35 45, fax 93 301 41 33, Carrer de la Canuda 4)*. Rooms without bath cost 2700/5000 ptas. If you can afford them, the best rooms are the doubles (with shower and toilet), which are extremely roomy and bright and cost 6000 ptas.

Hostal-Residencia Rembrandt (Map 4; ☎/fax 93 318 10 11, Carrer de la Canuda 23), is extremely popular so it's wise to book ahead. The rooms are good and cost 3000/5000 ptas without bath, or 4000/7000 ptas with bath.

Hostal Paris (Map 4; ☎/fax 93 301 37 85, Carrer del Cardenal Casañas 4) has 42 mostly large rooms in a rambling, shambolic old place. Singles without bath can start as low as 3000 ptas, and the most you'll pay is 7500 ptas for a double with bathroom. The place is basic and often full of backpackers.

Hostal Galerias Maldà (Map 4; ☎ 93 317 30 02, Carrer del Pi 5), upstairs in the arcade, is a rambling family house with 21 rooms, some of them huge. It's one of the cheapest places in town, at 1500/3000 ptas, and has one great single set in a kind of tower.

Hostal Fontanella (Map 3; ☎/fax 93 317 59 43, Via Laietana 71) is a friendly, immaculately clean place, with 10 (in some cases smallish) rooms costing 3000/5000 ptas or 4000/6900 ptas with bathroom.

Pensión Fernando (Map 4; ☎ 93 301 79 93, Carrer de l'Arc del Remedio 4), is on Carrer de Ferran, in spite of the address. You have the option of dorms here, at 2300 ptas per person (if you get lucky you'll be in a room with its own shower and toilet). At least one of these rooms is designed for wheelchair access too. There are lockers in the dorm rooms (which start at four beds). Otherwise, you can take a double or triple for 7000/8500 ptas. You can catch some rays on the roof.

Smack in the heart of the Call (the old Jewish quarter) is *Hotel Call* (Map 4; ☎ 93 301 11 23, fax 93 301 34 86, Carrer de l'Arc de Sant Ramon del Call 4). The rooms are comfortable and all have bath and phone; some, however, are terribly small. Still, they are OK value at 3425/4815 ptas.

Pensió Colom 3 (Map 4; ☎ 93 318 06 31, Carrer de Colom 3), almost on Plaça Reial, is an unofficial hostel with double bunks in dorms for 1500 ptas. It also has doubles/triples for 8000/10,800 ptas, or 9100/12,100 ptas with private shower and toilet – they are overpriced. The place has washing machines and pool tables.

If you want a nice double on the square, head instead to *Pensión Villanueva* (Map 4; ☎ 91 301 50 84, Plaça Reial 2). Prices start at 2500/3500 ptas for basic singles/doubles and range up to 7500 ptas for the best rooms, spacious doubles with own bath and looking onto the square.

Hotel Barcelona House (Map 4; ☎ 93 301 82 95, fax 93 412 41 29, Carrer dels Escudellers 19) is a newish place in the middle of the Gothic action. It has reasonable, comfortable rooms. The doubles are quite OK at 8667 ptas, while the singles are less inspiring for 3745 ptas.

Hostal Levante (Map 4; ☎ 93 317 95 65, Baixada dè Sant Miquel 2), off Plaça de Sant Miquel, is a large, bright place with rooms of all shapes and sizes. Smallish singles start at 3500 ptas, while doubles without/with bath go for 5500/6500 ptas. Try for the room with the balcony. These people have some apartments nearby too, which can work out well for groups of four or more – ask at reception.

Casa Huéspedes Mari-Luz (Map 4; ☎ 93 317 34 63, Carrer del Palau 4) is another fine budget option. The bright, sunny rooms with wooden beams in the ceiling are well maintained and the management chirpy. The place has a genuinely social atmosphere. There are rooms sleeping four or more at 2000 ptas per person, and doubles for 5500 or 5800 ptas.

Lone travellers have a hard time of it in many Barcelona digs, but *Pensión Alamar* (Map 4; ☎ 93 302 50 12, Carrer de la Comtessa de Sobradiel 1) seems to specialise in them. It has only one double among the 13 small but well-kept rooms. You pay 2500 ptas per person, which is fair.

Moving a little farther towards the waterfront, *Hostal El Cantón* (Map 4; ☎ 93 317 30 19, Carrer Nou de Sant Francesc 40) is another good low-budget bet. Singles/doubles/triples without own bath cost 2000/4000/5700 ptas. With own bath, you are looking at 2600/5800/7800 ptas. Some rooms are spacious with sparkling new bathrooms, fan, fridge and balcony.

El Raval *Hotel Peninsular* (Map 4; ☎ 93 302 31 38, fax 93 412 36 99, Carrer de Sant Pau 34) is a bit of an oasis on the fringe of the Barri Xinès. Once part of a convent, it has a plant-draped atrium extending the full height and most of the length of the hotel. The 80 rooms are clean and (mostly) spacious but otherwise nothing particularly special. You can start at 3500/6000 for rooms without bath or 5000/7500 ptas with bath.

Hostal Residencia Òpera (Map 4; ☎ 93 318 82 01, Carrer de Sant Pau 20) is a bit tatty but it's worth trying if other places are full. Rooms are 3500/5000 ptas, or 4000/6000 ptas with bath.

A much better option, but one that is perenially full and nudging up into the mid-range price bracket, is **Hostal Mare Nostrum** *(Map 4; ☎ 93 318 53 40, fax 93 412 30 69, Carrer de Sant Pau 2)*. Bright doubles without/with own bath cost 7500/8975 ptas plus IVA. It has a couple of singles for 5850 ptas.

La Ribera **Pensión Lourdes** *(Map 4; ☎ 93 319 33 72, Carrer de la Princesa 14)* has about 20 clean rooms for 3500/4700 ptas. Doubles with bath cost 6700 ptas.

L'Eixample A few cheapies are spread strategically across this upmarket part of the city north of Plaça de Catalunya.

Hostal Goya *(Map 2; ☎ 93 302 25 65, fax 93 412 04 35, Carrer de Pau Claris 74)* has 12 nice, good-sized rooms at 3100/4500 ptas. Doubles with private shower and toilet cost 5600 ptas.

You should check out **Hostal Oliva** *(Map 2; ☎ 93 488 01 62, fax 93 488 17 89, Passeig de Gràcia 32)* just for the quaint old lift, which you'll want to take up to the 4th floor. The rooms are basically well kept, but some of those without bath have little room for anything but the bed. Rooms are 4000/6200 ptas, doubles with bath are 7200 ptas.

In a leafier location is **Hostal Neutral** *(Map 2; ☎ 93 487 63 90, fax 93 487 68 48, Rambla de Catalunya 42)*. Doubles with own bath cost 6530 ptas; those without are 5460 ptas. There are no singles.

Pensión Aribau *(Map 3; ☎ 93 453 11 06, Carrer d'Aribau 37)* offers reasonable rooms for 3500/6500 ptas. The singles only have a washbasin but do come with a TV, while the doubles have shower, toilet, TV and even a fridge.

PLACES TO STAY – MID-RANGE

All rooms in this range have private bathrooms.

La Rambla

Hotel Continental *(Map 4; ☎ 93 301 25 70, fax 93 302 73 60, Rambla de Canaletes 138)* has 35 pleasant, well-decorated rooms, all with cable TV, microwave, fridge, safe and fan. Room rates, including a good breakfast, start at 6900/9000 ptas in summer and rise for doubles with Rambla

views. Seems OK to us, but some readers have reported being disappointed.

Hotel Cuatro Naciones *(Map 4; ☎ 93 317 36 24, fax 93 302 69 85, La Rambla 40)* has adequate rooms for 7490/10,700 ptas, which includes breakfast and IVA. It was built in 1849 and was once (a long time ago) Barcelona's top hotel. Buffalo Bill preferred it to a wagon when he was in town back in 1889.

Hotel Oriente *(Map 4; ☎ 93 302 25 58, fax 93 412 38 19, La Rambla 45)* is famous for its modernista design and has a fine sky-lit restaurant and other public rooms, but staff can be offhand. The bedrooms are slightly past their prime but still comfortable, with tiled floors and bathrooms, safes and TV. Rooms, pushing the limits of mid-range pricing, are 10,7000/17,120 ptas plus IVA.

Barri Gòtic

Hotel Roma Reial *(Map 4; ☎ 93 302 03 66, fax 93 301 18 39, Plaça Reial 11)* has decent rooms, all with bath, at 6000/9000 ptas in high season.

At **Hotel Jardi** *(Map 4; ☎ 93 301 59 00, Plaça de Sant Josep Oriol 1)* doubles with a balcony over the lovely square cost around 8000 ptas. At the time of writing some rooms were being refurbished, including the singles. It is a good little hotel and may well be better when the work is finished.

Hotel Nouvel *(Map 4; ☎ 93 301 82 74, fax 93 301 83 70, Carrer de Santa Anna 18-20)* has some elegant modernista touches and good rooms with air-con and satellite TV for 10,300/15,750 ptas plus IVA. Prices include breakfast.

El Raval

Hotel Mesón de Castilla *(Map 3; ☎ 93 318 21 82, fax 93 412 40 20, Carrer de Valldonzella 5)* has some lovely modernista touches – stained glass and murals in its public rooms, Gaudíesque window mouldings – and 56 good, quaintly decorated rooms for 11,600/14,800 ptas with breakfast plus IVA.

Hotel España *(Map 4; ☎ 93 318 17 58, fax 93 317 11 34, Carrer de Sant Pau 9-11)* is famous for its two marvellous dining rooms designed by Domènech i Montaner. One has big sea-life murals by Ramon Casas, the other has floral tiling and a wood-beamed roof. The 60-plus simple but comfortable rooms cost 5700/10,800 ptas, including breakfast.

Not as interesting but quite a reasonable option is *Hotel Principal (Map 4; ☎ 93 318 89 70, fax 93 412 08 19, Carrer de la Junta del Comerç 8)*, where functional rooms with TV, air-con and safe cost 7900/10,200 ptas. Breakfast is included. It runs *Hotel Joventut* virtually next door at the same rates.

L'Eixample
A fine choice for a bit of old-fashioned style is *Hotel Gran Via (Map 2; ☎ 93 318 19 00, fax 93 318 99 97, Gran Via de les Corts Catalanes 642)*, with 53 good-sized rooms at 10,000/14,000 ptas plus IVA and a big, elegant lounge opening onto a roof terrace. Breakfast is available for 1100 ptas.

PLACES TO STAY – TOP END
Someone has neglected to tell these people that inflation in Spain is running at under 3%. In a little more than two years some hotels have lifted their official rates by as much as 50%! If you get lucky and turn up when businesspeople aren't in town, you can get some good offers – always ask. You must add 7% IVA to the rates below, except where otherwise indicated.

La Rambla
The top hotel on La Rambla is the elegant *Le Meridien (Map 4; ☎ 93 318 62 00, fax 93 301 77 76)* at No 111. Its top-floor presidential suite is where the likes of Michael Jackson, Madonna and Julio Iglesias stay. Standard singles/doubles are 38,000/42,000 ptas, but occasionally it puts on specials at 26,000 ptas per room (single or double use).

Barri Gòtic
Hotel Suizo (Map 4; ☎ 93 310 61 08, fax 93 310 40 81, Plaça de l'Àngel 12) is old on the outside but quite modern within and has a restaurant and snack bar. Rooms are comfortable, if unspectacular, and cost 14,250/18,500 ptas plus IVA.

Hotel Colón (Map 4; ☎ 93 301 14 04, fax 93 317 29 15, Avinguda de la Catedral 7) is a better choice (if you can afford it) for its location facing the cathedral. The 146 comfortable and elegant rooms cost 17,500/26,300 ptas.

El Raval
Hotel San Agustín (Map 4; ☎ 93 318 16 58, fax 93 317 29 28, Plaça de Sant Agustí 3) has some character, if only because of its location on a quiet square. Rooms, all with air-con, heating and satellite TV, cost 12,500/17,500 ptas, including breakfast.

L'Eixample
Hotel Balmes (Map 2; ☎ 93 451 19 14, fax 93 451 00 49, Carrer de Mallorca 216) is a good, modern hotel with white bricks much in evidence in the interior. Average-sized rooms with air-con, nice tiled bathrooms and satellite TV are comparatively good value at 14,500/24,400 ptas.

Hotel Majèstic (Map 2; ☎ 93 488 17 17, fax 93 488 18 80, Passeig de Gràcia 70) is a sprawling, comfortable place with a nice line in modern art on the walls and a rooftop swimming pool. The 300-plus rooms, with air-con and satellite TV, range up to 30,000/36,000 ptas.

Comtes (or Condes) de Barcelona Hotel (Map 2; ☎ 93 488 22 00, fax 93 488 06 14, Passeig de Gràcia 73-75) is one of Barcelona's best hotels. It has two separate buildings facing each other across Carrer de Mallorca. The older one occupies the Casa Enric Batlló, built in the 1890s but now stylishly modernised. The air-con, soundproofed rooms have marble bathrooms. Rooms start at 29,000/31,000 ptas.

Hotel Ritz (Map 2; ☎ 93 318 52 00, fax 93 318 01 48, Gran Via de les Corts Catalanes 668) is the city's top choice for old-fashioned elegance, luxury, individuality and first-class service. It's been going since 1919. Room rates (regardless of whether single or double occupancy) start at 45,000 ptas. A one-bedroom suite with tiled step-down 'Roman bath' costs 140,000 ptas.

One of the classiest addresses in town is *Hotel Claris (Map 2; ☎ 93 487 62 62, fax 93 487 87 36, Carrer de Pau Claris 150).* Of course you pay for the pleasure, to the tune of 36,000/42,900 ptas. Suites cost up to 125,000 ptas. Breakfast is another 2800 ptas.

Port Olímpic

Barcelona's most fashionable, if rather impersonal, lodgings is at *Hotel Arts Barcelona (Map 1; ☎ 93 221 10 00, fax 93 221 10 70, Carrer de la Marina 19-21),* in one of the two sky-high towers that dominate the Port Olímpic. It has over 450 rooms and charges from 50,000 ptas for a double.

LONG-TERM RENTALS

The Universitat de Barcelona, Gran Via de les Corts Catalanes 585 (Map 3) and the British Council (Map 1; see Information earlier in this chapter) have notice boards with ads for flat shares. Young people and students should check out the options at Punt d'Informació Juvenil, Carrer de Calàbria 147 (Map 1).

The free English-language monthly *Barcelona Metropolitan* (see Newspapers & Magazines in the Facts for the Visitor chapter) carries rental classifieds.

Rooms can come as cheap as 25,000 ptas a month, but for something halfway decent, not too far from the centre, you're looking at a minimum of 35,000 ptas. You need to add bills (gas, electricity, water, phone and *comunidad,* ie, building maintenance charges).

PLACES TO EAT

Barcelona is packed with good places to eat. Menus may be in Catalan or Spanish, or both; some places have foreign-language menus too. Specifically Catalan food tends to be a bit expensive in Barcelona, but you won't regret having at least one Catalan meal while you're here (see the boxed text 'Catalan Cuisine' in the Catalunya chapter for a rundown on some typical dishes and words you'll encounter on Catalan menus).

Barcelona folk usually eat lunch between about 2 and 4 pm and don't start a dinner out until 9 or 10 pm. Most restaurants stop serving between 11 pm and midnight. Many have a weekly closing day and some stay

shut throughout August, when locals abandon the city in droves. Telephone numbers are given for places where it may be worth booking ahead.

Places To Eat – Budget

La Rambla *Viena (Map 4; Rambla dels Estudis 115)* is a popular cafe with stools around a central counter and good *barretas* (baguettes) for 300 to 500 ptas.

Cafè de l'Òpera (Map 4; ☎ 93 317 75 85, La Rambla 74), opposite the Liceu opera house, is La Rambla's most interesting cafe, with elegant 1920s decor. It gets busy at night (see Bars under Entertainment), but is quieter for morning coffee and croissants.

Barri Gòtic This area is peppered with good eateries, some of them excellent value.

Restaurants Self-Naturista (Map 4; Carrer de Santa Anna 13) is a popular self-service vegetarian restaurant with a four-course lunch *menú del día* (daily set meal) for 965 ptas. Mains don't cost more than 700 ptas.

Carrer de la Mercè, running roughly west from the main post office, is a good place to hunt around for great little northern Spanish *tascas* (bars) and *sidrerías* (cider houses). Most of these are run by immigrants from Galicia and Asturias. *Tasca El Corral* (Map 4), at No 19, and *Sidrería La Socarrena* (Map 4), at No 21, are both worth checking out, but there are many others. *Bar Celta* (Map 4), No 16, is cheap – you can fill up on tapas for under 1000 ptas.

A cross between a cafe of a century ago and hippy hang-out, *La Cereria (Map 4; Baixada de Sant Miquel 3–5)* is a cooperative that offers some tasty vegetarian cooking, great desserts and low prices. The fruit shakes are good too.

La Verónica (Map 4; Carrer d'Avinyò 20) shines out like a beacon around here, its red decor and bright white lighting hard to miss. It serves reasonable pizzas at affordable prices in an atmosphere that could be described as fashionably camp. There is a lunch *menú* for 1000 ptas.

Pastry Shops & Coffee Bars Tempting pastry and/or chocolate shops, often combined with coffee bars, abound. There's a special concentration along Carrer la Llibreteria and Baixada de la Llibreteria, north-east off Plaça de Sant Jaume. Among the least resistible are (all on Map 4): *Santa Clara* (*Carrer de la Llibreteria 21*) and *La Colmena*, on the corner of Baixada de la Llibreteria and Plaça de l'Àngel. Two places with particularly good coffee in this area are *Bon Mercat*, on the corner of Baixada de la Llibreteria and Carrer de la Freneria, and *Il Caffè di Roma*, on Plaça de l'Àngel, which is part of a chain you'll see all over town.

Xocolateria La Xicra (*Map 4; Plaça de Sant Josep Oriol 2*) has great cakes, various coffees, teas and *xocolata* (hot chocolate; 250 ptas) so thick it's listed on the menu under *postres* (desserts). Nearby, two other good places to sit down for a coffee and croissant are *Granja La Pallaresa* (*Map 4; Carrer de Petritxol 11*) and *Croissanterie del Pi* (*Map 4; Carrer del Pi 14*).

A great little place to sip a wide variety of teas and herbal infusions is *Salterio* (*Map 4; Carrer de Sant Domènec del Call 4*), just in off Carrer de Ferran.

International Cuisine The Bagel Shop (*Map 4; Carrer de la Canuda 25*), just in off La Rambla, is the only place in town where your lox and cream cheese bagel will be the genuine article. It is also open for Sunday hangover breakfast (not bad at 700 ptas).

Sushi-Ya (*Map 4; Carrer d'En Quintana 4*) is a simple place for cheap Japanese food. The sushi set meal costs 1175 ptas, which is hard to argue with in terms of price and you can take food away. Don't expect top Japanese cuisine, but it makes an affordable change.

Wagamama (*Map 4; Carrer d'Escudellers 39*) is a cool new place to get into good noodle dishes (up to 900 ptas) until 1 am daily. It also does weird and wonderful salads and mixed fruit drinks.

Takeaway Felafel & Kebabs Disco-Bar Real (*Map 4*), on the corner of Plaça Reial and Carrer de Colom, has a takeaway

counter doing good felafel for 250 ptas. *Buen Bocado* (*Map 4; Carrer dels Escudellers 31*) has felafel for 300 ptas and shwarma for 425 ptas. It's open evenings only, until 2 am. The nameless *felafel & kebab takeaway* (*Map 4*), on Carrer dels Escudellers just north of Carrer dels Obradors, charges a tad less.

El Raval *Restaurant Els Tres Bots* (*Map 4; Carrer de Sant Pau 42*) is grungy but cheap, with a *menú* for 875 ptas. Along the same street at No 31, *Restaurante Pollo Rico* has a downstairs bar where you can get a quarter chicken, an omelette or a veal steak with chips, bread and wine, from 500 ptas. There's a more salubrious but only slightly more expensive upstairs restaurant.

Bar Kasparo (*Map 4; Plaça de Vicenç Martorell 4*) is a relaxed Australian-run place where you can get great mixed salads and other healthy light food – perfect in summer on this quiet pedestrianised square.

Another hip little establishment is *Ra* (*Map 4; ☎ 93 301 41 63, Plaça de la Gardunya*), which looks like a beach bar that got lost and ended up in the car park. It offers a vaguely vegetarian menu, with a couple of meat options thrown in. The food is OK but unexceptional. It is, however, cheap (*menú* for 995 ptas) and the atmosphere decidedly groovy.

The charming *El Convent* (*Map 4; ☎ 93 302 31 12, Carrer de Jerusalem 3*), elegantly lodged in what was once a religious institution, offers a good *menú* of 965 ptas. The *ensalada de arroz con gambitos* (rice salad with shrimps) is a tasty first course.

International Cuisine Kashmir Restaurant Tandoori (*Map 4; Carrer de Sant Pau 39*) does tasty curries and biryanis from around 800 ptas. It is one of a growing number of curry houses around here, reflecting the wave of mainly Pakistani migration into El Raval.

La Ribera *Comme-Bio* (*aka La Botiga; Map 4; Via Laietana 28*) is a modern, chemical-additive-free vegetarian restaurant and wholefood shop. Its good, four-course *menú*

(1125 ptas) includes a help-yourself salad bar; many a la carte dishes, including pizzas and spinach-and-Roquefort crepes, cost around 900 ptas, or you can go for a set dinner menu for 1850 ptas. There's a branch at Gran Via de les Corts Catalanes 603 (Map 3).

Lluna Plena (Map 4; Carrer de Montcada 2) is an unclad-brick, cellar-style place with good Catalan and Spanish food, open Tuesday to Sunday. It's packed for its four-course, 1050-ptas lunch *menú*. It's closed on Sunday night and Monday.

Restaurant L'Econòmic (Map 3; Plaça de Sant Agustí Vell 13) is a popular local hang-out where a full set lunch comes in at 1000 ptas, unless you want to try the classier 3000 ptas version.

International Cuisine *Café Kafka (Map 3; Carrer de La Fusina 7)* offers a strange mix of food. Its Sudanese chef prepares Arab dishes, while the Filipino cook does a range of South-East Asian style food. Prices are moderate.

L'Eixample A good place to start a visit to L'Eixample is at the top cafeteria at *El Corte Inglés* department store on Plaça de Catalunya (Map 3). It's reasonably priced and has tremendous views.

Restaurants Bar Estudiantil (Map 3), on Plaça de la Universitat, does economical *plats combinats*, eg, chicken, chips and *berenjena* (aubergine), or *botifarra* (beans and red pepper), each for around 600 ptas. This place is open until late and is a genuine student hang-out.

L'Hostal de Rita (Map 2; Carrer d'Aragó 279), a block east of Passeig de Gràcia, is an excellent mid-range restaurant. The 995 ptas four-course lunch *menú* is a good deal. A-la-carte mains are 700 to 1000 ptas. Expect to queue. The same people own *Restaurant Madrid Barcelona (Map 2; Carrer d'Aragó 282)*, virtually over the road. Mains come in under 1000 ptas, although if you have wine and dessert you are likely to end up with a bill of 2000 ptas. It is so popular that they set up little cardboard stools outside for customers who are waiting for a table.

Tapas, Snacks & Coffee You'll find a number of glossy but informal tapas places near the bottom end of Passeig de Gràcia (Map 2). At No 24 is *Quasi Queviures (Qu Qu)*, with a big choice, including sausages and hams, pâtés and smoked fish. Many tapas cost over 400 ptas, but portions are decent. At No 28 is *Ba-Ba-Reeba*, similar but less Catalan. *Cerveseria Tapa Tapa* at No 44, on the corner of Carrer del Consell de Cent, is another big, bright place with a great range of tapas from 250 ptas. Some of these places can feel a little barn-like and are owned by the same people.

Lizarran (Map 2; Carrer de Mallora 257) is a lively spot serving reasonable tapas. It is part of a chain but, as chains go, the quality isn't bad.

Gràcia *Bar Candanchu (Map 2; ☎ 93 237 73 62, Plaça de Rius i Taulet 9)* has a restaurant with many plats combinats and paella for 1250 ptas. *Mario Pizza*, on the same square, does pizzas for 900 to 1100 ptas.

A good homy Lebanese place is *Sannin (Map 1; ☎ 93 285 00 51, Carrer de l'Encarnació 44)*. A full meal of old faves such as shwarma, hummus, tabouleh, dessert and drinks will not cost you much more than 1500 ptas.

Restaurant Chains There are a few local restaurant chains where you can get a quick, decent snack or meal with minimum effort. A few of the branches are listed below.

Bocatta – sells hot and cold baguettes with a big range of fillings, mostly for 360 to 695 ptas. Some branches are at La Rambla 89 (Map 6); Carrer de Santa Anna 11 (Map 6); Plaça de Sant Jaume (Map 6); the corner of Carrer de Comtal and Carrer d'En Amargòs (Map 6) and Rambla de Catalunya between Carrer de Mallorca and Carrer de València (Map 2); most branches open 8 am to midnight daily.

Pans & Company – provides similar fare and prices to Bocatta. Branches are at La Rambla 123 (Map 6), Carrer de Ferran 14 (Map 6), and on Carrer dels Arcs off Plaça Nova (Map 6), Ronda de la Universitat 7 (Map 4), Rambla de Catalunya 13 (Map 5), Passeig de Gràcia 39 (Map 2) and Carrer de Provença 278 (Map 2).

Pastafiore – pizza and pasta: a half (media) pizza is 395 to 575 ptas but you'll need a whole *(entera)* one for 550 to 865 ptas if you're hungry; pasta is around 475 to 675 ptas but tends to be less appetising (any resemblance to Italian food is purely coincidental). Branches are at Rambla de Canaletes 125 (Map 6), Carrer de Provença 278 (Map 2) and Travessera de Gràcia 60 (Map 2).

Self-Catering There's great fresh food of all types at the *Mercat de la Boqueria* on La Rambla (Map 6), open 8 am to 8 pm Monday to Saturday. In La Ribera (Map 6), *Mercat de Santa Caterina*, which has been temporarily shifted to Passeig de Lluís Companys, is another good shopping choice. In Gràcia there's a big covered *food market* at the corner of Travessera de Gràcia and Carrer de la Mare de Déu dels Desemparats.

Champion (Map 4), near the northern end of La Rambla, is a convenient central supermarket.

Places to Eat – Mid-Range

Opening your purse wide will improve your options greatly. At the places listed below you can expect to pay anything from 2000 to 3500 ptas for a full evening meal with all the trimmings.

Plaça de Catalunya *Café Zurich (Map 4; ☎ 93 317 91 53, Carrer de Pelai 39)*, actually right on the square, has been resuscitated after years of closure. It is an old-style cafe, great for the morning paper but a little more expensive than the average cafe.

Barri Gòtic A Basque favourite is *Irati (Map 4; Carrer del Cardenal Cassañes 17)*. Its lunch *menú* is 1500 ptas, or you can enjoy the great tapas and a zurrito of beer, or six (but watch how your debts mount!).

Mesón Jesús (Map 4; ☎ 93 317 46 98, Carrer dels Cecs de la Boqueria 4), between Plaça de Sant Josep Oriol and Carrer de la Boqueria, is a cosy place with a homy ambience. It does a good 1400 ptas three-course *menú*. It's closed Saturday night and Sunday.

Can Culleretes (Map 4; Carrer d'En Quintana 5) is Barcelona's oldest restaurant, founded in 1786. It's still going strong,

with old-fashioned decor and good Catalan food. A three-course *menú,* including half a bottle of wine, will cost around 2500 ptas.

Les Quinze Nits (Map 4; Plaça Reial 6) is a stylish, bistro-like restaurant, on the borderline between smart and casual, with a long menu of good Catalan and Spanish dishes at reasonable prices. Three courses with wine and coffee typically come to about 2500 ptas. The problem is you almost always have to queue for ages and, while the place is good, it is not *that* good!

El Taxidermista (Map 4; Plaça Reial 8) is a rather slick new joint offering Les Quinze Nits some competition. The cooking demonstrates a little Mediterranean sparkle and the lunch *menú* is not bad at 1200 ptas. In the evening you're looking at about 3000 ptas. The kitchen closes by midnight but the place stays open as a cafe until 2.30 am. It closes altogether on Monday.

La Fonda Escudellers (Map 4), on the corner of Carrer dels Escudellers and Passatge dels Escudellers, is run by the same people as Les Quinze Nits and has a similar ambience and standards. You will be directed efficiently to one of the three floors from the entrance and the food is better than in many places around town that charge double.

El Paraguayo (Map 3; Carrer del Parc 1) is a great place for succulent slabs of meat bigger than your head. Try the *entraña;* the word means 'entrails' but the meal is in fact a juicy slice of prime beef folded over onto itself and accompanied by a herb sauce. The *dulce de leche* (a South American version of caramel) is to die for. Expect to pay around 2000 ptas per head.

El Raval Urban revival is bringing new life into this area, one of the poorest quarters of old Barcelona. Several tempting places have popped up, attracting a hip, young clientele.

Salsitas (Map 4; Carrer Nou de la Rambla 22) is the place to go for your post-binge brunch a la East Village. Eggs Benedict anyone? It's open from the unlikely time of 8 am to 1 pm weekend mornings.

At *Rita Blue (Map 4; Plaça St Agustí 3)* be prepared to wait at the bar of this pleasant designer restaurant with a whiff of New York in the air. The food is a tempting mix of Mediterranean dishes with a hint of the exotic. For instance, you could order Mexican *fajitas* with tandoori chicken. The lighting is perfect and the service efficient. Expect to pay up to 3000 ptas per head.

Poble Sec The recently renovated ***Restaurant Elche*** *(Map 1; Carrer de Vila i Vilà 71)* does some of Barcelona's best paella and good *fideuá* (paella made with noodles instead of rice). Several varieties are on offer, mostly around 1300 to 1800 ptas per person (minimum of two people).

La Ribera For a bit of a splurge on superb, mainly Catalan and French cooking, you can't do much better than ***Senyor Parellada*** *(Map 4; Carrer de l'Argenteria 37)*, an informally chic restaurant. Mains start at around 2000 ptas. You might start with *carpaccio de salmó* (thin strips of garnished uncooked salmon), followed by *anec amb figues* (duck with figs). Book for dinner.

Centre Cultural Euskal Etxea (Map 4; Placeta de Montcada 1) is a fine San Sebastián-style bar where you can wash down the scrummy tapas with glasses of the Basque wine, *txacoli*. If you plan to make this your main meal, be prepared to part with 2000 to 3000 ptas.

You'll struggle to get into ***L'Ou Com Balla*** *(Map 4; ☎ 93 310 53 78, Carrer dels Banys Vells 20)* without a reservation. It presents a sometimes exquisite choice of local, sort-of-Moroccan and more-or-less French dishes in an inviting space with low lighting and well-chosen ambient music. A meal can cost about 3500 ptas.

International Cuisine Restaurante Bunga Raya (Map 4; Carrer dels Assaonadors 7) makes a nice change with its Malaysian and Indonesian cooking. It has a *menú* for 1795 ptas.

Gades (Map 4; Carrer de l'Esparteria 10) is a smart address for fondue, of which it does nearly a dozen varieties for 1700 ptas. The bare brick walls and vaults lend the place an elegantly muted atmosphere.

L'Eixample *Centro Asturiano (Map 2; Passeig de Gràcia 78)* is a great little club tucked away up on the 1st floor. It opens its doors to the lunchtime rabble for the solid 1200-ptas *menú*. The open-air interior patio is a wonderful spot to eat, but you can go inside too.

International Cuisine At *Thai Gardens (Map 2; Carrer de la Diputació 273)* you can pop in for a limited lunch *menú* for 1500 ptas or try the more extensive evening spread for 4500 ptas.

Gràcia *Taverna El Glop (Map 2; ☎ 93 213 70 58, Carrer de Sant Lluís 24)* is a rustic spot specialising in *torrades*, grilled meats and salads. Locals say it's a bit passé and it has taken to opening branches elsewhere in town, but the food remains good. A meal with drinks costs 2500 to 3000 ptas. It's closed on Monday.

La Singular (Map 2; ☎ 93 237 50 98, Carrer de Franciso Giner 50) does fantastic salads (with salmon, tuna or pâté) as mains. If you throw in a few tapas and have wine and coffee, you'll be looking at 2500 ptas per head. It's closed on Wednesday.

Port Vell & La Barceloneta Fronting the Palau de Mar is a line of al fresco dining options mostly specialising in (finer) seafood. One of the best is *La Gavina* (Map 3), where you can expect to pay around 4000 ptas per head for a full meal with wine. When it's in form, its fideuás are scrummy.

Restaurant Set (7) Portes (Map 4; ☎ 93 319 30 33, Passeig d'Isabel II 14) is a classic, founded in 1836. The old-world atmosphere is reinforced by the decor of wood panelling, tiles, mirrors and plaques naming some of the famous – such as Orson Welles – who have eaten here. Paella (1475 to 2225 ptas) is the speciality. It's near-essential to book.

La Barceloneta has some good seafood restaurants. One of the best along this strip is *Puda Can Manel (Map 3; Passeig de Joan de Borbó 60-61)*. The paella is fine at 1400 ptas per head, the *crema catalana* for dessert not so hot. All up you will pay around 3500 ptas per head.

Port Olímpic The harbour here is lined on two sides by dozens of restaurants and tapas bars, extremely popular in spring and summer. They are not cheap and mostly rely on the frenetic portside activity for atmosphere. One of the more economical places is *La Taverna del Cel Ros* (Map 1), which does a reasonable fideuá for 1375 ptas. The irritating thing around here is the touting waiters – seriously good eateries don't need to tout for business.

Tibidabo Plaça del Doctor Andreu at the foot of the Tibidabo funicular is a good place to halt on your way to or from Tibidabo. The best views are from *Mirablau Terrazza* (Map 1), an open-air cafe by the tramvia blau stop. A couple of more expensive restaurants across the street are the only alternative.

Places to Eat – Top End

Barri Gòtic *Els Quatre Gats* (Map 4; Carrer de Montsió 3 bis) was a turn-of-the-20th-century artists' lair now reincarnated as a fairly expensive restaurant with somewhat dismissive service. Starters/snacks such as *esqueixada*, or *escalivada amb torrada,* are close to 1000 ptas, and mains cost close to 3000 ptas. Just have a drink if you just want to sample the atmosphere.

Les Quatre Barres (Map 4; ☎ 93 302 50 60, Carrer d'En Quintana 6) serves up excellent Catalan food – 3000 or 4000 ptas for a meal with drinks. It offers a set lunch at 1380 ptas. It is closed all day Sunday and Monday night.

Los Caracoles (Map 4; ☎ 93 302 31 85, Carrer dels Escudellers 14) started life as a tavern in the 19th century and is one of Barcelona's best-known restaurants – although it's now frequented by tourists rather than by the celebrities whose photos adorn its walls. It's still good and lively and offers a big choice of seafood, fish, rice and meat. Try the snails.

La Ribera *Cal Pep* (Map 4; ☎ 93 310 79 61, Plaça de les Olles 8) has great tapas and a small dining room with good seafood where a three-course Catalan meal with drinks will be around 3500 ptas. It is closed

Cool Cats of the 1900s

Els Quatre Gats was opened in 1897 by four Barcelonese who had spent time in Paris artistic circles: the modernista artists Ramon Casas and Santiago Rusiñol, and their friends Miquel Utrillo and Pere Romeu who, among other things, were deeply interested in shadow puppetry. Romeu, the manager, was a colourful character equally devoted to cabaret and cycling.

The name Els Quatre Gats is Catalan for 'the four cats', and alludes both to the cafe's four founders and to Le Chat Noir, an artistic cafe in Montmartre, Paris. Idiomatically, it means 'a handful of people, a minority' – no doubt about how its avant-garde clientele saw themselves. Situated in the first Barcelona creation of the modernista architect Josep Puig i Cadafalch, Els Quatre Gats quickly became an influential meeting, drinking and cavorting place of young artists, writers, actors, musicians and their circles.

It published its own magazine and staged exhibitions, recitals and, of course, shadow puppet shows. Picasso's first exhibition was here in 1900, and included drawings of many of the customers. Els Quatre Gats closed in 1903. Later it was used as an art gallery, before its present incarnation as a restaurant.

on Sunday, holidays and at lunchtime on Monday.

L'Eixample You could easily miss *Tragaluz* (Map 2; ☎ 93 487 01 96, Passatge de la Concepció 5), but don't. It serves inventive Mediterranean cuisine (with an Italian leaning) and mouth-watering desserts – try the *tarta de manzana con helado de dulce de leche* (apple pie with caramel ice cream). A meal with wine costs about 5000 ptas per head.

Barcelona's first Japanese restaurant is still one of its best. *Yamadori* (Map 3; ☎ 93 453 92 64, Carrer d'Aribau 68) will set you back about 5000 ptas. It is closed on Sunday.

Gràcia *Botafumeiro* (Map 2; ☎ 93 218 42 30, Carrer Gran de Gràcia 81) is reputedly a place where the shellfish is about as good as it gets in all Barcelona. It would want to be, as you will abandon the best part of 10,000 ptas per head for the pleasure.

ENTERTAINMENT

Barcelona's entertainment bible is the weekly Spanish-language magazine *Guía del Ocio* (125 ptas), which comes out on Thursday and lists almost everything that's on in the way of music, film, exhibitions, theatre and more. You can pick it up at most newsstands. An alternative is *La Agenda de Barcelona* (225 ptas).

Bars

Barcelona's bars run the gamut from wood-panelled wine cellars to bright waterfront places and trendy designer bars. Most are at their liveliest from about 10 pm to 2 or 3 am, especially from Thursday to Saturday, as people get into their night-time stride.

La Rambla *Cafè de l'Òpera (Map 4; La Rambla 74)*, opposite the Liceu opera house, is the busiest and classiest place on an otherwise largely tacky strip. It has been in action since at least 1929 and was founded in 1876. It is pleasant for an early evening tipple before getting serious.

Barri Gòtic The smell of dope in *B.O.2 (Map 4; Carrer de Sant Domènec del Call 14)* can be so thick that knives would be useless. Still, if you want to swallow beer to the accompaniment of old rock concert videos, this is not a bad little dive to skive around in until about 3 am. A quite different option open until the same time is *Paradise (Map 4)*, on Carrer del Paradis, a little reggae hideaway open from Wednesday to Saturday.

Glaciar (Map 4; Plaça Reial 3) gets busy with a young crowd of foreigners and locals in the evening and stays open until 2 or 3 am.

Tiny **Bar Malpaso** (Map 4) on Carrer d'En Rauric, just off Plaça Reial, is packed at night with a young, casual crowd and plays great Latin and African music – it takes a while to get into gear. Another hip low-lit place with a more varied, gay-leaning clientele is *Schilling (Carrer de Ferran 23)*. Mixed drinks cost about 700 ptas at both.

The decor at *Al Limón Negro (Map 4; Carrer dels Escudellers Blancs 3)* keeps changing, but it remains a laid-back place for a few tipples until well into the night.

A few yards closer to the waterfront you can raise the red lantern at *Shanghai (Map 4; Carrer de N'Aglá 9)*, a humming but cosy place for a beer, or sake.

Thiossan (Map 4; Carrer del Vidre 3) is a cool Senegalese haunt where you can get a bite to eat or just sit in mellow content listening to the African rhythms and allowing soothing ales to do their work.

Zoo (Map 4; Carrer dels Escudellers 33) is a busy little watering hole in the heart of the Barri Gòtic. It will cater to foreigners' desires for *sangría* but the place gets a few locals in too.

Dot (Map 4; Carrer Nou de Sant Francesc 7) is generally open until about 3 am, a little later on Friday and Saturday, and each night the musical theme changes, from 'easy listening' to 'space funk' on Friday and drum 'n' bass on Saturday.

Bar Center Point (Map 4; ☎ 619-35 39 45, Passeig de Colom 11) is an odd little bar down near the old port. During the week it stays open until 3 am but on Friday and Saturday keeps happening until 6 am. On occasion it gets in a DJ and the session has been known to go on into broad daylight.

El Raval Don't miss *Bar Marsella (Map 4; Carrer de Sant Pau 65)*, which opened its doors in 1820 and still specialises in *absenta* (absinthe), a beverage hard to find because of its supposed narcotic qualities.

Nearby is *The Quiet Man (Map 4; Carrer del Marquès de Barberà 11)*, a relaxed Irish pub attracting both locals and foreigners. There's live music some nights.

Another good place is *Casa Almirall (Map 3; Carrer de Joaquim Costa 33)*, which has been going since the 1860s; it's dark and intriguing (although less so since it was spruced up in early 2000), with modernista decor and a mixed clientele. *Bar Pastís (Map 3; ☎ 93 318 79 80, Carrer de*

Santa Mònica 4) is a tiny old bar with a French cabaret theme (lots of Piaf in the background).

L'Ovella Negra (Map 4; Carrer de les Sitges 5), or The Black Sheep, is a noisy, fun, barn-like tavern with a young crowd.

Café Que Pone Muebles Navarro ('Cafe where the Sign says Navarran Furniture'; Map 3; Carrer de la Riera Alta 4-6) is an art gallery-cum-lounge-cum-bar where you can get great cheesecake. It's an odd place but worth a look. It is open until midnight, closed Monday.

If by 2.30 am, when all or most of these places have shut their doors, you still need a drink and you don't want a club or disco, your best bet (except on Sunday) is the *London Bar (Map 4; Carrer Nou de la Rambla 36).* It's open until 5 am and occasionally stages some off-the-wall music acts (a bottled beer costs about 500 ptas).

La Ribera *El Xampanyet (Map 4; Carrer de Montcada 22)* is the city's best-known *cava* (Catalan champagne) bar – a small, cosy place with tiled walls and good tapas as well as cava by the glass.

Next door at No 20, the baroque magnificence of the *Palau de Dalmases* is matched only by the plush luxury inside. The snag is price – a glass of no-name wine will cost 1000 ptas!

El Nus (Map 4; Carrer dels Mirallers 5) is a small, dim, chic bar in the narrow old streets near the Església de Santa Maria del Mar, done out with pictures of its Maharishi-lookalike owner – good for a quiet drink after dinner.

Along and near Passeig del Born (Map 4), which links the Església de Santa Maria del Mar and the former fresh produce market El Born, you'll find stacks of bars. Worth a try are *El Copetín,* No 19, for cocktails and *Miramelindo,* No 15 – a spacious tavern where you can actually hear yourself talk as well as drink.

Mudanzas (Map 4; Carrer de la Vidrieria 15) has been around for a lot longer. It's a popular little bar and quite often you can hear live music here. Around the corner, shady Plaça de les Olles is a charming little hideaway square in summer when the *terrasses* are in operation.

In a class of its own is the nearby wine bar *La Vinya del Senyor (Map 4),* on Plaça de Santa Maria del Mar. Come here to taste a selection of wines and cavas, accompanied by simple snacks.

If you should head north off Passeig del Born, you probably would never think to trudge up Carrer del Rec. Do it. At No 49 is *Borneo (Map 4),* a laid-back bar with wide windows onto the street.

L'Eixample In general it is safe to say that the 19th-century expanse that is l'Eixample is not a good place to go looking for nightlife. One or two options are worthwhile, however.

La Bodegueta (Map 2; Rambla de Catalunya 100) is a classic wine cellar. Bottles and barrels line the walls and stools surround marble tables.

La Fira (Map 2; Carrer de Provença 171) is a designer bar with a difference. You enter through a hall of distorting mirrors and inside you'll find that everything is fairground paraphernalia. It sounds corny but the atmosphere is fun.

Gràcia *Café del Sol (Map 2; ☎ 93 415 56 63, Plaça del Sol 16)* and *Mirasol (Map 2; ☎ 93 238 01 13)* opposite at No 4 are lively bars. The former has a vaguely bohemian crowd, tapas and tables outside.

Café Salambó (Map 2; Carrer de Torrijos 51) is a gentle designer haunt imitating a village bar, with benches at low tables, and has an upper level with pool tables. There's food too – 1150 ptas for a three-course *menú.*

Farther up the hill are bars and cafes with potential, around the corner of Carrer de Torrijos and Carrer de la Perla. A block north, *Café La Virreina (Map 2; ☎ 93 237 98 80)* on the leafy Plaça de la Virreina is a relaxed place with a mixed-age crowd, 1970s rock music, cheap hot *bocadillos,* and tables outside.

Montjuïc The Poble Espanyol has several bars that get lively. The most original is *Torres de Ávila (Map 1; ☎ 93 424 93 09),* inside the tall entrance towers themselves. Created by the top Barcelona designer Javier Mariscal (he was responsible for the Olympics mascot Kobi in 1992), it has several levels and all sorts of surreal touches, including an egg-shaped room and glass lifts that you fear will shoot you through the roof. It's open 10 pm to 4 am.

Western Gràcia/Avinguda Diagonal
The area around Carrer de Marià Cubí gets busy with locals on weekends. It's a little on the *pijo* (well-off kids) side, but can be fun all the same. And it's not likely to be filled with tourists! Don't bother earlier in the week, as the area tends to be dead.

Mas i Mas (Map 2; Carrer de Marià Cubí 199) is one of the area's best known drinkeries. Another must is *Universal*, across the road at No 182. It is open until 4.30 am Monday to Saturday.

Live Music
There's a good choice most nights of the week. Many venues double as bars or clubs. In the latter case, if you paid to get in to see an act, the dancing afterwards will come free. Starting times are rarely before 10 pm, more often around midnight. Entry charges range from free to 1500 ptas or so – the higher prices often include a drink.

To see big-name acts, either Spanish or from abroad, you will probably pay more. They often perform at venues such as the 17,000-capacity *Palau Sant Jordi (Map 1)* on Montjuïc or the *Teatre Mercat de les Flors (Map 1)*, at the foot of Montjuïc.

Barri Gòtic *Barcelona Pipa Club (Map 4; Plaça Reial 3)* generally has jazz from Thursday to Saturday at around midnight (usually 1000 ptas plus drinks). It's like someone's apartment inside and stays open until 2 or 3 am.

Harlem Jazz Club (Map 4; Carrer de la Comtessa de Sobradiel 8) is a stalwart stop on the Barcelona jazz circuit, although it sometimes gets in other acts too, including some rock and Latin.

Jamboree (Map 4; Plaça Reial 17) offers varied jazz and funk most nights. Entry

costs up to 2000 ptas (which generally includes a drink).

Sidecar (Map 4; Carrer de Heures 4-6), just off Plaça Reial, presents pop and rock bands of various denominations several nights a week, usually starting about 11 pm and winding up about 3 am. Entry ranges up to 1000 ptas.

La Ribera *El Foro (Map 3; Carrer de la Princesa 53)* has jazz, tango and other music sessions from Wednesday through to the weekends, usually kicking off at 11 pm.

Poble Sec *Club Apolo (Map 3; Carrer Nou de la Rambla 113)* is the place for world music – chiefly African, Latin and Spanish – several nights a week around 10.30 pm (2000 ptas for big-name bands), followed by live salsa or (on Friday and Saturday) a disco.

Western Gràcia/Avinguda Diagonal
La Boîte (Map 2; Avinguda Diagonal 477) offers jazz or blues, with the occasional jam session several nights a week at midnight (1200 to 2500 ptas).

La Cova del Drac (Map 1; ☎ 93 200 70 32, Carrer de Vallmajor 33) is a good spot for jazz sessions most nights of the week. Entry is free but you must swallow at least one slightly overpriced drink, which can be as much as 1600 ptas. A taxi is the easiest way here. It's closed on Monday.

Clubs & Discos
Barcelona's discos come alive from about 2 or 3 am until 5 or 6 am, and are best on Friday and Saturday nights. Some have live bands, often starting about midnight, to fill the place before the real action begins. Cover charges range from nothing to as much as 3000 ptas. It depends partly on how busy the place is and whether the bouncers like your look. If you go early, you'll often pay less. Drinks are expensive – anything up to 800 ptas for a beer.

Barri Gòtic *Jamboree (see under Live Music earlier)* becomes a crowded dance scene from around 1.30 am, after the live stuff finishes. It has two spaces – one for Latin rhythms, one for rock – until 5 am or so. Entry is free, up to 1500 ptas.

Karma (Map 4; Plaça Reial 10) is a young, student-type basement place with good music open from around 11 pm to 4 am. You usually pay 1000 ptas, which covers a drink.

El Raval *Moog (Map 4; Carrer de l'Arc del Teatre 3)* is a fun disco – upstairs Latin and dance hits from as far back as the 1970s; downstairs strobe lights and techno. It's open until about 7 am on weekends and entry is 1000 ptas (as are the mixed drinks!).

La Ribera *Luz de Luna (Map 3; Carrer del Comerç 21)* is a sassy salsa place where early in the week you can sip on piña coladas and other South American mixes and dance on the luridly decorated dance floor. Midweek, it fills up from around 2 am but closes by about 4 am. Friday and Saturday you can shake and wiggle until 6 am. Cocktails cost around 600 ptas.

Woman Caballero (Map 3) is the latest reincarnation of a Barcelona classic, the former Fellini in the basement of Estació de França. The action starts at 2 am on weekends and holidays and DJs from all over the country and abroad spin everything from techno to 'minifunk' and 'industrial minimalism'. Entry is 2000 ptas.

Port Vell A bevy of bars and discos open in the Maremàgnum complex (Map 1) until the wee hours. In July and August, most of the action is here and spreads along the waterfront. One of the places to watch for is *Boîte Nayandei*.

L'Eixample *Nick Havanna (Map 2; Carrer del Rosselló 208)* is a big 1980s 'designer bar' with a video bank at one end of the dance space and glass-backed urinals flushed by veritable cascades of water. It's open nightly from 11 pm to 4 or 5 am, often with bands or salsa/merengue classes at midnight. Entry is free but drink prices are cheeky.

Satanassa (Map 3; Carrer d'Aribau 27) is an 'antidesign' haunt of androgynous people

(with a notable gay leaning), with gaudy erotic murals; open from about 11 pm to 4 or 5 am. It's free.

Velvet (Map 2; Carrer de Balmes 161) is a smallish designer bar and disco inspired by the film *Blue Velvet*, with 1960s music. It is busy with a fairly straight crowd. Entry is free.

Zoo Club (Map 2; Carrer de Balmes 51) is relatively new on the Barcelona scene. The standard fare is house but it's an accessible club that attracts a heterodox clientele. It opens at 11.30 pm and keeps hopping until 5 am from Wednesday to Saturday nights. Entry is generally 2000 ptas.

Around Avinguda Diagonal *Otto Zutz (Map 2; Carrer de Lincoln 15)*, west of Via Augusta, is for beautiful people (bouncers will decide how beautiful you are) and those who favour wearing black. A beer costs 800 ptas.

La Boîte (see under Live Music) becomes a club after the nightly jazz or blues session.

The Music Box (Map 1; Avinguda Diagonal 618) is farther west, and is a favourite with the Carrer de Marià Cubí bar crowd. This thumping disco hits its straps from about 2 to 5 am (early in the week is not so hot).

Gràcia *KGB (Map 1; Carrer de Ca l'Alegre de Dalt 55)* maintains a hard-rock warehouse-type scene and stays open until 8 am for tireless all-nighters.

Tibidabo *Mirablau (Map 1; Plaça del Doctor Andreu)* is a bar with great views and a small disco floor that keeps going until about 5 am.

El Clot *Savannah (Map 1; Carrer de la Muntanya 16)* has good dance music nightly until midnight on Sunday, to 3 am Tuesday to Thursday and to 5 am Friday and Saturday.

Gay & Lesbian Venues

Three good gay bars, virtually one on top of the other, are *Punto BCN (Map 3; Carrer de Muntaner 63-65)*, *Dietrich (Map 3; Carrer* del Consell de Cent 255) and **Este Bar** (Map 3; Carrer del Consell de Cent 257), around the corner. Punto BCN is a relaxed place to meet a 30-something plus crowd, while Este Bar is perhaps a tad more self-conscious. Dietrich is more of a theatre cafe, often with very camp entertainment. It is a big, friendly space and open until about 3 am. This local concentration of bars (and some clubs – see later) has earned this part of town the sobriquet of 'Gaixample'.

Café de la Calle (Map 2; Carrer de Vic 11) is a cosy meeting place for lesbians and gay men. **Antinous** (Map 4; Carrer Josep Anselm Clavé 6) is a gay bookshop-cum-cafe.

A good lesbian bar is **Bahía** (Map 2; Carrer de Seneca 12), open until about 2.30 am. Another nearby is **Member's** (Map 2; ☎ 93 237 12 04, Carrer de Seneca 3). Both are open to all comers. More exclusively lesbian is **La Rosa** (Map 1; ☎ 93 414 61 66, Passatge de Brusi 39).

Clubs & Discos The two top gay discos are **Metro** (Map 3; Carrer de Sepúlveda 185) near Plaça de la Universitat, and **Martin's** (Map 2; Passeig de Gràcia 130). Metro attracts some lesbians and heteros as well as gay men; it's packed for its regular Monday-night cabarets. Martin's is gay men only. Both are open from midnight to 5 am and have 'dark rooms'.

Popular with a young, cruisy gay crowd is **Arena** (Map 3; Carrer de Balmes 32). It has a dark room, opens at midnight and closes around 5 am. Around the corner, **Arena Clasic** (Map 3; Carrer de la Diputació 233) is a little more sedate. **Arena VIP** (Map 3; Gran Via de les Corts Catalanes 593) is a more mixed mainstream place with a gay flavour. It opens at midnight and you will probably leave about dawn.

Classical Music & Opera

Guía del Ocio has ample listings, but the monthly Informatiu Musical leaflet has the best coverage of classical music (as well as other genres). You can pick it up at tourist offices and the Palau de la Virreina arts information office (Map 4; ☎ 93 301 77 75) at La Rambla de Sant Josep 99, which also

sells tickets for many events. Recitals take place all over the city and beyond, in theatres, museums, monasteries and so on.

Amid much pomp and circumstance Barcelona's great opera house, **Gran Teatre del Liceu** (Map 4; ☎ 93 485 99 13, La Rambla 51-59), reopened in September 1999, more than five years after being destroyed by fire. Apart from opera, you can see world-class dance companies strut their stuff, or attend classical music concerts and recitals. Tickets can cost anything from 500 to 1000 ptas for the cheapest seats, and up to 11,000 ptas for the best spot for a night at the opera. You will need to book well in advance for the big shows. You can do so through ServiCaixa on ☎ 902-33 22 11. Take a peek at the Liceu's Web site at www.liceubarcelona.com.

The chief venue for classical and choral music is **Palau de la Música Catalana** (Map 4; ☎ 93 295 72 00, Carrer de Sant Pere més alt 11) in La Ribera, which has a busy and wide-ranging program. You could easily find yourself paying from 5000 to 15,000 ptas for prestigious international performances.

In the late 1990s, Barcelona's impressive new home for serious music lovers, **L'Auditori** (Map 1; ☎ 93 247 93 00, Carrer de Lepant 50), swung into action. It puts on plenty of orchestral, chamber, religious and other musical events throughout the year.

The easiest way to get hold of tickets for most of the above venues and other theatres throughout the city is through the Caixa de Catalunya's Tel-Entrada service on ☎ 902-10 12 12, or on the Internet at www.telentrada.com. There's also a ticket office (venta de localidades) on the ground floor of Le Corte Inglés on Plaça de Catalunya (Map 3) and another at the FNAC store on the same square.

To get half-price on some tickets, you can buy them personally at the Caixa de Catalunya desk in the tourist office at Plaça de Catalunya. To qualify you must purchase the tickets in person no more than three hours before the start of the show you wish to see. The system is known as Tiquet-3. Shows for which you can get such tickets are marked with an asterisk in the Guía del Ocio.

Cinemas

Foreign films, shown with subtitles and original soundtrack rather than dubbed, are marked 'v.o.' *(versión original)* in movie listings. Cinemas to check for these (all on Map 2 except where indicated) include:

Alexis (☎ 93 215 05 06) Rambla de Catalunya 90

Arkadín (☎ 93 405 22 22) Travessera de Gràcia 103

Casablanca (☎ 93 218 43 45) Passeig de Gràcia 115

Icària-Yelmo (Map 1; ☎ 93 221 75 85) Carrer de Salvador Espriu 61

Renoir-Les Corts (Map 1; ☎ 93 490 55 10) Carrer de Eugeni d'Ors 1

Verdi (☎ 93 237 05 16) Carrer de Verdi 32

The *Filmoteca* (*Map 2;* ☎ *93 410 75 70, Avinguda de Sarrià 3*) specialises more in film seasons that concentrate on particular directors, styles and eras of film.

A ticket usually costs 600 to 750 ptas but most cinemas have a weekly *día del espectador* (viewer's day; often Monday or Wednesday) when they charge 400 to 600 ptas.

Theatre

Theatre is nearly all in Catalan or Spanish (*Guía del Ocio* specifies which). For all that's happening in theatre, head for the information office in Palau de la Virreina. Look for the many leaflets and the monthly listings guide, *Teatre BCN.*.

Teatre Lliure (*Map 2;* ☎ *93 218 92 51, Carrer de Montseny 47*) in Gràcia is dedicated to theatre in Catalan.

Artenbrut (*Map 2;* ☎ *93 457 97 05, Carrer del Perill 9-11*) concentrates more on new and rising directors. Performances are usually in Catalan and occasionally in Castilian. *Teatre Malic* (*Map 3;* ☎ *93 310 70 35, Carrer de la Fusina 3*) is a relatively small spot that offers a packed program including music, alternative theatre and a mix of better-known local talent and emerging genius.

Teatre Tantarantana (*Map 3;* ☎ *93 285 79 00, Carrer de les Flors 22*), apart from staging all sorts of contemporary theatre, also puts on kids' shows, including pantomimes, puppet shows and the like. These shows start at 6 pm.

Originally destined to become *the* home of Catalan theatre, Ricard Bofill's ultra-neoclassical *Teatre Nacional de Catalunya* (*Map 1;* ☎ *93 306 57 06, Plaça de les Arts 1*) opened its doors in 1997. So far it has put on a mixed bag of not always exciting theatre, but it is worth keeping an eye on the program.

Teatre Victòria (☎ *93 443 29 29, Avinguda del Paral.lel 67-69*) often stages ballet and contemporary dance but otherwise is used by well-known companies such as Tricicle. This trio of comic mimes has been doing the rounds with its version of 'intelligent humour' for 20 years. The good thing about these guys is that anyone can enjoy the fun because language is not an issue.

Dance

Sardana The *sardana,* Catalunya's national dance, is danced every week – except sometimes in August – on Plaça de la Seu (Map 4) in front of the cathedral at 6.30 pm Saturday and noon Sunday. These are not shows for tourists but feature ordinary Catalans doing something they enjoy. The dancers join hands to form ever-widening circles, placing their bags or coats in the centre. The dance is intricate but, in true Catalan style, hardly flamboyant. The steps and the accompanying brass and reed music are rather sedate, at times jolly, at times melancholy, rising to occasional crescendos, then quietening down again. It's a bit of an acquired taste.

Flamenco Although quite a few important flamenco artists grew up in the *gitano* barrios of Barcelona, seeing good performances of this essentially Andalucian dance and music here is surprisingly difficult. A few tacky *tablaos* (tourist-oriented flamenco performances) are scattered about. If this is the only way you can see it, perhaps it's better than nothing. *El Tablao de Carmen* (☎ *93 325 68 95, Carrer dels Arcs 9*) is in the Poble Espanyol (Map 1), while the *Cordobés* (*Map 4;* ☎ *93 317 66 53*) is at La Rambla 35. Book ahead.

SPECTATOR SPORTS
Football
Barcelona Football Club has not only one of Europe's best teams, Barça, but also one of its best stadiums, the 120,000 capacity Camp Nou (Map 1). Games are quite an occasion as long as the opposition is good enough to fire up the home team and the crowd. Check the daily press for upcoming games. Tickets, available at the stadium and through some banks, cost from around 3000 to 8000 ptas – the cheapest are in the one small standing section, a long, long way above the pitch. For more information, call ☎ 93 496 36 00. The city's other club, Espanyol, based at the Estadi Olímpic on Montjuïc (Map 1), traditionally plays a quiet second fiddle (in the top division) to Barça, although lately the players have been improving their game. A local derby, or better still a match against arch-rivals, Real Madrid, is a guarantee that sparks will fly, although getting tickets can be difficult.

Bullfights
Death in the Afternoon is not a favourite Catalan theme but there are some fights on summer Sunday afternoons at the Plaça de Braus Monumental (Map 1), on the corner of Gran Via de les Corts Catalanes and Carrer de la Marina. The 'fun' usually starts at 6 pm. Tickets are available at the arena 10.30 am to 2 pm and 6 to 7 pm Wednesday to Saturday, and from 10 am Sunday, or by calling ☎ 902-33 22 11. Prices range from 2500 to 12,000 ptas.

SHOPPING
Barcelona's obsession with style is, needless to say, reflected in its shops. There are enough chic (and expensive) boutiques and trendy shops to keep the fashion-conscious happy (or worried) for weeks.

Most of the mainstream stores can be found on a shopping 'axis' that looks something like the hands of a clock set at 10 to six. From the waterfront it leads up La Rambla through Plaça de Catalunya and on up Passeig de Gràcia. At Avinguda Diagonal you turn left. From here as far as Plaça de la Reina Maria Cristina (especially the final stretch from Plaça de Francesc Macià) the Diagonal is jammed with places where you can empty your bank account. The T1 Tombbus service has been laid on for the ardent shopper.

The best shopping areas in central Barcelona are Passeig de Gràcia and the streets to its south-west (including the Bulevard Rosa arcade, just north of Carrer d'Aragó; Map 2), and Barri Gòtic streets such as Carrer de la Portaferrissa, Carrer de la Boqueria, Carrer del Call, Carrer de Ferran, and around Plaça de Sant Josep Oriol (all of these are on Map 4).

Department store bargain-hunters should note that the winter sales officially start on or around 10 January and their summer equivalents on or around 5 July.

Art Galleries
Along Carrer de Montcada (Map 4) are several galleries, the biggest being Galeria Maeght at No 25. You'll also find half a dozen small galleries and designer stores on Carrer del Doctor Dou, Carrer d'Elisabets and Carrer dels Àngels (Map 4).

The classiest concentration of galleries – about a dozen of them – is on the short stretch of Carrer del Consell de Cent between Rambla de Catalunya and Carrer de Balmes (Map 3).

Clothing & Fabrics
If you are after international fashion, Avinguda Diagonal is the place to look. Calvin Klein (Map 2) is at No 484, Giorgio Armani (Map 2) at Nos 490 and 620, Gianni Versace (Map 1) at No 606 and Gucci (Map 2) at No 415. Max Mara fans will want to head for Passeig de Gràcia 23 (Map 2).

Loewe (Map 2), at Avinguda Diagonal 570, is one of Spain's leading and oldest fashion stores, founded in 1846. There's another branch in the modernista Casa Lleo Morera (Map 2) on Passeig de Gràcia.

Zara is another well-known local name for women's fashion. It is a chain and you'll find several across town, including branches in l'Illa del Diagonal shopping complex (Map 1) and Passeig de Gràcia 16 (Map 2).

Crafts

If you want to take a look at high-quality Catalan crafts *(artesania)* to get some inspiration for future shopping expeditions, pop into the Centre Català d'Artesania (Map 2; ☎ 93 467 46 60) at Passeig de Gràcia 55.

Design

Vinçon (Map 2), Passeig de Gràcia 96, has the slickest designs in furniture and household goods, both local and imported.

Markets

The large Els Encants Vells (The Old Charms; Map 1) flea market (also known as the Fira de Bellcaire) is held every Monday, Wednesday, Friday and Saturday from 8 am to 7 pm (8 pm in summer) next to Plaça de les Glòries Catalanes.

In the Barri Gòtic, there's a crafts market in Plaça de Sant Josep Oriol (Map 4) on Thursday and Friday, an antiques market in Plaça Nova on Thursday (Map 4), and a coin and stamp collectors' market in Plaça Reial on Sunday morning (Map 4). On the western edge of El Raval, the Mercat de Sant Antoni (Map 3) dedicates Sunday morning to old maps, stamps, books and cards.

Music

One of the biggest record stores is Planet Music (Map 2), with more than 50,000 CDs, at Carrer de Mallorca 214. It has several other branches around town.

Several small shops specialising in indie and other niche music can be found on or around Carrer de les Sitges and especially on Carrer dels Tallers (El Raval), which boasts a dozen music stores.

Shoes

There's a gaggle of relatively economical shoe shops on Avinguda del Portal de l'Àngel, off Plaça de Catalunya (Maps 3 & 4).

Camper (Map 2), Carrer de València 249, something of a classic shoe merchant in Spain, has a good range.

GETTING THERE & AWAY

For some agencies offering cheap air fares and youth and student train and bus tickets,

see the Travel Agencies section earlier in this chapter.

Air

The airport (☎ 93 298 38 38) is 14km southwest of the centre at El Prat de Llobregat. Barcelona is a big international and domestic destination, with direct flights from North America as well as many European cities.

Tickets can be bought at almost any travel agency. Iberia (Map 2; ☎ 902-40 05 00) is at Passeig de Gràcia 30; Spanair (24 hours ☎ 902-13 14 15) and Air Europa (☎ 902-40 15 01) are at the airport. Other airline numbers include Alitalia (☎ 902-10 03 23), Delta Airlines (☎ 93 412 43 33), easyJet (☎ 902-29 99 92), KLM (☎ 93 379 54 58), Lufthansa (☎ 93 487 03 52) and TWA (☎ 93 215 84 86).

For more information on flights and air fares, see the Air sections in the Getting There & Away and Getting Around chapters.

Bus

The main intercity bus station *(estació d'autobusos)* is the modern Estació del Nord at Carrer d'Alí Bei 80, 1.5km northeast of La Rambla and 1½ blocks from the Arc de Triomf metro (Map 1). Its information desk (☎ 93 265 65 08) is open 7 am to 9 pm daily.

A few services – most importantly some international buses and the few buses to Montserrat – use Estació d'Autobusos de Sants beside Estació Sants train station (Map 1).

International The main international services are run by Eurolines/Julià Via (☎ 93 490 40 00) from Estació d'Autobusos de Sants, and by Eurolines/Linebús (both ☎ 93 265 07 00) from Estació del Nord.

Three to five weekly departures head for London (24 to 26 hours, 14,075 ptas). One leaves most days for Paris (15 hours, 11,975 ptas). Eurolines/Julià Via also has services at least three times weekly to Amsterdam, Brussels, Florence, Geneva, Montpellier, Nice, Perpignan, Rome, Toulouse, Venice and Zürich, and twice a week to several cities in Morocco.

Domestic You can ride buses to most large Spanish cities. A plethora of companies operate to different parts of the country, although many come under the umbrella of Enatcar. For schedule information call ☎ 93 245 88 56.

Departures from Estació del Nord include the following, with journey time and fare (where frequencies vary, the lowest figure is usually for Sunday):

departure	daily	hours	cost
Almería	2	12¾ to 13½	7120 ptas
Granada	3	13 to 14¼	7915 ptas
Madrid	11 to 18	7 to 8	3400 ptas
Salamanca	3	11½	6415 ptas
Sevilla	1 or 2	16	9135 ptas
Valencia	5 to 10	4½	2900 ptas
Zaragoza	11	4½	1655 ptas

For buses to other places in Catalunya, see the relevant sections in the Catalunya chapter.

Train

The main international and domestic station is Estació Sants, on Plaça dels Països Catalans, 2.5km west of La Rambla (Map 1).

Only a handful of services, including one to Madrid, now use Estació de França, on Avinguda del Marquès de l'Argentera, 1km east of La Rambla (Map 3).

Other useful stations for long-distance and regional trains are Catalunya on Plaça de Catalunya (Map 3), and Passeig de Gràcia, on the corner of Passeig de Gràcia and Carrer d'Aragó (Map 2), 10 minutes' walk north of Plaça de Catalunya.

Information It's advisable to book at least a day or two ahead for most long-distance trains, domestic or international. There's a Renfe information and booking office in Passeig de Gràcia station, open 7 am to 10 pm daily (9 pm Sunday). You'll find some lockers on Via (Platform) 2.

At Estació Sants, the Informació Largo Recorrido windows provides information on all trains except *cercanías* (suburban trains). The station has a *consigna* (left-luggage office), which is open 5.30 am to 11 pm (400 or 600 ptas for 24 hours), and a

tourist office, a telephone and fax office, a hotel reservations office, currency exchange booths (open 8 am to 9.30 pm daily), and ATMs.

Estació de França has a train information office and consigna (open 6 am to 11 pm daily).

International For details on getting to Barcelona by rail from London and Paris, see the Getting There & Away chapter.

Direct overnight trains connect Barcelona with Zürich (13 hours) and Milan (12¾ hours) at least three days a week. From those two cities you can then make further connections to major destinations elsewhere in Italy and into Germany.

A direct Talgo service also connects Montpellier with Barcelona (4½ hours, 245FF or 6400 ptas in 2nd class). A couple of other slower services (with change of train at Portbou) also make this run. All stop in Perpignan.

From Estació Sants, eight to 10 trains a day run to Cerbère (2½ hours) and four to five to Latour-de-Carol (3½ hours). From these stations, there are several onward connections to Montpellier and Toulouse respectively.

Domestic There are trains to most large Spanish cities, with the usual huge range of train types and fares. Most services depart from Estació Sants (a handful stop at Estació de França and/or Passeig de Gràcia). For sample fares, see the Getting Around chapter.

Car & Motorcycle

Autopistas (tollways) head out of Barcelona in most directions, including the A-19 to the southern Costa Brava; the A-16 to Sitges; the A-18 to Manresa (with a turn-off for Montserrat); and the A-7 north to Girona, Figueres and France, and south to Tarragona and Valencia (turn off along the A-2 for Lleida, Zaragoza and Madrid). All these have tolls (eg, around 1500 ptas to La Jonquera near the French border); the toll-free alternatives, such as the N-II north to Girona, Figueres and France, and west to Lleida and beyond, or the N-340 to Tarragona, tend to be busy and slow.

Rental If you haven't organised a rental car from abroad, local firms such as Julià Car, Ronicar and Vanguard are generally cheaper than the big international names. From these companies, a typical small car like a Ford Ka or Fiat Punto should cost from around 2800 ptas per day plus 25 ptas per kilometre, plus IVA. For unlimited kilometres, rental costs are around 18,000 ptas for three days or 35,000 ptas a week, plus IVA. You pay insurance on top, which can come to around 1500 ptas a day. Special low weekend rates (ie, from Friday lunchtime or afternoon to Monday morning) are worth looking into. Rental firms (several have branches scattered about town) include:

Avis (Map 2; ☎ 902-13 55 31, ☎ 93 237 56 80) Carrer de Córsega 293-295, l'Eixample
Europcar (Map 2; ☎ 902-10 50 30) Gran Via de les Corts Catalanes 680
Hertz (Map 2; ☎ 902-40 24 05, ☎ 93 270 03 30) Carrer d'Aragó 382-384, l'Eixample
Julià Car (Map 3; ☎ 93 402 69 00) Ronda de la Universitat 5, l'Eixample
National/Atesa (Map 3; ☎ 902-10 01 01, ☎ 93 323 07 01) Carrer de Muntaner 45, l'Eixample
Ronicar (Map 1; ☎ 989-06 34 73) Carrer d'Europa 34-36, Les Corts
Vanguard (Map 2; ☎ 93 439 38 80) Carrer de Londres 31, l'Eixample

Avis, Europcar, Hertz and several other big companies also have desks at the airport, Estació Sants train station and Estació Nord bus terminus.

Vanguard also rents out motorcycles. If you want something decent for touring outside Barcelona, you'll be looking at around 12,000 ptas a day (plus 16% IVA).

Boat
Balearic Islands Passenger and vehicular ferries to the Balearic Islands, operated by Trasmediterránea, dock at Moll de Barcelona wharf in Port Vell (Map 1). Information and tickets are available from Trasmediterránea (☎ 902-45 46 45) or from travel agencies. Buquebús (☎ 902-41 42 42) is a high-speed car ferry that does the trip to Palma de Mallorca in 3¼ hours.

For information on schedules and fares, see the introductory Getting There & Away section in the Balearic Islands chapter.

Italy There are departures from Barcelona on Tuesday, Thursday (both at 10 pm) and Sunday (2 am). Going the other way, departures are on Monday (10 pm), Wednesday and Friday (both at 9 pm). An airline-style seat costs from L113,000 one way in the low season to L167,000 in the high season. A car costs anywhere from L161,000 to L256,000 one way, depending on the size of the vehicle and time of year. The trip lasts about 17 hours.

In Genoa, Grimaldi (☎ 010 58 93 31, fax 010 550 92 25) is at Via Fieschi 17/17a. The ferry terminal is at Via Milano (Ponte Assereto). You can book direct via phone, through a travel agency, at the docks (if there is space) or online at www.grimaldi.it. In Barcelona, where you can book through any travel agency, the boat docks at Moll de San Beltran (Map 1).

GETTING AROUND
The metro is the easiest way of getting around and reaches most places you're likely to visit (although not the airport). For some trips you need buses or FGC suburban trains. The main tourist office on Plaça de Catalunya gives out the comprehensive *Guia d'Autobusos Urbans de Barcelona*, with a metro map and all bus routes. For public transport information, you can call ☎ 010 or ☎ 93 412 00 00 (☎ 93 205 15 15 for FGC trains only). For information on disabled facilities, call ☎ 93 486 07 52.

Targetas
Targetas are multiple-trip transport tickets and offer worthwhile savings. They are sold at most city-centre metro stations. Targeta T-10 (825 ptas) gives you 10 rides on the metro, buses and FGC trains. Each ride is valid for an hour and permits you to make changes between metro and FGC lines. The Targeta T-10 (1325 ptas) is similar but gives you 75 minutes for each ride and allows you to transfer between metro, FGC and bus. Targeta T-DIA

(625 ptas) gives unlimited metro, bus, FGC, Renfe and night bus travel in one day.

A plethora of other options exist, including monthly passes for unlimited use of all public transport at 5550 ptas. For this you need to get a Targetren ID card, available at the Centres d'Atenció al Client. The Targeta T-50/30 (for 50 trips within 30 days; 3500 ptas) and discounted tickets/passes for seniors and students are further possibilities.

If you plan to move around a lot over a short period with buses, metro and FGC trains, the three- and five-day Abonament tickets are good value at 1600/2400 ptas.

If you take the Aerobús from the airport, you can get an all-in ticket for the bus and unlimited use of Barcelona's buses and metro for three days (2000 ptas) or five days (2500 ptas).

Fines

The fine for being caught without a ticket on public transport is 5000 ptas.

To/From the Airport

Rodalies trains run from the airport to Estació Sants (Map 1) and Catalunya station on Plaça de Catalunya (Map 3) every 30 minutes from 6.13 am to 10.41 pm daily. It takes 16 minutes to Sants and 21 minutes to Catalunya (355 ptas to either place). Departures from Sants to the airport are from 5.43 am to 10.13 pm; from Catalunya they're five minutes earlier.

The A1 Aerobús service runs from the airport to Plaça de Catalunya via Estació Sants every 15 minutes from 6 am to midnight weekdays (from 6.30 am on weekends and holidays). Departures from Plaça de Catalunya are from 5.30 am to 11.15 pm weekdays (6 am to 11.20 pm on weekends and holidays). The trip takes about 40 minutes – depending on traffic – and costs 500 ptas.

Cheaper suburban buses (Buses EA and its night version, the EN) leave every 80 minutes for Plaça d'Espanya. The trip takes about an hour and costs 150 ptas.

A taxi to/from the centre, a half-hour ride, is about 2500 ptas.

Bus

Buses run along most city routes every few minutes from 5 or 6 am to 10 or 11 pm. Many routes pass through Plaça de Catalunya and/or Plaça de la Universitat (both on Map 3). After 11 pm, a reduced network of yellow *nitbusos* (night buses) runs until 3 or 5 am. All nitbus routes pass through Plaça de Catalunya and most run every 30 to 45 minutes. A single fare on any bus costs 150 ptas.

Bus Turístic This bus service covers two circuits (24 stops) linking virtually all the major tourist sights. Tourist offices, TMB offices and many hotels have leaflets explaining the system. Tickets, available on the bus, are 2000 ptas for one day of unlimited rides, or 2500 ptas for two consecutive days. Frequency of buses varies from 10 to 30 minutes, depending on the season, from 9 am to 7.45 pm.

Tickets entitle you to discounts of up to 300 ptas on entry fees to more than 20 attractions, the tramvia blau (Barcelona's last surviving tram), funiculars and cable cars, as well as shopping discounts and a meal at KFC and Pizza Hut (oh great!). The discounts don't have to be used on the day(s) you use the bus.

Tombbus The T1 Tombbus route has been thought out for shoppers and runs regularly from Plaça de Catalunya up to Avinguda Diagonal, along which it proceeds west to Plaça de Pius XII (Map 1), where it turns around. On the way you pass such landmarks as El Corte Inglés (several of them), Bulevard Rosa, FNAC and Marks & Spencer. Tickets are 180 ptas.

Train

FGC Suburban Trains Suburban trains, run by the Ferrocarrils de la Generalitat de Catalunya, include a couple of useful city lines. One heads north from Plaça de Catalunya. A branch of it will get you to Tibidabo and another within spitting distance of the Monestir de Pedralbes.

The other FGC train line heads to Manresa from Plaça d'Espanya and is less likely to be of use (except for the trip to Montserrat).

These trains run 5 am to 11 or 11.30 pm Sunday to Thursday, and 5 am to 2 am Friday and Saturday. Rides within the city are 150 ptas.

Rodalies/Cercanías These Renfe-run local trains serve towns around Barcelona, as well as the airport.

Metro

The metro has five lines, numbered and colour-coded, and is easy to use. A single ride is 150 ptas and tickets are available from machines and staffed booths at most stations. At interchange stations, you just need to work out which line and direction you want. The metro runs from 5 am to 11 pm Monday to Thursday; 5 am to 2 am Friday, Saturday and the day before public holidays; 6 am to midnight Sunday; 6 am to 11 pm on other holidays; and 6 am to 2 am on holidays immediately preceding another holiday. Line 2 has access for the disabled and some stations on other lines have lifts.

Car & Motorcycle

An effective one-way system makes traffic flow fairly smoothly, but you'll often find yourself flowing the way you don't want to go, unless you happen to have an adept navigator and have a map that shows one-way streets. Parking can also be tricky and expensive if you choose a parking garage. It's better to leave your car alone while you're here and to use Barcelona's public transport.

Taxi

Taxis charge 300 ptas flag fall plus meter charges. These work out to about 105 ptas per kilometre (30 ptas more from 10 pm to 6 am and all day Saturday, Sunday and holidays). A further 300 ptas is added for all trips to/from the airport, and 125 ptas for luggage bigger than 55x35x35cm. The trip from Estació Sants to Plaça de Catalunya, about 3km, is about 700 ptas. You can call a taxi on ☎ 93 225 00 00, ☎ 93 330 03 00, ☎ 93 266 39 39 or ☎ 93 490 22 22. General information is available on ☎ 010.

Radio Taxi Móvil (☎ 93 358 11 11) has disabled-adapted taxis.

Catalunya (Cataluña)

North, south and west of Barcelona spreads a land of such diversity that, although its farthest-flung corner is no more than 200km (six hours by bus) from Barcelona, you could spend weeks exploring it and still feel you'd barely begun. The Costa Brava, for all its dreary concrete pockets of mass tourism, still has the wild beauty that drew visitors there in the first place. Inland, the Pyrenees rise to mighty 3000m peaks from a series of green and often remote valleys, dotted with villages that retain a palpable air of the Middle Ages. These mountains provide some magnificent walking and good skiing.

Excitement runs thinner in the flat far west and south, but there's enough to keep you happily exploring for days, from the wetlands of the Ebro delta to the historic cities of Tarragona and Lleida. Throughout Catalunya (Catalonia in English) the sense of difference from the rest of Spain is intense, not only in the use of the Catalan language (although everyone speaks Castilian too) but in the unusual festivals, the cuisine and constant reminders of the region's unique history. Among the latter, the wealth of superb Romanesque and Gothic buildings speak with greatest eloquence of Catalunya's distinct past. It doesn't take long to understand why so many people here think of themselves as Catalans first and as Spaniards, if at all, a distant second.

Accommodation

Room and camping ground prices in this chapter are for the high season – July and August, plus around January to March in ski resorts – when it's often advisable to ring ahead to ensure a room. Most establishments charge around 10% or 20% less at other times; some more expensive places drop rates by almost half in the low season.

Catalunya has a wide network of *cases de pagès*, the local name for *casas rurales*, which provide economical and good accommodation in country areas.

Highlights

- Exploring the coves and beaches near Palafrugell or Begur
- Cadaqués, a magical Costa Brava village haunted by the memory of Salvador Dalí
- Sunrise or sunset at beautiful Cap de Creus, the easternmost point of mainland Spain
- The Teatre-Museu Dalí in Figueres, a voyage through one of the 20th century's strangest minds
- Riding the *cremallera* narrow-gauge railway up to the Vall de Núria
- Walking in the Parc Nacional d'Aigüestortes i Estany de Sant Maurici
- A visit to the weird, rock-pillar mountain of Montserrat
- A night or two on the town at Sitges, Spain's most outrageous resort

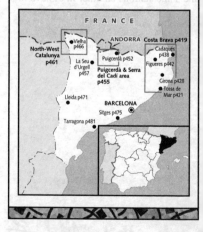

Youth Hostels The 26 member hostels of Catalunya's official youth hostel network, Xarxa d'Albergs de Joventut, share a central booking service (☎ 93 483 83 63, fax 93 483 83 50) at Turisme Juvenil de Catalunya, Carrer de Rocafort 116-122, Barcelona

CATALUNYA (CATALUÑA)

(metro: Rocafort). Nearly all hostels in Catalunya outside Barcelona are Xarxa (and REAJ/HI) hostels.

At Xarxa hostels you need an HI card. With a few minor exceptions, all have the same price structure: if you're under 25 or have an ISIC, B&B is 1675/1900/2250 ptas in low/mid/high season; otherwise it's 2200/2500/2800 ptas respectively. Lunch or dinner costs 850 ptas and sheets 350 ptas. For 300 ptas you can stay in the hostel during the day. There's no cheaper rate for bed without breakfast. High and low seasons vary from hostel to hostel and are specified

where hostels are mentioned in this chapter. The Christmas (25 December) and Semana Santa (in March/April) holidays and all long weekends are high season everywhere.

Getting Around

A good network of Renfe *trens regionals* (regional trains) fans out across Catalunya from Barcelona. There are three types of tren regional: a Catalunya Exprés is the fastest, with limited stops and 1st-class as well as 2nd-class carriages; a Delta stops more often and is 2nd class only; and a plain Regional, also 2nd class only, stops

Catalan Cuisine

Catalans love their food, and with good reason, for it nudges Basque cuisine for the title of Spain's best. Its variety and originality stem mainly from Catalunya's geographical diversity, which is the source of fresh, quality seafood, meat, poultry, game, fruit and vegetables. These can come in unusual and delicious combinations: meat with seafood (a genre known as *mar i muntanya*, literally, 'sea and mountain'), poultry with fruit, and fish with nuts. You'll probably eat more truly Catalan food away from Barcelona, where it tends to be expensive.

The essence of Catalan food lies in its sauces for meat and fish. These sauces may not be mentioned on menus as they're so ubiquitous. There are five main types: *sofregit*, of fried onion, tomato and garlic; *samfaina*, sofregit plus red pepper and aubergine or zucchini (courgette); *picada*, based on ground almonds, usually with garlic, parsley, pine or hazel nuts, and sometimes breadcrumbs; *allioli*, garlic pounded with olive oil, often with egg yolk added to make a mayonnaise; and *romesco*, an almond, tomato, olive oil, garlic and vinegar sauce, also used as a salad dressing.

Catalans find it hard to understand why other people put mere butter on bread when *pa amb tomàquet*, bread slices rubbed with tomato, olive oil and garlic, is so easy. They eat it with almost everything and prefer their *entrepans* (bocadillos) this way, too.

And some old standbys you may have come to rely on elsewhere in Spain are here too, only with different names. Try asking locals why a *sandwich mixto* (humble toasted cheese and ham sandwich) is known in Catalunya as a *bikini*. And try asking for a bikini outside Catalunya!

Most main courses are meat or fish with a sauce and potatoes. There are some good stews too. You can wash it all down with good Catalan wine, including *cava*, the inexpensive local version of champagne. Here are some typical dishes:

Starters

amanida Catalana – Catalan salad; almost any mix of lettuce, olives, tomatoes, hard-boiled eggs, onion, chicory, celery, green pepper and garlic, with fish, ham or sausage, dressed with mayonnaise or vinaigrette

calçots amb romesco – calçots, a type of long onion, are delicious as a starter with romesco sauce

escalivada – red peppers and aubergines (sometimes with onions and tomatoes) grilled, peeled, sliced and served lukewarm, dressed with olive oil, salt and garlic

esqueixada – salad of shredded salted cod *(bacallà)* with tomato, red pepper, onion, white beans, olives, olive oil and vinegar

Main Dishes

arròs a la cassola or *arròs a la Catalana* – Catalan paella, cooked in an earthenware pot, without saffron

botifarra amb mongetes – pork sausage with fried white beans

cargols – snails; a religion in parts of Catalunya; popular stewed with rabbit *(conill)* and chilli

escudella – a meat, sausage and vegetable stew with the liquid, mixed with noodles or rice, served as a soup, followed by the rest as a main course known as *carn d'olla*

fricandó – a pork and vegetable stew

mandonguilles amb sipia – meatballs with cuttlefish, a subtly flavoured *mar i muntanya* combination

pollastre amb escamerlans – chicken with shrimps, another amphibious event

sarsuela (zarzuela) – a Barcelona invention of mixed seafood cooked in sofregit with various seasonings

Catalan Cuisine

Desserts

crema Catalana – a cream custard with a crisp burnt sugar coating

mel i mató – honey and fresh cream cheese, simple but delicious

music – a serving of dried fruit and nuts with a glass of sweet muscatel wine

Other good things to look out for include *ànec* (duck), *oca* (goose) and *canalons* (Catalan cannelloni). *Fideuas* (noodles) are usually served with tomato and meat/sausage or fish sauces. Wild mushrooms are a Catalan passion – people disappear into the forests in autumn to pick them. There are many, many types; the large succulent *rovellons* are a favourite. Here are more words (with, where they differ, their Spanish equivalents) to help you with Catalan-only menus:

Catalan	Spanish	English
ametller	almendra	almond
anyell	cordero	lamb
bou	carne de vaca	beef
caldereta		a seafood stew
carxofe	alcachofa	artichoke
castanya	castaña	chestnut
ceba	cebolla	onion
costella	chuleta	cutlet
cranc	cangrejo	crab
entrepan	bocadillo	filled bread roll
farcit	relleno	stuffed
formatge	queso	cheese
fregit	frito	fried
fuet		a thin dried pork sausage
gelat	helado	ice cream
llagosta	langosta	lobster
llenties	lentejas	lentils
llet	leche	milk
llonganissa	longaniza	pork sausage
oli	aceite	oil
orxata	horchata	tiger nut drink
ostra		oyster
ous	huevos	eggs
pastis	pastel	cake
pebre	pimienta	pepper
peix	pescado	fish
pernil de la comarca		country-cured ham
pops	pulpo	octopus
rap	rape	monkfish
suquet		seafood stew
torrada	tostada	open toasted sandwich
truita	trucha	trout
truita	tortilla	omelette
xai	cordero	lamb

everywhere. Exprés fares are about 15% higher than the others.

The Portbou, Lleida and Tarragona lines are also served by Renfe long-distance trains, with fares sometimes as much as twice those on trens regionals.

For some places closer to Barcelona, such as Montserrat, Sant Sadurní d'Anoia and Sitges, the best services are often *rodalies,* the Catalan version of *cercanías* (local trains servicing big cities' suburbs and nearby towns). Places off the railways are served by buses, often including direct services from Barcelona. In general there are more buses in summer than winter, and more on weekdays than at the weekend and on holidays. On some routes fares go up by around 15% at the weekend and on holidays. Fares in this chapter are basic weekday fares – check on weekend increases as you go.

Costa Brava

The Costa Brava, stretching from Blanes, 60km north-east of Barcelona, to the French border, ranks with the Costa Blanca and Costa del Sol as one of Spain's three great holiday *costas*. Don't let that put you off. It has its share of awful concrete development, English breakfasts and *Konditoreien,* but as the name 'Rugged Coast' suggests, it also offers some spectacular stretches.

Nestling in the hilly country – green and covered in umbrella pine in the south, barer and browner in the north – are a number of attractive old, country towns. A little farther inland are the bigger towns of Girona (Gerona in Castilian), with a sizable medieval centre, and Figueres (Figueras), famous for its bizarre Teatre-Museu Dalí, the foremost of a series of sites associated with the eccentric surrealist artist Salvador Dalí.

Diving

The ruggedness of the Costa Brava continues under the sea to provide some of the best diving in Spain. Diving centres with certified instructors operate at a dozen or more places. The Illes Medes off L'Estartit are a group of protected islets with probably the most diverse sea life along the Spanish coast.

Other top diving spots include the Illes Formigues, rocky islets off the coast between Palamós and Calella de Palafrugell with waters down to 45m, and Els Ullastres, which has three underwater hills off Llafranc with some sheer walls and depths to 54m.

Getting There & Away

Direct buses from Barcelona go to most towns on and near the Costa Brava. The railway between Barcelona and the coastal border town of Portbou runs inland most of the way, through Girona and Figueres. From Girona and Figueres there are fairly good bus services to the coast.

In summer, you could take an alternative approach to the southern Costa Brava from Barcelona by a combination of rodalia train and boat (see Getting There & Away in the Tossa de Mar section).

The A-7 *autopista* (tollway) and the toll-free N-II highway both run from Barcelona via Girona and Figueres to the French border a few kilometres north of La Jonquera. The A-19 autopista follows the N-II up the coast as far as Blanes. Other roads run up the coast and inland to Girona and Figueres.

TOSSA DE MAR
postcode 17320 • pop 4016

Curving around a boat-speckled bay guarded by a headland crowned with medieval defensive walls and towers, Tossa de Mar is a white village of crooked, narrow streets onto which tourism has tacked a larger, modern extension of straighter, wider ones. In July and August it's hard to reach the water's edge without tripping over oily limbs, but it is heaven compared with its bigger neighbour 12km to the south-east, Lloret de Mar – a real concrete and neon jungle of Piccadilly pubs, *Bierkeller* and soccer chants.

Tossa was one of the first places on the Costa Brava to attract foreign visitors – a small colony of artists and writers gravitated towards here in the 1930s. The painter Marc Chagall dubbed it the 'Blue Paradise'.

CATALUNYA

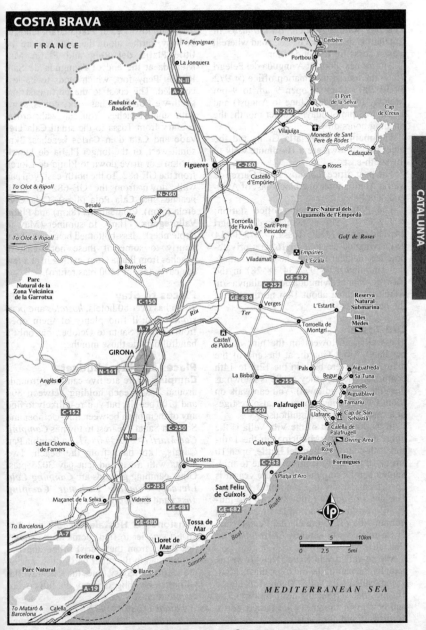

COSTA BRAVA

FRANCE

To Perpignan

To Perpignan

Cerbère

Portbou

La Jonquera

N-II

A-7

Embalse de
Boadella

El Port
de la Selva

Llançà

Cap
de Creus

N-260

Vilajuïga

Monestir de Sant
Pere de Rodes

Cadaqués

Figueres

C-260

Castelló
d'Empúries

Roses

To Olot & Ripoll

N-260

Besalú

Riu Fluvià

Parc Natural dels
Aiguamolls de l'Empordà

To Olot & Ripoll

Torroella
de Fluvià

Sant Pere
Pescador

Golf de Roses

Banyoles

Viladamat

Empúries

L'Escala

Parc
Natural de la
Zona Volcánica
de la Garrotxa

C-150

GE-632

Reserva
Natural
Submarina

GE-634

Verges

Riu Ter

L'Estartit

Illes
Medes

GIRONA

A-7

Castell
de Púbol

C-252

Torroella
de Montgrí

Anglès

N-141

Pals

Aiguafreda

Sa Tuna

La Bisbal

C-255

Begur

Fornells

Aiguablava

C-152

GE-660

Palafrugell

Tamariu

Cap de Sant
Sebastià

Santa Coloma
de Farners

N-II

C-250

Llafranc

Calella de
Palafrugell

Diving Area

Calonge

Palamós

Cap
Roig

Illes
Formigues

Llagostera

C-253

Platja d'Aro

G-253

Sant Feliu
de Guíxols

Route

Maçanet de la Selva

Vidreres

GE-681

GE-682

To Barcelona

A-7

GE-680

Tossa de
Mar

Boat

Lloret de
Mar

Tordera

Summit

Blanes

MEDITERRANEAN SEA

Parc Natural

A-19

0   5   10km

0   2.5   5mi

To Mataró &
Barcelona

Calella

LP

Orientation & Information

The bus station (*estació d'autobusos* in Catalan) is beside the GE-682 road where it leaves Tossa for Lloret de Mar.

Almost next door, at Avinguda del Pelegrí 25, is the tourist information office (☎ 972 34 01 08), which is open 9 am to 9 pm Monday to Saturday (June to August) and 10 am to 1 pm Sunday. In other months the opening hours drop.

The main beach, Platja Gran, and the older part of town are a 10-minute walk to the south-east.

The post office *(correos)* is on Carrer de Maria Auxiliadora, one block east of Avinguda del Pelegrí.

The Policía Nacional (police station; ☎ 972 34 01 35) is at Avinguda del Pelegrí 14. The Centre Mèdic Tossa (☎ 972 34 14 48), Avinguda del Pelegrí 16, is a private-practice medical clinic. The state clinic is the Ambulatori (☎ 972 34 18 28) in the Casa del Mar at Avinguda de Catalunya s/n, which is located about 1km north-west of the old town.

Old Tossa

The walls and towers on the pine-dotted headland, Mont Guardí, at the end of the main beach, were built in the 12th to 14th centuries. The area they girdle is known as the Vila Vella (old town). You can walk on Mont Guardí, where there are also vestiges of a castle, and a far (lighthouse).

In the lower part of the Vila Vella is the interesting Museu Municipal in the 14th- and 15th-century Palau del Batlle, open 10 am to 10 pm daily from mid-June to mid-September. During the rest of the year it is open from 10 am to 1 pm and 3 to 6 pm Tuesday to Sunday (500 ptas). In the museum are mosaics and other finds from a Roman villa off Avinguda del Pelegrí, and Tossa-related art including *El Violinista* by Chagall.

The so-called Vila Nova (New Town) is actually the part of the old town that is north of the walled Vila Vella. Much of its tangle of lanes dates from the 18th century. The real new town stretches a lot farther north, north-west and north-east.

Beaches & Coves

The main town beach, Platja Gran, tends to be busy. Farther along the same bay are the little Platja del Reig and Platja Mar Menuda at the end of Avinguda de Sant Ramon Penyafort, which tends to be less crowded. The coast to the north-east and south-west of Tossa has rocky coves, some with small beaches. You can walk cross-country from Tossa to the small Cala Llevado and Cala d'En Carlos beaches, 3km south-west, or the longer Platja de Llorell (3.5km), or drive down to Platja de Llorell from the GE-682. To the north-east, you can walk down from the GE-682 to small beaches like Cala Pola (4km), Cala Giverola (5km), Cala Salions (8km) and Platja Vallpregona (11km). In summer (May to September), glass-bottomed boats run about hourly to some of these north-eastern beaches from Platja Gran, calling in at a few sea caves (about 1100 ptas return).

Places to Stay

Tossa has over 80 hotels, *hostales* and *pensiones*. You'll find plenty of them open from Semana Santa to October, but only a handful outside those months.

Places to Stay – Budget

Camping There are five camping grounds around Tossa, each holding between 800 and 1700 people, but you're unlikely to find any of them open between mid-October and Semana Santa. Nearest to town is *Camping Can Martí* (☎ 972 34 08 51) on Rambla Pau Casals, 1km back from the beach. Two adults with a car and tent pay 3025 ptas. Other camping grounds are *Camping Cala Llevado, Camping Turismar, Camping Tossa* and *Camping Pola*.

Pensiones & Hostales In July and August it's easier to find rooms in the streets just down from the tourist office and bus station than in the older part of town or on the seafront. In busy times the lone traveller will often be obliged to pay the full cost of double rooms.

Fonda Lluna (☎ 972 34 03 65, Carrer de la Roqueta 20), also called Can Lluna, is good value at 2000/4000 ptas for small singles/doubles with bath, and breakfast included.

Pensión Can Tort (☎ 972 34 11 85, Carrer del Portal 1) has sizable doubles with breakfast for 6000 ptas with bath. **Hostal Tonet** (☎/fax 972 34 02 37, Plaça de l'Església s/n), where doubles with bath cost up to 6000 ptas plus IVA, is open all year.

A dozen or so pensiones and hostales lie scattered about within three blocks of the tourist office. **Hotel Ros** (☎ 972 34 02 11, Avinguda del Pelegrí 27) has good rooms with bath for up to 5500 ptas for a double.

Comparable places include **Hostal Isabel** (☎ 972 34 03 36, Carrer de Sant Vicenç 3); **Hostal Anna** (☎ 972 34 06 44, Carrer de Tomàs Barber s/n); and **Hostal Horta Rosell** (☎ 972 34 04 32, Carrer de Pola 29).

A few blocks towards the old town, **Pensión Carmen** (☎ 972 34 05 26, Carrer de Sant Miquel 8), with signs also saying Pensión Pepi and, for good measure, Pensión Carmen-Pepi, has decent doubles only, with shower, for 4950 ptas. The place is built around a charming courtyard.

A decent beachfront *hostal* is **Hostal Del Mar** (☎ 972 34 00 80, Passeig del Mar 13)

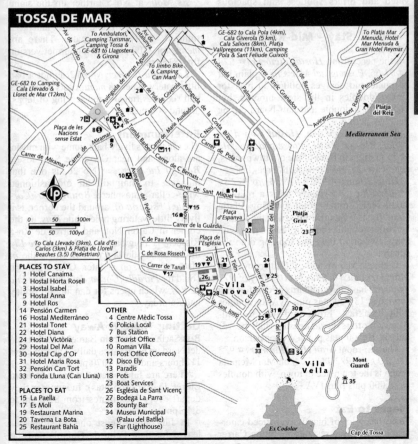

TOSSA DE MAR

CATALUNYA

PLACES TO STAY
1 Hotel Canaima
2 Hostal Horta Rosell
3 Hostal Isabel
5 Hostal Anna
9 Hotel Ros
14 Pensión Carmen
16 Hostal Mediterráneo
21 Hostal Tonet
22 Hotel Diana
24 Hostal Victòria
29 Hostal Del Mar
30 Hostal Cap d'Or
31 Hotel Maria Rosa
32 Pensión Can Tort
33 Fonda Lluna (Can Lluna)

PLACES TO EAT
15 La Paella
17 Es Molí
19 Restaurant Marina
20 Taverna La Bota
25 Restaurant Bahía

OTHER
4 Centre Mèdic Tossa
6 Policia Local
7 Bus Station
8 Tourist Office
10 Roman Villa
11 Post Office (Correos)
12 Disco Ely
13 Paradis
18 Pots
23 Boat Services
26 Església de Sant Vicenç
27 Bodega La Parra
28 Bounty Bar
34 Museu Municipal (Palau del Batlle)
35 Far (Lighthouse)

with rooms for about 4000/5500 ptas. If you can't find a room there, the owners have another place, *Hostal Mediterráneo (☎ 972 34 00 99, Carrer Nou 3),* back in from the beach. The front part of the hostal is a refurbished centuries-old house with exposed timber beams in the ceiling and some charm. Doubles only cost 5500 ptas.

Hotel Maria Rosa (☎ 972 34 02 85, Carrer del Pont Vell 4) is a meticulously well-kept little house where smallish but welcoming rooms cost 5500 ptas.

Hotel Canaima (☎ 972 34 09 95, Avinguda de la Palma 24) has been largely renovated and offers spotless and spacious rooms for up to 3775 ptas per person.

Places to Stay – Mid-Range & Top End

On the beachfront, *Hostal Victòria (☎ 972 34 01 66, Passeig del Mar s/n)* is plain but adequate and charges 3500/4400 ptas for singles/doubles in the slow months, but 11,800 for a double and half-board during the busy period.

The more attractive, *Hostal Cap d'Or (☎/fax 972 34 00 81, Passeig de la Vila Vella 1),* right in front of the old town walls, charges 4725/9450 ptas, with breakfast.

Hotel Diana (☎ 972 34 18 86, fax 972 34 11 03, Plaça d'Espanya 6) is a relaxed, small-scale, older hotel fronting Platja Gran. It has a Gaudí fireplace in the lounge and offers doubles costing 15,100 ptas with sea views or 13,000 ptas looking onto the square.

On Platja Mar Menuda, the 40-room *Hotel Mar Menuda (☎ 972 34 10 00, fax 972 34 00 87)* has high standards of comfort and service at 13,700 ptas plus IVA for doubles with breakfast. From mid-July to mid-August it offers *media pensión* (half-board) only at 10,500 ptas plus IVA per person.

The 166-room *Gran Hotel Reymar (☎ 972 34 00 00, fax 972 34 15 04)* on Mar Menuda beach is the top place in town, with doubles at 28,000 ptas plus IVA.

Places to Eat

Tossa has a lot of bland, overpriced eateries. The al fresco restaurants lining Carrer del Portal are nicely sited and do some good fish and seafood, but are expensive for what you get.

Restaurant Bahía (Passeig de Mar 19) does some of the better food along the Tossa waterfront, with a *menú del día* (daily set meal) for 1925 ptas.

On Carrer de Tarull, beside the church in the old town, *Restaurant Marina* at No 6 offers a fairly good *menú* for 1400 ptas and also does some economical specials such as chicken, chips, salad and beer for 500 ptas. *Taverna La Bota,* with a nice garden, is next door and has a simpler *menú* for 1200 ptas.

Es Molí, at No 5 farther up the same street, serves up classier local cooking, including good prawns and *fideuas,* and has a tranquil, shady garden patio. There are *menús* for 2700 ptas and a gourmet version for 4815 ptas.

La Paella (Carrer Nou 12) is not a bad little eatery, where a *menú* costs 1300 ptas and *raciones* (meal-sized serving of tapas) around 800 ptas.

Entertainment

The old town's lively bars, some with music, are along and near Carrer de Sant Josep. *Bodega La Parra*, at No 26, is one that manages to maintain an old-fashioned wine-cellar atmosphere. *Bounty Bar (Carrer de l'Església 6),* around the corner, is a lively little watering hole while *Pots,* on the corner of Carrer Nou and Carrer de Rosa Rissech, is a big barn of a place. *Disco Ely* off Avinguda de la Costa Brava is the *in* place to carry on at later. Otherwise you could try *Paradis (Carrer del Pou de la Vila 12-14),* which opens for dancing on Friday and Saturday.

Getting There & Away

Bus Sarfa runs to/from Barcelona's Estació del Nord up to 10 times daily. The trip takes 1¼ hours and costs 1070 ptas.

There are fairly frequent buses to/from Lloret de Mar (165 ptas): in summer they depart every 30 minutes from 8.45 am to 8.45 pm.

In July and August one all-stops bus leaves for Sant Feliu de Guíxols daily at

10.40 am, returning at 7 pm (420 ptas). From Sant Feliu there are Sarfa buses to Girona, Palafrugell, Torroella de Montgrí and L'Escala (most several times daily).

Two or three buses daily run direct between Tossa and Girona in July and August; otherwise there's one daily on school days at 7.30 pm (540 ptas). Year round there are more frequent connections to Girona from Lloret de Mar.

Car & Motorcycle From Barcelona, the A-19 autopista, which takes you almost to Blanes, saves a weary trudge on the toll-free N-II. To the north, the 23km stretch of the GE-682 to Sant Feliu de Guíxols is a great drive, winding its way up, down and around picturesque bays. On this road Rose Macaulay, author of *Fabled Shore* (1950), 'met only one mule cart, laden with pine boughs, and two very polite *guardias civiles*'.

Boat In June, July and August two boat services offer a scenic way of reaching Tossa, or of taking an outing from it. Crucetours (☎ 972 37 26 92), Viajes Marítimos (☎ 608 93 64 76) and Dolfi-Jet (☎ 972 37 19 39) run boats several times a day between Blanes, Lloret de Mar and Tossa (one to 1½ hours), with stops at a few in-between points. A few of the services continue to/from Calella, 12km south of Blanes (*not* Calella de Palafrugell farther north), and/or Palamós, north of Tossa, again with intermediate stops (including Sant Feliu de Guíxols). You could catch one of the frequent suburban rodalia trains from Barcelona's Catalunya station to Calella or Blanes, then transfer to the boat. A return boat ticket to Tossa is generally 1950 ptas from Calella or 1350 ptas from Sant Feliu de Guíxols. In many places the boats simply pull up at the beach (in Tossa, at Platja Gran) and tickets are sold at a booth there.

Getting Around
Jimbo Bike (☎ 972 34 30 44), Avinguda de Pau Casals 12, rents out mountain bikes for 3000 ptas, or 500 ptas an hour.

PALAFRUGELL & AROUND
postcode 17200 • pop 17,564

The 21km reach of coast from Sant Feliu de Guíxols to Palamós is unattractively built up all the way, but north of Palamós begins one of the most beautiful stretches of the Costa Brava. The town of Palafrugell, 5km inland, is the main access point for a cluster of attractive beach spots.

East of Palafrugell are Calella de Palafrugell, Llafranc and Tamariu, once fishing villages squeezed into small bays and now three of the Costa Brava's most charming, low-key and low-rise little resorts. Even in July and August they remain relatively laid-back, although accommodation is on the expensive side (Palafrugell itself has some cheaper rooms). Begur, 7km north-east of Palafrugell, is an interesting village with a cluster of less developed beaches nearby.

Palafrugell
Palafrugell, a pleasant enough town, is the main transport, shopping and service hub for the area.

Orientation & Information The C-255 Palamós-Girona road passes through the western side of Palafrugell, a 10-minute walk from the central square, Plaça Nova. The tourist office (☎ 972 30 02 28) is at Carrer del Carrilet 2 beside the C-255. It's open from at least 10 am to 1 pm and 5 to 7 pm Monday to Saturday and until 1 pm Sunday and holidays. In July and August, it's open 9 am to 9 pm Monday to Saturday.

The Sarfa bus station is at Carrer de Torres Jonama 67-69, five minutes' walk from the tourist office.

Museu del Suro The Museu del Suro, dedicated to the important local cork industry, is one block east of Carrer de Pi i Margall at Carrer de la Tarongeta 31. It's open 5 to 9 pm Tuesday to Saturday, and in summer the hours extend to include 10 am to 1 pm Tuesday to Saturday and 10.30 am to 1.30 pm Sunday.

Places to Stay *Fonda L'Estrella* (☎ 972 30 00 05, Carrer de les Quatre Cases 13-17), 1½

CATALUNYA

blocks west of Plaça Nova, is a pleasant, cool, old-fashioned house where singles/doubles with shared bathrooms are 2600/4800 ptas.

Two blocks in the opposite direction from the plaça, *Residència Familiar* (☎ 689-269538, Carrer de Sant Sebastià 29) is ordinary but good and clean with doubles at up to 4600 ptas. The good *Hostal Platja* (☎ 972 30 05 26), across the street at No 34, has a nice courtyard, and rooms with bath for 3200/6000 ptas. It's open all year.

Getting There & Away Sarfa (☎ 972 30 06 23) runs buses to/from Barcelona's Estació del Nord (two hours, 1635 ptas) seven to 13 times daily and to/from Girona (one hour, 550 ptas) up to 15 times daily. Sarfa also has a few daily services north to Begur, Torroella de Montgrí, L'Escala and Figueres (1½ hours), and in July and August only two daily buses to Lloret de Mar and Tossa de Mar (two hours).

Calella de Palafrugell

The southernmost of the three Palafrugell resorts, Calella is also the most spread out. Its low buildings are strung Aegean-style around a bay of rocky points and small beaches, with a few fishing boats still hauled up on the sand. The tourist office (☎ 972 61 44 75), down near the seafront at Carrer de les Voltes 4, is open 10 am to 1 pm and 5 to 8 pm Monday to Saturday and 10 am to 1 pm Sunday and holidays, April to October.

Things to See & Do Apart from plonking on one of the beaches, you can stroll along nice coastal footpaths north-east to Llafranc (20 or 30 minutes), or south to Platja del Golfet beach close to Cap Roig (about 40 minutes). Atop Cap Roig, the **Jardí Botànic de Cap Roig** is a beautiful garden of 1200 Mediterranean species, set around the early 20th-century castle/palace of Nikolai Voevalsky, a tsarist colonel who fled the Russian Revolution. The garden is open 8 am to 8 pm daily in summer and 9 am to 6 pm in winter (300 ptas).

Special Events Calella stages probably the Costa Brava's biggest summer *cantada*

de havaneres sing-song. Havaneres are strangely melancholy songs from the Caribbean that became popular among Costa Brava sailors in the 19th century, when Catalunya maintained busy links with Cuba. Havaneres are traditionally accompanied by the drinking of *cremat,* a rum, coffee, sugar, lemon and cinnamon concoction that you set alight briefly before quaffing. Traditionally, Calella's cantada is held in August.

Places to Stay & Eat *Camping Moby Dick* (☎ 972 61 43 07, Carrer de la Costa Verde 16-28), in the village, has room for 470 people. *La Siesta Camping* (☎ 972 61 51 16) has a shady site by the Palafrugell road 1.25km back from the beach, with space for 2000. Both open from April to September. Moby Dick charges 2355 ptas plus IVA, for two adults, a tent and a car; at La Siesta it's 3525 ptas plus IVA.

Hostería del Plancton (☎ 972 61 50 81, Carrer de Codina 12) has the best-value rooms in any of the three Palafrugell resorts – follow the signs to Església de Sant Pere. Unfortunately it's only open June to September. Good, clean, little rooms, some with balconies and all sharing bathrooms, are 2200 ptas per person.

Tambucho (Plaça de Sant Pere 1), just back a little from the beach, is a relaxed restaurant where you can eat well by candlelight – it serves a reasonable *fondue bourguignon.* Mains cost from 1800 to 2500 ptas. Overlooking the beach is *Les Voltes (Les Voltes 7),* with a pleasant outside dining area beneath the arches from which the restaurant takes its name, offers fairly standard Catalan dishes for similar prices to those at Tambucho.

Getting There & Away Buses from the Sarfa station in Palafrugell run to La Siesta Camping, then Calella, then Llafranc, then back to La Siesta and Palafrugell, a return trip of 30 minutes (145 ptas). They leave every half-hour or so from 7.40 am to 8.30 pm in July and August; the service is progressively reduced to three or four buses a day from November to February.

Llafranc

postcode 17211 • pop 172

Barely 2km north-east of Calella de Pala-frugell and now merging with it along the roads back from the rocky coast between them, Llafranc has a smaller bay but a longer stretch of sand, is a bit more fashionable and lively, and gets more crowded. The tourist office (☎ 972 30 50 08), a kiosk on Carrer de Roger de Llúria just back from the western end of the beach, is open June to September, the same hours as Calella de Palafrugell's office.

Things to See & Do From the **Far de Sant Sebastià** lighthouse and **Ermita de Sant Sebastià** hermitage, up on Cap de Sant Sebastià, the cape to the east of the town, there are tremendous views in both directions along the coast. It's a 40-minute walk up: follow the steps from the harbour and the road up to the right. You can walk on to Tamariu, but check with the tourist office about the most scenic of the several routes available.

Places to Stay & Eat *Camping Kim's* (☎ 972 30 11 56) is in a pine wood on Camí de la Font d'en Xeco, about 750m back from the beach. It's open from April to September and charges 2900 ptas for a site and car parking space.

Residencia Montaña (☎ 972 30 04 04, Carrer de Cesàrea 2), off Plaça del Promontori, is not a bad deal at all. Double rooms cost up to 6300 ptas plus IVA.

Pensió Celimar (☎ 972 30 13 74, Carrer de Carudo 12), also off Plaça del Promontori, is more modern, stays open all year round and has doubles with bath for 6500 ptas plus IVA.

La Pasta (Carrer de Cipsela 1) is popular for its pizzas and salads, which start at around 800 ptas. The waterfront is lined with restaurants, but none are overly inspiring – you're paying for the sea views. Tucked away a block from the waterfront is a more genuine eating experience, *La Sal (Carrer de Perre Pascuet 2)*. Seafood is the name of the game and you can eat well for around 3500 ptas.

Getting There & Away See the Calella de Palafrugell section for information on bus services. The Llafranc bus stop is on Carrer de la Sirena, up the hill on the Calella side of town.

Tamariu

postcode 17212 • pop 89

Three or four kilometres north up the coast from Llafranc as the crow flies, and nearly twice as far by road, Tamariu is smaller and attracts a quieter, more select crowd. Its beach has some of the cleanest waters on Spain's Mediterranean coast. The tourist office (☎ 972 62 01 93), in the middle of the village on Carrer de la Riera, is open 10 am to 1 pm and 5 to 8 pm Monday to Saturday and 10 am to 1 pm Sunday and holidays, April to October.

Places to Stay & Eat *Camping Tamariu* (☎ 972 62 04 22), about 1km back from the beach on Carrer de la Riera, is open from May to September and charges 2640 ptas plus IVA, for two adults, a tent and a car.

Hotel Sol d'Or (☎ 972 30 04 24, Carrer de la Riera 18), 500m nearer to the beach, is open from June to September. Doubles with bath are 6550 ptas plus IVA. *Hotel Es Furió* (☎ 972 62 00 36, Carrer del Foraió 5-7) is just back from the beach and has spacious, cheerfully decorated doubles for up to 11,400 ptas (as little as 7000 ptas in slow periods). The beachfront is lined with seafood eateries – *Restaurant Royal* is one of the best and serves a reasonable seafood fideuá for about 2000 ptas.

Getting There & Away Sarfa buses from Palafrugell run to Tamariu (15 minutes, 145 ptas) three or four times daily, from mid-June to mid-September only.

A rough road will take you on to Aiguablava (see Beaches near Begur later).

Begur

postcode 17255 • pop 2700

The **castle** *(castell)*, dating from the 10th century, on a rock above the village, is still pretty much in the state in which it was left by Spanish troops who wrecked it in 1810

CATALUNYA

to impede the advance of Napoleon's army. Dotted around the village are half a dozen towers built for defence against 16th- and 17th-century pirates. There's a tourist office (☎ 972 62 45 20) at Avinguda del Onze de Setembre 5.

Places to Stay The pine-shaded *Camping Begur* (☎ 972 62 32 01), open from April to September, is about 2km south on the road from Palafrugell. *Hotel Rosa* (☎ 972 62 30 15, Carrer de Forgas i Puig 6), a few steps towards the castle from the church, has nice rooms with bath; doubles with buffet breakfast cost up to 7060/10,915 ptas in low/high season.

Getting There & Away Sarfa (☎ 972 62 24 26) is at Plaça de Forgas 6 and runs three daily buses to Barcelona (2¼ hours) via Palafrugell. On weekdays one Sarfa bus runs to Girona.

Beaches near Begur

You can reach a series of smallish beaches, on an enticing stretch of coast, by turning east off the Palafrugell road 2km south of the centre of Begur. About 2km down is a turn-off to the black-sand beach of **Platja Fonda** (1km). Half a kilometre farther on is the turn-off to **Fornells** (1km), a small village on one of the most picturesque bays of the whole Costa Brava, with a marina, beach and incredibly blue waters.

The large but friendly *Hotel Aiguablava* (☎ 972 62 20 58, fax 972 62 21 12), overlooking most of this, has doubles for 14,800 ptas plus IVA (closed mid-November to mid-February). *Hotel Bonaigua* (☎ 972 62 20 50, fax 972 62 20 54), back up the street a little, charges 10,800 ptas plus IVA (closed October to late April). Back up at the Fornells turn-off, *Restaurant Ondina* (☎ 972 62 30 52), open from April to October, has four rooms at 8000 ptas a double, plus IVA.

One kilometre on from the Fornells turn-off is **Aiguablava**, with a slightly bigger and busier beach, and *Parador Nacional de la Costa Brava* (☎ 972 62 21 62, fax 972 62 21 66) enjoying lovely views back across

the Fornells bay. Doubles start at 19,500 ptas plus IVA.

Another road from Begur leads 2km east to **Aiguafreda**, a beach on a lovely cove backed by pine-covered hills, and, a bit farther south, the slightly more built-up **Sa Tuna** beach. If you fancy staying, try *Hostal Sa Rascassa* (☎ 972 62 42 47), at Cala d'Aiguafreda 3, Aiguafreda. It has doubles for up to 12,000 ptas, including breakfast.

Getting There & Away A Bus Platges (beach bus) service runs from Plaça de Forgas in Begur between late June and mid-September.

CASTELL DE PÚBOL

The Castell de Púbol at La Pera, just south of the C-255 and 22km north-west of Palafrugell, forms the southernmost point of north-eastern Catalunya's 'Salvador Dalí triangle', whose other elements include the Teatre-Museu Dalí in Figueres and the Cadaqués area where the artist spent much of his life.

Dalí bought the Gothic and Renaissance mansion, which includes a 14th-century church, in 1968 and gave it to his wife, Gala, who lived here without him until her death. Local lore has it that the notoriously promiscuous Gala was still sending for young village men almost right up to the time she died in 1982, aged 88. On her death, Dalí himself moved into Púbol, but abandoned it after a fire, which nearly burnt him to a crisp in 1984, to live out his last years at Figueres.

The castle was renovated by Dalí in his inimitable style, with lions' heads staring from the tops of cupboards, statues of elephants with giraffes' legs in the garden and a stuffed giraffe staring at Gala's tomb in the crypt. The strength of the artist's passion for Gala is shown by motifs and reminders of her all over the castle. A visit is in effect a tour of the couple's tortured relationship. The blue bedroom in which Dalí nearly burnt to death now has a bright red fire extinguisher standing ready in the corner. There are many sumptuous beds in other rooms. In the garage is the blue Cadillac in which Dalí took Gala for a last drive round the estate – after she died.

Take the time to have a look around the village as well – it's a little gem of sand-coloured stone houses all huddled together.

The mansion is open from mid-March to the end of October only. From mid-June to mid-September the hours are 10.30 am to 7.15 pm daily. For the remaining months it opens until 5.15 pm daily, but is closed Monday (700 ptas, seniors and students 500 ptas). Sarfa buses between Palafrugell and Girona run along the C-255.

GIRONA
postcode 17080 • pop 71,858
Northern Catalunya's largest city, Girona (Gerona in Castilian) sits in a valley 36km inland from Palafrugell. Its impressive medieval centre, which seemingly struggles uphill above the Riu Onyar, is a powerful reason for making a visit.

The Roman town of Gerunda lay on the Via Augusta, the highway from Rome to Cádiz (Carrer de la Força in Girona's old town follows part of the line of the Via Augusta). Taken from the Muslims by the Franks in AD 797, Girona became capital of one of Catalunya's most important counties, falling under the sway of Barcelona in the late 9th century. Its wealth in medieval times produced many fine Romanesque and Gothic buildings, which have survived repeated attacks and sieges through the centuries.

Orientation
The narrow streets of the old town climb above the eastern bank of the Riu Onyar and are easy to explore on foot. Several road and footbridges link it to the new town across the river. The train station is 1km to the south-west, on Plaça d'Espanya off Carrer de Barcelona, with the bus station behind it on Carrer de Rafael Masó i Valentí.

Information
The tourist office (☎ 972 22 65 75) is towards the southern end of the old town, at Rambla de la Llibertat 1. It's open 8 am to 8 pm weekdays; until 2 pm and 4 to 8 pm Saturday; and 9 am to 2 pm Sunday. Another

office operates at the airport, but only when charter flights are due.

There are branches of La Caixa bank, with ATMs, on Carrer dels Abeuradors off Rambla de la Llibertat and on Carrer Nou just across the Riu Onyar. The main post office is at Avinguda de Ramon Folch 2, also across the river.

The Policía Nacional, Carrer de Sant Pau 2, is at the northern end of the old town; the Policía Municipal are at Carrer de Bernat Bacià 4. The Hospital de Santa Caterina (☎ 972 18 26 00) is at Plaça de l'Hospital 5.

Two good bookshops in the old town for maps and local guides are Les Voltes, on Plaça del Vi, and Geli, at Carrer de la Argenteria 18.

Catedral
The fine baroque facade of the cathedral stands at the head of a majestic flight of steps rising from Plaça de la Catedral. Most of the building, however, is much older than its exterior might lead you to conclude. Repeatedly rebuilt and altered down the centuries, it has Europe's widest Gothic nave (23m). The cathedral's museum, through the door marked 'Claustre Tresor', contains the masterly Romanesque *Tapís de la Creació* (Tapestry of the Creation) and a Mozarabic illuminated *Beatus* manuscript from AD 975. The 500 ptas fee for the museum also admits you to the beautiful 12th-century Romanesque cloister, whose 112 stone columns have some fine, although rather weathered, carving. From the cloister you can see the 13th-century Torre de Carlemany bell tower, also Romanesque. The cathedral is open 10 am to 2 pm and 4 to 7 pm (morning only on Sunday). From October to April it shuts on Monday.

Museu d'Art
Next door to the cathedral, in the 12th- to 16th-century Palau Episcopal, the art museum's collection ranges from Romanesque woodcarvings to early-20th-century paintings. It's open 10 am to 6 pm (to 7 pm in summer) Tuesday to Saturday, and until 2 pm Sunday and holidays (300 ptas).

CATALUNYA

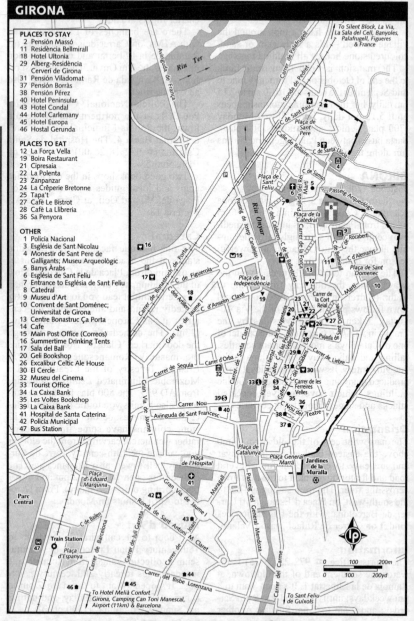

GIRONA

PLACES TO STAY
2 Pensión Massó
11 Residència Bellmirall
18 Hotel Ultonia
29 Alberg-Residència
   Cerverí de Girona
31 Pensión Viladomat
37 Pensión Borràs
38 Pensión Pérez
40 Hotel Peninsular
43 Hotel Condal
44 Hotel Carlemany
45 Hotel Europa
46 Hostal Gerunda

PLACES TO EAT
12 La Força Vella
19 Boira Restaurant
21 Cipresaia
22 La Polenta
23 Zanpanzar
24 La Crêperie Bretonne
25 Tapa't
27 Cafè Le Bistrot
28 Cafè La Llibreria
36 Sa Penyora

OTHER
1 Policía Nacional
3 Església de Sant Nicolau
4 Monestir de Sant Pere de
   Galligants; Museu Arqueològic
5 Banys Àrabs
6 Església de Sant Feliu
7 Entrance to Església de Sant Feliu
8 Catedral
9 Museu d'Art
10 Convent de Sant Doménec;
   Universitat de Girona
13 Centre Bonastruc Ça Porta
14 Cafe
15 Main Post Office (Correos)
16 Summertime Drinking Tents
17 Sala del Ball
26 Geli Bookshop
26 Excalibur Celtic Ale House
30 El Cercle
32 Museu del Cinema
33 Tourist Office
34 La Caixa Bank
35 Les Voltes Bookshop
39 La Caixa Bank
41 Hospital de Santa Caterina
42 Policía Municipal
47 Bus Station

To Silent Block, La Via,
La Sala del Cell, Banyoles,
Palafrugell, Figueres
& France

Riu Ter
Avinguda de França
Avinguda del Ter

Carrer de Palafrugell
Ronda de Pedret
C de Sant Pau
Plaça de Sant Pere
C de Bellaire
C de Santa Llúcia
Plaça del Rei Martí
Passeig Arqueològic
Plaça de Sant Feliu
Pujada de la Catedral
Plaça de la Catedral
Rocaberti
C d'Alemanys
Plaça de Sant Domenec
Carrer de la Força
Carrer de Bellmirall
Passeig de Josep Canalejas
Riu Onyar
C de Ballesteries
C dels Calderers
Passeig de la Devesa
Carrer de Bonastruc de Porta
C dels Abeuradors
C de Figuerola
Plaça de la Independència
Carrer de Santa Clara
Gran Via de Jaume I
C d'Anselm Clavé
Carrer de l'Argentería
Carrer de la Cort Reial
Carrer de la Llibertat
Carrer d'Orba
Carrer de Sèquia
Carrer de les Ferreries Velles
Rambla de la Llibertat
Carrer de Liebre
Pujada de
Plaça Generàl Marrà
Jardines de la Muralla
Gran Via de Jaume I
Avinguda de Sant Francesc
Carrer Nou
Plaça de Catalunya
Plaça de l'Hospital
Maragull
Parc Central
Plaça d'Eduard Marquina
Passeig del General Mendoza
C de Bailén
Ronda de Sant Antoni M Claret
Carrer de Juli Garreta
Carrer de Barcelona
Train Station
Plaça d'Espanya
Carrer del Carme
Carrer del Bisbe Lorenzana
To Hotel Melià Confort
Girona, Camping Can Toni Manescal,
Airport (11km) & Barcelona
To Sant Feliu
de Guíxols

0   100   200m
0   100   200yd

Església de Sant Feliu

Girona's second great church is downhill from the cathedral. The 17th-century main facade, with its landmark single tower, is on Plaça de Sant Feliu, but the entrance is around the side. Put 100 ptas in the slot inside the door to light up the interior. The nave has 13th-century Romanesque arches but 14th- to 16th-century Gothic upper levels. The northernmost of the chapels at the far western end of the church is graced by a masterly Catalan Gothic sculpture, Aloi de Montbrai's alabaster *Crist Jacent* (Recumbent Christ).

Banys Àrabs

The 'Arab baths' on Carrer de Ferran Catòlic are, although modelled on earlier Muslim and Roman bathhouses, actually a 12th-century Christian affair in Romanesque style. It's the only public baths yet discovered from medieval Christian Spain where, in reaction to the Muslim obsession with water and cleanliness, washing almost came to be regarded as ungodly. The baths contain a changing room, the *apodyterium*, followed by the *frigidarium* and *tepidarium*, with respectively cold and warm water, and the *caldarium*, a kind of sauna. Opening hours in summer are 10 am to 7 pm Tuesday to Saturday and until 2 pm Sunday and holidays (200 ptas). The rest of the year it's open 10 am to 2 pm daily, but closed Monday.

Passeig Arqueològic

Across the street from the Banys Àrabs, steps lead up into lovely gardens that follow the city walls up to the 18th-century Portal de Sant Cristòfol gate, from which you can walk back down to the cathedral.

Monestir de Sant Pere de Galligants

Down across the little Riu Galligants, this 11th- and 12th-century Romanesque monastery has another lovely cloister with some marvellous animal and monster carvings on the capitals of its pillars. The monastery houses Girona's **Museu Arqueològic** (Archaeology Museum), whose exhibits range from prehistoric to medieval times and include Roman mosaics and some medieval Jewish tombstones. Opening hours are 10.30 am to 1.30 pm and 4 to 7 pm (in winter 10 am to 2 pm and 4 to 6 pm) Tuesday to Saturday and 10 am to 2 pm Sunday and holidays (300 ptas).

Església de Sant Nicolau

This pretty little Lombard-style 12th-century Romanesque church in front of the Monestir de Sant Pere de Galligants is unusual in that it has an octagonal tower, and three apses laid out in a trefoil plan.

The Call

Until 1492, Girona was home to Catalunya's second most important medieval Jewish community (after Barcelona), and its Jewish quarter, the Call, was centred on Carrer de la Força. For an idea of medieval Jewish life and culture here, visit the **Centre Bonastruc Ça Porta**, entered from a narrow alley off the upper side of Carrer de la Força. Named after Jewish Girona's most illustrious figure, a 13th-century Cabbalist philosopher and mystic, the centre – a warren of rooms and stairways around a courtyard – has exhibitions and a cafe, and is a focus for studies of Jewish Spain. It's open 10 am to 8 pm (to 6 pm in winter) and until 3 pm Sunday and holidays (200 ptas).

Passeig de la Muralla

You can walk along a good length of the top of the city walls, the Passeig de la Muralla, from Plaça de Josep Ferrater i Mora, just south of the Universitat de Girona building at the top of the old town, down to Plaça del General Marvà near Plaça de Catalunya. This southern part of the old town dates from the 13th century onwards – a bit younger than the more northerly area around the cathedral, where the Roman and early medieval towns stood.

Museu del Cinema

The Casa de les Aigües houses Spain's only cinema museum. The Col.lecció Tomàs Mallol includes not only displays tracing the history of cinema, but a parade of hands-on items for indulging in shadow games, optical illusions and the like – it's

Catalan Romanesque Architecture

Catalunya, through its contacts with southern France and northern Italy, was the first part of Spain affected by the wave of Romanesque architecture and art that rippled across Western Europe from about the 10th century. A blend of ancient Roman traditions and Carolingian experimentation, the Romanesque style was at first disseminated chiefly by master builders from Byzantine-influenced Lombardy in northern Italy.

Typical features of the simple early-Romanesque churches were massive masonry to support barrel vaults; tall, square bell towers; aisles separated by lines of pillars joined by semicircular arches; semicircular arches round doors and windows; semicircular apses; and blind arcades and pilasters on outside walls.

From the end of the 11th century, stonemasons began to deck Catalan churches with increasing amounts of sculpture (notably on the capitals of columns), and bigger churches started to appear, with up to five aisles and apses, transepts and some fine cloisters.

Catalunya has over 2000 surviving Romanesque buildings. They're much more numerous in what's known as Catalunya Vella (Old Catalunya) – roughly north of a line from Sitges to Tremp – which was taken from the Muslims in the 9th century, than in the southern Catalunya Nova (New Catalunya), which remained in Muslim hands till the mid-12th century.

great for kids. The museum is open 10 am to 8 pm Tuesday to Sunday from May to September. The rest of the year it opens until 6 pm Tuesday to Saturday and 11 am to 3 pm Sunday, closed Monday (500 ptas).

Places to Stay – Budget
The nearest camping ground is *Camping Can Toni Manescal (☎ 972 47 61 17),* Fornells de la Selva, 7km south of Girona. It only holds 140 people but is open all year. Rates are 475 ptas per person, per car and 950 ptas per tent.

Girona has a good modern youth hostel, *Alberg-Residència Cerverí de Girona (☎ 972 21 80 30, Carrer dels Ciutadans 9),* which is well placed in the old town.

Several pensiones and hostales lurk in the old town. In July and August the better ones fill up quickly. *Pensión Pérez (☎ 972 22 40 08, Plaça de Bell.lloc 4)* has a gloomy entrance stairway but clean, adequate singles/ doubles for 1700/2900 ptas. The owners have another cheap place, *Pensión Borràs*, with the same phone number, around the corner at Travessera d'Auriga 6.

Pensión Massó (☎ 972 20 71 75, Plaça de Sant Pere 12) offers doubles with shared baths for 3000 ptas; the sign just says 'Habitacions'.

One of the nicest cheaper places in the old town is *Pensión Viladomat (☎ 972 20 31 76, Carrer dels Ciutadans 5).* Comfortable rooms without bath are 2000/4000 ptas, and there are a few doubles with bath for 6000 ptas.

The fairly modern *Hotel Peninsular (☎ 972 20 38 00, Carrer Nou 3),* just west of the Riu Onyar, has 68 rooms at 3000/5900 ptas with shared bath, or 5500/7200 ptas with bath, plus IVA. *Hostal Gerunda (☎ 972 20 22 85, Carrer de Barcelona 34),* near the train station, has functional doubles with private bath for 3700 ptas.

Places to Stay – Mid-Range & Top End
The attractive little *Residència Bellmirall (☎ 972 20 40 09, Carrer de Bellmirall 3)* is in a lovely medieval building with rooms for 4970/7920 ptas, or 5280/ 8580 ptas with shower and toilet, including breakfast.

Everything else in this price range is in the new town west of the Riu Onyar. *Hotel Condal (☎ 972 20 44 62, Carrer de Joan Maragall 10)* and *Hotel Europa (☎ 972 20 27 50, fax 972 20 03 56, Carrer de Julí Garreta 21)* both have doubles from 6000 to 6500 ptas. *Hotel Ultònia (☎ 972 20 38 50, fax 972 20 33 34, Gran Via de Jaume I 22)* is ugly on

CATALUNYA

the outside but has well-equipped doubles at 11,000 ptas plus IVA (except in August, when prices shoot up to 14,000 ptas).

Top of the tree are the modern *Hotel Melià Confort Girona* (☎ 972 40 05 00, fax 972 24 32 33, Carrer de Barcelona 112), where a double costs 14,500 ptas plus IVA, and *Hotel Carlemany* (☎ 972 21 12 12, fax 972 21 49 94) on Plaça de Miquel Santaló, with doubles for 15,500 ptas plus IVA.

Places to Eat

The *cafes* under the arcades on Rambla de la Llibertat and nearby Plaça del Vi are good places to soak up a bit of atmosphere.

Tapa't, on Carrer de la Cort Reial, has a great range of tapas from 325 ptas. You can tuck into some vegetarian goodies at *La Polenta (Carrer de la Cort Reial 6)*, where mains cost up to 1200 ptas. Another vegie option, although not exclusively so, is *Sa Penyora (Carrer Nou del Teatre 3)*.

A great little Basque tavern and restaurant is *Zanpanzar (Carrer de la Cort Reial 10-12)*. It's usually packed with locals and offers *pintxos* (Basque tapas) and some fine meat dishes. Round off with *goxua intxaursaltsarekin*, a Basque tart consisting of biscuit, apple and an amazing nut sauce. Expect to fork out about 3000 ptas per head.

For tempting savoury and sweet crepes, head for *La Crêperie Bretonne (Carrer de la Cort Reial 14)*. This is the local branch of a popular eatery in Perpignan (southern France).

Cafè Le Bistrot, on Pujada de Sant Domènec, one of the most picturesque stairways in the old town, is a treat. Vaguely bohemian, it serves salads, *pizzes de pagès* (good, little bread-based pizzas) and crepes for between 500 and 700 ptas. Also nice is the calm *Cafè La Llibreria* (Carrer de les Ferreires Velles), serving light meals such as lasagne or escalivada for 700 ptas or green salads for up to 600 ptas.

La Força Vella (Carrer de la Força 4) has a four-course *menú* for 1500 ptas. Much better lit and easily more inviting is *Cipresaia (Carrer de Blas Fournàs 2)*, where you can tuck into paella and fideuá.

Plaça de la Independència in the new town is a popular munching area. The busy *Boira Restaurant (Plaça de la Independència 17)* is an old stalwart. It serves reasonable Catalan dishes and you should be lightened by not much more than 2500 ptas for a full meal.

Entertainment

Students make the nightlife here, so in summer things tend to calm down. Thursday is the big night, as most people head for the coast on weekends.

The old town has lots of good bars and cafes for evening *copas* (drinks) along Rambla de la Llibertat and around Carrer de Carreras Peralta. A seemingly nameless *cafe (Carrer de les Ballesteries 23)* stays open longer than some and is a popular spot overlooking the river. If the Irish theme is your thing, try *Escalibur Celtic Ale House (Carrer de la Cort Reial)*. *El Cercle (Carrer del Ciutadans 8)* is a charming place for a quiet drink carved out of a medieval warren of stone arches and timber.

You can keep going until 3 am or so near the river just north of the old town, where streets such as Carrer de Palafrugell and Ronda de Pedret harbour several lively and varied music bars. On the former, *Silent Block (Ronda de Pedret 20)* is good, while *La Via (Ronda de Pedret 66)* is also busy.

In summer, a series of drinking tents *(las carpas)* go up in the park west of the railway line. Across the road, the cyber-techno *Sala del Ball (Carrer del Riu Güell 2)* is Girona's dance destination on Thursday nights. For dancing, you can also try *La Sala del Cel (Ronda de Pedret 118)*.

Getting There & Away

Air Girona's airport (☎ 972 47 43 43), 11km south of the centre just off the A-7 and N-II, is devoted to summer charter flights for Costa Brava tourists.

Bus Barcelona Bus (☎ 972 20 24 32) runs to/from Barcelona's Estació del Nord (1¼ hours, 1450 ptas) and Figueres (50 minutes, 580 ptas) three to seven times daily. Sarfa (☎ 972 20 17 96) runs buses to most parts

CATALUNYA

of the Costa Brava. TEISA (☎ 972 20 02 75) runs eight services daily (four on Sunday) to Besalú (50 minutes, 385 ptas) and Olot (1¼ hours, 670 ptas).

Train Girona is on the railway between Barcelona, Figueres and Portbou on the French border. There are around 20 trains a day to Figueres (30 to 40 minutes, 330 to 380 ptas) and Barcelona (1½ hours, 790 to 910 ptas), and about 15 to Portbou and/or Cerbère (515 to 595 ptas). A few trains a day travel through to Montpellier in France, or beyond.

Getting Around
There's no airport bus service. You can call a taxi on ☎ 972 20 10 20 or ☎ 972 22 23 33.

Parking in the old town is fraught, but you can leave your metal steed in several parking areas across the river.

BESALÚ
postcode 17850 • pop 1991
In the 10th and 11th centuries, pretty Besalú was the capital of an independent county that stretched as far west as Cerdanya, before it came under Barcelona's control in 1111.

Most picturesque of all is the view of the village across the tall, crooked 11th-century **Pont Fortificat** (fortified bridge*)*, with its two tower-gates, from the southern side of the Fluvià.

The tourist office (☎ 972 59 12 40) on the arcaded central square, Plaça de la Llibertat, is open 10 am to 2 pm and 4 to 7 pm daily, but from June to mid-October only. It hands out a decent map-brochure, sells 100 ptas tickets for the **Miqvé** (a 12th-century Jewish ritual bath by the river) and offers worthwhile guided visits to the Miqvé, the bridge and the Romanesque **Església de Sant Vicenç**, otherwise normally closed. Have a look at the 11th-century Romanesque church of the **Monestir de Sant Pere**, with an unusual ambulatory (walkway) behind the altar, and the 12th-century Romanesque **Casa Cornellà**.

Places to Stay & Eat
There are three good little places to stay. *Habitacions Venència (☎ 972 59 12 57, Carrer Major 8)* has singles/doubles for 2600/4500 ptas. *Fonda Siqués (☎ 972 59 01 10, fax 972 59 12 43, Avinguda del President Lluís Companys 6)* offers doubles with bath for up to 6500 ptas. *Residència Marià (☎ 972 59 01 06, Plaça de la Llibertat 7)* has doubles with bathroom, TV and heating (handy in winter) for 4500 ptas.

Restaurant Can Quei, facing the Església de Sant Vicenç, has a three-course *menú* for 1400 ptas, including wine. An old favourite is *Restaurant Pont Vell*, by the bridge, where good Catalan mains can cost up to 1850 ptas. The classiest operation is *Els Fogons de Can Llaudes (Prat de Sant Pere 6)*, opposite the Monestir de Sant Pere. It's set in an elegant stone former chapel and offers imaginative twists on old themes. Mains range from 125 to 2850 ptas. You'd pay the latter for the *solomillo*, a tender loin slab of beef bathed in a raisin-based sauce.

Getting There & Away
The N-260 road from Figueres to Olot meets the C-160 from Girona at Besalú. See the Girona and Figueres sections for information on TEISA bus services to Besalú and on to Olot. The stop in Besalú is on the main road just west of Fonda Siques.

TORROELLA DE MONTGRÍ
postcode 17257 • pop 8020
On the Riu Ter about 30km north-east of Girona and 15km north of Palafrugell, the agreeable old town of Torroella de Montgrí is the funnel through which travellers to L'Estartit must pass. The tourist office (☎ 972 75 19 10) is on the Carretera de l'Estartit.

Things to See
About 100m south of the porticoed central square, Plaça de la Vila, in an old mansion at Carrer Major 28, the **Museu del Montgrí** will tell you about local history and archaeology, and a bit about the Illes Medes off L'Estartit. It's open 10 am to 2 pm and 6 to 9 pm (5 to 7 pm October to March) Monday to Saturday and 11 am to 2 pm Sunday and holidays (closed Tuesday and holidays from October to March). Entry is free.

Three blocks north of Plaça de la Vila is the **Església de Sant Genís**, which is mainly

15th-century Gothic (with fine ceiling tracery), but has an 18th-century baroque main facade at the western end.

Overlooking the town from the top of the 300m limestone Montgrí hills to the north, the impressive but empty **Castell de Montgrí** was built between 1294 and 1301 for King Jaume II in his efforts to bring to heel the disobedient counts of Empúries, to the north. There's no road and by foot it's a 40-minute climb from Torroella. Head north from Plaça del Lledoner along Carrer de Fàtima, at the end of which is a sign pointing you to the castle.

Places to Stay & Eat

Pensió Mitjà (☎ 972 75 80 03, *Carrer de l'Església 14*) is open all year but December and is a block north of Plaça de la Vila. It has bare but decent singles/doubles with bath and TV for 2600/5200 ptas. It serves food too.

The *cafes* on Plaça de la Vila are the best place for snacks and people-watching.

Getting There & Away

Ampsa (☎ 972 75 82 33), at Plaça d'Espanya 19 (three blocks west, then two south, from Plaça de la Vila), runs buses about hourly to L'Estartit from June to September and about half that during the rest of the year. The same company runs two to four trips daily to Girona (one hour). Sarfa (☎ 972 75 90 04), at Passeig de Catalunya 61 (three blocks east, then one north, from Plaça de la Vila), has three or four daily buses running to Barcelona's Estació del Nord (1¾ hours), Palafrugell (25 minutes) and Figueres (1¼ hours).

VERGES

postcode 17142 • pop 1127

About 15km east of Girona, this town has little to offer, but if you happen to be in the area on Holy Thursday (Easter) make an effort to see the rather macabre evening procession *Dansa de la Mort*. People dressed up as skeletons dance the Dance of Death through the streets in a festivity that seems to have little to do with the Last Supper! The fun usually starts about 10 pm. Girona-Torroella buses pass through here.

L'ESTARTIT & THE ILLES MEDES

postcode 17258 • pop 915

L'Estartit, 6km east of Torroella de Montgrí, has a long, wide beach of fine sand but nothing over any other Costa Brava package resort – except for the Illes Medes (Islas Medes). The group of rocky islets barely 1km offshore are home to some of the most abundant marine life on Spain's Mediterranean coast.

The main road in from Torroella de Montgrí is called Avinguda de Grècia as it approaches the beach; the beachfront road is Passeig Marítim, at the northern end of which is the tourist office (☎ 972 75 19 10).

Illes Medes

The shores and waters around these seven islets, an offshore continuation of the limestone Montgrí hills, have been protected since 1985 as a Reserva Natural Submarina (underwater natural reserve), which has brought a proliferation in their marine life and made them Spain's most popular destination for snorkellers and divers. Some 1345 vegetable and animal species have been identified here. There's a big bird population too; one of the Mediterranean's largest colonies of yellow-legged gulls (8000 pairs) breeds here between March and May.

Kiosks by the harbour at the northern end of L'Estartit beach offer snorkelling and glass-bottomed boat trips to the islands. Other glass-bottomed trips go to a series of caves along the coast to the north, or combine these with the Medes. A two-hour snorkelling trip to the Illes Medes costs anything up to 2500 ptas per person. Trips go frequently every day from June to September and, depending on demand, in April, May and October. Snorkelling, diving and other activities all tend to cost more in the peak months of July and August.

Diving

The range of depths (down to 50m), and the number of underwater cavities and tunnels around the Illes Medes contribute much to their attraction. On and around rocks near the surface are colourful algae and sponges as well as octopuses, crabs and various fish.

CATALUNYA

Below 10m or 15m, cavities and caves harbour lobsters, scorpion fish and large conger eels and groupers. Some groupers and perch may feed from the hand. If you get down to the sea floor you may see angler fish, thornback rays or marbled electric rays.

At least half a dozen outfits in L'Estartit can take you out scuba diving, at the Medes or off the mainland coast –the tourist office has lists of them. It's worth shopping around before taking the plunge. If you're already a qualified diver, a single two-hour trip usually costs up to 4200 ptas per person. If you need to rent all the gear, the extra cost will be somewhere between 2000 and 3500 ptas. Night dives are possible too (usually about 4500 ptas). If you're a novice, you can do a one-day introductory course costing around 7000 ptas or a full, five-day PADI Open Water Diver course for 40,000 to 60,000 ptas.

Places to Stay

Apart from the eight camping grounds in and around the town, budget accommodation doesn't really exist unless you're on a package. Two of the camping grounds, *La Sirena* (☎ 972 75 15 42, *Avinguda de la Pletera s/n*) and *Les Medes* (☎ 972 75 18 05, *Paratge Camp de l'Arbre)*, are open year round.

Some of the better options are opposite the harbour at the northern end of the beach. *Hotel Les Illes* (☎ 972 75 12 39, *fax 972 75 0086, Carrer de Les Illes 55)* has singles/doubles with bath for 5426/7585 ptas with breakfast. A cheap if very plain deal is *Pensió Santa Clara* (☎ 972 75 17 67, *fax 972 75 06 41, Passeig Marítim 18)*, where rooms cost 3600/6600 ptas.

Places to Eat

The northern end of Passeig Marítim, by the roundabout, is swarming with eateries. These places are all pretty similar, presenting a mix of basic Spanish fare and chicken-and-chips-style meals.

For something with a little more class, try *Restaurant Robert* (*Passeig Marítim 59)*. The nearly century-old house set in luxuriant gardens looks like it should be in the Swiss Alps. It ain't cheap though and the budget conscious might want to stick to the lunch *menú* for 1750 ptas – or settle for chicken and chips elsewhere.

Getting There & Around

Ampsa buses to Torroella de Montgrí (about one hourly) and Girona (three or four daily) go from Passeig Marítim, 150m south of the tourist office. Sarfa runs to Barcelona three or four times daily.

L'ESCALA

postcode 17130 • pop 5942

L'Escala, on the coast 11km north of Torroella de Montgrí, is a pleasant medium-sized resort on the southern shore of the Golf de Roses. It's close to the ancient town of Empúries (Ampurias in Castilian) and, a few kilometres farther north, the wetlands of the Parc Natural dels Aiguamolls de l'Empordà.

Orientation & Information

If you arrive by Sarfa bus, you'll alight on L'Escala's Plaça de les Escoles, where you'll find the tourist office (☎ 972 77 06 03) at No 1. It's summer hours are 9 am to 8 pm Monday to Saturday and 10 am to 1 pm Sunday. Empúries is 1km around the coast to the north-west of the town centre.

Empúries

Empúries was probably the first, and certainly one of the most important, Greek colonies on the Iberian Peninsula. Early Greek traders, pushing on from a trading post at Masilia (modern Marseille in France), set up a new post around 600 BC at what is now the village of Sant Martí d'Empúries, then an island. Soon afterwards they founded a mainland colony nearby, which forms part of the site you visit today. The colony came to be called Emporion ('market') and remained an important trading centre, and conduit of Greek culture to the Iberians, for centuries.

Empúries was also the place where, in 218 BC, Roman legions landed in Spain to cut off Hannibal's supply lines in the Second Punic War. About 195 BC they set up a military camp and by 100 BC had added a town. A century later it had merged with the

Greek one. Emporiae, as the place was then known, was abandoned in the late 3rd century AD, after raids by Germanic tribes. Later, an early Christian basilica and cemetery stood on the site of the Greek town, before the whole place, after over a millennium of use, disappeared altogether, to be rediscovered by archaeologists at the turn of the 20th century.

Many of the ancient stones now laid bare don't rise more than knee-high. You need a little imagination – and perhaps the aid of a taped commentary (300 ptas from the ticket office) – to make the most of it.

The Site In spring and summer the site is open from 10 am to 8 pm, with a pedestrian entrance from the seafront promenade in front of the ruins; just follow the coast from L'Escala to reach it. At other times it's open until 6 pm and the only way in is the vehicle approach from the Figueres road, about 1km from central L'Escala. Entry is 400 ptas.

The **Greek town** lies in the lower part of the site, closer to the shore. Main points of interest include the thick southern defensive walls; the site of the Asklepion, a shrine to the god of medicine, with a copy of his statue found here; and the Agora (town square), with remnants of the early Christian basilica and the Greek Stoa (market complex), beside it.

A small **museum** (the Museu d'Arqueologia in Barcelona has a bigger and better Empúries collection) separates the Greek town from the larger Roman town on the upper part of the site. Highlights of the **Roman town** include the mosaic floors of a 1st-century-BC house; the Forum; and the strong 1st-century-BC walls, said to have been built by Julius Caesar. Outside the walls are the remains of an oval amphitheatre.

A string of brown-sand beaches stretch along in front of the site. On one stands a Greek stone jetty.

Places to Stay
Camping The nearest camping ground to the centre of L'Escala is the small *Camping La Escala* (☎ 972 77 00 84, Camí d'Ample 21), about 700m south of La Platja. It is

open from mid-April to late September. There are four other sites 2km to 4km east of the centre in the Riells and Montgó areas of town, and a further half-dozen or so along or near the beach a few kilometres north of Empúries.

Youth Hostel *Alberg d'Empúries* (☎ 972 77 12 00, Les Coves 41) is just south of the Empúries ruins. It has room for 68 people, in dorms of six beds or more. Midseason rates are charged from April to mid-September.

Hostales, Pensiones & Hotels A good bet, although often booked up in high season, is *Hostal Mediterrà* (☎ 972 77 00 28, fax 972 77 45 93, Carrer de Riera 22–24), a block west of Carrer del Pintor Joan Massanet. Singles/doubles with shower cost 2560/5125 ptas in summer. Equally good is *Pensió Torrent* (☎ 972 77 02 78), at No 28, with rooms at 2000/4350 ptas. Singles are hard to come by in summer.

A step up in quality is *Hostal El Roser* (☎ 972 77 02 19, fax 972 77 45 29, Carrer de l'Església 7), on the first street on the right as you go down Carrer de Santa Mà'ima from Plaça de les Escoles. Good-sized modern rooms with TV and bath are 3750/5900 ptas plus IVA. In high season half-board costs 5200 ptas per person.

On Passeig de Lluís Albert, 10 minutes' walk east along the seafront from La Platja, *Hotel Voramar* (☎ 972 77 01 08), at No 2, has rooms for 5200/9845 ptas plus IVA, and *Hotel Bonaire* (☎ 972 77 32 33), at No 4, has them for 5313/10,625 ptas plus IVA for B&B.

Places to Eat
L'Escala is famous for its *anchoas* (anchovies) and fresh fish, both of which are likely to crop up on *menús*.

The seafront restaurants are mostly expensive but, if your wallet is fat enough, try *Els Pescadors* (☎ 972 77 07 28, Port d'En Perris 5), the next bay west from La Platja (five minutes' walk), which serves superb baked and grilled seafood, *suquet* (seafood stew) and rice dishes. You will pay from 3000 to 4000 ptas per head unless you opt

CATALUNYA

for the *menú* at 2200 ptas. *L'Olla* and *Volanti*, also on Port d'En Perris, both serve pizzas for around 700 to 950 ptas.

A really cute place for simple *torrades* (open toasted sandwich) with various toppings and other light meals is the attractively decorated *Café dell'Arte* (☎ 972 77 44 96, Carrer de Calvari 1), a few minutes' walk in from the seafront.

Getting There & Away

Sarfa has one bus from Barcelona (via Palafrugell) on weekdays (1½ hours), rising to three on Sunday. Five buses a day run to Figueres (50 minutes) and two to Girona (one hour).

PARC NATURAL DELS AIGUAMOLLS DE L'EMPORDÀ

This natural park preserves the remnants of marshes that once covered the whole coastal plain of the Golf de Roses, an important site for migrating birds. Bird-watchers have spotted over 100 species a day in the March-May and August-October migration periods, which bring big increases in the numbers of wading birds and even the occasional flamingo, glossy ibis, spoonbill or rare black stork. There are usually enough birds around to make a visit worthwhile at any time of year.

The best place to head for is the El Cortalet information centre (☎ 972 45 42 22), 1km east off the Sant Pere Pescador-Castelló d'Empúries road. Marked paths lead to a 2km stretch of beach and a number of *aguaits* (hides) where you can view saltwater marshes and their bird life. From the top of the Observatori Senillosa, a former silo, you can see out across the whole park. The paths are always open, but morning and evening are the best times for watching birds (and mosquitoes!). The information centre is open 9.30 am to 2 pm and 4.30 to 7 pm (3.30 to 6 pm from mid-September to mid-June).

The nearest places to El Cortalet that you can reach by bus are Sant Pere Pescador, 6km south (served by four or five Sarfa buses daily from L'Escala and Figueres), and Castelló d'Empúries, 4km north.

CASTELLÓ D'EMPÚRIES
postcode 17486 • pop 4000

This old town was the capital of Empúries, a medieval Catalan county that maintained a large degree of independence up to the 14th century. At the heart of the narrow streets in the old part of town you'll find Plaça dels Homes, with a tourist office (☎ 972 15 62 33) in a 14th-century building.

The finest monument is the **Església de Santa Maria** on Plaça de Jacint Verdaguer, a large 13th- and 14th-century Gothic church with a fine Romanesque bell tower remaining from an earlier church on the site.

Places to Stay & Eat

Hotel Canet (☎ 972 25 03 40, fax 972 25 06 07, Plaça del Joc de la Pilota 2), a modernised 17th-century mansion in the centre, has elegant singles/doubles with bath and breakfast for 6000/8000 ptas and a swimming pool in an interior courtyard. Its *restaurant* is reasonably priced.

In the newer part of town to the south there are several options. *Hostal Ca L'Anton* (☎ 972 25 05 09, Carrer de Santa Clara 23) has rooms for 3500/5140 ptas and *Pensió/Fonda Serratosa* (☎ 972 25 05 08, Carrer de Santa Clara 14) charges 2400 ptas per person, plus IVA.

For your grumbling tummy, head to *El Portal de la Gallarda* on the street of the same name, about 50m away from the left flank of the church. It's partly set behind a Romanesque gate and you can snack on torrades (500 ptas) in the garden.

Getting There & Away

Sarfa runs up to 15 buses each day to Figueres (15 minutes), about three to Cadaqués (50 minutes), three daily to/from Girona (45 minutes) and up to four to Barcelona's Estació del Nord (1½ hours).

CADAQUÉS & AROUND
postcode 17488 • pop 1878

If you have time for only one stop on the Costa Brava, you can hardly do better than Cadaqués. Little more than a whitewashed village round a rocky bay, it and the surrounding area have a special magic – a fusion of wind, sea, light and rock – that isn't dissipated even by the throngs of mildly fashionable summer visitors.

A portion of that magic owes itself to Salvador Dalí, who spent family holidays in Cadaqués in his youth and lived much of his later life at nearby Port Lligat. The empty moonscapes, odd-shaped rocks and barren shorelines that litter Dalí's paintings weren't just a product of his fertile imagination. They're strewn all round the Cadaqués area in what Dalí termed a 'grandiose geological delirium'.

The country here is drier than farther south. The sparseness continues to dramatic Cap de Creus, 8km north-east of Cadaqués, lending itself to some coastscapes of almost (ahem) surreal beauty.

Thanks to Dalí and other luminaries, Cadaqués pulled in an artistic, offbeat and celebrity crowd for decades. One visit by the poet Paul Éluard and his Russian wife, Gala, in 1929 caused an earthquake in Dalí's life: he broke with his family, ran off to Paris with Gala (who was to become his lifelong obsession and, later, wife) and joined the surrealist movement. In the 1950s, after Dalí's success in the USA, the crowd he attracted was more jet-setting – Walt Disney, the Duke of Windsor and Greek ship-owner Stavros Niarchos. In the 1970s, Mick Jagger and Gabriel García Márquez turned up. Today the crowd is neither so creative nor so famous – and a lot bigger – but Cadaqués' atmosphere remains.

Information

The tourist office (☎ 972 25 83 15) is at Carrer del Cotxe 2. It's open 10 am to 2 pm and 4 to 7 pm (closed Wednesday afternoon and Sunday). The Policía Local (☎ 972 15 93 43) are a few steps behind the tourist office, on Carrer del Vigilant. There's a hospital (☎ 972 25 88 07) on Carrer de Guillem Bruguera, just west of the church.

The Town

Cadaqués is perfect for wandering, either around the town or along the coast. The 16th- and 17th-century **Església de Santa Maria**, with a gilded baroque *retablo*, or

altarpiece), is the focus of the older part with its narrow hilly streets.

There are two art museums worth visiting in Cadaqués. The **Centre d'Art Perrot-Moore**, off Carrer del Vigilant, was founded by Dalí's secretary and focuses on Dalí and Picasso. It was closed in 2000 and there was no clear indication when it might reopen. The **Museu de Cadaqués**, Carrer de Narcís Monturiol 15, includes Dalí among other local artists. It is generally open 11 am to 1.30 pm and 3 to 8 pm daily, and the cost of entry depends on the temporary exhibition being held.

Beaches

Cadaqués' main beach, and several others along the nearby coast, are small, with more pebbles than sand, but their picturesqueness and beautifully blue waters make up for that. Overlooking Platja Llaner on the southern side of the bay is Dalí's parents' holiday home; out the front is a statue by Josep Subirachs dedicated to Federico García Lorca, in memory of his 1920s stay.

Port Lligat

Port Lligat, a 1.25km walk from Cadaqués, is a tiny settlement around another lovely bay, with fishing boats pulled up on its beach. The **Casa Museu Dalí** here began as a fisherman's hut and was steadily altered and enlarged by Dalí, who lived here, apart from a dozen or so years abroad during and around the Spanish Civil War, from 1930 to 1982. It's the house with a lot of little white chimney pots and two egg-shaped towers, overlooking the western end of the beach.

Visits must be booked (☎ 972 25 80 63) and you are allowed a grand total of about 30 minutes inside as you are guided through. From mid-June to mid-September the house is open 10.30 am to 9 pm daily. From mid-March to mid-June and from mid-September to early January it's open until 6 pm, closed Monday. The rest of the year it's shut. Entry is 1300 ptas, students and seniors 800 ptas.

Cap de Creus

Cap de Creus is the most easterly point of the Spanish mainland and a place of sublime, rugged beauty. With a steep, rocky coastline indented by dozens of turquoise-watered coves, it's an especially wonderful place to be at dawn or sunset. Atop the cape stand a lighthouse and a good, mid-priced *restaurant*.

Walking

There are infinite possibilities: out along the promontory between Cadaqués and Port Lligat; to Port Lligat and beyond; along the southern side of the Cadaqués bay to the Far de Cala Nans lighthouse; or over the hills south of Cadaqués to the coast east of Roses. For a full day's outing you could walk to the Monestir de Sant Pere de Rodes and back, possibly via El Port de la Selva (see the following section, Cadaqués to the French Border); the Cadaqués tourist office can give you directions.

Places to Stay

Let's get one thing straight – Cadaqués, especially in high season, is anything but cheap. *Camping Cadaqués (☎ 972 25 81 26),* about 1km from central Cadaqués on the road to Port Lligat, has room for about 500 people and can get crowded. Two adults with a tent and car pay 2880 ptas plus IVA. It is open from Semana Santa to September.

Fonda Vehí (☎ 972 25 84 70, Carrer de l'Església 5), near the church, has singles/doubles with shared baths for 2200/4000 ptas. It tends to be booked up for July and August.

Hostal Marina (☎ 972 25 81 99, Carrer de Frederic Rahola 2) is probably a better bet, with doubles at up to 5500 ptas with washbasin only or 8000 ptas with private bath.

Hotel Ubaldo (☎ 972 25 81 25, Carrer de la Unió 13), towards the back of the old part of town, has good rooms with bath, some with balcony, for 8935/11,745 ptas plus IVA.

Hotel Playa Sol (☎ 972 25 81 00, fax 972 25 80 54, Platja Pianc 5), on the eastern side of the bay, has doubles/triples for up to

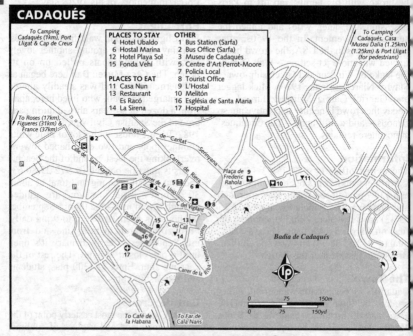

CADAQUÉS

PLACES TO STAY
4 Hotel Ubaldo
6 Hostal Marina
12 Hotel Playa Sol
15 Fonda Vehí

PLACES TO EAT
11 Casa Nun
13 Restaurant Es Racó
14 La Sirena

OTHER
1 Bus Station (Sarfa)
2 Bus Office (Sarfa)
3 Museu de Cadaqués
5 Centre d'Art Perrot-Moore
7 Policía Local
8 Tourist Office
9 L'Hostal
10 Melitón
16 Església de Santa Maria
17 Hospital

To Camping Cadaqués (1km), Port Lligat & Cap de Creus

To Camping Cadaqués, Casa Museu Dalia (1.25km) (1.25km) & Port Lligat (for pedestrians)

To Roses (17km), Figueres (31km) & France (37km)

Avinguda de Caritat

Carrer de Serinyana

Carrer de Riera

Plaça de Frederic Rahola

Carrer de la Unió

C del Vigilant

Portal d'Amunt

C del Call

Carrer de la Riba

Badia de Cadaqués

To Café de la Habana

To Far de Cala Nans

0 75 150m
0 75 150yd

CATALUNYA

22,000/27,400 ptas plus IVA. Loners can take a double for 18,200 ptas. Rooms have air-con, satellite TV and breakfast is included. There's a nice pool area too.

In Port Lligat, *Residencia/Aparthotel Calina (☎ 972 25 88 51),* close to the small beach, offers a range of pleasant modern rooms and one-room apartments ranging up to 12,500 ptas.

Places to Eat
The eastern part of the central beachfront is lined with spots proffering uninspired *menús* for up to 1500 ptas, or pizzas for about 800 ptas.

Restaurant Es Racó (Carrer del Dr Callis 3) serves a fine *parrillada de pescado* (mixed seafood grill) for 2200 ptas per person. Its balcony overlooking the western half of the beach catches some breeze. *Fonda Vehí's* 2nd-floor restaurant serves three-course *menús* for 1250 to 1500 ptas plus IVA.

La Sirena, in a quiet little patio off Carrer del Call, is a romantic little eating hideaway. The blue-on-white decor is fine and transports you to a dream-like Mediterranean setting.

Casa Nun (Plaça del Port Ditxos 6) is another stylish bijou restaurant set back on a dainty square. From the tables outside you can look out over the Mediterranean. Prices are mid-range for local standards – around 2000 ptas for a main.

Entertainment
L'Hostal, facing the beachfront *passeig,* has live music on many nights. One night in the 1970s Dalí called it the *'lugar más bonito del mundo'* ('the most beautiful place on earth'). The beachfront *Melitón* bar has a fine *terraza* (terrace) but with prices to match. *Cafe de la Habana* can get lively, too.

Getting There & Away
Sarfa (☎ 972 25 87 13) has buses to Castelló d'Empúries and Figueres (one hour) up to eight times daily (three in winter), to Girona (1½ hours) three times daily (one in winter) and to Barcelona (2¼ hours) two to five times daily.

CADAQUÉS TO THE FRENCH BORDER
If you want to prolong the journey to France, **El Port de la Selva**, **Llançà** and the border town **Portbou** are pleasant enough minor beach resorts-cum-fishing towns, all with a range of accommodation.

A more spectacular stop is the **Monestir de Sant Pere de Rodes**, a classic piece of Romanesque architecture looming 500m up in the hills south-west of El Port de la Selva, with great views. Founded in the 8th century, it later became the most powerful monastery between Figueres and Perpignan in France. The great triple-naved, barrel-vaulted basilica is flanked by the fine square Torre de Sant Miquel bell tower and a two-level cloister. The monastery is open 10 am to 8 pm daily (closed Monday) from June to the end of September. The rest of the year it closes at 5.30 pm (300 ptas, students 150 ptas, free on Tuesday).

Getting There & Away
The monastery is on a back road over the hills between Vilajuïga, 8km to its west, and El Port de la Selva, 5km north-east. Each town is served by three or four Sarfa buses from Figueres daily, but there are no buses to the monastery. Vilajuïga is also on the railway between Figueres and Portbou.

FIGUERES
postcode 17600 • pop 33,600
Twelve kilometres inland from the Golf de Roses, Figueres (Figueras in Castilian) is a humdrum town (some might say a dive) with a single attraction: Salvador Dalí. In the 1960s and 1970s Dalí created here, the town of his birth, the extraordinary Teatre-Museu Dalí. Whatever your feelings about old Salvador, this is worth every minute you can spare.

Orientation
From the bus and train stations, on Plaça de l'Estació, it's a 10-minute walk north-west to the central boulevard, the Rambla. Teatre-Museu Dalí is 200m north of the Rambla, with most of the sleeping and eating options concentrated within a few blocks nearby.

CATALUNYA

Information

The tourist office (☎ 972 50 31 55) on Plaça del Sol is open 9 am to 9 pm Monday to Saturday and until 3 pm Sunday from June to mid-September. Otherwise its hours are 8.30 am to 3 pm and 4.30 to 7.30 pm weekdays, and 9.30 am to 1.30 pm and 3.30 to 7.30 pm Saturday (closed Sunday).

There's no shortage of banks or ATMs in the central area. American Express (☎ 972 50 91 00), Carrer de Peralada 28, is at Viatges Figueres.

The post office is on Carrer de Santa Llogaia. You can get online at a couple of places along Carrer de Sant Antoni. Bar Arcadia (☎ 972 67 38 91), at No 7, is open 9 am to 10 pm daily, but closed Sunday. Down the road at Pizz@fono (☎ 972 67 71 77), a takeaway pizza joint at No 27, you can navigate until 11 pm.

The Policía Nacional are on Carrer de Pep Ventura. A Creu Roja (Red Cross; ☎ 972 50 17 99) post is at Carrer de Santa Llogaia 67 and there's a hospital on Ronda del Rector Aroles.

Teatre-Museu Dalí

Salvador Dalí was born in Figueres in 1904. Although his career took him for spells to Madrid, Barcelona, Paris and the USA, he remained true to his roots and lived well over half his adult life at Port Lligat, on the coast east of Figueres. Between 1961 and 1974 Dalí converted Figueres' former municipal theatre, ruined by a fire at the end of the civil war in 1939, into the Teatre-Museu Dalí. 'Theatre-museum' is an apt label for this multidimensional trip through one of the most fertile (or disturbed) imaginations of the 20th century, full of surprises, tricks and illusions, and containing a substantial portion of his life's work. 'The museum should not be considered as a museum, it is a gigantic surrealist object, everything in it is coherent, there is nothing that escapes my net of understandings,' explained its creator with characteristic modesty. Those searching for meaning or explanations for a lot of its seemingly haphazardly distributed contents might beg to differ.

Even outside, the building aims to surprise, from the collection of bizarre sculptures outside the entrance on Plaça de Gala i Salvador Dalí to the pink wall along Pujada del Castell, topped by a row of Dalí's trademark egg shapes and what appear to be female gymnast sculptures.

Inside, the ground floor (level 1) includes a semicircular garden area on the site of the original theatre stalls. In its centre is a classic piece of weirdness called *Taxi Plujós* (Rainy Taxi), composed of an early Cadillac – said to have belonged to Al Capone – and a pile of tractor tyres, both surmounted by statues, with a fishing boat balanced precariously above the tyres. Put a coin in the slot and water washes all over the inside of the car. The Sala de Peixateries (Fish Shop Room) off here holds a collection of Dalí oils including the famous *Autoretrat tou amb tall de bacon fregit* (Self-Portrait with Fried Bacon) and *Retrat de Picasso*. Beneath the former stage of the theatre is the crypt, with Dalí's plain tomb.

The stage area (level 2), topped by a glass geodesic dome, was conceived as Dalí's Sistine Chapel. The large egg-head-breasts-rocks-trees backdrop was part of a ballet set, one of Dalí's many ventures into the performing arts. If proof were needed of Dalí's acute sense of the absurd, *Gala mirando el Mar Mediterráneo* (Gala looking at the Mediterranean Sea) would be it. The work appears from the other end of the room, with the help of coin-operated viewfinders, to be a portrait of Abraham Lincoln. Off this room is the Sala del Tresor, where paintings such as *La panera del pa* (The Breadbasket) show that Dalí was a master draughtsman, too.

One floor up (level 3) you come across the Sala de Mae West, a living room whose components, viewed from the right spot, make up a portrait of Ms West: a sofa for her lips, twin fireplaces for nostrils, impressionist paintings of Paris for eyes. On the top floor (level 5) is a room containing works by other artists from Dalí's own collection, including El Greco's *Sant Pau* (St Paul).

In 2000, the museum acquired the Owen Cheatham collection of 37 magnificent jewels designed by Dalí. It was planned to have them housed in a separate annex of the museum by the end of the year.

The museum is open 9 am to 7.15 pm daily from July to September and for most of this period there are night sessions from 10 pm to 12.30 am. Queues are long on summer mornings. From October to June it's open 10.30 am to 5.15 pm daily (closed Monday until the end of May, on 1 January and 25 December). Entry is 1000 ptas, and 1200 ptas for the summer night sessions.

Other Things to See & Do

The **Museu de l'Empordà** at Rambla 2 combines Greek, Roman and medieval archaeological finds with a sizable collection of art, mainly by Catalan artists but there are also some works on loan from Prado in Madrid. It is open 11 am to 7 pm Tuesday to Saturday, and 10 am to 2 pm Sunday and holidays (closed Monday) from mid-June to mid-September. During the remainder of the year the hours are 11 am to 1.30 pm and 3 to 7 pm, and until 1.30 pm Sunday (300 ptas).

At Rambla 10, the **Museu de Joguets**, Spain's only toy museum, has more than 3500 Catalunya- and Valencia-made toys from the pre-Barbie 19th and early 20th centuries. It opens 10 am to 1 pm and 4 to 7 pm Monday and Wednesday to Saturday, and 11 am to 1.30 pm Sunday and holidays (closed Tuesday). From July to September, it's also open 5 to 7 pm Sunday. It closes mid-January to the end of February. Entry is a rather hefty 750 ptas.

The large 18th-century **Castell de Sant Ferran** stands on a low hill 1km north-west of the centre. Built in 1750, it saw almost no action in the following centuries. After abandoning Barcelona, Spain's Republican

Dalí – the Last Decades

Salvador Dalí's life, itself never short on the surreal, seemed to tip over the edge during the time the Figueres theatre-museum was getting under way.

Having won huge success in the USA in the 1940s (and earned the anagram Avida Dollars) Dalí returned to his roots. In 1948 he came with Gala, the lover to whom he was obsessively devoted and who was the subject of many of his paintings, to live at Port Lligat near Cadaqués. In 1958 Dalí and Gala were married in a secret Catholic ceremony.

By the late 1960s, according to Colm Tóibín's *Homage to Barcelona* (1990), the couple had 'a whole court of helpers, hangers-on, advisers, secretaries and sexual performers'. Dalí bought the Castell de Púbol near Girona and in 1970 gave it to Gala, who was now enjoying a string of young lovers. He masochistically contracted never to visit the castle unless she summoned him, which she rarely did (although she phoned daily).

In 1975 Dalí, ever a glutton for outrage, sent the dying Franco a telegram of congratulations on the execution of five prisoners, a gesture that provoked widespread disgust and for which many people never forgave him. Subsequently, he became increasingly depressed and inaccessible; a prisoner himself, some say, of Gala and/or the 'minders' enriching themselves at his expense.

MICK WELDON

On Gala's death in 1982, Dalí moved into Púbol himself, but he almost died in a fire two years later. Frail and malnourished, he retired to the Torre Galatea, a tower adjoining the theatre-museum at Figueres (and now part of it), hardly ever leaving his room before he died in 1989. His tomb is part of the theatre-museum.

government held its final meeting of the civil war on 1 February 1939 in the dungeons. It is open 10.30 am to 2 pm daily, but until 8 pm from July to mid-September (350 ptas).

Places to Stay – Budget

Camping Pous (☎ 972 67 54 96), north of the centre on the N-II towards La Jonquera, is small and charges 2000 ptas for site, car and two adults. It closes in December. Don't sleep in the Parc Bosc Municipal – people have been attacked there at night.

Alberg Tramuntana (☎ 972 50 12 13, Carrer d'Anicet de Pagès 2) is two blocks west of the tourist office. This youth hostel holds only 50 people but is open nearly all year; mid-season rates are charged from April to mid-September. Rates are 475 ptas per person, per car and 950 ptas per tent.

Habitacions Bartis (☎ 972 50 14 73, Carrer de Méndez Núñez 2), on the way into the centre from the bus and train stations, has adequate singles/doubles for 1700/2700 ptas plus IVA.

Bar La Vinya (☎ 972 50 00 49, Carrer de Tints 18), three short blocks east of the Teatre-Museu Dalí, has bare rooms up the street on Carrer de la Muralla for 1200/2400 ptas.

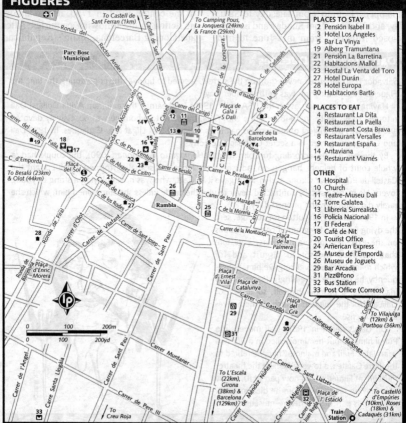

FIGUERES

PLACES TO STAY
2 Pensión Isabel II
3 Hotel Los Ángeles
5 Bar La Vinya
19 Alberg Tramuntana
21 Pensión La Barretina
22 Habitacions Mallol
23 Hostal La Venta del Toro
27 Hotel Durán
28 Hotel Europa
30 Habitacions Bartis

PLACES TO EAT
4 Restaurant La Dita
6 Restaurant La Paella
7 Restaurant Costa Brava
8 Restaurant Versalles
9 Restaurant España
14 Antaviana
15 Restaurant Viarnés

OTHER
1 Hospital
10 Church
11 Teatre-Museu Dalí
12 Torre Galatea
13 Llibreria Surrealista
16 Policía Nacional
17 El Federal
18 Café de Nit
20 Tourist Office
24 American Express
25 Museu de l'Empordà
26 Museu de Joguets
29 Bar Arcadia
31 Pizz@fono
32 Bus Station
33 Post Office (Correos)

Pensión Isabel II (☎ 972 50 47 35, Carrer d'Isabel II 16) has reasonable rooms with bath for 2800 ptas. *Hostal La Venta del Toro (☎ 972 51 05 10, Carrer de Pep Ventura 5)* has bare but adequate doubles for 3700 ptas, or one with shower for 4000 ptas. *Habitacions Mallol (☎ 972 50 22 83)*, along the street at No 9, charges 2000/3450 ptas.

A better quality place to sleep is *Pensión La Barretina (☎ 972 67 64 12, Carrer de Lasauca 13)*, where comfortable rooms with bath cost 3500/6000 ptas.

Hotel Los Ángeles (☎ 972 51 06 61, Carrer de Barceloneta 10) is good value with roomy singles/doubles for 4180/6000 ptas plus IVA. *Hotel Europa (☎ 972 50 07 44, Ronda de Firal 37)* is another respectable mid-range hotel. Rooms with bath are 3950/5950 ptas plus IVA.

Places to Stay – Mid-Range
Hotel Durán (☎ 972 50 12 50, fax 972 50 26 09, Carrer de Lasauca 5), just off the top end of the Rambla, has a bit more style. Comfortable singles/doubles are 6900/9900 ptas plus IVA.

Places to Eat
Carrer de La Jonquera, just down the steps east of the Teatre-Museu Dalí, is lined with cheapy restaurants, among them are *Restaurant España (Carrer de La Jonquera 20)*, *Restaurant Versalles (Carrer de La Jonquera 18)* and *Restaurant Costa Brava (Carrer de La Jonquera 10)*, offering basic three-course *menús* starting at 1150 ptas. *Restaurant La Paella*, two short blocks east on Carrer de Tins, serves one for 1250 ptas. None is a great culinary experience, but they are quick and easy.

A quality leap upwards is *Restaurant La Dita (Carrer de la Muralla 7)*, where you can try a mix of Mediterranean dishes and a few vegetarian options for up to 1000 ptas.

Restaurant Viarnés (Pujada del Castell 23) offers traditional local cooking, with the emphasis on seafood. Mains cost from 1500 ptas to 2500 ptas. The nearby *Antaviana (Carrer de Llers 5)* is another of the Mediterranean cooking crowd. It has a lunch *menú* for 1200 ptas.

The excellent restaurant of *Hotel Durán (Carrer de Lasauca 5)* is a big step up, serving Catalan and Spanish specialities like *conill rostit amb cargols* (roast rabbit with snails). You won't get much change from 3500 ptas.

Entertainment
Two of the grooviest cafe-bars in town are next to one another on Carrer del Mestre Falla – *Café de Nit* and *El Federal*. In fact this street hosts pretty much all Figueres' 'nightlife'. Locals tend to get a taxi to Empuriabrava on the coast to strut their stuff.

Getting There & Away
Bus Barcelona Bus (☎ 972 50 50 29) runs to Girona (50 minutes, 500 ptas) seven times a day, and on to Barcelona six times a day (2¼ hours, 1750 ptas).

Sarfa serves Castelló d'Empúries 10 to 20 times daily (150 ptas) and Cadaqués (one hour, 500 ptas) up to eight times daily. TEISA runs to Besalú (315 ptas) and Olot (590 ptas) two or three times daily.

Train Figueres is on the railway between Barcelona, Girona and Portbou on the French border, and there are regular connections to Girona (30 to 40 minutes, 330 to 380 ptas in 2nd class), Barcelona (2¼ hours, 1125 to 1290 ptas) and to Cerbère and the French border (about 25 minutes, 295 ptas).

The Pyrenees

The Pyrenees in Catalunya aren't as high as those in neighbouring Aragón, but still encompass some awesomely beautiful mountains and valleys.

Above all, the Parc Nacional d'Aigüestortes i Estany de Sant Maurici is a jewel-like area of lakes and dramatic peaks in the north-west. Aside from the natural beauty of the mountains and valleys and the obvious attractions of walking, skiing and other activities, the Catalan Pyrenees and their foothills also have a rich cultural heritage, notably many lovely Romanesque churches and monasteries, often tucked away in

CATALUNYA

surprisingly remote valleys. These are mainly the product of a time of prosperity and optimism in these regions in the 11th and 12th centuries, after Catalunya had broken ties with France in AD 988 and as the Muslim threat from the south receded.

Skiing

Baqueira-Beret in the Val d'Aran is one of Spain's biggest and best ski resorts. La Molina near Puigcerdà is also good, and there are several other smaller ones.

Trekking

The Pyrenees provide magnificent walking and trekking areas. You can undertake strolls of a few hours or day walks that can be strung together into treks of several days. Nearly all of these can be done without camping gear, with nights spent in villages or *refugis,* mountain refuges that offer basic dorm accommodation and often meals. It is

Walking in the Pyrenees

The best season for walking in the high Pyrenees is from late June to early September. Earlier than that, snow can make things difficult, and avalanches are possible. Later, the weather can turn poor. It can get very hot even at high altitudes in high summer, but nowhere in the Pyrenees is the weather reliable; even in July and August you can get plenty of rainy days and cloud – and cold at high altitude.

The Pyrenees are to be respected and anyone heading into the hills should be suitably fit, experienced and properly equipped for any conditions. This book suggests a number of walks, of varying length and toughness, but it is *not* a trekking or walking guide. The same can be said of other mountain areas covered in the course of the book.

For detailed route descriptions and advice on equipment and preparation, consult other sources such as those mentioned in the Maps, Books and Activities sections in the Facts for the Visitor chapter. Local advice from tourist offices, park rangers, mountain refuges and other walkers is also invaluable.

important to plan ahead and make sure you have secured a place to sleep in refuges Telephone numbers are given in this chapter – otherwise check with tourist offices.

Most the refuges mentioned in this chapter are run by two Catalan alpine clubs based in Barcelona, the Federació d'Entitats Excursionistes de Catalunya (FEEC; ☎ 93 412 07 77), and the Centre Excursionista de Catalunya (CEC; ☎ 93 315 23 11). A night in a refuge costs up to around 1300 ptas Normally FEEC refuges allow you to cook CEC ones don't. Moderately priced meals are often available.

The coast-to-coast GR-11 long-distance path traverses the entire Pyrenees from Cap de Creus on the Costa Brava to Hondarribia on the Bay of Biscay. Its route across Catalunya goes by way of La Jonquera, Albanyà, Beget, Setcases in the upper Ter valley, the Vall de Núria, Planoles, Puigcerdà Andorra, south of Catalunya's highest peak Estats (3143m), over to the Parc Naciona d'Aigüestortes i Estany de Sant Maurici, then on to the southern flank of the Val d'Aran and into Aragón.

Other Activities

The Riu Noguera Pallaresa around Llavorsí and Sort has some of Spain's most exciting white water and is a centre not just for **rafting, canoeing** and **hydrospeed** (water-tobogganing) but for several other adventure sports too. The world white water rafting championships will be held here in 2001, the first time Spain will have hosted the event.

You can go **horse riding** almost anywhere – there are *hípicas* (riding stables) all over the place. Mountain bikes are, by Spanish standards, relatively easy to rent in the Pyrenees. There's boundless scope for **climbing** – Pedraforca in the Serra del Cadí offers some of the most exciting ascents.

OLOT

postcode 17800 • pop 27,644
The hills around Olot are little more than pimples, but the pimples are the volcanoes of the Parc Natural de la Zona Volcànica de la Garrotxa. Admittedly they're extinct or

Fun in the sun, Sitges (Catalunya)

Seaside Tarragona (Catalunya)

View of Gósol from a nearby abandoned village (Catalunya)

Harbour view of white-washed Cadaqués (Catalunya)

Teatre-Museu Dalí, Figueres

Benasque (Aragón)

Mountainous Andorra offers great winter skiing and summer walking.

Keen walkers in the Parc Nacional de Ordesa y Monte Perdido (Aragón)

'¡Coliflor, coliflor!' (Catalunya)

dormant, but one erupted as recently as 11,500 years ago.

Information

The best town map is given out by the Patronat Municipal de Turisme (☎ 972 26 01 41), at Carrer del Bisbe Lorenzana 15, opposite the bus station. It's open 9 am to 3 pm and 5 to 8 pm weekdays, and 10 am to 2 pm weekends. From late September to late June, the hours become 9 am to 2 pm and 4 to 7 pm weekdays, 10 am to 2 pm and 5 to 7 pm Saturday, and 11 am to 2 pm Sunday.

The Casal dels Volcans (☎ 972 26 62 02) concentrates on information about the Parc Natural de la Zona Volcànica de la Garrotxa. It's in the Jardí Botànic on Avinguda de Santa Coloma de Farners, 1km southwest of Plaça de Clarà. Its hours are 9 am to 2 pm and 4 to 6 pm (5 to 7 pm from July to September) weekdays, from 10 am Saturday, and 10 am to 2 pm Sunday.

Things to See & Do

The **Museu Comarcal de la Garrotxa**, at Carrer de l'Hospici 8, covers Olot's growth as an early textile centre and includes a collection of local 19th-century art. It's open 11 am to 2 pm and 4 to 7 pm (closed Tuesday, Sunday and holiday afternoons).

The **Jardí Botànic**, a botanical garden of Olot-area flora, contains the interesting **Museu dels Volcans**, covering local flora and fauna as well as volcanoes and earthquakes. It opens 10 am to 2 pm and 5 to 7 pm (4 to 6 pm from September to June). It is closed Tuesday, Sunday and holiday afternoons.

Four **volcanoes** stand sentry on the fringes of Olot. Head for Volcà Montsacopa, 500m north of the centre, or Volcà La Garrinada, 1km north-east of the centre. Both have paths climbing to their craters.

Places to Stay & Eat

Camping Les Tries (☎ 972 26 24 05, *Avinguda de Pere Badosa s/n*), on the eastern edge of town, is open from Semana Santa to October. *Torre Malagrida* (☎ 972 26 42 00, *Passeig de Barcelona 15*) is a youth hostel in an unusual early 20th-century modernist building. The high season, price-wise, is March to September.

The central *Hostal Residència Garrotxa* (☎ 972 26 16 12, *Plaça de la Móra 3*) offers bare but big singles/doubles with private shower for 1875/3745 ptas plus IVA. *Pensión Narmar* (☎ 972 26 98 07, *Carrer de Sant Roc 1*), near Plaça Major, has good, modern rooms starting at 2900 ptas for singles without bath and 5000 ptas for doubles with bath. Prices include breakfast.

Aparthotel Perla D'Olot (☎ 972 26 23 26, *fax 972 27 04 74, Avinguda de Santa Coloma de Farners 97*) has 30 rooms with kitchen, bathroom and TV for 3250/6955 ptas plus IVA.

Pensión Narmar runs a restaurant with main dishes starting at 750 ptas, which include trout and chicken, and a *menú* for 1100 ptas. If you have transport and want to head where the locals go for good Catalan cooking, try *Els Ossos* (☎ 972 26 61 34), 2.5km out of town on the road to Santa Pau. The *ànec amb peres* (duck cooked in pears) is delicious. You'll shed close to 4000 ptas.

Getting There & Away

Bus TEISA (☎ 972 26 01 96) runs buses to: Barcelona two to four times a day (two to 2½ hours, 1855 ptas); Girona via Besalú, eight times daily (1¼ hours, 670 ptas, three on Sunday); and Figueres via Besalú, three times daily (one hour, 605 ptas). Other destinations include Ripoll and Camprodon.

Car & Motorcycle The easiest approach from Barcelona is by the A-7 and C-152. The N-260 runs west to Ripoll and east to Besalú and Figueres, passing Olot on a northerly ring road.

PARC NATURAL DE LA ZONA VOLCÀNICA DE LA GARROTXA

The park surrounds Olot on all sides but the most interesting area is between Olot and the village of Santa Pau, 10km south-east.

Volcanic eruptions began here about 350,000 years ago and the most recent one, at Volcà del Croscat, happened 11,500 years ago. In the park are about 30 volcanic cones, up to 160m high and 1.5km wide. Together with the lush vegetation, a result of fertile

CATALUNYA

soils and a damp climate, these create a landscape of unusual beauty. Between the woods are crop fields, a few hamlets and scattered old stone farmhouses.

Information

The main information office for the park is the Casal dels Volcans in Olot. Another is the Centre d'Informació Can Serra (☎ 972 19 50 74), beside the GE-524 Olot-Banyoles road 4.5km from the middle of Olot.

Santa Pau

The old part of the village, perched picturesquely on a rocky outcrop, contains a porticoed plaza, the Romanesque Església de Santa Maria, and a locked-up baronial castle.

Castellfollit de la Roca

This village on the N-260, 8km north-east of Olot, stands atop a crag composed of several layers of petrified lava – it's most easily viewed from the road north of the village.

Walking

Several good marked walks, which you can complete in less than a day, allow you to explore the park with ease. Inquire at the park information offices about routes.

Places to Stay & Eat

Just off the GE-524 and close to the most inter esting parts of the natural park are two pleasant, small country camping grounds: *Camping La Fageda* (☎ 972 27 12 39), 4km

---

An International Language

As a result of Catalunya's role in the Reconquista in the Middle Ages, the Catalan language (català) is also the first language of most people in the Balearic Islands and nearly half those in Valencia, areas that were taken from the Muslims by Catalunya in the 13th century.

Catalan is also spoken in a narrow strip of Aragón bordering Catalunya – and in the French district of Roussillon, a wedge spreading east from Andorra to the Mediterranean, including the city of Perpignan (Perpinyà in Catalan). Roussillon was ruled from Barcelona for most of the Middle Ages until the Treaty of the Pyrenees in 1659, which set the current French-Spanish border. Farther afield, the residents of the town of Alghero in Sardinia (L'Alguer in Catalan) speak Catalan too, a remnant of Catalunya's medieval empire. And so, back in the Pyrenees, do the people of Andorra, always closely connected with Catalunya. Much to Catalans' delight, Andorra's recent entry to the United Nations has meant that Catalan is now heard there too.

Like all languages, Catalan has its dialects. The main distinction is between western and eastern Catalan; the former is used in Andorra, western and far southern Catalunya and the Catalan-speaking parts of Aragón and Valencia; the latter in the rest of the Catalan world. Expert ears go on to subdivide these into a total of 12 sub-dialects! Valencians prefer to call their sub-dialect valencià rather than català, while in the Balearic Islands you may hear of languages called mallorquí, menorquí and eivissenc – actually the Catalan sub-dialects used in Mallorca, Menorca and Ibiza, respectively.

The 'language question' has plagued relations between Barcelona and Madrid for some years now. In 1998, after much heated debate, Catalunya passed the Ley de la Lengua, which seeks to enshrine the use of the language in all official activities and promote its use in everyday life. Castellano speakers fear it is an attempt to marginalise them, and Jordi Pujol's enemies on the right and left have used every opportunity to take him to task on the issue. A simple fact of life is that Catalan is hard to do without if you want to work anywhere in the public sector or in business in Catalunya.

The issue is just as vexing elsewhere. Catalanists in the Balearic Islands fear that the language is being swamped by the waves of foreign tourists and mainlanders, whose lingua franca (where there is one!) is Spanish. In Valencia, with a higher non-Catalan speaking population than Catalunya, the authorities have tried to steer a middle course: when Catalan and Valencian officials meet (and relations between the two comunidades could be better) it is not unusual to hear the former chatting in Catalan and the latter replying in Spanish!

---

from the middle of Olot, and *Camping Lava* (☎ 972 68 03 58), 7km out. *Restaurant Can Xel*, about halfway between the two on the GE-524, serves meals. Wild camping is banned throughout the Garrotxa district, which stretches from east of Besalú to west of Olot, and from the French border to south of Sant Feliu de Pallerols.

In Santa Pau, there are 10 quaint old rooms with bath at *Bar-Restaurant Cal Sastre* (☎ 972 68 00 49, Cases Noves 1) on Placeta dels Balls in the old part of the village. Doubles start at around 7000 ptas.

RIPOLL
postcode 17500 • pop 10,953

Ripoll, 30km from Olot in the next valley west, is a shabby industrial town of 12,000 people. But it can claim, with some justice, to be the birthplace of Catalunya. At its heart, in the Monestir de Santa Maria, is one of the finest pieces of Romanesque art in Spain.

In the 9th century, Ripoll was the power base from which the local strongman, Guifré el Pilós (Wilfred the Hairy), succeeded in uniting several counties of the Frankish March along the southern side of the Pyrenees. Guifré went on to become the first Count of Barcelona. In AD 879, to encourage repopulation of the Pyrenees valleys, he founded the Monestir de Santa Maria, the most powerful monastery of medieval Catalunya.

Orientation & Information
The tourist office (☎ 972 70 23 51) is on Plaça del Abat Oliba, by the Ribes de Freser–Sant Joan de les Abadesses road, which runs through the north of town. It's open 9.30 am to 1.30 pm and 4 to 7 pm. The Monestir de Santa Maria is virtually next door.

Monestir de Santa Maria
Following its founding in AD 879, the monastery grew rapidly rich, big and influential. From the mid-10th to mid-11th centuries, under famous abbots such as Arnulf and Oliba, it was Catalunya's spiritual and cultural heart. A great five-naved basilica was built, and adorned in about 1100 with a stone portal that ranks among the high points of Romanesque art. The decline began in the 12th century, when Poblet replaced Ripoll as the burial place of Catalan royalty. The monks were evicted during 19th-century anticlerical reforms and two fires left the basilica in ruins by 1885, after which it was restored in rather gloomy imitation of its former glory. The most interesting feature inside now is the restored tomb of Guifré el Pilós.

You can visit the basilica and its great portal, now protected from atmospheric decay by a wall of glass, 8 am to 1 pm and 3 to 8 pm daily (free). A chart near the portal (in Catalan) helps to interpret the feast of sculpture: a medieval vision of the universe, from God the Creator, in the centre at the top, to the month-by-month scenes of daily rural life on the innermost pillars.

Down a few steps to the right of the doorway is the monastery's beautiful *claustre* (cloister), which is open 10 am to 1 pm and 3 to 7 pm daily (100 ptas). It's a two-storey affair, created in the 12th to 15th centuries.

Museu Etnogràfic de Ripoll
Next door to the Monestir de Santa Maria, this museum, housed in part of the medieval Església de Sant Pere, covers local crafts, industries and religious art. It's open 9.30 am to 1.30 pm and 3 to 7 pm (to 6 pm, late September to late March). Entry costs 300 ptas.

Places to Stay & Eat
The friendly *Hostal Paula* (☎ 972 70 00 11, Carrer de Berenguer 8) is barely a stone's throw from the Monestir de Santa Maria. Its 11 modern rooms with sparkling bathrooms are 3320/5325 ptas for a single/double. *Hostal del Ripollès* (☎ 972 70 02 15, Plaça Nova 11) has quite decent rooms for 4500/6500 ptas, with some looking over the square.

There are a few nondescript eating places in the centre of Ripoll. Locals prefer *Can Villaura* (Carretera de Barcelona s/n), just outside the town centre. It has a broad menu and serves local fare.

Getting There & Away
The bus and train stations are almost side by side on Carrer del Progrés, 600m south-east

CATALUNYA

CATALUNYA

of the centre. Connections with Barcelona, Ribes de Freser and Puigcerdà are all better by train than bus. About 12 trains a day run to Barcelona (two hours), up to nine to Ribes de Freser (20 minutes) and five to Puigcerdà (1¼ hours).

VALL ALTO DEL TER

From Ripoll, this upper part of the Riu Ter valley reaches north-east to the pleasant small towns of Sant Joan de les Abadesses and Camprodon (950m), then north-west to the modest Vallter 2000 ski centre (2150m), just below the French border. The area is a more pleasant overnight stop than Ripoll and from the upper reaches there are some excellent walks to the Vall de Núria.

The C-151 road leaves the Ter valley at Camprodon to head over the 1513m Collado d'Ares into France.

Information

Sant Joan de les Abadesses has one tourist office (☎ 972 72 05 99) and Camprodon has two (☎ 972 74 09 36 and ☎ 972 74 00 10).

Things to See

Sant Joan de les Abadesses Worth a look in Sant Joan de les Abadesses are the restored 12th-century **bridge** over the Ter, and the **Museu del Monestir** on Plaça de l'Abadessa. This monastery, another Guifré el Pilós foundation, began life as a nunnery but the nuns were expelled in 1017 for alleged licentious conduct. Its elegant 12th-century church contains the marvellous *Santíssim Misteri*, a 13th-century polychrome woodcarving of the descent from the cross, composed of seven life-size figures. Also remarkable is the Gothic retablo of Santa Maria La Blanca, carved in alabaster. The elegant 15th-century late-Gothic cloister is charming. The monastery complex is open 10 am to 2 pm and 4 to 6 pm daily (to 7 pm in May, June and September). In July and August it opens from 10 am to 7 pm daily, and from November to mid-March hours reduce dramatically (200 ptas).

Beget Capping the end of a long and winding mountain lane that trails off here into a heavily wooded valley, this hamlet is a joy to behold. The 12th-century Romanesque church is accompanied by an implausible array of roughly hewn houses, all scattered about stone-paved lanes. Through it gushes a busy mountain stream. Beget is on the GR-11 walking route.

Skiing

Lying at 2150m in an impressive mountain bowl about 1km from the French border, **Vallter 2000** (☎ 972 13 60 75) is the easternmost Pyrenean ski resort and snow can be unreliable. It has 14 pistes of all grades, nine lifts and a ski school. A day's lift pass is 3300 ptas. You can rent gear at the resort or in Setcases or Camprodon.

Walking

The fit and well equipped can undertake excellent full-day walks west from the topmost part of the Ter valley to the Vall de Núria, 10km to 12km away as the crow flies. Get the Editorial Alpina *Puigmal* mapguide. Shorter walks are also possible.

Places to Stay

There are many accommodation options, including camping grounds near Sant Joan and Camprodon, and the good *Camping Conca de Ter* (☎ 972 74 06 29), at Vilallonga de Ter, 5km north-west of Camprodon. It's open all year, charging 2780 ptas plus IVA, for two adults with a car and tent.

Hostal Janpere (☎ 972 72 00 77, Carrer del Mestre Andreu 3), in Sant Joan de les Abadesses, has good rooms with private bath costing 3000 ptas per person.

Camprodon is a popular base for walkers and skiers. *Can Ganansi* (☎ 972 74 01 34, Carrer de Josep Morera 9), 100m south of the central Plaça d'Espanya, has doubles with bath and TV for up to 6000 ptas.

North-west up the valley from Camprodon, the villages of Vilallonga de Ter, Tregurà de Dalt (5km up a steep side road, 12km from Camprodon) and Setcases (11km) have at least one pensión or hostal each. Setcases has half a dozen.

You can stay in two places in Beget. *El Forn* (☎ 972 74 12 30, Carrer de Josep

Duñach 'En Feliça' 9) is a well-kept cosy house. Doubles cost 9600 ptas. Full board is 7500 ptas per person. A little more basic but fine is **Can Joanic** (☎ 972 74 12 41, Carrer de Bell Aire 14), with doubles at 5000 ptas.

Places to Eat

You'll find a few cheap and (sometimes) cheerful little restaurants in central Camprodon and other towns – often the menú won't exceed about 1200 ptas. Some local favourites are a little less obvious to find for the uninitiated and require your own wheels (or a taxi). **Restaurant El Serrat** (☎ 972 13 60 19) is a delightful, rustic sort of place in the town of Tregurà. It's good for country cooking. Both of the little hotels in Beget have inviting restaurants.

Getting There & Away

Güell i Güell runs around seven buses daily from Ripoll to Sant Joan de les Abadesses (15 minutes) and Camprodon (40 minutes). The only daily bus north-west from Camprodon, as far as Setcases (30 minutes), leaves in the early afternoon and returns soon after. TEISA runs a couple of buses daily from Olot to Sant Joan de les Abadesses and Camprodon. There are no buses to Rocabruna or Beget.

VALL DE NÚRIA & RIBES DE FRESER

Around AD 700, the story goes, Sant Gil (St Giles) came from Nîmes to live in a cave in an isolated mountain valley 26km north of Ripoll, preaching the Gospel to shepherds. Before he left four years later, apparently fleeing Visigothic persecution, Sant Gil hurriedly hid away a wooden Virgin and child image he had carved, a cross, his cooking pot and the bell he had used to summon the shepherds. They stayed hidden until 1079, when an ox miraculously led some shepherds to the spot. The statuette, the Mare de Déu de Núria, became the patron of Pyrenean shepherds and Núria's future was assured. The first historical mention of a shrine here was made in 1162.

Sant Gil would recoil in shock if he came back today. The large, grey sanctuary complex

squatting at the heart of the valley is an eyesore and the crowds would make anyone with hermitic leanings run a mile. But otherwise Núria remains almost pristine, a wide, green, mountain-ringed bowl that is the starting point for numerous walks. Getting there is fun too, either on foot up the Gorges de Núria – the green, rocky valley of the thundering Riu Núria – or by the little cremallera (ratchet) railway from Ribes de Freser, which rises over 1000m on its 12km journey up the same valley.

The Legend of Comte Arnau

Sant Joan de les Abadesses is one of many places in the country north of Ripoll associated with perhaps the strangest of Pyrenean legends: that of Comte Arnau, the wicked medieval Count of Mataplana, who cheated his workers of their due payments of wheat and had more than his quota of lust for local womanhood. The insatiable count, it seems, came by tunnel to Sant Joan from Campdevànol, 10km west, for covert trysts with the abbess and other nuns. When the abbess, his favourite, died, her pious replacement barred him from the convent, but, thanks to help from the devil, he still got in – and carried on.

Eventually, Arnau fell in love with a local lass, whose only refuge was the nunnery at Sant Joan. Arnau forced his way into the convent to find his beloved dead, from fear and misery, it's surmised. Her corpse, however, revived just long enough to give the count a good ticking-off for his misdeeds. Overcome by remorse, Arnau retired to the Serra de Mogrony, where, condemned to eternal misery for his sins, his tortured soul still wanders, returning on thundery nights (and, some say, under a full moon) to the convent: a horrific vision on horseback with a pack of balefully howling dogs.

If you visit Sant Joan or other villages in the region in summer, you might be lucky enough to catch one of the occasional re-enactments of bits of the Arnau legend. Or you can look at his supposed residence, the Castell de Mataplana, at Gombrèn, about 11km north-west of Ripoll on the GE-401.

CATALUNYA

Orientation

Unless you're walking to Núria across the mountains, you must approach from the small town of Ribes de Freser, on the N-152 14km north of Ripoll. The cremallera starts at Ribes-Enllaç station, just off the N-152 at the southern end of Ribes, and makes two stops on the way to Núria: at Ribes-Vila station, near the northern end of Ribes after 1km, and at the village of Queralbs (1200m) after 6km. There's a road from Ribes to Queralbs, but from there on it's the cremallera or your feet.

Information

Núria's tourist office (☎ 972 73 20 20), open 8.30 am to 6.30 pm daily (to 8 pm July to September), is in the sanctuary complex.

Ribes de Freser's tourist office (☎ 972 72 77 28) is at Plaça de l'Ajuntament 3.

Santuari de Núria

The large 19th- and 20th-century building dominating the valley contains a hotel, restaurants and exhibition halls as well as the *santuari* itself, which holds the sacred *símbols de Núria*. The santuari has the same opening hours as the information office. The Mare de Déu de Núria sits behind a glass screen above the altar and is in the Romanesque style of the 12th century, so either Sant Gil was centuries ahead of his time or this isn't his work! Steps lead up to the bell, cross and cooking pot (all dating back to at least the 15th century). To have a prayer answered, put your head in the pot and ring the bell while you say it.

Walking & Skiing

Get Editorial Alpina's *Puigmal* map-guide before you come to Núria if you plan on doing some walking. If you want to walk up to Núria, you can avoid the first unexciting 6km from Ribes de Freser by taking the cremallera (or road) to Queralbs, saving your energies for the steepest and most spectacular part of the approach – about three hours up. Or take the cremallera up and walk down!

From the Vall de Núria, you can cap several 2700m to 2900m peaks on the main Pyrenees ridge in about 2½ to four hours

walking each (one way). The most popular is Puigmal (2913m).

In winter, Núria is a small-scale ski resort with 10 short runs.

Places to Stay & Eat

Wild camping is banned in the whole Ribes de Freser–Núria area.

Núria Behind the sanctuary there's a cheap and basic *zona d'acampada (bookings ☎ 972 73 20 20),* which is a camping area with limited facilities.

Alberg Pic de l'Àliga (☎ 972 73 20 48) is a youth hostel up at the top of the cable car *(ecabina)* on the eastern side of the valley. It has 138 places in dorms of four to 14. High-season prices apply all year except April, October and November. The cable car runs 9 am to 6.35 pm daily (to 8.15 pm July to September) and also 9.30 to 10 pm Friday and Saturday.

Hotel Vall de Núria (☎ 972 73 20 00) in the sanctuary building has 65 comfortable singles/doubles with bath and TV ranging from 6550/8770 ptas (weekdays most of the year) to 11,680/15,180 ptas (August). It is closed in May and December, but runs some apartments that open all year. In the sanctuary building, *Autoservei* self-service cafeteria and *Bar Finistrelles* both have starters in the 600 ptas region and main courses for around 1000 ptas. The hotel restaurant has a *menú* for 2200 ptas. A shop in the sanctuary building sells food. The bar and restaurant are closed during slow periods, but the Autoservei is generally open daily.

Ribes de Freser *Fonda Vilalta (☎ 972 72 70 95, Carrer de Cerdanya 6)* has a variety of basic but clean doubles at 3200, 4200 (views and shower) or 5200 ptas (views and full bathroom). Three lower mid-range hotels, with doubles at up to 7250 ptas, are on Carrer de Sant Quintí.

Queralbs This delightful hamlet of stone houses with slate roofs makes a prettier base. Try for a room at *Pensió L'Avet (☎ 972 727 377, Carrer Major 7),* which is the only option (often open only at weekends). It's a pleasant old house with six doubles at 5000 ptas. The guy who runs it isn't always about, so make sure you don't leave your passport with him as you may find him hard to track down when you want to leave.

The town is short on eating options, however, so bring your own during slow periods or have a car to get to another town.

Getting There & Away

Transports Mir runs between Ripoll and Ribes de Freser, with two or three buses a day on weekdays, and one on Saturday.

About six Renfe trains a day run to Ribes-Enllaç from Ripoll (20 minutes) and Barcelona (2¼ hours).

The cremallera (☎ 972 73 20 20), a narrow-gauge electric-powered cog-wheel railway operating since 1931, runs from Ribes-Enllaç to Núria and back six to 12 times a day, depending on the season. Some services connect with Renfe trains at Ribes-Enllaç.

The cremallera ride is about 45 minutes one way and all trains stop at Ribes-Vila and Queralbs. It's a spectacular trip, particularly after Queralbs, as the train winds up the Gorges de Núria. The one-way/return fare from Ribes to Núria is 1375/2200 ptas.

PUIGCERDÀ

postcode 17520 • pop 6580 • elev 1202m

Just 2km from the French border, Puigcerdà (puh-cher-**da**) is not much more than a way station, but it's a jolly little one, particularly in summer and during the ski season. A dozen Spanish, Andorran and French ski resorts lie within 45km.

At a height of 1200m, Puigcerdà is capital of the district of Cerdanya, which, with French Cerdagne across the border, occupies a low-lying basin between higher reaches of the Pyrenees to the east and west. Cerdanya and Cerdagne, once a single Catalan county, were divided by the Treaty of the Pyrenees in 1659 but still have a lot in common. It's in areas like this that you have the strongest sense of being neither in Spain nor in France, but in Catalunya.

Orientation & Information

Puigcerdà stands on a small hill, with the train station at the foot of its south-western side. A few minutes' climb up some flights of steps takes you to Plaça de l'Ajuntament, off which is the tourist office (☎ 972 88 05 42), at Carrer de Querol 1. It's open 9 am to 1 pm and 4 to 7 pm Tuesday to Friday (morning only on Tuesday), and 10 am to 1.30 pm and 4.30 to 7.30 pm Saturday.

You'll find plenty of banks on the main plaças. The post office is at Avinguda del Coronel Molera 11. The Guàrdia Urbana (municipal police; ☎ 908-831160) are in the ajuntament on Plaça de l'Ajuntament. The Hospital de Puigcerdà (☎ 972 88 01 50) is centrally located at Plaça de Santa Maria 1.

Things to See

Despite being seriously damaged in the civil war, the town centre retains a relaxed and old-fashioned air. Of the 17th-century **Església de Santa Maria**, only the tower remains; the rest fell victim to the civil war. The 13th-century Gothic **Església de Sant Domènec**, on Passeig del 10 d'Abril, was also wrecked in the war, but was rebuilt. It contains 14th-century Gothic murals that somehow survived. The **Estany** (lake) in the north of town, created back in 1380 for irrigation, is surrounded by turn-of-the-20th-century summer houses built by wealthy Barcelona families.

Places to Stay

Camping Stel (☎ 972 88 23 61) on the Llívia road is open all year and charges 3510 ptas plus IVA, for two adults with a car and tent.

Outside the train station, **Hostal Estación** (☎ 972 88 03 50, Plaça de l'Estació 2) has plain but adequate singles/doubles with private bath for 3000/5000 ptas plus IVA.

Up in town, the friendly **Hostal Alfonso** (☎ 972 88 02 46, Carrer d'Espanya 5) is a bit better at around 6000 ptas for large doubles with bath. **Hostal La Muntanya** (☎ 972 88 02 02, Avinguda del Coronel Molera 1) is clean, if a little hospital-ward like, and charges 5000 ptas a double. Singles are hard to come by in either place.

CATALUNYA

Hotel Sala (☎ 972 88 01 04, Carrer d'Alfons I 17) has straightforward rooms without bath for 2500/5000 ptas. For a little more comfort (ie, private bathroom), you pay 3500/6500 ptas.

Hotel Del Lago (☎ 972 88 10 00, fax 972 14 15 11, Avinguda del Dr Piguillem s/n), near the Estany, has old-fashioned style and a nice garden for 7000/9500 ptas a room plus IVA.

Top of the tree is **Hotel Avet Blau** (☎ 972 88 25 52, fax 972 88 12 12, Plaça de Santa Maria 14), a fine old mansion overlooking the centre of the village. Comfortable doubles cost up to 14,000 ptas plus IVA.

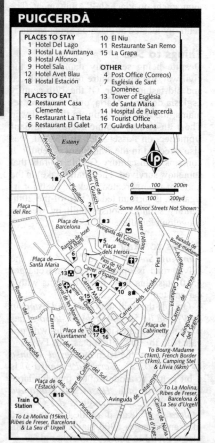

PUIGCERDÀ

PLACES TO STAY
1 Hotel Del Lago
3 Hostal La Muntanya
8 Hostal Alfonso
9 Hotel Sala
12 Hotel Avet Blau
18 Hostal Estació

PLACES TO EAT
2 Restaurant Casa Clemente
5 Restaurant La Tieta
6 Restaurant El Galet

10 El Niu
11 Restaurante San Remo
15 La Grapa

OTHER
4 Post Office (Correos)
7 Església de Sant Domènec
13 Tower of Església de Santa Maria
14 Hospital de Puigcerdà
16 Tourist Office
17 Guàrdia Urbana

Places to Eat

For cheap, no-nonsense food you could do worse than **El Niu** (Carrer d'Alfons I 15), where the 1200 ptas menú appears to be just two courses, but is actually three (one of which is usually trout) with wine thrown in, too. Another straightforward option is **Restaurante San Remo** (Carrer de Ramón Cosp 9), with a 1100 ptas menú.

Restaurante Casa Clemente (Avinguda del Dr Piguillem 6) has a more interesting menú for 1650 ptas and a range of other dishes. **Restaurant La Tieta** (Carrer dels Ferrers 20) is an intimate, cavernous place where you can choose from an interesting menu. The carpaccio de salmón is good at 1400 ptas.

Restaurant El Galet (Plaça de Santa Maria 8) is a welcoming little dining option with warm timber ceiling and a menu of Catalan dishes at moderate prices.

La Grapa (Carrer de Querol 4) is a cocktail and cava bar that also offers an appetising range of munchies, from salads and crepes through to torrades and cheese platters.

Getting There & Away

Bus Alsina Graells runs two daily buses (one at weekends) to Barcelona (three hours) via the 5km Túnel del Cadí; two or three to La Seu d'Urgell (one hour); and one to Lleida (3½ hours). They stop at the train station. The tourist office has timetables.

The quickest way to Andorra is by train to Latour-de-Carol, then by bus, a journey of 2¼ to 2¾ hours. See the Andorra chapter for information on the bus connections. You can also reach Andorra la Vella by changing buses in La Seu d'Urgell.

Train About six trains a day run to Ribes de Freser, Ripoll and Barcelona (3¼ hours, 1125 ptas). Five in each direction make the seven-minute hop over the border to Latour-de-Carol in France, where they connect with trains from Toulouse or Paris, and with the narrow-gauge Train Jaune ('yellow train') down the Têt valley to Perpignan. Puigcerdà station has details on the French trains.

Car & Motorcycle From Barcelona, the A-18 autopista feeds into the C-1411, which approaches Puigcerdà through the Túnel del Cadí. Bicycles are not allowed in the tunnel, which is a tollway.

The N-152 from Ribes de Freser climbs west along the northern flank of the Rigard valley, with the pine-covered Serra de Mogrony rising to the south, to the 1800m Collado de Toses pass, then winds down to Puigcerdà.

The main crossing into France is at Bourg-Madame, immediately east of Puigcerdà, from where roads head to Perpignan and Toulouse.

AROUND PUIGCERDÀ
Llívia
postcode 17527 • pop 975 • elev 1224m
Six kilometres east of Puigcerdà across flat farmland, the little town of Llívia is a piece of Spain in France. Under the 1659 Treaty of the Pyrenees, Spain ceded 33 villages to France, but Llívia was a 'town' and so, together with the 13 sq km of its municipality, remained a Spanish possession.

The interest of Llívia's tiny medieval nucleus, near the top of the town, centres on the **Museu Municipal** at Carrer dels Forns 4 and the 15th-century Gothic **Església de Nostra Senyora dels Àngels**, just above the museum. There's a tourist office (☎ 972 89 63 13) in the museum and both open 10 am to 1 pm and 3 to 6 pm (to 7 pm, April to September) Tuesday to Saturday (and Monday in July and August), and in summer 10 am to 2 pm Sunday. The museum (150 ptas) is in what's claimed to be Europe's oldest pharmacy, the Farmacia Esteva, which was founded in 1415. The church contains an 18th-century baroque retablo and a processional cross given to Llívia by Carlos I. From the church you can walk up to the ruined **Castell de Llívia** where, during the short-lived period of Islamic dominion in the Pyrenees, the Muslim governor Manussa enjoyed a secret dalliance with Lampègia, daughter of the Duke of Aquitaine (or so legend has it).

You can stay here if you want and dine on the balconies of *Restaurant Can Ventura (Plaça Major 1),* a ramshackle building

dating to 1791. The food is delightful, traditional Catalan fare, with mains costing around 2000 ptas.

At the time of writing, one or two Alsina Graells buses and one TEISA bus a day connected Puigcerdà train station with Llívia. Otherwise, it's not a long walk, and the road is flat and quiet. You only cross about 2km of France before entering the Llívia enclave and, apart from a couple of French road signs, you'd hardly know you'd left Spain.

La Molina & Masella
These two ski resorts lie either side of Tosa d'Alp (2537m), about 15km south of Puigcerdà. La Molina is one of Catalunya's biggest and most popular ski centres. Altogether it has 31 pistes of all grades, totalling 27km, at altitudes of 1600m to 2537m. The resort straggles about 4km up the hill from La Molina proper, where the train station is, to 'Supermolina', where some lifts start and you'll find the information and bookings office (☎ 972 89 20 31).

Masella (☎ 972 14 40 00) has some long forest runs among its 37 pistes totalling 49km. The majority are blue or red. The lift system is more limited than La Molina's. A one-day pass costs 4100 ptas.

Both resorts offer equipment rental and ski schools (La Molina has three).

Places to Stay *Alberg Mare de Déu de les Neus (☎ 972 89 20 12)* is a youth hostel in the bottom part of La Molina, near the train station. It has 148 places in rooms ranging from doubles to a 38-person dorm. Mid-season prices are charged from December to April and in July and August. High-season rates are applied on most winter weekends.

Other accommodation is mostly on the expensive side and many skiers stay in Puigcerdà or even farther afield. *Hostal 4 Vents (☎ 972 89 20 97, Pista Standard s/n),* about halfway up the hill to Supermolina, has doubles for about 10,000 ptas but only opens in winter (like most places here). *Hotel Adserà (☎ 972 89 20 01)* is another option at about the same price.

CATALUNYA

CATALUNYA

Getting There & Away La Molina is on the Barcelona-Ribes de Freser-Puigcerdà railway, with about six trains a day each way. In the ski season there's a bus service from Puigcerdà. Most people come by car; the easiest route from Barcelona is by the A-18 autopista and the C-1411 through the Túnel del Cadí.

SERRA DEL CADÍ

The N-260 runs west along the wide Riu Segre valley from Puigcerdà to La Seu d'Urgell, with the Pyrenees climbing away northward towards Andorra, and one of the finest pre-Pyrenees ranges, the Serra del Cadí, rising steep and high along the southern side. Although this face of the Cadí – rocky and fissured by ravines known as *canales* – looks daunting enough, the range's most spectacular peak is Pedraforca (2497m), a southern offshoot with probably the best rock climbing in Catalunya. Pedraforca and the main Cadí range also offer some excellent mountain walking for those suitably equipped and experienced.

The dramatic scenery, attractive villages and some unpaved roads in among the hills (passable for non-4WD vehicles in dry conditions) make the area well worth a visit.

Orientation

The area around Pedraforca is most easily reached from the C-1411, along the B-400, which heads west 1.5km south of Guardiola de Berguedà. Pedraforca looms mightily into view about halfway to the village of Saldes, which sits 1215m high at its foot, 15km from the C-1411. The main Cadí range runs east to west about 5km north of Saldes. The Refugi Lluís Estasen (see Places to Stay & Eat) is under the northern face of Pedraforca, 2.5km north-west of Saldes. You can reach it by footpath from Saldes or by a partly paved road that turns north off the B-400 about 1km west of Saldes. Park at the Mirador de Gresolet, from where it's a 10-minute walk up to the refuge.

Information

The Parc Natural del Cadí-Moixeró's main Centre d'Informació (☎ 93 824 41 51) is in Bagà, a pleasant little village (walk down to the stone bridge across the stream) on the C-1411, 4km north of Guardiola de Berguedà. The office is open 9 am to 1.30 pm and 3.30 to 6.30 pm weekdays, 10 am to 2 pm and 4 to 6.30 pm on Saturday, and until 2 pm Sunday and holidays. The office is a mite inconveniently placed at Carrer de la Vinya 1, on the Gisclareny road on the western edge of Bagà.

In Saldes, the Centre d'Informació Massís del Pedraforca (☎ 93 825 80 05) is open 11 am to 2 pm and 5 to 7 pm daily June to September, but otherwise on weekends only. It has information on the Saldes and Pedraforca area only.

Walking

Pedraforca The name means 'Stone Fork' and the approach from the east makes it clear why. The two separate rocky peaks, northern Pollegó Superior (2497m) and southern Pollegó Inferior (2400m), are divided by a saddle called L'Enforcadura. The northern face, rising near vertically for 600m, has some classic rock climbs; the southern has a wall that sends alpinists into raptures.

Pedraforca is also possible for walkers, but certainly exhilarating. From Refugi Lluís Estasen you can reach the Pollegó Superior summit in about three strenuous hours – either southwards from the refuge, then up the middle of the fork from the south-eastern side (a path from Saldes joins this route); or westwards up to the Collada del Verdet, then south and east to the summit. The latter route has some hairy precipices and requires a good head for heights. It's not suitable for coming down: you must use the first route.

Other Walks Walkers can ascend Comabona (2530m), towards the eastern end of the main Cadí ridge, in about four or five hours from the Refugi Lluís Estasen. Puig de la Canal del Cristall (2563m) and Puig de la Canal Baridana (2647m), the highest in the range, are longer walks that may require a night in the hills.

There are various routes of one to two days right across the Cadí, from Saldes,

Refugi de Lluís Estasen or Gósol, to the Segre valley. If you want to stay overnight in the mountains, the FEEC's small **Refugi Prat d'Aguiló** (☎ *973 25 01 35*), at 2037m on the northern slopes, has room for up to 38 and a kitchen.

Gósol

The B-400 continues paved from Saldes to the pretty stone village of Gósol, 6km farther west. The original Gósol (the Vila Vella), which dated back to at least the 9th century, is now abandoned on the hill south of the present village. Picasso spent some of

1906 painting in Gósol and the village has a museum just off the *plaça major* with a section devoted to him.

Tuixén & Beyond

An unpaved road west from Gósol climbs the 1625m Coll de Josa pass then descends past the picturesque hamlet of Josa del Cadí to Tuixén (1206m), another attractive village on a small hill. From Tuixén, scenic paved roads lead north-west to La Seu d'Urgell (36km) and south to Sant Llorenç de Morunys (28km), which is on a beautiful cross-country road from Berga to Organyà.

PUIGCERDÀ & SERRA DEL CADÍ AREA

Places to Stay & Eat

Saldes & Around There are at least four camping grounds along the B-400 between the C-1411 and Saldes, some open year round. In Saldes, *Can Manuel (☎ 93 825 80 41)* on the plaza offers accommodation with half-board only, which costs 3600 ptas per person.

The FEEC's *Refugi Lluís Estasen (☎ 93 822 00 79)*, near the Mirador de Gresolet (see Orientation earlier), is open year-round with 100 places, meals and a warden in summer, and about 30 places in winter. When the refuge is full you can sleep out-side, but not in a tent.

Gósol *Hostal Cal Francisco (☎ 973 37 00 75)*, by the road at the eastern end of the village, has singles/doubles for 2700/5000 ptas.

Tuixén The friendly *Can Farragetes (☎ 973 37 00 34, Carrer del Coll 7)* has doubles with bath for 3200 ptas and food in the bar. There are a couple of other places nearby.

Getting There & Around

Berga, Guardiola de Berguedà and Bagà are all on the Alsina Graells bus routes from Barcelona to Puigcerdà and La Seu d'Urgell via the Túnel del Cadí. There's a bus between Guardiola de Berguedà and Ripoll once or twice daily, Monday to Saturday.

Getting to Saldes, Gósol or Tuixén basically requires your own transport or an itchy hitching thumb. This is feasible along the B-400 as far as Saldes or Gósol in July or August, or on the weekend during the other summer months, but there won't be much traffic at other times.

LA SEU D'URGELL

postcode 25700 • pop 10,661

The lively valley town of La Seu d'Urgell (la **se**-u dur-**zhey**) is Spain's gateway to Andorra, 10km north. It's a pleasant place to spend a night, with a fine medieval cathedral.

When the Franks evicted the Muslims from this part of the Pyrenees in the early 9th century, they made La Seu a bishopric and capital of the counts of Urgell. It has been an important market and cathedral town since the 11th century and has also played a key role in the history of Andorra (see the Andorra chapter).

Orientation & Information

The main axis runs north-south under the names Avinguda de les Valls d'Andorra, Avinguda de Pau Claris, Carrer de Sant Ot and Passeig de Joan Brudieu, with the old part of town to its east.

The tourist office (☎ 973 35 15 11) is at the northern entrance to town, at Avinguda de les Valls d'Andorra 33. It's open 9 am to 9 pm from July to mid-September. Otherwise, it's open 10 am to 2 pm and 4 to 7 pm Monday to Saturday. You can also get some info at the Consell Comarcal (☎ 973 36 01 55), Passeig de Joan Brudieu 15. It opens weekdays in the morning only.

The Policía Municipal (☎ 973 35 04 26) are in the Casa de la Ciutat (town hall), at Plaça dels Oms 1. There's a hospital (☎ 973 35 00 50) at the southern end of Passeig de Joan Brudieu.

Llibreria Ribera de Antich on Carrer de Sant Ot is a good source of maps and local guides.

Catedral de Santa Maria & Museu Diocesà

Looming on the southern side of Plaça dels Oms, the 12th-century *seu* (cathedral) is one of Catalunya's outstanding Romanesque buildings despite various remodellings. It is one of more than a hundred Romanesque churches lining what has come to be known as the Ruta Románica from Perpignan (France) to the Urgell district.

The fine western facade, through which you enter, is decorated in typical Lombard style. The inside is dark and plain but still impressive, with five apses, some murals in the south transept, and a 13th-century Virgin and child sculpture in the central apse.

From inside the cathedral you can enter the good Museu Diocesà. This encompasses the fine cloister and the 12th-century Romanesque Església de Sant Miquel, as well as some good medieval Pyrenees church murals, sculptures and altarpieces and a rare

10th-century Mozarabic *Beatus* (illustrated manuscript of the Apocalypse).

The cathedral and museum are open 10 am to 1 pm and 4 to 6 pm Monday to Saturday, and 10 am to 1 pm Sunday. On Sunday morning only the cloister is open. Entry to the church is free. Entry to the cloister and Església de Sant Miquel is 150 ptas, or 350 ptas if you want to see the museum too (which is well worthwhile).

Places to Stay

Camping En Valira (☎ 973 35 10 35), in the north of town on Avinguda del Valira, has room for 1200 people at 2300 ptas for two adults with a car and tent.

The modern youth hostel *Alberg La Valira* (☎ 973 35 38 97, Carrer de Joaquim Viola Lafuerza 57), 800m west of the centre, has spacious public areas and 100 places in eight-bunk dorms. The mid-season is March to mid-September. There's little other cheap accommodation.

By contrast there are lots of good lower mid-range hotels. *Hotel Avenida* (☎ 973 35 01 04, Avinguda de Pau Claris 18) is a good bet, with bright singles/doubles for up to 3600/5300 ptas or 3975/6750 ptas plus IVA. The more expensive ones are bigger and recently renovated.

On a fairly quiet street, *Residència Duc d'Urgell* (☎ 973 35 21 95, Carrer de Josep de Zulueta 43) has nice modern rooms with TV and bath for 4700/6700 ptas. *Hotel Andria* (☎ 973 35 03 00, Passeig de Joan Brudieu 24) has sizable rooms with a certain antiquated charm, but generally offers half-board only at up to 7900 ptas per person. The bigger 56-room *Hotel Nice* (☎ 973 35 21 00, Avinguda de Pau Claris 4-6) is a better deal, with smart rooms for 5675/7675 ptas.

La Seu's *Parador* (☎ 973 35 20 00, Carrer de Sant Domènec s/n), built around the restored cloister of the 14th-century Sant Domènec convent, is suitably luxurious with doubles at 15,000 ptas plus IVA.

CATALUNYA

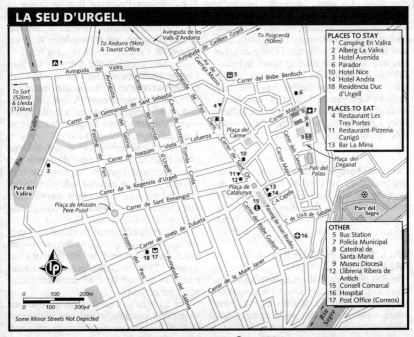

LA SEU D'URGELL

PLACES TO STAY
1 Camping En Valira
2 Alberg La Valira
3 Hotel Avenida
6 Parador
10 Hotel Nice
14 Hotel Andria
18 Residència Duc
d'Urgell

PLACES TO EAT
4 Restaurant Les
Tres Portes
11 Restaurant-Pizzeria
Canigó
13 Bar La Mina

OTHER
5 Bus Station
7 Policia Municipal
8 Catedral de
Santa Maria
9 Museu Diocesà
12 Llibreria Ribera de
Antich
15 Consell Comarcal
16 Hospital
17 Post Office (Correos)

Some Minor Streets Not Depicted

Places to Eat

Bar La Mina (☎ 973 35 10 51, Passeig de Joan Brudieu 24) serves good pizzas for 775 ptas and a range of mains starting at 900 ptas. Its outside tables are a fine place to watch the world go by. *Restaurant-Pizzeria Canigó (☎ 973 35 10 43, Carrer de Sant Ot 3)* has a wide range of options. The *parrillada de carne* (mixed meat grill) is good value at 1200 ptas.

A homely little place is *Restaurant Les Tres Portes (☎ 973 35 29 07, Carrer de Garriga i Massou 7),* where you can chow down to mains from 1200 to 1800 ptas in the garden.

The *Hotel Avenida, Hotel Nice* and *Hotel Andria* offer Catalan and Spanish food, with *menús* at around 1650 ptas.

Getting There & Away

Bus The bus station is on the northern edge of the old town. Alsina Graells (☎ 973 35 00 20) runs four or five buses daily to Barcelona (3½ hours, 2475 ptas; two each via Solsona and Ponts, and one, which does not run on Sunday, via the Túnel del Cadí); three to Puigcerdà (one hour); and two to Lleida (2½ hours, 1150 ptas). La Hispano Andorrana runs up to seven buses daily to Andorra la Vella (30 minutes, 340 ptas). Hispano Igualadina has one bus daily to Tarragona (3¼ hours). Two buses a day crawl along in all-stops mode to Sort from 1 July to mid-September. Otherwise, they run on weekdays only. The trip costs 500 ptas.

Car & Motorcycle The N-260 heads 6km south-west to Adral, then turns off west over the hills to Sort. The C-1313 carries on south to Lleida, threading the towering Tresponts gorge about 13km beyond Adral.

VALL DE LA NOGUERA PALLARESA

The Riu Noguera Pallaresa, running south down a dramatic valley about 50km west of La Seu d'Urgell, is Spain's best-known white-water river. The main centres for white-water sports are the town of **Sort** and the villages of **Rialp** and **Llavorsí**. You'll find firms to take you rafting, hydrospeeding, canoeing and kayaking or, when you feel like getting out of the river, canyoning, trekking, climbing, mountain biking, horse riding and *ponting* (involving dangling by a rope from bridges).

The tourist office (☎ 973 62 10 02) in Sort is at Avinguda dels Comtes del Pallars 21.

Walking

The Vall de Cardós and Vall Ferrera, heading back into the hills north-east of Llavorsí, lead to some remote and, in parts, tough mountain walking country along and across the Andorran and French borders, including Pica d'Estats, the highest peak in Catalunya. Lonely Planet's *Walking in Spain,* and Editorial Alpina's *Pica d'Estats* and *Montgarri* will help you find your way around this area.

White-Water Rafting

The Noguera Pallaresa has no drops of more than grade 4 (on a scale of 1 to 6), but it's exciting enough to attract a constant stream of white-water fans from April to August. It's at its best in May and June.

The best stretch is the 14km or so from Llavorsí to Rialp, on which the standard raft outing lasts one to 1½ hours and costs 4500 to 5000 ptas per person. A quicker surge down the same stretch on a hydrospeed costs 7000 ptas. Other longer rides down to Sort and beyond will cost more.

At least one company, Yeti Emotions (☎ 973 62 22 01), at Carrer de Borda Era d'Alfons s/n in Llavorsí, organises a high grade trip for experienced rafters only farther upstream. Two other rafting companies also operate from Llavorsí and you will find still more based in places like Sort.

You can do adventure-weekend packages combining rafting with other activities (such as mountain-bike excursions) for around 12,000 to 26,000 ptas (the cost depends in part on type of accommodation and time of year).

For all trips you need to bring your own swimming costume, towel and change of clothes. All other gear is generally provided.

Places to Stay

Llavorsí is the most pleasant base, much more of a mountain village than Rialp or Sort. *Camping Riberies* (☎ 973 62 21 51) has a good riverside site and charges 575 ptas per person, per tent and per car, but is open from mid-June to mid-September. *Camping Aigües Braves* (☎ 973 62 21 53), about 1km north by the river, costs the same.

Hostal del Rey (☎ 973 62 20 11), *Hostal La Noguera* (☎ 973 62 20 12) and *Hotel Lamoga* (☎ 973 62 20 06) all overlook the river. They charge 4800, 6000 and 7725 ptas respectively for doubles with bath.

Getting There & Away

Alsina Graells runs one daily bus (at 7.30 am) from Barcelona to Sort, Rialp, Llavorsí (5½ hours) and Esterri d'Àneu (3450 ptas). From June to October it continues to the Val d'Aran. The return bus leaves Llavorsí at 1.55 pm. Alsina Graells also has a daily bus (except on Sunday) between Lleida and Esterri d'Àneu (2030 ptas) via Sort, Rialp and Llavorsí. From Llavorsí you catch this at 5.40 am, and can change at La Pobla de Segur.

PARC NACIONAL D'AIGÜESTORTES I ESTANY DE SANT MAURICI & AROUND

Catalunya's only national park extends 20km east to west and only 9km from north to south, but packs in more beauty than most areas 100 times its size. The product of glacial action over two million years, it's essentially two east-west valleys at 1600m to 2000m altitude lined by jagged 2600m to 2900m peaks of granite and slate. Against this backdrop, pine and fir forests, and open bush and grassland – bedecked with wild flowers in spring and early summer – combine with some 200 *estanys* (small lakes) and countless streams and waterfalls to create a wilderness of rare splendour.

The national park, whose boundaries were extended in 1996 to cover 141.2 sq km, lies at the core of a wider wilderness area, whose outer limit is known as the *zona perifèrica* and includes some magnificent high country to the north and south. The total area covered is 408.5 sq km and is monitored by park rangers.

Although the park's main valleys are easily accessible and there are numerous marked walking routes, off the main trails it's not hard to lose your way, and the peaks themselves are mainly for mountaineers. The whole park is normally under snow from December to April.

Chamois are relatively abundant. In summer they prefer to stick to high altitudes, but you may spot some lower down when they feed in the early morning and evening. Deer are more common at lower altitudes. Spectacular birds include the capercaillie and golden eagle.

Apart from its natural wonders, the region also contains a cluster of Catalunya's most charming Romanesque churches, in the Boí and Taüll area.

Orientation

Approaches One main approach to the park is from the village of Espot (1320m), 4km east of its eastern boundary. An 8km paved road leads west up to Espot from the C-147 road 12km north of Llavorsí.

The other main approach – and in summer the easier one if you're dependent on buses – is from the L-500, which heads north-east off the N-230 Lleida-Vielha road 2km north of El Pont de Suert. From there it's 15km to the turning for Boí (1km east), then a farther 1.5km to the turning for the park, which begins 4km east.

Walkers can also enter the park by passes from the Vall Fosca to the south and the Val d'Aran to the north.

The Park The two main valleys are those of the Riu Escrita in the east and the Riu de Sant Nicolau in the west. The Escrita flows out of the park's largest lake, the 1km-long Estany de Sant Maurici. The Sant Nicolau's main source is Estany Llong, 4km west of Estany de Sant Maurici across the 2423m Portarró d'Espot pass. Three kilometres downstream from Estany Llong, the Sant Nicolau runs through a particularly beautiful stretch known as Aigüestortes (Twisted Waters).

Apart from the valley openings at the eastern and western ends, virtually the whole perimeter of the park is mountain crests, with numerous spurs of almost equal height reaching in towards the centre. One of these, from the south, ends in the twin peaks Els Encantats (2746m and 2733m), towering over Estany de Sant Maurici.

Maps & Guides Editorial Alpina's map-guides are adequate, although they don't show every single trail. *Sant Maurici – Els Encantats* covers the eastern half of the park and its approaches; *Vall de Boí* covers the western half and its approaches; *Montsent de Pallars* covers the Vall Fosca; and *Val d'Aran,* naturally, covers the Val d'Aran. A better map of the whole area is the Institut Cartogràfic de Catalunya's *Parc Nacional d'Aigüestortes i Estany de Sant Maurici,* scaled at 1:25,000 – but even it is not perfect. The help of guides can be enlisted at the Espot and Boí information offices.

Information

Tourist Offices National park information offices in Espot (☎ 973 62 40 36) and Boí (☎ 973 69 61 89) are open 9 am to 1 pm and 3.30 to 7 pm daily. The tourist office (☎ 973 69 40 00) in Barruera, on the L-500 10km up from the N-230, is a good source of information on the area around the western side of the park. It's open 10 am to 2 pm and 4 to 7 pm Monday to Saturday (closed on holidays). There are other tourist offices south of the park in El Pont de Suert (☎ 973 69 06 40), La Torre de Capdella (☎ 973 25 22 31) and La Pobla de Segur (☎ 973 68 02 57).

Money Boí has a Caixa de Catalunya ATM just up the road from the Pensió Pey. In Espot and Barruera are branches of La Caixa bank.

Park Rules Private vehicles cannot enter the park. From Espot, they can go to the park entrance; on the western side they must stop about 2.5km short of the park on the approach from the L-500. Jeep-taxis, however, offer easy transport into the park from Espot and Boí (see Getting Around).

Wild camping is not allowed in the park, nor is swimming or other 'aquatic activities' in the lakes and rivers. Hunting, fishing, mushroom picking and just about every other kind of potentially harmful activity are banned. Between the limit of the park core and that of the zona perifèrica, most such activities are allowed, but subject to control (to avoid such problems as overfishing).

Romanesque Churches

The Vall de Boí south-west of the park is dotted with some of Catalunya's loveliest little Romanesque churches. Two of the finest are at Taüll, 3km east of Boí. **Sant Climent de Taüll** at the entrance to the village, with its slender six-storey bell tower, is a gem, not only for its elegant, simple lines but also for the art that graced its interior until the works were transferred to museums in the 20th century. The central apse contains a copy of a famous 1123 mural, which resides in Barcelona's Museu Nacional d'Art de Catalunya. At its centre is a Pantocrator whose rich Mozarabic-influenced colours, and expressive but superhuman features, have become a virtual emblem of Catalan Romanesque art. Other art from this church has found its way to museums as far away as Boston, USA! The church is supposedly open 10.30 am to 2 pm and 4 to 8 pm daily – but don't count on it.

Santa Maria de Taüll, up in the old village centre with a five-storey tower, is also well represented in the Barcelona museum, but lacks the *in situ* copies that add to the interest of Sant Climent.

Other Romanesque churches in the area are at Boí, Barruera, Durro, Erill la Vall, Cardet and Coll.

Trekking

The park is crisscrossed by plenty of paths, ranging from well marked to unmarked, enabling you to pick routes and circuits to suit yourself.

East-West Traverse You can walk right across the park in one day. The full Espot to Boí (or vice-versa) walk is about 25km and

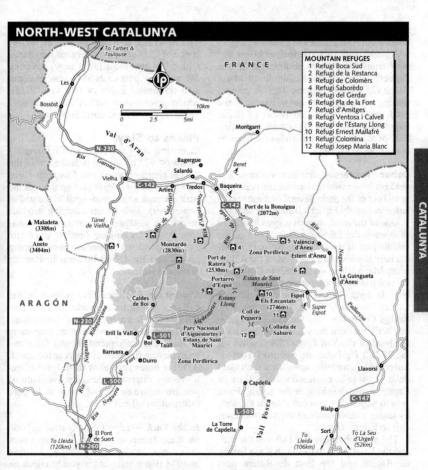

NORTH-WEST CATALUNYA

MOUNTAIN REFUGES
1 Refugi Boca Sud
2 Refugi de la Restanca
3 Refugi de Colomèrs
4 Refugi Saboredo
5 Refugi del Gerdar
6 Refugi Pla de la Font
7 Refugi d'Amitges
8 Refugi Ventosa i Calvell
9 Refugi de l'Estany Llong
10 Refugi Ernest Mallafré
11 Refugi Colomina
12 Refugi Josep Maria Blanc

CATALUNYA

takes nine hours, but you can shorten this by using jeep-taxis to/from Estany de Sant Maurici and/or Aigüestortes. Espot (1300m) to Estany de Sant Maurici (1900m) is 8km (two hours). A path then climbs to the Portarró d'Espot pass (2423m), where there are fine views over both of the park's main valleys. From the pass you descend to Estany Llong and Aigüestortes (1820m; about 3½ hours from Estany de Sant Maurici). Then you have around 3.5km to the park entrance, 4km to the L-500 and 2.5km south to Boí (1260m) – a total of about three hours.

Shorter Treks Numerous good walks of three to five hours return will take you up into spectacular side valleys from Estany de Sant Maurici or Aigüestortes.

From the eastern end of Estany de Sant Maurici, one path heads south 2.5km up the beautiful Monastero valley to Estany Monastero (2171m), passing Els Encantats on the left. Another goes 3km north-west up by Estany de Ratero to Estany Gran d'Amitges (2350m). From Planell Gran (1850m), 1km up the Sant Nicolau valley from Aigüestortes, a path climbs 2.5km south-east to Estany Gran de Dellui (2370m). You can descend to Estany Llong (3km) – about four hours from Aigüestortes to Estany Llong.

A good walk of three to four hours one way from Espot goes south-west up the Peguera valley to the Refugi Josep Maria Blanc (2350m) by Estany Tort. A marked turning to the right just out of Espot, on the road up to the small ski resort of Super Espot, points the way. This walk is the first half of the route to the Refugi Colomina (see Other Traverses).

Other Traverses Serious walkers and trekkers have many options for extended trips in and out of the park. Several of these are detailed in Lonely Planet's *Walking in Spain*.

One of the most attractive areas to head to or from is the lake-rich basin south of the middle part of the park. The Refugi Colomina here is about four hours from the Refugi Josep Maria Blanc via the 2630m Collada de Saburó pass, or about seven hours from Estany de Sant Maurici by the more difficult Coll de Peguera (2726m). You can reach the Refugi Colomina from the south by a half-day walk up from the village of Capdella at the head of the Vall Fosca, 20km north off the N-260 La Pobla de Segur-El Pont de Suert road. (Capdella, sometimes spelt Cabdella, is not to be confused with La Torre de Capdella, which is 8km farther south.) From July to September you can shorten the walk by taking a cable car from the Sallente reservoir to Estany Gento.

The most obvious route between the park and the Val d'Aran to the north is via Estany de Ratera and the Port de Ratera pass (2530m) over to the Refugi de Colomers (2125m), in a fine lake-strung valley – a not-too-long day from Estany de Sant Maurici. From the Refugi de Colomers it's about 10.5km down the Vall de l'Aiguamotx, mostly by a partly paved road, to Tredòs. A slightly longer alternative, diverging at Port de Ratera, is via the Refugi de Saborèdo (2310m) and the Ruda valley (east of the Aiguamotx). There are also good, more westerly routes using the Refugi Ventosa i Calvell at the head of Vall de Boí and the Refugi de la Restanca on the Aran side (see the Val d'Aran section later).

Skiing
The Boí-Taüll ski resort (☎ 973 69 60 44) is one of Catalunya's more promising areas, with 51 pistes (most fairly easy) covering 39km. A day pass costs 3975 ptas. You can also ski around Espot (☎ 973 414 19 26), which gives you a further 32 pistes over 38km. A day skipass costs 3600 ptas.

Places to Stay
Camping At Espot, the small *Camping Solau* (☎ 973 62 40 68) is at the top of the village (open all year) and *Camping Vora-park* (☎ 973 62 41 08) is 1km up towards the park entrance (open mid-April to the end of September). Two bigger camping grounds below the village have summer-only seasons. At Taüll, *Camping Taüll* (☎ 973 69 61 74) is open all year. There are three camping grounds on the L-500 between El Pont de Suert and Boí.

Mountain Refuges Five refuges in the park and seven more inside the zona perifèrica provide accommodation for walkers. In general they tend to be staffed from early or mid-June to September, and for some weeks in the first half of the year for skiers. At other times several of them leave a section open where you can stay overnight; if you are unsure call ahead or ask at the park information offices.

In the Park You don't usually need to book for these except in August. The Espot park office can contact the Mallafré, Amitges and JM Blanc refuges for you to check on availability.

Refugi Ernest Mallafré (☎ 973 25 01 18), sometimes called *Refugi Sant Maurici*, near the eastern end of Estany de Sant Maurici (1885m), is run by the FEEC and has 24 places, with meals available. *Refugi d'Amitges* (☎ 973 25 00 07), at Estany Gran d'Amitges (2380m) in the north of the park, is run by the CEC and has 66 places. Meals are available.

Refugi de l'Estany Llong (☎ 629-37 46 52), near Estany Llong (2000m), is run by the national park, with 40 places and a kitchen. *Refugi Josep Maria Blanc* (☎ 93 423 23 45), near Estany Tort (2350m), is run by the CEC, with 40 places and meals available when staffed.

In the north-west of the park, the CEC's **Refugi Ventosa i Calvell** (☎ 973 29 70 90) has 80 places.

Zona Perifèrica South of the park by Estany de Colomina, **Refugi Colomina** (☎ 973 68 10 42) is run by the FEEC and has 40 places, and meals available, when staffed.

Refugi de Colomèrs (☎ 973 64 05 92), north of the park in the lovely Circ de Colomèrs (2130m), is run by the FEEC, with 40 places, and meals available when staffed. **Refugi Saborèdo** (☎ 973 25 30 15), north of the park in the lake-strewn Circ de Saborèdo (2310m), is run by the FEEC and has 21 places. The FEEC's **Refugi de la Restanca** (☎ 608- 036559) has 80 places.

Hostales & Hotels The villages of Espot, Boí and Taüll have a range of accommodation options.

Espot The following places are all near the centre of this small village. The friendly, family-run **Residència Felip** (☎ 973 62 40 93) has clean singles/doubles with shared bathroom for 2000/4000 ptas (3000/5000 ptas in July and August), including breakfast. **Casa La Palmira** (☎ 973 62 40 72, Carrer de Marineta s/n) has rooms with bath for 2400/4800 ptas. **Hotel Roya** (☎ 973 62 40 40, Carrer de Sant Maurici s/n) has rooms with shower or bath for 5000/8000 ptas. The big **Hotel Saurat** (☎ 973 62 41 62, Carrer de Sant Martí s/n) has doubles for up to 9500 ptas plus IVA.

Boí On the small village square, **Pensió Pey** (☎ 973 69 60 36) has doubles for 6500 ptas plus IVA. In peak summer season it charges 5000 ptas per person for half-board. **Hostal Fondevila** (☎ 973 69 60 11), on the right as you enter the village, has similar prices.

Cases de pagès have cheaper rooms with shared baths. To find **Casa Cosan** (☎ 973 69 60 18) and its nice garden, head down into the village from the square, bear right and ask. The seven rooms are just 1600 ptas

per person. **Casa Guasch** (☎ 973 69 60 42) charges 2350 ptas per person; take the lane along the right side of the Pensió Pey, then fork right down the hill.

Taüll Although 3km uphill from Boí, Taüll is more picturesque and a nicer place to stay. **Restaurant Sant Climent** (☎ 973 69 60 52), on the road into the village from Sant Climent church, is a new stone building with singles/doubles for 1500/3000 ptas, or 2000/4000 ptas with private bath.

Casa Chep (or Xep; ☎ 973 69 60 54), up in the village on Plaça de Santa Maria, has rooms for 1800/3600 ptas, and a kitchen is available.

Elsewhere There are hostales and/or cases de pagès in Barruera, El Pont de Suert, Capdella and La Torre de Capdella.

Places to Eat

Espot has a couple of supermarkets and Boí has one small one. Some of the best food can be had at **Restaurant Juquim** on the main square. Its *menú* is varied and costs 1750 ptas.

In Boí, **Pensió Pey** serves *menús* for 1800 ptas or bocadillos and other snacks. Right opposite the Sant Climent church in Taüll, **Restaurant Mallador** is set in a tumbledown house with a leafy garden – a perfect place for lunch.

Getting There & Away

Bus La Pobla de Segur, a staging post on some approaches, can be reached by bus from Barcelona (twice daily) and by bus or train from Lleida. For further information you can ring tourist offices or the Alsina Graells bus company in La Pobla de Segur (☎ 973 68 03 36).

Espot Daily Alsina Graells buses from Barcelona, Lleida and La Pobla de Segur to Esterri d'Aneu (and in summer to the Val d'Aran) will stop at the Espot turning on the C-147, from where you have an 8km uphill walk (or hitch) to Espot.

Boí From June to mid-September, an Alsina Graells bus from La Pobla de Segur and El

CATALUNYA

Pont de Suert stops daily at Barruera and the Boí turn-off *(el Cruce de Boí)* on the L-500. The rest of the year it runs on Friday only. At the time of writing the bus left La Pobla de Segur at 9.30 am and El Pont de Suert at 11.15 am. The southbound return bus stops at the Boí turn-off about 2 pm. Both buses connect at El Pont de Suert with Alsina Graells buses from Lleida. You can also get from Boí to Vielha, or vice versa, in one day with a change at El Pont de Suert.

Taxi For a taxi in Boí call ☎ 973 69 60 15 or ☎ 973 69 60 36. In Espot call ☎ 973 62 41 05.

Getting Around

Once you're close to the park, the easy way of getting inside it is by jeep-taxi from Espot or Boí. Fleets of these things, whose drivers congregate loudly in local bars in their off-duty moments, run a more or less continuous shuttle service between Espot and Estany de Sant Maurici, and between Boí and Aigüestortes, saving you, respectively, 8km and 10km of walking. The one-way fare for either trip is 600 ptas per person and the services run from outside the park information offices in Espot and Boí (from July to September 8 am to 7 pm, other months 9 am to 6 pm). You can also do several excursions with these taxis, for instance to the Estany Negre or the Estanys d'Amitges. Prices hover around 1700 ptas for this kind of trip.

VAL D'ARAN
pop 7000

This lush green valley, Catalunya's northern-most outpost, is almost entirely surrounded by spectacular 2000m-plus mountains. Its only natural opening is northwards to France, to which it gives its river, the Riu Garona (Garonne), flowing down to Bordeaux. Thanks to this geography, Aran's native language is not Catalan but Aranese *(aranés),* a dialect of Occitan or the *langue d'oc,* the old Romance language of southern France. Most Aranese, however, switch happily into Catalan, Castilian or French.

Despite this northward orientation, Aran has been tied politically to Catalunya since

1175, when Alfonso II took it under his protection to forestall the designs of rival counts on both sides of the Pyrenees. In 1312, following one of many French takeover bids, the Aranese voted by popular referendum to stay with Catalunya – perhaps because in practice this meant a large degree of independence. A major hiccup came with the Napoleonic occupation from 1810 to 1815.

For all its intriguing past, however, the Val d'Aran is in danger of being overrun by tourism, which since the opening of the Baqueira-Beret ski resort in 1964 has replaced farming and herding as the economic mainstay. A valley that 30 years ago probably was still a pocket of scattered stone villages centred on quaint, pointy-towered Romanesque churches is being swamped by ski-apartment development. That said, most of the villages retain an old-fashioned core, and from Aran's pretty side valleys walkers can continue over the mountains in any direction, notably southwards to the Parc Nacional d'Aigüestortes i Estany de Sant Maurici.

The Val d'Aran is some 35km long and is considered to have three parts: Naut Aran (Upper Aran), the eastern part, aligned east-west; Mijaran (Middle Aran) around Vielha; and Baish Aran (Lower Aran), where the Garona flows north-east to France. Despite Baqueira-Beret, Naut Aran is still the most attractive area, and the pleasant village of Salardú is a base for some of the best outings.

Editorial Alpina's *Vall d'Aran* is a useful aid here.

Walking & Trekking

One nice shortish walk, if you have a vehicle to get to Beret (some 8km north up a hairpin road from Baqueira), is the 5km from Beret along the headwaters of the Riu Noguera Pallaresa to the abandoned village of Montgarri, with a 16th-century shrine.

More spectacular routes head south up into the mountains on the northern fringes of the Parc Nacional d'Aigüestortes i Estany de Sant Maurici. The following three can all be done part of the way by vehicle, and end at mountain refuges for those who want to linger or head on over into the national park.

From the village of Tredòs, slightly east of and below Salardú, a road ascends the valley of the Riu d'Aiguamotx. You can get a car about 8km up, to a level of about 1850m. From there it's a 2.5km walk up to the Refugi de Colomers at 2125m, set in a beautiful lake-strewn bowl. From the refuge there are easy marked circuit walks of two and four hours.

Or from Tredòs you could head southeast up the valley of the Riu de Ruda to the Refugi Saborèdo, some 12km up at 2310m, in another fine lake-dotted cirque. This route is motorable about two-thirds of the way.

If you happen to stop at Arties, call in at *Hotel Valarties* (☎ 973 64 43 64, *Carrer Major 3*). Set in a house that is a heterodox mix of local building tradition and tarty avant-garde, it houses a *restaurant* known to skiers and walkers for miles around. You can stay too if you want, with doubles up to 9400 ptas in high season.

From Arties, 3km west of Salardú, it's 8km up the Riu de Valarties valley to the Refugi de la Restanca. It's drivable for about the first 4.5km; from there you must walk the steeper part, about 3.5km, up to the refuge at 2000m. From the refuge you can walk for about one hour south-west up to the lake Estany de Mar, amid extremely rugged scenery at 2250m, or spend a day climbing and descending 2830m Montardó (to the east), which has magnificent views.

The Refugi de Colomers and Refugi de la Restanca are a short day's walk from each other, on the GR-11. From Restanca the GR-11 heads about five hours' west to the *Refugi Boca Sud* (☎ 973 69 70 52), near the southern end of the Túnel de Vielha. From there it's two days (with a night's camping) past the Maladeta massif over to Benasque in Aragón.

Getting There & Away

The N-230 from Lleida and El Pont de Suert reaches Aran through the 5.25km Túnel de Vielha (built in the 1940s and showing its age), then heads north from Vielha to the French border at Eth Pont de Rei. Continuing as the French N-125, it reaches the Toulouse-Pau road at Montréjeau, 46km from the border.

From the Esterri d'Àneu in the Vall de la Noguera Pallaresa, the C-142 crosses the 2072m Port de la Bonaigua pass – which may be closed in winter – into Naut Aran, along which it proceeds to meet the N-230 at Vielha.

Two Alsina Graells buses daily run between Barcelona and Vielha (3555 ptas) via Lleida and El Pont de Suert. The leg from Lleida to Vielha (1510 ptas), where there is usually a half-hour layover, takes three hours. From June to October a daily Alsina Graells bus connects Barcelona and Vielha (same price) via La Pobla de Segur, Llavorsí, the Espot turning on the C-147, Port de la Bonaigua and Salardú (the total journey time is about seven hours). At the time of writing the southbound departure from Vielha was at 11.44 am.

A local bus service connects Vielha with Baqueira, Eth Pont de Rei and intervening villages from four (weekends) to nine times a day.

Vielha

postcode 25530 • pop 3896

Vielha is Aran's junction town and the Aranese spelling of its name is more common than the Catalan and Castilian version, Viella.

Information The Val d'Aran's main tourist office (☎ 973 64 01 10), Carrèr de Sarriulèra 5, is open 10 am to 1 pm and 4.30 to 7.30 pm. There are banks along Avenguda de Castièro and Avenguda deth Pas d'Arró. The post office is at Carrèr de Sarriulèra 4. The Mossos d'Esquadra (Catalunya regional police; ☎ 973 64 20 44) are 2km from the centre along the N-230 highway to France. There's a hospital (☎ 973 64 00 66) on Carrèr deth Espitau, off Avenguda deth Pas d'Arró.

Things to See The small old quarter is around Plaça dera Glèisa and across the little Riu Nere just west of the square. The **Glèisa de Sant Miquèu** church on Plaça déra Glèisa is a mix of 12th- to 18th-century styles, with a 13th-century main portal. It contains some notable medieval artwork, especially the 12th-century *Crist de Mijaran*, an almost life-sized wooden bust thought to have been part of a Descent from the Cross group. The

CATALUNYA

Musèu dera Val d'Aran at Carrèr Major 11 tells the interesting tale of Aran's history up to the present. It's open 5 to 8 pm Tuesday to Friday, 10 am to 1 pm and 5 to 8 pm Saturday, and until 1 pm Sunday (200 ptas).

Places to Stay For some of the cheaper places, head down Passeig dera Llibertat, north off Avenguda de Castièro just west of Plaça dera Glèisa. *Hostal El Ciervo* (☎ *973 64 01 65, Plaça de Sant Orenç 3),* just off Passeig déra Llibertat, has ageing but adequate singles/doubles for 2500/4000 ptas, or 3500/5000 ptas with private bath. On Camin Reiau, a north-east extension of Passeig dera Llibertat, *Pensión Puig* (☎ *973 64 00 31),* at No 6, with no sign except a 'P', has doubles for 2800 ptas; *Casa Vîcenta* (☎ *973 64 08 19),* at No 7, is much better at 5500 ptas for doubles with bath and breakfast.

For a bit more comfort, *Hotel Urogallo* (☎ *973 64 00 00, Avenguda del Castièro 7), Hotel Arán* (☎ *973 64 00 50),* at No 5, and

Hotel Riu Nere (☎ *973 64 01 50, Carrèr de Sant Nicolau 2)* have doubles with bath ranging from 5000 to 6500 ptas in low season and 9000 to 12,000 ptas in high season.

Petit Hotel des Arts (☎ *973 64 18 48, Carrèr dera Palha 15)* is a rather spick-and-span bijou sort of place with attractive doubles for 8100 ptas.

Places to Eat *El Curné (Plaça de Sant Orenç)* is a cosy little bar and restaurant in a charming old house where mains start at about 1000 ptas.

Restaurant All i Oli (Carrèr Major 9) is one of the costlier places in town with a *menú* for 2500 ptas. Anyone for snails?

An unassuming little place is *Bar Espres (Passeig dera Llibertat 3),* where the staff will sell you Aranese products or whip you up a quick tapa or two to try the wares.

Restaurant El Serrano (Carrer de Sant Nicolau 2) serves some reasonable Aranese dishes. The traditional local broth *olla aranesa* goes for 750 ptas a pop.

Salardú

postcode 25598 • pop 1200 • elev 1270m
Nine kilometres east of Vielha, Salardú's little nucleus of old houses and narrow streets has largely resisted the temptation to sprawl. If you come in May, June, October or November, however, you'll find only a few hotels open. The tourist office (☎ 973 64 57 26) is by the car park near the middle of the village and open in summer only. Otherwise, call the Ayuntamiento on ☎ 973 64 40 30. In the apse of the village's 12th- and 13th-century church, admire the 13th-century *Crist de Salardú* crucifixion carving.

Places to Stay & Eat *Xalet-Refugi Juli Soler Santaló* (☎ *973 64 50 16),* just above the main road towards the east end of the village, has dorm places for 1500 ptas and bunk rooms at 2400 ptas per person, plus a kitchen and cafeteria. You may find yourself being obliged to pay 4400 ptas per person for half-board.

The large youth hostel nearby, *Alberg Era Garona* (☎ *973 64 52 71),* has room for 180 people; the high season is December to

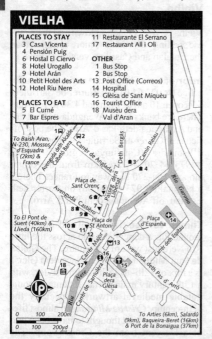

VIELHA

PLACES TO STAY	11 Restaurante El Serrano
3 Casa Vicenta	17 Restaurant All i Oli
4 Pensión Puig	
6 Hostal El Ciervo	OTHER
8 Hotel Urogallo	1 Bus Stop
9 Hotel Arán	2 Bus Stop
10 Petit Hotel des Arts	13 Post Office (Correos)
12 Hotel Riu Nere	14 Hospital
	15 Glèisa de Sant Miquèu
PLACES TO EAT	16 Tourist Office
5 El Curné	18 Musèu dera
7 Bar Espres	Val d'Aran

To Baish Aran,
N-230, Mossos
d'Esquadra
(2km) &
France

Plaça de
Sant Orenç

To El Pont de
Suert (40km) &
Llieda (160km)

Plaça
d'Espanha

Plaça de
St Antoni

Avenguda Castièro

Carrèr Major

Avenguda deth Espitau

Carrèr deth Espitau

Avenguda deth Pas d' Arró

Plaça
dera
Glèisa

Carrèr de Samuàra

Riu Nere

Riu Garona

Camin Reiau

Carrèr de Anglada

Passeig dera Llibertat

Carrèr de Anglada

Deth Bergàs

Cabeç Baratt dera Alcalde

0   100   200m
0   100   200yd

To Arties (6km), Salardú
(9km), Baqueira-Beret (16km)
& Port de la Bonaigua (37km)

April, and July and August. In the centre, **Refugi Rosta** (☎ *973 64 53 08, fax 973 64 58 14, Plaça Major 1*) is an 18th-century place full of character and with dorm bunks for 1925 ptas per person and double rooms for 4600 ptas in July and August or 5600 ptas in the ski season (prices include breakfast). It's closed at most other times. There's a great wood-panelled bar where you can eat sausage, pâté or crepes for 500 to 750 ptas, and a good dining room.

Baqueira-Beret

Baqueira (Vaquèira in Aranese), 3km east of Salardú, and Beret, 8km north of Baqueira, form Catalunya's premier ski resort, favoured by the Spanish royal family, no less! Its good lift system gives access to 47 varied pistes totalling 77km (more than any other Spanish resort), amid fine scenery at between 1500m and 2510m. A one-day lift pass is 4600 ptas.

In summer the Bosque and Mirador chair lifts open from July to September to carry you from Baqueira almost to the top of Cap de Baqueira (2500m). There's nowhere cheap to stay in Baqueira, and nowhere at all at Beret. Many skiers stay down the valley in Salardú, Arties or Vielha. Information on packages is available from Baqueira-Beret's Central de Reservas (☎ 973 64 44 55, fax 973 64 44 88), at Apartado 60, 25530 Vielha.

The cheapest five-day packages start at around 30,000 ptas per person, including room, breakfast and lifts. The price-tag depends on where and when – you could easily find yourself paying 200,000 ptas per person for a good apartment at New Year (the most expensive moment).

West of Barcelona

The mountain and monastery of Montserrat and the Penedès wine-growing area are within day-trip distance of Barcelona.

MONTSERRAT

Montserrat (Serrated Mountain), 50km northwest of Barcelona, is a 1236m mountain of truly weird rock pillars, shaped by wind, rain and frost from a conglomeration of limestone, pebbles and sand that once lay under the sea. With the historic Benedictine Monestir de Montserrat, one of Catalunya's most important shrines, cradled at 725m on its side, it makes a great outing from Barcelona.

The most dramatic approach is by the cable car that swings high across the Llobregat valley from Montserrat-Aeri station, served by regular trains from Barcelona. From the mountain, on a clear day, you can see as far as the Pyrenees, Barcelona's Tibidabo and even, if you're lucky, Mallorca.

Orientation & Information

The cable car from Aeri de Montserrat arrives on the mountain just below the monastery. Just above the cable-car station is a road. To the left is the information office (☎ 93 877 77 77), open 10 am to 6 pm daily. A minor road doubles back up to the left to the lower station of the Funicular de Sant Joan. The main road curves round and up to the right, passing the Cel.les (see Places to Stay & Eat), to enter Plaça de Santa Maria at the centre of the monastery.

Monestir de Montserrat

The monastery was founded in 1025 to commemorate a 'vision' of the Virgin on the mountain. Wrecked by Napoleon's troops in 1811, then abandoned as a result of anticlerical legislation in the 1830s, it was rebuilt from 1858. Today a community of about 80 monks lives here. Pilgrims come from far and wide to venerate La Moreneta (the Black Virgin), a 12th-century Romanesque wooden sculpture of Mary with the infant Jesus, which has been Catalunya's patron since 1881.

The two-part **Museu de Montserrat** on Plaça de Santa Maria has an excellent collection ranging from an Egyptian mummy and Gothic retablos to art by El Greco, Monet, Degas and Picasso. It's open 9.30 am to 6 pm daily (600 ptas, students 400 ptas).

From Plaça de Santa Maria you enter the courtyard of the 16th-century **basilica**, the monastery's church. The basilica's facade, with its carvings of Christ and the 12 Apostles, dates from 1900 to 1901, despite its 16th-century plateresque style. Opening times when you can file past the image of the Black Virgin, high above the basilica's main altar, vary according to season. The church is open 8 am Sundays and holidays and 9 am on other days. It remains open to 8 pm in summer (July-September) but tends to close earlier in the rest of the year. Follow the signs to the Cambril de la Mare de Déu, to the right of the main basilica entrance.

The **Montserrat Boys' Choir**, or Escolania, reckoned to be Europe's oldest music school, sings in the basilica at 1 and 7 pm Monday to Saturday, and at 1 pm only Sunday, except in July. The church fills up quickly, so try to arrive early. It is a rare treat, as the choir does not perform often outside Montserrat – five concerts a year and a world tour every two.

On your way out have a look in the room across the courtyard from the basilica entrance, which is filled with gifts and thank-you messages to the Montserrat Virgin from people who give her the credit for all manner of happy events. The souvenirs range from plaster casts to wedding dresses.

The Mountain

You can explore the mountain above the monastery on a web of paths leading to some of the peaks and to 13 empty and rather dilapidated hermitages. The **Funicular de Sant Joan** (580/925 ptas one way/return) will carry you up the first 250m from the monastery. If you prefer to walk, the road past the funicular's bottom station will lead you up and around to its top station in about one hour (3km).

From the Sant Joan top station, it's a 20-minute stroll (signposted) to the **Sant Joan hermitage**, with fine westward views. More exciting is the hour's walk north-west along a path marked with occasional blobs of yellow paint to Montserrat's highest peak, **Sant Jeroni**, from which there's an awesome sheer drop on the northern side. The walk takes you across the upper part of the mountain, with a close-up experience of some of the weird rock pillars. Many have been given names: on your way to Sant Jeroni look over to the right for La Prenyada (The Pregnant Woman), La Mòmia (The Mummy), L'Elefant (The Elephant), the phallic Cavall Bernat and El Cap de Mort (The Death's-head).

Places to Stay & Eat

For accommodation options call ☎ 93 877 77 77. A small camping ground, 300m along the road past the lower Sant Joan funicular station, is open from Semana Santa to October. The cheapest rooms are in the *Cel.les de Montserrat*, which has three blocks of simple apartments for two to 10 people. A two-person apartment costs up to 5990 ptas in high season. You must stay for a minimum of two days (a week in July and August). Overlooking Plaça de Santa Maria is the comfortable *Hotel Abat Cisneros*, with rooms starting at 6725/11,650 ptas in high season.

The *Snack Bar* near the top cable-car station has straightforward meals, bocadillos and snacks, as does *Bar de la Plaça* in the Abat Oliva cel.les building. *Cafeteria Self-Service*, near the car park, has great views but is dearer. *Hotel Abat Cisneros* has a four-course *menú* for 2900 ptas.

KATE NOLAN

The statue of the Black Virgin attracts pilgrims to the Monestir de Montserrat.

CATALUNYA

Getting There & Away

Bus There's a daily bus with the Julià company to the monastery from Estació d'Autobusos de Sants in Barcelona at 9 am (plus 8 am in July and August), returning at 5 pm (1400 ptas).

Train & Cable Car The alternative is a trip by train and cable car. FGC trains run from Plaça d'Espanya station in Barcelona to Montserrat-Aeri up to 18 times a day. Get the R5 train. Return tickets for 1905 ptas include the cable car between Montserrat-Aeri station and the monastery. The cable car runs (about every 15 minutes) 9.25 am to 1.45 pm and 3 to 6.45 pm Monday to Saturday. The whole trip takes a little over an hour. The price for the cable car alone is 625/950 ptas (one way/return).

FGC offers various all-in-one tickets. Return-trip tickets costing 2800 ptas include the train trip, cable car to/from Montserrat-Aeri, two metro rides and unlimited use of the funiculars. For 4100 ptas you can have all this, plus the museum entrance fee and a modest dinner at the self-service restaurant.

There has long been talk of constructing a new cremallera railway up the hill from Monistrol. One of these steep incline lines ran from 1892 to 1957 and planners hope a new one would cut down the car and bus traffic to what is, with 2.5 million visitors a year, Catalunya's second most visited spot.

From Montserrat-Aeri, trains continue north to Manresa, from which there are three trains daily west to Lleida and one or two Alsina Graells buses daily north to Berga, Guardiola de Berguedà, Puigcerdà and (except on Sunday) La Seu d'Urgell.

Car & Motorcycle Probably the most straightforward route by car from Barcelona is by Avinguda Diagonal, Via Augusta, the Túnel de Vallvidrera and the A-18. Turn on to the BP-1213, just past Terrassa, and follow it 18km north-west to the C-1411. Then head 2km south on this road to Monistrol de Montserrat, from where a road snakes about 7km up the mountain.

SANT SADURNÍ D'ANOIA & VILAFRANCA DEL PENEDÈS

Some of Spain's best wines come from the area centred on these towns. Sant Sadurní d'Anoia, a half-hour train ride west of Barcelona, is the capital of *cava* (Spanish bubbly). Vilafranca del Penedès, 12km down the track, is the heart of the Penedès DO, which produces noteworthy light, still whites. Visitors are welcome at numerous wineries; there'll often be a free glass or two included in the tour, and plenty more for sale, but if you fancy a full-scale tasting you should ring ahead.

Sant Sadurní d'Anoia
postcode 08770 • pop 9343

A hundred or so wineries around Sant Sadurní produce 140 million bottles of cava a year – something like 85% of the entire national output. Cava is made by the same method as French champagne. Freixenet (☎ 93 891 70 00), the best-known cava company, is based right next to the train station at Carrer de Joan Sala 2. Free tours are given at 9, 10 and 11.30 am and 3.30 and 5 pm Monday to Thursday; in December there are also tours Friday morning, Saturday and Sunday.

Codorníu (☎ 93 818 32 32) is at Can Codorníu, at the entry to the town by road from Barcelona. Manuel Raventós, head of this firm back in 1872, was the first Spaniard successfully to produce sparkling wine by the champagne method. The Codorníu headquarters, a modernist building, is open for free visits 9 am to 5 pm weekdays and until 1 pm weekends.

Vilafranca del Penedès
postcode 08720 • pop 28,925

Vilafranca is larger than Sant Sadurní and more interesting. The tourist office (☎ 93 892 03 58) on Plaça de la Vila is open 9 am to 1 pm and 4 to 7 pm Tuesday to Friday, and 10 am to 1 pm Saturday. In summer it also opens 5 to 8 pm Saturday and 10 am to 1 pm Sunday.

A block north, the mainly Gothic **Basilica de Santa Maria** faces the combined **Museu de Vilafranca** and **Museu del Vi** (Wine

CATALUNYA

Museum) across Plaça de Jaume I. The museum, a fine Gothic building, covers local archaeology, art, geology and bird life, and also has an excellent section on wine, at the end of which you're treated to a free copa. It's open 10 am to 2 pm and 4 to 7 pm (9 am to 9 pm in summer) Tuesday to Saturday, and 10 am to 2 pm Sunday and holidays (400 ptas). A statue on Plaça de Jaume I pays tribute to Vilafranca's famous *castellers* (human-castle builders), who do their thing during Vilafranca's lively *festa major* (main annual festival) at the end of August.

Vilafranca's premier winery is Torres (☎ 93 817 74 87), 3km north-west of the town centre on the BP-2121 road near Pacs del Penedès. The Torres family revolutionised Spanish local wine-making in the 1960s by introducing new temperature-controlled, stainless-steel technology and French grape varieties. They helped produce much lighter wines than the traditional heavy Spanish plonk. Torres is open for visits 9 am to 6 pm Monday to Saturday, and until 1 pm Sunday and holidays. Most other Penedès wineries are, like Torres, out of town.

Getting There & Away

Up to three rodalies trains an hour run from Barcelona's Estació Sants to Sant Sadurní and Vilafranca. By car, take the A-2, then the A-7. From Sitges, both places are a short drive inland, or a longer train journey involving a change at Coma-ruga. Two or three buses a day connect Vilafranca with Sitges too.

LLEIDA
postcode 25080 • pop 112,207
Much of western Catalunya is flat and drab, but if you're not in a hurry Lleida (Lérida) is a likeable place with a long and varied history. It's also the starting point of several routes towards the Pyrenees.

Orientation

The centre spreads around the southern side of a hill dominated by the old cathedral, La Seu Vella, with Carrer del Carme, Carrer de Sant Joan, Plaça de Sant Joan and Carrer Major forming a mainly pedestrianised axis

from north-east to south-west. The train station is at the north-eastern end of Rambla de Ferran, with the bus station 1.25km away on Carrer de Saracíbar, off Avinguda de Madrid.

Information

Turisme de Lleida's Centre d'Informació i Reserves (☎ 902-25 00 50), Carrer Major 31 bis, is the municipal tourist office. It opens 11 am to 8 pm (to 1.30 pm Sunday) and is the best place for city info. For tips on the rest of Lleida province you can try the Oficina Turismo de la Generalitat (☎ 973 27 09 97), Avinguda de Madrid 36, which is open 10 am to 2 pm and 3.30 to 6 pm weekdays. Another good place for provincial information is the Patronato Intercomarcal (☎ 973 24 54 08), Rambla de Ferran 18. It's open 8 am to 3 pm weekdays.

The main post office is on Rambla de Ferran. The Policía Nacional station (☎ 973 24 40 50) is at Cerrer de Sant Martí s/n.

If you're heading for the Pyrenees, Caselles, at Carrer Major 46, has some material on the mountains. For material on just about any subject concerning Catalunya that you care to name, try the Llibreria de la Generalitat, at Rambla d'Aragó 43.

La Seu Vella

Lleida's 'old cathedral' towers above all else in position and grandeur. It stands within a *recinte* (compound) of defensive walls erected between the 12th and 19th centuries.

The main entrance to the recinte (open 8 am to 9 pm, free) is from Carrer de Monterey on its western side, but during the cathedral's opening hours you can use the extraordinarily ugly *ascensor* (lift) from above Plaça de Sant Joan (60 ptas).

The cathedral was built in sandy-coloured stone in the 13th to 15th centuries on the site of a former mosque (Lleida was under Muslim control from AD 719 to 1149). It's a masterpiece of the Transitional style, although it only recently recovered from 241 years use as a barracks, which began as Felipe V's punishment for the city's opposition in the War of the Spanish Succession.

A 70m octagonal bell tower rises at the south-western end from the cloister, whose windows have exceptionally fine Gothic tracery. The spacious but rather austere interior, used as stables and dormitories during the military occupation, has a forest of slender columns with carved capitals.

The cathedral is open from 10 am to 1.30 pm and 3 to 5.30 pm (4 to 7.30 pm from June to September) Tuesday to Saturday, and until 1.30 pm Sunday and public holidays (400 ptas).

Above the cathedral are remains of the Islamic fortress and residence of the Muslim governors, known as the Castell del Rei or La Suda.

Carrer Major & Around

A 13th-century Gothic mansion **La Paeria** has housed the city government almost since its inception. The 18th-century neoclassical **La Seu Nova** on Plaça de la Catedral was built when La Seu Vella was turned into a barracks.

Opposite is the **Hospital de Santa Maria**, with a Gothic courtyard. It now houses the **Museu Arqueològic**, which includes Iberian and Roman finds from the Lleida region. Museum hours change throughout the year. It's open noon to 2 pm and 5.30 to 8.30 pm Tuesday to Saturday (October to

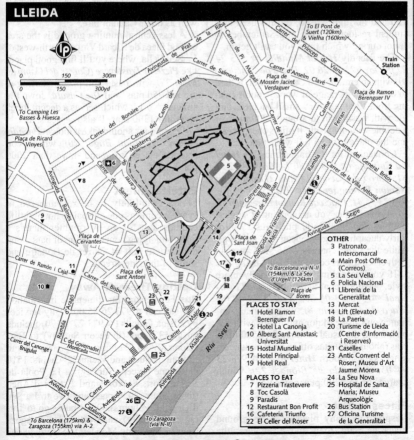

LLEIDA

PLACES TO STAY
1 Hotel Ramon Berenguer IV
2 Hotel La Canonja
10 Alberg Sant Anastasi; Universitat
15 Hostal Mundial
17 Hotel Principal
19 Hotel Real

PLACES TO EAT
7 Pizzeria Trastevere
8 Toc Casolà
9 Paradís
12 Restaurant Bon Profit
16 Cafeteria Triunfo
22 El Celler del Roser

OTHER
3 Patronato Intercomarcal
4 Main Post Office (Correos)
5 La Seu Vella
6 Policía Nacional
11 Llibreria de la Generalitat
13 Mercat
14 Lift (Elevator)
18 La Paeria
20 Turisme de Lleida (Centre d'Informació i Reserves)
21 Caselles
23 Antic Convent del Roser; Museu d'Art Jaume Morera
24 La Seu Nova
25 Hospital de Santa Maria; Museu Arqueològic
26 Bus Station
27 Oficina Turisme de la Generalitat

May). In June it opens a little longer and the remaining months only 11 am to 2 pm.

Carrer dels Cavallers and Carrer de la Palma climb from Carrer Major up through the old part of town. The **Antic Convent del Roser** at Carrer dels Cavallers 15, with an unusual three-storey cloister, houses the **Museu d'Art Jaume Morera** and its collection of work by Lleida-associated artists.

Places to Stay

Camping Les Basses (☎ 973 23 59 54), at Km 5 on the N-240 to Huesca, charges 625 ptas per person, per tent and per car. Lleida's youth hostel, *Alberg Sant Anastasi* (☎ 973 26 60 99, Rambla d'Aragó 11), has room for 120 and no high season, but it's used as a student residence from mid-September to June, during which time you can't get in.

The friendly *Hostal Mundial* (☎ 973 24 27 00, fax 973 24 26 02, Plaça de Sant Joan 4), with an entrance on Carrer Major, is hard to beat, with its range of worthy rooms costing from 1200 ptas for a small but clean single with washbasin to around 3200 ptas for a double with own bath. It offers cheap meals and the place is often full with students.

Convenient for the train station are *Hotel La Canonja* (☎ 973 23 80 14, fax 973 22 25 81, Carrer del General Britos 21) and *Hotel Ramon Berenguer IV* (☎ 973 23 73 45, fax 973 23 95 41, Plaça de Ramon Berenguer IV 2). At the former you are looking at singles/doubles for 2400/4500 ptas plus IVA for fairly uncaptivating but clean and quiet digs, while the latter charges 4635/5875 ptas. In both cases rooms come with own bath.

If you're looking for marginally more style, one good central option is *Hotel Principal* (☎ 973 23 08 00, fax 973 23 08 03, Plaça de la Paeria 8), with its main entrance on Carrer Major and rooms with TV, phone and the usual features for 5500/6800 ptas (about 1000 ptas off on weekends). Another is the modern *Hotel Real* (☎ 973 23 94 05, Avinguda de Blondel 22), which charges up to 8200 ptas plus IVA.

Places to Eat

Despite the many pleasant cafes around Plaça de Sant Joan and elsewhere, the downtown options for an actual meal are limited. *Cafeteria Triunfo* on Carrer Major has a *menú* for 950 ptas.

The cheapest food deal in town is *Restaurant Bon Profit* (Carrer dels Cavallers 37). The area is home to many black and North African migrants, and the eatery serves up all sorts of mains, including couscous, starting at 500 ptas.

Lleida is Catalunya's snail-eating capital. So many *cargols* are swallowed during the annual Aplec del Cargol snail feast, held on a Sunday in early May, that some have to be imported. *El Celler del Roser* (Carrer del Cavallers 24) serves the slithering things *a la llauna* (baked on tin over hot coals), as well as other Catalan fare.

A less central hunting ground is the area around Plaça de Ricard Vinyes, north-west of La Seu Vella, where you'll find good places like *Pizzeria Trastevere* (Carrer del Camp de Mart 27) with pasta and pizzas starting at around 950 ptas, and *Toc Casolà*, down the street at No 12, which serves a decent lunch *menú* for 1300 ptas. It also serves snails.

Vegetarians should take a look at *Paradis* (Carrer de Joan Baget 20), where you shouldn't need to spend more than 2000 ptas a head.

Entertainment

Lleida is unlikely to be remembered in years to come as one of Spain's hot nightlife capitals, but for an overnighter there's a fairly satisfying concentration of bars along the western half of Carrer de Bonaire and some of the side streets.

Getting There & Away

Bus For general bus timetable information you can call ☎ 973 26 85 00. Daily services by Alsina Graells (☎ 973 27 14 70) include up to 13 buses (three on Sunday) to Barcelona (2¼ to 2¾ hours, 2045 ptas); two to El Pont de Suert and Vielha (2¾ hours, 1510 ptas); one (except Sunday) to La Pobla de Segur, Sort, Llavorsí and Esterri d'Àneu (three hours, 2030 ptas) and two to La Seu d'Urgell (2½ hours). Other buses go to Tarragona (six daily), and westward to Zaragoza (four or five daily Monday to Saturday; one

Sunday) and Barbastro and Huesca (four to six daily).

Train Lleida is on the Barcelona-Zaragoza-Madrid line. Around 20 trains daily run to Barcelona, most taking about two hours, although some dawdle for four. Second-class fares start at 1260 ptas. Up to 10 daily trains head to Zaragoza (around 1¾ hours, 1405 ptas) and five to Madrid. Other direct services run to Tarragona (1¼ hours, from 660 ptas, 10 daily) and La Pobla de Segur (two hours, 660 ptas, three daily).

Car & Motorcycle The quickest routes to Barcelona, Tarragona and Zaragoza are by the A-2, but you can avoid tolls by taking the N-II to Zaragoza or Barcelona or the N-240 to Tarragona. The main northward roads are the C-1313 to La Seu d'Urgell, the N-230 to Vielha and the N-240 to Barbastro and Huesca (in Aragón).

CONCA DE BARBERÀ

This hilly, green, back country district comes as a refreshing surprise in the otherwise drab flatlands of south-western Catalunya. Vineyards and woods succeed one another across green rolling hills, studded by occasional medieval villages and monasteries.

Monestir de Poblet

The jewel in the crown is doubtless this imposing fortified monastery, founded by Cistercian monks from southern France in 1151.

The walls of this abbey devoted to Santa Maria, as much as a defensive measure, also symbolised the monks' isolation of themselves from the vanities of the outside world. Within the triple line of walls stand out several magnificent buildings. But before you get inside you must pass between the powerful towers flanking the Porta Reial.

Inside, the Gothic **Capilla de Sant Jordi** is also known as 'la dorada', because bronze panels on the chapel were made over with gold to impress the visiting emperor Felipe II in 1564. In the **Palau del Rei Martí**, the most captivating element are the exquisitely crafted Gothic windows. The oldest part of

this sprawling abbey is the **cloister**, a Transitional work showing clearly enough its Romanesque origins.

Without doubt, it is the haughty **iglesia** that most impresses itself on the memory. Begun in 1161, it is the largest Cistercian church in Spain. The high altar is presided over by a magnificent alabaster retablo.

The monastery is open 10 am to 12.30 pm and 3 to 6 pm (to 5.30 pm in winter); 500 ptas, students 300 ptas. Hour-long guided tours (in Catalan and/or Spanish) start every 15 to 30 minutes.

Of six Vibasa buses (☎ 902-10 13 63) from Tarragona to Montblanc and L'Espluga de Francolí, three also stop at the monastery. Regular trains from Barcelona to Tarragona via Reus (line Ca4) stop at Montblanc and L'Espluga de Francolí, a 40-minute walk to the monastery.

Around Monestir de Poblet

It is worth spending time exploring the vicinity. **L'Espluga de Francolí**, 2.5km away from the monastery along a pleasant tree-lined country road that makes walking tempting, is a bright little town with several small hotels.

More interesting still is **Montblanc**, 8km away. Still surrounded by medieval battlements, this one-time royal residence is jammed with medieval jewels, including a Gothic royal mansion and a couple of churches from the same era, as well as some vestiges of its Romanesque origins. The winding cross-country drive to **Prades** also takes you through lovely country.

If monasteries are your thing, the less imposing **Monestir de Santes Creus**, east of Montblanc, and **Vallbona de les Monges**, to the north, are also worth searching out.

Southern Catalunya

Sitges, 35km south-west of Barcelona, is the wildest resort on the Catalan coast. From there to the Valencian border stretches the Costa Daurada (Golden Coast), a series of less exciting resorts along a mainly flat coast varied only by the delta of the Río

Ebro, which protrudes 20km out into the Mediterranean. Along the way, however, is the old Roman capital of Tarragona and the modern extravaganza of Port Aventura – Spain's answer to EuroDisney.

SITGES
postcode 08870 • pop 17,600

Sitges attracts everyone from jet-setters to young travellers, honeymooners to week-ending families, Barcelona night owls to an international gay crowd. The beach is long and sandy, the nightlife thumps until break-fast and there are lots of groovy boutiques if you need to spruce up your wardrobe. In winter Sitges can be dead, but it wakes up with a vengeance for *carnaval,* when the gay crowd puts on an outrageous show.

Sitges has been fashionable in one way or another since the 1890s, when it became an avant-garde art world hang-out. It has been one of Spain's most anti-conventional, anything-goes resorts since the 1960s. One thing it isn't, however, is cheap. You'll struggle to find a room for under 5000 ptas, food is pricey and a mixed drink can easily set you back 1000 ptas.

Orientation

The main landmark is the Església de Sant Bartomeu i Santa Tecla parish church, atop a small rocky elevation that separates the 2km-long main beach, to the south-west, from the smaller, quieter Platja de Sant Se-bastià, to the north-east. The old part of town climbs gently inland from the church area, with the train station some 500m back, at the top of Avinguda d'Artur Carbonell.

Information

The tourist office (☎ 93 894 42 51, fax 93 894 43 05), Carrer de Sínia Morera 1, is open 9 am to 9 pm daily in July and August. In other months, it's open 9 am to 2 pm and 4 to 6.30 pm weekdays, and 10 am to 1 pm Saturday. To book accommodation in advance, you can also call (from within Spain) ☎ 902-10 34 28. The office's Web site is at www.sitgestur.com.

You can occasionally pick up the *Plano Gay de Sitges,* a free map of gay-oriented

bars, hotels, restaurants and shops, at several spots around town including Parrots Pub, on Plaça de la Industria.

Several banks and ATMs grace Plaça del Cap de Vila and surrounding streets in the old town. The post office is on Plaça d'Es-panya. The Policía Local (☎ 93 811 76 25) is at Plaça d'Ajuntament, behind the parish church. The Hospital Sant Joan (☎ 93 894 00 03) is on Carrer del Hospital in the upper part of town.

Museums

The **Museu Cau Ferrat** on Carrer de Fonol-lar was built in the 1890s as a house-cum-studio by Santiago Rusiñol, a co-founder of Els Quatre Gats in Barcelona, and the man who attracted the art world to Sitges. In 1894 Rusiñol reawakened the public to the then unfashionable work of El Greco by parading two of the Cretan's canvases in from Sitges train station to Cau Ferrat. These are on show along with the remainder of Rusiñol's large art and crafts collection, which includes paintings by the likes of Picasso, Ramon Casas (another of the 'four cats') and Rusiñol himself.

Next door, the **Museu Maricel del Mar** houses art and artisanry from the Middle Ages to the 20th century. The museum is part of the Palau Maricel, a stylistic fantasy built around 1910 by Miquel Utrillo (yet another 'cat'). The **Museu Romàntic**, at Carrer de Sant Gaudenci 1, recreates the lifestyle of a 19th-century Catalan landowning family and contains a collection of several hundred antique dolls.

All three museums are open 10 am to 1.30 pm and 3 to 6.30 pm Tuesday to Friday, 10 am to 7 pm Saturday and until 3 pm Sunday. Entry to each costs 500 ptas, or you can get an all-in ticket for 900 ptas.

Beaches

The main beach is divided by a series of breakwaters into sections with different names. A pedestrian promenade runs its whole length. In high summer, especially on the weekend, the end nearest the parish church gets jam-packed. Crowds thin out slightly towards the south-west end. Sitges also has two nude beaches – one exclusively gay – about 20 minutes' walk beyond the Hotel Terramar at the far end of the main beach. To reach them, you have to walk along the coast past a sewage plant, over a hill and along the railway a bit.

Special Events

Carnaval in Sitges is a week-long riot of the extrovert, ambiguous and exhibitionist, capped by an extravagant gay parade on the last night. June sees the Sitges International Theatre Festival, with a strong experimental leaning. Sitges' festa major in late August

features a huge firework show on the 23rd. Early October is the time for Sitges' International Fantasy Film Festival.

Places to Stay

Sitges has over 50 hotels and hostales, but many close from around October to April, then are full in July and August. If you haven't booked ahead, it's not a bad idea to ask the tourist office to ring around for you, especially if you arrive late in the day.

Camping *Camping El Rocà (☎ 93 894 00 43, Avinguda de Ronda s/n)* is north of the

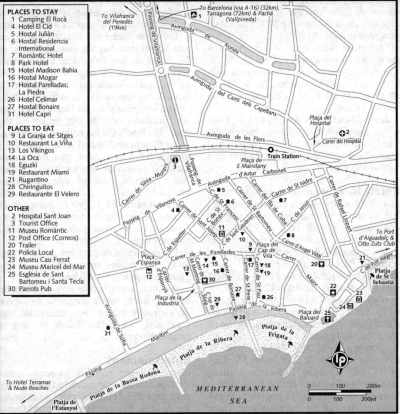

SITGES

PLACES TO STAY
1 Camping El Rocà
4 Hotel El Cid
5 Hostal Julián
6 Hostal Residencia International
7 Romàntic Hotel
8 Park Hotel
15 Hotel Madison Bahía
16 Hostal Mogar
17 Hostal Parelladas; La Piedra
26 Hotel Celimar
27 Hostal Bonaire
31 Hotel Capri

PLACES TO EAT
9 La Granja de Sitges
10 Restaurant La Viña
13 Los Vikingos
14 La Oca
18 Eguzki
19 Restaurant Miami
21 Rugantino
28 Chiringuitos
29 Restaurante El Velero

OTHER
2 Hospital Sant Joan
3 Tourist Office
11 Museu Romàntic
20 Post Office (Correos)
22 Trailer
23 Policía Local
24 Museu Cau Ferrat
25 Museu Maricel del Mar
25 Església de Sant Bartomeu i Santa Tecla
30 Parrots Pub

railway line, 1km from the beach. It has room for 600 people and charges 695 ptas per adult, car and tent. *Camping El Garrofer* (☎ 93 894 17 80) and *Camping Sitges* (☎ 93 894 10 80) are out of town off the C-246.

Hostales One friendly place that's popular with travellers is *Hostal Parellades* (☎ 93 894 08 91, Carrer de les Parellades 11). It has singles without shower for 2700 ptas and doubles with private bathroom for 5300 ptas.

Hostal Julià (☎ 93 894 03 06, Avinguda de Artur Carbonell 2), near the train station and tourist office, has garish wallpaper but good-sized rooms, with shared baths, for 4675/6000 ptas. Close by, *Hostal Residència Internacional* (☎ 93 894 26 90, Carrer de Sant Francesc 52) has eight sizable and clean doubles for 5000 ptas (6000 ptas with private shower).

One place that's open all year round is the quirky *Hostal Bonaire* (☎ 93 894 53 26, Carrer de Bonaire 31), where rooms with bathroom cost 5000/6000 ptas. *Hostal Mogar* (☎ 93 811 00 09, Carrer de Bonaire 2) has similar prices.

Hostal Sant Joan (☎ 93 894 13 50, Carrer de Joan Tarrida 16) is not a bad choice. The rooms on offer are fairly spacious and quiet, have their own bathroom and cost 5000/8300 ptas.

Hotels *Hotel Madison Bahía* (☎/fax 93 894 00 12, Carrer de les Parellades 31-33) has friendly management and singles/doubles/triples with bath at 7900/9800/11,800 ptas (prices drop by a third or more in low season). All 25 rooms have exterior windows. *Park Hotel* (☎ 93 894 02 50, fax 93 894 08 93, Carrer de Jesús 12-14) is a slight step up with rooms at 8900/12,600 ptas.

Hotel El Cid (☎ 93 894 18 42, fax 93 894 63 35, Carrer de Sant Josep 39) is an understated place with reasonable, modern rooms for 5200/8400 ptas.

Romàntic Hotel (☎ 93 894 83 75, fax 93 894 81 67, Carrer de Sant Isidre 33) comprises three adjoining 19th-century villas, sensuously restored in period style, with a leafy dining courtyard. It's popular with gay visitors, although not exclusively so. There are about 60 rooms with shower costing up to 12,825 ptas.

On the seafront near the parish church, *Hotel Celimar* (☎ 93 811 01 70, fax 93 811 04 03, Passeig de la Ribera 20) has rooms for 10,750 to 17,750 ptas plus IVA. *Hotel Capri* (☎ 93 811 02 67, fax 93 894 51 88, Avinguda de Sofia 13-15) is a good family-run place with doubles at 14,500 ptas plus IVA.

Places to Eat

You'll be lucky to find a *menú* for less than 1200 ptas. The self-service *Los Vikingos* (Carrer del Marques de Montroig 7-9) in the thick of the action, serves tolerable pasta, pizza and seafood starting at 850 ptas. *La Oca* (Carrer de les Parellades 41) is popular for its pizzas starting at 725 ptas and grilled chicken at 385 ptas for a quarter-bird.

Carrer de Sant Pau has a string of good restaurants including the Basque *Eguzki* at No 3, which has good tapas and a mixed menu of seafood and meat mains from 1000 to 1800 ptas. *Restaurant Miami*, at No 11, has a decent four-course *menú* for 1875 ptas.

The best thing about *La Piedra* (Carrer de les Parellades 7) is the big terrace out the back. The food's OK but nothing marvellous.

La Granja de Sitges (Carrer de les Parellades 4) is a lively tapas spot. *Restaurant La Viña* (Carrer de Sant Francesc 11) also has a range of generous tapas starting at around 500 ptas.

Restaurante El Velero (Passeig de la Ribera 38) is a fairly classy fish and seafood joint with most mains costing 1500 ptas or more.

For real seaside dining you could munch away on expensive tapas at the two *chiringuitos* on Passeig de la Ribera.

A calmer area to eat is over on Platja de Sant Sebastià, where *Rugantino* (Carrer del Port Alegre 21) serves pizza, pasta, and meat and vegetarian dishes starting at around 900 ptas.

Entertainment

Much of Sitges' nightlife happens on one short pedestrian strip packed with humanity right through the night in summer: Carrer del 1er de Maig, Plaça de la Industria and Carrer

View of Olite from the Palacio Real (Navarra)

DAMIEN SIMONIS

DUSHAN COORAY

DAMIEN SIMONIS

Spa town of Arnedillo (La Rioja)

Cathedral of San Sebastián (Basque Country)

The Puente Romano, a medieval bridge spanning the Río Sella, Cangas de Onis (Asturias)

Multicoloured boats and buoys at the Cantabrian port town of Castro Uriales

Picos de Europa (Cantabria)

Stone huts in the Picos de Europa (Asturias)

del Marques de Montroig, all in a short line off the seafront Passeig de la Ribera.

Carrer del 1er de Maig – or Calle del Pecado (Sin Street) – vibrates to the volume of 10 or so disco-bars all trying to outdo each other in decibels. They start to fill at about midnight. Plaça de la Industria and Carrer del Marques de Montroig have the bars and cafes where people sit, drink and watch other people. All you have to do is cruise along, see what takes your fancy and try not to bust your budget (more easily said than done).

If you're in need of a change of location, head round the corner to Carrer de les Parellades, Carrer de Bonaire or Carrer de Sant Pere, where there's more of much the same. Carrer de Sant Bonaventura has a string of gay bars, mostly behind closed doors. *Trailer* (*Carrer del Ángel Vidal 36*) is a popular gay disco.

Some distance from the centre of town are some of the big discos, such as *Pachá* in Vallpineda, and the local branch of Barcelona's *Otto Zutz Club*, in Port d'Aiguadolç where you will also find other bars along the waterfront.

Getting There & Away
Four rodalies trains an hour, from about 6 am to 10 pm, run from Estació Sants to Sitges, taking 30 minutes and charging 335 ptas. Three trains a day leave Sitges for Tarragona (one hour), where you can change for Port Aventura, Valencia and beyond.

The best road from Barcelona is the A-16 tollway. In Sitges itself, the traffic usually makes it quicker to walk than drive. You can call taxis on ☎ 93 894 35 94 or ☎ 93 894 13 29.

TARRAGONA
postcode 43080 • pop 112,795
Tarragona was first occupied by the Romans, who called it Tarraco, in 218 BC. In 27 BC Augustus made it the capital of his new Tarraconensis province (roughly all modern Spain) and stayed here till 25 BC while directing campaigns in Cantabria and Asturias. Tarragona was abandoned when the Muslims arrived in AD 714, but reborn as the seat of a Christian archbishopric in

1089. Today it's a mainly modern city, but its rich Roman remains and fine medieval cathedral make it an absorbing place.

Tarraco, An Archaeological Guide by Xavier Aquilué and others will help you unravel Tarragona's ancient history and complicated archaeology; one place selling it is the Museu Nacional Arqueològic de Tarragona (MNAT).

Orientation
The main street is Rambla Nova, which runs roughly north-west from a cliff-top overlooking the Mediterranean. A couple of blocks to the east, and parallel, is Rambla Vella, which marks the beginning of the old town and, incidentally, follows the line of the Via Augusta, the Roman road from Rome to Cádiz.

The train station is half a kilometre south-west of Rambla Nova, near the seafront, and the bus station is about 2km inland, just to the west off Plaça Imperial de Tàrraco.

Information
The main town tourist office (☎ 977 24 50 64), at Carrer Major 39, is open from 10 am to 2 pm and 4.30 to 7 pm weekdays, and until 2 pm weekends and holidays (extra hours from July to September). There's also a regional tourist office (☎ 977 23 34 15), Carrer de Fortuny 4, which opens 9.15 am to 2 pm and 4 to 7.30 pm Monday to Saturday (closed Saturday afternoon). Several info booths scattered about town open 10 am to 2 pm weekends and in summer.

Several countries have consulates in Tarragona. The main post office is on Plaça Corsini.

The Guàrdia Urbana (municipal police; ☎ 977 24 03 45) are at Carrer de Pare Palau 7. There's a hospital (☎ 977 23 27 14) on Passeig de Torroja.

Things to See & Do
All the city's monuments are closed Monday except the cathedral. You will soon come to notice that, aside from the cathedral, the theme is decidedly Roman. Pick up the handy *Ruta Arqueològica Urbana* brochure from the tourist office. It details

CATALUNYA

CATALUNYA

Of Giants, Dragons & Human Castles

DAMIEN SIMONIS

The Castellers de Barcelona making a 'quatre de vuit'

As befits a people of such independent traditions, Catalans get up to all sorts of unusual tricks at *festa* time.

Fire and fireworks play a big part in many Spanish festivals, but Catalunya adds a special twist with the *correfoc* (fire-running), in which devil and dragon figures run through the streets spitting fireworks at the crowds. (Wear protective clothes if you intend to get close!) Correfocs are often part of the *festa major* – a town or village's main annual festival. Many of these are in July or August.

Also usually part of the festa major fun are the *sardana* (Catalunya's national round-dance), all sorts of costumed local dances, and *gegants,* splendidly attired and lifelike 5m-high giants who parade through the streets or dance in the squares to the sound of old-fashioned instruments. Giants usually come in male-female pairs: a medieval king and queen, a Muslim sultan and a Christian princess. Almost every town and village has its own – sometimes just one pair, sometimes five or six. They're usually accompanied by an entourage of grotesque 'dwarfs' (otherwise known as *capgrossos,* or bigheads).

On La Nit de Sant Joan, 23 June, big bonfires burn at crossroads and on town squares in a combined midsummer and St John's Eve celebration. Fireworks go on all night. But Catalunya's supreme fire festival is the Patum in the otherwise unexceptional Pyrenean foothill town of Berga. An evening of dancing and firework-spitting angels, devils, mule-like monsters, dwarfs, giants and men covered in grass culminates in a kind of mass frenzy of fire and smoke

---

more than 30 locations throughout the old town where Roman remains can be viewed, some of them in shops and restaurants. If they are not too busy with customers, shop owners are generally happy for individuals to drop by and take a look.

Catedral Sitting grandly at the top of the old town, Tarragona's cathedral is a treasure house deserving 1½ hours or more if you're to do it justice. Built between 1171 and 1331 on the site of a Roman temple, it combines Romanesque and Gothic features, as typified by the main facade on Pla de la Seu. The entrance is by the cloister on the north-western side of the building.

The cloister has Gothic vaulting and Romanesque carved capitals, one of which

shows rats conducting what they imagine to be a cat's funeral, until the cat comes back to life! The rooms off the cloister house the Museu Diocesà, with an extensive collection extending from Roman hairpins to some lovely 12th- to 14th-century polychrome woodcarvings of a breastfeeding Virgin.

The interior of the cathedral, over 100m long, is Romanesque at the north-eastern end and Gothic at the south-west. The aisles are lined with 14th- to 19th-century chapels and hung with 16th- and 17th-century tapestries from Brussels. The arm of St Thecla, Tarragona's patron saint, is normally kept in the Capella de Santa Tecla on the south-eastern side. The choir in the centre of the nave has 15th-century carved walnut stalls. The marble main altar was carved in the

Of Giants, Dragons & Human Castles

that has been likened to a medieval vision of hell. The 'real' Patum happens on Corpus Christi (the Thursday following the eighth Sunday after Easter Sunday) although there are watered-down versions on the next two or three days.

An activity demanding rather more calm and order, but still emotive, is the building of *castells,* human castles. This tradition is strongest in southern and central Catalunya: Valls, Vilafranca del Penedès and Terrassa have three of the most famous groups of *castellers.* The golden age was the 1880s, when castells of *tres de nou* and *quatre de nou* ('three of nine' and 'four of nine', ie, nine storeys of three people and nine storeys of four people) were achieved.

There are all sorts of permutations in the construction of the castell: those built without a *pinya, folre* or *manilles* – extra rings of support for the first, second and third storeys – are particularly tricky and termed *net* (clean). A completed castell is signalled by the child at the top (the *anxaneta*) raising their arm – a cue for tumultuous applause and cheering from the onlookers. A castell that manages to dismantle itself without collapsing is *descarregat.* Especially difficult is a *pilar,* a tower of one person per storey. The best pilar ever done was eight storeys, a *pilar de vuit.*

Since the 1980s the practice has experienced a revival, which is threatening to break all-time records for degrees of difficulty. Building castells is a sort of sport and competitions are held, often at festes majors. Festivals where you can expect to see castellers include: Vilafranca del Penedès, at the end of August; Tarragona, in the last week of September or early October; El Vendrell, mid-October; and Valls, on the first Sunday after 21 October.

A *castell* is completed by putting a child at the top.

13th century with scenes from the life of St Thecla.

The cathedral opens 10 am to 7 pm Monday to Saturday (closed Sunday and holidays) from July to mid-October, 10 am to 2 pm from mid-November to the end of March, and until 1 pm and 4 to 7 pm the rest of the year. The 300 ptas charge includes a detailed booklet.

Museu d'Història de Tarragona This museum comprises four separate Roman sites around the city and the 14th-century noble mansion now serving as the **Museu Casa Castellarnau**, at Carrer dels Cavallers 14.

Start with the **Pretori i Circ Romans** on Plaça del Rei, which includes part of the vaults of the Roman circus, where chariot races were held. The circus, 300m long, stretched from here to beyond Plaça de la Font. Near the beach is the well-preserved **Amfiteatre Romà**, where gladiators battled each other, or wild animals, to the death. In its arena are the remains of 6th- and 12th-century churches built to commemorate the martyrdom of the Christian bishop Fructuosus and two deacons, whom they say were burnt alive here in AD 259.

By Carrer de Lleida are remains of the **Fòrum Romà**, dominated by several imposing columns. The north-western half of this site was occupied by a judicial basilica (where legal disputes were settled), from which the rest of the forum stretched downhill to the south-west. Linked to the site by a footbridge is another excavated area with a stretch of Roman street. This forum was the hub of public life for the Roman town but was less important, and much smaller, than the provincial forum, the navel of all Tarraconensis province.

The **Passeig Arqueològic** is a peaceful walk round part of the perimeter of the old town between two lines of city walls; the inner ones are mainly Roman while the outer ones were put up by the British in the War of the Spanish Succession.

All these places are open 9 or 10 am to 9 pm Tuesday to Saturday, and until 3 pm Sunday (June to September). In other months, they tend to be open 10 am to 1.30 pm and 4 to 6.30 pm Monday to Saturday, and 10 am to 2 pm Sunday and holidays. The cost of entry for each element is 300 ptas.

Museu Nacional Arqueològic de Tarragona

This carefully presented museum on Plaça del Rei gives further insight into Roman Tarraco, although most explanatory material is in Catalan or Castilian. Exhibits include part of the Roman city walls, frescoes, sculpture and pottery. A highlight is the large, almost complete *Mosaic de Peixos de la Pineda* showing fish and sea creatures. In the section on everyday arts you can admire ancient fertility aids including an outsize stone penis, symbol of the god Priapus.

The museum is open 10 am to 8 pm Tuesday to Saturday and until 2 pm Sunday and holidays. For the rest of the year the weekday times change to 10 am to 1.30 pm and 4 to 7 pm. Entry costs 400 ptas and entitles you to enter the museum at the **Necròpolis Paleocristians**. This large Christian cemetery of late-Roman and Visigothic times is on Passeig de la Independència on the western edge of town and boasts some surprisingly elaborate tombs. Unfortunately only its small museum was open at the time of writing.

Roman Aqueduct

The Aqüeducte Romà, 4km inland on the N-240 Lleida road, is a fine stretch of two-tiered aqueduct 217m long and 27m high. Bus No 5 to Sant Salvador from Plaça Imperial de Tàrraco, running every 10 to 20 minutes, will take you there.

Museu d'Art Modern

This modest art gallery at Carrer de Santa Anna 8 is at its most interesting when temporary exhibitions take place. It opens 10 am to 8 pm Tuesday to Saturday (with a lunch break of two hours from 3 pm Saturday) and 11 am to 2 pm Sunday. Entry is free.

Beaches

The town beach, **Platja del Miracle**, is reasonably clean but can get terribly crowded. **Platja Arrabassada**, 1km northeast across the headland, is longer, and **Platja Llarga**, beginning 2km farther out, stretches for about 3km. Bus Nos 1 and 9 from the Balcó stop on Via Augusta go to both (110 ptas). You can get the same buses along Rambla Vella and Rambla Nova.

Places to Stay

There are eight camping grounds on or close to the beach within 11km north-east of the city along the N-340. Nearest is *Camping Tàrraco* (☎ 977 23 99 89), behind Platja Arrabassada, but others, such as *Camping Las Palmeras* (☎ 977 20 80 81) at the far end of Platja Llarga, are better. Most grounds close from October to March. The only one that doesn't is the *Camping Tamarit Park* (☎ 977 65 01 28), 4km farther beyond La Palmeras.

Plaça de la Font in the old town has three adequate pensiones (one closed at the time of writing). *Pensión Forum* (☎ 977 23 17 18), at No 37, charges 2500/5000 ptas for small, clean singles/doubles with own shower and toilet. *Hostal Noria* (☎ 977 23 87 17), at No 53, is a bit better value at 2700/4600 ptas but is often full.

Habitaciones Mariflor (☎ 977 23 82 31, Carrer del General Contreras 29), in a drab block near the train station, has clean rooms with shared baths for 2100/4000 ptas.

Hotel España (☎ 977 23 27 12, Rambla Nova 49) is a well-positioned but unexciting one-star hotel where rooms with bath cost 3300/6000 ptas plus IVA. The three-star *Hotel Lauria* (☎ 977 23 67 12), at No 20, is a worthwhile splurge at 5500/8500 ptas plus IVA, with a good location and a pool.

Less inspired in terms of location but comfortable is *Hotel Urbis* (☎ 977 24 01 16,

CATALUNYA

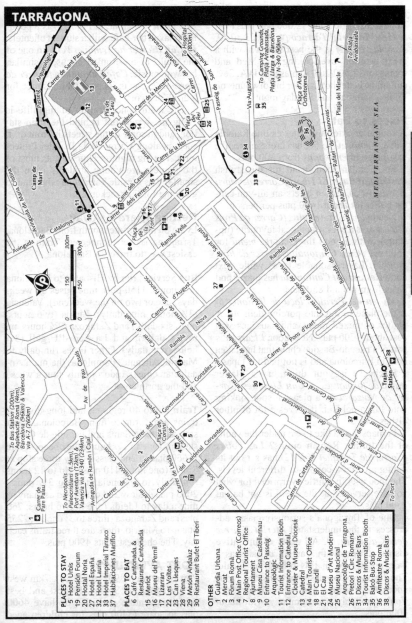

TARRAGONA

PLACES TO STAY
5 Hotel Urbis
19 Pensión Forum
20 Hostal Noria
27 Hotel España
32 Hotel Lauria
33 Hotel Imperial Tarraco
37 Habitaciones Mariflor

PLACES TO EAT
6 Café Cantonada &
  Restaurant Cantonada
15 Merlot
16 Museu del Pernil
17 Lizarran
22 Les Voltes
23 Can Llesques
28 Viena
29 Mesón Andaluz
30 Restaurant Bufet El Tiberi

OTHER
1 Guàrdia Urbana
2 Mercat
3 Fòrum Romà
4 Main Post Office (Correos)
7 Regional Tourist Office
8 Ajuntament
9 Museu Casa Castellarnau
10 Entrance to Passeig
   Arqueològic
11 Tourist Information Booth
12 Entrance to Catedral,
   Cloister & Museu Diocesà
13 Catedral
14 Main Tourist Office
18 El Candil
21 El Cau
24 Museu d'Art Modern
25 Museu Nacional
   Arqueològic de Tarragona
26 Pretori i Circ Romans
31 Discos & Music Bars
34 Tourist Information Booth
35 Balcó Bus Stop
36 Amfiteatre Romà
38 Discos & Music Bars

euro currency converter €1 = 166pta

fax 977 24 36 54, Carrer de Reding 20). Rooms cost up to 9500/12,000 ptas plus IVA.

Hotel Imperial Tàrraco (☎ 977 23 30 40, Rambla Vella 2) is the best in town, with a great position overlooking the Med and rooms for 12,500/16,050 ptas plus IVA. Several of the better hotels offer big discounts on Friday, Saturday and Sunday nights.

Places to Eat

A couple of cafes and eateries line Rambla Nova. *Viena*, at No 50, has croissants and a vast range of *entrapans* from 300 ptas.

For Catalan food, head for the stylish *Restaurant Bufet El Tiberi (Carrer de Martí d'Ardenya 5),* which offers an all-you-can-eat buffet for about 1450 ptas per person.

Nearby, *Mesón Andaluz (Carrer de Pons d'Icart 3)* is a backstreet local favourite (upstairs), with a good three-course *menú* for 1500 ptas. *Café Cantonada (Carrer de Fortuny 23)* has reasonable tapas while next door, *Restaurant Cantonada* has pizzas and pasta from around 850 ptas.

Museu del Pernil (Plaça de la Font 16) is the place to dig into porcine delights. A platter of mixed meats and sausages will cost about 1700 ptas. Next door, *Lizarran* is part of a pseudo-Basque chain that has taken hold in Barcelona and is not bad for tapas.

If cheese is your thing, try a platter *(taula de formatges)* at *Can Llesques (Carrer de Natzaret 6),* a pleasant spot looking onto Plaça del Rei. It serves a lot of other dishes too.

Perhaps you'd like to eat under the vaults of the former Roman circus? *Les Voltes (Carrer de Trinquet Vell 12)* has set out its dining area on a couple of different levels. The food itself is a little overpriced for what you are served, but the *menú* is not bad at 1500 ptas.

One of Tarragona's seriously classy addresses is the understated *Merlot (Carrer dels Cavallers 6)*. All sorts of inventive dishes starting with Catalan classics as a base are served in this refreshing locale. The heavy exposed stone walls are lightened by paintings and other decoration. You'll probably part company with about 4000 ptas.

Entertainment

El Candil (Plaça de la Font 13) is a popular, relaxed bar-cafe with a student clientele. *El Cau (Carrer de Trinquet Vell),* in one of the vaults of the Roman circus, is similar, but with music. *Café Cantonada (Carrer de Fortuny 23),* with its pool table, is nice for a drink or two.

The main concentration of nightlife is along the waterfront behind the train station, and in some of the streets in front of it, such as along Carrer de la Pau del Protectorat. The big night is Thursday, as most of the punters are young students from the small towns outside Tarragona who tend to go home for the weekend.

Getting There & Away

Lying on main routes south from Barcelona, Tarragona is well connected. Train is the easiest way to travel to Barcelona.

Bus Services run by Hispania to Barcelona (1½ hours, 1150 ptas, nine buses on weekdays, one or two on the weekend), Valencia (3½ hours, nine daily); Lleida (two hours, up to six daily) and Zaragoza (2¾ hours, up to six daily); and La Seu d'Urgell (3¼ hours, one daily). Other buses run daily to Madrid, Alicante, Pamplona, the main Andalucian cities, Andorra (only four a week) and the north coast.

Train Up to 40 regional and long-distance trains a day run to/from Barcelona. Most stop at Estació Sants and Passeig de Gràcia stations (one to 1½ hours; the cheapest fare is 660 ptas in 2nd class). Only three stop at Sitges (one hour, 410 ptas). Up to 12 trains run daily to Valencia (two to 3½ hours, 2095 ptas in slow 2nd class) and as many as nine a day to Lleida (one to two hours, 760 ptas) and Zaragoza (three to 3¾ hours, 2255 ptas). To Madrid, there are three trains each day. The cheapest costs 4900 ptas.

PORT AVENTURA

Port Aventura (☎ 902-20 22 20), 7km west of Tarragona, is Spain's biggest and best funfair-adventure park. If you have 4600 ptas to spare (3400 ptas for children aged five to 12), it makes an amusing day out, especially if you have ankle-biters.

In 1998 Universal Pictures Studios bought up the park and began filling it with Americanisms that may or may not appeal. Woody Woodpecker is the new mascot of a park that is billed as a 'world of fun for all ages'. Rocky & Bullwinkle, that famous Catalan pair, have also been catapulted to star status in the park. Sarcasm aside, the park has plenty of spine-tingling rides and other attractions. The big new addition is a virtual submarine created by Universal at a staggering cost of 4.5 million ptas.

The funfair is only open from Semana Santa to the end of October, 10 am to 8 pm weekdays (to 10 pm weekends); to midnight from around mid-June to mid-September. Night tickets, valid from 7 pm, are 3400 ptas.

Trains run to Port Aventura's own station, about 1km walk from the site, several times a day from Tarragona (375 ptas return) and Barcelona (1305 ptas return). By road, take exit 35 from the A-7, or the N-340 from Tarragona. Parking is 600 ptas.

TORTOSA
postcode 43500 • pop 29,600
Home to Iberian tribes 2000 years ago, Tortosa has seen them all come and go: Greeks, Romans, Visigoths and Muslims. The town was on the northern front line between Christian and Muslim Spain for four centuries.

A tourist booth (☎ 977 44 25 67), Avinguda de la Generalitat, is open 10 am to 1.30 pm and 4 to 8 pm Tuesday to Saturday, and until 1.30 pm Sunday. Another booth opens similar hours on Carrer de Ferran Arasa.

The old town, concentrated in the western end of the city north of the Ebro, is watched over by the imposing **Castell de la Suda**, where a small medieval Arab cemetery has been unearthed and in whose grounds now stands a fine *parador* (☎ 977 44 44 50). The Gothic **catedral** (or Seu) dates to 1347 and contains a pleasant cloister and some baroque additions. It's open 9 am to 1 pm and 4 to 8 pm. Other attractions include the **Palau Episcopal** and the lovely **Jardins del Príncep**, perfect for a stroll.

About the cheapest place to stay is *Hostal Virginia* (☎ 977 44 41 86, Avinguda de la Generalitat 133), where singles/doubles with bath cost up to 3300/4500 ptas.

The train and bus stations are opposite each other on Ronda dels Docs. There are two daily buses (one to 1½ hours, 785 ptas) but more regular trains to Tarragona. Trains also run to Vinarós (Valencia). Up to six buses run daily to Barcelona (two hours, around 1000 ptas), and two to four run into the Ebro Delta area (see the following section). Lleida is about two hours away by bus (up to four daily services).

EBRO DELTA
The delta of the Río Ebro (Delta de l'Ebre in Catalan), formed by silt brought down by the river, sticks 20km out into the Mediterranean near Catalunya's southern border. Dotted with reedy lagoons and fringed by dune-backed beaches, this flat and exposed wetland is northern Spain's most important water-bird habitat. The October-November migration season sees the peak bird population, with an average of 53,000 ducks and 15,000 coots, but they're also numerous in winter and spring. Ten per cent of all water birds wintering on the Iberian Peninsula choose to park themselves here.

Nearly half the delta's 320 sq km are given over to rice-growing. Some 77 sq km, mostly along the coasts and around the lagoons, form the Parc Natural Delta de l'Ebre.

Orientation
The delta is a seaward-pointing arrowhead of land with the Ebro flowing eastwards across its middle. The town of Deltebre straggles about 5km along the northern bank of the river at the centre of the delta. Deltebre's western half is called Jesús i Maria and the eastern half La Cava. Facing Deltebre on the southern bank is Sant Jaume d'Enveja. Roads crisscross the delta to Deltebre and beyond from the towns of L'Ampolla, Amposta and Sant Carles de la Ràpita, all on the N-340. Three ferries *(transbordadors),* running from early morning until nightfall, link Deltebre to Sant Jaume d'Enveja. They charge 50 ptas per

pedestrian and 300 ptas for a car with two people.

Information

The tourist office (Centre d'Informació; ☎ 977 48 96 79) is at Carrer de Martí Buera 22, Deltebre. Adjoining is an Ecomuseu, with displays describing the delta environment and an aquarium-terrarium of delta species. Hours for both are 10 am to 1 pm (2 pm weekdays) and 3 to 6 pm (closed Sunday afternoon). Entry to the museum is 200 ptas.

There's another information office, with a bird museum, at La Casa de Fusta, by L'Encanyissada lagoon about 10km south-west of Deltebre. Hours there are 10 am to 2 pm and 3 to 6 pm (closed Monday).

Other offices are in Sant Carles de la Ràpita, Amposta and L'Ampolla.

Things to See & Do

A good way to explore the delta is by **bicycle** and you can rent one for about 1300 ptas a day at several places in Deltebre.

Early morning and evening are the best times for **bird-watching**, and good areas include L'Encanyissada and La Tancada lagoons and Punta de la Banya, all in the south of the delta. L'Encanyissada has two observation towers and La Tancada one (others are marked on a map you can pick up at the Centre d'Informació). La Tancada and Punta de la Banya are generally the best places to see the greater flamingoes, the delta's most spectacular birds. Almost 2000 of the birds nest here, and since 1992 the delta has been one of only five places in Europe where they reproduce. Punta de la Banya is joined to the delta by a 5km sandspit with the wide, long and sandy Platja de l'Eucaliptus beach at its northern end.

Olmos (☎ 977 48 05 48) is one of a couple of companies that run daily tourist **boat trips** from Deltebre to the mouths of the Ebro

and the Illa de Buda at the delta's tip. Trips last 1½ hours and cost around 800 ptas per person. Boats go daily, but the frequency depends on the season: in summer both companies do several trips a day.

Places to Stay

Camping Mediterrani Blau (☎ 977 47 90 46), on Platja de l'Eucaliptus, is open from April to September with room for 240 people in a small eucalyptus grove, charging 500 ptas plus IVA, per adult, per car and per tent. It has a restaurant. There are two more camping grounds, open all year, at Riumar, 10km east of Deltebre.

Restaurant Can Salat (☎ 977 48 02 28, Carrer de Adrià VI 1) is in the centre of La Cava and has a few adequate rooms, and charges 2000 ptas per person. *Delta Hotel (☎ 977 48 00 46, fax 977 48 06 63, Avinguda del Canal, Camí de la Illeta s/n),* on the northern edge of Deltebre by the road to Riumar, has nice modern singles/doubles costing up to 5950/9850 ptas (including breakfast) plus IVA and a good restaurant.

The most pleasant places to eat are out by Riumar and the mouth of the river. *Restaurante Galach,* by the Llacuna Garxal (the end of the road as it were), serves Ebro specialities, which include *anguilas* (eels), *angules* (baby eels) and shellfish.

There are several places to stay in Sant Carles de la Ràpita, a pleasant fishing town with a marina.

Getting There & Away

The delta is easiest to get to and around with your own wheels, but it is possible to reach it by bus or a train-bus combination.

Autocars Hife (☎ 902-11 98 14) runs to Jesús i Maria and La Cava from Tortosa (one hour) up to four times daily (twice on Saturday, Sunday and holidays), and from Amposta (30 minutes) once or twice daily.

Andorra

The Catalan-speaking principality of Andorra (population 66,000), whose mountainous territory comprises only 464 sq km, nestles in the Pyrenees between Catalunya (Cataluña) and France. Although it *is* tiny, this political anomaly contains some of the most dramatic scenery and best skiing in the Pyrenees. And in summer there's plenty of good walking in the higher, more remote parts of the principality. There's relatively little of historical interest other than a handful of Romanesque churches.

Facts about Andorra

HISTORY

By tradition, Andorra's independence is credited to Charlemagne, who captured the region from the Muslims in AD 803. In 843 Charlemagne's grandson, Charles II, granted the Valls d'Andorra (Valleys of Andorra) to Sunifred, Count of Urgell, whose base was La Seu d'Urgell, in Catalunya. From the counts, Andorra later passed to the bishops of Urgell, also based in La Seu. In the 13th century, after a succession dispute between the bishops and the French counts of Foix to the north, Andorra's first constitutional documents, the Pareatges, established a system of shared sovereignty between the two rivals. This feudal setup created a peculiar political equilibrium that saved Andorra from being swallowed by its powerful neighbours despite recurrent tension between the co-princes down the centuries.

Since the 1950s Andorra has developed as a centre for skiing and duty-free shopping – the latter business grew out of the smuggling of French goods to Spain during the Spanish Civil War and Spanish goods to France in WWII (Andorra remained neutral in both). These activities have brought not only wealth, foreign workers and eight million visitors a year, but also some unsightly develop-

FRANCE

ANDORRA

Andorra la Vella pp494-5

SPAIN

ment and heavy traffic for several kilometres either side of the capital, Andorra la Vella.

GEOGRAPHY

Andorra, in the heart of the Pyrenees, is essentially a pair of major valleys and their surrounding mountains. It measures 25km from north to south at its maximum and 29km from east to west. Most of its 40 or so towns and hamlets – some with just a few dozen people – are in the valleys. The main river, the Riu Gran Valira, is formed near the capital, Andorra la Vella, by the confluence of the Valira d'Orient and the Valira del Nord.

Pic de Coma Pedrosa (2942m) in western Andorra is the highest mountain. The lowest

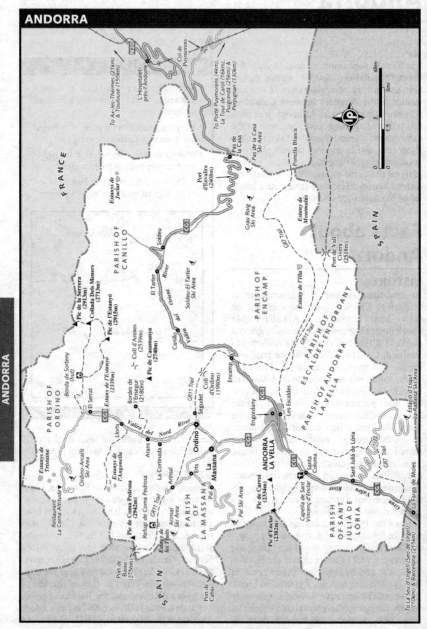

ANDORRA

point, on the Spanish frontier at La Farga de Moles, is 838m above sea level. Andorra's mountain peaks remain snowcapped until early July or later.

GOVERNMENT & POLITICS

For seven centuries Andorra was a 'co-princedom', with sovereignty vested in two 'princes': the French president, who inherited the job from France's pre-Revolutionary kings (who had taken it over from the counts of Foix), and the bishop of La Seu d'Urgell.

Then in March 1993, 75% of the 9123 native Andorrans who were eligible to vote (less than one-sixth of the population) voted in a referendum to establish Andorra as an independent, democratic 'parliamentary co-princedom'. The new constitution placed full sovereignty in the hands of the Andorran people, although the co-princes continue to function as joint heads with much reduced powers and the country retains its full name of Principat (Principality) d'Andorra.

The country's elected parliament, the Consell General (General Council), took over from the Consell de la Terra (Land Council), which had run the show since 1419. It has 28 members – four from each of the seven parishes – who meet three or four times a year. The Consell General appoints a *cap de govern* (prime minister) who chooses ministers whose programs in turn have to be approved by the Consell. The liberal Marc Forné, cap de govern since 1994, is due for re-election in 2001.

Women were given the vote as late as 1970 and all Andorran citizens over 18 can now vote. Andorra is a member of the United Nations and of the Council of Europe, but not a full member of the EU.

Of Andorra's seven parishes *(parròquies)*, six have existed since at least the 9th century. The seventh, Escaldes-Engordany, was created in 1978 by dividing the fast-growing parish of Andorra la Vella.

ECONOMY

The Andorran economy is based on cheap tax-free shopping, tourism and banking. The most important components of the agricultural sector, which makes up only 1.2% of total economic activity, are tobacco growing and cattle raising.

POPULATION & PEOPLE

Only about a quarter of Andorra's 66,000 inhabitants, almost two-thirds of whom live in Andorra la Vella and its suburbs, are Andorran nationals. The rest are Spaniards (about 30,000), Portuguese (5000), French (5000) and others. Until the 1950s Andorra's population was only 6000 or so.

LANGUAGE

The official language is Catalan, but nearly everyone speaks Spanish too. Local lore has it that everyone speaks Catalan, Spanish and French, but plenty of Andorrans know only a smattering of French and some Spanish residents have little Catalan. Young people and those working in tourism speak basic to good English. For Catalan pronunciation and handy phrases, see the Language chapter at the back of the book.

Facts for the Visitor

TOURIST OFFICES

There are two tourist offices in Andorra la Vella and several other smaller ones around the country. Andorra's tourist offices or tourism representatives abroad include the following:

France (☎ 01 42 61 50 55, fax 01 42 61 41 91) 26 Ave de l'Opéra, 75001 Paris
Germany (☎ 030-415 49 14) Finsterwalder Strasse 28, D-13435 Berlin
Spain (☎ 91 431 74 53) Calle Alcalá 73, 28001 Madrid
(☎ 93 200 07 87) Carrer de Marià Cubí 159, 08021 Barcelona
UK (☎ 020-8874 4806) 63 Westover Rd, London SW18 2RF
USA (☎ 847-674 30 91) 6800 Knox Ave, Lincolnwood, IL 60646

VISAS & DOCUMENTS

Visas are not necessary; the authorities figure that if Spain or France let you in, that's good enough for them. But bring your passport or national ID card with you.

ANDORRA

EMBASSIES & CONSULATES
Andorran Embassies & Consulates

Andorra has embassies in France and Spain:

France (☎ 01 40 06 03 30) 30 Rue d'Astorg, 75008 Paris

Spain (☎ 91 431 7453) Calle Alcalá 73, 28001 Madrid

Embassies & Consulates in Andorra

France and Spain maintain reciprocal diplomatic missions in Andorra.

France
Embassy: (☎ 82 08 09) Carrer les Canals 38-40
Consulate: (☎ 86 91 96) Carrer de la Sobrevia
Spain
Embassy: (☎ 80 00 30) Carrer Prat de la Creu 34

CUSTOMS

For information about duty-free allowances for goods entering Spain or France from Andorra, pick up the leaflet *Traveller's Duty Free Allowance* from a tourist office. Allowances include 5L of still wine; either 1.5L of spirits or three litres of lighter spirits or sparkling wine and 300 cigarettes. Checks for smugglers are rigorous on the Spanish border.

MONEY

Andorra, which has no currency of its own, will continue to use pesetas (ptas) and French francs (FF) until the euro kicks in on 1 January 2002. Except in Pas de la Casa on the French border, where the franc is king, prices are usually noted in pesetas and euros. The exchange rate for francs in shops and restaurants is seldom in your favour.

Exchange Rates

country	unit	franc		peseta
Australia	A$1	=	3.78FF	=	108 ptas
Canada	C$1	=	4.46FF	=	127 ptas
euro	€1	=	5.82FF	=	166 ptas
France	10FF	=	–	=	253 ptas
Germany	DM1	=	2.97FF	=	85 ptas
Ireland	IR£1	=	7.39FF	=	211 ptas
Japan	¥100	=	6.15FF	=	175 ptas
Morocco	Dr10	=	6.92FF	=	170 ptas
New Zealand	NZ$	=	2.81FF	=	80 ptas
Portugal	100$00	=	3.27FF	=	83 ptas
Spain	100 ptas	=	3.50FF	=	–
UK	UK£1	=	9.51FF	=	271 ptas
USA	US$1	=	6.55FF	=	187 ptas

POST & COMMUNICATIONS
Post

Andorra has no post office of its own. France and Spain each operate a separate postal system with their own Andorran stamps. Until the advent of the euro, those issued by La Poste (France) are in francs while the Spanish ones are in pesetas. They're valid only for items posted within Andorra – and needed only for international mail since letters for destinations within the country go free. You can't use regular French or Spanish stamps.

International mail (except letters to Spain) is better routed through the French postal system. There are two kinds of postboxes but if you use the wrong one your letter will be transferred.

Letters to Andorra la Vella marked 'Poste Restante' go to the town's French post office. There's a charge of about 3FF per letter. The best way to get a letter to Andorra (except from Spain) is to address it to 'Principauté d'Andorre via FRANCE'.

Telephone

International Andorra's country code is ☎ 376. To call Spain from Andorra, dial ☎ 00-34 followed by the local number. To call France, dial ☎ 00-33 (☎ 00-33-1 for the Paris area), then the local number.

Directory assistance (☎ 111 for numbers within Andorra, ☎ 119 for international information) has operators who speak Catalan, Spanish and French. Cheap rates for international calls apply between 9 pm and 7 am plus all day Sunday. During off-peak hours, a three-minute call to Europe costs 210 ptas (306 ptas to the US or Australia). Reverse-charge (collect) calling is not available in Andorra.

Public Telephones Public telephones take pesetas (francs in Pas de la Casa) or an Andorran *teletarja*. These telephone cards worth 50, 100 and 150 units are widely sold

ANDORRA

at tourist offices and tobacconists and cost 500/900/1350 ptas.

Email and Internet Access

You can log on at Punt Internet (☎ 86 36 71, fax 86 64 71, ☻ info@internet.ad) on the 5th floor of Carrer Bonaventura 39, a short stroll from the bus station. It's open 10 am to 1 pm and 3.30 to 9 pm weekdays (4 to 8 pm Saturday, August and September), and charges 1000 ptas per hour.

MEDIA

Andorra has three radio stations: the government-run Ràdio Nacional Andorra (RNA, 94.2 MHz) plus Ràdio Valira (93.3 Mhz) and Radio Andorra Uno (96.0 Mhz), both private. You can see Spanish and French TV, along with the local ATV station.

The principality's main daily paper is the conservative Catalan language *Diari d'Andorra*.

TIME

Andorra, like most of Europe, is two hours ahead of GMT/UTC from the last Sunday in March to the last Sunday in October, and one hour ahead at other times.

ELECTRICITY

The electric current is 220V at 50 Hz.

HEALTH

Visitors must pay for all medical care in Andorra.

USEFUL ORGANISATIONS

For information on weather and snow conditions in winter, call ☎ 84 88 52 (Spanish), ☎ 84 88 53 (French) or ☎ 84 88 51 (Catalan). Call ☎ 84 88 84 for information about road conditions in Spanish, French and Catalan.

DANGERS & ANNOYANCES

The country's minimal legislation to protect the consumer is often not enforced. Also, there's no grading system for hotels, which sometimes fail to post their prices. Some have tariffs which differ wildly between low and high season.

Roads follow the floor of the tight valleys and long traffic jams can clog Andorra la Vella's main arteries. And Andorran drivers must rank among Europe's most reckless; they hurtle around the tight mountain bends as if propelled by some collective death wish.

Emergency telephone numbers include: police ☎ 110; fire or ambulance ☎ 118; medical emergency ☎ 116; and mountain rescue service ☎ 112.

BUSINESS HOURS & PUBLIC HOLIDAYS

Shops in Andorra la Vella are generally open 9.30 am to 1 pm and 3.30 to 8 pm daily except (in most cases) Sunday afternoon.

Public holidays fall on 1 January, Good Friday, 8 September and 25 December.

ACTIVITIES
Skiing

Downhill Andorra, with five downhill ski resorts *(estaciós d'esquí)*, boasts the best skiing and snowboarding in the Pyrenees. And its ski passes are considerably cheaper than those of most other European resorts. For up-to-the-minute information, contact one of the capital's two tourist offices or Ski Andorra (☎ 86 43 89, fax 86 59 10, ☻ skiand@andornet.ad).

The biggest, best and most expensive are the linked resorts of Pas de la Casa-Grau Roig and Soldeu-El Tarter in the east. Arinsal, Pal and Ordino-Arcalís, more limited and often windier, are in the north-west.

Skiing is good for all levels – especially so for beginners and intermediates. The season normally lasts from December to April, depending on snow conditions, which in the past decade have not been reliable (all resorts have snow making machines).

Prices for lift passes and ski school (and often accommodation too) rise at peak times: all weekends; 23 December to 7 January; 10 February to early March (when French schools enjoy their winter break) and Easter week. You can get a five-day pass for all resorts for 15,450 ptas (low season) or 18,300 ptas (high season).

Ski school costs from 3600 to 4250 ptas an hour for individual tuition, 4000 to 4500 ptas

ANDORRA

for four hours of group classes, or 10,100 to 12,500 ptas for 15 hours of group classes.

The hire of ski gear varies between 1200 and 1600 ptas per day for skis, poles and boots (5200 to 7250 ptas for five days). Snowboards go for 2500 to 3000 ptas per day and 10,500 to 13,500 for five days.

Ski Touring If you're an experienced off-pister, the choice is extensive. With 26 mountain shelters you shouldn't need a tent. However, an all-seasons sleeping bag is essential, plus ice axe, food and camping stove (some huts lack cooking facilities). One popular route, taking about six days, starts in Aixirivall, just east of Sant Julià de Lòria in southern Andorra, and goes anti-clockwise around the country to the Pal ski station. This should only be attempted by experienced ski tourers.

There's also a cross-country skiing centre with 15km of marked forest trails at La Rabassa in the south.

Walking

The tranquillity of Andorra's unspoiled back country, where more than 50 lakes lie hidden among the soaring mountains, begins only a few hundred metres from the bazaar-like bustle of the capital.

The best season for walking is June to September, when temperatures climb well into the 20°Cs, although they drop to around 10°C at night. June can be wet.

The GR-11 trail, which traverses the Spanish Pyrenees from Mediterranean to Atlantic, enters Andorra by the Port de Vall Civera pass (2518m) in the south-east and crosses to the challenging Port de Baiau pass (2756m) in the north-west.

Walkers can sleep for free in any of 26 mountain refuges *(refugis)* dotted around the high country (see Accommodation for details).

The most up-to-date and accurate maps are a series of four covering the whole of this small country. Produced at 1:25,000 by the Spanish IGN, *Llorts* (No 183-I) and *Andorra La Vella* (No 183-III) are out and available while Nos 183-II and 183-IV were in the pipeline at the time of writing.

Tourist offices give out a very useful booklet (*Sport Activities* in English) with 52 recommended walks from 15 minutes to eight hours and over a dozen mountain bike routes.

ACCOMMODATION

Andorra, which survives on 'touro euros', isn't an easy place to find budget accommodation. Most visitors come as members of an organised group – and, indeed, if you're happy to stay in one place, the cheapest option, especially during the ski season, is to sign up for a package. All major tour operators in Britain, for example, offer Andorra as a destination.

Hotels are fullest in July and August and from December to March. During this time some places put prices up substantially and others don't take in independent travellers.

There are no youth hostels in Andorra. The 26 refugis do not require reservations. All are some distance from the road and all except one are unstaffed and free. Most have bunks, fireplaces and drinkable water but no cooking facilities. Invest 200 ptas in the *Mapa de Refugis i Grans Recorreguts*, a map that pinpoints them all.

Ask at any tourist office for their comprehensive free brochure, *Hotels, Restaurants, Apartaments i Cámpings*. Be warned, however, that while the rest of the information is reliable, the prices it quotes are merely indicative.

SHOPPING

With low customs duties and no sales tax, Andorra is famous for cheap electronic goods, sports gear, photographic equipment, shoes, clothing, perfume, petrol and, above all, alcohol, cigarettes and French dairy products. Shops selling these goods cluster in Andorra la Vella, Pas de la Casa and near the Spanish border. Visitors from Spain and France come for the shopping, although potential savings are no longer what they were. Shopping around, you'll pay around 25% less than in Spain or France.

If you're after particular photographic or electronic equipment, you can probably find it. But if you don't know what you want, Andorra is not such a great place to shop since most places sell a bit of everything, and salespeople know little about the merchandise.

Some shops add a surcharge if you pay by credit card. Some warranties are valid only in the country of purchase, so read the fine print. Beware of confusion, unintentional or otherwise, that may result from shifting between pesetas, francs and your home currency.

Getting There & Away

The only way into Andorra – unless you trek across the mountains – is by road. One of the two roads climbs from La Seu d'Urgell in Spain, 20km south of Andorra la Vella. The other enters Andorra at Pas de la Casa on the eastern border with France, then crosses the spectacular 2408m Port d'Envalira, the highest road pass in the Pyrenees, en route to Andorra la Vella. It's approached along the French N-22, which takes off south-west from the main N-20. Both entry routes have bus services.

Petrol is about 15% cheaper than in Spain and 25% cheaper than in France; petrol stations cluster near the borders.

The nearest major airports are at Barcelona (225km south) and Toulouse (180km north). Both are linked to Andorra by bus or a train-bus combination.

Schedules of some of the following bus and train services are subject to seasonal change. Check with the company or any Andorran tourist office.

BUS & TRAIN
Spain
La Hispano Andorrana (☎ 82 13 72) runs five to eight buses daily between La Seu d'Urgell and Carrer Doctor Nequi in Andorra la Vella (30 minutes, 345 ptas).

Alsina Graells (☎ 82 73 79) has up to seven buses daily between Barcelona's Estació del Nord and Andorra la Vella's bus station on Carrer Bonaventura Riberaygua (four hours, 2435 to 2715 ptas).

Novatel Autocars (☎ 86 48 87, e novatel@ andornet.ad) has three runs daily (3500 ptas) between Andorra la Vella's bus station and Barcelona's El Prat airport. Eurolines (☎ 86 00 10) has four services daily (2800 ptas) between Andorra (departing from the car park of Hotel Diplomàtic) and Barcelona's Sants bus station. Three of these originate from/continue to El Prat airport (3300 ptas).

Samar/Andor-Inter (☎ 82 62 89) runs three times weekly between Andorra and Madrid (nine hours, 4700 ptas) via Zaragoza (2300 ptas).

An interesting alternative is to take the 9.18 am train from Barcelona's Sants station to Latour-de-Carol in France, from where a connecting bus leaves for Andorra at 1.15 pm – a total journey from Barcelona of 5½ hours for about 2500 ptas. In the reverse direction, there's no such convenient connection; better to take a direct bus to Barcelona. See also the France section following.

France
Autocars Nadal (☎ 82 11 38), in association with the French company Espace Fram, has two buses a day (four hours, 2750 ptas) on Monday, Wednesday, Friday and Sunday, linking Toulouse's Gare Routière (bus station) and Andorra la Vella. Services to Toulouse continue to the town's airport, starting point for the evening bus to Andorra, which departs at 6 pm, then calls by the Toulouse bus station.

By rail, the most convenient option is to take a train from Toulouse to either L'Hospitalet (2¼ to 2¾ hours) or Latour-de-Carol (2½ to 3¼ hours), both in France. From Latour-de-Carol station, daily Hispano Andorrana buses (1125 ptas) leave for Andorra at 10.30 am and 1.15 pm. In the reverse direction, one departs from Andorra la Vella at 7.30 am, while the second and last of the day leaves at 10.30 am. The early one allows you to connect with frequent trains to Toulouse and Barcelona and, less frequently, to Perpignan.

From L'Hospitalet, buses leave daily for Andorra la Vella at 7.35 am and 7.45 pm. In the reverse direction, they leave from the Andorran capital at 5.45 am, 1.30 pm (summer only) and 5 pm. In high summer, there's a supplementary daily service from L'Hospitalet, departing at 5 pm. On Saturdays, as many as five buses run from L'Hospitalet as far as Pas de la Casa.

If you're picking up a bus mid-route – at Soldeu for instance – get to the stop in good time, as they sometimes go through earlier than scheduled.

Getting Around

BUS
Buses run along the principality's three main roads. For details, see individual destinations and also Getting There & Around at the end of the Andorra la Vella section.

Ask at a tourist office for the free brochure, Línies Regulars de Transport Públic de Passatgers, which gives current timetables for the eight bus routes radiating from the capital.

CAR & MOTORCYCLE
The speed limit is 40km/h in populated areas and 90km/h elsewhere. Two problems are the recklessness of local drivers (see Dangers & Annoyances) and Andorra la Vella's horrendous traffic jams. It's possible to bypass the worst of the latter by taking Avinguda de Salou, which becomes Avinguda de Tarragona, around the southern side of town. If you're driving between the parishes of Ordino or La Massana and those of En Camp or Canillo, avoid this motorist's nightmare by taking the scenically striking route over the Coll d'Ordino. However, snow blocks this alternative for much of the winter.

Andorra la Vella

pop 23,000 • elev 1029m
Andorra la Vella (Vella, meaning 'old', is pronounced 'vey-yah'), the capital and only real town of the principality, lies in the Riu Gran Valira valley, surrounded by mountains of up to 2400m. The town is mainly engaged in retailing duty-free electronics and luxury goods. With the mountains, the constant din of jackhammers and 'mall' architecture, you could almost be in Hong Kong, were it not for the snowcapped peaks and lack of noodle shops!

Orientation
Andorra la Vella is strung out along one main street, whose name changes from Avinguda Príncep Benlloch to Avinguda Meritxell to Avinguda Carlemany. The little Barri Antic (historic quarter) around the Antic Carrer Major (the old high street) is split by this heavily trafficked artery. The town merges with the once separate villages of Escaldes and Engordany to the east and Santa Coloma to the south-west.

Information
Tourist Offices The helpful municipal tourist office (☎ 82 71 17) on Plaça de la Rotonda is open 9 am to 1 pm and 4 to 8 pm daily (to 7 pm on Sunday, continuously until 9 pm in July and August). It sells stamps and phone cards.

The national tourist office (☎ 82 02 14, fax 82 58 23) is just off Plaça Rebés. It's open 10 am (9 am, July to September) to 1 pm and 3 to 7 pm Monday to Saturday plus Sunday morning.

Money Crèdit Andorrà, Avinguda Meritxell 80, has a 24-hour banknote exchange machine that accepts 15 currencies.

American Express is represented by Viatges Relax (☎ 82 20 44, fax 82 70 55, ⓔ relaxtravel@viatgesrelax.com), a travel agency at Carrer Mossén Tremosa 2. It's open 9 am to 1 pm and 3.30 to 7 pm weekdays.

Post & Communications La Poste (☎ 82 04 08), the French post office, at Carrer Pere d'Urg 1, functions from 8.30 am to 2.30 pm weekdays and 9 am to noon Saturday. It accepts only French francs.

Conversely, Correus i Telègrafs, the Spanish post office (☎ 82 02 57) accepts only pesetas. (This particular piece of Ruritanian silliness – they're the only institutions not to deal in both currencies – will cease in 2002, when both will use euros). At Carrer

ANDORRA

Joan Maragall 10, it at least observes the same hours as its French counterpart.

You can make international telephone calls from street pay phones or from the Servei de Telecomunicacions d'Andorra (STA; ☎ 86 01 23) at Avinguda Meritxell 110, which also has a fax service. It's open 9 am to 9 pm daily.

Bookshops Casa del Llibre, at Carrer Fiter Rossell 3, sells a reasonable selection of books, some in English. For readers of Spanish, French or Catalan, Llibreria Jaume Caballé (☎ 82 94 54), Avinguda Fiter Rossell 31, has a splendid collection of second-hand and new travel books. It also carries a comprehensive range of maps but has few titles in English.

Medical Services & Emergency The modern Hospital Nostra Senyora de Meritxell (☎ 87 10 00) is just west of the Caldea.

The main police station (*servei de policia/despatx central*; ☎ 82 12 22) is at Carrer Prat de la Creu 16.

Barri Antic
The small Barri Antic was the heart of Andorra la Vella when the principality's capital was little more than a village. The narrow cobblestone streets around the Casa de la Vall are flanked by attractive stone houses.

Casa de la Vall Casa de la Vall (House of the Valley), constructed in 1580 as the home of a wealthy family, has served as Andorra's parliament building since 1702. The monument in the plaça in front commemorates the new constitution of 1993. Downstairs is **El Tribunal de Corts**, the country's only courtroom. The **Sala del Consell**, upstairs, is one of the cosiest parliament chambers in the world. The **Chest of the Seven Locks** (Set Panys) once held Andorra's most important official documents; it could be opened only if a key-bearing representative from each of the seven parishes was present.

Free, heavily subscribed guided tours (available in English) are given 9.30 am to 1 pm and 3 to 7 pm Monday to Saturday (daily in August). It's advisable to book

(☎ 82 91 29) at least a week ahead in summer to ensure a place. That said, individuals can often be squeezed in at the last minute.

Església de Sant Esteve Andorra la Vella's parish church dates from the 11th century but, apart from the Romanesque apse, has been largely modernised. Some of the paintings date back to the 13th century.

Plaça del Poble
This large public square just south of Plaça Rebés occupies the roof of the Edifici Administratiu Govern d'Andorra, a modern government office building. Affording good views, it's a popular local gathering place, especially in the evening. The lift in the south-eastern corner whisks you down to the car park below on Carrer Prat de la Creu 58.

Caldea
In Escaldes, what looks like a large, futuristic cathedral is actually the Caldea spa complex (☎ 80 09 95), Europe's largest and a fine place for a spot of soothing relaxation after exertions in the mountains. Fed by hot springs, its heart is a 600-sq-metre lagoon kept at a constant 32°C. A series of other pools, plus Turkish baths, saunas, jacuzzis and hydromassage are all included in the three-hour entrance ticket (2950 ptas). Caldea is a 10-minute walk upstream from Plaça de la Rotonda. It is open 10 am to 11 pm daily (last entry at 9 pm).

Places to Stay – Budget
Camping *Camping Valira* (☎ 82 23 84, Avinguda de Salou) charges 525 ptas per person, per tent and per car and has a small indoor swimming pool. *Camping Riberaygua* (☎ 82 66 99) and *Camping Santa Coloma* (☎ 82 88 99), both in Santa Coloma about 2.5km south-west of Plaça Guillemó, have similar prices.

Hostales, Pensiones & Hotels *Residència Benazet* (☎ 82 06 98, Carrer la Llacuna 21) is excellent value. It has large rooms with washbasin for up to four people at 1400 ptas per person. Nearby on Plaça Guillemó, spruce singles/doubles with shower at

ANDORRA

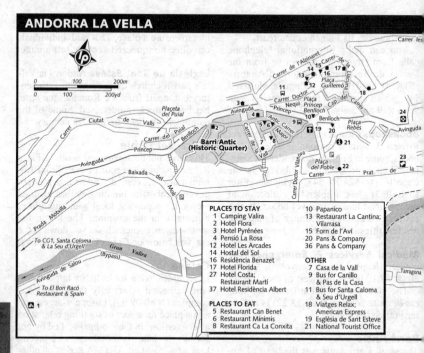

ANDORRA LA VELLA

PLACES TO STAY	
1	Camping Valira
2	Hotel Flora
3	Hotel Pyrénées
4	Pensió La Rosa
12	Hotel Les Arcades
14	Hostal del Sol
16	Residència Benazet
17	Hotel Florida
27	Hotel Costa; Restaurant Martí
37	Hotel Residència Albert

PLACES TO EAT	
5	Restaurant Can Benet
6	Restaurant Minimis
8	Restaurant Ca La Conxita
10	Papanico
13	Restaurant La Cantina; Vilarrasa
15	Forn de l'Aví
20	Pans & Company
36	Pans & Company

OTHER	
7	Casa de la Vall
9	Bus for Canillo & Pas de la Casa
11	Bus for Santa Caloma & Seu d'Urgell
18	Viatges Relax; American Express
19	Església de Sant Esteve
21	National Tourist Office

ANDORRA

the friendly *Hostal del Sol* (☎ 82 37 01) cost 2000/3900 ptas.

Also in the Barri Antic, *Pensió La Rosa* (☎ 82 18 10, Antic Carrer Major 18) has plain rooms for 2000/3500 ptas plus triples, quads and a veritable dorm sleeping six for 1500 ptas per person.

Hotel Costa (☎ 82 14 39, Avinguda Meritxell 44), badly signed and on the 3rd floor, has basic but clean rooms for 1700/3000 ptas. *Hotel Residència Albert* (☎ 82 01 56, Avinguda Doctor Mitjavila 16) has recently had a face-lift. Good value singles/doubles/triples, the majority with bathroom, cost 2700/4500/6000 ptas.

Places to Stay – Mid-Range & Top End
Hotel Les Arcades (☎ 82 13 55, Plaça Guillemó 5) has rooms with bathroom and TV for 5000 ptas.

The delightful *Hotel Florida* (☎ 82 01 05, fax 86 19 25, e aran@solucions.ad), one

block from Plaça Guillemó, has equally modern rooms for 5425/7850 ptas (6750/9500 ptas on the weekends), which includes breakfast.

At *Hotel Pyrénées* (☎ 86 00 06, fax 82 02 65, e ph@mypic.ad) rooms cost 5000/8250 ptas; you're required to take half-board in high season. Just off the same street, *Hotel Flora* (☎ 82 15 08, fax 86 20 85, e flora@andornet.ad) has immaculate singles/doubles/triples for 6500/9500/13,000 ptas, including breakfast. Both hotels have a tennis court, swimming pool and dedicated garage (1000 to 1300 ptas per night).

Nearly all hotels in this category hike their prices by 20% or more in the high season (essentially August and major Spanish or French public holidays), when advance reservations are essential.

Places to Eat
Self-caterers will enjoy wandering the aisles of the well-stocked supermarket on

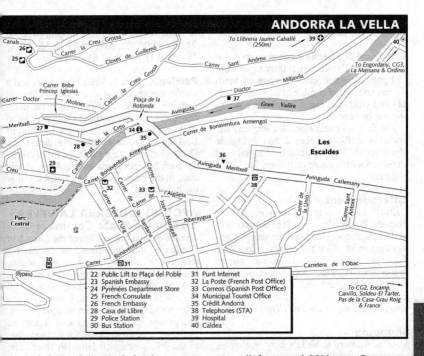

ANDORRA LA VELLA

22	Public Lift to Plaça del Poble	31	Punt Internet
23	Spanish Embassy	32	La Poste (French Post Office)
24	Pyrénées Department Store	33	Correos (Spanish Post Office)
25	French Consulate	34	Municipal Tourist Office
26	French Embassy	35	Crèdit Andorrà
28	Casa del Llibre	38	Telephones (STA)
29	Police Station	39	Hospital
30	Bus Station	40	Caldea

ANDORRA

the 2nd floor of the *Pyrénées* department store at Avinguda Meritxell 21.

Restaurants *Restaurant La Cantina* on Plaça Guillemó is a friendly place where you can expect huge servings. An *amanida variada* (mixed salad) as an entree is almost big enough to make you forget about any main course. These start at around 800 ptas or you can choose from its 1200 ptas *menú del día* (daily set meal). Next door, try the friendly *Vilarrasa*, which has good-value two/three-course *menús* for 950/1450 ptas. Just off the square, *Forn de l'Aví* has an excellent *menú* for 850 ptas and does hunky *platos combinados* for 725 to 850 ptas. With its wide selection of breads and sticky cakes, plus great coffee, it's also a good place to start the day.

There is a trio of great places in the heart of the Barri Antic. *Restaurant Ca La Conxita* (☎ 82 99 48, *Placeta de Monjó 3*) is a bustling little family business where you can see the staff preparing your hearty meal. You can

eat well for around 2500 ptas. *Restaurant Can Benet* (☎ 82 89 22, *Carrer Major 9*), where main dishes cost between 1600 and 2300 ptas, is also delightful. A couple of doors away and in the same price bracket, *Restaurant Minim's* serves primarily French dishes in an equally pleasant ambience.

The *restaurant* of Hotel Pyrénées (see Places to Stay) serves Catalan, French and Spanish dishes amid sparkling chandeliers and two-tone tablecloths. Platos combinados go for a very reasonable 625 to 1400 ptas.

Restaurant Martí, upstairs at Avinguda Meritxell 44, has *menús* for 1200 ptas and 1550 ptas and platos combinados from 650 ptas.

The best place for real Catalan cooking is the decidedly upmarket *El Bon Racó* (*Avinguda de Salou 86*) on Santa Coloma's main street about a kilometre west of Camping Valira. Meat – especially *xai* (lamb) – roasted in an open hearth is the speciality, but you might also try *escudella*, a stew of chicken, sausage and vegetables. Expect to part with close to 3000 ptas for a full meal with wine.

Fast Food & Snacks *Papanico*, on Avinguda Príncep Benlloch, has tasty *tapas* from 250 ptas each and does a range of sandwiches and platos combinados. Fun at midday and vibrant at night, it's also a place to see and be seen.

The Spanish chain *Pans & Company* has branches at Plaça Rebés 2 and Avinguda Meritxell 91. They're good for hot and cold baguettes with a range of fillings for 350 to 500 ptas.

Entertainment
Cultural events sometimes take place at Plaça del Poble, where you'll find Andorra la Vella's theatre and its music academy. Contact the tourist office for details of festivals, dance performances etc. These intermittent events apart, once the shops have closed Andorra is fairly moribund. For details on the handful of discos and the like scattered about town, buy a copy of *Guia de l'Oci* (175 ptas).

Shopping
Most of Andorra la Vella's duty-free shops are strung along the eastern part of Avinguda Príncep Benlloch, the length of Avinguda Meritxell and into its continuation, Avinguda Carlemany in Escaldes. Hours are normally 9 am to 1 pm and 4 to 8 pm, though the big stores work through the break lest they miss a buck or two. On Saturdays and in July and August, when the eager hordes pour in, shops remain open 9 am to 9 pm daily (until 7 pm on Sunday, the nominal day of rest).

Getting There & Around
Buses to La Seu d'Urgell via Santa Coloma and Sant Julià leave from the stop on Carrer Doctor Nequi. Those for all other destinations within Andorra and French train stations just over the border (see the Getting There & Away section earlier in this chapter) pass by the bus stop on Avinguda Príncep Benlloch.

Long distance buses arrive and depart from the main bus station.

Call ☎ 86 30 00 to order a taxi in Andorra la Vella. To hire a car ring Europcar (☎ 82 00 91, fax 82 06 42), Avis (☎ 87 18 55, fax 87 18 45) or Hertz (☎ 82 64 04, fax 86 70 40).

Parking Andorra la Vella is compact and a traffic nightmare; you're much better off walking. Vehicles with non-Andorran number plates can stay without charge for up to 48 hours in the car park at the junction of Baixada del Moli and Carrer Prat de la Creu. Otherwise, stick your car in the multi-storey car park beneath Plaça del Poble or, at less cost, in the large open-air park just north of the bus station.

AROUND ANDORRA LA VELLA
Església de Santa Coloma
The pre-Romanesque form of the Church of Santa Coloma, mentioned in documents from the 9th century and Andorra's oldest, has been much modified over the centuries. The four-storey, free-standing circular bell tower was raised in the 12th century. All the church's 12th-century Romanesque murals, except one entitled *Agnus Dei* (Lamb of God), were taken to Berlin for conservation in the 1930s and still languish there. The church is 2.5km south-west of Plaça Guillemó along the main road to Spain.

Walking
The **Rec del Solà** (1100m) is an almost flat, 2.5km path that follows a small irrigation canal running along the hillside just north of Andorra la Vella. Another walk heads southeastwards from Carretera de la Comella up to the **Refugi de Prat Primer** (2250m), where you can stay overnight. The ascent takes you about three hours from Andorra la Vella.

From Carrer dels Barrers in Santa Coloma, a path leads north-west up the hill to **Capella de Sant Vicenç d'Enclar** (20 minutes), once the site of an important castle. A trail continues up the valley to **Bony de la Pica** (2405m) on the Spanish border, from which you can follow the crest north-east to **Pic d'Enclar** (2383m) and **Pic de Carroi** (2334m), which overlooks Santa Coloma from the north – a fairly exacting one-day walk there and back.

North-Western Andorra

La Massana, 6km north of Andorra la Vella, is the gateway to the ski centres of Arinsal and Pal. From La Massana, the CG3 continues north into the mountainous Parròquia d'Ordino, arguably the country's most beautiful parish, with slate and fieldstone farmhouses, gushing streams and picturesque old bridges. It has plenty of fine walks and in winter it is possible to ski at the Ordino-Arcalís ski area.

LA MASSANA
pop 3000 • elev 1253m

The village of La Massana, much less attractive than its smaller neighbours a few kilometres north, has a number of hotels and some good restaurants.

The tourist office (☎ 83 56 93) is on Plaça del Quart at the junction of the CG3 and the road to Arinsal and Pal. It's open 9 am to 1 pm and 3 to 7 pm daily.

Places to Stay

La Massana is a little too brash and noisy and not close enough to either the skiing or walking action to make a great base. It can be a backup if places farther into the mountains are full.

Camping Santa Catarina (☎ 83 50 65) is in a grassy field next to a rushing stream just outside La Massana by the CG3. It's open from late-June to mid-September. Charges are 385 ptas per person and 350 ptas each per tent and car. The rather dreary *Hotel Palanques* (☎ 83 50 07) is La Massana's cheapest option. On the corner of the CG3 and Carrer Major, it has singles/doubles with shower for 3000/4500 ptas.

Places to Eat

You can get pizzas from 800 ptas at *Pizzeria el Vesuvio* on the main road just north of Hotel La Massana. *Restaurant Cal Cristobal*, much more gastronomically exciting, specialises in grills, with main dishes between 1000 and 1500 ptas. To get there,

climb the steps opposite the Esso garage on the CG3 a little north of the Pizzeria.

Just outside the village are two of Andorra's better restaurants: *La Borda de l'Aví*, 500m north of the tourist office on the road to Arinsal, and *La Borda Raubert*, 1km beyond. Both are rustic places with open hearths and offer grills, Andorran specialities and good wine selections.

Getting There & Away

Buses between Andorra la Vella and Ordino pass through La Massana about every half hour from 7 am to 9 pm.

ARINSAL & PAL SKI AREAS

Arinsal (☎ 83 58 22, fax 83 62 42), 5km north-west of La Massana, has good skiing and snowboarding for beginners and intermediates and a lively après-ski scene. Pal (☎ 83 62 36, fax 83 59 04), 7km from La Massana, has gentler slopes that make it ideal for families. Both the more-exposed Pal and Ordino-Arcalís (see later in this section) ski areas can be considerably colder than those of eastern Andorra.

Skiing

Arinsal has 13 lifts (including a new cabin lift to hurtle you up from the village), 28km of pistes and a vertical drop of 1010m. Lift passes cost 2800/3300 ptas a day in low/high season; for three days it's 7500/9000 ptas.

Pal has 12 lifts, 35km of pistes and a vertical drop of 578m. Lift passes cost 3000/3700 ptas per day in low/high season. Three-day passes are 7500/9000 ptas.

Walking

From Aparthotel Crest at Arinsal's northern extremity, a trail leads north-west then west to **Estany de les Truites** (2260m). *Refugi de Coma Pedrosa* (☎ 32 79 55), Andorra's only staffed mountain refuge (open from June to late September), is just above this natural lake. The cost per night is 1100 ptas, and it does snacks and meals (dinner 1800 ptas). The steepish walk up to the lake takes around 1½ hours. From here, it's about a further 1½ to two hours to the highest point in Andorra, **Pic de la Coma Pedrosa** (2964m).

ANDORRA

Other Activities

From July to mid-September, the long chair lift opens at Pal. Here you can hire mountain bikes (around 2800 ptas a day) and go horse riding (1700 ptas an hour).

Places to Stay

The large, well-equipped *Camping Xixerella* (☎ 83 66 13) between Pal and Arinsal is open all year and has an outdoor swimming pool. Rates are 500 to 600 ptas each per adult, tent and car.

In Arinsal, the recently renovated *Hostal Pobladó* (☎ 83 51 22, fax 838 79, ℮ hospoblado@andornet.ad) beside the new cabin lift is friendliness itself. With a lively bar, which offers Internet access on the side, its rooms cost 4400 ptas (6100 ptas with bathroom), including breakfast. *Hotel Coma Pedrosa* (☎/fax 83 51 23), also welcoming and popular with skiers and summer walkers, has rooms for 5500 ptas. More upmarket, *Hotel Solana* (☎ 83 51 27, fax 83 73 95) has large rooms with bathroom for 6500/9000 ptas. Pal has no accommodation.

Places to Eat

As a change from the plentiful snack and sandwich joints, try *Refugi de la Fondue*, up the hill towards the main chair lift, which does cheese or meat *fondue* dishes. Although *Restaurant el Moli* bills itself as Italian – and indeed offers the usual staple pastas and pizzas (both 900 to 1200 ptas) – it also has more exotic fare such as pork stirfry (1575 ptas) and Thai green chicken curry (1650 ptas).

Entertainment

In winter, Arinsal fairly throbs after sunset. In summer, it can be almost mournful. When the snow's around, call by *Surf* near the base of the cabin lift. At once pub, dance venue and restaurant, it specialises in Argentinian dishes of juicy grilled meat (1250 to 2200 ptas). *Rocky Mountain*, similarly all-embracing, has a gringo menu with dishes such as T-bone steak and 'New York-style cheesecake'. *Quo Vadis*, a late-night bar popular with English skiers, occasionally has live music.

Getting There & Away

Buses leave from Andorra la Vella for Arinsal (185 ptas) via La Massana at 9.30 am, 1 and 6.15 pm. There are also over 10 buses daily between La Massana and Arinsal and four linking La Massana and Pal. In winter, Skibus (325 ptas) runs five services daily between La Massana and Arinsal plus five between the latter and Pal. For some of these services, you need to change in Erts.

ORDINO

pop 1000 • elev 1300m

Ordino is large as local villages go but despite recent development (holiday homes and English-speaking residents abound) it retains its Andorran character, with most building still in local stone.

Orientation & Information

The tourist office (☎ 73 70 80) is within the Centre Esportiu d'Ordino beside the CG3. It's open 9 am to 1 pm and 3 to 7 pm daily (morning only on Sunday).

Museu d'Areny i Plandolit and Museo Postal de Andorra

This ancestral home of one of Andorra's great families, the Areny Plandolits, was built in 1633. Modified in the mid-19th century, it's now a museum (☎ 83 69 08), which offers half-hour guided visits in Spanish or Catalan of its richly furnished interior.

In the same grounds, Museo Postal de Andorra is far from nerdy. It has an interesting 15-minute audiovisual presentation (available in English) and a comprehensive collection of stamps issued by France and Spain specifically for Andorra (see Post & Communications in Facts for the Visitor of this chapter).

Entry to each museum costs 300 ptas. Both are open 9.30 am to 1.30 pm and 3 to 6.30 pm Tuesday to Saturday plus Sunday morning.

Walking

From the hamlet of Segudet, just east of Ordino, a path goes up through fir woods to the **Coll d'Ordino** (1980m), reached in about 1½ hours. **Pic de Casamanya** (2740m), where you can enjoy expansive panoramas, is some two hours north from the col.

Places to Stay & Eat
The cavernous *Hotel Casamanya (☎ 83 50 11, fax 83 84 76)* has singles/doubles for 4000/7000 ptas. Better value for money is the small, family-run *Hotel Santa Bàrbara de la Vall d'Ordino* with rooms for 5500/8000 ptas. Rooms at the splendid top-end *Hotel Coma* fluctuate from a low season 4500/9000 ptas to high-season prices of 9000/13000 ptas.

Bar Restaurant Quim has a basic *menú* at 1350 ptas. Next door, *Restaurant Armengol* offers a *menú* for 1500 ptas and a wide range of plentiful a la carte meat dishes.

Getting There & Away
Buses to/from Andorra la Vella (130 ptas) run about every 30 minutes daily from 7 am to 9 pm.

VALL D'ORDINO
The tiny, partly Romanesque **Església de Sant Martí** in **La Cortinada** has 12th-century frescoes in remarkably good condition. Opposite is a small working water-powered flour and sawmill, which is open from June to November.

Exhilarating trails lead from the small settlements that nestle beside the CG3, north of Ordino.

Walking
A track leads west from **Llorts** (1413m) up the Riu de l'Angonella valley to a group of lakes, the **Estanys de l'Angonella** at about 2300m. Count on three hours to get there.

From slightly north of the even smaller settlement of **El Serrat** (1600m), a secondary road leads 4km east to the Borda de Sorteny mountain refuge (1969m). From there, a trail goes south-east to **Estany de l'Estanyó** (2339m). Another heads east up to the Collada dels Meners pass (2713m, about 1½ hours), from where you can go north to **Pic de la Serrera** (2913m, 30 minutes) or a couple of hours south and west via **Pic de la Cabaneta** (2863m) to **Pic de l'Estanyó** (2915m), Andorra's second highest summit. In about eight hours from Borda de Sorteny you could bag all three peaks and continue via the Coll d'Arenes pass (2539m) and Pic

de Casamanya to the Coll d'Ordino, enjoying great views along the way.

From **Arans** (1385m), a trail goes north-eastward to **Bordes de l'Ensegur** (2180m), where there is an old shepherd's hut.

Places to Stay
Some 200m north of Llorts, *Camping Els Pardassos (☎ 85 00 22)*, one of the most beautiful camping grounds in Andorra, is surrounded by forested mountains and has its own spring. Open from mid-June to mid-September, it costs 325 ptas per person, per tent and per car. *Hotel Vilaró (☎ 85 02 25)*, just south of the village, has singles/doubles with washbasin and bidet for 2200/4000 ptas.

At *Hotel Sucará* in La Cortinada, rooms are 3500/5200 ptas outside August and the ski season, when half-board (7200 ptas per person) is obligatory. Renowned locally for its rich Catalan and Andorran cuisine, it has good-value *menús* for 1600 ptas and 2500 ptas.

Getting There & Away
Buses to El Serrat (240 ptas) leave from Andorra la Vella at 1 and 8.30 pm. The small communities in the valley are also served by buses linking Ordino and Arcalís.

ORDINO-ARCALÍS SKI AREA
The slopes of the Ordino-Arcalís ski area (☎ 85 01 21, fax 85 04 40) in Andorra's far north-western corner are better for beginners and intermediates. A number of the rugged peaks in this beautiful area reach 2700m and provide challenging and spectacular summer walking. There's no accommodation in Arcalís.

Orientation & Information
Restaurant La Coma (2200m) at the end of the paved road (closed in winter) is a useful landmark. From there, the Creussans chairlift, opened in 2000 and the highest in Andorra, whisks you up to 2625m.

Skiing
In winter, Ordino-Arcalís has enough snow and a decent selection of runs but can be cold and windy. There are 14 lifts covering 26km of pistes at elevations between

ANDORRA

1940m and 2625m. A lift pass costs 2950/7350 ptas for one/three days in the low season (3700/9200 ptas in high season).

Walking
The trail behind Restaurant La Coma leads eastwards across the hill, then north and over the ridge to a group of beautiful mountain lakes, **Estanys de Tristaina**. The walk to the first lake takes about 30 minutes.

Places to Eat
Restaurant La Coma functions from December to early May and late June to early September. Open 10 am to 6 pm daily during these months, it offers snacks and a full menu.

Getting There & Away
In the ski season there are 10 buses daily (125 ptas) between Ordino and the ski station. In summer, four buses go as far as El Serrat (not Sunday) and continue as far as Arcalís on request.

Eastern Andorra

The best skiing in Andorra is here, at Soldeu-El Tarter and Pas de la Casa-Grau Roig.

ENCAMP
The town of Encamp houses the **Museu Nacional de l'Automòbil** (National Automobile Museum; ☎ 83 22 66). Beside the CG2, it has about 100 vintage cars plus antique motorcycles and bicycles. It's open 9.30 am to 1.30 pm and 3 to 6 pm Tuesday to Saturday plus 10 am to 2 pm Sunday (300 ptas).

Most of the **Església Sant Romà de les Bons**, about 1km north of Encamp, dates from the 12th century. The Romanesque frescoes in the apse are reproductions of the originals, which are in Barcelona's Museu Nacional d'Art de Catalunya.

To the right of the CG2, 3km north of Encamp, the austere **Santuari de Nostra Senyora de Meritxell** looms over the highway. Designed by the internationally renowned Catalan architect Ricardo Bofill it replaces the original shrine to Andorra's patron, which was destroyed by fire in 1972.

Buses run from Andorra la Vella to Encamp (110 ptas) every 20 or 30 minutes between 7 am and 9.30 pm.

In winter, Funicamp, the long bubble lift at the northern end of En Camp, gives access to the Grau Roig and Pas de la Casa snowfields, thus saving you a 25km drive over the Port d'Envalira.

Information
The tourist office (☎ 73 10 00, fax 83 18 78) is beside the CG2, 100m south of Encamp's town hall, a striking smoked-glass cube. It's open 9 am to 1 pm and 3.30 to 6 pm Monday to Saturday.

CANILLO
Canillo, 7 km west of Soldeu and El Tarter and considerably more tranquil than either, makes a good base for a skiing or summer activity holiday, offering canyon clambering, guided walks, a *vía ferrata* climbing gully and climbing wall, the year-round Palau de Gel with ice rink and swimming pool, and endless possibilities for walking (including an easy, signed nature walk that follows the valley downstream from Soldeu). The helpful tourist office (☎ 85 10 02) is on the main road at the east end of the village. A little beyond is the splendid 11th-century Romanesque church of Sant Joan de Caselles.

Places to Stay
For the moment – although the introduction of a bubble lift giving direct access to the Soldeu-El Tarter ski slopes may bring a change – accommodation in Canillo is markedly less expensive than higher up the valley. And, in contrast to places in the bigger resorts, prices of the hotels we've selected remain constant year-round.

Of Canillo's five camping grounds, *Camping Santa Creu* (☎ 85 14 62) is the greenest and, since it's the farthest from the highway, the quietest. *Hotel Casa Nostra* (☎ 85 10 23) has simple rooms for 2500 ptas (3250 ptas with shower, 3750 ptas with full bathroom). *Hotel Pellissé* (☎ 85 12 05, fax 85 18 75), east of town opposite the Sant Joan church, has decent singles/doubles for 2750/4400 ptas while *Hotel Canigó*

(☎ 85 10 24, fax 85 18 24) does comfortable rooms at 3000/5000 ptas.

SOLDEU-EL TARTER SKI AREA

Soldeu and El Tarter, both popular with British skiers, are separate villages 2km apart whose ski lift systems interconnect. Each has a small tourist office (☎ 85 24 92 in Soldeau, ☎ 89 05 01 in El Tarter), which are open from December to April plus July and August, at the base of the ski lifts. For skiing information, ring ☎ 85 11 51. Soldeu has the bulk of the accommodation and facilities.

Skiing

The skiing here gets better each time we visit. With the grafting of a new bubble lift and ski area above Canillo in 2001, 23 lifts will connect 86km of runs with a vertical drop of 850m. Skiing is similar to that at Pas de la Casa except that here black runs into the villages are steeper and more picturesque. Also, the slopes, wooded in their lower reaches, are often warmer than the more-exposed ski areas of Pas de la Casa and Grau Roig.

Lift passes for one/three days cost 3650/8580 ptas in low season, 4200/10,050 ptas in high season.

Walking

You'll find a week's worth of walks around Canillo and Soldeu in Lonely Planet's *Walking in France*.

Andorra has great ski slopes for mastering new snowboarding moves.

Other Activities

From mid-July to the end of August, two chair lifts rise up to 2400m from El Tarter, where you can hire a mountain bike, take it aboard and whizz down again.

Places to Stay & Eat

Most places to stay are full to bursting with groups and are expensive for the independent traveller. The cosy *Hotel Naudi* (☎ 851 148, fax 852 022) with its welcoming bar and restaurant has singles/doubles for 6000/8500 ptas, year round.

Residència Supervalira (☎ 85 10 82, fax 85 10 62), 2.5km north of Soldeu, has off-hand service and rooms for 3500/5000 ptas outside the ski season, when they would otherwise cost 6250 ptas.

In the top-end bracket, *Sport Hotel* (☎ 87 86 00, fax 87 06 66, ☻ sporthotels@ andorra.ad) charges 9000 ptas per person in the low season (11,000 ptas in high season), including breakfast.

On the main street, the cheerful *restaurant* of Hotel Bruxelles does well-filled sandwiches (450 to 575 ptas), whopping burgers and a tasty *menú* for 1175 ptas. *Restaurant Fontanella* does a range of Italian specialities, plus the usual pizzas and pastas. *Snack-Bar Bonell*, 50m south of the cabin lift station, has rather overpriced platos combinados and pizzas and more reasonably priced daily specials (575 to 825 ptas).

Entertainment

The night scene at Soldeu-El Tarter gets hopping in winter. *Pussy Cat* and its neighbour, *Fat Albert*, both one block from the main drag, rock until far too late to allow any impressive skiing the next day. *Piccadilly Pub*, by the Sport Hotel, is a clone of a British pub that occasionally has bands. *Capital Discoteca*, with free entry on Tuesday, Wednesday and on weekends, is a busy dance hangout.

Getting There & Around

Buses run from Andorra la Vella to El Tarter and Soldeu (40 minutes, 375 ptas) 9 am to 8 pm hourly. In winter, there are free shuttle buses (just flash your ski pass) between

ANDORRA

MARTIN HARRIS

Canillo and the two upper villages. These run approximately hourly (with a break from noon to 3 pm) until 11 pm.

All three villages are also on the route of buses between Andorra la Vella and the French railheads of Latour-de-Carol and L'Hospitalet (see the Getting There & Away section earlier in this chapter).

PAS DE LA CASA-GRAU ROIG SKI AREA

The linked ski stations of Pas de la Casa and Grau Roig lie either side of the Port d'Envalira pass. Grau Roig, with just one hotel, is on the western side of the col, 2km south of the CG2. Pas de la Casa, on the French border and largest of the Andorran ski resorts, is an architecturally bleak place with numerous shops catering principally to French visitors. In high season, especially the French winter school holiday from mid-February to early March, it's near impossible to get a bed and lift queues can be frustratingly long.

Information

Pas de la Casa's tourist office (☎ 85 52 92, fax 85 62 75), opposite the Andorran customs station, is open 9 am to 7 pm daily except Sunday afternoon.

Skiing

Skiing and snowboarding are well suited to all levels. The combined ski area (☎ 87 19 00) has a network of 29 lifts and 100km of pistes. Lift passes cost 3700/8800 ptas for one/three days in low season and 4200/10,000 ptas in high season.

Other Activities

In winter, for a magnificent bird's-eye view of the Pyrenees and Andorra in its entirety, you can take a 10-minute helicopter flight from Grau Roig with Helitrans (☎ 866 566). At 6000 ptas, a chopper doesn't come cheap and require a minimum of four people.

Places to Stay

During the winter ski season and, to a lesser extent, July and August, it's almost impos-

sible to find reasonably priced accommodation since so many hotels are occupied partially or fully by tour companies.

One of the most reasonable places to stay – remembering all is relative – is *Hotel/Aparthotel Condor* (☎ 855 708, fax 855 578, Carrer Bearn 14), where, according to season, singles/doubles/triples cost from 4400/6600/ 8500 to 6850/11,750/14,000 ptas.

At *Hotel la Montanya* (☎ 855 318, fax 855 898, e pimand@hotmail.com, Carrer Catalunya 12), singles/doubles with breakfast start at 6300/7600 ptas in low season and 8900/12,800 ptas in high season.

Hotel Casado (☎ 855 219, fax 855 498, Carrer Catalunya 23) has rooms with breakfast for 7000/9000 ptas in low season and 10,300/13,000 ptas in high season.

Places to Eat

In Pas de la Casa, you can eat sandwiches and burgers until they ooze out of your ears. For more substantial fare, try the battery of restaurants around the base of the ski slopes.

If you fancy something more subtle, visit *Restaurant La Cabanya*, co-located with Hotel/Aparthotel Condor, which has *menús* for 1300 ptas and 2150 ptas. *Bar Restaurant Cava Roca*, beside the Parking Central, does a great *menú* for 1400 ptas and has a wide selection of a la carte meat dishes.

Entertainment

During the ski season, Pas de la Casa, considerably larger than its Andorran competitors, throbs after dark. Dance away your bruises at *West End* and *Billboard*. *Milwaukee* also packs in the après ski crowd.

Getting There & Away

From Andorra la Vella, only one bus a day goes to Pas de la Casa (620 ptas), leaving at 9 am and returning at 11.30 am. Pas de la Casa is also on the bus routes between Andorra la Vella and the French railheads of L'Hospitalet and Latour-de-Carol, the latter two no more than 12km away (see the Getting There & Away section earlier in this chapter).

Aragón

Sparsely populated Aragón is flanked by several worlds: France, Catalunya (Cataluña), Valencia, the Basque region of Navarra and the north-eastern reaches of Spain's Castilian heartland. Few foreigners explore Aragón but it has some of Spain's most varied and spectacular scenery and is full of history and wonderful old castles, monasteries and other buildings. The *mudéjar* architecture in Zaragoza (Saragossa) and Teruel stands out, as does the Romanesque work, chiefly in the north.

Aragón's northern strip, taking in the highest and some of the most spectacular parts of the Pyrenees, offers a wealth of walking and skiing that could easily extend to the French side of the frontier. Along the valleys and down into the lower pre-Pyrenees hills is a surprising mix of canyons, pretty villages, lonely castles and venerable monasteries.

The one big city, Zaragoza, is not Spain's most beautiful or fascinating, but it has a warmth and a collection of monuments and sights that may make you linger longer than you planned.

Central Aragón consists mainly of a forlorn series of treeless depressions and high plateaus. It was the scene of some of the nastiest fighting in the civil war, and the two sides could hardly have chosen a more comfortless place to do combat. However, you then come up against the mysterious mountain regions of the south, peppered with isolated and picturesque villages.

Various local culinary specialities are much touted, but really there's little to differentiate average Aragonese from Castilian cooking. *Ternasco* (lamb's ribs) is a standard local dish, while ham shavings make an occasional appearance as the millionth variation on the Spanish pig theme.

Though overshadowed by the fame of neighbouring La Rioja and Navarra in the wine production game, Aragón doesn't produce a bad drop. Of the four areas at work, wines from the Cariñena zone just south of Zaragoza are among the best.

In medieval times, Aragón was the northernmost salient of Muslim territory, with semi-independent governors in Zaragoza ruling over the Ebro valley and the Pyrenees foothills. The Christian kingdom of Aragón, from small Pyrenean beginnings, managed to drive the Muslims out by 1200. Aragón and neighbouring Catalunya had been united by royal marriage in the 12th century, and the resulting Crown of Aragón, as it was called, became one of the Iberian Peninsula's great medieval kingdoms, albeit dominated by Catalunya.

ARAGÓN

503

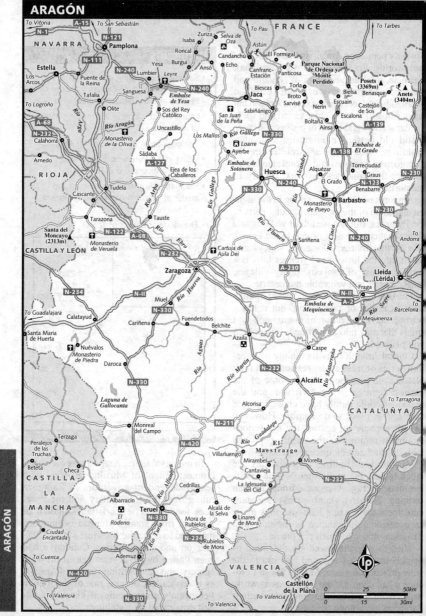

ARAGÓN

The union of the Crown of Aragón with Castile in the 15th century under their respective monarchs Fernando and Isabel (Ferdinand and Isabella, the Catholic Monarchs) effectively gave birth to what we know as Spain. Ranking with Fernando El Católico as Aragón's most famous son is Francisco Goya, born near Zaragoza in 1746. Goya's artistic oeuvre is well represented in Aragón.

Skiing

Aragón is well endowed with ski resorts, mainly along the Pyrenees in the north. The tourist offices in Zaragoza, Huesca and Jaca have information but you're generally better off arranging a package rather than turning up under your own steam. The downhill version is the most popular, but cross-country skiing is gaining a higher profile.

Walking

Aragón's mountains are, if anything, more popular in summer than in winter, with innumerable options for walking – anything from gentle rambles of a few hours to two-week treks. A network of long-distance trails (Grandes Recorridos, or GRs) is marked throughout the northern strip of Aragón and on into neighbouring regions and France. The coast-to-coast GR-11, along the mountain line just south of France, crosses through much of the most spectacular Aragón Pyrenees, but there are plenty of other routes. As always, some paths are in good shape and clearly marked, while others, even stretches of some main routes, can be difficult to follow.

The optimum time to lace up your walking boots is from mid-June to early September. Even then the Pyrenean weather can be unpredictable, so serious walkers need to come prepared for most contingencies. Mid-July to mid-August is the peak summer holiday period in Spain, when the more popular parks and paths can become very crowded.

We refer to a number of mountain refuges (refugios) in this chapter, but there are others. Refuges offer basic accommodation for walkers and climbers: some are staffed and serve meals; others are empty shacks providing nothing but shelter. Refuges are often full, so unless you have booked ahead (which is always advisable), go ready to camp. The Federación Aragonesa de Montañismo in Zaragoza (☎ 976 22 79 71) can provide some information on mountain refuges and routes.

When walking in the mountains, it's essential to go well prepared, and that includes asking ahead about path and weather conditions, and water sources and shelter along your route.

The best maps for walkers in the Aragón Pyrenees are those produced by Aragonese publisher PRAMES, at scales between 1:25,000 and 1:50,000. Editorial Alpina maps, widely available, are an acceptable substitute, though they have their inaccuracies. All these maps cost around 600 or 700 ptas. Lonely Planet's *Walking in Spain* is a good companion if you plan any serious outings in the Pyrenees. Walkers should also see the boxed text 'Walking in the Pyrenees' in the Catalunya chapter.

Other Activities

Climbing, canyoning, caving, paragliding, white-water rafting, mountain biking and horseback riding are all options in Aragón, mainly in the Pyrenees. We've provided a few tips; tourist offices have more information on firms that organise these activities.

Accommodation

The *Guía de Servicios Turísticos de Aragón,* available from main tourist offices, contains full lists of hotels, *hostales* (budget hotels), camping grounds, *casas rurales,* mountain refuges and other accommodation. Recently it has been published in three separate parts devoted to different types of accommodation.

Room prices in this chapter are for the high season, from about July to mid-September in most places. You'll pay between 5% and 30% less at other times.

Emergency

Throughout Aragón you can telephone ☎ 112 should you be in need of the police, an ambulance or urgent medical attention. The calls are free.

ARAGÓN

Central Aragón

ZARAGOZA

postcode 50080 • pop 594,000

The regional capital is home to almost exactly half Aragón's population, the result of an intense drift from country to city since the 19th century. Long an important crossroads on one of Spain's most important waterways, the Río Ebro, Zaragoza is today a major centre of industry and transport.

Most of the city has grown up in the past 100 years and a lot of it is grey apartment blocks lining straight streets. But the old centre (though it somehow doesn't feel so old) definitely rewards a day or two's exploration. Intriguing archaeological remains, fine art and artisanry, and hundreds of bars and restaurants are among the attractions.

On a bad day it can get blowy, and locals call the north wind that seems to tear right through you 'El Cierzo'. Fortunately, this is not a permanent phenomenon, so Zaragoza has avoided that unfortunate sobriquet, 'the Windy City'.

History

The Romans founded the colony of Caesaraugusta (of which 'Zaragoza' is a corruption) in 14 BC. As many as 25,000 people came to live in the prosperous Roman city. In Muslim times Zaragoza was capital of Upper March, one of Al-Andalus' border territories, governing much of the Ebro valley and pre-Pyrenees. In 1118 it fell to Alfonso I 'El Batallador' (The Battler), of the emerging Christian kingdom of Aragón, of which it immediately became capital.

Centuries later, Zaragoza put up unusually stiff resistance under Napoleonic siege, although it had to capitulate in 1809. Industrial growth late in the 19th century made it a centre of militant trade unionism, but in 1936, when the civil war began, the Republicans had no time to organise themselves and Zaragoza was quickly put under Nationalist control. The country's main military academy was set up here under General Franco in 1928. (It still functions, beside the Huesca road north of the city.)

Orientation

The core of old Zaragoza lies on the southern bank of the Río Ebro, the outline of its former walls marked by Avenida de César Augusto and El Coso. Much of what there is to see, and a good choice of hotels, restaurants and bars, lie within the old city limits. To the south, several great avenues stretch into the 20th-century city, where the extensive Parque Primo de Rivera provides a green oasis. The train station, called El Portillo, is about 1.5km south-west of the old centre. A dozen bus stations (estaciones de autobuses) are scattered around.

In the old centre, the huge Plaza del Pilar, dominated by Zaragoza's great churches, gives way southward to a labyrinth of lanes and alleys, the heart of which is known as El Tubo.

Information

The helpful Oficina Municipal de Turismo (☎ 976 20 12 00), in a black glass cube on Plaza del Pilar, is open 10 am to 8 pm daily. There's a second office (☎ 976 43 88 29) at El Portillo train station.

The main post office (correos) is at Paseo de la Independencia 33. A central Internet/email service is Change, at Calle de Florencio Jardiel 3, which charges 275/350/500 ptas for 15/30/60 minutes online.

Librería General (☎ 976 22 44 83), Paseo de la Independencia 22, stocks road and walking maps, guidebooks and some novels in English and French.

Lavandería Casa (☎ 976 21 75 67), Calle de Pedro María Ric 37, will wash and dry 3kg for 1500 ptas in three or four hours.

Hospital Miguel Servet (☎ 976 76 55 00) is on Paseo de Isabel la Católica, south of the centre. The Policía Local are based on Calle de Domingo Miral, also south of the centre.

Plaza del Pilar

Plaza del Pilar and its eastward and westward continuations form a single open space 500m long, lined by important buildings.

Basílica de Nuestra Señora del Pilar

One day while preaching in Spain, Santiago (St James the Apostle) is supposed to have beheld a vision of the Virgin Mary, descended from the heavens atop a marble pillar. This she left behind and around it was built a chapel. At least that's the story of the *pilar* around which was later built the overwhelming baroque edifice on Plaza del Pilar, designed in 1681 by Francisco de Herrera. The towers were not completed until the early 20th century. The main dome is accompanied by 10 smaller ones, all decorated with tiles of blue, green, yellow and white.

The Capilla Santa, the oval chapel in which the pillar is enshrined, is a pink marble structure at the eastern end of the church. A tiny oval-shaped portion of the legendary pillar is accessible on the west side of the Capilla Santa, and it's to kiss this that pilgrims arrive in Zaragoza daily by the busload.

The basilica's single greatest piece of fine art is the alabaster altarpiece by Damián Forment from Valencia, done in the early 16th century well before the present church was started. It stands roughly in the middle of the basilica, facing west. Goya painted *La Reina de los Mártires* (Mary, Queen of Martyrs) in a cupola above the north aisle, immediately east of the entrance to the cathedral's museum.

The basilica is open 6 am to 8 pm daily (free), and the museum from 9 am to 2 pm and 4 to 6 pm daily (150 ptas).

La Lonja This fairly plain but finely proportioned Renaissance-style building east of the basilica, between the 18th-century Palacio Arzobispal and the 20th-century *ayuntamiento* (city hall), was constructed in the 16th century as a trading exchange. The medallions on its exterior depict kings of Aragón and other historical personages. The Lonja is now an exhibition hall, usually open 10 am to 2 pm and 5 to 9 pm Tuesday to Saturday, 10 am to 2 pm Sunday.

Museo del Foro de Caesaraugusta The unassuming trapezoid on Plaza de la Seo, the eastern extension of Plaza del Pilar, is the modern entrance to part of ancient Caesaraugusta's forum, which is now well below ground level.

What you see underground are the remains of shops, porticoes, a great *cloaca* (sewerage system) and a limited collection of artefacts. Sections of lead pipes used to channel water to the city's populace are a reminder of the Romans' genius for engineering. All of this dates from between 14 BC and about AD 15. A good audiovisual show, presented on the hour in Spanish, breathes life into the old crockery.

The forum is open 10 am to 2 pm and 5 to 8 pm Tuesday to Saturday, 10 am to 2 pm Sunday (300 ptas, students 200 ptas, over-65s free). You can also buy a 600-ptas ticket (students 400 ptas, over-65s free), which covers the Puerto Fluvial and Termas Públicas museums (see later) as well as the Foro.

La Seo The Catedral de San Salvador, known as La Seo, rises on the eastern side of Plaza de la Seo (enter from Plaza de San Bruno at the far end). Built between the 12th and 17th centuries on the site of Muslim Zaragoza's central mosque (which in turn stood on the site of the Roman forum's temple), La Seo is a smorgasbord of architectural styles from Romanesque to baroque. The north-western facade is an Aragonese mudéjar masterpiece deploying classic dark brickwork and colourful ceramic decoration in a series of eye-pleasing geometrical patterns.

The interior, reopened in 1998 after 18 years of restoration work and still squeakily clean, is essentially Gothic though many of the elaborate chapels are baroque. The artistic highlight is the 15th-century main altarpiece in polychromed alabaster.

Visiting hours are 10 am to 2 pm (until 1 pm Saturday, to noon Sunday) and 5 to 7 pm (4 to 6 pm in winter) daily except Monday. Entry is free. La Seo's **Museo de Tapices** has a noted collection of 14th- to 17th-century Flemish and French tapestries (200 ptas).

Other Roman Remains

The small **Museo del Puerto Fluvial** on Plaza de San Bruno displays remains of the Roman city's river-port installations, with a film every hour. The **Museo de las Termas Públicas**, at Calle San Juan y San Pedro 3-7,

ARAGÓN

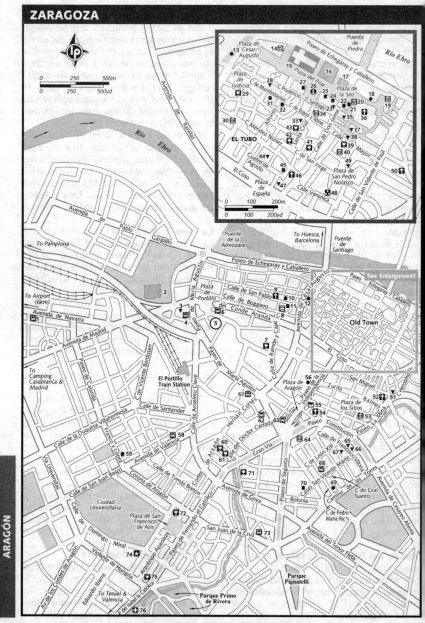

ZARAGOZA

ZARAGOZA

PLACES TO STAY
10	Hotel Posada de las Almas
11	Hotel San Blas
21	Hotel Tibur
22	Hotel Vía Romana
24	Hostal Ambos Mundos
25	Hostal Plaza
27	Hotel Las Torres
31	Fonda Manifestación
32	Fonda Satué
45	Pensión La Peña
59	Albergue Juvenil Baltasar Gracián
70	Pensión La Dama

PLACES TO EAT
3	Restaurante Casa Emilio
23	La Milagrosa
28	Cafetería Picolo
33	Casa Juanico
35	Casa Amadeo
37	Vitorinos II
38	Cervecería Mapy, El Lince
44	Pascualillo
47	Casa Lac
49	La Calzorras
51	Restaurante la Retama
65	Restaurante El Mangrullo
66	Churrasco
67	Risko Mar

OTHER
1	Autobuses Cinco Villas & Autobuses Conda Bus Station (Cinco Villas, Pamplona, San Sebastián Buses)
2	Aljafería
4	Samar Buil Bus Station (Fuendetodos Buses)
5	Plaza de Toros
6	Viajes Viaca Bus Station (Basque Country, Cantabria, Asturias, León Buses)
7	Sphinx
8	Oasis
9	Iglesia de San Pablo
12	Mercado Central
13	Roman Walls
14	Change
15	Basílica de Nuestra Señora del Pilar
16	Ayuntamiento
17	La Lonja
18	Palacio Arzobispal
19	Museo del Puerto Fluvial
20	Museo del Foro de Caesaraugusta
26	Oficina Municipal de Turismo
29	Bar Corto Maltés
30	Museo de Pablo Gargallo
34	Museo Camón Aznar
36	La Seo
39	La Casa del Loco
40	Museo de las Termas Públicas
41	Chastón
42	Café El Prior
43	Café Praga
46	Iglesia de San Gil
48	Teatro Romano
50	Iglesia de La Magdalena
52	Iglesia de San Miguel
53	Museo de Zaragoza
54	Iglesia de Santa Engracia
55	Post Office (Correos)
56	Librería General
57	Ágreda/Oscense Bus Station
58	Ágreda Automóvil Buses to/from Cariñena, Daroca
60	Troppico
61	Morrison
62	Automóviles Zaragoza Bus Station (Calatayud, Monasterio de Piedra Buses)
63	Airport Bus
64	Espacio Goya
68	Therpasa Bus Station (Tarazona, Soria Buses)
69	Lavandería Casa
71	Morrissey
72	Loch Ness Scottish Pub
73	Tezasa Bus Station
74	Policía Local
75	Kitsch
76	Hospital Miguel Servet

houses remains of the Roman baths. Both these have the same hours and prices as the Museo del Foro except that the Termas Públicas opens at 11 am Tuesday to Saturday. The **Teatro Romano** (Roman Theatre) on Calle Verónica is being prepared for opening as a museum, too. A short stretch of **Roman walls** extends north from the Mercado Central.

Aljafería

Despite all the changes it has undergone, the Aljafería remains the greatest Muslim era edifice outside the province of Andalucía. Originally built as a pleasure dome for Zaragoza's Muslim rulers, chiefly in the 11th century, it was never intended as a serious defensive installation. From the 12th century, Zaragoza's Christian rulers made alterations, and in 1486 the Inquisition

moved in to the main square tower, the Torre del Trovador. At the end of the 15th century, Fernando and Isabel tacked on the new palace. Later it was used as a hospital and barracks, at the same time being allowed to decay. From the 1940s to 1990s restoration was carried out and in 1987 Aragón's parliament *(Cortes)* established itself here.

Once through the main gate, cross the first courtyard, a 14th-century mudéjar creation, into a second, the Patio de Santa Isabel, which was the central courtyard of the Muslim palace. Here you are confronted to the north and south by the opulence and geometric mastery of Muslim architecture, with arches like fine lacework. Opening off the northern porch is the Muslim palace's small, octagonal *oratorio* (prayer room). A magnificent horseshoe-arched doorway leads

ARAGÓN

into the *mihrab* (prayer niche indicating the direction of Mecca). The oratorio's finely chiselled floral motifs, inscriptions in Arabic from the Qur'an and pleasingly simple cupola are impressive examples of high Muslim art.

As though by way of a riposte, the Catholic Monarchs' palace, upstairs, has its own treasures, especially the beautiful mudéjar work of the *artesonado* ceilings.

During Semana Santa and from 15 April to 15 October the Aljafería is open 10 am to 2 pm and 4.30 to 8 pm daily except Friday morning and Thursday. At other times of the year, it closes at 6.30 pm and all of Sunday afternoon. Entry was free at the time of writing but there were plans to introduce a charge. Parking nearby is virtually impossible.

Churches

Several minor churches are worth a quick look. The **Iglesia de San Pablo** has a delicate mudéjar tower and a retablo by Damián Forment. The **Iglesia de La Magdalena**, **Iglesia de San Miguel** and **Iglesia de San Gil** boast further mudéjar towers. The 16th-century **Iglesia de Santa Engracia** is notable for its intricately carved Renaissance entrance and two early Christian sarcophagi from AD 340 in its underground crypt, believed to contain bones of martyrs killed by the Romans.

Museums

Museo de Zaragoza The main part of this museum is devoted to archaeology and fine arts and is on Plaza de los Sitios. On display are artefacts from prehistoric to Muslim times and an important collection of Gothic art, as well as a dozen paintings by Goya from different stages of his career. Hours are 10 am to 2 pm and 5 to 8 pm Tuesday to Saturday, 10 am to 2 pm Sunday (free). The museum's Aragonese ethnology and ceramics sections are in Parque Primo de Rivera.

Museo Camón Aznar This eclectic collection of Spanish art from the 16th to the 20th centuries, including a room of Goya etchings and half a dozen paintings attributed to El Greco, spreads over the three storeys of the Palacio de los Pardo, a Renaissance mansion at Calle de Espoz y Mina 23. It's open 9 am to 2.15 pm and 6 to 9 pm Tuesday to Friday, and shorter hours on Saturday and Sunday (100 ptas).

Espacio Goya The 'Goya Space' is the Ibercaja bank's collection of a dozen Goya paintings, exhibited in a lovely plateresque courtyard, the Patio de la Infanta, at Calle San Ignacio de Loyola 16. Among them are a self-portrait of Goya aged 20 and a colourful sketch for his famous *El Dos de Mayo*. Opening hours are 8.30 am to 2.30 pm and 6 to 9 pm weekdays, 11 am to 2 pm and 6 to 9 pm Saturday (free).

Museo de Pablo Gargallo This is a representative display of sculptures by Pablo Gargallo (1881–1934), possibly Aragón's most gifted artistic son after Goya. The works, mostly done in the early 20th century, are housed in the 17th-century Palacio Argillo on Plaza de San Felipe. It's open 10 am to 2 pm and 5 to 9 pm Tuesday to Saturday, 10 am to 2 pm Sunday (free).

JANE SMITH

Goya, a native of Aragón, was Spain's greatest artist of the 18th century and early 19th century.

Organised Tours

A variety of walking tours are given in Spanish by the Oficina Municipal de Turismo, on Saturdays and Sundays all year. From Easter to late summer there are extra tours and some may be available in English or French.

Special Events

The city's biggest event is the Fiestas del Pilar, a week of celebrations around 12 October.

Places to Stay – Budget

Camping & Hostels *Camping Casablanca* (☎ 976 75 38 70), a few kilometres out to the south-west, opens from April to mid-October. Turn off the N-II from Madrid at about Km 317 and head towards Valdefierro. From the city centre, Avenida de Madrid leads out to the N-II. The cost is 625 ptas per person/tent/car.

The HI *Albergue Juvenil Baltasar Gracián* (☎ 976 55 13 87, Calle Franco y López 4) is open all year except August. Cost is 1100/1500 ptas for the under/over 26s.

Fondas, Hostales & Pensiones Zaragoza is bursting with *fondas*, hostales and hotels of most categories. But many of the cheap places are true dumps, so look out.

A good choice in the heart of El Tubo is *Pensión La Peña* (☎ 976 29 90 89, Calle de Cinegio 3), with singles/doubles for 1500/3000 ptas. It has a decent little *comedor* (dining room).

The friendly *Fonda Manifestación* (☎ 976 29 58 21, Calle de la Manifestación 36) has just three rooms but they're clean, and cost 2500/3500 ptas. Just along the street is the *Fonda Satué* (☎ 976 39 07 09, Calle de Espoz y Mina 4), which offers doubles for 2600 ptas.

There are two hostales right on Plaza del Pilar, each with some rooms overlooking the plaza. *Hostal Plaza* (☎ 976 29 48 30, Plaza del Pilar 14) has comfy singles/doubles with shower and toilet for 4300/4900 ptas plus IVA (the singles are small but OK), and doubles with bath for 5900 ptas plus IVA. *Hostal Ambos Mundos* (☎ 976 29 97 04, Plaza del Pilar 16) is tattier but kept reasonably clean. Rooms with

shower are 2250 ptas per person; doubles with bath and a plaza view are 4700 ptas.

A clean and friendly place in the new part of town is *Pensión La Dama* (☎/fax 976 22 39 99, Calle del Doctor Casas 20). Singles/doubles are 2200/3500 ptas; doubles with shower are 5000 ptas.

Places to Stay – Mid-Range & Top End

Hotel Posada de las Almas (☎ 976 43 97 00, fax 976 43 91 43, Calle de San Pablo 22) has been going since 1705 but few of the rooms (3800/6500 ptas plus IVA) have any of the character you might expect. The same people run *Hotel San Blas* (☎ 976 43 96 22, Calle de San Pablo 19) across the street, where doubles are 5200 ptas.

Several comfortable small or medium-sized hotels are within a stone's throw of Plaza del Pilar. The fairly characterless *Hotel Las Torres* (☎ 976 39 42 50, fax 976 39 42 54, Plaza del Pilar 11) offers singles/doubles for 6000/7500 ptas plus IVA. The doubles are fine, but the singles can be poky. *Hotel Vía Romana* (☎ 976 39 82 15, fax 976 29 05 11, Calle de Don Jaime I 54-56) includes breakfast in its prices of 6300/8000 ptas plus IVA on Friday, Saturday and Sunday nights, and 6700/9000 ptas plus IVA on other nights. *Hotel Tibur* (☎ 976 20 20 00, fax 976 20 20 02, Plaza de la Seo 2) is a nice place with pretty rooms for 7750/9800 ptas plus IVA.

Places to Eat

The *cafes* along Plaza del Pilar can't be beaten for location but beware the 200-ptas mark-up for every item you eat at an outside table. A block back from the plaza, the bright *La Milagrosa* (Calle de Don Jaime I 43) serves *bocadillos* (filled rolls) and *raciones* (meal-sized serves of tapas) for 300 to 700 ptas, and inexpensive breakfasts. *Cafetería Picolo* on Calle Prudencio serves decent *platos combinados* from 800 ptas and its kitchen cooks until 1 or 2 am.

The narrow streets and small plazas south-west of La Seo harbour some brilliant tapas bars, perfect for cooling off with a beer and a bite on a warm evening.

ARAGÓN

On Plaza Santa Marta *Cervecería Mapy*, *Vitorinos II* and *El Lince* are all appealing; the latter specialises in excellent (but not cheap) seafood tapas. Nearby, the tight little bar *Casa Amadeo (Calle Jordán de Urries 3)* provides seafood raciones for as little as 600 ptas. Tantalising larger-than-tapa specialities for 500 to 600 ptas at *La Calzorras*, on Plaza de San Pedro Nolasco, include *tostadas* with smoked salmon and Cabrales cheese. Another string of *tapas bars* a little farther south-east, on Calle Heroísmo, is popular with a younger crowd.

In El Tubo, *Pascualillo (Calle de la Libertad 5)* has a good *menú del día* (daily set meal) for an inexpensive 1000 ptas. The antique *Casa Lac (Calle de los Mártires 12)*, going since 1825, has a faint touch of fading class and serves salads and fish dishes for 650 to 975 ptas. Meat dishes start at 800 ptas. *Casa Juanico (Calle de la Santa Cruz 21)* is a popular old-style tapas bar with a comedor in the back.

Restaurante Casa Emilio (Avenida de Madrid 5), near the Aljafería, is a simple sort of place with moderately-priced, home-cooked meals, where you'll find few tourists. Several daily *menús* range from around 800 to 2500 ptas.

For classier eating, head for Calle de Francisco Vitoria in the new town, 1km south of Plaza del Pilar. *Risko Mar*, at No 16, is one of the city's best-known fish restaurants but it's pricey, with set meals (for a minimum of two people) costing 4250 and 6200 ptas plus IVA per person. Across the street, the tavern-like *Churrasco* offers a wide variety of meat and fish and is similarly expensive – but it does do an excellent-value three-course lunch *menú*, with wine, for 1300 ptas plus IVA. *Restaurante El Mangrullo*, at No 17, does Argentine food, with main dishes between 1000 and 2000 ptas.

Vegetarians should head for *Restaurante la Retama (Calle de la Reconquista 4)*. Varied salads, starters and main dishes range between 600 and 1500 ptas, or there's a 1200-ptas *menú*. It's open 1.30 to 3.30 pm Wednesday to Saturday, and 9 to 11.30 pm Monday to Saturday.

Entertainment

Bars Drinking and good company are just as important a pleasure in Zaragoza as in any other big Spanish city.

El Tubo and the adjacent Mercado Central area have no shortage of options. *Bar Corto Maltés (Calle del Temple 23)* is one of a string of rather cool places on a lane near the Mercado Central. This area is popular with Zaragoza's many students. *Chastón (Plaza de Ariño 4)* is a relaxed little bar playing recorded jazz. Nearby on Plaza de la Santa Cruz, bare, blue *Café Praga* sprawls onto the plaza in the warm months. *La Casa del Loco (Calle Mayor 10)* stages live rock bands some nights.

Farther south – about halfway to the university – Calle del Doctor Cerrada and nearby streets are absolutely packed with bars, some full of adolescents, others with Caribbean sounds and a 20s and 30s crowd. *Morrissey (Gran Vía 33)* gives a stage to varied local bands from 10 pm Thursday to Saturday (free entry). *Morrison (Calle Ricla 8)* usually has DJs the same nights and sports Australian-theme decor. It's a pity the only Aussie liquid on offer is overpriced cans of Foster's. On the subject of ethnic drinking places, Zaragoza possesses not only a lot of Irish bars but also a few English pubs and even the excellent *Loch Ness Scottish Pub (Calle Baltasar Gracián 31)*, with a respectable selection of Scottish and English beers at around 500 ptas a *pinta* – it's worth the trip just for the corny decor.

Clubs & Discos For drinks and casual dancing, *Café El Prior (Calle de la Santa Cruz 7)* is a good place to start.

The long-standing variety cafe-theatre *Oasis (Calle de Boggiero 28)* is currently going very strong as a venue for popular drag queen shows – open from around 11 pm on Friday and Saturday. *Troppico (Calle Dato 21)* is a popular bar with plenty of room to dance to its Latin American rhythms.

Kitsch (Paseo de Fernando El Católico 70) purveys electronic dance noise, open until about 5 am on weekends.

Sphinx, on Calle de Ramón y Cajal, is a gay nightspot.

Shopping
The main shopping streets spread either side of Paseo de la Independencia. Shops in and around El Tubo sell the usual kitsch as well as ceramics from various parts of Aragón.

Getting There & Away
Air Zaragoza airport (☎ 976 71 23 00) has direct scheduled Iberia flights to/from Madrid and Barcelona daily and Frankfurt (Germany) most days. Air Europa flies to/from Palma de Mallorca and Santiago de Compostela.

Bus Zaragoza has a dozen bus stations, each serving different destinations. The most important is at Paseo de María Agustín 7 (☎ 976 22 93 43). From here Ágreda Automóvil operates at least 15 buses a day to/from Madrid (3¾ hours, 1750 ptas) and Barcelona (3½ hours, 1655 ptas); and Alosa/La Oscense runs up to 15 times to/from Huesca (one hour, 715 ptas) and a few times to/from Jaca (2¼ hours, 1500 ptas). Alosa also has a Saturday and Sunday service from mid-June to early September to/from Lourdes, France (6½ hours) via Huesca, Jaca, Pau and Tarbes.

Tezasa (☎ 976 27 61 79), Calle Juan Pablo Bonet 13, serves Teruel and Valencia. Check destination sections in this chapter for other addresses, and our map for locations. The tourist offices hand out a full list of bus company details.

Train All trains use the shiny El Portillo station. Zaragoza is an important junction, with up to 14 trains daily serving Madrid (three to 4½ hours, 3100 to 4000 ptas) and Barcelona (3½ to 5¼ hours, 2900 to 4100 ptas), but most days there's just one to/from Valencia (5½ hours, 2525 ptas). Trains also run to/from several Aragonese towns (see destination sections) and many other parts of Spain, even as far away as Galicia and Andalucía.

Getting Around
Airport buses (☎ 976 34 38 21) to/from Plaza de Aragón link with flights. Bus No 22 links El Portillo train station to Plaza de España, which is served by almost all routes.

AROUND ZARAGOZA
The following places can be reached by bus, but having your own transport is ideal.

Cartuja de Aula Dei
This Carthusian monastery about 10km north of Zaragoza contains a series of frescoes painted by the young Goya in 1774, depicting the lives of Christ and the Virgin Mary. Until recently, because of monastic rules, only men were allowed in. Then, after a campaign by women in Zaragoza, the government funded building of a tunnel so that visitors of either sex could get to the paintings without being seen by the monks. But the monks, who clearly value their privacy, now restrict visits to the last Saturday of each month, when one group of 20 or 30 people is allowed in. The waiting list is two years long; if you want to join it, call ☎ 976 71 49 34.

Muel & Cariñena
The N-330 south towards Teruel passes through Cariñena country – home of Aragón's premier viticultural industry. Along the way, peek into the **Ermita de la Fuente** in Muel, 19km before Cariñena, which sports paintings of saints by Goya.

There are many **bodegas** on the main road into Cariñena. If you decide to linger, *Hostal Iliturgis (☎ 976 62 04 92, Plaza de Ramón y Cajal 1)* has comfortable doubles without/with bathroom for 3500/4500 ptas.

Fuendetodos
Some of the greatest start small. One such was Francisco Goya y Lucientes, who was born in this insignificant hamlet, 24km east of Cariñena, in 1746. The **Casa Natal de Goya** stayed in his family until the early 20th century, when the artist Ignacio Zuloaga found and bought it. Partly destroyed during the civil war, the three-storey abode – a little less humble than the legends make out – has been restored. Down the road, the **Museo del Grabado de Goya** contains an impressive collection of the artist's engravings and is well worth a visit. Both are open 11 am to 2 pm and 4 to 7 pm Tuesday to Sunday. The combined ticket costs 300 ptas. *El Capricho de Goya (☎ 976 14 38 10,*

ARAGÓN

Paseo Vista Alegre 2) has doubles with bath for 5500 ptas, and a restaurant. Samar Buil (☎ 976 43 43 04) at Calle de Borau 13, Zaragoza, runs daily buses to Fuendetodos.

Belchite

This town, or rather the twin towns that constitute Belchite, must be one of the most eloquent reminders of the destruction wrought in the civil war. The ruins of the old town, replaced by a new village next door, have been left standing as a silent memorial. A few kilometres west stands the strangely neglected 18th-century **Santuario de Nuestra Señora del Pueyo**.

WEST OF ZARAGOZA
Tarazona
postcode 50500 • pop 10,500

West of Zaragoza on the N-122, the dimly lit, serpentine streets of Tarazona's crumbling old town are a remarkable reminder of the Muslim era, though most of its main monuments date from later times. Well before Muslim times, Turiaso, as it was then known, was the scene of a famous victory by a small band of Roman soldiers over a far greater Celtiberian army.

The tourist office (☎ 976 64 00 74), in an outside corner of the cathedral, is open 10 am to 2 pm and 4.30 to 7.30 pm daily (shorter hours in winter).

Things to See The **catedral**, closed for restoration, is a mixed bag of Romanesque, Gothic, mudéjar and Renaissance styles. The mudéjar cloisters are particularly pretty.

Nearby, the **Plaza de Toros Vieja** (Old Bullring) is an octagonal affair made up of 32 houses built in the 1790s as a private housing initiative – with entertainment thrown in.

The rest of Tarazona's sights are within the twisting cobbled ways of the medieval 'high part' of the town, on the other side of the Río Queiles (really just a ditch). From all around you can see the slender mudéjar tower of the **Iglesia de Santa María Magdalena**. The **Palacio Episcopal** opposite was a Muslim fortified palace. Farther north on Plaza de España is the richly decorated 16th-

Lest We Forget

In the summer of 1937, Republican forces fought a savage battle with Franco's troops for control of the small town of Belchite. By the time they had finished, the elegant houses along the Calle Mayor, along with the town's two churches, mostly built of the narrow bricks typical of *mudéjar* architecture, had been thoroughly blasted. The Torre del Reloj (clock tower) was left leaning precariously, the clock face blown away. In March the following year Nationalist forces marched back in as the seesaw war in this heavily fought-over part of Spain swung back in Franco's favour. By now the town's populace lived in a labyrinth of wreckage, struggling to keep life going in the midst of disaster. The Franco government judged the town too far gone to be rebuilt, and decided to build it afresh next door. That plan was not completed until 1954 – a long wait for people living in such misery. Today, it is an eerie experience to wander past the shell-shocked buildings down silent streets, where for a time life and death led a tragic coexistence.

century **ayuntamiento**, one of whose large reliefs is believed to represent Hercules.

Places to Stay & Eat The three places to stay are all of decent standard and provide rooms with bath. *Hostal Palacete de los Arcedianos* (☎/fax 976 64 23 03, Plaza Arcedianos 1), in the old part of town, is the least expensive, with doubles for 5000 ptas in high season. *Hotel Ituri Asso* (☎ 976 19 91 66, Calle Virgen del Río 3), right on the river, has good singles/doubles with bath for 5000/8100 ptas. *Hotel Brujas de Becquer* (☎ 976 64 04 04, Carretera de Zaragoza s/n), on the way out towards Zaragoza, charges 4400/6250 ptas.

Both hotels have decent restaurants, or you could try the ternasco at *El Galeón* (Avenida de la Paz 1), just off the centre.

Getting There & Away Therpasa on Avenida de Navarra runs up to seven buses daily to/from Zaragoza (Calle del General

Sueiro 22, ☎ 976 22 57 23) and Soria. The Zaragoza trip (765 ptas) takes 1¼ hours. For Pamplona and the Monasterio de Veruela you need to go to a different stop on Avenida de la Estación. Both streets branch off Plaza de San Francisco in the centre.

Around Tarazona

The fortified walls of the **Monasterio de Veruela**, founded in the 12th century, are more reminiscent of a Castilian castle than a monastery. Long inhabited by Jesuits, it now belongs to Zaragoza's provincial government. The cold Gothic church is flanked by a charming cloister, with a lower, Gothic level surmounted by a Renaissance upper gallery. Inside the complex is a small wine museum. The monastery is open 10 am to 2 pm and 4 to 7 pm Tuesday to Sunday (shorter hours in winter), for 300 ptas. Several buses come here from Tarazona.

If you have time and a vehicle, take a spin to the **Parque Natural de la Dehesa del Moncayo**, on the flank of the 2300m-plus Sierra del Moncayo. The park information centre (☎ 976 19 21 25) is at Agramonte.

Calatayud

postcode 50300 • pop 17,400

There are only a few points of interest in this busy, dusty town that is just off the N-II Zaragoza-Madrid highway. Head for the mazy old town and search out the **Iglesia de Santa María**, with a fine plateresque portal and mudéjar bell tower. The **Iglesia de San Pedro**'s tower on Rua de Eduardo Dato looks as though it's about to topple into the street – which would upset the storks which nest on it! The **castle ruins** above the town are extensive, but not among the country's best.

There are several cheap and basic places to stay in the centre, such as *Pensión La Perla* (☎ 976 88 13 40, Calle de San Antón 17) with singles/doubles for 1600/2850 ptas. *Hotel Calatayud* (☎ 976 88 13 23), on the Zaragoza road at the north-eastern edge of town, has quality doubles for 8920 ptas plus IVA. Automóviles Zaragoza (☎ 976 21 93 20) runs regular buses between Zaragoza (at Calle de Almagro 18) and Calatayud's bus station, hidden in a building on Calle de Ramón y Cajal in the town centre. There are also three daily buses from Calatayud to Madrid. Several trains run to/from Zaragoza and Madrid.

Monasterio de Piedra

The one-time Cistercian Monasterio de Piedra and the soothing park surrounding it tend a little to the Disneyesque. Founded in 1194 and moved to its present site in 1218, the monastery was abandoned in the 1830s. Now in private hands and partly restored to house a posh hotel, much of it remains a shell. The park, with its waterfalls and caves, is pleasant but the whole experience reeks of the artificial. Entry, including a guided visit to the monastery, costs 1000 ptas. The park is open from 9 am until dusk; monastery tours are given from 10 am to 1.30 pm and 3 to 7 pm.

Hostal San Sebastián (☎ 976 87 04 96, Carretera Cillas-Alhama Km 37.7), in Nuévalos, 3km north of the monastery, has decent rooms for 2500 ptas per person. Singles/doubles at the *Hotel Monasterio de Piedra* (☎ 976 84 90 11, fax 976 84 90 54) in the monastery cost 7500/12,000 ptas plus IVA.

Automóviles Zaragoza (see the preceding Calatayud section) runs buses from Zaragoza to the monastery at 9 am on Tuesday, Thursday and Saturday, and every day in summer, for 1125/2250 ptas one-way/return. One or two daily buses from Calatayud run to Nuévalos, but not right to the monastery.

EAST OF ZARAGOZA

Few stops suggest themselves on the often disconsolate plains and plateaus east of Zaragoza.

Fraga

postcode 22520 • pop 12,000

The old core of this town, by the N-II towards Lleida (Lérida) in Catalunya, makes an intriguing stroll. Its centrepiece is the much-remodelled 12th-century **Iglesia de San Pedro**, seemingly growing out of the steep streets. *Cobertizos,* the galleries that allow passage between houses above the streets, cast deep shadows over the dishevelled maze below. Head uphill from the

ARAGÓN

church for views across the *casco histórico,* the wide Río Cinca valley and the chain of parched hills to the west.

Accommodation is only in the new town. *Hostal Trébol (☎ 974 47 15 33, Avenida de Aragón 9),* within walking distance of the old town, has doubles with bath for 6000 ptas in high season, and serves meals.

The bus station is just west of the river on Avenida de Aragón. Up to 10 buses daily head to Lleida, three to Zaragoza and one to Barbastro and Huesca. Some take roundabout routes and there is hardly a bus anywhere on Sunday.

Pyrenees & the North

As you turn north from parched Zaragoza province, a hint of green tinges the landscape. Although the town of Huesca lies in a basin, the Pyrenees foothills are not far off.

Aragón's section of the Pyrenees is the most rewarding on the Spanish side of the range, with half a dozen decent ski resorts and some great walking, especially in the Parque Nacional de Ordesa y Monte Perdido and the north-east. See this chapter's introductory Skiing and Walking sections for some background information. There are many ways to approach the area, with several main routes clawing up through the valleys and some crossing into France.

HUESCA
postcode 22080 • pop 54,600
Known to the Romans as Osca and to its Muslim masters of nearly four centuries as Wasqa, Huesca was conquered by Christian Aragón in 1095, becoming its capital until it was superseded by Zaragoza in 1118. Huesca has an interesting medieval centre with that down-at-heel feel of many Aragonese towns. It's a good starting point for exploring the north.

As in many places across Spain, the decision to expel the Jews in 1492 and the subsequent dispersal of the Muslims struck a blow from which the flourishing trading

town never recovered. During the civil war Huesca was besieged by Republican forces for a long time, but never taken.

Orientation & Information
The old part of Huesca sits on a slight rise, with the bus station a short walk downhill. The train station is a few hundred metres farther south.

The helpful tourist office (☎ 974 29 21 70), in the ayuntamiento, is open 9 am to 2 pm and 4 to 8 pm daily. From July to September an information kiosk operates on Plaza de Navarra.

There are plenty of banks in the centre. Banesto and Banco Santander on Plaza de Navarra have ATMs. The post office is on the corner of Calle del Coso Alto and Calle de Moya.

The main police station (☎ 974 24 54 00) is on Plaza de Luis Buñuel. The Hospital General San Jorge (☎ 974 21 11 21) is on Avenida Martínez de Velasco, 1km southwest of Plaza de Navarra.

Plaza de la Catedral & Around
This leafy square at the heart of the old town *(casco antiguo)* is presided over by a venerable Gothic **catedral**, built between the 13th and 16th centuries. The main portal, richly carved with disciples, saints and other figures, was fashioned by a master artisan known as Gyllem Inglés (William English), in 1327. Inside, the cathedral is unusually bare, but it does have a large, 16th-century, alabaster retablo by Damián Forment. Entry is free. The **Museo Diocesano** next door exhibits religious art and artisanry from around Huesca diocese – open daily except Sunday (200 ptas). The 16th-century **ayuntamiento** across the square is another Aragonese gem. A little way north on Plaza Universidad, the octagonal **Museo Provincial** incorporates an old Aragonese royal palace where the infamous 'Bell of Huesca' episode took place (see the boxed text). The museum's interesting collection includes portraits and engravings by Goya and archaeological finds from Huesca province. It's open 10 am to 2 pm and 5 to 8 pm, except Saturday afternoon and Sunday.

Iglesia de San Pedro El Viejo

Huesca's real gem is 250m south-east of Plaza de la Catedral. The church of San Pedro itself is an understated 12th-century Romanesque masterpiece. But it's the cloister that's particularly worth a close look, with beautiful Romanesque capitals attributed to the same *maestro* who carved those at San Juan de la Peña (see the Monasterio de San Juan de la Peña section later in this chapter). The fourth and fifth monarchs of Aragón, Alfonso I El Batallador (1104–34) and Ramiro II (1134–37), lie here in the Panteón Real, a chamber off San Pedro's cloister. It was the marriage of Ramiro's daughter Petronilla to the Count of Barcelona that united the provinces of Aragón and Catalunya; most subsequent Aragonese monarchs were buried at the Monestir de Poblet in Catalunya. The church and convent are open 10 am to 2 pm and from about 6 to 8 pm daily.

Parque Municipal de Miguel Servet

The newer part of town has few saving graces apart from this well-manicured, shady park.

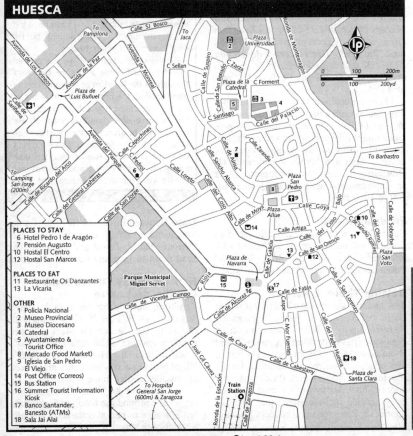

HUESCA

PLACES TO STAY
6 Hotel Pedro I de Aragón
7 Pensión Augusto
10 Hostal El Centro
12 Hostal San Marcos

PLACES TO EAT
11 Restaurante Os Danzantes
13 La Vicaria

OTHER
1 Policía Nacional
2 Museo Provincial
3 Museo Diocesano
4 Catedral
5 Ayuntamiento & Tourist Office
8 Mercado (Food Market)
9 Iglesia de San Pedro El Viejo
14 Post Office (Correos)
15 Bus Station
16 Summer Tourist Information Kiosk
17 Banco Santander; Banesto (ATMs)
18 Sala Jai Alai

Organised Tours

The tourist office gives free guided tours of the town in English and Spanish at 11 am Monday to Saturday and 10 am Sunday.

Places to Stay & Eat

Camping San Jorge (☎ 974 22 74 16, Calle Ricardo del Arco s/n), 1km west of the old town centre, opens from April to mid-October, charging 525 ptas plus IVA per adult, per tent and per car.

Pensión Augusto (☎ 974 22 00 79, Calle de Aínsa 16) has adequate singles/doubles for 2000/3000 ptas. *Hostal El Centro* (☎/fax 974 22 68 23, Calle de Sancho Ramírez 3) has pleasant rooms with shower and TV for 3200/4600 ptas. *Hostal San Marcos* (☎/fax 974 22 29 31, Calle de San Orencio 10) has good rooms for 4500/6500 ptas. The classy *Hotel Pedro I de Aragón* (☎ 974 22 03 00, fax 974 22 00 94, Avenida del Parque 34) charges 9620/16,270 ptas plus IVA.

There's excellent-value food but only three tables (and a bar) at *La Vicaria (Calle de San Orencio 9)*, where the 1200-ptas *menú* might give you prawn and mushroom *revuelto* followed by a big *churrasco*, dessert, wine and bread. *Restaurante Os Danzantes (Calle de Sancho Ramírez 18)* is an unpretentious spot doing *raciones* for 700 to 1000 ptas.

Entertainment

Calle del Padre Huesca, Calle de San Lorenzo and nearby streets are loaded with *late-night bars*. *Sala Jai Alai (Calle del Padre Huesca 65)* sometimes has live bands.

Getting There & Away

Bus The bus station (☎ 974 21 07 00) is at Calle del Parque 3, just off Plaza de Navarra. Up to 15 daily buses run to/from Zaragoza (Paseo de María Agustín 7) and about four each to/from Jaca (1¼ hours, 800 ptas), Barbastro (50 minutes), Lleida (Lérida; 2¼ hours) and Barcelona (4¼ hours). Other destinations with at least one daily service include Benasque, Biescas, Panticosa, Pamplona and (except Sunday) Fraga.

The Bell of Huesca

Ramiro II of Aragón (1134–37), known as 'El Monje' (The Monk), preferred the monastic life, but when his brothers all died childless and he found himself king by default, any otherworldly principles he might have had were rapidly jettisoned in favour of a desire to hang on to his earthly throne. Ramiro's difficulty was that the Aragonese nobility, unable to believe that a monk could make a good king, held him in scant respect and just wouldn't do what he wanted them to. Ramiro sent for advice from the abbot of the French monastery he had recently left. The abbot silently led Ramiro's messenger into the monastery's kitchen garden, where he proceeded to cut down all those cabbages that had grown too tall, commenting 'I'm saying nothing, but tell King Ramiro what you have seen'.

Ramiro understood well. He announced that he would forge a bell to be heard throughout the kingdom of Aragón. Then he summoned all the nobility to court – and as the first few arrived at his palace in Huesca, he had an executioner chop their heads off. He arranged the heads in a circle on the floor – all except one, which he swung from the ceiling on a cord. This 'bell of Huesca' was more than enough to convince the remaining lords that Ramiro was a monarch to be respected.

Train Between three and five trains a day run to/from Zaragoza, with one each to/from Madrid, Teruel and Valencia. Two head north to Jaca and Canfranc-Estación.

NORTH-WEST OF HUESCA

Castillo de Loarre

Rambling and haughty on its rocky perch, this castle (☎ 974 38 26 27) was perfectly placed to keep watch for Muslim raiders racing across the wheat plains to the south. It was raised in the 11th century by Sancho VII of Navarra and is uncannily reminiscent of crusader castles in the Middle East.

A labyrinth of dungeons, tunnels and towers, in and around the living rock, has been left in a state of partial restoration, giving it a suitably untamed feeling. You can climb two of the towers for magnificent views and get to the Romanesque church's crypt via trapdoors before the altar. The castle is open 10 am to 8 pm daily in July and August down to 11 am to 2.30 pm daily except Monday and Tuesday in winter. Entry is free.

The castle is a 5km walk, hitch or drive from the small village of Loarre, where the *Hospedería de Loarre* (☎ 974 38 27 06, *Plaza Miguel Moya 7),* in a 17th-century building, has pleasant singles/doubles for 4750/7500 ptas and a good, medium-to-expensive restaurant. *Camping Castillo de Loarre* (☎/fax 974 38 27 23, *Carretera del Castillo s/n)* is closer to the castle. Two daily buses run to Loarre village from Huesca, and one from Jaca.

Los Mallos
After a boring patch along the Huesca-Pamplona road, you come to a pretty stretch along the Río Gállego north of Ayerbe. On the eastern bank, bizarre rock formations known as Los Mallos (The Mallets) rise up – they wouldn't look out of place in the Grand Canyon. For a closer look, head for **Riglos**.

ALQUÉZAR & AROUND
Alquézar
postcode 22145 • pop 310
The dramatic canyons of the Río Vero and other rivers cutting through the Sierra de Guara north of the Huesca-Barbastro road are Europe's prime location for 'canyoning' (*descenso de barrancos* in Spanish), which involves following canyons downstream by whatever means are appropriate – this can be walking, abseiling, jumping and sometimes even diving.

The main base is the picturesque little village of Alquézar, 20km north-west of Barbastro. Alquézar is well worth a detour even if you don't want to descend a canyon. Its narrow streets and stone buildings have a timeless quality despite the wave of modern canyon tourism. The rocky hill on which the village stands is topped by the Colegiata de Santa María, a large 16th-century church, some of the monastery buildings of which date back to the 11th century (open daily except Tuesday).

Several agencies in Alquézar, such as Avalancha (☎ 974 31 82 99), and several of the places to stay there, offer guided canyoning trips. Costs range between 5500 and 6950 ptas a day per person, depending on how many people go (assuming a minimum of two). The main season is from mid-June to mid-September and there are outings for all levels, including complete beginners.

Places to Stay & Eat
Camping Alquézar (☎ 974 31 83 00), just outside the village, is open year-round. *Camping Alquézar Río Vero* (☎ 974 31 83 50),* down by the Río Vero about 4km towards Barbastro, opens from April to October. Several *albergues* (hostels) in the village offer beds or bunks for around 1300 ptas per person. A step up is the charming *Casa Jabonero* (☎ 974 31 89 08, *Calle Mayor 8),* with doubles for 3800 ptas. *Fonda Narbona* (☎/fax 974 31 80 78, *Calle Baja 19)* charges 4800 ptas and has a lovely terrace restaurant. There are also two good mid-range hotels. Meals are available at most places to stay and several restaurants.

Getting There & Away
Autocares Cortés (☎ 974 31 15 52) usually runs a bus to Alquézar from Barbastro about 2 pm daily except Sunday.

If you're heading north from Alquézar, the road through Colunga up to Aínsa is a fantastic drive through pre-Pyrenean canyons.

BARBASTRO & AROUND
Barbastro
postcode 22300 • pop 15,000
An ancient town, Barbastro spent some 350 years as one of Muslim Spain's most northerly outposts. Today it's a scruffy spot, although the old area around Plaza del Mercado has some atmosphere and the 16th-century cathedral has a main altarpiece partly done by the Renaissance master Damián Forment. In more recent times, the founder of the Catholic movement Opus Dei, Josemaría Escrivá (1902–75), grew up at Plaza del Mercado 11.

The tourist office (☎ 974 30 83 50), open 10 am to 2 pm and 4.30 to 8 pm Tuesday to

ARAGÓN

Saturday, is by the bullring and displays and sells local Somontano wines. There are about 10 places to stay. *La Sombra* (☎ *974 31 10 64, Calle de Argensola 9)* has simple rooms for 1000 ptas per person. *Hotel Clemente* (☎ *974 31 01 86, Calle Corona de Aragón 5)* has large, sparkling clean singles/doubles with bath for 5000/7000 ptas plus IVA. Both these and several other options are within a short stroll of the traffic lights towards the east end of town where the Benasque and Lleida (Lérida) roads diverge.

Daily departures from the bus station (☎ 974 31 12 93) include at least two to Barcelona, five to Monzón and Lleida (Lérida), three to Huesca, one to Benasque and one (except Sunday and holidays) to Fraga.

Monasterio de Pueyo

Six kilometres west of Barbastro on the main highway from Huesca, the hill-top Monasterio de Pueyo commands unlimited vistas in all directions. For that alone it's worth a stop if you're motorised, but there's also a quaint chapel. In July 1936, 20 monks were shot here by Republican militia.

Monzón

postcode 22400 • pop 14,650

Enemies riding against Monzón must have been fazed by the impregnable **castle** walls rising proudly above its jumbled streets. It was the Muslims who built Monzón's first great fortress, taken for Aragón by Sancho Ramírez in 1089. The Knights Templar took it over in 1143 and used it mostly as a convent and centre of education. After the order of knights fell, the fortress decayed under the effect of several sieges over the 16th to 19th centuries, but it has now been partly restored, as has the 12th-century town church, the **Colegiata de Santa María del Romeral**. The castle is open 11.30 am to 1 pm and 3 to 5 pm Tuesday to Saturday, and 10 am to 2 pm Sunday (200 ptas).

There are a number of scruffy pensiones across from the train station. Monzón's premier choice is the more central *Hotel Vianetto* (☎ *974 40 19 00, Avenida de Lérida 25),* with rooms from 4000/6500 ptas plus IVA and a good restaurant.

Numerous trains between Zaragoza, Lleida (Lérida) and Barcelona stop here, and buses run to/from Barbastro, Lleida, Huesca and Fraga.

Torreciudad

The spiritual centre of the Catholic movement Opus Dei (see the boxed text 'Opus Dei' in the Religion section of Facts about Spain) overlooks the grand El Grado reservoir, north-east of Barbastro. A religious complex of unusual artistic taste, the Santuario de Torreciudad opened in 1975, the year of the death of Opus' founder, Josemaría Escrivá. Beatified in 1992 (unusually quickly), Escrivá may soon become a saint.

Much ink has been spilled in attack on or defence of Opus Dei. It has 83,000 members worldwide (28,000 in Spain). Professionals who are members are encouraged to continue their careers rather than become clerics – making them useful contributors to the Opus coffers, said to be substantial. The text by which Opus members lead their spiritual lives is the 999 aphorisms of Escrivá's *El Camino* (The Way). Enthusiastic members practise mortification of the flesh as one means of attaining holiness.

Torreciudad is open to visitors (without dogs or exposed shoulders and not wearing shorts) 9 am to 7 pm or later, daily; the *santuario* (the main church) closes 2 to 4 pm. Buses from Barbastro and Huesca run to El Grado. You have to get a taxi or make your own way from there.

THE NORTH-EAST

The highest peaks in the Pyrenees rise in the north-east corner of Aragón and even in midsummer they can be covered in a blanket of snow and ice. The growing village of Benasque, in a broad, green valley with rocky mountains rising on three sides, is a well-equipped base for forays into the hills. Walkers have almost limitless options, and climbers have a wide choice of peaks and routes. Hostales and camping grounds abound, and they don't come more beautifully situated.

ARAGÓN

The approach gets exciting as the A-139/N-260 threads its way through the Congosto de Ventamillo, a narrow defile carved by the crystal-clear Río Ésera. North of the defile, the village of Castejón de Sos is a paragliding centre with a range of accommodation.

Benasque
postcode 22440 • pop 1400 • elev 1140m

In this happening nerve centre of the Valle de Benasque, the typical grey-stone and ragged slate tile roofs of old Benasque (known locally as Benás) have been swamped by new construction, mostly in keeping with the style of the area. Walkers, climbers and skiers flock here not only as a jumping-off point for fresh-air activities but also for the weekend nightlife.

Information The tourist office (☎ 974 55 12 89), on Calle San Pedro, is open 9 am to 2 pm and 4 to 7 pm daily except some low-season Sundays. It can provide some information on shorter walking routes. The Parque Natural Posets-Maladeta, which provides the north-east Aragón mountains with some environmental protection, has its visitor centre (☎ 974 55 20 66) 1km from Benasque just off the Anciles road. The centre is open daily from 23 June to 14 September, but weekends and holidays only at other times of year.

Barrabés Esquí Montaña, by the A-139 as it skirts Benasque, sells a truly vast array of outdoors equipment, plus maps and guidebooks. There's a ski and climbing gear rental shop 350m north along the main road. Vit's shop on Plaza Mayor rents climbing equipment too, and mountain bikes.

Casa de la Montaña (☎ 974 55 20 94), on Avenida de los Tilos opposite Hotel Ciria, and the Compañía de Guías Valle de Benasque (☎ 974 55 13 36), at Avenida Luchon 19, offer guides and instruction for climbing, trekking and other activities.

Places to Stay & Eat There are several camping grounds near the A-139 north of Benasque. Of these *Camping Aneto* (☎ 974 55 11 41) is closest (3km away) and open all year, while *Camping Plan de Senarta*, 2.5km farther north is utterly bucolic and costs only about 300 ptas per person, tent or car, but lacks drinking water and most other facilities.

One of the better budget choices in town is *Pensión Barrabés* (☎ 974 55 16 54, Calle Mayor 3) with singles/doubles at 1700/3300 ptas. *Pensión Solana* (☎ 974 55 10 19, Plaza Mayor 5), nearby, has doubles for 2500 ptas (5500 ptas with bath). *Hotel Ciria* (☎ 974 55 16 12, fax 974 55 16 86, Avenida de los Tilos s/n) has good rooms for 4700/7500 ptas plus IVA (6200/10,500 ptas plus IVA in August and Semana Santa). Up at the top end of the village *Hotel San Marsial* (☎ 974 55 16 16, Carretera de Francia s/n) is a cosy, family-run hotel. In summer doubles range from 9100 to 13,300 ptas plus IVA, including breakfast.

A number of places in Benasque serve pizzas for around 1000 ptas. A fun place to hang out is *Pepe & Company*, opposite Pensión Barrabés. It has pizzas, Spanish food, snacks and ice creams. The *cafetería* of Hotel Ciria serves generous platos combinados for around 1000 ptas in its.

Getting There & Away Two buses run Monday to Saturday, and one on Sunday, between Huesca and Benasque (three hours) via Barbastro. Buses from Lleida (Lérida) connect with these at Barbastro.

Cerler
Six kilometres east of Benasque stands Aragón's easternmost ski resort, based on the Pico de Cerler (2409m). On offer are 38 varied runs totalling 45km, and there are ski hire outlets in the town. With only two expensive hotels and one hostal here, you're probably better off staying in Benasque.

Walking & Climbing
From early July to late September a bus runs about four times daily between Benasque and La Besurta, 16km north in the upper Ésera valley, for 600/1000 ptas one-way/return. It stops at camping grounds on the A-139 north of Benasque and you can use it to get to/from many of the walks mentioned

ARAGÓN

below. In 2000 the last buses left Benasque at 3.30 pm and La Besurta at 9.30 pm.

The best maps for north-east Aragón are PRAMES' *Ribagorza: Mapa Excursionista, Mapa Excursionista: Valle de Benasque & Valle de Gistaín* and *Maladetas*.

For some useful hints, see this chapter's introductory Walking section.

Near Benasque Several trails, from an hour to a day long, start from Benasque itself or nearby villages such as Eriste and Sahún. Ask the tourist office for its pamphlet *El Placer de Caminar* detailing 15 such walks.

Valle de Vallibierna This valley runs south-eastwards up from the A-139 about 5.5km north of Benasque. On foot, take the track towards Camping Ixeia which leaves the A-139 just before the Puente de San Jaime (or Chaime) bridge, 3km out of Benasque. You're now on the GR-11, which after a couple more kilometres diverges up into the Vallibierna valley. It's then about 2½ hours' walk (an ascent of 600m) to the *Refugio Coronas*, a small fishers' refuge with no facilities. Three groups of mountain lakes, the Lagos (or Ibons) de Coronas, Llosas and Vallibierna, can each be reached in under two hours from the refuge.

GR-11 to Bielsa Westbound, the GR-11 leaves the A-139 just after the Puente de San Jaime and it's an easy three-hour walk (600m ascent), up the Valle de Estós to the *Refugio de Estós (☎/fax 974 55 14 83)*. This good 185-bunk refuge is attended all year and serves meals and drinks. A further five or so hours brings you, via the 2592m Puerto de Gistaín (or Chistau) pass and some superb views of the Posets massif, to the excellent *Refugio de Viadós (☎ 974 50 61 63)*, staffed from about 1 July to 20 September. Good-value dinners are 1300 ptas. Viadós is a base for climbs on **Posets** (3369m) – about six hours to the summit. The GR-11 continues some six hours west to the hamlet of Parzán in the Bielsa valley, before heading into the Parque Nacional de Ordesa y Monte Perdido. Bielsa, 4km south

of Parzán, is an unattractive village but with several *hostales* and *hotels*. Autocares Bergua (☎ 974 50 00 18) runs a bus from Bielsa to Aínsa at 6 am Monday, Wednesday and Friday.

Upper Ésera Valley & Maladeta Massif
The A-139 continues paved for about 12km north from Benasque. About 10km from Benasque, an unpaved side-road to the east leads 6km along the pretty upper Ésera valley, ending at a spot called La Besurta, with a hut serving drinks and some food. A little under halfway from the A-139 to La Besurta is *Llanos del Hospital (☎ 974 55 20 12, e info@llanosdelhospital.com)*, with a bar, restaurant and a variety of accommodation from bunks at 1400 ptas plus IVA, to comfy singles/doubles for 6200/9800 ptas plus IVA including breakfast. The summer bus shuttles back and forth between La Besurta and Llanos del Hospital during the hours when it's not going to or from Benasque.

An exacting trail from Llanos del Hospital heads north-east and upwards to Peña Blanca and from there winds steeply to the 2445m Portillón de Benasque pass on the French frontier. This should take fit walkers about 2½ hours. You could return via a visit to the Port de la Picada, another pass to the east – or another 3½ hours north would take you down past the Boums del Port lakes to the French town of Bagnères-de-Luchon.

From La Besurta there are great southward (and upward) views of the Macizo de la Maladeta (Maladeta Massif), which is a hard-to-resist challenge for experienced climbers. This forbidding line of icy peaks, with glaciers suspended from the higher crests, culminates in Aneto (3404m), the highest peak in the Pyrenees. *Refugio de la Renclusa (☎ 974 55 21 06)*, staffed and serving meals from early June to late September, is a 40-minute walk up from La Basurta. From here climbers can reach the top of Aneto in a minimum of five hours. The massif offers other peaks including Maladeta (3308m). From La Besurta or La Renclusa, walkers can follow paths southeastwards beneath the Maladeta massif, leading ultimately into Catalunya.

ARAGÓN

AÍNSA

postcode 22330 • pop 1650

The wide, cobbled, hill-top Plaza Mayor of the medieval village of Aínsa (L'Aínsa in the local dialect) draws a disconcerting number of tour buses each day – with good reason, as Aínsa is one of the prettiest places in northern Aragón, definitely worth a stop on the way to France or the Parque Nacional de Ordesa y Monte Perdido.

The wonderfully helpful tourist office (☎ 974 50 07 67), at Avenida Pirenaica 1 by the traffic lights in the lower, newer part of the village, is open 9 am to 9 pm daily in summer (10 am to 2 pm and 4.30 to 8.30 pm Tuesday to Saturday in other seasons). Aguas Blancas (☎ 974 51 00 08), at Avenida Sobrarbe 4 down the street, rents rafting and climbing equipment and organises a wide range of adventure trips in the area – from rafting or canoeing on rivers flowing out of the Pyrenees to climbing, horse riding or mountain biking.

The **Iglesia de Santa María**, a restored Romanesque church, rises just off the south-eastern corner of the Plaza Mayor. It has a pleasing little Gothic cloister and a belfry you can climb. The belfry served as part of the town defences during the civil war when the whole area suffered heavy damage. The **castle** and fortifications off the far end of the plaza mostly date from the 17th century, though the main tower (which contains an eco-museum open in Semana Santa and summer) is 11th century.

The massive rocky mountain **La Peña Montañesa** (2291m) dominates the landscape north-east of Aínsa. You can climb it in about 3½ hours by a path starting near the Monasterio de San Victorián to its south.

Places to Stay & Eat

The best place to stay in Aínsa is **Habitaciones La Botiga** (☎ 608-39 97 90 or 974 50 00 95), opposite the south door of the church. Spotless singles/doubles cost 3000/ 4500 ptas – try to book ahead as this appears to be the only accommodation in the old part of town. Otherwise, there's a hive of places within a short walk of the traffic lights in the lower town. **Hostal Dos Ríos** (☎ 974 50 01 06, Avenida Central 2) charges 4200/5600 ptas plus IVA.

About half the houses around the Plaza Mayor function as restaurants and most have outside tables – a superb place to eat in the cool of a summer evening. **Casa Albas – La Brasería** is a good choice, with main dishes from 950 ptas. If you feel like splashing out, **Bodegas del Sobrarbe**, just off the plaza but with a nice patio, is recommended. Mains are 1800 ptas or more, or there's a *menú* for 2500 ptas plus IVA.

Getting There & Away

Autocares Cortés (☎ 974 31 15 52) runs buses from Barbastro bus station to Aínsa (one hour) at 11 am daily except Sunday from mid-July to the end of August, and at 7.45 pm daily except Sunday all year. Returning, these leave from Aínsa at 3.10 pm and 7 am respectively. For further services, see the later Parque Nacional de Ordesa y Monte Perdido and the earlier GR-11 to Bielsa sections.

PARQUE NACIONAL DE ORDESA Y MONTE PERDIDO

At 156 sq km, this national park doesn't cover a huge area, but it and adjacent areas contain arguably the most spectacular scenery in the whole Spanish Pyrenees, and present several days' worth of fine walks for walkers of most levels. The park's 'spine' is a chain of limestone peaks running along the French border, with a south-eastward spur that includes Monte Perdido (3355m), the third-highest peak in the Pyrenees. From these heights descend a series of deep valleys, most of them gouged out by glaciers and headed by bowl-like glacial cirques *(circos)*. Chief among the valleys are Pineta (east), Escuaín (south-east), Añisclo (south), Ordesa (south-west), Bujaruelo (west) and Gavarnie (north). This last one, on the French side, has the sheerest, most dramatic cirque of all.

The depth of the valleys gives rise to a range of vegetation at different altitudes within each one. Typically the valley bottoms are full of lush green forest – birches, boxwoods, willows, firs, ashes – giving way to pines higher up, some of them clinging to

ARAGÓN

the sheer cliffs which rise to the high mountain zone above, where edelweiss, gentians and other wild flowers add colour.

Chamois (*rebeco* in Spanish but often called *sarrio* in Aragón) hop around the park's upper reaches in herds of up to 50. In the skies fly the rare and ugly lammergeier or bearded vulture *(quebrantahuesos)* and the more common golden eagle. But by far the most common animal in the park is *Homo sapiens*. So popular are the more accessible zones that severe restrictions have been placed on vehicle access in summer (see Park Rules under Information later).

Park staff bluntly advised us not to come at all during the peak of the Spanish holiday season from about 4 to 20 August.

Orientation

The main jumping-off point for the park is the village of Torla, 3km south of the southwest corner of the national park. From Torla you can drive (by paved road) as far as Pradera de Ordesa, a lawn-like area in the Valle de Ordesa with a big car park and an overpriced cafeteria, 5.5km inside the park – but see Park Rules later for seasonal vehicle restrictions. If you have no vehicle,

PARQUE NACIONAL DE ORDESA Y MONTE PERDIDO

and you're not there when the shuttle bus runs (see Park Rules later), it's a walk of about 7km from Torla to Pradera de Ordesa by an agreeable path starting by the Hostal Bella Vista, on the main road in Torla.

The Bujaruelo valley, just outside the park's western boundary, is accessed by an unpaved road veering north from the park entrance on the road from Torla.

From Escalona, 11km north of Aínsa on the A-138, a minor paved road heads northwest across to Sarvisé on the N-260 a few kilometres south of Torla. This road crosses the southern tip of the park, heading up the dramatic valley of the Río Bellos for a while and giving access to the spectacular Cañón de Añisclo (the upper reaches of the Bellos valley).

A 12km paved road runs up the Valle de Pineta from Bielsa.

Maps The best are PRAMES' *Parque Nacional de Ordesa y Monte Perdido y Valle de Añisclo* and Editorial Alpina's *Ordesa y Monte Perdido* (both 1:40,000). PRAMES includes detailed descriptions of 15 walks. You should be able to ferret out at least one of the maps in Torla.

Information

The Centro de Visitantes El Parador (☎ 974 48 64 21) is 2km inside the park, just off the road from Torla to Pradera de Ordesa. It has worthwhile displays and friendly staff provide leaflets on walks and answer questions – open 9 am to 2 pm and 3.30 to 6 pm daily, April to November only. There's also a year-round park information office in Torla (☎ 974 48 64 72), by the main road at the north end of the village. Further park information centres are in Escalona, Tella and Bielsa, and there are summer-only tourist offices in Torla (☎ 974 30 40 25), at Avenida de Ordesa 4, and Bielsa (☎ 974 50 11 27) in the Plaza Mayor.

If you need to use an ATM, or change money, you can do so in Torla.

Park Rules The exact details of restrictions on vehicle access to ease the peak-season crush change from time to time. At the time of writing, private vehicles may not drive from Torla to Pradera de Ordesa during Semana Santa, July, August or September. At these times, a shuttle bus (250/375 ptas one-way/return) covers the route instead, stopping only at the visitor centre. The shuttle service is limited to a maximum 1800 people a day. When this number is reached (which can happen by midday in August), no more people will be bussed into the park that day.

During the same periods, a one-way system is enforced on part of the Escalona-Sarvisé road. From the Puyarruego turning, 2km out of Escalona, to a point about 1km after the road diverges from the Bellos valley, only north-westward traffic is allowed. South-eastward traffic uses an alternative more southerly road. It's possible that a shuttle bus may be introduced here too, instead of the one-way system.

There are no restrictions on people walking into the park, including from Torla, at any time.

Free camping is allowed only above certain altitudes (ranging from 1800m to 2500m depending which part of the park you're in), in small tents pitched at sunset and taken down at sunrise. Swimming in rivers or lakes, mountain biking and horse riding are banned.

Walks & Climbs

If you fancy crossing the whole park from east to west, Lonely Planet's *Walking in Spain* will guide you from the Valle de Bielsa to the Valle de Bujaruelo in three to four days.

Circo de Soaso One of the easier walks leads along the Valle de Ordesa to the Circo de Soaso, a rocky balcony whose centrepiece is the Cola del Caballo (Horsetail) waterfall. From the eastern end of the Pradera de Ordesa, take the path that crosses the Río Arazas and climbs steeply up through the woods on the southern side of the valley. This hardest part of the walk, called the Senda de los Cazadores (Hunters' Path), in which you ascend 600m, takes a bit over an hour. Then it's level or downhill all the way along the Faja de Pelay path, high on the southern side of

ARAGÓN

the valley, to the *circo*. Return by the path along the bottom of the valley, passing several charming waterfalls as you go. The whole circuit takes about seven hours. Doing it in reverse is not recommended because descending the Senda de los Cazadores at the end of the day can put quite a strain on tired limbs.

Refugio de Góriz & Monte Perdido Fit walkers can climb a series of steep switch-backs (part of the GR-11 long-distance path) to the top of the Circo de Soaso and on up to the *Refugio de Góriz* (☎ 974 34 12 01) at 2195m. This 96-place refuge, attended and serving meals all year, makes an obvious base for the ascent of Monte Perdido. Book ahead for both meals and sleeping space. For July and August, book a month ahead. A lot of people end up simply camping nearby. You'd need ice axe and crampons to make the peak.

Circo de Cotatuero & Faja Racón Leave Pradera de Ordesa eastwards by the path signed 'Cascadas', then within 1km head north from the Ordesa valley at a junction by a small shrine. Follow the signs for Cotatuero and after a couple of hours on a fairly steep zig-zag path you reach a bridge and tiny shelter below the Circo de Cotatuero's highly impressive 200m waterfall.

A westward path marked 'Circo de Carriata' from the Circo de Cotatuero takes you along the Faja Racón, a high-level route to the Circo de Carriata, about 3km west. From the latter a path descends to Casa Oliván on the main road, about 600m west of the Pradera car park. This whole circuit takes about five hours.

Brecha de Rolando The sturdy-hearted may climb the wall of the Circo de Cotatuero by a set of iron pegs installed back in 1881 (no special equipment is needed, except an unshakeable head for heights). From here you are about 2½ hours' march from La Brecha de Rolando (or Roldán; 2807m) – a dramatic, often very windy gap in the mountain wall on the French frontier (also reachable by a three-hour path from the Refugio de Góriz). The descent from the Brecha on the French side is via a glacier and crossing into France this way requires experience, ice axe, crampons and adequate clothing.

Walks from the Valle de Bujaruelo The GR-11 describes a 6km arc up the pretty Bujaruelo valley to San Nicolás de Bujaruelo. From there an east-north-eastward path leads in about three hours (with a 950m ascent) up to the Puerto de Bujaruelo pass, on the border with France. You are now in the French Parc National des Pyrénées, and in about two hours can descend to Gavarnie village. Experienced wielders of ice axes and crampons have the option of heading south-east and upwards from the pass to the French Refuge des Sarradets and from there back into Spain via the Brecha de Rolando (see earlier in this chapter).

Other destinations from San Nicolás include the mountain tarns Ibón de Lapazosa and Ibón de Bernatuara, each 2½ to three hours up to the north-east, or Panticosa (about eight hours' walking to the north-west).

Southern Gorges The karstic **Cañón de Añisclo** is a gaping wound in the mountain fabric carved out – unlike the glacial valleys farther north – by the erosive action of water on limestone. More adventurous walkers can start from the Refugio de Góriz and descend the gorge from the north, but it's easier to take a day walk from the southern end – feasible if you have a vehicle. Some 12km from Escalona on the road to Sarvisé, a broad path with signs to about a dozen destinations leads down to the dramatic Puente de San Úrbez, then on up the canyon. You can walk as far north as La Ripareta and back in about six hours.

Descending into the smaller-scale but still dramatic **Gargantas de Escuaín** gorge, to the east, takes about an hour from the semi-abandoned hamlet of Escuaín, reached by a minor road leaving the Escalona-Sarvisé road just outside Escalona.

Places to Stay & Eat
Torla Standing above the Río Ara with a backdrop of the national park's mountains,

ARAGÓN

the stone village of Torla has not yet lost too much of its charm to holiday building. With so many places to stay, getting a bed is tricky only in the monster season of July-August, when booking well ahead is mandatory. There are three *camping grounds* on or near the road from Torla to the national park (all closed from November to March).

Refugio L'Atalaya (☎ 974 48 60 22) and *Refugio Lucien Briet* (☎ 974 48 62 21), both on Calle de Francia in the village, have dorm beds for 1000 ptas, and half-board for around 2800 ptas. Otherwise, about the cheapest place is *Hostal Alto Aragón* (☎ 974 48 61 72, Calle de Capuvita 11), where high-season doubles with bath are 5500 ptas plus IVA. The same people run *Hotel Ballarín* (☎ 974 48 61 55), across the street, which costs 6500 ptas plus IVA. The good *Hotel Villa de Torla* (☎ 974 48 61 56, Plaza Nueva 1) and several other places have very similar rates.

All the above places have restaurants. You can stock up on supplies in supermarkets seven days a week.

Valle de Bujaruelo About 3.5km up the valley, *Camping Valle de Bujaruelo* (☎ 974 48 63 48), open from Semana Santa to some time in October, has a refugio with bunks for 1400 ptas as well as camping and a restaurant. A farther 3km up, in a particularly nice spot and open for similar seasons, are *Camping San Nicolás de Bujaruelo* (☎ 974 48 64 28) and the friendly *Mesón San Nicolás de Bujaruelo* (☎ 974 48 60 60), with dorm beds for 1000 ptas.

South of Torla There are plenty of alternatives should Torla be full – or should you just fancy a different village. The cheapest place in **Broto**, a pleasant place on the N-260 3km south of Torla, is *Hostal Español* (☎ 974 48 60 07, Avenida de Ordesa 20), where doubles with bath are 4000 ptas. Among a handful of lodgings in **Sarvisé**, the next village south, the cosy *Hotel Casa Frauca* (☎ 974 48 61 82), on the main road, has doubles for 5000 ptas.

In tiny **Nerín**, 3km from the Cañón de Añisclo, *Albergue Añisclo* (☎ 974 48 90 10) offers lodging for 1000 ptas a person and does meals too.

Biescas Biescas, 24km west of Torla on the approach from Jaca and Huesca, and also on the most direct road from Zaragoza and Huesca to France (Vallée d'Ossau), is not a bad spot to stop. *Habitaciones Las Heras* (☎ 974 48 50 27, Calle de Agustina de Aragón 35) has the cheapest beds, with singles/doubles for 2300/3500 ptas. *Hotel Casa Ruba* (☎/fax 974 48 50 01, Calle Esperanza 20), in the centre, is nicer, at 5300 ptas plus IVA for doubles with bath.

East of the Park The villages of **Escalona** and **Bielsa** both have several inexpensive hostales. The upper reaches of the Valle de Pineta, which is headed by a very impressive cirque, harbour two *camping grounds* and the always-attended *Refugio de Pineta* (☎ 974 50 12 03), with meals, as well as the luxurious *Parador de Bielsa* (☎ 974 50 10 11), where singles/doubles are 13,200/16,500 ptas plus IVA. All these places are accessible by the road up the valley from Bielsa.

Getting There & Away

Hudebús (☎ 974 21 32 77) runs a daily bus from the town of Sabiñánigo, on the N-330 between Huesca and Jaca, at 11 am, to Biescas (11.15 am), Torla (noon) and Aínsa (1 pm). It heads back from Aínsa at 2.30 pm, reaching Torla at 3.30 pm, Biescas at 4.20 pm and Sabiñánigo at 4.30 pm. Late afternoon services run between Sabiñánigo, Biescas and Torla (but not Aínsa) on Sundays and school-term Fridays all year, and daily in July and August.

A daily Alosa bus leaves from Zaragoza (Paseo de María Agustín 7) at 8.30 am, stops in Huesca at 9.45 am and arrives in Sabiñánigo at 10.35 am – just in time for you to catch the Torla bus. From Huesca there are also buses to Biescas, at 9.45 am daily and 5.15 pm daily except Sunday. From Jaca, probably the best bet is the 10.10 am bus (except Sunday) to Sabiñánigo, a 20-minute ride.

It's advisable to confirm schedules before travelling. Tourist offices can usually

ARAGÓN

help. Sabiñánigo's bus station number is ☎ 974 48 00 45.

For buses to Aínsa from farther south, see the earlier Aínsa & Around section. Aínsa-Bielsa buses are covered in the earlier GR-11 to Bielsa section.

JACA
postcode 22700 • pop 14,700
Occupied by the Muslims and later the Franks, Jaca became capital of the nascent kingdom of Aragón in about 1035 under Ramiro I, retaining this status for 60 years until Aragón conquered Huesca. Tourism and skiing farther north have brought recent prosperity to Jaca. On winter weekends it's an aprés-ski-cum-lager-lout fun town.

Information
The well informed tourist office (☎ 974 36 00 98) is at Calle del Regimiento de Galicia 2. It's open 9 am to 2 pm and 6.30 to 8 pm weekdays, 9 am to 1.30 pm and 5 to 8 pm Saturday, and 10 am to 1.30 pm Sunday from 1 July to 15 September. In other seasons it opens daily except Sunday. There are plenty of banks, including a couple on Calle Mayor.

Ski Jaca 2000 (☎ 974 35 54 62), Avenida de Francia 31, rents ski equipment.

Things to See
The **catedral** is a fine building, although tinkering has obscured much of its original French-style Romanesque grace. The real attraction lies in the **Museo Diocesano** in its cloister, which has assembled a remarkable collection of frescoes and sculpture from churches throughout the region – a rare chance to observe the evolution of religious art from 12th century Romanesque through to 15th century Late Gothic. The museum is open 11 am to 1.30 pm and 4 to 6.30 pm daily except Monday. The 300 ptas charge is well worth it.

Addicts of all things Romanesque may want to see the carved stone sarcophagus of Doña Sancha, Ramiro I of Aragón's daughter, in the **Iglesia de San Salvador y San Ginés**.

The 16th-century star-shaped **Ciudadela**, which houses an army academy, can be visited on a guided tour from 11 am to noon

and 6 to 8 pm daily (afternoon hours may change a little with the seasons), when the soldiers briefly drop their guard. To the west, the well-preserved medieval **Puente de San Miguel** spans the Río Aragón.

Special Events
Jaca puts on its party gear for the week-long Fiesta de Santa Orosia, its patron saint, which starts on 23 June. If you want to see medieval jousts, visit on the first Friday of May, when Jaca celebrates a victory over Muslims in 760.

Places to Stay
There are few cheap options, and the town can fill up in peak periods, particularly summer, Easter and holiday weekends.

Camping Peña Oroel (☎ 974 36 02 15), a couple of kilometres east on the road to Sabiñánigo, opens for Easter and from mid-June to mid-September.

In town, *Hostal París (☎ 974 36 10 20, Plaza de San Pedro 5)* is one of the few places suitable for a low budget. High-season singles/doubles are 2500/4000 ptas plus IVA. *Hostal Somport (☎ 974 36 34 10, Calle de Echegaray 11)* is clean and reliable. Rooms cost 3500/4500 ptas, or 5500 ptas for doubles with bathroom.

Most other places charge around 5500/8000 ptas in high season but if things are not *too* busy they may come down a bit, even in August. *Hotel Pradas (☎ 974 36 11 50, Calle del Obispo 12)* is reasonable value at 4300/7500 ptas. *Hotel La Paz (☎ 974 36 07 00, Calle Mayor 41)* is a bright place charging 5000/8000 ptas plus IVA. Another good, established hotel is *Hotel Mur (☎ 974 36 01 00, Calle de Santa Orosia 1)*, at 5500/8500 ptas.

Places to Eat
The wood-ceilinged *Asador La Fragua* on Calle de Gil Berges is a popular grill house with a *menú* for 1500 ptas plus IVA. *Mesón Serrablo (Calle del Obispo 3)* is a rather classier and dearer version of much the same thing. The *cafetería* at Hotel Pradas does platos combinados for 800 ptas. *Casa Fau* on Plaza de la Catedral is a typically good tapas bar.

Entertainment

A bevy of youthful nocturnal *bars* lines Calle de Gil Berges and trickles off into the neighbouring lanes.

Getting There & Away

The bus station (☎ 974 35 50 60) is handily located on Plaza de Biscós. Four to five buses go daily to Sabiñánigo and Huesca, three or four to Zaragoza, and one or two to Pamplona (1¾ hours, 865 ptas). Up to five head up the valley as far as the ski slopes at Astún and one or two daily wind over to Panticosa and El Formigal, via Biescas.

The train station is a half-hour walk north-east of the town centre, with two trains daily south to Huesca and Zaragoza and two north to Canfranc-Estación.

CANFRANC-ESTACIÓN

postcode 22880 • pop 535 • elev 1200m

Not to be confused with the even less pleasant Canfranc-Pueblo to the south, Canfranc-Estación is, as they say, the end of the line. Trains (two a day to/from Zaragoza via Huesca and Jaca) don't go beyond this un-exciting tourist stop, 25km north of Jaca, but the trip up the Río Aragón valley is pretty and between one and three daily buses cross to the Vallée d'Aspe and Oloron-Ste-Marie in France.

The tourist office (☎ 974 37 31 41) is at Plaza del Ayuntamiento 3.

Albergue Pepito Grillo (☎ *974 37 31 23, Avenida Fernando El Católico 2*) charges 1400 ptas for a bed. *Hotel Ara* (☎ *974 37 30 28, Plaza del Ayuntamiento 2*) is an inexpensive hotel option, with doubles at 3400 ptas, or 4700 ptas with bathroom.

CENTRAL ARAGÓN SKI RESORTS

To book accommodation in any of these resorts (highly recommended), you can call the resort information numbers given below.

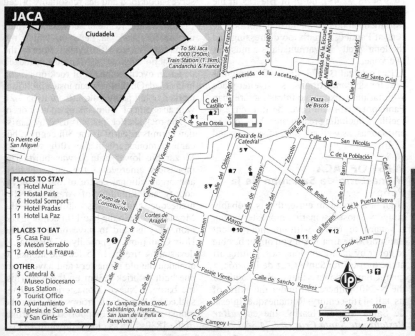

JACA

PLACES TO STAY
1 Hotel Mur
2 Hostal París
6 Hostal Somport
7 Hotel Pradas
11 Hotel La Paz

PLACES TO EAT
5 Casa Fau
8 Mesón Serrablo
12 Asador La Fragua

OTHER
3 Catedral & Museo Diocesano
4 Bus Station
9 Tourist Office
10 Ayuntamiento
13 Iglesia de San Salvador y San Ginés

ARAGÓN

Candanchú & Astún

Aragón's westernmost and longest estab-lished ski resort is just 34km north of Jaca. Some 49km of widely varied pistes make it appealing to most grades of skiers. Al-though there are only four hotels or pen-siones, you can also stay in *Apartamentos Loma Verde* (☎ 974 37 32 37). The small town is reasonably well equipped with gen-eral stores and ski hire shops.

One advantage of Candanchú is that an-other good resort, Astún, is just 3km east. The 36km of pistes there are largely for cap-able skiers. Astún's only hotel, *Hotel Eur-opa* (☎ 974 37 33 12), charges up to 21,000 ptas per double, but there are several sets of apartments.

Astún-Candanchu's joint information and reservations number is ☎ 974 37 30 38, and the Web site is at www.astun.com.

Panticosa & El Formigal

The comparatively small Panticosa resort (☎ 974 48 72 48), north of Biescas in the Gállego valley, has a bigger counterpart, El Formigal, about 10km farther north. The runs at Panticosa aren't too distressing and the long, pretty Mazarranuala is a must for everyone.

El Formigal (☎ 974 49 00 00), a regular host for ski competitions, is a livelier place with far more extensive infrastructure than Panticosa. Here you have the full range of facilities, including restaurants, bars, discos and saunas, as well as 56km of ski runs and 23 lifts.

WEST OF JACA
Monasterio de San Juan de la Peña

High in a mountain eyrie, this is probably Aragón's most fascinating monastery – but it's hard to reach without independent transport. You might be able to cover by Jaca-Pamplona bus, getting off at the turn-off for **Santa Cruz de la Serós**, a quaint tumbledown village 4km south of the N-240, gathered in under the skirts of its tall, 11th-century Romanesque Iglesia de Santa María. Nearby, the cosy *Bar Restaurante Santa Cruz* (☎ 974 36 19 75)

> ### Tunnel Vision
>
> Candanchú is just inside Spain's border with France and is reached from either country by a steep, winding road loaded with switchbacks and great views. But if you're just passing through (so to speak), you'll soon be steered through the new Somport Tunnel, expected to open in 2001. This controversial EU-aided project has caused an outcry from ecologists, who argue that construction of the 9km tun-nel, along with the inevitable widening of its approach roads, will not only disfigure the beautiful Vallée d'Aspe on the French side but also adversely affect the remaining half-dozen native Pyrenees bears (which live hereabouts), as well as various species of eagle and other birds. The expected cost, well over US$1000 million, has multiplied from original estimates and opponents say the average time-saving for vehicles will be only 16 minutes.

serves good food and has reasonably priced rooms with bath.

From Santa Cruz de la Serós a road winds up the Sierra de la Peña on which the monastery stands. It's nearly 7km to the Monasterio Viejo (Old Monastery), tucked under an overhanging lip of rock on a bend in the road. On foot you can instead follow a marked uphill path of 4km (the GR-65.3.2), with an ascent of 350m, taking an hour or so.

The rock shelter, perhaps used by Chris-tian hermits as early as the 8th century, be-came a monastery in the 10th, when its Mozarabic lower church was built. The monastery emerged as the early spiritual and organisational centre of the medieval county and kingdom of Aragón. A Ro-manesque church was built above the Mozarabic one in the late 11th century. The monastery is said to have once held the Holy Grail (now supposedly in Valencia). A devastating fire in 1675 led the monks to abandon the old monastery and have a new one built in brick 1.3km up the hill. This, the baroque Nuevo Monasterio, was later sacked by Napoleonic troops and, after the monks misguidedly supported the Carlists in the 1830s, it was closed down in 1835.

ARAGÓN

The first three kings of Aragón – Ramiro I (1036–64), Sancho Ramírez (1064–94) and Pedro I (Peter I, 1094–1104) – were among those buried at the Monasterio Viejo. Although the Panteón Real (Royal Mausoleum), constructed here in 1770, dislodged some of the tombs of those it was supposed to honour, you can see the original tombs from another room in the monastery. The greatest highlight is the Romanesque cloister, with marvellous carved 12th- and 13th-century capitals depicting Genesis and the life of Christ.

Entry to the old monastery is 400 ptas and the ticket includes the Iglesia de Santa María at Santa Cruz de la Serós. Hours for both places are the same, varying a bit with the seasons and years. Expect them to be open 10 am to 2.30 pm and 3.30 to 8 pm daily from June to August, and from 11 am to 2 pm and 4 to 5.30 pm daily except Monday in winter. In spring and autumn they open daily but for shorter hours than in summer. You can call ☎ 974 35 51 19 or ☎ 974 34 81 95 to check exact times.

The Nuevo Monasterio is closed but it's well worth the extra climb: nearby are a cafe-kiosk, a visitor centre, and the Balcón de los Pirineos, a lookout point with marvellous views both of the Pyrenees and, usually, of members of the local vulture and eagle population wheeling around the air in front of you. You might even see a lammergeier.

Sos del Rey Católico
postcode 50680 • pop 940

About 80km west of Jaca, this small town takes its name from a son of whom any place would be proud: Fernando II of Aragón, born here in 1452. He married Isabel I of Castile and together, as Los Reyes Católicos (the Catholic Monarchs), the couple finished off the Reconquista and united Spain. The old medieval town, which could do with a little loving care, is a fascinating little spider's web of twisting, cobbled lanes and claustrophobic houses atop a hill on the rim of the Aragonese wheat plains. The Castillo de la Peña Feliciano crowns the hill top and the Gothic Iglesia de San Esteban below it is

worth a peek. Fernando is said to have been born in the Palacio de Sada, one of several mansions scattered about the centre.

Fonda Fernandina (☎ 948 88 81 20, Calle Emilio Álfaro s/n) offers basic singles/ doubles for 2000/3300 ptas. The mid-range *Hostal Las Coronas (☎ 948 88 84 08, Calle Pons Sorolla 1)* has doubles with bath for 7000 ptas. There's also an expensive *parador*.

Sos is the northernmost of the Cinco Villas (Five Towns) just inside Aragón's border with Navarra, which were declared *villas* by Felipe V (Philip V) in the 18th century. The other four, in what's otherwise a very thinly populated region, are Uncastillo, Sádaba, Ejea de los Caballeros and Tauste. With a variety of monumental old buildings, they form a potentially interesting alternative route between, say, Zaragoza and Pamplona.

A bus to Sos del Rey Católico and Sanguesa leaves at 7 pm (except Sunday and holidays) from Zaragoza train station.

NORTH-WEST OF JACA
Valle de Echo
Less spectacular than the territory farther to the east, the Valle de Echo nonetheless boasts some charming old stone villages and culminates, at its northern end, in the beautiful Selva de Oza forest.

A bus leaves from Jaca at 6.30 pm Monday to Saturday for Echo and Siresa, returning from Siresa at 6.25 am and Echo at 6.45 am. There are no buses farther up the valley.

Echo The biggest village in the valley, Echo (Hecho; population 670) is a surprising warren of solid stone houses with steep roofs and flowery balconies. It was briefly the seat of the County of Aragón in the 9th century. The only 'sight' is the **Museo Etnológico**, with displays characteristic of rural life in the area. It's on Calle Aire, near the church.

You couldn't do better than stay at *Pensión Casa Blasquico (☎ 974 37 50 07, Plaza del Palacio 1),* which is almost totally obscured by verdant flora. The charming rustic and varied rooms, with bath, costing between

ARAGÓN

6000 and 8000 ptas plus IVA a double, rest above the highly proclaimed *Restaurante Gaby*. If it's full, there are two bland *hostales* and a *hotel*, plus the year-round *Camping Valle de Echo* (☎ 974 37 53 61).

Siresa A couple of kilometres up the road to the north, Siresa (population 130) is another hamlet typical of the region and is dominated by the formidable Iglesia de San Pedro. The clean *Albergue Siresa* (☎/fax 974 37 53 85, ⓔ albsiresa@arrakis.es, Calle Reclusa s/n) is open year round, provides bunk-and-breakfast for 1350 ptas, with other meals available, rents mountain bikes and has a library. *Hotel Castillo d'Acher* (☎ 974 37 53 13, Calle La Virgen s/n) has singles/doubles with bath and TV for 5000/6000 ptas and can also provide 4000-ptas doubles in *casas rurales*. A few kilometres north on the road to the Selva de Oza, the colourful *Hospedería Usón* (☎ 974 37 53 58) stands in splendid isolation with fine rooms for 4500/6000 ptas.

Selva de Oza North of Siresa the scenery is particularly lovely as the road parallels the Río Aragón Subordán which bubbles its way through thick woodlands. It's 12km to the sprawling but attractively located *Camping Selva de Oza* (☎ 974 37 51 68), open mid-June to mid-September, with a restaurant. The road continues a few kilometres farther to meet the GR-11 path en route between Candanchú and Zuriza, and at least half a dozen mountain peaks sit in an arc to the north for strenuous day assaults.

Valle de Ansó

As with the Valle de Echo, the main interest for walkers is at the northern end of the valley, but Ansó village is an enticing stop on the way up. The bus from Jaca to Echo continues to Ansó (arriving at 8.10 pm and returning at 6 am). No buses go farther up the valley.

Ansó The rough-hewn stone houses here repeat the pretty picture of Echo, but on a smaller scale. Ansó (population 540) could make an ideal base for exploring the region, especially if you have your own transport.

Posada Magoria (☎ 974 37 00 49, Calle Milagros 32), just below the church, is an early 20th-century house beautifully renovated with period furnishings. The six rooms, with bath, cost 3100/6200 ptas for singles/doubles (singles may have to pay the double price in August). In the *comedor* you can savour good vegetarian cooking with home-grown ingredients.

Four cheaper *hostales*, all with restaurants, also compete for custom. *Bar Zuriza* is a great old drinking establishment with a wide selection of beers, tapas and local cider.

Zuriza Fifteen kilometres north from Ansó, Zuriza is little more than a camping ground and glorified refugio. *Camping Zuriza* (☎ 974 37 01 96), open all year, is popular – it's worth booking ahead for peak periods and busy weekends. It also has a handful of double rooms for 4500 ptas (6000 ptas with bathroom) and a restaurant. A rough but driveable track leads 5km farther north to the 100-place *Refugio Linza* (☎ 974 37 01 12), attended all year and with a bar.

Walks of varying duration and difficulty abound, as do opportunities for climbing and caving. The GR-11 passes right through Zuriza. You could follow it west to Isaba (Navarra), about 9km away via a stiff climb over 2050m Ezkaurre. Eastwards, it's a bit farther to the Selva de Oza (see earlier) via the 1958m Collado Petraficha pass. A couple of peaks on the border with France, Sobarcal (2249m) and Petrechema (2360m), attract a lot of attention (the latter is a trickier ascent than the former). Both can be done as day excursions from the Linza refuge, or even from Zuriza.

The South

Vast sweeps of the country immediately south of Zaragoza are dreary plains or bald, uninviting ridges, but farther south and east you run into more dramatic country with some intriguing towns and villages. Teruel is a storehouse of some of the best mudéjar architecture you'll find anywhere, and nearby Albarracín is a medieval treat.

DAROCA

postcode 50360 • pop 2350

Daroca lies low in a valley just below the N-234 Calatayud-Teruel highway. On the hills either side of town rise the crumbling remnants of its once extensive walls. Some of the original 114 towers have been restored, but most have disappeared. Calle Mayor, the main street, is marked at either end by monumental gates. About midway along it and up to the west lies the main square, Plaza de España, dominated by the Iglesia Colegiata de Santa María. Restructured in the 16th century, this large church is mainly in Renaissance style, although it preserves a 12th-century Romanesque apse and the bell tower is mudéjar.

The best place to stay is *Pensión Ruejo* *(☎ 976 80 09 62, Calle Mayor 88),* towards the southern end of the main street. It has singles/doubles for 2000/3500 ptas and doubles with bath for 4500 ptas, plus a ground-floor bar and a pub in the courtyard behind.

Buses stop outside Mesón Félix bar, at Calle Mayor 104. Two or three a day run to/from Zaragoza (Ágreda Automóvil; Avenida de Valencia 20) and Teruel. An early morning bus goes to Calatayud weekdays.

LAGUNA DE GALLOCANTA

Some 20km south of Daroca and a similar distance west of Calamocha on the N-234, this is Spain's largest natural lake, about 15 sq km in area (though it can almost dry up in summer). It's an important winter home for many thousands of cranes and water fowl. A Centro de Interpretación (☎ 978 72 50 04) with information and exhibitions, on the Tornos-Bello road at the south-east end of the lake, is open 10 am to 2 pm and 4 to 8 pm weekends.

TERUEL

postcode 44080 • pop 29,300

This compact provincial capital contains a handful of the most ornate and striking mudéjar monuments in the country. Its hill-top casco merits a few hours of your time at least. Teruel makes a decent stopover between Zaragoza and Valencia, or indeed between north-east Castilla-La Mancha and the coast.

History

During the 11th century, Teruel was for a while part of the Muslim *taifa* (small kingdom) based in nearby Albarracín. Taken for Christendom by Alfonso II of Aragón in 1171, Teruel was an operational base for Jaume I of Aragón in his 1230s campaign to wrest Valencia from Muslim hands.

Orientation & Information

The train station is downhill on the western edge of the old town, and the modern bus station on the eastern edge. From either it's a short walk into the centre. Several hostales cluster near the cathedral in the heart of the old town.

The tourist office (☎ 978 60 22 79) is at Calle de Tomás Nogués 1. Its basic hours are 8 or 9 am to 2 pm and 5 to 7.30 pm daily except Sunday, but it's open until 9 pm Tuesday to Saturday and 10 am to 2 pm Sunday, from July to September.

The post office is at Calle de Yagüe de Salas 19. You'll find plenty of banks around Plaza del Torico. There's a Centro de Salud (clinic) on Calle Joaquin Arnau. The local police (☎ 978 60 21 78) are in the ayuntamiento on Plaza Catedral.

Catedral & Museo de Arte Sacro

Viewed from outside, the cathedral of Teruel is like a brick wedding cake, decorated with brightly coloured ceramic tiles – a rich example of the mudéjar imagination at work. Work on the cathedral began in 1176. The mudéjar bell tower, erected in the 12th and 13th centuries and tinged with a little Romanesque, is the most appealing exterior feature. Inside, the recently restored roof of the nave is a mudéjar artesonado marvel from the late 13th century, systematically covered with paintings which add up to a complete medieval cosmography – from musical instruments, hunting scenes and peasants to coats of arms, bishops and Christ's crucifixion. Guided tours are given every 45 minutes or so from 11 am to 2 pm (until noon on Sunday) and 4 to 8 pm daily (300 ptas). It's advisable to be there an hour or more before closing time.

ARAGÓN

Behind the cathedral is the Museo de Arte Sacro (Museum of Sacred Art) with an extensive collection of Christian painting and sculpture from Romanesque to baroque times.

Other Mudéjar Monuments

Of Teruel's three other mudéjar bell towers, the **Torre de El Salvador**, an early 14th century fantasy of brick and ceramics built around an old Muslim minaret, is the most impressive. You can climb up by stairways occupying the gap between the inner and outer towers from 11 am to 2 pm and 5 to 8 pm (until 9 pm in August) daily, for 250 ptas.

The **Torre de San Martín**, at the end of Calle de los Amantes, is similar in dimensions and form, but a little more worn around the edges.

The other tower is the **Torre de San Pedro** on the Iglesia de San Pedro, to which is attached the celebrated **Mausoleo de los Amantes** (Mausoleum of the Lovers). The latter holds the mummified remains of Isabel and Diego, 13th-century star-crossed lovers who supposedly died of grief at seeing their love frustrated; they lie with their heads tilted towards each other (see the boxed text 'Diego & Isabel'). The mausoleum is open 10 am to 1.50 pm and 5 to 7.20 pm daily (50 ptas).

Museo Provincial

The Provincial Museum on Plaza Polanco is housed in the 16th-century Casa de la Comunidad, a fine work of Renaissance architecture. The archaeological displays are a highlight but exhibits range through to contemporary art. It's open 10 am to 2 pm and 4 to 7 pm Tuesday to Friday, 10 am to 2 pm Saturday and Sunday (free).

Special Events

On the nearest weekend to 14 February, thousands of townspeople don medieval dress for a gala and reenactment of the Diego

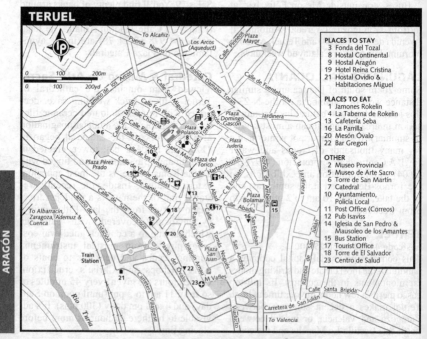

TERUEL

Scale
0   100   200m
0   100   200yd

PLACES TO STAY
3 Fonda del Tozal
8 Hostal Continental
9 Hostal Aragón
19 Hotel Reina Cristina
21 Hostal Ovidio & Habitaciones Miguel

PLACES TO EAT
1 Jamones Rokelin
4 La Taberna de Rokelin
13 Cafetería Seba
16 La Parrilla
20 Mesón Óvalo
22 Bar Gregori

OTHER
2 Museo Provincial
5 Museo de Arte Sacro
6 Torre de San Martín
7 Catedral
10 Ayuntamiento, Policía Local
11 Post Office (Correos)
12 Pub Isaviss
14 Iglesia de San Pedro & Mausoleo de los Amantes
15 Bus Station
17 Tourist Office
18 Torre de El Salvador
23 Centro de Salud

and Isabel legend. The Día de San Cristóbal (St Christopher's Day; 10 July) is the hub of the week-long Feria del Ángel festivities, in celebration of Teruel's foundation.

Places to Stay

An inexpensive place with character is *Fonda del Tozal* (☎ 978 60 10 22, Calle del Rincón 5). You pay from 1500/3000 to 2800/4500 ptas for singles/doubles in varied rooms with low, wood-beam ceilings, but make sure the linen is clean. Nearby, the comfortable, clean *Hostal Aragón* (☎ 978 60 13 87, Calle de Santa María 4) offers rooms for 2150/3200 ptas plus IVA, or 3200/4860 ptas plus IVA with bath. *Hostal Continental* (☎ 978 60 23 17, Calle de Juan Pérez 9), also good, has rooms for 2300/3500 ptas (3000/5500 ptas with bath).

For significantly more luxury in the central area, it's a big price jump to the *Hotel Reina Cristina* (☎ 978 60 68 60, fax 978 60 53 63, Paseo del Óvalo 1), which charges 10,500/15,950 ptas plus IVA.

Down near the train station, *Habitaciones Miguel* (☎ 978 60 04 31, Camino de la Estación 6) has four basic but very clean rooms with very clean shared bathrooms, for 3000 ptas single or double. *Hostal Ovidio* (☎ 978 60 28 66), in the same building but with reception next door in Casa La Amalia bar, charges 3000/4000 ptas (3500/6500 ptas with bath).

Places to Eat

Spain is pretty obsessed with all things porcine, and Teruel is no exception, going to great lengths to promote its local jamón. *Virutas de jamón* (ham shavings) is one form in which it arrives at your table.

One of the best places to try Teruel ham is *La Taberna de Rokelin* (Calle Tozal 33), a narrow bar with a beautiful rack of smoked pig hocks. It's linked to a shop just along the street, *Jamones Rokelin*, which has an impressive selection of smoked meats, sausages and cheeses. Load up here for a week's worth of picnics.

Cafetería Seba on Calle Ramón y Cajal is a bustling breakfast spot that serves good bocadillos.

Diego & Isabel

Isabel de Segura and Juan Diego de Marcilla fell in love as teenagers but Isabel's self-important parents considered Diego too poor to marry her. They did give him five years to win his fortune, however, and off he went to fight the heathen, amassing sufficient loot to return to Teruel to claim Isabel's hand on the day the five years were up. He was just too late. Earlier that very day, Isabel's parents had married her off to a nobleman from Albarracín. The grief-stricken Diego managed to see Isabel that night and asked for one last kiss. His request refused, he promptly expired at her feet. At his funeral in the Iglesia de San Pedro the following day, Isabel, dressed in mourning, stepped forward to give Diego the kiss he had pined for, then she, too, promptly died. So astounded and moved were the townspeople that they decided to bury the two lovers together in the church where Isabel had died. The bodies, it is said, were later transferred to what is now their mausoleum.

Bar Gregori (Paseo del Óvalo 6), with some outdoor tables, is a popular and good spot for tapas and raciones. *Mesón Óvalo* (Paseo del Óvalo 2) is good for a heartier meal, combining the traditional and the innovative, with local ingredients. It has *menús* for 1495 and 2595 ptas plus IVA. *La Parrilla* (Calle San Esteban 2), in Teruel's bar zone, is another good place to get a hearty meal; *carnes a la brasa*, salads and asparagus dishes start around 900 ptas.

Entertainment

Most of the late-night excitement takes place in the bars on and around Plaza Bolamar. The spacious ground-floor bar at *Fonda del Tozal* is active and has live music some nights. For a more relaxed drink or coffee, *Pub Isaviss* is at the lower end of Plaza del Torico.

Getting There & Away

From the modern bus station (☎ 978 60 10 14) on Ronda de Ambeles, four or more

ARAGÓN

daily buses run to/from Zaragoza (2½ hours, 1130 ptas) and Valencia (two hours, 1160 ptas); up to three each to/from Madrid (4½ hours, 2415 ptas) and Barcelona (6½ hours, 3250 ptas); and one except Sunday and holidays to/from Cuenca (1180 ptas). For more local services see destination sections.

Teruel is on the railway between Zaragoza (2¾ hours, 1405 ptas) and Valencia (2½ hours, 1125 ptas), with two or three trains each way daily.

RINCÓN DE ADEMUZ

The Rincón de Ademuz (Ademuz Corner) is a mountainous detached piece of Valencia province sandwiched between the provinces of Teruel and Cuenca (Castilla-La Mancha). It makes a picturesque alternative route between Teruel town and Valencia or Cuenca provinces. The most spectacular stretch is the rough and winding 17km of the old N-330A road, south from the town of Ademuz (a steep but unremarkable little place) to Santa Cruz de Moya. Starting along the deepening gorge of the upper Río Turia, the road crosses into Castilla-La Mancha in quite spectacular fashion. This section (and Ademuz itself) are bypassed by the main N-330, so if you want to follow it you need to head into Ademuz via Torrebaja – or if you're coming from the south, through Manzaneruela to Santa Cruz de Moya.

The N-420 west from the Rincón de Ademuz skirts the southern hills of the Serranía de Cuenca en route to Cuenca. The first 15km or so are a bit of an adventure owing to the road's poor condition.

The large *Hostal Casa Domingo (☎ 978 78 20 30, Avenida Valencia 1),* on the N-330A in Ademuz, has decent rooms with bath and TV at 2535/4650 ptas plus IVA, and a restaurant. It's also the stop for buses to/from Teruel (one a day except Sunday) and Valencia via the N-330A (twice daily, weekdays).

ALBARRACÍN

postcode 44100 • pop 1060 • elev 1170m

The crenellated walls climbing above the medieval town of Albarracín, 38km west of

Teruel, dramatically announce its proximity as you approach. Built on steep, rocky height carved out by a meander of the Río Guadalaviar, Albarracín was from 1012 to 1104 the seat of a tiny Islamic state ruled by the Banu Razin, a Berber dynasty. Later, from 1170 to 1285, it was an independent Christian kingdom under the Azagra family, sandwiched between Castile and Aragón. It's a wonderfully dramatic-looking place in a remote setting, with impressive buildings clinging to steep slopes. The cool, narrow streets are even today in the best tradition of the Arab medina, with centuries-old buildings leaning and bulging alarmingly over them.

Information

The tourist office (☎ 978 71 02 51) at Calle Diputación 4, just off Plaza Mayor, is open 10 am to 2 pm and 4 to 7 pm daily, except Sunday afternoon and Monday. You'll find the post office and a couple of banks with ATMs on or just off Plaza Mayor.

Things to See

The cathedral, with its cupola typical of the Spanish Levant, has an elaborate gilded altarpiece. The Palacio Episcopal to which it's connected houses the **Museo Diocesano**, with 16th-century paintings, tapestries, and religious *objets d'art*. The cathedral (free) and museum (300 ptas; guided visits only) both open 10.30 am to 2 pm and 4 to 6 pm (until 8 pm in August) daily.

The castle near the southern end of town and the Torre del Andador near the top of the walls both date from the 9th century, when Albarracín was already an important Muslim military post.

Best of all, simply enjoy exploring the streets and walls. Nearly every brick, stone, slab of concrete and slap of mortar in the place is in some earthy shade of red or pink, making for wonderful plays of colour against the green of its gardens, particularly in the evening.

Places to Stay & Eat

The pleasant, small and shady *Camping Ciudad de Albarracín (☎ 978 71 01 97)* is 2km from the heart of town, off the Bezas oad, charging just 375 ptas for each person, ent and car. It closes from November to March. Of many places in town, *Hostal Olimpia* (☎ 978 71 00 83, Calle San Anto- *nio 5),* right by the bus stop, has some cheerful singles/doubles with bath for 3300/5500 ptas, and rooms with shared baths for 2500/4000 ptas. *Mesón del Gallo* (☎ 978 71 00 32, Calle de los Puentes 1), around the corner, charges 4000/6500 ptas for decent rooms with bath and TV.

A few steps up from Plaza Mayor in the heart of the old town, cosy *Casa de Santiago* (☎ 978 70 03 16, Subida a las Torres 11) has eight charming rooms at 5400/7900 ptas plus IVA. Perhaps best value of all is *Habita- ciones Los Palacios* (☎ 978 70 03 27, Calle Palacios 21), where spotless rooms with bal- cony, bath and gorgeous views are 2500/ 4500 ptas. On foot, it's 250m past the Casa de Santiago (start along Calle de Santiago); in a vehicle (from the Teruel direction), pass through the tunnel under the town then take the first road up to the right.

Several places to stay have restaurants, and there are more eateries in the streets off Plaza Mayor. *La Taberna*, on the square it- self, does good raciones (most under 1000 ptas) and tapas. *Bar Aben Razin*, nearby, is an atmospheric place for a drink.

Getting There & Away
Daily except Sunday and holidays, Auto- transportes Teruel buses leave from Teruel for Albarracín at 3.30 pm, and from Albar- racín for Teruel at 9 am.

EL RODENO
The back road leading south-east from Al- barracín towards Bezas passes near a series of Neolithic rock paintings known as the Conjunto de Arte Rupestre El Rodeno de Albarracín, among pretty, boulder-strewn and wooded countryside. There are 12 lots of paintings in all, in four or five groups, up to 1.4km off the road from turnings between 3.5 and 5km from the edge of Albarracín. The Albarracín tourist office has a small map showing the sites, and signs and ex- planatory plaques along the way point you to them. The clearest – showing bulls,

horses and deer – are those at Los Toricos del Navazo. No buses run this way, but if it's not too hot you can walk by part of the GR-10 long-distance path. This diverges left from the Bezas road on the south edge of Albarracín, about 100m south of a fork iden- tifiable by its GR-10 information panels.

ALBARRACÍN TO CASTILLA-LA MANCHA
For those with a vehicle, a couple of routes suggest themselves from Albarracín into Castilla-La Mancha. The A-1512 west from Albarracín reaches a fork after 7km. The way to the left leads across the varied and pretty Montes Universales and on across the Serranía de Cuenca towards Cuenca via the dramatic Río Júcar gorge.

The right fork takes you through the Sierra de Albarracín into Guadalajara province. You could follow several routes, but perhaps the most scenic is the one via Checa, Terzaga, Peralejos de las Truchas and the Hoz de Beteta (Beteta Gorge) to- wards the Alcarria area of Cuenca and Guadalajara provinces. See also the Castilla-La Mancha chapter.

EL MAESTRAZGO
The series of sparsely populated sierras stretching east of Teruel and into the Valen- cia region present a smorgasbord of bleak rocky peaks and dramatic gorges, among which the small pueblos seem to be left to their own devices. The area around Can- tavieja, Villarluengo and Castellote forms the Aragonese part of El Maestrazgo, a medieval knightly domain centred on Sant Mateu in Castellón province (see El Maes- trazgo in the Valencia chapter).

Unless you have a lot of time, you need a vehicle to explore El Maestrazgo. Buses serve most places but rarely more than once daily, and often not at all on week- ends. The following is a route drivers might take through El Maestrazgo from Teruel. There are year-round tourist offices in Can- tavieja (☎ 964 18 52 43) and Alcañiz (☎ 978 83 12 13).

A few kilometres out of Teruel, the A-226 forks off the northbound N-420. A 40km

ARAGÓN

drive through largely inhospitable country brings you to dishevelled little **Cedrillas**, with castle ruins and a mudéjar church.

Farther east along the A-226 the wind-swept heights give way to some spectacular scenery, especially as you wind down from the 1700m Puerto de Villaroya pass. It's 65km from Cedrillas to **Cantavieja**, reputedly founded by Hannibal. It became a seat of the Knights Templar and in the Carlist wars during the 19th century was heavily damaged. The best preserved (and partly restored) part of town is the porticoed Plaza del Ayuntamiento.

The cheaper of the two places to stay is *Pensión Julián (☎ 964 18 50 05, Calle García Valiño 6)*, with no-frills doubles for 3000 ptas, and home-cooked meals. If you're heading for Morella in the Valencian Maestrazgo – a destination well worth seeking out – the A-226 north-east from Cantavieja will take you there via the interesting medieval town of **Mirambel** (see El Maestrazgo in the Valencia chapter).

Thirteen kilometres south-east of Cantavieja, **La Iglesuela del Cid** is worth a quick visit to see its church and old ayuntamiento. *Casa Amada (☎ 964 44 33 73, Calle Fuente Nueva 10)* has singles/doubles for 3000/4100 ptas and a good restaurant.

Back west of Cantavieja, the A-1702 tacks north for an attractive drive past the precariously located **Villarluengo** and, a few kilometres farther on, the weird rock formations of the **Órganos de Montoro**, forming the valley walls of the Río Guada-

lope. *Hostal La Trucha (☎ 978 77 30 08* with a beautiful riverside location at La Fábricas, about 10km north of Villarluengo has singles/doubles for 7800/12,000 pta plus IVA.

Another 30km north you leave El Maestrazgo and hit the N-211, along which yo can head west to the Teruel-Zaragoza roa or north-east to **Alcañiz**, with an oversize castle (now a parador) which for centurie was the Aragonese base of the Knights c Calatrava. Of equally exaggerated dimer sions is the Iglesia de Santa María L Mayor, dwarfing Plaza de España with it huge baroque portal. Of a dozen or so ho tels and hostales, the fairly central *E Trillero (☎ 978 83 10 26, Plaza de Sant Domingo 1)* offers doubles for 3400 ptas.

Getting There & Away

One of the more useful bus services is the pm (weekdays) bus from Teruel to La Igle suela del Cid (three hours, 1040 ptas) vi Cedrillas and Cantavieja, by Altaba (☎ 96 44 10 42). The return bus leaves from L Iglesuela at 6 am. From Monday to Satur day, an early morning bus leaves from Can tavieja for La Iglesuela and Morella (th bus returns from Morella at 6 pm). O weekdays, there's also a bus from Can tavieja to Villarluengo and Alcorisa an vice-versa. At Alcorisa you can connect fo Alcañiz, which is served by buses to/from Teruel, Barcelona, Zaragoza, Morella an other places, although in most cases only once or twice daily.

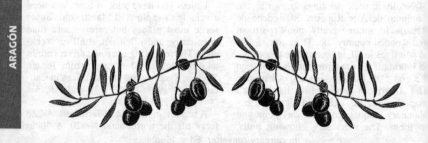

Camino de Santiago

CAMINO DE SANTIAGO

Pilgrims' Progress

Nowadays it's not only the faithful who walk the Camino de Santiago, the way of St James' pilgrim route (or, rather, routes) to Santiago de Compostela in Galicia. Many walk, cycle or even drive the Camino as a simple travel exercise.

Plenty, however, still do it in a religious context and have the option of staying overnight in *albergues* (pilgrims' refuges). In this case, you need to get a record booklet (available at albergues along the Camino) in which you collect date stamps as you go.

The refuges are free, with priority going to walkers and stays generally limited to one night. However it is customary to leave 300 to 500 ptas for maintenance. Some are closed in winter and most of them are rudimentary. Accommodation is in bunk beds in mixed-sex dorms. Some have no hot water or even shower curtains in the basic bathrooms.

The greatest distance between refuges is the 23km from Ponferrada to Villafranca del Bierzo in León province. Since the Camino is becoming increasingly popular with walkers, competition for a bed (let alone a room) can be quite tough. Walkers sometimes find themselves obliged to push on to the next refuge or seek out hotels (perhaps off the trail).

Those who complete at least 100km on foot or 200km on bicycle can, on arrival in Santiago, pick up the *compostela,* a document testifying that the bearer has completed at least part of the Camino as a pilgrim (rather than as a tourist).

There are plenty of guidebooks dedicated to the subject of the Camino de Santiago (see the Books section in the Facts for the Visitor chapter). Tourist offices along the Camino also hand out or sell maps, brochures, booklets, lists of refuges and other information pertinent to the pilgrim. Lonely Planet's *Walking in Spain* features a good section on the Camino.

The most useful and accurate map is *El Camino de Santiago* by Edilesa (Leon, 1999). It costs 400 ptas and is available en route. The various routes are marked with yellow arrows, blue metal signs with

Title page: A stone musician on the wall o the Santo Domingo de la Calzada cathedral, west of Logroño (Photographer: David Peevers)

CAMINO DE SANTIAGO

NANCY FREY

yellow conch shells or with metal or ceramic shells set into concrete. Bus timetables and other local information is posted at refuges.

Many of the Camino destinations mentioned below are covered in greater detail in their respective regional chapters: Basque Country, Navarra & La Rioja, Castilla y León and Galicia.

Routes to Santiago de Compostela

The **Camino Francés**, which is described in greater detail later, is what most people have in mind when talking of the Camino de Santiago. Historically, this was without a doubt the most well-travelled though certainly not the only route. Also popular was the **Camino del Norte**, which follows the Basque, Cantabrian and Asturian coasts before turning inland at Ribadeo (Galicia). The **Vía de la Plata** brought pilgrims north from southern Spain via Salamanca and Zamora along an old Roman trade route. The **Camino Portugués** crosses into Galicia at Tuy before continuing north,

while the **Camino Inglés** saw pilgrims landing at numerous ports in north-western Galicia – including O Parrote (near La Coruña), Ferrol and Neda – and then proceeding via Pontedeume and Betanzos to hook up with the Camino Francés at Sigüeiro.

DAVID PEEVERS

Above: Part of the Camino de Santiago in the Pyrenees before Roncesvalles (Navarra)

ght: A sign for pilgrims along the Camino de Santiago

The Camino Francés

The main road to Santiago de Compostela enters Spain just north of Roncesvalles in the Navarran

St James the Moor-Slayer

Queen Lupa was more than a little suspicious when two Palestinian refugees landed in her territory, near Padrón in northern Galicia, with the decomposing and headless body of a Christian martyr, and requested permission to bury him. The apostle Santiago (St James), son of Zebedee, is by tradition thought to have preached in Spain, turning up in Zaragoza at one point. Herod Agrippa had him executed on his return to Jerusalem and Santiago's followers whisked the body to Jaffa, from where they let Providence guide them on a miraculous sea voyage to Spain.

The good queen sent the pair on to the nearest Roman governor in Finisterre, who promptly incarcerated them. Before the Romans had a chance to kill Santiago's disciples, they were freed by an angel and returned to Queen Lupa. Impressed by this and other exploits, she eventually converted to Christianity. Santiago was buried and a small mausoleum was erected (its remains are now located beneath the main altar in the cathedral in Santiago de Compostela) to mark the spot. There he remained forgotten until the year 813, when a hermit named Paio (Pelayo) rediscovered the tomb with the help of a supernatural light showing him the way.

Things were tough for Spain's Christians in those days, with most of the country in Muslim hands. Santiago soon featured in many legends, miraculous tales and visions, his spirit appearing on battlefields and cheerfully cutting down Moors left and right. For this latter activity he became known as Santiago Matamoros (St James the Moor-Slayer).

Understandably, his figure became of prime symbolic importance in Spain and the word soon spread across Europe. By the 11th century, streams of pilgrims were descending on Santiago, mostly crossing the Pyrenees at Roncesvalles and walking 750km west via Pamplona, Logroño and León. A French priest, Amérique Picaud, wrote what might be considered the first guidebook to the Camino de Santiago. His *Liber Sancti Jacobi* (also known as the Codex of Calixtus), divides the route from the Pyrenees to Santiago into 13 stages.

In the 12th century, the Castilian and Aragonese monarchs upgraded the Camino (Pilgrim's Way). At the same time, a group of Castilian knights formed a new military order with a religious bent, the Orden de Santiago, which, apart from taking an active part in the Reconquista, also saw aiding and protecting pilgrims as part of its duty. The pilgrimage route also became an important commercial conduit across northern Spain, stimulating local trade.

The route's current revival as a tourist activity is just as important for the local economy today. There's no shortage of people on the Camino in the warmer months with the telltale staff and scallop shell, the latter originally being a practical device for sipping water from streams along the way.

Pyrenees, then travels west for 750km through the regions of Navarra, La Rioja, Castilla y León and Galicia. En route it passes countless hamlets as well as such major historical cities as Pamplona, Logroño, Burgos and León.

Pretty much all the albergues and information centres for pilgrims are along the Camino Francés, but signs and references to the Camino de Santiago proliferate over north-western Spain, making it a collective term for the various caminos.

The Camino Francés is intertwined with asphalted roads, meaning you can drive bits of the old route, and of course all the main towns are linked by road. The route is at its most rewarding, however, when it leaves the highway and becomes a minor back road or walkers' trail. Covering the entire route by public transport is difficult as not all destinations are served by bus or train. Even if they are, service is often sporadic and limited to weekdays.

Roncesvalles to Viana (Map 1)

The principal Camino route enters Spain at the pass through the Pyrenees just north of Roncesvalles. It then makes its way through rural and partly forested landscapes to **Pamplona** before proceeding south-west to **Puente la Reina** on the Río Arga. A beautiful bridge – the pilgrims' bridge – spans the river at this point, where a secondary camino from Aragón joins the main route. Of major interest further west are **Estella** (Lizarra) and, just beyond, the Monasterio de Irache. Other stops worth a look include **Torres del Río** and **Viana**, where the Camino leaves Navarra to enter La Rioja at the Hermitage of Las Cuevas.

MAP 1   NAVARRA & LA RIOJA

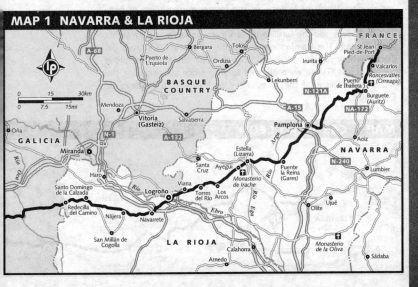

Logroño to Santo Domingo de la Calzada (Map 1)

In La Rioja, the Camino passes through countryside characterised by orchards, farmlands and vineyards. Its capital is **Logroño**, historically an important stopover, although smaller towns a bit further west are actually richer in architectural treasure. Worthwhile sites include **Nájera**, but even more so the Monasteries of Yuso and Suso in **San Millán de Cogolla** and the cathedral in **Santo Domingo de la Calzada**.

Redecilla del Camino to Villafranca del Bierzo (Map 2)

The Camino enters Castilla y León 54km east of Burgos at the tiny settlement of Redecilla del Camino. About half of the Camino Francés (374km) travels through the Castilian plain, cutting across the provinces of Burgos, Palencia and León. The landscape is fairly easy to navigate but also rather monotonous with plains of cereal crops only occasionally interrupted by low rises and winding streams. It is well protected from the capriciousness of Atlantic weather by the Cordillera Cantábrica, although the long, dark winters can be uncomfortably cold.

Apart from the provincial capitals of Burgos, Palencia and León, the route is littered with numerous other interesting waystations. In **Frómista** (Palencia), the Romanesque Iglesia de San Martín has long been a pilgrim's must-see, and the churches of San Tirso and San Lorenzo in **Sahagún** (León) are two more gems.

The cathedral and Palacio de Gaudí in **Astorga** (León) mark a unique juxtaposition of the very best of classic religious architecture and modern flights of fantasy. At the former mining town of **Ponferrada** (León), the castle of the Knights Templar as well as the Iglesia de San Andrés and the Basilica de la Virgen de la Encina are sights worth seeing. The Camino leaves Castilla y León at Villafranca del Bierzo, where pilgrims too weak to cope with the more strenuous stretch across Galicia were allowed to stop while still receiving the same absolution as if they'd travelled all the way to Santiago de Compostela.

MAP 2 CASTILLA Y LEÓN

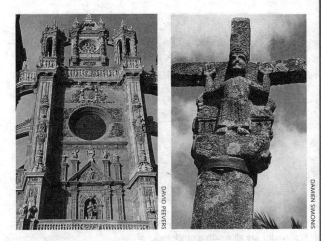

DAVID PEEVERS

DAMIEN SIMONIS

O Cebreiro to Santiago de Compostela (Map 3)

Those pilgrims with true grit – the ones who didn't give up at Villa-franca del Bierzo – face the formidable task of climbing to the mountain pass of Pedrafita do Cebreiro (1109m), the main gateway to Galicia in the Cordillera Cantábrica mountain chain.

From here it is another 5km to **O Cebreiro**, a tiny, wind-battered settlement of stone houses high above a patchwork of green valleys. In amongst the huddle of houses and a couple of *pallozas* (traditional circular, thatch-roofed houses) remains an 11th-century church. Many walkers actually begin here, as the Galician stretch is, overall, the most beautiful and intriguing.

About 10km on, the Camino crosses its highest point in Galicia, the Alto do Poio (1335m). From here it's downhill for 14km to sleepy **Triacastela**, near the Río Oribio. At this point the route forks. The main road dips south via Samos on the way to Sarriá, 23km west, while the original Camino travels along narrow, wooded paths to the north, past small farming hamlets and the odd wayside chapel, meeting the highway at Sarriá. The latter route is slightly shorter and easier.

If you follow the main road, a stop at **Samos** with its imposing Benedictine monastery is a must. The original 6th-century complex was replaced in the 12th century by another, which in turn was destroyed by fire and rebuilt in the Gothic style in the 16th century. Fire struck again in 1951, killing one person and devastating anything not made of stone; only the 18th-century church remained unharmed. The place was rebuilt one more time, and the exquisite cloister gardens must be among the most lovingly maintained in all Iberian Christendom (closed Sunday afternoon and Monday; 300 ptas).

Twelve kilometres on is **Sarriá**, a town grown too big to be charming, although the older hilltop area is vaguely interesting. The castle,

Above left: The plateresque main facade of Astorga's cathedral dates back to 1471.

Above right: This *cruceiro* at Melide, dating back to the 14th century, is the oldest in Galicia.

OLIVER STREWE

the Convento de La Magdalena and the churches of Santa Mariña and El Salvador are all worth a quick look.

Better than Sarriá as an overnight stop is **Portomarín**, in spite of the fact that the original village was flooded by the damming of the Río Miño in 1963. The 13th-century Iglesia de San Nicolás, with an impressive rose window, was transferred to the new town where it joined other salvaged buildings on the central square.

There's little to detain you at **Palas de Rei**, the next town on the Camino, so push on for another 15km to **Melide**, home to the oldest *cruceiro* (14th century) in Galicia. This stands outside the unassuming Gothic Iglesia de San Pedro on the main road before you reach the centre. As you exit Melide, you'll pass the Iglesia de Santa María, a fine example of the Romanesque.

If you have the time and inclination, detour north from Melide. The Cistercian monastery of **Sobrado de los Monjes** (Sobrado dos Monxes), which forms the hub of an otherwise humdrum hamlet, came close to falling into irrecoverable disrepair in the years following its expropriation in 1834. In 1954, however, a small band of Cistercians

Above: In Santiago de Compostela (Galicia), tr the flat, dense *tarta de Santiago*, or St James cake, decorated with an icing-sugared outline of a sword and baked by local nuns.

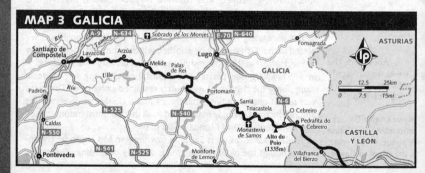

MAP 3 GALICIA

Where to Stay Along the Camino de Santiago

Aside from the various albergues, most towns and villages along the Camino offer accommodation, from rustic *casas rurales* to luxurious *paradors*. A few options are listed below. For details on places to stay in the larger cities – including Pamplona, Logroño, León, Burgos, Astorga, Ponferrada, Palencia and Santiago de Compostela – refer to the regional chapters.

Puente la Reina
Hotel Rural Bidean (☎ 948 34 04 57, Calle Mayor 20) has gorgeous singles/doubles stuffed with antiques for 4000/7000 ptas with private bath; breakfast is included. Rooms 34 and 35 have skylights with views of the tower of Iglesia de Santiago.

Estella
Camping Lizarra (☎ 948 55 17 33) lies on the river at the edge of town and is open year round. *Fonda Izarra* (☎ 948 55 06 78, Calle de la Calderería 20) has basic doubles for 4000 ptas. *Pensión San Andrés* (☎ 948 55 41 58, Plaza de Santiago 58) has plain rooms with washbasin for 1800/3500 ptas and others with bath for 3500/5000 ptas. *Hostal Cristina* (☎ 948 55 04 50, Calle de Baja Navarra 1), near the main square, charges 4500/7000 ptas for rooms with bath.

Santo Domingo de la Calzada
Hospedería Cisterciense (☎ 941 34 07 00, Calle Echegoyen 2) has comfortable rooms with private bath for 3150/5660 ptas. The imposing *Parador* (☎ 941 34 03 00, fax 941 34 03 25) occupies the former hospice built by Santo Domingo himself; even St Francis of Assisi is said to have stopped over once. The stunning lobby features Gothic arches and coffered ceilings and exudes a distinctly palatial feel. Rooms, luxuriously appointed and sporting warm colour schemes, cost 14,000/17,500 ptas (less in low season).

Frómista
Pensión Marisa (☎ 979 81 00 23, Plaza de Obispo Almaraz 2) offers good clean rooms for 2200/3300 ptas and also provides meals.

Sahagún
The central *Hospedería Benedictina* (☎ 987 78 00 78, Avenida Doctores Bermejo y Calderón 8) has nice rooms with shower and toilet for 3000/5800 ptas.

O Cebreiro
Hospedería O Cebreiro (☎ 982 36 71 25) next to the church has comfortable rooms for 3300/4300 ptas; there's also a great restaurant. Failing that, *Mesón Antón* (☎ 982 15 13 36) has a couple of nice rooms for the same price.

Portomarín
Mesón de Rodríguez (☎ 982 54 50 54) has a decent restaurant and rooms for 3000/4000 ptas.

returned and much has been restored. The church's ornate Galician baroque facade contrasts with its rather austere interior. The bare Claustro de los Peregrinos, the first cloister you enter in the complex, was completely rebuilt in 1972. The Claustro de los Medallones, erected in the mid-18th century to replace its 12th-century Romanesque forerunner, takes its name from the 'medallions' (containing busts) that line the porticoes. Off this, the kitchen contains a huge 13th-century chimney flue. Possibly the most incongruous elements inside the church are the much-neglected choir stalls, jammed in here when it was decided not to lodge them in the Santiago cathedral, as originally intended. The monastery complex is open daily (200 ptas).

Back on the Camino, you'll pass through **Lavacolla**, where pilgrims used to wash in the river before cresting the last hill before Santiago, **Monte do Gozo** (or Monxoi). The first to reach the top and to spot the distant spires of the Catedral de Santiago was proclaimed 'king' of the group. After enjoying this satisfaction, only a few kilometres separate weary walkers from that final personal victory of completing the pilgrimage to Santiago de Compostela.

DUSHAN COORAY

Left: The lavish baroque facade of the Catedral del Apóstol, Santiago de Compostela (Galicia)

Basque Country, Navarra & La Rioja

The territories of the Basque people, which take in the three provinces of the Basque Country (País Vasco in Spanish) and Navarra, as well as the abutting parts of south-western France, together form a remarkable historical anomaly. Descended from a people who, according to some theories, predate even the earliest Indo-European invasions of Europe in prehistoric times, the Basques have retained a language whose origins still puzzle linguists and a sense of separateness that has been the bane of everyone from the Muslims through Charlemagne to Franco.

A mountainous, green interior, often shrouded in Atlantic mists, presents a soothing, beautiful counterpoint to the rugged coast and its cosmopolitan centres. People are drawn here for myriad reasons: the sophisticated seaside life of San Sebastián, the surfing, Bilbao's striking Museo Guggenheim, the (in)famous festivities at the running of the bulls in Pamplona, and the lush countryside. The area's proximity to France is also an attraction.

Created as a separate region in 1978, La Rioja is for most people synonymous with wine. The vineyards of the Ebro valley form a kind of buffer zone between Basque territories and the broad expanse of Castilla to the south.

Across the Basque Country and, to a lesser extent, in Navarra, the Basque names for towns are gaining the upper hand over Castilian versions, which in many cases only pose minor variations in spelling anyway. In this guide, Basque has been favoured in all cases except for the provincial capitals, which are still better known by their Castilian names.

Highlights

- San Sebastián, Spain's culinary capital and home to some of the region's liveliest tapas bars (tied with Bilbao)
- El Bosque Pintado de Oma, for its original approach to art and for challenging one's perception of reality
- Exploring Bilbao's spectacular Museo Guggenheim
- La Rioja, source of some of the world's finest wines
- Pamplona, for keeping alive the spirit of Hemingway and staging the world's best-known *encierro* (running of the bulls)
- Driving around and getting lost in the lush alpine countryside of the Navarran Pyrenees

Basque Country

The Basque Country is made up of three provinces: Guipúzcoa (Gipuzkoa in the Basque language), Álava (Araba) and Vizcaya (Bizkaia, and hence Biscay in English) which together form the Comunidad Autónoma Vasca (CAV). In the Basque language (called *euskara*), the Basque Country is known as Euskadi, a term coined by nationalists at the end of the 19th century, though some prefer the classic term

BASQUE COUNTRY, NAVARRA & LA RIOJA

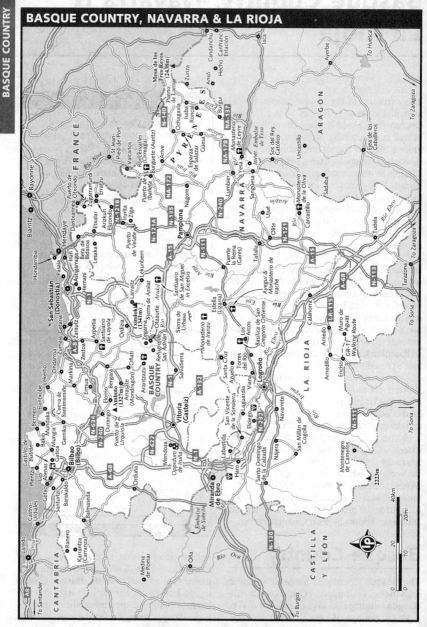

Euskal Herri (or Euskal Herria – the final 'a' means 'the').

History

Throughout much of the Middle Ages rival warlords fought constantly for control over Basque territory, and the expanding Castilian crown only gained sovereignty with some difficulty. Neighbouring Navarra in fact constituted a separate kingdom until 1512.

Still, Navarra and the three provinces were able to extract broad autonomy arrangements, known as the *fueros,* from Madrid. These were first repealed by Napoleon in the early 19th century. The modern idea of a centralised state was anathema to more conservative Basques, who tended to support the reactionary Don Carlos during the Carlist wars (see The 19th Century under History in the Facts about Spain chapter). The colour red was associated with the Carlists, and has since come to symbolise Basque assertions of separateness.

At the close of the Second Carlist War in 1876 all provinces but Navarra were stripped of their coveted fueros, although a measure of economic autonomy remained. This of course alienated the many Basques who had sided with liberal Madrid, and by the end of the century their resentment had taken shape in the form of nascent Basque nationalism. The Basque Nationalist Party (PNV) was formed in 1894, but support was never uniform, as Navarra and the province of Álava had a considerable Castilian contingent.

When the Republican government in Madrid proposed the possibility of home rule to the Basques, the regions of Navarra and Álava both declined the offer. Navarra in particular, with the bulk of its fuero rights intact, had little to gain. The remaining provinces liked the idea, and when the Spanish Civil War erupted in 1936, they sided with the Republicans. Conservative rural Navarra and Álava supported Franco, so of course it was Vizcaya and Guipúzcoa that paid the heaviest price for backing the wrong horse. In fact, Navarra managed to retain its fuero rights in spite of Franco's penchant for ultra-centralised government.

ETA In 1961 a small group of Basque separatists known as Euskadi Ta Askatasuna (ETA; the name stands for Basque Homeland and Freedom) carried out its first terrorist attack. Their goal: to carve an independent Basque state out of Basque territories in northern Spain and southern France. Thus began a cycle of violence and repression that has continued to this day, despite Franco's death and the granting of wide-ranging autonomy in the early 1980s and 1990s. Its political wing, Herri Batasuna (HB), constitutes a small but vocal parliamentary force. In certain municipalities it holds the balance of power.

A lull in the early 1990s and an ETA cease-fire in 1998 have changed little. On 3 December 1999 the group ended the cease-fire and began killing again. From January 2000 until the time this book went to press, ETA had assassinated 19 victims and attempted several other attacks in their most furious campaign in years. The main, but by no means only, targets have been Basque Partido Popular politicians and members of the Guardia Civil.

As the killing and related street violence in many Basque towns continue, reactions become more hardline. The PP run central government and most opposition parties have ruled out dialogue with HB as long as it refuses to condemn the violence. The PNV, which has ruled the Basque Country in coalition with other nationalist groupings since autonomy was granted, has found itself increasingly isolated and vacillating. In September HB withdrew its parliamentary support, leaving the PNV in minority control. At the same time, Spanish and French police operations led to the arrest of Iñaki de Rentería, believed to be the terrorist group's operational boss, and around 30 other ETA suspects. The police successes have not stopped the killing however.

When this book was sent to print, pressure was growing on the PNV to call early elections in the wake of no-confidence motions brought by the PP and Basque socialists. Some skeptics believe the PP is attempting to turn the tense situation to its electoral advantage. None of the events since the cease-fire was broken augur well for the future.

Language

In the modern autonomous region of the Basque Country the *ikurriña* (Basque flag) flies everywhere, and pride in Basque identity has thankfully not only expressed itself in violence, but also in language. Suppressed by Franco, the idiom is being studied by a growing number of young Basques, although it's rarely used in everyday discourse.

You may in fact never hear a word of Basque spoken throughout your stay in the Basque Country, though there are Basque radio and TV stations. In Guipúzcoa province especially, the zeal to promote it is leading to the elimination of Spanish in one of its most useful forms – signs. Street signs usually show both the Castilian and the Basque names, but the Castilian has often been spray-painted over! This can cause some confusion, especially if you're driving.

Bear in mind that many Castilian words are also written slightly differently in the Basque Country. *Tx* often replaces *ch, b* replaces *v,* and *k* takes over from the hard Castilian *c.* The letter *g* is always pronounced hard in Basque. For more information on the Basque language, turn to the Language chapter at the back of the book.

Signs in Basque

Basque words which commonly appear on signs include:

Basque	English & Spanish
ERDIALDEA	city centre
ERDIA	centre
JATETXEA	restaurant
KALEA	street *(calle)*
KALE NAGUSIA	main street *(calle mayor)*
KOMUNA/K	toilet/s
KONTUZ!	caution/beware!
NEKAZAL TURISMOA	*casa rural*
ONGI ETORRI	welcome
TURISMO BULEGOA	tourist office

Food

Basque cuisine is generally regarded as Spain's finest. Catalans might dispute that, but if you can wangle your way into one of the private Basque gastronomic societies (traditionally all-male affairs) you'll certainly be in food heaven. They emerged mainly in San Sebastián, formed by groups of chefs cooking for each other and friends.

San Sebastián is home to Spain's greatest tapas (often known as *pintxos* in the Basque Country) – just entering some bars is enough to get you salivating. Apart from beer and cider, the traditional plonk of the region is a slightly tart, young white wine called *txacoli.*

The classics of Basque cooking are simple enough, and seafood is the staple ingredient. Famous dishes include *bacalao al pil pil* (salt cod cooked with garlic and chillies), *merluza a la vasca* (hake in green sauce), *chipirones en su tinta* (cuttlefish in their own ink) and *chuletas de buey* (enormous beef chops). What has really brought the area's restaurants to grandeur is the flood of nouvelle cuisine influences that have taken hold in San Sebastián especially. Led by such chefs as Juan Mari Arzak, the Basque country's more imaginative cooks have, since the 1970s, made a name for themselves in Spain and abroad with what is commonly called the *nueva cocina vasca,* a tasty genre in constant evolution.

Sport

The Basques indulge in a rather odd assortment of sports, ranging from grass-cutting and log-chopping through to caber-tossing and tug-of-war. The most famous is *pelota vasca* (or *jai-alai* in Basque), a form of handball played on a walled court known as a *frontón.* There is also a version involving the use of a *txistera,* a kind of hand-held basket which allows the ball to be slung with disconcerting velocity at the wall. You can often see local teams whacking away at the town frontón.

The traditional game is played with the bare hand, but there are up to 20 variants of the sport, now played in one form or other all over the world. Fourteen variants are accepted at world championship level. The

MARTIN HARRIS

The Basque Country is home to the energetic game of *pelota vasca*, or *jai-alai*.

resort surrounded by the low green hills of Guipúzcoa (Gipuzkoa in Basque), the province of which it is the capital, San Sebastián (Donostia) is a mere stone's throw from France.

Although at first you could be forgiven for drawing comparisons with its French Basque cousin, Biarritz, the two could not be further apart in atmosphere. Where the latter has a rather reserved quality, San Sebastián's Parte Vieja (old town) boasts possibly the greatest concentration of bars per square metre in Spain.

Although in many people's minds Bilbao has a bad reputation for street confrontations between the police and ETA sympathisers, San Sebastián is, if anything, worse. Bands of young members hurling bottles and rocks at the local autonomous police (the Ertzaintza) are not an uncommon sight – although not common enough to put you off a visit.

bare-handed version, *esku huska,* is played in several different ways, with court and ball sizes, and rules, varying. The txistera version is the newest, and the French Basques have a variant involving use of a smaller catch-hurl scoop called a *joko garbi.* The five-a-side game *rebot* is supposedly the hardest in which to score properly. Some export versions are odder still, such as *xari,* an Argentine derivation in which a string racquet is employed.

Cycling is wildly popular and drivers in the region should pay heed to entire squadrons of cyclists on the roads.

Emergency
The general telephone number for all emergency situations (police, ambulance, fire) in the Basque Country is ☎ 088. There are also local numbers, some of which are noted in this chapter.

SAN SEBASTIÁN
postcode 20080 • pop 182,000
Forming a half-moon around the beautiful bay of La Concha, San Sebastián is the most Basque of Basque cities and at the same time a captivating crossroads. A seaside

History
Long little more than a fishing village privileged by its position on a protected bay at the mouth of the Río Urumea, San Sebastián was later the Kingdom of Navarra's principal outlet to the sea. By the 16th century, it had become a prosperous trade centre specialising first in the export of Castilian wool and other products to France, the Low Countries and England, and later benefiting from burgeoning commerce with the Americas. Disaster came with the Peninsular War, during which Anglo-Portuguese forces virtually razed the city in 1813 after wresting it from French hands. The city you see today is, not surprisingly, largely a product of the years following the withdrawal of Napoleon's troops from Spain.

Orientation
The heart of San Sebastián beats in the Parte Vieja, squeezed below Monte Urgull on the eastern spur of the Bahía de la Concha. Bars, restaurants and many of the cheaper *hostales* (budget hotels) are bunched up in this narrow grid of car-free lanes, with more hotels scattered in the Centro district to the immediate south. Just across the Río Urumea, in

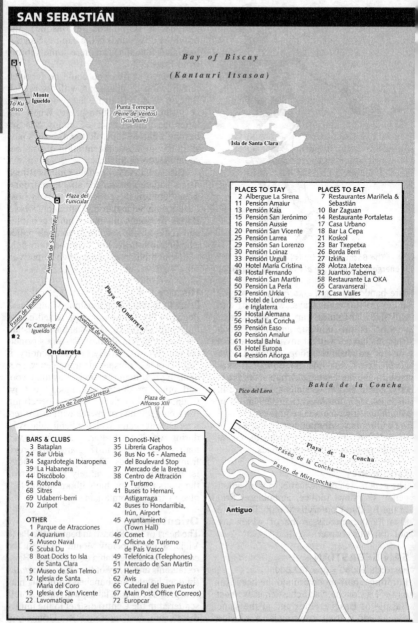

SAN SEBASTIÁN

Bay of Biscay

(Kantauri Itsasoa)

Monte
Igueldo

To Ku
disco

Punta Torrepea
(Peine de Ventos)
(Sculpture)

Isla de Santa Clara

Plaza del
Funicular

Avenida de Satrústegui

Paseo de Igueldo

To Camping
Igueldo

Avenida de Satrústegui

Playa de Ondarreta

Ondarreta

Avenida de Zumalacárregui

Plaza de
Alfonso XIII

Pico del Loro

Bahía de la Concha

Paseo de la Concha

Playa de la Concha

Paseo de Miraconcha

Antiguo

PLACES TO STAY
2 Albergue La Sirena
11 Pensión Amaiur
13 Pensión Kaia
15 Pensión San Jerónimo
16 Pensión Aussie
20 Pensión San Vicente
25 Pensión Larrea
29 Pensión San Lorenzo
30 Pensión Loinaz
33 Pensión Urgull
40 Hotel María Cristina
43 Hostal Fernando
48 Pensión San Martín
50 Pensión La Perla
52 Pensión Urkia
53 Hotel de Londres
   e Inglaterra
55 Hostal Alemana
56 Hostal La Concha
59 Pensión Easo
60 Pensión Amalur
61 Hostal Bahía
63 Hotel Europa
64 Pensión Añorga

PLACES TO EAT
7 Restaurantes Mariñela &
   Sebastián
10 Bar Zaguan
14 Restaurante Portaletas
17 Casa Urbano
18 Bar La Cepa
21 Koskol
23 Bar Txepetxa
26 Borda Berri
27 Izkiña
28 Alotza Jatetxea
32 Juantxo Taberna
58 Restaurante La OKA
65 Caravanserai
71 Casa Valles

BARS & CLUBS
3 Bataplan
24 Bar Urbia
34 Sagardotegia Itxaropena
39 La Habanera
44 Discóbolo
54 Rotonda
68 Sitres
69 Udaberri-berri
70 Zuripot

OTHER
1 Parque de Atracciones
4 Aquarium
5 Museo Naval
6 Scuba Du
8 Boat Docks to Isla
   de Santa Clara
9 Museo de San Telmo
12 Iglesia de Santa
   María del Coro
19 Iglesia de San Vicente
22 Lavomatique

31 Donosti-Net
35 Librería Graphos
36 Bus No 16 - Alameda
   del Boulevard Stop
37 Mercado de la Bretxa
38 Centro de Attración
   y Turismo
41 Buses to Hernani,
   Astigarraga
42 Buses to Hondarribia,
   Irún, Airport
45 Ayuntamiento
   (Town Hall)
46 Comet
47 Oficina de Turismo
   de País Vasco
49 Telefónica (Telephones)
51 Mercado de San Martín
57 Hertz
62 Avis
66 Catedral del Buen Pastor
67 Main Post Office (Correos)
72 Europcar

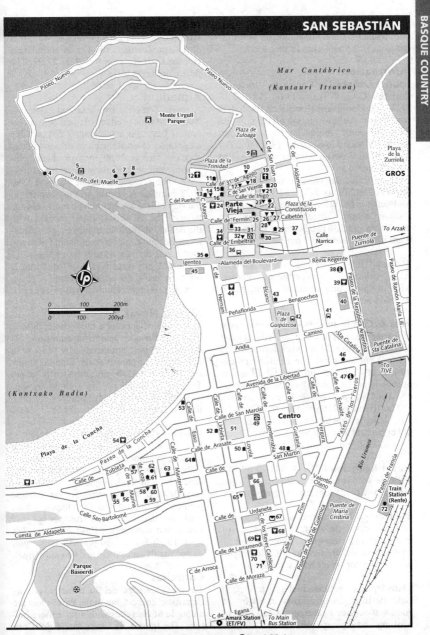

SAN SEBASTIÁN

Mar Cantábrico
(Kantauri Itsasoa)

Paseo Nuevo

Paseo Nuevo

Playa
de la
Zurriola

GROS

Monte Urgull
Parque

Plaza de
Zuloaga

Plaza de la
Trinidad

Paseo del Muelle

C del Puerto

Parte
Vieja

Plaza de la
Constitución
Calbetón

Calle Narrica

To Arzak

Puente de
Zurriola

Reina Regente

Alameda del Boulevard

Paseo de la República Argentina

Paseo de Ramón María Lili

Puente de
Sta Catalina

To
TIVE

Plaza
de
Guipúzcoa

Bengoechea

Peñaflorida

Sta Catalina

Camino

Andia

(Kontxako Badia)

Avenida de la Libertad

Centro

Río Urumea

Paseo de los Fueros

Paseo de Francia

Calle de San Marcial

Playa de la Concha

Paseo de la Concha

Calle de Arasate

San Martín

Valentín
Olano

Train
Station
(Renfe)

Calle San Bartolomé

Cuesta de Aldapeta

Urdaneta

Puente de
María
Cristina

Puente de Árbol de Guernica

Parque
Basoerdi

Calle de Larramendi

C de Arroca

Calle de Moraza

Cuesta de Egaña

Amara Station
(ET/FV)

To Main
Bus Station

0   100   200m
0   100   200yd

the district of Gros, is the Renfe train station, while the main bus station (estación de autobuses) is about 1km farther south.

Information

Tourist Offices The Centro de Attración y Turismo (CAT; ☎ 943 48 11 66, fax 943 48 11 72), at Boulevard Reina Regente 8, has comprehensive information on the city and the province of Guipúzcoa. It's open 8 am to 8 pm Monday to Saturday (9 am to 2 pm and 3.30 to 7 pm in winter) and 10 am to 1 pm Sunday.

The Oficina de Turismo de País Vasco (☎ 943 02 31 50, fax 943 02 31 51), Paseo de los Fueros 1, has information about the entire Basque Country. Office hours are from 9 am to 1.30 pm and 3.30 to 6.30 pm weekdays and 9 am to 1 pm and 3 to 7 pm weekends.

Money There are plenty of banks with ATMs scattered all over the city centre, with a particular concentration along Avenida de la Libertad.

Post & Communications The main post office (correos) is at Calle de Urdaneta and open 8.30 am to 8.30 pm weekdays and 9.30 am to 2 pm Saturday. The Telefónica locutorio is at Calle de San Marcial 29 and is open 9.30 am to 2 pm (10 am to 2 pm weekends) and 4 to 8.30 pm (to 8 pm weekends).

The friendly Donosti-Net (☎ 943 42 58 70), Calle de Embeltrán 2, is the most central cybercafe and charges 250/350/550 ptas for 15/30/60 minutes of access.

Travel Agencies TIVE (☎ 943 27 69 34), Calle de Tomás Gros 3 in the Gros district, can help with student travel arrangements.

Bookshops Newsstands on Avenida de la Libertad stock the current day's issue of many foreign newspapers. Librería Graphos, on Alameda del Boulevard at Calle Mayor, is excellent for travel books and maps.

Laundry Lavomatique, in the Parte Vieja at Calle de Iñigo 14, is a rarity in Spain – a good self-service laundrette. A full load of washing and drying costs about 1000 ptas.

Medical Services & Emergency The Hospital de Gipuzkoa (☎ 943 45 40 00) is at Alto de Zorroaga s/n. For an ambulance, call the Cruz Roja on ☎ 943 27 22 22. The police are on ☎ 091.

Aquarium

A recent complete overhaul and expansion has turned what used to be a mediocre aquarium at best into a fascinating display. Ten large tanks re-create habitats of hundreds of species of tropical fish, morays, sharks, poisonous varieties and many other finned creatures. The original museum building from 1928 introduces visitors to the denizens of the Bay of Biscay, including conger eels and triggerfish. All this is supplemented with themed exhibits on naval history, pirates, famous Basque explorers and fishing gear and methods. Feedings usually take place at 11 am and 4 pm weekdays. The aquarium is open 10 am to 10 pm daily (until 8 pm in winter; 1100 ptas, children half-price).

Museo Naval

Visit this museum for a more in-depth look into the Basque seafaring tradition, although it is best appreciated by those with at least basic Spanish skills. Summer hours are 10 am to 1.30 pm and 5 to 8.30 pm Tuesday to Saturday (4 to 7.30 pm in winter), and 11 am to 2 pm Sunday (200 ptas, free on Thursday).

Museo de San Telmo

Housed in a former monastery with a nice cloister, this moderately interesting museum features paintings ranging from the Renaissance through the baroque to the 19th century, with a heavy emphasis on Basque painters. A highlight is the chapel, whose walls are decorated with frescoes by José María Sert chronicling Basque history. It's open 10.30 am to 1.30 pm and 4 to 8 pm, closed Sunday afternoon and Monday (free).

Churches

The city's **Catedral del Buen Pastor** is of little artistic interest, but in the Parte Vieja are a couple of churches with a little more history. The **Iglesia de Santa María del Coro** stands out for its churrigueresque facade, while the 16th-century **Iglesia de San Vicente** is the city's oldest standing house of worship.

Monte Urgull
You can walk to the top of Monte Urgull, topped by low castle walls and a grand statue of Christ, by taking a path from Plaza de Zuloaga. The views across the Bahía de la Concha and the city are wonderful.

Monte Igueldo
The views from the summit of Monte Igueldo are better still. You can save your legs by catching the funicular to the **Parque de Atracciones** (amusement park). Drivers must pay 160 ptas per person for parking. At the foot of the hill, at Punta Torrepea right in the bay, is Eduardo Chillida's intriguing abstract iron sculpture *Peine de Vientos* (Wind Combs).

Beaches & Isla de Santa Clara
The placid Playa de la Concha and its westerly extension, the Playa de Ondarreta, are among the best city beaches in Spain, although both get rather crowded. To get away from the masses, you can swim out to platforms anchored in the bay or, if you're really fit, all the way to the Isla de Santa Clara. Landlubbers can hop aboard the boats that run to the island every half-hour from June to September (350 ptas). The Playa de la Zurriola (also known as Playa de Gros), east of the Río Urumea, is less crowded and popular with both swimmers and surfers.

Diving
The Scuba Du dive shop (☎ 943 42 24 26), Paseo del Muelle 23, runs diving courses (CMAS and PADI) and hires out gear.

Organised Tours
Donosti Tour is a bus tour that allows you to hop on and off at any of the 27 stops as often as you wish over one day. Tickets, which include headphones for commentary in your choice of language, are sold on the bus and cost 1200 ptas. In season, buses run hourly from 10 am to 9 pm, but service is severely curtailed in winter. For further information, contact the CAT office.

Special Events
Among San Sebastián's top drawing cards are the International Jazz Festival in July and the two-week Festival de Cine (film festival), held annually in the second half of September since 1957. Other major fiestas are the Festividad de San Sebastián on January 20, and *carnaval* in mid-February.

Places to Stay
As in much of northern Spain, July and August can be trying months for searching out accommodation in San Sebastián. Arrive early or call ahead and be aware that summer prices often rise sharply. Prices given here are for high season; lower rates apply the rest of the year.

Places to Stay – Budget
Camping & Hostels The nearest camping ground, *Camping Igueldo* (☎ 943 21 45 02), is open year round but is a rather long way west of the city out beyond Monte Igueldo. It is served by bus No 16 with several stops in the city centre, including Alameda del Boulevard and the cathedral (115 ptas).

Albergue La Sirena (☎ 943 31 02 68, fax 943 21 40 90, e udala-youthhostel@ donostia.org, Paseo de Igueldo 25) is San Sebastián's HI (Hostelling International) hostel. Bunk beds and breakfast cost 2000/ 2255 ptas for juniors/seniors (less from mid-October to May). The midnight curfew is extended to 2 am weekends.

Pensiones & Hostales The old quarter is almost as replete with *pensiones* as it is with bars – which is great for stumbling home, but can be disturbing if you want to sleep. Unless noted, rooms in this category come with shared facilities.

Parte Vieja Pensión Aussie (☎ 943 42 28 74, Calle San Jerónimo 23), indeed run by an Australian expatriate, works pretty much like a hostel. Beds in two- to four-bed rooms, some quite nicely decorated, are 2000 ptas. It's popular with backpackers, as is *Pensión San Vicente* (☎ 943 42 29 77, Calle de San Vicente 7), which charges 3000/5000 ptas for its rather bare-bones single/double rooms. *Pensión San Jerónimo* (☎ 943 28 64 34, *Calle San Jerónimo 25)* has doubles only for 5000 ptas.

Consider yourself lucky to score a room at *Pensión San Lorenzo* (☎ 943 42 55 16, *Calle de San Lorenzo 2)*. Completely redecorated rooms with attached new bathrooms have more than a touch of style and cost just 3500 ptas per double. Other assets include metered Internet access and kitchen use (low season only).

Another good bet is *Pensión Loinaz* (☎ 943 42 67 14, *Calle de San Lorenzo 17)*, which has friendly, English-speaking proprietors, updated bathrooms and rooms for 4000/5500 ptas.

Pensión Larrea (☎ 943 42 26 94, *Calle de Narrika 21)* has been recommended by travellers. It is simple but pleasant and has rooms for 2500/5000 ptas. *Pensión Urgull* (☎ 943 43 00 47, *Calle de Esterlines 10)* is quiet and amiable and has comfortable rooms with washbasin for 3000/5000 ptas.

Pensión Amaiur (☎ 943 42 96 54, *Calle de 31 de Agosto 44)* is as pretty as a picture and has doubles for 6000 ptas, although you may be able to bargain them down a little.

Centro The *Pensión La Perla* (☎ 943 42 81 23, *Calle de Loyola 10)* has excellent rooms with shower and toilet, with some overlooking the cathedral, for 3500/5500 ptas. Keeping it in the family, *Pensión Urkia* (☎ 943 42 44 36, *Calle de Urbieta 12)* is run by the sister of La Perla's proprietor, is just as good and charges the same prices.

Pensión Añorga (☎ 943 46 79 45, *Calle de Easo 12)* comes recommended for its motherly owner and good-sized rooms costing 4000/5000 ptas, or 6500 ptas with bath. *Hostal Fernando* (☎ 943 42 55 75, *Plaza de Guipúzcoa 2)* is not a bad spot on one of the city's more attractive squares. Simple but clean rooms with washbasin, however, are a bit overpriced at 4500/6200 ptas.

Pensión Amalur (☎ 943 46 08 61, *Calle de San Martín 43)* offers functional double rooms with shower for 5000 ptas and also has a few with full bath for 7000 ptas.

Places to Stay – Mid-Range

Rooms in this category all have private facilities. If Calle de San Martín were a bough, it would be bending under the weight of its hotels. Towards the eastern end, *Pensión San Martín* (☎ 943 42 87 14, *Calle de San Martín 10)* has squeaky-clean doubles for 7800 ptas. *Hostal La Concha* (☎ 943 45 03 89, *Calle de San Martín 51)* rents out nicely decorated doubles for 7000 ptas.

A step up is *Hostal Alemana* (☎ 943 46 25 44, fax 943 46 17 71, *Calle de San Martín 53)*, a friendly place with well-equipped singles/doubles costing 9000/11,000 ptas. You can get drinks and snacks in the salon. If it's full, you might also consider *Hostal Bahía* (☎ 943 46 92 11, *Calle de San Martín 54)*. It's not quite as good value as Alemana, but has comfortable rooms for 9900/11,500 ptas.

In the same neighbourhood is *Pensión Easo* (☎ 943 45 39 12, *Calle San Bartolomé 24)*, a worthwhile contender with a range of pleasantly furnished rooms, the nicer of which cost 7200/9000 ptas. Back in the Parte Vieja, *Pensión Kaia* (☎ 943 43 13 42, *Calle del Puerto 12)* has good rooms for 8560 ptas.

Places to Stay – Top End

Hotel Europa (☎ 943 47 08 80, fax 943 47 17 30, *Calle de San Martín 52)* is a relative bargain, with singles/doubles sporting all the trimmings for 13,500/23,400 ptas – and that also includes breakfast. Enter from Calle Triunfo.

Hotel de Londres e Inglaterra (☎ 943 44 07 70, fax 943 44 04 94, *Calle de Zubieta 2)* oozes old-world charm and otherwise impresses with its waterfront location. Singles/doubles cost 19,800/23,000 ptas.

Luxury is taken *very* seriously at *Hotel María Cristina* (☎ 943 42 49 00, fax 943 42 39 14, *Oquendo 1)*, where prices soar to a stratospheric 45,000/74,500 ptas.

Places to Eat

In San Sebastián you will experience some of the tastiest cuisines in Spain. The choice of venues seems virtually limitless and it is here that the art of the bar snack (tapas, or pintxos) has been refined, with tray after tray of mouthwatering goodies lining the bars. Eating in this way is not the cheapest way to fill your stomach, but it sure is a lot of fun!

If you want to stock up to make your own meals, go where the locals go – the underground *Mercado de la Bretxa*, which also has a supermarket (open until 9 pm). Another busy market in the centre is the *Mercado de San Martín* on Calle de San Marcial.

Tapas Bars The Parte Vieja is crammed with delightful tapas bars. You're likely to find your personal favourite, but here are a few places to get you started.

Bar Txepetxa (☎ 943 42 22 27, Calle Pescadería 5) has won numerous awards for its *anchoa* (anchovy) pintxos, listed on a board behind the bar and made to order. Suits, construction workers and pimply teens all rub shoulders at *Juantxo Taberna* (☎ 943 42 74 05, Calle de Embeltrán 6), famous for its cheap, super-sized *bocadillos* and pintxos. *Borda Berri* (Calle Fermín Calbetón 12) is another worthy contender, as is *Bar La Cepa* (☎ 943 42 63 94, Calle de 31 de Agosto 7).

South of the cathedral, *Casa Valles* (☎ 943 45 22 10, Calle de los Reyes Católicos 10) is an unpretentious place where pintxos, *raciones* and substantial bocadillos are consumed at long communal tables.

Restaurants Just west of the cathedral, at the end of Calle San Bartolomé, is *Caravanserai*, a trendy bistro with stylish North African-inspired decor. The extensive menu runs the gamut from burgers to pasta to sandwiches, mostly priced under 1000 ptas.

For seafood by the sea, a string of places have set up by the fishing harbour, including *Restaurante Mariñela* (☎ 943 42 73 83) and *Restaurante Sebastián* (☎ 943 42 58 62) on Paseo del Muelle. Both are only open from June to September and charge around 1300 to 2000 ptas for main courses.

In the Parte Vieja, *Izkiña* (☎ 943 42 25 62, Calle Fermín Calbetón 4) and *Alotza Jatetxea* (☎ 943 42 07 82) across the street

at No 7 are among the few places that do a *menú del día* (daily set meal) for dinner (2500 ptas). Both also have respectable pintxos selections.

Bar Zaguan (Calle de 31 de Agosto 31) is low on charm *and* price: the set lunch costs just 950 ptas and *platos combinados* go for as little as 700 ptas. Better food is on the plate at tiny, low-key *Koskol* (Calle de Iñigo 5). For 1000 ptas you get exceedingly generous portions; the *ensalada mixta* is a meal in itself, and the fried anchovies with garlic are divine.

Casa Urbano (Calle de 31 de Agosto 17) is a more upmarket choice and an old favourite with a well-entrenched reputation for quality seafood. Mains cost around 2500 ptas and the set lunch is 3000 ptas. *Restaurante Portaletas* (☎ 943 42 42 72, Calle del Puerto 8) is popular with locals. Dining takes place beneath heavy timber beams. The set lunch is 1500 ptas, and mains start at 1500 ptas as well.

A fun vegetarian place is *Restaurante La OKA* (☎ 943 46 38 84, Calle de San Martín 43), open for lunch daily (plus Saturday dinner). Prices range from 650 to 1000 ptas per plate.

One of the country's most acclaimed chefs, Juan Mari Arzak, cooks up his world-renowned Basque nouvelle cuisine at *Arzak* (☎ 943 27 84 65, Alto de Miracruz 21). Expect to pay top peseta (10,000 ptas and up) for a full dinner. Reservations are obligatory.

Entertainment

Bars San Sebastián has two good areas for bar activity – the Parte Vieja and around Calle de los Reyes Católicos.

Parte Vieja The Parte Vieja is crawling with all sorts of bars. The area comes to life from about 8 pm virtually every day of the week, although weekends are predictably more intense. Late-night bars rock on when the tapas bars close, with Calle de la Pescadería and Calle de Fermín Calbetón being two of the busier streets. It is difficult to single out particular bars, as they're all full of merry-makers. *Bar Urbia* (Calle del Puerto 7) is a downstairs dance bar that attracts a mixed crowd. If you'd like to have a swig of Basque cider *(sidra),* head for *Sagardotegia Itxaropena* (☎ 943 42 45 76, Calle de Embeltrán 16).

Calle de los Reyes Católicos The other easily accessible concentration of nocturnal activity is down by Calle de los Reyes Católicos, just south of the cathedral. *Udaberriberri,* at Calle de Larramendi, has a cool ground-floor bar and a rather hysterical Spanish music karaoke scene downstairs. A few doors down is *Zuripot (Larramendi 9),* small and smoky and with a distinctly anarchistic vibe. Check out the brightly pigmented canvases with surreal imagery. *Sitres (Calle de Sánchez Toca 3)* is the place of choice for some head-banging heavy metal.

Clubs & Discos One of the better-known discos is *Ku,* a taxi ride away near the Monte Igueldo funicular. Closer to the centre, *Bataplan* and *Rotonda* are both on the beach promenade; dress to kill and be prepared to drop about 2000 ptas to get in. *Discóbolo* on Alameda del Boulevard is the nearest disco to the Parte Vieja. *La Habanera,* in the basement of the Cafe Rock in the Teatro Arriaga, does sizzling Latin rhythms and there's no cover charge.

Getting There & Away
For details on crossing the border with France, see the Irún section later in this chapter.

Air The city's airport (☎ 943 64 12 67) is 22km out of town, near Hondarribia. There are regular flights to Madrid and occasional charters to major European capital cities.

Bus The main bus station, a 20-minute walk south of the Parte Vieja, is between Plaza de Pío XII and the river. A bewildering number of ticket offices huddle just north of it along Avenida de Sancho el Sabio and Paseo de Vizcaya. Local bus No 28 connects the station with the city centre.

Continental Auto runs nine times daily to Madrid (3800 ptas) via Vitoria (925 ptas) and Burgos (1855 ptas). Vibasa has three buses daily to Barcelona (3350 ptas).

La Roncalesa has up to 10 buses daily operating to Pamplona (790 ptas) and six to Zaragoza (2420 ptas). PESA has halfhourly services to Bilbao along the *autopista* (tollway) from 6.30 am to 10 pm (1120 ptas). It also sends a few buses along the coast as far as Lekeitio (705 ptas) and has twice-daily buses to Biarritz and Bayonne in France.

Turytrans buses serve many major European destinations. Enatcar has weekday buses to Sevilla (7800 ptas) via Salamanca (3750 ptas).

Buses to Hondarribia, Irún and the airport depart from Plaza de Guipúzcoa (Bus I; 175 ptas), while Buses A1 and G1 travel to Hernani and Astigarraga (125 ptas) from the stop on Calle de Echalde.

Train The main Renfe train station is just across the Río Urumea on Paseo de Francia, on a line linking Paris to Madrid. There are five services daily to Madrid (eight hours, 6400 ptas). Trains to Barcelona run twice a day (8¼ hours, 5000 ptas).

Other Spanish cities, including Alicante, Salamanca and La Coruña are served as well, as is Lisbon (in Portugal).

There is only one direct train to Paris, but you can pick up plenty more from the French border town of Hendaye. It is served every half-hour by the private railway company Eusko Tren/Ferrocarril Vasco (ET/FV; international passes not valid), on a line nicknamed 'El Topo' (the Mole). Trains depart from Amara station, about 1km south of the city centre. They also stop in Pasaia and Irún. Another ET/FV line heads west to Bilbao (2¾ hours, 900 ptas) via Zumaia, Zarautz and Durango.

Car & Motorcycle The A-8 autopista passes through San Sebastián to Bilbao in the west and into France (where it becomes the A-63) to the east. You can avoid the toll on the virtually parallel N-634. Hugging the coast, it's considerably more scenic but also rather slow. The main route south is the N-1, which runs to Madrid via Vitoria. The A-15 to Pamplona veers off the N-1 just south of San Sebastián.

Rental Several major companies are represented by agencies in San Sebastián, including Avis (☎ 943 46 15 27), Calle del Triunfo 2; Europcar (☎ 943 32 23 04) in the Renfe train station; and Hertz (☎ 943 46 10 84), Calle de Zubieta 5.

Bicycle You can rent bicycles and mountain bikes at Comet (☎ 943 42 66 37), Avenida de la Libertad 6. The cost is 2500/3000 ptas per half-day/day or 14,000 ptas per week.

EAST OF SAN SEBASTIÁN
Pasaia
postcode 20110 • pop 18,300

Pasaia (Pasajes) has the largest port in the province of Guipúzcoa, right where the Río Oiartzun empties into the Atlantic. While the new part of town is asphyxiated by a clot of highway bypasses, one neighbourhood, the Pasai de San Juan, still maintains a great degree of charm. Victor Hugo spent the summer of 1843 here and you can still see the house where he stayed. The single street and the area immediately around the central square are lined with pretty houses and colourful balconies. It is accessible only by boat from San Pedro or by road via the town of Lezo. Pasaia itself is on the El Topo train route (see the Irún section) and also served by buses from San Sebastián.

Irún
postcode 20300 • pop 53,300

A more nondescript introduction to Spain you could hardly get, so you'd best move straight on to Hondarribia or San Sebastián.

If you do find yourself obliged to stay, there are half a dozen relatively cheap places within a stone's throw of the trains. *Pensión Los Fronterizos (☎ 943 61 92 05, Calle de Estación 7)* is a perfectly clean and central place where single/double rooms with shower and toilet are just 2800/4000 ptas (more in summer).

Getting There & Away To shuttle between Irún and Hendaye in France, take the half-hourly train (known as 'El Topo' – 'the Mole') for 115 ptas from the ET/FV station on Paseo de Colón – look for the 'Eusko Tren' sign. In the other direction, El Topo goes to San Sebastián, or you can take a *cercanía* (suburban train) from the Renfe station, five minutes' walk to the south.

Frequent buses connect Irún (there's a stop on Paseo de Colón) with San Sebastián (Plaza de Guipúzcoa) and Hondarribia.

Long-distance trains from the Renfe station run to Madrid, Barcelona, Alicante, Galicia and other destinations. Long-distance buses also depart from here.

Up to 10 trains daily leave the SNCF station in Hendaye for Paris (six of them high-speed TGVs). Other trains serve Pau, Lille and Bordeaux, and there is a daily train to Rome via Ventimiglia.

Hondarribia
postcode 20280 • pop 13,500

Hondarribia (Fuenterrabía in Castilian), founded by the Romans and the scene of several sieges throughout its history, has managed to preserve its charming old city. Although it has a character all its own, the whiff of France, lying just across the bay, is also perceptible in the reserved orderliness of the place.

The tourist office (☎ 943 64 54 58), Calle de Javier Ugarte 6, is open 9 am to 1.30 pm and 4 to 6.30 pm weekdays and 10 am to 2 pm Saturday.

You can enter the partly intact old town walls through the Puerta de Santa María, traditionally the main gate. Past the Gothic Iglesia de Santa María de la Asunción you arrive in the expansive Plaza de Armas, dominated by the sumptuous parador (see Places to Stay & Eat). Cross the plaza and work your way downhill to the modern part of town and the tourist office. East (right) of here, a wide harbourside promenade invites strolling, while straight ahead is La Marina, Hondarribia's most scenic quarter. Its main street, Calle San Pedro, is flanked by typical fisherfolk houses, their facades painted bright green or blue and their wooden balconies gaily decorated with flower boxes. This is where you'll find several restaurants, cafes and small stores. The best beaches are north of the centre.

Places to Stay & Eat The *Albergue Juan de Elkano* (☎ 943 64 15 50, fax 943 64 00 28), on Foroko Igoera, and *Camping Faro de Higuer* (☎ 943 64 10 08, Paseo del Faro 58) are both a bit east of the centre.

In town, the cheapest option is *Hostal Álvarez Quintero* (☎ 943 64 22 99, Beñat Etxepare Kalea 2), near the tourist office, where singles/doubles with private facilities cost from 3700/4900 ptas. Those with more dosh have a tempting range of options in the old town *(casco antiguo)*, starting with the homy and postcard-pretty *Hotel San Nikolas* (☎ 943 64 42 78, Plaza de Armas 6), where doubles go for 7250 ptas.

For a special treat, ensconce yourself at the grand *Parador El Emperador* (☎ 943 64 55 00, fax 943 64 21 53), a fortress with origins in the 12th century but turned into a palace by Carlos V. Behind the foreboding battle-scarred facade, a breezy inner courtyard, festooned with flowers, gives access to the luxurious rooms. Antiques and tasteful decor grace the public areas. The price tag? Singles cost 12,000 to 15,000 ptas and doubles 15,500 to 19,500 ptas.

The old town has oodles of eating places, though none is particularly cheap. In the new part of town, *Bar Maitane*, just behind the tourist office, is popular with locals, has good bar snacks and serves up low-priced meals.

Getting There & Away Buses leave from near the post office for Irún, San Sebastián and occasionally across the border to Hendaye.

SOUTH OF SAN SEBASTIÁN
Walking in the Hills
Ordizia, 30km south of San Sebastián and served by frequent buses, is the best base from which to visit the hills to the east. The popular 1½ hour walk up to the top of Monte Txindoki, one of the highest peaks (1341m) in the Sierra de Aralar, begins from the village of **Larraitz**, about 8km to the east (follow the signs for Zaldibia). A few buses make the run from Ordizia on weekends only. More ambitious walkers head for other peaks farther into the chain and even make for the Santuario de San

Miguel in Excelsis – a good day's strong hiking to the south-east in Navarra.

Push on south from Ordizia to Zegama and the hamlet of **Otzaurte** just beyond, and you can pick up a stretch of the GR-12 trail heading 5km westwards to the Refugio de San Adrián and a **natural tunnel** of the same name (higher up from the refuge). This medieval pilgrim route once linked the heart of Spain with the rest of Europe. Traces of an early medieval highway can still be seen on the approach to the tunnel – inside which rests a small chapel. The road then emerges from the tunnel and continues southwards.

Trains serve Otzaurte from Vitoria. The refuge supposedly is open on weekends and in summer, but it's a little unreliable.

The Interior
The hills rising to the south between San Sebastián and Bilbao are dotted with several towns offering an appealing variety of architectural monuments, all settled into a luxuriant green backdrop reminiscent of Tuscany – but much more affordable. There is plenty of accommodation, with *nekazal turismoas* (agrotourism homes) spread throughout the area.

Santuario de Loyola Just outside Azpeitia (12km south of the A-8 motorway) lies the portentous Santuario de Loyola, dedicated to St Ignatius, the founder of the Jesuit order. This sumptuous baroque spectacle seems oddly incongruous with its rural setting. Inside, the circular basilica is laden with dark grey marble and plenty of carved ornamentation. The house where Loyola was born in 1490 is conserved in one of the two great wings of the *santuario* (shrine). It is open 10 am to 12.30 pm and 3.30 to 7 pm daily, but you can generally wander into the church any time that services are not on.

Bergara Bear south-west from Azpeitia along the Río Urola, and a delightful back road (GI-3750) winds through the hills to the rather scraggly town of Bergara. The main square and Iglesia de San Pedro in the old quarter retain just enough reminders of a prosperous past to merit a stop.

Basque Cider House Rules

The lush green hinterland just in from the coast, far removed from worldly San Sebastián, has long been home to a liquid tradition most pleasing to the palate. The cider produced here looks deceptively like apple juice – it's flat and slightly bitter – but with an alcoholic kick. The best place to look is in and around the towns of Hernani and Astigarraga. Most cider houses stay open only during cider production, which usually lasts from January to Easter. They then bottle the surplus and most close the doors to their bars and restaurants.

If you happen to be in town in those months, you could treat yourself to a ritual cider house dinner. This is an evening-filling culinary extravaganza built around a giant beef chop, preceded by a *bacalao* (cod) omelette and capped off by a dessert of cheese, quince jelly and walnuts. Dinners start around 10 pm and cost from 3000 to 4000 ptas, including all the cider you can guzzle. It's a hugely popular outing, so be sure to make reservations, especially on weekends.

When drinking the cider, it's important to keep in mind the local etiquette: *'gutxi eta maiz'*, which translates as 'little and often'. Rather than filling up the entire glass (you do this yourself), pour only a little bit and drink it right away. Letting the cider sit spoils the fresh taste.

A well-signposted series of half a dozen *sagardotekis* (the Basque term for cider houses) lies along a 2km winding, hilly road off the narrow highway connecting Hernani to Astigarraga (3km apart). Getting *to* the area from San Sebastián is easy, with Buses A1 and G1 departing frequently from Calle de Echalde (125 ptas). Service back into town, though, stops at about 9 pm, so you'd need to catch a taxi. There are no lodging options in cider house country.

If you're travelling outside of cider season, you can also indulge in this kind of meal at sagardotekis in most larger towns.

Oñati

One of the most enticing towns in rural Basque Country, Oñati is a short hop from Bergara down the GI-627. A Renaissance gem is the **Universidad de Sancti Spiritus**, where for 350 years alumni were schooled in philosophy, law and medicine until its closure in 1902. Highlights are the plateresque facade and *múdejar* courtyard. Nearby is the **Iglesia de San Miguel**, a Late Gothic confection whose cloister was built over the river. The church faces onto the main square, Foruen Enparantza, dominated by the eye-catching baroque *ayuntamiento* (town hall). The tourist office (☎ 943 78 34 53), open daily, is also here.

Hostal Echeverria (☎ 943 78 04 60, Zuazola 15) has singles/doubles with washbasin for 2500/3800 ptas. Stretch just a bit more and you can live in rural luxury at the agroturismo *Arregi* (☎ 943 78 08 24, Garagaltza 19), 2km south of town. Double rooms at this splendid home cost just 5000 ptas with bath.

For inventive cuisine, try *Itturitxo Jatetxea (Atzeko Kalea 32)*. The scrumptious *menú* costs 1100 ptas for lunch and 1500 ptas for dinner.

There are frequent buses to San Sebastián, Bilbao and Vitoria.

Arantzazu About 10km south of Oñati, the **Santuario de Arantzazu** is a Franciscan-run religious complex where the patron saint of Gipuzkoa is worshipped. Considered the most important example of modern architecture in the Basque Country, it is a collaboration of major regional architects and sculptors, including Eduardo Chillada, who designed the entrance doors.

The road up and the setting are themselves worth the trip, and the whole area lends itself to some nice walks – the Oñati tourist office can sell you a collection of route maps.

ALONG THE COAST

The coast road out of San Sebastián snakes its way past some spectacular ocean scenes, with cove after cove stretching west and verdant fields suddenly dropping away in rocky shafts to the sea. Fairly regular buses from San Sebastián run as far as Lekeitio, and agroturismos and camping grounds are plentiful.

Getaria
postcode 20808 • pop 2350
If surfing is your thing, you may want to stop in the resort town of **Zarautz**, 23km west of San Sebastián, which hosts a round of the World Surfing Championship every September.

Otherwise, bypass this holiday haven and pull in at Getaria, a small medieval fishing settlement huddled in the shadow of El Ratón (the Mouse), the distinctive islet visible long before you enter the town. The sober mass of the 14th-century Gothic **Iglesia de San Salvador** stands sentinel over the port, which in 1522 saw the return of its most illustrious son, Juan Sebastián Elcano, after more than three years spent in the first successful circumnavigation of the globe. He had joined Magellan's expedition in 1519 – its aim to find a passage to India across the Atlantic and Pacific. Magellan and most of the fleet perished, but Elcano crawled back to Spain with just 18 other survivors. Getaria is also the birthplace of Cristóbal Balenciaga, the famous haute couture fashion designer, who died in 1972.

A couple of local homes offer cheap beds, and the **Pensión Guetariano** (☎ 943 14 05 67) has singles/doubles with shower and toilet for 5000/6500 ptas. Several harbour-front restaurants grill up the fresh catch of the day, which washes down well with a glass of crisp, locally produced txakoli wine.

Zumaia
A few kilometres farther west, Zumaia has sprawled itself out to accommodate summer beach-goers aplenty. The Playa de Izturun is wedged in among cliffs while, a couple of kilometres east of the town centre, the Playa de Santiago is a more open strand. Next to the latter stands the **Museo de Zuloaga**, housed in the Basque artist Ignacio Zuloaga's (1870–1945) one-time studio. It contains some of his important works, as well as a handful by other headliners, including Goya and El Greco. The museum is open 4 to 8 pm Wednesday to Sunday.

Mutriku
The picturesque fishing village of Mutriku is clamped by a steep rocky vice cut into the coast, its streets winding tortuously down to a small harbour. **Restaurante Zumalage**, up above the eastern end of town, affords great views. Four **camping grounds** surround the town, largely because of the fine beach of **Saturrarán**, a few kilometres west.

Inland to Markina
A few kilometres west of Saturrarán, the BI-633 turns south just before Ondarroa to reach, after about 10km, the pretty town of Markina. Its main claim to fame is being the home of pelota, and the local frontón is even known as the Universidad de la Pelota!

Another 5km south lies the birthplace of Simón Bolívar, the great early-19th-century South American independence fighter. A **museum** here dedicated to his exploits is open 10.30 am to 1 pm Tuesday to Friday and noon to 2 pm weekends. Hourly buses between Ondarroa and Bilbao stop at Iruzubieta, from where it's a 2km walk.

Lekeitio
postcode 48280 • pop 7560
Back on the coast, another 12km west of Ondarroa brings you to this attractive fishing town. Of the two beaches, the one just east of the river is nicer. The harbourside is dominated by the Late Gothic **Iglesia de Santa María de la Asunción**.

Unfortunately, accommodation is scarce, driving prices up. In summer, advance bookings are mandatory. Alternatively, you could try **Camping Endai** (☎ 94 684 24 69), on Playa Mendexa, a few kilometres back east (during summer only). The waterfront and back streets of the old town teem with bars and snack joints.

Elantxobe
Sticking to the 'coast road' unfortunately does not mean hugging the cliffs, although occasionally you get some great views. The tiny hamlet of Elantxobe is worth a look,

seemingly glued onto the almost perpendicular rock walls cascading down to the sea. A couple of buses run from Gernika daily except Sunday.

Urdaibai Reserva de la Biosfera

Just west of Elantxobe, the Río Oka spills into the Bay of Biscay, its last 10km forming an estuary that was given Biosphere Reserve status by Unesco in 1984. It is home to hundreds of bird species and is also a stop on the migratory route between Europe and Africa. Sprawling over 220 sq km, it encompasses 22 towns and villages, including Gernika, Mundaka and Bermeo. On its eastern and northern edges, respectively, are the expansive sandy beaches of **Laga** and **Laida**.

Gernika

postcode 48300 • pop 15,500

Gernika (Guernica) occupies a special place in Basque history, for it was here that, until 1876, an independent Basque parliament held its legislative meetings beneath an ancient oak tree. But to most, the town is etched more deeply into consciousness as the tragic victim of the massive systematic bombing by Hitler's Legión Condor, at the request of Franco, on 26 April 1937. Almost 2000 people died in the attack, which took place during the busy Monday afternoon market, still held today. The massacre was later immortalised in Picasso's nightmare vision *Guernica*. The painting is housed in the Reina Sofía gallery in Madrid, though there's talk about moving it here or to the Guggenheim in Bilbao.

The events of that day are chronicled in detail in the interesting **Gernika Museoa** in the central Foru Plaza. Aside from photographs, documents and scale models, there are also copies of *Guernica* sketches and displays about other cities destroyed by war, including Hiroshima, Warsaw and Dresden. Display panels are also in English. Museum hours are from 11 am to 2 pm and 4 to 7 pm daily (closed Sunday afternoon); 350 ptas. A couple of blocks north, on Calle Allende Salazar, is a nice ceramic-tile version of *Guernica*.

On the same street is the **Euskal Herriko Museoa**, housed in the 18th-century Palacio

de Montefuerte. The museum, with its comprehensive exhibitions on Basque history and culture, is open 10 am to 2 pm and 4 to 7 pm Tuesday to Saturday, and 10 am to 1.30 pm Sunday; free.

The pleasant gardens behind it lead to the **Casa de Juntas**, where the provincial government has met since 1979. Inside is a monumental, modern stained-glass window depicting historic scenes. In the garden is the famous **Oak Tree**, now a mere stump sheltered by a neoclassical gazebo. Just north is the peaceful **Pueblos de Europa** park, with sculptures by Eduardo Chillada and Henry Moore.

Gernika is an easy day trip from Bilbao by ET/FV train from Atxuri station (one hour). There's a tourist office (☎ 94 625 58 92) at Artekale 8. Hotels are scarce and include *Hotel Boliña (☎ 94 625 03 00, Barrencalle 3)*, which has singles/doubles with bath for 5500/6500 ptas.

Cueva de Santimamiñe

The grotto of Santimamiñe is a crowd-pleaser for its impressive stalactites, stalagmites and well-preserved prehistoric cave paintings. Guided tours (maximum 15 people) start at 10 and 11.15 am, and 12.30, 4.30 and 6 pm, and are very popular, so arrive early or inquire about organised trips at the Gernika tourist office. There is no public transport, although the Gernika-Lekeitio bus can drop you at Kortezubi, from where it's a 40-minute walk. If you're driving, take the BI-638 to Kortezubi, then turn off to the BI-4244 just before reaching the town.

El Bosque Pintado de Oma

Near the grottoes is one of the region's most unusual and enchanting attractions, the 'Painted Forest' of Basque artist Agustín Ibarrola. Aided by several of his students, he has adorned dozens of trees in the Oma valley with rainbows, outlines of people and colourful abstract shapes. While at first they seem disjointed, a closer look reveals an intentional composition, with several trees together forming a complete picture. Each visitor is invited to recompose the images and to discover their own visions. See if you can spot the two motor-cyclists!

The Bosque is accessible by bike, car or on foot. Follow the directions to the Cueva de Santimamiñe, but turn off the BI-4244 onto a marked forest road before reaching the caves.

Mundaka
postcode 48360 • pop 1640

The legend of one of the world's longest left-handers still attracts surfers the world over to this pretty but pretentious little estuary town 10km north of Gernika. They may well want to track down Craig, who came in the early 1980s and hasn't been able to drag himself away since, at his Mundaka Surf Shop. He rents out gear and also gives surfing lessons.

Food and accommodation are hopelessly overpriced in this town, even in the low season. Your best bet is *Camping Portuondo* (☎/*fax 94 687 77 01,* e *recepcion@camp ingportuondo.com),* which has lovely terraced grounds and charges 585 ptas per person plus 1250 ptas for tent/caravan and car. It also has several nice bungalows with full kitchens starting at 10,500 ptas (sleeping up to four).

Buses and ET/FV trains connecting Bilbao with Bermeo stop here.

Bermeo
postcode 48370 • pop 17,900

A stone's throw up the coast, this fishing port looks appealing at first, but turns out to be a rather sprawling and gritty place. Those interested in commercial fishing could poke their noses into the **Museo del Pescador** (closed Monday and Sunday afternoon). The tourist office (☎ 94 617 91 54) is at Askata-sun Bidea 2, on the waterfront. Buses and ET/FV trains run to Bilbao.

The coast road west of Bermeo offers some tantalising glimpses of the rugged and at times forbidding Basque coast. A few kilometres beyond Bermeo, the **Ermita de San Juan de Gaztelugatxe** juts out to sea from an odd lick of land. The minor fishing village of **Bakio**, around the tip, has an attractive beach.

BILBAO
postcode 48080 • pop 360,000

Bilbao (Bilbo in Basque), the capital of Vizcaya (Bizkaia) province, is the largest Basque city and is quickly becoming one of the region's most popular. An ambitious urban renewal plan has given the city not only a spanking new Metro line but, best of all, the spectacular Museo Guggenheim, a wonder of contemporary architecture and an extraordinary gallery of modern art. Its arrival in 1997 helped catapult Bilbao out of its postindustrial slumber, brought on in the 1970s by the collapse of the steel industry, once the backbone of its economy.

Central Bilbao's businesslike and sober air is reminiscent of many a French provincial capital, its architecture reflecting the bourgeois boom days of the mid-19th and early 20th centuries. Hang around for an evening, though, and any comparisons with stuffy French cities disappear in a whirlwind of frenzied partying in Las Siete Calles – the nucleus of the medieval *casco viejo* (old town). Here the Spanish propensity for raucous night-long revelry is taken for a serious spin – there is nothing sober about a weekend night out in Bilbao.

History

Bilbao was granted the title of *villa* (a city statute) in 1300 and medieval *bilbaínos* went about their business in the bustle of Las Siete Calles and on the wharves of San Antón and Abando. As the boats got bigger and the business more sophisticated, the quays moved farther towards the coast and the city grew. Conquest of the Americas stimulated trade growth and by the late 19th century the area's skyline was crimped by the slender smoke stacks of furnaces and smelters. Bilbao's golden age was fed by steelworks, shipbuilding yards and chemical plants before it was hit by the crises that have affected all of Europe's heavy industries in recent decades. Commerce remains buoyant, however, and the city sees itself increasingly as a centre of learning and culture, to which its two universities and several good museums attest.

Orientation

The nerve-centre of Bilbao, the casco viejo, lies bundled up on the right bank of the Ría de Bilbao, also sometimes known as the Río Nervión, which it becomes upriver. Hotels, restaurants and bars cluster here among Siete Calles. The main train stations are just over the river in an area known as El Ensanche, while bus stations are scattered farther across this part of town. The Museo Guggenheim and Museo de Bellas Artes, west of the centre, and the Basílica de Begoña, to the east, are about the only sights requiring more than a shortish walk from the casco viejo.

Information

Tourist Offices The friendly, English-speaking tourist office (☎ 94 479 57 60, fax 94 479 57 61), Paseo del Arenal 1, is open 9 am to 2 pm and 4 to 7.30 pm, from 10 am Sunday, closed weekend afternoons. Ask for the free bimonthly *Bilbao Guía,* with entertainment listings plus tips on restaurants, bars and nightlife. A smaller information kiosk by the Museo Guggenheim operates from 11 am to 2 pm and 4 to 6 pm daily except Monday (5 to 7 pm Saturday).

Money Banks, many with ATMs, abound in central Bilbao. American Express (☎ 94 444 48 58) is represented by Viaca at Calle Alameda Recalde 68.

Post & Communications The main post office on Alameda de Urquijo is open 8.30 am to 8.30 pm weekdays, and 9.30 am to 2 pm on Saturday. There's a Telefónica locutorio at Calle de Barroeta Aldámar 7, open 9 am to 9 pm weekdays and 10.30 am to 1.30 pm and 5 to 9 pm on Saturday.

For Internet access, go to El Señor de la Red at Calle de Rodríguez Arias 69, which charges 350 ptas per hour and is open until 10 pm (to 1 am weekends). Other places include Euskalfont at Calle de Licenciado Poza 53 and Master PC at Alameda de Recalde 14.

Bookshops Librería Camara (☎ 94 422 19 45), at Calle de Euskalduna 6, has a huge selection of international newspapers and magazines.

Medical & Emergency Services For an ambulance, call the Cruz Roja on ☎ 94 422 22 22. The Hospital Civil de Basurto (☎ 94 441 87 00) is on Calle de Gurtubay, with the Policía Nacional nearby at Calle de Luis Briñas 14. Call ☎ 092 in emergencies.

Museo Guggenheim

Bilbao's showpiece and an instant tourist magnet from its opening in September 1997, the Museo Guggenheim is perhaps even more remarkable for its architecture than its contents. Designed by US architect Frank Gehry, this fantastical, swirling structure was inspired in part by the anatomy of a fish and the hull of a boat – both elements of Bilbao's past and present economy, which are used to project a fresh image into the 21st century. Indeed the museum blends right into the river on which it sits, incorporating a nearby bridge and railroad line into its sphere of aesthetic influence.

It's well worth wandering around the entire thing to appreciate the extraordinary imagination behind it, and to catch the different colours reflected by the titanium and glass shell, meant to resemble fish scales. The interior makes wonderful use of space, with light pouring in through a central glass atrium, which has the loftiness of a cathedral. There's an emphasis on organic lines, so that the visitor doesn't feel overwhelmed by hallucinogenic grandeur. Of course, this all came at a price: US$100 million for the building alone.

Inside, the permanent exhibit of modern and contemporary painting and sculpture is still fairly small and housed in galleries 305 to 307. Artists represented include Picasso, Braque, Mondrian, Rothko, Klee and Kandinsky. All the other galleries are used for high-calibre temporary exhibits, usually showcasing the works of avant-garde artists. Of special note is the so-called 'Fish Gallery' on the ground floor, which at 130m is longer than a football pitch. It's bisected by Richard Serra's 1996 enormous site-specific steel *Snake* – walk through it and check out the aural effects it can create.

The museum is open 10 am to 8 pm daily (on Monday in July and August only);

BASQUE COUNTRY

BILBAO

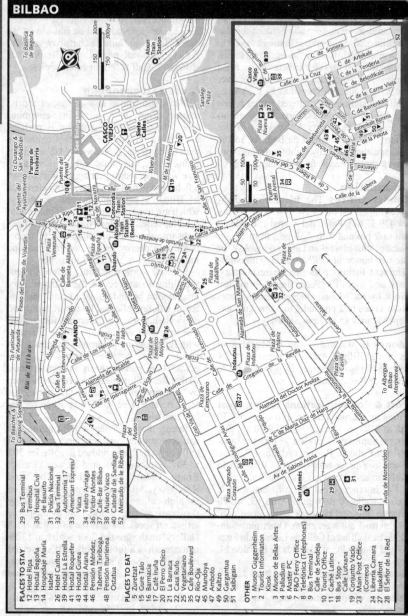

1200 ptas, students half-price. Given its popularity (it had 1.3 million visitors in its first year), try to arrive early to avoid long queues. Free guided tours in English, which provide a wonderful means of comprehending the building and some of its more bizarre contents, take place at 4 pm. Sign up 30 minutes before at the information desk. Taped self-guided tours are available for an additional 600 ptas.

Funicular de Artxanda
For intriguing perspectives of the Museo Guggenheim and a sweeping city panorama, take this historic funicular up the Artxanda hill. It operates daily every 15 minutes until 10 pm (until 11 pm on summer weekends; 110 ptas).

Museo de Bellas Artes
Just 300m up the street from the Museo Guggenheim, Bilbao's Fine Arts Museum has amassed an impressive collection in its own right – from Gothic sculptures to 20th-century pop art – since its inception in 1908. Headliners include classic Spanish artists like El Greco, Zurbarán, Goya and Van Dyck, as well as 20th-century international masters such as Gauguin and Bacon. Basque artists, including the sculptor Chillida, are represented as well. World-class temporary exhibits usually supplement the permanent displays. The museum is open 10 am to 1.30 pm and 4 to 7.30 pm Tuesday to Saturday, and 10 am to 2 pm Sunday (600 ptas, students half-price).

Casco Viejo
Bilbao's old town, loaded with bars and restaurants, is in itself a 'sight'. While wandering, take note of the **Teatro Arriaga**, the arcaded Plaza Nueva, and the recently spiffed up Gothic **Catedral de Santiago**, with its lovely Renaissance cloister. The **Museo Vasco** is a proud and well-executed display of archaeological findings from the Basque region, enhanced by exhibits about local livelihoods and pastimes, such as fishing, shipbuilding, sheep farming, metalworking and pottery. Hours are from 10.30 am to 1.30 pm and 4 to 7 pm, closed Sunday afternoon

and Monday (300 ptas, students half-price). The entrance is on Calle de María Múñoz.

After a long uphill walk to the east you'll come to the monumental **Basílica de Begoña**, home of the city's patron saint and an interesting crossover from Gothic to Renaissance contours.

Organised Tours
Guided 90-minute walking tours in English of the casco viejo operate Tuesday, Thursday and Saturday at 10.30 am from the tourist office at Paseo del Arenal (500 ptas).

Special Events
Carnaval, held in February, is celebrated with particular vigour, but Bilbao's grandest fiesta begins on the first Saturday after 15 August and is known as the Aste Nagusia (Big Week). Traditional parades and music mix with a full program of cultural events over 10 days.

About 25km north of Bilbao, Getxo hosts the first of a trio of week-long international jazz festivals held in the Basque Country in July (Vitoria is next, followed by San Sebastián).

Places to Stay – Budget
Camping & Hostels The nearest place to camp is the pleasant *Camping Sopelana* (☎ 94 676 21 20), by the beach in the town of the same name – it's on the Metro line. Prices are 545 ptas each per person and tent and 425 ptas per car.

Albergue Bilbao Aterpetxea (☎ 94 427 00 54, fax 94 427 54 79, e aterpe@albergue .bilbao.net, Carretera Basurto-Kastrexana Errep 70) is a 10-minute direct bus ride (No 58) away from the action. Prices range from 1900 ptas per person in a six-bed dorm to 2500 ptas for a single room, including breakfast. Rates drop slightly in low season.

Pensiones & Hostales The casco viejo brims with affordable lodging options, although things may get a bit noisy on weekends. Better ask for a room facing away from the street.

Pensión Méndez (☎ 94 416 03 64, Calle de Santa María 13) is about as central as you can get and it's quite cheap too, at 3000/4000 ptas for singles/doubles with shared facilities. The friendly *Hostal Roquefer (☎ 94 415 07 55, Calle de la Lotería 2)* has rooms with washbasin for 3000/5000 ptas and others with bath for 5000/6000 ptas.

Hostal La Estrella (☎ 94 416 40 66, fax 94 416 70 66, Calle de María Múñoz 6) is a charming, brightly painted little place. Rooms with washbasin go for 2700/4800 ptas and those with bath are 4000/6500 ptas. *Hostal Gurea (☎/fax 94 416 32 99, Calle de Bidebarrieta 14)* is another solid choice with rooms costing 3250/4500 ptas with bath. Nearby *Hostal Arana (☎ 94 415 64 11, fax 94 4156 12 05, Calle de Bidebarrieta 2)* is popular with international travellers and has slightly worn rooms costing 4500/5500 ptas with washbasin or 5500/6600 ptas with full bath.

On the other side of the river, *Hospedaje María Isabel (☎ 94 424 85 66, Calle de la Amistad 5)* is characterless but cheap at 3000/4500 ptas. *Hostal Begoña (☎ 94 423 01 34, Calle de la Amistad 2)*, just down the street, is another reliable if unexciting option. Rooms without bath start at 3000/4800 ptas, those with start at 3500/6000 ptas.

Places to Stay – Mid-Range & Top End

Natural wood, stone and antiques collaborate to create the soothing decor of *Pensión Iturrienea Ostatua (☎ 94 416 15 00, fax 94 415 89 29, Calle de Santa María 14)*. Snug singles/doubles with bath are 6500/9000 ptas. *Hotel Ripa (☎ 94 423 96 77, Calle de Ripa 3)*, just across the river, is also fine but can get a little noisy. You pay 6000/8000 ptas.

A landmark in its own right, *Hotel Carlton (☎ 94 416 22 00, fax 94 416 46 28, Plaza Federico Moyúa 2)* is well situated near the Guggenheim and Gran Vía shopping. Graceful rooms with a full range of amenities cost 16,000/26,500 ptas.

Places to Eat

Some of Bilbao's better restaurants offer what's called a *menú bit,* a lunch or dinner special that allows you a taste of haute cuisine without assaulting the bank account.

Bilbao Guía includes a list of these. Many of Bilbao's bars, including some of those listed later under Entertainment, have a restaurant attached, usually out the back. To pack your own, the *Mercado de la Ribera* in the casco viejo, allegedly the largest food market in Europe, has three storeys of meat, fish, cheese and produce.

Restaurants – Casco Viejo A good place for a cheap meal is *Rio-Oja (Calle de Perro 6),* which is usually packed with locals swilling 50-pta glasses of wine and chowing down on *cazuelitas,* small portions of fish, stew or other dishes.

Less frenetic is *Kaltzo (Calle Barrenkale Barrena 7),* a comfortable upstairs dining room, which does set three-course lunches *and* dinners for 2000 ptas. It's closed Sunday night and Monday. Other contenders on the same street are *Saibigain (☎ 94 415 01 23, Calle Barrenkale Barrena 16)* and *Gargantua (Calle Barrenkale Barrena 3).*

Mandoya (☎ 94 415 02 28, Calle de Perro 3-5) is a fine restaurant specialising in meat and seafood (it even has its own lobster hatchery). The *menú* is 3500 ptas. *Amboto (☎ 94 415 61 48, Calle de Jardines 2)* is a rustic establishment with traditional Basque dishes. Expect to spend about 4000 ptas for a three-course meal with drinks.

Restaurants – El Ensanche *Gure Talo (Calle del Príncipe 1)* is an earthy place serving up good Basque food and it's popular with Bilbaínos. The set lunch costs 950 ptas. *Zuretzat (☎ 94 424 85 05, Calle de Iparraguirre 7),* near the Guggenheim, is perfect for refuelling after a morning of art and architecture. The pintxos are killer and it's decorated with hats from museum construction crew members.

La Barraca (☎ 94 410 20 21, Calle García Salazar 12) specialises in paella, while *Vegetariano (☎ 94 444 55 98, Alameda de Urquijo 33)* cooks up meatless lunches daily except Sunday for 950 ptas.

Casa Rufo (☎ 94 443 21 72, Calle Hurtado de Amézaga 5) is an extraordinary place – an intimate *comedor* (dining room) behind a gourmet food store. Prices for the inventive Basque cooking average 4000 ptas. Being 'discovered' by Frank Gehry is what propelled *El Perro Chico* (☎ 94 415 05 19, Calle de Aretxaga 2) into the trendiness stratosphere. The theatrical decor is one asset, but the chef delivers substance as well – at a price. Reservations are a good idea here, and also at Casa Rufo.

Cafes Bilbao is graced with several fine old cafes. *Café Iruña*, on the corner of Calle de Colón de Larreátegui and Calle Berástegui, going strong since 1903, is probably the most celebrated. Its fairy-tale decor was inspired by the Alhambra in Granada. If you like this kind of style, also check out *Barmacia (Calle Villarías 3)*.

The Art Deco *Cafe Boulevard (Calle del Arenal 3)* is Bilbao's oldest coffeehouse (1871). Come here for breakfast specials, platos combinados or pintxos, all at great prices.

The porticoed Plaza Nueva is another good spot for coffee and people-watching.

Entertainment
Bilbao is a good place to catch a stage show or concert, with two main theatres and its own symphony orchestra. Consult *Bilbao Guía* for the latest events schedule.

Bars There are several areas to search out nightlife, but the most obvious is the central Siete Calles. That said, it can be extremely crowded, rowdy and adolescent. Calle de Barrenkale is probably the most concentrated scene of drinking and post-tipple lunacy in the country.

On a Saturday night, you'll be lucky to elbow your way into *Cafe-Bar Bilbao* (☎ 94 415 16 71, Plaza Nueva 6), which has some of the most creative pintxos in town. Nearby *Victor Montes (Plaza Nueva 8)* is a worthy competitor; it has more traditional decor and attracts an older crowd. *Taberna Txiriboga (Calle de Santa María 13)* is a curious mix – a kind of Basque nationalist-cum-gay crowd hangs out here.

There is a line of bars along La Ripa, between the Puente del Ayuntamiento and the Puente del Arenal. The zone around the intersection of Calle de Licenciado Poza and Calle de Gregorio de la Revilla is another fruitful hunting ground.

Clubs & Discos The *Palladium* (☎ 94 424 61 65, Calle de Iparraguirre 11) is a happening bar with a disco in the basement and occasional live music as well. Cover is usually 1000 ptas.

Conjunto Vacío (Muelle de la Merced 4) is the haunt of the young *bacalao* (techno) set and open 9 pm to 9 am on Friday and Saturday. A fun place to go Cubano is *Caché Latino (Muelle de Ripa 3)*, where fiery salsa and merengue dominate the turntables. It also does dance lessons; it's open nightly.

Getting There & Away
Air Airlines flying into Bilbao airport include Iberia, British Airways (and its low-cost spin-off Go), Lufthansa, Sabena, Crossair, Air Nostrum and Air Europa. Cities served include Madrid, Barcelona, London and Paris.

Bus Just about every town in the Basque Country and the rest of Spain is served from Bilbao, but there is a bewildering number of bus stations.

Most companies are based at the Termibus station in the south-western corner of town (metro: San Mamés). La Unión's destinations include Vitoria (675 ptas), Pamplona (1580 ptas) and Logroño (1475 ptas). Alsa Turytrans goes to Irún (1125 ptas), Santander (925 ptas) and Oviedo (2575 ptas). Pesa has services every 30 or 60 minutes to San Sebastián (1020 ptas) and also serves Durango-Elorrio and Oñati.

Buses to Madrid (3400 ptas), Barcelona (4850 ptas), León and Burgos are operated by Ansa Grupo and leave from Calle de Autonomía 17.

Bizkaibus has destinations throughout the rural Basque Country, including coastal communities like Lekeitio and Bermeo, and mostly uses the terminal at Calle de Sendeja. Some of its buses, though, including the one to the port of Santurtzi, leave from Calle Lutxana. Call ☎ 94 420 81 32 for details.

Train Renfe's Abando station sends out four trains daily to Madrid (6¼ hours, 5800 ptas) and two to Barcelona (nine hours, 4900 ptas). Other cities served include Valladolid (four hours, 2800 ptas) and Burgos (2½ hours, 2000 ptas).

Next door is the rather fancy Concordia train station used by the FEVE private rail company for trains west into Cantabria and Asturias.

ET/FV offers regional services from Atxuri station. There are trains to Bermeo (1¼ hours) via Gernika (one hour) and Mundaka (1¼ hours). Another line heads to San Sebastián (2¾ hours, 900 ptas) via Durango, Zarautz and Zumaia.

Car & Motorcycle The A-68 autopista leads directly south and is the quickest way to make for Vitoria, Burgos and Madrid. The A-8 autopista west to Santander is not a tollway, but you pay heading east to San Sebastián. In all cases there are alternative highways that, in general, are slower but more picturesque.

Boat P&O ferries leave for Portsmouth from Santurtzi, about 14km north-west of Bilbao's city centre. The voyage takes about 35 hours from England and 29 hours the other way. Service is restricted from November to March. From Portsmouth, sailings are on Tuesday and Saturday at 8 pm, and from Bilbao they leave Monday and Thursday at 12.30 pm.

The range of fares is confusing, depending on season and other factors. Always ask about special family, group, promotional or return fares.

In general, figure on a one-way foot passenger fare of 12,900 ptas in low season (up to 30,000 ptas in August). Standard return fares are about one-third higher. Cabins range from 8250 to 67,500 ptas each way.

The cost of taking a vehicle up to 5m long and 1.83m high ranges from 37,600 to 83,750 ptas, including driver. Motorcycles and scooters cost from 22,300 to 50,000 ptas, including rider, while bicycles cost from 1600 to 5000 ptas. All prices are each way.

Inquiries and bookings can be made at P&O's office (☎ 94 423 44 77, fax 94 423

54 96), Calle de Cosme Echevarrieta 1, or by calling ☎ 0990-980980 in the UK.

Santurtzi can be reached by cercanía from Abando station (155 ptas) or by Bizkaibus No 3115 from the Calle Lutxana stop (145 ptas).

Getting Around

Central Bilbao is eminently walkable and even from the casco viejo to the Guggenheim should take no more than 20 minutes. Bizkaibus No 3247 runs to the airport from Calle de Sendeja every 40 minutes (140 ptas).

Metro Designed by British star architect Sir Norman Foster (and dubbed 'Fosterito' by locals), Bilbao's Metro opened in 1997 and is the most modern underground/subway system in the world. It runs to the north coast from a number of stations on both sides of the river and makes getting to the beaches nearest Bilbao relatively simple. Tickets within the central area are 140 ptas; going all the way to the northern terminus of Plentzia is 195 ptas.

AROUND BILBAO
Beaches

If you want something relatively close you can try **Las Arenas**, which is good for tanning but a bit polluted. For swimming, **Azkorri**, a bit farther north, is better, while **Ereaga** is popular with surfers. **Sopelana** is nice too; its Playa Salvaje section is set aside for nudists. Better beaches still are east of Plentzia. The Bilbao Metro runs to Algorta (165 ptas) and Plentzia (195 ptas).

A worthwhile stop en route to the beaches is the newly restored **Puente Colgante**, the world's first transporter bridge at its opening in 1893. It links Getxo and Portugalete. A platform, suspended from the actual bridge high above, is loaded with up to six cars plus foot passengers and then silently glides over the Río Nervión to the other bank. Rides are 35 ptas per person each way. You can also take a lift up to the superstructure at 46m and walk across the river and back (not for the vertigo-prone) for some great views (500 ptas). The nearest Metro stop is Areeta (165 ptas).

Castillo de Butrón

This sugary fortified pile with crenellated towers, surrounded by a moat and set in a dreamy park, is the quintessential fairy-tale castle. Located a few kilometres west of the village of Gatica (Gatika) and roughly 20km north-east of Bilbao, it was built in the 14th century as the bastion of the Basque Butrón clan, but has recently been turned into a tourist attraction. Groups of rowdy school kids romp past sickly looking wax mannequins of soldiers, prisoners and fair damsels, and the scene is completed with audiovisual tall tales and a tacky souvenir stall. If you've got children, this could be just the ticket. It's open 10.30 am to 8 pm daily (11 am to 6.30 pm in winter); 700 ptas, or 900 ptas with tour of living quarters.

If you're not driving, you could take the Metro to Larrabasterra, then change to the bus (direction: Munguía), which leaves from Calle de Akilino Arriola 71, about 500m from the Metro station, every 90 minutes (weekdays only).

Durango & Elorrio

The industrial town of Durango has few drawing cards, although the Iglesia de Santa Ana has an interesting blend of Renaissance, Gothic and Herrerian styles. The real attraction is the Duranguesado, the mountainous area around the city. The drive south to the Puerto de Urquiola pass is festooned with spectacular lookouts. Climbers make for the summit of Amboto (1327m), 5km east of the pass.

It seems that at one stage just about everyone in nearby Elorrio was a VIP, if the number of mansions bearing family crests is anything by which to judge. Calle de San Balentin Berrio-Otxoa in particular is loaded with the impressive facades of past greatness. It spills onto the delightful Plaza Gernikako Arbola, dominated by the austere 15th-century Basílica de la Purísima Concepción. Opposite is the local frontón, while less sport-inclined people pass the time in neighbouring cafes.

Apart from an expensive hotel, you could try one of three local agroturismos. *Arabio Azpikoa* (☎ 94 658 33 42, Arabio Kalea 8)

and *Galartza Barrena* (☎ 94 658 27 07, Zenita Kalea 1) both have doubles for 4000 ptas. *Berriolope* (☎/fax 94 682 06 40, Berrio Kalea 10) charges 5500 ptas but that gives you private facilities.

Regular buses and the ET/FV train, coming from either Bilbao or San Sebastián, stop in Durango, from where buses run every hour or so to Elorrio.

VITORIA

postcode 01080 • pop 207,000

Capital not only of the southern Basque province of Álava (Araba in Basque) but of the entire Basque Country, Vitoria (Gasteiz) is a strange mix of sober, businesslike city and ebullient student enclave. This cocktail is, of course, given that special Basque twist, with enough ETA posters and graffiti to remind you of its presence, and you could easily stumble across a game of pelota down at the frontón on Plaza de los Fueros.

History

Nueva Vitoria was founded in 1181 by the Navarran king Sancho VI (El Sabio) on the site of the old Basque village of Gasteiz. It later swapped hands between the Castilian and Navarran crowns. The expansion that began in the 18th century picked up pace in the 20th with the growth of industry. The city was named capital of the Basque Country in 1979.

Orientation

The old city centre – casco viejo – is composed of narrow lanes arranged more or less as a series of concentric circles around a slight hill-top swell. A 10-minute walk south brings you to the train station, while the bus station lies a few blocks to the east of the centre. Hotels of all categories are spread out between the two, with a handful in the old city itself.

Information

The friendly tourist office (☎ 945 13 13 21, e turismo-bulegoa@ej-gv.es), in the Parque de la Florida, is open 9 am to 1.30 pm (to 1 pm weekends) and 3 to 7 pm daily. The smaller municipal office (☎ 945 16 15 98, fax 945 16 11 05), Calle de Eduardo Dato 11, has more convenient hours, from 10 am to 7 pm (weekends to 2 pm).

Banks abound in the newer part of town between the train station and Plaza de España. The main post office is on Calle de las Postas. Nirvana Net (☎ 945 12 84 77) at Manuel Iradier 19 offers Internet access.

Hospital de Santiago (☎ 945 25 36 00) is on Calle de la Paz (corner of Olaguíbel), with the Policía Nacional nearby. For an ambulance call the Cruz Roja on ☎ 945 22 22 22.

Walking Tour

While not blessed with outstanding sights, Vitoria's charms are easily assimilated during a walking tour of the medieval casco viejo and the neoclassical commercial town centre. Excluding museum visits, the loop should take 60 to 90 minutes. Museums mentioned here are free and open 10 am to 2 pm and 4 to 6.30 pm Tuesday to Friday, 10 am to 2 pm Saturday and 11 am to 2 pm Sunday.

Start at Plaza de la Virgen Blanca, dedicated to the White Virgin, the city's patron saint. The square is lorded over by the **Iglesia de San Miguel** and anchored by a monument to Wellington's victory over the French in 1813.

From here, plunge into the casco viejo along Calle Herrería to the north-west. You'll soon pass the 14th-century **Iglesia de San Pedro**, the city's oldest church, en route to the Torre de Doña Oxtanda, which houses the **Museo de Ciencias Naturales** (Natural Science Museum). Continue to the end of Calle Herrería, then veer right to the bottom of Calle de la Correría and **El Portalón**, a classic 15th-century brick and timber edifice. The building opposite, a former armory and now the **Museo de Arqueología**, is in much the same style.

Walking uphill will take you to the **Catedral de Santa María**, a veritable gallery of classical art (including works by Caravaggio and Rubens) but, alas, closed for restoration. Most likely, all you'll get is a glimpse of its magnificent Gothic portico.

Head south on Calle de Fray Zacarías Martínez, passing the dignified **Palacio de Escoriaza-Esquivel** and its plateresque portal before hooking a left on Calle de Gasteiz to Calle de la Cuchillería. Here, in the Palacio de Bendaña (1525), is the **Museo Fournier de Naipes** (Card Museum), with its impressive collection of historic playing cards. Not far beyond, down Calle de la Cuchillería, is the Gothic-era **Casa del Cordón**, used for temporary exhibits.

Work your way back downhill to the porticoed Plaza de España, the heart of neoclassical Vitoria. Head south on Calle de Eduardo Dato, then right (west) on Calle de General Alava to the **Basque Parliament Building** (1853) in the Parque de la Florida.

From here, you could detour south of the park to the elegant Calle de Fray Francisco de Vitoria, where you'll find lined up the **Museo de Bellas Artes**, with paintings and sculpture from the Gothic to the modern; the **Museo de Armería**, with suits of armour and the like; and the **Palacio de Ajuria-Enea** (1920), residence of the *lehendakari* (president of the regional government).

Otherwise, continue west to the neo-Gothic **Catedral de María Inmaculada**. North of here, along Calle Vicente Goicoetxea, stands the monumental **Palacio de la Provincia**, from where Calle Diputación Foral de Alava leads back south to Plaza de la Virgen Blanca.

Special Events

Vitorianos let their hair down for the Fiestas de la Virgen Blanca from 4 to 9 August. A jazz festival is held in July.

Places to Stay

Vitoria's *Albergue Juvenil* (☎/fax 945 14 81 00) is on Calle de Escultor Isaac Díez (corner of Salvatierrabide), about 800m south-west of the train station, and charges 1950/3250 ptas for juniors/seniors.

Plenty of pensiones in and around the casco viejo offer similar or better rates. These include *Casa de Huéspedes Antonio* (☎ 945 26 87 95, Calle de la Cuchillería 66), where snug but comfortable singles/doubles cost 1500/3000 ptas; and *Pensión Mari* (☎ 945 27 73 03, Calle de Prudencio María de Verastegui 6), which has doubles only for

VITORIA

PLACES TO STAY
7 Casa de Huéspedes Antonio
19 Pensión Mari;
   Pensión Balzola
30 Hostal Amárica
31 Hotel Dato

PLACES TO EAT
11 Hirurak
13 Bar El 7
17 Salburua
32 La Huerta
33 Naroki

OTHER
1 Taberna del Tuerto
2 El Portalón & Restaurante
   El Portalón
3 Museo de Arqueología
4 Catedral de Santa María
5 Museo de Ciencias Naturales

6 Palacio de Escoriaza-Esquivel
8 Fournier Card Museum
9 Iglesia de San Pedro
10 Sherezade
12 Casa del Cordón
14 Iglesia de San Miguel
15 Main Post Office
16 Policía Nacional
18 Bus Station
20 Hospital de Santiago
21 Municipal Tourist Office
22 Palacio de la Provincia
23 Basque Parliament Building
24 Catedral de María
   Imaculada
25 Provincial Tourist Office
26 Museo de Bellas Artes
27 Palacio de Ajuria-Enea
28 Museo de Armería
29 Nirvana Net
34 Baco

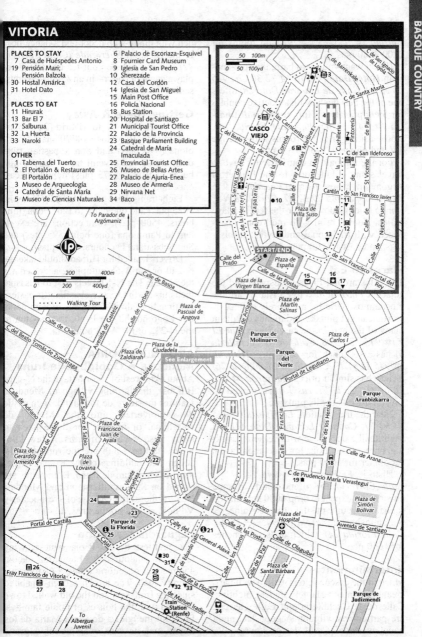

3500 ptas. In the same building is *Pensión Balzola* (☎ 945 25 62 79) with rooms for 2700/4000 ptas.

If you want your own bath, the spic-and-span *Hotel Dato* (☎ 945 14 72 30, fax 945 23 23 20, Calle de Eduardo Dato 28) offers one of the best deals, with attractive doubles for 5990 ptas. If it's full, try *Hostal Amárica* (☎ 945 13 05 06, Calle Florida 11), whose asking price for rooms with satellite TV and phone is 5750/6500 ptas.

For the ultimate in comfort, you have to travel some 15km north to the hamlet of Argómaniz, whose palatial *Parador* (☎ 945 29 32 00, fax 945 29 32 87, Carretera N-1, Km 363) looks down over the fertile Álava plains. Rooms brim with mod cons juxtaposed with traditional and stylish furnishings, and cost 15,000 ptas.

Places to Eat

The cafes around Plaza de España and the adjacent Plaza de la Virgen Blanca are the most atmospheric for a leisurely coffee.

You can get pintxos and menús del día at many of the bars in the casco viejo. *Bar El 7* (☎ 945 27 22 98, Calle de la Cuchillería 3) has a set lunch for 1300 ptas. *Hirurak* (☎ 945 28 81 47, Calle de la Cuchillería 26) nearby has similar prices. *Salburua* (☎ 945 28 64 60, Calle Fueras 19) has picked up several awards for its pintxos.

Near the train station, *La Huerta* (☎ 945 14 94 51, Calle de Eduardo Dato 41) is a traditional cider house with seasonal cooking, numerous options for vegetarians and a set dinner for 3000 ptas.

Historic *El Portalón* (☎ 945 14 27 55, Calle Correría 15) offers quality Basque cuisine, but expect to drop 6000 ptas and up for a three-course meal. For better value, try the atmospheric *Naroki* (☎ 945 23 15 40, Calle Florida 24), which does set lunches for 1650 ptas.

Entertainment

Much of the casco viejo is wall to wall bars, creating an intense, largely student, nightlife. Calle de la Cuchillería and Calle Herrería are particularly vibrant. A good late-night haunt is *Baco* (Calle de los Fueros 39).

Taberna del Tuerto in El Portalón is a dark den with pirate-ship decor and a dance floor in the back. At *Sherezade* (Calle Correría 42) you can imbibe your tea or coffee – or play a game of chess – in an Arabian Nights' setting.

Getting There & Away

Nine buses daily go to Madrid (2870 ptas) and four to Barcelona (4370 ptas). Pamplona (890 ptas) and San Sebastían (985 ptas) are served several times daily, while buses to Bilbao (675 ptas) depart at least once hourly.

Eight trains daily go to Madrid (5½ hours, 4025 ptas) and one daily to Barcelona (nine hours, 4500 ptas). Connections are excellent to Pamplona (one hour, 595 ptas) and San Sebastián (1¾ hours, 1175 ptas).

Drivers headed for Bilbao should take the N-240 or the A-68 autopista, accessed via the N-622. The N-1 travels east to Alsasua, then cuts north to San Sebastián. Its eastern continuation, the N-240 goes to Pamplona. For Logroño, hit the E-80, then switch to the N-232 or the A-68 autopista.

AROUND VITORIA
Mendoza & Oppidum de Iruña

About 6km west of Vitoria (take the N-1 for Burgos), the farming village of Mendoza features the Torre de los Mendoza, a castle now converted into the Museo de Heráldica, of interest for those keen to study Basque coats of arms. A few kilometres farther south are the ruined walls, streets and buildings of the Roman settlement of Oppidum de Iruña. Both sights are closed on Sunday afternoon and Monday. Nearby, the Roman bridge of Trespuentes y Villodas should not be missed.

Laguardia & Around

The prettiest of the Rioja wine-growing towns is undoubtedly Laguardia, about 45km south of Vitoria along a picturesque country road. The area has been inhabited since the Iron Age, and the old walled town is filled with the houses of noble families. Look for the Iglesia de Santa María de los Reyes and its rare example of a grand

Gothic doorway, with its polychrome colouring intact. Virtually every house in town has a basement wine cellar, and bars and *bodegas* serve the local drinks for as little as 50 ptas a glass. For more information on wine, see under Wine Region in the La Rioja section later in this chapter.

Of the handful of places to stay, none is cheap. *Hostal Pachico Martinez (☎ 941 60 00 09, fax 941 60 00 05, Calle Sancho Abarca 20),* in a historic building, has comfortable doubles with satellite TV for 7350 ptas. There's also *Hostal Marixa (☎/fax 941 60 01 65)* nearby, which asks 5500/8950 ptas for its singles/doubles. A few slow buses connecting Vitoria and Logroño daily pass through Laguardia.

You'll find plenty of interesting little villages if you have a vehicle to tour around in. Headed for Haro in La Rioja, the road west from Laguardia passes through **San Vicente de la Sonsierra**, whose remaining castle walls spill off their hill-top perch. Views across the plains are marvellous and an impressive medieval bridge spans the Río Ebro below. Continuing on, **Labastida** straggles up a small hillside capped by the Ermita del Cristo, with a fine Romanesque portal.

Navarra

Several Spains intersect in Navarra (Nafarroa in Basque). The fiercely independent traditions of the Basques here have their special flavour in the historical fueros, or autonomous rights, long exercised by the Navarrese and resurrected today – the region is in fact officially known as the Comunidad Foral de Nafarroa.

The Navarrese are strong on symbolic points – red dominates the region's coat of arms. The Policía Foral have bright red cars, motorbikes and uniforms. In the Navarran Pyrenees everyone seems to paint doors and window frames red; when villages celebrate local fiestas, half the locals wear the traditional Basque white trousers and tops with red scarves, and red geraniums seem to be the main form of floral decoration in the ubiquitous window box.

The soft greens and bracing climate of the Navarran Pyrenees lie like a cool compress across the sunstruck brow of the south, which is all stark plains, cereal crops and vineyards, sliced up by high, forbidding sierras. Navarra is pilgrim territory – for centuries the faithful have used the pass at Roncesvalles to cross from France on their way to Santiago de Compostela (see the special section 'Camino de Santiago'). Here too armies have crossed to and from Spain, but not always with success: Roland's retreating Frankish forces were harried and decimated by Basques in 778, leaving behind little but one of the great *gestes* (epic poems) of early medieval French literature, *La Chanson de Roland*.

Although many associate Navarra exclusively with the running of the bulls in Pamplona, the region's real charm is in its small towns, many in possession of fine monuments ranging from Romanesque to Renaissance.

PAMPLONA
postcode 31080 • pop 182,500

Pamplona (Iruña, Iruñea), capital of the fiercely independent-minded Navarrese, is an attractive display of centuries-old middle-class wellbeing set behind the remains of its once haughty city walls. A fine cathedral is the jewel in the crown, but the footloose wanderer will get pleasure from simply meandering along narrow streets or relaxing in the vast green belt on the western edge of the inner city.

On 6 July, all hell breaks loose as Spain's best known bull fest, the Fiesta de San Fermín (or Sanfermines) kick-starts the city into a frenzy of drinking and mayhem. The running of the bulls *(el encierro),* made famous by Hemingway in his 1926 novel *The Sun Also Rises,* is accompanied by a stampede of visitors from all over the world bent on having such a good time they are unlikely to remember much of it at all. For more details, see the boxed text 'The Running of the Bulls' in this chapter.

History
The Romans called the city Pompaelo, after its founder Pompey the Great. They were

succeeded by the Visigoths and briefly by the Muslims, but by the 8th century Pamplona formed the nucleus of an independent power – the future kingdom of Navarra. It reached the height of its glory under Sancho III in the 11th century, and its position on the Camino de Santiago assured it prosperity. In 1936, under Franco, Pamplona and indeed the rest of Navarra sided with the Nationalists.

Orientation
The compact old city centre is marked off to the north and east by the Río Arga and what remains of the old defensive walls and to the west by parks and the former citadel. The main square, Plaza del Castillo, roughly marks the division between old and new in the south. Everything, including the bullring, is a short walk away. Much of the cheaper accommodation is west of Plaza del Castillo and near the central bus station. The train station is less centrally located north-west of the city centre.

Information
Tourist Offices Pamplona's excellent tourist office (☎ 948 20 65 40, fax 948 20 70 34) on Plaza de San Francisco has English-speaking staff and information about everything in Navarra. Hours are from 10 am to 2 pm and 4 to 7 pm weekdays. In July and August, it's also open Saturday morning.

Money There are several banks with exchange services and ATMs along Paseo de Sarasate. During the Sanfermines, they're open mornings only.

Post & Communications The main post office is on Paseo de Sarasate (corner of Calle de Vínculo). There's a tiny telephone locutorio on Plaza de Castillo, open nightly to 11 pm. To go online, there's Net Iruña (☎ 948 26 01 51) at Calle de Esquiroz 28 near the university.

Medical Services & Emergency The main police station is on Calle del General Chinchilla. The Hospital de Navarra (☎ 948 42 21 00) is on Calle de Irunlarrea. The

emergency number for all services, including ambulances, is ☎ 112.

Catedral
Pamplona's main house of worship stands on a rise just inside the city ramparts. Its single most outstanding feature is the Gothic cloister in the French style. Inside the church are buried in splendour Carlos III of Navarra (the Noble) and his wife Doña Leonor. The **Museo Diocesano** occupies the former refectory (dining room) and kitchen, and houses the usual assortment of religious art, including some fine Gothic woodcarvings.

The cathedral, cloister and museum are visited on tours offered from 10.30 am to 1.30 pm and 4 to 7 pm, except Saturday afternoon and Sunday (500 ptas). The cathedral gates are open just before and after Mass, allowing you to sneak a free look inside.

City Walls
The most intact section of the wall encloses the north-eastern corner of the old town, perched high above a gentle river bend. You can climb the ramparts from behind the cathedral. Farther around to the left is the Portal de Francia, once the main gateway into Pamplona.

Museo de Navarra
Housed in a former medieval hospital, this museum contains a mildly interesting and eclectic collection of archaeological finds, including a Roman mosaic, and art, including a Goya. It is open 10 am to 2 pm and 5 to 7 pm Tuesday to Saturday, and 11 am to 2 pm Sunday and holidays (300 ptas).

Ciudadela & Parks
The walls and bulwarks of the grand fortified citadel – the star-shaped Ciudadela – can barely be made out for all the grass and trees in what now constitutes a park. Gates are open 7.30 am to 10 pm daily. Just north of here are three more parks, allowing for extensive strolling.

Places to Stay
During Sanfermines all hotels as much as triple their normal rates and it is next to

The Running of the Bulls

The Fiesta de San Fermín, or Sanfermines, has its origins in medieval legend. Fermín, son of a recently Christianised Roman governor of Pamplona, went off to spread the word in Gaul, ending up imprisoned and decapitated in Amiens for his trouble. No one really knows when he became the patron saint of Navarra and Pamplona, but his feast day was set on 7 July in 1591. A 15th-century wooden statue of the saint is hauled around the city in solemn procession at 10 am on 7 July.

The fiesta is an almost nonstop cacophony of music, dance, fireworks, processions and, of course, bullfights. The fights take place at 6.30 pm each day from 7 to 14 July. The day starts early – at 6.45 am bands march around town with the aim of waking everyone from their slumbers to launch them into another day of festivity and abandon. Although the festivities begin on 6 July, the first running of the bulls doesn't take place until the following morning. This is not some one-off tradition peculiar to Pamplona. The running of the bulls, or *el encierro*, always preceded the day's bullfights for the simple reason that you had to get the bulls to the ring somehow. Then, as now, the *toros bravos* (fighting bulls) were accompanied by *toros mansos* (quiet bulls) and herded from behind. How or when this exercise became a dangerous diversion remains unknown. Nowadays in many cities the bulls are often transported by truck to the *plaza de toros* (bullring), but plenty of smaller Spanish towns celebrate the encierro as an integral part of the fiesta.

In Pamplona, every morning from 7 to 14 July the bulls are let loose from the Coralillos de Santo Domingo and charge across the square of the same name (a good vantage point). They continue up the street, veering onto Calle de los Mercaderes from Plaza Consistorial and sweeping right onto Calle de la Estafeta for the final charge to the ring. The brave or the foolish – called *mozos* – depending on one's point of view, race madly with the bulls, aiming to keep close – but not too close. The total course is some 800m long and the race lasts little longer than three minutes. The spectacle is followed by a tamer version when *vaquillas* (small cows) are let loose in the streets to chase (or be chased by) other spectators.

The entire ethos of the *corrida*, or bullfight, is steeped not only in measuring the valour of man against beast, but also in the skill, some would say art, of the fight. To a certain extent, the same can be said of the encierro. Every year, people are hurt and sometimes killed in encierros, not only in Pamplona but across the country. This is largely because the majority of those who run are full of bravado (or drink, or both) but have little idea of what they are doing. It is difficult to recommend this activity, but plenty participate anyway. Try to run with someone experienced, and above all do not get caught near bulls that have been separated from the herd. Keep ahead of the herd and you should be all right.

To participate you must enter the course before 8 am from Plaza de Santo Domingo and take up your position. Around 8 am two rockets are fired. The first announces that the bulls have been released from the corrals. The second lets you know they are all out and running. The first truly dangerous point is where Calle de los Mercaderes leads into Calle de la Estafeta. Here many of the bulls crash into the barriers because of the sheer speed at which they attempt to take the turns, and this is where at least some bulls are likely to be separated from the herd. A bull thus separated and surrounded by charging humans is probably rather more frightened than the people. And 500kg or more of frightened bull make for an unpredictable and dangerous animal.

Another particularly dangerous stretch comes towards the end, where Calle de la Estafeta slopes down into the final turn to the Plaza de Toros. A third rocket goes off when all the bulls have made it to the ring, and a final one when they have been rounded up in the stalls where they will await the fight. If you want to watch a fight and fail to get tickets in advance at the ring, you'll usually find scalpers selling cheaper seats for around 1000 ptas.

The whole shebang winds up at midnight on 14 July with a candlelit procession, known as the Pobre de Mí, which starts from Plaza Consistorial.

NAVARRA

PAMPLONA

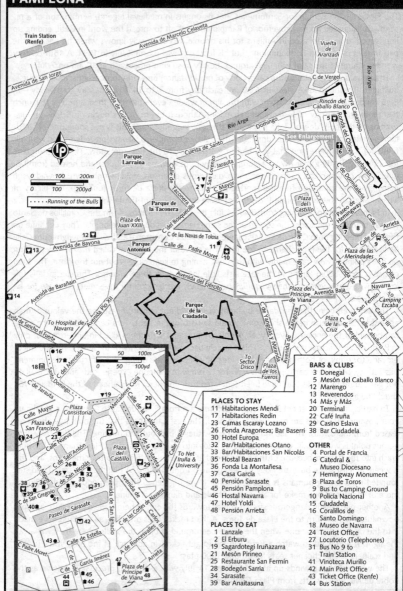

Train Station (Renfe)

Vuelta de Aranzadi

Río Arga

C de Vergel

Rincón del Caballo Blanco

Avenida de Marcelo Celayeta

Avenida de San Jorge

Avenida de Guipúzcoa

Playa Caparroso

Ronda del Obispo Barbazán

Río Arga

Domingo

4

5

6

Cuesta de Santo

Parque Larraina

0   100   200m
0   100   200yd

····· Running of the Bulls

Calle de Taconera

Calle de San Lorenzo

Calle de Jarauta

C de Mayor

1
2

C Mayor

3

Parque de la Taconera

Plaza del Castillo

Paseo de Hemingway

Calle Arrieta

8

7

9

C de Olite

Calle de San Ignacio

Plaza de las Merindades

C de Dormitalería

Plaza de Juan XXIII

C del Bosquecillo

C de las Navas de Tolosa

12

13

Avenida de Bayona

Parque Antoniuti

Calle de Padre Moret

10

Avenida del Ejército

Avenida de Barañain

14

Avda de Sancho el Fuerte

Avenida Pío XII

To Hospital de Navarra

Parque de la Ciudadela

15

Avenida del Príncipe de Viana

Avenida Baja

C de Yanguas y Miranda

Avenida de Zaragoza

Plaza de los Fueros

To Sector Disco

Plaza de la Cruz

C de Bergamín

C de San Fermín

Carlos III

Navarra

To Camping Ezcaba

Enlargement (inset map)

16

17

18

C del Mercado

Santo Domingo

0   50   100m
0   50   100yd

C de Jarauta

Mercaderes

Calle de la Calderería

19

20

Calle Mayor

Plaza Consistorial

Plaza de San Francisco

22

21

Calle Nueva

23

24

26

C de San Antón

25

27

28

Plaza del Castillo

29

To Net Iruña & University

C de San Nicolás

33

32

38

37

34

31

35

39

36

C de San Gregorio

40

41

Paseo de Sarasate

42

43

C Padre Moret

C de Tudela

C de Estella

Calle de Estella

García Jiménez

47

44

45

46

48

Plaza del Príncipe de Viana

C de Roncesvalles

C de las Cortes de Navarra

Carlos III

Avenida de San Ignacio

BARS & CLUBS
3   Donegal
5   Mesón del Caballo Blanco
12 Marengo
13 Reverendos
14 Más y Más
20 Terminal
22 Café Iruña
29 Casino Eslava
38 Bar Ciudadela

PLACES TO STAY
11 Habitaciones Mendi
17 Habitaciones Redin
23 Camas Escaray Lozano
26 Fonda Aragonesa; Bar Baserri
30 Hotel Europa
32 Bar/Habitaciones Otano
33 Bar/Habitaciones San Nicolás
35 Hostal Bearan
36 Fonda La Montañesa
37 Casa García
40 Pensión Sarasate
45 Pensión Pamplona
47 Hostal Navarra
47 Hotel Yoldi
48 Pensión Arrieta

PLACES TO EAT
1   Lanzale
2   El Erburu
19 Sagardotegi Iruñazarra
21 Mesón Pirineo
25 Restaurante San Fermín
28 Bodegón Sarria
34 Sarasate
39 Bar Anaitasuna

OTHER
4   Portal de Francia
6   Catedral &
    Museo Diocesano
7   Hemingway Monument
8   Plaza de Toros
9   Bus to Camping Ground
10 Policía Nacional
15 Ciudadela
16 Coralillos de
    Santo Domingo
18 Museo de Navarra
24 Tourist Office
27 Locutorio (Telephones)
31 Bus No 9 to
    Train Station
41 Vinoteca Murillo
42 Main Post Office
43 Ticket Office (Renfe)
44 Bus Station

impossible to get a room without booking ahead. Touts will often greet you at the train station or tourist office at this time, offering rooms in private houses.

Otherwise, you can join the throngs sleeping in the parks. People choosing this option should be aware that they are a prime target for thieves who are expert at slitting sleeping bags and whipping out anything from inside, apart from yourself. It's best to leave most belongings in the *consigna* (left-luggage office) at the bus or train stations.

Even if you base yourself outside Pamplona, you may still have to put up with a night in the park if you are relying on public transport and want to be in town in good time for the early morning running of the bulls.

Places to Stay – Budget
Camping The nearest camping ground, *Ezcaba* (☎ 948 33 03 15), is on the banks of the Río Ulzama, about 7km north on the N-121. It's open year round and charges 525 ptas each per person, tent and car. A bus service runs four times daily from just near the Plaza de Toros. Look for the Montañesa bus to Arre/Oricain.

Fondas, Pensiones & Hostales Plenty of cheap *fondas* (inns) and pensiones lurk in Pamplona's old centre. All places in this category have basic rooms with shared bath costing between 2000 and 3000 ptas for singles and 3500 to 4500 ptas for doubles.

Contenders lined up on bustling Calle San Nicolás, one of Pamplona's main arteries for food and drink, include *Fonda Aragonesa* (☎ 948 22 34 28, Calle San Nicolás 32), *Habitaciones San Nicolás* (☎ 948 22 13 19, Calle San Nicolás 13) and *Habitaciones Otano* (☎ 948 22 50 95, Calle San Nicolás 5). Otano also has a few doubles with bath for 5500 ptas.

Calle San Gregorio is the western continuation of San Nicolás and a bit quieter. This is where you'll find *Fonda La Montañesa* (☎ 948 22 43 80, Calle San Gregorio 2) and *Casa García* (☎ 948 22 38 93, Calle San Gregorio 12).

Near the tourist office, *Camas Escaray Lozano* (☎ 948 22 78 25, Calle Nueva 24)

has small but clean rooms and is probably the best value in this range. Right by the indoor market and next to the bull-running route is *Habitaciones Redin* (☎ 948 22 21 82, Calle del Mercado 5).

Places to Stay – Mid-Range
Habitaciones Mendi (☎ 948 22 52 97, Calle de las Navas de Tolosa 9) has large rooms with TV and bath, but it's not as clean as one might hope. Still, it's not a bad deal at 4000/6000 ptas for singles/doubles.

Near the bus station you'll find several clean and comfortable places that all look much the same inside. Best of these is *Pensión Arrieta* (☎ 948 22 84 59, Calle de Arrieta 27), whose lovely rooms come with TV and ceiling fans. The bathroom is down the hall and rates are 4000/5000 ptas.

Tiny *Pensión Pamplona* (☎ 948 22 99 63, Calle de Tudela 5) has small rooms with TV, but they're a bit expensive at 4000/5500 ptas. Two doors down, *Hostal Navarra* (☎ 948 22 51 64, fax 948 22 34 26, Calle de Tudela 9) has had a recent make-over and offers clean rooms with satellite TV (BBC reception), minibar and music system. The proprietor speaks English and charges 5140/7000 ptas for rooms with bath.

Another good bet is *Pensión Sarasate* (☎/fax 948 22 30 84, Paseo de Sarasate 30), which charges 4000/5000 ptas for pleasant, if smallish, rooms with private facilities. A step up is *Hostal Bearan* (☎/fax 948 22 34 28, Calle de San Nicolás 25), which has 17 comfortable rooms with TV, phone and bath for 5500/6500 ptas.

Places to Stay – Top End
A Pamplona institution since the 1920s, *Hotel Yoldi* (☎ 948 22 48 00, Avenida de San Ignacio 11) has hosted celebs from Hemingway to Charlton Heston. It usually charges 11,000/16,000 ptas, but on weekends rates plummet to just 7400/8000 ptas.

Offering a similar level of comfort, the *Hotel Europa* (☎ 948 22 18 00, fax 948 22 92 35, Calle de Espoz y Mina 11) also has bargain weekend rates of 5000/7850 ptas, but otherwise charges a more unforgiving 6900/14,625 ptas.

Places to Eat

Bar Anaitasuna (☎ *948 22 79 56, Calle de San Gregorio 58)* has uncluttered, modern decor and changes clientele and ambience throughout the day – from the newspaper-reading breakfast crowd to the late-night *marcha* (action). There's a daily *menú* for 1600 ptas and platos combinados cost around 1000 ptas.

Farther east, Calle San Nicolás is a veritable restaurant row. For the most innovative and creative pintxos in town, belly up to the bar at *Baserri* (☎ *948 22 20 21, Calle San Nicolás 32)*. There's even a menu listing the morsels that have garnered awards, and the wine selection here is tops too. Almost as good is *Otano* (☎ *948 22 26 38)* across the street. If you don't want to eat standing up, there are quite a few tables in the back. Its *patatas bravas* are outstanding.

Also here is the upmarket *Restaurante San Fermín* (☎ *948 22 21 91, Calle San Nicolás 44)*, a Pamplona classic with a set lunch for 3000 ptas and excellent *menestra de verdures,* a kind of vegetable stew, for 900 ptas. The popular *Bar San Nicolás* *(Calle San Nicolás 13)* does a Basque set meal for 1700 ptas. For meatless fare, make for the vegetarian *Sarasate (Calle San Nicolás 23)*.

Calle Estafeta is right on the bull-running route and has its share of cosy, timber-laden establishments serving traditional dishes. *Bodegón Sarria (Calle Estafeta 50)* draws an older crowd with its substantial, mostly meat-based meals. It's an atmospheric place with a great collection of black-and-whites of Hemingway gracing the walls. *Mesón Pirineo* (☎ *948 22 20 45, Calle Estafeta 41)* is similar and has a lunch *menú* for 1600 ptas. If you pick carefully, you can also put together a three-course a la carte meal for about 2300 ptas.

For more options, wander over to the more downmarket Calle de San Lorenzo. *El Erburu* (☎ *948 22 51 69, Calle de San Lorenzo 19)* has a *menú* for 1500 ptas, and *Lanzale* (☎ *948 22 10 71, Calle de San Lorenzo 31)* charges just 1150 ptas. Both are unassuming places heavily frequented by a local elbow-on-the-table crowd.

Sagardotegi Iruñazarra (☎ *948 22 51 67, Calle de los Mercaderes 15)* is a cider house offering the full traditional meal for 3000 ptas. If consuming what seems like half a cow is too much, you could opt for the tasty platos combinados from 1000 ptas.

If you need to stock up on vast amounts of good Navarran wine, *Vinoteca Murillo* (☎ *948 22 10 15)*, on the corner of Calle de San Gregorio and Plaza de San Nicolás, will fill 5L containers for 990 ptas.

Entertainment

Thanks to a student population of about 20,000, Pamplona has a lively after-dark scene all year. On Friday and Saturday nights, you may have to shoehorn your way into some of the more popular establishments.

Cafes & Bars The cafes on Plaza del Castillo with their French-style awnings are a great place to start the day, or end it. *Café Iruña* (☎ *948 21 15 64)*, at No 44, with its frilly Belle Epoque decor, is one of Pamplona's grande dames and a nice spot for coffee or an aperitif. *Casino Eslava* at the opposite end offers more reservedly modern chic.

Upstairs at *Bar Ciudadela* (☎ *948 21 04 49, Calle de la Ciudadela 3)* you can sip a drink on little balconies in summer. Better still is the outdoor *Mesón del Caballo Blanco,* just inside the city walls north of the cathedral. Calle de Jarauta is wall to wall bars (of the loud and late variety).

Clubs & Discos Most of Pamplona's dance venues are a walk or short taxi ride south and west of the old city centre in the general direction of the university. *Reverendos (Calle de Monasterio de Velate 5)* and *Más y Más (Avenida Bayona 45)* pull in techno fiends, while *Marengo (Avenida Bayona 2)* and *Sector (Calle Abejeras 11)* get the crowds going with Latin rhythms and international dance music. Doors at these places are usually open after 11 pm Thursday to Saturday, and cover tends to be around 1000 ptas.

Back in the old town, *Donegal (Calle de San Francisco 30)* and *Terminal (Calle de Calderería 19)* host local rock bands on some nights.

Getting There & Away

Bus Buses depart from the main bus station, on Avenida de Yangüas y Miranda, to most towns throughout Navarra, though service is restricted on Sunday.

Up to eight buses run daily to Bilbao (1580 ptas), and about 10 each go to Vitoria (900 ptas) and San Sebastián (790 ptas). Four daily head for Madrid (3220 ptas) and two to Barcelona (2190 ptas). Regional destinations include Olite, Javier, Estella, Logroño, Tudela, Soria and Puente La Reina.

Train Pamplona's train station is north of town but conveniently connected to the centre by bus No 9 every 15 minutes. Tickets are also sold at the Renfe agency (☎ 948 22 72 82) at Calle Estella 8 (closed Sunday).

There are two trains daily to Madrid (five hours, 5700 ptas) and three to Barcelona (seven hours, 4400 ptas). San Sebastián is served up to four times daily (two hours, 1600 ptas).

Car & Motorcycle The A-15 autopista connects Pamplona with San Sebastián to the north and Zaragoza in the south, although the N-121 is a more scenic – and free – alternate proposition. Several pretty routes, including the N-135, lead east into the Pyrenees and on to France. The N-240 west heads to Vitoria and Burgos, while its eastern continuation goes to Aragón. For Logroño take the N-111.

EAST OF PAMPLONA

South-east along the N-240, a handful of interesting towns and a grand monastery lying virtually on the southern rim of the Pyrenees together form a worthwhile excursion or stopover before heading on into Aragón. Buses are infrequent, however, and accommodation is pricey.

Sangüesa

postcode 31400 • pop 4580

The biggest town in eastern Navarra and once an important stop on the pilgrim route to Santiago de Compostela for those crossing from France, Sangüesa retains a sense of its past. Coming from Pamplona, you cross the Río Aragón and immediately on the left are

Navarra's Casas Rurales

Navarra has a particularly well-organised set of *casas rurales*. These are often beautifully looked-after houses in mountain villages and are popular in peak periods – reservations are recommended. You can recognise the casas rurales by one of two small plaques – one has 'CR' in white on a dark green background; the more modern one, in brown, olive green and white, displays the letter 'C' and the outline of a house.

Pick up a copy of the *Guía de Alojamientos de Turismo Rural*, available from most tourist offices in Navarra, which lists all the private homes and farmsteads that rent out rooms. The standards are often higher and rates lower than in your average hostal.

There is a central reservations switchboard on ☎ 948 22 93 28.

presented with one of the premier examples of Romanesque religious art in Navarra, the **Iglesia de Santa María** with its octagonal tower. Entry is through an exquisite 12th-century portal. Immediately opposite is the tourist office, which organises guided tours of the town's main sights upon request. Simpler, but with its own charm, is the **Iglesia de Santiago**, which shows signs of the transition to the Gothic.

Sangüesa is not a bad place to spend the night since it has more life than any of the nearby pueblos and a sufficient assortment of minor monuments and mansions to keep you interested. There's camping at *Cantolagua* (☎ 948 43 03 52) on Camino de Cantolagua; *Pensión Las Navas* (☎ 948 87 07 00, Calle de Alfonso el Batallador 7), near the ayuntamiento, has singles/doubles for 3000/5000 ptas. It also has decent food.

Buses run daily to Pamplona.

Javier

postcode 31411 • pop 158

From Sangüesa, it's 11km north-east to Javier (or Xavier), where the patron saint of Navarra, San Francisco Xavier, was born in 1506. The town, a forgettable grid of dead streets, lies downhill from the Jesuit-owned

Castillo de Javier. An evocative piece of medieval architecture, it houses a small museum whose eclectic collection includes 14th-century Japanese kimonos decorated with scenes from the life of the saint who was a missionary in the Far East. There's also a chapel with macabre murals depicting the Dance of Death. The castle's opening hours are from 9 am to 12.40 pm and 4 to 6.40 pm daily (to 5.40 pm in winter); entry is free.

Javier's two hotels have a monopoly on food and beds and are overpriced, but if you must stay, *Hotel El Mesón* (✆ 948 88 40 35) is the cheaper one at 4900/6600 ptas for singles/doubles. A daily bus passes through from Pamplona and Sangüesa en route for Huesca, while another heads up the Valle de Roncal.

Yesa & the Monasterio de Leyre
postcode 31410 • pop 293

If you have wheels and no luck with rooms in Sangüesa, skip those in Javier and try here. *Hostal El Jabalí* (✆ 948 88 40 42) on the Jaca road, for instance, charges 3000/4000 ptas for single/double rooms with washbasin.

About 5km north lies the **Monasterio de Leyre** (or Leire), set in the shadow of the Sierra de Leyre, virtually the last mountain range before the Pyrenees. A religious community was first established here in the 9th century. By the 12th century it had become a powerful Cluniac bastion, looming large in the religious and cultural life of all Navarra and pretty much in command of all the pilgrim-route passes from France. By the time the Cistercian reform was introduced in the 13th century, the monastery was beginning to lose influence. In 1836 the monks were kicked out, and over the next 100 years local shepherds used the monastery to shelter themselves and their flocks. In 1954, when the Benedictines moved in, they found themselves confronted by the enormous task of restoration.

The early Romanesque crypt is the most fascinating part of the complex. It is a three-nave structure with a low roof; its squat columns and vaguely horseshoe-shaped arches are unique to the monastery. The Romanesque cloister was destroyed after the expulsion of the Cistercians, but the 12th-century main portal of the church is a fine example of Romanesque artistry at its most challenging and is rich in symbolism. Much of the church is, however, built in the early-Gothic style.

The monks sell recordings of themselves performing Gregorian chants. If you can make it to the 9 am Mass or 7 pm vespers service, you can hear the real thing. The monastery is open 10.15 am to 2 pm and 3.30 to 7 pm daily (250 ptas).

There's an early morning bus from Yesa to Pamplona as well as one to Huesca. You might also be able to pick up the daily service connecting Pamplona and the Valle de Roncal. Virtually no buses run on Sunday, and none at all from Yesa to the monastery.

WEST OF PAMPLONA
The N-111 is the main route west out of Pamplona, winding gently to Logroño along the Camino de Santiago. Dotted with a handful of charming villages and especially bursting with colour after the spring rains, it is one of the more enticing stretches for those walking the Camino. Virtually every town has a pilgrims' hostel. Buses regularly run between Pamplona and Logroño along this route.

Puente la Reina
postcode 31100 • pop 2125

It is at Puente la Reina (Gares) that pilgrims approaching from Roncesvalles to the north and Aragón to the east have for centuries joined together to take the one main route west to Santiago de Compostela. Their first stop here was the late-Romanesque **Iglesia del Crucifijo**, erected by the Knights Templar and still containing one of the finest Gothic crucifixes in existence. From here the narrow Calle Mayor leads to the **Iglesia de Santiago**, sporting an interesting, if somewhat eroded, Romanesque portal with múdejar touches. Inside is an especially beautiful sculpture of the saint. The town's namesake bridge, the six-arched medieval **Puente la Reina** at the end of Calle Mayor, remains the nicest way to cross the Río Arga and continue on the Camino.

For information on places to stay, see the special section 'Camino de Santiago'.

Estella

postcode 31200 • pop 12,750 • elev 483m

The highlight on this route is the picturesque town of Estella (Lizarra), huddled on the bend of the tree-shaded Río Ega. It makes a good base for excursions in the vicinity and is certainly the best place to end up for the night.

Seat of the Carlists in the 19th century, the village of Lizarra acquired its Castilian name in 1090 when Sancho Ramírez (king of Navarra and Aragón) made it the primary reception point for the growing flood of pilgrims along the Camino.

Every year from 31 July to 8 August, Estella hosts a *feria* (fair) with its own running of the bulls – not nearly as hyped as Pamplona's but equally thrilling.

The extremely helpful tourist office (☎ 948 55 40 11), on Calle de San Nicolás 1, is right in among the most important monuments on the south-western bank of the river. It's open 10 am to 8 pm Monday to Saturday (to 5 pm from October to Easter) and Sunday to 2 pm year round.

The most important monument is just opposite: the 12th-century cliff-top **Iglesia de San Pedro de la Rúa**, whose fortified tower lords over the town. The tourist office gives tours in English (325 ptas), or you can view the cloister by climbing the steps farther along the street. Guided tours of the entire town with English commentary cost 600 ptas.

Adjacent to the tourist office is the **Palacio de los Reyes**, a rare example of Romanesque civil construction, containing a small art museum. Across the river and overlooking the town is the **Iglesia de San Miguel**. Its most interesting feature is the Romanesque north door.

Estella has numerous hotels and eateries. For details, see the special section 'Camino de Santiago'.

Monasterio de Irache

About 3km south-west of Estella, near Ayegui, this ancient Benedictine monastery has undergone many changes over the centuries. Its most alluring features are the 16th-century plateresque cloister and the Puerta Especiosa, decorated with delicate sculptures. It is open 9.30 am to 1.30 pm and 5 to 7 pm, closed all day Monday and Tuesday afternoon (free). It is supposed to be the future home of a museum of Navarran ethnography. Virtually next door you can taste some local reds at the Bodega de Irache.

Los Arcos & Torres del Río

The only point of interest in Los Arcos is the **Iglesia de Santa María** and its Gothic cloister. If you need to stay, try *Hotel Mónaco* (☎ 948 64 00 00, Plaza del Coso 22), where singles/doubles are 2750/3950 ptas.

The road on this stretch twists and turns through rolling country to Torres del Río, whose little gem is the octagonal 12th-century Romanesque **Iglesia del Santo Sepulcro**.

Viana

Only about 10km short of Logroño, Viana is a quiet spot with the mansions of noble families peppered around its old centre. The Gothic **Iglesia de Santa María** has an outstanding Renaissance doorway.

NORTH OF PAMPLONA

If you're headed for San Sebastián, the coast and/or France from Pamplona, you have several options. The quickest dash north can be made up the A-15. A preferable and dawdling route would see you pushing straight up north along the N-121A (keep alert for the right exit from Pamplona by car, as it's a little confusing). The initial stretch is pretty enough, but there's little to stop for until you wind over the **Puerto de Velate** pass. From here you could follow the same highway along the valley known as the **Regata de Bidasoa**.

Valle del Baztán & Regata de Bidasoa

If you're in no bust-a-gut hurry, consider making a detour up the lush Valle del Baztán to the north-east. Minor roads take you past charming little villages such as **Ziga** (which has a 16th-century church and, about 1km farther north, a beautiful lookout point) and **Irurita** (with another fine church) before reaching the valley's biggest town, **Elizondo**, on the N-121B. Although not the prettiest of the Baztán pueblos, this can make a convenient base for exploring the area, and there is plenty of accommodation.

Casa Jaén (☎ 948 58 04 87) is a *casa rural* with cute little doubles for 3800 ptas. About 10km out of town, *Casa Urruska* (☎ 948 45 21 06) is in a more tranquil, rural setting and offers singles/doubles with bath for 2800/4200 ptas.

The bus station is on the main road and buses go to Pamplona and San Sebastián up to three times daily, stopping in many of the smaller villages up and down the valley.

Beyond Elizondo, a particularly lovely road climbs eastwards through the enchanting villages of **Arizkun** and **Erratzu** to the French border pass of Puerto de Izpegui. Coming the other way, this is without doubt one of the prettiest introductions to Spain from France. You'll find two *casas rurales* with doubles for 3700 ptas in Arizkun, plus three more and a *camping ground* (☎ 948 45 31 33) in Erratzu.

Back on the N-121B, turn northwards for the Puerto de Otxondo and the border crossing into France at Dantxarinea. Just before the border a minor road veers west to **Zugarramurdi**, whose main claim to fame is its caves. For centuries they have been known as the **Cuevas de Las Brujas** (Witches' Caves). A trail snakes around and through a huge rock tunnel (300 ptas). A few kilometres away are more caves, this time with the odd stalactite and stalagmite, at Urdazubi-Urdax.

There are two welcoming *casas rurales*, each charging 4000 ptas per double, in Zugarramurdi. One bus daily (except Sunday) goes to Elizondo.

From Zugarramurdi you could now follow a tiny back road south to Mugairi (Oronoz), putting you back on the N-121A and into the Regata de Bidasoa. The first worthwhile stop from there heading north along the N-121A is a few kilometres off to

the east at **Etxalar** (Echalar). The churchyard is sprinkled with traditional tombstones in the shape of small discs. A little farther north and off to the west, **Lesaka** is noted for its Iglesia de San Martín de Tours and the so-called *casherna,* a medieval tower in the village centre. Last stop before the coast is **Bera de Bidasoa**, with an atmosphere virtually indistinguishable from that of French Pyrenees towns. Its ayuntamiento and 15th-century church are impressive. All these towns have casas rurales.

SOUTH OF PAMPLONA
Olite
postcode 31390 • pop 3050

The extensive medieval defensive castle complex known as the **Palacio Real**, which completely dominates the small town of Olite, was built on the site of what was originally a fortified Roman *praesidium* (garrison). It served as the residence of the Navarran kings until the union with the kingdom of Castille in 1512. The bulk of what you see today was built by Carlos III of Navarra a hundred years earlier with the help of master craftsmen from around Europe. The centrepiece of the rambling, crenellated structure is the Gran Torre, one of a straggle of round towers and annexes. Integrated into the castle is the **Iglesia de Santa María la Real**, with its astonishingly detailed Gothic portal.

The castle is open 10 am to 2 pm and 4 to 7 pm daily (until 8 pm in July and August, to 6 pm in winter); 400 ptas, plus an optional 200 ptas for a taped self-guided tour.

Olite makes for a nice place to spend a night – if you've got money to spare. *Hotel Casa Zanito* (☎ 948 74 00 02) on Rúa Revillas and *Hotel Merindad de Olite* (☎ 948 74 07 35, Rúa de la Judería 11) both charge around 6500/8500 ptas for fully-equipped singles/doubles. There's also a *parador* (☎ 948 74 00 00, fax 948 74 02 01, Plaza de los Teobaldos 2) with rooms starting at 11,600/14,500 ptas.

Buses between Olite and Pamplona stop 3km north in the rambling old city of **Tafalla**. There's little to detain you there save for the dominating Iglesia de Santa María.

Ujué

Some 19km east of Tafalla (there is another back road from Olite too, via San Martín de Unx), this tiny medieval village balances atop a hill looking out over the plains around it. The icing on the cake, as it were, is the hybrid **Iglesia de Santa María**, a fortified church of mixed Romanesque-Gothic style. Several *casas rurales* offer affordable beds.

Monasterio de la Oliva

Off another side road to the east of the main Pamplona-Zaragoza highway lies the quiet backwater of **Carcastillo**. Two kilometres farther on, the formidable Monasterio de la Oliva was begun by the Cistercians in the 12th century. Its austere church gives onto a particularly pleasing Gothic cloister. There are two or three buses daily between Pamplona and Carcastillo.

Tudela

postcode 31500 • pop 26,460

An ancient city that was in Muslim hands for some 400 years, Tudela is well worth a wander, with its twisting street layout serving as a reminder of its Islamic past. There is a tourist office (☎/fax 948 84 80 58) opposite the cathedral.

Most people set out to explore the town from the brightly decorated Plaza de los Fueros. From here, take Calle de Yangüas y Miranda through the arch and at the next square take a right into Calle de las Carnicerías. This leads to the **catedral**, a sober 12th-century Gothic structure built of stone and brick. The western Puerta del Juicio is particularly striking, its many sculpted figures looking decidedly uneasy about their participation in the Last Judgment. There are some good altarpieces inside, and if you're lucky you can get into the beautiful Romanesque cloister. In 1993, traces of the central mosque that had preceded the cathedral were identified adjacent to it.

Perhaps the quirkiest of Tudela's attractions is its 13th-century **bridge** over the Río Ebro. To get to it, follow Calle del Portal eastwards (downhill) from the cathedral past the 12th-century **Iglesia de la Magdalena**

and then head out the scruffy town gate (topped by the railway line). The Spaniards call a botch job a *chapuza,* and this bridge, with its arches all different shapes and sizes, seems to fit the bill perfectly. Yet seven centuries later, it still works fine! The Ebro flows mightily by, quite unperturbed by the lack of symmetry above it.

Of the other churches in Tudela, the **Iglesia de San Nicolás** still sports a fine Romanesque tympanum featuring lions above one of its doors. It's at the end of Calle Rúa. Take time to wander the streets, as there are some fine old mansions, many with Aragonese-style awnings *(aleros)* jutting out from the roof; the **Palacio del Marqués de San Adrián** at Calle de Magallón 10 is an impressive example.

Places to Stay & Eat *Hostal Remigio* (☎ 948 82 08 50, Calle de Gaztambide 4), just off Plaza de los Fueros, offers doubles with washbasin for 3800 ptas and others with bath for 5100 ptas. It also has a venerable old dining room.

Getting There & Away Tudela is on the Pamplona-Zaragoza railway, and buses operate from next to the train station, southeast of centre.

THE PYRENEES

The Navarran Pyrenees are a rich playground for outdoor enthusiasts as well as for pilgrims on the Camino de Santiago, which enters Spain from France in Valcarlos. Walkers should refer to the boxed text 'Walking in the Pyrenees' in the Catalunya chapter. Trekkers and skiers alike should note a couple of emergency numbers in case they get into serious trouble on the Navarran or French side of the mountains. Call ☎ 088 in Navarra or ☎ 17 in Aquitaine (France).

To France via Roncesvalles

As you bear north-east out of Pamplona along the N-135 and ascend into the Pyrenees, the yellows, browns and olive green of lower Navarra begin to give way to a more luxuriant vegetation.

Burguete This spotless mountain village straddling the main road was a favourite getaway for Hemingway – it's worlds apart from its dusty counterparts farther south. There is a fair spread of accommodation, including *Casa Vergara* (☎ 948 76 00 44), which charges 4800 ptas for doubles with bath, and *Hostal Juandeaburre* (☎ 948 76 00 78, Calle de San Nicolas), which is good value at 2200/3800 ptas for singles/doubles with washbasin. *Camping Urrobi* (☎ 948 76 02 00), open from April to October, is a few kilometres south. For eating out, *Restaurante Tikipolit*, on the main drag, has tasty mains for around 1000 ptas. There is also a supermarket and a bank.

Roncesvalles A few kilometres farther north, Roncesvalles (Orreaga) is little more than a monastery complex sitting within a mountain pass which for centuries has been a major Pyrenees crossing point for pilgrims on the Camino de Santiago. The 13th-century Gothic **Real Colegiata de Santa María** church contains a much revered silver-covered statue of the Virgin. Also of interest is the cloister (rebuilt in the 17th century), and more particularly the chapterhouse with its beautiful star-ribbed vaulting. This contains the tomb of King Sancho VII (El Fuerte) of Navarra, the apparently 2.25m-tall victor in the Battle of Las Navas de Tolosa fought against the Muslims in 1212.

The attached museum contains many paintings, books and objects donated by wealthy pilgrims over the years. Also nearby is the 12th-century Capilla de Sancti Spiritus. All sites are open 10.30 am to 1.10 pm and 4 to 5.40 pm daily (longer in summer). Entry to the cloister, chapterhouse and museum is 300 ptas. Guided tours (500 ptas) cover all these, plus the tomb of Sancho VII. A few steps away is the excellent tourist office, open until 5 or 6 pm daily, closed Sunday afternoon.

HI members can try the *Albergue de la Juventud* (☎ 948 76 00 15), housed in an 18th-century hospital where pilgrims used to take respite. Of the two hotels, the highly regarded *Hostal La Posada* (☎ 948 76 02 25) has singles/doubles with bath for 5200/6500 ptas.

The afternoon bus (daily except Sunday) from Pamplona via Burguete stops here.

Puerto de Ibañeta & Valcarlos From Roncesvalles, the road climbs to the Puerto de Ibañeta, the pass where Roland, Charlemagne's nephew, and his men were attacked – a modern memorial marks the spot (see the boxed text 'Roland's Swan Song'). From here you have magnificent views across into France. The last town before the frontier is Valcarlos, a sleepy but pretty spot.

Casa Etxezuria (☎ 948 79 00 11), on the main road heading towards France, is a private house with delightful doubles for 3800 ptas (2000 ptas for single occupancy). The owner has a couple of other places nearby.

From Valcarlos, you'll know you've crossed the border when you pass the Campsa petrol station – it is well worth pursuing the road on to St Jean Pied-de-Port.

Into the Backblocks If little villages and quiet country roads are an attraction, there is plenty of scope for losing yourself in the area east of the main Roncesvalles road. A couple of kilometres south of Burguete, the NA-202 branches off east to Garralda. Push on to **Arive**, a charming hamlet on the crossroads of several country lanes. From here, you could continue east to the Valle del Salazar (see the following section), or go south along the Río Irati past the fine Romanesque church near Nagore, or take a loop north-east through the Bosque de Irati forest, which again would eventually bring you to the Valle del Salazar, at Ochagavía. The forest, full of elms, beeches and lime trees, is one of Europe's most extensive, inviting you to drop your vehicle and head off for a hike.

Valle del Salazar
The NA-178 veers north-east off the N-240 through the sleepy town of **Lumbier**, only worth a stop for its medieval bridge and the beautiful gorge *(foz)* of the same name. Flanked by steep walls, it follows the flow of the Río Aragon to the remains of a Roman bridge. Farther up, the road crosses paths with another nice gorge, the Foz de Arbayún. Just after you see the sign, swing right for the platform that affords splendid vistas. Those with binoculars will be able to see flights of eagles.

Many of the hamlets that line the road north contain some gems of medieval handiwork, and in some cases their quiet cobbled streets and little plazas are equipped with the odd bar or cafe. Among the candidates are **Güesa**, nearby **Igal**, **Sarriés** and particularly **Esparza**, with its mansions, medieval bridge and restored Iglesia de San Andrés. A bus runs the length of the Salazar valley from Pamplona to Ochagavía.

Ochagavía Busier than the rest of the valley, this Pyrenean town lying astride the narrow Río Zatoya sets itself quite apart from the villages farther south. Grey stone and slate are the main building materials in the old centre and the place has a sober dignity reinforced by the looming presence of the Iglesia de San Juan Evangelista.

This is a popular base for walkers and even skiers, so many local families have opened up their homes as *casas rurales* – there are no fewer than 12 of them. There is also a year-round *camping ground (☎ 948 89 01 84)*.

A lively place for a meal or drink is *Iratxo Bar*, the first place to the left on the main drag when you arrive from the south.

Heading North The smaller of the two roads north from Ochagavía winds 24km over the Pyrenees into a dead end in the Bosque de Irati, where you can embark on some pleasant, solitary walks.

For France you take the N-140 north-east from Ochagavía into the Sierra de Abodi and cross at the Puerto de Larrau (1585m), a majestically bleak pass where you won't even realise you've crossed the frontier north until you're already over. Four kilometres short of the border is a restaurant and bar for skiers. Day-trippers come here to ski, but there are no lifts or other facilities.

Valle del Roncal
This easternmost valley in the Navarran Pyrenees is in most respects also the most attractive. Its mountain territory is Navarra's most spectacular, although for skiing and alpine splendour, the neighbouring Aragónese Pyrenees have more to offer. One bus leaves Pamplona daily except Sunday, passing through all these towns on its way to Uztárroz. It returns early in the morning.

Burgui The gateway to this part of the Pyrenees is Burgui. Its Roman bridge over the Río Esca, combined with its huddle of stone houses, is an evocative introduction to the rural Pyrenean towns farther upstream. Nice as it is, you should really push on upriver for Roncal or Isaba. Be warned, however, that these can get crowded in summer. If you need to stay in Burgui, *Hostal El Almadiero* (☎ 948 47 70 86) on Plaza Mayor is the only game in town, with doubles ranging from 5000 to 6400 ptas, depending on the month.

Roncal This brooding, tightly knit village boasts a 16th-century parish church, but it is the cobblestone alleyways twisting between dark stone houses that lend the village its charm.

The tourist office (☎ 948 47 51 36), on the main road towards the Isaba exit from town, can provide photocopies of walking maps. It's open in summer only (closed Sunday afternoon). There is one bank and even a ski-hire outlet here.

Although Isaba, farther north, makes a better base, you could do a lot worse than to choose one of the four casas rurales in the centre of Roncal as a place to stay. *Casa Pili* (☎ 948 47 51 35) and *Casa Txarpa* (☎ 948 47 50 68) are both traditional houses in the centre of the village and charge 3400 ptas per double with shared bath.

Isaba The village of Isaba is another popular base for walkers and skiers, lying on the confluence of the Río Belagua and the Río Uztárroz, which together flow into the Río Esca. There are a few banks with ATMs and a tourist office (☎ 948 89 32 51).

Of the eight casas rurales, the better ones are *Casa Catalingarde* (☎ 948 89 31 54) and *Casa Francisco Mayo* (☎ 948 89 31 66), both with doubles at 3500 ptas. *Camping Asolaze* (☎ 948 89 30 34) is at Km 6 on the road to France. A good restaurant is the *Tapia*, just out of the old centre on the road to Roncal. You can eat well for 1500 ptas or less.

North of Isaba The *Refugio Belagua*, 19km north of Isaba, is a handy base for trekkers in summer and skiers in winter. It operates a restaurant and bar, and has some bunks to throw a sleeping bag onto. There is no bus up this way.

Walking
In addition to numerous local walking trails, those with more time can follow the GR-12 long-distance trail across the best Navarra has to offer. You will need a sleeping bag and all-weather gear, even in summer. Starting in Burguete, head north to Roncesvalles, cross the Puerto de Ibañeta and steer eastwards to Fábrica de Orbaitzeta. You may need to head south to the town of Orbaitzeta proper to get a bed (there are three casas rurales).

The next day would take you through the Bosque de Irati to Las Casas de Irati; you may be able to stay in the *Casa del Guarda* (a kind of warden's house) but be prepared to camp (free). The following stage sees you climbing to the bare heights of the Puerto de Larrau (ask at the restaurant-bar 4km south of the French border about bunk beds). The trail then cuts across the Sierra de Abodi and you can reach the Belagua refugio in about five hours' march.

The final trek takes you to the highest mountain in Navarra, La Mesa de los Tres Reyes (2438m), from where the easiest thing to do is descend to the town of **Zuriza** at the top end of the Valle de Ansó, in Aragón (see the Valle de Ansó section of the Aragón chapter).

La Rioja

Mention the word Rioja and thoughts turn to some of the best red wines produced in Spain. The bulk of the vineyards line the Río Ebro around the town of Haro, extending into neighbouring Navarra and the Basque province of Álava (Araba). A lesser-known fact is that La Rioja was also a major stomping ground of dinosaurs, with much fossilised evidence still in existence (see the boxed text 'In the Footsteps of Big Feet' later in this chapter). The Camino de Santiago also passes through La Rioja and constitutes the area's other main attraction.

LOGROÑO
postcode 26080 • pop 120,800
Although Logroño is an important agricultural, industrial and commercial centre, it also owes some of its wealth to its position on the Río Ebro and the Camino de Santiago.

There is not a helluva lot to see, but the old centre is really quite enjoyable and it's not a bad place for an overnight stop and a little bar-hopping.

History
It was the Muslim armies in the 8th century that gave Logroño its name. In the Middle Ages Logroño was the object of a dispute between the crowns of Castile and Navarra, but its fortunes declined in the 18th century. By 1861, when the walls were torn down to permit expansion, things were looking up and La Rioja's agricultural riches were reflected in the prosperity of the capital.

Orientation
If you arrive at the train or bus station, head up Calle del General Vara de Rey until you reach the Espolón, a large, park-like square. The tourist office is here and the old town starts just a bit farther north. A bed, food and drink can all be easily found in the vicinity.

Information
The slick and friendly tourist office (☎ 941 29 12 60, fax 941 29 16 40), in the Espolón square, is usually open 9 am to 2 pm Monday to Saturday, but from June to October it's also open afternoons and Sunday morning. The main post office is in the old quarter on Plaza San Agustín 1.

Things to See
The **Catedral de Santa María Redonda** started life as a Gothic church, a fact easily overlooked when your gaze is held by the voluptuousness of the churrigueresque towers added in the 18th century. Closer to the river and right on the pilgrims' route through the city is the predictable **Iglesia de Santiago**. Above one of the portals is a somewhat uncared-for equestrian statue of the church's patron saint. Take a look at the impressive main entrance to the **Iglesia de San Bartolomé** too.

A stroll around the old town and down to the river is a pleasant diversion, or you could pop in to see the free art exhibits in the **Museo de la Rioja** (closed Sunday afternoon and Monday).

LOGROÑO

PLACES TO STAY	OTHER
4 Hostal Marqués de Vallejo	1 Iglesia de Santiago
5 Hostal La Numantina	2 Iglesia de San Bartolomé
9 Casa de Huéspedes Villar	3 Catedral de Santa María Redonda
11 Pensión Bilbaína	7 Tourist Office
	8 Bus Station
PLACES TO EAT	10 Café/Bar Moderno
6 La Piazza	12 Noche y Día
16 Lorenzo	13 Main Post Office
18 El Muro	14 Café Eldorado
	15 Panadería El Paraíso
	17 Museo de la Rioja
	19 Mercado San Blas

Special Events
Try to be in Logroño for the week-long Fiesta de San Mateo starting on 21 September. This also doubles as a harvest festival, for which all of La Rioja comes to town to celebrate and to watch the grape-crushing ceremonies in the Espolón. Another party day is 11 June, when the Fiesta de San Bernabé is held.

Places to Stay
Logroño and budget accommodation seem to be mutually exclusive, a couple of fondas in the old quarter notwithstanding. *Pensión*

euro currency converter €1 = 166pta

LA RIOJA

Bilbaína (☎ 941 25 42 26, Calle Gallarza 10), run by a young couple, has quite decent doubles with shower for 3500 ptas. *Casa de Huéspedes Villar (☎ 941 22 02 28, Calle de Martínez Zaporta 7)* is really a big apartment in a well-maintained 1911 building. The crotchety owner lets out large and cosy doubles for 3000 ptas per person. *Hostal La Numantina (☎ 941 25 14 11, Calle de Sagasta 4)* has decor from the disco decade and overpriced singles/doubles for 4000/6200 ptas with bath. For more comfort, you'll need to dig deeper to stay at *Hostal Marqués de Vallejo (☎ 941 24 83 33, Calle del Marqués de Vallejo 8),* which has rooms with bath and TV for 6500/9500 ptas.

In the Footsteps of Big Feet

Dinosaurs tramped about most of Spain, but far and away their favourite stomping ground was La Rioja – long before wine was an attraction. Hikers looking for something a little different could choose to follow a route dotted with traces of this prehistoric passing trade. The section of the long-distance walking route GR-93 between the villages of Enciso, about 10km south of the spa village of Arnedillo, and Muro de Aguas, about 15km east of Enciso, has eight fossil prints of dinosaurs along the way, signposted and with explanations posted in Spanish. In Valdecevillo, for example, you can see the footprints left by an enormous carnivorous biped. Other such fossils can be seen scattered about the area along different tracks. You'll be accompanied overhead by Leonado (griffon) vultures along the 20km route, which lies about midway between Logroño and Soria (Castilla y León). The most attractive place to stay around here is Arnedillo.

ERROL HUNT

Places to Eat

The area around Calle de San Agustín and Calle de Laurel is jammed with tapas bars and restaurants. For great *pinchos morunos* (the Spanish version of kebabs) at 100 ptas a stick and cheap drinks, try *Lorenzo,* an unpretentious stand-up bar on Travesía de Laurel. *El Muro (☎ 941 20 64 68, Calle Bretón de los Herreros 34-36)* is a cosy place for tapas or a meal – the set lunch for 1500 ptas or 1950 ptas is excellent. *La Piazza (☎ 941 22 33 83),* on Avenida de la Rioja, is a trendy Italian restaurant with bright decor and a sensible menu featuring pizza, pasta and salads all priced around 1000 ptas.

Mercado San Blas has fresh fruit and vegetables, and for irresistible pastries and breads, head to *Panadería El Paraíso* on Calle Agustín.

Entertainment

Café/Bar Moderno (☎ 941 22 00 42, Plaza de Franco Martínez Zaporta 9) is something of a local institution, with old men playing dominoes and drinking wine amid black-and-white photos of the good old days. *Café Eldorado (Calle de Portales 80)* sometimes provides live music to accompany your beer. Popular *Noche y Día (Calle de Portales 63)* has clever decor and is a good cafe-bar for hanging out any time of day.

Getting There & Away

Up to five buses leave daily for Burgos (865 ptas) via Santo Domingo de la Calzada (380 ptas). Six buses daily head north for Bilbao (1475 ptas), while five services go to Madrid (2515 ptas). Other destinations such as Vitoria, Pamplona, Haro and Calahorra are regularly served as well.

By train, Logroño is connected to Zaragosa up to nine times daily (2¼ hours, 1265 ptas) and once to Madrid (5½ hours, 4100 ptas); four trains each go to Bilbao (2¾ hours, 2000 ptas) and Burgos (three hours, 2600 ptas).

The A-68 autopista from Zaragoza to Bilbao skirts Logroño to the south. The N-111 heads north-east to Pamplona and south to Soria, while the N-120 reaches west for Burgos.

WINE REGION

Spain's best-known wines come from La Rioja – the vine has been cultivated here since Roman times. When talking wine, the name 'La Rioja' really refers to the banks of the Río Ebro. Much is in fact made on the Basque side of the river, known as La Rioja Alavesa (from the southern Basque province of Álava). The region produces reds, rosés and whites.

The bulk of the reds are designed to be aged and some of the best years include 1995, 1994 and 1982. Wines produced around Laguardia, on the Basque side, are fruity and soft and can only be grown in this part of La Rioja because of its unique microclimate. Protected by the Sierra de Cantabria from the worst of the bitter northern cold and blessed with an ochre soil different from the red earth of the south bank, vines here produce a result quite distinct from elsewhere in the region.

Most of the La Rioja wine is bought up and marketed by big concerns, but small family bodegas are reasserting themselves. Wine tasting for passing tourists is not common in Spain. Most bodegas reserve such activity for people in the business. Here again, things are changing a little, and some smaller bodegas will open their doors to curious passers-by, although it's best to call ahead for an appointment.

Exploring the Rioja region will almost inevitably take you across the border into the Basque Country and La Rioja Alavesa. See Laguardia & Around in the Basque Country section earlier in this chapter.

Haro

postcode 26200 • pop 8780
Haro is the capital of La Rioja's wine-producing region. There's not a whole lot of interest here, although the compact old quarter leading off Plaza de la Paz has some intriguing alleyways with bars and wine shops, and it makes a good enough base from which to scoot into the vineyards.

The tourist office (☎ 941 30 33 66) is downhill from Plaza de la Paz on Plaza de Florentino Rodríguez and is open 10 am to 2 pm and 4 to 7 pm daily in summer (mornings only on Sunday and in winter).

The **Museo del Vino** (or Estación Enológica), near the bus station on Calle de Cira Anguciana, houses a detailed display on how wine is made. It is open 10 am to 2 pm and 4 to 8 pm daily, closed Sunday afternoon (300 ptas, free on Wednesday).

Check at the tourist office for wineries open to the public; Bodega Muga, just after the railway bridge on the way out of town, sometimes gives guided tours. You can also pick up various bottles of local wines at shops, such as Todos los Vinos de Rioja, which certainly has many wines, if not the 'all' that its name claims. It's just off the main square on Calle de San Martín. There are more stores on Calle de Santo Tomás.

Places to Stay & Eat A few budget places are on Calle de la Vega just off the square, such as the creaky *Hostal Aragón (☎ 941 31 00 04, Calle de la Vega 9),* where singles/doubles start at 2000/3000 ptas. Better value are the bright, clean rooms above *Restaurante La Peña (☎ 941 31 00 22, Calle de la Vega 1),* which cost the same (more with bath). Some overlook Plaza de la Paz. The restaurant itself comes recommended, with a *menú* for 1100 ptas.

For a classier meal washed down with fine Rioja wines, try *Restaurante Beethoven (☎ 941 31 00 18, Calle de Santo Tomás 10).* Mains cost from about 1500 to 2000 ptas. Highly recommended is the rustic *Terete (☎ 941 31 00 23, Calle de General Franco 26),* which serves traditional fare on butcher-block tables.

Getting There & Away Regular trains and buses connect Haro with Logroño and Vitoria, and buses additionally serve Bilbao, Santo Domingo de la Calzada and Laguardia.

MONASTERY ROUTE

The area west of Logroño harbours a handful of monasteries, all important stops on the Camino de Santiago. Buses make the trip from Logroño at least once daily, although the most efficient way of getting from one monastery to the next is to go under your own steam.

Nájera

postcode 26300 • pop 7150

The main attraction of this town is the Gothic **Monasterio de Santa María la Real**, and in particular its fragile-looking early-16th-century cloisters. Inside the church you can see splendid choir stalls with imaginative carvings and a pantheon of tombs containing the remains of kings of Castile, León and Navarra. It is open 10 am to 1 pm and 4 to 6 pm Tuesday to Sunday, closing a little later in summer (200 ptas).

San Millán de Cogolla

If you hit the back roads south-west of Nájera you will, after about 16km, reach the two remarkable monasteries in the hamlet of San Millán de Cogolla, framed by a beautiful valley. The **Monasterio de Yuso**, sometimes a bit presumptuously called El Escorial de La Rioja, contains numerous treasures in its museum. A highlight are the remains of the 6th-century hermit San Millán, contained within a shrine whose delicate ivory carvings depict scenes from the saint's life. Also of note are the lavishly decorated, barrel-vaulted sacristy, the library with its rare manuscripts and the church with paintings by Juan Rizzi.

A short distance away is the equally interesting **Monasterio de Suso**. It is built above the caves where San Millán once lived, and was consecrated in the 10th century. Much of the original Mozarabic architecture survives, despite numerous alterations. It is widely believed that, in the 13th century, a monk named Gonzalo de Berceo penned the first-ever written Castilian words here. He is buried in one of the chapels.

Both monasteries are open 10.30 to 1.30 pm and 4 to 6.30 pm (slightly shorter hours in winter), closed Monday (400 ptas).

Santo Domingo de la Calzada

postcode 26250 • pop 5700

This fascinating little town gets its name from a feisty 11th-century hermit who, having been rejected by two local monasteries, simply built his own hermitage on the site of the present-day town. Watching a steady stream of pilgrims struggle through here

Of Pilgrims, Fowl & Miracles

The most curious 'decoration' in the cathedral of Santo Domingo is that of a live white rooster and hen kept in a special niche as a reminder of the saint's sideline as a miracle worker. The tall tale is that, once upon a time, a young German pilgrim, overnighting at the local inn, snubbed the advances of the innkeeper's daughter. To get back at him, she hid a piece of silver in his satchel, then denounced him to the authorities as a thief. The poor guy was quickly convicted and hanged, but when his parents came to say farewell to their dead child, they found him still alive: he had been saved by the intercession of Santo Domingo. When told of this, the disbelieving local ruler (*corregidor*) exclaimed that the lad was about as alive as the roast chook he was about to tuck into. Upon which, the hen and rooster on his plate leapt off his plate and started to crow!

MICK WELDON

along a worn Roman path en route to Santiago de Compostela inspired him to construct a new road, a bridge and a hospital (now a parador). The king rewarded his efforts by constructing a church, which became a cathedral in 1232.

As you enter the **Catedral de Santo Domingo de la Calzada**, you may well be greeted by a rooster's resounding 'kikeriki' (see the boxed text 'Of Pilgrims, Fowl &

Miracles' in this chapter). Turn your attention to the oldest section, the Romanesque eastern end, which has some particularly nice carved sandstone pilasters. Their expressive simplicity contrasts with the overwhelming detail of the main altar by Damián Forment and the elaborate mausoleum of the saint topped by an alabaster canopy. The actual remains of Santo Domingo are buried in the crypt beneath. Also of note is the cloister, with exhibits on the Camino de Santiago and various paintings and sculptures. The cathedral/museum is open 10 am to 6.30 pm daily (250 ptas, free on Sunday).

Places to stay are listed in the special section 'Camino de Santiago'. Buses leave the square for Burgos (66km west) and Logroño (48km east).

SOUTH OF LOGROÑO

A couple of picturesque routes suggest themselves if you're heading south for Soria in Castilla y León. One is along the N-111 which, after a boring start, picks up as it follows deep canyon walls along the Río Iregua into the sierras that mark Soria province off from the flatlands of central La Rioja. Several pretty villages, including

Villanueva de Cameros, line the lower half of the route. About halfway to Soria you could turn west for Montenegro de Cameros and then drop south for Vinuesa and the Laguna Negra (see Around Soria in the Castilla y León chapter).

Another good route to Soria is to head south-east of Logroño to Calahorra, on the N-232. Of Roman origin, Calahorra overlooks the Río Ebro and its tributary Río Cidacos, upon which dwells a moderately interesting Gothic cathedral. The sacristy, chapterhouse and museum are all worth a look. Guided tours operate from 9 am to 1 pm and 5 to 8 pm daily (free). If you want to spend the night, *Hostal Teresa* (☎ 941 13 03 32, Calle de Santo Domingo 7) has worn but adequate singles/doubles with facilities for 2100/4300 ptas.

From Calahorra, head south-west towards Arnedo, and then follow the Río Cidacos through quite dramatic country. The small, traditional spa town of Arnedillo, gathered up in a fold of the valley, is in a pretty location ideal for a night or two if you plan to do a spot of walking in the area. The road starts to climb after entering Soria province and is frequently blocked by snow during winter.

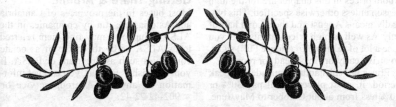

Cantabria & Asturias

For all they hold in common, the neighbouring regions of Cantabria and Asturias, stretching west from the Basque Country, throw up some striking differences.

Established as a province only late in the 18th century, Cantabria was, until after Franco's demise, merely an extension of Castilla la Vieja (Old Castile). Asturias, on the other hand, has a long history of independence and, along with Galicia, was exclusively Celtic territory before the arrival of the Romans. Asturians take pride, too, in inhabiting the sole patch of Spain untouched by the Muslims. Asturias, they say, is the real Spain; the rest is simply *tierra de la Reconquista* – reconquered land.

The two regions share a coastline of alternating sheer cliffs, sandy beaches and tiny protected coves. Their lifestyles and history have been in great measure determined by the chain-mail strip of highlands and mountains that forms their natural southern boundary, the Cordillera Cantábrica. The green and often misty hills, meadows and pastures descending from these mountains to the Bay of Biscay could not stand in greater contrast to the parched Castilian *meseta* (tableland) south of the *cordillera*.

The mountains reach their greatest heights and grandeur in the Picos de Europa, a northern spur of the cordillera straddling south-east Asturias, south-west Cantabria and the north of Castilla y León. The Picos are allotted a section to themselves at the end of this chapter.

Accommodation

Room prices in this chapter are for the high season unless otherwise specified. This typically means August and the second half of July. As well as high prices, at this time you face a lot of *'Completo'* (House Full) signs, so arrive early or ring ahead for rooms.

Prices fall substantially outside this peak period. In most places you'll pay 30% or 40% less from about October to May/June.

Highlights

- Walking in the Picos de Europa mountains
- Enjoying the convivial *sidrerías* (cider bars) – and cider – of Asturias
- The enchanting towns of Santillana del Mar and Comillas
- Discovering little beaches and coves, especially around Llanes in Asturias
- Studying the pre-Romanesque churches of Asturias
- Touring the bars of Santander
- Sitting down to an Asturian *fabada* – the ideal food for the chilly mountain climate
- Eating, drinking and touring the eclectic museums in gutsy Gijón

Getting There & Around

Most buses in the provinces of Cantabria and Asturias are run by companies in the ALSA group. You may find them referred to as ALSA or by the name of associate companies such as Turytrans or EASA. If your Spanish is up to it, you can get information on any ALSA group service on ☎ 902-42 22 42.

As for trains, as well as Renfe (Spanish National Railways), there's the independent company FEVE, whose network stretches from Bilbao across Cantabria and Asturias to Ferrol in Galicia. Bicycles and surfboards can be transported in FEVE guards' vans, but you can't use rail passes on FEVE trains.

Trains running east-west or west-east tend to be FEVE, while Renfe tends to concentrate on services to/from Castilla y León, Madrid and other regions farther south and east.

Cantabria

The Romans reported having a hard time dealing with the Cantabrians, a people of obscure origins who inhabited coastal and mountain areas beyond the limits of modern Cantabria. From 29 to 19 BC, the fortunes of war fluctuated, but in the end Rome carried the day and the subdued coastal tribes were absorbed into imperial Hispania.

Until the constitution of 1978 created the region of Cantabria, the area had, unlike the Basque Country to the east and Asturias to the west, long been regarded simply as a coastal extension of Castile and as its direct gateway to what was confidently known as the Mar de Castilla (Castilian Sea).

Cantabria's chief attractions are natural, from the eastern flank of the Picos de Europa through the evergreen rural hinterland, to the rippled coastline and its sprinkling of pretty beaches and coastal towns. Santander, the capital, boasts fine beaches and a thumping nightlife, while Santillana del Mar and Comillas to the west are among the region's prettiest towns.

Cantabria's official tourism Web site, at http://turismo.cantabria.org, has a lot of useful material in English and Spanish.

Emergency
In Cantabria, you can call ☎ 112 (free) for the fire brigade, police or an ambulance.

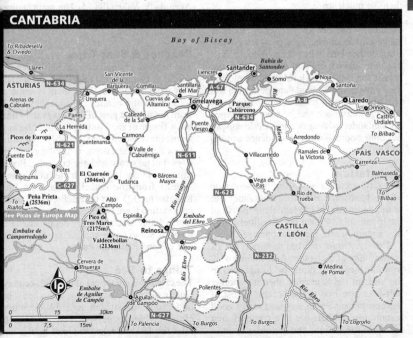

SANTANDER

postcode 39080 • pop 192,000

Most of modern Santander, with its bustling centre, clanking port and shapeless suburbs, stands in somewhat drab contrast to its pretty beaches, particularly the old-world elegance of El Sardinero, which is reminiscent of the French resort of Biarritz, albeit without much of the ritz.

A huge fire raged through the city in 1941, but what's left of the 'old' centre is certainly a lively source of entertainment for the palate and liver and has an atmosphere well worth stopping to savour. All up, however, Santander is a good deal more staid than its resort cousin, San Sebastián.

History

When the Romans landed on the beaches here in 21 BC, they named the place Portus Victoriae (Victory Harbour) and indeed, within two years they had finally vanquished the Cantabrian tribes that had given them so much strife.

From that time, Santander, as the city eventually became known, led a modestly successful existence as a port. Its heyday came rather late, when King Alfonso XIII began to make a habit of spending summer here in the 1900s. The locals were so pleased they gave him the Magdalena peninsula and built him a little palace there. Everyone who wanted to see and be seen converged on Santander, giving rise to a *belle époque* building boom – most in evidence around El Sardinero.

Orientation

The city stretches along the northern side of the handsome Bahía de Santander out to the Península de la Magdalena. North of the peninsula, Playa del Sardinero, the city's main beach, faces the open sea.

The ferry, train and bus terminals are all within 300m of each other. A 10-minute walk in a north-easterly direction brings you to the heart of old Santander, then it's another half-hour stroll on to the beaches. Most of the cheaper places to stay and many good restaurants and bars are in a compact area taking in the stations and the old quarter.

Information

Tourist Offices The Oficina Municipal de Turismo (☎ 942 21 61 20), in the Jardines de Pereda, is open 9.30 am to 1.30 pm and 4.30 to 7.30 pm weekdays, 10 am to 1 pm Saturday. The Cantabria regional tourist office on Plaza de Velarde (also known as Plaza Porticada) is open 9 am to 9 pm daily from about 1 July to 15 September, and 9 am to 1 pm and 4 to 7 pm daily at other times.

Money Banks cluster especially in the newer part of central Santander around Avenida de Calvo Sotelo.

Post & Communications The main post office *(correos)* is on Avenida de Calvo Sotelo, facing the Jardines de Pereda. Emailers can choose from several places including Insistel at Calle Méndez Núñez 8

Medical Services & Emergency The Hospital Valdecilla (☎ 942 20 25 20) is at Avenida de Valdecilla 25. The main station *(comisaría)* of the Policía Nacional is on Plaza de Velarde.

Beaches & Boat Trips

The beaches on the Bahía de Santander are a little more protected than the main strand, **Playa del Sardinero**. The latter is quite a walk from the centre, so catch bus No 1 from outside the post office. **Playa del Puntal**, a finger of sand jutting out into the bay from the eastern side roughly opposite Playa de la Magdalena, is idyllic on calm days (but take care with the currents). Boats sail there every 15 to 30 minutes in July and August from the Estación Marítima Los Reginas for 325 ptas return. From the same boat station there are one-hour summer bay tours (700 ptas) and a year-round passenger ferry to Somo (with another sandy beach), just beyond Playa del Puntal.

Things to See

The **catedral** is composed of two 13th-century Gothic churches, one above the other. The upper one, off which is a 14th-century cloister *(claustro),* was heavily rebuilt after the 1941 fire. In the lower Iglesia del

SANTANDER

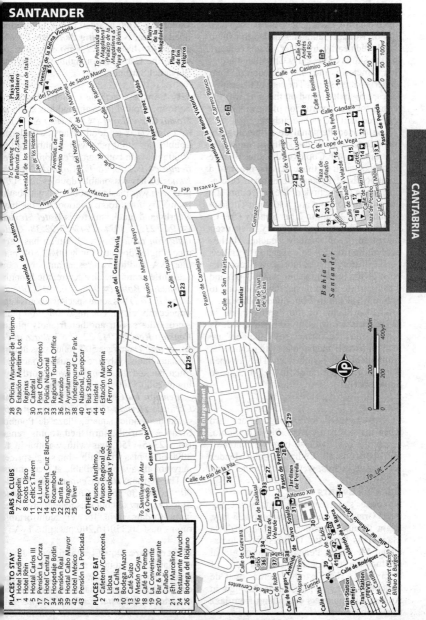

PLACES TO STAY
1 Hotel Sardinero
4 Hotel Rhin
5 Hostal Carlos III
17 Pensión La Corza
27 Hotel Central
34 Hospedaje Botín
35 Pensión Real
39 Hostal Cabo Mayor
42 Hotel México
43 Pensión La Porticada

PLACES TO EAT
2 Cafetería/Cervecería Lisboa
3 La Caña
10 Bodega Mazón
13 Café Suizo
16 Mesón Goya
18 Café de Pombo
19 La Conveniente
20 Bar & Restaurante Cañadío
21 ¡Eh! Marcelino
24 Restaurante Marucho
26 Bodega del Riojano

BARS & CLUBS
7 Zeppelin
8 Roots Disco
11 Celtic's Tavern
12 La Luna
14 Cervecería Cruz Blanca
15 Rocambole
22 Santa Fe
23 Dragon
25 Oliver

OTHER
6 Museo Marítimo
9 Museo Regional de Arqueología y Prehistoria
28 Oficina Municipal de Turismo
29 Estación Marítima Los Reginas
30 Catedral
31 Post Office (Correos)
32 Policía Nacional
33 Regional Tourist Office
36 Mercado
37 Ayuntamiento
38 Underground Car Park
40 National, Europcar
41 Bus Station
44 Insistel
45 Estación Marítima (Ferry to UK)

CANTABRIA

Santísimo Cristo (open 8 am to 1 pm and 4 to 8 pm daily), glass panels reveal excavated bits of Roman Santander under the floor. Displayed nearby are silver vessels containing the skulls of the early Christian martyrs San Emeterio and San Celedonio, Santander's patron saints. The care of these holy relics, originally found on this site, was the reason for the construction of the monastery that preceded the cathedral here.

The **Museo Regional de Arqueología y Prehistoria**, at Calle de Casimiro Sainz 4, is of some interest. Copies and photos of cave paintings, such as those at Altamira, and a hotchpotch of ancient Cantabrian bric-a-brac make up the bulk of the collection. It's open 10 am to 1 pm and 4 to 7 pm Tuesday to Saturday, 11 am to 2 pm Sunday (free).

If seafaring is your thing, try the **Museo Marítimo**, near the bay beaches. It has everything from a whale skeleton to models on the history of Cantabrian sea lore. It's open 10 am (11 am in summer) to 1 pm and 4 to 6 pm (to 7 pm in summer) Tuesday to Saturday, 11 am to 2 pm Sunday (free).

The parklands of the **Península de la Magdalena**, crowned by the Palacio de la Magdalena, the former royal palace, are nice for a stroll and popular with picnickers, but the mini-zoo is rather sad. They're open 8 am to 8.30 pm daily (to 10 pm June to September).

Surfing

Surfers emerge in force along El Sardinero when the waves are right. Playa de Somo, across the bay, can also be good. Three or four shops on Calle Cádiz and Calle Méndez Núñez sell boards, wetsuits and other gear.

Special Events

Santander's big summer fiesta is the Semana Grande, a week of fun around 25 July. Right through summer, the Palacio de la Magdalena hosts the Universidad Internacional Menéndez Pelayo, a kind of global get-together for specialists in all sorts of disciplines. The Festival Internacional de Santander is a sweeping musical review in August which covers everything from jazz to chamber music.

Places to Stay

Camping The nearest camping ground open all year is *Camping Bellavista* (☎ 94. 39 15 30, Avenida del Faro s/n), out towards the Cabo Mayor lighthouse beyon Playa del Sardinero.

City Centre Several low-budget spots ca be found around the train and bus stations *Hostal Cabo Mayor* (☎ 942 21 11 81, Call de Cádiz 1) is as good as any, with basi doubles for 5000 ptas with washbasin an 7000 ptas with bathroom. *Pensión La Por ticada* (☎ 942 22 78 17, Calle de Ménde Núñez 6) has reasonable doubles for 500 ptas with washbasin or 6000 ptas with bath room. Try for a room overlooking the bay Nearby and much smarter is *Hotel Méxic* (☎ 942 21 24 50, fax 942 22 92 38, Call Calderón de la Barca 3), which has ver nice singles/doubles for 8000/12,800 pta plus IVA, and its own restaurant.

A little nearer the city centre, the friendl *Hospedaje Botín* (☎ 942 21 00 94, Calle d Isabel II No 1) has some spacious rooms kep impeccably clean, costing 3500/5900 ptas Across the street, another friendly place *Pensión Real* (☎ 942 22 57 87, Plaza de l Esperanza 1) charges 5000/6000 ptas durin Semana Santa, July and August. In fact, it' often booked out then, but well worth try ing at 2000/3500 ptas in other months.

Pensión La Corza (☎/fax 942 21 29 5 Calle de Hernán Cortés 30) is nicely lo cated on a quiet square, Plaza de Pombo Sizable, quirkily furnished rooms rang from 2375/4750 ptas with washbasin t 3000/6000 ptas with bath – but single price may not always be available at peak times

The 41-room *Hotel Central* (☎ 942 22 2 00, fax 942 36 38 29, Calle General Mol 5) is a century old but was recently restore in up-to-date style. Its very comfortabl rooms cost 10,350/16,200 ptas plus IVA.

El Sardinero Down by fashionable Play del Sardinero, quite a few of the cheape places close in the low season. One goo choice, open from Semana Santa to the en of October, is *Hostal Carlos III* (☎/fax 94 27 16 16, Avenida de la Reina Victoria 135)

where rooms with bath and TV cost 6500/8500 ptas plus IVA.

Those with fur-lined bathing costumes may be able to afford the chichi old-style glamour of the *Hotel Sardinero* (☎ *942 27 11 00, Plaza de Italia 1)*, where rooms are 13,400/18,800 ptas plus IVA. The recently restored *Hotel Rhin* (☎ *942 27 43 00, Avenida de la Reina Victoria 153)* is another very comfortable place, costing 13,700/21,000 ptas plus IVA.

Places to Eat

Bodegas & Restaurants Atmospheric old *bodegas* account for many of the best places to eat. The word implies a wine cellar, or a bar specialising in wine, but in these cases they act as restaurants too. The dark *Bodega del Riojano (Calle del Río de la Pila 5)* is stacked floor to ceiling with wine racks creaking under the load of dusty bottles. It's open until midnight and serves straightforward but tasty dishes, particularly of the day's catch. It's not cheap, though, with most mains over 1800 ptas. Less expensive is *Bodega Mazón (Calle de Hernán Cortés 57)*, jammed with great lumbering wine vats and serving varied *raciones* (meal-sized serves of tapas) from 600 to 1600 ptas. *Mesón Goya (Calle Daoíz y Velarde 25)* is in a similarly traditional mould, though the focus is a bit more on food and a bit less on wine. There's a large choice of meals, with a grilled beef fillet, for instance, costing only 800 ptas.

The bodega of our dreams, however, is *La Conveniente (Calle Gómez Oreña 9)*. It has no name outside. Inside, you enter something akin to a set of caverns, with high stone walls, wooden pillars and beams, long wooden tables, and more wine bottles than you may ever have seen in one place before. A pianist tinkles on a balcony high against one wall. To eat, you might go for a *tabla* (board) of seven or eight cheeses for 1900 ptas, or a *ración* of pâté for 850 ptas, or that classic accompaniment to Spanish wine, *jamón serrano* (cured ham). For something lighter, order *bocadillucos,* little hot rolls with tasty fillings.

The bright tile decor of *¡Eh! Marcelino,* on the corner of Calle de Santa Lucía and Calle de Pizarro, makes it a welcoming place and ideal for snacking and doing the bar-fly thing.

One of the most innovative places in town is *Bar & Restaurante Cañadío (Plaza de Cañadío 15)*. A full meal *a la carta* in the restaurant at the back would leave you little change from 5000 ptas, but raciones in the bar (600 to 1400 ptas) will still give you a taste of the exquisite cooking here, from some original salads and *revueltos* to *bacalao* croquettes or *chipirones encebollados* (small squids done in onions).

For good fish, head east over to *Restaurante Marucho* (☎ *942 27 30 07, Calle Tetuán 21)*, one of a few modest-looking seafood eateries on this street. Marucho is small, unassuming and often packed – testimony to the quality of its food. Main dishes start around 1700 ptas.

In El Sardinero, *La Caña (Calle de Joaquin Costa 45)* has a good *menú del día* (daily set meal) for 1400 ptas.

Cafes The waterfront promenades brim with cafes. *Café Suizo (Paseo de Pereda 28)* is pricey, but it has a great range of sandwiches and ice-cream desserts. *Café de Pombo (Calle de Hernán Cortés 21)*, on Plaza de Pombo, is a classy and soothing but not exorbitant spot for breakfast, ice cream, crepes, tea or sandwiches.

Down near Playa del Sardinero, *Cafetería/Cervecería Lisboa* on Plaza de Italia has a very large *terraza* (terrace) and is a bit of a Santander institution.

Entertainment

The municipal tourist office produces a summer what's-on guide.

An enjoyable first port of call in your investigation of after-dark Santander might be *Cervecería Cruz Blanca*, on the corner of Calle de Hernán Cortés and Calle de Lope de Vega. It has 29 mostly non-Spanish beers in bottles and a few more on tap. A little farther east, *Celtic's Tavern* Irish pub on Calle Gándara is popular with young foreigners, while *La Luna (Calle General Mola 35)* is a lively music bar with a slightly older crowd, and keeps going late.

CANTABRIA

Santa Fe (Calle de Valliciergo 2) is a favourite with a broad age range, often spilling onto the street outside. *Zeppelin* is just one of a half-dozen cafe-bars around the junction of Calle de Valliciergo and Paseo de Menéndez Pelayo. The heavily mood-lit *Oliver (Paseo de Menéndez Pelayo 14)* is the perfect place for a sleek late-night cocktail to mellow jazz tunes.

Plaza de Cañadío is home to several *bares de copas* where you can enjoy an outdoor beer in the evening – but it will probably cost you 250 ptas.

Calle del Río de la Pila and its immediate neighbourhood also teem with *bars* of all descriptions.

A popular late-night dance spot is the rock music bar *Rocambole (Calle de Hernán Cortés 10)* – it often goes on until dawn and one some nights stages live blues. For a different rhythm, try *Roots Disco* near the top of Calle Gándara. *Dragon (Calle Tetuán 32)* is a gay men's club, with cabaret on weekend nights.

Getting There & Away

Air The airport is about 5km south of town at Parayas. A handful of daily flights serves Madrid and Barcelona.

Bus From the bus station *(estación de autobuses;* ☎ 942 21 19 95), Continental-Auto runs six buses daily to/from Madrid (3300 ptas) via Burgos (1350 ptas). ALSA/ Turytrans runs east to Bilbao (1½ hours) up to 13 times daily, and to San Sebastián (2½ hours, 1790 ptas), Irún and the French border (3½ hours) up to six times. Westward, ALSA/ Turytrans goes up to six times to San Vicente de la Barquera, Llanes, Ribadesella, Arriondas, Oviedo (three hours, 1710 ptas) and Gijón. Daily ALSA group buses also serve Valladolid (four hours, 1385 ptas), Salamanca, Palencia, Pamplona, Zaragoza and Barcelona. For destinations within Cantabria, see the relevant town sections.

Train There are two train stations. Renfe has three trains most days to/from Madrid (by day 5½ hours, 4300 ptas; overnight 8¾ hours, 5300 ptas) via Palencia, Valladolid and Ávila. A couple more trains serve Palencia and Valladolid, and about nine head to/from Reinosa.

FEVE, next door, runs two trains daily to/from San Vicente de la Barquera, Llanes, Ribadesella, Arriondas and Oviedo (4¼ hours, 1685 ptas) and three to/from Bilbao (2½ hours, 925 ptas).

Car & Motorcycle Heading west, take the A-67 for Torrelavega for a quick getaway. The N-623 to Burgos – a pretty route – is the main road south.

Hertz has a car-rental office inside the Brittany Ferries terminal; Europcar and National are beside the Renfe train station.

Boat Brittany Ferries (☎ 0870 536 0360 in the UK) operates a twice-weekly car ferry from Plymouth to Santander (24 hours sailing time), from mid-March to mid-November. For two people with a car, they quoted us return fares of UK£692/822 with seat/cabin in July, and UK£462/560 in April.

In Spain, reservations can be made by calling ☎ 942 36 06 11. You can also buy tickets at Santander's Estación Marítima (ferry terminal) itself.

AROUND SANTANDER

Coastal Walk

The town of **Liencres**, about 10km west of Santander, could be the starting point for a nice coastal walk. About 4km south-west of Liencres is **Playa de Valdearenas**, with probably the most impressive dunes on Spain's north coast. From here paths run along or near the coast, via more beaches and some impressive rock outcrops, at least as far as **Playa de Arnía**, about 2km north-east of Liencres. You can drive to both beaches and to a couple of spots between, and frequent buses go to Liencres from Santander bus station. Sea birds breed in the dunes area in spring.

Parque de la Naturaleza de Cabárceno

A bizarre landscape 15km south of Santander, forged by the erosion of limestone and human mining activity, is the unusual setting for an 8-sq-km open-air zoological park with

400-odd animals from around the globe. The Parque Cabárceno opens from about 9.30 am to 8 pm daily (1200 ptas, children 900 ptas). The park is best seen from its 30km of paved roads, so it's ideal to have your own vehicle (take exit No 8 from the N-635 Bilbao road to approach it). Otherwise, you could ask at Santander tourist offices about regular tours to Cabárceno, for around 2500 ptas.

Puente Viesgo
postcode 39670 • pop 550
The valley town of Puente Viesgo, 25km south of Santander on the N-623 to Burgos, is 1.5km downhill from the impressive Cueva del Castillo. In addition to a labyrinth of stalactites and stalagmites, this cave contains a series of prehistoric wall paintings of varied animals that, while not as breathtaking as those at Altamira (see Western Cantabria later in this chapter), is still well worth inspecting. The cave is open 9 am to noon and 3.15 to 6.30 pm Tuesday to Sunday (9 am to 2 pm Wednesday to Sunday, November to March). Visits are by 45-minute guided tour costing 300 ptas. In summer it's advisable to book a day ahead by calling ☎ 942 59 84 25.

The cheapest place to stay is *Hostal La Terraza* (☎ 942 59 81 02) at the turn-off from the highway to the caves. It charges 3000 ptas plus IVA for singles or doubles but is only open in July and August.

Regular buses (260 ptas) run to Puente Viesgo from Santander bus station.

EASTERN CANTABRIA
The 95km stretch of coast between Santander and Bilbao offers jaded citizens of both cities several seaside escape hatches. Some, such as Noja, are little more than beaches fronted by endless rows of holiday flats. The pick of the bunch is undoubtedly Castro Urdiales, 35km short of Bilbao.

Santoña
The fishing port of Santoña is dominated by two forts, the Fuerte de San Martín (sometimes open as an exhibition hall) and, farther north, the abandoned Fuerte de San Carlos. You can take a pleasant walk around the forts area, or plonk yourself down on sandy Playa de San Martín.

Buses run to/from Santander and other coastal towns, and a passenger ferry crosses the estuary to the western end of Laredo beach.

Playa de Oriñón
One of the nicer beaches along this coast is at Oriñón, 14km east of Laredo. Popular on summer weekends, the broad sandy strip is set deep behind protective headlands, making the water calm and *comparatively* warm. In contrast, you'll find a chilly sea and some surfable waves on the windward side of the western headland. All-stops buses between Santander and Castro Urdiales can drop you nearby.

Castro Urdiales
postcode 39700 • pop 10,700
The haughty Gothic Iglesia de Santa María de la Asunción, open 4 to 6 pm daily, stands out above the harbour and the tangle of narrow lanes that make up the medieval centre of Castro Urdiales. The church shares its little headland with the ruins of what was for centuries the town's defensive bastion, now home to a lighthouse. Of the two beaches, the westerly Playa de Ostende is the more attractive.

Castro makes a pleasant overnight stop. At weekends in particular, it's pretty lively. One inexpensive place is *Hostal La Marina* (☎ 942 86 13 45, Calle de la Plazuela 20), where singles/doubles with washbasin cost 2500/4500 ptas. Six of the nine rooms have harbour views. Several other small places are scattered about the old centre, but most tend to open in summer only. A dependable place farther east is *Hostal La Mar* (☎ 942 87 05 24, Calle de la Mar 27), where bright, functional rooms with bathroom are 4500/7000 ptas.

La Pizzeria di Stefano, at the western end of Playa de Ostende, serves excellent thin-crust pizzas for 1200 to 1750 ptas. There's good-value fare at *Fast Food Serman* (Avenida Constitución 4), facing the harbour. *Platos combinados* start at 800 ptas, and there are big *bocadillos* (filled

CANTABRIA

CANTABRIA

rolls) from 450 ptas. More traditional fare abounds in *mesones* and *tabernas* all over the old centre.

ALSA/Turytrans (☎ 942 86 32 55), at Calle Leonardo Rucabado 2, runs about 10 daily buses to/from Santander (one hour) and Bilbao (30 minutes). Bizkaibus has more frequent buses to/from Bilbao, stopping at Bar La Ronda at the corner of Calle La Ronda and Calle Benito Pérez Galdós.

Eastern Valleys

Short on specific sights but rich in some of Cantabria's least spoiled rural splendour, the little-visited valleys of eastern Cantabria are great for exploring, especially if you have a vehicle. Plenty of routes suggest themselves, so what follows is by way of example only.

From Puente Viesgo (see Around Santander earlier), take the S-580 south-east and make for Vega de Pas. The town is of minimal interest, but the drive is quite something. The views from the **Puerto de Braguía pass** in particular are stunning. From Vega de Pas you could continue south-east, briefly crossing into Castilla y León, before turning north again at Río de Trueba, then following the Río Miera down through San Roque de Riomiera towards Santander.

Another option from Río de Trueba is to take the BU-571 road up over the Puerto de la Sía pass towards Arredondo. This road is full of switchbacks, a couple of mountain passes and isolated little farmhouses. The drive along the Río Gándara and Río Asón, farther east again, is just as rewarding. You'll find places to stay in **Ramales de la Victoria** and **Ampuero**.

SOUTHERN CANTABRIA

Wonderful views of high peaks and deep river valleys flanked by patchwork quilts of green await the traveller penetrating into the Cantabrian interior. Every imaginable shade of green seems to have been employed to set this fairy-tale stage, strewn with warm stone villages and held together by a network of narrow, often poorly maintained country roads.

Reinosa

postcode 39200 • pop 12,850

Reinosa, the main town in southern Cantabria, is drab, with little to stop for except perhaps a look at the mansions *(casonas)* and other buildings around the central Plaza de España. But the **Colegiata de San Pedro** in Cervatos, 5km south, is one of Cantabria's finest Romanesque churches. If it's winter and you're itching for a whizz down a white slope, you could head 27km west to the small ski station of **Alto Campóo**, which has a youth hostel and one rather expensive hotel.

Reinosa's tourist office (☎ 942 75 52 15) is at Avenida del Puente de Carlos III No 23, near the bridge. Ask for information on walking routes *(senderos)* if a little rambling in the area appeals to you (see Western Valleys in the Western Cantabria section for one possibility).

If you get stuck in Reinosa, *Hostal Sema (☎ 942 75 00 47, Calle de Julióbriga 14)* is handy to the train and bus stations and has singles/doubles for 2200/4200 ptas. The part of Avenida del Puente de Carlos III between the bus station and the Río Ebro is jammed with bars, snack joints and the odd restaurant. The most atmospheric is *Pepe de los Vinos,* near the tourist office.

The train and bus stations are adjacent. Around nine trains a day head to/from Santander and five to/from Palencia and Valladolid. Buses serve Santander (frequently) and other destinations along the Cantabrian coast and run south into Castilla y León and to several local villages including Polientes (three daily) and San Martín de Elines.

Along the Río Ebro

The Río Ebro, one of Spain's major rivers, rises about 10km west of Reinosa, fills the Embalse del Ebro reservoir and then meanders south and east into Castilla y León. You can follow the river's course along minor roads out of Reinosa.

Head first towards Arroyo on the southern bank of the lake (you will pass the ruins of Roman Julióbriga). Just before Arroyo, turn right (south). You will pass the Monasterio de Montes Claros, then descend to Arroyal de los Carabeos and finally hit a T-junction where the S-614 meets the S-621. About 13km east is **Polientes**, where you'll find banks, a petrol station and a couple of places to stay. Along or just off the S-621, several small medieval chapels hewn from the rock can be visited. The best example, the Iglesia de Santa María de Valverde, is actually about 10km *west* of the T-junction. East of the T-junction there are chapels at **Campo de Ebro** and, beyond Polientes, **Cadalso** and **Arroyuelos**.

Across the Ebro from Arroyuelos, **San Martín de Elines** has a fine Romanesque church and marks the end of the line for a daily bus from Reinosa via Polientes. With your own transport you can push on for Orbaneja del Castillo (see Routes North of Burgos in the Castilla y León chapter).

WESTERN CANTABRIA
Santillana del Mar
postcode 39330 • pop 1030

You could easily drive through this medieval jewel and never know what lies off the main road. Declared a national monument in 1899, Santillana has preserved its lovely ancient stone buildings and cobbled streets so well that it appears almost artificial, with a public face given over almost entirely to a thriving tourist trade. Shops hawk everything from Cantabrian cheese and Asturian cider to cowbells and Mexican sombreros.

Jean-Paul Sartre was one illustrious guest to remark on Santillana, but since all other guidebooks quote him on the subject, we won't. Locals themselves have something to say about it: *'Santillana es la villa de las tres mentiras – no es santa, no es llana y no tiene mar'* (Santillana is the town of the three lies – it is not holy, it is not flat and it does not have a sea).

Information You'll find a tourist information office (☎ 942 81 82 51) on the very handsome Plaza Mayor, along with a post office, telephones and a bookshop. Banks abound.

Things to See A stroll along the cobbled main street past solemn nobles' houses, some with magnificent coats of arms, leads you to the exquisite 12th-century Romanesque **Colegiata de Santa Juliana**. The chief drawing card inside this former collegiate monastery is the cloister, a formidable storehouse of Romanesque artisanry, with its lines of twin columns surmounted by capitals carved with a huge variety of figures and motifs. The sepulchre of Santa Juliana, an early Christian martyr (and the real source of the name Santillana), stands in the centre of the church. This saint was supposedly tortured to death by her husband for not wanting to renounce her faith, in Turkey in the 3rd century AD. The monastery and town grew up around her relics which somehow found their way here later. The colegiata is open 9.30 am to 1 pm and 4 to 7.30 pm daily, with shorter hours in winter (300 ptas).

A little way down the main street is the **Museo de la Inquisición**, with instruments of medieval barbarity on show that can leave you feeling a little queasy. It's open 10 am to 9 pm daily (600 ptas).

Places to Stay About 500m west on the Comillas road, *Camping Santillana* (☎ 942 81 82 50) is open all year and has good facilities including a pool, tennis court and cabins for those who lack tents.

Bolos

Every Cantabrian village has its *bolera*, a long, rectangular, sandy area, probably with a few benches or terraces for spectators, where the game of *bolos* is played. Bolos is a kind of cross between ten-pin bowling and the French *boule*. Players hurl large, heavy wooden balls through the air attempting to knock down nine wooden skittles arranged in a square. Wherever and whenever it's played, knots of onlookers gather, and this is indeed a sport taken seriously. Pages of Cantabrian newspapers are devoted to results, reports and league tables. There's even a Liga Nacional (National League) – a curious concept for a sport that barely seems to exist outside Cantabria, but perhaps no odder than the notion of a World Series played exclusively by baseball teams from the USA and Canada!

At least 30 varied places with rooms are scattered about the old part of town, around the Campo de Revolgo park across the main road, and along the main road towards Santander. Some don't have single rooms but will charge a reduced rate to lone travellers if business is slow. Some close from November to February.

The friendly *Hospedaje Octavio* (☎ 942 81 81 99, Plaza de las Arenas 4), just behind the Colegiata, has charming singles/doubles with timber-beam ceilings and private bathrooms for 3500/5500 ptas, and a couple of rooms with shared bathrooms for a little less. Back along the main street, *Posada El Cantón* (☎ 942 84 02 74, Calle Carrera 2) and *Posada Santa Juliana* (☎ 942 84 01 06, Calle Carrera 19) are also attractive, rustic-style little places offering rooms for 8000 ptas (single or double).

The first house on the left as you go up Camino de los Hornos from Plaza Mayor, with a simple *Habitaciones* sign, has two good doubles sharing a bathroom, for 3500 ptas each (a bit more in August). *La Casa del Organista* (☎ 942 84 03 52, e organist@ arrakis.es, Camino de los Hornos 4) has particularly attractive rooms for 12,000 ptas.

A good place on Campo de Revolgo is *Posada González* (☎ 942 81 81 78, Calle La Robleda 13), charging 6000 ptas per room. *Posada Araceli* (☎ 942 84 01 94, Campo de Revolgo 20) has rooms with bath for 4000/6000 ptas plus IVA.

Hotel Altamira (☎ 942 81 80 25, fax 942 84 01 36, Calle del Cantón 1), in a 16th-century building in the old part of town, has well-appointed rooms for 7125/11,500 ptas plus IVA. For an even classier stay, head for the luxury *parador* (☎ 942 81 80 00) on Plaza Mayor, charging 14,000/17,500 ptas plus IVA.

Places to Eat The nearest restaurant to the Colegiata, *Casa Cossío*, serves a good range of seafood, meat and *tortillas*, and has a *menú* for 1150 ptas. *Restaurante Altamira*, attached to the hotel of the same name, has a *menú* for 1750 ptas. There are several snack places if you want to keep it simple.

Getting There & Away Autobuses La Cantábrica (☎ 942 72 08 22) runs four times a day on weekdays, and twice at weekends, from Santander bus station to Santillana (45 minutes, 270 ptas), Comillas (one hour, 425 ptas) and San Vicente de la Barquera (1½ hours, 500 ptas). Extra buses run in July and August.

Cuevas de Altamira

Lots of hot air from the yearly flood of tourists to the prehistoric caves of Altamira, 2km south-west of Santillana, led to the inevitable result. The world-famous wall paintings of bison, horses, deer and other beasts have been closed since 1977 to all but 30 visitors daily – to protect the already damaged images from the moisture caused by, well, too much breathing.

However the new Museo de Altamira at the site, which was expected to open in 2001, includes life-size replicas of the caves which should go a long way towards satisfying many people's curiosity.

To see the famous art itself, which was painted, carved and scratched on the cave walls around 12,000 BC, you need to write at least three years in advance to the Centro de Investigación de Altamira, 39330 Santillana del Mar, Cantabria, Spain. For further information, call ☎ 942 81 80 05 or fax 942 84 01 57. Entry for the patient few is 400 ptas (students half-price; minimum age 13).

Comillas
postcode 39520 • pop 1870

Comillas offers the attractive combination of a charming old centre, a handful of interesting monuments and a couple of good nearby beaches. One result is that you can all but forget about trying to find a bed here in high summer without a reservation.

The tourist office (☎ 942 72 07 68) is near the centre at Calle de María de Piélago 2. Signs to it tend to use the French 'Tourisme'. In July and August it's open 10 am to 2 pm and 4 to 8 pm daily; in other months 11 am to 1 pm and 4.30 to 7 pm Monday to Saturday, 11 am to 1 pm Sunday and holidays.

Things to See Antoni Gaudí left few reminders of his genius beyond Catalunya

(Cataluña) but, of those that he did, the 1885 **Capricho de Gaudí** in Comillas is easily the most flamboyant, if modest in stature. The building, originally a summer house for the Marqués de Comillas, is liberally plastered with ceramic sunflower motifs on a green background. It's now an expensive restaurant: you can look at the exterior from 11 am daily.

The *capricho* (caprice) was one of several buildings commissioned from leading Catalan *modernista* architects by the first Marqués de Comillas, who had been born here as plain Antonio López, made a fortune in Cuba and returned to beautify his home town. In the same hillside parklands stand the neo-Gothic **Capilla Panteón de los Marqueses de Comillas** and the wonderful **Palacio de Sobrellano**, both designed by Joan Martorell. With the palacio, Martorell truly managed to out-Gothic real Gothic. You can visit it during seasonally varying hours which always include 10 am to 1.30 pm and 4 to 6 pm (daily from June to September; Wednesday to Sunday otherwise).

Martorell also had a hand in the **Universidad Pontificia** on the hill opposite. Lluís Domènech i Montaner, another Catalan modernista, contributed the medieval flavour to this elaborate building, a former seminary, whose grounds you can stroll from 11 am daily.

Comillas' compact medieval centre is full of its own little pleasures. **Plaza del Generalísimo Franco** is its focal point, a sloping cobbled square flanked by the town hall, the Iglesia de San Cristóbal and old sandstone houses with flower-bedecked timber balconies.

Places to Stay Grassy *Camping Comillas* (☎ 942 72 00 74), on the eastern edge of town, opens from June to September, and in July and August employs a finely located clifftop area over the road.

About the cheapest rooms are at *Pensión La Aldea* (☎ 942 72 03 00, La Aldea 5), near the tourist office, with simple singles/doubles for 2500/4000 ptas. It's open from mid-June to end-September, and weekends only the rest of the year.

The ramshackle *Hostal Fuente Real* (☎ 942 72 01 55, Barrio Sobrellano 19), in a lane just behind the Capricho de Gaudí (signposted), has rooms for 2000/4000 ptas (closed October to May).

A big step up is *Hostal Esmeralda* (☎ 942 72 00 97, fax 942 72 22 58, Calle Antonio López 7), near the eastern end of town. Attractive rooms with bath cost 7000/11,000 ptas plus IVA, and there's a good, not over-expensive restaurant. Nearby, the *Casal del Castro* (☎ 942 72 00 36, Calle de San Jerónimo s/n) is a period-furnished, 17th-century mansion that could compete with the better paradores. Rooms are 8900/12,600 ptas plus IVA.

Places to Eat The *Bar El Galeón*, across the street from Pensión La Aldea, does decent medium-priced food, and has a *menú* for 1500 ptas. A cute little place (try for a table by the window upstairs) is *Restaurante El Pirata* on Calle del Marqués de Comillas, the street below the Palacio de Sobrellano. It has a *menú* for 1300 ptas.

At *Capricho de Gaudí* (☎ 942 72 03 65) you'd be lucky to get away with paying less than 5000 ptas per head for a full meal. There are heaps more *eateries* on Plaza de José Antonio Primo de Rivera, next door to Plaza del Generalísimo Franco (Comillas does not lean to the left when naming its plazas).

El Secaderu, down on the town beach, does an excellent two-person *paella* for 4000 ptas (order an hour or two ahead), and seafood dishes for 800 to 1600 ptas.

Getting There & Away Comillas is served by the same buses as Santillana del Mar (see that section earlier). The stop is on Calle del Marqués de Comillas, almost beside the driveway to the Palacio de Sobrellano and Capricho de Gaudí.

Around Comillas
Of several beaches around Comillas, the long, sandy **Playa de Oyambre**, 5km west, is decidedly superior – so much so that the road gets choked on summer weekends. There are a few hotels on the road from

CANTABRIA

Comillas, and two year-round camping grounds behind the beach.

A little farther west, the wilder and less crowded **Playa de Merón** and its continuation **Playa del Rosal** stretch 3km to the estuary at San Vicente de la Barquera. Heed warning signs about currents here.

San Vicente de la Barquera
postcode 39540 • pop 3100

San Vicente was an important fishing port throughout the Middle Ages and later became one of the so-called Cuatro Villas de la Costa – converted by Carlos III (Charles III) into the province of Cantabria in 1779.

Today, streams of lorries and, in summer, holiday traffic pour through the largely modern town and across the low arches of the 15th-century Puente de la Maza. Towering above it all is the craggy outcrop that contains what remains of the old town. East of the estuary a string of good beaches begins (see Around Comillas).

There's a summer-only tourist office (☎ 942 71 07 97) at Avenida del Generalísimo 20, and several banks along the same main street.

Apart from a few remnants of the old city walls and castle (castillo), the one outstanding monument is the largely 13th-century **Iglesia de Santa María de los Ángeles**. Though Gothic, it sports a pair of impressive Romanesque doorways. Inside, the life-like statue of 16th-century Inquisitor Antonio del Corro, who is shown reclining on one elbow, reading, is deemed by those who know to be the best example of Renaissance funerary art in Spain.

Camping del Rosal is on the beach just across the estuary. Of the handful of places in town, about the cheapest is *Hostería La Paz* (☎ 942 71 01 80, Calle del Mercado 2), just off the central Plaza de José Antonio, with singles/doubles starting at 2900/4700 ptas. *Pensión Liébana* (☎ 942 71 02 11, Calle Ronda 2), just up the steps in front of the Hostería La Paz, is a good deal. Rooms with bathroom and TV are 4500/5500 ptas plus IVA.

There is no shortage of choice for food. The *Restaurante Maruja* (Avenida del Generalísimo 22) is a long-established posh seafood spot. A little scruffier and easier on the wallet is the nearby *Restaurante Las Redes* at No 24. Both have tables set up out the back, overlooking the estuary.

San Vicente bus station, at the eastern end of town by the bridge, is served by the same buses as Santillana del Mar (see that section), as well as half a dozen ALSA services linking Oviedo, Arriondas, Ribadesella, Llanes, Santander, Bilbao and beyond. Autobuses Palomera services stop here en route between Santander, Panes, Potes and Fuente Dé (see Picos de Europa later in this chapter).

Western Valleys

Generally ignored by holiday-makers concentrating their attention on the Picos de Europa farther west, the valleys of the Río Saja and, next over to the west, the Río Nansa make a soft contrast to the craggy majesty of the Picos.

People starting from the Picos might well take the following route: a narrow, winding way snakes up high and eastwards from La Hermida, on the Río Deva. It is a beautiful drive and there is a small *pensión* in **Quintanilla**. The village of **Puentenansa** (with banks and bars) forms a crossroads. The S-224 southwards follows the Río Nansa upstream: along the way, a short detour east leads to the attractive hamlet of **Tudanca**, where accommodation includes *La Cotera* (☎ 942 74 65 03), a *casa rural* with doubles for 4000 ptas. The S-224 eventually meets the C-627, on which you can head south to Cervera de Pisuerga (see the Montaña Palentina section in the Castilla y León chapter) or north-west back to the Picos.

To proceed east you'll have to retrace your steps to Puentenansa through **Carmona**, a village with many fine stone mansions. When you reach the village of Valle de Cabuérniga and the Río Saja, head south towards Reinosa. The views are magnificent. The hamlet of **Bárcena Mayor**, about 9km east off the main road, is a popular spot with a couple of *casas rurales* to stay in and great *mesones* where you can eat cheaply and well. Locals often walk there from Reinosa (see Southern Cantabria) on weekends. Leaving about 7.30 am gives them ample time to enjoy the trail and arrive at Bárcena Mayor for lunch, where you should try *cocido montañés,* the local bean, cabbage, meat and sausage stew.

Asturias

'*Ser español es un orgullo,*' the saying goes, '*ser asturiano es un título*'. If being Spanish is a matter of pride, to be called Asturian is a title, or so some of the locals will have you think.

Ever since King Pelayo warded off the Muslims in the Battle of Covadonga in 722 and laid the foundations of Christian Spain's 800-year comeback, Asturians have thought of themselves – or been seen to think of themselves – as a cut above the rest of the peninsula's inhabitants.

Be that as it may, the Reconquista's slow southward progress left Asturias increasingly a backwater. As a concession, Juan I of Castilla y León made Asturias a principality *(principado)* in 1388 and to this day the heir to the Spanish throne holds the title Príncipe de Asturias. Annual awards in the prince's name to personalities of distinction are Spain's rough equivalent of the Nobel prizes.

Although Oviedo and other towns have their moments, the area's real beauty lies beyond the cities. Much of the grand Picos de Europa mountain range is on Asturian territory, and towns such as Llanes and Luarca make great bases for exploring the riches of the Asturian coast. For the art and architecture buff, Asturias is the land of pre-Romanesque – modest but unique survivals of early medieval building and decoration.

Bucolically green though much of it is, Asturias also has its gritty industrial side. The Oviedo-Gijón-Avilés triangle is the heart of industrial Asturias.

Traditional Asturian food is simple, peasant fare. The best known is the *fabada asturiana,* a hearty bean dish jazzed up with bits of meat and sausage. Mountain streams teem with salmon, always a treat for fish-lovers. Another tasty dish you may come across in western Asturias is *repollo relleno de carne* – cabbage stuffed with meat.

ASTURIAS

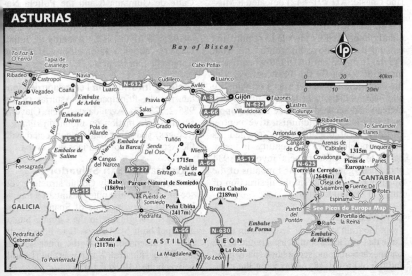

ASTURIAS

Bable

You may notice that some place names and other words in Asturias crop up in a variety of spellings. A common example is 'u' where you might expect 'o' at the end of a word. Another is 'Cai' instead of 'Calle' (street). These are manifestations of Bable, the Asturian dialect. Bable is alive enough to have newspapers written in it, but not used in schools such as Galician, Basque or Catalan. Nor is it distinct enough from Castilian Spanish to be classified as a language rather than a dialect.

OVIEDO
postcode 33080 • pop 192,000

The modern part of Asturias' capital, with its elegant parks and shopping streets, is agreeably offset by what remains of the old town *(casco antiguo)*. Out in the periphery, the hum and heave of factories is a reminder that Oviedo is a key producer of textiles, pharmaceutical products, metal goods, sugar and chocolate.

History

When the Asturian king Alfonso II El Casto (the Chaste; AD 791–842) defeated a Muslim detachment that had all but destroyed the small town of Oviedo, he was sufficiently impressed by the site to rebuild and expand it, and move his court here from Pravia. It stayed until AD 910 when it was moved to León. By the 14th century, with the declaration of Asturias as a principality and the construction of the cathedral, Oviedo had secured its place as an important religious and administrative centre. Around 1600 the university opened its doors and in the 19th century industry began to take off. A miners' revolt in 1934 and a nasty siege in the first months of the Spanish Civil War led to the destruction of much of the old town.

Orientation

From the train station, Oviedo's main drag, Calle de Uría, leads south-east straight to the Campo de San Francisco, a huge shady park, and the old town. If you arrive at the main bus station, head along Calle de Fray Ceferino to get to Calle de Uría. A good collection of restaurants, cafes and bars waits to be discovered in and near the narrow, mainly pedestrianised streets of the old town.

Information

Tourist Offices The main tourist office (☎ 985 21 33 85) is at Plaza de Alfonso II El Casto 6. The opening hours are 9.30 am to 1.30 pm and 4 to 6.30 pm weekdays and 9 am to 2 pm Saturday in summer (June to September). The Oficina Municipal de Turismo (☎ 985 22 75 86), on the Campo de San Francisco, is also helpful. It's open 10.30 am to 2 pm and 4.30 to 7.30 pm weekdays, and 11 am to 2 pm weekends.

Money Calle de Uría is lined with banks, most with user-friendly ATMs.

Post & Communications You'll find the main post office on Calle de Alonso Quintanilla. L@ser, at Calle de San Francisco 9, offers a public Internet/email service.

Medical Services & Emergency The Policía Municipal (☎ 985 22 26 40) are at Calle de Quintana 6 and the Policía Nacional have a station on Calle del General Yagüe. The Hospital Central de Asturias (☎ 985 10 61 00) is on Avenida de Julián Clavería about a kilometre west of the Campo de San Francisco.

Walking Information Federación de Montañismo del Principado de Asturias (☎/fax 985 25 23 62), Avenida de Julián Clavería s/n, has information on mountain *refugios* (refuges) and other matters connected with the Asturian part of the Picos de Europa.

Catedral de San Salvador

In a sense, the mainly Gothic structure you see today forms the outer casing of a many-layered history in stone of Spanish Christianity. Its origins lie in the Cámara Santa, a chapel built by Alfonso II to house holy relics. The chapel is now the inner sanctuary of the cathedral, which was chiefly built between the 14th and 16th centuries.

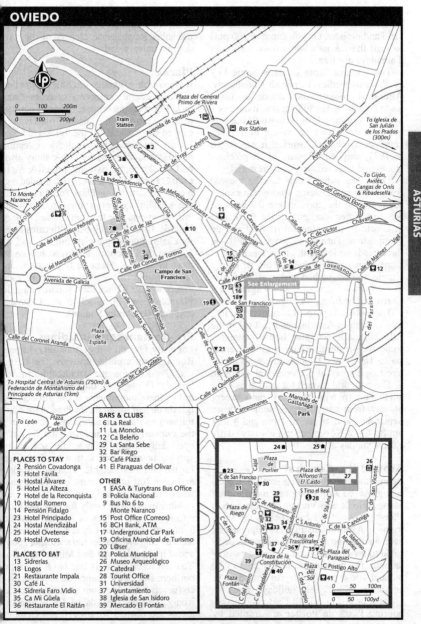

ASTURIAS

OVIEDO

Plaza del General Primo de Rivera

Train Station

ALSA Bus Station

To Iglesia de San Julián de los Prados (300m)

To Gijón, Avilés, Cangas de Onís & Ribadesella

Avenida de Santander

C Campoamor

Calle de Fray Ceferino

Avenida de Pumarín

Avenida del General Elorza

To Monte Naranco

C de la Independencia

Calle de Melquíades Álvarez

Calle de Uría

Calle de Caveda

Calle de la Independencia

Calle de Ventura Rodríguez

C de Gil de Jaz

C de Central Yagüe

Calle del Matemático Pedrayes

Calle del Marqués de Teverga

Calle del Marqués de Cervantes

Avenida de Galicia

Campo de San Francisco

Calle del Conde de Toreno

Paseo del Bombé

Calle de Santa Susana

Plaza de España

Calle del Coronel Aranda

Calle de Covadonga

Calle de la Vallina

C de Víctor Chávarri

C de la Luna

Calle de Jovellanos

Calle de Martínez Vigil

C del Paraíso

C de Alonso Quintanilla

Calle Argüelles

C de San Francisco

See Enlargement

To Hospital Central de Asturias (750m) & Federación de Montañismo del Principado de Asturias (1km)

Calle de Calvo Sotelo

Calle de Clabo Noval

Calle del Rosal

Calle de Quintana

C Marqués de Gastañaga Park

Calle de Campomanes

To León

Plaza de Castilla

BARS & CLUBS
6 La Real
11 La Moncloa
12 Ca Beleño
29 La Santa Sebe
32 Bar Riego
33 Café Plaza
41 El Paraguas del Olivar

OTHER
1 EASA & Turytrans Bus Office
8 Policía Nacional
9 Bus No 6 to Monte Naranco
15 Post Office (Correos)
16 BCH Bank, ATM
17 Underground Car Park
19 Oficina Municipal de Turismo
20 L@ser
22 Policía Municipal
26 Museo Arqueológico
27 Catedral
28 Tourist Office
31 Universidad
37 Ayuntamiento
38 Iglesia de San Isidoro
39 Mercado El Fontán

PLACES TO STAY
2 Pensión Covadonga
3 Hotel Favila
4 Hostal Álvarez
5 Hotel La Alteza
7 Hotel de la Reconquista
10 Hostal Romero
14 Pensión Fidalgo
23 Hotel Principado
24 Hostal Mendizábal
25 Hotel Ovetense
40 Hostal Arcos

PLACES TO EAT
13 Sidrerías
18 Logos
21 Restaurante Impala
30 Café JL
34 Sidrería Faro Vidío
35 Ca Mi Güela
36 Restaurante El Raitán

Plaza de Porlier

Plaza de Alfonso II El Casto

Cajal

C de San Francisco

C Ramón

C de Alamirano

C San Antonio

C de Santa Ana

C de Cimadevilla

C de Fruela

C Jesús

C de Magdalena

C del Fierro

C de Mon

Plaza de Riego

Plaza de la Constitución

Plaza Fontán

Plaza del Sol

Plaza de Trascorrales

Plaza del Paraguas

Plaza del Postigo Alto

S Tirso el Real

C de la Canóniga

C Ildefonso Martínez

C de San Vicente

Inside, a 400 ptas ticket gives you access to the Cámara Santa, Museo Diocesano and cloister. Or you can pay 200 ptas to visit the Cámara Santa only. Visits on Thursdays are free.

The Cámara Santa contains some key symbols of medieval Spanish Christianity. Alfonso II presented the Cruz de los Ángeles to Oviedo in AD 808 – it is still the city's symbol. A century later, Alfonso III donated the Cruz de la Victoria, which in turn became the symbol of Asturias. It was stolen in 1977, stripped of many of its precious stones and later recovered and restored.

These and other items can be viewed from the Sala Apostolar, whose remarkable sculptures of the apostles are the work of Maestro Mateo, designer of the Pórtico de la Gloria in the cathedral of Santiago de Compostela. Turning to leave, you'll see three heads sculpted out of a single block of stone above the doorway. This strikingly simple and anguished piece of work depicts, from left to right, the Virgin Mary, Christ and St John on Calvary.

The cloister is pure 14th-century Gothic, rare enough in Asturias, and just off it the *sala capitular* (chapter house) contains some well-restored Flemish Gothic choir stalls. The Museo Diocesano houses an interesting display of ecclesiastical artefacts.

The cathedral is open for tourist visits 10 am to 8 pm (to 6 pm Saturday) daily except Sunday from early July to some time in September, and 10 am to 1 pm and 4 to 7 pm (to 6 pm November to February) daily except Sunday at other times.

Around the Catedral

Behind the cathedral is the small but interesting **Museo Arqueológico**, in the former Monasterio de San Vicente at Calle de San Vicente 3. Artefacts from across the spectrum of Asturian history are represented here, but the Roman mosaic and rooms dedicated to pre-Romanesque art are of particular note. The museum is open 10 am to 1.30 pm and 4 to 6 pm Tuesday to Saturday, 11 am to 1 pm Sunday and holidays (free).

Plaza de Alfonso II El Casto and neighbouring Plaza de Porlier are fronted by several elegant palaces dating from the 17th and 18th centuries. A little farther west is the sober Renaissance cloister of the now defunct **universidad**.

Plazas

It's enjoyable to indulge in a little exploration of the old centre's nooks and crannies. **Plaza de la Constitución** occupies a barely perceptible rise close to the heart of old Oviedo, capped at one end by the Iglesia de San Isidoro and fronted by an eclectic collection of old stores, cafes and the 17th-century town hall. To the south, past the attractive **Mercado El Fontán** food market, the arcaded and recently smartened-up **Plaza Fontán** has passages leading under the houses to surrounding streets and the leafy Plaza de Daoíz y Velarde. Both are equipped with cafes ideal for chatting or people-watching.

Plaza de Trascorrales, almost hidden to the north-east of Plaza de la Constitución, has a couple of pleasant restaurants (see Places to Eat). Other little squares include Plaza de Riego, Plaza del Sol and Plaza del Paraguas (Umbrella Square).

Pre-Romanesque Buildings

For many, Oviedo's key attraction is its pre-Romanesque architecture (see the boxed text 'Pre-Romanesque Architecture in Asturias'). The biggest, oldest and most central of these monuments is the 9th-century **Iglesia de San Julián de los Prados** (or Santullano) on Plaza de Santullano, just above the *autovía* (toll-free highway) to Gijón. It's open daily except Monday for seasonally varying hours: check with a tourist office for the current timetable. Visits are guided and cost 200 ptas, except on Wednesday when they're free and unguided.

More evocative, if only for their position up on the rural slopes of Monte Naranco 3km north-west of the city centre, are the **Palacio de Santa María del Naranco** and, 200m above it, the **Iglesia de San Miguel de Lillo**. You can reach them by bus No 6 from the northern side of the Campo de San Francisco (get its timetable from a tourist office as it only goes a few times daily). The two monuments are open 9.30 am (10 am October

Pre-Romanesque Architecture in Asturias

More or less cut off from the rest of Christian Europe by the Muslim invasion, the small, rough-and-tumble kingdom that emerged in 8th-century Asturias gave rise to a style of art and building distinct not only in Spain, but in all of Europe.

The 14 buildings, mostly churches, that survive from the two centuries of the Asturian kingdom take some inspiration from other sources but are unique. Those in and near Oviedo are representative of the best pre-Romanesque you'll find. Typical of all is their straight profile – no curves and cylinders here. The semicircular arches found to a greater or lesser extent in all the pre-Romanesque churches are an obvious forerunner to a style that would later triumph in northern Spain and across much of Europe – Romanesque. Another precursor to the Romanesque style is the complete vaulting of the nave.

Roman and Visigothic elements *are* visible. In many cases the bases and capitals of columns, with their Corinthian or floral motifs, were simply cannibalised from earlier structures. Another adaptation, which owes something more to developments in Muslim Spain, was the use of lattice windows. They appear purely as a design effect, since their eastern progenitors were inspired by the desire to maintain privacy from the outside world – hardly an issue in a church.

The **Iglesia de San Julián de los Prados**, in Oviedo, is the largest remaining pre-Romanesque church, and one of the oldest, built under Alfonso II. It is flanked by two porches – another very Asturian touch – and the inside is covered with frescos. The **Iglesia de Santa María de Bendones**, just outside Oviedo, also dates from the days of Alfonso II. Restored in the 1950s after severe civil war damage, it is unique for its extra-wide nave, a result of Roman influence. On Monte Naranco, also just outside Oviedo, the tall, narrow **Palacio de Santa María del Naranco** and the **Iglesia de San Miguel de Lillo** were built for Ramiro I (842–50), Alfonso II's successor, and mark an advance in Asturian art. An outstanding feature of the decoration in the former is the *sogueado*, the sculptural motif imitating rope used in its columns. Other decoration was influenced by Byzantine and Near Eastern art. The large windows are a pointer to later Gothic solutions in church architecture. San Miguel's unusual, very vertical appearance is a result of two-thirds of the church having been destroyed in the 14th century.

ASTURIAS

to March) to 1 pm and 3 to 7 pm (to 5 pm October to March) daily except Sunday and Monday afternoons. Visits are guided and cost 250 ptas, except on Monday when they're free and unguided. Also up here is a visitors centre with worthwhile explanatory displays on pre-Romanesque architecture.

Another pre-Romanesque gem, the church of **Santa María de Bendones**, 5km southeast of the city on the AS-242 towards Tudela Veguín, was closed to visitors at the time of research.

Special Events

Oviedo's biggest fiesta is that of San Mateo, celebrated in the third week of September and climaxing around the 21st. Carnaval, in February or March, is also a good time to sample street festivities.

Places to Stay

Oviedo is liberally sprinkled with hotels of most grades. You'll find plenty of places near the train station and more just north of the old town.

Pensión Covadonga (☎ 985 21 06 21, Calle Campoamor 30), near the train station, has just a handful of very basic but clean singles/doubles for 1500/3000 ptas. *Hostal Álvarez* (☎ 985 25 26 73, Calle de la Independencia 14) provides decent rooms with bath and TV for 3500/5500 ptas. *Hostal Romero* (☎ 985 22 75 91, Calle de Uría 36), under the same ownership, has good-sized rooms for about 2000 ptas more.

Hostal Mendizábal (☎ 985 22 01 89, Calle de Mendizábal 4), neatly located just off Plaza de Porlier, has mostly clean rooms with shared bathroom for 3000/4500 ptas, and

ASTURIAS

doubles with bath for 5000 ptas. The solid **Pensión Fidalgo** (☎ 985 21 32 87, Calle de Jovellanos 5) has three rooms with shared bathroom for 4000/5500 ptas, as well as three doubles with private shower for 7000 ptas.

Hostal Arcos (☎ 985 21 47 73, Calle de Magdalena 3), ideally located within stumbling distance of some of Oviedo's best watering holes, has doubles for 5900 ptas with bathroom, or 4000 ptas without.

A grade better, **Hotel La Alteza** (☎ 985 24 04 04, Calle de Uría 25) charges 7500 ptas plus IVA for singles or doubles in high summer, but 3700/5600 ptas plus IVA most of the year, for clean rooms with bath and TV. It has a little cafe. **Hotel Favila** (☎ 985 25 38 77, Calle de Uría 37) is of similar standard, charging 6500/8000 ptas plus IVA. It has a reasonably priced restaurant.

Hotel Ovetense (☎ 985 22 08 40, Calle de San Juan 6) is comfortable, with rooms for 5500/8000 ptas. Heading into luxury class is **Hotel Principado** (☎ 985 21 77 92, Calle de San Francisco 6), with rates of 11,500/16,000 ptas plus IVA. Top of the heap is the opulent **Hotel de la Reconquista** (☎ 985 24 11 00, fax 985 24 11 66, Calle de Gil de Jaz 16), where doubles are 29,950 ptas plus IVA.

Places to Eat

Restaurants The **Restaurante Impala** (Calle de Cabo Noval 10) does good Asturian food at reasonable prices. The set lunch is good value at 1200 ptas.

Restaurante El Raitán (Plaza de Trascorrales 6) is an atmospheric place where a satisfying meal will probably set you back about 3000 ptas. Next door is their rather classy version of a chigre, or traditional tavern. **Logos** (Calle de San Francisco 10) is a good grill restaurant with a touch of class and a set lunch for 1800 ptas (1400 ptas in the bar).

Lunchers up on Monte Naranco should check out **Parrilla Buenos Aires**, about a kilometre up the hill from the Palacio de Santa María, with unbeatable views over Oviedo.

Cafes & Bars Plaza de Porlier has a couple of nice cafes for your morning coffee. And

the dark woodwork of **Café JL** (Calle de Ramón y Cajal 16) makes it a cosy alternative when the sun's not shining; ensconce yourself upstairs. The lacework of squares around the old town is loaded with cafes to suit all tastes. Plaza del Paraguas in particular can be pleasant in summer.

For lunchtime pinchos (snacks) and a beer, locals tend to converge on the bars along Calle del Rosal.

Ca Mi Güela (Calle de Mon 9) has an excellent-value set lunch for 1200 ptas. More is said below about **sidrerías** (cider houses), but it's worth noting that you can get a square meal in most of them, as well as tippling on fermented apples. Those on Calle de la Gascona typically serve raciones of seafood, fish, meat, cheese or revueltos (scrambled eggs) priced between 600 and 2200 ptas. A slightly upmarket option, specialising in seafood, is **Sidrería Faro Vidio** (Calle de Cimadevilla 19).

Entertainment

If you're after no-frills drinking Asturian-style, check out the **sidrerías**. Calle de la Gascona is a classic street lined with about eight lively, no-nonsense sidrerías, but you'll soon start turning them up all over town.

Ca Beleño (Calle de Martínez Vigil 4) is a well-established spot for enjoying Celtic music, whether of Asturian, Galician or Irish extraction (occasionally live).

The narrow pedestrian streets of the old town are thronged with people having a great time inside, and outside, dozens of music bars at weekends. Calle de Mon has many of the rowdier and later-opening spots. **El Paraguas del Olivar** at No 14 is a slightly psychedelic joint, but if it's not your scene there's plenty of choice. **La Santa Sebe** (Calle de Altamirano 6) provides space for a little dancing, and a platform for occasional live bands. On Plaza de Riego, **Bar Riego**, with lots of tables outside, is good for quieter conversation, while **Café Plaza** is a livlier music bar. Other streets to explore are Calle Ildefonso Martínez and Calle de la Canóniga.

Central Oviedo is not richly blessed with all-night dance-till-you-drop places. One reasonably handy place to check out is *La Moncloa (Calle de Covadonga 28). La Real (Calle de Cervantes 19)* provides late-night weekend sessions of techno, house and, of course, technohouse.

Getting There & Away

Air The Aeropuerto de Asturias is at Ranón, 43km north-west of Oviedo and 39km west of Gijón. Iberia flies daily nonstop to/from Madrid and Barcelona and a few days a week direct to/from London and Paris. Spaniar flies to/from Madrid.

Bus The main ALSA bus station (☎ 958 96 96 96) is at Plaza del General Primo de Rivera 1, but the entrance is unmarked – look for what appears to be an arcade. From here buses run to destinations over much of Spain, including about 12 daily to Madrid (5¼ hours, 3825 ptas) and six or more daily to León (1½ hours). Buses also run to Valladolid, Salamanca, Barcelona, Sevilla and various cities in Galicia – there are three or more daily to/from La Coruña (six hours, 3165 ptas) and Santiago de Compostela (7½ hours, 3740 ptas).

ALSA services within Asturias include half a dozen daily to/from Villaviciosa (one hour), a couple to/from Cudillero (1¼ hours), and six or more to/from Luarca (1½ hours, 1000 ptas), Navia, Tapia de Casariego, Castropol (1520 ptas) and over the border to Ribadeo in Galicia (three hours, 1700 ptas). Direct services charge up the motorway to Gijón (30 minutes, 255 ptas) every few minutes from 7 am to 10.30 pm. International buses go as far afield as Lisbon, Paris, Brussels, London and Zürich.

The other main bus terminal is that of EASA and Turytrans at Calle de Jerónimo Ibrán 1 (☎ 985 29 00 39). From here, about six buses a day run to places such as Rib-adesella (1½ hours, 805 ptas), Llanes (two hours, 1050 ptas), Santander (three hours, 1710 ptas), Bilbao (five hours, 2575 ptas) and San Sebastián (six hours, 3470 ptas). Buses to Arriondas, Cangas de Onís and Covadonga (see Picos de Europa later in this chapter) also go from here.

Train The one station serves both rail companies, Renfe and FEVE. The best way to Gijón is by Renfe *cercanías* (suburban trains), which run from early morning until after 10 pm and take 35 minutes. Five daily Renfe trains serve León (two hours, 1700 to 2300 ptas), continuing either to Valladolid and Madrid or to Burgos, Pamplona and Barcelona.

FEVE runs four daily trains to/from Arriondas (1½ hours), Ribadesella (1¾ hours) and Llanes (2¼ hours), with two continuing to Santander (4¼ hours, 1685 ptas). Westward, FEVE runs three times daily to Cudillero (1¼ hours), Luarca (2¼ hours) and Navia, with two continuing to Tapia de Casariego, Ribadeo, Viveiro and Ferrol (6½ hours, 2470 ptas).

Getting Around

Up to eight buses daily run to the Aeropuerto de Asturias (40 minutes, 740 ptas) from the main ALSA bus station, timed to coincide with departing flights; these also bring arriving passengers into town.

GIJÓN
postcode 33200 • pop 259,000

Bigger, busier and gutsier than Oviedo, Asturias' largest city Gijón (khi-**hon**) produces iron, steel, chemicals and oil, as well as being the main loading terminal for Asturian coal. Many *gijoneses* think their city should be the regional capital and some go to the trouble of buying cars in Girona, Catalunya, to have a 'GI' number plate instead of one with 'O' (for Oviedo). To confuse matters further, those writing in the local dialect spell the place 'Xixón' anyway!

In the past decade or so Gijón has gone to some trouble to make itself attractive by pedestrianising and cleaning up old streets, creating new parks and waterside walks and opening some interesting museums. Allied to its people's *joie de vivre* and a big summer entertainment programme, this makes the place well worth some of your time.

Information

The Asturias regional tourist office (☎ 985 34 60 46), Calle del Marqués de San Esteban

ASTURIAS

1, is open 9.30 am to 1.30 pm weekdays, 9 am to 2 pm Saturday. In summer several extra information booths open around the city. The central post office is on Plaza de Seis de Agosto. The Policía Local (☎ 985 18 11 00) are at Calle San José 2, south of the centre. The main general hospital is the Hospital de Cabueñes (☎ 985 18 50 00), 4km east of the centre.

Things to See & Do

The ancient core of Gijón is concentrated on the headland known as **Cimadevilla**. At the top of this, what used to be a fortified military zone has been converted into something of a park. Wrapped around the landward side of the hill is a fine web of narrow lanes, small squares and dead ends. Plaza de Jovellanos is dominated by the 16th-century house of the 18th-century Enlightenment politician Gaspar Melchor de Jovellanos, now housing the **Museo Jovellanos** devoted mainly to Asturian art and Jovellanos himself.

To the east, underneath Campo Valdés, are the town's **Termas Romanas** (Roman Baths), built in the 1st to 4th centuries AD. West of here is the harmonious square **Plaza Mayor**, with porticoes on three sides and

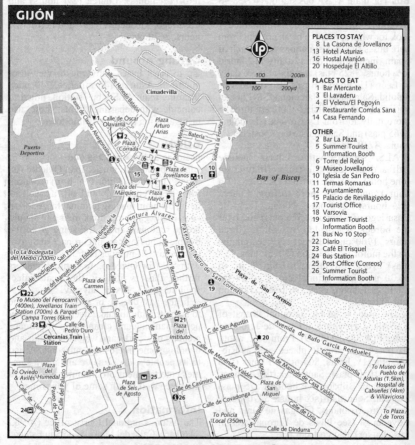

GIJÓN

PLACES TO STAY
8 La Casona de Jovellanos
13 Hotel Asturias
16 Hostal Manjón
20 Hospedaje El Altillo

PLACES TO EAT
1 Bar Mercante
3 El Lavaderu
4 El Veleru/El Pegoyín
7 Restaurante Comida Sana
14 Casa Fernando

OTHER
2 Bar La Plaza
5 Summer Tourist Information Booth
6 Torre del Reloj
9 Museo Jovellanos
10 Iglesia de San Pedro
11 Termas Romanas
12 Ayuntamiento
15 Palacio de Revillagigedo
17 Tourist Office
18 Varsovia
19 Summer Tourist Information Booth
21 Bus No 10 Stop
22 Diario
23 Café El Trisquel
24 Bus Station
25 Post Office (Correos)
26 Summer Tourist Information Booth

the 19th-century ayuntamiento on the fourth. A little farther west, the impressive 18th-century **Palacio de Revillagigedo** is now a lively contemporary arts centre, staging exhibitions, music, dance and theatre. The **Torre del Reloj**, just behind it, houses a six-floor exhibition on Gijón's history.

The **Museo del Ferrocarril de Asturias** (Asturias Railway Museum), in Gijón's old Renfe station on Plaza de la Estación del Norte, a few minutes' walk west of the centre, explores the key role played by railways in Asturian history, with 50 locomotives and carriages and heaps more chuff-chuff paraphernalia.

The **Museo del Pueblo de Asturias**, on a large woodland site 2km east of the centre, is an Asturian ethnographic museum with several traditional buildings, one containing the **Museo de la Gaita** (Bagpipe Museum) with Asturian and international pipes and other Asturian musical instruments. Take No 10 from Plaza del Instituto to the Grupo Cultura Covadonga stop, about 400m from the museum.

Parque Campa Torres, on the Cabo Torres headland 6km north-west of the centre, is Gijón's birthplace – a Roman and pre-Roman archaeological site where you can examine remains of dwellings, wells and cisterns.

For swimming, **Playa de San Lorenzo** is a surprisingly good, clean city beach.

Special Events

Between late June and the end of August Gijón finds some excuse for a fiesta almost every week, from the late June Semana Negra (Black Week), supposedly dedicated to police and science fiction novels, to the late August Fiesta de la Sidra Natural (Natural Cider Festival). All these events feature copious and varied music, partying and other fun. The biggest week of all is Semana Grande (early to mid-August).

Places to Stay

Plenty of places of most standards are scattered about the centre of the new town, south-east and north-east of the train station. A good spot overlooking the port is *Hostal Manjón* (☎ 985 35 23 78, Plaza del Marqués

Gijón Museums

All Gijón museums are closed on Monday. Opening hours on other days vary from place to place and season to season, but the typical timetable is 10 am to 1 pm and 5 to 8 pm Tuesday to Saturday, 11 am to 2 pm Sunday. Tourist offices have lists of current hours. All museums are free on Tuesday, in fact most are free every day, the exceptions being the Termas Romanas, Museo del Ferrocarril and Parque Campa Torres, each costing 350 ptas (200 ptas for students, youth card holders, under-16s and seniors).

1). Singles/doubles cost 3500/5800 ptas plus IVA, or slightly more with bath.

Closer to Playa de San Lorenzo, *Hospedaje El Altillo* (☎ 985 34 33 30, Calle de Capua 17) has rooms with bath at 7000 ptas a double.

Hotel Asturias (☎ 985 35 06 00, Plaza Mayor 12) is one of two hotels in Cimadevilla. Comfortable rooms cost 13,650 ptas plus IVA per double. The other is *La Casona de Jovellanos* (☎ 985 34 20 24, Plaza de Jovellanos 1), where doubles are 12,600 ptas plus IVA in high season but 7000 ptas plus IVA in low season.

Places to Eat

The newer part of the centre, south of Cimadevilla, offers many eating options, but the most atmospheric area to eat in is Cimadevilla. Just off Plaza Mayor is a series of lively little sidrerías, most with outside tables, including *Casa Fernando*. Varied raciones range from 900 ptas, and among the more unusual local specialities are *oricios* (sea urchins), *llámpares* (limpets) and *centollos* (spider crabs). Farther up Cimadevilla, *Restaurante Comida Sana* (Plaza de los Remedios 1) offers many vegetarian dishes between 900 and 1200 ptas. *El Veleru/El Pegoyín* has good varied fare with main dishes starting around 1400 ptas. On the wide Plaza Arturo Arias, the popular *El Lavaderu* serves a four-course *menú* for 1000 ptas. *Bar Mercante*, on short Cuesta del Cholo, serves inexpensive raciones and offers great sunsets.

Entertainment

Gijón is a lively place after dark towards the end of the week. The *sidrerías* mentioned in Places to Eat are fun, and farther up in Cimadevilla, spots around Plaza Corrada such as *Bar La Plaza* are the hub of a good music bar scene.

In the newer part of town, streets such as Calle de San Bernardo, Calle de la Corrida and Calle de los Moros also have plenty of good sidrerías, cafes and bars. *Varsovia (Paseo del Muro de San Lorenzo 18),* facing the beach, is one particularly popular spot; you can dance downstairs and chat upstairs. To the west is *Café El Trisquel (Calle de Pedro Duro 12),* which is a Celtic music haven, with tables out the back – serving very good pancakes too. *Diario (Calle de Rodríguez San Pedro 25),* nearby, is good for a quieter drink to mainly jazz sounds. For yet other rhythms, try *La Bodeguita del Medio (Calle de Rodríguez San Pedro 43),* one of several salsa spots in the vicinity.

A Blessing from on High

Asturias' climate is great for growing apples – many of which are put to very good use in the production of some excellent cider *(sidra)*. Cider-drinking for Asturians is a particularly gregarious and enjoyable activity – and if Asturias has a national sport, it has to be cider-pouring. In *sidrerías* throughout Asturias you'll see drinkers, waiters and bartenders pouring cider from bottles held high overhead into glasses held close to horizontal near ground level. The object of this appears to be to instil some fizz into the drink, and the essence of the activity is to do it with maximum nonchalance, preferably while looking in another direction entirely and holding a slurred conversation with someone in yet a third direction. The percentages of cider that actually enter the glass or are splashed over the pourer's and bystanders' clothes are, by comparison, of slight importance. Expert *escanciadores* (pourers) get to compete against each other in a competition held during the Fiesta de la Sidra Natural, staged each August in Gijón.

Getting There & Away

Bus For most destinations, buses are the best bet. The ALSA bus station (☎ 985 34 27 11) is on the corner of Calle Magnus Blikstad and Calle de Llanes, near Plaza del Humedal. From here, frequent buses go to Oviedo, and about 12 daily run to Madrid (5¾ hours, 4075 ptas), six or more to León (two hours) and two to Barcelona (12½ hours, 4850 ptas). Half a dozen buses head east to the French border via Ribadesella, Llanes, Santander (3½ hours), Bilbao and San Sebastián (6½ hours). Westward, three or more go to Cudillero (1½ hours, 560 ptas), Luarca, Navia, Tapia de Casariego and Castropol, and one to Ribadeo (3¼ hours, 1780 ptas). Two or more go to Santiago de Compostela (eight hours) and other Galician cities. Other places served daily include Valladolid, Salamanca, Sevilla and the same international destinations as from Oviedo.

Train The main station, on Plaza del Humedal, is known as Cercanías, which is a little confusing as it isn't only used by *cercanías* (suburban trains). The other station, Jovellanos, is 600m west and less convenient.

Renfe (☎ 985 17 02 02) provides frequent cercanías to/from Oviedo (35 minutes), and long-distance trains three times daily to/from Madrid (6½ to 9¼ hours, 4600 to 5800 ptas) and twice daily to Barcelona. All five long-distance trains stop at León. The overnight train to/from Madrid uses Jovellanos station only, but all other Renfe trains stop at both stations.

FEVE (☎ 985 34 24 15), using Cercanías station only, runs frequent cercanías to/from Pravia (1¼ hours) and Cudillero (1¾ hours). Two or three each day connect in Pravia with FEVE trains to/from Luarca, Navia, Tapia de Casariego, Castropol, Ribadeo (four hours from Gijón), Viveiro and Ferrol (Galicia).

EASTERN COAST

With the magnificent Picos de Europa rising up just 15km inland in places, Asturias' eastern coast attracts a good number of Spanish holiday-makers over the summer. A string of pretty beaches and coves provides a tempting counterpoint to the mountains.

Villaviciosa & Around
postcode 33300 • pop 8000

Apart from the Iglesia de Santa María, a 13th-century Late Romanesque structure, Villaviciosa's pretty centre is mostly a child of the 18th-century. Calle García Caveda, the main street, is lined with noble houses, mostly in good condition. A helpful tourist office (☎ 985 89 17 59) in Parque Vallina is open in summer only.

The town is a good base for church-lovers. The surrounding area is fairly sprinkled with often diminutive places of worship bearing Romanesque or even pre-Romanesque features. Many are for aficionados only, but one that shouldn't be missed is the pre-Romanesque **Iglesia de San Salvador de Valdediós**, about 9km south-west, off the road to Pola de Siero. It was built in AD 893 as part of a palace complex for Alfonso III in what Asturians dubbed 'God's Valley', but archaeologists have failed to find any remnant beyond this simple church.

Next door are the Romanesque **Iglesia y Monasterio de Santa María**, of the Cistercian persuasion. They're open for guided visits (200 ptas) from 11 am to 1 pm and 4 to 6 pm daily except Monday from May to October, and 11 am to 1 pm daily except Monday in other months. Oviedo-bound buses from Villaviciosa can drop you at Ambás, from which it's about a 2km walk. Another fine Romanesque church is the **Iglesia de San Juan de Amandi**, 1.5km south of Villaviciosa.

Facing the open sea on the western side of the Ría de Villaviciosa is the minute port of **Tazones**, where Carlos I (Charles I) supposedly first landed in Spain in 1517. It's quite a popular spot and in summer gets a little crowded. The eastern side of the *ría* (estuary) is covered by the golden sands of the **Playa de Rodiles**. Surfers might catch a wave here in late summer or early autumn.

Places to Stay & Eat At Playa de Rodiles, the inexpensive *Camping La Ensenada* stays open all year.

There are a few cheapish places in Villaviciosa. *Café del Sol (☎ 985 89 11 30, Calle del Sol 27)* offers singles/doubles for 2400/4000 ptas (5000 ptas for doubles with bath). *Hotel Neptuno (☎ 985 89 13 02, Plaza de Obdulio Fernández 8)*, next to the bus station, charges 4500/6000 ptas plus IVA with bath.

There are several mid-range options on Calle García Caveda and elsewhere, but for a real treat try *La Casona de Amandi (☎ 985 89 01 30)*, a 19th-century farmhouse in Amandi, 1.5km south of Villaviciosa. Doubles with their original Isabelline furnishings cost up to 13,900 ptas plus IVA. On the food front, head for *Casa Milagros* on Calle General Campomanes. The *salmon a la ribereña* (salmon in a rich sauce), for 1100 ptas, is delicious.

In Tazones, the waterfront *Hotel Imperial (☎ 985 89 71 16)* has rooms for 6500/7500 ptas. *Seafood* is the speciality in Tazones, although the restaurants are pricey.

Getting There & Away Around seven ALSA buses a day go to/from Oviedo (one hour, 430 ptas), Gijón (45 minutes, 300 ptas), Lastres and Ribadesella (one hour, 390 ptas). From early July to early September buses run to Playa Rodiles. The bus station is behind Bar El Ancho on Plaza de Obdulio Fernández.

Lastres

Apart from a few sandy beaches, the only worthwhile stop along the 40km stretch between Villaviciosa to Ribadesella is the precarious cliff-side fishing village of Lastres, a scruffier version of Cudillero (see the Western Coast section) with a couple of 16th-century churches thrown in.

Ribadesella
postcode 33560 • pop 4000

Unless you've booked in advance, stay away from here on the first weekend after 2 August when the place goes mad over the Río Sella canoe festival (see Arriondas later in this chapter). Otherwise, Ribadesella is a low-key resort. Its two halves, split by the Sella's estuary, are joined by a bridge. The western half has a good, long, fairly clean beach, Playa de Santa Marina, while the old town and fishing harbour are on the eastern side.

ASTURIAS

The tourist office (☎ 985 86 00 38) is just north of the eastern end of the Sella bridge. It is open 10 am to 10 pm daily in July and August; otherwise, 10 am to 1 pm and 4 to 8 pm Tuesday to Saturday, 11 am to 4 pm Sunday.

Cueva de Tito Bustillo Those who missed out on the real thing at Altamira can make up for it a little by visiting the Cueva de Tito Bustillo, a short distance south of the western end of the Sella bridge (signposted). The **cave drawings** here, mostly of animals (especially horses), are roughly 12,000 years old. The cave is open 10 am to 4.15 pm Wednesday to Sunday, April to mid-September only, with a group allowed in every 25 minutes. Entry is 330 ptas (students 165 ptas). There's a limit of 385 visitors daily, so turn up early in August.

Activities A couple of firms can set you up with canoe trips on the Sella (see Arriondas later in this chapter), rent you bikes, take you caving or canyoning and so on. Turaventura (☎ 985 86 09 22), at Avenida Palacio Valdés 14, has been around a few years (it no longer rents bikes, though). Another is Trasgu Aventura (☎ 985 86 02 23), Avenida Palacio Valdés s/n.

Places to Stay & Eat *Camping Los Sauces* (☎ 985 86 13 12) on Carretera de San Pedro, 1.4km past the western end of Playa de Santa Marina, is open from mid-June to late September. In Sebreño, 1km inland from the Gijón road, *Camping Ribadesella* (☎ 985 85 82 93), with its own pool, charges a little more and is open from Easter to the end of September.

A bed (in rooms of four or six) at the hostel *Albergue Roberto Frassinelli* (☎ 985 40 02 05), on Calle de Ricardo Cangas and fronting Playa de Santa Marina, costs 1500 ptas, including breakfast. You don't need an HI card. Otherwise, there's not too much cheap accommodation.

In the older, eastern part of town, *Hotel Covadonga* (☎ 985 86 02 22, Calle Manuel Caso de la Villa 6) has ageing but spacious rooms for 5000/7000 ptas with bathroom and 4000/5500 ptas with washbasin, and a

reasonable restaurant with seafood from 900 to 2400 ptas.

There are plenty of newer, more expensive places on the western side of town, many of them right on Playa de Santa Marina, including *Hotel La Playa* (☎ 985 86 01 00, Paseo de la Playa 42) and *Hotel Ribadesella Playa* (☎ 985 86 07 15, Calle de Ricardo Cangas 3), both in old mansions, with doubles for 10,000 and 11,500 ptas plus IVA respectively.

For food, try the busy sidrerías on Paseo del Muelle on the eastern side of the river. One, *El Tarteru* at the end of the street, provides fish raciones from 800 ptas.

Getting There & Away Around half a dozen daily ALSA/EASA/Turytrans buses run each day to/from Villaviciosa, Arriondas, Oviedo (1½ hours, 805 ptas), Gijón and, eastward, Llanes, San Vicente de la Barquera, Santander, Bilbao and San Sebastián. The bus station is on Paseo del Cobayo, about 300m south of the bridge on the eastern side of town. FEVE provides six trains daily to/from Llanes and Arriondas, four or five to/from Oviedo (1¾ hours) and two to/from Santander. An ALSA bus from Llanes to Madrid and vice-versa, daily in July and August (once weekly in other months) links Ribadesella with Cangas de Onís.

Ribadesella to Llanes

Several little beaches and coves await discovery between Ribadesella and Llanes by those with transport and time. About 10km short of Llanes, **Playa de San Antolín** is an open and comparatively unprotected beach where you might pick up the odd wave. More interesting for some will be the nearby Benedictine **Monasterio de San Antolín de Bedón**, founded in the 11th century. You'll be lucky to find anyone in the surrounding half-dozen houses to let you inside the Romanesque church which is its main feature. The unkempt setting makes up for it though.

Llanes

postcode 33500 • pop 5000

Inhabited since ancient times, Llanes was long an independent-minded town and whaling port with its own charter awarded by Alfonso IX of León in 1206. Today, though marred by nascent urban spread, it's one of northern Spain's more popular holiday destinations – a handy base for some pretty beaches and with the Picos de Europa close at hand.

The tourist office (☎ 985 40 01 64) is in La Torre, a tower left over from Llanes' 13th-century defences, in a lane off Calle Alfonso IX. It's open 10 am to 2 pm and 4 to 6.30 pm weekdays, 10.30 am to 1.30 pm Saturday.

Things to See & Do Of the two town beaches, the **Playa de Toró** to the east is infinitely preferable to the tiny **Playa del Sablón**.

If you're interested in **organised trips** into the Picos de Europa, caving, canoeing or horse riding, see what Naturas (☎ 985 40 22 00), at Calle Mayor 14, or Senda (☎ 985 40 24 30) on Calle Castillo have to offer.

The Gothic church **La Basílica** on Plaza de Cristo Rey is worth a look. It was begun in 1240.

Places to Stay Finding a room in July or August is difficult – and lone travellers will be lucky indeed to get a single.

Camping Entre Playas (☎ 985 40 08 88), just near Playa de Toró, is open from June to September. The HI *Albergue Juvenil Juventudes (☎/fax 985 40 07 70, Calle Celso Amieva 7)* has 40 twin rooms at 825 ptas per person. It's open all year.

Pensión La Guía (☎ 985 40 25 77, Plaza de Parres Sobrino 1), in a 300-year-old house, is centrally located and its nice, remodelled rooms with bathroom go for 7000 ptas single or double in high season but 2000/4000 ptas for singles/doubles in low season. *Hospedaje Casa del Río (☎ 985 40 11 91, Avenida de San Pedro 3)* is a good place with rooms for 2750/5500 ptas with washbasin, or 7500 ptas a double with bath and TV.

Places to Eat A trio of lively, medium-priced *marisquerías* (seafood eateries) line up beside the unimpressive Río Carrocedo, just upstream of the main street through the heart of the town. Raciones start at about 750

ptas. Otherwise, the narrow Calle de Manuel Cué has some more mainstream restaurants. *Restaurante Siete Puertas* is an upmarket place where you'll pay around 3000 or 4000 ptas for two courses with drinks – but it has a *menú* for 1250 ptas. If it's just a cider and tapas you want, try *El Bodegón*, the big old sidrería on Plaza de la Magdalena near the Siete Puertas' other entrance.

Getting There & Away Llanes is served by the same buses and trains as Ribadesella. The bus station is on Calle La Bolera, east of the river.

Beaches near Llanes
The little beaches and coves either side of Llanes form one of the most appealing coastal stretches this side of Santander. Particularly worth noting is the long **Playa Ballota**, a few kilometres east of Llanes. It is hemmed in by green cliffs and accessible by dirt track; part of it is for nudists. **Playa de la Franca**, farther towards Cantabria, is also nice and has a summer *camping ground*. About 7km west of Llanes is the village-cum-understated holiday resort of **Barro**. Its main beach is a little bigger than the average cove and not too crowded. You can stay at the friendly little *Hostal La Playa (☎ 985 40 07 66)*, where singles/doubles cost up to 5500/8500 ptas plus IVA.

WESTERN COAST
Cudillero
postcode 33150 ● pop 2000
Cudillero is the most picturesque fishing village on the Asturian coast, and it knows it. The houses, painted varying pastel shades, cascade down to a tiny port on a narrow inlet. Near the harbour, half a dozen restaurants compete for custom. Despite its touristy feel, Cudillero *is* cute and pretty laid-back. The nearest beach is **Playa de Aguilar**, a fine, sandy strand a 3km drive or road-walk later. A few kilometres west of Cudillero are **Playa Concha de Artedo** and the small but pretty **Playa de San Pedro**.

Cudillero's tourist office (☎ 985 59 01 18), open in summer only, is on Plaza de San Pedro.

The closest camping ground is *L'Amuravela* (☎ 985 59 09 95) at El Pito, 1km east. *Camping Cudillero* (☎ 985 59 06 63) is at Playa de Aguilar. Both open from some time in June to some time in September and get packed in August.

Accommodation in Cudillero itself is limited. *Pensión El Camarote* (☎ 985 59 12 02, Calle García de la Concha 4) and *Pensión Álver* (☎ 985 59 00 05, Calle García de la Concha 8), about 600m back from the harbour along Cudillero's single street, are small places both charging 6000 ptas for doubles with bathroom in August. They close at least half the year.

The stone-built, 11-room *La Casona de Pío* (☎ 985 59 15 12, Calle Riofrío 3), just back from the port, has new, very comfortable singles/doubles with a rustic touch for 8000/10,000 ptas plus IVA, and a good restaurant. If these fail, there are a few alternatives around the upper edges of the village and along the Oviedo road.

There's no shortage of eateries, but a meal with wine is likely to cost you about 3000 ptas wherever you try. *Restaurante El Remo*, beside the port, is a reliable seafood place.

A few ALSA buses from Oviedo and Gijón stop at Cudillero and most continue as far as Artedo. FEVE trains (the station is about 3km inland) come several times a day from Gijón and three times from Oviedo. Westward, FEVE runs two or three times daily to Cadavedo, Luarca, Navia and on along the coastal line as far as Ferrol (Galicia).

Where Am I?

Two little ways in which Asturias differs from most of the rest of Spain are that its word for municipality is *concejo*, not *municipio*, and that municipalities are often *not* named after their main town or village. This can be troublesome if for instance you're trying to find a hostal in an accommodation directory that's organised by municipalities. You'll find Arenas de Cabrales, Bulnes, Carreña, Poncebos and Sotres all listed under the concejo of Cabrales. Arriondas will be under Parres, Niserias under Peñamellera Alta, and Luarca under Valdés.

Luarca
postcode 33700 • pop 3000

Larger and more dishevelled than Cudillero, the fishing village of Luarca will appeal to lovers of seaside decay. This is one of those places that, simply because it is carved in two by a stream equipped with a handful of bridges, gets the tourist trade talking about the 'Venice of...' – in this case, Asturias. It's an interesting little place with a pretty harbour filled with small fishing boats and a couple of beaches; Venice, however, it's not.

The summer-only tourist office (☎ 985 64 00 83) is at Calle Olavarrieta 27.

Beaches The **Playa de Cueva**, set back from a dramatic headland 7km east and occasionally throwing up some decent surf, is a better beach than Luarca's own. From nearby **Cabo Busto** you can get some measure of the Asturian coast's wildness. Pebbly **Playa de Cadavedo**, farther east, is pleasant.

Places to Stay & Eat Luarca has a fair range of accommodation. Friendly *Pensión Moderna* (☎ 985 64 00 57, Calle del Crucero 2), near the central Plaza de Alfonso X, has large, clean rooms for 4500 ptas (single and double) in high season, and 1500/2500 ptas for singles/doubles in low season. *Hostal Oria* (☎ 985 64 03 85, Calle del Crucero 7) is a little classier. Doubles are 5000 ptas with shared bathroom, 7000 ptas with private bath.

Hotel La Colmena (☎ 985 64 02 78, Calle de Uría 2), close by, is reasonable value with rooms costing 5000/8000 ptas plus IVA in high season. The most enticing option in the more expensive range is *Hotel Báltico* (☎ 985 64 09 91, Paseo de Muelle 1), overlooking the port. Doubles cost up to 10,000 ptas plus IVA. The hotel's restaurant has a wide menu.

Direct your search for food to the waterfront. The well-priced sidrería *El Ancla* (Paseo del Muelle 14) has raciones and will do you a *media-ración* of about 16 delicious *mejillones picante* (chillied mussels) for 450 ptas, or a generous tabla of tasty Asturian cheeses for 1500 ptas. *Mesón de la*

Mar, farther along, is a huge, popular and more expensive seafood establishment, with some tables right on the harbourside. Its *menú* is 1800 ptas.

Getting There & Away Around six daily ALSA buses run to/from Oviedo (1½ hours, 1000 ptas) and on along the coast as far as Ribadeo, Galicia. A few come from Gijón too. A daily bus (two in summer) runs to/from Madrid via Lugo and Astorga. The station of FEVE (☎ 985 64 05 52) is a couple of kilometres out of town. Three daily trains run to/from Cudillero and Oviedo, and two trains run along the coast to/from Ferrol (Galicia).

Navia
Twenty kilometres west of Luarca is Navia, another busy port. Rather than hang about, cross the estuary (a modest version of Galicia's grander *rías* to the west) and take a sharp left along what becomes Río Navia towards Coaña (see under Coaña & the Río Navia in the Inland Western Asturias section).

Tapia de Casariego
postcode 33740 • pop 3000
This welcoming fishing haven makes a pleasant lunch stop if you're driving, but little more. The best of the unspectacular beaches is **Playa de Represas**, where you may be able to get a wave. There are several surf shops in town.

The most convenient and cheapest places to stay are *Hotel La Ruta* (☎ 985 62 81 38) and *Hotel Puente de los Santos* (☎ 985 62 81 55), facing each other across the main road and both with singles/doubles for around 5000/8000 ptas (but about half that in low season).

For nutrition, try **Maxin's Bar** *(Calle del Arquitecto Villanil 7)*, which offers platos combinados for 600 ptas or a set lunch for 1000 ptas. Otherwise, *La Marina*, down by the small harbour, is popular.

Castropol
postcode 33760 • pop 400
The Ría de Ribadeo marks the frontier between Asturias and Spain's north-western-most region, Galicia. Spanning the broad mouth of this, the first of the many grand estuaries that slice into Galicia's coast, is the Puente de los Santos.

You could detour a few kilometres south to the whitewashed village of Castropol, on a rise above the eastern side of the ría. *Hotel Casa Vicente* (☎ 985 63 50 51), at the northern entrance to the village, is a tranquil alternative to staying in Ribadeo, across in Galicia. Singles/doubles cost 3300/5500 ptas plus IVA. The road south to Lugo is a little-travelled back route into Galicia.

INLAND WESTERN ASTURIAS
Although well off the beaten track and mostly difficult to reach unless you're driving, there's some beautiful country in south-west Asturias. Even just passing through on alternative routes into Castilla y León or Galicia can be rewarding.

Salas
postcode 33860 • pop 3000
Drivers heading between Oviedo and Luarca could take, instead of the standard highways, the pretty N-634, which snakes up and down lush valleys north-west from Oviedo. At Salas, 45km from Oviedo, it soon becomes clear that the town's most famous son was Grand Inquisitor Fernando de Valdés Salas, who also founded Oviedo's university in the 16th century. His **castle** has been converted into a hotel (you can climb the tower next door), and his elaborate alabaster tomb stands inside the nearby **Colegiata de Santa María**.

Though not the cheapest place in town, *Hotel Castillo de Valdés Salas* (☎ 985 83 22 22) makes an attractive stop, with doubles for 8000 ptas plus IVA. Its restaurant is the best choice too.

Regular ALSA buses run to/from Oviedo.

Senda del Oso
The Senda del Oso (Path of the Bear) is a 20km concrete walking trail between the villages of Tuñón and Entrago, south-west of Oviedo, created by the Asturian government along the course of a former mine railway through fields, riverbank woodlands, villages and canyons. It passes through the

ASTURIAS

Monte del Oso, where you should be able to see Paco and Tola, two Asturian bears orphaned by a hunter in 1989, now living in semi-liberty in a 40,000-sq-m compound. A 1km detour from Proaza village leads to the Casa del Oso, a museum on the history and defence of the brown bear. ALSA runs at least three buses daily from Oviedo to both end-points of the path, enabling you to do it in a day trip from the city.

Parque Natural de Somiedo

If you fancy exploring some dramatic mountain country that few foreigners know of, consider this 300-sq-km protected area on the northern flank of the Cordillera Cantábrica. Composed of five valleys descending from the 2000m-plus heights of the cordillera's sometimes snow-covered ridge, the park is characterised by lush woodlands and high pastures dotted with thatched shepherds' shelters. It's also the major bastion of Spain's small remaining brown bear population.

Each of the valleys has a number of varied marked walking trails, which you can find out about at the park information centre (☎ 985 76 37 58) in the hamlet of Pola de Somiedo, open 10 am to 2 pm and 4 to 8 pm daily. Pola also has a bank, supermarket and half a dozen cheap and midrange places to stay. One of the best walking areas is the Valle de Lago, whose upper reaches contain a number of glacial lakes and high summer pastures. There is a *camping ground* and a pair of *pensiones* in Valle de Lago hamlet, a good starting point for walks, 8km south-east of Pola de Somiedo.

ALSA runs two daily buses from Oviedo to Pola de Somiedo.

Cudillero to Castilla y León

The road up through Pola de Somiedo and across the 1486m Puerto de Somiedo pass is one of the more scenic routes from Asturias into Castilla y León. Starting from the coast, a good approach for drivers is from Soto del Barco, 7km east of Cudillero. Follow the AS-16 up the placid valley of the Río Nalón then the AS-15 up the Río Narcea, veering south on the AS-227 for Pola de Somiedo.

For another good route across the cordillera, stay on the AS-15 to Soto de los Infantes. The wooded hills on either side of the valley begin to acquire stature here and 8km past Soto the Embalse de la Barca formed by the dammed Río Narcea matches them. If you're looking for somewhere to spend the night, a turn-off west just before the misnamed Puente del Infierno (Hell's Bridge) leads to Pola de Allande, a peaceful village dominated by the lugubrious 16th-century Palacio de Peñalba-Cienfuegos. *Hostal La Nueva Allandesa* (☎ 985 80 73 12, Calle de Donato Fernández 3) has modern singles/doubles for 5000/7000 ptas.

Back on the AS-15, you pass the Monasterio de Corias before reaching Cangas del Narcea, a rather large and modern place although not without some charm. The AS-213 south from here takes you into Castilla y León by the spectacular Puerto de Leitariegos (1525m). From the pass it's about 80km to Ponferrada – or you could loop around to the east and re-enter Asturias by the Puerto de Somiedo!

Coaña & Río Navia

The small town of Coaña lies about 4km inland of Navia along the Río Navia. A couple of kilometres beyond is the Castro de Coaña, one of the best preserved Celtic settlements in northern Spain. It is open 11 am to 2 pm and 4 to 7 pm Tuesday to Sunday from April to September, but 11 am to 1.30 pm and 4 to 5 pm in other months (200 ptas).

From the castro, a poor road snakes its way high above the cobalt blue Río Navia, through classic Asturian countryside – meadows alternating with rocky precipices – to Lugo in Galicia, crossing some of Galicia's least visited and wildest territory, around the town of Fonsagrada.

Picos de Europa

These jagged, deeply fissured mountains straddling Asturias, Cantabria and the north-east of León province amount to some of the finest walking country in Spain, offering plentiful short and long outings for striders of all levels, plus lots of scope for climbers and cavers too.

Beginning only 15km from the coast, and stretching little more than 40km from east to west and 25km north to south, the Picos still manage to encompass enough spectacular mountain and gorge scenery to ensure a continual flow of visitors from all over Europe and beyond. They comprise three limestone massifs: the eastern Macizo Ándara, with a summit of 2444m; the western Macizo El Cornión, rising to 2596m; and the particularly rocky Macizo Central or Macizo Los Urrieles, reaching 2648m.

The 647-sq-km Parque Nacional Picos de Europa, created in 1995, covers all three massifs and is Spain's second biggest national park. It greatly extended its 169-sq-km precursor, the Parque Nacional de la Montaña de Covadonga, which had been created as Spain's first national park back in 1918.

Virtually deserted in winter, the area is full to bursting in August and you should always try to call ahead, whether you are heading for a hotel or a refugio.

Orientation

The main access towns for the Picos are Cangas de Onís in the north-west, Arenas de Cabrales in the central north, and Potes in the south-east. Paved roads lead from Cangas south-east up to Covadonga, Lago de Enol and Lago de la Ercina; from Arenas south up to Poncebos then east up to Sotres and Tresviso; and from Potes west to Espinama and Fuente Dé. The mountains are roughly bounded on the western side by the Río Sella and the N-625 Cangas de Onís–Riaño road; on the north by the AS-114 Cangas de Onís–Arenas de Cabrales–Panes road; and on the east by the Río Deva and the N-621 Panes-Potes road.

Maps & Guidebooks The best maps of the Picos, sold in shops in Cangas de Onís, Potes and elsewhere for 600 to 700 ptas each, are Adrados Ediciones' *Picos de Europa* (1:80,000), *Picos de Europa Macizos Central y Oriental* and *Picos de Europa Macizo Occidental* (1:25,000). Lonely Planet's *Walking in Spain* describes, in far more detail than we have room for here, a nine-day circuit through much of the Picos' finest scenery which can be joined or left at several points. In Spanish, the walking and climbing guides by Miguel Ángel Adrados are recommended. The same guy has also written a route guide for mountain bikers that includes the Picos, *Cordillera Cantábrica – Ciclo-Travesías*.

Information

The national park's main information office is Casa Dago(☎ 985 84 86 14), Avenida de Covadonga 43 in Cangas de Onís, which is open 8 am to 9 pm daily in July, August and September, and 9 am to 2 pm and 4 to 6.30 pm daily in other months (except that it closes Saturday and Sunday in December, January and February). Basic information on walks in the mountains and accommodation is available here. The national park has further information offices in Camaleño on the Potes–Fuente Dé road (☎ 942 73 32 01) and in Posada de Valdeón (☎ 987 74 05 49). Local tourist offices, which can usually provide information on nearby sections of the park as well as on their own towns, are mentioned in the following sections.

Cangas de Onís, Arenas de Cabrales and Potes all have good supermarkets, and banks which open about 8.30 am to 2 pm weekdays. At least Cangas and Potes have ATMs too.

When to Go The weather across northern Spain is similar to what you'd find in the UK, Ireland or Brittany, and in the Picos it's notoriously changeable. You could begin a walk in brilliant sunshine, only to be enveloped in a chilly pea-soup fog a few hours later. But the south-eastern end of the Picos is generally drier than farther north and west.

Try to avoid August, when most of Spain is taking its holidays and finding rooms is near impossible. July is not far behind. May, June and September are about the best times to visit – more tranquil and just as likely to be sunny as August. If you want to sleep in refugios in August, you should try to book ahead. In fact, most serious walkers and climbers choose September, as it tends to be the driest month – an important consideration in the

PICOS DE EUROPA

PICOS DE EUROPA

PICOS DE EUROPA

mountains. Drivers too should beware of bad weather. Conditions can become extremely dangerous, especially in winter, when chains are often needed.

What to Bring For the walks mentioned here, you don't need special equipment. But sun protection (hats, creams, sunglasses, adequate covering of clothes) is essential, as is a water bottle – sources of drinkable water are irregular at best. Walking boots are advisable, if not absolutely necessary on every route, and even on a sunny day you should take some items of warmer clothing and even a waterproof jacket. For any treks or climbs off established tracks, you'll need the appropriate gear and experience.

Guided Walks The national park offers several free guided walks of between three and six hours, every day in July, August and September. Routes vary according to the day of the week; pick up a program at an information office. Guides usually speak Spanish only.

Fauna Although some wolves and the odd brown bear still survive in the Picos, you're highly unlikely to see either. Far more com-

Warning

The Picos de Europa are not the highest mountains in Spain, but walkers and climbers should come armed with a dose of respect. In particular, those attempting the tougher routes must bear several factors in mind: the weather is notoriously changeable, and mist, rain, cold and snow are common problems. Higher up, few trails are marked and there is virtually no animal life or vegetation. Water sources are infrequent. Paying insufficient attention to these details has cost several lives over the years and you don't want to join the statistics. National park information offices and tourist offices will readily give you a list of mountain safety tips.

mon is the chamois *(rebeco)*, a kind of cross between antelope and mountain goat. Around 6500 of them skip around the rocks and steep slopes. Deer, foxes, badgers, wild boar, hedgehogs, squirrels and martens, in various quantities, inhabit the more wooded areas.

A variety of eagles, hawks and other raptors fill the skies above the Picos, but you'd be truly lucky to catch sight of the majestic golden eagle *(águila real)* or the huge scavenging griffon vulture *(buitre leonado)* or Egyptian vulture. Choughs, with their unmistakable caws, accompany walkers at the highest altitudes.

Getting There & Around

Trying to taste the main delights of the Picos by public transport can be a frustrating matter, if you're not hanging around long enough to crisscross them on foot.

Bus & Train Just a few bus and train services – mostly summer only – will get you into the hills or to the edge of them. Timetable details change from time to time but the broad outlines of the following services are likely to be maintained.

Oviedo-Arriondas/Cangas/Arenas/Panes
From Oviedo, ALSA/EASA runs at least 13 times daily to Arriondas and 10 or more times to Cangas de Onís (one to 1¾ hours,

700 ptas). Between two and four of the Cangas buses continue to Carreña and Arenas de Cabrales, and one or two go on to Niserias and Panes (2½ hours from Oviedo). Frequencies in the opposite direction are similar. At Panes you can switch to/from buses running between Santander and Potes. The last (some days the only) westward bus from Panes leaves at 5.25 pm.

Arriondas is also on the FEVE railway between Oviedo, Ribadesella, Llanes and Santander.

Oviedo/Gijón/Arriondas/Enol/Cangas–Covadonga At least four ALSA/EASA buses daily go to Covadonga from Cangas de Onís (20 minutes, 120 ptas) and three from Arriondas. In summer, services are more frequent (up to 10 daily from Cangas). On weekends and holidays, three run from Oviedo to Covadonga (875 ptas); on other days, change in Arriondas or Cangas. From Gijón there's a daily bus to Covadonga (three hours) via Villaviciosa from June/July to early September. The last bus down from Covadonga is at 8 pm in summer, and 6 pm (7.15 pm weekends and holidays) in other seasons.

From early July to early September about five buses a day travel from Covadonga up to Lago de Enol (30 minutes) and back. The first leaves from Covadonga at 10 am and the last leaves from the lake at 6.30 pm.

Llanes/Cangas/Oseja–Madrid An ALSA bus from Llanes to Madrid and vice versa, daily in July and August (and on Sunday southbound, Friday northbound in other months), stops in Ribadesella, Arriondas, Cangas de Onís, Oseja de Sajambre, Riaño and Valladolid. The Cangas-Madrid trip (3805 ptas) takes seven hours.

Otherwise, to travel between Cangas and Ribadesella or Llanes you need to transfer at Arriondas, which is linked by about 10 buses daily and three or more FEVE trains to/from the pair of coastal towns. There's also a Cangas-Oseja service on weekdays.

Poncebos & Posada de Valdeón From about early July to early September frequent buses run between Arenas de Cabrales and

Poncebos. In the same period, a daily ALSA bus runs in the morning from Gijón, Oviedo and Llanes to Posada de Valdeón, then in the afternoon/evening from Poncebos back to Llanes, Oviedo and Gijón. The idea is that people can walk the 8km road along the Cares valley from Posada de Valdeón to Caín, then along the gorge path to Poncebos, and be picked up at the end. Contact local bus stations or ALSA (☎ 902-42 22 42) for current details.

There's also a daily bus from León to Posada de Valdeón (all year), but no buses go to Caín.

Arenas-Llanes ALSA/EASA buses between Arenas de Cabrales and Llanes operate three times a day on weekdays during school terms.

Santander-Panes/Potes/Fuente Dé Autobuses Palomera (☎ 942 88 06 11) runs from Santander bus station via San Vicente de la Barquera to Panes, Urdón, La Hermida, Lebeña and Potes, and back, two or three times daily. Santander to Potes takes about 2½ hours. For those needing to connect in Panes with buses to/from Arenas de Cabrales and Cangas de Onís, the last Potes-bound bus leaves Panes at 7 pm (5.30 pm on nonsummer weekends), and the last Santander-bound bus leaves Panes at 6.25 pm (a few minutes' later on nonsummer weekends).

From late June to mid-September buses run from Potes to Turieno, Baró, Camaleño, Cosgaya, Espinama and Fuente Dé (45 minutes) at 1 pm daily and 8.15 am weekdays, with an extra weekday service at 8 pm in July and August. Buses leave Fuente Dé for Potes at 5 pm daily, 9 am weekdays, and 8.45 pm weekdays in July and August, with the first two continuing to Santander.

Potes-León From July to September, a bus to León leaves daily from Bar Pipo next to the Hostal Picos de Europa on Calle San Roque in Potes.

Taxi An alternative to the buses for getting around the Picos area is taxis. Apart from regular taxis that stick to the better roads –

Taxis Pidal (☎ 985 84 51 77) in Arenas de Cabrales is one firm offering a 24-hour service – there are several 4WD taxi services which can manage some of the mountain tracks. One of the latter is operated by Casa Cipriano (see Sotres later in this chapter); another is Taxi Emiliano Martínez (☎ 987 74 26 09) in Soto de Valdeón, useful for the southern side of the Picos.

A regular taxi costs around 3500 ptas from Cangas de Onís to the Lagos de Covadonga, and about 2500 ptas from Arenas de Cabrales to Sotres or Potes to Fuente Dé.

WESTERN PICOS
Arriondas
postcode 33540 • pop 2500

Arriondas is the traditional starting point for easy and popular canoe trips down the pretty Río Sella to Llovio (16km). At least half a dozen agencies in town will rent you a canoe and the necessary equipment, show you how to paddle and bring you back from Llovio at the end. The standard charge is 3000 ptas per person. Agencies in Cangas de Onís offer much the same deal, including transport from and back to Cangas.

This stretch of the Sella is not a white-water affair, but a pleasant outing that for most people lasts around five hours including picnic stops. It's easily at its busiest on the first Saturday after 2 August when tens of thousands of people converge on Arriondas to witness 1500 or so canoes start a downriver trip to Ribadesella together, in the Descenso Internacional del Sella, a major international canoeing event.

Arriondas' *Camping Sella* (☎ 985 84 09 68), open at Easter and from mid-June to mid-September, charges around 2200 ptas for two adults with a car and tent. The *Albergue de Arriondas* youth hostel (☎ 985 84 12 82, Calle del Barco 12) is open all year. There are a couple of *hostales* and a two-star *hotel* too.

Cangas de Onís
postcode 33550 • pop 4000

Good King Pelayo, after his victory at Covadonga, moved about 12km down the hill to settle the base of his nascent Asturian kingdom at Cangas in AD 722. Cangas' big moment in history lasted 70 years or so, until the capital was moved elsewhere. Its second boom time seems to have arrived with the late 20th-century invasion of Picos de Europa tourists. In August especially the largely modern town is full to bursting with trekkers, campers, holiday-makers and not a few people desperately searching for a room – a common story throughout eastern Asturias in high summer.

Cangas makes a reasonable base, although as usual you'll be better placed if you have a vehicle.

Information The tourist office (☎ 985 84 80 05), at Jardines del Ayuntamiento 2, just off the main street, Avenida de Covadonga, is open 10 am to 10 pm daily in July and August. The rest of the year, opening hours are 10 am to 2 pm and 4 to 7 pm Tuesday to Saturday, 10 am to 2 pm Sunday. Casa Dago (see Information in the Picos de Europa section) provides national park information. Cangas has a fair smattering of banks with ATMs. Aventura Montaña, at Calle San Pelayo 31, sells walking and climbing gear.

Things to See The so-called **Puente Romano** spanning the Río Sella is almost certainly medieval, but no less impressive for all that. From it hangs a copy of the Cruz de la Victoria, the symbol of Asturias which resides in Oviedo cathedral. Not far off, the tiny, old-looking **Capilla de Santa Cruz** was actually built in 1931 on what has been a sacred site for several millennia. Inside (if you find it open), you can see a megalithic tomb in the crypt. The first Christian church was built here in AD 437. **Parque de Naturaleza La Grandera** at Soto de Cangas, 3km east on the Covadonga road, offers the chance to see in captivity bears, wolves, birds of prey and other Spanish wildlife that you'd be lucky to see in the wild – open daily most of the year.

Activities Los Cauces (☎ 985 94 73 18), Avenida de Covadonga 23, offers a range of activities including canoe descents of the Río Sella (see the Arriondas section earlier), horse riding (1700 ptas for one hour),

canyoning (5000 ptas for two or three hours), caving (3000 ptas for two or three hours), and walking and climbing in the mountains. Cangas Aventura (☎ 985 84 92 61), Avenida de Covadonga s/n, next door, and the Hotel Monteverde (☎ 985 84 80 79), around the corner at Calle Sargento Provisional 5, offer similar activities.

Places to Stay The friendly *Hospedaje Principado* (☎ 985 84 83 50, Avenida de Covadonga 6) is one of a handful of small pensiones near the Puente Romano. Clean singles/doubles cost 2500/5000 ptas. Almost next door, *Pensión Reconquista* (☎ 985 84 82 75, Avenida de Covadonga 6) has doubles for 6000 ptas. *Pensión El Chófer* (☎ 985 84 83 05, Calle de Emilio Laria 10) is reasonable value with rooms at 3000/5000 ptas.

Several one-star hotels offer comfy if plain rooms with bath and TV at fair prices. Among them are *Hotel Los Robles* (☎ 985 94 70 52, fax 985 94 71 65, Calle San Pelayo 8), charging 8000/9000 ptas plus IVA (3000/4500 ptas plus IVA in low season). *Hotel Monteverde* (☎ 985 84 80 79, Calle Sargento Provisional 5) and *Hotel Plaza* (☎ 985 84 83 08, La Plaza 7) are a little cheaper, charging 5500/7850 ptas plus IVA and 4000/7000 ptas plus IVA, respectively.

For a little more comfort, try *Hotel Los Lagos* (☎ 985 84 92 77, Jardines del Ayuntamiento 3), almost next door to the tourist office. Doubles are 13,000 ptas plus IVA.

Places to Eat A good bet is *Sidrería Restaurante Mario* (Avenida de Covadonga 19). It serves raciones under 1000 ptas and numerous tempting main dishes between 1000 and 2500 ptas. There's plenty of wine as well as cider. Two more good places within a couple of doors are the slightly pricier *Los Arcos*, and *Restaurante Torreón* where pizzas and platos combinados are 1000 to 1200 ptas. The *cafe* at Hotel Los Robles serves good omelette rolls for breakfast.

Getting There & Away The ALSA bus office (☎ 985 84 81 33) and stop is on Avenida de Covadonga, opposite Jardines del Ayuntamiento.

Covadonga

The importance of Covadonga, 11km south-east of Cangas de Onís, lies in what it represents rather than what it is. Somewhere hereabouts, in approximately AD 722, the Muslims received their first defeat, at the hands of King Pelayo, who set up the Asturian kingdom considered the beginning of the Reconquista – a mere 800-year project.

The place is an object of pilgrimage, for in a cave here, the **Santa Cueva**, the Virgin supposedly appeared to Pelayo's warriors before the battle. Weekend and summer queues of the faithful or superstitious lined up to get into the cave, now with a chapel installed, are matched only by the ceaseless line of cars crawling past to get up to the Lagos de Covadonga. The **Fuente de Siete Caños** spring, by the pool below the cave, is supposed to assure marriage within one year to those who drink from it. Landslides destroyed much of the area in the 19th century and the main church here now, the **Basílica de Covadonga**, is a neo-Romanesque affair built between 1877 and 1901. Opposite the basilica is the **Tesoro de la Santina**, a museum filled with all sorts of items, mostly donations by the illustrious faithful – open from 11 am to 2 pm and 4 to 7.30 pm daily.

Hospedería del Peregrino (☎ 985 84 60 47) is a pleasant mid-range accommodation possibility. Doubles with shared bath are 5000 ptas in June. Its restaurant is a little pricey, with a *menú* for 1500 ptas. About nine mid-range hotels are scattered along the road between Cangas de Onís and Covadonga.

Lagos de Covadonga

In summer, don't be deterred from joining the almost unbroken line of vehicles crawling the 12km uphill from Covadonga to these two beautiful little lakes. Most of the day-trippers don't get past patting a few cows' noses near the lakes, so walking here is as enjoyable as anywhere else in the Picos. Some days in August the road is closed when traffic reaches saturation point.

Lago de Enol is the first lake you reach. A few hundred metres away are *Refugio Vega de Enol (☎ 985 84 85 76)*, open all year with bunks for 500 ptas and reasonably priced food, and a *zona de acampada*, where you can camp free for up to three nights (but with no water or toilet facilities). It's just over 1km from Lago de Enol to Lago de la Ercina; they're linked not only by the paved road but also by a footpath via the Centro de Visitantes Pedro Pidal (open 10 am to 6 pm daily, Semana Santa to mid-December) which has information and displays on the Picos and a bookshop. There are rustic restaurants near both lakes (the Ercina one is cheaper), which are both closed in winter. Bathing in the lakes is banned.

When mist descends, the lakes, surrounded by the green pasture and bald rock that characterise this part of the Picos, take on an eerie appearance.

Walks from the Lakes Two classic and relatively easy trails begin and end at the lakes. The first leads about 7km south-east, with an ascent of 600m, from Lago de la Ercina to the **Vega de Ario**, where the *Refugio Marqués de Villaviciosa (☎ 639-81 20 69)*, attended and with meal service daily from May to October and at weekends year-round, has bunk space for 40 (1000 ptas). The last stages around the Vega Robles are marked with splodges of yellow paint, and the reward for about 2½ hours' effort is some magnificent views across the Cares gorge to the Macizo Central of the Picos.

The alternative walk takes you roughly south from Lago de Enol, passing the Refugio Vega de Enol, to the *Refugio de Vegarredonda (☎ 985 92 29 52)*, and on to the **Mirador de Ordiales**, a lookout point over a 1km sheer drop into the Valle de Angón. It's about a 3½-hour walk (one way) – relatively easy along a mule track as far as the refugio, then a little more challenging on up to the mirador. The 68-place refugio (1000 ptas per bunk) is attended, and has meals available all year.

Desfiladero de los Beyos

The N-625 south from Cangas de Onís follows the Río Sella upstream through one of the most extraordinary defiles in Europe. The road through the Desfiladero de los Beyos gorge is a remarkable feat of engineering.

Towards its southern end you cross from Asturias into Castilla y León.

Oseja de Sajambre
postcode 24916 • pop 380

Once inside the province of León you soon strike Oseja de Sajambre, an average sort of place with magnificent views across the gorge. *Hostal Pontón* (☎ 987 74 03 16), on the main road, has singles/doubles for 3750/4750 ptas plus IVA, and doubles with bathroom for 5750 ptas plus IVA. You'll probably also be able to find someone renting rooms privately. There are a couple of *restaurants* and grocery *shops*.

Soto de Sajambre
postcode 24916 • pop 100

A better base for walking is this much prettier village by a freshwater stream, 4km north of Oseja de Sajambre. *Hostal Peñasanta* (☎ 987 74 03 95, Calle Principal s/n) charges 4000 ptas for doubles (5500 ptas with bathroom) and can organise horse-riding excursions. You can also usually rent a private room.

Walks from Soto de Sajambre include La Senda del Arcediano, a very scenic trip of five or six hours north to Amieva, manageable by most walkers, and a more difficult trail eastwards to Posada de Valdeón.

Embalse de Riaño

The road south from Oseja de Sajambre to the beautiful Embalse de Riaño is a worthwhile drive, and the reservoir itself, with its stunning rocky backdrop, is a delight to the eyes, although there was much controversy over its creation. In 1987 the valley was flooded and its inhabitants evacuated with paltry compensation. The town of Riaño is pretty characterless as a result.

CENTRAL PICOS

A star attraction of the Picos' central massif is the gorge that divides it from the western Macizo El Cornión. The popular Garganta del Cares (Cares Gorge) trail can be crowded in summer but the walk is worthwhile. This part of the Picos also has plenty of less heavily tramped walking paths and climbing challenges once you've 'done' the Cares.

You can approach the area from several directions, but for many it will be easiest to come from the north. Arenas de Cabrales and Poncebos are obvious bases.

Carreña

This unassuming town on the Río Casaño, some 25km east of Cangas de Onís by the AS-114, has a couple of banks. There are a few fairly cheap places to stay on the main road here if you have no luck farther on in Arenas. *Hostal Cabrales* (☎ 985 84 50 06) is a friendly little place where singles/doubles with bathroom are 2500/4000 ptas plus IVA. *Casa Corro* (☎ 985 84 52 15) and *Casa Ramón* (☎ 985 84 50 39) charge a little more. Lone travellers will probably have to pay for double occupancy in the high season.

Arenas de Cabrales
postcode 33554 • pop 1000

Another 5km east, Arenas de Cabrales (or just plain Arenas), lies at the confluence of the Río Cares and Río Casaño. The busy main road is lined with hotels, restaurants and bars, and just off it lies a quiet little tangle of tranquil squares and back lanes.

Orientation & Information Buses stop next to the tourist office (☎ 985 84 64 84), which is a kiosk on the main road in the middle of town at the junction of the Poncebos road. The tourist office is open in summer (9 am to 2 pm and 4 to 9 pm daily), at Easter and on long weekends, and is well equipped with information. Maps of the Picos are available at newsstands. You'll find a post office, bank and ATM on the main street.

Turismo Activo Picu Urriellu (☎ 985 84 64 75), on the main road at the eastern end of town, offers guided mountain trips, caving, canyoning and other activities.

Places to Stay The good *Camping Naranjo de Bulnes* (☎ 985 84 65 78) has a nice green riverside site 1.5km east of the centre on the Panes road. It opens March to October, charging around 2500 ptas for two adults with a car and tent. Arenas has about 10 pensiones, hostales and hotels. *Pensión Covadonga* (☎ 985 84 65 66), just off the main road opposite the tourist office, has doubles from 2500 to 3500 ptas without private bath and 3000 to 4500 ptas with, depending on season. Outside August, single occupancy is usually 1000 ptas less.

Pensión El Castañeu (☎ 985 84 65 73, Barrio El Castañeu), on a quiet little square behind Pensión Covadonga, has one small single for 2000 ptas, and doubles with bathroom for 5000 ptas. *Hotel Naranjo de Bulnes (☎ 985 84 65 19, fax 985 84 65 20, Carretera General s/n)* is a comfortable mid-range spot with rooms for 3000/6000 ptas plus IVA (add 50% in August).

Places to Eat The restaurant in *Hotel Picos de Europa* has a good *menú* for 1500 ptas. *Restaurante Cares,* west along the main road, is a little cheaper at 1300 ptas. Pensión El Castañeu has a modestly priced *restaurant* with a varied menu. You could eat well a la carte for less than 2000 ptas.

Garganta del Cares

Nine kilometres of well-maintained path high above the Río Cares between Poncebos and Caín constitute, perhaps unfortunately, the most popular mountain walk in Spain; in August the experience is akin to London's Oxford Street on a Saturday morning. If you do arrive with the holiday rush, try not to be put off – the walk is a spectacular excursion between two of the Picos' three massifs. If you're feeling fit (or need to get back to your car), it's quite possible to walk the whole 9km and back as a (somewhat tiring) day's outing. It takes about seven hours plus stops.

Poncebos This straggle of buildings is exclusively dedicated to Picos tourism. A road turning uphill just above the Pensión Garganta del Cares leads 1.5km up to the hamlet of **Camarmeña**, where there's a lookout with views to the Naranjo de Bulnes in the Macizo Central. A few metres up the Sotres road just below Poncebos is the lower end of a **funicular railway** tunnel up to the hamlet of Bulnes, which is inaccessible by road. Work on this needless-to-say controversial project was stalled at the time of writing, but it may open by 2001. While most Bulnes villagers not surprisingly welcome the idea, other mountain-lovers fear the effects of such easy public access on the Picos environment.

Say Cheese

Northern Spain, with its damp climate helping lots of grass grow and supporting herds of dairy cattle (rare elsewhere in the country), makes greater quantities of, and more varied, cheese than other regions. A plate or board of, say, Asturian cheeses provides a delicious range of flavours and textures. The Picos de Europa produces a particularly high number of traditional cheeses, and the Cabrales *concejo* (municipality), along the central northern rim of the Picos and running up to mountain villages such as Tielve and Sotres, is home to one of the most celebrated of all Spanish cheeses, a powerful bluey-green creation much appreciated by connoisseurs. The basic raw material of *queso de Cabrales* is untreated cows' milk, particularly that milked in May, June and July. Traditionally, this is mixed with lesser quantities of goats' and/or sheep's milk, though these are included in less than 20% of cheeses nowadays. The cheese is matured for up to four months in mountain caves.

It's the penicillium fungus that gives the cheese its characteristic hue and a creamy consistency – not to mention a rather strong odour. In this case the bite is every bit as powerful as the olfactory bark, as a good Cabrales cheese tends to have considerable kick. The last Sunday of August is the day Cabrales celebrates its cheese, with Arenas de Cabrales hosting cheese-making demonstrations, a cheese judging (with the winning cheese being auctioned off for as much as 200,000 ptas), a folklore festival – and thousands of free Cabrales cheese bocadillos.

You can distinguish a genuine Cabrales from imitators by its label, which will show a five-pointed green leaf with the crucial wording 'Denominación de Origen Cabrales' and 'Consejo Regulador'.

For more information on cheese, see the special section 'Eating & Drinking in Spain'.

The closest beds to Garganta del Cares trail are at *Pensión Garganta del Cares* (☎/fax 985 84 64 63), which has singles/doubles with shared bathroom for 2000/4000 ptas and with private bathroom for 2500/5000 ptas. Platos combinados here cost from 450 to 800 ptas. Next door is *Hotel Mirador de Cabrales* (☎ 985 84 66 73, fax 985 84 66 85), where doubles cost from 5000 to 11,000 ptas plus IVA, depending on season. *Hostal Poncebos* (☎ 985 84 64 47), 500m down the road towards Arenas, has adequate doubles without/with its own bath for 6000/10,000 ptas plus IVA in high season; it also has an inexpensive restaurant.

Garganta del Cares Walk By doing the walk from north to south, you save the best until last. Follow the 'Senda de Cares' sign pointing uphill about 750m up the road from the top end of Poncebos. The initial stages involve a steady climb upwards in the wide and mostly bare early stages of the gorge. After about 3km you'll reach some abandoned houses and probably a makeshift drinks stand. A little farther and you are over the highest point in the walk. Within a kilometre or so you should encounter another drinks stand (they lug the stuff up on horseback).

As you approach the regional boundary with Castilla y León, the gorge becomes narrower and its walls thick with vegetation, creating greater contrast with the alpine heights above. The last stages of the walk are possibly the prettiest, and as you descend nearer the valley floor, you pass through a series of low (and wet) tunnels to emerge at the end of the gorge among the meadows of Caín. Along the way, there are several paths – most of them on the slippery side – leading down to the river, which you can follow for stretches.

Caín If you're coming from the south, the trailhead is at Caín, where the rickety (and picturesque) road from Posada de Valdeón ends. *Casa Cuevas* (☎ 987 74 27 20) is open all year and charges 2800 ptas for basic doubles with washbasin. There are at least two other places to stay, plus a couple of

bars and restaurants. You'll find further places to stay at the string of villages south of Caín, including Cordiñanes and Posada de Valdeón.

Sotres

A side road leads off eastwards at first, then south, from Poncebos to little Sotres, the highest village in the Picos at 1045m and starting point for a number of good walks. Casa Cipriano offers a professional mountain and caving guide service.

Pensión La Perdiz (☎ 985 94 50 11) in Sotres charges 2500/4000 ptas for singles/doubles with private bath (less without). The two top rooms have balconies and wonderful views. Across the road, *Casa Cipriano* (☎ 985 94 50 24, fax 985 94 50 63) has bunks for 1000 ptas as well as rooms at 6500 ptas a double with bath (5500 ptas without) in high season. *Albergue Peña Castil* (☎ 985 94 50 49) has good, clean bunk rooms for 1100 or 1300 ptas per person (the higher price is for rooms with a door). All three places have restaurants, and there's a shop. No public transport runs here.

Walks around Sotres A common route takes you east to the village of **Tresviso** and on to **Urdón**, on the Potes-Panes road. As far as Tresviso (10km) it's a paved road but the final 6km are a dramatic foot-only trail, the **Ruta de Tresviso**, snaking 850m down to the Desfiladero de la Hermida. Doing this in the upward direction, starting from Urdón, is at least as popular. An alternative track winds off the Sotres-Tresviso road and down via the hamlet of Beges to La Hermida, also in the Desfiladero de la Hermida.

Many walkers head west from Sotres to **Pandébano**, about 90 minutes away up on the far side of the Duje valley. From Pandébano it's possible to see the 2519m rock finger called **El Naranjo de Bulnes** (also called Pico Urriello), something of an emblem of the Picos de Europa and a classic challenge for climbers. The Naranjo's first recorded ascent, by the shepherd Gregorio Pérez and Pedro Pidal, the Marqués de Villaviciosa, in 1904, was the birth of Spanish rock-climbing.

Few walkers can resist the temptation of getting even closer to El Naranjo. It's possible to walk in around three hours from Pandébano to the **Vega de Urriello**, at the foot of the north-western face of the mountain, where the 96-place *Refugio de la Vega de Urriellu (☎ 985 94 50 24 or ☎ 985 92 52 00)* is attended, with meal service, all year (1000 ptas per bunk).

Otherwise, you can descend about an hour west to **Bulnes**. This remote settlement (see Poncebos earlier) is divided into two parts, Barrio del Castillo and La Villa. All the amenities are in La Villa, including the *Albergue de Bulnes (☎ 985 84 59 43)*, with 20 bunks, showers and meals, and *Pensión Casa Marcelino (☎ 985 84 59 34)*. You can also get to Bulnes by walking south-east up from Poncebos (about 1¼ hours).

South from Sotres, you can walk to Vegas de Sotres (which from afar looks like a village but is only used for animal shelter) and the Fuente Dé cable car or Espinama (see the Eastern Picos section). This track is also suitable for 4WD vehicles.

Niserias

East of Arenas de Cabrales, the AS-114 follows the Río Cares downstream towards Panes, through an attractive gorge much of the way. There are several places with accommodation. A particularly pretty spot on a bend in the Cares is *Casa Julián (☎ 985 41 57 79)* in Niserias, about 15km from Arenas. Rooms cost 4500/8000 ptas plus IVA. The restaurant does great salmon dishes. *La Tahona de Besnes (☎/fax 985 41 57 49)* is a beautifully renovated set of old stone bakery buildings in a leafy river valley 1.75km north of Niserias (take the Alles road and follow signs). It provides attractive double rooms for between 8000 and 9000 ptas in high season, and more expensive apartments, and has a good restaurant. You horse ride here too.

EASTERN PICOS
Panes

Panes is the junction town where the AS-114 from Cangas and Arenas meets the N-621 running from the coast to Potes, the main access point for the south-eastern

Picos. It has a range of accommodation should you need to stay overnight. Buses to/from Arenas, Cangas and Oviedo stop at Bar La Cortina on the edge of town on the Arenas road; buses to Potes and Santander stop at Bar Comportu on the main street.

Desfiladero de la Hermida

The N-621 south from Panes follows the Río Deva and soon enters the impressive Desfiladero de la Hermida gorge. You cross into Cantabria here at Urdón, the bottom end of the Ruta de Tresviso path (see Walks around Sotres earlier), 2km before the hamlet of **La Hermida**. There's not much at La Hermida but the bubbling Deva, the Picos looming to the west and a couple of *pensiones*.

Lebeña

About 7km south from La Hermida, this spot warrants visiting. A kilometre east of the N-621 stands the 10th-century Mozarabic **Iglesia de Santa María de Lebeña**. The horseshoe arches in the bell tower are a telltale sign of the architectural style of the place – not often seen this far north in Spain. Inside, the floral motifs on the columns are Visigothic, while below the main retablo lies a Celtic stone engraving. They say the big yew tree outside was planted 1000 years ago.

If you want to stay in this peaceful location, *Casa de Labranza El Agero (☎ 942 74 43 37)*, on the main road just north of the Lebeña turning, charges 5500 ptas for good doubles with bath. In low season you can negotiate down for single occupancy. There's a restaurant here too.

Potes
postcode 39570 • pop 1400

Fairly overrun in peak periods but with some charm in the old centre (much restored after considerable damage during the civil war), Potes is a popular staging post on the south-eastern edge of the Picos. Many of its inhabitants ride on tourism's coat-tails.

Information The tourist office (☎ 942 73 07 87), located on Calle Independencia behind the big parish church at the centre of own, is open 10 am to 2 pm and 4 to 7 or 5 pm daily.

Potes has several banks with ATMs, and a couple of big supermarkets for stocking up on supplies before heading into the mountains.

Things to See Right in the centre of town, the squat **Torre del Infantado** was built as a defensive tower in the 15th century and is now the town hall, having served for a long time as a prison. The 14th-century **Iglesia de San Vicente Mártir** next to the tourist office, deconsecrated in the 19th century, is a nice example of rustic Gothic architecture.

Activities Several activities outfits are based in Potes. Picos Awentura (☎/fax 942 73 21 61), at Calle Cervantes 3, for instance, will take you paragliding (8500 ptas for a 10- to 15-minute beginner's flight) or horse riding, canyoning or canoeing (all between 3500 and 5000 ptas for three to four hours). Turismo Activo La Liébana (☎ 942 73 10 00), Calle Independencia 4, offers combined 4WD and walking trips in the Picos. One possible itinerary combines Fuente Dé and the Garganta de Cares walk in one day.

Places to Stay *Camping La Viorna (☎ 942 73 20 21)* is about 1km from Potes en route to Fuente Dé (take the turn-off for the Monasterio de Santo Toribio). It has its own restaurant and pool, and opens from April to October.

A relatively cheap place in town with spacious rooms, some overlooking the Torre del Infantado, is *Hostal Lombraña (☎ 942 73 05 19, Calle del Sol 2)*. From July to September, doubles cost 4500 ptas plus IVA with private bath or 3800 ptas plus IVA without. Lower prices for single occupancy depend on how busy it is.

Restaurante El Fogón de Cus (☎ 942 73 00 60, Calle del Capitán Palacios 2) has a little pensión upstairs with seven small but spotless and pretty rooms for around 4000/5000 ptas. The pick of the bunch is *Casa Cayo (☎ 942 73 01 50, fax 942 73 01 19, Calle Cántabra 6)*, with helpful service and excellent rooms (some wood-beamed and overlooking the river) for 3000/6000

ptas. *Hostal Rafa (☎ 942 73 09 24)*, around the corner from the post office on the main road, has attractively furnished rooms with bath for 4500 ptas single or double (2200/3800 ptas for singles/doubles from October to May).

For more class, try *Hotel Valdecoro (☎ 942 73 00 25, Calle Roscabao 5)*, with rooms for 4400/8000 ptas. It's at the entrance to town coming from Panes.

Places to Eat The wood-beamed *El Bodegón* on Calle San Roque, about 300m in the Panes direction from the bridge in the middle of town, prepares probably the best-value food: ham with eggs and chips, or trout or chicken are all 700 to 800 ptas. Casa Cayo has an excellent *restaurant*, where you can eat well for about 2000 ptas. *Restaurante El Fogón de Cus* serves good local fare. Fish and meat mains start at 1700 ptas but there's also a *menú* for 1750 ptas.

Potes to Fuente Dé

There are quite a lot of places to stay along and near the 23km road from Potes to Fuente Dé. Turieno, 3km from Potes, has *Camping La Isla (☎/fax 942 73 08 96)*, open from Semana Santa to October, and a few small *hostales*. At **Baró**, 4km past Turieno, *Camping San Pelayo (☎ 942 73 30 87)* has a swimming pool. Between here and Cosgaya (see later in this section), you'll find several other possible places to bunk down. **Camaleño**, 1km past Baró, has a national park information office.

Monasterio de Santo Toribio de Liébana The Liébana valley, of which Potes is in a sense the 'capital', lies wedged between the south-eastern side of the Picos de Europa and the main spine of the Cordillera Cantábrica. The valley was repopulated in the 8th century with Christians from Spain's meseta by Alfonso I of Asturias, putting it on the frontline between Muslim Spain and what little there was at that stage of its Christian opponent.

One thing the new settlers brought with them was the Lígnum Crucis, a purported piece of Christ's cross supposedly transported from Jerusalem by Bishop Toribio of Astorga in the 4th century. The holy relic has been housed ever since in the Monasterio de Santo Toribio de Liébana, 3km west of Potes (signposted off the Fuente Dé road).

The relic, which according to tradition features the hole made by the nail that passed through Christ's left hand, is an extraordinary magnet for the faithful. It's kept inside a crucifix of gold-plated silver, which is housed in a lavish 18th-century baroque chapel, off the monastery's austere Gothic church (dating from 1256). The monastery's typical opening hours are 10 am to 1 pm and 3.30 to 8.30 pm daily.

Cosgaya This small town 14km from Potes is a nice spot to rest and relax. *Mesón Cosgaya (☎ 942 73 30 47)* has six doubles with bath and TV for 5500 ptas. In a classier range are *Hotel Del Oso Pardo (☎ 942 73 30 18)*, with rooms for 6800/8600 ptas plus IVA, and *Hotel Del Oso (also ☎ 942 73 30 18)*, over the road, charging 8100/9100 ptas plus IVA.

Espinama This is the last stop of any significance before Fuente Dé and probably makes a more appealing base if you have your own transport. You should be able to find 4WD taxis to take you up into the hills. One 4WD track from here leads about 7km north and uphill to the Refugio de Áliva (see the following section) and on to Sotres.

There's a surprising choice of decent places to stay on or just off the main road through Espinama – you can't miss them. *Hotel Máximo (☎ 942 73 66 03)* has rooms for 3700/6000 ptas and is possibly the pick of the crop; it has a good restaurant as well. *Hostal Remoña (☎ 942 73 66 05)* has doubles for 5500 ptas. The almost new, stone-built *Hospedaje Sobrevilla (☎ 942 73 66 69)* has doubles with bath for 6000 ptas.

Another attractive option is *Hostal Puente Deva (☎ 942 73 66 58)*, with rooms for 3400/5000 ptas plus IVA. *Hostal Nevandi (☎ 942 73 66 13)* has good rooms for 3500/5000 ptas plus IVA. All the places mentioned have restaurants.

Fuente Dé & the Teleférico

At 1078m, Fuente Dé lies at the foot of the stark southern wall of the Macizo Central. In four minutes the *teleférico* (cable car ☎ 942 73 66 10) here whisks people 762m to the top of that wall, from where walkers and climbers can make their way deeper into the central massif.

Be warned that during the high season (especially August) you can wait for hours at the bottom before your numbered ticket comes up (numbers are called out on a PA system). Coming down again, you simply join the queue and wait – OK on a sunny summer's day, but otherwise a little unpleasant if the queue's long. One-way return tickets cost 800/1300 ptas, and the service runs from 9 am to 8 pm during Semana Santa and summer, and 10 am to 6 pm at other times. It's closed from about 10 January to 28 February.

Walking & Climbing It's a walk of 3.5km from the top of the teleférico to the Refugio de Áliva (see Places to Stay & Eat), or you can catch one of the private 4WD shuttles that do the trip for 300 ptas per person. From the refugio, two trails descend into the valley that separates the central massif from its eastern cousin. The first winds its way some 7km south down to Espinama, while the other will get you north to Sotres via Vegas de Sotres. 4WDs cover the Sotres and Espinama routes if there is a demand.

Other possibilities for the suitably prepared include climbing Peña Vieja (2613m) and making your way across the massif to the Naranjo de Bulnes. This requires proper equipment and experience – Peña Vieja has claimed more climbers' lives than any other mountain in the Picos. Less exacting is the route of about two hours leading north-west from the cable car, passing below Peña Vieja by marked trails to the tiny *Refugio Cabaña Verónica (☎ 942 7 00 07 or ☎ 942 75 52 94)* at 2325m near Horcados Rojos. The refugio is attended with meals available, all year but has room for only about four people (600 ptas) and no running water.

Paragliding Alas Cantabria (☎ 942 73 61 25), actually based in Vega de Liébana, organises beginner flights on paragliders at Fuente Dé. Beginners are accompanied by an instructor.

Eagle Show If it looks like you'll have a long wait for the cable car in July, August or September, check to see if **La Montaña de las Águilas** is in operation. At the time of writing, this performance by low-flying eagles, buzzards and other birds of prey was staged at 1, 4 and 6.30 pm. It's a rare chance to see these birds, including the majestic golden eagle, trained to swoop in over the audience and pick up their reward of meat. The organisers use the money to promote rehabilitation of injured birds and increase awareness of the dangers many of these species face.

Places to Stay & Eat There is an adequate camping ground, *El Redondo* (☎ 942 73 66 99), which also has refugio-style accommodation for 20, about 100m from the Montaña de las Águilas. Otherwise, Fuente Dé has two hotels: *Hotel Rebeco* (☎ 942 73 66 01), an old stone house with comfy doubles for 8800 ptas plus IVA, and *Parador de Fuente Dé* (☎ 942 73 66 51), with singles/doubles for 10,800/13,500 ptas plus IVA. Dining options are limited to the hotel restaurants and some tourist cafes – *Cafetería Fuente Dé* is reasonable value, with a 1300-ptas *menú*.

Refugio de Áliva (☎ 942 73 09 99) is actually a 27-room hotel set 1700m high, with restaurant, cafe and even a solarium (see Walking & Climbing in this section). It's open June to September only. Doubles, with bath, are 7500 ptas.

Galicia

If the regions of Spain were identified by colour, Galicia's might well be green tinged with grey. In the same way that Andalucía wears its dazzling whitewash and Castilla-La Mancha bathes in the burnt red and dusty olive green of its sun-scorched plains, so the characteristic granite walls and ubiquitous slate rooftops on a verdant rural background seem symbolic of Galicia. Without doubt, the often inclement weather contributes to the impression. You've always got to be ready for rain in Galicia.

The wild coastline, battered by the Atlantic, is sliced up and down its length by a series of majestic *rías* (inlets or estuaries). Eastern Galicia is separated from the *meseta* (central tableland) by the western end of the Cordillera Cantábrica and associated ranges. Galicia's southern boundary is the Portuguese border, demarcated for a long stretch by Galicia's main river, the Río Miño. Frenetic deforestation has unfortunately stripped much of Galicia of its indigenous trees, mostly replaced by eucalyptus.

Most travellers in Galicia make a beeline for Santiago de Compostela, and no one can blame them. This melancholy medieval city-shrine is one of Spain's most engaging urban centres. Beyond it, however, lies plenty more. The popular Rías Bajas and less well-known Rías Altas are dotted with coves, beaches and enticing villages, and you'll see some of Spain's wildest coast towards Cabo Ortegal in the north-west. Of the numerous other towns that could go on a must list, Pontevedra stands out.

Though the roads between Galicia's major cities and towns have improved by leaps and bounds in the past few years, opportunities still abound for getting lost. Some minor roads and many villages simply aren't marked on even good atlases, while meaningful road signs are as scarce as hen's teeth in out-of-the-way places.

Highlights

- Completing the Camino de Santiago walk from the French border to Santiago de Compostela
- The magnificent Catedral de Santiago de Compostela
- Some of Spain's best and most varied seafood, washed down with a crisp Ribeiro white
- Exploring the spectacular *rías* (estuaries) along the coast
- Gazing over the Atlantic from the heights of Cabo Ortegal and Cabo Finisterre
- *Pimientos* (peppers) of Padrón
- Stretching out on the beaches around Cedeira
- Catching a *curro*, or round-up of wild horses
- The pretty town of Tuy, on the Río Miño, just across from the Portuguese fortress town of Valença

La Coruña p651

Lugo p679

◉ Santiago de Compostela p642

Pontevedra p664   Orense p676

● Vigo p670

P O R T U G A L

History

Inhabited since at least 3000 BC, by the Iron Age Galicia was populated by Celts living in *castros,* villages of circular stone

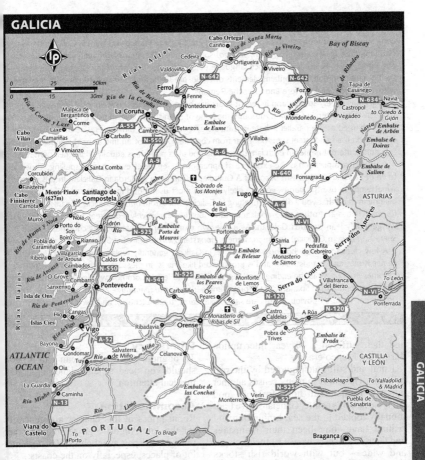

GALICIA

huts surrounded by a defensive perimeter. The arrival in the 1st century BC of the Romans, who seem to have mingled tolerably well with the locals, gave the area its name, initially Gallaecia. Ruled by a Germanic tribe, the Suevi, for most of the 5th and 6th centuries AD, before the Visigoths asserted themselves here, Galicia was barely touched by the 8th-century Muslim invasion. By 866 it was under the control of the Christian kingdom of Asturias.

The big event in the area's medieval history was the 'rediscovery' of the grave of Santiago Apóstol (St James the Apostle) in

813, at what would become Santiago de Compostela. The site became a rallying symbol for the Reconquista, but by the time this was completed in 1492, Galicia had become an impoverished backwater in which the centralist-minded Catholic Monarchs Fernando and Isabel (Ferdinand and Isabella) had already begun to supplant the local tongue and traditions with Castilian methods and language. Galicia had even staged a rare peasants' revolt in the 1460s. The first signs of the *Rexurdimento,* a reawakening of the Galician consciousness, did not surface until late in the 19th century,

euro currency converter €1 = 166pta

Travelling in Tongues

Long suppressed during the Franco years (strange, really, since Franco was born in Galicia), the Galician language (galego or, in Spanish, gallego) sounds much like a cross between Castilian Spanish and Portuguese. Basically a Romance language (ie, a latter-day version of the language spoken by the Romans, Latin), it also contains elements of Celtic, pre-Celtic and Germanic tongues from peoples who inhabited Galicia before and after the Romans.

Galician is widely spoken and in recent years has been pushed as the main local language. News broadcasts are often in Galician. Although the issue of Spanish vs Galician usage is not quite as politically charged as the parallel debate in Catalunya, it does present difficulties. Use of Galician is increasing on road and street signs but is far from consistent. You'll often find a street signposted with two quite different names in each language. Map and atlas publishers equally all go their own ways.

A further complication is the existence of apparent discrepancies even in local spelling. Thus the town of La Guardia (Spanish) becomes A Guardia, A Guarda or A Garda in Galician. In this chapter we attempt to use the names you are likely to find most useful during your travels. This means – bearing in mind that you'll often be heading to Galician cities from outside Galicia – Spanish spellings for many cities and other geographical features, but not exclusively. For street names and the like we generally lean towards Galician. As a rule, we name monuments such as churches (iglesia in Spanish, igrexa in Galician) and monasteries (monasterio vs mosteiro) in Spanish.

A few clues to those who know Spanish: 'x' in Galician generally replaces 'g' or 'j' (so Junta becomes Xunta and Juan is Xoan) and is pronounced like the 's' in pleasure; 'o' replaces 'ue' (puente becomes ponte); while the ending 'eiro' replaces 'ero' and 'erio'. Common words you'll come across include praza (plaza in Spanish), praia (playa) and perhaps xeral (general) – as in Hospital Xeral. Three useful, not-quite-so-obvious words are saida, exit; caixa, the bill (check); and pechado – closed!

---

and then suffered a 40-year interruption during the Franco era.

Rural and still much ignored by the rest of Spain, Galicia is in many senses another country. Rather than hope for any good from the nation's centre, Galicians have traditionally looked to the sea. Emigration and fishing have long been their mainstays and Galicia's fishers have cast their nets far and wide – but with world fish stocks falling and international conflict over fishing rights growing, Galicia's fleet finds itself staring at an uncertain future. Much as in England's Cornwall, smuggling is an integral part of Galicia's seafaring lore, but the growth of drug-running from South America has led to fears that Galicia is becoming 'another Sicily'.

Internet Resources

Turgalicia (www.turgalicia.es), the official tourism Web site of the Xunta de Galicia (the regional government), is pretty informative – and comes in seven languages.

Emergency

Throughout Galicia you can call ☎ 061 should you need an ambulance or urgent medical attention.

Accommodation

Room prices in this chapter are generally for the July-August high season. At other times you'll pay as much as 30% less in a lot of places, especially on the coasts.

Food & Drinks

When stomachs grumble in Galicia, thoughts turn to seafood. Although some may feel the quality is higher in Portugal, there is no doubt that you can eat better here than in much of the rest of Spain. And as a rule, eating out is generally cheaper in Galicia. Pulpo (octopus) is a staple, but there are plenty of options (see the boxed text 'Galician Food Fare'). The fact that Galicia's biggest export has traditionally been labour, in particular to Argentina, is well reflected in its modern eating habits. Nowhere else in

Spain will meat-eaters feel so happy, for this is the territory of the *churrasco* – slabs of grilled meat or ribs accompanied by a slightly tangy sauce.

Galicia produces some fine wines. The Ribeiro wines, mostly from around Ribadavia, count among their number a clean, crisp white and a decent red. Mencia is also a pleasing red. For a robust white, the Condado label is recommended – its grapes are grown around the lower Miño. Rosal is a more expensive drop from La Guardia, while the Albariño is considered the prince of Galician tipples. Occasionally you'll be served wine in small, shallow ceramic cups.

Always served in more conventional glasses is Estrella de Galicia beer, brewed in La Coruña and about the best Spain has to offer. Galicians also brew several versions of *orujo*, a breath-catching firewater along the lines of *aguardiente* (a grape-based liqueur, like the Italian *grappe*).

Santiago de Compostela

postcode 15780 • pop 87,000

There can be few cities in the world as beautiful as Santiago that are founded on the basis of so preposterous a story. The corpse of Santiago Apóstol (St James), the myth relates, was transported in a stone boat to the far side of Spain by two disciples after his execution in Jerusalem in AD 44. They landed at Padrón and, so they say, managed to bury Santiago in a spot 17km inland.

In 813 the grave was supposedly rediscovered by a religious hermit following a guiding star (hence the second part of the city's name, a corruption of the Latin Campus Stellae, 'Field of the Star'). The saint's purported grave became a welcome rallying symbol for Christian Spain, and work began on a church above his remains. The myth gained strength in following centuries, and Santiago de Compostela became a quietly impressive city. It has improved with both age and the various architectural additions

Galician Food Fare

Here is an introductory vocabulary to Galician food:

almejas – clams

anguilas – small eels from the Río Miño

caldo gallego – broth with cabbage or turnip, potato and usually a token clump of meat

caldeirada de pescado – a hotpot of potato and different types of fish

chinchos – various tiny fried fish

chipirones – chopped squid cooked in its own ink

chocos/choquitos – a variation on the squid theme

cigalas – crayfish

empanada/empanadilla – something like a pasty; the most common version is done with tuna and tomato and is very tasty. An *empanada a la gallega* contains *chorizo* (sausage), onion and occasionally other vegetables. An *empanadilla* is the bite-size snack version.

gambas – prawns; most commonly done *al ajillo* (with garlic) or *a la plancha* (lightly grilled)

mejillones – orange mussels, mostly bred on the odd web-like platforms called *bateas*, which you see all over most of the rías

pimientos de Padrón – small green peppers cooked in loads of garlic, with the occasional seriously hot one thrown in

pulpo a la gallega – the Galician dish; basically, boiled octopus bits

vieiras – scallops

xoubas/xoubiñas – sardines

zorza – a local equivalent of kebabs

made after the initial wave of enthusiasm for the pilgrimage around the 12th century.

Apart from the undisputed splendour of its gold-tinged (at least when the sun's out) monuments and the charm of its medieval

GALICIA

SANTIAGO DE COMPOSTELA

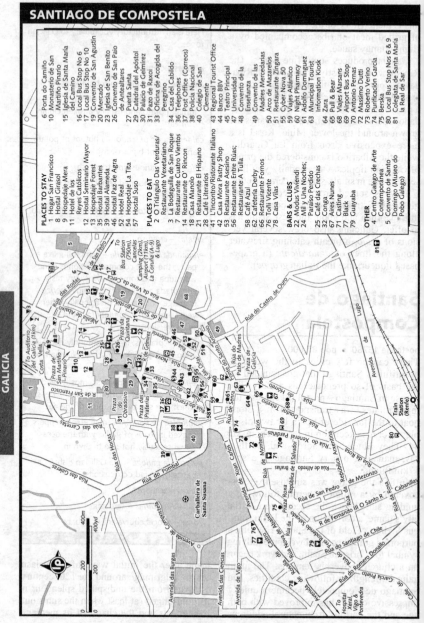

PLACES TO STAY
1 Hogar San Francisco
8 Hostal Girasol
9 Hospedaje Mera
11 Hotel de los Reyes Católicos
12 Hostal Seminario Mayor
13 Hospedaje Forest
35 Hostal Barbantes
39 Hostal Alameda
46 Hotel Real
52 Hotel Paz de Agra
54 Hospedaje La Tita
55 Hostal Suso

PLACES TO EAT
2 O Triángulo Das Verduras;
Restaurante Vexetariano
7 La Bodeguilla de San Roque
14 Restaurante Cuatro Vientos
17 Restaurante O' Rincon
18 Casa Manolo
21 Restaurante El Hispano
28 Café Literarios
41 L'Incontro/Ristorante Italiano
42 Casa Mora Pastry Shop
53 Restaurante Asesino
56 Restaurante Entre Rúas;
Restaurante A Tulla
58 Café Azul
62 Cafetería Derby
76 Toñi Vicente
78 Casa Vilas

BARS & CLUBS
22 Modus Vivendi
24 Mil y Una Noches;
Paraíso Perdido
25 Café das Crechas
32 Conga
71 Aires Nunes
77 Casting
79 Guayaba

OTHER
4 Centro Galego de Arte
Contemporánea
5 Convento de Santo
Domingo (Museo do
Pobo Galego)
6 Porta do Camiño
10 Monasterio de San
Martiño Pinario
15 Iglesia de Santa María
del Camino
16 Local Bus Stop No 6
17 Local Bus Stop No 10
19 Convento de San Agustín
20 Mercado
23 Iglesia de San Benito
26 Convento de San Paio
de Antealtares
27 Puerta Santa
29 Catedral del Apóstol
30 Palacio de Gelmirez
31 Pazo de Raxoi
33 Oficina de Acogida del
Peregrino
34 Casa del Cabildo
36 Telephones
37 Post Office (Correos)
38 Policía Nacional
40 Colegio de San
Clemente
43 Regional Tourist Office
44 Banco BBV
45 Teatro Principal
47 Universidad
49 Convento de la
Enseñanza
49 Convento de las
Madres Mercedarias
50 Arco de Mazarelos
51 Restaurante Zingara
55 Cyber Nova 50
59 Viajes Atlántico
60 Night Pharmacy
61 Adolfo Domínguez
63 Municipal Tourist
Information Kiosk
64 Zara
65 Pull & Bear
68 Viajes Marsans
69 Airport Bus Stop
70 Antonio Pernas
72 Massimo Dutti
73 Roberto Verino
74 Purificación García
75 Berska
80 Local Bus Stop Nos 6 & 9
81 Colegiata de Santa María
la Real de Sar

streets, Santiago de Compostela is a lively city full of bars and with, in summer especially, a packed program of concerts, theatre and exhibitions.

History

Although the history of Santiago de Compostela virtually begins with the story of Santiago Apóstol, the region had long been inhabited by Visigoths, Romans and Celts. In any event, Alfonso II, the Asturian king, soon turned up to have the first church erected in honour of the saintly discovery.

By 1075, when the Romanesque basilica was begun and the pilgrimage was becoming a major European phenomenon, Santiago de Compostela had already been raided on various occasions by the Normans and Muslims. The worldly Bishop Diego Gelmírez added numerous churches to the city in the 12th century, when homage paid to its saint brought in a flood of funds, used to build much of the present city.

The following couple of centuries were marked by internecine squabbling between rival nobles, damped down when Fernando and Isabel managed to turn more attention to internal affairs after the conclusion of the Reconquista. After backing the wrong horse by siding with the Carlists in the 1830s, Santiago de Compostela slipped into the background. Only since the early 1980s has the city, as capital of the autonomous region of Galicia and a rediscovered tourist target, really begun to emerge.

Orientation

Santiago's compact old centre (casco antiguo) is virtually all pedestrianised. The Renfe train station is about a 15-minute walk downhill from the centre, while the bus station (estación de autobuses) lies about the same distance to the north-east. Local city buses pass both and take you to Praza de Galicia on the southern fringe of the old town. Most of the monuments and accommodation can be found in the old town, whose more important streets include Rúa Nova, Rúa do Vilar and Rúa do Franco.

Information

Tourist Offices The regional tourist office (☎ 981 58 40 81), Rúa do Vilar 43, is open 10 am to 2 pm and 4 to 7 pm weekdays, 11 am to 2 pm and 5 to 7 pm Saturday, and 11 am to 2 pm Sunday. There's also an excellent municipal-run information kiosk (☎ 981 58 44 00) on Praza de Galicia (handy if you arrive by train). Its hours are 10 am to 2 pm and 5 to 8 pm weekdays.

Money There are banks dotted about the centre of town. A handy one is Banco BBV at Rúa do Vilar 33.

Post & Communications The main post office (correos) lines Travesía de Fonseca and is open 8.30 am to 8.30 pm Monday to Saturday. There are pay phones outside, and on Rúa Nova, plus more scattered about town. Cyber Nova 50, Rúa Nova 50, provides Internet access 9 am to 1 am weekdays, 10 am to 1 am weekends.

Oficina de Acogida del Peregrino

People who have walked all or part of the Camino de Santiago as pilgrims and want the certificate to prove it can head for this 'pilgrims' reception office' (☎ 981 56 24 19) in the Casa del Deán, Rúa do Vilar 1. It's open 9 am to 9 pm daily.

Medical Services & Emergency The Policía Nacional station (☎ 981 58 19 44) is on Avenida de Rodrigo de Padrón. The Hospital Xeral (☎ 981 95 00 00) is west of the town centre on Travesa da Choupana. There is a night pharmacy where Rúa das Orfas meets Canton de Toral.

Catedral del Apóstol

Those who have chosen to trudge the Camino de Santiago will hardly be disappointed on finally entering Praza do Obradoiro to behold the Catedral del Apóstol's lavish baroque western facade. Before this was built in the 18th century, the less overwhelming but artistically unparalleled **Pórtico de la Gloria** (Porta da Gloria in Galician) – now behind the baroque facade – was the first scene to greet weary pilgrims.

GALICIA

The bulk of the Romanesque cathedral was built between 1075 and 1211. Much of the 'bunting' – the domes, statues, pyramids and endless flourishes – came later.

There is little doubt that construction of the baroque icing on the essentially Romanesque cake muted the impact of the Pórtico de la Gloria, which was put in place in the 12th century. But it has also been something of a blessing, protecting the sculptures of Maestro Mateo and his team from the elements. The main figure in the central archway is Christ risen. At his feet and hands are the four Evangelists, and around them angels with the crown of thorns and other instruments connected with Jesus' passion. Below Christ's feet is represented Santiago, and the tradition says that below him is the figure of Maestro Mateo. Bump your head on it three times and you're supposed to acquire some of his genius; the problem is that his bust appears, if at all, on the other side, facing the altar, while the popular but mistaken head belongs to Samson. Another tradition calls for a brief prayer of thanksgiving as you place your fingers in the five holes created near Samson's head by the repetition of this very act by millions of the faithful over centuries.

The remarkably life-like figures that dominate the columns on the right side of the portico are the remaining apostles, while those to the left represent Old Testament prophets. Almost nothing remains of the portico's original colouring.

Approaching the churrigueresque **altar mayor**, you may notice an opening and stairs on the left side. Head down here to contemplate what you are assured is the tomb of Santiago. You emerge on the right side and a little farther on see another entrance with steps going up. Follow the crowds up and embrace the 13th-century statue of Santiago. There was a time when pilgrims would lift a gold crown from the statue's head and put it on their own, exchanging it briefly for their own more humble hats.

You may catch one of the special Masses where the greatest dispenser of incense in the world, the *botafumeiro,* is swung heftily across the length of the transept by an expert team of *tiraboleiros* using an ingenious pulley system – an unforgettable sight.

You really need to make more than one visit to cope with the cathedral's remarkable riches. It is open all day.

Museo Catedralicio To the right of the Pórtico de la Gloria is the entrance to the Museo Catedralicio which occupies the *claustro* (cloister). The entry ticket also includes a visit to the *cripta* (crypt), beneath the Pórtico de la Gloria, and *tesoro* (treasury) in the Capilla de San Fernando, on the southern side of the cathedral's nave. You can pay for your ticket, and begin your visit, in the crypt or treasury if you wish.

The museum spreads over several floors of the cloister, which replaced the Romanesque original in the 16th century and is a successful mix of Late Gothic and plateresque. It has an impressive collection of religious art, including Romanesque sculptures, tapestries, a library, and not a few images of Santiago. The ground-floor rooms are devoted to archaeological finds related to early Christianity in Galicia, and the various stages in the cathedral's development from shrine to the complex structure of today. Maestro Mateo's original stone *coro* (choir stall) has been reconstituted and occupies a large room; you can watch a video about the reconstruction in an adjacent room!

The crypt is notable for its 12th-century architecture and rich decoration, while the main item of the treasury is the 16th-century silver and gold-plated processional monstrance.

The museum (cloister, crypt and treasury) is open 10.30 am to 1.30 pm and 4 to 6.30 pm daily (500 ptas).

Palacio de Gelmírez

On the cathedral's north flank, the Palacio de Gelmírez was built for the bishop of the same name in 1120 and subsequently altered. Worth seeking out in this Gothic adjunct is the **Sala de Banquetes**, the main dining hall. The exquisite little busts around the walls depict happy feasters and musicians, as well as the odd king and juggler.

GALICIA

Diego Gelmírez's biggest contribution to Santiago de Compostela was to resuscitate the myth of the Battle of Clavijo. Supposedly Santiago had joined Ramiro I in this fiesta of Moor-slaying in 844, for which the grateful king promised to dedicate the first fruits of every harvest to the saint. Few historians believe the battle ever took place, but Gelmírez turned the myth into one of his city's biggest revenue sources for centuries after his demise.

The palacio is open 10 am to 1.30 pm and 4 to 7.30 pm daily, except public holiday afternoons (200 ptas).

Around the Catedral

However much the cathedral dominates the heart of Santiago de Compostela, the area around it is rich in other architectural jewels. The northern end of Praza do Obradoiro is closed off by the Renaissance **Hotel de los Reyes Católicos**, built by Fernando and Isabel with some of the loot from Granada to shelter the poor and infirm. It now shelters the well-off instead, as a *parador* (luxury hotel). Fronting the western side of the square is the elegant 18th-century **Pazo de Raxoi**, in French neoclassical style and now housing the town hall.

A stroll around the cathedral takes you through some of the city's most inviting squares. To the south is **Praza das Praterías** (Silversmiths' Square), the centre of which is marked by the Fuente de los Caballos (1829). Up the steps is the only original facade of the cathedral, a Romanesque masterpiece.

Following the cathedral walls you enter **Praza da Quintana**, split into two parts by a low staircase. The lower part, *dos mortos,* was once a cemetery. Facing onto it is the **Puerta Santa** (Holy Door) of the cathedral, opened only in Holy Years when the Feast of Santiago (25 July) falls on a Sunday. Keep following the walls northwards and you will reach Rúa da Azabachería.

Rising up on the far side is the huge Benedictine **Monasterio de San Martiño Pinario**. The classical facade hides a couple of extensive cloisters inside, built in the 17th century. Behind them (and best approached

from Praza de San Martiño) is the monastery's captivating church, an elaborate piece of baroque on which construction began in 1611. The church's towers were never finished, their construction apparently blocked by officials of the cathedral anxious not to see any shadows cast on its greater glory.

Beyond the Old Town

Just north-east of the old town, the former Convento de Santo Domingo stands out, an impressive baroque structure that now houses the **Museo do Pobo Galego**. The most singular feature is the triple spiral staircase, off which lie the rooms of the museum. These contain various displays on different aspects of Galician life and arts, covering everything from the fishing industry through music and crafts to traditional costumes. The museum is open 10 am to 1 pm and 4 to 7 pm Monday to Saturday and 11 am to 2 pm on Sunday (free).

Facing it is the **Centro Galego de Arte Contemporánea**, hosting temporary exhibitions of modern art and open 11 am to 8 pm Tuesday to Sunday (free).

About 1km south down Rúa do Patio de Madres stands, precariously (it suffers a pronounced tilt), the Romanesque **Colegiata de Santa María la Real de Sar**. Part of the beautiful cloister, supposedly designed by Maestro Mateo, can still be admired, and there's a small museum containing mainly religious art and Romanesque sculpture. It's open 10 am to 1 pm and 4 to 7 pm Monday to Saturday (100 ptas).

Organised Tours

One-day bus tours (6000 ptas, including lunch) are organised through various hotels and travel agencies. The tours are pretty busy affairs – designed for those with more money than time – covering the Rías Bajas, Rías Altas, Vigo and Portugal, and Finisterre. Inquire at Viajes Marsans (☎ 981 56 44 17), Rúa do Hórreo 44.

Special Events

July is the month to be in Santiago de Compostela. The 25th is the Feast of Santiago

GALICIA

and simultaneously Galicia's 'national' day. The night before, Praza do Obradoiro comes alight with the *fogo do Apóstolo*, a spectacular fireworks display that dates to the 17th century and culminates in the *quema de la fachada mudéjar* (literally 'burning of the mudéjar front'), a mock burning of the cathedral facade. Despite growing fears for the safety of the real cathedral, this spectacular performance continues. However, the emphasis is changing from exhilarating pyrotechnics to more sedate plays of light.

The Santiago festivities see processions and lots of people getting about in traditional costume, and the town authorities organise numerous concerts, notably in Praza da Quintana, and other cultural activities.

Places to Stay

Santiago is crawling with accommodation. In the old town, many bars advertise rooms for rent *(habitaciones)* and the number of tiny hostelries *(hospedajes)* should be reassuring. Touts frequently intercept new arrivals at the train and bus stations. All this means that you should rarely have trouble finding a place. If you can't find anything in the old town, there are plenty of options on and around Praza de Galicia, between the old town and the train station.

Places to Stay – Budget

Camping *Cancelas Camping* (☎ 981 58 02 66), on Rúa 25 de Xulo, is 2km southeast of the city centre. The cost for two adults, a tent and a car is 2400 ptas. Bus No 9, with stops at the train station and Praza de Galicia, heads out here.

Hospedajes & Hostales A good option – especially if you can get a top-floor double – is the friendly, English-speaking *Hospedaje Forest* (☎ 981 57 08 11, *Callejón de Don Abril Ares 7).* Singles/doubles start at 1600/2900 ptas. There's one bathroom for each two rooms, although a couple of rooms now have private showers. A quiet option is *Hospedaje La Tita* (☎ 981 58 39 81, *Rúa Nova 46),* with clean rooms with shared bathrooms for 2000/4000 ptas.

Friendly *Hostal Girasol* (☎ 981 56 62 87, *Porta de la Peña 4),* at the northern end of the old town, has reliable doubles for 4300 ptas, or 5300 ptas with bath. Virtually across the road, welcoming *Hospedaje Mera* (☎ 981 58 38 67, *Porta da Peña 15)* offers decent rooms with bath, some with pleasant views, for 4300/5500 ptas (3800/4900 ptas in low season).

Near both the university and the market, an attractive option is *Hostal Paz de Agra* (☎ 981 58 90 45, *Rúa da Calderería 37).* Rooms in this homy, spotless old house are 2500/4000 ptas with shared bath, 3500/5000 ptas with private bath. Inquire around the corner at Restaurante Zíngara on Rúa de Cardenal Payá. Right in the hub of the old town, the small *Hostal Suso* (☎ 981 58 66 11, *Rúa do Vilar 65)* is popular, with doubles with bath, TV etc, for 5350 ptas (4280 ptas in low season).

Hostal Barbantes (☎ 981 58 10 77, *Rúa do Franco 1)* has a lovely position overlooking little Praza de Fonseca. Singles/doubles/triples with bath cost 4000/5350/7500 ptas.

Places to Stay – Mid-Range

In a good position just below the leafy Carballeira de Santa Susana is the friendly *Hostal Alameda* (☎ 981 58 81 00, *Rúa de San Clemente 32),* with doubles for 5200 ptas plus IVA, or 7000 ptas with private bath. There's a large underground car park nearby.

Hostal Seminario Mayor (☎ 981 58 30 08, *Praza da Inmaculada 5)* has somewhat bare rooms but offers a rare experience – a stay inside the Monasterio de San Martiño Pinario. Singles/doubles/triples cost 4334/6688/8820 ptas including breakfast, mostly with private bath, but the 123 rooms are only available July to September, when student lodgers are away. Viajes Atlántico (☎ 981 56 90 40), on Plaza de Fuente Rabirra, handles inquiries out of season.

Along the same lines but a step or two up in class and comfort is *Hogar San Francisco* (☎ 981 57 24 63, fax 981 57 19 16, *Campiño de San Francisco 3),* in the monastery of the same name, where singles/doubles start at

7100/10,500 ptas plus IVA. *Hotel Real* (☎ 981 56 92 90, fax 981 56 92 91, Rúa da Calderería 49) has good-sized rooms with all mod cons for 7500/10,500 ptas, including breakfast.

Places to Stay – Top End

Hotel de los Reyes Católicos (☎ 981 58 22 00, fax 981 59 02 87) is itself one of Santiago's prime monuments, closing off the northern flank of Praza do Obradoiro (see Around the Catedral earlier). In keeping with its exalted past, guests pay rather splendid prices: 26,500 ptas plus IVA for a double – but what a double!

Places to Eat

There are countless places to eat to suit all pockets in Santiago. Do-it-yourselfers should visit the city's majestic *mercado* (market), along Rúa de Santo Agostiño in the south-east of the old town. If you choose to eat in one of the old-town restaurants that display seafood in their windows, be aware that you generally pay for this fine fare by weight and it is *not* cheap.

Restaurants *Restaurante O'Rincon (Rúa da Algalia de Arriba 21)* is a tiny spot where you'll get simple but filling *raciones* (meal-sized serves of tapas) for a few hundred pesetas. For a full and solid meal with wine and dessert for less than 1000 ptas, try *Restaurante Cuatro Vientos (Rúa de Santa Cristina 19)*. Popular with readers of travel guides is *Casa Manolo (Rúa Travesa 27)*, which has a tasty and good-value *menú del día* (daily set meal) of two courses, dessert and bread for 750 ptas.

A couple of medium-priced and popular places that come up with some good dishes are *Restaurante Entre Rúas* and *Restaurante A Tulla*, next to each other in the tiny square on Entrerúas, a laneway linking Rúa do Vilar and Rúa Nova. *Menús* at A Tulla are 1350 and 1650 ptas.

For a *parrillada de pescados* (fresh fish grill), head for *Restaurante El Hispano* on Rúa de Santo Agostiño, opposite the market – you can't get much closer to the raw ingredients!

A long-time institution in Santiago de Compostela is *Restaurante Asesino (Praza da Universidade 16)*. Prices are moderate and the decor pretty. The 1600-ptas *menú*, with plenty of choice, is good value. There are several more places to eat on and around this plaza.

L'Incontro/Ristorante Italiano (Rúa do Franco 50) does reasonable Italian food in a relaxed setting; there's a huge outdoor eating area if you want to dine *al fresco*. Home-made pastas are around 1000 ptas, and pizzas from 925 to 1850 ptas.

There are a couple of good possibilities in the San Roque area, on the north-eastern rim of the old town. *O Triángulo Das Verduras/Restaurante Vexetariano (Praza das Penas 2 baixo)* does very good vegetarian dishes prepared with organic ingredients. Most dishes are less than 1000 ptas.

In the same area, *La Bodeguilla de San Roque (Rúa San Roque 13)* has an eclectic menu of excellent, moderately priced dishes. Try the *revoltos revueltos* (scrambled eggs) with local greens and prawns (825 ptas) and the *pan tomate* (toasted rolls brushed with crushed tomato and garlic; 225 ptas).

Just south of the old town, *Restaurante Fornos (Rúa do Hórreo 24)*, near Praza de Galicia, is pricey but has a solid local reputation. Starters cost from 800 to 1800 ptas and mains from 2000 ptas.

If you want to really splash out, Avenida de Rosalía de Castro is home to a couple of prime targets. *Casa Vilas (Avenida de Rosalía de Castro 88)* is a staunch bastion of the best in Galician cuisine. Famous people from Fidel Castro to Pope John Paul II have tucked in here. You're looking at 5000 ptas per head at least. Similarly expensive is the nouvelle-cuisine specialist *Toñi Vicente (Avenida de Rosalía de Castro 24)*.

For takeaway dessert or a daytime sweet fix, pop in to *Casa Mora (Rúa do Vilar 60)*.

Cafes A coffee will cost you about 175 ptas in most places, but 125 ptas in the simple bars. A breakfast of fruit juice, coffee and toast can be had for about 400 ptas in the smaller places. *Café Literarios* on Praza da

GALICIA

Quintana is a laid-back place in a great location but it only has pastries for breakfast. Coffees are served in nice big glasses. The brasher sidewalk cafes along Rúa do Franco and Rúa do Vilar and on the main squares charge excessively.

Virtually on the border of the old and new towns, *Cafetería Derby (Rúa das Orfas 29)* is one of Santiago's oldest cafes and something of an institution. *Café Azul* on Porta Faxeira, at the southern end of Rúa do Franco, is right in the thick of things and extremely popular for a tea or coffee (185 ptas) and a spot of people-watching.

Another hugely popular spot is *Bar/Cafetería Suso (Rúa do Vilar 65)*, attached to the hostal of the same name and with tables out front.

Entertainment

Try to get hold of *Compostelán*, a local monthly student news rag. It has comprehensive listings of restaurants, bars and nightlife.

Bars & Live Music If you want to hear traditional Celtic music, Galician-style, head for *Café das Crechas (Vía Sacra 3)*. Sometimes the music's live, other times you'll have to make do with recordings. *Mil y Una Noches* and *Paraíso Perdido*, both on the tiny square on Rúade San Paio de Antealtares, are bars equally good for a coffee or drinks later in the evening. The latter is one of Santiago's oldest bars. A touch farther south, the street hits Praza de Feixoo – here are at least five bars, including *Modus Vivendi* which often has live music. *Conga (Rúa da Conga 8)*, in the centre of the old town, has live Latin and Brazilian music or jazz some nights.

Tunas – traditionally university students dressed up in medieval garb and busking towards the end of the academic year – seem to be a year-round phenomenon in Santiago. The tradition is an old one and the music, when played well, is entertaining.

Clubs & Discos More drinking and dancing goes on in the new town. Cafes, bars and *discotecas* are spread through the

---

Dancing to Their Own Tune

Perhaps it is in Galicia's rich tradition of folk music that the Galicians' Celtic strains come most vividly to the fore. Although the sounds and rhythms differ noticeably from those played by their cousins in Brittany, Ireland and Scotland, the links between them all are impossible to deny. Most readily recognisable is the *gaita* (Galician bagpipes), of which there are several versions. Summertime in Santiago is a good time to catch buskers playing traditional Galician tunes. There is quite an inventory of instruments at the disposal of folk musicians. In addition to the standard gaita, *tamboril* (big drum) and *violín*, there is a range of simple wood instruments, including the *pito* (whistle); the *pandereita* (tambourine); *buguinas* (small ceramic trumpets); the *birrimbao* (Jew's harp); *ferriños* (triangles); *castañolas* and *tarrañolas* (both variations on castanets); and the *zanfona*, a string and key instrument vaguely along the lines of an accordion.

Possibly the best internationally known Galician traditional music group is the very polished Milladoiro. Pallamallada is a Santiago group that does a mix of instrumental and vocal pieces based on traditional popular music. Uxía is a powerful female vocalist very roughly of the Enya genre. A more staid artiste is Amancio Prada, actually from the province of León, whose folk interpretations are in Galician and Castilian.

---

streets around Praza Roxa (Red Square). Explore Rúa de Fernando III o Santo, Rúa Nova and Rúa de Frei Rodendo Salvado. *Black (Avenida de Rosalía de Castro s/n)* is a popular *disco* for those aged 25 plus, as is *Casting*, downstairs in Hotel Melia Araguaney on Rúa de Alfredo Brañas – on Wednesday and Thursday it attracts students while Friday and Saturday fetch an older crowd. *Aires Nunes (Rúa do Doutor Teixeiro 15)*, in Hotel Maycar, is apparently one of the last stops on an all-night trek. For more of a Latin American touch, have a look in at *Guayaba (Rúa de Frei Rodendo Salvado 16)*.

GALICIA

Concerts The modern *Auditorio de Galicia* (☎ 981 57 38 55) on Praza da Música en Compostela, north of the centre, and the central *Teatro Principal*, on Rúa Nova, host concerts, art exhibitions and other cultural events, especially crammed into the summer months. The *ayuntamiento* (town hall) also sponsors similar events elsewhere throughout town, such as in the church of the former Convento de Santo Domingo.

Shopping

Santiago's old town is littered with shops selling the characteristic local jet or jet-and-silver jewellery. The pieces are ornate and generally very beautiful. There's plenty of Galician lace here too. See also the boxed text 'Galicia a la Moda'.

Getting There & Away

Air Lavacolla airport (☎ 981 54 75 00) is 11km south-east of Santiago. There are up to seven flights daily to Madrid and three to Barcelona with Iberia (☎ 981 59 75 50). For Málaga you need to change in Madrid; for the Balearic Islands, in Barcelona. Air Europa (☎ 981 59 49 50) flies to Barcelona, Málaga and international destinations, always with a stop or connection in Madrid.

Bus Santiago's modern bus station (☎ 981 58 77 00) is, along with La Coruña's, Galicia's main bus terminus. It's on Rúa de Rodriguez Viguri, north-east of the centre. The Castromil line (☎ 981 58 90 90) runs regular services south to Vigo (925 ptas) via Pontevedra, south-east to Orense, west to Noia, south-west to Cambados and O Grove, and north to La Coruña (835 ptas).

Enatcar/Dainco (☎ 981 57 45 37) has at least two buses daily running to Barcelona (8½ hours, 8000 ptas), two buses to Salamanca (7½ hours, 3600 ptas), and one to Sevilla, Cádiz and Algeciras. ALSA (☎ 981 58 61 33) runs four buses daily to Madrid (nine hours, 5135 ptas). Several international services run by ALSA originate in La Coruña and stop in Santiago and/or Pontevedra en route to Paris, Belgium, Holland, Switzerland and Germany.

Galicia a la Moda

While Santiago's old town has a fair population of students wearing typically ethnic-inspired garb, if you take a wander into modern Santiago's main shopping area, between Rúa de Senra and Rúa de República Argentina, you'll notice that it's unusually full of fashionable boutiques.

It may come as a bit of a surprise that designers from remote Galicia take a lead nationally – and, to some extent, internationally – on the fashion catwalks. Leading Spanish designers such as Adolfo Domínguez (whose Santiago shop is at Rúa de Senra 108), Antonio Pernas, Purificación García and Roberto Verino (all to be found on Rúa do Xeneral Pardiñas) are all *gallegos*.

But to check out the latest styles of the biggest Galician success story of all, you need to look a little more widely. Berska (Praza Roxa 6), Massimo Dutti (Rúa de Montero Ríos 24), Pull & Bear (Rúa do Doutor Teixeiro 3) and Zara (Praza de Galicia 3) are the Santiago branches of four more mass-market fashion chains that total over 1000 shops worldwide – all belonging to one adoptive Galician, Amancio Ortega.

Ortega's flagship is Zara, accounting for three-quarters of his shops. Providing women with the most up-to-date dress trends at affordable prices has made Ortega an extremely wealthy man. He was estimated by *El Mundo* newspaper in 1999 to be worth around 800,000 million pesetas (about US$4,400 million), which would make him easily Spain's richest person.

He's also highly secretive. He managed to completely avoid having his photo published till 1999, when he was well into his 60s. Born around 1936, probably in Castilla y León, Ortega was working as a messenger at a La Coruña shirtmaker's at the age of 14, and started his own dressing-gown maker's in 1963. The 12,000-employee empire that grew from that, the third-biggest clothing company in the world (after Gap of the USA and Sweden's HM), is still based in La Coruña, on the Sabón industrial estate.

GALICIA

Train From Santiago's station (☎ 981 52 02 02), you can reach Madrid (Chamartín station) on a daily Talgo (7¾ hours, 5900 ptas) or a night train (nine hours, 5900 ptas). Both stop at Zamora (4100 ptas). Two trains daily head to Barcelona via León (3600 ptas) and Zaragoza.

Trains run almost hourly from 6.25 am to 11.30 pm north to La Coruña (one hour, 515 ptas) and south to Vigo (two hours, 790 ptas) via Pontevedra (one hour, 515 ptas). There are at least two daily to Orense. For Tuy, on the Portuguese border, you need to change at El Redondela de Galicia, between Pontevedra and Vigo.

Car & Motorcycle Santiago is on the A-9 *autopista* (tollway) between La Coruña and Vigo. Cost for the 66km from Santiago to La Coruña is 590 ptas. Parallel, slower and free is the N-550.

Getting Around

To/From the Airport An almost hourly bus service runs between Lavacolla airport and the centre (220 ptas) with stops at the bus station and Rúa do Xeneral Pardiñas, a block south-west of Praza de Galicia. Taxis charge 2200 ptas.

Around Town Santiago de Compostela is walkable, although it's a hike to the train and bus stations. A public bus system runs *around* the old town. Bus No 10 (every 20 minutes from 6 am to 10.30 pm) runs from the bus station to Praza Roxa via Praza de Galicia. You could get out at Rúa de San Roque or Praza de Galicia. Bus Nos 6 and 9 pass near the train station and go to Praza de Galicia.

La Coruña & the Rías Altas

Often more intemperate and certainly much less visited than the west-facing coast of Galicia (the Rías Bajas), the northern coast is peppered with pleasant surprises. La Coruña is a busy and surprisingly attractive port city with decent beaches. There are

plenty of smaller towns and fishing villages worth exploring too – plus some of the most impressive coast in all Galicia.

LA CORUÑA

postcode 15080 • pop 252,000

La Coruña (A Coruña in Galician) has only in recent years been overtaken by Vigo as Galicia's biggest city. It remains the region's most go-ahead, outward-looking urban centre. It has a liberal-republican tradition at variance with the conservatism of the remainder of Galicia, and its port has kept it open to the rest of the world. It has also been a gateway for those outward bound – everyone from Galician emigrants to the doomed Armada of 1588.

Initially a Celtic port on the tin route to the British Isles, the site was later occupied by the Romans, who in the 2nd century AD built the lighthouse known as the Torre de Hércules. Nothing much is known of La Coruña's subsequent history until 991, when the port was put under control of the Church in Santiago.

Britain looms large on La Coruña's horizon. Felipe II embarked here for England to marry Mary Tudor in 1554, and 34 years later the ill-fated Armada also weighed anchor in La Coruña. The following year Sir Francis Drake tried to occupy the town but was seen off by María Pita, a heroine whose name lives on in the town's main square. Napoleon's troops occupied La Coruña for the first six months of 1809. Their British opponents were able to 'do a Dunkirk' and evacuate, but their commander, General Sir John Moore, died in the covering Battle of Elviña and was buried here.

Orientation

The Renfe train station and the bus station are a couple of kilometres south-west of the heart of town. La Coruña gets interesting along a fairly narrow isthmus and the large headland to its east and north. The old part of town (the *ciudad vieja*) is huddled together in the southern tip of the headland, while the Torre de Hércules caps the headland's northern extreme. Most offices, hotels, restaurants and bars are in the newer,

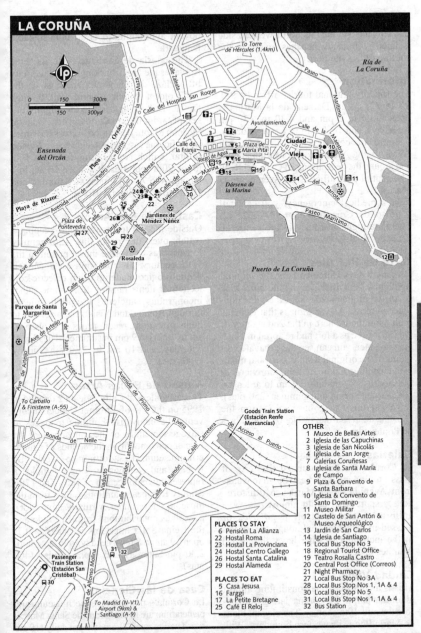

LA CORUÑA

To Torre de Hércules (1.4km)

Ría de La Coruña

Ensenada del Orzán

Playa de Riazor

Plaza de Pontevedra

Parque de Santa Margarita

To Carballo & Finisterre (A-55)

Ciudad Vieja

Ayuntamiento

Plaza de María Pita

Jardines de Méndez Núñez

Dársena de la Marina

Rosaleda

Puerto de La Coruña

Goods Train Station (Estación Renfe Mercancías)

Passenger Train Station (Estación San Cristóbal)

To Madrid (N-VI), Airport (9km) & Santiago (A-9)

OTHER
1 Museo de Bellas Artes
2 Iglesia de las Capuchinas
3 Iglesia de San Nicolás
4 Iglesia de San Jorge
7 Galerías Coruñesas
8 Iglesia de Santa María de Campo
9 Plaza & Convento de Santa Barbara
10 Iglesia & Convento de Santo Domingo
11 Museo Militar
12 Castelo de San Antón & Museo Arqueológico
13 Jardín de San Carlos
14 Iglesia de Santiago
15 Local Bus Stop No 3
18 Regional Tourist Office
19 Teatro Rosalía Castro
20 Central Post Office (Correos)
21 Night Pharmacy
27 Local Bus Stop No 3A
28 Local Bus Stop Nos 1, 1A & 4
30 Local Bus Stop No 5
31 Local Bus Stop Nos 1, 1A & 4
32 Bus Station

PLACES TO STAY
6 Pensión La Alianza
22 Hostal Roma
23 Hostal La Provinciana
24 Hostal Centro Gallego
26 Hostal Santa Catalina
29 Hostal Alameda

PLACES TO EAT
5 Casa Jesusa
16 Farggi
17 La Petite Bretagne
25 Café El Reloj

GALICIA

euro currency converter €1 = 166pta

predominantly 19th-century part of town that fills the isthmus. Its north-western side is lined with sandy beaches, while to the south-east lies the port.

Information

The friendly regional tourist office (☎ 981 22 18 22) on the Dársena de la Marina is open 9 am to 2 pm and 4.30 to 6.30 pm weekdays, and 10.30 am to 1 pm Saturday.

There are countless banks, many with ATMs, lining Avenida de la Marina and on and around the pedestrianised Calle del Real. The central post office is on Avenida de la Marina.

In a medical emergency, you can call ☎ 061 or the Cruz Roja on ☎ 981 22 22 22. There's a night pharmacy in the centre on Calle del Real.

Torre de Hércules

One myth says Hercules built the original lighthouse here after slaying the cruel king of a tribe of giants who kept the local populace in terror. All we *know* is that Romans built a lighthouse here in the 2nd century. It was later used as a fort and restored in 1792. As you enter, you can see the excavated remains of the original Roman base and medieval meddling. Climb to the top for views of the city. It is open daily 10 am to at least 6 pm, later in spring and summer (250 ptas).

To get there take bus No 3 from the Dársena de la Marina, or No 3A from Plaza de Pontevedra.

Galerías

La Coruña has been dubbed the 'city of glass'; to find out why, head down to waterfront Avenida de la Marina. Multistorey houses sport what could almost pass as a uniform protective layer of *galerías* or glassed-in balconies – although the effects of the inclement weather have diminished their aesthetics.

Ciudad Vieja

This is a compact zone constituting almost all of that part of La Coruña dating from before the mid-19th century. The elegant Plaza de María Pita is its western boundary. With porticoes on three sides, the city's flamboyant **ayuntamiento** is an unmistakable landmark.

The **Iglesia de Santiago**, with its three Romanesque apses backing on to the pretty little Plaza del General Azcarraga, is the city's oldest church. A short walk through the labyrinth brings you to the slightly unkempt **Jardín de San Carlos**, where General Sir John Moore lies buried. Across the street, war aficionados can look over the **Museo Militar**, which houses arms from the 18th to the 20th centuries. It is open 10 am to 2 pm and 4 to 7 pm Monday to Saturday, and 10 am to 2 pm Sunday (free).

Castelo de San Antón

Outside the old town walls and keeping a watch over the port, this 12th-century fortress was converted into a prison in the 18th century. It now houses a **Museo Arque-ológico** made up of an eclectic collection of items ranging from some rather incongruous ancient Egyptian pieces through Roman and Visigothic artefacts to items from more recent times. It is open 10 am to 7 pm (to 9 pm in summer) Tuesday to Saturday, and 10 am to 2.30 pm Sunday (300 ptas).

Museo de Bellas Artes

This art gallery at Calle Zaleata 2 opened in 1995 on the site of a former Capuchin convent. The innovative building manages to salvage something of the atmosphere of the former convent within the bounds of a modern museum. In addition to works by Rubens and etchings by Goya, it holds a representative collection of 16th- and 17th-century European paintings (taken from the museum's forerunner, virtually next door), as well as contributions from El Prado and the Reina Sofía museums in Madrid. It is open 10 am to 8 pm Tuesday to Friday, until 2.30 pm Saturday and 2 pm Sunday (400 ptas).

Casa de las Ciencias

La Coruña's popular science museum and planetarium are in the Parque de Santa Margarita. They're open 11 am to 9 pm daily (10 am to 7 pm in winter). Entry to the museum is 300 ptas, to the planetarium 200 ptas.

Beaches

Aside from the protected city beaches (Playa de Riazor and Playa del Orzán), several others stretch away along the 30km sweep of coast west of the city. In summer, buses run out from the city to the long, sandy Playa de Baldaio.

Places to Stay

There is no shortage of lower-range hotels in La Coruña. Calle de Riego de Agua is a good spot to look, as it's in the heart of the most interesting part of town and surrounded by streets with some of the best eating in La Coruña. Friendly *Pensión La Alianza* (☎ 981 22 81 14, Calle de Riego de Agua 8), one of four little places on the street, charges 2200/3800 ptas for average singles/doubles with shared bathrooms.

Hostal Roma (☎ 981 22 80 75, Rúa Nueva 3) is another cheapie, offering basic doubles for women only at 3100 ptas. Virtually around the corner, *Hostal Centro Gallego* (☎ 981 22 22 36, Calle Estrella 2) has recently upgraded rooms with TV and bathroom for 3000 ptas per person.

A step up is *Hostal La Provinciana* (☎ 981 22 04 00, Rúa Nueva 7-9), which has rooms for 4500/6500 ptas plus IVA in high season. The reliable *Hostal Santa Catalina* (☎ 981 22 66 09, Travesía de Santa Catalina 1) has comfy rooms at 3900/6500 ptas plus IVA.

A little farther from the centre is the extremely pleasant *Hostal Alameda* (☎ 981 22 70 74, Calle de la Alameda 12). Doubles with bath, TV etc range from 4900 to 7500 ptas, depending on season and demand.

Places to Eat

The narrow lanes stretching west of Plaza de María Pita are the first place to make for in search of good food. Calle de la Franja in particular is lined with options. *Casa Jesusa* (Calle de la Franja 8) offers a tasty set lunch usually composed of seafood (the *empanadillas* are especially good) for 1350 ptas. Calle Estrella and Calle de los Olmos

are also rich hunting grounds – you'll see plenty of octopuses in the windows. *Café El Reloj*, opposite Hostal Santa Catalina, has a great atmosphere at office workers' breakfast time.

For a dessert with a difference, try the crepes at *La Petite Bretagne* (Calle de Riego de Agua 13). It also serves savoury crepes and a wonderful range of exotic salads. *Farggi* (Calle de Riego de Agua 5) is good for breakfast and sticky things; it's closed Sunday.

Although you pay a little over the odds for your coffee, the cafes on Plaza de María Pita are an unbeatable choice for people-watching. Just as good is the Avenida de la Marina.

Entertainment

You'll find plenty to drink with your tapas in the central streets already mentioned. If you're more interested in drinking than eating, try one of the 50 or so watering holes crammed into the streets off Playa del Orzán. As the night wears on, Calle de Juan Florez is also worth checking out, as are many of its side streets.

Teatro Rosalía Castro, on Calle de Riego de Agua, is the place for classical music concerts and other cultural events.

Getting There & Away

Air La Coruña's Alvedro airport (☎ 981 18 72 00) is 9km south of the centre. Iberia and Air Europa have several flights daily to Madrid, and Iberia flies twice most days to Barcelona.

Bus There are plenty of buses to most destinations throughout Galicia and several beyond. Castromil (☎ 981 24 91 92) runs up to nine buses daily to Vigo via Santiago de Compostela and Pontevedra. There are several more buses daily just to Santiago. IASA has regular services daily to Lugo, Ferrol (775 ptas), and Betanzos (245 ptas). IASA also runs at least two buses daily to Orense, or you can change at Santiago.

For international buses, see the Santiago de Compostela section earlier. For further information, you can call the bus station on ☎ 981 23 90 99.

GALICIA

Train From 8 am to midnight (more or less on the hour), trains head from the train station (☎ 981 15 02 02) south to Santiago de Compostela (515 ptas), Pontevedra (1030 ptas) and Vigo (1305 ptas). There are two trains daily to Madrid (Chamartín), and two to Barcelona via Zaragoza. The twice-daily train to Ferrol (1½ hours, 515 ptas) stops at Betanzos (400 ptas).

Car & Motorcycle The A-9 tollway is the quickest south-eastward road out of La Coruña. Before this reaches Betanzos another tollway heads north to Fenne, just short of Ferrol (La Coruña–Fenne costs 415 ptas); the A-9 heads down to Vigo (1130 ptas, 155km) via Santiago de Compostela and Pontevedra. The N-550 to Santiago is prettier, and free, but slower.

Getting Around

Four buses head from the bus station to the airport from Monday to Saturday (200 ptas). A taxi costs around 600 ptas.

Local bus No 5 links the train station with central La Coruña, while Nos 1, 1A and 4 stop outside the bus station en route to the centre.

RÍAS ALTAS

Although the Rías Altas and surrounding countryside, east of La Coruña, are less extensive and visited less often than the Rías Bajas, in many respects they have quite an edge over their more popular counterpart. For starters, they are not nearly as populated, retaining a greater natural attraction. And when the weather is good, many beaches on this stretch are every bit as good as anything you'll find to the south. A handful of enticing little towns such as medieval Betanzos and Pontedeume are handsomely accompanied by some of the most dramatic coast you will see in all Galicia – that of the Serra de la Capelada and Cabo Ortegal.

Buses are fairly frequent along the main roads at least as far east as Viveiro, and trains heading for Asturias follow a similar route. Off the main roads bus services are rarer, but with a little patience, you can get to a lot of places.

Betanzos
postcode 15004 • pop 11,900

Just 24km east of La Coruña, Betanzos can be seen as a small-scale Toledo of the north, decidedly flavoured *a la gallega* with its multistorey houses glassed in by classic white galerías. Re-sited here in 1219, medieval Betanzos was long a busy port until eclipsed by La Coruña. Lately it has made valiant – and fairly successful – efforts to stave off the tangible effects of economic depression.

The tourist office (☎ 981 77 00 11), in the same building as the Museo das Mariñas on Rúa de Emilio Romay, has a map and list of hospedajes. It's open 10 am to 1 pm and 4 to 8 pm weekdays, 10 am to 2 pm Saturday.

Several banks are located on or near the sprawling main square, Praza dos Irmáns García Naveira. The post office is on Paseo de Alfonso IX, near the square.

The Celtic settlement *(castro)* that predated the town was located in what is now Praza da Constitución, flanked notably by the neoclassical ayuntamiento and Gothic Iglesia de Santiago. More interesting is the small Praza de Fernán Pérez de Andrade, with the pretty Gothic churches of **Santa María do Azogue** and **San Francisco**. Inside the latter is the tomb of Fernán Pérez de Andrade, the noble who founded a monastery in nearby Ferrol in the 14th century, supported by the beautiful family emblems in stone – a bear and a wild boar.

The **Museo das Mariñas** (☎ 981 77 19 46) contains a lot of curios, including fragments of medieval sculpture and a display of traditional Galician costumes (225 ptas). It opens the same hours as the tourist office (see earlier) in the same building.

The Fiesta de San Roque, held annually on 16 August, is marked at midnight by the sending up of a huge, 'home-made', paper hot-air balloon.

Places to Stay & Eat *Hostal Barreiro* (☎ 981 77 22 59, Rúa de Argentina 6) has simple singles/doubles for 1400/2300 ptas. Doubles with bath are 2500 ptas. *Hotel Los Angeles* (☎ 981 77 15 11, Rúa dos Anxeles 11) charges 5500/7000 ptas plus IVA for comfy rooms.

Opposite the main square, Travieso do Progreso, the lane between Café La Goleta and a pharmacy, is the focus of Betanzos' culinary life. *O' Pote (Travieso do Progreso 9)* and the **Mesón O' Progreso** at the end of the same lane are decent. The parallel lane Venela do Campo has more tapas bars, while the cafes on the main square are popular for breakfast. You can quench a thirst at *Cervecería Old Inn*, just off the small Praza de Domingo, which has a fair selection of Irish and German beers.

Getting There & Away The easiest way in and out of Betanzos is by bus. Bus information is posted on the window of Café Maino on Praza dos Irmáns García Naveira. Regular services to/from La Coruña operate from Praza dos Irmáns García Naveira. Less frequent buses head to Lugo and Ferrol. Buses to Madrid, Asturias and the Basque Country leave from Rúa de Emilio Romay.

The closest of the town's two train stations, Betanzos Cidade, is north of the old town, just across the Río Mendo. Two trains daily go to Ferrol and La Coruña.

Pontedeume
postcode 15007 • pop 4500

Founded in 1270, this hillside feudal bastion, while scruffier than Betanzos to the south, is an appealing stop with the advantage of having a beach close by the town's fishing port. Rúa Real, the porticoed main street leading off the roundabout at the entry to town from the Betanzos direction, climbs past a cheerful little square (in front of the *concello*, or town hall) up to the 18th-century Iglesia de Santiago. Winding down the hill from here are numerous lanes characterised by Galician galerías. Down on the waterfront, near the market, rises the **torreón** (main tower) of what was once the Palacio de Andrade, named after the local feudal lord.

Fonda Martís (☎ 981 43 06 37, Rúa Real 23) has spartan singles/doubles in the heart of things for 1500/2500 ptas. Rúa Real is also lined with taverns and eateries. At *Bar Cañiza (Rúa Real 28)* you can try a *queimada* (a warmed aguardiente).

Ferrol
postcode 15400 • pop 85,000

For a town with rather leftist leanings, it is a small irony of history that Franco was born here in 1892. Under his rule the town was known as El Ferrol del Caudillo, and his equestrian statue still dominates Plaza de España. The house he was born in is at Calle María 136. Otherwise, there is little to excite in a town that has been badly hit by the decline of its shipyards in the past few decades. The tourist office (☎ 981 31 11 79) is at Calle Magdalena 12, three blocks inland from the port.

If you decide to take a look at the town centre, head for Calle de Pardo Bajo for food and lodgings. *Hostal Aloya (☎ 981 35 12 31, Calle de Pardo Bajo 28)* is a reliable place to stay, with doubles for 5030 ptas in high season. Otherwise, check out some of the cheaper hospedajes on the same street. In between them is crammed a selection of restaurants and bars. *Restaurante Côté (Calle de Pardo Bajo 24),* oddly enough for a port town, has better meat than fish dishes.

Regular buses run south to Santiago de Compostela (1100 ptas) via Betanzos, and to Viveiro and Vigo (2000 ptas) via Pontevedra (1600 ptas). Two buses run daily to Madrid. For more information, call ☎ 981 32 47 51. Two daily Renfe trains connect Ferrol with La Coruña (515 ptas) via Betanzos, and three or four FEVE trains head east to Viveiro and Ribadeo, two continuing to Oviedo.

Cedeira
postcode 15350 • pop 7600

If possible, give Ferrol a miss and make for Cedeira, 38km up the coast. En route, don't miss, after about 16km, the beautiful sweep of beach at Valdoviño where, in August, there is an international windsurfing competition.

Cedeira sits on a stream that spills into the pretty Ría de Cedeira. The older nucleus of this little town fronts the river with traditional glassed-in galerías, while across two parallel bridges on the modern side of town is a pleasant, sheltered beach. Better still is the estuary to the south, the **Ría de Esteiro**,

GALICIA

where you'll find a still more appealing beach, popular with free-campers. Cedeira's tourist office (☎ 981 48 21 87) is in the old town on Calle Ezequiel López and is open 10 am to 1 pm and 5 to 8 pm daily, June to September only.

Places to Stay & Eat There are a few hostales to choose from. *Habitaciones El Puente (☎ 981 48 00 87, Calle Ortigueiro 1)* has clean singles/doubles for 1500/3000 ptas – and more rooms in a place in the new town *(Calle de los Excombatientes 2)* at the same price (look for the 'Habitaciones El Puente' sign on the Ferrol side of the bridge crossed by the main road).

Hostal Brisas (☎ 981 48 10 54, Arriba da Ponte 19), right by the main bridge, has large, clean but musty rooms with bath and TV for 3000/4500 ptas. *Hostal Avenida (☎ 981 49 21 12, Calle Cuatro Caminos 66)*, on the approach to town from the Ferrol direction, is a step up, with rooms from 6000 to 9000 ptas depending on the season.

The pretty *Hospedería Cordobelas (☎ 981 48 06 07)*, clearly signposted at Esteiro, a couple of kilometres south of town, has attractive doubles with bath for 6000 ptas most of the year, 9000 ptas July to September.

A very popular place for excellent raciones (ranging from 450 to 1200 ptas) and a beer is *Mesón Muiños Kilowato (Avenida a Moreno 12)*, along the waterfront of the old town. *Cafetería Pinza (Praza de Galicia 1)* does breakfasts, juices and pastries all year round.

Getting There & Away By bus, you'll need to change in Ferrol. Regular buses also connect Cedeira with Cariño to the north-east.

Serra de la Capelada
North from Cedeira things only get better. On the road to San Andrés de Teixido, you exchange the ever-changing horizons of the rías for higher, wilder ground. The Serra de la Capelada is heavily wooded and instead of milestones, the winding road is regularly marked by spectacular *miradores* (lookouts) over some of the sheerest Atlantic

coast in Europe. Windy even on a hot summer day, this territory can be downright fear-inspiring in the midst of a winter storm.

Wild horses still mingle here with cattle, and early June tends to be the main time for the *curro*, the festive rounding up and breaking in of these free-spirited animals (see the boxed text 'Galician Round-Up' later in this chapter).

San Andrés de Teixido Along a particularly pretty stretch of coast, this hamlet is renowned as a sanctuary of relics of St Andrew. Spaniards flock to see the sanctuary and fill up a few bottles with spring water from the so-called **Fuente de la Suerte** (Lucky Spring). The result of this is a predictable line of kitsch tourist stalls – enough to make you wonder if there's anyone out in the surrounding fields. Don't let this put you off. Anyone with a vehicle should take this route for the views – before, in and after the village. Buses from Cedeira to Cariño occasionally stop in.

Cabo Ortegal Another 20km or so northeast, Cabo Ortegal is the mother of Spanish capes. Great stone shafts drop sheer into the ocean from such a height that the waves crashing onto the rocks below seem pitifully – and deceptively – benign. The cape is 3.5km beyond the soulless fishing town of **Cariño**. Travellers without their own wheels can get buses to Cariño from Ferrol, Cedeira and Ortigueira, and there are a couple of *hostales* if you need one.

Cariño to Viveiro
From Cariño the road roughly follows the curves of the Ría de Ortigueira southwards to the Río Mera. The area is rich in waterbird life and the only town of any consequence is **Ortigueira**, a not unattractive but hardly captivating fishing town on the bus route and the FEVE railway between Ferrol and Viveiro. One time when it's worth being here is during the annual Mundo Celta music festival, usually held in the first week of August.

Otherwise, you'll be happier if you continue north-east to **O Barqueiro**, a Galician fishing village as you might imagine one, again on the Ferrol-Viveiro bus route and railway. White houses capped with slate-tile roofs cascade down to a small protected port. There's little to do but watch the day's catch come in, but that's the point – this is the real thing. There are a couple of places to stay down on the waterfront. Try *Hostal La Marina* (☎ 981 41 40 98), which has doubles only with bath for 5000 ptas.

Free-campers should push on up to **Porto de Vares (Bares)**, 2km past Vila de Vares. The place is smaller and boasts a pair of beaches (the one closer to town is more protected). *Restaurante La Marina*, with a terrace overlooking the beach, does acceptable seafood and paella. A very pretty side road leads to **Cabo Estaca de Vares** (you can't miss the windmills), Spain's most northerly point.

Beaches The coast eastwards to Viveiro is broken up by several decent beaches. It is wise to choose one at least 5km from Viveiro, or you'll have to put up with comparatively built-up stretches.

Viveiro
postcode 27850 • pop 5600
Behind the grand **Puerta de Carlos V** (the most impressive of Viveiro's three remaining medieval gates) lies a straggle of cobbled lanes and plazas where very little seems to have changed since the town was rebuilt after a fire in 1540. Directly up the road past Praza Maior is the **Iglesia de Santa María do Campo**, displaying Romanesque and Gothic features. Nearby is a bad-taste reproduction of Lourdes, while to the north the 14th-century **Iglesia de San Francisco** is the most interesting of Viveiro's buildings.

A wooden tourist kiosk, open June to September, is opposite the small bus station on Avenida Ramón Canosa (north along the waterfront from the Puerta de Carlos V).

The welcoming *Fonda Nuevo Mundo* (☎ 982 56 00 25, Rúa de Teodoro de Quirós 14), one of several modest hostelries inside the old town, is a good, clean deal. Singles/doubles cost 1700/3500 ptas – try for a

room in one of the galerías. There are more *hostales* and a couple of *camping grounds* on the beaches outside town, particularly at Praia de Covas.

For a decent seafood meal, try *Bar Serra (Rúa de Antonio Bas 2)*. The area around Placiña da Herba presents a few appetising options. *Mesón O' Tunel (Rúa Fernández Victorio 6)* has good tapas. For a late-night drink, Rúa Pérez das Mariñas and Rúa Almirante Chicarro are promising.

FEVE trains between Ferrol and Ribadeo or Oviedo call into Viviero but buses are more frequent. Six buses run most days to La Coruña (1635 ptas) and Ferrol (985 ptas), four head to Lugo (1155 ptas) and a couple on weekdays to Ribadeo (625 ptas).

Mondoñedo
postcode 27740 • pop 5600
Compared with the natural spectacles of north-western Galicia's Atlantic coast, the offerings east of Viveiro cut a poor figure. For much of the trip towards Asturias the road lies well inland from the coastline and what beaches there are pale before their cousins farther west and east. The towns of Cervo, Sargadelos, Burela and Foz are all pretty drab and best examined from the comfort of whatever transport you're in.

By contrast, a detour inland from Foz down the Río Masma to Mondoñedo is rewarding. First settled in the 5th century by a group of restless migrants from Brittany, Mondoñedo became an important religious centre and long a provincial capital in the old Kingdom of Galicia. Its slightly down-at-heel appearance today in no way diminishes its interest.

The tourist office (☎ 982 50 71 77) is just off Praza de España, near the impressive cathedral. Also fronting the old square are the Palacio Episcopal, next to the cathedral. The **Fonte Vella** (Old Fountain) that you can see just south of the square was built in 1548.

Pensión La Tropicana (☎ 982 52 10 08, Rúa de Lodeiro Piñeiroa 8) is the closest accommodation to the centre of town; doubles cost 4000 ptas.

There are several buses operating to Foz and Lugo.

GALICIA

Ribadeo & Around

Aside from the odd mediocre beach, there is little to keep you waiting along the coast between Foz and **Ribadeo**. The best thing about this frontier town is its ría, a broad expanse and an obvious natural frontier between Galicia and Asturias. The impressive **Puente de los Santos** crosses the waterway that, becoming the Río Eo farther inland, continues to mark the regional frontier for some 30km south. A busy little place, Ribadeo contains nothing much to see or do. If you get stuck, the area around the central Praza de España is awash with hotels of every type.

Two daily FEVE trains run to/from Oviedo via several spots on the Asturian coast; three or four run to/from Ferrol. A few daily buses head to/from Luarca, Lugo and (except weekends) Viveiro.

The Costa da Morte

On one of those not-so-frequent hot, sunny days, you could be forgiven for thinking that the tales of danger surrounding this stretch of the Atlantic seaboard – the 'Death Coast' – are greatly exaggerated. But the idyll can undergo a rapid metamorphosis when ocean mists blow in and envelop the whole region.

The A-55 tollway from La Coruña bypasses the beginning of the Costa da Morte, running inland to Carballo (245 ptas). From Carballo, a reasonable road heads north-west to Malpica de Bergantiños, passing through Buño, known for its ceramics. The minor, coastal road out of La Coruña passes a few ocean beaches such as Playa de Barrañán and Playa de Sorrizo where you must be mindful of the currents. The Costa da Morte begins at the unassuming point of Caión.

Getting There & Away

As elsewhere along Galicia's coasts, your own vehicle is the best means of exploring the ins and outs of the Costa da Morte. But Transportes Finisterre (☎ 981 58 04 57),

in Santiago de Compostela, provides a passable bus service to many places, with Carballo an important hub. Its services include:

Camariñas – a daily bus from Santiago de Compostela; buses from La Coruña via Carballo
Carballo – up to 30 daily buses from La Coruña (470 ptas)
Corme – same buses as for Malpica de Bergantiños
Finisterre – four daily buses from La Coruña (1540 ptas); up to three from Santiago de Compostela
Laxe – two daily buses from Carballo (maybe fewer on weekends)
Malpica de Bergantiños – two daily buses on weekdays and one on weekends from La Coruña (650 ptas); one from Santiago de Compostela on weekdays (1060 ptas)

MALPICA DE BERGANTIÑOS
postcode 15113 • pop 2800

Malpica has a sandy beach on one side and a busy port on the other. The main attraction is the liveliness of the village centre and its bars and eateries, several of which overlook the beach. Off the coast you can see the **Islas Sisargas**, where various bird species, mostly types of seagull, nest. *Hostal JB* (☎ 981 72 02 66) on Rueiro da Praia has lovely, comfortable rooms, some virtually overhanging the beach. Singles/doubles with TV and bath are 4000/5000 ptas in July and August. *Hostal Panchito* (☎ 981 72 30 07), on Praza de Anselmo Villar Amigo, has decent rooms without the views for about the same price. For a place to eat, hunt around the various bars squeezed in just back from the beach. *Pizzería Vagalume*, right on the beachfront, does respectable pizzas from 700 to 1300 ptas.

CORME & AROUND

Climb Corme's steep, winding streets from the waterfront and you'll notice how its fishing-port feel gives way to that of the agricultural hinterland (known as Corme Aldea) – quite a complementary arrangement. Although most of the buildings are modern, the place has some of its old *pueblo* atmosphere and a serviceable nearby beach.

If the latter does not meet your expectations, move south to **Praia Hermida**, an attractive and uncrowded ocean strand. Harder to reach without your own transport but just as pleasant is **Praia Balarés**. Perhaps not so nice is a growing side industry here, as in other Galician ports. In 1996 a fishing vessel was impounded with 2600kg of cocaine – the biggest haul by Spanish authorities then on record.

LAXE & AROUND
If you're driving down the coast, make first for **Ponteceso**, a local crossroads. Nearby **Laxe** (population 3000) has a white sandy beach but, like quite a few of these fishing towns, its mostly modern buildings deprive it of character. If you need to stay, *Hostal Bahía (☎ 981 72 82 07, Avenida Generalísimo 24)* has clean singles/doubles with bath for 5000/6000 ptas in high season.

For something a little easier on the eye, dare to penetrate the unsignposted maze of roads south of Laxe that should eventually get you to the wilder **Praia de Traba**. Or take a two-day 40km coastal walk from Laxe to Camariñas, as outlined in Lonely Planet's *Walking in Spain,* with an overnight stop in **Camelle** where there are a couple of places to stay and eat. *A Molinera (☎ 981 71 04 92, Calle Principal 79)* has self-catering apartments at 5000 ptas for two.

Just west of Camelle is **Arou**, a little-visited fishing village with a couple of pleasant swimming areas – especially if you follow the track along the coast. In Arou you'll find *señoras* working on lace and probably get better prices than in Camariñas along the coast.

A lousy track leads off from near Arou towards **Ensenada de Trece**, a not-overly-visited beach. After 10km the track passes the **Cemeterio de los Ingleses** (English Cemetery) in which are buried the few recovered bodies from an 1890 shipwreck in which 170 British cadets drowned.

CAMARIÑAS
postcode 15123 • pop 7400
In essence a modern fishing village, Camariñas attracts a steady trickle of mainly Span-

ish tourists. The place has something of a reputation for *encajes* (lacework) and you may see women making the stuff in strategic locations for passers-by.

Apart from the craftwork and walking possibilities (see Laxe earlier), the other reason to pass this way is to take a look at **Cabo Vilán**, an impressive cape with a 25m lighthouse, 5km north-west of the town. The Atlantic storms are put to good use with the modern windmills of the Parque Eólico.

Camariñas has a couple of hostales. *Hostal Dársena (☎ 981 73 62 63)* on Calle Alcalde Patiña has comfortable rooms at 4000 ptas for doubles, and isn't a bad place to try seafood. Another is the *4 Vientos (Calle Molino de Viento 81),* a 500m walk south from town.

MUXÍA & AROUND
Getting to and from Camariñas you'll pass through Ponte do Porto, on the Río Grande. The coastal road south for Os Muiños passes the pretty hamlet of **Cereixo** and heads down a narrow, shaded road. Along here, near Leis, you'll find one of the most inviting beaches along the Costa da Morte, **Praia do Lago**. The sand fronts the ocean and also a quiet river. There are a couple of camping grounds and at least one hostal.

From Os Muiños the road passes the Romanesque **Monasterio de San Xián de Moraime**, built over a Roman settlement.

Muxía (population 1590) itself is nothing special, but you can head out to the **Punta da Barca**, which affords good views of the coast. The rocks in front of the baroque Santuario de Nuestra Señora de la Barca are the scene of a popular *romería* (festive pilgrimage) in September. *Hostal La Cruz (☎ 981 74 20 84, Avenida de Calvo Sotelo 53)* has singles/doubles for 5000/7000 ptas in high season.

FINISTERRE & AROUND
Those poking their noses about the Costa da Morte will probably want to make it to Galicia's version of England's Land's End, Cabo Finisterre (Cabo Fisterra in Galician). The towns on the approach, such as **Corcubión**, **Sardiñeiro** and **Finisterre**, are not very

GALICIA

attractive, though the tree-lined road is more appealing.

From Finisterre town (population 2890) it's another 3.5km to **Cabo Finisterre**, where Spain stops and the Atlantic begins. To the right on the way out of town is the 12th-century **Iglesia de Santa María das Areas**, a mix of Romanesque, Gothic and baroque. The westernmost shelter for pilgrims en route to Santiago de Compostela once stood just opposite. The best views of the coast are to be had by climbing up the track to Monte Facho and Monte San Guillermo. The area is laced with myth and superstition, and they say childless couples used to come up here to increase their efforts to conceive.

Corcubión has a few hostales should you need one. *Ruta Finisterre* camping ground (*☎ fax 981 74 63 02*) near Sardiñeiro is not a bad place for the night. There is a reasonable beach across the road and another one a couple of kilometres farther on, stretching almost to the town of Finisterre.

Pensión Casa Velay (*☎ 981 74 01 27*), just off the main square in the older part of Finisterre, has decent doubles for 2800 ptas (3800 ptas with bath). The owners also run a pleasant *restaurant* with sea views, or you could hang around *Bar Tito* on the main square for snacks and beer.

TOWARDS THE RÍAS BAJAS

The southernmost stretch of the Costa da Morte has its moments. Two kilometres north-west of **Ézaro** and 25km from Cabo Finisterre, the coast road passes a mirador with breathtaking views over the Atlantic. Lonely Planet's *Walking in Spain* describes a walk up to A Moa (627m), the highest point of nearby Monte Pindo, with even better views. The walk starts and ends at **O Pindo** (El Pindo), a cute fishing village set back on a shallow, tranquil bay. Here *Hospedaje La Morada* (*☎ 981 77 48 70*) has singles/doubles for 3500/5000 ptas.

Another 10km south and you reach Playa de Carnota, a long, sandy beach – usually not too crowded, and fine if the wind isn't up. **Carnota** town, towards the southern end of the beach, is renowned as home to Galicia's longest *hórreo* (grain store) – 34.5m

long, it was built late in the 18th century (for more details, see the boxed text 'Of Grain Stores & Crossroads' later in this chapter).

Rías Bajas

The four great estuaries of Galicia's south, the Rías Bajas (Rias Baixas), are without doubt the grandest of all the rías that indent the length of the Galician coast, and they are justifiably well known. There are plenty of beaches and several relatively low-key resorts, and in summer good weather is a better bet here than farther north. You may be a little disappointed about how dully built-up some stretches of the rías are, but there are enough pretty villages and stretches of beautiful shore to keep most of us happy. Throw in the Islas Cíes, the lovely medieval town of Pontevedra and the more harried centre of Vigo, and you have a travelling mix that is hard to beat.

Getting to and around the Rías Bajas is, as usual, easiest with your own wheels, but bus services do enable you to reach most places, occasionally with the aid of a bit of foot or thumb work. Santiago de Compostela is a good enough stepping-off point for the northern rías; Pontevedra and Vigo are the main hubs for the south. Though the following sections start at the inland end of each ría and work outwards, if you have a vehicle an appealing option is simply to follow the coast round from one ría to the next.

RÍA DE MUROS Y NOIA
Noia
postcode 15200 • pop 14,800

Noia is worth visiting for its old centre, which preserves some reminders of its glory days: in particular, the main entrance and rose window of the 15th-century Gothic **Catedral de San Martiño**. Nearby is the highly evocative **Casa de Costa**, whose four arches date back to at least the mid-14th century. The former **Iglesia de Santa María La Nova**, a short walk from the old centre, was built in 1327 and today, together with its cemetery, forms a unique museum of headstones and funerary art. It is open 11 am to 1.30 pm and 6.30 to 8 pm Tuesday to Friday and 11 am to 1.30 pm weekends.

There are several places to stay, to suit all budgets. *Hospedaje Marico (☎ 981 82 00 09, Rúa de Galicía s/n),* on the road to Santiago and near the old part of town, is a good deal at 2000/3500 ptas for singles /doubles with shared bath (doubles with bath cost 4000 ptas). For snacks and drinks, you cannot beat *Tasca Típica,* right in the Casa de Costa, with tables spilling out under the arches.

Several daily buses run here from Santiago and on to Muros. A couple of buses also serve Padrón.

Muros
postcode 15250 • pop 11,250
Out towards the western end of the northern side of the ría, and on an attractive driving route to/from the Costa da Morte, Muros is perhaps not quite as wonderful as the travel literature makes out. Founded in the 10th century, it was long an important port for Santiago de Compostela. Today it lives mainly from fishing and a passing tourist trade.

From the main seaside square dominated by the ayuntamiento, follow Calle Real vaguely in the direction of Santiago. Along the way are some attractive porticoes, the odd *cruceiro* (crucifix; see the boxed text 'Of Grain Stores & Crossroads' later in this chapter), a couple of ageing churches and an overly extravagant mercado. Apart from the pleasure of having a beer or meal on the waterfront, that's about all there is to the place, apart from a couple of nice beaches west of the town.

South Shore
The main attraction here, if the weather is good, is the long series of beaches – such as Aguieira, one of the first you encounter. The village of **Porto do Son** makes a relaxed stop. For food and lodgings, try *Hostal O Chinto* on Avenida de Galicia, by the port. Doubles with shared bathrooms are 4000 ptas, and there's good seafood in the bar below.

On a headland near **Baroña** are the remains of a Celtic settlement, signposted from the roadside cafe. The beach nearby, **Arealonga**, is for nudists.

RÍA DE AROUSA
Padrón
postcode 15900 • pop 4000
The hottest thing to come out of Padrón is peppers. That's right, *pimientos de Padrón* – shrivelled little green things that taste very good, but beware the odd *very* hot one. Franciscan friars first imported them from Mexico in the 16th century, and the whole area now grows them to meet the high demand.

This town where Santiago's corpse supposedly arrived in Galicia (see the Santiago de Compostela section earlier) is struggling valiantly to make a tourist attraction of itself, putting most effort into the Galician poet Rosalía de Castro, who died here in 1885. The **Casa y Museo de Rosalía**, just behind the train station, contains memorabilia and is one stop in the so-called Ruta Rosaliana that has been mapped out in various locations throughout this region. It's open 10 am to 2 pm and 4 to 8 pm Tuesday to Sunday (in winter 10 am to 1.30 pm and 4 to 7 pm).

The very pretty *Hostal del Jardín (☎ 981 81 09 50, Rúa de Salgado Araujo 3)* is opposite the park on the road to the train station. Spacious singles/doubles are 3000/ 5000 ptas plus IVA in high season.

Padrón is fairly well linked by bus to Santiago de Compostela and Pontevedra; there are also regular services to/from Noia, Cambados and O Grove.

North Side
There's little that is attractive about the northern side of the Ría de Arousa (Ria de Arosa). An exception, however, for those with a motor vehicle, is *Casa da Posta de Valmaior (☎ fax 981 86 25 48)* at Cespón Boiro, a few kilometres north-east of the rather awful town of Boiro. This country home is a wonderful place to stay and an ideal country base for exploring the rías. Its lovely singles/doubles cost 3700/7000 ptas

GALICIA

in high season. It is *turismo rural* at its best, and is well signposted off the N-550 between Boiro and Padrón.

Out near the western end of the ría, **Ribeira** is a drab and drizzly fishing town, and has virtually nothing to recommend it.

If you're driving, you might just want to detour to the **Dolmen de Axeitos**, a well-preserved megalithic monument. It's signposted off the road between Ribeira and Xuño.

Catoira
postcode 36612 • pop 3700

About 15km from Padrón down the Río Ulla's southern side, which shortly after widens into the Ría de Arousa, stand the **Torres do Oeste** at Catoira. These towers are what remains of Castellum Honesti, the early medieval castle that was the key in protecting (not always successfully) Santiago de Compostela against Norman landings. On the first Sunday of every August, a Viking landing is staged here as an excuse for a boisterous fiesta.

Caldas de Reyes
postcode 36650 • pop 9100

This old spa town on the N-550 between Padrón and Pontevedra – or a diversion inland from Villagarcía de Arousa – is something of a curiosity. At one end of the cobbled Calle Real stands a small medieval bridge, while on the Río Umia, the two spa hotels, or *balnearios,* still function. It is worth having a peek inside *Hotel Acuña (☎ 986 54 00 10, Calle de Herrería 2).* You can have a bath if you want to, but generally guests here are under medical supervision. The whole place exudes a mouldy 19th-century feeling. The other balneario, *Hostal Dávila (☎ 986 54 00 12, Calle de Laureano Salgado 11),* is even more dilapidated. Just outside it is As Burgas, a small spa water fountain.

Hostal Buceta (☎ 986 54 00 31, Calle de José Salgado 34) is something of an ageing piece as well, with singles/doubles with bath at 4000/5000 ptas. *Taberna O' Muiño* is an old, run-down riverside bar and grill.

Isla de Arousa

Back by the water, you could drive straight past **Vilanova de Arousa** (although it has a few reasonable beaches) and make for the Isla (Illa) de Arousa, an island connected to the mainland by a long, low bridge. The small town on the island lives mainly from fishing and the whole place has a low-key profile. Some of the beaches facing the mainland are very pleasant and protected, with comparatively warm water. The southern part of the island forms the **Parque Natural Carreirón** where you'll find sand dunes, marshlands, a lake and associated ecosystems, with abundant bird life.

Camping Salinas (☎ 986 52 74 44) is open from June to September on the island's Playa de Xastelas and there are several year-round camping grounds, plus a few lower mid-range hotels, around Vilanova. The occasional bus runs between here and Pontevedra.

Cambados
postcode 36630 • pop 12,600

Founded by the Visigoths and a victim of constant harrying by Vikings in the 9th and 10th centuries, Cambados is today a peaceful seaside town. From the north you enter by the magnificent **Praza de Fefiñáns**, bordered on two sides by a grand 17th-century *pazo* (mansion) and on another by the 18th-century Iglesia de San Benito. Several appealing little streets branch off the plaza, and nearby another pazo has been converted into a parador. There's a tourist office on Paseo da Calzada beside the parador, and a wooden tourist kiosk on Avenida de Galicia, behind the bus station which faces the waterfront on Paseo Marítimo in the newer part of town.

If you have a car, a pretty inland excursion via San Salvador de Meis will take you to the Cistercian **Monasterio de Santa María de Armenteira**, founded in 1162.

Places to Stay & Eat *Hostal Pazos Feijoo (☎ 986 54 28 10, Calle de Curros Enríquez 1)* is one street inland from the bus station. Singles/doubles with bathroom and TV are 4000/6000 ptas. *Parador El Albariño (☎ 986*

54 22 50, fax 986 54 20 68, Paseo da Calzada s/n) charges 12,000/15,000 ptas plus IVA in high season.

O Meular on Rúa Caracol, off Calle de Curros, is a good spot for a drink. *Restaurante/Café/Marisquería Mar de Arousa* on Avenida de Galicia, near the bus station, serves up good-value fare. For something more special, take a walk up Rúa Príncipe, the cobblestoned street beside the parador, to Praza de Fefiñáns, and take your pick.

Cambados is in the heart of Albariño wine country, and Praza de Fefiñáns is swarming with *bodegas, bars* and pretty good *restaurants* flogging what can be a very good drop.

Getting There & Away At least three buses daily head to/from Pontevedra and Santiago de Compostela. There are also regular bus services to/from Villagarcía and O Grove.

O Grove
postcode 36980 • pop 10,700
How you react to O Grove may depend on the weather. It's a strange mix of England's Blackpool and some of Italy's Adriatic 'family' resorts. In summer you'll find little more than hotel blocks, mainly unexciting restaurants, mediocre nightclubs, a fairground and Galicia's unpredictable climate. In winter most of the above is closed, and the weather is worse.

Still, it could make a lunch stop on your way through the area, and there are several beaches around the little peninsula it stands on. Nature enthusiasts can enjoy a visit to the **Centro de Visitantes A Siradella**, above the town in a forested area, which has excellent displays related to the district's plentiful marine and bird life, and the cultivation of *mariscos* (shellfish). Its opening hours are 10 am to 2 pm and 4.30 to 8 pm daily in summer, 10 am to 2 pm Monday to Saturday for the rest of the year.

In steady weather, a number of companies run trips out to sea, largely to look at the **bateas** – platforms that look like miniature oil rigs, where *mejillones* (mussels), *ostras* (oysters) and *vieiras* (scallops) are

cultivated. Tours (1½ hours, 1600 ptas) include a seafood tasting. Other trips, run by Cruceros Rías Bajas for one (see Sanxenxo later in this chapter), go to Ribeira and around the Isla de Arousa.

As for the island of **A Toxa**, connected to O Grove by a bridge, this one-time natural beauty spot has been irreparably spoiled by holiday-makers and builders with more money than sense. The place is crawling with 'classy' hotels and holiday apartments.

Places to Stay & Eat Should you want to stay, the only potential problem times are August and summer weekends. For the cheap options, head for Praza do Corgo (beside the port), where you'll also find the ayuntamiento, a car park, and in summer, a tourist information kiosk. *Hostal María Aguiño (☎ 986 73 11 87, Rúa de Pablo Iglesias 26),* on one of the streets going inland from the plaza, has decent singles/doubles for 4000/4500 ptas in July and August, 2500/3500 ptas at other times. Across the road, *Residencia Marisé (☎ 986 73 08 40, Rúa de Pablo Iglesias 23)* has clean rooms for 2500/4500 ptas.

When hunger strikes, the restaurants around Praza do Corgo are OK, and *Taberna O' Pescador (Rúa de Pablo Iglesias 9)* is a popular and reasonably priced seafood joint. The Italian restaurant *Casa de Pasta,* attached to Hostal María Aguiño, has an impressive list of home-made pastas and salsas.

Getting There & Away Buses run to/from Cambados, Sanxenxo, Pontevedra, Padrón, Santiago de Compostela and elsewhere. The stop is on Calle Beirama, in front of the port.

PONTEVEDRA
postcode 36080 • pop 69,000
Galicia's smallest provincial capital is perhaps its most striking. It has managed to preserve intact a classic medieval centre backing on to the Río Lérez – ideal for simply wandering around and poking one's nose into all sorts of nooks and crannies.

GALICIA

History

Known to the Romans as Ad Duos Pontes, Pontevedra reached the height of its glory in the 16th century, when it was the biggest city in Galicia and an important port. The *Santa María,* the flagship of Columbus' journey of discovery, was built here, and a local legend that the Genoese explorer was born in Pontevedra persists to this day. In the 17th century the city began to decline in the face of growing competition in the ría and the silting up of its port. Its 1719 sacking by the British did not help matters. In spite of it all, Pontevedra was made provincial capital in 1835 despite fierce opposition from Vigo, and tourism is proving a healthy boon.

Orientation

The historic centre, or *zona monumental* as the local authorities refer to it, is clearly confined within a circle formed by Rúa do Arzobispo Malvar, Rúa de Michelena, Rúa de Cobián Raffignac, Rúa de Padre A Carballo and the Río Lérez, itself forded by two bridges (not the original *duos pontes* of the Roman name, though they may be in the same places). The walls have gone, but the

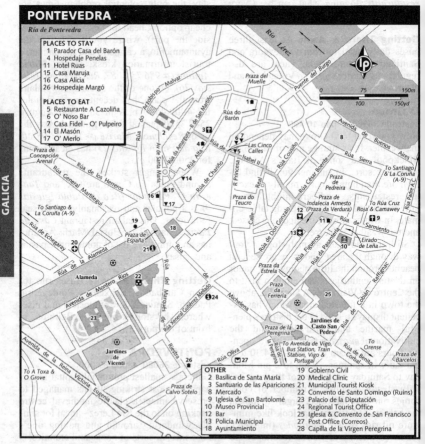

PONTEVEDRA

Ría de Pontevedra

PLACES TO STAY
1 Parador Casa del Barón
4 Hospedaje Penelas
11 Hotel Ruas
15 Casa Maruja
16 Casa Alicia
26 Hospedaje Margó

PLACES TO EAT
5 Restaurante A Cazoliña
6 O' Noso Bar
7 Casa Fidel – O' Pulpeiro
14 El Masón
17 O' Merlo

OTHER
2 Basílica de Santa María
3 Santuario de las Apariciones
8 Mercado
9 Iglesia de San Bartolomé
10 Museo Provincial
12 Bar
13 Policía Municipal
18 Ayuntamiento
19 Gobierno Civil
20 Medical Clinic
21 Municipal Tourist Kiosk
22 Convento de Santo Domingo (Ruins)
23 Palacio de la Diputación
24 Regional Tourist Office
25 Iglesia & Convento de San Francisco
27 Post Office (Correos)
28 Capilla de la Virgen Peregrina

boundaries remain the same. Inside this area you'll find several hotels, all your eating and drinking needs and much of what you'll want to see. Banks and other offices lie on or near Rúa de Michelena, the main drag of the newer town.

Information

The tourist office (☎ 986 85 08 14) is at Calle del General Mola 3, also called Rúa Xeneral Gutiérrez Mellado. The opening hours in summer are 10 am to 2.15 pm and 5.15 to 8.45 pm Tuesday to Saturday, 11 am to 1 pm Sunday. There's a municipal tourist kiosk on Praza de España, open daily in summer.

There are plenty of banks on Rúa de Michelena, near the tourist office. The main post office is on Rúa Oliva and is open 8.30 am to 8.30 pm weekdays.

The Policía Municipal are on Praza de Indalecio Armesto (Praza da Verdura). In an emergency, call them on ☎ 092. The Policía Nacional (☎ 091) are at Rúa de Joaquín Costa 19. There's a walk-in medical clinic on Rúa de Echegaray.

Zona Monumental

Starting on the south-eastern edge of the zona monumental, you can't miss the distinctive curved facade of the Capilla de la Virgen Peregrina, an 18th-century baroque/neoclassical caprice with a distinctly Portuguese flavour. Virtually across the street, lie Praza da Ferrería and the adjoining Praza da Estrela. The former, colonnaded on one side and displaying an eclectic collection of buildings dating as far back as the 15th century, was once the scene of the town's bullfights. Set back from Praza da Ferrería in its own gardens is the Iglesia de San Francisco, believed by some to have been founded personally by St Francis of Assisi when on pilgrimage to Santiago de Compostela. What was the adjacent convent is now the local tax office.

Head down Rúa da Pasantería and you emerge in the Eirado da Leña, one of Pontevedra's most enchanting little corners, partly colonnaded and with a cruceiro in the middle. Just off it lie the main buildings of

the Museo Provincial, two baroque palaces that were joined by an arch in 1943. The collection ranges from Bronze Age finds, through to the work of contemporary Galician artists. In summer the museum is open 10 am to 2.15 pm and 5 to 8.45 pm Tuesday to Saturday; in winter 10 am to 1.30 pm and 2.30 to 8 pm Tuesday to Saturday, 11 am to 1 pm Sunday (free).

North-east of the Museo Provincial rises the baroque facade of the Jesuit Iglesia de San Bartolomé. A block west of the Eirado da Leña is Praza da Verdura, so called because of the luxuriant trees that fill what is officially known as Praza de Indalecio Armesto.

Farther west, the area known as Las Cinco Calles is a hub of Pontevedra nightlife. The tiny square where the five lanes converge is marked by a cruceiro. From here you can wander north to the Río Lérez and the bustling mercado, if renovations are finished. Take a look at the parador along the way – it's housed in the venerable, neoclassical Pazo del Barón de Maceda.

West up Rúa de Isabel II stands the Basílica de Santa María, a mainly Gothic church with a whiff of plateresque and Portuguese Manueline influences. It's open 10 am to 9 pm daily. On the way up is the signposted Santuario de las Apariciones, a chapel and lodgings where Lúcia of Fátima, the famous early-20th-century child visionary from Fátima in Portugal, resided and where the Virgin Mary is said to have appeared to her.

New Town

The elegant Alameda and Jardines de Vicenti spread south-west of the medieval centre and together form modern Pontevedra's green lung. Alongside them are the ruins of the 15th-century Convento de Santo Domingo, which also house part of the Museo Provincial's archaeological collection.

Places to Stay

There are about half a dozen places to stay in the old town. *Hospedaje Penelas (☎ 986 85 57 05, Rúa Alta 17)* has small but decent

GALICIA

singles/doubles with shared bath for 2500/4000 ptas in July and August, 2000/3000 ptas the rest of the year. *Hospedaje Margó* (☎ *986 85 26 94, Rúa del Marqués de Riestra 4),* just outside the old town, is nothing special, but has cheap rooms for 2500/3000 ptas in summer.

Much better located are *Casa Alicia* (☎ *986 85 70 79, Avenida de Santa María 5)* and *Casa Maruja* (☎ *986 85 49 01, Praza de Santa María 12)* around the corner. The former has only four homy doubles for around 3000 ptas, while the latter charges from 2500/4000 ptas for spotless rooms, some with private bath.

For those with a little more dosh to fling around, the elegant and popular *Hotel Ruas* (☎ *986 84 64 16, fax 986 84 64 11, Rúa de Padre Sarmiento 37)* provides rooms with bath, TV etc from 3500/6500 to 4500/8000 ptas plus IVA, depending on season.

At the top of the tree is one of Spain's more appealing paradores, *Parador Casa del Barón* (☎ *986 85 58 00, fax 986 85 51 00, Rúa do Barón 19).* Rooms here cost 12,000/15,000 ptas plus IVA at the height of the tourist season.

Places to Eat

The hub of Pontevedra's eating and drinking is the Cinco Calles area in the old town. You could keep yourself well occupied in the streets converging on Praza de Rogelio Lois, handily marked by a cruceiro. Look for the boiling tubs of chopped-up octopus at *Casa Fidel – O' Pulpeiro (Rúa de San Nicolás 7).* You can also eat cheaply at *O' Noso Bar (Rúa de San Nicolás 5). Restaurante A Cazoliña,* right on the little square, is more expensive.

O' Merlo (Avenida de Santa María 4) has an excellent 1000-ptas *menú.* Around the corner *El Masón (Rúa Alta 7)* is a slicker city-centre-type place serving delicious food; try the *brochetas de rape y langostinos* (1475 ptas).

Dessert is important in Pontevedra, and the town is known for its pastries, particularly its *tarta a las almendras,* an almond-topped cake you can find in many pastry shops around Rúa de Michelena.

Entertainment

The best places for coffee and people-watching are the cafes along the squares. Praza da Ferrería probably wins on this score. For drinking of a more nocturnal kind, head first for the pocket of bars on Rúa do Barón, and then, for some heftier *marcha* (action), up the road to Rúa de Charino – you'll soon get a feel for what's right for you. There is a nameless and popular *bar* on Praza da Verdura. If it's nightclubs you're after, try *Camawey (Rúa Cruz Roja 8),* open 1 to 4 am Thursday to Saturday, or check out the clubs on Rúa de Benito Corbal.

Getting There & Away

The bus station (☎ 986 85 24 08) is located a couple of kilometres south-east of the centre on Rúa Calvo Sotelo. At least 20 buses daily head for Santiago de Compostela, some stopping in Padrón, others heading ultimately for La Coruña and following the quicker A-9. Other buses serve Vigo, Orense, Lugo and Ferrol and smaller places on the Rías Bajas such as O Grove, Portonovo, Cangas and Moaña.

The train station (☎ 986 85 13 13) is by the bus station. Pontevedra is on the Vigo–La Coruña line, and there are almost hourly connections with those cities and Santiago de Compostela.

Getting Around

Local circle line buses run from the bus and train stations to Praza de España (the *gobierno civil* building).

RÍA DE PONTEVEDRA
Monasterio de San Juan de Poio

Just north-west of Pontevedra and 3km short of Combarro, the town of Poio is dominated by its grand monastery. This was long a Benedictine stronghold – the first church here may have been built in the 7th century – but the Benedictines abandoned the site in 1835, to be replaced 55 years later by the Mercedarios (roughly translated, the Fathers of Mercy). The gardens of the 16th-century Claustro de las Procesiones are gathered around a baroque fountain. You can visit two cloisters and the

GALICIA

church from 10 am to 1.30 pm and 4.30 pm to 8 pm daily, except Sunday morning. Within the complex, *Hospedería de Poio* (☎ 986 70 00) is open from Semana Santa/Easter to November; singles/doubles cost 2000/4600 ptas.

Combarro
postcode 36993 • pop 1300
Nothing could stand in greater contrast to the organised amusement of Sanxenxo, farther west along the northern shore of the ría, than the fishing village of Combarro. Although hardly indifferent to the tourist dollar, Combarro has managed to retain some measure of its original character. It is best known for the string of hórreos along and near the waterfront Rúa do Mar – a tranquil spot for a leisurely lunch. A tourist office operates 10 am to 2 pm and 4 to 9 pm daily.

There are at least three cheapish hostales along the main road from Pontevedra. *Hostal La Parada* (☎ 986 77 01 41, *Avenida de la Cruz 21*) has singles/doubles for 1700/3000 ptas, slightly more in July and August. Just up the road, *Hotel Xeito* (☎ 986 77 00 39, *Avenida de la Cruz 35*) has rooms at 5000/7000 ptas in July and August, 3000/5000 ptas in low season. You could enjoy well-prepared tapas or a full meal at the *Restaurante Alvariñas*, on Rúa do Mar.

The C-550 west towards Sanxenxo is fairly liberally laced with *hostales* and a few *camping grounds*.

La Unión company runs buses via Combarro en route from Pontevedra to O Grove.

Sanxenxo
postcode 36960 • pop 15,000
Sanxenxo (Sangenjo), farther west, is about as close as Galicia comes to emulating the holiday *costas* on the Mediterranean. Its best beach, **Praia de Silgar**, is fine and sandy, if crowded in summer. The town itself, however, has little to offer in the way of sights. A tourist office (☎ 986 72 02 85), Rúa de Madrid s/n, is open 10 am to 2pm and 4 to 9 pm daily July to mid-November.

One possible diversion is to take a boat to the **Isla de Ons**, beyond the mouth of the ría. Cruceros Rías Bajas (☎ 986 73 13 43),

based at Rúa Reboredo 76, O Grove, organises return trips from Sanxenxo and Portonovo from mid-July to mid-September. In Sanxenxo, buy tickets at the port, just east of Praia de Silgar.

As far as accommodation goes, late July to early September is the most difficult period, although in practice the main problem is elevated prices. Out of high season, quite a few places have moderately priced rooms. *Hotel Cucos* (☎ 986 72 01 64, *Rúa de Carlos Casas 17*) near Praia de Silgar has doubles ranging seasonally from 5350 to 8560 ptas. Slightly cheaper is the nearby *Hostal Casa Román* (☎ 986 72 00 31, *Rúa de Carlos Casas 2*).

For food and drink, you're best off trekking down the road a couple of kilometres west to **Portonovo**, where you'll find more *tapas* bars and *seafood* places than you can poke a stick at.

Buses between Pontevedra and O Grove stop here.

Playa de la Lanzada
The road swings around northwards from Sanxenxo towards O Grove past the longest beach in the Ría de Pontevedra – La Lanzada. There is a string of *camping grounds* and several *hostales* around here, but the beach is free of the resort feel. (But it's *not* deserted and remote!) Surfers may find the odd decent wave, although it is generally better for windsurfers. Buses between Pontevedra and O Grove will drop you on Playa de la Lanzada.

South Side
Don't be put off by the road from Pontevedra to Marín. It's an ugly business that bears little resemblance to what lies beyond Marín, a foul industrial port and home to the country's naval academy.

Hio & Around A few kilometres southwest of Aldán, the cluster of houses that constitutes Hio has its focal point in Galicia's most remarkable cruceiro. This was sculpted last century from a single block of stone and the great passages of Christian teaching, from Adam and Eve's sinful errors through

GALICIA

to the taking down of Christ from the cross, are narrated up its length.

A couple of kilometres on are a few tranquil beaches at **Vilanova**, while south of Hio, on the Ría de Vigo, are **Praia de Nerga**

Of Grain Stores & Crossroads

Away from the famous facades, Galicia is studded with a wealth of 'popular architecture' quite specific to the region. Most common of all is the *cruceiro*, a crucifix usually bearing a statue of Christ on one side and a distraught Virgin Mary on the other. The more ornate ones represent key scenes from the Bible. In both cases they are most commonly found at crossroads – where they served an orientational function for wayfarers in the days before street signs – and in churchyards. The bulk of them have been erected over the centuries by various religious orders and they are said to possess a protective power. They frequently became objects for local cult 'worship' of particular saints.

The simple 14th-century cruceiro of Melide, along the Camino de Santiago, is the oldest in existence, while the complex 19th-century one at Hio (Ría de Pontevedra), depicting the taking down of Christ from the cross, was carved from a single block of granite and is judged by those in the know to be the most beautiful.

The other odd-looking construction you'll see all over the place is the *hórreo*. Generally made of granite, and sometimes partly of wood, these rectangular structures have for centuries served as grain stores. Sitting on squat stilts, the hórreo serves to keep grain easily accessible and dry. Some, like the one in Carnota, are extremely long, generally a reflection of the owners' wealth. Your average family hórreo, nowadays more often than not used as a junk shed and somewhere to hang clothes, is of more modest proportions. If you cross the regional border into Asturias, you will immediately notice that the Asturians have their own version, a square-based wooden affair, sometimes with a tiled roof and quite often a sort of mini-veranda all the way around.

and **Praia de Barra**. Part of the latter is for nudists, and although both are good they can get windy. The reward for covering 5km of mostly dirt track from Hio to Cabo de Home is great views of the Islas Cíes and the Atlantic.

Hio is a peaceful base, and served by buses from Cangas. *Hostal Stop* (☎ 986 32 94 75, *Rúa Iglesiario 71)*, near the famous cruceiro, has rooms for as little as 1500/2300 ptas in winter, 3000/5000 ptas in summer. There are also *rooms* in Vilanova.

RÍA DE VIGO

It's enjoyable to drive along the northern bank of the ría, which is magnificent in parts. You can see serried ranks of bateas (see O Grove earlier) and observe Vigo in the distance. But except for the far western area around Hio – see the preceding Ría de Pontevedra section – this area is not one of Galicia's best.

Cangas and Moaña, along the northern shore, are served by buses from Pontevedra and Vigo and by frequent ferries from Vigo.

Drivers on the old N-550 down the east side of the ría could make a quick diversion east to the well-preserved **Castillo de Soutomaior**.

Moaña

The town has a modest Romanesque church. If you have transport, head a few kilometres inland to the **Mirador de Cotorredondo**, a lookout commanding magical views over both the Ría de Vigo, with its imposing suspension bridge, the Puente de Rande, and the Ría de Pontevedra.

Cangas

A bustling but ill-ordered port also passing for a resort, Cangas is arguably the ría's least attractive feature. Its big moment in history was a tragic one. In 1617 a band of several thousand Saracens (possibly Algerians) landed nearby and proceeded to sack the whole area in grand style. Such was the thoroughness of the slaughter, the story goes, that quite a few women went mad and became witches – some good *(meigas)* and others bad *(brujas)*. The Inquisition took things in hand, and so a number of these witches ended up burning at the stake. There is little of specific interest to see, although you could while away an hour or two strolling around the back streets of the port. There's a tourist information booth at the port.

If you feel some irresistible urge to stay the night, head for the eastern end of Praia de Rodeira (about a 2km walk from the bus station and port). *Hostal Playa* (☎ *986 30 36 74, Avenida de Orense 78)* has singles/doubles for 5900/6850 ptas in high season.

VIGO

postcode 36200 • pop 280,000

Arriving from anywhere else in Galicia, Vigo, a traffic-choked and chaotic city, can come as a shock. Its long port is protected from Atlantic disturbances by the Islas Cíes and once boasted a busy passenger terminal. These days, the farthest you'll get from Vigo by sea is the Islas Cíes, though big cruise liners drop in. The small, tangled nucleus of old Vigo exerts a fascination in a down-and-out sort of way, and hanging about the port and nearby cafes on a sunny afternoon is not unpleasant, but overall this city may disappoint given its wonderful setting.

People only started to notice Vigo in the Middle Ages as it began to overtake Bayona as a major port. Sir Francis Drake thought it sufficiently interesting to take control for a few days in 1589. In 1702 the English were back with their Dutch allies to sink a galleon fleet bearing gold from the Americas near where the Puente de Rande crosses the narrowest neck of the ría today.

Orientation

The Renfe train station is about 800m south-east of the town centre. Between the two you'll find plenty of accommodation, although for eating and drinking you're best off hunting around the old town area. From the station, Rúa Urzaiz and its pedestrianised continuation, Rúa do Príncipe, lead you to the centre and port. The bus station is on Avenida de Madrid, south of Praza de España.

Information

Tourist Offices Vigo has two main tourist offices. The excellent regional tourist office (☎ 986 43 05 77) on the Muelle de Trasatlánticos, by the Estación Marítima (ferry terminal), is open 9.30 am to 2 pm and 4.30 to 6.30 pm weekdays, 10 am to noon Saturday. The municipal tourist office, on the 10th floor of the tall concello building on Praza do Rei, is open 9 am to 2 pm and 4.30 to 6.30 pm weekdays and 10 am to 12.30 pm Saturday. Other offices open in summer on Praza de España, Praza da Estación (train station) and at the airport for incoming flights.

Money There is no shortage of banks, mostly with ATMs, particularly around Rúa do Príncipe.

Post & Communications You'll find the main post office on Rúa da Victoria; you can make phone calls here.

Medical Services & Emergency Call ☎ 091 in a police emergency. There is a national police station at Rúa de Luís Taboada 3. The nearest hospital to the city centre is the Hospital Xeral (☎ 986 81 60 00), near Praza de España.

Old Town

Praza da Constitución, lined by elegant old houses seated above arcades, marks the entrance to the old town *(casco antiguo)* from the bustling thoroughfares of downtown Vigo. Take Rúa dos Cesteiros north and you'll come upon the **Iglesia Colegiata de Santa María**, a neoclassical construction of 1816. Nearby **Praza da Pedra** hosts a sad-looking, off-the-back-of-a-boat market where the *ostreiras* (oyster catchers) hawk their slithery wares in the morning. Rúa Real is the old town's main street, on or near which you'll find a fair selection of taverns.

Parque do Castro

Directly south (and uphill) of the old town you can wander in this park for a little peace and quiet, and have a look at the **castillo**

GALICIA

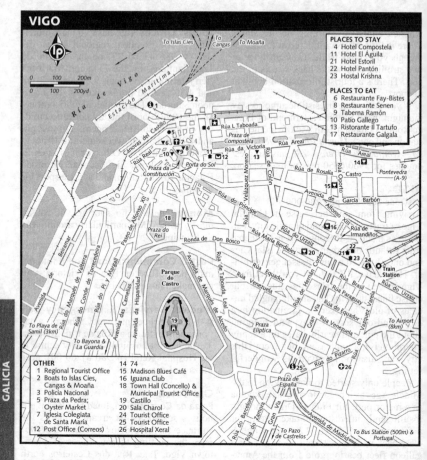

VIGO

PLACES TO STAY
4   Hotel Compostela
11 Hotel El Águila
21 Hotel Estoril
22 Hotel Pantón
23 Hostal Krishna

PLACES TO EAT
6   Restaurante Fay-Bistes
8   Restaurante Senen
9   Taberna Ramón
10 Patio Gallego
13 Ristorante Il Tartufo
17 Restaurante Galgala

OTHER
1   Regional Tourist Office
2   Boats to Islas Cíes,
    Cangas & Moaña
3   Policía Nacional
5   Praza da Pedra;
    Oyster Market
7   Iglesia Colegiata
    de Santa María
12 Post Office (Correos)
14 74
15 Madison Blues Café
16 Iguana Club
18 Town Hall (Concello) &
    Municipal Tourist Office
19 Castillo
20 Sala Charol
24 Tourist Office
25 Tourist Office
26 Hospital Xeral

that formed part of the town defences built under Felipe IV.

Beaches

The best beaches within reach are to the south-west at **Playa de Samil** and, farther on, **Canido**. Local bus Nos 15, 16 and 27 pass Samil beach; No 10 goes to the beach at Canido.

Places to Stay

Around the Train Station There's a host of hotels around the train station, not distressingly far from the centre. *Hotel Pantón*

(☎ 986 22 42 70, Rúa de Lepanto 18) has singles/doubles with bathroom and TV for 3300/5900 ptas plus IVA. *Hotel Estoril* (☎ 986 43 61 22, Rúa Lepanto 12) has good rooms for 2500/3500 ptas most of the year, 3000/6000 ptas in high season. Close by, *Hostal Krishna* (☎ 986 22 81 61, Rúa do Urzaiz 57) has modern and spacious, if unspectacular, rooms for 2000/3000 ptas out of season, but doubles only, for 4500 to 6500 ptas, in July and August.

Around the Old Town In the heart of the old town is a sprinkling of generally

GALICIA

run-down and poor-value *casas de huéspedes* (marked by blue 'CH' signs) and *fondas*.

Rooms with bath and TV at *Hotel El Águila* (☎ 986 43 13 98, *Rúa do Victoria 6*) have rates that vary seasonally from 3200/4000 to 4000/5900 ptas. *Hotel Compostela* (☎ 986 22 82 27, *Rúa García Olloqui 5*) is a step up in price and a few paces closer to the port. Comfortable rooms cost 6400/9200 ptas plus IVA in July and August.

Places to Eat

The winding lanes and blind alleys of old Vigo are laced with tapas bars and eateries of all descriptions – part of the fun is looking around. *Taberna Ramón (Rúa dos Cesteiros 2A)* is a cheap, spit-and-sawdust place off Praza da Constitución – itself a pleasant spot for a morning coffee. *Patio Gallego (Rúa dos Cesteiros 7)* has a decent set lunch for 1100 ptas; *Restaurante Senen (Rúa da Palma 3)* is similar, as is *Restaurante Fay-Bistes (Rúa Real 7)*, which has a set lunch for 1000 ptas and good tapas.

If you want a change, *Ristorante Il Tartufo (Praza de Compostela 16)* is hard to beat for quality Italian food. The pasta is made on the premises and most dishes are around 1000 ptas. Vegetarians can enjoy a variety of inexpensive dishes, all under 1100 ptas, at *Restaurante Galgala (Rúa Placer 4)*, near the concello building.

Entertainment

On the weekends in particular, head for Rúa Real in the old town. Here and in the surrounding lanes is a fair smattering of taverns.

The *zona de marcha*, or nightlife area centres on the area around the train station. You'll find a few busy places on little lanes such as Rúa de Churruca (try *Iguana Club*) and Rúa de Irmandiños.

A late-night drinking place that attracts a mixed crowd is *74 (Rúa Areal 74)*. *Madison Blues Café (Rúa Oporto 26)* has live music some nights. For Galician folk music, try *Sala Charol* (☎ 986 22 30 30, *Rúa María Berdiales*). In summer, the Playa de Samil area also gets busy late at night.

Getting There & Away

Air Vigo's Peinador airport (☎ 986 26 82 00) is about 10km east of town. Iberia flies to/from Bilbao, Barcelona, Madrid and Valladolid. Air Europa and Spanair also have flights.

Bus From the bus station (☎ 986 37 34 11) on Avenida de Madrid, well south of the centre, you can pick up services to all the main Galician destinations (with the Castromil line) as well as long-distance ones such as Madrid (with AutoRes) and Barcelona and the Basque Country (both with Vibasa). ATSA runs plenty of buses to destinations south such as Bayona, Tuy and La Guardia. La Unión runs a few buses to the southern parts of the Rías Bajas.

Train There are three trains daily to Madrid (5900 ptas), one or two to Barcelona via Oviedo (6500 ptas), and one to Irún on the French border. Regular services run to Santiago de Compostela (690 ptas), Pontevedra (345 ptas) and La Coruña (1500 ptas), and three daily to Orense (1100 to 1500 ptas). Two trains run daily to Porto, Portugal. For more information, call the station on ☎ 986 43 11 14.

Car & Motorcycle The A-9 tollway runs to La Coruña via Pontevedra (340 ptas) and Santiago.

Boat Ferries to Cangas sail about every half-hour 6.30 am to 10.30 pm, and Moaña ferries go hourly; it costs 250 ptas to either place. For ferries to Islas Cíes, see the Islas Cíes section following.

Getting Around

Vigo has a fairly decent local bus system. From Porta do Sol, No 9 goes to the airport and Nos 21, 14 and 7 stop close to the bus station.

ISLAS CÍES

The best beaches in the Rías Bajas aren't really in the rías at all. Rather, you need to head out for the Islas (Illas) Cíes. Of the three islands, access to one is for private

GALICIA

boats only. The other two, Isla de Monte Faro and Isla de Monte Agudo, are linked by a white sandy crescent that also forms a lagoon known as Lago dos Nenos. The little archipelago forms a 9km breakwater that protects Vigo and its harbour from the Atlantic's fury. Together with the Islas de Ons and Sálvora to the north and a couple of other Galician islets, the Islas Cíes are on the verge of being declared the **Parque Nacional de Islas Atlánticas**.

You can only visit the islands on weekends from Semana Santa/Easter to mid-June, or daily from mid-June to the end of September, and numbers are strictly limited. To stay overnight you must book for the island *camping ground* at the Estación Marítima (☎ 986 43 83 58) in Vigo – places are limited to 800 people daily. You pay a 1000-ptas reservation fee for the camping voucher, and you can then organise a return boat ticket for the day you require. Without the camping voucher, you must get a same-day return ticket. Camping costs 575 ptas per person and per tent plus IVA. At the camping ground, the 1000-ptas reservation fee will be used as a credit towards your overall camping costs.

The return boat ticket costs 2000 ptas and four boats daily are scheduled from Vigo. While it is also possible to get a boat to the islands from Bayona, you can only arrange camping from Vigo. For boat information, call ☎ 986 22 52 72.

The South

THE COAST
Bayona
postcode 36209 • pop 10,100

On 1 March 1493, the caravel *Pinta* came into view off Bayona, bearing the remarkable news that Columbus had made it to the Indies. In fact, as would later become clear, he and his band had bumped into something quite different – the Americas. In those days Bayona (Baiona) was an important trading port. Later it was eclipsed by Vigo, and in the 17th century its population dropped to 150. Today it is one of Galicia's premier summer resorts, but understated compared with its Mediterranean counterparts.

There is a tourist information booth (☎ 986 68 70 67) just before the gateway to the parador and city walls. It's open 10.30 am to 2 pm and 4 to 8 pm daily.

The mighty **walls** stretching round the pine-covered western side of town were erected between the 11th and 17th centuries. It costs 100 ptas to walk into the grounds (500 ptas to drive in), and it's worth it. In the placid harbour, a remake of the *Pinta* serves as a small **Museo Flotante**. On the way west out of town is the unlovely 15m stone statue of the Virgen de la Roca, finished in 1930. You can climb up inside the statue (if it's open) and take in the views from the boat-shaped lookout in her hand.

For beaches, head out on the coast road to Vigo, north-east. First up is **Praia Ladeira**, but better is the **Praia América**, a couple of kilometres farther on. Most Vigo buses call in at these beaches. On the way, at **A Ramallosa**, you'll notice a wonderful old medieval bridge (often mistaken for a Roman one). There was a time when women three months pregnant came here to perform superstitious rites to assure themselves of an easy birth.

Places to Stay & Eat A couple of camping grounds are open in summer. *Bayona Playa* (☎ 986 35 00 35), at Sabaris on Praia Ladeira, charges 690 ptas per person, 490 ptas per tent, 760 ptas per car.

Some of the cheapest rooms are at *Hospedaje Kin* (☎ 986 35 56 95, Rúa de Ventura Misa 29) – inquire in the cafe of the same name at No 53. Singles/doubles start at 2000/3000 ptas, with doubles going up to 5000 ptas. Or try *Hostal Mosquito* (☎ 986 35 50 37, Calle Ciudad de Vigo 1), which has doubles for 2500 ptas. *Hostal Santa Marta* (☎ 986 35 70 45, Barrio del Burgos s/n) is more expensive at 5000 ptas a double.

The cobbled lanes in the centre of town, including Rúa de José Antonio, Rúa do Conde and Rúa de Ventura Misa, are full of restaurants, tapas bars and watering holes. Try the *Freiduría Jaqueyvi (Rúa José Antonio 2)*.

Galician Round-Up

The length of Galicia's Atlantic coast is dotted with pastures favoured by semiwild horses, particularly in the hills south and east of Bayona, but also in the north around Cabo Ortegal. Locals occasionally head out to round the horses up in what becomes a day-long fiesta, or *curro*. You'll need to ask around for information about when and where they are on. At the time of writing, curros were held in the following villages, but there are bound to be others:

June
  Torroña (south of Bayona), first Sunday
  Mougas (south of Bayona), second Sunday
  Morgadanes (east of Bayona), third Sunday
  San Cibrán (east of Bayona), fourth Sunday

July
  Curota, Pobra do Caramiñal, second Sunday

August
  Galiñeiro (near Gondomar, east of Bayona), last Sunday

Getting There & Away Frequent buses north for Vigo and south towards La Guardia (A Guarda) leave from beside the entrance to the port. Most of the latter also go to Tuy. In summer you can get boats to the Islas Cíes (see that section earlier in this chapter).

Oia

postcode 36390 • pop 3100
About 20km south of Bayona, a small cove giving shelter to some fishing boats is presided over by the majestic baroque facade of the **Monasterio de Santa María de Oia**. Although the present facade was erected in 1740, the monastery church dates from the 16th century, when it was remodelled.

La Guardia

postcode 36780 • pop 6200
A ramshackle and unlovely port, La Guardia (A Guarda, A Garda) is nevertheless in a

prime position, sitting just north of where the Río Miño enters the Atlantic. There is a tourist information office (☎ 986 61 18 50) on Calle de Rosalía de Castro.

The treat here is to head south out of the town centre up Monte de Santa Tecla (50 ptas per person if you drive up). On the way up you can inspect a Celtic castro, where a couple of the primitive circular dwellings have been restored. At the top is a small museum with some Celtic finds, open 10 am to 6 pm daily in summer and 5 to 7 pm in winter (free). Even better than all that are the wonderful views up the Miño, across to Portugal and out over the Atlantic.

A few kilometres south of La Guardia you'll find a beach at **Camposancos**, just inside the heads of the Río Miño, although you'd be much better off on the other side of the river and on an ocean beach in Portugal.

Places to Stay & Eat The best place to choose is the *Hotel Pazo de Santa Tecla* (☎ 986 61 00 02), up on top of the mountain. Average singles/doubles with bath cost 3600/4650 ptas plus IVA. The best feature of the hotel is the view. There's also a restaurant here.

There are several undistinguished budget hotels in the town itself. *Hostal Celta* (☎ 986 61 09 11, Calle de Pontevedra s/n) has basic rooms for 2700/4000 ptas, and slightly better ones with own bath for 3000/4300 ptas. *Hostal Martirrey* (☎ 986 61 03 49, Calle de José Antonio 8) charges up to 2800/4400 ptas for its rooms in high season.

Hunt around the centre of town for *tapas bars* – most of what you eat will have been caught that day.

Getting There & Away ATSA has regular buses to Vigo via Bayona, and some to Tuy. In summer, buses run to the Camposancos beaches.

A ferry crosses from Camposancos to Caminha in Portugal (from where you can get to the first in a string of sandy ocean beaches on the way south to Viana do Castelo). The cost is 50 ptas per person and 450 ptas per car.

GALICIA

RÍO MIÑO
Tuy

postcode 36700 • pop 15,200

Tuy (Tui) is a gem, a pretty old town sitting on the Río Miño. Especially popular in summer when its little bars come alive, it is ideally situated by a bridge across to Portugal's equally interesting Valença. Some of Portugal's best northern beaches are just 35km away. A fair crowd of Portuguese day-trippers fill Tuy on weekends, and Spaniards reciprocate in Valença.

Called Tude by the Romans, Tuy later for a short while hosted the court of the Visigothic king Witiza (702–10). Tuy was subsequently attacked several times by Spain's Muslim invaders and Norman raiders. Later still, it found itself on the frontline during various wars between Spain and Portugal.

The tourist office (☎ 986 60 17 89), on Avenida de Portugal, is in a kiosk about 1km before the Portuguese frontier.

Things to See The brooding, fortress-like **catedral** dominates Tuy's small medieval centre. Completed in 1287, it was much altered in the 15th century and the extra stone bracing was added after the Lisbon earthquake in 1755. The main 13th-century portal is opulently decorated with sculptures in a style typical of many Galician churches. If you want to visit the cloister and Museo Catedralicio, and climb the Torre de Sotomayor, the ticket will cost you 300 ptas. The cathedral is open 9.30 am to 1.30 pm and 4 to 7 pm weekdays, 1 to 10 pm Saturday and Sunday.

Opposite, stands the **Museo Diocesano**, with a modest archaeology collection; it's open 10.30 am to 1.30 pm and 4 to 8 pm Tuesday to Sunday (200 ptas).

The surrounding steep, narrow lanes all afford tempting glimpses of Portugal across the Miño. They shelter a pair of cruceiros and chapels, including the **Capilla de San Telmo** (St Elmo), which contains relics of the patron saint of sailors.

Beyond the old town centre, the pleasant riverside walk around the **Convento de San Domingo** is enticing. The monastery church's baroque facade hides a largely 14th-century interior.

While here, take a look at the charming Portuguese fortress town of **Valença**, just across the century-old Puente Internacional. With border formalities nonexistent, it makes a pleasant diversion even if you don't want to go any farther into Portugal.

Places to Stay You'll find a couple of simple places to stay in the centre of town – but they fill up quickly in August. *Hostal Generosa (☎ 986 60 00 55, Calle de Calvo Sotelo 37)* has singles/doubles for 2100/3000 ptas. *Hostal Cruceiro do Monte (☎ 986 60 09 53, Carretera de Bayona 23)* has a good reputation and offers decent rooms with bath for 3500/4500 ptas. Or you could try *Hostal Alonso (☎ 986 63 90 54)* on Calle Baños Caldelas de Tuy, where doubles are 3700 ptas. *Parador de Tuy (☎ 986 60 03 09, fax 986 60 21 63, Avenida de Portugal s/n)* has rooms for 12,000/15,000 ptas plus IVA.

Places to Eat There are several inviting places in the area immediately around the cathedral. Try the *Jamonería* on Plaza del Generalísimo or *Pizzeria di Marco* on Calle de Seijas. The streets between the cathedral and the river are laced with great drinking establishments. A good one with views of the river is *Pub Zuriza* on Calle de Cuenca.

Getting There & Away Buses stop along Paseo de Calvo Sotelo, the main road through town. ATSA has regular services to Vigo and La Guardia, and you can also get to Bayona and Pontevedra. On weekdays a few buses go to Valença.

The train station, north of the centre, is on the line between Vigo and Porto (Portugal), with two trains daily each way. More trains run to Porto from Valença. For other destinations such as León, Bilbao, and other cities in Galicia, you'll need to get to the train station at Guillarey (Guillarei), a few kilometres east. It's probably easier to make for Vigo first.

Goyán

About 20km south-west of Tuy, Goyán (Goián) has a car ferry to Vila Nova de Cerveira in Portugal every 30 minutes (350 ptas plus 100 ptas per passenger).

GALICIA

Ribadavia

postcode 32400 • pop 1850

About 80km up the Miño from Tuy towards Orense, Ribadavia is in the heart of Ribeiro wine country. It was once Galicia's most important Jewish settlement. Even after Fernando and Isabel, the Catholic Monarchs, decided to expel Jews in 1492, most managed to hang on, either converting to Christianity or fleeing temporarily to Portugal and returning after the hue and cry had died down.

The tourist booth (☎ 988 47 12 75), on Praza Maior, is open 9.30 am to 3 pm and 5 to 9 pm Monday to Saturday and 10.30 am to 3.30 pm and 5 to 8 pm Sunday in summer.

It is a pleasure to wander around the medieval town centre, characterised by a patchwork of uneven little cobbled squares, lined with heavy stone arcades and galerías. The **Barrio Judío** (Jewish Quarter) is signposted and the usually indifferent weather lends the area a melancholy air. Nearby Praza de García Boente is fronted by the **Casa de la Inquisición**. Of the several churches dotted about the town, the Romanesque **Iglesia de Santiago** and **Iglesia de San Juan** stand out. The remains of the castle date from the 15th century.

There's nowhere much to stay in the centre of this surprisingly big town, unless you get lucky with a cheap room at *Bar Celta* (☎ 988 47 08 67, Praza da Fonte de Prata 8). *Hostal Vista Alegre* (☎ 988 47 12 86, Avenida Rodríguez de la Fuente 14) is a possibility at 1500 ptas per person. *Hostal Evencio 2* (☎ 988 47 10 45, Avenida de Rodríguez Valcarcel 30), out of town, has singles/doubles for 2500/5000 ptas. To eat and drink in a tavern atmosphere, dive into the gloomy and cavernous *Bar O Xudío* (Rúa de Caula 10), between Praza Maior and Praza da Magdalena.

Regular buses run to Orense from a station nearby. Two or three trains daily run to Vigo and Orense from a station just over the Río Avia.

Celanova

Drivers crossing southern Galicia have the option of bypassing Orense in favour of the C-531 through Celanova. The route from Ribadavia to Celanova via Cortegada is a marvel of green – mostly Ribeiro vines – and of curves. Celanova, once you reach it, is a nondescript sort of place except for the massive, recently restored **Monasterio de San Rosendo** on Praza Maior. The complex includes an impressive church, two handsome cloisters and a tiny 10th-century Mozarabic chapel, the **Oratorio de San Miguel**, as well as, nowadays, a school and municipal offices.

The East

With the notable exception of the well-trodden Camino de Santiago, Galicia's deep interior is little visited. Of its cities, Orense has a surprisingly attractive, compact centre, while Lugo's main claim to fame is its Roman walls. Away from the towns, nothing human-made can match the natural splendour of the Sil Gorge.

ORENSE

postcode 32080 • pop 107,000

Orense (Ourense in Galician) may well be the first Galician city encountered by travellers arriving from neighbouring Castile. First impressions are of an unexciting sprawl of apartment blocks, but give it a chance, for at Orense's core is a wonderful old town bursting with life.

History

Orense was a Roman settlement of some importance. The Visigoths raised a cathedral here but the Muslims destroyed the place during several raids. Repopulated by Sancho II of Castile in 1071, the town eventually began to take off as a trade centre. Orense's considerable Jewish population, having contributed generously to the campaign against Granada, was rewarded in 1492 with expulsion – an order that the local branch of the Spanish Inquisition was particularly scrupulous in executing. Essentially an ecclesiastical town, it declined for centuries until the arrival of the railway in 1882.

GALICIA

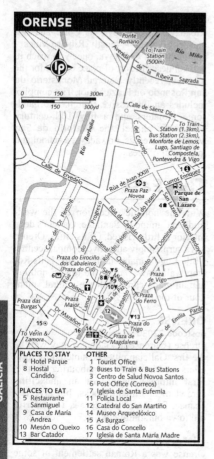

ORENSE

```
0    150    300m
0    150    300yd
```

Ponte Romano
Avenida de la Ribeira Sagrada
Río Miño
To Train Station (500m)
Calle de Sáenz Díez
Río Barbaña
Calle del Correo
To Train Station (1.3km), Bus Station (2.3km), Monforte de Lemos, Lugo, Santiago de Compostela, Pontevedra & Vigo
Calle de Ervedelo
Rúa de Juan XXIII
Curros Enríquez
Praza Paz Novoa
Parque de San Lázaro
Calle de Fleming
Progreso
Rúa do Paseo
Rúa do Capitán Eloy
Rúa do Santo
Manuel Bedoyo
Calle de Cardenal Quiroga
Domingo
Praza do Eirociño dos Cabaleiros (Praza do Cid)
Rúa San Miguel
Praza de Vigo
Calle de Obispo
Rúa de Lepanto
Praza do Ferro
Praza das Burgas
Praza Maior
Dr Marañón
Praza do Trigo
Calle de Emilia Pardo
To Verín & Zamora
Praza de Magdalena

PLACES TO STAY
4 Hotel Parque
8 Hostal Cándido

PLACES TO EAT
5 Restaurante Sanmiguel
9 Casa de María Andrea
10 Mesón O Queixo
13 Bar Catador

OTHER
1 Tourist Office
2 Buses to Train & Bus Stations
3 Centro de Salud Novoa Santos
6 Post Office (Correos)
7 Iglesia de Santa Eufemia
11 Policía Local
12 Catedral do San Martiño
14 Museo Arqueolóxico
15 As Burgas
16 Casa do Concello
17 Iglesia de Santa María Madre

GALICIA

Orientation

The train station, on Plaza de la Estación, is 500m north of the Río Miño, and the bus station, at Carretera de Vigo 1, a farther 1km north-west. On foot you can approach the city centre across the Ponte Romano, a mostly medieval bridge constructed in place of an older Roman one. Head for the Catedral do San Martiño, around which unfolds the old town (casco antiguo). Rúa do Capitán Eloy marks the northern boundary of this old part of the centre, the life of which is played out on Praza Maior, Praza do Trigo and Praza do Ferro.

Information

The tourist office (☎ 988 37 20 20), at Rúa Curros Enríquez 1, is open 9 am to 9 pm daily in summer (less hours during winter).

There's no shortage of banks along Rúa Curros Enríquez and its continuation, Rúa do Paseo. The Policía Local (☎ 988 38 81 38) are just by the cathedral. The handiest medical clinic, Centro de Salud Novoa Santos (☎ 988 38 55 80), is at Rúa de Juan XXIII 6-8.

Casco Antiguo

A leap of about 1000 years and a walk south into the old town brings you to the **Catedral do San Martiño**, a rather gloomy 13th-century church whose main feature is the Pórtico do Paraíso, a Gothic copy of Santiago de Compostela's Pórtico de la Gloria.

Around the cathedral spreads a web of charming little squares and alleyways, inviting exploration by day or night. Sloping **Praza Maior** is the grandest, hemmed in by arcaded walkways, above which stand out the elegant galerías of private houses. At one end of the plaza are the dignified Casa do Concello (town hall) and, next door, Orense's **Museo Arqueolóxico** (Archaeological Museum), which is open daily except Monday.

As Burgas

Since the Romans arrived on the scene, Orense's thermal waters have been a blessing for the sick and tired, or simply those with sore feet. The steaming mineral waters gush out in fountains on Praza das Burgas, and the water is still used for heating in the surrounding houses.

Places to Stay

The choice area is around the cathedral. *Hostal Cándido* (☎ 988 22 96 07, Rúa dos Irmáns Villar 25), one of four places on this narrow street or adjacent Rúa San Miguel, has singles/doubles with bath for 2500/3800 ptas. *Hotel Parque* (☎ 988 23 36 11, fax 988 23 96 36, Parque de San Lázaro 24), though outside the old city, is a good bet for something a little more comfortable. Rooms with bath and TV are 3210/5350 ptas.

Places to Eat

The streets and squares around the cathedral are bursting with restaurants, tapas bars, cafes and watering holes. For simple Galician and Spanish dishes, head for *Bar Catador* on Rúa dos Fornos; main dishes are 700 to 900 ptas. Orense's top restaurant is *Restaurante Sanmiguel (Rúa San Miguel 18)*; the 1400-ptas *menú* in its attached cafe allows you to enjoy its cooking without breaking the bank. On nearby Praza do Eirociño dos Cabaleiros (Praza do Cid), *Casa de María Andrea* serves another excellent lunch *menú* (1350 ptas). Next door, *Mesón O Queixo* is a jolly spot specialising in great cheese tapas.

Getting There & Away

Several buses a day run to all Galicia's other main cities. The trip to Santiago de Compostela takes 2½ hours (1190 ptas). Daily buses also go to most other regions of Spain, including five or more to Madrid (six hours, 3525 ptas). Up to six daily head to Feces (930 ptas) on the Portuguese border (south of Verín), where they connect with buses to Chaves, from where there are buses to many Portuguese destinations. Five buses a week go from Orense to Viana do Castelo and Vila do Conde (five hours) on the Portuguese coast north of Porto.

A few trains a day run to Santiago de Compostela (1¼ to two hours, 945 to 2000 ptas), Vigo, Pontevedra, La Coruña and León. Others head for Zamora, Ávila, Madrid (six hours, 5100 ptas) and Barcelona.

Getting Around

Local bus Nos 1, 3, 6, 8, 12, 15 and 33 run between the train station and Parque de San Lázaro in the centre. Nos 6 and 12 also serve the bus station.

CASTILLO DE MONTERREI

The N-525 south-east of Orense crosses several low ranges on the way to Castilla y León. Outside Verín the N-532 diverges south to Feces on the Portuguese border. If you have your own transport, it's worth detouring to the Castillo de Monterrei, in a commanding position just west of Verín. Its main tower offers spectacular views on all sides. The castle is open 10.30 am to 1.30 pm and 4 to 7 pm Wednesday to Sunday (free).

RÍO SIL

The N-120 north-east from Orense follows the Río Miño, a pretty stretch but nothing compared to what's in store if you turn off east at Os Peares. Here the Miño meets the Río Sil, and the ensuing 15km make for a spectacular drive along the upper levels of the **Gargantas del Sil** (Sil Gorges). The Orense-Monforte railway also follows the gorge for a few kilometres.

The road ends in a T-junction with another minor road. If you turn right (west) here (towards Orense), after 5km you'll reach the **Monasterio de San Esteban (Mosteiro de Santo Estevo) de Ribas de Sil**. Some of this huge complex, with three cloisters, dates from the 10th century, although much has been stripped bare. The monastery is normally open from about 10 am to 2 pm and 5 to 7 or 8 pm daily, but at the time of writing was closed for construction of a hotel on the premises. The hotel is likely to open, and the monastery to reopen to visitors, in late 2001.

Two buses daily except Sunday from Orense to Parada do Sil stop at the monastery and could also drop you at the T-junction mentioned above.

From the monastery those with a vehicle have the option of heading back eastward past the T-junction and on towards Castilla y León. It's a picturesque route through woods and across high, windswept heath, with the Sil Gorges never far away. **Castro Caldelas** has a nice castle; shame about the town, but there are a couple of hostales if you need one. Twenty-seven kilometres north-east of Pobra de Trives, your road meets the N-120 again.

MONFORTE DE LEMOS

postcode 27400 • pop 20,000

Inhabited before the Romans appeared and later converted into the medieval Mons Forti, this dishevelled place, north-east of Orense, has made a living as Galicia's principal rail junction since 1883. It's actually

GALICIA

quite interesting if you should be caught between trains.

Long before you reach the town centre you'll see the **Torre del Homenaje**, the most intact part of the 13th-century castle at the top of the *monte forte*. Across the river from the town centre stands the proud **Colegio de Nuestra Señora la Antigua**, which once housed a Jesuit seminary.

Should you decide to stay, head for the 16th-century bridge over the Río Cabe. *Hostal Puente Romano* (☎ 982 41 11 68, Plaza Doctor Goyanes 7) has singles/doubles with bath for 2140/3745 ptas. There are a few *cafes* and *eateries* around the bridge and river.

Many trains crossing Galicia call in here. Several buses a day head north to Lugo and south-west to Orense, and a few east to Ponferrada and León (the station is near the centre).

SERRAS DO COUREL & DOS ANCARES

North of the Río Sil along Galicia's eastern border, these two remote ranges form the beginnings (or end) of the Cordillera Cantábrica. With abundant wildlife and flora, they make good walking territory and four outings in them are described in Lonely Planet's *Walking in Spain*. The Ponferrada-Lugo road (A-6) and the Camino Francés of the Camino de Santiago both pass between the two ranges.

CAMINO DE SANTIAGO

The main route of the Camino de Santiago, the Camino Francés, crosses the middle of Galicia en route from Castilla y León to Santiago de Compostela. For information on a couple of spots you might detour to if you're travelling in this region, see the special section 'Camino de Santiago' earlier in this book.

LUGO

postcode 27080 • pop 80,000
Lugo has impressive Roman walls and makes an interesting stop for a few hours, but is not the most tantalising place in Galicia to linger.

The Romans established Lucus Augusti over a Celtic castro in the 1st century BC. The walls went up three centuries later, but failed to keep out the Suevi in 460, or indeed the Muslims 300 years later. Until well into the 19th century the city gates were closed at night and tolls were charged to bring in goods from outside.

Orientation & Information

Whether you arrive in Lugo by train or bus (the latter is more convenient), you will end up not too far outside the circuit of Roman walls.

The tourist office (☎ 982 23 13 61) is in an arcade at Praza Maior 27–29. You'll find several banks and ATMs on nearby Rúa da Raiña and Praza de Santo Domingo. The Policía Local (☎ 982 29 71 10) are on Praza da Constitución, a few steps from the bus station. The Hospital Xeral Calde (☎ 982 29 60 00) is at Rúa Doutor Ochoa s/n, about 600m west of the old town. Be aware that the area between the cathedral and the Porta do Carmen is an unsavoury red-light zone.

Roman Walls

More than 2km round and up to 15m high, the Roman walls enclosing Lugo are the best preserved of their kind in all of Spain, if not the world. You can climb atop them – one convenient access point is the Porta de Santiago (Gate of Santiago) near the cathedral – and walk right around the town.

Catedral

Back on the ground inside the Porta de Santiago, the imposing grey cathedral might not at first glance seem a basically Romanesque-Gothic structure, but it was begun in 1129, inspired by the cathedral in Santiago de Compostela. Work went on until the 14th century, and a neoclassical layer was coated on later still. The northern doorway, however, remains obviously Romanesque. Inside, the walnut choir stalls are a baroque masterpiece. The cathedral is open 8 am to 8.30 pm daily.

Museo Provincial

Considered Galicia's best museum, the Provincial Museum at Praza do Soedade 6

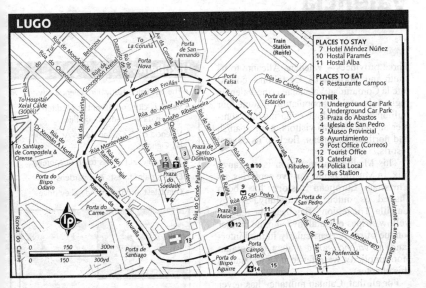

LUGO

PLACES TO STAY
7 Hotel Méndez Núñez
10 Hostal Paramés
11 Hostal Alba

PLACES TO EAT
6 Restaurante Campos

OTHER
1 Underground Car Park
2 Underground Car Park
3 Praza do Abastos
4 Iglesia de San Pedro
5 Museo Provincial
8 Ayuntamiento
9 Post Office (Correos)
12 Tourist Office
13 Catedral
14 Policia Local
15 Bus Station

includes what remains of the Convento de San Francisco – a Gothic cloister and the convent kitchen and refectory. The collections range from pre-Roman gold jewellery and Roman mosaics, to Galician art from the 15th to 20th centuries. The museum is open 10.30 or 11 am to 2 pm and 4.30 or 5 to 8 pm Monday to Saturday, 11 am to 2 pm Sunday, closed Saturday afternoon and Sunday in July and August (free).

Places to Stay & Eat

Hostal Alba (☎ 982 22 60 56, Rúa de Calvo Sotelo 31) has simple singles/doubles with shared baths for 1610/3210 ptas. The friendly *Hostal Paramés* (☎ 982 22 62 51, Rúa do Progreso 28) is a good choice at 2800/4500 ptas for rooms with bath and TV. If you want something classier within the walls, you've got to jump to the *Hotel Méndez*

Núñez (☎ 982 23 07 11, Rúa da Raiña 1), charging 7000/9100 ptas in summer.

Rúa Nova is full to bursting with tapas bars and restaurants. You can get a good seafood meal for around 2000 ptas at *Restaurante Campos (Rúa Nova 4)*.

Getting There & Away

Several buses a day run to Santiago de Compostela (two hours, 930 ptas), La Coruña (1½ hours, 1025 ptas), Ponferrada and Madrid (six hours, 4170 ptas). Two or three head for Orense, Pontevedra, Vigo, León, Ribadeo and Luarca on the north coast, and across Asturias, Cantabria and the Basque Country.

Up to five trains run north-west to La Coruña (two hours, 865 to 1600 ptas) and south to Monforte de Lemos. One or two of the latter continue across Castilla y León to Madrid or Barcelona.

GALICIA

Valencia

Three provinces – Valencia, Alicante to its south and, northwards, Castellón – constitute la Comunidad Valenciana (the Valencia region). Its resident population of some four million more than doubles during high summer and holidays as visitors, both Spanish and northern European, flock to its coastal resorts.

This Mediterranean region is a strange mix. In Muslim hands for five centuries, its Christian European history has been shaped as much by Catalunya as by Castilla. The region's flag bears the red and yellow stripes of Catalunya and the mother tongue of many (particularly in the hinterland) is *valenciano,* a dialect of Catalan (for simplicity we refer to it as Catalan in this chapter).

For all that, Catalan militancy has never been as strong here as in its northern neighbour. True, more and more street signs and place names now appear in Catalan but it's a political gesture – and often as not the Castilian name figures too.

Valencia, the capital, is famed for its exuberant nightlife and the wild Las Fallas festival.

To the north along the Costa del Azahar is a string of low-key resorts and several worthwhile attractions, including the historic town of Sagunto.

Too much of the Costa Blanca, south of Valencia, is a Spanish horror story. The ghastly tourist developments reach their dubious pinnacle in a kind of Manhattan on Med – the infamous Benidorm. But the story isn't all bad. Like beachcombers with a metal detector, the patient traveller will uncover a few gems along the coast that have retained their charm – the old towns of Jávea and Altea in particular. And many of the beaches are indeed beautiful, even if the people you rub shoulders with are mainly splotchy Dutch, Brits and Germans.

Inland, west of the A-7 coastal motorway, lies another world. Mountains buckle towards the rough and ready interior of

Highlights

- The Las Fallas festival in Valencia city
- Valencia city and Alicante's Mediterranean dawn-to-dusk nightlife
- Valencia city's Ciudad de las Artes y de las Ciencias
- The medieval fortress town of Morella
- Elche's palm forests and gardens
- Guadalest and the inland valley drive

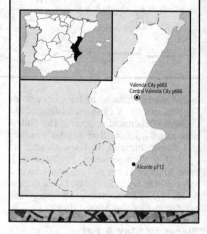

Valencia City p683
Central Valencia City p686

Alicante p712

Aragón, Castilla-La Mancha and Murcia. Castles abound. The drive to Guadalest is particularly stunning. Other towns to take in include Morella and Játiva, while Elche's endless palm groves are a potent reminder of Valencia's Islamic heritage.

Other mementoes of Islamic settlement are the names of towns, cities and rivers. One beginning with 'Al' (Arabic for 'the') is a giveaway – Alicante is an example, as are those starting with 'Beni' (such as Benicasim), meaning 'sons of' or 'folk of'. And, as elsewhere in southern Spain, 'guad' at the beginning of a name is a deformation of the Arabic *wadi,* meaning river valley.

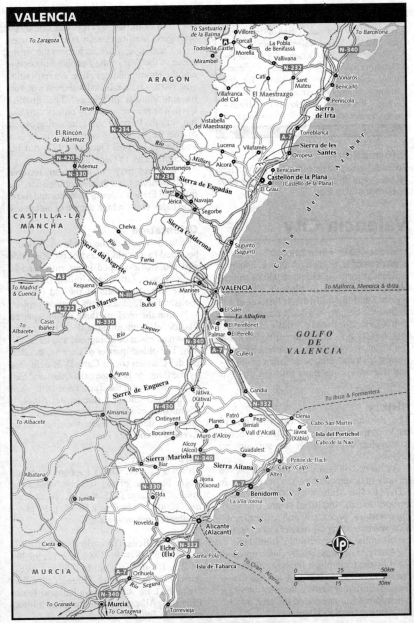

VALENCIA

To Zaragoza
To Santuario de la Balma
Villores
Forcall
To Barcelona
Todolella Castle
La Pobla de Benifassá
Mirambel
Morella
Vallivana
N-340
Catí
Sant Mateu
Vinaròs
Benicarló
ARAGÓN
El Maestrazgo
Peñíscola
Villafranca del Cid
Teruel
N-234
Sierra de Irta
El Rincón de Ademuz
Vistabella del Maestrazgo
Río
Torreblanca
N-420
Ademuz
Lucena
Vilafamés
Sierra de les Santes
N-330
Millars
Alcora
Oropesa
Montanejos
Benicasim
Sierra de Espadán
Castellón de la Plana
(Castelló de la Plana)
CASTILLA-LA MANCHA
Viver
Navajas
El Grau
Jérica
Chelva
Segorbe
Sierra Calderona
Río
Sierra del Negrete
Turia
Sagunto (Sagunt)
To Madrid & Cuenca
A-3
Requena
Chiva
VALENCIA
To Mallorca, Menorca & Ibiza
N-III
Manises
N-322
Sierra Martes
Buñol
El Saler
La Albufera
Casas Ibáñez
N-330
Xuquer
El Perellonet
To Albacete
Río
Palmar
El Perelló
GOLFO DE VALENCIA
N-340
A-7
Cullera
Ayora
Sierra de Enguera
Játiva (Xàtiva)
Gandia
To Ibiza & Formentera
Almansa
N-430
Patró
Pego
To Albacete
Ontinyent
Planes
Beniali
Denia
Cabo San Martín
Bocairent
Muro d'Alcoy
Vall d'Alcalá
Jávea (Xàbia)
Isla del Portichol
Cabo de la Nao
Alcoy (Alcoi)
Guadalest
Sierra Mariola
N-340
Sierra Aitana
Peñón de Ifach
Albatana
Biar
Calpe (Calp)
Villena
Jijona (Xixona)
Altea
N-330
A-7
Benidorm
Jumilla
Elda
La Vila Joiosa
Costa Blanca
Novelda
Alicante (Alacant)
Cieza
Elche (Elx)
N-332
Santa Pola
To Oran, Algeria
MURCIA
A-7
Orihuela
Isla de Tabarca
Río Segura
N-340
0   25   50km
0   15   30mi
To Granada
Murcia
To Cartagena
Torrevieja

euro currency converter €1 = 166pta

Warning – Creeping Catalan

The tendency to replace Castilian street signs with the Catalan equivalent is bound to be a source of confusion. Occasionally we use the Catalan version, where it's clearly the dominant one, but since Castilian (for the moment at any rate) remains fairly common – and is the version every local understands – we have elected to stick with it in most cases.

Information

To email any tourist office in the Valencia region, type **e** touristinfo.*name of town*@turisme.m400.gva.es.

Valencia City

postcode 46003 • pop 800,000

Spain's third-largest city, Valencia comes as a pleasant surprise. Home to *paella* and the Holy Grail, it's also blessed with great weather and the mid-March festival of Las Fallas, the country's wildest party.

It's a vibrant, friendly, mildly chaotic city that boasts an outstanding fine arts museum, an accessible old quarter, Europe's newest cultural and scientific complex – and one of Spain's most exciting nightlife scenes.

History

The Romans founded 'Valentia' on the banks of the Río Turia in 138 BC and began to develop irrigation for the surrounding regions.

As Rome collapsed, the Visigoths moved in, only to be expelled by Muslim cohorts in AD 711. The Arabs made Valencia a rich agricultural and industrial centre, establishing ceramics, paper, silk and leather industries and extending the network of irrigation canals in the rich agricultural hinterland.

Muslim rule was briefly interrupted in 1094 by the triumphant rampage of the legendary Castilian knight El Cid. The Christians definitively retook the city in 1238, when Jaime I incorporated the area into his burgeoning Catalan kingdom.

Valencia's Golden Age was in the 15th and 16th centuries, when it was one of the strongest Mediterranean trading centres. Like Catalunya, Valencia backed the wrong horse in the War of the Spanish Succession and the Bourbon king Felipe V's retribution was swift – he abolished Valencia's *fueros,* or autonomous privileges. The Spanish Civil War proved similarly unlucky, as siding with the Republicans (and acting as seat of the Republican government from November 1936 until October 1937) did not endear the city to General Franco.

The fueros may not have been restored but, benefiting from the decentralisation that followed Franco's death, Valencia and its region today enjoy a high degree of autonomy.

Orientation

The 'action' part of the city is an oval area bounded by the old course of the Río Turia and the sickle-shaped inner ring road of Calles Colón, Játiva and Guillem de Castro. These trace the walls of the old city, demolished in 1865 as a job-creation project.

Within the oval are three major squares: Plazas del Ayuntamiento, de la Reina (also known as Plaza de Zaragoza) and de la Virgen. The oldest quarter of the city, the Barrio del Carmen (or El Carmé), is delimited by the Plaza de la Virgen, the Quart and Serranos towers and the Turia river bed.

The train station, Estación del Norte, is 250m south of Plaza del Ayuntamiento. The main bus station is beside the river bed on Avenida Menéndez Pidal.

Information

To get a grip on what's happening around town, buy one of the weekly 'what's-on' guides: *La Turia* (175 ptas), *Valencia Semanal* (200 ptas) or *Que y Donde* (150 ptas), available from newsstands.

Tourist Offices The main tourist office is at Calle Paz 48 (☎ 96 398 64 22, fax 96 398 64 21). It's open 10 am to 6.30 pm weekdays (to 2 pm Saturday). Three smaller ones are at the train station, town hall and Teatro Principal. All are well endowed with information in English.

VALENCIA

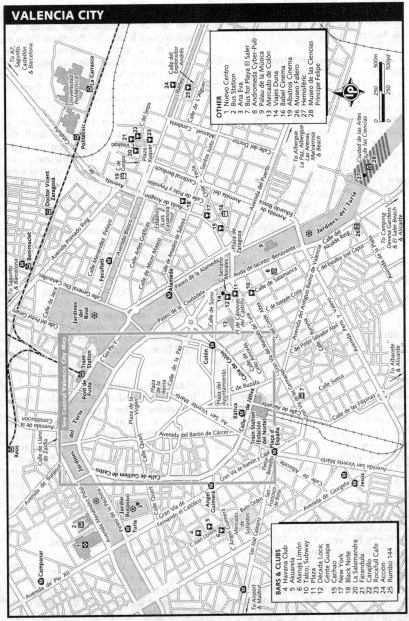

VALENCIA CITY

OTHER
1 Nuevo Centro
2 Bus Station
3 Ana Eva
6 Bus for Playa El Saler
8 Andromeda Cyber-Pub
9 Palau de la Música
13 Mercado de Colón
14 Viajes Duna
16 Babel Cinema
19 Albatros Cinema
26 Museo Fallero
27 Hemisféric
28 Museo de las Ciencias
   Príncipe Felipe

BARS & CLUBS
4 Havana Club
5 Akuarela
6 Maruja Limón
10 Talco; Subway
11 Plaza
12 Década Loca;
   Gente Guapa
15 Cachao
17 New York
18 Black Note
20 La Salamandra
21 Farándula
22 Carajillo
23 Rocafull Cafe
24 Acción
25 Rumbo 144

See Central Valencia City Map

To A7,
Sagunto,
Castellón &
Barcelona

To Sagunto
& Barcelona

To Albergue
La Paz, Albergue
Las Arenas,
Malvarrosa
& Beach

To Camping
Dunas; Devesa's
& El Saler Beach
& Alicante

To Albacete
& Alicante

To Airport
& Madrid

Money American Express is represented by Viajes Duna (☎ 96 374 15 62), Calle Cirilo Amorós 88.

Post & Communications The neo-baroque main post office *(correos)* building is on Plaza del Ayuntamiento. Poste restante is on the 1st floor.

Among several cybercafes in town is the noisy, 48-terminal Www.confederacion.com (yes, that's the name) at Calle Ribera 8, just off Plaza del Ayuntamiento. It charges 500 ptas per hour. Also central is Cyberdrac, Calle Paz 33, open weekdays and charging 500 ptas per half-hour. If you're a bedtime reader or just fancy clicking on with a *copa*, visit Andromeda Cyber-Pub, Calle Salamanca 37, open 6 pm to 3.30 am (2.30 am in winter); it charges 500 ptas per hour.

Bookshops Valencia has two good predominantly English-language bookshops: the English Book Centre, Calle Pascual y Genís 16, and Eurollibre, Calle Hernán Cortés 18.

Laundry There are two central laundrettes: at Plaza del Mercado 12, close to the covered market, and Calle Pelayo 11, near the train station.

Medical Services & Emergency In a medical emergency, call ☎ 085. To find your nearest all night pharmacy, call ☎ 900-16 11 61 (toll free). The general hospital (☎ 96 386 29 00) is on Avenida del Cid in the west of the city. The Policía Nacional (☎ 96 351 08 62) are at Gran Vía de Ramón y Cajal 40.

Museo de Bellas Artes

The Museo de Bellas Artes (Fine Arts Museum) ranks among Spain's best, with works by El Greco, Goya, Velázquez, Ribera, Ribalta and artists such as Sorolla and Pinazo of the Valencian impressionist school. Across the river, on Calle de San Pío V, it's open 10 am to 2.15 pm and 4 to 7.30 pm Tuesday to Saturday, and continuously on Sunday (free).

Catedral

The cathedral is a microcosm of the city's architectural history: the Puerta del Palau on Plaza de la Virgen is Romanesque; the dome, tower and Puerta de los Apóstoles are Gothic; the presbytery and main entrance on Plaza de la Reina are baroque; and there are a couple of Renaissance chapels inside.

In the flamboyant Gothic Capilla del Santo Cáliz, right of the main entrance, is what's claimed to be the **Holy Grail**, the chalice from which Christ sipped during the Last Supper. Beyond it is the **museum**, open 10 am to 1 pm and 4.30 to 7 pm (to 6 pm December to February) daily (200 ptas). The next chapel south, La Capilla de San Francisco de Borja, has a pair of particularly sensitive Goyas.

Left of the main portal is the entrance to the **Miguelete bell tower**, open 10 am to 12.30 pm and 4.30 to 7.30 pm daily except Monday; entry is 200 ptas. Clamber up the 207 steps of its spiral staircase for great 360° views of city and skyline.

As for the past thousand years, the **Tribunal de las Aguas** (Water Court) meets every Thursday at noon outside the cathedral's Plaza de la Virgen doorway. Here, local farmers' irrigation disputes are settled in Catalan.

Plaza de la Virgen

Beside the cathedral is the church of **Nuestra Señora de los Desamparados**. Above the altar is a highly venerated statue of the Virgin, patroness of the city. Opposite is the handsome 15th-century Gothic – and much amended – **Palau de la Generalitat**, seat of government for the Valencia region. The reclining figure in the central fountain represents the Río Turia while the eight maidens with their gushing pots symbolise the main irrigation canals flowing from it.

Cripta de la Cárcel de San Vicente Mártir

The crypt of a Visigoth chapel, reputedly prison to the 4th-century martyr San Vicente, is nearby on Plaza del Arzobispo.

Although the crypt itself isn't particularly memorable, it's well worth taking in the free 25-minute multimedia show, which presents Valencia's history and the saint's life. Make reservations at the **Palacio del Marqués de Campo** – itself worth a browse – just opposite and ask for a showing in English.

L'Almoina

Immediately north of the crypt is the large archaeological site of L'Almoina, the heart of 'Valentia', the Roman town. There's an English version of both the introductory pamphlet and information panels, and a 15-minute video (in Spanish), shown four to six times daily except Monday. Entry is free.

Palacio del Marqués de Dos Aguas

This baroque palace on Calle Poeta Querol, to the south of Plaza de la Reina, has an extravagant 18th-century alabaster facade. Inside, the **Museo Nacional de Cerámica** displays ceramics from around the world – and especially the renowned local production centres of Manises, Alcora and Paterna. It's open 10 am to 2 pm and 4 to 8 pm Tuesday to Saturday plus Sunday morning; free entry.

Plaza del Mercado

Facing each other across Plaza del Mercado are two magnificent buildings, each a masterpiece of its era. Pop into the 15th-century Gothic **Lonja**, an early Valencian commodity exchange, now a Unesco World Heritage site, with its striking colonnaded hall. And set aside time to prowl the **Mercado Central**, Valencia's *modernista* covered market (see also Self-Catering in Places to Eat), constructed in 1928 and a swirl of smells, movement and colour. (An even finer modernista building is the **Mercado de Colón** on Calle Cirilo Amorós, no longer, alas, used as a market).

Torres de Serranos and Torres de Quart

Two imposing, twin-towered stone gates are all that remain of the old city walls. Once the main exit to Barcelona and the north, the well-preserved, 14th-century Torres de Serranos overlook the bed of the Río Turia. They're open 9.15 am to 2 pm and 4.15 to 6 pm Tuesday to Saturday plus Sunday morning (free). Farther west, the 15th-century Torres de Quart look westwards, towards Madrid. Up high, you can still see the pockmarks caused by French cannonballs during the 19th-century Napoleonic invasion.

Ciudad de las Artes y de las Ciencias

South-east of the city centre, the aesthetically stunning City of Arts & Sciences, largely designed by local architect Santiago Calatrava, promises to become Valencia's premier attraction. Already open is the **Hemisfèric** (☎ 96 399 55 77), at once planetarium, IMAX cinema and laser show; entry is 1100 ptas to each.

An interactive science museum, the **Museo de las Ciencias Príncipe Felipe** (☎ 902-100 031; 1000 ptas), is scheduled to open in 2001, to be followed by the **Parque Oceanográfico**, a series of lakes, lagoons and islets illustrating coastal marine life, then the **Palacio de las Artes**, a multifunctional arts complex. Take bus No 13, 14, 15 or 18 from the city centre.

Parks & Gardens

The **Jardines del Turia** in the former river bed are a 6km-long lung of green, a glorious mix of playing fields, cycling, jogging and walking paths, plantations, fountains, lawns and playgrounds (see Lilliputian kids scrambling over a magnificent, ever-patient Gulliver east of the Palau de la Música).

Reaching down to them are the **Jardines del Real** (Royal Gardens, commonly called Los Viveros), another lovely spot for a stroll. Within them are the new **Museo de Ciencias Naturales** (Natural Science Museum) and a small **zoo**.

The **Jardín Botánico** on Calle Quart, established in 1802, is Spain's first botanical gardens. With mature trees and plants and an extensive cactus garden, it's a shady, tranquil place to relax. It's open 10 am to 6 pm (9 pm in summer) daily except Monday (50 ptas).

VALENCIA

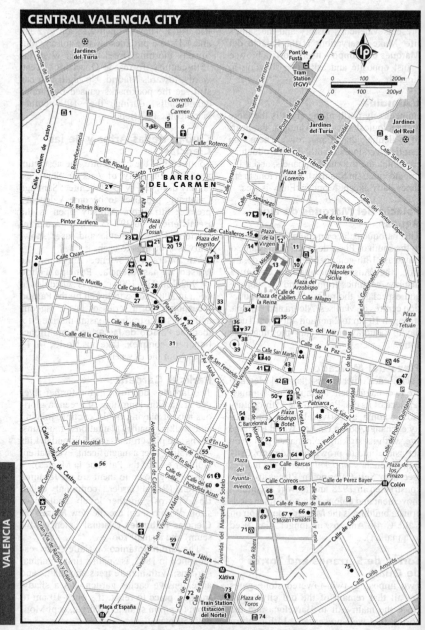

CENTRAL VALENCIA CITY

VALENCIA

CENTRAL VALENCIA CITY

PLACES TO STAY
27 Hostal El Rincón
28 Hospedería del Pilar
33 Hostal Antigua Morellana
34 Habitaciones Reina
43 Hotel Inglés
48 Pensión París
51 Hotel Astoria Palace
52 Hostal Moratín
54 Hotel Londres
62 Hotel Reina Victoria
63 Hostal-Residencia Universal
65 Hotel Continental
69 Hostal Castelar
70 Hostal-Residencia Alicante

PLACES TO EAT
2 La Lluna
14 Restaurante El Generalife
16 Seu-Xerea; S'Horabaixa
37 Horchatería el Siglo
38 Horchatería de Santa Catalina
50 La Utielana
55 Pizzería La Vita é Bella
59 Las Añadas de España
67 Cervecería-Restaurante Pema

BARS AND CLUBS
17 Café de las Horas
18 Café-Bar Negrito
19 Fox Congo

20 Johnny Maracas
21 San Jaume
22 John Silver
23 Café Montesinos
25 Café Bolsería
26 Café Infanta
35 Finnegan's
41 Cervecería Madrid

OTHER
1 Instituto Valenciano de Arte
   Moderno (IVAM)
3 Ergobike
4 Centro del Carmen (IVAM)
5 Museo del Siglo XIX
6 San Carlos e Iglesia de la
   Santísima Cruz
7 Torres de Serranos
8 Museo de Ballas Artes
9 Palacio del Marqués de
   Campo
10 Cripta de la Cárcel de San
   Vicente
11 L'Almoina
12 Nuestra Señora de los
   Desamparados
13 Cathedral
15 Palau de la Generalitat
24 Torres de Quart
29 Laundry
30 Iglesia de los Santos Juanes

31 Mercado Central (Food
   Market)
32 La Lonja de los Mercaderes
36 Iglesia de Santa Catalina
39 Plaza Redonda
40 Iglesia de San Martín
42 Palacio del Marqués de Dos
   Aguas &
   Museo Nacional de Cerámica
44 Iberia Office
45 Colegio del Patriarca
46 Cyberdrac
47 Regional Tourist Office
49 Iglesia de San Juan de la Cruz
53 Filmoteca & Teatro Rialto
56 Casa de la Cultura &
   Municipal Library
57 Police Station
58 Iglesia de San Agustín
60 Town Hall
61 Municipal Tourist Office
64 Teatro Principal & Municipal
   Tourist Office
66 English Book Centre
68 Post Office
71 Www.confederacion.com
   (internet)
72 Laundry
73 Tourist Office
74 Museo Taurino
75 Eurollibre

Beaches

Valencia city's beach is the broad **Playa de la Malvarrosa**, east of the town centre, bordered by the **Paseo Marítimo** promenade and a string of restaurants. One block back, lively bars and discos thump out the beat in summer. Take bus No 19 from Plaza del Ayuntamiento, No 1 or 2 from the bus station or Gran Vías, or the high-speed tram from Pont de Fusta or the Benimaclet Metro junction.

Playa El Salér, 10km south, is backed by shady pine woods. Autocares Herca (☎ 96 349 12 50) buses run hourly (every half-hour in summer) from the junction of Gran Vía de las Germanias and Calle Sueca (30 minutes, 150 ptas).

Other Attractions

Off Plaza de la Reina is **Iglesia de Santa Catalina**, its striking 18th-century baroque belfry one of the best-known landmarks in the city. Nearby, stalls in the small circular **Plaza Redonda** sell bits and bobs, buttons and bows, clothes and locally made crafts and ceramics.

South of here, the **Estación del Norte** is another impressive modernista building. Opened in 1917, the train station's entrance hall is decorated with ceramic mosaics and murals – and 'bon voyage' in mosaic in more languages than you've probably ever heard.

The **Instituto Valenciano de Arte Moderno (IVAM)**, beside Puente de las Artes, just north-west of the centre, houses an impressive permanent collection of 20th-century Spanish art and hosts excellent temporary exhibitions. IVAM (pronounced 'ee-bam') is open 10 am to 7 pm daily except Monday (350 ptas, free on Sunday).

Side by side nearby, and just off Plaza del Carmen, are the **Museo del Siglo XIX** (Museum of the 19th Century), a branch of the

VALENCIA

Bellas Artes museum, and the **Centro del Carmen**, an annexe of IVAM. Entry to both is free.

The bijou **Colegio del Patriarca** museum on Plaza del Patriarca has works by El Greco, Juan de Juanes and Ribalta. It's open 11 am to 1.30 pm daily (100 ptas).

The small **Museo Taurino**, behind the Plaza de Toros just south of the centre, holds a collection of bullfighting memorabilia; entry is free.

The **Museo Fallero** on Plaza del Monte-olivete, south-east of the town centre, is dedicated to the festival of Las Fallas (see Special Events). *Ninots* are near-life-sized figurines that strut and pose at the base of each falla. And the *ninot indultat* ('reprieved' or 'exempted') is the only one from among thousands to be saved from the flames each year. Entry is 300 ptas.

Organised Tours

Valencia Bus Turístico (☎ 96 342 03 14) runs 90-minute city tours with a recorded commentary in eight languages. Buses leave from Plaza de la Reina every two hours from 10.30 am until 6.30 pm (1000 ptas).

A cheaper, if less comprehensive, option is EMT bus No 5, El Interior, which will take you around the circumference of the town's inner oval (see Orientation earlier in this section) for the standard 125 ptas fare. It too bills itself as a *Bus Turístico* and its TV monitors indicate major sights as you pass them.

Ergobike (see Bicycle in the Getting Around section) organises friendly one- to three-hour tours around town on recumbent bikes – an easily acquired skill if you can ride a normal bicycle.

Special Events

Las Fallas Las Fallas de San José is an exuberant, anarchic swirl of fireworks, music, festive bonfires and all-night partying. If you're in Spain between 12 and 19 March, don't miss it.

The *fallas* are huge sculptures of papiermâché on wood – with, increasingly, environmentally damaging polystyrene – built by teams of local artists. Each neighbourhood sponsors its own falla, and when the town wakes to the *plantà* (overnight construction of the fallas) on the morning of the 16th, over 350 have been erected. Reaching up to 15m in height, with the most expensive costing over 20 million pesetas, these grotesque, colourful effigies satirise celebrities, current affairs and local customs.

Round-the-clock festivities include street parties, paella-cooking competitions, parades, open-air concerts, bullfights and nightly free firework displays. Valencia considers itself the pyrotechnic capital of the world and each day from 1 to 19 March a *mascletà* (over five minutes of deafening thumps and explosions) shakes the window panes of Plaza del Ayuntamiento at 2 pm. After midnight on the final day each falla goes up in flames – backed by yet more fireworks.

Other Festivals & Events The suburb of La Malvarrosa celebrates Semana Santa

A giant (pre-bonfire) *falla* at Las Fallas de San José festival in Valencia

(Holy Week) with elaborate processions. On the Sunday after Easter, the Fiesta de San Vicente Ferrer sees colourful parades and miracle plays performed around town. On the second Sunday in May, the effigy of the Virgen de los Desamparados, patron of the city, makes the short journey across the Plaza de la Virgen to the cathedral, hemmed in by fervent believers struggling to touch her.

The festival of Corpus Christi, held in June, was first celebrated here way back in 1355. Each 24 June, Día de San Juan and midsummer's day, thousands spend the evening on the Playa de la Malvarrosa and take part in a traditional cleansing ceremony where you wash your feet in the ocean and write your bad habits on a piece of paper, which you throw onto a bonfire.

The Feria de Julio in July features a packed program of performing arts, brass band competitions, concerts, bullfights, fireworks and a 'battle of the flowers'.

Every October Valencia hosts a festival of Mediterranean cinema, while the 9th marks the Día de la Comunidad, commemorating the city's 1238 liberation from the Arabs.

Places to Stay – Budget

Camping The nearest camping ground, *Devesa Gardens* (☎/fax 96 161 11 36), is 13km south of Valencia, on Carretera el Saler. Open year round, it's a 15-minute walk from El Saler beach and charges 2000 ptas for two people, a tent and car.

Hostels *Alberge Las Arenas* (☎/fax 96 356 42 88, e arenahostel@ctv.es, Calle Eugenia Viñes 24) is a fairly tatty place but it's friendly, a pebble's throw from the beach and within earshot of Malvarrosa's wild summer nightlife. Open year round, it has a kitchen for guest use. Dorm beds cost 850/1250 ptas for juniors/seniors. Take bus No 32 from Plaza del Ayuntamiento to the end of the line.

Albergue La Paz (☎ 96 369 01 52, Avenida del Puerto 69) is normally a student hostel. But from July to September, B&B is open to all and costs 1500/1900 ptas for juniors/seniors. Take bus No 19 from Plaza del Ayuntamiento or No 2 from the Torres de Serranos.

Hostales & Pensiones There are a few scruffy *hostales* (budget hotels) around the western side of the train station, but the budget options in the Barrio del Carmen or around Plaza del Ayuntamiento are better value.

Barrio del Carmen Hospedería del Pilar (☎ 96 391 66 00, Plaza del Mercado 19) is a rambling hostal with clean, basic singles/doubles/triples at 1600/2995/3900 ptas (2140/3850/4815 ptas with shower).

Nearby, the vast ***Hostal El Rincón*** (☎ 96 391 79 98, Calle de la Carda 11) is one of Valencia's oldest and best-known hostales. Most singles/doubles are small and dim, costing 1500/2800 ptas. It also has eight spacious, renovated rooms with bathroom and air-con – excellent value at 2000/3600 ptas. On Plaza de la Reina, ***Habitaciones Reina*** (☎ 96 392 18 92) is very basic but well placed and cheap with doubles at 2400 ptas.

Around Plaza del Ayuntamiento At ***Pensión París*** (☎/fax 96 352 67 66, Calle Salvá 12, 1st & 3rd floors) the rooms and corridor bathrooms are spotless. Singles/doubles/triples cost 2500/3600/5400 ptas (doubles/triples with shower 4200/6000 ptas). The few doubles with full bathroom are 4800 ptas.

Recently renovated ***Hostal Moratín*** (☎/fax 96 352 12 20, Calle Moratín 15, 4th & 5th floors) is quiet and welcoming. Singles/doubles with shower are 2900/4500 ptas (3500/5500 ptas with bathroom) while fancier triples with bathroom are 10,500 ptas.

Hostal-Residencia Universal (☎/fax 96 351 53 84, Calle Barcas 5, 2nd to 4th floors) is run by the same family as Pensión Paris (and to similar standards). Basic rooms are 2300/3600/5100 ptas (doubles with shower 4200 ptas).

Hostal Castelar (☎/fax 96 351 31 99, Calle de Ribera 1) has singles/doubles at

VALENCIA

2500/4500 ptas (3000/5000 ptas in high season). All rooms sport a TV, some have showers and the front ones have excellent views of the Plaza del Ayuntamiento. Across the road at *Hostal-Residencia Alicante (☎/fax 96 351 22 96, Calle de Ribera 8, 2nd floor)* colourfully tiled hallways lead to rooms with shower at 3000/4000 ptas (3500/5000 ptas with bathroom). All rooms have TV.

Places to Stay – Mid-Range

Newly opened *Hostal Antigua Morellana (☎/fax 96 391 57 73, Calle En Bou 2)*, in a renovated 18th-century building, has cosy singles/doubles with bathroom at 4000/6000 ptas.

Just off Plaza del Ayuntamiento, popular *Hotel Londres (☎ 96 351 22 44, fax 96 352 15 08, Calle de Barcelonina 1)* has cosy singles/doubles/triples from 4700/8500/10,600 ptas.

Hotel Continental (☎ 96 353 52 82, fax 96 353 11 13, e continental@contitel.es, Calle Correos 8) is a modern, friendly place where singles cost 7000 to 9000 ptas and doubles 9000 to 15,000 ptas, according to season. All rooms have air-con and satellite TV.

Places to Stay – Top End

Since Valencia is a business centre, big hotels struggle to fill rooms on weekends. Many offer fat weekend discounts of up to one-third. There are three good choices in the heart of town.

Hotel Reina Victoria (☎ 96 352 04 87, fax 96 352 27 21, e hreinavictoriavalencia@husa.es, Calle de Barcas 4) is a grand old place which has been comprehensively renovated. Singles/doubles/triples are usually 12,600/15,200/19,600 ptas.

Singles/doubles at *Hotel Inglés (☎ 96 351 64 26, fax 96 394 02 51, e melia.confort .ingles@solmelia.es, Calle del Marqués de Dos Aguas 6)*, also with character and a recent face-lift, are 21,650/24,000 ptas. Its discounted doubles rate of 12,300 ptas at weekends and during most of July and August is especial value for money.

More self-consciously modern, *Hotel Astoria Palace (☎ 96 398 10 00, fax 96 398 10 10, e info@hotel-astoria-palace.com, Plaza de Rodrigo Botet 5)* has rooms at 25,250/31,800 ptas.

Places to Eat

Valencia is the capital of *la huerta,* a fertile coastal agricultural plain which supplies the city with a diverse range of fresh produce.

Rice is the staple of much Valencian cuisine – and basis of the dish Valencia exported to the world: *paella.* You'll encounter plenty of other rice dishes too, including *arroz a banda* (rice and seafood cooked in a fish stock), *arroz negro* (rice with squid, including its ink) and *arroz al horno* (rice baked in the oven). Then there's *fideuá,* a paella made with noodles instead of rice.

Valencianos normally eat rice only at lunchtime, when locals in their hundreds head for Las Arenas, just north of the port, where a long line of restaurants all serve up the real stuff. For around 1500 ptas enjoy a three-course, waterfront meal. At *La Pepica (☎ 96 371 03 66, Paseo Neptuno 6),* more expensive than its competitors, Ernest Hemingway, among other luminaries, once strutted. In this same seafront area, *La Lonja del Pescado Frito (☎ 96 355 35 35, Calle Eugenia Viñes 243),* an unadorned shed right beside the Eugenia Viñes tram stop, is unbeatable value for fresh fish. It's open for dinner daily except Monday plus lunchtime at weekends (open weekends only in winter). Grab an order form as you enter and fill it in at your table.

You could also try a glass of *horchata,* an opaque local drink made from pressed *chufas* (tiger nuts), into which you dip large finger-shaped buns called *fartons;* both name and taste are to savour. Two traditional horchata houses are *Horchatería de Santa Catalina* and *Horchatería el Siglo*, both on Plaza de Santa Catalina.

There are several worthwhile places just off Plaza de la Virgen. *Restaurante El Generalife (Calle Caballeros 5)* has an excellent-value *menú del día* (daily set meal) for 1200 ptas. More subtle, *Seu-Xerea (☎ 96 392 40 00, Calle del Conde de Almodóvar 4)* has an inventive a-la-carte menu with dishes both international and rooted in Spain, and does a warmly recommended lunchtime *menú* at 2200 ptas. It's closed at Saturday lunchtime and Sunday. Next door, the cuisine at *S'Horabaixa* (☎ 96 391 21 77) has a Mallorcan slant. With its cosy decor, it's popular for salads and open sandwiches; it's open evenings only and closed Monday.

Around Plaza del Ayuntamiento, *Pizzeria La Vita é Bella (Calle d'En Llop 4)* occupies a tastefully restored draper's shop. A cosy cafe-bar with good pizzas and pastas (700 to 1200 ptas), it also does mouth watering home-made ice creams. It's well worth tracking down the excellent-value *La Utielana* (☎ 96 352 94 14), tucked away just off Calle Prócida. You can eat well at this unpretentious place for around 1500 ptas; it's closed Saturday night and Sunday.

Calle Mosén Femades, a pedestrian street one block south-east of Plaza del Ayuntamiento, has a cluster of superb upmarket seafood restaurants. If the high prices deter you, head for *Cervecería-Restaurante Pema* (☎ 96 352 66 50, Calle Mosén Femades 3), where you can have anything from a simple tapa to a full-blown meal. Its weekday lunch *menú* at 1100 ptas, including a drink and coffee, ranks among central Valencia's best deals.

Tiny *La Lluna* (☎ 96 392 21 46, Calle San Ramón 23), a popular vegetarian place in the Barrio del Carmen with a *menú* at 900 ptas, has simple, good-value vegetarian food; it's closed Sunday. Altogether more sophisticated – and more pricey – is *Ana Eva* (☎ 96 391 53 69, Calle Turia 49) with tasteful decor and a delightful patio. Count on 2000 to 2500 ptas per head; it's closed Sunday evening and Monday.

Self-Catering A visit to the magnificent central covered market, *Mercado Central*, on Plaza del Mercado, is a must, even if you only browse (open until 2 pm daily except Sunday). For the best in local cheeses and meats – at a price – visit *Las Añadas de España (Calle Játiva 3)*.

Entertainment

Fuelled by a large student population and an overdeveloped sense of competitiveness with Madrid and Barcelona, Valencia has a reputation as one of Spain's best nightlife scenes. For many visitors, Valencia's 'party long and hard' attitude is the motivation for coming.

The **Barrio del Carmen** has the grungiest and grooviest collection of bars. The other major area is around the **university**. Along Avenidas Aragón and Blasco Ibáñez and around Plaza de Xuquer are enough bars and discos to keep you busy beyond sunrise.

Other areas worth checking out are around the **Mercado de Subastos** and **Plaza de Cánovas**. In summer, Malvarrosa, north of the port, and El Perellonet, some 20km south, come alive with disco fever.

Bars & Pubs Valencia is well equipped with places to enjoy a *copa* or two.

Barrio del Carmen 'El Carmé' has everything from upmarket designer bars and yuppie pubs to grungy thrash-metal haunts and squat punk bars. At weekends, Calle Caballeros, the main street, seethes with people seeking out *la marcha* ('the action').

Plaza del Tossal has some of the most sophisticated bars this side of Barcelona. *Café Bolsería* is a stylish upstairs-downstairs job that attracts a well-dressed crowd of 30-somethings. Opposite, *Café Infanta* is a swanky, stylish bar. On the northern side, the smaller *Café Montesinos* has a quiet upstairs area, while the 1st floor of *San Jaume*, a converted pharmacy, is all quiet crannies and poky passageways.

From here, head eastwards along Calle Caballeros to *Johnny Maracas* at No 39, a suave salsa place with fishtanks on the bar. At No 35, *Fox Congo* has a cool marble bar, patchwork suede benches, scrap-metal montage ceilings – and glass-walled toilets.

At *Cafe-Bar Negrito*, a block south on Plaza del Negrito, the crowd and music spill out onto the square.

Bars north of Plaza del Tossal along Calle Alta are cheaper, with tables on the street. At No 8 is *John Silver*, low, dark and named after the monopode old pirate himself (his wooden leg hangs behind the bar).

VALENCIA

Other Areas Just north of Plaza de la Virgen is *Café de las Horas (Calle Conde de Almodóvar 1)*, a wonderfully baroque place with tapestries, classical music and candelabras dripping wax. On Plaza de la Reina, *Finnegan's* – one of Valencia's several Irish bars – is a popular meeting place for English speakers.

Near the Mercado de Subastos just west of the town centre, the intersection of Calle Juan Lloréns and Calle Calixto III is very much the 'in' area. Drop into modish *Akuarela*, the smaller *Maruja Limón* or *Havana Club*.

Just east of the centre, Plaza de Cánovas, tamer and more upmarket, attracts a younger crowd. *Plaza* is a stylish corner bar on the square itself. Around the corner are a string of places along Calle Serrano Morales: *Década Loca* at No 7 does the retro '60s thing, while *Gente Guapa* next door is a salsa dance bar. Among the bars on Calle de Salamanca, just south, *Talco* and *Subway* are both worth dropping into.

Live Music Smoke-darkened paintings by local artists hang from the downstairs walls of atmospheric *Cervecería Madrid (Calle de la Abadía de San Martín 10)*. Upstairs, it's jazz (usually weekends only), courtesy of the owner on piano and his friends. *Black Note (Calle Polo y Peyrolón 15)* has jazz, blues and soul sessions most nights, while *Roxy (Avenida de San Vicente Mártir 200)*, well south of the train station, has live pop and rock.

Clubs & Discos A handful of discos are scattered around the centre but if you really want to experience life after 3 am in Valencia, head for the zone along and around Avenida Blasco Ibáñez, towards the university (500 to 600 ptas by taxi from the centre).

Plaza de Xuquer, where students pack the bars, is the place to go early on. Bars worth checking out include *La Salamandra*, *Farandula*, *Carajillo* and *Rocafull Cafe*. Don't discount Avenida de Aragón, where new bars are opening by the month. *New York* has funky music, while at *Cachao (Calle Periodista Ros Belda 5)* it's salsa; it even offers lessons.

Around 3 am the stayers, with cash to splash, move on to the big discos along Blasco Ibáñez. Most discos have cover charges of between 600 and 1200 ptas, although discounted passes are often available from local bars.

If you're into South American salsa and reggae, head for the funky *Rumbo 144 (Avenida Blasco Ibáñez 146)*. Most other places, including *Acción Disco* across the road, are dominated by *bacalao* dance music.

Theatre & Opera The *Teatro Principal (☎ 96 351 00 51, Calle Barcas 15)* is Valencia's main venue for opera and the performing arts. The *Palau de la Música (☎ 96 337 50 20)*, a huge, glass-domed concert hall above the Jardines del Turia, hosts mainly classical music recitals.

Cinemas On the 4th floor of the Teatro Rialto building on Plaza del Ayuntamiento, the *Filmoteca (☎ 96 399 55 77)* screens undubbed classic, art-house and experimental films. Entry is 200 ptas – one of Valencia's best bargains.

Two multiscreen cinemas show undubbed films: *Albatros (☎ 96 393 26 77)*, on Plaza Fray Luis Colomer, and *Babel (☎ 96 362 67 95, Calle Vicente Sancho Tello 10)*. Movies are cheaper on Monday.

Getting There & Away

Air Aeropuerto de Manises (☎ 96 159 85 00) is 10km west of the centre. Regular flights connect Valencia with Madrid, Barcelona, Palma de Mallorca and Ibiza, and there are daily scheduled flights to London, Brussels, Frankfurt, Paris and Milan. There are no cut-price carriers, however, so if your budget's tight, fly from Alicante, which has several cheapo charter flights daily to major European cities.

Bus The bus station (☎ 96 349 72 22) is beside the river bed on Avenida de Menéndez Pidal. Bus No 8 connects it to Plaza del Ayuntamiento.

AutoRes runs 10 to 12 buses to Madrid daily (2875 to 3175 ptas). There are five to

10 buses to/from Barcelona daily (2900 ptas) and up to nine motorway runs to Alicante (2¼ hours, 1980 ptas), some of which pass by Benidorm (1¾ hours, 1510 ptas).

Train From Estación del Norte (☎ 96 352 02 02 or 902-24 02 02), there are up to 10 Alaris express trains daily to/from Madrid (3½ hours, 5700 ptas) via Albacete and three regional services via Cuenca (5½ hours, 2945 ptas).

A dozen daily trains (mostly 4500 ptas) make the three- to five-hour haul north to Barcelona via Tarragona, including the high-speed Euromed (5100 ptas, five daily). Up to eight trains head daily to Alicante (1½ to two hours, 1400 to 3200 ptas).

Most of the frequent northbound trains stop at Sagunto (30 minutes, 325 ptas) and Castellón (up to one hour, 550 ptas). There are also trains to Gandía (one hour, 550 ptas) every 30 minutes – hourly at weekends.

Boat In summer, Trasmediterránea (reservations ☎ 902-45 46 45) operates daily car and passenger ferries to Mallorca and Ibiza and has a weekly run to Menorca. During the rest of the year, sailings are less frequent (see the Balearic Islands chapter for more details). Buy your ticket at the Estación Marítima (☎ 96 367 39 72) or any travel agency.

Getting Around

Valencia has an integrated bus, tram and metro network. EMT buses ply town routes while MetroBus serves outlying towns and villages. Tourist offices stock maps for EMT and Metro services.

To/From the Airport Trains (20 minutes, 125 ptas) run from Estación del Norte to Manises Aeropuerto station every half-hour (hourly at weekends). MetroBus (45 minutes, 125 ptas) takes a roundabout route from the bus station, bay No 51, to the airport every 10 minutes. A taxi into the centre costs around 1800 ptas.

Bus EMT (☎ 96 352 83 99) buses run until about 10 pm with night services continuing on seven routes until around 1 am. Tickets

cost 125 ptas, a one-day pass is 500 ptas and a 10-trip *bono* 700 ptas.

Tram & Metro The smart high-speed tram is a pleasant way to get to the beach, paella restaurants of Las Arenas and the port. Pick it up at Pont de Fusta or where it intersects with the Metro at Benimaclet.

Metro lines serve the outer suburbs. The closest stations to the centre are Ángel Guimerá, Xàtiva (for the train station), Colón and Pont de Fusta.

Car Major car-hire companies include Europcar (airport ☎ 96 152 18 72, train station/town ☎ 96 351 90 55) and Avis (airport ☎ 96 152 21 62, train station/town ☎ 96 352 24 78).

Reliable local – and normally substantially cheaper – companies operating from Valencia airport include Javea Cars, Solmar and Victoria Cars. For details of each, see Getting Around in the Alicante section.

Street parking can be a real pain. There are large subterranean car parks beneath Plazas de la Reina and Alfonso el Magnánimo and on Calle Laura, just off Calle Colón.

Taxi Call Radio-Taxi (☎ 96 370 33 33) or Valencia Taxi (☎ 96 357 13 13).

Bicycle Ergobike (☎ 96 392 32 39), on Calle Museo, just off Plaza del Carmen, rents out town bikes and recumbents (see also Organised Tours).

Around Valencia City

Some of the most popular day excursions from Valencia include visits to the Roman ruins at Sagunto, the beach resort of Gandia and the inland town of Játiva (see later in this chapter for details).

LA ALBUFERA

About 15km south of Valencia, La Albufera is a huge freshwater lagoon separated

VALENCIA

from the sea by a narrow strip of sand dunes and pine forests known as La Devesa. The lake and surrounding areas are a breeding ground and sanctuary for migrating and indigenous birds and have been protected as a nature park. Keen birdwatchers flock to the Parque Natural de la Albufera to count kingfishers, mallards, white herons, coots and red-crested pochards, among others.

The unspoiled sections of La Albufera have a serene beauty and the area is noted for its spectacular sunsets. You can take a boat trip on the lagoon, joining the local fisherfolk who use distinctive flat-bottomed boats and nets to harvest fish and eels from the shallow waters.

Surrounded by rice fields, La Albufera was the birthplace of paella. The villages of **El Palmar** and **El Perellonet** boast some excellent restaurants that specialise in paella and other rice and seafood dishes.

Autocares Herca buses for Playa El Salér (see Beaches in the Valencia City section) are also good for La Albufera and continue to either El Perellonet (the majority) or El Palmar.

Costa del Azahar

Stretching north from Valencia is the Costa del Azahar – the orange blossom coast. Backed by a mountainous hinterland, its coastal plain is a green sea of orange groves, from whose headily scented flowers the region takes its name.

Getting There & Away

The Valencia-Barcelona railway follows this coast and regional trains stop at all main towns. There are at least 15 daily trains to Castellón (550 ptas). Seven trains daily call at Benicasim, three at Oropesa and eight at Benicarló/Peñíscola and Vinaròs.

Fares differ considerably from stop-at-every-station *cercanías* and *regionales* to the swifter InterCity. Valencia-Benicasim, for example, is 700 ptas by regional and 1800 ptas by InterCity.

SAGUNTO
postcode 46500 • pop 58,200

Sagunto (Sagunt in Catalan), 25km north of Valencia, was a thriving Iberian community as early as the 5th century BC, when the settlers fortified their hill town with stone walls and traded with Greeks and Phoenicians.

In 219 BC Hannibal besieged the town for eight months. The inhabitants were eventually wiped out and their town destroyed, an event that led to the Second Punic War between Carthage and Rome. Rome won, named the town Saguntum and set about rebuilding it.

Sagunto is usually visited as a day or half-day excursion from Valencia.

Orientation & Information

The Roman ruins are atop an inland hill behind the new town. From the train station beside the highway it's a 10-minute walk to the tourist office (☎ 96 266 22 13) on Plaza del Cronista Chabret. From here, a further 15-minute uphill walk through narrow streets – passing beside the judería, the former Jewish quarter – brings you to the Roman theatre and castle of all ages.

Things to See

You could easily spend a day exploring the castle complex. The **Roman theatre** was built into the hillside during the 1st century AD. Centuries of use and disuse had left it in poor shape, but the controversial modern 'restoration' is in questionable taste. Still, the acoustics remain outstanding, and the theatre is the main venue for Sagunto's three-week, open-air August arts festival.

Higher up, the old stone walls of the **castle** wind around the hillside for almost a kilometre. Mostly in ruins, the rambling complex's seven sections each represent a different period in Sagunto's long history.

Both castle and theatre are free and open 10 am to 6 pm (7.30 pm in summer) Tuesday to Saturday plus Sunday to 2 pm.

Down in the town, other monuments include the ruins of the 4th-century **Templo de Diana**, the adjacent **Iglesia de Santa María**, which features Gothic and baroque doorways, and the 17th-century **Ermita de la Sangre**.

Getting There & Away
There are frequent trains between Valencia and Sagunto (325/535 ptas one way/return), and Autobuses Vallduxense runs a half-hourly service (300 ptas) from Valencia's bus station.

CASTELLÓN (CASTELLÓ) DE LA PLANA
postcode 12005 • pop 136,000
Like many Spanish cities Castellón's outskirts are drab and industrial, so the centre comes as quite a pleasant surprise to the few tourists who visit.

It's a prosperous commercial centre and university town with a good fine arts museum, some interesting monuments and fine examples of modernista architecture.

Orientation & Information
Plaza Mayor marks the centre of Castellón. The train station is almost 1km north-west, on the far side of leafy Parque Ribalta. The accommodation hub, Puerta del Sol, is 200m south-west of the square. The tourist office (☎ 964 35 86 88), Plaza María Agustina 5, is open 9 am to 2 pm and 4 to 7 pm weekdays (continuously in July and August) plus 10 am to 2 pm Saturday.

Buses to the beaches north of El Grau leave from Plaza Borrull (300m south of Plaza Mayor). Those to/from Valencia operate from Plaza del País Valenciano (700m south-west of Plaza Mayor). For both Valencia and resorts to the north, trains are swifter and more frequent than buses.

Things to See
Castellón's under-visited **Museo de Bellas Artes** (☎ 964 35 97 11), on the corner of Calles Caballeros and Gracia, displays an eclectic collection, its large ceramics section focusing on the region's major industry; entry is free. Also worth a visit is the **Museo Etnológico de la Diputación** on Calle de Sanchis Abella just east of Plaza Mayor. Both are open 10 am to 2 pm and 4 to 6 pm weekdays (9 am to 2 pm only mid-

July to mid-September) and 10 am to 12.30 pm Saturday.

Art-lovers will enjoy a visit to the chapel of the **Convento de Capuchinas** on Calle de Núñez de Arce, which houses 10 fine paintings by Zurbarán. It's usually open 2 to 6 pm daily (free).

From Plaza Mayor, bordered by the early 18th-century town hall and bustling covered market, thrusts the long finger of **El Fadrí** (1604), an octagonal bell tower and symbol of the city. Beside the tower is the reconstructed **Concatedral de Santa María**, which was virtually demolished in the civil war.

In the centre of the adjacent **Plaza de Santa Clara** is a sculpture by Llorens Poy depicting Castellón's history.

Four kilometres east of the centre is **El Grau de Castellón**, a harbour that handles this industrial region's exports as well as the local fishing fleet. Castellón's beaches start north of here.

Places to Stay & Eat
At *Pensión La Esperanza* (☎ 964 22 20 31, Calle Trinidad 37), spotless singles/doubles above a bar-restaurant cost 2100/3635 ptas. *Hotel-Residencia del Real* (☎/fax 964 21 19 44, Plaza Real 2) has pleasant rooms with '70s decor, TV, phone and air-con from 5000/6850 ptas.

Julivert (☎ 964 22 37 26, Calle Caballeros 41), open lunchtime and Friday evening only, does a three-course *menú* with a vegetarian option for 1100 ptas. Nearly opposite, and barely 30m north of the Museo de Bellas Artes, *Lizarran* (☎ 964 22 69 70, Calle Caballeros 18) offers Basque cuisine with a wide range of soups, salads and tapas. Around the corner, *Comidas La Brasa* (☎ 964 23 51 17, Calle de la Gracia 7) has a good *menú* for 1150 ptas.

BENICASIM
postcode 12004 • pop 10,000
Benicasim (Benicàssim in Catalan) has been a popular resort since the 19th century, when wealthy Valencian families built summer residences here. It's still the best of the Costa del Azahar coastal playgrounds, despite the addition of 21st-century tourism trimmings.

VALENCIA

Unlike the Costa Blanca, it isn't completely overrun by foreigners. A high 80% of visitors are Spanish and many people from Madrid, Valencia and Castellón own summer apartments here.

Orientation & Information
Benicasim's beaches and accompanying development stretch for 6km along the coast. The main tourist office (☎ 964 30 09 62), Calle del Médico Segarra 4, is 1km inland in the old town, within the *ayuntamiento* (town hall). It's open 9 am to 2.30 pm daily; during summer two other offices function along the beachfront.

Things to See & Do
Those 6km of broad beach are the main attraction. Inland are the **Aquarama water park** (☎ 964 30 33 21), open 11 am to 7 or 8 pm June to September, and several **golf courses**.

Backing Benicasim and approximately 6km inland is the **Desierto de las Palmas**, a mountain range with a Carmelite monastery (1694) at its heart. Now a nature park and far from being a desert (for the monks it meant a place for 'mystic withdrawal'), it's a green, popular outdoor activities area. From **Monte Bartolo**, its highest point at 728m, there are staggering, wrap-around views.

Special Events
In early August thousands of young people gather for the annual Festival Internacional de Benicasim, now one of Spain's top outdoor music fests, which also embraces a festival of short films, dance and alternative theatre.

Places to Stay & Eat
Benicasim's eight *camping grounds* are all within walking distance of the beaches.

The youth hostel, *Albergue Argentina* (☎ 964 30 27 09, Avenida Calle Ferrandis Salvador 40), on the seafront, is a whopping, whitewashed complex with two pools and 140 bunks. Beds are 800/1100 ptas for juniors/seniors. Forget it in July and August, when it's always booked solid.

The best budget option is *Hostal el Forcat* (☎ 964 30 50 84, Avenida Castellón 20) in the old town. Rooms with bathroom above a rather seedy bar cost 2500 ptas per person year round. Open from March to September, *Hotel Avenida* (☎ 964 30 00 47, fax 964 30 00 79, Avenida Castellón 2), 100m away, is an appealing mid-range hotel with a pool and shady courtyard. Mid-July to mid-September, B&B (that second B is compulsory) costs between 3550 and 4700 ptas per person. The rest of the time, singles/doubles are good value at 3900/4850 ptas.

A plethora of economical *eateries* line Calle de Santo Tomás (the old town's main street).

Entertainment
Particularly on weekends and during summer, Benicasim has a vibrant nightlife. Along Calle de los Dolores in the old town, you'll find a good collection of bars, including *Pay Pay, Cactus, Bumerang* and *Campus*.

OROPESA
It's a fine scenic drive from Benicasim to Oropesa (Orpesa) along a narrow road winding around the rocky coastline. With its two main beaches of **Morro de Gos** and **La Concha**, this small resort is a relatively tranquil alternative in the high season to seething Peñíscola and Benicasim, to the north and south. The main tourist office (☎ 964 76 66 12) is on Plaza París beside Playa de la Concha and there's another at Avenida de la Plana 1 in the old town.

PEÑÍSCOLA
postcode 12598 • pop 4700
Peñíscola's old town, all narrow, cobbled streets and whitewashed houses, perches on a rocky, fortified promontory jutting into the sea. Its 13th-century **castle** (200 ptas) was built by the Knights Templar on Arab foundations and later became home to Pedro de Luna ('Papa Luna', the deposed Pope Benedict XIII). Although it's often open longer, the castle is officially open from 9.30 am to 1 pm and 4.30 to 6 pm.

VALENCIA

There's also a recently inaugurated **Museu de la Mar** (Maritime Museum), open 10 am to 2 pm daily year round; afternoon hours are from 4 pm and vary according to season.

The old town is pretty as a postcard – and just as commercial, with dozens of souvenir and ceramics shops and clothes boutiques catering to the ascending hordes of tourists. By stark contrast, the modern high-rises sprouting northwards along the coast are mostly leaden and charmless. But the **Paseo Marítimo promenade** makes pleasant walking and the beach, one of the best around, is being extended a further 3km northwards.

The main tourist office (☎ 964 48 93 92) is at the south end of the Paseo Marítimo and there are a couple of others near the port and the beach.

Places to Stay & Eat

Welcoming *Chiki Bar (☎ 964 48 02 84, Calle Mayor 3)*, in addition to its engaging name, offers great value. Modern double rooms with bathroom are 4000 ptas (5000 ptas in high season) and its restaurant, open from Easter to October, does reasonable set-price meals.

Hotel-Restaurante Simo (☎ 964 48 06 20, e simo@peniscola.net, Calle Porteta 5), at the base of the old town, offers singles/ doubles with sea views and bathroom ranging from 4000/5000 ptas to 6400/8000 ptas in August.

Paseo Marítimo, the main waterfront promenade, is lined with *restaurants* specialising in local seafood (and high prices).

Getting There & Around

There are buses every half-hour between Peñíscola, Benicarló and Vinaro. Alternatively, hire a bike from Alquiler Dos Ruedas (☎ 670 45 72 27), Avenida Papa Luna 27, 150m south of the Peñíscola Palace hotel.

VINARÒS
postcode 12004 • pop 21,000

Unlike its sybaritic neighbours, Vinaròs is a working town whose port is still used commercially and by in-shore fishing boats. A fairly grim, dreary place, Vinaròs' redeeming feature is its fairly small but sandy beaches.

Iglesia Arciprestal on Plaza del Ayuntamiento is an interesting baroque church with a tall bell tower and elaborate main doorway decorated with candy-twist columns. From here, pedestrianised Calle Mayor takes you to the covered market, tourist office (☎ 964 45 33 34) and Playa del Fortí beach.

Pensión Casablanca (☎ 964 45 04 25, Calle de San Pascual 8), two blocks north of the tourist office, has presentable budget singles/doubles from 1700/3000 ptas; it's open from March to September. You've plenty of eating choices on the waterfront, most specialising in seafood.

Inland Valencia

In Valencia the difference between holiday *costa* and interior is, perhaps appropriately, marked by a motorway. Just head west of the A-7 and you find yourself in a different world – a truly Spanish one. The few tourists who venture away from the coast are richly rewarded. By far the easiest way to explore the region is with your own transport, although you can reach most of the main centres by bus or train.

Pick up the parchment-coloured series of fold-out map-brochures covering inland areas. Produced by the Comunidad Valenciana and packed with interesting information, they're available from provincial tourist offices in several languages, including English.

Cycling & Walking

The area is particularly popular with cyclists (on- and off-road) and walkers. The long-distance GR-7 walking trail crosses the Els Ports and La Tinença de Benifassà districts, while the GR-10 and GR-36 pass through the Alto Palancia region. Particularly in the Maestrazgo, there are many other shorter blazed day and half-day routes.

EL MAESTRAZGO

Straddling north-western Valencia and south-eastern Aragón (see the Aragón chapter), El Maestrazgo (El Maestrat in Catalan)

VALENCIA

is a mountainous land, sparsely dotted by ancient *pueblos* huddling on rocky outcrops, cones and ridges, as if seeking protection from warrior enemies and insulation from the area's harsh winters.

One such pueblo, Sant Mateu, was chosen in the 14th century by the *maestro* (hence the name El Maestrazgo) of the Montesa order of knights as his seat of power.

The area is a world away from the coastal resorts and little visited by non-Spaniards. Ask at local tourist offices for *Guía de Alojamientos del Maestrazgo,* a complete guide to accommodation from four-star hotels to *casas rurales* to camping grounds in both the Valencian and Aragonese sectors.

Morella

postcode 12300 • pop 2850 • elev 1000m
The fairy-tale town of Morella, commanding the southern corner of El Maestrazgo, is an outstanding example of a medieval fortress. Perched on a hill top, crowned by a castle and enclosed by a wall over 2km long, it's one of Spain's oldest continually inhabited towns.

Orientation & Information The town's walls are broken only by the seven entrance gates. Calle de la Muralla runs around the inner perimeter, but the rest of the town is a confusing, compact jumble of narrow streets, alleys and stairs.

The tourist office (☎ 964 17 30 32), closed Sunday afternoon and Monday, is just behind the Torres de San Miguel, twin 14th-century towers flanking the main entrance gate.

Things to See Morella's **castle**, although in ruins, remains imposing. You can almost hear the clashing of swords and clip clop of horses that were a part of fortress life. A strenuous climb is rewarded by breathtaking views of the town and surrounding countryside. The castle grounds are open 10.30 am to 6.30 pm daily (to 7.30 pm May to August); entry is 300 ptas.

The old town is best explored on foot. There are three small museums in the towers of the ancient walls: the **Museo Tiempo de Imagen** has a collection of old black and white photos of Morella; the **Museo Tiempo de Dinosaurios** presents a handful of dinosaur bones – the Maestrazgo's remote hills have been a treasure trove for palaeontologists – and a video (in Spanish); and the **Museo Tiempo de Historia** charts Morella's history. The **Museo del Sexenni** in the Sant Nicolau church evokes the atmosphere of this major fiesta (see Special Events). Entry to each costs 300 ptas or you can buy a combined ticket, including entry to the castle, for 1000 ptas.

The Gothic **Basílica de Santa María la Mayor** has two elaborately sculpted doorways on its south facade. Inside are a fine choir and altarpiece and the **Museo Arciprestal** (100 ptas).

Also worth seeing are the 14th-century **ayuntamiento**, the **Real Convento de San Francisco** – through whose tranquil cloister you pass to reach the cathedral – and several impressive manorial houses, such as the **Casa de la Cofradía de Labradores** (Farmer's Guild).

On the outskirts of town stand the arches of a 13th-century **aqueduct**.

Special Events Morella's major festival is the Sexenni, held every six years during August (the next is in 2006) in honour of the Virgen de Vallivana. Visit the Museo del Sexenni (mentioned earlier) to get the flavour of this major celebration. Annually in August, there's a baroque music festival, starring the huge organ in the Basílica de Santa María la Mayor.

Places to Stay The cheapest option is friendly *Fonda Moreno* (☎ 964 16 01 05, Calle de San Nicolás 12), which has six quaint, basic doubles at 2350 ptas.

Freshly refurbished *Hostal El Cid* (☎ 964 16 01 25, Puerta de San Mateo 2) has spruce singles/doubles with bathroom for 3400/5500 ptas. The ones at the front have magnificent views over the valley. Around the corner and just as trim is *Hotel La Muralla* (☎ 964 16 02 43, Calle de la Muralla 12), where rooms with bathroom cost 3600/5100 ptas, including breakfast. Both raise their prices by a modest 500 ptas during August.

Hotel Cardenal Ram (☎ 964 17 30 85, fax 964 17 32 16, e hotelcardenalram@ ctu.es, Cuesta de Suñer 1), all ancient stone floors, high ceilings and antique furniture, occupies a wonderfully transformed 16th-century cardinal's palace. Rooms with all facilities are 5350/8550 ptas.

Places to Eat The upstairs restaurant at *Fonda Moreno* (see Places to Stay) does a hearty menú for 950 ptas.

Once-famous *Restaurante Casa Roque* (☎ 964 16 03 36, Calle de Segura Barreda 8) these days lives on its fading laurels. All the same, its menú at 1350 ptas remains good value. Even better is the menú – 1250 ptas and rich in local dishes – of *Restaurante Vinatea* (☎ 964 16 07 44, Calle Blasco de Alagón 17). Order a plateful of the scrummy garbanzos en salsa de almendra (chick peas in almond sauce; 600 ptas); it's closed Monday.

The peaceful garden of *Restaurante Marqués de Cruïlles* (☎ 964 16 09 90) on Carrer de l'Hospital, just opposite the castle entrance, makes a restful drinks stop. It also offers mainly regional cuisine and has a fine menú at 1700 ptas. It's closed Tuesday evening and Wednesday.

Getting There & Around On weekdays, Autos Mediterráneo (☎ 964 22 05 36) runs two buses a day to/from both Castellón and Vinaròs. There's also one Saturday bus to/from Castellón.

Drivers can leave their vehicles in the large car park (300 ptas) just north of the main San Miguel gate.

Els Ports

Morella is the ancient capital of Els Ports, the 'mountain passes'. This north-eastern corner of Valencia offers some outstanding scenic drives and strenuous cycling excursions, as well as excellent possibilities for walkers and mountain climbers.

On the Forcall road, 4.5km west of town, the upmarket *Hotel Fábrica de Giner* (☎ 964 17 31 42, fax 964 17 31 97), occupying a renovated textile factory, has singles/doubles for 10,600/11,650 ptas. In the former workers housing of the same 19th-century industrial complex is Morella's *Youth Hostel* (☎ 964 16 01 00, fax 964 16 09 77), where a bed costs 1100 ptas and half-board 1900 ptas.

Forcall, 9km farther west, is a quiet village at the confluence of the Ríos Caldés and Cantavieja. Each weekend closest to 17 January, the Fiesta de San Antón (also known as 'La Santantonà'), a winter festival celebrating fire, briefly dispels the prevailing calm as local youths sprint through a blazing tunnel. On opposite sides of the Plaza Mayor stand two fine, renovated, 16th-century Aragonese palaces. One has been converted into an elegant hotel, *Hotel-Restaurante Palau dels Osset-Miró* (☎ 964 17 75 24, fax 964 17 75 56), where rooms, with original features, cost 11,000/15,000 ptas. Half-board (an extra 3600 ptas per person) is compulsory on weekends.

Beyond your budget? Then check in at *Hostal Aguilar* (☎ 964 17 11 06), Forcall's most easterly building, where rooms with bathroom, central heating and TV offer unbeatable value at 2000/3500 ptas (3000/5000 ptas in August).

Back on Plaza Mayor, *Mesón de la Vila* (☎ 964 17 11 25), with its attractive terracotta floors, stone arches and whitewashed walls, does a copious, excellent-value menú for 1300 ptas, even if the service is short on smiles.

At the end of Calle San Vicente, at the western limit of the village, is a fine nevera (ice house), sunk in 1638.

To the north is the tiny whitewashed village of **Villores**, while to the west stands the medieval castle of **Todolella**.

Mirambel
postcode 44141 • pop 145

If you want to see what a small, walled medieval town looks like without the usual modern-day add-ons, Mirambel's the place. Even though you penetrate only 2.5km into Aragón, you'll notice the switch in local chat from Catalan to Castilian.

Created by order of the Knights Templar in 1243, Mirambel boasts several magnificent Aragonese mansions. The town served

VALENCIA

as the headquarters of the Carlist forces in Valencia, Aragón and Murcia in the 19th century, its population reaching the dizzy heights of 950. Today only 150 remain, many of whom appeared as extras in Ken Loach's film *Land and Freedom,* which used Mirambel as its main location.

In the modest *Fonda Guimera (☎ 964 17 82 69, Calle de Agustín Pastor 28),* singles/doubles with bathroom cost 2000/3500 ptas and there's a cafe beneath.

Santuario de la Balma

For the unbelievers among you, an excursion 12km north of Villores to this sanctuary dedicated to Nuestra Señora de la Balma should be instructive. This extraordinary chapel is set inside the rock face – from which juts out a belfry. Behind the main altar is a forest of offerings to Our Lady – wax limbs, baby clothes, bridal dresses, military berets and so on – accompanied by notes of thanks to the Virgin for her protection or intercession. Attached to the sanctuary is a bar-restaurant (a scrummy plate of frogs' legs costs 650 ptas).

Tinença de Benifassà

Tinença de Benifassà is the collective name of seven isolated hamlets in the northernmost reaches of Valencia. Often snowbound in winter, they belonged in feudal times to the vast **Monasterio de Santa María de Benifassà**. The convent is still in use, and the nuns open their church to visitors between 1 and 3 pm every Thursday.

Around 7km south-west is **La Pobla de Benifassà**, featuring distinctive local stone houses fronted by timber balconies. *Hotel Tinença de Benifassà (☎ 977 72 90 44, Calle Mayor 50),* set in a restored villa, has 10 attractive singles/doubles with heating and TV at 7700/9600 ptas.

Most other villages in the area, including **Bellestar**, **Fredes** and **Coratxá**, are uninhabited in winter.

Catí

About 35km south-east of Morella is the well-preserved medieval village of Catí, famous for its cheeses.

Up in the mountains 5km away, the tiny spa village of **L'Avellá** is no more than a dozen buildings, a 16th-century chapel and a plant for bottling the spring water. *Fonda Miralles (☎ 964 76 50 51)* is a simple hostal, open from July to September.

Sant Mateu
postcode 12004 • pop 1800

Farther east and 5km south of the N-232 is Sant Mateu, ancient capital of the Maestrazgo. Its impressive mansions and elaborate facades are reminders of the town's more illustrious past and former wealth, based upon the wool trade. Bars and cafes surround the colonnaded Plaza Mayor, from where signposts point to four municipal museums: the **Museo Paleontológico**, **Museo Arciprestal** of religious art, **Museo Histórico-Etnológico**, co-located with the tourist office and town hall in a fine 15th-century building, and the new **Museo les Presons** in the former jail.

The tourist office (☎ 964 41 66 58) is just off the Plaza Mayor at Calle del Historiador Betí 6.

Places to Stay & Eat *Hotel-Restaurante La Perdi (☎ 964 41 60 82, Calle del Historiador Betí 9)* has modern, comfortable singles/doubles with bathroom, TV and heating at 3000/5000 ptas (1000 ptas more from mid-July to mid-September); its restaurant has a good *menú* for 900 ptas. Cheaper but less welcoming, *Hostal el Cubano (☎ 964 41 63 95, Calle del Historiador Betí 26)* has rooms with bathroom for 2650/4000 ptas.

On a rocky hillside east of Sant Mateu is *Restaurante Mare de Déu (☎ 964 41 60 44)*. A monastery until the civil war (take a peep at its over-the-top baroque chapel), it's now a warren of barrel-vaulted, whitewashed dining areas. Sadly, neither the food – albeit reasonably priced – nor the service is what such a magnificent site merits. The restaurant's open daily July to September and at weekends during the rest of the year. Follow the signs from Sant Mateu's Plaza Mayor.

Getting There & Away Weekday buses link San Mateu and Vinaròs (one hour, four daily), Castellón (up to two hours, three daily)

n old *señora* among grapevines (Galicia)

La Coruña (Galicia)

OLIVER STREWE

DAMIEN SIMONIS

ishing boats bobbing in the Costa da Morte port of Laxe (Galicia).

DAMIEN SIMONIS

Forested hills, jagged rock and terraced fields, near Selle (Valencia)

Church near the Plaza de la Iglesia, Altea (Valencia)

Murals depicting past harvests, Requena (Valencia)

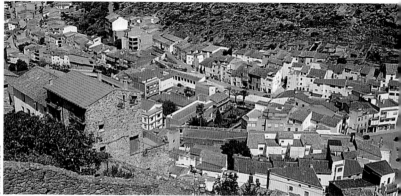

View of Vilafamés from the town's hill-top Muslim castle (Valencia)

and Morella (1¼ hours, two daily). On Saturday, there's one bus to Castellón and Morella.

VILAFAMÉS
postcode 12006 • pop 1450

What draws visitors to Vilafamés, a hillside town 26km north of Castellón, is its excellent **Museo Popular de Arte Contemporáneo** on Calle de Arriba. Within the 15th-century Palacio del Batlle – worth a visit in its own right – is an excellent, highly eclectic collection of contemporary paintings and sculpture. The museum is open 11 am to 1 pm and 5 to 7 pm weekdays, 11 am to 2 pm and 4 to 7 pm weekends (300 ptas).

The small old town is an agreeable clutter of whitewashed houses and civic buildings in rust-red stone. The 18th-century **Iglesia de la Asunción** features some unique ceramic artworks. From Plaza de la Sangre, stone steps take you up to the **castle**, with its Muslim foundations, rebuilt circular turret and sensational panoramas.

Hotel El Rullo (☎ 964 32 93 84, Calle de la Fuente 2), 200m below the museum, has eight rooms with bathroom and great views at 2000 per person, including breakfast. Down the road, you can get a *menú* for 1100 ptas at *Meson El Rullo*.

MONTANEJOS
postcode 12448 • pop 465

It's a spectacular drive from Castellón up the Río Mijares gorges to this popular resort and spa village, surrounded by craggy, pine-clad mountains. The warm springs of the nearby **Fuente de Los Baños** and the cool, fresh mountain air attract hordes of mainly Spanish visitors in summer. The village, uninteresting in itself, is a popular base for mountain sports. The tourist office (☎ 964 13 11 53) is within the Balneario (spa) on Carretera Tales.

Places to Stay

To meet friendly, outdoor folk, choose *Refugio de Escaladores* (☎ 964 13 13 17, ℮ erlopsas@teleline.es), where a dorm bed with breakfast costs 1200 ptas. There's also limited camping space (500 ptas per person). It's closed mid-January to March.

Most hotels open only in summer and on weekends. The upmarket *Hotel Rosaleda del Mijares* (☎ 964 13 10 79, fax 964 13 11 36, Carretera Tales 28), open year round, has singles/doubles from 4500/6950 ptas (6300/8550 ptas in high summer).

ALTO PALANCIA

Don't go out of your way, but if you happen to be heading along the N-234 (linking Sagunto and Teruel as it follows the upper reaches of the Río Palancia), there are some worthwhile short stop-offs.

Segorbe, 33km north-west of Sagunto, is the main town of the valley, with an impressive cathedral with a tranquil cloister. Inside one of the alcoves is a small museum, open 11 am to 1 pm (200 ptas). And you thought the running of the bulls in Pamplona was interesting? In the first week of September it's run here too – on horseback! The tourist office (☎ 964 71 32 54) is beside the municipal car park.

Navajas, shaded by cypress and palm trees, is surrounded by orchards, almond and olive groves, and loads of springs. Note the charming tiled and pastel-painted summer villas, built during the 19th century by rich Valencians.

Municipal *Camping Altamira* (☎ 964 71 32 11) is open daily from mid-July to mid-October (weekends only during the rest of the year). *Hostal el Jardín de Estornell* (☎/fax 964 71 11 98, Calle Valencia 1), open year round, has fully equipped double rooms from 5900 ptas.

Jérica is dominated by an unusual *mudéjar* tower, but has little else going for it. In and around **Viver**, a couple of kilometres away, over 50 springs gurgle and spurt. Nearby is *Camping Villa de Viver* (☎ 964 14 13 34).

REQUENA
postcode 46340 • pop 15,000

On the N-111 highway 71km west of Valencia, Requena is a bustling commercial centre from whose heart rises a little, walled, medieval town, established by the Muslims in the 8th century. Requena's former wealth came from silk; at one time it

VALENCIA

La Tomatina

MICK WELDON

Buñol? It'll make you see red.

If you happen to be in Valencia on the last Wednesday in August, you can participate in one of Spain's messiest and most bizarre festivals. Held in the town of Buñol (about 40km west of Valencia on the N-111 highway and the Madrid railway), La Tomatina is, believe it or not, a tomato-throwing festival.

Buñol is an otherwise drab industrial town; its outskirts are overshadowed by a massive, smoke-belching cement factory, while the old town is dominated by a crumbling 12th-century stone castle.

The festival's origins are obscure, but who cares. And while it mightn't last long, it attracts up to 30,000 visitors to a town that normally has just 9000 inhabitants.

Here's how it goes: just before noon on the day of the festival, truckloads of ripe, squishy tomatoes (125,000kg is one estimate) are delivered to (thrown at) the waiting crowd, and for the next hour or so everyone joins in a frenzied, cheerful and anarchic tomato war. The most enthusiastic participants chant *'tomate, tomate, queremos tomate!'* ('tomato, tomato, we want tomato!')

After being pounded with pulp, expect to be sluiced down with hoses by the local fire brigade.

Fun, fun, fun! The lunacy takes place on the town's main square and Calle del Cid.

At 1 pm an explosion signals the end and the change into their stash of fresh clothes. Most people come for the day, arriving on the morning train from Valencia and heading back in the afternoon.

---

had 800 active looms, making this tiny town Spain's fourth-biggest producer. Nowadays it's primarily wine country, producing robust reds and sparkling *cavas*.

In late August/early September, Requena's Fiesta de la Vendimia brings revellers from far around to participate in this hearty bacchanal celebrating the end of the grape harvest.

The tourist office (☎ 96 230 38 51) is near the entrance to the old town at Calle de García Montés s/n.

Things to See

Enter the old quarter beside the 10th-century Muslim **Torre del Homenaje**. Within the town walls are the Gothic **Santa María** and **San Salvador** churches, each with a magnificent main portal, and sturdy manorial houses such as the **Casa del Arte Mayor de la Seda** (silk guild house), **Casa del Corregidor** (mayor's house) and **Palacio del Cid**.

The **Museo Municipal** (open 11 am to 2 pm daily except Monday; 300 ptas) is in the **Convento Carmelito** near Plaza Consistorial in the new town. Possibly more interesting is what lies below ground. Plaza de la Villa (Plaza Albornoz) in the old town hides in its intestines a network of interlinked **cuevas** (cellars), once used as storerooms and, during strife, hideouts. Guided visits leave from the tourist office on the hour five times daily at weekends.

Places to Stay & Eat

Pensión Bar Cantarranas (☎ 96 230 50 80, Calle de García Montés 43) has good singles/doubles at 1500/3000 ptas (2000/4000 ptas with bath). Downstairs is a bar-restaurant where you can eat well for about 1000 ptas.

Hotel Avenida (☎ 96 230 04 80, Calle de San Agustín 10), just off Avenida del Arrabal, has rooms with bath and TV from 3000/4800 ptas.

If you can't visit the cuevas, eat at *Mesón La Villa* (☎ 96 230 12 75, *Plaza de Albornoz 13)* and ask your hosts to let you see theirs – briefly used by the local branch of the Inquisition for the cheerful business of torturing heretics.

Getting There & Away

Requena is on the Valencia-Madrid railway. Seven trains run daily to/from Valencia (505/825 ptas one way/return) and three to Madrid.

JÁTIVA

postcode 03009 • pop 25,000

Játiva (Xàtiva in Catalan), snug at the base of the Serra Vernissa mountain range 50km south of Valencia, has a fascinating history.

The nearby Cova Negra (Black Cave) revealed relics over 30,000 years old and a Neanderthal skull. In the 11th century the Muslims built Europe's first paper manufacturing plant here. After the Reconquista, Játiva became Valencia's second-largest city. It was the birthplace of the Borgia Popes Calixtus III and Alexander VI, but its glory days ended in 1707 when Felipe V's troops torched most of the town.

Information

The tourist office (☎ 96 227 33 46) is at Alameda de Jaime I 50, the shady main drag. It's open 10 am to 1.30 pm and 4 to 6 pm (mornings only on weekends, closed Monday).

Things to See & Do

Most of Játiva's monuments are south and uphill from the Alameda. The **Museo del Almudín** houses a fine collection of archaeological relics and artworks, including the famed portrait of Felipe V, hung upside down in retribution for his pyrotechnic assault. It's open 10 am to 2 pm and 4 to 6 pm Tuesday to Saturday, mornings only on weekends and June to September (free).

In the heart of town, the 16th-century **Colegiata Basílica** (Collegiate Church) and its rich treasures (open 10.30 am to 1.30 pm Monday to Saturday) merit a visit.

It's a long climb to the **castle**, from where the views are marvellous. On the way, stop by the 18th-century **Ermita de San José** and **Iglesia de Sant Feliu** (1269), Játiva's oldest church. The castle grounds are open 10 am to 7 pm (to 6 pm in winter) daily except Monday (free).

Places to Stay & Eat

Accommodation is limited. Three generations of the same family have run *Fonda El Margallonero* (☎ 96 227 66 77, *Plaza del Mercado 42)*. It has simple rooms at 1400 ptas per person and a popular, bustling restaurant (open at lunchtime only, closed Sunday) with *menús,* strong on traditional cooking, at 1300 ptas and 2000 ptas.

A charming alternative for those with fatter wallets is *Hostería de Mont Sant* (☎ 96 227 50 81, *fax 96 228 19 05,* **e** *montsant@ servidex.com)* on the road to the castle. It has 15 beautifully appointed rooms with full facilities. Views over the town and valley are superb, the restaurant is first class and guests can enjoy the fine gardens and swimming pool. Singles/doubles cost from 13,900/16050 ptas.

Casa la Abuela (☎ 96 228 10 85, *Plaza de la Bassa 6)* is renowned for its a-la-carte regional cuisine and does a good *menú* for 2000 ptas.

Getting There & Away

Train and bus stations are on Avenida del Cavaller Ximén de Tovia. The train's your best bet. Frequent local services connect Játiva with Valencia (435 ptas, every half-hour) and most Valencia-Madrid trains stop here too. You can also reach Alicante (1020 to 2300 ptas, three daily) and Gandía (change in Silla; 435 ptas, frequent).

VILLENA

postcode 03203 • pop 31,500

Villena, on the N-330 between Alicante and Albacete, is an upbeat town with a couple of worthwhile attractions, some fine restaurants and swanky bars.

Head for Plaza de Santiago, bordered by the tourist office (☎ 96 580 38 04) and, within the fine 16th-century **Palacio Municipal**, the **Museo Arqueológico**. The pride of its collection are 60 priceless gold

VALENCIA

Fiestas de Moros y Cristianos

More than 80 towns and villages throughout Valencia hold their own Fiesta de Moros y Cristianos (Moors and Christians festival) to celebrate the Reconquista, the region's liberation from Arab rule.

The biggest and best-known is Alcoy's, when, in April, hundreds of locals dress up in elaborate traditional costumes representing different 'factions' – Muslim and Christian soldiers, slaves, guild groups, town criers, heralds, bands – and march through the streets in spectacular and colourful processions with mock battles.

A wooden fortress is erected in the main plaza, on which the various processions converge from different directions. Tradition dictates who goes where when, but standing in the crowd it all feels incredibly chaotic with processions coming at you from every direction.

It's an exhilarating spectacle of sights and sounds: soldiers in shining armour, white-cloaked Muslim warriors carrying scimitars and shields, turban-topped Arabs, scantily clad wenches, brass bands, exploding blunderbusses, fireworks displays and confetti showering down on the crowds from above.

Each town has its own variation on the format of the festival, steeped in traditions that allude to the events of the Reconquista. For example, Villena's festival (5–9 September) features midnight parades, while Villajoyosa (24–31 July) re-enacts the landing of Muslim ships on the beaches. Some other major festivals are those held in Bocairent (1–5 February), Biar (10–13 May) and Ontinyent (end August).

artefacts weighing over 10kg and dating from around 1000 BC. It's open 9 am to 2 pm weekdays and entry is free. Facing it, the **Iglesia de Santiago** has a flamboyant, impressively restored interior. Perched high above the town, the **Castillo de la Atalaya** is splendidly lit at night.

Villena celebrates its Moros y Cristianos fiesta from 5 to 9 September (see the boxed text 'Fiestas de Moros y Cristianos').

Hotel-Restaurante Salvadora *(☎ 96 580 09 50,* e *hrsalvador@arrakis.es, Avenida*

de la Constitución 102) has pleasant singles/doubles with all facilities for 3800/5700 ptas.

ELDA

Foot fetishists shouldn't miss the **Museo de Calzado** (Shoe Museum; ☎/fax 96 538 30 21) in Elda, which vies with Elche for the title of shoemaking capital of Spain. Above the mezzanine floor with its row upon row of Heath Robinson drills, stamps and sewing machines, it's wall-to-wall footware – boots through the ages, shoes and slippers from around the world, fanciful designs that must have been agony to wear and donated cast-offs from matadors, flamenco dancers, King Juan Carlos and Queen Sofia and other well-shod great and good. This temple to leather is open 10 am to 1 pm and 4 to 8 pm Tuesday to Saturday, plus Sunday morning (400 ptas).

NOVELDA

If you're a fan of Art Nouveau and *modernismo,* make the 25km pilgrimage from Alicante to Novelda's wonderful **Casa-Museo Modernista** (☎ 96 560 02 37), Calle Mayor 24. A bourgeois mansion completed in 1903, its stained glass, soft shapes in wood, period furniture and magnificent spiralling wrought-iron staircase take the breath away. It's open 9.30 am to 2 pm and 4.30 to 6 pm weekdays plus 11 am to 2 pm Saturday (free).

Peek too inside No 6 – these days the municipal library – and admire the exterior of the Cruz Roja (Spanish Red Cross) building at Plaza del Ayuntamiento.

ALCOY
postcode 03203 • pop 61,000

For 51 weeks a year, there's little to entice you to the lugubrious town of Alcoy (Alcoi), 50km south of Játiva – and everything to draw you here in the third week of April. Then, it's time for Alcoy's annual Moros y Cristianos festival (see the boxed text 'Fiestas de Moros y Cristianos'), the Valencia region's most colourful event after Valencia's Fallas.

Friendly ***Hostal Savoy*** *(☎ 96 554 72 72, Calle Casablanca 9),* one block south of the main Plaza de España, is markedly the cheaper of only two accommodation options in town. Singles/doubles with bathroom cost 3900/5500 ptas.

There are four to five trains daily to Valencia (1¾ hours, 945 ptas) via Játiva. From the nearby bus station, four to six services run to Valencia, at least 10 to Alicante and a couple a day to Gandia.

CENTRAL VALLEYS
Vall de Gallinera & Vall d'Alcalá

A few kilometres north of Alcoy, a judicious right (east) turn at Muro d'Alcoy sends you down winding valley roads past a series of pueblos, mostly of Muslim origin (look for village names beginning with *Beni* – eg, Benisivà, Benialí and Benissili – a sure-fire indicator). You're in the heart of Valencia's cherry-growing country and the Vall de Gallinera is especially rich in the juicy red fruit. The second half of March, when the trees are in blossom, is sensational. **Planes**, watched over by the ruins of an old castle, merits a short stop.

A tempting detour about halfway between Muro d'Alcoy and Pego leads down a second valley, the Vall d'Alcalá. The village of the same name is 5.5km down the road, and on the way you'll pass hill-top **Margarida**.

There's a modest *camping ground* (☎ 96 551 43 33) with a cafe-restaurant at Vall d'Alcalá, open from Easter to mid-October, and *Casa Rural Almasera* (☎ 96 551 42 32) in Margarida with singles/doubles for 4000/6000 ptas, including breakfast.

Guadalest

A still more spectacular route runs west from the coast just south of Calpe towards Alcoy. It's well worthwhile, even if you get no farther than the old Muslim settlement of Guadalest, about halfway along and dominated by the Castillo de San José, reached by a natural tunnel. This is about the only place in inland Valencia that tour buses have unfortunately discovered in force.

ELCHE
postcode 03200 • pop 192,000

Just 20km south-west of Alicante, Elche (Elx in Catalan) is renowned for the Misteri d'Elx, its annual mystery play (see the

---

Misteri d'Elx

The Misteri d'Elx, a two-act lyric drama dating from the Middle Ages, is performed annually in the Basílica de Santa María in Elche.

One distant day, according to legend, a casket was washed up on Elche's Mediterranean shore. Inside were a statue of the Virgin and the 'Consueta', the plot of a mystery play describing Our Lady's death, assumption into heaven and coronation.

The story tells how the Virgin, realising that death is near, asks God to allow her to see one last time the apostles, who arrive one by one from distant lands. In their company, she dies at peace. Once received into paradise, she is crowned Queen of Heaven and Earth to swelling music, the ringing of bells, cheers all round and – hey, we're in the Valencia region – spectacular fireworks.

The mystery's two acts, La Vespra – the eve of her death – and La Festa – the celebration of her assumption and coronation – are performed in Catalan by the people of Elche themselves on 14 and 15 August respectively (with public rehearsals the three previous days).

If your visit doesn't coincide with the real thing, you can see a multimedia presentation – complete with a virtual apostle – in the Museu Municipal de la Festa, Carrer Major 27 (about a block west of the basilica). Lasting 35 minutes, it's repeated several times daily and has an optional English commentary (500 ptas). The museum, which also contains relevant paraphernalia, is open 10 am to 1 pm and 4.30 to 8.30 pm Tuesday to Saturday plus Sunday morning.

---

boxed text), and its extensive palm groves, first planted by the Muslims and now the most extensive in Europe. Their irrigation systems converted the region into a rich agricultural district that produces citrus fruit, figs, almonds, dates and cotton to this day.

Orientation & Information

The town is divided by the Río Vinalopó, with the older town on the eastern side.

VALENCIA

Most of the parks and monuments are in the old town. The tourist office (☎ 96 545 27 47) is on the south-eastern corner of the Parque Municipal. It is open 10 am to 7 pm weekdays and 10 am to 2 pm weekends.

The train and bus stations are beside each other on Avenida de la Libertad (also called Avenida del Ferrocarril), north of the centre. From either, exit and take a left, then take the first left down Paseo de la Estación (which leads to the Parque Municipal, tourist office and town centre).

Things to See

Palm groves – in all, around a quarter of a million trees – dominate the city and its environs. Some are pretty dishevelled, but both the **Parque Municipal** and newly spruced-up **Parque de Palmeras del Filet de Fora** are pleasant to stroll through. The **Huerto del Cura** is a lovely private garden with tended lawns, colourful flowerbeds and a freakish eight-pronged palm tree. Opposite the hotel of the same name, the garden is open 9 am to 6 pm daily (300 ptas).

The narrow streets of the old Vila Murada (walled city) are also worth a wander.

At the recently renovated 12th-century **Arab Baths** on Plaza de Santa Lucia, there's an impressive free audiovisual presentation with optional English soundtrack. They're open 9.30 am to 1.30 pm and 4.15 to 7.30 pm Tuesday to Saturday (morning only Sunday).

The baroque **Basílica de Santa María** is used for performances of the Misteri d'Elx (see the boxed text), while the east wing of the 15th-century **Palacio de Altamira** is home to the small **Museo Arqueológico Municipal**, open 10 am to 1 pm and 4 to 7 pm daily except Monday (100 ptas). Farther south on Carrer Major de Raval is the **Museo de Arte Contemporáneo**.

The Alcúdia archaeological site is 2km south of the town centre. Core hours at its excellent **Museo Arqueológico** (☎ 96 545 36 03) are 10 am to 1 pm and 4 to 7 pm Tuesday to Saturday plus Sunday morning. On this site was unearthed the emblematic Dama de Elche, a masterpiece of Iberian art (see the Museo Arqueológico Nacional section in the Madrid chapter). The museum displays the rich findings from a settlement that was occupied continuously from Neolithic to late Visigoth times; entry is 100 ptas.

Places to Stay & Eat

Budget choices are very limited. One little gem is the friendly, spotlessly clean **Hotel Faro** (☎ 96 546 62 63, Camí dels Magros 24), where simple singles/doubles will cost you 1800/3600 ptas (2000/4000 ptas July to September).

Do yourself a favour – save up, come on a weekend and book into the magnificent **Hotel Huerto del Cura** (☎ 96 545 80 40, Calle de la Puerta de la Morera 14). Set in lush gardens and shaded by huge palms, it has tennis courts, a gym, sauna, solarium, a wonderful kidney-shaped pool and spa, and bungalow-style rooms – you're right in the city centre but it feels like a tropical island. During the week it's popular with business-people and pricey at 14,450/19,100 ptas. But on Friday, Saturday and Sunday (and for most of August), rates drop to 10,700/12,850 ptas. The hotel restaurant, **Els Capellans**, concentrates on local cuisine.

If you prefer to eat more modestly, the cosy **Bar Los Extremenos** on Carrer de la Mare de Déu serves great tapas.

Getting There & Away

Elche is on the Alicante-Murcia railway, with 17 to 24 trains daily to both Alicante (235 ptas) and Murcia (325 ptas).

AM Molla has buses operating every half-hour to Alicante (205 ptas) on weekdays (fewer at weekends) and plenty to Santa Pola (260 ptas).

ORIHUELA

postcode 03360 • pop 51,000
On the banks of the Río Segura, Orihuela, set at the base of a barren mountain of rock, is the district capital of the Vega Baja region. It's quite a dull place apart from the old quarter, which has several interesting Gothic, Renaissance and, especially, baroque buildings.

The tourist office (☎ 96 530 62 94) is at Calle Francisco Die 25.

VALENCIA

Things to See

Orihuela's old quarter includes half a dozen buildings, registered as national monuments, with a bewildering and uncoordinated range of opening times.

The 16th-century **Convento de Santo Domingo**, which functioned as a university until the early 19th century, has fine Renaissance cloisters. Built on the site of a mosque, the 14th-century Catalan-Gothic **Catedral de San Salvador** houses the **Museo Diocesano de Arte Sacra**, with a religious art collection, including Velázquez's *Tentación de Santo Tomé* (Temptation of St Thomas).

The **Iglesia de las Santas Justa y Rufina** has a Renaissance facade and a Gothic tower graced with gargoyles. Also noteworthy are the baroque **Palacio Episcopal**, the 14th-century **Iglesia de Santiago Após-tol** (100 ptas) and, crowning the mountain, the ruins of a castle originally constructed by the Muslims.

Places to Stay & Eat

Hostal-Residencia Rey Teodomiro (☎ 96 674 33 48, Avenida de Teodomiro 10) has singles/doubles with bathroom, TV, air-con and heating for 3750/6450 ptas.

Try some of the distinctive local dishes such as *cocido con pelotas* (meat stew with dumplings) and *arroz con costra* (a baked rice dish topped with an egg crust).

Getting There & Away

The train station is a five-minute walk from the centre at the end of Avenida de Teodomiro. Orihuela is on the Alicante-Murcia railway. The bus station is on Avenida Doctor García Rogel, a little north of the Convento de Santo Domingo.

If you're driving, avoid claustrophobia in Orihuela's narrow streets by leaving your vehicle in the large Entrepuentes car park beside the river.

Costa Blanca

Alicante and the 'White Coast' are among Europe's most heavily visited regions. If you want a secluded beach in midsummer,

stay away. But if you're looking for a lively social life, good beaches and a suntan…

It isn't all concrete and package deals. Although the original fishing villages have long been engulfed by the sprawl of resorts, holiday villas and skyscrapers, a few kernels of old towns have survived. Particularly attractive (everything is relative) are Jávea and Altea – and they're better still out of season. During July and August your chances of finding accommodation anywhere are limited if you haven't reserved. Out of season many places close but those remaining open usually charge substantially less than in high summer and during national holidays.

Most buses linking Valencia and Alicante head straight down the motorway, some making a stop in Benidorm. A few, however, call by other intervening towns. Renfe trains connect Valencia with Gandia, while FGV narrow-gauge trains ply the scenic route between Denia and Alicante, stopping at all pueblos en route.

GANDIA

postcode 46700 ● pop 59,000

Gandia, 65km south of Valencia, is a tale of two cities. The main town, once home to a branch of the Borja dynasty (more familiar to most people as the infamous Borgias), is a prosperous commercial centre.

Four kilometres away on the coast, Playa de Gandia has so far avoided the tawdriness of too many Costa Blanca resorts. Its long, broad, sandy beaches are groomed daily by a fleet of tractors and backed by medium-rise hotels and apartments. It's a popular and predominantly Spanish resort with a well-merited reputation for great summer nightlife.

Information

The main tourist office (☎ 96 287 77 88) is in town opposite the train station. Core weekday hours are 10 am to 1 pm and 4.30 to 6.30 pm, plus Saturday morning. The Playa de Gandia tourist office (☎ 96 284 24 07), beside the beach on Paseo Marítimo, is open daily in summer but only Sunday 10 am to 1 pm the rest of the year.

VALENCIA

Things to See & Do

Chief among Gandia's historic buildings is the magnificent **Palacio Ducal de los Borja** (☎ 96 287 12 00), the 15th-century home of Duque Francisco de Borja and adorned with a collection of his personal belongings. One-hour guided tours in Spanish, with an accompanying leaflet in English, take place at 11 am and 6 pm (5 pm in winter) weekdays, plus Saturday morning (250 ptas).

There are two excellent Rutas Ecoturísticas (Ecotourism Routes). The 12km **Racó del Duc** walking and cycling trail follows an old railway line through unspoiled countryside between the villages of Vilallonga (8km south of Gandia) and L'Orxa. **Entre Senill i Borrò** is a 13km walking trail through coastal marsh and dunes from Gandia town to the coast. Both tourist offices have brochures in Spanish describing the routes.

Places to Stay

Gandia has a couple of camping grounds. *Camping la Naranja* (☎ 96 284 16 16), on Camino Assagador de Morant, is closer to the beach. *Camping L'Alquería* (☎ 96 284 04 70) is situated 1km inland but has a pool in compensation.

Some 5km south of Gandia beside Playa de Piles is the excellent beachfront youth hostel, *Albergue Mar i Vent* (☎ 96 283 17 48). Closed late December and January, it charges 800/1100 ptas for juniors/seniors. Take La Amistad bus from opposite the train station.

Highly recommended *El Nido* (☎ 96 284 46 40, Calle de Alcoy 22) is a friendly hostal near the beach where bright singles/doubles cost 3800/5500 ptas (up to 5500/8500 ptas in July and August). Its restaurant has filling *menús* at 1300 and 1500 ptas. Nearby, *Week-end* (☎ 96 284 00 97, Calle Mare Nostrum 45), above a small, pleasant bar, has rooms for 3200/5350 ptas (4300/8550 ptas June to mid-September).

Modern *Hotel La Alberca* (☎/fax 96 284 51 63, Calle de Cullera 8), 300m from the beach, has comfortable, excellent-value rooms at 3200/5350 ptas (4300/7500 ptas in high season).

Up in town, *Hotel La Safor* (☎ 96 286 40 11, fax 96 286 41 79, **e** scampturia@tpi .infomail.es, Carretera de Valencia 40) has good singles/doubles/triples with bathroom and air-con from 3750/6450/9650 ptas (5000/9000/12850 in August).

Entertainment

There's great summer nightlife at Playa de Gandia, with bars, including *Paco Paco Paco*, *Mama Ya Lo Sabe* and *La Década*, clustered around Plaza del Castell, barely 300m inland from the beach. After they close (around 3 am), head for one of the discos that bop till dawn: *Coco Loco* is on the corner of Paseo Marítimo and Calle de Galicia, while *La Arasa* is just south of the tennis club.

Getting There & Around

Trains run between Gandia and Valencia (one hour, 550 ptas) every half-hour (hourly at weekends). The stylish new bus station and train station are located together. La Marina Gandiense buses for Playa de Gandia (125 ptas, every 20 minutes) stop opposite the train station.

DENIA

postcode 03700 • pop 30,000

Denia is a big, popular, pricey resort dominated by a large boat harbour.

Orientation & Information

The tourist office (☎ 96 642 23 67) is near the waterfront at Glorieta del Oculista Buigues 9. It's open 9.30 am to 1.30 pm and 4.30 to 7.30 pm daily (not Sunday afternoon). Both the train station and ferry terminal are no more than 100m from it. From the latter, ferries operate to Palma de Mallorca and Ibiza City (Balearia Lines) and San Antonio, Ibiza (Trasmediterránea plus Pitra and Balearia Lines). For more details, see the Balearic Islands chapter. Call ☎ 902-191 068 for information and reservations.

From the station seven trains a day follow the scenic route south to Alicante (2¼ hours, 995 ptas) via Calpe (340 ptas) and Benidorm (550 ptas). See also Getting There & Away in the Alicante section.

VALENCIA

Places to Stay

Right in front of the train station, *Hotel Costa Blanca* (☎ 96 578 03 36, Calle del Pintor Llorens 3) has singles/doubles from 4900/9500 ptas. Three blocks inland, *Hostal El Comercio* (☎ 96 578 00 71, Calle de la Via 43) with fewer frills has fully equipped rooms from 3700/4650 ptas (5000/7900 ptas in July and August).

XÀBIA

postcode 03730 • pop 22,000

Jávea, or Xàbia (the Catalan form, preferred by locals), with one-third of its resident population and over two-thirds of its annual visitors being non-Spanish, isn't the best place to meet the locals. This said, it's gentle, laid-back and well worth a visit early in the season, when the sun shines but the masses haven't arrived.

It's in three parts: the attractive old town (3km inland), El Puerto (the port) and the beach zone of El Arenal, which is lined with pleasant bar-restaurants. Just south, the promontory of **Cabo La Nao** offers spectacular views and tiny **Granadella** has a small, relatively uncrowded beach.

The main tourist office (☎ 96 579 43 56, fax 96 579 63 17) is in the old town's charming Plaza de la Iglesia and there are branches beside the port and in El Arenal.

Bookworld (☎ 96 646 22 53), Avenida Amanecer de España 13, carries a good range of books in English.

Places to Stay

There are two possibilities for camping: *Camping El Naranjal* (☎ 96 579 29 89), about 10 minutes' walk from the beach at El Arenal, and *Camping Jávea* (☎ 96 579 10 70, e camjavea@arrakis.es, Camino de la Fontana 2).

The pleasant port area has some reasonably priced accommodation. On the foreshore 200m south, *Pensión La Marina* (☎ 96 579 31 39, Avenida de la Marina Española 8) has bright singles/doubles with full bathroom or shower for 4000/7000–8000 ptas. Outside the summer season, all rooms are a bargain 3000 ptas. *Hotel Miramar* (☎/fax 96 579 01 02, Plaza Almirante Bastarreche 12) has cosy

rooms with air-con from 4000/7000 ptas (1500 ptas more from July to September).

In the old town, the clean if slightly shambolic *Hostal Levante* (☎ 96 579 15 91, Calle Maestro Alonso 5), a block behind Bookworld, has basic rooms for 2700/4500 ptas (5500 ptas with shower, 6500 ptas with bathroom).

Places to Eat

There's plenty of choice around the beach area. In the old town, two good options just off Plaza de la Iglesia are *Tasca La Rebotica* (☎ 96 579 28 55, Carrer de Sant Bertomeu 8), which does a daily rice special and has a good selection of tapas, and *Tasca Tonis* (☎ 96 646 18 51, Carrer Major 2).

Getting Around

You can rent a bike for 1000/5000 ptas per day/week from Bike Centre (☎/fax 96 646 11 50), Avenida Lepanto 21.

CALPE

postcode 03710 • pop 14,500

The Gibraltaresque **Peñon de Ifach**, a giant molar protruding from the sea, dominates the seaside resort of Calpe (Calp). The rock is a protected area through which a popular and fairly strenuous trail – allow a good 45 minutes – ascends towards the 332m summit. From its limit at the end of a dark tunnel, you can soak up the great views.

Two large bays sprawl either side of the Peñon: Playa Arenal on the southern side is backed by the old town, while Playa Levante to the north has most of the more recent development.

Information

The main tourist office (☎ 96 583 85 32) is on Plaza del Mosquit (in the old town and 200m from Plaza de la Constitución). It's open 9 am to 2 pm and 4.30 to 7.30 pm weekdays plus Saturday morning. There are others on Avenida de los Ejércitos Españoles (the ring road) and beside the port.

Places to Stay

Camping Ifach (☎ 96 583 04 77) and *Camping Levante* (☎ 96 583 22 72), both on

VALENCIA

Avenida de la Marina, are a brief walk from Playa Levante.

There are a couple of good-value places to bed down. *Pensión Centrica (☎ 96 583 55 28)* on Plaza de Ifach, just off Avenida Gabriel Miró, has pleasant, simple rooms for 1500 ptas per person. A stone's throw from the beachfront, neat *Hostal Crespo (☎ 96 583 39 31, Calle de la Pinta 1)* has eight doubles with bathroom (four rooms with sea views) ranging from 4000 to 6000 ptas. It's open from Easter to October.

Places to Eat

There are plenty of restaurants and bars around Plaza de la Constitución and along the main Avenida de Gabriel Miró. Attractive *Restaurante El Pati* at No 34 has a *menú* for 1600 ptas. A couple of blocks towards the waterfront, *La Cambra (☎ 96 583 06 05, Calle Delfín 2)*, all agreeably antique wood and tile, specialises in rice dishes (1300 to 1800 ptas) and has a rich a-la-carte selection; it's closed Sunday.

ALTEA

Altea, separated from Benidorm only by the thick wedge of the Sierra Helada, could be a couple of moons away. Its beaches are mostly pebbles and rock – and that's what's saved it so far from mass tourism, though the pile drivers are beginning to pound. The beaches and harbour are backed by a pleasant foreshore promenade and a strip of low-key development. The whitewashed old town, perched on a hill top overlooking the sea, retains its charm despite having been systematically gentrified.

Altea's tourist office (☎ 96 584 41 14), on the beachfront at Calle San Pedro 9, is open 10 am to 2 pm and 5 to 7 pm weekdays plus Saturday morning (also Sunday morning July to September).

Up in the old town, *Hostal Fornet (☎ 96 584 30 05, Calle Beniardá 1)* has comfy single/double rooms from 2140/3400 ptas (3425/4280 ptas with bathroom). Off Plaza de la Iglesia and especially down Calle Major, there's a profusion of cute little restaurants, many open evenings only except in high summer. On the square itself,

Trattoria dels Artistes remains a good Italian restaurant.

BENIDORM
postcode 03500 • pop 56,500

It's easy to be snobbish about Benidorm, who long ago sold her birthright to cheap package tourism (nearly five million visitors annually), and indeed many of the horror tales are true. The 5km of white sandy beaches *are* backed by hideous concrete high-rises and its streets *are* thronged with lumpy tourists toting plastic beach toys. But Benidorm, though violated most summer nights by louts from northern Europe, still manages to retain a certain dignity. The foreshore is magnificent as the twin sweeps of Playa del Levante and the longer Playa del Poniente beach meet beneath Plaza del Castillo, where the land juts into the bay like a ship's prow.

In winter, it's predominantly a haven for elderly northern European tourists. But during summer it's for all ages – and becomes one of Spain's premier disco hot spots with a club scene to rival Ibiza's.

Information

The main tourist office (☎ 96 585 32 24) is in what's left of the old town at Calle Martínez Alejos 16 and there are three other branches around the resort.

You can go Net-surfing at Cyberc@t Cafe, Calle Ruzafa 1, an underground cavern of a place, open 10 am to 2 am daily.

Things to See & Do

Terra Mítica (Mythical Land; ☎ 902-40 45 40) on Benidorm's outskirts opened in August 2000 as the Costa Blanca's answer to Disney and to Port Aventura in Catalunya. A fun day out, especially if you're on holiday with children, it's Mediterranean in theme with areas devoted to ancient Egypt, Greece, Rome, Iberia and the Mediterranean islands. Entry varies from 2500/3500 ptas per child/adult to 3300/4600 ptas, according to season.

Side by side, **Aqualandia** (☎ 96 586 01 00) – entry 1375/2375 ptas for children/adults, open from May to October – and **Mundomar** (☎ 96 586 91 01) – entry 1150/1975 ptas, open year round, with parrots, dolphins, sea lions, even bats – are each worth a full day. You can buy a combined ticket, which can be used on different days, for 1900/3475 ptas.

Should Benidorm's frenetic pace get you down, pick up a free copy of *Routes Across Sierra Helada* from the tourist office, pull on your walking shoes and take one of the walks into the hills to the north of town, for superb seascapes and views of the bay.

Places to Stay
Since almost everyone's on a package deal, Benidorm's accommodation comes expensive for the independent traveller. Our recommendations are all in the old town.

Hotel Nou Calpí (☎/fax 96 681 29 96, ✉ hotelnoucalpi@hotmail.com, Plaza Constitución 5) has freshly refurbished singles/doubles with full bathroom for 2700/5000 ptas (3000/6500 ptas July to October), including breakfast.

Hostal La Santa Faç (☎ 96 585 40 63, fax 96 681 22 48, ✉ hotelsantafaz@ctv.es, Calle Santa Faç 18), also recently renovated, has singles/doubles/triples with all facilities, including air-con, for 7500/10,700/16,100 ptas. It's open from April to October only.

Major hotels can be reasonable value out of season. *Hotel Colón* (☎/fax 96 585 04 12, Paseo de Colón 3) has winter singles/doubles with balcony and sea views for 4500/6500 ptas, rising to 6500/10,000 ptas in August. *Hotel Bilbaíno* (☎/fax 96 585 08 04, ✉ bilbaino@arrakis.es, Avenida Virgen del Sufragio 1), on the beachfront, charges from 4500/7500 to 7000/13,300 ptas.

Places to Eat
Good places with local cuisine are as rare as space in summer to spread your beach towel. For fish and seafood, visit long-established *Restaurante-Bar Enrique* (☎ 96 586 09 35, Calle Ricardo 3). For rice dishes and other Spanish selections, try *Aitona* (☎ 96 585 30 10, Calle Ruzafa 3), which does a good *menú* for 1400 ptas. For Benidorm's biggest concentration of local and Spanish regional restaurants and tapas bars, take your pick from those lining Calle Santo Domingo at the Plaza de la Constitución end. Drift into *La Cava Aragonesa*, which has a magnificent selection of tapas and fat canapes and serves good wine by the glass.

ALICANTE
postcode 03080 • pop 285,000
Alicante (Alacant) is the Valencia region's second-largest town. Dynamic and brimming with fresh projects, it has transformed itself in less than a decade from a rather seedy port to an attractive town which improves with every visit. And unlike its coastal neighbours, it's a real town, living for much more than tourism alone. Fit in a minimum of one night to experience its frenetic – and very Spanish – nightlife.

Orientation
Palm trees shade pedestrian Explanada de España, rich in cafes and running parallel to the harbour. Around Catedral de San Nicolás are the narrow streets of El Barrio (the old quarter), which has most of the cheaper accommodation options and the best nightlife. El Barrio is bordered by the Rambla de Méndez Núñez; to its south-west are the post office and bus and train stations.

Information
There are no fewer than five tourist offices around town. The main, regional one (☎ 965 20 00 00, fax 96 520 02 43) is at Rambla de Méndez Núñez 23, while the principal municipal ones are at the bus station and town hall.

Alicante's main post office (incorrectly shown on older town maps) is at the intersection of Calle Alemania and Calle Arzobispo Loaces.

Things to See & Do
The 16th-century **Castillo de Santa Bárbara** overlooks the city. A lift, reached by a footbridge opposite Playa del Postiguet, ascends deep within the mountain (400 ptas return). The castle is open 10 am to 8 pm daily (9 am to 7 pm October to March); entry is free. Inside is the **Colleción Capa**, a permanent display of contemporary Spanish sculpture; entry is 100 ptas.

VALENCIA

ALICANTE

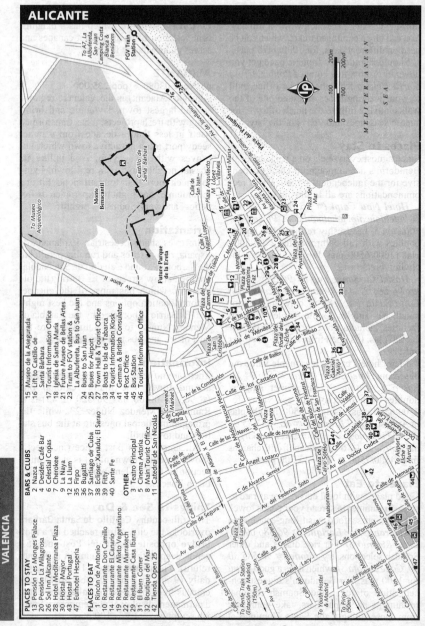

PLACES TO STAY
13 Pensión Les Monges Palace
20 Pensión La Milagrosa
26 Sol Inn Alicante
28 Hotel Mediterranea Plaza
30 Hostal Mayor
43 Hostal Portugal
47 Eurhotel Hesperia

PLACES TO EAT
1   Rincón de Antonio
10 Restaurante Don Camillo
14 Restaurante El Canario
19 Restaurante Mixto Vegetariano
22 Restaurante Marrakech
29 Restaurante Casa Ibarra
31 El Buen Comer
32 Boutique del Mar
42 Tienda Open 25

BARS & CLUBS
2   Nazca
4   Desdén Café Bar
6   Celestial Copas
7   Cherokee
9   La Naya
12 La Llum
35 Firpo
36 Bugatti
37 Santiago de Cuba
38 Eclipse; Xanadu; El Sarao
39 Fitty
40 Sante Fe

OTHER
3   Teatro Principal
5   Cinema Astoria
8   Main Tourist Office
11 Catedral de San Nicolás
15 Museo de la Asegurada
16 Lift to Castillo de
    Santa Bárbara
17 Tourist Information Office
18 Iglesia de Santa María
21 Future Museo de Bellas Artes
23 Tram to FGV station &
    La Albufereta, Bus to San Juan
24 Buses to San Juan
25 Buses for Airport
27 Town Hall & Tourist Office
33 Boats to Isla de Tabarca
34 Tourist Information Kiosk
41 German & British Consulates
44 Post Office
45 Bus Station
46 Tourist Information Office

The **Museo de la Asegurada**, in Alicante's oldest building on Plaza Santa María, houses an excellent collection of modern art, including a handful of works by Dalí, Miró and Picasso. It's open 10 am to 2 pm and 5 to 9 pm Tuesday to Saturday plus Sunday morning (10 am to 2 pm and 4 to 8 pm from October to April); entry is free.

On the same plaza, the **Iglesia de Santa María** has a flamboyant, 18th-century facade and ornate, gilded altarpiece, both contrasting with the nave's Gothic simplicity of line.

At the time of writing, the **Museo Arqueológico** was in store, pending its transfer to a new permanent home off Calle Doctor Sapena. Also in preparation was the new **Museo de Bellas Artes**, Alicante's fine-arts museum, which will occupy an 18th-century mansion on Calle Gravina.

Kontiki (☎ 96 521 63 96) runs boat trips from the harbour to the popular **Isla de Tabarca**, 11 nautical miles south (1800 ptas return). The island has quiet beaches offering good snorkelling and scuba diving, plus a couple of hotels.

A huge industrial port and ritzy boat harbour take up most of central Alicante's foreshore. Immediately north is the sandy beach of **Playa del Postiguet**. Larger and less crowded beaches are at **Playa de San Juan**, easily reached by buses No 21 and 22.

Special Events

Alicante's major festival is the Fiesta de Sant Joan, spread either side of 24 June, when Alicante stages its own version of Las Fallas (see Special Events in the Valencia City section), with fireworks and satirical effigies going up in smoke all over town.

Places to Stay – Budget

Camping About 10km north of Alicante on Campello's outskirts, *Camping Costa Blanca* (☎ 96 563 06 70), 200m from the beach, has a good pool and cafe. It charges 2820 ptas for two people, tent and car in high season.

Youth Hostels The large *Albergue Juvenil La Florida* (☎ 96 511 30 44, Avenida de Orihuela 59) is 2km west of the centre on a busy main road. Normally a student residence, it functions as a youth hostel from July to September. Facilities are good, and juniors/seniors pay 800/1100 ptas for a bed in a single or double room; meals are available.

Hostales & Pensiones There are several cheap hostales in El Barrio. Thoroughly recommended is *Pensión Les Monges Palace* (☎ 96 521 50 46, Calle de Monges 2) – that 'Palace' is a recent appendage since it upgraded! Walls of the cosy guest sitting room are hung with tapestries and artworks (look for the Dalí). All rooms, costing 3900/4200/5000 ptas with washbasin/shower/full bathroom, are individually and tastefully decorated, and have heating, satellite TV and air-con (700 ptas supplement). There's also a private garage (900 ptas).

Basic, no-frills *Pensión La Milagrosa* (☎ 96 521 69 18, Calle de Villavieja 8) has clean rooms for 1500 to 2000 ptas per person according to season. There's a small guest kitchen and roof terrace and some rooms overlook Plaza de Santa María. *Hostal Mayor* (☎ 96 520 13 83, Calle Mayor 5) has pleasant singles/doubles/triples with full bathroom at 3000/6000/9000 ptas (cheaper in low season).

Opposite the bus station, *Hostal Portugal* (☎ 96 592 92 44, Calle de Portugal 26) is a slightly old-fashioned place with clean, spacious singles/doubles for 2600/3900 ptas (4800 ptas with bathroom).

Places to Stay – Mid-Range and Top End

Sol Inn Alicante (☎ 96 521 07 00, fax 96 521 09 76, ✉ sol.alicante@solmelia.es, Calle de Gravina 9) is a modern, stylish three-star place with rooms for 9600/11,350 ptas (cheaper on weekends).

Eurohotel Hesperia (☎ 96 513 04 40, fax 96 592 83 23, ✉ eurohotel@adv.es, Calle del Pintor Lorenzo Casanova 33) has rooms for 13,500/15,500 ptas midweek (a bargain 8000/9600 ptas at weekends).

At brand new, couldn't-be-more-central *Hotel Mediterranea Plaza* (☎ 96 521 01 88, fax 96 520 67 50, Plaza del Ayuntamiento 6) rooms are 15,950/20,200 ptas

VALENCIA

from June to September (9650/13,900 ptas weekends and the rest of the year).

Places to Eat

Restaurante El Canario (Calle de Maldonado 25) is a no-frills local eatery with a hearty *menú* for 950 ptas. Nearby, *Restaurante Mixto Vegetariano (Plaza de Santa María 2)* is a simple low-ceilinged place with vegetarian and – paradoxically – meat *menús* from 1000 ptas. You can choose or combine dishes from both.

Restaurante Casa Ibarra (Calle de Rafael Altamira 19), one of several budget places around Plaza del Ayuntamiento, does a *menú* for 1300 ptas. It also has plenty of tapas ('squids to the Roman' is the engaging translation of one seafood dish) plus fish and grilled meat options. *El Buen Comer (☎ 96 521 31 03, Calle Mayor 8)* has a fancy, upstairs, a-la-carte restaurant. Downstairs and on the street terrace, there's a great selection of more modest dishes. Try the *parrillada de pescado*, grilled fish and seafood, for 1300 ptas.

It's unusual to strike good Italian food in Spain. An exception is *Restaurante Don Camillo (Plaza del Abad Penalva 2)*, where pasta dishes range up to 975 ptas.

For the best in local seafood dishes, try the stylish *Boutique del Mar (☎ 96 520 60 09, Calle de San Fernando 16)*. It offers *arroz negro*, *arroz a banda* or *arroz marinera* (1100 to 1300 ptas) and seafood dishes (450 to 1300 ptas). The midday *menú* costs 1550 ptas while the more elaborate *menú especial* is 2250 ptas.

For great atmosphere head up to the *Rincón de Antonio*, on Calle de Rafael in the Barrio de Santa Cruz. Here on the steep, stepped lane above Plaza del Carmen is local life – *alicantinos* enjoying themselves on the street.

For Moroccan food, *Restaurante Marrakech (☎ 96 521 37 63, Calle de Gravina 15)* is a good, if a tad expensive, bet. Hearty *tajines* (a North African stew) go for around 1250 ptas.

Highly regarded *Piripi (☎ 96 522 79 40, Calle de Oscar Esplá 30)* is the place to go for stylish tapas or fine rice and seafood dishes. Expect to pay about 3500 ptas per head.

Self-Catering Browse around the huge, two-storey *covered market* on Avenida de Alfonso X El Sabio. Out of hours, *Tienda Open 25* is a 24-hour store on Calle del Pintor Lorenzo Casanova.

Entertainment

Bars & Discos The old quarter around Catedral de San Nicolás is wall-to-wall bars and what follows is but a taster of places where you can eliminate grey matter and/or dance yourself into oblivion. Most bars stay open until 2 am early in the week and until 4 or 5 am at weekends.

On Calle de los Labradores is *La Naya*, a cocktail bar with paintings by local artists. The heavenly (and weird) *Celestial Copas* on Calle de San Pascual has a kitsch collection of religious art/junk and great music. Farther up on Calle de San Tomás, look out for *Cherokee* at No 8 and the nearby *Desdén Café Bar*. On the corner of Calle de Montengon and Calle del Padre Maltés, tiny *La Llum* is a sweatbox dance-bar that goes wild late in the night.

Nazca, on the corner of Calle de Argensola and Calle de Cienfuegos, plays mainly Spanish dance music and has a roof terrace if it's all getting too claustrophobic.

The area farther west between Rambla de Méndez Núñez and Avenida del Doctor Gadea is a more concentrated but equally hectic option.

People and pounding music spill out of *Santiago de Cuba* onto its open-air terrace on Explanada de España. There's more action a block back along Calle de San Fernando. *Santa Fe* on the corner of Avenida del Doctor Gadea is a sophisticated place to kick off the evening. A few steps east, any pretensions are left behind in a blur of mixed drinks and dancing. *Fitty* at No 57 is happening, and if for any reason it ain't you can try neighbours *Eclipse*, *Xanadu* or *El Sarao*.

Just off Plaza Gabriel Miró, the popular *Bugatti* is a slick disco with a dress code and 1000 ptas cover charge. It's open nightly except Monday until dawn (don't turn up before 3 am).

If the average partying age of about 18 is making your grey hair feel luminous – and you happen to like salsa – *Firpo (Calle de San Francisco 28)* might be your place.

During summer the disco scene at Playa de San Juan gets thumping. In fact, there are dozens of discos all along the coast from Alicante to Denia. 'Night trains' run by FGV ferry partygoers along this notorious section of *la ruta bakalao,* running hourly between 11 pm and 7 am during July and August. *Búhobus* (the 'Night Owls Bus') is a similar service running as far as San Juan.

Theatre & Cinema *Cinema Astoria (☎ 96 521 56 66)* 'mini twin', on Plaza del Carmen, screens undubbed films. Alicante's main venue for the performing arts is the *Teatro Principal (☎ 96 520 23 80, Calle del Teatro 16).*

Getting There & Away

Air Alicante's El Altet airport, gateway to the Costa Blanca, offers frequent flights (information ☎ 96 691 91 00) to major centres, including Palma de Mallorca, Ibiza City, Barcelona and Madrid. There are flights, both scheduled and charter and often at discount prices, to many European destinations.

Bus From the bus station (☎ 96 513 07 00), there are up to nine motorway buses daily to Valencia (1980 ptas) and others, much slower, which pass through Costa Blanca coastal towns such as Benidorm (440 ptas) and Calpe (640 ptas). Other long-distance destinations include Granada (5¾ hours, 3410 ptas, five daily), Madrid (five hours, 3345 ptas, eight daily), Barcelona (eight hours, 4650 ptas, nine daily) and Almería (4½ hours, 2570 ptas, three daily).

Train Alicante has two train stations. Destinations from the main Renfe Estación de Madrid (☎ 902-24 02 02) include Madrid (four hours, 4700 ptas, six daily), Valencia (1½ to two hours, 1400 to 3200 ptas, up to eight buses daily) via Villena and Játiva,

Barcelona (4½ to 5½ hours, 5800 to 6800 ptas, six daily) and Murcia (1½ hours, 1540 to 575 ptas, up to 20 daily) via Orihuela. The high-speed Euromed train to Valencia and Barcelona (see the Getting Around chapter) leaves three times daily.

Estación de la Marina, the Ferrocarriles de la Generalitat Valenciana (FGV) station (☎ 96 526 27 31), is at the far north-eastern end of Playa del Postiguet. A narrow-gauge service, commonly called the *trenet* (little train), follows a coastal route, at times scenically stunning, northwards as far as Denia (995 ptas) via Playa de San Juan (125 ptas), Benidorm (445 ptas) and Calpe (680 ptas). Trains run hourly until 8 pm as far as Altea and every two hours to Denia. For details of summer night trains, see the earlier Entertainment section.

Boat There is a ferry connection (☎ 96 514 15 09) to Oran (Algeria), but until things calm down there you'd be mad to get aboard.

Getting Around

El Altet airport is 12km south-west of the centre. Alcoyana runs buses every 40 minutes between Plaza del Mar and the airport, passing by the west side of the bus station.

Reliable local car-hire companies operating from the airport include Javea Cars (☎ 96 579 3312, fax 96 579 60 52, Ⓔclients@ javeacars.com), Solmar (☎ 96 646 10 00, fax 96 646 01 09, Ⓔ solmar@solmar.es) and Victoria Cars (☎ 96 579 27 61, fax 96 583 20 00, Ⓔ victoriacars@ctv.es).

An experimental tram service runs from Plaza del Mar to La Albufereta, passing by Estación de la Marina.

To call a taxi, ring ☎ 96 591 05 91 or ☎ 96 510 16 11.

SANTA POLA
postcode 03130 • **pop 16,000**
Santa Pola, 20km south of Alicante, sprawls around its harbour, base of the local fishing fleet and haven to hundreds of pleasure vessels. From here pleasure boats leave for the popular **Isla de Tabarca**, just 3.5 nautical miles offshore (1300 ptas return).

VALENCIA

Most of Santa Pola's beaches are backed by jungles of concrete but the sandy **Gran Playa**, **Playa Lisa** and **Santa Pola del Este** are still worth a visit.

In the centre of town on Plaza de la Glorieta, the well-preserved 16th-century **Castillo-Fortaleza de Santa Pola** fortress stands besieged by 20th-century high-rise architecture. Around its stark courtyard are a small chapel, bar and the **Museo del Mar**, a small maritime museum, open 11 am to 1 pm and 4 to 7 pm Tuesday to Saturday plus Sunday morning (100 ptas).

The tourist office (☎ 96 669 22 76) is at the entrance to town beside El Palmeral park.

Places to Stay

One kilometre west of town on the C-3317 highway to Elche, *Camping Bahía de Santa Pola* (☎ 96 541 10 12), open year round, has a bar-restaurant, pool and shop.

Hostal-Restaurante Michel (☎ 96 541 18 42, fax 96 541 19 42, Calle Felipe 11) has pleasant singles/doubles with TV and aircon for 4000/5500 ptas, including breakfast (in summer 6100 ptas, doubles only). Nearby at *Hostal-Restaurante Picola* (☎ 96 541 18 68, Calle de Alicante 66), rooms with TV and ceiling fan are 3745/5000 ptas (4500/5500 ptas in summer).

Three-star *Hotel Polamar* (☎ 96 541 32 00, fax 96 541 31 83, @ polamar@acceso sis.es), right on the Playa de Levante beachfront, has singles/doubles/triples for 6100/9950/14,450 ptas (8150/13,150/17,550 in summer). Ask for a room with sea views.

TORREVIEJA
postcode 03180 • pop 36,000

A heavily developed resort with a high proportion of northern European visitors, Torrevieja retains a twinkle or two of its former charm – such as the elegant casino just west of the tourist office – and has good beaches, some reasonable restaurants and a lively nightlife. The tourist office (☎ 96 570 34 33), on the waterfront at Plaza de Capdepont, is open 9 am to 1 pm and 4 to 7 pm weekdays plus 10 am to noon Saturday. Just to its south is a large parking area and the jetty from which boats leave for the day trip to Tabarca Island (Tuesday and Thursday, daily in summer; 2400 ptas).

Places to Stay

The nearest camping ground is *Camping La Campana* (☎ 96 571 21 52), 4.5km south of town on the Cartagena road.

Friendly *Hostal Reina* (☎ 96 670 19 04, Avenida del Doctor Gregorio Marañón 22) has rather shabby singles/doubles/triples, with a minuscule bathroom, for 2140/3425/4900 ptas.

Spruce *Hostal Belén* (☎ 96 570 56 85, Calle Apolo 45) is excellent value. Singles/doubles with bathroom, TV, air-con and heating cost 2400/4400 ptas (2900/5500 ptas in high season).

Five blocks west of the bus station and one east of Hostal Belén, *Hotel Cano* (☎ 96 670 09 58, Calle de Zoa 53) has modern rooms with bathroom and TV for 4300/5900 ptas (5350/8000 ptas in summer). One star up, *Hotel Madrid* (☎ 96 571 00 38, Calle Villa Madrid 15) near Hostal Reina charges 6800/9000 ptas (more in summer) for comfortable rooms with all facilities, including breakfast.

Places to Eat

Plenty of restaurants clustered around the waterfront offer cheap meals and international menus. One block back from the beachfront, the *Restaurante Vegetariano (Calle de Pedro Lorca 13)* is a little vegetarian haven run by a Spanish-Australian couple offering salads, sandwiches and tasty pizzas.

Getting There & Away

The bus station is 500m inland on Calle de Antonio Machado. There are four buses daily to Madrid (3615 ptas) via Albacete (1675 ptas) and Villena (815 ptas). Autocares Costa Azul has frequent buses to both Cartagena (545 ptas) and Alicante (420 ptas).

VALENCIA

Balearic Islands (Islas Baleares)

Floating out in the Mediterranean, the Balearics (Illes Balears in Catalan) are invaded every summer by a massive multinational force of hedonistic party animals and sunseekers, as well as a minority of quieter species. This is hardly surprising when you consider what's on offer – fine beaches, relentless sunshine, good food and wild nightlife.

What *is* surprising is that, despite all this, the four main islands – Mallorca (sometimes known in English as Majorca), Menorca (Minorca), Ibiza and Formentera – have, to a degree, maintained their individuality and links with the past. Beyond the bars and beaches are Gothic cathedrals, Stone Age ruins, fishing villages, spectacular bushwalks, endless olive and almond groves and orange orchards. Tourism hasn't *completely* consumed these islands, although many locals are increasingly sick of the yearly influx of lager louts and cocaine-snorting clubbers.

Including all the islets, the islands have a combined area of 5040 sq km and a population of 796,483. Mallorca is by far the largest in area (3640 sq km) and population (638,874), more than half of which lives in Palma.

Place names and addresses in this chapter are in Catalan, the main language spoken (with slight regional variations). The major exceptions are Ibiza and Ibiza City – both are called Eivissa in Catalan.

History
Archaeologists believe the first human settlements in the Balearic Islands date from around 5000 BC. An abundance of prehistoric relics and monuments uncovered on the islands show that these communities constructed houses of stone, practised basic agriculture, domesticated animals, performed ritual burials and manufactured pottery, tools and jewellery.

The Balearics were regular ports of call for ancient Phoenician traders. They were

Highlights

- Walking in Mallorca's Serra de Tramuntana mountains
- Palma's enormous cathedral, and the old quarter (Mallorca)
- Scenic drives and small villages along Mallorca's north-west coast
- Sunrise at the Sanctuari Puig de Maria (Mallorca)
- Ibiza's amazing discos and bars
- The limpid blue waters of Menorca's tranquil beaches
- Formentera's beaches and walking and cycling trails
- Menorca's ancient monuments

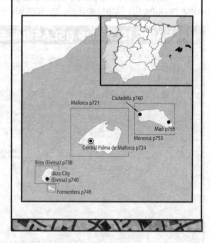

followed by the Carthaginians, who founded Ibiza City in 654 BC and made it one of the Mediterranean's major trading ports. Next came those compulsive road-builders the Romans, who, in turn, were conquered by the Visigoths.

The Muslims, who invaded the islands in the 8th century, left a lasting legacy – you can see it in the appearance and customs of the local people, in their traditional dress, and in much of the island's architecture.

The Muslim domination lasted more than three centuries. The Christian Reconquista was led by Jaume I of Catalunya and Aragón, who took Palma de Mallorca in 1229 and sponsored the invasion of Ibiza in 1235. Menorca was the last to fall: Alfonso III took it in 1287 in a nasty Vietnam-style campaign, completing the islands' incorporation into the Catalan world.

After their initial boom as trading centres and Catalan colonies, the islands had fallen on hard times by the 15th century. Isolation from the mainland, famines and frequent raids by pirates contributed to the decline. During the 16th century, Menorca's two major towns were virtually destroyed by Turkish forces and Ibiza City's fortified walls were built. After a succession of bloody raids, Formentera was abandoned.

The Balearics fared poorly in warfare. After backing the Habsburgs in the Spanish

War of Succession, Mallorca and Ibiza were occupied by the victorious Bourbon monarchy in 1715. Menorca, on the other hand, was granted to the British along with Gibraltar in 1713 under the Treaty of Utrecht. British rule lasted until 1802, with the exception of the Seven Years War (1756–63), during which the French moved in to Menorca.

Brief moments of recovery subsequently proved illusory and the rot was only truly stopped from the 1950s with the advent of mass tourism. The islanders now enjoy – by some estimates – the highest standard of living in Spain.

This has proven something of a double-edged sword. The quick peseta has become king; construction and hotel mafias have made a killing on some of the costas while farming and most other pillars of the economy have fallen by the wayside.

The foreign invasion isn't just seasonal either. One estimate puts more than a fifth of all property on the island of Mallorca in

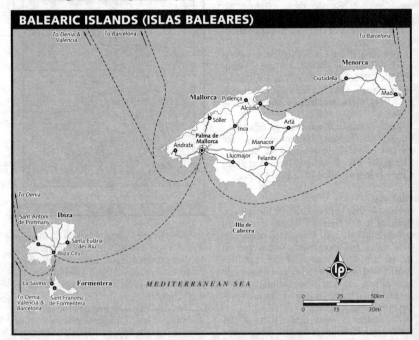

BALEARIC ISLANDS (ISLAS BALEARES)

foreign hands, mostly German. The influx has completely warped the local housing market. Prices for farm cottages that Spaniards wouldn't consider paying for decent flats in central Madrid or Barcelona are the norm. In fact, even Germans looking at real estate windows (all prices in marks and *then* pesetas!) can be heard to mutter *'Wahnsinn!'* ('madness!').

Still, even now stories abound of northern Europeans simply popping up in some inland Mallorcan village (forget the coast – you pay downtown Manhattan prices there now) and asking around if anything is for sale. When told of the asking price, they simply double or triple and pay in cash (the house back home may well be mortgaged to the hilt!). Of course the trend cuts most Mallorcans out of the running altogether.

Planning

Summer (June, July and August) is the silly season in the Balearics. In July and August you'll have to put up with crowded beaches, higher prices and a shortage of accommodation. On the other hand, you can also expect plenty of sunshine, warm water and great nightlife.

To avoid the crowds and save money, come in May-June or September-October. Winter (December, January and February) can be a peaceful time but the lack of beach weather keeps most people away and many hotels and other businesses shut between November and April (Easter).

Accommodation

Most beds are in resorts tailored to the package tourism industry, but *hostales* and other cheaper hotels cater for independent travellers.

Accommodation on the islands is more expensive than on the mainland, especially in summer, but occasional bargains can be found. Prices in this chapter are for the high (silly) season. In some cases they drop considerably in slower periods.

Getting There & Around

Air Scheduled flights from major cities on the Spanish mainland are operated by

---

Taxing Tourism

Amid much heated debate and in spite of the irreducible opposition of hotel associations, the Govern Balear (the island's regional government) decided in June 2000 to apply an *ecotasa* (ecological tax) to all visitors, even locals who for whatever reason end up staying in hotels. The tax will probably go into effect in 2001. How much it will cost seems a complicated matter. It has been priced in euros and will range from 25c per person per day in a country house *(casa rural)* to two euros per person per day in five-star hotels. The funds will be directed to projects aimed at protecting the islands' sorely tried environment – or at least that's what the official cant would have us believe. The tax is all part of a growing backlash against the massive and generally low-quality tourism that since the 1960s has made the Balearics the wealthiest part of the country.

---

several airlines, including Iberia, Air Europa and Spanair. The cheapest and most frequent flights leave from Barcelona and Valencia.

Standard one-way fares from Barcelona are not great value – hovering around 10,000 ptas to Palma de Mallorca and costing more to the other islands. However, it is possible to get a fixed-date return, valid for up to a month, for 13,000 ptas with Spanair. Booking at least four days ahead brings the price down to about 10,000 ptas. In the low season the occasionally truly silly offer, such as 4000 ptas one way, comes up.

From Valencia a one-way flight to Palma (15,900 ptas) costs marginally more than to Ibiza (15,000 ptas).

When on the islands, keep your eyes peeled for special deals to the mainland. At the time of writing one-way flights in June to Sevilla were going for 14,900 ptas, to Málaga for 10,900 ptas and to Alicante for 7500 ptas.

Inter-island flights are expensive (given a flying time of less than 30 minutes), with a trip from Palma de Mallorca to Maó or Ibiza costing 9400 ptas (return flights cost double). There are no direct flights from Ibiza to Maó. If you book far enough in advance the price comes down. Iberia and Air Europa are the main operators, with up to around 10 flights a day between Palma and Ibiza or Maó.

In July 2000, Aebal (a subsidiary of Spanair) began a new inter-island service with ultramodern Boeing 717 jets making three flights a day between Palma and Ibiza/Maó. Prices are similar to those of the competing airlines.

Charter flights from Europe are usually sold as a package including accommodation. If you're looking for a cheap deal check with travel agencies, as spare seats on charter flights are often sold at discounted prices. In summer masses of charter and regular flights converge on Palma de Mallorca and Ibiza. From the UK, easyJet can get you there for anything from UK£25 each way (plus taxes), while German charter airlines such as Air-Berlin and LTU shuttle in thousands of passengers from cities all over Germany daily.

If your main goal in Spain is the Balearic Islands, it makes *no* financial sense to fly via the mainland.

Boat Buquebús (☎ 902-41 42 42) is a sleek high-speed ferry that rockets from Barcelona to Palma de Mallorca and back twice daily in just 3¾ hours. One-way tickets start at 9100 ptas (double for a return). You can frequently get cheaper return flights.

Otherwise, Trasmediterránea (☎ 902-45 46 45) is the major ferry company for the islands, with offices in (and services between) Barcelona, Ibiza City, Maó, Palma de Mallorca and Valencia. Tickets can be purchased through any travel agency or online at www.trasmediterranea.com. Timetables and fares change quite a lot from year to year, but the following will give you an idea of what's available.

Scheduled services are: Barcelona-Palma (eight hours, seven to 21 services weekly); Barcelona-Maó (nine hours, two to eight services weekly); Barcelona–Ibiza City (9½ hours or 14½ hours via Palma, three to six services weekly); Valencia-Palma (8½ hours,

six to 11 services weekly); Valencia–Ibiza City (seven hours, six to seven services weekly); Palma–Ibiza City (4½ hours, one or two services weekly); and Valencia-Maó (6½ hours, one service weekly).

Prices quoted later are for one-way fares during summer; fares in low and mid-season are cheaper.

Standard fares from the mainland (Barcelona or Valencia) to any of the islands are 6920 ptas for a 'Butaca Turista' (seat); a berth in a cabin ranges from 11,410 ptas (four share) to 18,690 ptas (twin share) per person. Taking a small car costs 19,315 ptas. Cheaper fares are available for students with ID (ISIC or Euro<26), seniors over 60 and groups of more than 20. Alternatively, if you don't mind booking fixed-date return fares up to a week in advance, it is possible to get reductions with so-called 'mini' and 'estrella' tickets (see the Getting Around chapter). Always ask about discount options.

Inter-island services (Palma–Ibiza City and Palma-Maó) both cost 3540 ptas for a Butaca Turista and 9875 ptas for a small car. Similar discount fares to those described above are available on these services.

During summer (peak services from late June to early September), Trasmediterránea also operates the following 'Fast Ferry' services (prices quoted are for a Butaca Turista): Barcelona-Palma (4¼ hours, 8990 ptas, up to eight services weekly); Valencia-Palma (six hours, 6920 ptas, four services weekly); Valencia–Ibiza City (3¼ hours, 6920 ptas, up to seven services weekly); Palma–Ibiza City (2¼ hours, 5750 ptas, up to seven services weekly); and Denia (on the mainland between Valencia and Alicante) to Sant Antoni de Portmany, Ibiza (four hours, 6200 ptas, up to three services a day).

Another company, Balearia (☎ 902-16 01 80), operates two or three daily ferries from Denia to Sant Antoni de Portmany and one to Ibiza City (four hours, 6295 ptas). Another service links Ibiza to Palma (three hours, 3245 ptas).

Iscomar (☎ 902-11 91 28) has from one to four daily car ferries (depending on the season) between Ciutadella on Menorca and Port d'Alcúdia on Mallorca (4400 ptas).

Cape Balear (☎ 902-10 04 44) operates up to three fast ferries daily to Ciutadella (Menorca) from Cala Ratjada (Mallorca) in summer for around 8000 ptas return. The crossing takes 75 minutes.

For details of ferries between Ibiza and Formentera, see the Formentera section.

Mallorca

In 1950 the first charter flight landed on a small airstrip on Mallorca, the largest of the Balearic Islands. By 1999 the number of annual visitors had topped nine million – most in search of the three 's's: sun, sand and sea.

There is more to the place. Palma de Mallorca, known as Palma, is the main centre and a charming stop. The north-west coast, dominated by the Serra de Tramuntana mountains, is a beautiful region of olive groves, pine forests and small villages, with a spectacularly rugged and rocky coastline.

Most of Mallorca's best beaches are on the north and east coasts and, although many have been swallowed up by tourist developments, you can still find the occasional exception.

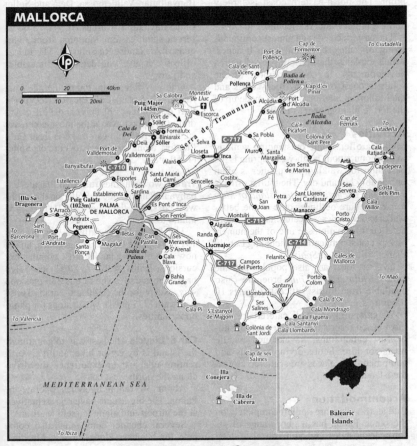

Orientation

The capital, Palma de Mallorca, is on the southern side of the island on a bay famous for its brilliant sunsets.

Locals refer to what lies beyond the capital as the *part forana*, the 'part outside'. A series of rocky coves and harbours punctuate the short south-western coastline. Offshore from the island's westernmost point is the large, uninhabited island of Sa Dragonera.

The spectacular Serra de Tramuntana mountain range runs parallel with the north-western coast and includes the mountain of Puig Major (1445m), Mallorca's highest point. The north-eastern coast is largely made up of two bays, the Badia de Pollença and the larger Badia d'Alcúdia.

The eastern coast is an almost continuous string of sandy bays and open beaches, which explains the densely packed tourist developments. In contrast, most of the southern coast is lined by rocky cliffs and the Mallorcan interior is largely made up of the fertile plain known as Es Pla.

Activities

Mallorca offers some outstanding walking in the mountainous north-west. Spring is the best time for walking, as summer is often unbearably hot and dry. The tourist office's *20 Hiking Excursions on the Island of Mallorca* brochure outlines some of the better walks and includes a locater map. For more detailed information see one of the numerous specialist publications, including Lonely Planet's *Walking in Spain*.

Cycling tours are also popular and the handy *Cicloturismo Guía* brochure (also available from tourist offices) suggests 10 itineraries.

Water sports are well catered for and most beach resorts have a selection of sailboards, catamarans, kayaks and paddle boats for hire. Scuba-diving schools and equipment-hire places are scattered around the island.

Accommodation

Budget travellers are not left completely on the outer. Palma has a good range of affordable hostales and you can also sleep cheaply in about half a dozen monasteries around the island – ask for a list at the Consell de Mallorca tourist office (see the Information section later).

Getting Around

Bus Most of the island is accessible by bus from Palma. A dozen different companies' buses depart from Plaça de Espanya and the surrounding streets. A new bus station is being built about half a kilometre to the north-east.

Bus Nord Balear (☎ 971 49 06 80) serves towns along the north-west coast, including Banyalbufar, Valldemossa, Deià and Sóller and has departures from Carrer del Arxiduc Lluís Salvador 1. Darbus (☎ 971 75 06 2) serves south-eastern Mallorca from Avinguda d'Alexandre Rosselló 32. The tourist offices can give you details of timetables and fares.

One-way fares from Palma include Cala Ratjada (925 ptas), Ca'n Picafort (595 ptas), Port d'Alcúdia (590 ptas) and Port d'Andratx (440 ptas). About the most expensive single bus ride you can make is from Ca'n Picafort along the coast to Port de Sóller (1250 ptas).

Train Two train lines run from Plaça d'Espanya in Palma – one to Sóller on the north-west coast and the other (☎ 971 75 22 45) inland to Inca.

The Palma-Sóller railway was built in 1912 to replace the local stagecoach, and is now one of the island's most popular excursions. Trains (☎ 971 75 20 51) leave five or six times daily. The fare is 380 ptas one way, except for the 10.40 am 'Parada Turística' train (735 ptas!), which stops for photo opportunities.

Car & Bicycle The best way to get around the island is by car or bike, and it's worth renting one just to experience the drive along the north-west coast.

About 30 rental agencies operate in Palma. The big league have representatives at the airport and along Passeig Marítim. Several cheaper companies also compete for business along Passeig Marítim, including Iber-Auto (☎ 971 28 54 48) at No 13 and Entercar (☎ 971 73 94 50) at No 11.

One of the best deals is Hasso (☎ 971 26 02 19), Camí de Ca'n Pastilla 100, not far from the airport. If you can live without a radio and air-con, you could get an Opel Corsa for as little as 3500 ptas all inclusive. Hasso is on the No 17 airport bus route and has a reservations desk at the airport.

You can rent bicycles at Royal Rent (☎ 971 26 64 25), Camí Ca'n Pastilla 110, near the airport. It also rents motorbikes.

Taxi You can get around the island by taxi, but it's costly. Prices are posted at central points in many towns. You're looking at around 9000 ptas from the airport to Cala Ratjada.

Boat Palma and the major resorts and beaches around the island are also connected by numerous boat tours and water-taxi services. The tourist office's *Excursiones En Barca* brochure details some of these. Cruceros Iberia (☎ 971 71 71 90) organises trips right around the island. Call or inquire at the tourist office.

PALMA DE MALLORCA
postcode 07080 • pop 319,181

Palma de Mallorca is the islands' only true city and a highly agreeable spot to explore for a day or two before you head off around the island.

Central Palma's old quarter is an attractive blend of tree-lined boulevards and cobbled laneways, Gothic churches and baroque palaces, designer bars and slick boutiques. It's a stylish city that buzzes by day and sizzles by night.

That's the good news. The bad news is that it's also crammed to the hilt with tourists and tacky souvenir shops. And you'll have to take a bus to get to the beaches, where you'll discover the endless sprawl of high-rise development that has engulfed the bay.

Orientation
Central Palma stretches from the harbour to Plaça d'Espanya, home to the train and bus

terminals (the airport bus stops here too). It also has a tourist office and frequent buses run to the central Plaça de la Reina (a 20-minute walk).

From the harbour and ferry terminals, Avinguda d'Antoni Maura runs north up to Plaça de la Reina and through the old quarter. On the western side is Palma's main restaurant and nightlife zone, while on the eastern side are the Palau de l'Almudaina and the cathedral. The broad boulevard of Passeig d'es Born continues north up to Plaça del Rei Joan Carles I; Avinguda de Jaume III, which runs westwards from here, is the heart of the commercial district. Farther east is the large open space of Plaça Major from where another wide boulevard, Passeig de la Rambla, continues north-westwards.

Information
Tourist Offices The main municipal tourist office (Turisme; ☎ 971 72 40 90) is in a pedestrian walkway just off the north-eastern end of Carrer del Conquistador at Carrer de Sant Domingo 11. It is open 9 am to 8.30 pm on weekdays and 9 am to 1.30 pm on Saturday. Staff seem to be a little tired of tourists, guidebook writers or both, and getting information is hard going.

Their colleagues at the municipal tourist office (☎ 971 75 43 29) in the Parc de les Estacions (in one of the railway buildings) off Plaça d'Espanya keep much the same hours and seem equally disinterested.

The Consell de Mallorca's tourist office (☎ 971 71 22 16), covering the whole island and more agreeably staffed, is at Plaça de la Reina 2. Opening hours are 9 am to 8 pm weekdays and 10 am to 2 pm Saturday. It also operates a less encouraging branch at the airport (☎ 971 78 95 56).

Of the many tourist mags on sale, perhaps *Mallorca Tourist Info* (600 ptas at newsstands) is the most useful, with town maps for places all over the island and a few helpful insights. German readers might look out for *Mallorca Magazin*.

Foreign Consulates Numerous countries maintain consular agencies here, a few of

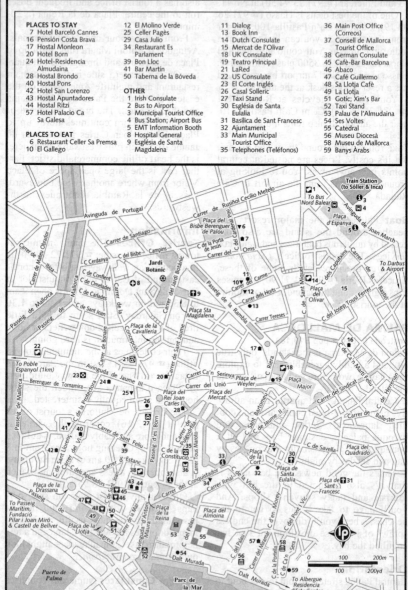

CENTRAL PALMA DE MALLORCA

PLACES TO STAY
7   Hotel Barceló Cannes
16 Pensión Costa Brava
17 Hostal Monleon
20 Hotel Born
24 Hotel-Residencia
    Almudaina
28 Hostal Brondo
40 Hostal Pons
42 Hotel San Lorenzo
43 Hostal Apuntadores
44 Hostal Ritzi
57 Hotel Palacio Ca
    Sa Galesa

PLACES TO EAT
6   Restaurant Celler Sa Premsa
10 El Gallego

12 El Molino Verde
25 Celler Pagès
29 Casa Julio
34 Restaurant Es
    Parlament
39 Bon Lloc
41 Bar Martin
50 Taberna de la Bóveda

OTHER
1   Irish Consulate
2   Bus to Airport
3   Municipal Tourist Office
4   Bus Station; Airport Bus
5   EMT Information Booth
8   Hospital General
9   Església de Santa
    Magdalena

11 Dialog
13 Book Inn
14 Dutch Consulate
15 Mercat de l'Olivar
18 UK Consulate
19 Teatro Principal
21 LaRed
22 US Consulate
23 El Corte Inglés
26 Casal Solleric
27 Taxi Stand
30 Església de Santa
    Eulalia
31 Basílica de Sant Francesc
32 Ajuntament
33 Main Municipal
    Tourist Office
35 Telephones (Teléfonos)

36 Main Post Office
    (Correos)
37 Consell de Mallorca
    Tourist Office
38 German Consulate
45 Cafè-Bar Barcelona
46 Abaco
47 Café Guillermo
48 Sa Llotja Cafè
49 La Llotja
51 Gòtic; Xim's Bar
52 Taxi Stand
53 Palau de l'Almudaina
54 Ses Voltes
55 Catedral
56 Museu Diocesà
58 Museu de Mallorca
59 Banys Àrabs

which have been marked on the Central Palma map.

Money You'll find plenty of banks on Avinguda de Jaume III and Passeig d'es Born.

Post & Communications Palma's post office *(correos)* is at Carrer de la Constitució 6. There is a telephone office marked Teléfonos on Carrer de Paraires, which is open 9 am to 8 pm daily. To go online, try LaRed (☎ 971 71 35 74), Carrer de la Concepció 5. It's open seven days.

Bookshop Book Inn is a good English-language bookshop just off Passeig de la Rambla at Carrer dels Horts 22. For English or German books also try Dialog, Carrer del Carme 14.

Medical Services The main Hospital General (☎ 971 72 84 84) is up by the Jardi Botanic.

Catedral
Palma's enormous cathedral (or La Seu) is often likened to a huge ship moored at the city's edge. Construction work on what had been the site of the main mosque started in 1230 but wasn't completed until 1600. This awesome structure is predominantly Gothic, apart from the main facade (replaced after an earthquake in 1851) and parts of the interior (renovated in *modernista* style by Antoni Gaudí at the beginning of the 20th century).

Entry is via a small, three-room museum, which holds a rich collection of religious artwork and precious gold and silver effects, including two amazing candelabras.

The cathedral's interior is stunning in its sense of spaciousness, with a series of narrow columns supporting the soaring ceiling and framing three levels of elaborate stained-glass windows. The front altar's centrepiece, a twisting wrought-iron sculpture suspended from the ceiling and periodically lit with fairy lights, has been widely acclaimed, mainly because it was Gaudí's handiwork. Some think it looks awkward and out of place. The cathedral and museum

are open 10 am to 6 pm weekdays (10 am to 3 pm from November to March) and 10 am to 2 pm Saturday (500 ptas).

Palau de l'Almudaina
In front of the cathedral stands the Palau de l'Almudaina, a Muslim castle converted into a residence for the Mallorcan monarchs at the end of the 13th century. It is still occasionally used for official functions when King Juan Carlos is in town, but at other times you can join the hordes and wander through an endless series of cavernous and austere stone-walled rooms and inspect a collection of portraits of Spanish monarchs, Flemish tapestries and antique furniture. The palace is open 10 am to 6.30 pm weekdays (10 am to 2 pm and 4 to 6 pm between October and March) and 10 am to 2 pm Saturday (450 ptas).

Museu de Mallorca
A more interesting way to spend your time and money is to visit the Museu de Mallorca at Carrer de la Portella 5. This converted 15th-century palace holds an impressive collection of archaeological artefacts, religious art, antiques and ceramics. Upstairs there is a great portrait gallery of local identities and painters. Opening hours are 10 am to 2 pm and 5 to 8 pm Tuesday to Saturday (10 am to 1 pm and 4 to 6 pm from October to March), and 10 am to 2 pm Sunday (300 ptas).

Banys Àrabs
The Arab baths near the Museu de Mallorca are the only extant monument to the Muslim domination of the island. All that remains are two small underground chambers, one of which has a domed ceiling supported by columns. Interestingly, each of the columns is topped by a different capital: the Muslims were great recyclers and the capitals came from demolished Roman buildings. The adjacent courtyard is pleasant. The baths are open 9 am to 7 or 8 pm (200 ptas).

Museu Diocesà
Palma's Museu Diocesà, close to the cathedral, houses a collection of religious art including paintings, ceramics and artefacts. It is

open 10 am to 1 pm and 5 to 8 pm weekdays (10 am to 1 pm and 3 to 6 pm from November to March), 10 am to 1.30 pm on weekends and holidays (300 ptas).

La Llotja

This gorgeous Gothic building, opposite the waterfront on Passeig de Sagrera, was built as a merchants' stock exchange and is now used for exhibitions. It's open 11 am to 2 pm and 5 to 9 pm Tuesday to Saturday, and 11 am to 2 pm Sunday.

Casal Solleric

This excellent art gallery at Passeig d'es Born 27 has a good cafe attached. It's open 10.30 am to 1.45 pm and 5.30 to 9 pm, closed Monday and Sunday afternoon (free).

Churches

Two of Palma's oldest churches are Església de Santa Eulalia and the nearby Basílica de Sant Francesc. The latter was begun in 1281 in Gothic style and its baroque facade was completed in 1700. Inside are the tomb of and monument to the 13th-century scholar Ramon Llull, while at the front of the church is a statue of Junípero Serra, the Franciscan missionary who founded many missions in California.

Other Attractions

On the western side of the city, Poble Espanyol is a copy of the village of the same name in Barcelona. It displays replicas of famous monuments and other buildings representative of a variety of Spanish architectural styles, not to mention souvenir shops galore. Farther south, the circular Castell de Bellver is an unusual 14th-century castle set in pleasant parklands.

Also worth visiting is the Fundació Pilar i Joan Miró, at Carrer de Joan de Saridakis 29 in Cala Major (about 4km south-west of the city centre). Housed in the artist's Palma studios, it exhibits a permanent collection of the works stored here at the time of his death. There are also temporary exhibitions and a shop selling Miró souvenirs, prints etc. It's open 10 am to 7 pm Tuesday to Saturday (to 6 pm from mid-September to mid-May), and 10 am to 3 pm Sunday and holidays (700 ptas).

Places to Stay

Central Palma is by far the best area to stay in. Avoid the string of glossy (and not-so-glossy) tourist hotels around the waterfront west of the centre – they're a long way from anything (except each other) and filled with package tourists.

Places to Stay – Budget

Nothing seems to have changed at *Hostal Pons* (☎ 971 72 26 58, Carrer del Vi 8) since the 1880s. The downstairs chambers are cluttered with antiques and artworks, and the quaint bedrooms all have timber bedsteads and rickety tiled floors. Amid such charm you can almost overlook the spongy beds and queues outside the (solitary) bathroom. Singles/doubles cost 2500/4500 ptas.

If you want somewhere more contemporary, *Hostal Apuntadores* (☎ 971 71 34 91, Carrer dels Apuntadors 8) is good. Rooms start at 2700/4200 ptas; doubles with private shower are 4800 ptas. Or you can get a bed in a dorm for 1800 ptas. Next door at No 6, the English-run *Hostal Ritzi* (☎ 971 71 46 10) has good security and comfortable rooms at 3500/5000 ptas with shower or doubles with shower/bath for 5500 ptas. Doubles with en suite bathroom are 7500 ptas. There are laundry and kitchen facilities and satellite TV in the lounge.

Hostal Monleon (☎ 971 71 53 17, Passeig de la Rambla 3) is a big old place with dim rooms from 2400/4200 ptas (2700/4800 ptas with shower and 3000/5300 ptas with full bathroom).

Pensión Costa Brava (☎ 971 71 17 29, Carrer de Ca'n Martí Feliu 16) is a backstreet cheapie with reasonable rooms from 2000/3300 ptas. On the downside, this area is somewhat seedy at night. *Hostal Brondo* (☎ 971 71 90 43, Carrer de Ca'n Brondo 1) is in a much better location, just off Plaça del Rei Joan Carles I. It has 10 clean rooms with bathrooms costing 5000/6000 ptas.

Palma's youth hostel, the *Albergue Residencia d'Estudiantes* (☎ 971 26 08 92), is at Carrer de la Costa Brava in S'Arenal, a crowded and heavily developed beach suburb 11km east of the centre. It is open from June to September only.

Places to Stay – Mid-Range

Hotel Barceló Cannes (☎ 971 72 69 43, Carrer del Cardenal Pou 8), close to Plaça d'Espanya, is an unexciting modern two-star place with rooms from 4500/7000 ptas to 6000/8000 ptas (plus IVA).

A good bet is *Hotel-Residencia Almudaina (☎ 971 72 73 40, fax 971 72 25 59, Avinguda de Jaume III 9).* It's an oldish hotel that was renovated in 1992. All rooms have air-con, heating, TV and phone; some have sea views. You pay 10,700/16,050 ptas, which includes breakfast.

The superb *Hotel Born (☎ 971 71 29 42, Carrer de Sant Jaume 3),* in the heart of the city, is set in an 18th-century palace. The rooms combine elegance and history with all the mod cons. B&B rates range up to 13,375/17,655 ptas.

Places to Stay – Top End

If you're lucky enough to get a booking and be able to afford it, stay at *Hotel San Lorenzo (☎ 971 72 82 00, fax 971 71 19 01, Carrer de Sant Llorenç 14)* in the old quarter. The hotel is in a beautifully restored 17th-century building and has its own bar, dining room and rooftop terrace with swimming pool. There are just six rooms and it costs 18,190 ptas for one of them.

The classiest act in town is *Hotel Palacio Ca Sa Galesa (☎ 971 71 54 00, fax 971 72 15 79, Carrer de Miramar 8).* It's an enchanting 16th-century mansion that has been tastefully turned into a luxury hotel. It has five doubles and two singles arranged around a cool patio garden, which cost up to 28,000/32,500 ptas.

Places to Eat

For a mess of eateries and bars catering to Palma's visitors, wander through the maze of streets between Plaça de la Reina and the port. Carrer dels Apuntadors is lined with restaurants and should have something to suit everyone, including seafood,

Chinese, Italian – there's even a few Spanish restaur-ants along here! Mostly they proffer unspectacular cooking, but they're substantially better than those lining Avinguda d'Antoni Maura (opposite the Palau de l'Almudaina).

Just off Plaça de la Llotja, *Taberna de la Bóveda* is a spacious tavern-restaurant with excellent food, reasonable prices and a lively atmosphere (which later transmogrifies into a classy bar). For starters try the delicious *pa amb oli* – bread smeared with tomato and olive oil and topped with your choice of anchovies (1200 ptas), chorizo or cheese (900 ptas).

For a simple cheap meal with the locals, head for *Bar Martín (Carrer de la Santa Creu 2).* There's a no-nonsense *menú del día* (daily set meal) for 950 ptas.

For not a lot more you can eat simply but well in the tiny *Celler Pagès (Carrer de Felip Bauçà 2).* The *menú* is 1250 ptas. Try the *sopa de pescado* (fish soup).

Away from the tourist streams nestle a couple of cheerful eateries frequented mainly by locals. *El Molino Verde (Carrer del Carme 21)* has a cheap set lunch at 900 ptas or a slightly more refined version at 1600 ptas. One of the most reassuring things about *El Gallego,* across the road at No 16, is the absence of a menu in any language but Spanish – a rare sight in Mallorca! The *menú* is 1125 ptas.

The solid *Casa Julio (Carrer de la Previsió 4)* is something of a workers' local. The place is packed for the lunchtime *menú* (1100 ptas) and closed for dinner.

Restaurant Es Parlament (Carrer del Conquistador 11), beside Palma's parliament building, has a gracious Victorian-era dining room with soaring ceilings and gilt-framed artworks. Main courses range from 1050 ptas (roast chicken) to 2750 ptas (Chateaubriand).

The rustic *Restaurant Celler Sa Premsa (Plaça del Bisbe Berenguer de Palou 8)* is something of a local institution, and a visit here is almost obligatory. It's a cavernous tavern filled with huge old wine barrels and has walls plastered with faded bullfighting posters. The food is hearty but basic and the *menú* costs 1335 ptas.

For vegetarian food, try **Bon Lloc** *(Carrer de Sant Feliu 7)*.

Entertainment

The old quarter is the city's most vibrant nightlife zone. Particularly along the narrow streets between Plaça de la Reina and Plaça de la Drassana, you'll find a huge selection of bars and pubs ranging from flashy tourist haunts to stylish bodegas. For complete info on what's happening in Palma and around the island, pick up a copy of the tri-weekly *Guía del Ocio* (200 ptas).

Abaco (Carrer de Sant Joan 1), behind a set of ancient timber doors, is the bar of your wildest dreams (with prices from your darkest nightmares). Inside, a Mallorcan patio and candle-lit courtyard are crammed with elaborate floral arrangements, cascading towers of fresh fruit and bizarre artwork, and bow-tied waiters fulfil your wishes while classical music soothes your ears. A cocktail can cost 2000 ptas.

Plenty of watering holes line Carrer dels Apuntadors. The atmospheric **Cafe-Bar Barcelona** at No 5 has live jazz and soul most nights in its somewhat cramped upstairs bar.

If you just want a quiet drink there are several stylish bars on Plaça de la Llotja. **Gotic** and **Xim's Bar** are both fronted by rows of outdoor tables, while on the opposite corner is the smooth and popular **Sa Llotja Cafe**. *Cafe Guillermo (Carrer de la Llotja de Mar 10)* is another pleasing location for a few quiet drinks. Or walk on to Plaça de la Drassana for tippling al fresco.

For the city's clubs you have to head west to the area around Passeig Marítim (or Avinguda de Gabriel Roca), Avinguda Joan Miró and Plaça de Gomila. On the latter square is one of Palma's longest survivors, **Tito's**. Spain's big name in clubbing, **Pachá** *(Passeig Marítim 42)*, has a branch here too. There's plenty of tack, including karaoke bars, music pubs, flamenco shows and, along S'Aigo Doka, a couple of topless bars.

S'Arenal and Magaluf, the amorphous tourist haunts, are full of bars and discos filled to bursting with the lobster-hued package tourist crowd.

Getting There & Away

The Sant Joan airport (☎ 971 78 90 00) is about 10km east of Palma. Trains and buses to other parts of the island depart from terminals at or near Plaça d'Espanya (see the earlier Mallorca Getting Around section for details).

Getting Around

Bus If you arrive by air, bus No 17 runs every half-hour between the airport and Plaça d'Espanya in central Palma (30 minutes, 300 ptas one way). Alternatively, a taxi will cost around 2000 ptas.

From the ferry terminal, bus No 1 runs around Passeig Marítim and then left up Avinguda d'Antoni Maura into central Palma.

EMT (☎ 971 71 13 93) runs some 22 local bus services around Palma and its bay suburbs. Single trip tickets cost 175 ptas, or you can buy a 10-trip card for 1500 ptas at the EMT information booth on Plaça d'Espanya. For the beaches at S'Arenal, you can catch the S'Arenal Exprés from the same square (250 ptas).

Taxi A couple of handy ranks for the city's characteristic black and cream coloured cabs have been marked on the map. Otherwise, you can call ☎ 971 75 54 40.

SOUTH-WEST COAST

A freeway skirts around the Badia de Palma towards Mallorca's south-west coast. Along the way you pass the resorts of Cala Major, Illetes and Palma Nova, which are basically a continuation of Palma's urban sprawl. From the inland town of Andratx, two turn-offs lead down to the coast: one to Port d'Andratx, the other to Sant Elm.

Port d'Andratx

postcode 07080 • pop 8333

Port d'Andratx is a glamorous little town set on low hills surrounding a narrow bay. The main road around the waterfront is lined with upmarket seafood restaurants.

Several dive schools are based here and you can rent boats and **scuba-diving** equipment at numerous outlets. You can also take boat trips around to Sant Elm and the island of Sa Dragonera.

Places to Stay & Eat On the waterfront, *Restaurante Las Palmeras (☎ 971 67 20 78, Avinguda de Mateo Bosch 12)* rents out good upstairs rooms with singles/doubles from 3000/6000 ptas. Some of the doubles have harbour views and shower.

A couple of hundred metres back from the harbour, *Hostal-Residencia Catalina Vera (☎ 971 67 19 18, Carrer de Isaac Peral 63)* is a lovely guesthouse retreat with rooms set around a tranquil garden courtyard. B&B starts from 4500/7500 ptas. If you want rooms with a bath, you will pay 5000/8500 ptas.

There's no shortage of good seafood eateries along the waterfront. These places have terrific outlooks but charge accordingly. If you're after somewhere more affordable you could try *Restaurante Es Porteño (Carrer de Isaac Peral 58),* a couple of blocks inland, which has a lunch *menú* for 950 ptas.

Sant Elm
The small seaside township of Sant Elm is a popular destination for day trips from Palma. The last part of the drive across from Andratx is a spectacular climb through attractive hills. If you'd rather walk this section, take a bus to Andratx. Walk number two on the *20 Hiking Excursions on the Island of Mallorca* brochure, available from most tourist offices on the island, starts from here and takes you to the coast via the village of S'Arracó and a ruined 16th-century castle.

Sant Elm's sandy beach is pleasant but can get crowded. Just offshore is a small rocky islet – within swimming distance if you've been in training. Farther north there's a small dock from where you can join a glass-bottomed boat tour or take a cruise across to the imposing and uninhabited island of **Sa Dragonera**, which is criss-crossed by good walking trails. You can join a daily cruise to the island (1500 ptas) or take the boat between Sant Elm and Port d'Andratx (700 ptas). For more information, call ☎ 971 75 70 65.

Places to Stay & Eat Several possibilities line the waterfront. *Hotel Aquamarin (☎ 971 23 91 05, fax 971 23 91 25, Carrer de Cal Conis 4),* a modern, circular, six-storey hotel, charges 3900/7700 ptas for B&B.

Most of the restaurants along the main foreshore road specialise in local seafood and are pricey. At *Bar Restaurante Flexa (Avinguda del Rei Jaume I 13),* you can sit on a balcony over the sea and tuck into a limited but decent *menú* for 1500 ptas.

NORTH-WEST COAST & SERRA DE TRAMUNTANA
Dominated by the rugged Serra de Tramuntana mountain range, Mallorca's north-west coast and its hinterland make up 'the other Mallorca'. No sandy beach resorts here. The coastline is rocky and largely inaccessible, the towns and villages are mostly built of local stone (as opposed to concrete) and the mountainous interior is much loved by walkers for its beautiful landscapes of pine forests, olive groves and spring wildflowers.

The main road through the mountains (the C-710) starts at Andratx and runs roughly parallel to the coast to Pollença. It's a stunning scenic drive and a popular cycling route, especially during spring, when the muted mountain backdrop of browns, greys and greens is splashed with the bright colours of yellow wattles and blood-red poppies. Plenty of *miradores* (lookout points) recommend themselves as stops to punctuate the trip. Unfortunately the trip can be a slow-going traffic nightmare during late spring and summer.

Estellencs
postcode 07192 • pop 338
Estellencs is a picturesque village of stone buildings scattered around the rolling hills below the Puig Galatzó (1025m) peak. It's a popular base for walkers and cyclists or for simply escaping Palma and relaxing. A rugged walk of about a kilometre leads down to the local 'beach', a rocky cove with crystal-clear water.

Places to Stay & Eat The popular and stylish *Hotel Maristel (☎ 971 61 85 29,*

Carrer de Eusebio Pascual 10) has comfortable rooms with all the mod cons, as well as a pool and a restaurant with fine views from its outdoor terrace. Singles/doubles cost 7500/11,000 ptas, with breakfast.

Otherwise, the owner of *Pizzeria Giardini* (☎ 971 61 85 96) has four rooms to rent out. He charges around 3500 ptas person if anything is available, which for much of the summer is by no means a given.

Estellencs is home to the excellent *Restaurant Son Llarg* (☎ 971 61 85 64), which specialises in *cuina mallorquina* (Mallorcan cuisine). Main courses such as *calamars amb salsa de ceba* (squid casserole Mallorcan-style) cost up to 2000 ptas.

Banyalbufar
postcode 07191 • pop 503

Farther north, Banyalbufar is slightly larger than Estellencs but similarly positioned high above the coast. Surrounded by steep, stone-walled terraces carved into the hillside, the town is home to a cluster of bars and cafes and three upmarket hotels.

Places to Stay & Eat Fronted by a traditional Mallorcan patio, *Hotel Baronia* (☎ 971 61 81 46, Carrer de Baronia 16) has 36 modern rooms with fine views and a great cliff-side swimming pool. It has doubles with breakfast for 8100 ptas or with *media pensión* for 12,400 ptas.

Hotel Mar i Vent (☎ 971 61 80 00, Carrer Major 49) has a similar setup but is more formal and quite a deal more expensive, with B&B at 12,000/15,000 ptas for singles/doubles.

Valldemossa
postcode 00717 • pop 1599

Valldemossa is an attractive blend of tree-lined streets, old stone houses and impressive new villas. It owes most of its fame to the fact that the ailing composer Frédéric Chopin and his lover George Sand spent their 'winter of discontent' here in 1838–39.

They stayed in the **Cartuja de Valldemossa**, a monastery that was turned into rental accommodation after its monks were expelled in 1835. Their stay wasn't an entirely happy experience and Sand later wrote *Un Hiver à Menorque* (Winter in Mallorca), which, if nothing else, made her perennially unpopular with Mallorcans (although you'll still find copies of it at some souvenir stands).

Tour buses and day-trippers now arrive in droves to visit the monastery. It's a beautiful building with lovely gardens and fine views. In the couple's former quarters are Chopin's piano (which, due to shipping delays, arrived only three weeks before their departure), his death mask and several original manuscripts. The monastery is open 9.30 am to 6 pm Monday to Saturday (to 4.30 pm from November to February), and 10 am to 1pm Sunday. Entry includes piano recitals (given eight times daily during summer) and entry to the local museum (1300 ptas).

Costa Nord, a new attraction in Valldemossa, is situated on the main road opposite the car park, a few minutes' walk from the Cartuja. See the boxed text 'Michael's Mallorca'.

The rest of the town is extremely charming, although the part nearest the Cartuja a little too heavily laden with expensive eateries and souvenir shops. From here a tortuous 7km drive leads down to **Port de Valldemossa**, where a dozen or so buildings (including two bar-restaurants) huddle around a rocky cove.

Places to Stay Most visitors make Valldemossa a day trip, but you can stay at the perfectly adequate and central *Hostal Ca'n Mário* (☎ 971 61 21 22, Carrer de Uetam 8) where rooms cost 3600/6100 ptas. This must be one of the only places in all Mallorca not to have lifted its prices a single peseta! God bless 'em.

Can Marroig
A few kilometres north of Valldemossa on the road to Deià is Can Marroig, one of Habsburg Archduke Luis Salvador's former residences (see the boxed text 'Michael's Mallorca'). It is a delightful, rambling mansion jammed with furniture and household items of the duke's era, including many of

Michael's Mallorca

In spring 2000 a longtime visitor and part-time resident of this part of the island, Hollywood's very own Michael Douglas, opened up his peculiar contribution to the propagation of Mallorcan culture. His (what should we call it?) show, Costa Nord, is basically made up of two parts. The first is a not uninteresting three-screen short 'documentary' on the history of this part of the island. It can also be seen as Douglas' tribute to a part of the world he is apparently quite enamoured with (no argument from us there). Next you are ushered into a mock-up of the master's quarters of the good ship *Nixe*.

The vessel belonged to one Archduke Luis Salvador (or Ludwig to his family in Austria), son of the 19th-century Habsburg ruler of Tuscany, Leopoldo II. Luis spent much of his life bobbing around on the Mediterranean in *Nixe* and writing learned treatises on an astounding number of places and subjects, including the island of Mallorca, which he came to live on and love. Indeed, he liked it so much he proceeded to buy as much of it as he could (or of the mountainous north at any rate).

In his commentary on Luis' life, Douglas seems to be urging his listeners to see his own passion for Mallorca in the same light as that of the good archduke. The Mallorcan government at any rate sees Douglas and his ilk as a powerful instrument for communicating to the world an image of Mallorca far removed from the cheap lager-holiday dream. If he and his show can help safeguard the beauty of the island and slow (if not halt) speculative development, then long may it prosper.

What to make of the show itself? It is instructive, but at the end you can't help asking yourself – is that it? Especially having forked out 1100 ptas for the pleasure. You too can see it from 9 am to 8 pm daily. It rewinds every 20 minutes, but as it's done in several languages, you may have to wait a little for yours to come up. When you're done, you can lounge in the cafe and look at the photos on the wall of Douglas and all his important friends.

---

his books and other odds and ends. The views from the balconies and garden are the stuff of dreams. You can also wander down to the **Foradada**, the strange hole-in-the-rock formation down by the water. It's about a 3km walk. You can swim, but beware the men o' war. The property is open 9.30 am to 8 pm, but is closed on Sunday (350 ptas).

Deià
postcode 07179 • pop 625
Deià is perhaps the most famous village on Mallorca. Its setting is idyllic, with a cluster of stone buildings cowering beneath soaring mountains and surrounded by steep hillsides terraced with vegetable gardens, vines and fruit orchards.

Such beauty has always been a drawcard and Deià was once a second home to an international artists' colony of writers, actors, actors etc. The most famous member was the English poet Robert Graves, who died here in 1985 and is buried in the town's hillside cemetery.

Now somewhat overrun by pretentious expats, travel writers and tourists, Deià still has something special and is worth experiencing, particularly if you can avoid the summer crowds.

Things to See & Do The C-710 passes though the town centre where it becomes the main street and is lined with bars and shops, expensive restaurants and ritzy boutiques. Several pricey **artists' workshops and galleries** flog locally produced work.

Up beside the church, the small **Museu Parroquial** has an interesting collection of religious effects, icons and old coins (100 ptas). There's also a privately run **Archaeological Museum & Research Centre** (open by appointment) with a collection of artefacts found in the Valldemossa area.

On the coast, **Cala de Deià** has some popular swimming spots and a couple of bar-restaurants. The steep walking track from town takes about half an hour; you can drive down, but in the high season this might take almost as long. Some fine walks criss-cross the area, such as the gentle **Deià Coastal Path** to Lluc Alcari (three hours return).

Places to Stay Surprisingly, Deià still has a couple of affordable places to stay. *Fonda Villa Verde (☎ 971 63 90 37, Carrer de Ramon Llull 19)* has been refurbished somewhat and offers charming singles/doubles with bathroom for 6000/8300 ptas. Views from the large sunny terrace are gorgeous and prices include breakfast.

Set on a hillside overlooking the town, *Hostal Miramar (☎ 971 63 90 84, Ca'n Oliver s/n)* is an appealing stone pensión with simple rooms. B&B costs 4500/8500 ptas (without bathroom). Doubles with bathroom cost 10,600 ptas.

Somewhat more expensive and in the old town is the superbly renovated *S'Hotel d'Es Puig (☎ 971 63 94 09, Carrer d'Es Puig 4)*. Its gorgeous rooms cost 10,500/15,200 ptas, including breakfast.

If you want to rub shoulders with the rich and famous, the place to stay is *La Residencia (☎ 971 63 90 11, fax 971 63 93 70, Son Moragues)*, or 'the Res' as its habitues like to think of it. A short stroll from the town centre, this former 16th-century manor house is now a luxurious resort hotel set in 12 hectares of manicured lawns and beautifully tended gardens. It's part of Richard Branson's empire and of course, there's also the pool, tennis court, restaurant and grill-bar. B&B starts from a mere 26,000/41,000 ptas, plus IVA (ouch!).

Places to Eat The diverse collection of eateries along the main street includes a couple of affordable pizzerias and several expensive restaurants that claim to specialise in local cuisine.

One of the pizzerias is the rather pleasant *La Posada (Carrer del Archiduc Luis Salvador 9)*, where pizzas and many other dishes come in at under 1000 ptas.

Lluc Alcari

On the coast 3km north of Deià is the secluded *Hotel Costa d'Or (☎ 971 63 90 25)*, a popular mid-range hotel with 32 rooms, a swimming pool and a sun terrace with fine views of the coast. It's a 15-minute walk through a pine forest down to the hotel's beach. Singles/doubles cost 5700/10,300 ptas with breakfast.

Sóller

postcode 07100 • pop 11,207

Sóller's station is the terminus for the Palma-Sóller railway, one of Mallorca's most popular and spectacular excursions (see Mallorca's Getting Around section).

The town sprawls across a flat valley beneath soaring and jagged outcrops of the Serra de Tramuntana. It's a pleasant place with attractive old buildings, lush gardens and open plazas, but be prepared to cope with thick crowds of visitors during the day. Sóller is a preferred base for walkers.

The main square, Plaça de la Constitució, is 100m downhill from the train station. It's surrounded by bars and restaurants and is home to the **ajuntament** (town hall) and the tourist office (☎ 971 63 02 00), which is open from 9.30 am to 1.30 pm Monday to Saturday. Also here is the large 16th-century **Església Parroquial de San Bartolomé**, with a beautiful Gothic interior and a modernist facade.

Most visitors take a ride on one of Sóller's open-sided ex-San Francisco trams, which shuttle 2km down to Port de Sóller on the coast (115 ptas). They depart from the train station every 30 minutes between 6 am and 9 pm.

Places to Stay & Eat Beside the train station, *Hotel El Guía (☎/fax 971 63 02 27, Carrer del Castañer 2)* is a good place to meet other walkers. Its bright rooms feature timber trim and modern bathrooms. Room prices are 5405/8415 ptas, which includes breakfast.

Nearby (go past El Guía and turn right), the cosy *Casa de Huéspedes Margarita (☎ 971 63 42 14, Carrer Reial 3)* has just seven rooms with big old beds and shared bathrooms. Singles/doubles/triples cost 2800/3800/4500 ptas.

Celler Ca's Carreté (Plaça d'América 4), in an old cart workshop a little farther down

Fisherman at work in Mallorca's Port de Sóller (Balearic Islands)

Bougainvillea (Ibiza)

Where rocky cliffs drop into clear blue water, Ibiza (Balearic Islands)

Station of the cross (Mallorca)

Dusk in Ibiza city, looking deceptively quiet (Balearic Islands)

DAMIEN SIMONIS

The village of Binibèquer (Menorca)

DAMIEN SIMONIS

Too busy sunning to ride the paddle boats (Ibiza)

INGRID RODDIS

The remains of the Teatro Romano in Cartagena, believed to date back to 1 BC (Murcia)

hill and west of the tram line, has a rough and rustic feel and is a warm place to eat local food. You'll pay about 2500 ptas for a full dinner with wine.

Port de Sóller

Every day Port de Sóller is invaded on all fronts by hordes of tourists. They descend from the mountains by the bus load, sail around from Palma in dozens of cruise boats and trundle down on trams from nearby Sóller.

Why? Beats us. The harbour itself is quite scenic – the waterfront is lined with cafes and restaurants (and souvenir shops) and a fleet of boats run excursions to Sa Calobra, Deià, Sant Elm and Illa sa Dragonera. But the 'beach' is grubby and any lingering charm has long since been swept away by the flood of tourists.

Biniaraix & Fornalutx

From Sóller it's a pleasant 2km drive, pedal or stroll through narrow laneways up to the tiny village of Biniaraix.

From there, another narrow and scenic route continues north up to Fornalutx, taking you through terraced groves crowded with orange and lemon trees. Fornalutx is a pretty village of distinctive stone houses with green shutters, colourful flower boxes and well-kept gardens. Many of the homes are owned by expatriates but it's a far cry from the (comparative) hustle and bustle of Sóller.

Hostal Fornalutx (☎ 971 63 19 97, *Carrer de l'Alba 22*) is a delightfully converted former convent just off the main street. It costs 8500 ptas per person, including breakfast.

Sa Calobra

The 12km road from route C-710 across and down to the small port of Sa Calobra is one of the most spectacular and hair-raising scenic drives you'll ever take. The serpentine road has been carved through the weird mountainous rock formations, skirting narrow ridges before twisting down to the coast in an eternal series of hairpin bends.

If you come in summer you won't be alone. NATO would be proud to organise such an operation. Divisions of buses and fleets of pleasure boats disgorge battalion after battalion of tireless tourists. It makes D-Day look like play lunch and all that's missing are the choppers playing *The Ride of the Valkyrie*. Instead a couple of Peruvian musicians keep the tempo going over the ubiquitous loud-speaker system. Drinks are drunk, ice-creams gobbled, cheap junk purchased. And wave after wave, they just keep coming.

It is hard to know who is crazier – the bus drivers who negotiate the road down (and back up) with their load of human lobsters, or the occasional cyclists who scream down (we don't even want to contemplate what it must be like getting back up).

From the northern end of the road a short walking trail leads around the coast and through a series of long tunnels to a river gorge, the **Torrent de Pareis**, and a small cove with some fabulous (but crowded) **swimming** spots.

Sa Calobra is really quite pretty. It must be wonderful on a quiet, bright mid-winter morning...sigh. One bus a day comes from Ca'n Picafort via Pollença and the Monestir de Lluc. It returns at 3 pm. There is no bus on Sunday.

Monestir de Lluc

Back in the 7th century, a local shepherd claimed to have seen an image of the Virgin in the sky. Later, a similar image appeared on a rock. 'It's a miracle,' everyone cried and a chapel was built near the site to commemorate it.

A monastery was established here after Jaume I conquered Mallorca. Since then thousands of pilgrims have come every year to pay homage to the 14th-century **statue of the Virgin of Lluc**, known as La Moreneta because of her dark complexion.

The present monastery, a huge austere complex, dates from the 18th century. Off the central courtyard is the entrance to the **Basílica de la Mare de Déu**, which contains the statue. It is open 10 am to 5 pm. There is also a museum with archaeological bits and bobs and a modest art collection (300 ptas).

Places to Stay & Eat The monastery's accommodation section, *Santuari de Lluc* (☎ *971 87 15 25, fax 971 51 70 96)*, has 97 rooms and is popular with school groups, walkers and pilgrims. Singles/doubles start at 2400/3700 ptas. The downstairs rooms are dark and best avoided. Several restaurants and cafeterias cater to your tummy's demands.

Getting There & Away Buses connect twice daily with Inca and Pollença. From Inca there are regular bus and train connections to Palma.

Pollença
postcode 07460 • pop 13,450
Next stop on the Mallorcan pilgrimage is this attractive inland town. The devout and hardy come here to climb up **Calvari** (Calvary), 365 stone steps leading from the town up to a hill-top chapel and small shrine; the rest of us drive up the back road. Either way, the views from the top are great.

Otherwise, the central Plaça Major is a good place to relax. **Cafe Espanyol** has open-air tables shaded by big old plane trees, and an interesting collection of old photos of Mallorcan life inside.

Places to Stay A couple of kilometres south on the road to Palma, *Santuari del Puig de Maria* (☎ *971 18 41 32)* has rooms. Built during the 14th and 15th centuries, this former monastery is now a somewhat chaotic retreat. Neither the food nor the accommodation are anything to write home about, but the setting and views are spectacular, particularly if you manage to rise at dawn. A cell costs 1000 ptas per person – call ahead.

From the turn-off (signposted 2km south of Pollença on the Palma road), a narrow road leads two-thirds of the way up the hill; from there you'll have a steep 10 minute climb up a rocky path to the monastery.

Cala de Sant Vicenç
Actually a series of little jewel-like *calas* (coves), this is a tranquil little resort in a magnificent setting. Yes, the inevitable

English breakfast and German bratwurst problem is in evidence, but it's minimal compared with the big beaches farther to the south-east. And the water is so limpid you feel you could see to the centre of the world.

A small cluster of hotels, holiday apartments and eateries keep people housed and fed. Among them is the quirkily arranged and decorated *Hostal Mayol* (☎ *971 53 04 40, fax 971 53 42 69)*, with rooms and breakfast starting at around 4500/8000 ptas. The place has a pool and some rooms look out over the sea. Buses connect with Pollença.

Port de Pollença
On the northern shores of the Badia de Pollença, this resort is popular with British families, soothed by fish 'n' chips and pints of ale.

Sailboards and yachts can be hired on the beaches and boats run to the fine beaches of Platja de Formentor. South of town, the bay's shoreline becomes rocky and the beaches less attractive.

Places to Stay There are plenty of hotels and apartments. *Hostal-Residencia Paris* (☎ *971 86 40 17, Carrer de Magallanes 18)* is inland from the beach but not a bad deal with singles/doubles (all with bathroom) costing 4000/5400 ptas, which includes a buffet breakfast.

Cap de Formentor
A splendid drive (cyclists be warned: it is steep, narrow and often busy) leads from Port de Pollença out along this narrow, rocky promontory. Midway is *Hotel Formentor* (☎ *971 89 91 00)*, ritzy digs that have played host to the likes of Grace Kelly and Winston Churchill since 1926. Add yourself to the guest list for just 30,700/48,650 plus IVA.

Near the hotel and backed by shady pine forests, the sandy beaches of **Platja de Formentor** are among the island's best. At your disposal are a couple of exclusive beach bars, a golf course and a nearby horse-riding ranch.

From here it's another spectacular 11km out to the lighthouse on the cape that marks Mallorca's northernmost tip.

BADIA D'ALCÚDIA

The long beaches of this huge bay dominate Mallorca's north-eastern coast, its broad sweeps of sand stretching from Port d'Alcúdia to Ca'n Picafort.

Alcúdia
postcode 07400 • pop 10,581

Wedged between the two bays, busy Alcúdia was once a Roman settlement. Remnants of the Roman theatre can be seen and the old town is still partly protected by medieval walls. The tourist office organises walking tours of the town and publishes the handy *10 Excursions* booklet, which outlines some good walking and cycling tours to local destinations, including the **Parc Natural de l'Albufera** nature reserve and the ruins of the Roman city of **Pollèntia** – which are just outside one of the town's squat medieval gates.

Port d'Alcúdia
A large harbour dominates the town centre and imparts a chic maritime flavour, with boat trips leaving daily to Ca'n Picafort, Platja de Formentor and Port de Pollença. Flebasa has daily car-ferry services to Ciutadella (Menorca). The local tourist office (☎ 971 89 26 15) is at Avinguda de Joan Carles I 68.

South of the harbour, long, white, sandy beaches are backed by kilometres of apartments and big hotels slithering around the bay.

Places to Stay Budget options are limited. *Hostal Vista Alegre* (☎ 971 54 73 47, *Passeig Marítim 22*) is a friendly place with tidy singles/doubles with showers from 3500/5000 (no singles in summer).

Ca'n Picafort
A smaller version of Port d'Alcúdia, Ca'n Picafort is a package-tour frontier town and somewhat raw and soulless, but the beaches are pretty good.

Colònia de Sant Pere
Beyond Ca'n Picafort the road heads inland, but midway to Artà there's a turn-off leading 5km north towards the coast. Colònia de Sant Pere is an almost deadly quiet town with a tiny beach wedged between rocky coves and a few fishing boats bobbing in the sea.

Hostal Rocamar (☎/fax 971 58 93 12, *Carrer de San Mateo 9),* two blocks back from the beach, has comfortable singles/doubles with bathrooms and terraces for 5400/6600 ptas. If you stay less than four nights, the price is 7300/8500 ptas. It is the only accommodation in town.

EAST COAST
Most of the fine beaches along Mallorca's east coast have succumbed to the ravages of mass tourism. The northern half of this stretch of coastline is home to a series of concrete jungles that rival the worst excesses of the Costa del Sol on the mainland.

Farther south the coastline is corrugated with a series of smaller coves and ports, saving it from the same fate.

Artà
The inland town of Artà is dominated by the 14th-century hilltop fortress and **Església de San Salvador**. Also of interest is the **Museu d'Artà** on Plaça d'Espanya, which contains a small archaeological exhibition. The museum's open 10 am to 1 pm weekdays (200 ptas).

On the coast 10km south-east are the **Coves d'Artà**, said to be as impressive as Porto Cristo's Coves del Drac (see later). Tours of the caves are run every 30 minutes between 10 am and 7 pm (to 5 pm from October to June; 1200 ptas).

Cala Ratjada
postcode 07580 • pop 2545

Cala Ratjada is a heavily developed and busy resort particularly popular with Germans. The main streets are wall-to-wall souvenir shops and the pretty beaches are carpeted with sizzling flesh. A few kilometres inland, **Capdepera** is marked by the walls of the fortress enclave above the town.

For details of daily fast ferries to Ciutadella (Menorca), see Getting There & Around at the beginning of this chapter.

Places to Stay Your chances of finding accommodation here in July and August are next to nil. At other times, try *Hostal Gili (☎ 971 56 41 12, Carrer de Tamarells s/n)* overlooking the small bay of Son Moll a couple of kilometres to the south. It has a pool, sauna, bar and disco, with B&B costing 3500/6000 ptas for singles/doubles.

Cala Millor
Stretching along the east coast's largest bay, Cala Millor is a predominantly British resort with white-sand beaches backed by some of Mallorca's blandest and most intensive developments.

Porto Cristo
During the day, this place teems with day-trippers visiting the nearby underground caves. Porto Cristo is not good for your agoraphobia, but by late afternoon when the hordes have disappeared it can be quite nice. The town cradles a small sandy beach and boat harbour.

The **Coves del Drac** (Caves of the Dragon) on the southern outskirts of town are open 10 am to 5 pm daily. One-hour tours (1100 ptas) are held hourly on the hour, the 'highlight' being the classical music played by boat-bound musicians floating across a large subterranean lake. Nearby you can also visit Porto Cristo's large **aquarium**, which is open 10.30 am to 5 pm (11 am to 3 pm from November to March; 800 ptas).

Places to Stay Opposite the caves, *Hotel Sol i Vida (☎/fax 971 82 10 74, Avinguda de Joan Servera 11)* is a cheerful hostal with a pool, bar-restaurant and tennis court. Rooms with bathroom cost from 3800/6000 ptas for singles/doubles.

Portocolom
A tranquil village set on a generous harbour, Portocolom has managed to resist the tourist onslaught with a degree of dignity.

Various restaurants dot the long bay and within a couple of kilometres are some fine beaches, like the immaculate little cove of **Cala Marçal**. The cheapest place to stay is the no-nonsense *Pensión Portocolom (☎ 971 82 53 23, Ronda Cristóbal Colón 5)*, which charges 2100 ptas per person. Buses run to Portocolom from Palma via the inland farming town of **Felanitx**.

Cala d'Or
Once a quaint fishing village, Cala d'Or is now an overblown big-dollar resort. Its sleek new marina is lined with glisteningly expensive boats and the surrounding hills are crowded with blindingly whitewashed villas. Plenty of lifestyle, little substance.

Portopetro
Immediately south of Cala d'Or (and virtually joined to it by urban sprawl) is the smaller and more tranquil Portopetro. Centred on a boat-lined inlet and surrounded by residential estates, it has a cluster of harbourside bars and restaurants and a couple of small beaches nearby.

Cala Mondragó
Two kilometres south of Portopetro, Cala Mondragó is one of the most attractive beaches on the east coast. Sheltered by large rocky outcrops and fringed by pine trees, this protected sandy beach has a solitary bar surrounded by deck chairs and thatched umbrellas. Development is limited to a couple of houses and one large hostal, the five-storey *Hostal Playa Mondragó (☎/fax 971 65 77 52)*, which has good facilities, including a pool, bar and restaurant. It charges 3800 ptas per person per day (including breakfast).

Cala Figuera
Compared with much of the rest of the coast, this is a little gem. The fishermen here really still fish, threading their way down the winding inlet before dawn while the predominantly German tourists sleep off the previous night's food and drink. What has probably kept the place in one piece is the fact that the nearest beach, the equally

pretty little **Cala Santanyi**, is a few kilometres drive south-west. Nicer still is **Cala Llombards**, which you can walk to (scaling endless stairs) from Cala Santanyi or drive to via the town of Santanyi (follow the signs to Es Llombards and then Cala Llombards). Be warned though, the area *has* been 'discovered' – even born and bred locals seem German.

Some hostales and restaurants huddle along the southern side of the inlet. *Hostal-Restaurant Ca'n Jordi* (☎ *971 64 50 35, Carrer de la Virgen del Carmen 58)* has excellent rooms with bathroom, balcony and splendid views over the inlet from 3200/ 5000 ptas. The owners also rent out a few apartments and villas.

Several restaurants and bars dotted about town will keep your hunger and thirst at bay. A daily bus connects with Palma.

Colònia de Sant Jordi
On the south-east coast, the large resort town of Colònia de Sant Jordi is rather unexciting and the local beach is no great shakes either. Some good **beaches** lurk nearby, however, particularly Ses Arenes and Es Trenc (with a nudist strip), both a few kilometres up the coast towards Palma. The water at the latter is an impossible shade of blue and it's so popular that you pay 600 ptas to park your car here (250 ptas for motorbikes; free after 4 pm).

From Colònia de Sant Jordi itself you can take boat trips to the former prison island of **Cabrera**, where more than 5000 French soldiers died after being abandoned in 1809 towards the end of the Peninsular War. Cabrera and its surrounding islets now form the Parc Nacional Archipiélago de Cabrera.

THE INTERIOR
East of the Serra de Tramuntana, Mallorca's interior is a flat and fertile plain. Dominated by farmland and often unremarkable agricultural townships, it holds little of interest to the average beach-obsessed tourist. But for those with time, transport and an interest in discovering the traditional Mallorcan way of life, an exploration of the island's interior is highly rewarding.

Several of the major inland towns are well known for their specialised products. **Inca** holds a popular market each Thursday and has numerous factory outlets selling locally produced leather goods (check out the places along Gran Via de Colón and Avinguda del General Luque). Industrial **Manacor** has a thriving manufactured pearl industry (including the famous Majorica factory, since 1890) and many of the island's furniture manufacturers (it seems remarkable that a place so prosperous could be so ugly). **Felanitx** is known for its ceramics showrooms and factories.

Places to Stay
If you're interested in experiencing 'the other Mallorca', numerous rural properties, mountain houses and traditional villas around the island operate as upmarket B&Bs. Pick up the *Fincas* brochure at tourist offices or at the Associació Agroturisme Balear (☎ 971 72 15 08, fax 971 71 73 17, e agroturismo@mallorcanet.com), Avinguda de Gabriel Alomar i Villalonga 8a, in Palma.

Many of the properties are historic and often stylish country estates offering outstanding facilities, including swimming pools, tennis courts and organised activities and excursions. Prices for double rooms (often with room for three) range from about 10,000 to 25,000 ptas (there are a few expensive exceptions) a day.

Ibiza (Eivissa)

Ibiza is the most extreme of the islands, both in landscape and the people it attracts.

The Greeks called Ibiza and Formentera the Islas Pitiusas, or 'islands of pine trees'. The Ibizan landscape is harsh and rocky and the island receives little rainfall. Alongside the hardy pines, the most common crops are the traditionally Mediterranean olive, fig and almond trees.

A rugged coastline is interspersed with dozens of fine sandy beaches, most of them consumed by intensive tourist developments. A few out-of-the-way beaches remain but in

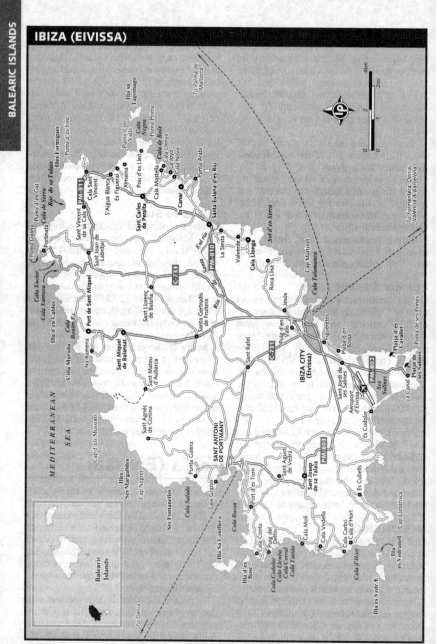

IBIZA (EIVISSA)

summer you won't be doing much solitary swimming.

The island's beaches and laid-back attitude first became a major drawcard in the flower-power heyday of the 1960s: while North America's hippies were 'California dreaming', their European counterparts were heading for Ibiza to tune in, turn on and drop out. It is hard to believe that in 1956 the island boasted a total of 12 cars!

Initially a resort for the hip and fashionable, Ibiza soon discovered the financial rewards of bulk tourism and started shipping in summer sunseekers by the thousand. Nowadays the island populace of 86,300 watches more than a million visitors a year – a strange blend of hippies, fashion victims, nudists, nightclubbers and package tourists – pour through. Official hopes rest with steering slowly away from the charter-flight lager louts and attracting a more culture-hungry set (with greater disposable income).

Ibiza's nightlife is renowned. The island, birthplace of the rave, is home to some of Spain's biggest and most famous discos, and its great summer club scene is complemented by a huge and diverse collection of bars.

Activities
Diving and sailing are both possible on Ibiza. You'll find plenty of schools for both activities in the main resorts – the tourist office has lists.

Accommodation
Of the five camping grounds around the island, only Camping Florida near Cala Nova is open year round. There are no grounds around the city.

Ibiza City has the most diverse range of accommodation, including good budget options, although in summer cheap beds are hard to come by. Santa Eulària also has several affordable places, but elsewhere bargains are few and far between.

As on the mainland, country homes *(casas rurales)* are beginning to win fans. For more information on the six or so of these attractive, quiet hideaways, approach the tourist office.

Getting Around
Bus Four bus companies operate services to different parts of the island (many run night buses in summer for party-goers):

Autobuses Empresas HF Vilas (☎ 971 31 16 01) Operates from Ibiza City to Santa Eulària d'es Riu, Es Canar, Cala Sant Vicent, Portinatx and other beaches on the east and north coasts. It also does the Santa Eulària–Sant Antoni de Portmany run.
Autobuses San Antonio (☎ 971 34 05 10) Operates between Ibiza City and Sant Antoni de Portmany.
Autobuses Voramar El Gaucho (☎ 971 34 03 82) Operates services from Ibiza City to the airport, Ses Salines, Platja d'en Bossa, Cala Llonga and Santa Eulària. It also services the south and south-west coasts from Ibiza City and Sant Antoni de Portmany.
Autocares Lucas Costa (☎ 971 31 27 55) Operates from Ibiza City to Santa Gertrudis, Sant Mateu, Sant Miquel de Balansat and Port de Sant Miquel.

Pick up a copy of the *Horario de Autobuses* (bus timetable) from tourist offices.

Car, Motorcycle & Bicycle If you are intent on getting to some of the more secluded beaches you will need to rent wheels.

The big operators have car rental desks at the airport, but smaller and often cheaper operators are scattered around the island: those in Ibiza City include Valentin (☎ 971 31 08 22), at Avinguda de Bartomeu Vicent Ramón 19, and Autos Isla Blanca (☎ 971 31 54 07), at Carrer de Felipe II. The latter will hire out a Renault Twingo for 18,000 ptas for three days all-inclusive.

Cyclists should ask for the tourist office's *Rutas en Mountain Bike* brochure, with seven suggested routes across the island.

IBIZA CITY (EIVISSA)
postcode 07800 • pop 31,500
Set on a protected harbour on the south-east coast of the island, Ibiza's capital is where most people arrive. It's a vivacious and popular place to stay: unlike other resorts around the island it's a living, breathing town with an interesting old quarter and numerous attractions. It's also a focal point for some of the island's best nightlife and the most diverse

range of cafes and restaurants. On the downside, it lacks good beaches, although you don't have to travel far if you want a swim. All in all, Ibiza City is an excellent base from which to explore the rest of the island.

Orientation

Most of the new city lies to the west, while the old centre and areas of most interest to visitors are immediately south of the harbour.

The old walled town, D'Alt Vila, is perched high on a hill top overlooking all. Between D'Alt Vila and the harbour lies the

Sa Penya area, a jumble of narrow streets and lanes lined with whitewashed shops, bars and restaurants – and a few accommodation options.

The broad Passeig de Vara de Rey is a favourite spot for the traditional sunset promenade. It runs westwards from Sa Penya to Avinguda d'Espanya, which in turn takes you out of the city towards the airport, 7km south-west.

Information

Tourist Offices Ibiza City's tourist office (☎ 971 30 19 00) is on Passeig des Moll

IBIZA CITY (EIVISSA)

PLACES TO STAY
4   Hostal-Residencia Ripoll
8   Hostal Sol y Brisa
10 Hotel Montesol
13 Casa de Huéspedes Navarro
17 Casa de Huéspedes L'Aduana
18 Hostal La Marina
19 Casa de Huéspedes Los Caracoles
24 Casa de Huéspedes La Peña
31 Hostal-Residencia Parque
39 Hotel El Corsario
40 Hotel El Palacio
41 La Torre del Canónigo

PLACES TO EAT
3   Lizarran
7   Pizzería da Franco er Romano
11 Restaurant Victoria
12 Ca'n Costa
28 Comidas Bar San Juan
32 La Brasa
33 Restaurante El Olivo
38 La Scala

OTHER
1   Autos Isla Blanca
2   Discobus Stop
5   Viajes Ibiza (American Express)
6   Valentin
9   Trasmediterránea Office
14 Change Booth & Disco Tickets
15 Tourist Office

OTHER (CONTINUED)
16 Estación Marítima (Ferry Terminal) for Palma de Mallorca, Barcelona & Valencia
20 Flash
21 Bar Mambo
22 The Rock Bar
23 Base
25 Samsara
26 Capricho Bar
27 Mercat de Verdures
29 Sunset Café
30 Iberia
34 Museu d'Art Contemporani
35 Dôme
36 Inkognitos
37 Anfora
42 Museu Arqueològic
43 Catedral

opposite the Estación Marítima (ferry terminal). The staff are friendly, multilingual and professional. Opening hours are 9.30 am to 1.30 pm and 5 to 7 pm weekdays; 10.30 am to 1.30 pm Saturday. There's another tourist office at the airport.

Money American Express is represented by Viajes Ibiza (☎ 971 31 11 11), Carrer de Vicent Cuervo 9.

Post & Communications The main post office is at Carrer de Madrid s/n. You can go online at Ibiform (☎ 971 31 58 69), Avinguda de Ignacio Wallis 8 (first floor). It's open 9 am to 2 pm and 4 to 9 pm weekdays. An hour costs 900 ptas, or less if you get a *bono* (pass) that allows you from two to 20 hours net time.

Medical Services & Emergency The Hospital Can Mises (☎ 971 39 70 00) is situated in the Barrio Can Mises, west of Ibiza City. There are three pharmacies along Carrer de Anibal – at any given time at least one of them is open. The Policía Nacional (☎ 971 30 53 13) are at Avinguda de la Pau s/n.

Sa Penya
When you arrive, take a stroll around Sa Penya. There's always something going on here. If you're into people-watching you'll be right at home: this small pocket must have one of the highest concentrations of exhibitionists and weirdos than anywhere else in Spain.

Shopping is a major pastime and Sa Penya is crammed with dozens of funky and trashy **clothing boutiques**. It's actually a surprisingly good place to shop around for clothes – the intense competition between the locally made gear and the imports keeps prices at an almost reasonable level. The so-called **'hippie markets'**, street stalls along Carrer d'Enmig and the adjoining streets, sell just about everything under the sun. The hippies aren't too numerous but the stalls that specialise in locally made arts and crafts are worth checking out.

D'Alt Vila
From Sa Penya you can wander up into D'Alt Vila, the old walled town. The Romans were the first to fortify this hill top, but the walls you see were raised by Felipe II in the 16th-century to protect against invasion by combined French and Turkish forces. A steep ramp leads from Plaça de sa Font in Sa Penya up to the **Portal de ses Taules** gateway, the main entrance to the old town. Above it hangs a commemorative plaque bearing Felipe II's coat of arms and an inscription recording the 1585 completion date of the fortification, which consists of seven artillery bastions joined by thick protective walls up to 22m in height.

Immediately inside the gateway is the expansive **Plaça de la Vila**, with its upmarket restaurants, galleries and shops. Up behind the plaza you can walk along the top of the walls and enjoy great views of the city, its harbour and the coast. Nearby, the **Museu d'Art Contemporani** is in an 18th-century powder store and armoury. It features constantly changing exhibitions of contemporary art. It is open 10 am to 1.30 pm Tuesday to Sunday (and 6 to 8 pm Tuesday to Friday in summer; 200 ptas).

A steep and well-worn route leads from Plaça de la Vila along narrow streets up to the **catedral**, which overlooks all from the top of the hill. It elegantly combines several styles: the original structure was built in the 14th century in the Catalan Gothic style, the sacristy was added in 1592 and major renovation work in baroque style took place during the 18th century.

Adjoining the cathedral, **Museu Arqueológic** houses a fine collection of ancient relics, mainly from the Phoenician, Carthaginian and Roman periods. It's open 10 am to 1 pm and 4 to 6 pm Tuesday to Saturday (10 am to 2 pm and 5 to 8 pm in summer), and 10 am to 2 pm Sunday (300 ptas, students half-price).

Beaches
The closest beach to Ibiza City is **Platja de Figueretes**, about 20 minutes' walk southwest of Sa Penya. In the next bay around to the north-east of Sa Penya is **Platja de**

Talamanca. These beaches are OK for a quick dip, although if you have time you'd be better off heading to the beaches at **Ses Salines** (see that section later).

Places to Stay – Budget

Quite a few reasonably priced hostales huddle around the port, although in midsummer cheap beds are as scarce as hen's teeth.

Sa Penya gets pretty rowdy at night; if you don't like the idea of staying in the heart of the nightlife zone there are a couple of quieter options a little way to the west. The friendly *Hostal Sol y Brisa* (☎ 971 31 08 18, Avinguda de Bartomeu Vicent Ramón 15) has clean singles/doubles with shared bathrooms from 3500/6000 ptas. Nearby, *Hostal-Residencia Ripoll* (☎ 971 31 42 75, Carrer de Vicent Cuervo 14) has similar rooms for 3800/5800 ptas.

Looking onto the waterfront (the entrance is at Carrer de Barcelona 7), *Hostal La Marina* (☎ 971 31 01 72) has good doubles with harbour views for 5000 to 7000 ptas depending on the season. They have also taken over a couple of other buildings in Carrer de Barcelona and converted them into lodgings at similar prices, *Casa de Huéspedes Los Caracoles* and *Casa de Huéspedes L'Aduana*. They can be contacted on the same phone number as Hostal La Marina. This is a noisy part of town so expect little sleep.

One of the most popular low-budget options is the friendly *Casa de Huéspedes La Peña* (☎ 971 19 02 40, Carrer de la Virgen 76). The 13 simple, tidy doubles with shared bathrooms cost up to 4000 ptas. The top rooms have great harbour views.

Casa de Huéspedes Navarro (☎ 971 31 07 71, Carrer de sa Creu 20, 3rd floor), in the thick of things, has 10 rooms at the top of a long flight of stairs. The front rooms have harbour views (but quite dark in summer) and there's a sunny rooftop terrace. This place charges 3500/6500 ptas.

Places to Stay – Mid-Range

Hostal-Residencia Parque (☎ 971 30 13 58, Carrer de Vicent Cuervo 3) is quieter and a bit more upmarket than most of the other hostales. Some of the rooms overlook the pleasant Plaça del Parque from above the cafe of the same name. Singles without bath cost 5000 ptas, while rooms, whether singles or doubles, with own bath cost anything from 8000 to 12,000 ptas.

Hotel Montesol (☎ 971 31 01 61, Passeig de Vara de Rey 2) is a comfortable one-star place. Rooms have their own bathroom, TV and phone – and most have views of the harbour or the old town. Singles/doubles cost up to 8700/16,300 ptas. The doubles are OK, but many of the singles are too poky for the price.

You could stay in Platja de Figueretes. Most of the hotels here cater for package tourists. The beach is nothing special but it's not a bad compromise if you need to be close to beaches and nightlife. *Hotel Marítimo* (☎ 971 30 27 08, fax 971 30 14 38, Carrer de Ramon Muntaner 48), right on the waterfront, is a decent two-star place with singles/doubles for 7500/11,770 ptas.

Places to Stay – Top End

Up in D'Alt Vila are the truly fine accommodation options. *Hotel El Corsario* (☎ 971 39 32 12, fax 971 39 19 53, Carrer de Ponent 5) is magically located with spectacular views of the town and harbour below. The rooms are straightforward but the sprawling mansion is loaded with character and the restaurant serves fine food (for fine prices). Doubles with breakfast range from an affordable 18,000 ptas to an extortionate 60,000 ptas for the best suite.

Hotel El Palacio (☎ 971 30 14 78, fax 971 39 15 81, Carrer de la Conquista 2) is designed for a generous wallet. Subtitled the 'Hotel of the Movie Stars', it is something of a private movie museum with a collection of signed photos, original movie posters and film awards, with seven rooms each paying homage to a different Hollywood star. The views are great, and there's a private courtyard with a bar and swimming pool. The Humphrey Bogart double is the cheapest at 34,000 ptas, and the Walt Disney room is the next up at 39,000 ptas (it has a nice terrace). The hotel is open from Easter to October.

Another fine option is **La Torre del Canónigo** (☎ 971 30 32 57, fax 971 30 78 43, Carrer Major 8). This 14th-century tower houses 10 gorgeous 'apartments' (doubles and suites), which were refurbished in 1999. They cost from 30,000 to 113,000 ptas(!) in August, depending on which one you choose.

Places to Eat

Plenty of bland and overpriced restaurants grace the streets of Sa Penya. Most serve up uniformly tasteless food and offer a similar selection – pizza, pasta, paella and seafood dishes – and many have touts who stand out the front thrusting menus at passers-by in an irritating attempt to lure them in.

Fortunately, a few exceptions are worth searching out. **Comidas Bar San Juan** (Carrer de Guillem de Montgri 8) is a simple, family-run operation with two small dining rooms. The decor ain't flash but the food is outstanding value, with main courses between 500 and 850 ptas – for dessert try the manzana al horno, a delicious baked caramelised apple.

The friendly **Ca'n Costa** (Carrer de sa Creu 19), a basement eatery, is another no-frills concern with good food at reasonable prices. It offers fish and meat mains for up to 1100 ptas.

Another good budget bet is **Restaurant Victoria** on the corner of Carrer de Riambau and Carrer de Guillem de Montgri. The dining room is stark, with linoleum floors and brown checked tablecloths, but the food is hearty and cheap with all main courses in the 500 to 950 ptas range.

If you want better Italian food than what's on offer in the port area, head for **Pizzería da Franco er Romano** (Avinguda de Bartomeu Vicent Ramon 15). Pizzas start at 700 ptas and the pasta dishes aren't bad.

Lizarran (Avinguda de Bartomeu Rosselló 15) is part of a Basque chain that has a firm foothold in Barcelona and has now made a hop across the sea. The tapas are good.

For somewhat more expensive fare you could try the leafy gardens of **La Brasa** (Carrer de Pere Sala 10), where fish, meat or rice mains will cost around 2200 ptas.

Most of Ibiza's more upmarket restaurants are in D'Alt Vila. There's a cluster of places just inside the entrance to the old town, spread along Plaça de Vila. **Restaurante El Olivo** is one of the best of these: main courses like pork fillet stuffed with goat's cheese and tarragon are around 2000 ptas.

If you're looking for somewhere intimate and romantic, head for the candle-lit **La Scala** (Carrer de sa Carrossa 6). The filete de avestruz con salsa 'cafe de Paris' (ostrich filet in a 'cafe de Paris' sauce – huh?), at just 2950 ptas, gives you an idea of what you might find here.

You can buy fresh fruit and vegies from the small open-air **Mercat de Verdures** on Carrer de ses Verdures, opposite the entrance to D'Alt Vila.

Entertainment

Sa Penya is the nightlife centre. Dozens of bars keep the port area jumping from around sunset until the early hours. After they wind down you can continue at one of the island's world-famous discos – if you can afford the outrageous cover charges or score a free pass, that is.

Bars Carrer de Barcelona, a pedestrian-only street that runs parallel with the harbour, is lined with an impressive collection of funky bars. Most have tall tables and stools out on the street and all pump out loud music and cold drinks.

You may soon come to notice something about them all. Apart from the expense of a tipple (an average 1500 ptas for a cocktail), they are all fronted by touts trying to drag you in for one said drinkie. If things are a little slack they will start trying to bribe you with cut-price entry to the clubs. If you want to go to a club, bargain like you're in a Middle Eastern souq – the savings can be worth the effort!

Less in your face are the bars farther east along Carrer de Garijo Cipriano, including **Bar Mambo** at No 10 and **Flash** at No 9. **The Rock Bar**, No 13, and its next door neighbour, **Base** at No 14, are particularly in with the clubbing crowd, as is **Dôme**

(Via de Alfonso XII 5), deeper inside Sa Penya. The latter is largely, but not exclusively, gay. Above all it is glam, and there are quite a few other attractive watering holes to try here.

If you're just after a quiet drink *Sunset Cafe* on Plaça del Parc is a good spot for much of the evening, although the place tends to crank up later at night as the odd celeb and clubland longtermers swing by.

To really glam it up you want to head out of town on the road to Sant Josep and wind up in *KM5,* the bar named after its highway location. There is a relaxed party atmosphere, several bars and a restaurant. It ain't cheap.

Don't be surprised if you receive unsolicited invitations from some attractive strangers. The local bar scene is highly competitive and lots of places employ slick and persuasive touts to 'invite' passers-by to join them for a drink, sometimes with the lure of free passes to the big discos.

Clubs & Discos Ibiza enjoys a reputation for having one of the best club scenes in Europe, and during the summer months the island is virtually a continuous party from sunset to sunrise and back again. Fuelled by an overdeveloped sense of competitiveness, the island's entrepreneurs have built a truly amazing collection of discos – huge, throbbing temples to which thousands of disciples flock nightly to pay homage to the gods of hedonism. Some of these places can hold 10,000 people or more.

Inevitably, the drugs business booms equally well. According to one estimate the trade is worth US$150 million.

A 'disco sunrise' is definitely part of the Ibiza experience and even if you're not a disco buff you should try to check out at least one of these unique entertainment megaplexes.

With the exception of Pacha (the only club to open year round), the major discos operate nightly between June and September and most open from around midnight till dawn, although things don't usually hot up until 3 am or later. Each has something different to offer and special theme nights,

fancy-dress parties, foam parties (where you are half-drowned in the stuff while you dance) and the like are regular features. Some places go a step or two further, putting on go-go girls, striptease acts and even live sex as a climax to the evening (or morning).

Entertainment Ibiza-style doesn't come cheap: most places charge between 4000 and 7000 ptas entry (and then sting you bigtime for drinks). If you hang around the right bars in Sa Penya you might score a flier that entitles you discounted entry (rarely more than 1000 ptas off, sometimes with a drink thrown in). These are handed out by club promoters, whose job it is to entice people with 'the look' (ie, bootiful people) to their discos. For free tickets or bigger discounts, you need to bargain with the bars in town that fleece you for your warm-up drinks.

The big names are: *Pacha,* on the northern side of Ibiza City's port; *Privilege* (formerly known as Ku) and *Amnesia,* both 6km out of Ibiza City on the road to Sant Antoni; *Es Paradis* in Sant Antoni itself; *El Divino,* across the water from the town centre (they put on boats and will refund taxis for groups of three or more); and *Space,* south of Ibiza City in Platja d'en Bossa. Head to Space when everywhere else is closed – it opens at 8 am and finishes up at 6 pm!

These are the physical locations, but club teams rotate around the venues. London's Ministry of Sound, the sexfabulous Manumission, Cream and others are what punters from clubland look out for. They each put together the entertainment and so make sure things never stay too samey in any given venue. To plug in a little more to the scene, look out for the free *Ministry in Ibiza* magazine in bars around town.

During summer, Ibiza's 'Discobus' service operates nightly from midnight until 6 am, doing circuits between the major discos, bars and hotels in Ibiza City, Platja d'en Bossa, Sant Rafel and Sant Antoni. They leave hourly on the hour or half hour, depending on where you get on. In Ibiza they leave from the waterfront on Avingunda de Santa Eulària.

Gay Bars & Clubs The gay scene is based towards the eastern end of Sa Penya, particularly along the far end of Carrer de la Virgen. At No 44, *Samsara* has live floor shows most nights at 12.30 pm and the *Capricho Bar* next door at No 42 is a popular watering hole. *Inkognitos*, in the shadow of the old city walls, is a busy gay bar. *Anfora (Carrer de Sant Carles 7),* in the D'Alt Vila, is a gay men's club open daily until dawn.

Getting There & Away
Ibiza's airport (Aeroport d'Eivissa; ☎ 971 80 90 00) is 7km south-west of the capital. Iberia (☎ 971 30 25 80) has an office in Ibiza City at Passeig de Vara de Rey 15.

Buses to other parts of the island generally depart from a series of stops along Avinguda d'Isidoro Macabich (the western continuation of Avinguda de Bartomeu Rosselló). Tickets can be bought from the bus companies' ticket booths or on board the buses. For more details, see Getting Around in the Ibiza section earlier.

Trasmediterránea has an office in Ibiza City on the corner of Avinguda de Bartomeu Vicent Ramon and Carrer de Ramon i Cajal. For information on inter-island ferries, see Getting There & Away at the beginning of this chapter.

Getting Around
Buses between the airport and Avinguda d'Isidoro Macabich operate hourly between 7.30 am and 10.30 pm (15 minutes, 125 ptas). Coming into town, get off when you see the old city walls rather than waiting to reach the terminus. A taxi from the airport should cost around 1800 ptas.

Ibiza's commercial centre is quite compact, with most places of interest lying within five to 10 minutes' walk of the harbour.

You may well want a taxi to get around the major nightclubs. You can call one on ☎ 971 30 70 00.

EAST COAST
Cala Llonga
A busy highway (C-733) speeds you north out of Ibiza City towards Santa Eulària on the east coast. Alternatively, you could take the slower but more scenic coastal road via Cala Llonga – take the turn-off to Jesús a couple of kilometres north-west of Ibiza City. This route winds through low hills and olive groves, with detours along the way to several beaches, including the pleasant Sol d'en Serra.

Cala Llonga is set on an attractive bay with high rocky cliffs sheltering a lovely sandy beach, but the town itself has many high-rise hotels.

Santa Eulària d'es Riu
postcode 07840 • pop 5901
Ibiza's third-largest town, Santa Eulària is a bustling and agreeable place with reasonable beaches, a large harbour and plenty of 20th-century tourist-resort architecture.

Orientation & Information The main highway, known as Carrer de Sant Jaume as it passes through the town centre, is a hectic traffic artery lined with souvenir shops and restaurants.

The tourist office (☎ 971 33 07 28) is just off the highway at Carrer de Marià Riquer Wallis 4. It is open 9.30 am to 1.30 pm and 5 to 7.30 pm weekdays and 9.30 am to 1.30 pm Saturday.

Places to Stay Modern hotels and apartments crowd the Santa Eulària beachfront, but a couple of blocks inland you'll find a cluster of affordable hostales. The excellent *Hostal-Residencia Sa Rota (☎ 971 33 00 22, Carrer de Sant Vincent 59)* has bright rooms with modern bath or shower. Singles/doubles cost 4700/7700 ptas. The three-storey *Hostal Rey (☎ 971 33 0210, Carrer de Sant Josep 17)* offers decent rooms with showers and balconies for 4000/ 7500 ptas.

The British-run *Ca's Català (☎ 971 33 10 06, Carrer del Sol s/n)* is a find. This 12-room hotel has the feel of a private villa, with its colourful flowerpots and sunny rooms overlooking a garden courtyard and swimming pool. Singles start at 5000 ptas and doubles range from 8500 (without bath) to 10,000 ptas (plus IVA).

Places to Eat Most of the restaurants and cafes along the beachfront are either overly expensive or pretty tacky. At *Mel's English Snack Bar* you can enjoy 'home cooking at its best', with choices such as beans on toast, shepherd's pie and chip butties. Nice one, Mel.

Four blocks back there are plenty of decent eateries along Carrer de Sant Vicent: the friendly folk at *Restaurante La Bota* at No 43 offer you a good *menú* for 990 ptas. At *El Naranjo (Carrer de Sant Josep 31)* you can enjoy fine seafood meals in a shady garden. A full dinner will cost you about 3500 ptas.

Getting There & Away The main bus stop is on Carrer del Doctor Curtoys; regular buses connect Santa Eulària with Ibiza City, Sant Antoni and the northern beaches. During summer there are also daily boat services from the harbour to Es Canar, Cala Llonga and other local beaches.

Santa Eulària to S'Aigua Blanca

North-west of Santa Eulària is the resort town of **Cala Nova**, which is heavily developed and probably best avoided, although there are several camping grounds nearby worth considering. The best is *Camping Cala Nova (☎ 971 33 17 74)*, 500m north of the main town. One kilometre south of Cala Nova and a short stroll from the popular Punta Arabi beach is *Camping Florida (☎ 971 33 16 98)*, open all year.

Farther north on the main road is the sleepy village of **Sant Carles de Peralta**. A good place to stop for a bite or a drink is the popular *Bar Anita*, opposite the church in the centre of town. Side roads lead off to the pleasant **Cala Llenya** and **Cala Mastella** beaches.

A kilometre farther along the main road a turn-off right leads to **Cala de Boix**, the only true black-sand beach in the Balearic Islands. This area is largely undeveloped and *Hostal Cala Boix (☎ 971 33 52 24)* is a good place to stay. All rooms have bathrooms and some have sea views. B&B costs 2500 ptas per person.

Back on the main road the next turning leads to the resort area of **Es Figueral**. A little farther a handwritten sign marks the turn-off to the lovely beaches of S'Aigua Blanca. Being a bit out of the way and little developed, these beaches are popular with Ibiza's 'young and restless' crowd, most of whom tend to forget to put on their swimsuits.

A couple of hundred metres back from the beachfront is the three-storey *Pensión Sa Plana (☎ 971 33 50 73)*, which is a laid-back place with a pool, outdoor courtyard and pool-side bar and barbecue. Each room has a bathroom and terrace. Singles/doubles cost around 5000/6500 ptas, including breakfast.

Cala Sant Vicent

The package-tour resort of Cala Sant Vicent is built around the shores of a protected bay on the north-east coast, a long stretch of sandy beach backed by a string of modern mid-rise hotels. It's not a bad place to stop for a swim if you happen to be passing by; you could join a boat trip to the islet of **Tagomago**.

NORTH COAST & INTERIOR
Cala Sant Vicent to Portinatx

The main road (PM-811) heads west from Cala Sant Vicent, passing by the unremarkable village of **Sant Vicent de sa Cala** before hitting the main north-south highway. From here you can head south to Ibiza City or north to Portinatx.

Portinatx
postcode 07820

Portinatx is the north coast's major tourist resort, with phalanxes of hotels around its three adjoining beaches – S'Arenal Petit, S'Arenal Gran and Platja Es Port. The beaches themselves are beautiful but unless you're looking for large crowds, beach toys or souvenirs there are better places to spend your time.

Cala Xarraca

This beach, just west of Portinatx, is worth a visit. Set in a picturesque, partly protected bay with a rocky shoreline and a dark-sand beach, development is limited to a solitary bar-restaurant overlooked by a couple of private houses.

This northern part of Ibiza contains some of the island's most attractive landscapes. If you need a break from the beaches the area's coastal hills and inland mountains are popular with bushwalkers and cyclists.

Sant Llorenç de Balafia

Between Portinatx and Ibiza City and just off the main highway, Sant Llorenç is a tiny village consisting of a cluster of houses and farms surrounding a typical whitewashed Ibizan church.

Sant Miquel de Balansat & Port de Sant Miquel

One of the largest inland towns, Sant Miquel is overlooked by a box-like 14th-century church but there isn't much else to the place.

Several kilometres north, Port de Sant Miquel is yet another overdeveloped resort town, dominated by the huge *Hotel Club San Miguel*, which has consumed an entire hillside above the admittedly fine beaches.

A turn-off to the right just before you enter town, coming from the south, takes you around a headland to the entrance to the **Cova de Can Marca**, a collection of underground caverns spectacularly lit by coloured lights. The caves are open daily for tours.

Beyond the caves, a *very* rough unsealed road continues 4km around the coast to the unspoiled bay of **Cala Benirrás**. A sealed road to Cala Benirrás leads off the Sant Joan-Sant Miquel road, midway between the towns.

Around the coast about 3km west of Port de Sant Miquel is Ibiza's famous cliff-top *Hotel Hacienda* (☎ *971 33 45 00, fax 971 33 46 06)*. If you can afford the hefty prices and want to rub shoulders with the rich and famous, this is *the* place to stay. Rates change seasonally. Singles cost 34,200 ptas during August, while standard rooms cost 45,500 ptas. Still more luxurious ones are 52,600 ptas. Add IVA to all prices. Rates cost substantially reduced in July.

Santa Gertrudis de Fruitera

If you blinked at the wrong time you could easily miss tiny Santa Gertrudis, south of Sant Miquel, which would be a shame. Clustered around the central Plaça de l'Església you'll find an unusual collection of art and craft galleries and antique and bric-a-brac shops, plus several good bars. The most famous of the latter is *Bar Costa*, and while you're here it's almost obligatory to try a *bocadillo completo* – a delicious warmed roll smeared with tomato and filled with *jamón serrano* and cheese.

Sant Rafel

Midway between Ibiza City and Sant Antoni de Portmany, Sant Rafel is home to a couple of Ibiza's biggest and best discos. By day, the town is known as a craft centre and has a pretty good collection of ceramics workshops, sculpture galleries, shops and markets.

WEST COAST
Sant Antoni de Portmany
postcode 07820 • pop 7642

Sant Antoni, widely known as 'San An', is big, tacky and about as Spanish as bangers and mash. The locals joke (somewhat sadly) that even soccer hooligans need holidays, and somehow they all seem to end up in San An. It's the perfect destination if you've come in search of booze-ups, brawls and hangovers.

You might turn up here to use the ferry service to/from Denia in Valencia, or to sample the notorious nightlife, which is wild, to say the least.

The tourist office (☎ 971 34 33 63) is at Passeig de ses Fonts s/n. Sant Antoni is connected with Ibiza City and the rest of the island by regular bus services. Boats run to local beaches like Cala Bassa and Cala Conta, as well as to Portinatx, Formentera and Denia.

Not far north of Sant Antoni are several pleasant and undeveloped beaches, such as **Cala Salada**, a wide bay with sandy shores backed by a pine forest. From here, a rough track continues north around the coast to the beach at **Ses Fontanelles**, but without a

BALEARIC ISLANDS

4WD this route isn't really passable. If you're keen, access from the main road is much easier.

Cala Bassa to Cala d'Hort

Heading west and south from Sant Antoni, you'll come to the rocky and popular bay of Cala Bassa. Not far back from the beach, *Camping Cala Bassa* (☎ 971 34 45 99) is an OK second-class camping ground open in summer. The next few coves around the coast also hide some very pretty beaches – Cala Conta (or Cala Comte) is one of the best. All are accessible by bus from Sant Antoni.

Farther south, **Cala Vedella** is a modest resort with a fine beach in the centre of town, backed by a couple of restaurants. A little farther south, Cala d'Hort has a spectacular setting overlooking two rugged rocky islets, Es Vedrá and Es Vedranell. The water here is an inviting shade of blue and the beach a long arc of sand sprinkled with pebbles and rocks. The developers still haven't ruined this place, and there's nothing here apart from two good bar-restaurants, one with a few rooms.

SOUTH COAST
Ses Salines

postcode 07640 • pop 3240

Platja de ses Salines and the adjacent **Platja d'es Cavallet**, at the southernmost tip of the island, are the best and most popular beaches within striking distance of Ibiza City. You can be here in half an hour on the local bus or quicker with your own transport. The area takes its name from the salt pans that have been exploited here since Carthaginian times.

If you're taking the bus from Ibiza City you'll be dropped at the western end of Ses Salines beside a small bar. Across the road on the other side of the sand dunes a long crescent-shaped bay stretches away into the distance, with a broad sandy beach broken by patches of rocks. These beaches are popular with Ibiza's party-hard crowd and there are four or five open-air beach bars spread around the bay. Each has a slightly different vibe and plays a different type of

music. The western end is more 'family oriented' and it seems that swimsuits become less common the farther east you go. Stroll on if the *au naturel* look appeals to you: Es Cavallet, the next bay around to the east, is Ibiza's official nudist beach.

Places to Stay *Hostal Mar y Sal* (☎ 971 39 65 84) is handy for the beach and has its own bar and restaurant; double rooms with bath are 5500 ptas (plus IVA) in summer.

Places to Eat All of Ses Salines' beach bars offer some type of food. About halfway along the beach, **Guaraná** is a funky tropical-style bar fronted by rows of banana lounges.

At the eastern end of the beach, **Sa Trincha** is more casual and considered the coolest place to be on this stretch of sand by those in the know. They serve up burgers, bocadillos, salads and fruit smoothies. They also do somewhat stronger drinks and when the DJ gets into gear things can get kind of wild and crazy.

Getting There & Away Autobuses Voramar El Gaucho runs eight to 10 buses daily to Ses Salines from Ibiza City (125 ptas).

Formentera

postcode (San Francesc Xavier) 07860 • pop 5323

A short boat ride south of Ibiza, Formentera is the smallest and least developed of the four main Balearic Islands. This idyllic island boasts fine beaches and some excellent short walking and cycling trails. It's a popular day trip from Ibiza and can get pretty crowded in midsummer, but most of the time it is still possible to find yourself a strip of sand out of sight and earshot of other tourists.

Formentera's predominantly flat landscape is rugged and at times bleak. The coast is alternately fringed with jagged rocky cliffs and beaches backed by low sand dunes. A handful of farmers scrape a living from the land in the centre and east

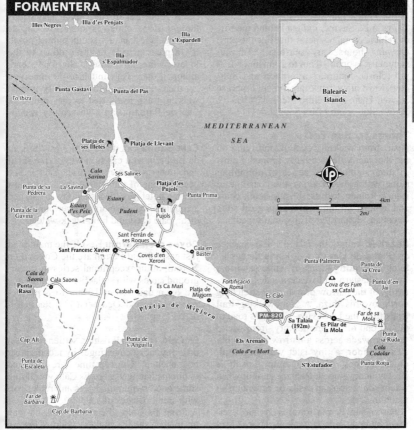

FORMENTERA

Illes Negres
Illa d'es Penjats
Illa s'Espardell
Illa s'Espalmador

Punta Gastavi
Punta del Pas

To Ibiza

MEDITERRANEAN SEA

Punta de sa Pedrera
La Savina
Cala Savina
Ses Salines
Platja de ses Illetes
Platja de Llevant
Platja d'es Pujols
Punta Prima

Estany d'es Peix
Estany Pudent
Es Pujols

Punta de la Gavina
Sant Ferrán de ses Roques
Sant Francesc Xavier
Coves d'en Xeroni
Cala en Baster

Punta Palmera
Punta de sa Creu
Cova d'es Fum sa Català
Punta d'en Jai

Cala de Saona
Punta Rasa
Cala Saona
Casbah
Es Ca Marí
Platja de Migjorn
Fortificació Romà
Es Caló
PM-820
Sa Talaia (192m)
Far de sa Mola
Es Pilar de la Mola
Punta sa Ruda

Cap Alt
Punta de s'Anguilla
Platja de Migjorn
Els Arenals
Cala d'es Mort
S'Estufador
Cala Codolar
Punta Rotja

Punta de s'Escaleta
Far de Barbaria
Cap de Barbaria

0   2   4km
0   1   2mi

Balearic Islands

---

but elsewhere the island is a patchwork of pine plantations, sun-bleached salt beds, low stone walls and vacant fields. The island lives off tourism and little incentive remains to work the unforgiving and little-watered land.

Orientation

Formentera is less than 20km across from east to west. Ferries arrive at La Savina, a functional harbour town wedged between two large salt lakes, the Estany d'es Peix and Estany Pudent (the aptly named Smelly Lake). Three kilometres south of La Savina

is the island's administrative capital, Sant Francesc Xavier, and another 5km south-west is Cap de Barbaria, the southernmost point. Es Pujols, the main tourist resort, is 3km east of La Savina.

The main road (PM-820) runs down the middle of the island, passing by the fine beaches of Platja de Migjorn along the south coast and through the fishing village of Es Caló (13km south-east of La Savina) before climbing to Sa Talaia, the island's highest point (192m). The eastern end of the island is marked by the Far de sa Mola lighthouse.

Information

Formentera's tourist office (☎ 971 32 20 57) is in La Savina, hidden behind the row of vehicle rental agencies that line the port. Opening hours vary seasonally; during summer it is open 10 am to 2 pm and 5 to 7 pm (closed Saturday afternoon and Sunday). Most of the banks are in Sant Francesc Xavier. There is a Centro Médico (☎ 971 32 23 69) 3km south of La Savina.

Things to See & Do

Apart from walking, cycling and lying on beaches, activities are fairly limited. Points of interest include a series of crumbling stone **watchtowers** along the coastline, a ruined **Roman fortress** on the south coast and another 40 minor **archaeological sites** (most are signposted off the main roads).

Beaches Among the island's best beaches are **Platja de Llevant** and **Platja de ses Illetes** – beautiful strips of white sand that line the eastern and western sides, respectively, of the narrow promontory stretching north towards Ibiza. A 2km walking trail leads from the La Savina–Es Pujols road to the far end of the promontory, from where you can wade across a narrow strait to **Illa s'Espalmador**, a tiny islet with beautiful, quiet beaches. The promontory itself is largely undeveloped. Be very careful when wading out – you can easily be caught up by incoming tides.

East of Sant Ferrán, towards Es Caló, a series of bumpy roads and unsealed tracks lead to the south coast beaches, known collectively as **Platja de Migjorn**. They are secluded and popular with nudists, despite their sometimes rocky and seaweed-strewn shorelines. Most of these beach settlements consist of a handful of houses and apartments, a couple of bar-restaurants and the odd hostal.

San Francesc Xavier Formentera's capital, San Francesc Xavier, is an attractive whitewashed village with some good cafes overlooking small, sunny plazas. The town's older buildings include a 14th-century chapel, an 18th-century fortress, and an interesting Ethnological Museum.

Cap de Barbaria A narrow sealed road heads south out of the capital and winds through stone-walled farmlands to Cap de Barbaria, the island's southernmost point. It's a pleasant ride or drive down to the lonely white lighthouse at the road's end, although there isn't much to do once you get there. From the lighthouse a 10-minute walking track leads east to the **Torre d'es Cap de Barbaria**, an 18th-century watchtower.

Cala Saona One-third of the way to Cap de Barbaria, you can turn west to the small and lovely settlement of Cala Saona. The beach is one of the island's best, with just one big hotel (see Places to Stay & Eat) and a couple of bar-restaurants overlooking the clear, pale aqua and blue-black waters.

Coves d'en Xeroni Beside the main road just east of Sant Ferrán are the Coves d'en Xeroni, an unexceptional series of underground caves with stalactites and all. They are open daily from 10 am to 8 pm between May and October (500 ptas, children 250 ptas).

Es Caló This small fishing settlement is set on a tiny rocky cove ringed by faded timber boat shelters. The coastline here is jagged but immediately west of Es Caló you'll find some good swimming holes and rock pools with small patches of sand.

From Es Caló, the road twists its way up to the island's highest point. Close to the top, **Bar-Restaurant El Mirador** offers spectacular views along the length of the island.

Eastern End The eastern end of the island is an elevated limestone plateau. It doesn't hold much interest: most of the coastline is only accessible by boat, and the interior is mainly taken up by pine stands and farms. A road runs arrow-straight to the island's eastern tip, passing through the nondescript town of Es Pilar de la Mola. At the end of the road stand the Far de sa Mola lighthouse and a monument to Jules Verne, who used this setting in one of his novels.

Places to Stay & Eat

Camping is prohibited on Formentera. And sad to say, most of the accommodation caters to package-tour agencies so is overpriced and/or booked out in summer. August and, to a lesser extent, July are the toughest months. While prices in August often border on the unreasonable, in many places they start falling in July and continue to deflate in other months. Prices given here are for August. Single rooms are as rare as hens' teeth in summer. In total, there are 45 hostales and hotels, from basic to five star, throughout the island. In addition, 73 blocks of flats, containing from three to 80-odd apartments, are on the books. Given the difficulties in the high summer months of finding anything without an advance booking, it might be an idea to contact the tourist office in advance to get a full accommodation list.

If you decide to stay longer, agencies in the main towns can help you rent an apartment, as can the tourist office.

Es Pujols Once a sleepy fishing village, Es Pujols has been transformed by Spain's tourism boom. Rows of sun-bleached timber boat shelters still line the beachfront, but nowadays they are overshadowed by modern hotels, apartments and restaurants, and tourism has all but replaced fishing as the town's main source of income. Nevertheless, the scale of development remains low-key compared with that on Ibiza or Mallorca. And if the town's sandy beaches are too crowded for your liking, more secluded options lie within easy striking distance.

Es Pujols has quite a few places to stay, but in high summer finding a room can still be near impossible.

Right on the beachfront, *Hostal Tahiti* (☎ 971 32 81 22, Carrer de Fonoll Marí 16) is a large, modern three-star place charging 7000/10,075 ptas for singles/doubles with B&B.

Several other hostales line Carrer de Miramar (the main street). *Hostal Voramar* (☎ 971 32 81 19), 100m inland, has double rooms for 9400 ptas.

Another cluster of hostales lurks a kilometre around the coast west of Es Pujols,

including *Hostal Sa Roqueta* (☎ 971 32 85 06), with doubles for 8350 ptas plus IVA.

Argentine food, which means lots of meat, seems popular hereabouts. Pop into *Gaucho (Carrer de Roca Plana 80)* – the *churrasco* is great for meat-eaters at 1900 ptas. Otherwise, take your pick from any of the waterfront joints.

Sant Francesc Xavier There's only one hostal here: the friendly *Restaurant-Casa Rafal* (☎ 971 32 22 05) on Carrer d'Isidoro Macabich has doubles for 7000 ptas, including breakfast. Out of the high season it lets some rooms out as singles.

Sant Ferrán de ses Roques Just 1.6km south of Es Pujols, this unassuming little town has a couple of decent budget hostales. The popular *Hostal Pepe* (☎ 971 32 80 33, Carrer Major 68) has 45 simple and breezy rooms with bath – B&B costs 3375/6090 ptas. The hostal's legendary bar has been a popular hippy hangout since the 1960s. On the main road, *Hostal Illes Pitiuses* (☎ 971 32 81 89) has modern rooms with bath costing up to 6500/8250 ptas in August.

La Savina Formentera's port town isn't the most thrilling place – if you go to the trouble of staying on the island you should head elsewhere. Still, if you get stuck *Hostal La Savina* (☎ 971 32 22 79) overlooks the Estany d'es Peix from Avinguda Mediterránea 22 (on the main road out of town). Doubles with lake views cost 9000 ptas. Otherwise, they are 7500 ptas, including breakfast.

Cala Saona The only accommodation is *Hotel Cala Saona* (☎ 971 32 20 30), a modernish if somewhat bland place with 116 air-con rooms, a pool, tennis courts, restaurant etc. Rooms (including breakfast) go for 12,250/18,000 ptas, plus IVA.

South Coast A spattering of hostales is spread along Formentera's south coast (otherwise known as Platja de Migjorn, which basically means South Beach).

Es Ca Marí is a small resort with a cluster of places to stay and reasonable beaches.

Hostal Ca Marí (☎ 971 32 81 80) is actually three hostales in one: their rooms and apartments all share a central bar, restaurant, pool and grocery shop. B&B rates are 6500/10,000 ptas.

Farther along the beach the exclusive *Hostal Santi (☎ 971 32 83 75)* has its own bar-restaurant and charges up to 12,500 ptas a double (plus IVA). Several hundred metres farther east, *Hostal Maysi (☎ 971 32 85 47)* charges 11,000 ptas a double.

Es Caló Overlooking a small rocky harbour, *Fonda Rafalet (☎ 971 32 70 16)* has good rooms (some with sea views) costing up to 5000/9000 ptas in August. It also incorporates a bar and a pricey seafood restaurant.

Across the (main) road, *Casa de Huéspedes Miramar (☎ 971 32 70 60)* has eight simple upstairs rooms sharing a communal bathroom. Nightly costs are 4000 ptas for doubles; the front rooms have sea views (and traffic noise), while the back rooms have bush views.

Es Pilar de la Mola Formentera's easternmost town has a handful of bars and restaurants. You can sit out the front of *Bar Can Toni* and watch the lighthouse-bound traffic go back and forth while you tuck into a good value meal (about 1400 ptas per head). Two kilometres farther east, near the lighthouse itself, the expensive *Bar Es Puig* specialises in mixed platters of hams, sausages and cheeses, herbal liquors and local wines.

Entertainment
Es Pujols has the only nightlife to speak of. In summer the town is pretty lively, with a cluster of bars along Carrer de Miramar that stay open until 3 or 4 am. Close to the beachfront, Carrer d'Espardell has a couple of popular watering holes, including the *Tennis Bar* and the small *Indiana Cafè*. Two good discos, *Magoos (Carrer de Roca Plana 31-35)* and *Tipic*, take you through until sunrise. The first is 100m in from the beach, while the other is by the town exit on the road to Sant Ferrán de ses Roques.

Getting There & Away
Balearia operates up to nine ferry services (one hour, 1250 ptas one way or 2300 ptas return) and up to 16 fast ferries (25 minutes, 2085 ptas one way) daily between Ibiza City and Formentera. The first ferry leaves Ibiza City at 7 am and the last returns from Formentera at around 8 pm.

Return fares for vehicles on the slower boats are 5000 ptas for a small car one way, 1225 ptas for motorbikes under 250cc and 350 ptas for a bicycle.

Inserco (☎ 971 32 22 10) runs two car-ferries daily. Prices are slightly higher than with Balearia. You may find one or two other companies compete with a handful of daily sailings.

Getting Around
Pedal power is the best way to get around this little island but Autocares Paya (☎ 971 32 31 81) runs a regular bus service connecting all the main towns.

If you need to hire transport you'll find rental agencies all over the island, including a string of places opposite the harbour in La Savina. Avis and Hertz have representatives here: local agencies include Moto Rent Mitjorn (☎ 971 32 22 55), Autos Isla Blanca (☎ 971 32 25 59) and Moto Rent La Savina (☎ 971 32 22 75). Daily rates are around 650 ptas for a bike, 900 ptas for a mountain bike, 1300 ptas for a motor scooter and up to 4000 ptas for motorbikes. A car is really superfluous on this tiny island, but they are available for rent at prices similar to those throughout the Balearics.

Menorca

Menorca, with a population of 70,206, is perhaps the least overrun of the Balearic Islands. In 1993 the island was declared a Biosphere Reserve by Unesco, with the aim of preserving important environmental areas such as the Parc Natural S'Albufera d'es Grau wetlands and its unique archaeological sites.

Not the island of choice for all-night party-goers, Menorca is probably the least

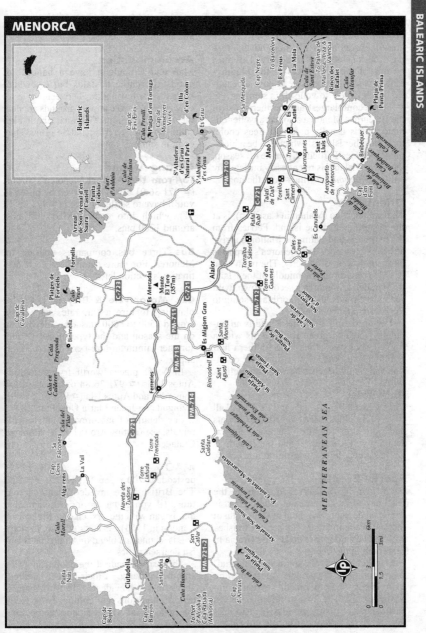

euro currency converter €1 = 166pta

affected of the islands. The untouched beaches, coves and ravines around its 216km coastline even allow the more adventurous the occasional sense of discovery! This must be one of the few places in the Mediterranean where it is possible to have a beautiful beach largely to yourself in summer.

The second-largest and northernmost of the Balearics, Menorca also has a wetter climate and is usually a few degrees cooler than the other islands –which can be a blessing in summer. Particularly in the off season, the 'windy island' is relentlessly buffeted by chilling *tramuntana* winds from the north.

Orientation

The capital, Maó (Mahón in Castilian), is at the eastern end of the island. Ferries from the mainland and Palma de Mallorca arrive at Maó's busy port, and Menorca's airport is 7km south-west of the city. The main road (C-721) runs along the middle of the island to Ciutadella, Menorca's second town, with secondary roads leading north and south to the resorts and beaches.

The northern half of the island is an undulating area of green rolling hills with a rugged, rocky coastline. The southern half is flatter and drier, with a smoother coastline and sandy beaches between high cliffs.

Activities

Maó, Ciutadella, Fornells and Es Castell all have yacht clubs. Many resorts have boats and sailboards for hire. There are several scuba-diving centres around the island, as well as a couple of horse-riding ranches.

Special Events

Each town has a festival to celebrate the feast day of its patron saint. The biggest is the Festa de Sant Joan, held in Ciutadella in the last week in June. The season finishes with the Festa de Mare de Déu de Gràcia in Maó on 8 September.

Menorca's festivals are steeped in traditions dating to the Middle Ages: jousting tournaments and other medieval games are common fare. The locals pride themselves particularly on their riding skills, and during the fiestas prancing horses are ridden

into the crowds, rearing on their hind legs and spinning in circles.

Accommodation

Maó and Ciutadella have a handful of good, affordable hostales but elsewhere bargains are few and far between.

Menorca's two camping grounds are near the resorts of Santa Galdana, about 8km south-west of Ferreries, and Son Bou. They open in summer only.

Getting Around

To/From the Airport Menorca's airport (☎ 971 36 01 50) is *not* served by buses so you'll have to settle for a taxi (☎ 971 36 71 11), which into central Maó will cost around 1200 ptas.

Bus Three bus companies operate on Menorca. For more details, see each destination's section later.

Car, Motorcycle & Bicycle If you're planning to hire a car, rates vary from around 3500 to 8000 ptas a day, depending on the season and the type of car. During summer minimum hire periods sometimes apply.

In Maó, places worth trying include Autos Valls (☎ 971 36 84 65), Plaça d'Espanya 13, and Autos Isla (☎ 971 36 65 69), Avinguda de Josep Maria Quadrado 28.

For details of motorcycle and bicycle rentals, see Getting Around under Maó and Ciutadella.

MAÓ

postcode 07700 • pop 21,541

The British have invaded Menorca four times (if you count the modest campaign that began with the first charter flight from London in 1953). As a result Maó, the capital, is an unusual blend of Anglo and Spanish characteristics.

The British made it the capital in 1713, and the influence of their almost hundred-year rule is still evident in the town's architecture, traditions and culture. Even today the majority of Maó's visitors come from Britain.

Maó's harbour is its most impressive feature and was the drawcard for the Brits. The deep, well-protected waters handle everything from small fishing boats to car ferries, cruise ships and tankers. The town was built atop the cliffs that line the harbour's southern shore. Although some older buildings remain, the majority of the architecture is in the restrained 18th-century Georgian style (note the sash windows!).

It's a pleasant and relaxed town and a good place to base yourself when you first arrive. Good beaches are a short bus ride away.

Information

Tourist Offices Menorca's main tourist office (☎ 971 36 37 90) is at Plaça de s'Esplanada 40. It is open 9 am to 7 pm weekdays, and 9.30 am to 1.30 pm Saturday.

Money American Express is represented by Viajes Iberia (☎ 971 36 28 48) at Carrer Nou 35, but at the time of writing they were looking for a new agent. Viajes Iberia will be able to tell you who the new agent is if it is no longer them.

Post & Communications Maó's post office is on the corner of Carrer del Bon Aire and Carrer de l'Església.

Medical Services & Emergency Hospital Verge del Toro (☎ 971 36 35 00) is at Carrer de Barcelona s/n. The Policía Nacional are at Carrer de la Concepció 1.

Old Quarter

Maó's main plaza is the large Plaça de s'Esplanada. A **craft and clothing market** is held here every Saturday.

The narrow streets to the east of here comprise the oldest part of Maó. The **Arc de Sant Roc**, a 16th-century archway at the top end of Carrer de Sant Roc, is the only remaining relic of the medieval walls that once surrounded the old city.

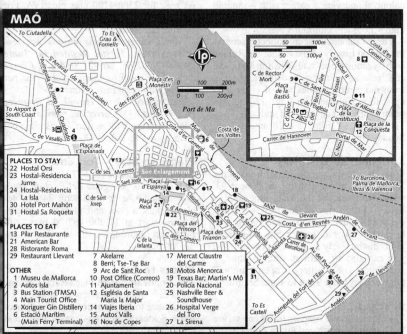

MAÓ

To Ciutadella
To Es Grau & Fornells
S'Arraval
Avinguda de Josep Ma (de Prieto i Caules)
To Airport & South Coast
C de Vasallo
C des Frares
C d'Isabel II
Plaça d'es Monestir
Plaça d'es
Port de Ma
Costa d'es General
Costa de ses Voltes
Plaça de s'Esplanada
C de ses Moreres
C de Sant Josep
C des Jordi
Plaça d'Espanya
Plaça Reial
C d'Anuncivay
Plaça del Princep
C des Comerç
C de la Infanta
Plaça des Trianon
Carrer de Concepció
Claustre del Carme
Ponent
Moll de Llevant
Costa d'en Reynés
Andén de Llevant
Carrer de Barcelona
Av del Port de Maó
To Barcelona, Palma de Mallorca, Ibiza & Valencia
To Es Castell
Avinguda del Fort de l'Eau
Andén
de Llevant
C de Rector Mort
Plaça de la Bastió
C de Sant Roc
C del Rosari
C d'Isabel II
C d'Alfous III
C de l'Església
C d'Alaior
C d'Alba
Plaça de la Constitució
Plaça de la Conquesta
Carrer de Hannover
Portal de Mar
Costa d'es General

PLACES TO STAY
22 Hostal Orsi
23 Hostal-Residencia Jume
24 Hostal-Residencia La Isla
30 Hotel Port Mahón
31 Hostal Sa Roqueta

PLACES TO EAT
13 Pilar Restaurante
21 American Bar
28 Ristorante Roma
29 Restaurant Llevant

OTHER
1 Museu de Mallorca
2 Autos Isla
3 Bus Station (TMSA)
4 Main Tourist Office
5 Xoriguer Gin Distillery
6 Estació Marítim (Main Ferry Terminal)
7 Akelarre
8 Berri; Tse-Tse Bar
9 Arc de Sant Roc
10 Post Office (Correos)
11 Ajuntament
12 Església de Santa Maria la Major
14 Viajes Iberia
15 Autos Valls
16 Nou de Copes
17 Mercat Claustre del Carme
18 Motos Menorca
19 Texas Bar; Martin's Mô
20 Policía Nacional
25 Nashville Beer & Soundhouse
26 Hospital Verge del Toro
27 La Sirena

Església de Santa Maria la Major, farther east on Plaça de la Constitució, was originally completed in 1287 but largely rebuilt during the 18th century. It houses a massive organ built in Barcelona and shipped across in 1810. On the northern end of this plaza is the **ajuntament**.

Plaça d'Espanya
Just off Plaça d'Espanya is the **Mercat Claustre del Carme**, where former church cloisters have been imaginatively converted into a market and shopping centre. From Plaça d'Espanya, the winding Costa de ses Voltes leads down to the harbour.

Museu de Mallorca
This former 15th-century Franciscan monastery off Plaça d'es Monestir has had a chequered history. From the time the Franciscans were obliged to abandon the premises in 1835 after Mendizábal's expropriations, the buildings embarked on a colourful and varied career path – ranging from nautical school and public library to high school and children's home.

The permanent museum collection covers the earliest history of the island, the Roman and Byzantine eras and Muslim Menorca, and includes paintings and other material from more recent times too. It is well set up with explanations in English. The museum is open 10 am to 2 pm and 5 to 8 pm, Tuesday to Saturday, and 10 am to 2 pm Sunday (free).

Xoriguer Gin Distillery
From the old quarter, head north up to the Xoriguer distillery at Moll de Ponent 93, where you can try the local gin, another legacy of the Brits. At the front is a liquor outlet and souvenir shop where visitors can help themselves to free samples. Menorcan gin is distinctively aromatic and very tasty; you can also try various strange liqueurs and tonics. The distillery is open 8 am to 7 pm weekdays and 9 am to 1 pm Saturday

Beaches
The closest decent beaches to the capital are **Es Grau** to the north and **Punta Prima** to the

south (you can sometimes catch small waves at the latter!). Both are connected to Maó by bus.

Organised Tours
Numerous operators offer boat cruises around the harbour. These can be a pleasant way to kill a few hours, but don't pay extra for the 'glass-bottomed boat trips': there isn't much to see down there.

Places to Stay – Budget
Hostal Orsi (☎/fax 971 36 47 51, Carrer de la Infanta 19) is run by a Glaswegian and his American wife who are a mine of information about the island. It's bright, clean and well located. Singles/doubles with a washbasin cost only 2600/4400 ptas in high season, while doubles with shower come in at 5100 ptas.

Hostal-Residencia La Isla (☎ 971 36 64 92, Carrer de Santa Catalina 4) is a large, family-run hostal with excellent rooms and *en suite* for 2300/4100 ptas plus IVA. For just 300 ptas extra per person, you get a continental breakfast.

Maó's other budget options are less praiseworthy. *Hostal-Residencia Jume (☎ 971 36 32 66, fax 971 36 48 78, Carrer de la Concepció 6)* charges 2800 ptas per person with breakfast in summer.

Farther south-east, *Hostal Sa Roqueta (☎ 971 36 43 35, Carrer del Carme 122)* is a long way from the action. It has plain but clean rooms at 2500/4500 ptas.

Places to Stay – Top End
Hotel Port Mahón (☎ 971 36 26 00, fax 971 35 10 50, Avinguda del Port de Maó) is a sleek four-star hotel with 74 marble-clad rooms, a pool and pleasant gardens. Rooms start at 11,000/16,000 ptas with breakfast. Doubles with sea views are 22,000 ptas.

Places to Eat
The *American Bar* on Plaça Reial is a spacious cafe fronted by open-air tables. It's a good place to linger over the newspaper or write postcards and has reasonable food with mains costing around 1200 ptas.

Maó's harbour is lined with restaurants and bars; most offer outdoor waterfront dining. A walk along here is a good way to work up an appetite while you decide where to eat.

Andén de Llevant, along the eastern end of the harbour, is home to Maó's most up-market restaurants – while you eat you can gaze enviously at the fleet of expensive yachts moored opposite. *Ristorante Roma (Andén de Llevant 295)* is a stylish Italian eatery; it's surprisingly good value with pizzas and pastas for around 900 ptas and several *menú* choices ranging from 1500 to 2300 ptas. Farther along at No 302 you can pretend you're on a Greek island rather than a Spanish one at *Restaurant Llevant*. Mains cost from 950 to 1500 ptas. For a mix of dishes ranging from gazpacho to felafel, you could try the wholesome food at *La Sirena*, at No 199.

Away from all the seaside chomping fun, *Pilar Restaurante (Carrer des Forn 61)* is a more intimate dining experience. The imaginative meals have a price – you are likely to be lightened to the tune of 4000 ptas per person.

Entertainment

Nightlife in Maó is low-key in comparison to Mallorca or Ibiza. Most of the bars and discos are down along the waterfront, but you'll need to wear your walking boots as they are well spread out.

Heading east along the Andén de Llevant, one of the first places you'll come to is the *Texas Bar*, a lively wood-panelled country and/or western joint at No 65 (yee-ha!); tacky but fun. It closes at 4 am but you can get in another tipple next door at *Martin's Mô*. Farther along, the *Nashville Beer & Soundhouse* is a large tavern featuring mainstream rock.

You'll find a string of places opposite the Estación Marítima. *Akelarre (Moll de Ponent 42)* is a hip place with a mixed crowd. *Berri (Costa d'es General 14)* is a dance bar playing standard rock faves, while *Tse-Tse Bar* next door is a funkier, upstairs place that doesn't get going until around 3 am.

Nou de Copes, in a laneway between the top of Costa de ses Voltes and the Claustre del Carme, is a popular little music bar with a cave-like interior carved out of the old walls above the harbour.

Getting There & Away

TMSA (☎ 971 36 03 61) buses depart from either the bus station at Avinguda de Josep Maria Quadrado 7 or from nearby Plaça de s'Esplanada. Six go to Ciutadella (560 ptas) via Alaior (160 ptas), Es Mercadal (270 ptas) and Ferreries (355 ptas). It also has regular services to the south-coast beaches, including Punta Prima (200 ptas).

Getting Around

Motos Menorca (☎ 971 35 47 86) at Andén de Llevant 35-36 hires out mountain bikes (1400 ptas per day), scooters and Vespas (from 3200 ptas per day).

THE INTERIOR – MAÓ TO CIUTADELLA

Menorca's main road, from Maó to Ciutadella, divides the island into north and south. It passes through the towns of Alaior, Es Mercadal and Ferreries, and along the way smaller roads branch off towards the beaches and resorts of the north and south coasts.

Many of the island's most significant archaeological relics are signposted off the main road (see the boxed text 'Menorca's Prehistoric Heritage').

The small town of **Alaior** is home to the (run-down) local cheese and shoe industries. Cheeses from the Quesos Coinga factory are sold all over Menorca, but if you're passing through you can visit the tasting and sales room at the front of the factory (Carrer des Mercadal 4); it's open 9 am to 1 pm and 5 to 8 pm weekdays (mornings only on Saturday).

In the centre of the island **Es Mercadal** is perhaps most notable as the turn-off for Fornells. You also turn here to get to **Monte El Toro**, Menorca's highest point (357m). A steep and twisting road leads to the summit, shared by a 16th-century church and Augustine monastery, a cluster of satellite

Menorca's Prehistoric Heritage

Menorca's beaches aren't its only attractions. The interior is liberally sprinkled with reminders of its rich and ancient heritage.

Many of the most significant sites and monuments are open to the public (and free!), although some are on private property and you'll need to ask permission before visiting.

Menorca's tourism promoters often liken the island to an open-air museum and the main sites have been made readily accessible to visitors – sometimes to their detriment. These places provide fascinating insights into the past, but most aren't as well presented as they could be. The major monuments are definitely worth a look, but many of the minor sites present little but crumbling ruins.

The monuments are linked to three main periods: the Pre-Talayotic Period (or cave era) from 2000 to 1300 BC; the Talayotic Period (or Bronze Age) from 1300 to 800 BC; and the Post-Talayotic Period (or Iron Age) from 800 to around 100 BC. Similarly, there are three types of structures: navetas, talayots and taulas.

Navetas, built from large rocks in the shape of upturned boat hulls, are thought to have been used as either tombs or meeting places – perhaps both.

Talayots, large stone mounds found all over the island, were perhaps used as watchtowers for each settlement.

Unique to Menorca, **taulas** are huge stone tablets precisely balanced in the shape of a 'T'. It has been suggested they could have

Prehistoric monuments near Binibèquer, south of Maó

been used as sacrificial altars but, as with Stonehenge, nobody is sure how these enormous slabs of stone were moved into position or what they signify.

Off the main road 3km west of Maó, the talayotic settlement known as **Talatí de Dalt** is one of the most interesting sites. It's about five minutes' walk from the car park to the main feature, a well-preserved taula. Unusually, it has an attached column, probably a second taula that fell here by accident.

About 4km farther along on the northern side of the road is the **Rafal Rubí**, a pair of well-preserved burial navetas.

The nearby **Torralba d'en Salord** is another talayotic settlement. It also features an impressive taula, but the rest of the settlement is in poor repair.

South of Alaior is the large **Torre d'en Gaumes** settlement, which now has its own car park, kiosk and a signposted walking trail that leads you around the site. It includes three talayots on a hilltop and a collection of circular dwellings.

Farther south on the coast at **Cales Coves** some 90 caves dug into the coastal cliffs were apparently used for ritual burials. More recently some of the caves have been homes to hippy colonies, and nearby the large **Cova des Xoroi** has been enterprisingly converted into a disco.

South of Ciutadella, **Son Catlar** is the largest talayotic settlement in the Balearic Islands. Its five talayots and the remains of its dwellings cover around six hectares. East of Ciutadella (near the 40km road marker), the **Naveta des Tudons** is a stone burial chamber that was restored in 1961.

The tourist office's excellent *Archaeological Guide to Menorca* (available in several languages to those with a serious interest in the subject) is a handy resource.

dishes and radio towers, and a statue of Christ (built to honour the islanders who died defending the Republican cause during the civil war). You can see right across the island in all directions and on a clear day as far as Mallorca.

Ferreries is Menorca's highest town. On Saturday morning the excellent Mercat de Ferreries is held, with stall-holders selling fresh produce as well as traditional Menorcan crafts and artworks. On other days there are few reasons to linger. The turn-off to the resort of Santa Galdana is just west of here.

CIUTADELLA
postcode 07760 • pop 21,785
Founded by the Carthaginians and known to the Muslims as Medina Minurqa, Ciutadella was virtually destroyed following the Turkish invasion of 1558 and much of the city was subsequently rebuilt during the 17th century. It was the capital of Menorca until the arrival of the British.

Known as Vella i Bella (the Old and the Beautiful), it's an attractive and distinctly Spanish city with a picturesque port and an historic old quarter. Its character is quite distinct from that of Maó, and its historic centre undoubtedly more appealing.

Information
Tourist Office Ciutadella's tourist office (☎ 971 38 26 93) is opposite the cathedral on Plaça d'es Born. During summer it's open 9 am to 1.30 pm and 5 to 7 pm weekdays, and 9 am to 1 pm Saturday.

Post & Communications The post office is at the southern end of Plaça d'es Born.

Things to See & Do
Ciutadella has few outstanding 'sights', which in a way is part of its appeal. It's an attractive town that simply goes about its business without too many concessions to tourism. It's a pleasure to explore the old quarter and port.

The main square, Plaça d'es Born, is surrounded by palm trees and gracious 19th-century buildings, including the post office, the **ajuntament**, and the **Palau Torresaura**.

In the centre of the square is a tall, thin obelisk, raised to commemorate those townsfolk who died trying to ward off the Turks on 9 July 1558.

Costa d'es Moll takes you down to the port from Plaça d'es Born. Heading in the other direction, the cobbled laneways and streets between Plaça d'es Born and Plaça d'Alfons III hold plenty of interest, with simple whitewashed buildings alongside ornate churches and elegant palaces. The pedestrian walkway of **Ses Voltes** (the arches), the heart of the commercial district, has a North African flavour and is lined with glamorous shops and boutiques, restaurants and smoky bars.

Architectural landmarks worth looking out for include the 14th-century **catedral**, built in Catalan Gothic (although with a baroque facade) style on the site of Medina Minurqa's central mosque (open 8 am to 1 pm and 6.30 to 9 pm); the baroque 17th-century churches **Església dels Socors** (which houses the Museu Diocesà) and **Església del Roser** (now used as an exhibition gallery); and impressive noble families' mansions such as **Palau Martorell** and **Palau Saura**.

A short walk north is the modest **Museu Municipal** in the Bastió de sa Font. It contains displays recounting the island's story from prehistory to medieval times. It's open 10 am to 2 pm Tuesday to Saturday (200 ptas).

Special Events
The Festa de Sant Joan de Ciutadella, held in the third week of June, is one of Spain's best-known and most traditional festivals. It features busy processions, prancing horses, performances of traditional music and dancing and lots of energetic partying.

Places to Stay – Budget
Hostal-Residencia Oasis (☎ 971 38 21 97, *Carrer de Sant Isidre 33)* is set around a spacious garden courtyard and has pleasant rooms, most with bathrooms. It charges up to 5500 ptas (no singles).

Cafe Ses Persianes (☎ 971 38 14 45), a hip little bar on Plaça d'Artrutx, has rooms upstairs at 4000 ptas a double.

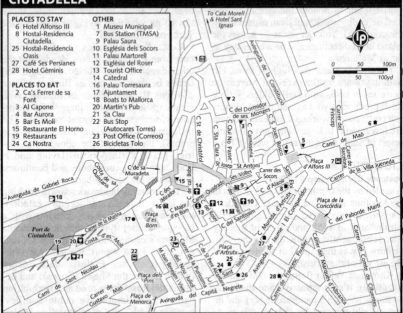

CIUTADELLA

PLACES TO STAY
6 Hotel Alfonso III
8 Hostal-Residencia Ciutadella
25 Hostal-Residencia Oasis
27 Café Ses Persianes
28 Hotel Gèminis

PLACES TO EAT
2 Ca's Ferrer de sa Font
3 Al Capone
4 Bar Aurora
5 Bar Es Molí
15 Restaurante El Horno
19 Restaurants
24 Ca Nostra

OTHER
1 Museu Municipal
7 Bus Station (TMSA)
9 Palau Saura
10 Església dels Socors
11 Palau Martorell
12 Església del Roser
13 Tourist Office
14 Catedral
16 Palau Torresaura
17 Ajuntament
18 Boats to Mallorca
20 Martin's Pub
21 Sa Clau
22 Bus Stop (Autocares Torres)
23 Post Office (Correos)
26 Bicicletas Tolo

Places to Stay – Mid-Range

Hotel Gèminis (☎ 971 38 46 44, fax 971 38 36 83, Carrer de Josepa Rossinyol 4) is a friendly and stylish two-star place. Excellent rooms with bathroom, TV, phone and heating cost from 5000/8000 ptas (plus IVA).

The well-located *Hostal-Residencia Ciutadella (☎/fax 971 38 34 62, Carrer de Sant Eloi 10)* is another good mid-range option. Cosy rooms with timber furniture, a phone and bathroom cost up to 6000/8900 ptas, including breakfast. Prices drop dramatically in low season.

If the other two are full, there's always the big and bland *Hotel Alfonso III (☎ 971 38 01 50, Camí de Maó 53)* on the main road into town. Rooms with bath cost 4100/8500 ptas (plus IVA).

Places to Stay – Top End

Hotel Sant Ignasi (☎ 971 38 55 75, fax 971 48 05 37, Carretera de Cala Morell s/n) is a fine retreat 3km outside Ciutadella. It boasts a pleasant garden, bar and pool. Prices for doubles and suites can range from 16,000 ptas plus IVA in low season to 36,000 ptas plus IVA at the height of summer.

Places to Eat

Ciutadella's small port is teeming with little restaurants and cafes, many of them set in the old city walls or carved out of the cliffs that line the waterfront. If you join the evening *paseo* you won't have any trouble finding somewhere to eat.

For coffee or drinks and a snack, try the singular *Bar Es Molí (Plaça de Alfons III)*, set in a mill. *Bar Aurora* on the same square is also OK. On a busy day the bars lining Ses Voltes are more fun.

The tucked away *Restaurante El Horno (Carrer d'es Forn 12)* is a cosy little place where you can dine equally well on seafood and meat dishes – most mains cost 1600 to 2200 ptas. A short stroll north are two other worthy options. *Al Capone (Carrer des*

Dormidor de sęs Monges 4) serves pizzas and solid Spanish cooking at modest prices. Nearby, *Ca's Ferrer de sa Font (Carrer del Portal de sa Font 16)* is a hushed, romantic place. You'll pay around 3000 ptas for a full meal.

For a simple set lunch or tapas, try *Ca Nostra (Carrer de St Pere Alcantara 35)*.

Entertainment

After dinner, check out *Sa Clau (Carrer de la Marina 199)* on the waterfront at the bottom of Costa d'es Moll. Set in the old city walls, it's a hip piano bar that features live jazz and blues.

Martin's Pub (Costa d'es Moll 20) pumps out throbbing *bakalao* music most nights until around 4 am.

Getting There & Away

TMSA (☎ 971 38 03 03) runs buses between Ciutadella and Maó; its depot is close to the centre at Carrer de Barcelona 8. Autocares Torres (☎ 971 38 47 20) serves the coast south of Ciutadella; its buses leave from Plaça dels Pins (from Plaça de Menorca in June).

Boats for Mallorca (Port d'Alcúdia and Cala Ratjada) leave from the northern side of the Port de Ciutadella.

Getting Around

Bicicletas Tolo (☎ 971 38 15 76), opposite Hostal-Residencia Oasis at Carrer de Sant Isidre 28, rents out mountain bikes (800 ptas per day) as well as Vespas and scooters (4800 to 9600 ptas for two days, depending on the model).

NORTH COAST

Menorca's north coast is rugged and rocky, dotted with small and scenic coves. It's much less developed than the south coast and, with your own transport and a bit of footwork, you'll discover some of the Balearics' best off-the-beaten-track beaches.

Maó to Fornells

The closest beach to the north of Maó, **Sa Mesquida**, isn't appealing. Farther north is **Es Grau**, a plain little village on an open

bay. The beach is OK and you can kick back at a couple of bar-restaurants.

Inland from Es Grau and separated from the coast by a barrier of high sand dunes is **Parc Natural S'Albufera d'es Grau**, the largest freshwater lagoon in the Balearic Islands. Home to many species of wetland birds and an important stopover for migrating species, S'Albufera and the surrounding countryside have been designated the 'nucleus zone' of Menorca's Biosphere Reserve, a natural park protected from the threat of development. **Illa d'en Colom**, a couple of hundred metres offshore, is considered part of the park. Boats splutter across to the island from Es Grau.

Continuing north, it's a great drive from Maó up to **Cap de Favàritx**, a narrow rocky cape at the top of the Parc Natural S'Albufera d'es Grau zone. The last leg of the drive is across a lunar-like landscape of black rock. At the end of the road a lighthouse stands watch while a relentless sea pounds the impassive cliffs.

South of the cape you can reach some fine sandy bays and beaches, including **Cala Presili** and **Platja d'en Tortuga**, on foot. If you park just before the gate to the lighthouse and climb up the rocks behind you, you'll see a couple of them.

Fornells

The picturesque whitewashed town of Fornells is on a large, shallow bay popular with windsurfers. A former fishing village, Fornells has been made famous by its waterfront seafood restaurants, most of which serve up the local speciality *caldereta de llagosta,* a lobster stew.

It's a nice place – perhaps too nice, to judge by the steady stream of white-shoed tourists. Another downside of its 'discovery' is that it's an expensive spot to eat or sleep in.

Things to See & Do If the sight of those fishing boats bobbing in the bay stirs the seawolf in your soul, you could always hire one of Servinautic's (☎ 971 37 66 36) small motor boats (they cost from 3000 ptas an hour) and go exploring. There's also a windsurfing school just south of town.

A couple of kilometres west at **Platges de Fornells**, the development frenzy has been unleashed on the coastal hills surrounding a small beach. The exclusive villas of the Menorca Country Club resort dominate this ritzy *urbanizació*.

If you want to escape the crowds, continue west to the beach of **Binimella**, from where you can walk around to the unspoilt beaches at **Cala Pregonda**.

Places to Stay *Hostal La Palma (☎/fax 971 37 66 34, Plaça S'Algaret 3)* offers the best value. Out the back of this bar-restaurant are cheerful rooms with bathrooms, balconies and views of the surrounding countryside. Singles (not available during summer) cost 4000 ptas and doubles are up to 7250 ptas.

Next door, *Hostal-Residencia S'Algaret (☎ 971 37 65 52)* is relatively overpriced at 7200/11,140 ptas. Fifty metres on is *Hostal Fornells (☎ 971 37 66 76, Carrer Major 17)*, a slick place with pool, bar and restaurant. Rooms (with breakfast) start at 7750/12,500 ptas and reach 8750/14,500 ptas if you want sea views. Add IVA to these prices, which can rise still further in the peak weeks of August. Prices drop heavily in the off season.

Places to Eat The restaurants along the foreshore are all pretty expensive and if you're here to try caldereta de llagosta, you're up for around 6000 ptas.

Should you be planning to lose that kind of fiscal mass, head for *Es Cranc (Carrer de Tramuntana 31)*, a couple of hundred metres north of the centre. It has a simple dining room, but it's less touristy than the waterfront places and the food is flavourful. Steak and seafood dishes mostly cost from 1400 to 2500 ptas. You could splash out on caldereta de llagosta (7000 ptas) or perhaps *paella de llagosta* (14,000 ptas for two people).

Near Ciutadella

Newly paved and well-signposted roads invariably lead to heavily developed *urbanizaciones*. If you find yourself bouncing along a narrow, pot-holed shocker lined with crumbling stone walls, it probably leads somewhere interesting.

A good example is the road from Ciutadella to **Cala Morell**. It's hard to find and bumpy as hell, but it leads to a low-key, tasteful development of whitewashed villas. Steep steps lead to the small port-beach, backed by a couple of bar-restaurants. A track leads around the cliffs to the **Cala Morell Necropolis**, burial caves hacked into the coastal cliffs in prehistoric times.

Instead of turning left to Cala Morell, you could also continue straight on to **La Vall**. At the end of the road you come to a set of gates, beyond which is a privately owned nature and wildlife park with a parking area, a small lake and pristine beaches. The owners charge 700 ptas entry per car. La Vall is open 10 am to 7 pm daily.

SOUTH COAST

Menorca's southern flank tends to have the better beaches – and thus the greater concentration of development. The recurring image is of a jagged coastline, occasionally interrupted by a small inlet with a sandy beach and backed by a growing cluster of gleaming white villas. Menorca has opted for small-scale developments in the 'Moorish-Mediterranean' style, largely modelled on the resort of Binibèquer (or Binibeca), south of Maó, designed by the architect Antonio Sintes in 1972.

Although comparatively easy on the eye, these resorts remain the domain of package tourists and time-share touts.

The rugged coastline south of Ciutadella gives way to a couple of smallish beaches at the resorts of **Santandria** and **Cala Blanca**. On the island's south-western corner looms the large resort of **Cala en Bosc**, a busy boating and diving centre. Not far east are the popular beaches of **Son Xoriguer**, connected to Ciutadella by frequent buses.

Between Son Xoriguer and Santa Galdana lies some of the least accessible coast in the south. A series of rough tracks and walking trails lead to the unspoiled beaches of **Son Saura**, **Cala en Turqueta** and **Es Castellet** de Macarelleta. Some of these pass through private property so you may need to ask permission to use them.

South-west of Ferreries is the big resort of Santa Galdana. Two-thirds of the way down this road, *Camping S'Atalai* (☎ 971 37 42 32) is a simple, pleasant camping ground shaded by pine trees.

Santa Galdana is just the place to go if karaoke bars, English pubs and mini-golf courses are your idea of a good holiday. In fairness, the beach is fine and the tack kept within bearable bounds. A walking track leads west around the coast to the popular **Macarella**, which has a couple of beach bars, and a little farther on is the previously mentioned Es Castellet de Macarelleta. To the east of Santa Galdana is **Cala Mitjana**, an excellent strand.

The resort of **Son Bou**, south of Alaior, boasts the island's longest beach and most depressing development. A few kilometres up the road towards Alaior is *Camping Son Bou* (☎ 971 37 26 05), a first-class place with everything from pool to horse riding and outdoor cinema.

Most of the coast south of Maó is more intensively developed. Regular buses sidle down to the resort of **Punta Prima**, which has a nice beach (you can even catch the occasional wave here!). West around the coast is **Binibèquer**, mentioned earlier. It is touted as a charming old fishing town. It has been given several coats of whitewash and turned into a tourist beehive *but* the curious houses and narrow lanes, not to mention the little boat harbour with its transparent water (fine for swimming), *are* attractive. A few kilometres farther west lies **Binidalí**. The village is no big deal and the beach small, but the water is so azure it makes you want to swim out of the inlet and into the open sea.

Murcia

Murcia remains one of Spain's least visited corners. Walled off to the west and south by the arid steppes and mountains of Andalucía and Castilla-La Mancha and to the north by the equally dry southern wedge of Valencia, it finds its only relief in the 250km of Mediterranean coastline called the Costa Cálida.

Its name derives from the Latin 'murtae' (mulberry). For centuries this tree provided a vegetarian diet for silkworms, exploited workers of a flourishing industry that lasted until well after WWII, when local silk could no longer compete against manmade fibres.

Long occupied by Muslims from North Africa, themselves no strangers to heat, Murcia inherited their systems of irrigation – waterwheels, aqueducts and *acequias,* or canals. This network helps to distribute the parsimonious 300mm annual rainfall, allowing at least some land to be cultivated intensively – especially for citrus crops and grapes in the El Guadalentín valley, fed by the Río Segura and Río Mula.

North of the Moratalla uplands, the region's highest, is La Puerta district, notable for its pine forest. In the middle of the province is the Segura valley, its ancient Muslim villages dotted around the rugged countryside and sheltered by the ochre rock of the Sierra de Ricote.

Local orchards and the associated canning industry are the main employers of those who live in the busy capital, also called Murcia. Cartagena, the second city, is one of the country's major ports. Inland, Lorca, in its time a frontier town between Christian and Muslim Spain, is famous for its spectacular Semana Santa processions.

The Parque Natural de Sierra Espuña draws climbers and walkers, while beach and sunseekers prefer the tepid waters of the Mar Menor.

MURCIA CITY
postcode 30005 • pop 350,000

Islamic Mursiya was founded in AD 825 by Abd ar-Rahman II, caliph of Córdoba on

Highlights

- Semana Santa celebrations in the town of Lorca
- Murcia's Catedral de Santa María
- Walking in the Parque Natural de Sierra Espuña
- A swim in the Mar Menor

Murcia City p766

Cartagena p769

the site of a Roman colony. Town and surrounding territories were reconquered in 1243 by Alfonso X of Castilla and León (who gave his name to one of Murcia's two *gran vías*). Over the years much of its borderland was picked off by neighbouring provinces until the region was reduced to its present size of 11,300 sq km in 1833.

Enriched by the silk industry and agricultural prosperity, Murcia city was at its grandest in the 18th century, when the magnificent baroque facade of the cathedral was built, together with the urban palaces of the nobility and the rising bourgeoisie.

Looted by Napoleonic troops in 1810 and later victim of plague and cholera, the city fell into decline during the 19th century. In 1936, during the Spanish Civil War, it was the scene of bitter fighting and many of its churches were burnt down.

Despite industrial growth on the outskirts, Murcia remains an attractive university city, with several important monuments still intact.

Orientation

The city centre is immediately north of the Río Segura and Puente Viejo (Old Bridge). The main commercial thoroughfare, Gran Vía del Escultor Francisco Salzillo (called simply 'La Gran Vía') runs north from the bridge.

All Murcia's major sights are within walking distance of each other. From the cathedral, the pedestrianised *calle mayor* (main street) of medieval and Renaissance Murcia (today Calle de la Trapería) runs north through the old town.

Information

Tourist Offices The tourist office (☎ 968 35 87 20), Calle del Plano de San Francisco 8, is open 10 am to 2 pm and 4 to 8 pm (5 to 9.30 pm in summer) Monday to Saturday plus Sunday morning. A tourist kiosk on Calle Maestro Alonso observes the same hours.

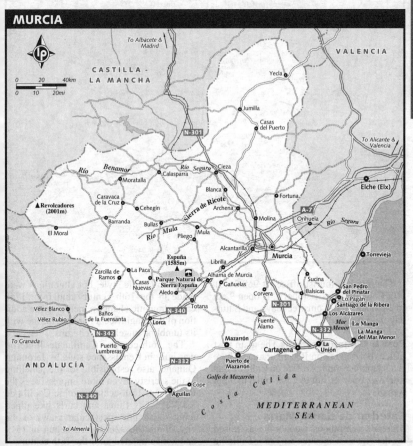

MURCIA

MURCIA

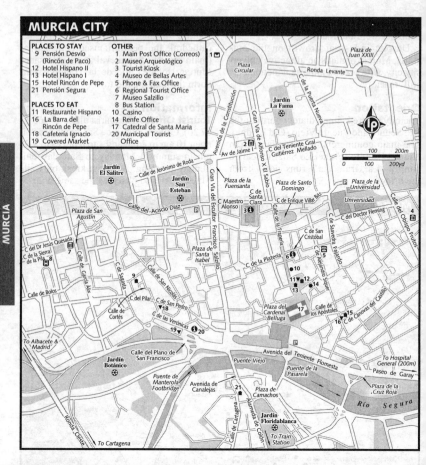

MURCIA CITY

PLACES TO STAY
9 Pensión Desvío
   (Rincón de Paco)
12 Hotel Hispano II
13 Hotel Hispano I
15 Hotel Rincón de Pepe
21 Pensión Segura

PLACES TO EAT
11 Restaurante Hispano
16 La Barra del
    Rincón de Pepe
18 Cafetería Ignacio
19 Covered Market

OTHER
1 Main Post Office (Correos)
2 Museo Arqueológico
3 Tourist Kiosk
4 Museo de Bellas Artes
5 Phone & Fax Office
6 Regional Tourist Office
7 Museo Salzillo
8 Bus Station
10 Casino
14 Renfe Office
17 Catedral de Santa María
20 Municipal Tourist
    Office

The regional tourist office (☎ 968 36 61 00), Calle de San Cristóbal 5, is open 9 am to 2 pm and 5 to 7 pm weekdays and Saturday morning.

Post & Communications The main post office *(correos)* is on Plaza Circular. There is a telephone and fax office on Calle de San Lorenzo, open 10 am to 2 pm and 6 to 9 pm weekdays.

Catedral de Santa María

Murcia's sumptuous cathedral was raised on the site of a mosque in 1358. Building began in Gothic style, but alterations were made in the 16th century and from 1748 came dramatic changes, including the addition of the magnificent baroque facade with its tumbling angels and cherubs.

The 16th-century Capilla de Junterón was built in Renaissance style by Jerónimo Quijano, also responsible for the panelling in the sacristy. Even more impressive is the flamboyant 15th-century gothic Capilla de los Vélez, its flutes and curls like piped icing sugar. For spectacular views of the city, climb the 92m tower, begun in 1519 and not completed until the 18th century.

In the 19th-century cloister and chapter-house, the museum includes a Roman sarcophagus, a delicate 18th-century silver monstrance and a fine 14th-century altarpiece by Bernabé de Módena.

Both the cathedral and museum are open from 10 am to 1 pm and 6 to 8 pm (5 to 7 pm during winter) daily. Entry to the museum is 200 ptas.

Casino

The casino, on Calle de la Trapería 22, opened as a gentlemen's club in 1847. Beyond the decorative facade, completed in 1901, are an Arab-style vestibule and patio. Don't miss the magnificent ballroom; pop 100 ptas in the slot for the 320 lamps of its candelabras to shimmer with light. It's open to nonmembers from 10 am to 9 pm daily (100 ptas).

Museums

The archaeological and Bellas Artes museums were closed for major renovations when we last passed by. Both are expected to re-open some time in 2001.

The **Museo Arqueológico**, Gran Vía de Alfonso X El Sabio 9, has a good collection of prehistoric, Roman and Islamic artefacts and some especially fine decorated Iberian pottery; free.

The **Museo de Bellas Artes**, Calle del Obispo Frutos 12, contains works by José de Ribero, Hernández Amores and Martínez Pozo and has a good selection of contemporary art; entry is free.

The **Museo Salzillo**, devoted to the Murcian sculptor Francisco Salzillo (1707–83), is in Ermita de Jesús, a baroque chapel at Plaza San Agustín 3. The museum displays his impressive *pasos*, figures carried in Semana Santa processions and his superb miniature Nativity figures – more than 500 of them clad in an eclectic mixture of middle eastern and 18th-century Murcian dress. The museum is open 9.30 am to 1 pm and 4 to 7 pm Tuesday to Saturday (weekdays in summer) plus 11 am to 1 pm Sunday (except in summer); entry is 500 ptas. The multilingual brochure has a section in not-quite English.

Places to Stay

Pensión el Desvío (or Rincón de Paco) (☎ 968 21 84 36, Calle Cortés 27), near the food market and as basic as you can get, has singles for 1500 ptas and doubles with bathroom for 2900 ptas.

In comparison, *Pensión Segura* (☎ 968 21 12 81, Plaza de Camachos 14), 200m south of the Puente Viejo, is luxurious. Its rooms, all with bathroom and TV, cost 3900 ptas.

Rooms at *Hotel Hispano I* (☎ 968 21 61 52, Calle de la Trapería 8) cost 3750/5350 ptas; it's closed in July and August. Around the corner at its fancier sister, *Hotel Hispano II* (☎ 968 21 61 52), singles/doubles with TV cost 5900/8000 ptas. The two hotels share parking facilities.

At the top of the range is *Hotel Rincón de Pepe* (☎ 968 21 22 39, fax 968 22 17 44, Calle de los Apóstoles 34). Doubles cost from 9700 ptas (during off-peak weekends) to 18,800 ptas.

Places to Eat

Cafetería Ignacio on Calle San Pedro has great tapas from 175 ptas and stickily satisfying cakes; it's closed Monday.

Snug between hotels Hispano I and Hispano II on Calle del Arquitecto Cerdán is the smart and warmly recommended *Restaurante Hispano*. It has a fabulous display of fresh fish and is much less expensive than it appears; a three-course *menú del día* (daily set meal) at the bar costs only 1000 ptas.

The Casino's *restaurant* on Calle de la Trapería has a four-course *menú* for 1100 ptas (lunchtime only).

Hotel Rincón de Pepe's *restaurant* is justifiably renowned throughout Spain. To really hit the spot and your credit limit, go for their *menú degustación* at 7500 ptas. But with main courses averaging around 2500 ptas, you don't have to fritter a fortune. Just around the corner, *La Barra del Rincón de Pepe*, with food from the same kitchen, has a *menú del día* for 1200 ptas. Go for their *picoteo Murciano*, a selection of local tapas for 2000 ptas.

A lively *covered market* is sandwiched between Calle de las Verónicas and Calle del Plano de San Francisco.

MURCIA

Entertainment

Most nightlife is concentrated around the university, particularly between Calle Saavedra Fajardo and the Museo de Bellas Artes. Later, move to the side streets off Gran Vía de Alfonso X El Sabio, between Plaza Circular and the Museo Arqueológico.

Getting There & Away

Bus There are frequent daily buses to Cartagena (415 ptas), seven to Alicante (600 ptas) via Orihuela, four to Almería (2150 ptas), five to Málaga (3830 ptas) and Barcelona (5315 ptas) and seven to Valencia (1855 ptas) via Elche. For information, call ☎ 968 29 22 11.

Train Renfe has a town office (☎ 968 25 21 54) at Calle Barrionuevo 4. There are eight trains daily to Cartagena (505 ptas by Regional, 1400 ptas by Talgo). Four run to Madrid (5200 ptas) via Albacete (2600 ptas). Up to 20 a day serve Alicante (540 to 575 ptas), from where options are greater for Valencia and Barcelona.

Getting Around

From the bus station, take bus No 3 into town; from the train station, Nos 9 or 11.

CARTAGENA

postcode 30200 • pop 175,000

In 223 BC, Hasdrubal marched into the Iberian settlement of Mastia at the head of his Carthaginian army and renamed it Carthago Nova. It continued to flourish under the Romans and under Muslim rule became the independent emirate of Cartajana. The Arabs improved agriculture and established its reputation for building warships before their expulsion in 1242.

In the latter part of the 20th century, Cartagena fell on hard times. Lead and pyrite mining, a staple of the economy since Roman times, all but ceased. The naval presence – particularly that of the American sixth fleet that periodically disgorges dollar-laden sailors on R&R – is less evident and the dingy approach to downtown, closed shops and dilapidated buildings all speak recession.

But the town is picking itself up. More sedate cruise passengers are replacing roustabout sailors. The redundant military hospital has been recycled as the campus of the spanking new Universidad Politécnica and, as tourism contributes more and more to the economy, Cartagena renews itself by digging into its past and stripping back more and more of its old quarter to reveal its long buried Roman heritage.

Information

The tourist office (☎ 968 50 64 83), Plaza del Almirante Bastarreche, is open 10 am to 1.30 pm and 5 to 7 pm weekdays and 10.30 am to 1 pm Saturday.

Things to See

At the western end of Paseo de Alfonso XII is the **Submarino Isaac Peral**, one of the oldest submarines in the world, built in 1888 by a local inventor who failed to interest the navy sufficiently to get funding for his schemes. Nearby, to the north-east, are the remains of the 13th-century **catedral** which recycled slabs and pillars from the adjacent **Teatro Romano** (built in 1 BC) and was devastated in its turn by aerial bombardment during the Spanish Civil War.

The **Museo Arqueológico Municipal**, Calle Ramón y Cajal 45, built on the site of the 4th-century Roman necropolis of San Antón, contains Carthaginian, Roman, Visigoth and Muslim antiquities. It is open 10 am to 1 pm and 4 to 6 pm Tuesday to Friday plus weekend mornings; entry is free.

The **Museo Naval**, Calle Menéndez Pelayo 8, is open 10 am to 3 pm and 4 to 6 pm Tuesday to Friday plus Saturday until 1.30 pm; free. The **Museo Nacional de Arqueología Marítima**, by the lighthouse on Dique (Jetty) de la Navidad, has a collection of relics recovered from the sea. It's open 10 am to 3 pm daily except Monday (400 ptas).

If architecture's your scene, pick up the excellent free pamphlet in English, *Cartagena Guide-Plan*. The information is accurate, even if the translation is sometimes a little wonky. Don't miss Modernista buildings such as Casa Cervantes, the Casino and Casa Llagostera (above Gran Bar) on Calle

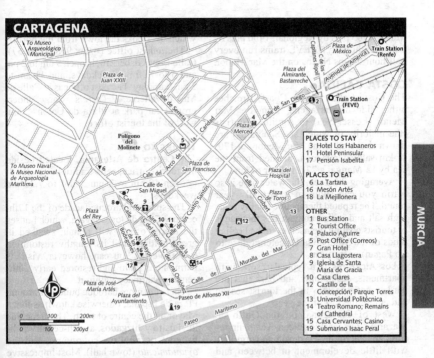

CARTAGENA

PLACES TO STAY
3 Hotel Los Habaneros
11 Hotel Peninsular
17 Pensión Isabelita

PLACES TO EAT
6 La Tartana
16 Mesón Artés
18 La Mejillonera

OTHER
1 Bus Station
2 Tourist Office
4 Palacio Aguirre
5 Post Office (Correos)
7 Gran Hotel
8 Casa Llagostera
9 Iglesia de Santa
   María de Gracia
10 Casa Clares
12 Castillo de la
   Concepción; Parque Torres
13 Universidad Politécnica
14 Teatro Romano; Remains
   of Cathedral
15 Casa Cervantes; Casino
19 Submarino Isaac Peral

MURCIA

Mayor, Gran Hotel and Casa Clares on the parallel Calle del Aire and the resplendent Palacio Aguirre on Plaza de la Merced.

For a sweeping view of town and the hills pincering the harbour, walk up through Parque Torres to the **Castillo de la Concepción**.

Places to Stay & Eat

All places, whatever their standard, tend to charge more in July and August.

Pensión Isabelita (☎ 968 50 77 35) on Plaza de José María Artés, has perfectly acceptable singles without/with bath for 1700/1900 ptas; doubles are 3000/3500 ptas.

Comfortable *Hotel Peninsular* (☎ 968 50 00 33, Calle de los Cuatro Santos 3) has singles/doubles with bathroom for 3200/5350 ptas.

Hotel Los Habaneros (☎ 968 50 52 50, Calle de San Diego 60) is a step up in luxury, with rooms for 5600/7100 ptas.

Most bars and restaurants are concentrated around the Plaza del Ayuntamiento,

Plaza de José María Artés and the side streets off Calle Mayor.

Virtually opposite Pensión Isabelita is *Mesón Artés*, where you can get a *menú* for 1000 ptas. Around the corner, the popular *La Mejillonera* specialises in fresh, reasonably priced fish and seafood (eg, a dozen prawns for 400 ptas). For more upmarket surroundings, try the *restaurant* in Hotel Los Habaneros, where the same four-course *menú* costs 1250 ptas at the bar or 2000 ptas in the restaurant.

La Tartana on Calle de la Morería Baja has great tapas and does a four course *menú* for 1300 ptas.

Getting There & Away

There are regular buses to Los Alcázares (285 ptas) and La Manga (300 ptas), both on the Mar Menor, and to Murcia (415 ptas). Northbound, eight daily buses serve Alicante (935 ptas) via Torrevieja (545 ptas) and Santa Pola (850 ptas).

For Renfe train destinations, change in Murcia (505 ptas by Regional, 1400 ptas by Talgo, eight daily). FEVE trains run every half hour to Los Nietos on the Mar Menor.

COSTA CÁLIDA

The Costa Cálida (Warm Coast) stretches either side of Cartagena, from the Mar Menor (Lesser Sea) to Águilas. Tourists (the majority of which are Spaniards) are drawn above all to the Mar Menor – a 170-sq-km saltwater lagoon, divided from the sea by **La Manga**, a 22km sliver of land.

Averaging 7m deep, the water here is so warm you can swim in it virtually year round. The reputed therapeutic quality of its high salt and iodine content has thousands of tourists coating themselves in the healing muds of the Mota de la Calcetera (close to Lo Pagán) every year.

Los Alcázares is a typical resort, with apartments, restaurants and bars that are hard to squeeze into in the tourist season and empty the rest of the year.

West of Cartagena, on the Golfo de Mazarrón, the coast is quieter. The main resorts are Puerto de Mazarrón and Águilas, with little development in between and some beautiful, unspoilt beaches.

LORCA

postcode 30800 • pop 75,000

Illurco was to the Romans merely a modest stopover on the road between the Pyrenees and Cádiz, but for the Visigoths it became a key bastion in the vain attempts to hold off Muslim armies probing northward. Captured around AD 780, it was from then known as Lurka.

On 23 November 1243, the very day his father, Fernando III, took Sevilla, the future Alfonso X El Sabio reconquered Lorca, although Muslims continued to raid it until the fall of Granada in 1492.

Nowadays, the town is an urban centre for the arid south-western corner of the Murcia region.

Orientation & Information

Lorca sits on the banks of the Río Guadalentín. Its old quarter lies between Calle Lope Gisbert and the 13th-century castle which overlooks the town from the north.

The tourist office (☎/fax 968 46 61 57), Calle Lope Gisbert 10, is open 9 am to 2 pm and 5 to 7.30 pm weekdays, and 11 am to 2 pm Saturday. The post office is at Calle de Musso Valiente 1. There's a large underground car park at Plaza de Colón, 200m west of the tourist office.

Things to See

The **Centro de Artesanía**, located beside the tourist office, sells traditional crafts. It is open 10 am to 2 pm and 4 to 7.30 pm weekdays.

The splendid baroque facade of the 17th-century **Casa de los Guevara**, which houses the tourist office, will remain swathed in green netting until its lengthy restoration is completed. You can, however, visit its harmonious patio and restored early 20th-century pharmacy within it.

There are more baroque buildings around **Plaza de España**, otherwise known as Plaza Mayor, in the centre of town. These include the **Pósito y Juzgados**, a 16th-century public granary, now the courthouse, and the *ayuntamiento* (town hall). Most impressive of all is the **Colegiata de San Patricio**, a collegiate church with a confident baroque facade and predominantly Renaissance interior. It is open 11 am to 1 pm and 4.30 to 6.30 pm daily.

Peculiar to Lorca are two small but extraordinary free museums – one for the Azules and another for the Blancos (see Special Events in this section) – featuring the magnificent embroidery used in the Semana Santa processions. The **Museo de Bordados del Paso Azul** at Calle de Nogalte 7 is open 11 am to 1 pm and 5.30 to 8.30 pm Tuesday to Friday plus Saturday morning.

The **Museo de Bordados del Paso Blanco**, inside the church on Plaza de Santo Domingo, is open much the same hours, weekdays. Nearby, the **Museo Arqueológico** in the grand 16th-century Casa de los Salazar just off Calle Santo Domingo, is open 11 am to 2 pm and 5 to 8 pm weekdays plus weekend mornings.

Special Events

Lorca is renowned throughout Spain for its Semana Santa celebrations, in which two brotherhoods – the Azules (Blues) and the Blancos (Whites) – have competed every year since 1855 to see who can put on the most lavish display.

Places to Stay & Eat

At the cheerful, spotless *Hostal del Carmen* (☎ 968 46 80 06, Rincón de los Valientes 3), rooms with bathroom and TV are 2000 ptas per person. It's in a tiny square just off Calle Nogalte, about 150m west of the Museo de Bordados del Paso Azul.

La Alberca (☎ 968 40 65 16), almost opposite the Museo Arqueológico on Calle Santo Domingo, has singles/doubles with bathroom and TV for 2500/4500 ptas and its own garage.

Down on the main drag in the eastern part of town, *Hotel Félix* (☎ 968 46 76 54, Avenida Fuerzas Armadas 146) has rooms with bathroom, air-con and TV for a bargain 3250/5350 ptas.

Two stars up, *Hotel Alameda* (☎ 968 40 66 00, Calle de Musso Valiente 8) has rooms with TV, air-con and independent parking for 5350/8050 ptas (1000 ptas per night).

Up another notch, *Jardines de Lorca* (☎ 968 47 05 99) on Alameda de Rafael Méndez offers rooms for 9100/11425 ptas plus IVA.

Cheery, no-frills *Rincón de los Valientes*, below and belonging to Hostal del Carmen, serves hearty local fare and has weekday *menús* from 900 ptas. *Casa Roberto (Calle de Musso Valiente 7)* is one of Lorca's more chic restaurants. Great anytime, it does a good weekday set lunch for 1500 ptas. On the highway, Hotel Félix has a rather spartan but reasonably priced *restaurant*.

Getting There & Away

Over 15 weekday buses run between Lorca and Murcia (600 ptas on the nonstop service) and at least six on weekends. There are four buses to both Almería (1125 ptas) and Granada (1845 ptas) and three to Alicante (1265 ptas), continuing to Valencia (2835 ptas) and Barcelona (5845 ptas).

At least 10 trains per day run to Murcia (525 to 575 ptas). The train and bus stations are beside each other about 200m south-west of the tourist office.

PARQUE NATURAL DE SIERRA ESPUÑA

A 40-minute drive south-west of Murcia towards Lorca, just north of the N-340, the Parque Natural de Sierra Espuña is a paradise for walkers and climbers, with over 250 sq km of unspoilt highlands and blazed trails.

Above the sprawling pine forests tower limestone formations, of which the most impressive is La Pared Sur del Valle de Leiva (the southern wall of the Leiva valley).

In the north-west of the park are 26 Pozos de la Nieve (Ice Houses). In them, snow was compressed into ice, then transported to nearby towns in the summer – a practice that lasted until the early 20th century.

Access to the park is best via Alhama de Murcia, where the small tourist office (☎ 968 63 35 12) can provide maps and information. Alternatively, visit the excellent Centro de Interpretación in the heart of the park. The nearby village of El Berro has a couple of restaurants and the friendly *Camping Sierra Espuña* (☎ 968 66 80 38).

MURCIA

Andalucía

This large region stretching across southern Spain is one of the country's most diverse and exciting. Andalucía's vibrant people are perhaps even more in love with fiestas, music, spectacle and fun than other Spaniards. This is the home of flamenco and some of the country's most spectacular festivities, a heartland of bullfighting and the birthplace of the guitar. Cities such as Sevilla, Granada, Málaga, Córdoba and Cádiz present not only a fascinating historic and artistic heritage but also a vibrant nightlife that often kicks on till dawn.

Geographically, Andalucía comprises two east-west mountain chains separated by the fertile valley of the Río Guadalquivir, plus coastal plains along the Mediterranean and Atlantic. Of the two mountain chains, the Sierra Morena rolls along Andalucía's northern borders, while the Cordillera Bética is a complicated mass of rugged *sierras* broadening out from the south-west to the east; it includes mainland Spain's highest peak, Mulhacén (3478m), in the Sierra Nevada south-east of Granada. This framework encompasses huge variety: the Sierra de Grazalema in the south-west, exposed to Atlantic winds, is the rainiest part of Spain; the deserts of Almería in the east are the driest. While inland cities such as Sevilla and Córdoba are notorious for their extreme heat in summer, snow lies on the heights of the Sierra Nevada nearly all year.

The coasts include not only the intensively developed Costa del Sol, but also, you'll be pleased to discover, some very beautiful and much less developed beaches on rugged Cabo de Gata and the Atlantic Costa de la Luz. Andalucía's hill country and its picturesque white villages present scenes of endlessly varied beauty and a wealth of excellent walking routes. (The best walking seasons are generally April to mid-June and September to mid-October.) With over 14,000 sq km protected as *parques nacionales* or *parques naturales,* Andalucía contains 60% of all environmentally protected land in Spain.

When it comes to festivals, Sevilla's Semana Santa processions at Easter are the most

Highlights

- Sevilla, the magical capital of the south
- Granada, with the Alhambra, Albayzín and a buzzing modern scene
- Beautiful, mountainous Parque Natural de Cazorla – Spain's biggest protected area
- The pretty patios and mesmerising Mezquita of Córdoba
- The mysterious Las Alpujarras valleys, beneath the snow-capped Sierra Nevada
- The isolated beaches and dramatic cliffs of Cabo de Gata, where semidesert meets the Mediterranean
- The Costa de la Luz – long, sandy, little-developed Atlantic beaches
- Walks in the spectacular, green Sierra de Grazalema
- Fiestas: Semana Santa or the Feria de Abril in Sevilla, *carnaval* in Cádiz, Málaga's August *feria,* the Horse Fair at Jerez de la Frontera, and many, many more

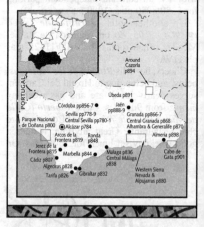

magnificent in the country; Cádiz's *carnaval* (carnival), Sevilla's Feria de Abril (April Fair) and Málaga's August feria are among the biggest parties you could ever hope to find; and the annual festive pilgrimage known as the Romería del Rocío is probably the largest religious (or quasi-religious) event in Europe. Nearly every Andalucian town and village holds its own Semana Santa processions, summer feria and a variety of other full-blooded celebrations through the year.

History

Around the 8th and 7th centuries BC the mysterious Tartessos civilisation flourished somewhere in western Andalucía. In Roman times Andalucía was the most civilised area in the empire west of Italy.

Andalucía was the obvious base for the Muslim invaders who arrived from Africa in AD 711. First Córdoba, until the 11th century, then Sevilla until the 13th, and finally Granada until the 15th century took turns as the leading city of Muslim Spain. Islamic civilisation lasted longer in Andalucía than anywhere else on the Iberian Peninsula and it's from the medieval name for the Muslim areas of the peninsula, Al-Andalus, that the name Andalucía comes. Andalucía's Islamic heritage includes such great buildings as the Alhambra in Granada, the Mezquita in Córdoba and the Alcázar and Giralda in Sevilla.

The Emirate of Granada, the last bastion of Al-Andalus, held out till 1492, when it fell to the Catholic Monarchs, Fernando and Isabel (Ferdinand and Isabella). Columbus' discovery of the Americas in the same year brought great wealth to Sevilla, and later Cádiz, the Andalucian ports through which most of Spain's trade with the new continent was conducted. But the Castilian conquerors killed off Andalucía's deeper prosperity by handing out great swathes of territory to their nobles, who set sheep to run on former food-growing lands.

By the late 19th century, rural Andalucía, especially the west, was a hotbed of anarchist unrest. During the Spanish Civil War Andalucía split along class lines and savage atrocities were committed by both sides. The hungry years after the war were particularly hungry in Andalucía, and between 1950 and 1970 some 1.5 million Andalucians left to find work in the industrial cities of northern Spain, and other European countries.

Since the 1960s, tourism and the overall improvement in the Spanish economy have made a difference. Andalucía's major cities today are bright, cosmopolitan places, its people increasingly well educated, and rural poverty has been dealt a blow by government aid. Yet unemployment, officially 27% in 1999, is still the highest in Spain.

For more on Andalucía's past, see History in the Facts about Spain chapter.

Medical Services & Emergency

Throughout Andalucía, you can call ☎ 061 for an ambulance.

Accommodation

Hotel and *hostal* (budget hotel) prices given in this chapter are generally for the high season (usually July and August, but in

---

Andalucian Youth Hostels

The 20-odd youth hostels affiliated to the official Andalucian youth hostel organisation, Inturjoven, are mostly good, modern places with a high proportion of twin rooms. Sheets are provided and most rooms have private bathrooms. Inconvenient curfews or daytime closing hours are rare. The hostels don't have cooking facilities but they do have *comedores* (dining rooms), usually serving all meals at good prices. Inturjoven has a central booking office (☎ 902-51 00 00, fax 95 503 58 48, e reservas@inturjoven.junta-andalucia.es), Calle del Miño 24, Los Remedios, 41011 Sevilla.

Inturjoven hostels have a fairly homogeneous price structure. Prices, including breakfast, are 1284/1605/1926 ptas in the low/medium/high season for under-26s, and 1605/2140/2461 ptas for people 26 and over. Most hostels have medium season from mid-June to mid-September and for certain short peak periods at other times of year, and low season the rest of the time. But the Almería, Córdoba, Granada, Málaga and Sevilla hostels have no low season. High-season rates only apply for certain short peak periods at these five and a few other hostels. Inturjoven hostels are also in the REAJ and HI (see Accommodation in the Facts for the Visitor chapter).

ANDALUCÍA

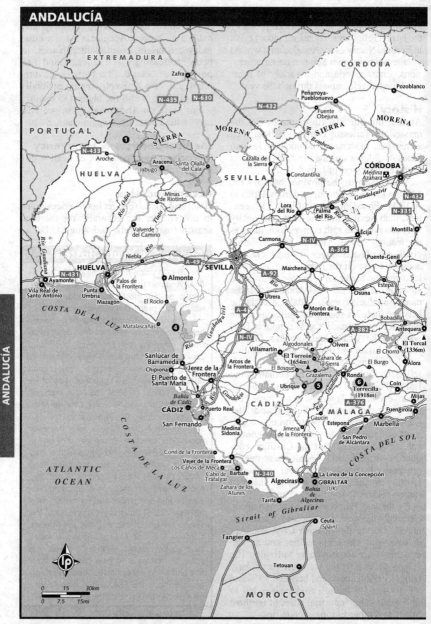

ANDALUCÍA

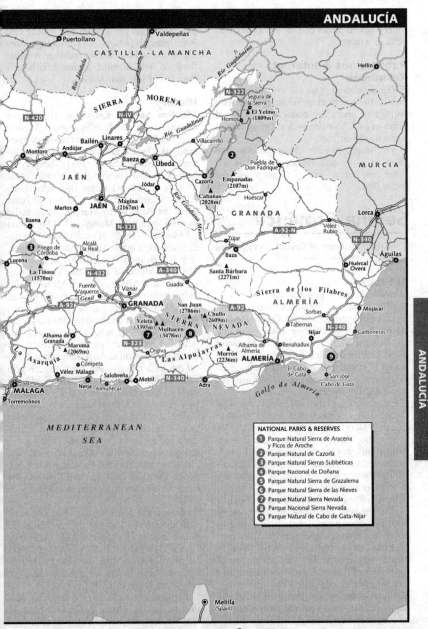

ANDALUCÍA

NATIONAL PARKS & RESERVES

1. Parque Natural Sierra de Aracena y Picos de Aroche
2. Parque Natural de Cazorla
3. Parque Natural Sierras Subbéticas
4. Parque Nacional de Doñana
5. Parque Natural Sierra de Grazalema
6. Parque Natural Sierra de las Nieves
7. Parque Natural Sierra Nevada
8. Parque Nacional Sierra Nevada
9. Parque Natural de Cabo de Gata-Níjar

some places it lasts as long as Easter to October). Room prices can fall by as much as 50% in winter.

Publications & Internet Resources

El Giraldillo and *¿Que Hacer?* are monthly publications covering all Andalucía with listings of upcoming concerts, fiestas and other events. You can pick them up free at some tourist offices.

You might like to check out the Web sites at www.andalucia.com and www.altur.com before you go, to get a taste for the region.

Sevilla Province

The wonderful city of Sevilla overshadows the rest of this province.

SEVILLA

postcode 41080 • pop 702,000

Sevilla, capital of the south, is one of the most exciting cities in Spain. One of the first people recorded as falling in love with the city was the Muslim poet-king Al-Mutamid in the 11th century. It still takes a stony heart not to be captivated by Sevilla's unique atmosphere – stylish and proud yet also relaxed and fun-loving.

Except along the banks of the Río Guadalquivir – navigable to the Atlantic Ocean 100km away – this is not a city of long vistas. Sevilla's dense centre unfolds more subtly as you wend your way through its narrow streets and small plazas. Its Catedral, Alcázar and Archivo de Indias are World Heritage Sites.

Sevilla has been throwing one of Spain's biggest parties, the Feria de Abril, every year for more than a century, and shortly before the feria it stages Semana Santa processions that are probably the most magnificent in the country. The city is also one of the homes of flamenco and bullfighting, and has wonderful nightlife. But above all, Sevilla has atmosphere. Being out among its happy crowds on a warm night is a not-to-be-forgotten experience.

Sevilla is expensive, though. You might pay 6000 ptas for a room that would cost 3000 ptas elsewhere. And prices go even higher around the two big festivals. Another thing to bear in mind is that Sevilla gets *very* hot in July and August.

History

Muslim Sevilla Known as Hispalis in Roman days, and Ishbiliya under Muslim rule, Sevilla was a significant town but overshadowed by Córdoba until the collapse of the Córdoba Caliphate in 1031. Then Sevilla became the most powerful of the *taifa* (small Muslim kingdom) states into which Al-Andalus broke up. By 1078 Sevilla ruled from the Algarve to Murcia. Its Abbadid dynasty rulers Al-Mutadid (1042–69) and Al-Mutamid (1069–91) presided over a hedonistic court in the Alcázar fortress-palace.

When Toledo fell to the Christians in 1085, Al-Mutamid asked the Muslim fundamentalist Almoravids of Morocco for help against the growing northern threat. The Almoravids came, defeated Castile's Alfonso VI, and returned to Morocco – but came back in 1091 to help themselves to Al-Andalus too. They persecuted Jews and Christians and ruled Al-Andalus from Marrakesh as a colony. But their austere grip soon weakened and by 1173 they had been displaced in both Morocco and Al-Andalus by a new strict Muslim sect, the Almohads.

The Almohad caliph Yacoub Yousouf made Sevilla the capital of his whole realm (which stretched as far as Tunisia) and built a great mosque where Sevilla's cathedral now stands. His successor, Yousouf Yacoub al-Mansour, added the Giralda tower and thrashed the Christian armies at Alarcos in 1195.

Reconquista The Christians bounced back with their pivotal victory at Las Navas de Tolosa, north-east of Jaén, in 1212. After this, Castile's Fernando III El Santo (Ferdinand III, the Saint) captured several major Andalucian cities, culminating in Sevilla, after two years' siege, in 1248.

Fernando brought 24,000 Castilian settlers to Sevilla, which, by the 14th century, was the most important Castilian city.

The Golden Age Following Columbus' discovery of the Americas in 1492, Sevilla was given a monopoly on Spanish trade with the new continent and rapidly became one of the richest, most cosmopolitan places in Europe – the *puerto y puerta de Indias* (port and gateway of the Indies). Lavish Renaissance and baroque buildings sprouted, and many stars of Spain's artistic golden age were based here: painters such as Zurbarán, Murillo and Juan de Valdés Leal (though Sevilla-born Velázquez left for Madrid), and sculptors such as Juan Martínez Montañés and Pedro Roldán.

The Not-so-Golden Age A plague in 1649 killed half Sevilla's population, and the Guadalquivir became less and less navigable for the increasingly big ships of the 17th century. In 1717 the Casa de la Contratación, which controlled commerce with America, was transferred to Cádiz. Another plague in 1800 killed 13,000 Sevillans. The 19th century brought limited industrialisation, but foreign Romantics were more attracted by Sevilla's air of faded grandeur.

20th Century Hopes of a recovery raised by Sevilla's first great international fair, the Exposición Iberoamericana of 1929, were dashed by the civil war. The city fell quickly to the Nationalists at the start of the war despite resistance in working-class *barrios* (districts). Numerous historic buildings were demolished in Franco's time, in the name of urban development.

Things looked up in 1982, with the coming to power in Madrid of the PSOE, led by *sevillano* Felipe González, and Sevilla received a huge boost from the 1992 Expo world fair. As well as millions of visitors that year, Sevilla got eight new bridges across the Guadalquivir, the new, super-fast AVE rail link to Madrid and thousands of new hotel rooms.

Orientation

Sevilla straddles the Río Guadalquivir, with most of the interest on the eastern side. The centre is a tangle of narrow old streets and small plazas, with the exception of wide, straight Avenida de la Constitución and broad Plaza Nueva at its northern end. The area between Avenida de la Constitución and the river is called El Arenal. Sevilla's major monuments – the cathedral, the Giralda tower and the Alcázar fortress-palace – are just east of Avenida de la Constitución. The quaint Barrio de Santa Cruz, east of the cathedral and Alcázar, has many budget lodgings. The real city centre (El Centro) is a bit farther north.

The main transport terminals are on the periphery of the central area: Santa Justa train station, 1.5km north-east of the cathedral; Plaza de Armas bus station *(estación de autobuses)*, 1km north-west of the cathedral; and Prado de San Sebastián bus station, 750m south-east of the cathedral.

Information

Tourist Offices The main tourist office is at Avenida de la Constitución 21 (☎ 95 422 14 04). Open 9 am to 7 pm weekdays, 10 am to 2 pm and 3 to 7 pm Saturday and until 2 pm Sunday (closed on holidays), it's often very busy. It has a list of over 30 foreign consulates in the city.

There are also two municipal tourist offices: one south of the centre at Paseo de las Delicias 9 (☎ 95 423 44 65), open 8.30 am to 2.45 pm weekdays; the other at Calle de Arjona 28 by the Puente de Triana (☎ 95 450 56 00), open 8 am to 8.45 pm weekdays and 8.30 am to 2.30 pm weekends. Further tourist offices are at the train station and airport.

Money There's no shortage of banks and ATMs in the central area. Santa Justa station has ATMs.

Post & Communications The main post office *(correos)*, at Avenida de la Constitución 32, is open 8.30 am to 8.30 pm weekdays and 9.30 am to 2 pm Saturday.

Sevilla has heaps of cybercafes and other public Internet and email services. A typical rate is 300 ptas per hour. They include Cibercafé Torredeoro.net (☎ 95 450 28 09), at Calle Núñez de Balboa 3A, and Sevilla Internet Center (☎ 95 450 02 75), at Calle Almirantazgo 2.

ANDALUCÍA

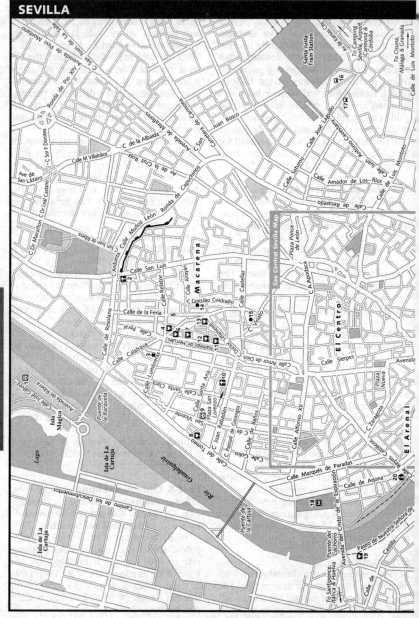

SEVILLA

Santa Justa Train Station

To Camping Sevilla, Airport, Carmona & Córdoba
To Osuna, Málaga & Granada
To Luis Montoto

See Central Sevilla Map

El Centro

Macarena

El Arenal

Isla Mágica

Isla de La Cartuja

Lago

Isla de La Cartuja

Río Guadalquivir

Camino de los Descubrimientos

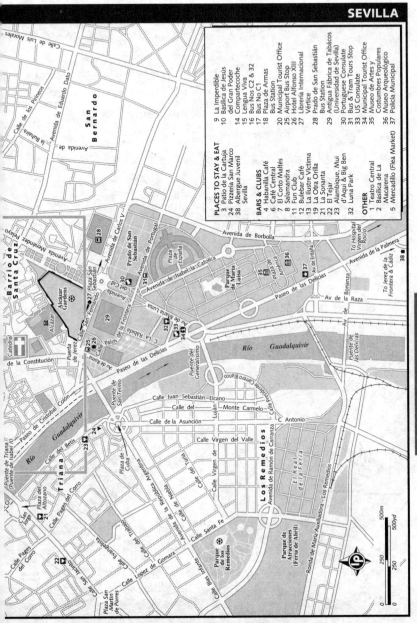

SEVILLA

PLACES TO STAY & EAT
3 Patio de la Cartuja
24 Pizzeria San Marco
38 Albergue Juvenil Sevilla

BARS & CLUBS
4 Habanilla Café
6 Café Central
7 El Corto Maltés
8 Salamandra
11 Fun Club
12 Bulebar Café
19 La Ilustre Víctima
21 La Otra Orilla
22 La Sonanta
23 Alambique, Mui d'Aquí & Big Ben
32 Luna Park

OTHER
1 Teatro Central
2 Basílica de La Macarena
5 Mercadillo (Flea Market)
9 La Imperdible
10 Basílica de Jesús del Gran Poder
14 Compartecoche
15 Lengua Viva
16 Bus Nos C2 & 32
17 Bus No C1
18 Plaza de Armas Bus Station
20 Municipal Tourist Office
25 Airport Bus Stop
27 Hotel Alfonso XIII
Librería Internacional Vértice
28 Prado de San Sebastián Bus Station
29 Antigua Fábrica de Tabácos (Universidad de Sevilla)
30 Portuguese Consulate
31 Bus & Tram Tours Stop
33 US Consulate
34 Municipal Tourist Office
35 Museo de Artes y Costumbres Populares
36 Museo Arqueológico
37 Policía Municipal

CENTRAL SEVILLA

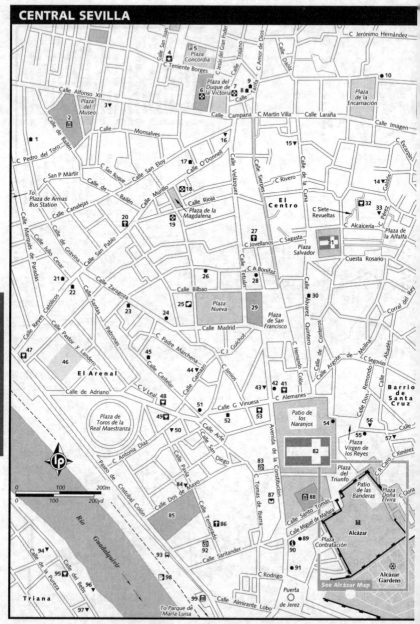

ANDALUCÍA

CENTRAL SEVILLA

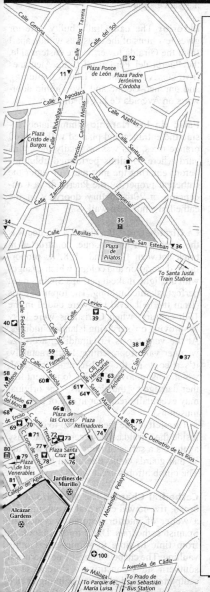

PLACES TO STAY
1 Hostal Romero
8 Hostal Pino
9 Hostal Unión
13 Las Casas del Rey de Baeza
17 Hostal Lis II
21 Hotel Becquer
22 Hotel Puerta de Triana
23 Hostal Central
30 Las Casas de los Mercaderes
38 Hostal La Montoreña
45 Hotel La Rábida
52 Hotel Simón
58 Hostal Goya
59 Hostal Córdoba
60 Pensión Fabiola
62 Las Casas de la Judería
63 Hostal Bienvenido
65 Pensión San Pancracio
66 Pensión Cruces
67 Pensión Vergara
71 Hotel Murillo
75 Huéspedes Dulces Sueños/Sweet Dreams
79 Hostería del Laurel

PLACES TO EAT
3 Bodegón Alfonso XII
11 El Rinconcillo
14 Sopa de Ganso
15 Restaurante San Marco
16 Patio San Eloy
33 Habanita
34 La Bodega Extremeña
36 Bodega Extremeña
43 Café de Indias
44 Bodega Paco Góngora
50 Mesón Serranito
56 Cervecería Giralda
57 Bodega Santa Cruz
61 Carmela
64 Bar Casa Fernando
68 Pizzeria San Marco
70 Café Bar Las Teresas
74 Restaurante Modesto
77 Restaurante La Albahaca
81 Corral del Agua
84 Mesón de la Infanta
94 Pizzeria O Mamma Mia
96 Kiosco de las Flores
97 Ristorante Cosa Nostra

BARS & CLUBS
32 El Mundo
39 La Carbonería
41 P Flaherty Irish Pub
47 Café Isbiliyya
48 Arena
49 A3
53 Hijos de E Morales
69 Bar Entrecalles
73 El Tamboril
78 Los Gallos
95 Café La Pavana

OTHER
2 Museo de Bellas Artes
4 Policia Nacional
5 Underground Car Park
6 El Corte Inglés
7 El Corte Inglés
10 Mercado de la Encarnación
12 Underground Car Park
18 El Corte Inglés
19 El Corte Inglés
20 Iglesia de la Magdalena
24 Renfe Office
25 British Consulate
26 CLIC
27 Capilla de San José
28 Halcón Viajes
29 Ayuntamiento
31 Parroquia del Salvador
35 Casa de Pilatos
37 LTC Map Shop
40 Australian Consulate
42 Librería Beta
46 Mercado del Arenal
51 Tintorería Roma
54 La Giralda
55 Usit Unlimited
72 French Consulate
76 Irish Consulate
80 Hospital de los Venerables Sacerdotes
82 Catedral
83 Sevilla Internet Center
85 Teatro de la Maestranza
86 Hospital de la Caridad
87 Post Office (Correos)
88 Archivo de Indias
89 Sevilla Mágica
90 Main Tourist Office
91 Librería Beta
92 Cibercafé Torredeoro.net
93 Bus & Tram Tours Stop
98 Cruceros Turísticos Torre del Oro
99 Torre del Oro
100 Centro de Urgencias

ANDALUCÍA

euro currency converter €1 = 166pta

Travel Agencies The student/youth travel agency Usit Unlimited (☎ 902-25 25 75) is at Calle Mateos Gago 2, Barrio de Santa Cruz.

Bookshops Librería Beta at Avenida de la Constitución 9 and 27 has guidebooks and novels in English, and maps. Librería Internacional Vértice, Calle San Fernando 33, has a large range of books in English, French and German.

LTC, Avenida Menéndez Pelayo 42-44, is a great map shop: stock up here if you're heading out to the remote areas.

Laundry Tintorería Roma, Calle Castelar 2C, will wash, dry and fold a load of washing in one hour for 1000 ptas. It's open 9.30 am to 1.30 pm and 5 to 8.30 pm weekdays, and 9 am to 2 pm Saturday.

Medical Services & Emergency There's a Centro de Urgencias (Emergency Medical Post; ☎ 95 441 17 12) on the corner of Avenida Menéndez Pelayo and Avenida Málaga. The main general hospital is the Hospital Virgen del Rocío (☎ 95 424 81 81) at Avenida Manuel Siurot s/n, 1km south of Parque de María Luisa. The Policía Municipal (☎ 95 461 54 50) are in the Pabellón de Brasil, Paseo de las Delicias 15; the Policía Nacional (☎ 95 422 88 40) are on Plaza Concordia.

Dangers & Annoyances Sevilla has a reputation for petty crime against tourists – pickpockets, bag-snatchers and the like.

Catedral & Giralda

After Sevilla fell to the Christians in 1248 its main mosque was used as a church until 1401, when in view of its decaying state the church authorities decided to knock it down and start again. 'Let us create such a building that future generations will take us for lunatics', they reputedly agreed. They certainly got themselves a big church. The main building (excluding the Patio de los Naranjos) is 126m long and 83m wide, one of the largest cathedrals in the world. It was completed by 1507 and was originally all Gothic, though work done after its central

dome collapsed in 1511 was mostly in Renaissance style.

Exterior The cathedral's bulky exterior gives few hints of the treasures within, apart from the Giralda tower on the eastern side, the Puerta del Perdón on Calle Alemanes (two survivors from the Islamic building), and one neo-Gothic and two Gothic doorways on Avenida de la Constitución.

Patio de los Naranjos Immediately inside the entrance and planted with over 60 orange trees, this was originally the courtyard where Muslims performed ablutions before entering the mosque. You enter the cathedral proper by the Puerta de la Concepción, a 20th-century doorway in the cathedral's northern wall.

La Giralda Over 90m high, La Giralda was the minaret of the mosque, constructed in brick between 1184 and 1198. Its proportions, decoration and colour, which changes with the light, make it perhaps Spain's most perfect Islamic building. The topmost parts (from the bell level up) were added in the 16th century, when Christians were busy 'improving on' surviving Islamic buildings. At the very top is El Giraldillo, a bronze weather vane representing Faith (actually, it's a copy of the 16th-century original, which was removed in 1997 to prevent further damage by the elements – the original may eventually reappear in one of Sevilla's museums).

Turn left inside the cathedral to climb up inside the Giralda. The ascent is quite easy as there's a series of ramps all the way up, so that guards could ride up on horseback. The climb affords great views.

Cathedral Chapels The sheer size of the broad, five-naved cathedral is obscured by a welter of interior decoration typical of Spanish cathedrals. Don't forget to look up from time to time to admire the Gothic vaulting. The chapels along the northern and southern sides constitute a storehouse of sculpture, stained glass and painting as rich as any church's in Spain. Near the western end of the northern side is the **Capilla de San Antonio** with Murillo's large 1666 canvas depicting the vision of St Anthony of Padua; thieves excised the kneeling saint in 1874 but he was found in New York and put back.

Columbus' Tomb Inside the cathedral's southern door stands the tomb of Christopher Columbus. The great sailor's remains – or rather, his probable remains, for no one's completely sure that the real ones didn't get mislaid somewhere in the Caribbean – were brought here from Cuba in 1899. The monument shows four pallbearers representing the kingdoms of Spain at the time of Columbus' 1492 voyage: Castile (carrying Granada on its spear), León, Aragón and Navarra.

Coro In the middle of the cathedral is the large *coro* (choir) with 117 carved Gothic-*mudéjar* stalls. The lower ones have marquetry representations of La Giralda. Vices and sins are depicted on the misericords.

Capilla Mayor East of the coro is the Capilla Mayor whose Gothic retablo is the jewel of the cathedral and reckoned to be the biggest altarpiece in the world. Begun by Flemish sculptor Pieter Dancart in 1482 and completed by others by 1564, this sea of gilded and polychromed wood holds more than 1000 carved biblical figures. At the centre of the lowest level is the 13th-century image of the Virgen de la Sede, patron of the cathedral.

Eastern Chapels Against the eastern wall of the cathedral are more chapels, which are usually roped off. The central Capilla Real (Royal Chapel) contains, in front of its altar, the silver and bronze tomb of Fernando III (he's mummified inside), and at the sides the tombs of Fernando's son, Alfonso X, and wife, Beatrice of Swabia.

Sacristía de los Cálices South of the Capilla Mayor is the entrance to a group of rooms with many of the cathedral's art treasures. The westernmost of these is the Sacristía de los Cálices, where Goya's 1817

painting of the Sevilla martyrs *Santas Justa y Rufina* (a pair of potters who died at the hands of the Romans) hangs above the altar. Also here is Martínez Montañés' masterly sculpture *El Cristo de la Clemencia* (1603).

Sacristía Mayor This large domed room east of the Sacristía de los Cálices is a plateresque creation of 1528–47: the arch over its portal has carvings of 16th-century foods. Pedro de Campaña's 1547 *Descendimiento* (Descent from the Cross), above the central altar at the southern end, and Zurbarán's *Santa Teresa*, to its right, are two of the cathedral's masterpieces. In a glass case are the city keys handed to the conquering Fernando III in 1248.

Cabildo This beautifully domed chapter house, in the south-eastern corner of the cathedral, was built between 1558 and 1592 to the designs of Hernán Ruiz, architect of the Giralda belfry. High above the archbishop's throne at the southern end is a Murillo masterpiece, *La Inmaculada*. Eight Murillo saints adorn the dome at the same level.

Entry The entry arrangements for the cathedral and Giralda change frequently, but current regulations are usually posted fairly clearly. At last check the entrance for non-group visitors was the Puerta del Perdón on the northern side of the building, and opening hours for the Catedral and Giralda were 11 am to 5 pm Monday to Saturday (700 ptas, or 200 ptas for students, pensioners and under-12s, with ID) and 2 to 7 pm Sunday (free).

Alcázar

Don't miss this intriguing, beautiful palace-fortress intimately associated with the lives and loves of many Muslim and Christian monarchs, above all the extraordinary Pedro I (1350–69), who perhaps loved Sevilla more than any other ruler but whose reign was confounded by bloody feuds in the ruling family. Pedro was known either as El Cruel or El Justiciero (the Justice-Dispenser), depending which side you were on.

ANDALUCÍA

ALCÁZAR

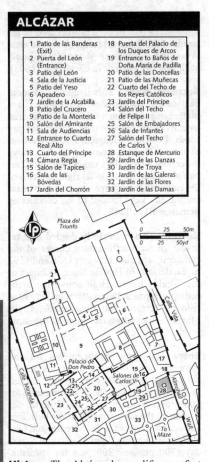

1 Patio de las Banderas (Exit)	18 Puerta del Palacio de los Duques de Arcos
2 Puerta del León (Entrance)	19 Entrance to Baños de Doña María de Padilla
3 Patio del León	20 Patio de las Doncellas
4 Sala de la Justicia	21 Patio de las Muñecas
5 Patio del Yeso	22 Cuarto del Techo de los Reyes Católicos
6 Apeadero	23 Jardín del Príncipe
7 Jardín de la Alcabilla	24 Salón del Techo de Felipe II
8 Patio del Crucero	
9 Patio de la Montería	25 Salón de Embajadores
10 Salón del Almirante	26 Sala de Infantes
11 Sala de Audiencias	27 Salón del Techo de Carlos V
12 Entrance to Cuarto Real Alto	28 Estanque de Mercurio
13 Cuarto del Príncipe	29 Jardín de las Danzas
14 Cámara Regia	30 Jardín de Troya
15 Salón de Tapices	31 Jardín de las Galeras
16 Sala de las Bóvedas	32 Jardín de las Flores
17 Jardín del Chorrón	33 Jardín de las Damas

History The Alcázar began life as a fort for the Córdoban governors of Sevilla in 913, and has been adapted and/or enlarged in almost every century since. Sevilla's prosperous 11th-century taifa rulers built themselves a palace called Al-Muwarak (The Blessed) in what's now the western part of the Alcázar. East of this, the Almohads added another palace in the 12th century around the Patio del Crucero. When Sevilla fell to the Christians in 1248, Fernando III moved into the Alcázar, dying here in 1252. His son, Alfonso X, replaced much of the Almohad palace with a Gothic

one, which has now become the Salones de Carlos V.

In 1364–66, Pedro I created the sumptuous mudéjar Palacio de Don Pedro, partly on the site of the old Al-Muwarak palace. The Catholic Monarchs, Fernando and Isabel, set up court in the Alcázar for several years as they prepared the conquest of Granada. The whole complex was further adapted and expanded by later rulers, who also created the Alcázar's beautiful gardens.

Patio del León This was the garrison yard of the Al-Muwarak palace. Off its south-eastern corner, the **Sala de la Justicia**, with beautiful mudéjar plasterwork, was built in the 1340s by Alfonso XI, who disported here with his mistress Leonor de Guzmán. Alfonso's sexual exploits left his heir Pedro I with five half-brothers and a severe case of sibling rivalry. Pedro had a dozen friends and relatives murdered in his efforts to stay on the throne. One of the half-brothers, Don Fadrique, met his maker right here in the Sala de la Justicia. The room gives on to the pretty **Patio del Yeso**, a 19th-century reconstruction of part of the 12th-century Almohad palace.

Patio de la Montería The rooms on the western side of this courtyard were part of the Casa de la Contratación founded by the Catholic Monarchs in 1503 to control American trade. The **Sala de Audiencias** contains the earliest known painting on the discovery of the Americas (by Alejo Fernández, 1530s), in which Columbus, Fernando El Católico, Carlos I (Charles I), Amerigo Vespucci and native Americans can be seen sheltered beneath the Virgin in her role as protector of sailors. Also here is a model of Columbus' ship, the *Santa María*.

Cuarto Real Alto The Alcázar is still a royal palace and the Cuarto Real Alto, the richly decorated set of rooms reserved for the Spanish royal family, can be visited by guided tour. Tickets (400 ptas) are sold, and the tours start, in the south-western corner of the Patio de la Montería. Around 12 half-hour tours, for 15 people, are given daily, alternately in Spanish and English. You can book in advance on ☎ 95 456 00 40. A highlight of the visit is Pedro I's bedroom, with marvellous mudéjar tiles and plasterwork.

Palacio de Don Pedro Whatever else Pedro I may have done, posterity owes him a big thank you for creating this palace.

When in 1364 Pedro decided to build himself a new palace in the Alcázar, his Muslim ally Mohammed V of Granada, the man chiefly responsible for the decoration of the Alhambra's Palacio Nazaries, sent along many of his best artisans to help. These were joined by Muslims and Jews from Toledo and Sevilla. Their work represented the best of contemporary architecture and design, and also drew on the traditions of the Almohads and caliphal Córdoba. What resulted is a unique synthesis of Iberian Muslim art.

Inscriptions on the palace's facade on the Patio de la Montería encapsulate the unusual nature of the enterprise. While one records that the building's creator was 'the very high, noble and conquering Don Pedro, by the grace of God king of Castile and León', another states repeatedly 'There is no conqueror but Allah'.

At the heart of the palace is the wonderful **Patio de las Doncellas**, surrounded by beautiful arches and with exquisite plasterwork and tiling. The doors at its ends are among the finest ever produced by Toledo's carpenters.

The beautiful Patio de las Doncellas, inside the Alcázar

JANE SMITH

The **Cámara Regia** on the northern side of the patio has two rooms with stunning ceilings and more wonderful plaster and tilework. The rear room was probably the monarch's bedroom. Just west is the small **Patio de las Muñecas**, the heart of the palace's private quarters, with delicate Granada-style decoration. The mezzanine and top gallery were built in the 19th century for Isabel II, using plasterwork brought from the Alhambra. The **Cuarto del Príncipe** to the north has superb ceilings and was probably the queen's bedroom.

The spectacular **Salón de Embajadores** (Hall of Ambassadors), off the western end of the Patio de las Doncellas, was Pedro I's throne room and incorporates much earlier caliphal-style door arches from the Al-Muwarak palace. Its fabulous wooden dome of multiple star patterns, symbolising the universe, was added in 1427. The dome's shape gives the room the alternative name Sala de la Media Naranja (Hall of the Half Orange). On its western side, the beautiful **Arco de Pavones** archway, with peacock motifs, leads into the **Salón del Techo de Felipe II**, with a Renaissance ceiling from 1589–91.

Salones de Carlos V Reached by a staircase from the Patio de las Doncellas, these are the much remodelled rooms of Alfonso X's 13th-century palace. It was here that Alfonso's intellectual court gathered and, a century later, Pedro I installed the mistress he loved to distraction, María de Padilla. The Sala de las Bóvedas is adorned with beautiful 1570s tiling, while the Salón de Tapices has a collection of huge 18th-century tapestries showing Carlos I's 1535 conquest of Tunis.

Patio del Crucero This patio outside the Salones de Carlos V's northern side was originally the upper level of the patio of the 12th-century Almohad palace. At first it consisted only of raised walkways, below which grew orange trees whose fruit could be plucked at hand height by the privileged folk strolling along the walkways. María de Padilla must have liked doing this because the patio is also known as the Patio de María de Padilla.

ANDALUCÍA

The patio's lower level had to be covered over in the 18th century after earthquake damage.

Gardens & Exit From the Salones de Carlos V you can head out into the Alcázar's large gardens *(jardines)*, a perfect place to relax. The gardens in front of the Salones de Carlos V and Palacio de Don Pedro were mostly brought to their present form in the 16th and 17th centuries, while those to the east, beyond a long Almohad wall, are 20th-century creations. From the little Jardín de las Danzas, a passage runs beneath the Salones de Carlos V to the so-called **Baños de Doña María de Padilla**, originally the lower level of the Patio del Crucero, with a grotto that replaced that patio's original pool (in which, judging by the name, María de Padilla must have liked to bathe).

From the new gardens you can leave the Alcázar via the **Apeadero**, a 17th-century entrance hall housing a collection of carriages, and the **Patio de las Banderas**.

Entry The entrance is the Puerta del León at the southern corner of Plaza del Triunfo. The Alcázar is open 9.30 am to 7 pm Tuesday to Saturday (to 5 pm from October to March) and until 5 pm Sunday and holidays. Entry is 700 ptas (free for students, pensioners and under-12s, with ID).

Archivo de Indias
Since 1785 this building on the western side of Plaza del Triunfo has been the main archive on Spain's American empire. It houses over 80 million pages of documents dating from 1492 through to the end of the empire in the 19th century. There are changing displays of fascinating maps and documents, open 10 am to 1 pm weekdays (free). The 16th-century building, by Juan de Herrera, was originally Sevilla's Lonja (Exchange) for American commerce.

Barrio de Santa Cruz
Sevilla's medieval *judería* (Jewish quarter), east of the cathedral and Alcázar, is today a tangle of quaint, winding streets and lovely plant-decked plazas. The judería came into

existence after the Reconquista and was emptied by a pogrom in 1391. Its most characteristic plaza today is Plaza de Santa Cruz, whose central cross, made in 1692, is one of the finest examples of Sevilla wrought-iron work. Plaza Doña Elvira is another quaint spot.

The 17th-century **Hospital de los Venerables Sacerdotes** on Plaza de los Venerables, a former residence for aged priests, is open most of the year for guided visits from 10 am to 2 pm and 4 to 8 pm daily (600 ptas). You visit the lovely central courtyard, old living quarters, several art exhibition rooms, and the church with murals by Valdés Leal and fine sculptures by Pedro Roldán.

El Centro
The real centre of Sevilla, north of the cathedral, is a densely packed zone of narrow, crooked streets, broken up here and there by plazas around which the city's life has revolved for aeons.

Plaza de San Francisco & Calle Sierpes
Site of a market in Muslim times, Plaza de San Francisco has been Sevilla's main public square since the 16th century and was once the scene of Inquisition burnings. The southern end of the **ayuntamiento** (town hall) here is encrusted with lovely Renaissance carving from the 1520s and '30s.

Pedestrianised Calle Sierpes, heading north from the plaza, is Sevilla's fanciest shopping street. Take a few steps along Calle Jovellanos to the **Capilla de San José**, an 18th-century chapel with breath-catchingly intense baroque ornamentation (open 8 am to 12.30 pm and 6.30 to 8.30 pm daily).

Plaza Salvador
This plaza was the forum of Roman Hispalis. It's dominated by the **Parroquia del Salvador** (open 6.30 to 9 pm daily), a big, red baroque church built between 1674 and 1712 on the site of Muslim Ishbiliya's original main mosque. On the northern side, the mosque's small patio remains, with a few half-buried Roman columns.

Casa de Pilatos
This finest of Sevilla's noble mansions, on Plaza Pilatos, is still occupied by the ducal Medinaceli family. This

extensive 16th-century building is a mixture of diverse architectural styles, with some beautiful tilework, *artesonado* ceilings and gardens, though the overall effect is not unlike that of the Alcázar. The Patio Principal, for instance, features intricate mudéjar plasterwork, 16th-century tiling, a Renaissance fountain and Roman sculpture. The staircase from here to the upper floor has the most magnificent tiles in the building, with a great golden artesonado dome above.

The Casa de Pilatos is open 9 am to 7 pm daily, at 500 ptas for each of the two floors – if time or money are short, skip the top floor.

Río Guadalquivir

A short walk west from the southern end of Avenida de la Constitución brings you to the eastern bank of the Guadalquivir, which is a pleasant place for a stroll.

Torre del Oro This 13th-century river bank Muslim watchtower, which once crowned a corner of the city walls, was supposedly covered in golden tiles, hence its name, 'Tower of Gold'. Inside is the small, crowded Museo Marítimo (Maritime Museum), open 10 am to 2 pm Tuesday to Friday and 11 am to 2 pm weekends, closed August (100 ptas).

Hospital de la Caridad A block back from the river at Calle Temprado 3, this hospice for the elderly was founded in the 17th century by Miguel de Mañara – by legend a notorious libertine who changed his ways after experiencing a vision of his own funeral procession. For the hospice's church he commissioned a collection of top-class 17th-century Sevillan art on the theme of death and redemption. Valdés Leal's frightening masterpieces *In Ictu Oculi* (In the Blink of an Eye) and *Finis Gloriae Mundi* (The End of Earthly Glory) face each other across the western end of the church, chillingly illustrating the futility of worldly success in the face of death.

Four Murillo paintings along the side walls illustrate the theme of redemption through mercy. They show Moses drawing water from the rock, the miracle of the loaves and fishes, St John of God (San Juan de Dios) caring for an invalid, and Isabel of Hungary curing the sick.

Mañara is buried in the crypt beneath the main altar, on which a masterly sculpture by Pedro Roldán illustrates the ultimate act of mercy, the burial of the dead – in this case, of Christ himself.

The Hospital de la Caridad is open 9 am to 1.30 pm and 3.30 to 6.30 pm Monday to Saturday, and until 1 pm Sunday and holidays (400 ptas).

Plaza de Toros de la Real Maestranza Sevilla's bullring on Paseo de Cristóbal Colón is one of the most elegant in Spain, and probably the oldest (building began in 1758). It was here and in the ring at Ronda that bullfighting on foot (instead of horseback) began in the 18th century. Interesting 300-ptas tours of the ring and its museum are given in English and Spanish, about every 20 minutes from 9.30 am to 2 pm and 3 to 6 or 7 pm daily (bullfight days: 10 am to 3 pm).

Museo de Bellas Artes The Fine Arts Museum, in a beautiful former convent at Plaza del Museo 9, does full justice to Sevilla's leading role in Spain's artistic golden age. The 17th-century Sevilla masters Murillo, Zurbarán and Valdés Leal are particularly well represented, but the museum also holds works by great artists who worked elsewhere such as El Greco and Ribera.

Highlights include Pedro Millán's 15th-century terracotta sculptures (Room I); El Greco's portrait of his son Jorge Manuel and Pedro Torrigiano's influential Renaissance sculpture *San Jerónimo Penitente* (Room II); paintings by Velázquez and Alonso Cano (Room III); Zurbarán's masterpiece *Apoteosis de Santo Tomás de Aquinas* and numerous Murillo paintings (Room V, formerly the convent church); Ribera's very Spanish-looking *Santiago Apóstol* and Zurbarán's disturbing little *Cristo Crucificado Expirante* (Room VI); and further major works by Zurbarán (Room X).

It's open 3 to 8 pm Tuesday, 9 am to 8 pm Wednesday to Saturday, 9 am to 2 pm Sunday

ANDALUCÍA

Semana Santa in Sevilla

Every day from Palm Sunday to Easter Sunday, large, richly bedecked images and whole life-size tableaux from the Easter story are carried from Sevilla's churches through the streets to the Catedral, accompanied by long processions that may take more than an hour to pass, and watched by vast crowds. These rites go back to the 14th century but they took on their present form in the 17th, when many of the images – some of which are supreme works of art – were created.

Semana Santa (Holy Week) in Sevilla, with its combination of splendour and anguish, spectacle and solemnity, and overriding adoration of the Virgin, can give a special insight into Spanish Catholicism.

The processions are organised by over 50 different *hermandades* or *cofradías* (brotherhoods, some of which include women), each normally with two *pasos* – as these sculptural representations of events from Christ's Passion are known. The first paso focuses on Christ; the second is an image of the Virgin. They are carried by teams of about 40 bearers called *costaleros,* who work in relays as each supports a weight of about 50kg. The pasos move with a hypnotic swaying motion to the rhythm of their accompanying bands and the commands of their *capataz* (leader), who strikes a bell to start and stop the paso.

Each pair of pasos has up to 2500 costumed followers, known as *nazarenos.* Many of these wear tall Ku Klux Klan-like capes that cover their heads except for eye slits, implying that the identity of the penitent is known only to God. The most contrite go barefoot and carry crosses.

From Palm Sunday to Good Friday, seven or eight hermandades leave their churches each day in the afternoon or early evening, and arrive between 5 and 11 pm at Calle Campana at the northern end of Calle Sierpes. This is the start of the *carrera oficial,* which all then follow, along Calle Sierpes, Plaza San Francisco and Avenida de la Constitución to the Catedral. They enter the Catedral at its western end and leave at the east, emerging on Plaza Virgen de los Reyes. They get back to their churches some time between 10 pm and 3 am.

The climax of the week is the *madrugada* (early hours) of Good Friday, when some of the most respected or popular hermandades file through the city. The first to reach the carrera oficial, about 1.30 am, is the oldest hermandad, El Silencio, which goes in complete silence. At about 2 am, comes Jesús del Gran Poder, whose 17th-century Christ, carved by Juan de Mesa, is one of the masterpieces of Sevillan sculpture. This is followed at about 3 am by La Macarena, whose Virgin is the most passionately adored of all. Created by an unknown sculptor in, it's believed, the mid-17th century, she's the city's supreme representation of the grieving yet hoping mother of Christ. Then comes El Calvario from the Iglesia de la Magdalena, followed by Esperanza de Triana and finally, at about 6 am, Los Gitanos, the *gitano* (gypsy) hermandad.

(free with EU passport or identity card, 250 ptas otherwise).

South of the Centre

Antigua Fábrica de Tabacos Sevilla's massive former tobacco factory on Calle San Fernando – workplace of Bizet's operatic heroine, Carmen – was built in the 18th century. It had its own jail, stables for 400 mules, 24 patios and even a nursery since most of its workers were women. Now part of the Universidad de Sevilla, it's an impressive if rather gloomy neoclassical building. It's open 8 am and 9.30 pm weekdays, and until 2 pm Saturday.

Parque de María Luisa & Plaza de España A large area south of the Fábrica de Tabacos was transformed for the 1929 Exposición Iberoamericana. It's spattered with all sorts of fancy and funny buildings, many of them harking back to Sevilla's eras of past glory. In its midst, the large Parque de María Luisa, with 3500 magnificent trees, is a fine respite from the hustle of the city.

Facing the park across Avenida de Isabel la Católica, Plaza de España is one of the city's favourite relaxation spots, with fountains and mini-canals. Around it is the most

Semana Santa in Sevilla

On the Saturday evening, just four hermandades make their way to the Catedral, and finally, on Easter Sunday morning, only one, the Hermandad de la Resurrección.

There are marked differences between the styles of the hermandades. City-centre hermandades, such as El Silencio, are traditionally linked with the bourgeoisie. They're austere, with little or no music, and wear black tunics, usually without capes. Hermandades from the working-class *barrios* (districts) outside the centre, such as La Macarena, have brass and drum bands accompanying more brightly bedecked pasos. Their nazarenos wear coloured, caped tunics, often of satin, velvet or wool. They have to come from farther away, and some are on the streets for more than 12 hours.

Programs giving each hermandad's schedule and route are widely available during Semana Santa. It's not too hard to work out which procession will be where and when, and pick one up in its own barrio or as it leaves or re-enters its church, which are always emotional moments.

Crowds along most of the carrera oficial make it hard to get much of a view there, unless you manage to get a seat. These are sold for between 1000 and 3000 ptas depending on where they are and when. But if you arrive early enough in the evening, you can usually get close enough to the cathedral to see plenty for free.

If you're not in Sevilla for Semana Santa, you can get an inkling of what it's about from some of the churches housing the famous images. The Basílica de La Macarena, Calle Bécquer 1, and the Basílica de Jesús del Gran Poder, on Plaza de San Lorenzo, are both in the north of the city, within about 600m of the Alameda de Hércules. The Iglesia de la Magdalena is farther south on Calle de San Pablo. All three churches are normally open daily from at least 9 to 11 am and 6.30 to 9 pm, and La Macarena has a museum too.

Sevilla's much adored sculpture of the Virgin

ANDALUCÍA

grandiose of the 1929 buildings, a semicircular brick-and-tile confection featuring Sevilla tilework at its gaudiest.

On Plaza de América in the southern end of the park is Sevilla's **Museo Arqueológico**, whose big collection includes a room of gold jewellery from the mysterious Tartessos culture and fine collections of Iberian animal sculptures and beautiful Roman mosaics. Facing it is the **Museo de Artes y Costumbres Populares**, with mockup workshops of local crafts such as guitarmaking, ceramics and wrought iron, and some beautiful old bullfighting and feria

costumes. Both museums are open 3 to 8 pm Tuesday, 9 am to 8 pm Wednesday to Saturday and 9 am to 2.30 pm Sunday and holidays (free with an EU passport or identity card, 250 ptas otherwise).

Isla Mágica

This large amusement park stands on the Isla de La Cartuja, a tongue of land between two branches of the Guadalquivir, north-west of the centre. Its theme is the 16th-century Spanish colonial adventure, and highlight rides include a roller-coaster with high-speed 360° turns, and the Iguazú in which you descend a

Brazilian jungle waterfall. Isla Mágica usually opens daily from about April to September, and some years at weekends and holidays in other months. Normal hours are 11 am to 11 pm, with an entry price of around 3400 ptas (2300 ptas for under-13s and over-60s), or 2300 ptas (1700 ptas) after 6 pm.

Isla Mágica uses part of the site of Expo 92. Other parts of the site are slowly being turned into a technology park, and others are sadly rotting away.

Bus Nos C1 and C2 (see Getting Around) go to Isla Mágica.

Courses

For information on Spanish-language courses at the university, contact the Instituto de Idiomas, Universidad de Sevilla (☎ 95 455 11 56, ⓔ idijsec@cica.es), Avenida Reina Mercedes s/n, 41012 Sevilla. Two private colleges we have heard good things about are CLIC (☎ 95 450 21 31), Calle Albareda 19, and Lengua Viva (☎ 95 490 51 31), Calle Viriato 22. The main tourist office can give you lists of others, and of dance and guitar schools. You'll also find ads in *El Giraldillo* and the *Alma 2000* flamenco magazine.

Organised Tours

The open-topped double-decker buses and converted trams of Sevilla Tour (☎ 95 450 20 99) make several daily city tours of about one hour, with earphone commentary in several languages. You can board on Paseo de Cristóbal Colón, 100m north of the Torre del Oro. Adult fare is 1500 ptas. The ticket is valid for 24 hours and you can hop off or on at Plaza de España or the Isla de La Cartuja. Sevirama/Guide Friday (☎ 94 456 06 93) operates similar tours from the same stops.

One-hour river cruises (1700 ptas) by Cruceros Turísticos Torre del Oro go at least hourly from 11 am to 7 pm from the Torre del Oro.

Special Events

Sevilla's Semana Santa processions (see the boxed text 'Semana Santa in Sevilla') and its Feria de Abril, a week or two later, are two of Spain's most famous and exciting festivals.

Feria de Abril Sevilla's April Fair, in the second half of the month, is a kind of release after the solemnity of Semana Santa. It takes place on a special *recinto* (site), El Real de la Feria, in the Los Remedios area west of the Guadalquivir. The ceremonial lighting of the feria grounds on the Monday night is the starting gun for six nights of eating, drinking, fabulous flouncy dresses, and music and dancing till dawn. Much of the recinto is occupied by private *casetas* (enclosures for associations and groups), but there are public casetas, too, where much the same fun goes on. There's also a huge fairground.

In the afternoons, from about 1 pm, those who have horses and carriages parade about the feria grounds in their finery (many of the horses are dressed up too). And it's during the feria that Sevilla's major bullfight season takes place.

Places to Stay

The summer prices we give can come down significantly from October to March, but typically rise at least 50% for Semana Santa and the Feria de Abril (a few places even triple their rates then). This spring *temporada extra* can last as long as two months at some hotels and you should definitely book ahead at this time. Accommodation in Sevilla is plentiful – the following is just a tiny selection – but always in demand.

Places to Stay – Budget

Camping About 6km out on the N-IV to Córdoba, just before Sevilla airport, is *Camping Sevilla* (☎ 95 451 43 79). It's open all year at 1790 ptas for two people with a car and tent, and runs a shuttle bus to/from Avenida de Portugal in the city.

Youth Hostels The Inturjoven *Albergue Juvenil Sevilla* (☎ 95 461 31 50, Calle Isaac Peral 2) has room for 277 in twins or triples. Take bus No 34 from opposite the main tourist office.

Hostales & Pensiones There are lots of places in the attractive Barrio de Santa Cruz, close to the cathedral, and north of Plaza Nueva.

Barrio de Santa Cruz Among several little places on Calle Archeros, friendly *Hostal Bienvenido* (☎ 95 441 36 55, Calle Archeros 14) has singles/doubles with shared bathrooms from 1900/3700 to 2200/4200 ptas. Just east, *Hostal La Montoreña* (☎ 95 441 24 07, Calle San Clemente 12) has clean, simple rooms at 2000/3000 ptas.

Friendly little *Huéspedes Dulces Sueños/ Sweet Dreams* (☎ 95 441 93 93, Calle Santa María La Blanca 21) has nice air-con rooms for 2000/4000 ptas, and singles with bath for 3500 ptas. *Pensión San Pancracio* (☎ 95 441 31 04, Plaza de las Cruces 9) has poky singles for 2000 ptas and bigger doubles for 3400 ptas (4000 ptas with bath). *Pensión Cruces* (☎ 95 422 60 41, Plaza de las Cruces 10) has a dorm room with beds at 1500 ptas, and singles/doubles at 2000/2500 to 4000/6000 ptas.

Pensión Vergara (☎ 95 421 56 68, Calle Ximénez de Enciso 11) consists of six brightly decorated rooms around the upper level of a 15th-century patio, at 2000/4000 ptas. Plants and skylights add to the cosy atmosphere.

Pensión Fabiola (☎ 95 421 83 46, Calle Fabiola 16), with a plant-filled courtyard, has simple, well-kept rooms for 3000/5000 ptas, and doubles with bath for 7000 ptas.

Hostal Goya (☎ 95 421 11 70, Calle Mateos Gago 31) has nice, clean rooms with private bathroom at 4300/6800 ptas, doubles with shower for 6000 ptas, and a pleasant sitting area.

North & West of Plaza Nueva Calle Gravina has several economical choices. Little *Hostal Romero* (☎ 95 421 13 53, Calle Gravina 21) offers clean, bare rooms with shared baths for 2000/3500 ptas.

Friendly *Hostal Unión* (☎ 95 422 92 94, Calle Tarifa 4) has nine good, clean rooms at 2000/3500 ptas, or 3000/4500 ptas with bath. *Hostal Pino* (☎ 95 421 28 10, Calle Tarifa 6), next door, is similarly priced.

Hostal Lis II (☎ 95 456 02 28, e lisII@ sol.com, Calle Olavide 5), which is in a pretty house, charges 2300/4500 ptas for basic rooms, or 5000 ptas for doubles with private bath.

Hostal Central (☎ 95 421 76 60, Calle Zaragoza 18) has well-kept, decent-sized rooms with bath for 4500/6500 ptas.

Places to Stay – Mid-Range
Barrio de Santa Cruz These first two places cut prices in July and August. *Hostería del Laurel* (☎ 95 422 02 95, e host-laurel@ eintec.es, Plaza de los Venerables 5) has 21 simple, attractive singles/doubles at 7000/9500 ptas plus IVA. *Hotel Murillo* (☎ 95 421 60 95, fax 95 421 96 16, Calle Lope de Rueda 7) has 57 less spic-and-span rooms for 4800/8300 ptas plus IVA.

Hostal Córdoba (☎ 95 422 74 98, Calle Farnesio 12) has nice air-con rooms for 5000/8000 ptas (7000/9500 ptas with a small shower room).

El Arenal This is a good, convenient location. *Hotel Simón* (☎ 95 422 66 60, fax 95 456 22 41, Calle García de Vinuesa 19), in a fine 18th-century house, has rooms at 6500/9500 ptas plus IVA. It's extremely popular, so book ahead. The bigger *Hotel La Rábida* (☎ 95 422 09 60, Calle Castelar 24) has good rooms at 6100/9300 ptas plus IVA.

North & West of Plaza Nueva At *Hotel Puerta de Triana* (☎ 95 421 54 04, fax 95 421 54 01, Calle Reyes Católicos 5), a good 65-room hotel in a modernised old house, doubles are 11,600 ptas plus IVA. *Patio de la Cartuja* (☎ 95 490 02 00, e patios@bbv.net, Calle Lumbreras 8-10), in an old patio building near the Alameda de Hércules, provides cosy apartments for 8800/11,000 ptas plus IVA (less in July and August).

Places to Stay – Top End
In the Barrio de Santa Cruz, *Las Casas de la Judería* (☎ 95 441 51 50, fax 95 442 21 70, Callejón de Dos Hermanas 7) is a group of charmingly restored old houses around several patios and fountains. Most of the 50-odd cosy singles/doubles cost 12,500/18,000 ptas plus IVA (less in July and August). Two other hotels in the same appealing small group, with similar rates, are in El Centro: *Las Casas de los Mercaderes* (☎ 95 422 58 58, Calle Álvarez Quintero 9-13) and *Las*

ANDALUCÍA

Casas del Rey de Baeza (☎ 95 456 14 96, *Plaza Cristo de la Redención 2*).

Farther west, *Hotel Becquer* (☎ 95 422 89 00, e hbecquer@arrakis.es, *Calle Reyes Católicos 4*) has 118 modern rooms for 13,000/15,000 ptas plus IVA.

Places to Eat
Sevilla is one of Spain's tapas capitals, with scores and scores of bars serving all sorts of tasty bites. To catch the city's atmosphere, you should certainly do some of your eating in bars.

Restaurants & Cafes Don't bother looking for dinner until at least 8 pm – very few kitchens get going for the evening before then.

Barrio de Santa Cruz & Around A good spot for breakfast is *Cervecería Giralda* (*Calle Mateos Gago 1*). Varied *tostadas* are from 120 to 480 ptas. The bustling *Café de Indias* (*Avenida de la Constitución 10*), opposite the cathedral, provides a large range of caffeine fixes starting at 150 ptas.

Hostería del Laurel (*Plaza de los Venerables 5*) has an atmospheric old bar with a wide range of good *media-raciones* (half portions of tapas), from 550 to 1500 ptas, and *raciones* (meal-sized serve of tapas). *Pizzeria San Marco* (*Calle Mesón del Moro 6*), in a refurbished Muslim bathhouse, is extremely popular for its pizzas and pastas at around 850 ptas (closed Monday).

Calle Santa María La Blanca has several busy places with outdoor tables: at the *Carmela* (*Calle Santa María La Blanca 6*) a media-ración of *tortilla Alta-Mira* (with potatoes and vegetables) is almost a meal for 700 ptas. Busy little *Bar Casa Fernando* around the corner serves good-value *platos del día* (plates of the day) for 500 ptas. *Restaurante Modesto* (*Calle Cano y Cueto 5*) specialises in seafood, with main dishes starting at 1200 ptas.

Corral del Agua (☎ 95 422 07 14, *Callejón del Agua 6*) has good, inventive food and its cool, green courtyard is great on a hot day, if you can get a table. Main courses (1900 to 2500 ptas) include good fish choices and varied dishes of the day.

Perhaps the best meals in this part of town are at *Restaurante La Albahaca* (☎ 95 422 07 14, *Plaza de Santa Cruz 12*), which provides such fare as roast wild boar with fig jam and apple puree. There's a *menú del día* (daily set meal) for 3500 ptas plus IVA.

El Arenal For a good selection of *platos combinados* from 800 ptas, try *Mesón Serranito* (*Calle Antonia Díaz 9*). Busy *Bodega Paco Góngora* (*Calle Padre Marchena 1*) serves a huge range of good seafood at decent prices – media-raciones of fish *a la plancha* (grilled) are mostly 675 ptas.

El Centro At *Restaurante San Marco* (*Calle de la Cuna 6*), in an 18th-century mansion, there's good pizza and pasta at around 1000 ptas.

Habanita (*Calle Golfo 3*), off Calle Pérez Galdós, nearby, serves a winning variety of Cuban, *andaluz* (Andalucian) and vegetarian food. Raciones are 700 to 1500 ptas and media-raciones are 350 to 800 ptas; it's closed winter Sunday evenings.

Bodegón Alfonso XII (*Calle Alfonso XII 33*), near the Museo de Bellas Artes, is excellent value with deals such as media-raciones of cheese, ham and spinach *revuelto* (scrambled) for 550 ptas.

Triana Calle del Betis on the western bank of the Río Guadalquivir, looking across to the city centre, has several very popular restaurants, including an Italian trio: *Pizzeria San Marco* (*Calle del Betis 68*), serving mostly pizzas and pasta at around 850 ptas; *Pizzeria O Mamma Mia* (*Calle del Betis 33*), which is slightly more economical; and the good *Ristorante Cosa Nostra* (*Calle del Betis 50*), with pizza for 650 to 1000 ptas and pasta for 650 to 1200 ptas. *Kiosco de las Flores*, on the river bank, is Sevilla's favourite *pescaito frito* (fried fish) eatery; it also serves raciones for around 1200 ptas.

Tapas Bars An evening of tapas-hopping round Sevilla's bars is one of the city's most enjoyable experiences. Most of these places open at lunchtime too.

Tapas in Sevilla

A few Sevilla tapas favourites to try out are:

caña de lomo – pork loin (can be expensive)

cazón en adobo – dogfish marinated in vinegar, salt, lemon and spices, then deep-fried (delicious)

espinacas con garbanzos – spinach and chick peas

papas aliñás – sliced potatoes and boiled eggs, with vegetable garnish and a vinaigrette dressing

pavía – battered fish or seafood

puntillitas – baby squid, usually deep-fried

Barrio de Santa Cruz On Calle Mateos Gago, *Bodega Santa Cruz*, a bar popular with visitors and locals, has a big choice of decent-sized tapas, most at 175 to 200 ptas. *Cervecería Giralda (Calle Mateos Gago 1)* has a wonderful variety of good tapas, some of which are pretty exotic, for 250 to 300 ptas. Some are tiny, though. *Café Bar Las Teresas (Calle Santa Teresa 2)* is an atmospheric old-style bar with good tapas from 150 to 275 ptas.

El Arenal A kind of tapas *haute cuisine* is served at *Mesón de la Infanta (Calle Dos de Mayo 26)*, with some delicious items composed of five or six complementary elements (250 to 400 ptas).

El Centro Near Plaza de la Alfalfa, *Sopa de Ganso (Calle Pérez Galdós 8)* offers innovative tapas combinations such as chicken and date brochette, and usually has vegetarian tapas options. It has great cakes too, and plays good music for its lively, youthful clientele.

On the corner of Calle Alfalfa and Calle Candilejo, tiny *La Bodega Extremeña* serves superb meat and cheese tapas and *montaditos* (small sandwiches) for 175 to 275 ptas – try *huevos codorniz jamón* (eggs with quail and ham). For succulent and generous tapas of meat *a la brasa* (chargrilled), head a few minutes east to another

Bodega Extremeña (Calle San Esteban 17); the *solomillo ibérico* (sirloin Iberian) is only 275 ptas.

Westward is the bright and busy *Patio San Eloy (Calle San Eloy 9)*, where *burguillos*, small *bocadillos* (filled rolls) with home-made bread, and good tapas of ham, cheese, smoked salmon, pork and more go for 175 to 215 ptas.

To the north, *El Rinconcillo (Calle Gerona 40)* is Sevilla's oldest bar, founded in 1670. The tapas, from *espinacas con garbanzos* (spinach with chickpea; 200 ptas) to *tortilla de jamón serrano* (ham omelette; 650 ptas), are straightforward but good.

Self-Catering Central Sevilla's two food markets are the *Mercado del Arenal* on Calle Pastor y Landero, and the *Mercado de la Encarnación* on Plaza de la Encarnación.

Entertainment

Several free publications have what's-on listings: look for *Casco Antiguo, El Giraldillo, Welcome & Olé* and *The Tourist*.

Bars Sevilla's vibrant bar and music scene really gets going at about midnight or 1 am on Friday and Saturday nights. But bars begin to fill from 10 pm most nights. In summer dozens of *terrazas de verano* (open-air late-night bars), many with live music, spring up beside the Guadalquivir.

Barrio de Santa Cruz There are some hugely popular bars just north of the cathedral: *P Flaherty Irish Pub (Calle Alemanes)* gets packed with locals and visitors alike – 600 ptas for your pint of Guinness.

In the heart of Santa Cruz, small bars such as *Bodega Santa Cruz*, on Calle Mateos Gago (see Places to Eat), and *Bar Entrecalles*, on Calle Ximénez de Enciso, can get pretty lively with a mixed crowd of visitors and locals.

El Arenal An old-fashioned *bodega* (winery-bar), *Hajjis de E Morales (Calle García de Vinuesa 11)* serves wine and sherry from the barrel in a large back room where old wine casks serve as tables. A little

ANDALUCÍA

farther west, around Calle de Adriano, the crowds (mostly young) some nights have to be seen to be believed. Busy music bars on Adriano with inexpensive drinks include *A3* and *Arena*.

Café Isbiliyya *(Paseo de Colón 2)* is a bustling gay music bar – mostly men – overflowing on to the street on busy nights.

El Centro From mid-evening to around 1 am, Plaza Salvador is a very popular spot for an open-air drink, with a student crowd and a couple of little bars selling carry-out drinks. Calle Pérez Galdós, off Plaza de la Alfalfa, has at least five throbbing music bars. You should find at least one to your fancy.

Alameda de Hércules Several excellent bars and some live music attract an offbeat crowd to this former red-light district north of the centre. *El Corto Maltés*, *Café Central* and the especially bohemian *Habanilla Café* are all busy pub-like places spilling out on to the street on the eastern side of the Alameda. *Bulebar Café (Alameda de Hércules 83)* is a relaxed place for a drink, with comfy old-fashioned furniture and a courtyard out the front.

There's an international crowd and always a buzz at *La Ilustre Víctima (Calle Doctor Letamendi 35)*, open daily until 2 am (4 am Friday and Saturday nights). The music and tapas are great, and beer costs 150 ptas.

Triana Calle del Betis, on the western bank of the Guadalquivir, has a string of lively bars, including *Alambique*, *Mui d'Aqui*, *Big Ben* and *Café La Pavana*, all playing good music and attracting an interestingly mixed crowd. They open at around 9 pm. *La Otra Orilla*, on Paseo de Nuestra Señora de la O, is a buzzing music bar with a great terrace overlooking the river.

Live Music *Almacén* bar (☎ 95 490 04 34), at La Imperdible arts centre, Plaza San Antonio de Padua 9, a few blocks west of the Alameda de Hércules, stages varied free music from around 11 pm Thursday to Saturday – from soul to psychedelic punks to beat-beat DJs.

Salamandra (☎ 95 490 28 38, Calle de Torneo 43), a little farther west, has varied bands – ethnic, Latin, blues – most often around 9 pm on Friday and Saturday; entry is usually 800 to 1200 ptas.

Fun Club (Alameda de Hércules 86) is a small dance warehouse open Thursday to Sunday. Live bands play Friday and/or Saturday from around 9.30 pm and entry is 500 to 1000 ptas, with drinks from 250 ptas.

Flamenco You're most likely to catch spontaneous atmosphere in one of the bars staging regular nights of flamenco or *sevillanas* with no entry charge. Quality is unpredictable!

In the Barrio de Santa Cruz, *La Carbonería* (☎ 95 421 44 60, Calle Levíes 18), with two large rooms, is thronged nearly every night with visitors and locals who've come to enjoy the scene and hear live music – nearly always flamenco – from about 11 pm to 4 am. A glass of wine is around 250 ptas. Jolly crowds pack into *El Tamboril* on Plaza de Santa Cruz to enjoy live sevillanas and rumba every night from 10 pm.

El Mundo (Calle Siete Revueltas 5), along a dark alley near Plaza Salvador, has flamenco on Tuesday at 11 pm.

In Triana, one of flamenco's birthplaces, there is live flamenco at 10 pm on Thursday at *La Sonanta* (Calle San Jacinto 31), and on Friday night at *El Tejar* (Calle San Jacinto 68).

Salamandra (mentioned earlier) has flamenco nights on Thursday at 11 pm, with an entry charge of 1500 ptas, including a drink.

Big-name flamenco artists make fairly frequent appearances at some of Sevilla's theatres, especially the *Teatro Central* (☎ 95 446 07 80), on Isla de La Cartuja, and the *Teatro de la Maestranza* (☎ 95 422 65 73, Paseo de Cristóbal Colón 22). Sevilla stages a major flamenco festival, the Bienal de Flamenco, in September of even-numbered years.

Hotels will steer you towards the expensive, tourist-oriented tablaos. These can lack atmosphere, but *Los Gallos* (☎ 95 421 69 81, Plaza de Santa Cruz 11) is a cut above the average. It stages two-hour shows

ANDALUCÍA

at 9 and 11.30 pm nightly for 3500 ptas, including one drink.

Clubs & Discos These come and go rapidly. People might think of going to one around 2 to 4 am on a weekend. The big noise at the time of writing was *Luna Park (Avenida de María Luisa s/n)*, with three separate halls, including one each for salsa and *bacalao* (Spanish techno).

Spectator Sports
Sevilla's Plaza de Toros bullring on Paseo de Cristóbal Colón holds 14,000 spectators. The season runs from Easter to October, with fights every Sunday, usually at 6.30 pm, and daily during the Feria de Abril and the preceding week. Up to late June/early July, nearly all fights are by fully fledged matadors and often only *sol* (sun) seats, starting at 3000 ptas, are available to those without season tickets. Most of the rest of the season, junior matadors fight young bulls: tickets start at 1500 ptas.

Shopping
The craft shops in the Barrio de Santa Cruz are inevitably tourist-oriented, but many sell excellent local ceramics.

Pedestrianised Calle Sierpes in the city centre is the heart of the fanciest shopping area, lined with shops devoted to a great range of everyday and luxury goods. El Corte Inglés department store occupies four separate buildings a little west, on Plaza de la Magdalena and Plaza del Duque de la Victoria. Farther north, Calle Amor de Dios and Calle Doctor Letamendi make for an interesting browse, with more alternative-style shops.

The large Thursday *mercadillo* (flea market) on Calle de la Feria is a colourful event that's well worth a visit. The Sunday morning mercadillo on the Alameda de Hércules is interesting too.

Getting There & Away
Air Sevilla airport (☎ 95 444 90 00) has quite a range of domestic and international flights. Iberia, Air Europa and Spanair all fly nonstop to/from Barcelona (from 16,500/18,500 ptas one way/return with Air Europa). Iberia also flies daily nonstop to/from London, Madrid, Valencia and Bilbao. British Airways flies to/from London nonstop.

The Iberia office (☎ 95 498 82 08) is east of the centre at Edificio Cecofar, Avenida de la Buhaira. Air Europa tickets are sold at Halcón Viajes (☎ 95 421 44 56), Calle Almirante Bonifaz 3. Spanair (☎ 95 444 90 33) is at the airport.

Bus From the Prado de San Sebastián bus station (☎ 95 441 71 11) on Plaza San Sebastián, there are nine or more buses daily to/from Córdoba (1¾ hours, 1225 ptas), Granada (three hours, 2400 ptas), Málaga (2½ hours, 1900 ptas), Jerez de la Frontera, Sanlúcar de Barrameda and Cádiz (1¾ hours, 1385 ptas), and a few to/from Ronda (2½ hours, 1335 ptas). This is also the station for Arcos de la Frontera, Tarifa, Algeciras, the Costa del Sol, Jaén, Valencia and Barcelona.

From the Plaza de Armas bus station (☎ 95 490 80 40), numerous buses run daily to/from Madrid (six hours, 2745 ptas), Huelva (1¼ hours, 900 ptas), Mérida (3¼ hours, 1700 ptas) and Zafra; and a few to/from El Rocío, Matalascañas, Cáceres (four hours, 2200 ptas), Salamanca and Galicia. To/from Lisbon there are five or more direct buses a week (eight hours, 4800 ptas). Daily buses run to/from places on Portugal's Algarve such as Faro, Albufeira and Lagos (4½ to six hours, 2135 to 2600 ptas).

Train Santa Justa station (☎ 95 454 02 02) is 1.5km north-east of the centre on Avenida Kansas City. The central Renfe ticket office, Calle Zaragoza 31, is open 9 am to 1.15 pm and 4 to 7 pm weekdays.

Fourteen super-fast AVE trains in each direction daily cover the 471km between Sevilla and Madrid in just 2¼ to 2½ hours, costing 8400 or 9900 ptas in the cheapest class *(turista)*; a few other trains take 3¼ to 3¾ hours for 6600 to 8300 ptas. AVEs reach speeds of 280km/h and if they arrive more than five minutes late, you get your money back (don't get excited: this happens very rarely).

ANDALUCÍA

Other trains from Sevilla include: about 20 daily to Córdoba (45 minutes to 1¼ hours, 1090 to 2800 ptas); up to 15 to Jerez de la Frontera and Cádiz (1½ to 2¼ hours, 1125 to 2100 ptas); three to five each to Granada (2¾ to 3½ hours, 2415 to 2665 ptas), Málaga (2¼ to 2½ hours, 2130 ptas), Huelva (1½ hours, 995 ptas) and Barcelona (10½ to 12½ hours, from 6300 ptas); two to Valencia (8½ hours, from 5300 ptas); and one each to Mérida (4½ hours, 1685 ptas), Cáceres and Jaén (three hours, 2225 ptas). For Lisbon (16 hours, 7000 ptas) you must change at Cáceres.

Car & Motorcycle If you're staying in the Barrio de Santa Cruz, you can usually park in streets such as Avenida de Cádiz, five minutes' walk away, east of Avenida Menéndez Pelayo.

Car rental is expensive. Try the local firms along Calle Almirante Lobo, off Paseo de Cristobal Colón.

Car Pooling Compartecoche (☎ 95 490 75 82), Calle González Cuadrado 49, is an intercity car-pooling service. Its service is free to drivers, while passengers pay an agreed transfer rate. Ring or visit between 10 am and 1.30 pm or 5 and 8 pm.

Getting Around
To/From the Airport Sevilla airport is about 7km from the centre off the N-IV Córdoba road. Amarillos Tour buses (☎ 902-21 03 17) make the 30-minute trip between the airport and the Puerta de Jerez, in front of Hotel Alfonso XIII, at least nine times daily (350 ptas one way). A taxi is about 2000 ptas.

Bus Bus Nos C1, C2, C3 and C4 follow circular routes linking the main transport terminals and the city centre. From Santa Justa train station the eastbound C1 follows a clockwise route via Avenida de Carlos V (close to Prado de San Sebastián bus station and the Barrio de Santa Cruz), Avenida de María Luisa, Triana, Isla Mágica and Calle de Resolana. No C2 follows the same route in reverse. Bus No 32, from the same stop as No C2, runs to/from Plaza de la Encarnación in El Centro.

The clockwise No C3 goes from Avenida Menéndez Pelayo (near Prado de San Sebastián bus station) to Puerta de Jerez, Triana, Plaza de Armas bus station, Calle de Resolana and Calle de Recaredo. The C4 does the same circuit anticlockwise except that from Plaza de Armas bus station it heads south along Paseo de Cristóbal Colón to Puerta de Jerez, instead of crossing the river to Triana. Bus fares are 125 ptas.

Bicycle Sevilla Mágica (☎ 95 456 38 38), Calle Miguel de Mañara 11B, near the main tourist office, rents out bikes for 2000 ptas a day, Monday to Saturday.

AROUND SEVILLA
Itálica
Itálica, 8km north-west of Sevilla on the north-western edge of the small town of Santiponce, was the first Roman town in Spain – founded in 206 BC for veterans of Rome's victory over Carthage at nearby Ilipa. Itálica was also the home town of the 2nd-century Roman emperors Trajan and Hadrian. The partly reconstructed ruins include one of the biggest of all Roman amphitheatres, a large public bathhouse, some excellent mosaics and a theatre. The site is open 9 am to 8 pm Tuesday to Saturday (to 5.30 pm October to March), 10 am to 3 pm Sunday and holidays (to 4 pm October to March). It's free with an EU passport or identity card; otherwise, 250 ptas.

Frequent buses run to Santiponce from Plaza de Armas bus station.

LA CAMPIÑA
This rolling, fertile area east of Sevilla is still mainly a land of huge agricultural estates, but the history and architecture of towns such as Carmona, Écija, Osuna and Estepa make them well worth a detour.

Carmona
postcode 41410 • pop 24,000
Carmona, fortified since the 8th century BC, is just off the N-IV, 38km east of Sevilla. Frequent buses from Sevilla (Prado de San Sebastián) stop on Paseo del Estatuto, 300m west of the old town. The

helpful tourist office (☎ 95 419 09 55), in the Puerta de Sevilla at the western end of the old town, is open 10 am to 6 pm Monday to Saturday and until 3 pm Sunday and holidays.

Things to See Carmona's **Necrópolis Romana** is at Avenida de Jorge Bonsor 9, just over 1km west of the Puerta de Sevilla. Here you can climb down into a dozen or more elaborate Roman tombs hewn from the rock. From 15 June to 15 September the necropolis is open 10 am to 2 pm Tuesday to Saturday; the rest of the year, hours are 9 am to 5 pm Tuesday to Friday and 10 am to 2 pm Saturday and Sunday (free for EU passport holders, 250 ptas for others).

The tourist office in the **Puerta de Sevilla**, the impressive fortified main gate of the old town, sells tickets (200 ptas) for the interesting upper levels of the gate, called the Alcázar de la Puerta de Sevilla, which includes an Almohad patio and traces of a Roman temple.

Up into the old town from here, the 18th-century **ayuntamiento** on Calle El Salvador (open 8 am to 3 pm weekdays) contains a large, very fine Roman mosaic. Nearby, Calle Martín López de Córdoba leads to the **Iglesia Prioral de Santa María**, built mainly in the 15th and 16th centuries in a typical Carmona combination of brick and stone. Its Patio de los Naranjos, originally a mosque's courtyard, has a Visigothic calendar carved in one of its pillars. It's open 10 am to 2 pm and 5 to 7 pm daily except Sunday morning and Monday (400 ptas).

Continuing along the same street you reach the **Puerta de Córdoba**, an originally Roman gate through which there are fine panoramas. South of here is the **Alcázar**, an Almohad fort that Pedro I turned into a country palace. Ruined by an earthquake in 1504, it was in part restored as a *parador* (historic luxury hotel) in the 1970s.

Places to Stay The small *Casa Carmelo* (☎ 95 414 05 72, Calle San Pedro 17), outside the Puerta de Sevilla, has doubles starting at 4000 ptas. *Pensión Comercio* (☎ 95 414 00 18, Calle Torre del Oro 56), just north

of the Puerta de Sevilla, is a lovely old building with 14 well-kept rooms for 2500/5000 ptas a single/double, or 6000 ptas for doubles with bath (about 25% more, March to May). *Parador Alcázar del Rey Don Pedro* (☎ 95 414 10 10, ℮ carmona@parador.es), in the Alcázar, has rooms at 14,800/18,500 ptas plus IVA.

Osuna
postcode 41640 • pop 17,000

Osuna, 91km from Sevilla just off the A-92, is a pleasant place with some impressive buildings, several of them created by the ducal family of Osuna, one of Spain's richest since the 17th century. The useful tourist office (☎ 95 582 14 00) is on the handsome Plaza Mayor.

Things to See Most impressive are the big buildings on the hill overlooking the centre. On the way up from Plaza Mayor, there's a **Museo Arqueológico**, which is open daily except Monday (300 ptas). Above here, the 16th-century **Colegiata de Santa María** church contains a wealth of sacred art, including several paintings by José de Ribera. It's open for guided tours from approximately 10 am to 1.30 pm and 4 to 7 pm daily except Monday (300 ptas). The visit includes the lugubrious Sepulcro Ducal, the Osuna family vault. Opposite is the **Convento de la Encarnación**, now a museum with mainly religious art and artefacts; open the same hours as the Colegiata (250 ptas).

Places to Stay *Hostal 5 Puertas* (☎ 95 481 12 43, Calle Carrera 79), five minutes' walk north of Plaza Mayor, has decent singles/doubles for 2500/5000 ptas (more in April and May). *Hostal Caballo Blanco* (☎ 95 481 01 84, Calle Granada 1), an old coaching inn across the street, charges 3500/6000 ptas, and has a restaurant.

Getting There & Away Half a dozen daily buses run to/from Sevilla (Prado de San Sebastián), four to/from Antequera and a few to/from Málaga. Three trains daily run to/from Sevilla, Antequera, Granada and Málaga.

ANDALUCÍA

Huelva Province

Andalucía's westernmost province includes most of the Parque Nacional de Doñana, whose famous wetlands are a bird habitat of huge international importance. The *lugares colombinos* (Columbus sites) east of Huelva city will fascinate anyone with a historical leaning. Also along Huelva's coasts are around half the excellent beaches of the Costa de la Luz. Aracena in the north is the focus of this beautiful hill-country district.

HUELVA

postcode 21080 • pop 140,000

The province's likeable but unspectacular capital, a port and industrial city, was probably founded by the Phoenicians as a trading settlement about 3000 years ago, but much of it was destroyed by the Lisbon earthquake of 1755.

Orientation

The central area is about 1km square, with the bus station on its western edge on Calle Doctor Rubio, and the train station on its southern edge on Avenida de Italia. Plaza de las Monjas is the central square; the main street, Avenida Martín Alonso Pinzón (also called Gran Vía), leads south-east from here, eventually becoming Alameda Sundheim.

Information

The tourist office (☎ 959 25 74 03), at Avenida de Alemania 12, a few steps from the bus station, is open 9 am to 7 pm weekdays and 10 am to 2 pm Saturday.

The Hospital General Juan Ramón Jiménez (☎ 959 20 10 88) is on the Ronda Exterior Norte ring road, 4km north of the centre. The Policía Local (☎ 959 21 02 21) are on Avenida Tomás Domínguez, opposite the main post office.

Museo de Huelva

At Alameda Sundheim 13, this museum is undergoing a long-term revamp, but its highlight section on prehistoric Huelva province

and Tartessos is already open. Exhibits include a reproduction of the Carambolo gold hoard found near Sevilla. The opening hours are 9 am to 8 pm Tuesday to Saturday and until 3 pm Sunday (free).

Places to Stay

Hostal Calvo (☎ 959 24 90 16, Calle Rascón 35), near the Mercado del Carmen fish market, has basic but clean singles/ doubles with shared baths for 1200/2400 ptas. **Pensión La Vega** (☎ 959 24 15 63, Paseo de la Independencia 15), near the cathedral, is better. Rooms are 1750/3500 ptas; doubles with bath are 4000 ptas.

Hotel Los Condes (☎ 959 28 24 00, Alameda Sundheim 14) has 54 air-con rooms with bath for 4500/7500 ptas plus IVA. The modern **Hotel Tartessos** (☎ 959 28 27 11, Avenida Martín Alonso Pinzón 13) has 112 comfy air-con doubles at 12,500 ptas plus IVA.

Places to Eat

Oh La La (Calle Berdigón 26), just south of Avenida Martín Alonso Pinzón, packs 'em in for its baguettes (300 to 475 ptas), and pizza and pasta (500 to 850 ptas). Nearby, **Los Encinares** (Calle Garcí-Fernández 5) serves excellent grills such as *brocheta de solomillo ibérico con patatas* (sirloin Iberian with potato; 1700 ptas).

To the north, Avenida Pablo Rado is lined with popular eateries, many of them with terrazas. Westward, **Camillo e Peppone** on Calle Isaac Peral serves up excellent pasta and pizza for 550 to 1000 ptas; it's open 1 to 4.30 pm and 9.30 pm to 1 am Thursday to Tuesday.

Entertainment

Late-night crowds flock to the bars and terrazas lining Avenida Pablo Rada and the bars in the streets south of the city's cathedral.

Getting There & Away

Bus From the bus station (☎ 959 25 69 00), frequent buses head to/from Sevilla (1¼ hours, 900 ptas), and three or four daily to Madrid. For Portugal, Transportes Agobe runs buses on Monday, Wednesday and Friday to Albufeira and Lisbon, and Damas has daily buses to Tavira, Faro, Albufeira and Lagos.

Train From the train station (☎ 959 24 56 14), three trains run daily to Sevilla (1½ hours, 995 ptas), and one to Madrid and Córdoba (two hours, 2400 ptas).

LUGARES COLOMBINOS

The small towns of La Rábida, Palos de la Frontera and Moguer, three key sites in the Columbus story, lie along the eastern bank of the Río Tinto estuary and can all be visited in a 40km return trip from Huelva. At least 10 buses daily travel from Huelva's bus station to La Rábida and Palos; some continue to Mazagón, but most to Moguer.

La Rábida

Columbus visited the **Monasterio de La Rábida** several times while planning his voyage, and won influential support from a monk here, Antonio de Marchena, and abbot Juan Pérez, a former confessor of Queen Isabel La Católica. Absorbing monk-guided tours of the monastery are given in simple Spanish, every 45 minutes from 10 am to 1 pm and 4 to 6.15 pm daily except Monday. You pay by donation at the end.

On the waterfront below the monastery is the **Muelle de las Carabelas** (Wharf of the Caravels), with replicas of Columbus' ships and an exhibition on his life. From 20 April to 20 September it's open 10 am to 2 pm and 5 to 9 pm Tuesday to Friday, and 11 am to 8 pm Saturday, Sunday and holidays. In other months, hours are 10 am to 7 pm daily except Monday (430 ptas).

Palos de la Frontera

Palos was the port where Columbus set sail and which provided two of his ships and more than half his crew, including cousins Vicente Yañez Pinzón and Martín Alonso Pinzón, captains of the ships *Niña* and *Pinta* respectively. Palos' access to the Tinto is now silted up.

Buses stop on the central plaza. The **Casa Museo Martín Alonso Pinzón**, a short walk uphill at Calle Colón 24, is open 10.30 am to 1.30 pm and 5 to 7.30 pm weekdays (free), was the home of the *Pinta's* captain. Farther along Calle Colón is the 14th-century **Iglesia de San Jorge**, open 10.30 am to 1 pm and 7 to 8 pm weekdays. Columbus and his men took communion here before embarking on 3 August 1492. In a park down the street is **La Fontanilla**, a well where Columbus' crew drew water. A plaque marks the site of the *embarcadero* from which they sailed.

Moguer

This pleasant small town provided many of Columbus' crew. It has a tourist office (☎ 959 37 23 77) at Calle Andalucía 5, a few steps off the central Plaza del Cabildo. The **Monasterio de Santa Clara** on Plaza de las Monjas, up the street almost opposite, is where Columbus kept vigil the night after his voyage. It's open for guided visits at 11 am, noon and 1, 5, 6 and 7 pm Tuesday to Saturday (300 ptas).

Moguer was also the birthplace of the 1956 Nobel literature laureate Juan Ramón Jiménez, who wrote of childhood wanderings here with his donkey in his famous *Platero y Yo* (Platero and I). The **Casa Museo Juan Ramón** at Calle Juan Ramón Jiménez 10, a five-minute walk from Plaza del Cabildo, is open for guided visits several times daily except Sunday afternoon and holidays (300 ptas).

Places to Stay

Just off Palos' central plaza, ***Pensión Rábida*** *(☎ 959 35 01 63, Calle Rábida 9)* has singles/doubles with shared bathroom at 1500/3000 ptas. Farther along the same street, the better ***Hotel La Pinta*** *(☎ 959 35 05 11, Calle Rábida 79)* charges 6000/ 10,000 ptas.

In Moguer, three central hostales, ***Hostal Platero*** *(☎ 959 37 21 59, Calle Aceña 4)*, ***Hostal Pedro Alonso Niño*** *(☎ 959 37 23 92, Calle Pedro Alonso Niño 13)* and ***Hostal Lis*** *(☎ 959 37 03 78, Calle Andalucía 6)*, all have doubles between 2600 and 3200 ptas.

ANDALUCÍA

PARQUE NACIONAL DE DOÑANA

The Parque Nacional de Doñana or Doñana National Park, one of Europe's most important wetlands, covers 507 sq km in the south-east of Huelva province and neighbouring Sevilla province. This World Heritage Site is not only a vital refuge for such endangered species as the pardel lynx and Spanish imperial eagle (with populations here of about 50 and 15 respectively), but also a crucial habitat for six million other birds that spend part of the year here.

Visiting the interior of the national park requires booking ahead for a guided tour.

These go from the Centro de Visitantes El Acebuche on the western side of the park (see later in this section) and from Sanlúcar de Barrameda (see Cádiz Province later in this chapter). However, there are also some interesting surrounding areas that you can visit freely, especially in the 540-sq-km Parque Natural de Doñana, comprising four discrete zones bordering the national park.

Since its creation in 1969 the national park has always had to battle agricultural and tourism schemes around its fringes that threaten its water supplies. But the biggest threat came in 1998 when a dam broke at a

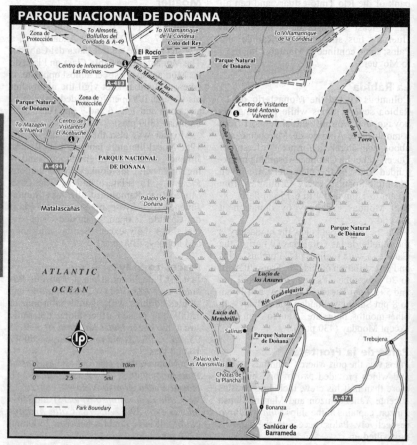

PARQUE NACIONAL DE DOÑANA

ANDALUCÍA

About 15 of the 130 remaining pairs of Spanish imperial eagles live in Parque Nacional de Doñana.

Doñana Ecosystems

Half the national park consists of *marismas* (marshes) of the Guadalquivir delta. The park contains only about one-tenth of the Guadalquivir marismas but most of those outside it have been drained or channelled for agriculture. The park's marismas are almost dry from July to October but in autumn they fill with water, attracting hundreds of thousands of water birds from the north to winter here, including an estimated 80% of Western Europe's wild ducks. As the waters sink in spring, other birds – greater flamingoes, spoonbills, storks, hoopoes, bee-eaters – arrive, many to nest. In summer they flock around the shrinking ponds, and in July, herons, storks and kites move in to feast on trapped perch.

Between the park's 28km Atlantic beach and the marismas is a band of moving sand dunes, up to 5km wide, which are blown inland at a rate of up to 6m a year. When dune sand reaches the marismas, it is carried back down to the sea, which washes it up on the beach where wind begins the cycle again. The beach and dunes make up 102 sq km of the park.

In other parts of the park, stable sand supports 144 sq km of *coto* (woodland and scrub), with an abundant mammal population, including deer, wild boar and semiwild horses.

heavy-metals mine at Aznalcóllar, 50km north, releasing nearly seven million cubic metres of water and mud loaded with acids and heavy metals into the Río Guadiamar, one of the chief waterways feeding Doñana's wetlands. Hastily erected dikes prevented the flood from entering all but a small corner of the national park, but biologists and environmentalists fear the effects may be felt for decades to come, through poisons entering Doñana's water table and the food chain of its birds and animals.

Getting There & Away

Damas runs three or more buses daily between Sevilla and Matalascañas at the south-western corner of the national park, via El Rocío at the north-western corner (1½ hours from Sevilla, 660 ptas). The El Rocío–Matalascañas road is also covered by three to six daily buses each way between Almonte and Matalascañas. All these will stop outside the Las Rocinas and El Acebuche national park centres.

You can travel between Huelva and El Rocío by changing buses at Almonte.

El Rocío
postcode 21750 • pop 690

El Rocío overlooks a section of the marismas at the north-western corner of the national park, which has water all year. Its sandy streets bear as many hoofprints as tyre marks, and are lined by rows of usually-empty verandaed buildings. But this is no ghost town: most of the houses belong to the 90-odd *hermandades* (brotherhoods) of pilgrim-revellers who converge on El Rocío every year for the Romería del Rocío (see the boxed text). Indeed, a fiesta atmosphere pervades the village most weekends as hermandades arrive to carry out lesser rituals.

Information There's a tourist office (☎ 959 44 26 84), open 10 am to 2 pm daily, at Avenida de la Canaliega s/n by the main road at the western end of the village. The Centro de Información Las Rocinas (see Things to See & Do) has national park information.

ANDALUCÍA

Things to See & Do The heart of the village is the **Ermita del Rocío**, the church housing the celebrated Virgen del Rocío, a tiny wooden image dressed in long, bejewelled robes. It's open from about 8 am to 9 pm daily, with people arriving to pay their respects every day.

In the **marismas**, deer and horses graze in the shallows and you might see a flock of flamingoes wheeling through the sky in a great pink cloud. The Spanish Ornithological Society's waterside **Observatorio Madre del Rocío** is open to the public 10 am to 2 pm and 4 to 7 pm Tuesday to Sunday (free).

The bridge over the river on the A-483, 1km south of the village, is another good viewing spot. Just past the bridge is the **Centro de Información Las Rocinas** (☎ 959 44 23 40), open 9 am to 3 pm and 4 to 7, 8 or 9 pm (depending on the season) daily. It has national park information and short paths to nearby bird-watching hides.

For a longer walk from El Rocío, head across the Puente del Ajolí at the north-eastern edge of the village and into the woodland ahead. This is the **Coto del Rey**, a large woodland zone where in the early morning or late evening you may spot deer or boar.

You can hire **horses** at various places in El Rocío.

Places to Stay & Eat Don't bother even trying for a room at Romería time. *Pensión Cristina* (☎ 959 44 24 13, Calle El Real 58), a short distance east of the Ermita, has reasonable singles/doubles with private bath for 3000/4000 ptas, and a restaurant where paella or venison and chips will cost you 700 ptas.

Hotel Toruño (☎ 959 44 23 23, Plaza Acebuchal 22), a little farther east, has 30 attractive air-con rooms with bath at 6260/8560 ptas. Some have marismas views. The larger *Hotel Puente del Rey* (☎ 959 44 25 75, Avenida de la Canaliega s/n), by the main road, charges 7275/9200 ptas for its rooms (more in August and during festive weekends).

There are several cafes, bars and restaurants around the village.

Romería del Rocío

The Romería del Rocío (Pilgrimage to El Rocío) is a vast festive cult that pulls people from all over Spain. This quintessentially Andalucian event is focused on one of Spain's holiest images, Nuestra Señora del Rocío, or La Blanca Paloma (White Dove), which has legendary origins from soon after the Reconquista.

Back in the 13th century, the story goes, a hunter from Almonte found her in a tree in the marismas. Carrying her home, he stopped for a rest, and the Virgin made her own way back to the tree. Before long a chapel was built where the tree had stood (El Rocío) and pilgrims began making for it. By the 17th century, hermandades were forming in nearby towns to make an annual pilgrimage to El Rocío at Pentecost, the seventh weekend after Easter (2–4 June in 2001, 18–20 May in 2002).

Today, over 90 hermandades, some of several thousand men and women, travel to El Rocío on foot, on horseback, and in gaily decorated covered wagons pulled by cattle or horses, using cross-country tracks.

In an atmosphere similar to Sevilla's Feria de Abril, participants dress in bright Andalucian costume and sing, dance, drink and romance their way to El Rocío. The total number of people in the village on this special weekend can reach a million or more.

The weekend comes to an ecstatic climax in the early hours of the Monday. Members of the hermandad of Almonte, which claims the Virgin for its own, barge into the church and bear her out on a float. Violent struggles ensue as others battle with the Almonte lads for the honour of carrying La Blanca Paloma. The crush and chaos is immense but somehow good humour survives and the Virgin is carried round to each of the hermandad buildings, finally being returned to the Ermita in the afternoon.

Centro de Visitantes El Acebuche

Twelve kilometres south on the A-483 from El Rocío, then 1.6km west, El Acebuche (☎ 959 44 87 11) is the national park's main visitors centre and the starting point for tours into the park. Open daily 8 am to 7, 8 or 9 pm, it also has footpaths to bird-watching hides overlooking a lagoon.

National Park Tours Trips in 20-person all-terrain vehicles from El Acebuche are the only way for ordinary folk to get inside the park from the western side. You need to book ahead on ☎ 959 43 04 32; for spring, summer and holiday times the trips can fill up over a month ahead, but otherwise a week or less is usually adequate. Bring binoculars if you can and, except in winter, cover up against mosquitoes or bring repellent. The trips go at 8.30 am year round, 3 pm in winter and 5 pm in summer, daily except Monday. They last about four hours, for 2750 ptas per person. Most guides speak Spanish only. The tour normally starts with a long beach drive, before moving inland. You can be pretty certain of seeing deer and boar, but ornithologists will probably be disappointed by the limited bird-observation opportunities.

Matalascañas & Mazagón
These two small resorts on the long, sandy beach running north-west from the national park towards Huelva provide alternative bases.

Matalascañas, at the south-western corner of the park, has a number of tall hotels and could hardly be in greater contrast to the Doñana wildernesses. There are a few hostales at the western end of town: *Hostal Rocío* (☎ 959 43 01 41, Avenida El Greco 60) has doubles with bath for 3745 ptas. The huge *Camping Rocío Playa* (☎ 959 43 02 40) is just above the beach, 1km west. One bus runs to/from Huelva via Mazagón on weekdays.

The fairly low-key Mazagón, 28km north-west of Matalascañas, is more pleasant. There are three year-round camping grounds between the main road and beach within 7km to its east, and a few hostales and hotels in the village.

WEST OF HUELVA
The coast between Huelva and the Portuguese border, 53km west, alternates between estuaries, wetlands, sandy Atlantic beaches, small and medium-sized resorts

(packed in the second half of July and August) and fishing ports. A few daily buses run from Huelva to all the places mentioned here. From Ayamonte there are buses to the Algarve and Lisbon.

Punta Umbría, Huelva's summer playground, stands on a point of land between the Marismas del Odiel and a good beach. Farther west, **La Antilla** fronts a wide beach that runs all the way from the Río Piedras to Isla Cristina. **Isla Cristina** has a sizable fishing fleet: its best beach is Playa Central, about 2km east of the centre. **Ayamonte** stands beside the broad Río Guadiana, which divides Spain from Portugal. A free road bridge crosses the river 2km north, but there's also a ferry from the town (525 ptas for a car and driver, 135 ptas for pedestrians).

Places to Stay
In La Antilla, at least six *hostales* are bunched near the beach on Plaza La Parada, with doubles between 5600 and 7500 ptas plus IVA in summer (but you'd be lucky to get a room in August).

In Isla Cristina, central *Hostal Gran Vía* (☎ 959 33 07 94, Gran Vía Román Pérez 10) has singles/doubles with bathroom for 4066/ 6420 ptas. The best hotels are along Camino de la Playa near Playa Central: *Hotel Paraíso Playa* (☎ 959 33 18 73), *Hotel Los Geranios* (☎ 959 33 18 00) and *Hotel Sol y Mar* (☎ 959 33 20 50), all with doubles for 9000 to 10,000 ptas plus IVA.

In Ayamonte, the central *Hotel Marqués de Ayamonte* (☎ 959 32 01 25, Calle Trajano 14) has adequate rooms with bath for 2675/5350 ptas.

MINAS DE RIOTINTO
postcode 21660 • pop 5000
This mining town 68km north-east of Huelva makes an unusual stop. Silver was being extracted locally well before the Phoenicians came here, and iron has been mined since at least Roman times. In the 19th century the British-dominated Rio Tinto Company turned the area into one of the world's great copper-mining centres. The mines returned to Spanish control in 1954.

Things to See & Do

The good **Museo Minero**, Plaza del Museo s/n, covers the geology and history of the mines. Pride of place goes to the Vagón del Maharajah, a luxurious carriage built for a tour of India by Britain's Queen Victoria and later used by Spain's Alfonso XIII to visit the mines. The museum is open 10 am to 7 pm daily (to 4 pm July to September); 300 ptas.

The museum is also the ticket office and reception centre for guided visits to the **Corta Atalaya**, 1km west of the town, claimed to be the world's biggest opencast mine (335m deep), and for rides on the **Ferrocarril Turístico-Minero** railway, with refurbished early-20th-century carriages and steam engine. From July to September, Corta Atalaya trips go hourly from 11 am to 3 pm daily (600 ptas), and train trips at 1 pm daily except Monday (1200 ptas); in other months, Corta Atalaya trips are hourly from 11 am to 6 pm (except 3 pm) daily, and train trips at 4 or 5 pm Saturday, Sunday and holidays. To check latest timetables, call ☎ 959 59 00 25.

About 1km north of Minas de Riotinto, the Aracena road passes the **Corta Cerro Colorado**, a vast opencast mine that was a hill a century ago.

Places to Stay & Eat

Hostal Galán (☎ 959 59 18 52, Avenida La Esquila 10), outside the Museo Minero, has doubles with bath at 4250 ptas plus IVA, and a decent restaurant and bar. *Hotel Santa Bárbara* (☎ 959 59 11 88, Cerro de los Embusteros s/n), on a hilltop at the eastern end of town, offers a pool and air-con doubles for 7356 ptas, including breakfast.

Getting There & Away

Three or more Damas buses daily run to/from Huelva (680 ptas). Casal has two buses to/from Aracena weekdays and one on Saturday, and two or more to/from Sevilla (Plaza de Armas) daily.

ARACENA

postcode 21200 • pop 6700

This main town of northern Huelva is an attractive, whitewashed place spreading beneath the Cerro del Castillo. The main tourist office is the Centro de Turismo Rural y Reservas (☎ 959 12 82 06) on Calle Pozo de la Nieve. The Centro de Visitantes Cabildo Viejo (☎ 959 12 82 25) on Plaza Alta, in the 15th-century former town hall, is the main information centre of the Parque Natural Sierra de Aracena y Picos de Aroche.

Things to See & Do

The **Gruta de las Maravillas** (Cave of Marvels), entered from Calle Pozo de la Nieve, ranks among Spain's most spectacular caves. It's open daily from 10.30 am to 1.30 pm and 2.30 to 6 pm, with visits by guided tour in Spanish; 900 ptas. The **Cerro del Castillo** hill is surmounted by a beautiful church and a ruined castle, both built around 1300.

Places to Stay

Camping Aracena (☎ 959 50 10 05), open all year, is 2.5km east of town, off the N-433.

The only budget beds are at the friendly *Casa Manolo* (☎ 959 12 80 14, Calle Barbero 6), just south of Plaza del Marqués de Aracena. Seven basic but adequate singles/doubles cost 2000/3400 ptas.

The central *Hotel Sierra de Aracena* (☎ 959 12 61 75, Gran Vía 21) has 43 rooms with bath at 4700/6950 ptas. *Finca Valbono* (☎ 959 12 77 11, Carretera de Carboneras Km 1), in the countryside 1km north of Aracena, provides comfy rooms for 6420/9360 ptas and *casitas* (apartments for up to four, with kitchen) at 10,700 ptas. It has a pool, riding stables and good restaurant.

Getting There & Away

Casal (☎ 959 12 81 96), on Avenida de Andalucía, runs three buses daily to/from Sevilla (Plaza de Armas; 1¼ hours, 770 ptas), and a daily bus to Rosal de la Frontera near the Portuguese border, where you can change to onward Portuguese buses. From the Casal station, Damas buses run daily to/from Huelva.

WEST OF ARACENA

The hills, verdant valleys and stone-built villages of Huelva's portion of the Sierra Morena form one of Andalucía's most surprisingly beautiful landscapes. Most of the villages grew up around fortress-like churches, or hilltop castles constructed to deter the Portuguese, who were pushed out by Castile in the 13th century, having themselves replaced the Muslims not very long before.

Linares de la Sierra, **Alájar**, **Fuenteheridos** and **Almonaster la Real** are all intriguingly old-fashioned places, and Almonaster's 10th-century Mezquita (mosque) is one of Spain's minor gems of Islamic architecture. Ham from **Jabugo** is acclaimed as the best in Spain (see the special section 'Eating & Drinking in Spain'), and the village has a line of bars and restaurants along Carretera San Juan del Puerto waiting for you to sample it. **Cortegana** and **Aroche**, two of the bigger places in the district, have impressive castles and churches. Nearly all these places have *hostales* with doubles between 2000 and 5500 ptas.

There's an extensive web of marked **walking trails** throughout the Parque Natural Sierra de Aracena y Picos de Aroche, particularly between Aracena and Aroche. You should be able to pick up enough maps and leaflets from tourist offices in Aracena and village ayuntamientos to find your way around.

Casal (see Getting There & Away under Aracena) runs daily buses from Aracena and Sevilla (Plaza de Armas) to nearly all these *pueblos* (villages). Two daily trains run from Huelva to Almonaster and Jabugo-Galaroza stations.

Cádiz Province

The province of Cádiz (**cad**-i, or even just **ca**-i) reaches from the mouth of the Río Guadalquivir to the Strait of Gibraltar and inland to the beautiful, green Sierra de Grazalema with its remote white towns and villages. It includes the historic port of Cádiz itself, the nearby triangle of 'sherry towns' (Jerez de la Frontera, Sanlúcar de Barrameda and El Puerto de Santa María) and the little-developed Atlantic beaches of the Costa de la Luz.

The proliferation of 'de la Frontera' place names here stems from the days of the Reconquista when, from the 13th to 15th centuries, the region was one of the *fronteras* (frontiers) of Christian-held territory. It retains an untamed feel today, with large tracts of sparsely inhabited sierra, windy coasts and big lowland ranches that breed famous fighting bulls.

CÁDIZ
postcode 11080 • pop 155,000

Few people think of Cádiz when they list the great cities of Andalucía, and yet this port is as famous and historic as almost any of them.

Past the desolate coastal marshes and industrial sprawl around Cádiz, you emerge into an 18th-century city of decayed grandeur, crammed on to the head of a peninsula like some huge, overcrowded Atlantic-going ship. Its people, called *gaditanos,* are a mostly unassuming and tolerant lot whose main concern is to make the best of life – whether staying out late in the sweltering summer months, or indulging in Spain's most riotous carnaval in spring.

History
Cádiz may be the oldest city in Europe. It was founded, tradition says, in 1100 BC by the Phoenicians, who called it Gadir. Later a naval base for the Romans, who heaped praise on its culinary, sexual and musical delights, Cádiz then faded into obscurity until 1262, when it was taken from the Muslims by Alfonso X.

Cádiz began to boom after Columbus found America. He sailed from here on his second and fourth voyages. Cádiz attracted Spain's enemies too: in 1587 England's Sir Francis Drake 'singed the King of Spain's beard' with a raid on the harbour that delayed the Armada, then in 1596 Anglo-Dutch attackers burnt almost the entire city.

Cádiz's golden age was the 18th century, when it enjoyed 75% of Spanish trade with the Americas and gave birth to Spain's first liberal middle class. In the Napoleonic Wars Cádiz was bombarded by British warships then, after Spain turned against Napoleon, endured a French siege from 1810 to 1812

ANDALUCÍA

(it was one of the few Spanish cities that never fell to the French).

The loss of the American colonies in the 19th century plunged Cádiz into a decline from which it's still recovering. It has Spain's highest unemployment (almost 40%).

Orientation

Breathing space between the huddled streets of the old city is provided by numerous plazas. From Plaza de San Juan de Dios, Calle Nueva, becoming Calle San Francisco, leads north-west towards Plaza de Mina. The train station is in the east of the old city on Plaza de Sevilla, with the main bus station (the Comes line) 800m north-west on Plaza de la Hispanidad. The 18th-century Puertas de Tierra (Land Gates) mark the eastern boundary of the old city.

Information

The municipal tourist office (☎ 956 24 10 01) at Plaza de San Juan de Dios 11 is open 9 am to 2 pm and 5 to 8 pm weekdays. On weekends, a kiosk opens on the plaza. The well-stocked regional tourist office (☎ 956 21 13 13) at Calle Calderón de la Barca 1, on Plaza de Mina, is open 9 am to 7 pm Tuesday to Friday and until 2 pm Saturday and Monday.

You'll find banks with ATMs on Avenida Ramón de Carranza and Calle San Francisco, north-west of Plaza de San Juan de Dios. The main post office is on Plaza de Topete. The Policía Local (emergency ☎ 092) have a station at Campo del Sur s/n. The Residencia Sanitaria hospital (☎ 956 27 90 11) is at Avenida Ana de Viya 21.

Torre Tavira

This highest and most important of Cádiz's old watchtowers (there were once 160), at Calle Marqués del Real Tesoro 10, is a fine place to get your bearings and a dramatic panorama. Its *cámara oscura* (movie projector) projects moving images of the city on to a screen. It's open 10 am to 6 pm (to 8 pm mid-June to mid-September) daily, with cámara oscura sessions (500 ptas) every 30 minutes.

Plaza de Topete

A couple of blocks south-east of the Torre Tavira, this plaza is bright with flower stalls and adjoins the large, covered Mercado Central (central market). It's also known by its old name, Plaza de las Flores (Plaza of the Flowers).

Museo Histórico Municipal

The City History Museum, Calle Santa Inés 9, contains a large, detailed 18th-century model of the city, made in mahogany and marble for Carlos III (Charles III), which would merit a visit even if there was nothing else here. It's open 9 am to 1 pm and 4 to 7 pm Tuesday to Friday (5 to 8 pm June to September), and 9 am to 1 pm weekends (free).

Oratorio de San Felipe Neri

Also on Calle Santa Inés, this is one of Cádiz's finest baroque churches. It was also the meeting place of the 1812 Spanish national *cortes* (parliament), which assembled while Cádiz was under French siege and adopted the liberal 1812 constitution that set the scene for a century of struggle between Spanish liberals and conservatives.

The oval interior has a beautiful dome. Murillo's *Inmaculada Concepción* (1680) has a place of honour in the main retablo. The church is open 10 am to 1.30 pm Monday to Saturday (150 ptas).

Oratorio de la Santa Cueva

This 1780s neoclassical church, attached to the Iglesia del Rosario on Calle Rosario, is a two-in-one affair, with the austere underground Capilla Baja contrasting with the lavish, oval Capilla Alta. Framed by three of the Capilla Alta's eight arches are Goya paintings depicting the Miracle of the Loaves and Fishes, the Guest at the Wedding, and the Last Supper. The church is open 10 am to 1 pm weekdays (free).

Museo de Cádiz

The city's major museum is on attractive Plaza de Mina. Pride of the ground-floor archaeology section is a pair of Phoenician white-stone sarcophagi carved in human

ANDALUCÍA

CÁDIZ

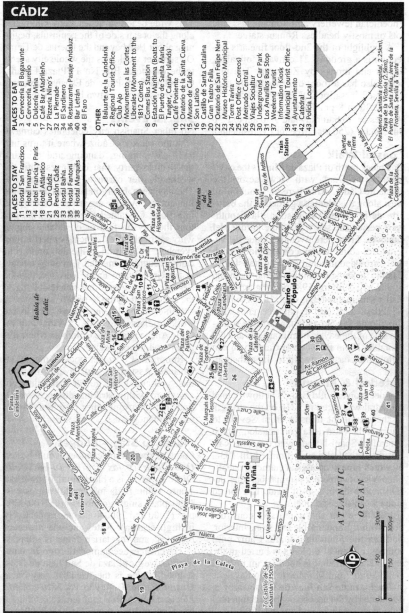

PLACES TO STAY
11 Hostal San Francisco
13 Hotel Imares
14 Hotel Francia y París
18 Hotel Atlántico
21 Quo Qádiz
28 Pensión Cádiz
33 Hostal Bahía
35 Hostal Fantoni
38 Hostal Marqués

PLACES TO EAT
3 Cervecería El Bogavante
4 Cervecería Aurelio
5 Dulcería Mina
17 Café Bar Madrileño
27 Pizzeria Nino's
32 La Pierrade
34 El Sardinero
36 Restaurante Pasaje Andaluz
40 Bar Letrán
44 El Faro

OTHER
1 Baluarte de la Candelaria
2 Regional Tourist Office
6 Club Ajo
7 Monumento a las Cortes Liberales (Monument to the 1812 Cortes)
8 Comes Bus Station
9 Estación Marítima (Boats to El Puerto de Santa María, Tangier, Canary Islands)
10 Café Poniente
12 Oratorio de la Santa Cueva
15 Museo de Cádiz
16 Son Latino
19 Castillo de Santa Catalina
20 Gran Teatro Falla
22 Oratorio de San Felipe Neri
23 Museo Histórico Municipal
24 Torre Tavira
25 Post Office (Correos)
26 Mercado Central
29 Viajes Socialtur
30 Underground Car Park
31 Los Amarillos Bus Stop
37 Weekend Tourist Information Kiosk
39 Municipal Tourist Office
41 Ayuntamiento
42 Catedral
43 Policía Local

ANDALUCÍA

likenesses. There are also some beautiful Phoenician jewellery and Roman glass, and lots of mostly headless Roman statues.

A highlight of the 2nd-floor fine arts collection is a group of 21 canvases of saints, angels and monks by Zurbarán. The museum also has a room of beautiful old puppets used in satirical theatre in Cádiz. It's open 2.30 to 8 pm Tuesday, 9 am to 8 pm Wednesday to Saturday and 9.30 am to 2.30 pm Sunday (250 ptas, free for EU residents).

Coastal Walk

One block north of Plaza de Mina is the city's northern seafront, with views across the Bahía de Cádiz. From here you could head west along the **Alameda** garden to the **Baluarte de la Candelaria** bastion, then southwest beside the sea wall to the **Parque del Genovés**. From here Avenida Duque de Nájera leads south to **Playa de la Caleta** beach (very crowded in summer). The star-shaped **Castillo de Santa Catalina** at the northern end of this bay, built in 1598 and for a long time Cádiz's main citadel, is open 10 am to 6 pm weekdays and until 1 pm weekends. The **Castillo de San Sebastián**, out on the southern side of the bay, is in military use and not visitable. From Playa de la Caleta you can follow the coast eastward to the cathedral.

Catedral & Around

The decision to build Cádiz's yellow-domed cathedral was taken in 1716 on the strength of the imminent transfer from Sevilla to Cádiz of the Casa de la Contratación, which controlled Spanish trade with the Americas. But the cathedral wasn't finished till 1838, by which time neoclassical elements had diluted Vicente Acero's original baroque design, and a drying-up of funds had forced cutbacks in size and quality.

It's still a big and impressive construction, with a grand marble and stone interior, lit from the 50m-high dome. Cádiz-born composer Manuel de Falla is buried in the crypt. The cathedral is open 10 am to 1 pm and 5.30 to 7 pm Monday to Saturday.

The **Plaza de San Juan de Dios** nearby is dominated by the neoclassical **ayuntamiento**, built at its southern end around 1800.

Playa de la Victoria

This wide beach stretches many kilometres along the ocean side of the peninsula, beginning about 1km beyond the Puertas de Tierra. On summer weekends the whole city seems to be out here. Bus No 1 'Plaza España-Cortadura' from Plaza de España runs along the peninsula one or two blocks inland.

Special Events

No other Spanish city celebrates carnaval with the verve of Cádiz, where it turns into a 10-day singing, dancing and drinking fancy-dress party that continues until the weekend after carnaval's normal Shrove Tuesday close. Everyone dresses up, and the fun, abetted by huge quantities of alcohol, is infectious. Costumed groups called *murgas* tour the city on foot or on floats, singing witty satirical ditties, dancing or performing sketches. In addition to the 300 or so officially recognised murgas, judged by a panel in the Gran Teatro Falla, there are also the *ilegales* – any group that fancies taking to the streets and trying to play or sing.

Some of the liveliest scenes are in the working-class Barrio de la Viña, and on Calle Ancha and Calle Columela where *ilegales* tend to congregate.

Rooms in Cádiz get booked months in advance. Assuming you haven't yet managed this, you could just go for the night from anywhere within striking distance. You'll find that plenty of other people do this – often in fancy dress.

Places to Stay – Budget

Cádiz's excellent independent youth hostel, *Quo Qádiz* (*☎/fax 956 22 19 39, Calle Diego Arias 1)*, is a block south of the Gran Teatro Falla. Beds in cheerful dorms cost 1000 ptas; singles/doubles are 2100/3200 ptas (2000 and 2000/4000 ptas respectively in high season). Rates include a decent breakfast, and vegetarian dinner is 550 ptas.

The cheaper accommodation mostly clusters just west of Plaza de San Juan de Dios. A good choice is the friendly, very clean *Hostal Fantoni* (*☎ 956 28 27 04, Calle Flamenco 5)*, with a roof terrace catching a bit of breeze. It has rooms for 2000/3700 ptas, and doubles with bath for 5500 ptas. *Hostal Marqués (☎ 956 28 58 54, Calle Marqués de Cádiz 1)* has slightly ageing but clean rooms, with balcony, for 2000/3500 ptas.

A bit farther north-west, *Pensión Cádiz (☎ 956 28 58 01, Calle Feduchy 20)* is a popular little place costing 2000/4000 ptas.

A good choice farther into the old city is *Hostal San Francisco (☎/fax 956 22 18 42, Calle San Francisco 12)*, with rooms starting at 2500/4250 ptas. Rooms at *Hotel Imares (☎ 956 21 22 57, Calle San Francisco 9)* are 3600/5800 ptas with bath; some are dank and airless, others bright and breezy.

Places to Stay – Mid-Range & Top End

Hostal Bahía (☎ 956 25 90 61, Calle Plocia 5), off Plaza de San Juan de Dios, has comfortable air-con rooms with TV at 6400/8300 ptas. *Hotel Francia y París (☎ 956 21 23 18, Plaza San Francisco 2)* is bigger (57 rooms) and more luxurious, at 8080/10,100 ptas plus IVA. Rooms at the seafront parador, *Hotel Atlántico (☎ 956 22 69 05, e cadiz@ parador.es, Avenida Duque de Nájera 9)* are 12,840/16,050 ptas.

Places to Eat

Naturally, Cádiz is strong on seafood, particularly *pescaíto frito* (fried fish) and shellfish. *Erizos* (sea urchins) are a local favourite. For exquisite seafood tapas (190 to 225 ptas), head for the bar at *El Faro (Calle San Felix 15)* in the Barrio de la Viña.

Plaza de San Juan de Dios If price is crucial, *Restaurante Pasaje Andaluz* has *menús* from 950 ptas and mains from 550 ptas. *El Sardinero* serves similar fare better but for almost twice the price. *Bar Letrán* has platos combinados from 550 to 1000 ptas. *La Pierrade (Calle Plocia 2)*, off the plaza, is a touch adventurous. The three-course *menú* (1200 ptas) might offer *mejillones* (mussels) *al Roquefort* or *brocheta de cordero* (lamb kebab), and includes wine and bread.

Plaza de Mina & Around At *Café Bar Madrileño*, on Plaza de Mina, there's a wide choice at reasonable prices, including salads

for 350 ptas and fish and seafood raciones from 800 ptas. *Dulcería Mina (Calle Antonio López 2)* has good pastries, baguettes and breakfasts (tea/coffee, juice and tostada for 300 ptas). It's hard to pass by the fresh seafood tapas at *Cervecería Aurelio (Calle Zorrilla 1)*. At the end of Calle Zorrilla, enjoy the bay views at *Cervecería El Bogavante* while tucking into good scrambled eggs, prawns and asparagus for 900 ptas, big salads (600 ptas), or fish or meat mains (900 to 1200 ptas).

Around Plaza de Topete On Calle Columela, *Pizzeria Nino's* serves tasty pizzas from 740 ptas, and pasta, Tex-Mex and burgers from 625 ptas. The *Mercado Central* sells *churros* (deep-fried doughnuts) that you can take to cafes to accompany hot chocolate for breakfast.

Entertainment

There's a great atmosphere in some of the old city's plazas on hot summer nights, with all ages out enjoying the relative cool. From midnight or so in summer the real scene migrates to the Paseo Marítimo along Playa de la Victoria. About 3km from the Puertas de Tierra, past the big Hotel Playa Victoria, you'll find lively music bars; a little farther along, on Calle Villa de Paradas, throngs of people stand in the street with *macetas* ('plantpots') of beer. A taxi there from the old city costs around 600 ptas. Until about 1.30 am you can take bus No 1 from Plaza de España.

In winter, the bars in the streets west of Plaza de España, such as Calle Dr Zurita, are among the liveliest, and the plaza itself is the setting for the Saturday night *movida* (action). *Club Ajo (Plaza de España 5)* is a popular hang-out open late from Thursday (when it has live music) to Sunday. *Café Poniente (Calle Beato Diego de Cádiz 18)* is a good gay bar.

Son Latino, on Plaza de la Mina, often has excellent live music from 11 pm.

Getting There & Away

Bus Most buses are run by Comes (☎ 956 21 17 63) from Plaza de la Hispanidad. At least 10 daily go to Sevilla (1¾ hours, 1385 ptas),

El Puerto de Santa María, Jerez de la Frontera and Tarifa; three or more to Arcos de la Frontera, Ronda and Málaga; and one or more to Córdoba and Granada.

Los Amarillos, with its stop by the southern end of Avenida Ramón de Carranza, runs up to 10 daily buses to El Puerto de Santa María and Sanlúcar de Barrameda, and two or three to Arcos de la Frontera and El Bosque. Tickets can be bought at Viajes Socialtur (☎ 956 28 58 52), Avenida Ramón de Carranza 31.

Train From the station (☎ 956 25 43 01) up to 35 trains run daily to/from El Puerto de Santa María and Jerez de la Frontera (40 minutes), and up to 15 to/from Sevilla (two hours, 1290 ptas). There are four trains daily to/from Córdoba, and two each for Madrid (five hours) and Barcelona.

Car & Motorcycle The A-4 *autopista* (tollway) from Sevilla to Puerto Real on the eastern side of the Bahía de Cádiz carries a toll of 900 ptas. The toll-free N-IV is much slower.

Boat Vapores Suardiaz (☎ 956 28 21 11) operates two ferries daily to/from Tangier (three hours). Fares are 3900 ptas per passenger and 9900 ptas per car. Trasmediterránea (☎ 956 45 46 45) operates a car ferry to the Canary Islands, leaving Cádiz on Saturday and arriving in Santa Cruz de Tenerife and Las Palmas 1½ and two days later, respectively. The one-way passenger fare is from 30,515 to 55,430 ptas.

EL PUERTO DE SANTA MARÍA
postcode 11500 • pop 69,000
This town, 10km north-east of Cádiz across the bay (22km by road), makes an interesting side trip, best enjoyed by taking the ferry *El Vapor*. It was here that Columbus met the owner of his flagship *Santa María*, Juan de la Cosa, who was his pilot in 1492. Later many palaces were built in El Puerto on the proceeds of American trade. Today it's one of Cádiz province's triangle of major sherry-making towns. It's a lively place with plenty of bars, and no lack of entertainment in summer.

Orientation & Information
The heart of the town is on the north-western bank of the Río Guadalete. *El Vapor* arrives dead centre at the Muelle del Vapor jetty, on Plaza de las Galeras Reales. The good tourist office (☎ 956 54 24 13) is 2½ blocks straight ahead at Calle Luna 22 – open 10 am to 2 pm and 6 to 7.30 pm daily. Calle Palacios, parallel to Calle Luna one block south-west, runs up to Plaza de España, seven blocks inland.

Things to See & Do
The four-spouted **Fuente de las Galeras Reales** (Fountain of the Royal Galleys), by the Muelle del Vapor, once supplied water to America-bound ships. The **Castillo San Marcos**, three blocks south-west along Avenida Aramburu de Mora, then a block inland, was built by Alfonso X after he took the town in 1260. Free tours are given on Saturday between 11 am and 1 pm. The **Fundación Rafael Alberti** at Calle Santo Domingo 25, 2½ blocks inland from the castle, has interesting exhibits on El Puerto native Rafael Alberti (1902–99), a painter, poet and communist politician of the Generation of 27. The impressive 15th- to 18th-century **Iglesia Mayor Prioral** dominates Plaza de España, a little farther inland (open 10 am to noon and 7 to 8.30 pm daily).

Phone ahead to visit either of El Puerto's best-known **sherry bodegas** (wineries). Osborne (☎ 956 85 52 11) provides tours in English at 10.30 am and Spanish at 11 am and noon, weekdays (300 ptas). Visits to Terry (☎ 956 54 36 90) are at 9.30 and 11 am and 12.30 pm, weekdays (325 ptas).

Pine-flanked **Playa de la Puntilla** beach is a half-hour walk south-west of the centre – or take bus No 26 south-west along Avenida Aramburu de Mora.

La Niña (☎ 956 85 57 28), a replica of one of Columbus' ships, makes daily **cruises** from the Muelle Pesquero (fishing pier) for 1000 ptas per person.

Special Events
El Puerto's early-May Feria de la Primavera is in largely dedicated to sherry, with about 180,000 half-bottles being drunk in a week.

ANDALUCÍA

Places to Stay

Camping Las Dunas (☎ 956 87 22 10), just behind Playa de la Puntilla, has shade and is open year round. Two adults with a car and tent pay 2330 ptas.

Hostal Santamaría (☎ 956 85 36 31, *Calle Pedro Muñoz Seca 38),* off Calle Palacios five blocks inland, has no name sign but good, clean singles/doubles at 1750/3500 ptas (2000/4000 ptas with bathroom). Friendly *Hostal Manolo* (☎ 956 85 75 25, Calle Jesús de los Milagros 18), a block inland from Plaza de las Galeras Reales, has rooms from 2500/4000 to 2900/4800 ptas.

Hotel Los Cántaros (☎ 956 54 02 40, *Calle Curva 6)* is a big step up in quality. Doubles are 12,840 ptas from mid-July to mid-September, but 8560 ptas or less at most other times. At *Hotel Monasterio San Miguel* (☎ 956 54 04 40, fax 956 54 26 04, *Calle Larga 27),* a converted 18th-century monastery, rooms start at 15,550/19,425 ptas plus IVA.

Places to Eat

Crowds flock to the *Romerijo*, a block north-east along Ribera del Marisco from Plaza de las Galeras Reales. One of the two buildings specialises in boiled fresh seafood, the other fries it; a quarter-kilogram of boiled prawns or fried *puntillitas* (miniature squid) costs 800 to 1200 ptas. Just behind here on Plaza de la Herrería, *La Herrería* has good food and good prices, with a nice little salad at 300 ptas and *pinchitos morunos* (Moroccan-style kebab) at 500 ptas a media-ración.

Restaurante El Resbaladero, in the handsome Antigua Lonja de Pescado (Old Fish Exchange) on Avenida Aramburu de Mora, provides air-conditioned comfort and a medium-to-expensive menu with lots of seafood.

Getting There & Away

Bus Buses run to Cádiz almost half-hourly on weekdays from the Plaza de Toros (bullring), three blocks south-west of the Plaza de España, and hourly, 8.30 am to 9.30 pm, from the train station. Weekend services are less frequent. For Jerez de la Frontera there are seven to 14 daily buses from the train station and a few from the Plaza de Toros. For Sanlúcar de Barrameda, four to 10 buses go from the Plaza de Toros.

Train El Puerto station (☎ 956 54 25 85) is a 10-minute walk north-east of the centre, beside the Cádiz-Jerez road. It's on the Cádiz-Sevilla line, half an hour from Cádiz, with up to 35 trains daily in each direction.

Boat *El Vapor* (☎ 956 87 02 70) sails from the Estación Marítima (ferry terminal) in Cádiz at 10 am, noon and 2 and 6.30 pm daily except Monday from February to November, with an extra trip at 8.30 pm in summer. Trips back from El Puerto are at 9 and 11 am and 1 and 3.30 pm, plus 7.30 pm in summer. The crossing takes 45 minutes (275 ptas one way).

SANLÚCAR DE BARRAMEDA
postcode 11540 • pop 60,000

Sanlúcar, 23km north-west of El Puerto de Santa María, is the northern tip of the sherry triangle and a likeable summer resort, looking across the Guadalquivir estuary to the Parque Nacional de Doñana.

Columbus sailed from Sanlúcar in 1498 on his third voyage to the Caribbean. So, in 1519, did the Portuguese Ferdinand Magellan, seeking – as Columbus had – a westerly route to the Asian spice islands. Magellan succeeded, thanks to the first known voyage round the bottom of South America, but was killed in the Philippines. His pilot Juan Sebastián Elcano completed the first circumnavigation of the globe by returning to Sanlúcar in 1522 with just one of the five ships, the *Victoria*.

Orientation

Sanlúcar stretches 2.5km along the south-eastern side of the estuary, fronted by a long, sandy beach. Calzada del Ejército, running inland from the seafront Paseo Marítimo, is the main avenue. A block beyond its inland end is Plaza del Cabildo, the central square. The Los Amarillos bus station is on Plaza La

ANDALUCÍA

Sherry

Sherry is fortified wine produced in the towns of Jerez de la Frontera, El Puerto de Santa María and Sanlúcar de Barrameda, plus five other areas in Cádiz province and Lebrija in Sevilla province. A combination of climate, chalky soils that soak up the sun but retain moisture, and a special ageing process called the *solera* system produce this unique wine.

The main distinction in sherry is between *fino* (dry and the colour of straw) and *oloroso* (sweet, dark and with a strong bouquet). An *amontillado* is an amber, moderately dry fino with a nutty flavour and a higher alcohol content than paler finos. An oloroso combined with a sweet wine results in a potent 'cream sherry'. A *manzanilla* – not strictly sherry but very similar – is an unfortified camomile-coloured fino from Sanlúcar de Barrameda; its delicate flavour is reckoned to come from sea breezes wafting into the bodegas.

Sherry, especially fino, goes brilliantly with many tapas, but it can also accompany a meal: manzanilla is great with seafood and an oloroso is good with red meat.

Once sherry grapes have been harvested, they are pressed and the resulting must is left to ferment. Within a few months a frothy veil of yeast called *flor* appears on the surface. The wine is transferred to the *bodegas* (wineries) in big barrels of American oak, which add to its flavour.

Wine enters the solera process when it is a year old. The barrels, about five-sixths full, are lined up in rows at least three barrels high: the barrels on the bottom layer, called the *solera* (from *suelo*, floor), contain the oldest wine. From these, around three times a year, 10% of the wine is drawn off. This is replaced with the same amount of wine from the barrels in the layer above, which is in turn replenished from the next layer. The wines are left to age for between three and seven years. A small amount of brandy is added to stabilise the wine before bottling, bringing the alcohol content to 16–18%, which stops fermentation. (This constitutes the 'fortification' of the wine.)

Sherry houses are often beautiful buildings in attractive gardens. A tour will take you through the bodegas where the wine is stored and aged, inform you about the process and the history of the sherry producers, and give you a bit of a tasting. You'll be given a demonstration of the use of a *venencia*, a long-handled cup for sampling sherry from the barrel. The venencia is expertly manipulated, with the sherry cascading from head height into a glass held at waist level.

ANDALUCÍA

Salle, 500m south-west of Plaza del Cabildo along Calle San Juan.

The old fishing quarter, Bajo de Guía, site of Sanlúcar's best restaurants and Doñana boat departures, is 750m north-east from Calzada del Ejército.

Information

The main tourist office (☎ 956 36 61 10) is situated towards the inland end of Calzada del Ejército. It's open 10 am to 2 pm and 6 to 8 pm (5 to 7 pm during winter) weekdays, and until 1 pm Saturday and summer Sundays.

The Centro de Visitantes Fábrica de Hielo (☎ 956 38 16 35) at Bajo de Guía has displays and information on the Parque Nacional de Doñana and related topics. It's open 9 am to 7 pm daily.

Walking Tour

A stroll around the monuments doesn't take long as few are open to visitors. From Plaza del Cabildo, cross Calle Ancha to Plaza San Roque and head up Calle Bretones to **Las Covachas**, a set of 15th-century wine cellars. Here the street becomes Calle Cuesta de Belén where you'll probably be able to look into the **Palacio de Orleans y Borbón**, a neo-mudéjar fantasy created for the Montpensier family in the 19th century, and now the ayuntamiento.

From the top of Calle Cuesta de Belén, a block to the left along Calle Caballeros is the 15th-century **Iglesia de Nuestra Señora de la O**, with a mudéjar facade and ceiling. Adjoining is the **Palacio de los Duques de Medina Sidonia**, home of the aristocratic family that once owned more of Spain than anyone else. Some 200m farther along the street is the 15th-century **Castillo de Santiago**, amid buildings of the Barbadillo sherry company. From the castle you can return directly downhill to the town centre.

Sherry Bodegas

Sanlúcar produces a distinctive sherry, *manzanilla* (see the boxed text 'Sherry'). Three bodegas give tours for which you don't need to book ahead. All start at 12.30 pm and cost 300 ptas. **La Cigarrera**, Plaza Madre de Dios – Monday and Tuesday; **Bodegas Barbadillo**, Calle Luis de Eguilaz 11, near the castle – Wednesday and Thursday; and **Pedro Romero**, Calle Trasbolsa 60 – Friday and Saturday.

Parque Nacional de Doñana

Viajes Doñana (☎ 956 36 25 40), Calle San Juan 20, operates 3½-hour guided tours (4700 ptas per person) into Doñana at 8.30 am and 4.30 pm Tuesday and Friday, leaving from Bajo de Guía. After the river crossing, the trip is by 20-person all-terrain vehicle, visiting much the same spots as the tours from El Acebuche (see Parque Nacional de Doñana earlier in this chapter). Book ahead and take mosquito repellent or cover up.

Once or twice daily except Monday, the boat *Real Fernando* makes 3½-hour trips on the Guadalquivir from Bajo de Guía. Despite brief stops in the national park and the Parque Natural de Doñana, these trips are not really designed for nature enthusiasts. Tickets (2200 ptas, or 1100 ptas for five-to-12 year olds) are sold at the Centro de Visitantes Fábrica de Hielo. Book on ☎ 956 36 38 13.

Special Events

The Sanlúcar summer gets going with a sherry festival, the Feria de la Manzanilla, in late May or early June, and blossoms in July and August with happenings like the Noches de Bajo de Guía flamenco season (late July), jazz and classical music festivals, and Sanlúcar's unique horse races, in which thoroughbred racehorses thunder along the beach during a couple of three- or four-day evening meetings in August.

Places to Stay

Book well ahead at holiday times. *Hostal La Blanca Paloma* (☎ 956 36 36 44, *Plaza San Roque 9*) has adequate singles/doubles for 3000/4500 ptas. *Hostal La Bohemia* (☎ 956 36 95 99, *Calle Don Claudio 1*) has better rooms with bath at 5500 ptas a double.

Hotel Posada de Palacio (☎ 956 36 48 40, *Calle Caballeros 11*), in the upper part of town, is a charming 18th-century mansion with 10 good-sized rooms for 6000/8000 ptas, and a restaurant. It closes for a couple of months in winter. *Hotel Los Helechos* (☎ 956 36 13 49, *Plaza Madre de Dios 9*), off Calle San Juan, has rooms with bath for 6420/8560 ptas. *Hotel Tartaneros* (☎ 956 36 20 44, *Calle Tartaneros 8*), another ex-mansion at the inland end of Calzada del Ejército, offers solidly comfy rooms for 6955/10,700 ptas.

Places to Eat

Spain holds few more idyllic dining experiences than watching the sun go down over the Guadalquivir while tucking into succulent fresh seafood at one of Bajo de Guía's restaurants facing the river, and washing it down with a glass or two of manzanilla. Just wander along and pick a restaurant that suits your pocket. At *Restaurante Virgen del Carmen* (*Bajo de Guía s/n*), for instance, most fish mains, *plancha* (grilled) or *frito* (fried), are 1000 to 1400 ptas. Don't skip the starters: *langostinos* (king prawns) and the juicy *coquines al ajillo* (clams in garlic), both 1000 ptas, are specialities. A half-bottle of manzanilla is 600 ptas.

Lots of cafes and bars, many serving manzanilla from the barrel, surround Plaza del Cabildo – *Casa Balbino* is a must for tapas. *Bar El Cura* (*Calle Amargura 2*), between Calle San Juan and Plaza San Roque, serves platos combinados for 500 ptas.

Entertainment

There are some lively music bars and *discotecas* on and around Calzada del Ejército and Plaza del Cabildo.

Getting There & Away

Los Amarillos (☎ 956 36 04 66) runs up to nine buses daily to/from El Puerto de Santa

ANDALUCÍA

María, Cádiz and Sevilla. Linesur (☎ 956 34 10 63), at Bar La Jaula behind the tourist office, runs at least seven daily to/from Jerez de la Frontera.

JEREZ DE LA FRONTERA
postcode 11480 • pop 182,000

Jerez, 36km north-east of Cádiz, is world-famous for its sherry, made from grapes grown on the area's chalky soil. Many people come here to visit its bodegas, but Jerez (heh-**reth** or, in andaluz, heh-**reh**) is also Andalucía's horse capital and one of the hotbeds of flamenco.

British money was largely responsible for the development of the wineries from around the 1830s. Jerez high society today is a mixture of andaluz and British due to intermarriage among sherry families over the past 150 years. Since the 1980s most of the wineries have been bought by multinational companies. Jerez reeks of money with lots of fancy shops, well-heeled residents, wide, spacious streets, old mansions and beautiful churches in its interesting old quarter. It puts on fantastic fiestas with sleek horses, beautiful people and flamenco, and hopes for a million visitors in 2002 when it hosts the World Equestrian Games.

History

The Muslims called the town Scheris, from which 'Jerez' and 'sherry' are derived. The drink was already famed in England in Shakespeare's time.

Jerez had its share of strife in the anarchic late 19th century: one day in 1891 thousands of peasants armed with scythes and sticks occupied the town for a few hours – succeeding only in bringing further repression.

The sherry industry has brought greater prosperity in more recent times. Jerez brandy, popular in Spain, is another profitable product.

Orientation

Jerez centres on the Alameda Cristina and Plaza del Arenal, which is connected by Calle Larga and Calle Lancería (both pedestrianised). Budget accommodation clusters east of Calle Larga, around Avenida de Arcos and Calle Medina. The old quarter is west of Calle Larga.

Information

The tourist office (☎ 956 33 11 50), at Calle Larga 39, has an energetic, multilingual staff with mountains of information. Its basic opening hours are 9 am to 3 pm and 4 to 7 pm weekdays, and 10 am to 2 pm and 5 to 7 pm Saturday.

There are plenty of banks and ATMs on and around Calle Larga.

Old Quarter

The obvious place to start a tour of the old town is the **Alcázar**, the 12th-century Almohad fortress south-west of Plaza del Arenal. Inside are the **Capilla Santa María la Real**, a chapel converted from a mosque by Alfonso X in 1264, the recently restored **Baños Arabes** (Arab Baths) and the 18th-century **Palacio Villavicencio**, whose tower has a cámara oscura providing a picturesque live panorama of Jerez accompanied by an interesting commentary, in English if you wish (sessions are every half-hour daily; 500 ptas).

The orange-tree-lined plaza outside the Alcázar overlooks the mainly 18th-century **catedral**, built on the site of Scheris' main mosque. Note its 15th-century mudéjar belfry, set slightly apart.

A couple of blocks north-east of the cathedral is Plaza de la Asunción, with the splendid 16th-century **Antiguo Cabildo** (Old Town Hall) and lovely 15th-century mudéjar **Iglesia de San Dionisio**.

North and west of here is the **Barrio de Santiago**, with a sizable gitano population. The barrio has churches dedicated to all four evangelists: the Gothic **Iglesia de San Mateo**, with mudéjar chapels, is on Plaza del Mercado, where you'll also find the **Museo Arqueológico**, with a 7th-century BC Greek helmet found in the Río Guadalete. The museum is open 10 am to 2 or 2.30 pm daily except Monday, plus 4 to 7 pm Tuesday to Friday from 1 September to 14 June (250 ptas).

Also in this area is the **Centro Andaluz de Flamenco** (Andalucian Flamenco Centre),

ANDALUCÍA

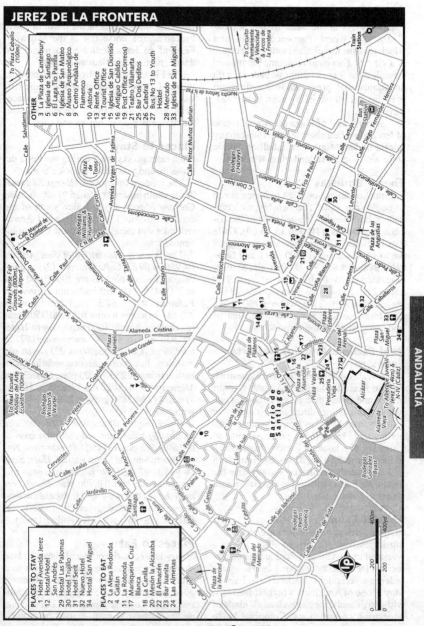

JEREF DE LA FRONTERA

OTHER
3 La Plaza de Canterbury
5 Iglesia de Santiago
7 El Laga Tio Parrilla
8 Iglesia de San Mateo
9 Museo Arqueológico
9 Centro Andaluz de Flamenco
10 Astoria
13 Renfe Office
14 Tourist Office
15 Iglesia de San Dionisio
16 Antiguo Cabildo
19 Post Office (Correos)
21 Teatro Villamarta
25 Bar Dos Deditos
26 Catedral
27 Bus No 13 to Youth Hostel
28 Mercado
33 Iglesia de San Miguel

PLACES TO STAY
1 Hotel Avenida Jerez
12 Hostal/Hotel San Andrés
29 Hostal Las Palomas
30 Hotel Trujillo
31 Hotel Serit
32 Nuevo Hotel
34 Hostal San Miguel

PLACES TO EAT
2 La Mesa Redonda
4 Gaitán
11 La Rotonda
17 Marisquería Cruz Blanca
18 La Canilla
20 Mesón la Alcazaba
22 El Almacén
23 Bar Juanita
24 Las Almenas

ANDALUCÍA

euro currency converter €1 = 166pta

in the Palacio de Pemartín on Plaza de San Juan. Jerez is at the heart of the Sevilla-Cádiz axis where flamenco began and which remains its heartland today. The centre is a kind of flamenco museum, library and school, open 9 am to 2 pm weekdays, with an audiovisual presentation hourly from 9.30 am to 1.30 pm in the main tourist seasons (free).

Just south-east of Plaza del Arenal is one of Jerez's loveliest churches, the 16th-century **Iglesia de San Miguel**, in Isabelline Gothic style with superb stained-glass windows.

Sherry Bodegas

For most bodegas you need to phone ahead to book your visit. The two biggest companies, both handily located west of the Alcázar, are **Domecq** (☎ 956 15 15 00), Calle San Ildefonso 3, with several tours from 9 am to 1 pm weekdays (400 ptas), and **González Byass** (☎ 956 35 70 00), Calle Manuel González s/n, visitable from at least 9.30 am to 2 pm and 4.30 to 6 pm weekdays (500 ptas), and 10 am to 2 pm weekends (600 ptas). The tourist office has a complete list of bodegas that welcome visitors.

Real Escuela Andaluz del Arte Ecuestre

The Royal Andalucian School of Equestrian Art, on Avenida Duque de Abrantes, trains horses and riders in dressage, and you can watch them going through their paces in training from 11 am to 1 pm Monday, Wednesday and Friday (1000 ptas). At noon on Thursday, plus noon on Tuesday from March to October and 10 am Thursday from April to June, there's an official show where the handsome horses perform to classical music (2000 to 3000 ptas).

Special Events

In April, Jerez stages a major indie/alternative music festival, 'Espárrago Rock', over a weekend at the Circuito Permanente de Velocidad (see Spectator Sports later).

Jerez's Feria del Caballo (Horse Fair) in May is one of Andalucía's biggest festivals, with music and dance as well as all kinds of equestrian competitions. Colourful horse parades pass through the Parque González Hontoria fairgrounds in the north of town. Preceding the horse fair is the two-week Festival de Jerez dedicated to music and dance, particularly flamenco dance.

The Fiestas de Otoño from mid-September to mid-October, celebrating the grape harvest, range from cultural events to horse races and dressage competitions, concluding with a massive parade of horses and carriages.

Places to Stay

Most rates go sky-high during the Feria del Caballo, and you need to book ahead.

The modern Inturjoven *Albergue Juvenil Jerez* youth hostel (☎ 956 26 97 88, Avenida Carrero Blanco 30) is 1.5km south of the centre. Bus No 13 from Plaza del Arenal will take you there; get off at the Campo Juventud stop.

The friendly *Hostal/Hotel San Andrés* (☎ 956 34 09 83, Calle Morenos 12) is a good choice. Singles/doubles are 2000/3000 ptas, or 2500/4500 ptas with bathroom. *Hostal Las Palomas* (☎ 956 34 37 73, Calle Higueras 17) has spacious rooms for 2000/3500 ptas (doubles with bath, 4000 ptas). *Nuevo Hotel* (☎ 956 33 16 00, 🄴 nuevohotel1927@ teleline.es, Calle Caballeros 23), in an old mansion, has roomy accommodation with bath starting at 2500/4000 ptas. *Hostal San Miguel* (☎ 956 34 85 62, Plaza San Miguel 4) costs 1800/3800 ptas, or 2500/ 5000 ptas with bath.

Hotel Trujillo (☎/fax 956 34 24 38, Calle Medina 3) has rooms with all mod cons at 6315/10,485 ptas (3745/5885 ptas from November to Semana Santa/Easter). *Hotel Serit* (☎ 956 34 07 00, Calle Higueras 7) has similar rooms for 7490/10,700 ptas. *Hotel Avenida Jerez* (☎ 956 34 74 11, Avenida Álvaro Domecq 10) has doubles for 15,000 ptas (30,000 ptas in April, May and October).

Places to Eat

Sherry is used to flavour local dishes and the sherry trade has introduced English and French elements into the local cuisine. A good, but pricey, place to try Jerez specialities is little *La Mesa Redonda (Calle Manuel de la Quintana 3),* north-east of the centre.

The restaurants on Pescadería Vieja, an alley off Plaza del Arenal that catches a refreshing breeze, are moderate to expensive. *Las Almenas* has three-course *menús* from 950 ptas. *Bar Juanita*, and *El Almacén (Calle Ferros 8),* round the corner, are local tapas haunts (shellfish are the thing) and good places to sample a fino. *Marisquería Cruz Blanca (Calle Consistorio 16)* has tables on pretty Plaza de la Yerba and serves great seafood tapas (175 to 300 ptas), including sensational sushi-style bacalao!

La Canilla (Calle Larga 8) is fine for a simple breakfast. Or, for a tostada and coffee (150 ptas) after 10 am, try *La Rotonda* at the northern end of Calle Larga.

Mesón la Alcazaba (Calle Medina 19), with a covered patio, has cheap and filling food; *menús* starting at 800 ptas offer plenty of choice, and a breakfast of coffee, *mollete* (soft bread roll) and fresh juice is 200 ptas.

For a splash-out meal at *Gaitán (Calle Gaitán 3),* expect to pay around 1500 ptas for starters such as seafood cocktails, and 1875 to 2500 ptas for main courses.

Entertainment
Check at the tourist office and watch for posters for upcoming events. *Diario de Jerez* newspaper has some what's-on information and the Teatro Villamarta on Calle Medina publishes a monthly program. The *Astoria*, an outdoor concert area on Calle Francos, has live music from blues to flamenco. *Bar Dos Deditos (Plaza Vargas 1)* has live music some nights, including blues; if there's something on, the crowd spills onto the pavement.

North-east of the centre just before the bullring, *La Plaza de Canterbury*, with loads of bars around a courtyard, attracts a young crowd. Between the bullring and Plaza Caballo is a small nightlife area centred on Calle Salvatierra, with bars and a couple of clubs for dancing until late at weekends and fiestas.

For flamenco, there are several *peñas* (clubs) in the Barrio de Santiago; the tourist office keeps a complete list. *El Laga Tío Parrilla*, on Plaza del Mercado, has more tourist-oriented flamenco performances at 10.30 pm and 12.30 am Monday to Saturday nights, but you may experience something more authentic there out of the main tourist seasons.

Spectator Sports
Jerez's racetrack, the Circuito Permanente de Velocidad, on the A-382 10km east of town, stages motorcycle races throughout the year including, in April or May, one of the *grands prix* of the World Motorcycle Championship. This is one of Spain's biggest sporting events with around 150,000 spectators.

Getting There & Away
Air Jerez airport (☎ 956 15 00 00) is 7km north-east of town on the N-IV. Iberia (☎ 956 18 43 94) and Air Europa fly daily to/from Madrid, and Iberia to/from Barcelona. The budget airline Buzz (☎ 91 749 66 33) began flights to/from London Stansted in 2000 with fares from UK£49 one way.

Bus The bus station (☎ 956 34 52 07) is on Calle Cartuja, about 1km south-east of the centre. Comes has buses for Cádiz (370 ptas, up to 19 daily), El Puerto de Santa María (up to five daily), Ronda (1320 ptas, four daily with one continuing to Málaga) and Córdoba (1950 ptas, one daily). Plenty of buses run to Sevilla (890 ptas) by Linesur-Valenciana and Comes. Linesur-Valenciana also runs to Sanlúcar de Barrameda hourly from 7 am to 9 pm. Los Amarillos serves inland towns with plenty to Arcos de la Frontera, and up to seven daily to El Bosque.

Train Jerez station (☎ 956 34 23 19), at the end of Calle Cartuja, is on the Cádiz-Sevilla line with plenty of trains in both directions. The central Renfe office is at Calle Larga 34.

ARCOS DE LA FRONTERA
postcode 11630 • pop 28,000

Arcos is 30km east of Jerez along the A-382 across wheat and sunflower fields, vineyards and orchards. Arcos' ridge-top old town, with the Río Guadalete meandering below, makes a striking sight. Arcos is said

ANDALUCÍA

to have a dark, sinister side: there are tales of strange vibes, madness and witchcraft. Whatever the truth of that, the old town is well worth exploring, with a street plan little changed since medieval times and some lovely post-Reconquista buildings.

History

In the 11th century Arcos was for a time an independent Muslim taifa until absorbed by Sevilla. In 1255 Alfonso X took the town and repopulated it with Castilians and Leonese. Some Muslims stayed but rebelled in 1261 and were evicted. In 1440 the town passed to the Ponce de León family, the Duques de Arcos. When the last duke died heirless in 1780, his cousin, the Duquesa de Benavente, took over his lands. She was partly responsible for replacing sheep farming with cereals, olives, vines and horse breeding as the area's dominant economic activities.

Orientation & Information

From the bus station on Calle Corregidora it's a 1km uphill walk to the old town: from Plaza España roundabout at the top of leafy Paseo de Andalucía, Paseo de los Boliches and Calle Debajo del Corral (becoming Calle Corredera) both head east up to the old town's main square, Plaza del Cabildo.

The tourist office (☎ 956 70 22 64) on Plaza del Cabildo, is open 10 am to 2 pm and 5 to 7 pm Monday to Saturday (to 6.30 pm Saturday) and 10.30 am to 12.30 pm Sunday, has lively staff. A tourist information kiosk on Paseo de Andalucía is open 10.30 am to 1.30 pm Monday to Saturday.

Banks and ATMs, on Calle Debajo del Corral and Calle Corredera, and the post office, on Paseo de los Boliches, are down to the west of the old town.

Things to See

Take a wander around Arcos' old town with its narrow cobbled streets, Renaissance buildings and whitewashed houses. **Plaza del Cabildo** is surrounded by fine old buildings and has a **mirador** (lookout) with panoramic views over the river and countryside – though its crowning glory, the **Castillo de los Duques**, dating from the 11th

century, is not open to the public. On the plaza's northern side, take a look at the **Basílica-Parroquia de Santa María**, begun in the 13th century. On the eastern side, the **parador**, with striking views from its restaurant and terrace, is a 1960s reconstruction of a 16th-century magistrate's house, the **Casa del Corregidor**.

On the streets east of here stand lovely buildings such as the 16th-century **Convento de la Encarnación** on Calle Marqués de Torresoto, with a Gothic facade. On Calle Núñez de Prado is the **Iglesia de San Pedro**, in 15th-century Gothic style but with an impressive baroque facade and bell tower (the latter is currently closed). Nearby, the 17th-century **Palacio Mayorazgo**, with a Renaissance facade, is now a senior citizens' centre.

The 15th-century Gothic/mudéjar **Palacio del Conde del Águila**, on Calle Cuesta de Belén, has the town's oldest facade.

Organised Tours

The tourist office organises hour-long guided tours (400 ptas) of the old town and its patios. Times are posted at the Paseo de Andalucía kiosk.

Special Events

Semana Santa processions at Easter through the town's old streets are dramatic. At the beginning of August, the three-day Fiesta de la Virgen de las Nieves includes late-night music on Plaza del Cabildo. On 29 September, during the feria dedicated to Arcos' patron saint San Miguel, there's a hair-raising running of the bulls.

Places to Stay

Camping Lago de Arcos (☎ 956 70 05 14), open year round with a good pool, is in El Santiscal near the Lago de Arcos reservoir north-east of the old town. The most straightforward route to drive from Arcos is by the A-382 and Carretera El Bosque y Ubrique. Turn left after the bridge across the dam. A local bus runs from Arcos.

Budget rooms are scarce. ***Hostal San Marcos*** *(☎ 956 70 07 21, Calle Marqués de Torresoto 6), a short walk from Plaza del Cabildo, has a handful of good, simple* singles/doubles with bath for 2500/4500 ptas, and a roof terrace. *Hostal Andalucía* (☎ 956 70 07 14), Polígono Industrial El Retiro, on the A-382 300m south-west of the bus station, offers large rooms with bath for 1605/3210 ptas, but it's above a car yard and backed by workshops.

If you can spend more, Arcos has some charming possibilities. *La Fonda Hotel* (☎ 956 70 00 57), on Calle Debajo del Corral, has well-equipped rooms with bath for 5350/8025 ptas. The friendly, attractive *Hotel Los Olivos* (☎ 956 70 08 11, Paseo de los Boliches 30) has rooms at 5350/9630 ptas. *Hotel El Convento* (☎ 956 70 23 33, Calle Maldonado 2), in a 17th-century convent east of Plaza del Cabildo, has great views. Tasteful rooms are 8560/10,700 ptas. Nearby in a converted mansion, *Hotel Marqués de Torresoto* (☎ 956 70 07 17, Calle Marqués de Torresoto 4) charges 8367/11,198 ptas.

Places to Eat
In the old town, the homy *Bar San Marcos* (Calle Marqués de Torresoto 6) serves platos combinados from 500 to 900 ptas, tapas around 200 ptas and a *menú* at 900 ptas. Opposite, the classy *El Convento* turns out

interesting fare – the three-course *menú* is 3000 ptas plus IVA. *Mesón Los Murales* (Plaza de Boticas 1), near Hotel El Convento, has a *menú* at 1000 ptas. The cave-like *Bar Alcaraván* (Calle Nueva 1), with tables under the castle walls, is good for tapas.

In the new town, there are a couple of options on Calle Debajo del Corral. *Café Bar El Faro*, No 14, has breakfasts at 225 ptas, main dishes from 500 to 1500 ptas and a *menú* at 900 ptas. At No 8, *Los Faraones* serves cheap breakfasts (150 ptas), platos combinados (600 ptas) and a *menú* (800 ptas) – plus excellent but pricier Arabic food, with some tasty vegetarian choices.

There are more eateries down by the river, below the castle.

Entertainment
In July/August, flamenco happens at Plaza del Cananeo, at the bottom of Calle Cadenas in the old town, from 10.30 pm Thursday.

Getting There & Away
Buses from Calle Corregidores on weekdays include 19 to Jerez, six to El Bosque, and a few each to Cádiz, Sevilla and Ronda. Fewer buses run on weekends.

ARCOS DE LA FRONTERA

PLACES TO STAY
5 La Fonda Hotel
6 Hotel Los Olivos
16 Hotel Marqués de Torresoto
17 Hostal & Bar San Marcos
20 Hotel El Convento

PLACES TO EAT
3 Café Bar El Faro
4 Los Faraones
9 Bar Alcaraván
18 El Convento
19 Mesón Los Murales

OTHER
1 Bus Station
2 Tourist Information Kiosk
7 Post Office (Correos)
8 Palacio del Conde de Águila
10 Castillo de los Duques
11 Tourist Office
12 Mirador
13 Parador, Casa del Corregidor
14 Basílica-Parroquia de Santa María
15 Convento de la Encarnación
21 Mercado
22 Palacio Mayorazgo
23 Iglesia de San Pedro

ANDALUCÍA

PARQUE NATURAL SIERRA DE GRAZALEMA

The mountainous Parque Natural Sierra de Grazalema in north-eastern Cádiz province, dotted with attractive white towns and villages, is one of Andalucía's greenest and most beautiful areas. Grazalema town has the highest measured rainfall in Spain, at 2153mm a year. This is fine walking country (best months: May, June, September, October), and there are opportunities for plenty of other activities from climbing and caving to paragliding.

The park extends into north-western Málaga province, where it includes the Cueva de la Pileta (see Around Ronda later in this chapter). A good overall map is the IGN/Junta de Andalucía *Sierra de Grazalema* (1:50,000), which with luck you'll find locally.

The northern flank of the Sierra del Pinar between Grazalema and Benamahoma supports a famous 3-sq-km *pinsapar,* Spain's best-preserved woodland of the rare Spanish fir (*pinsapo* in Spanish). Over 500 ibex inhabit the park, and around 100 pairs of griffon vulture live in the Garganta Verde and Garganta Seca Gorges.

Three of the park's best day walks are: the ascent of Torreon (1654m), the highest peak in Cádiz province; the route from Grazalema to Benamahoma via the pinsapar; and the trip into the Garganta Verde, a deep, lushly vegetated ravine south of Zahara de la Sierra.

All these are within a 30-sq-km *area de reserva* (reserve area), with entry rules that change occasionally. At the time of writing you needed a free permit from the El Bosque park office (see the following El Bosque section), which is attended 10 am to 2 pm Monday and Tuesday, as well as during its normal opening hours, for issuing permits. You can telephone in advance to arrange permits for specific days or arrange to collect your permit at Zahara or Grazalema. From January to June the Garganta Verde can only be visited with an authorised guide from Horizon or Pinzapo (see the Grazalema section). Lonely Planet's *Walking in Spain* describes these and further walks.

Getting There & Away

Los Amarillos runs up to seven buses a day to El Bosque from Jerez and Arcos, and two or three from Cádiz and Sevilla (Prado de San Sebastián). From El Bosque, except on Sunday, there's a 3.15 pm Los Amarillos bus to Grazalema. Return buses leave Grazalema at 5.30 am weekdays, and 7 pm Friday.

Los Amarillos also runs twice daily from Malaga to Ubrique via Ronda, Grazalema and Benaocaz.

Comes runs twice daily on weekdays between Ronda and Zahara de la Sierra, via Algodonales. There's no service between Zahara and Grazalema.

El Bosque
postcode 11670 • pop 1800

El Bosque, 33km east of Arcos across rolling country, is prettily situated below the wooded Sierra de Albarracín to the south-east. There's a take-off point for hang-gliders and paragliders in the Sierra de Albarracín. A pleasant 5km riverside path to Benamahoma starts beside El Bosque's youth hostel.

The natural park's main information centre (☎ 956 72 70 29) is at Avenida de la Diputación s/n, down a short lane off the A-372 at the western end of the village, opposite Hotel Las Truchas. It's open 10 am to 2 pm and 4 to 6 pm Wednesday to Sunday. El Bosque's large public swimming pool (350 ptas), with shade, is next door.

Places to Stay & Eat At *Camping La Torrecilla (☎/fax 956 71 60 95),* 1km south on the old road to Ubrique, two adults with one tent and a car pay 1750 ptas (closed 16 December to 31 January). The Inturjoven youth hostel, *Albergue Campamento Juvenil El Bosque (☎ 956 71 62 12, Molino de Enmedio s/n),* pleasantly sited by a stream, has a shady camping area (900 ptas per person, including breakfast) as well as double and triple rooms, most with bath. There's a swimming pool too. *Hostal Enrique Calvillo (☎ 956 71 61 05, Avenida Diputación 5),* near the park information office, has doubles with bath for 4500 ptas. *Hotel Las Truchas (☎ 956 71 60 61, Avenida Diputación 1)* has comfy singles/doubles with bath for 4600/7500 ptas plus IVA, and a restaurant terrace overlooking the village and countryside. Try trout, the local speciality.

Benamahoma

This small village, 4km east of El Bosque on the A-372 to Grazalema, has a trout farm and cottage industry of rush-backed chairs. You can walk to Zahara de la Sierra on dirt roads, a beautiful trip of 16km.

Camping Los Linares (☎ 956 71 62 75), 600m up Camino del Nacimiento at the back of the village, has cabins with bedding at around 4500 ptas for two, as well as camping. In winter it normally opens weekends and holidays only.

Grazalema

postcode 11610 • pop 2300

From Benamahoma the A-372 winds east over the Puerto del Boyar (1103m) to Grazalema. A haunt of nature lovers and artists, Grazalema is a neat, picture-postcard village (especially when dusted with snow), nestling into a corner of beautiful mountain country beneath the rock-climbers' crag Peñon Grande. Local products include pure wool blankets and rugs.

The tourist office (☎ 956 13 22 25), on the central Plaza de España, doubles as a crafts salesroom. It's open 10 am to 2 pm and 4 to 6 pm (6 to 8 pm in summer) Tuesday to Sunday. Unicaja bank, right by Plaza de España, has an ATM.

Things to See & Do Grazalema has a couple of lovely 17th-century churches, the **Iglesia de la Aurora** on Plaza de España and the nearby **Iglesia de la Encarnación**.

Horizon (☎ 956 13 23 63), Calle Agua 5, offers **guided activities** from climbing and bridge-jumping to bird-watching and walking, with minimum group size of four to six. Prices per person range from around 1700 ptas for a half-day walk to over 4000 ptas for some caving or canyoning trips. The office is open 11 am to 1 pm daily except Tuesday. Pinzapo (☎ 956 13 21 66), Calle Las Piedras 11, provides some similar activities.

Grazalema's public swimming pool, with good views, is by the El Bosque road at the eastern end of the village.

Camping Tajo Rodillo (see later) rents out mountain bikes for 1400 ptas per day.

Special Events Las Fiestas del Carmen, for a week in mid-July, include plenty of late-night music and dance performances. They end on a Monday with a bull-running through the streets.

Places to Stay & Eat At the top of the village beside the A-372 to El Bosque, *Camping Tajo Rodillo* (☎ 956 13 20 63) charges 1575 ptas for two adults, a tent and car. In winter you may only find it open on weekends and holidays.

In the centre, the good-value *Casa de las Piedras* (☎ 956 13 20 14, Calle las Piedras 32) has plenty of singles/doubles for 1500/3000 ptas, or 3600/4800 ptas with bath. Its restaurant, when open, serves hearty breakfasts and meals.

Villa Turística (☎ 956 13 21 62, El Olivar s/n), above the village to the north, has manicured lawns with a pool and great views. Rooms with all mod cons are 4925/8025 ptas; apartments are from 6850 ptas for one person to 18,085 ptas for four.

There are plenty of places to eat and drink on Calle Agua, off Plaza de España, among them *Bar La Posadilla* with good-value platos combinados for only 300 to 500 ptas. *Restaurante Cadiz El Chico (Plaza de España 8)* is good for a more expensive meal, with meat, fish and seafood from 600 to 1600 ptas.

Zahara de la Sierra

postcode 11688 • pop 1550

Topped by a crag with a ruined castle, Zahara is the most dramatically sited of the area's villages. It feels quite otherworldly if you've driven through mist from Grazalema via the vertiginous 1331m Puerto de los Palomas (Doves' Pass; but with more vultures than doves).

Zahara's recapture from the Christians by Abu al-Hasan of Granada in a night raid in 1481 sparked the last phase of the

ANDALUCÍA

Reconquista, which ended with the fall of Granada. In the late 19th century, Zahara was a hotbed of anarchism.

The village centres on Calle San Juan, a cobbled street with a church at each end. At one end of this, at Plaza del Rey 3, is a natural park information office (☎ 956 12 31 14), open from at least 9 am to 2 pm daily.

Things to See & Do There's a **mirador** (lookout) at one end of Calle San Juan, in front of the 18th-century baroque **Iglesia de Santa María de la Mesa**. You can climb to the 12th-century **castle** by a road behind this church – or by a path with steps from the main road below the village. Zahara's steep streets invite investigation, with vistas framed by tall palms or hot-pink bougainvillea.

Places to Stay & Eat *Camping Arroyomolinos* (956 23 40 79), 3km south-east of Zahara near the reservoir, charges 1000 ptas for two adults, a tent and a car. *Pensión Los Tadeos* (☎ 956 12 30 86, Paseo de la Fuente s/n) has a few basic doubles for 3000 ptas. *Hostal Marqués de Zahara* (☎ 956 12 30 61, Calle San Juan 3), a converted mansion, has comfy singles/doubles for 3750/5650 ptas. *Bar Nuevo* on this street offers homy, cheap food. *Hotel Arco de la Villa* (☎ 956 12 32 30, Camino Nazarí s/n) has 17 air-con rooms with good views, for 4925/8025 ptas, and a restaurant.

COSTA DE LA LUZ

The 90km coast between Cádiz and Tarifa can be windy, and its Atlantic waters are a shade cooler than the Mediterranean, but these are small prices to pay for an unspoiled, often wild shore, strung with long, white-sand beaches. Andalucians flock here in July and August, bringing a fiesta atmosphere to the normally quiet coastal settlements.

The three finest places to head for are the villages of Los Caños de Meca, Zahara de los Atunes and Bolonia. It's advisable to ring ahead for rooms in July and August. Between Los Caños and Zahara is **Barbate**, a drab town where you might need to change buses and which has the only tourist

office (☎ 956 43 39 62) in the district, at Plaza Onésimo Redondo s/n. Barbate's Comes station (☎ 956 43 05 94), on Avenida del Generalísimo, is served by up to 12 daily buses to/from Cádiz and one or two to/from Sevilla (Prado de San Sebastián), Tarifa and Algeciras.

Los Caños de Meca
postcode 11159 • pop 200

Los Caños, once a hippie hideaway, straggles along a series of sandy coves beneath a pine-clad hill 12km west of Barbate. It maintains its laid-back air even at the height of summer.

The road from Barbate emerges towards the eastern end of Los Caños' single street, which is mostly called Avenida Trafalgar. The main beach is straight in front of you. At the western end of the village a side road leads out to a lighthouse on a low spit of land with a famous name: Cabo de Trafalgar. Off here, Spanish naval power was terminated in a few hours one day in 1805 by a British fleet under Nelson. Further decent beaches stretch either side of Cabo de Trafalgar.

Places to Stay Three *camping grounds*, between 1km and 3km west from the Barbate road corner, open from about April to September and get pretty crowded in midsummer. They charge around 2000 to 2500 ptas for two people with a car and tent.

About 10 hostales are strung along Avenida Trafalgar, and there are more at Zahora, 2km west. Most are pretty similar and have decent rooms with bath.

The quieter end of the village is east from the Barbate road corner. *Hostal Fortuna* (☎ 956 43 70 75), about 200m along, has singles/doubles for 4000/6000 ptas (6000/8000 ptas in August). Farther on, the quaint, turreted *Hostal Los Castillejos* (☎ 956 43 70 19) has lingering hippie vibes and doubles from 5500 to 7500 ptas.

West from the Barbate road corner, *Hostal Miramar* (☎ 956 43 70 24, Avenida Trafalgar 100) boasts a pool and restaurant and has doubles for 6000 ptas in high season. Farther along, *Hostal El Ancla* (☎ 956 43 71 00) has doubles or triples with bath from 5000 ptas to 7000 ptas. Both places close in winter. Just past El Ancla, an 'Apartamentos y Bungalows' sign indicates *Casas Karen* (☎ 956 43 70 67, ⓔ *karen@jet.es, Fuente del Madroño 6), about 500m inland. Run by a dynamic young Englishwoman, this unusual accommodation ranges from a converted farmhouse to a *choza,* a traditional thatched dwelling. It caters mostly for weekly rentals, but one-night prices for doubles range from 6000 to 9000 ptas.

Places to Eat *Restaurante El Caña,* just east of the Barbate road corner, has a fine position above the beach. Most seafood is around 1300 ptas. It closes in winter. *El Pirata*, above the beach 200m west, is a good bet with salads from 300 ptas and seafood media-raciones at 500 or 600 ptas. In winter, if you find nowhere open in Los Caños village, try *Las Acacias* near the Trafalgar turning.

Entertainment In high summer, good bars include the cool *Bonano* next to Hostal Los Castillejos, *Café-Bar Ketama* opposite El Pirata, and a couple of places with music on the road out to Cabo de Trafalgar. *Sajoramí* restaurant-bar at Playa Zahora often has live rock, blues or flamenco on summer nights.

Getting There & Away On weekdays two buses each run to/from Barbate and Cádiz and one each to/from Sevilla (Prado de San Sebastián) and Zahara de los Atunes. Extra buses run from mid-June to early September, including Saturday and Sunday.

Zahara de los Atunes
postcode 11393 • pop 1000
Plonked in the middle of nothing except a broad, 12km, sandy beach, Zahara is an elemental sort of place. At its heart stands the crumbling old Almadraba, once a depot and refuge for the local tuna *(atún)* fishers, who were an infamously rugged lot. Cervantes wrote that no one deserved the name *pícaro* (scoundrel) unless they had spent two seasons fishing for tuna at Zahara. Today the nearest tuna fleet is at Barbate, but Zahara has become an almost fashionable Spanish

summer resort, with an old-fashioned core of narrow streets. It's a fine spot to let the sun, sea and wind – and, in summer, a spot of lively nightlife – batter your senses.

Places to Stay *Camping Bahía de la Plata* (☎ 956 43 90 40), near the beach at the southern end of Zahara, is open all year, charging 2490 ptas for two people with car and tent.

The cheapest rooms, and the most likely to have vacancies when everywhere seems full, are at *Hostal Monte Mar* (☎ 956 43 90 47, Calle Peñón 12), at the northern tip of the village. The rooms are fine, at 6500 ptas a double with its own bath. Little *Hotel Nicolás* (☎ 956 43 92 74, Calle María Luisa 13) has simple but attractive singles/doubles with TV and bath for 5350/7490 ptas, and a restaurant.

Hotel Doña Lola (☎ 956 43 90 09, Plaza Thompson 1) is a modern place in an old-fashioned style, with good doubles at 10,700 ptas. *Hotel Gran Sol* (☎ 956 43 93 01, Calle Sánchez Rodríguez s/n), with the prime beach position, has large, comfortable doubles at 12,500 ptas plus IVA.

Places to Eat Most restaurants are on or near Plaza de Tamarón near Hotel Doña Lola, and most offer similar lists of fish, seafood, salads, meat and sometimes pizzas. *Patio la Plazoleta* is a good choice, open to the air; a media-ración of *pez limón a la plancha* (grilled tuna with vegetables and lemon) is 800 ptas.

Entertainment In July and August a line of marquees and shacks along the beach south of the Almadraba serves as bars, discos and *teterías* (teahouses). They get busy from about midnight. Some have live flamenco or other music.

Getting There & Away Comes runs three daily buses weekdays (two on Saturday and Sunday) to/from Cádiz via Barbate, and one each on weekdays to/from Tarifa and to/from Sevilla (Prado de San Sebastián) via Los Caños de Meca. There are more buses from mid-June to September.

ANDALUCÍA

Bolonia
postcode 11391 • pop 100

This tiny village, 10km down the coast from Zahara and about 20km from Tarifa, has a fine white-sand beach, several restaurants and hostales, and the ruins of the Roman town of Baelo Claudia. The ruins include a theatre, a forum surrounded by temples and other buildings, and workshops that turned out the salted fish and garum that made Baelo Claudia famous in the Roman world (garum was a prized condiment made from fish entrails – an ancestor of the fish sauce of South-East Asian cuisine). The site is open 10 am to 6 pm Tuesday to Saturday (to 7 pm in spring, 8 pm in summer) and until 2 pm Sunday (250 ptas, free for EU citizens).

Accommodation, with summer prices for doubles with bathroom, includes *Hostal Bellavista (☎ 956 68 85 53),* in the centre at 6500 ptas; *Hostal Miramar (☎ 956 68 85 61),* at 4000 to 5500 ptas; and *Hostal Lola (☎ 956 68 85 36),* charging 4000 to 6000 ptas.

The road to Bolonia heads west off the N-340, 15km from Tarifa. Without wheels, it's a 7km hilly walk from the main road. You can also walk 8km along the coast from Ensenada de Valdevaqueros via Punta Paloma (see Tarifa).

TARIFA
postcode 11380 • pop 14,000

Even at peak times, Tarifa is an attractive, laid-back town. Relatively unknown until 15 or so years ago, it's now a windsurfing mecca, with some of the very best conditions in Europe for the sport. The beaches have clean, white sand, and inland the country is green and rolling. Then there's the old town to explore, with its narrow streets, whitewashed houses and cascading flowers. The only negative – though not for windsurfers or the hundreds of modern windmills inland! – is the wind; for much of the year, either the *levante* (easterly) or *poniente* (westerly) is blowing, which is ruinous for a relaxed sit on the beach and tiring if you're simply wandering around. August, however, can be blessedly still.

Tarifa takes its name from Tarik ibn Malik who led a Muslim raid in 710, the year before the main Islamic invasion of the peninsula. The Christians took the town in 1292.

Orientation
Two roads head into Tarifa from the N-340. The one from the north-west becomes Calle Batalla del Salado, ending at Avenida de Andalucía where the Puerta de Jerez leads through the walls into the old town. The one from the north-east meets Avenida de Andalucía at the Puerta de Jerez. The main street of the old town is Calle Sancho IV El Bravo. To the south-west protrudes the Punta de Tarifa, a military-occupied promontory that is the southernmost point of continental Europe.

Information
The tourist office (☎ 956 68 09 93) is near the top end of the palm-lined Paseo de la Alameda on the western side of the old town. It's open 10.30 am to 2 pm and 5 to 7 pm (6 to 8 pm in summer) weekdays, and summer Saturdays.

There are banks and ATMs on Calle Sancho IV El Bravo and Calle Batalla del Salado. Pandora's Papelería on Calle Sancho IV El Bravo provides Internet access. The Policía Local (☎ 956 61 41 86) are in the ayuntamiento on Plaza de Santa María. The Cruz Roja (Red Cross; ☎ 956 64 48 96) is at Calle Alcalde Juan Núñez 5.

International newspapers are sold at the News Stand on Calle Batalla del Salado.

Old Town
The mudéjar **Puerta de Jerez** was built after the Reconquista. Look in at the bustling **mercado** on Calle Colón before wending your way to the mainly 15th-century **Iglesia de San Mateo** at the end of Calle Sancho IV El Bravo. The streets south of the church are little changed since Islamic times. The **Mirador El Estrecho**, atop part of the castle walls, has spectacular views across to Africa.

The **Castillo de Guzmán**, extending west from here – but entered at its far end on Calle Guzmán – is named after the Reconquista hero Guzmán El Bueno. In 1294, when threatened with the death of his captured son unless he relinquished the castle to

Islamic forces trying to recapture Tarifa, he threw down his own dagger for the deed to be done. Guzmán's descendants became the Duques de Medina Sidonia (see Sanlúcar de Barrameda). The imposing fortress, originally built in 960 on orders of the Córdoban caliph Abd ar-Rahman III, is open 10 am to 2 pm and 4 to 8 pm daily (200 ptas). Tickets are sold in the stationery shop opposite the castle entrance. Inside, there are great views from the Torre de Guzmán El Bueno.

Beaches

The sheltered but tiny Playa Chica, on the isthmus leading out to Punta de Tarifa, is popular. From here Playa de los Lances stretches 10km north-west to the huge sand dune at Punta Paloma.

Activities

Aky Oaky (☎ 956 68 53 56), Calle Batalla del Salado 37, offers a range of organised activities (2500 to 7000 ptas), including caving, mountain biking, horse riding, diving, walking and visiting fighting-bull farms.

Windsurfing Conditions are often right on Tarifa's town beaches but most of the action occurs along the coast between Tarifa and Punta Paloma, 10km north-west. El Porro on Ensenada de Valdevaqueros, the bay formed by Punta Paloma, is one of the most popular spots as it has easy parking and plenty of space to set up.

You can buy new and second-hand gear in Tarifa at the shops along Calle Batalla del Salado. For board rental and classes you need to try places up the coast such as Club Mistral at the Hurricane Hotel (see Places to Stay), or Spin Out in front of Camping Torre de la Peña II, near El Porro. At Club Mistral board rental costs 2800 ptas per hour or 7500 ptas per day; a six-hour beginner's course is 19,500 ptas.

Competitions are held year round with two big events in summer: the World Speed Cup (July) and the World Cup (Formula 42) in July or August.

Horse Riding Hotel Dos Mares (☎ 956 68 40 35) and Hurricane Hotel (☎ 956 68 49 19), both on Playa de los Lances a few kilometres out of Tarifa, hire out horses with guides. An hour's ride along the beach costs about 3000 ptas.

Whale Watching Three-hour boat trips to track and watch dolphins and whales are run by Whale Watch España (☎ 956 62 70 13, 639-47 65 44), which has an office on Calle Sancho IV El Bravo. Trips cost 4500 ptas (3000 ptas for under-12s).

Bird-watching When the levante is blowing or there's little wind, the Tarifa area, including the spectacular Mirador del Estrecho lookout point 7km east on the N-340, is good for watching bird migrations across the Strait of Gibraltar (for more information on these migrations, see the Gibraltar section).

Places to Stay

Camping There are six year-round camping grounds on or near the beach between Tarifa and Punta Paloma, 10km north-west along the N-340. All of these grounds charge around 2200 ptas for two people with a tent and a car.

Hostales & Hotels It's best to phone ahead in August, when rooms can be tight. Most places cut prices 25% to 40% for much of the rest of the year.

In Town The attractive rooms at *Pensión Correo* (☎ 956 68 02 06, Calle Coronel Moscardó 9) cost from 2000 ptas per person. The lively, well-travelled owners of *Pensión Africa* (☎ 956 68 02 20, Calle María Antonia Toledo 12) offer bright, comfortable singles/doubles for 2500/4000 ptas with shared bath or 3500/5000 ptas with bath; all in an old house. Popular *Casa Facundo* (☎ 956 68 42 98, Calle Batalla del Salado 47) is geared to windsurfers. Rooms are 3000/4000 ptas (doubles with bath and TV: 6000 ptas).

Good, clean rooms with bath are 4000/8000 ptas at the friendly *Hostal Villanueva* (☎ 956 68 41 49, Avenida de Andalucía 11), built into the old city walls. Most rooms at the imaginatively restored *La Casa Amarilla*

ANDALUCÍA

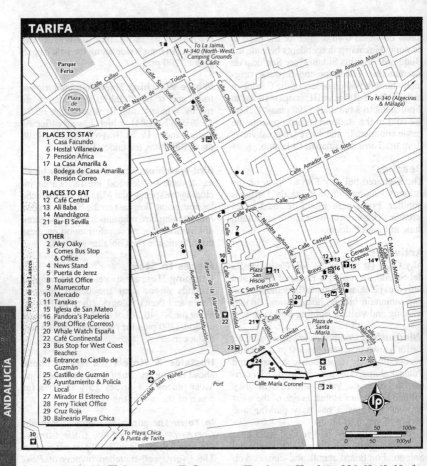

TARIFA

PLACES TO STAY
1 Casa Facundo
6 Hostal Villaneuva
7 Pensión Africa
17 La Casa Amarilla &
   Bodega de Casa Amarilla
18 Pensión Correo

PLACES TO EAT
12 Café Central
13 Ali Baba
14 Mandrágora
21 Bar El Sevilla

OTHER
2 Aky Oaky
3 Comes Bus Stop
   & Office
4 News Stand
5 Puerta de Jerez
8 Tourist Office
9 Marruecotur
10 Mercado
11 Tanakas
15 Iglesia de San Mateo
16 Pandora's Papelería
19 Post Office (Correos)
20 Whale Watch España
22 Café Continental
23 Bus Stop for West Coast
   Beaches
24 Entrance to Castillo de
   Guzmán
25 Castillo de Guzmán
26 Ayuntamiento & Policía
   Local
27 Mirador El Estrecho
28 Ferry Ticket Office
29 Cruz Roja
30 Balneario Playa Chica

(☎ 956 65 19 93, e lacasaamarilla@via
.goya.es, Calle Sancho IV El Bravo 9), have
a kitchenette and all have bath and cable TV;
doubles are 8560 ptas.

Along the Coast At least nine places are
dotted along the beach and the N-340
within 10km north-west of Tarifa, but none
is cheap. All have rooms with bath.

Hostal Millón (☎ 956 68 52 46), located 5km from the town centre, has a nice
little beachside garden, its own small restaurant, and reasonable doubles costing
12,000 ptas.

Hurricane Hotel (☎ 956 68 49 19, fax
956 68 03 29), in semitropical beachside
gardens 6km from town, has 33 large, comfy
rooms, two pools, a health club, a windsurfing school and board rental. Doubles are
19,260 ptas on the ocean side and 17,120
ptas on the land side, including an excellent
buffet breakfast.

The closest places to Punta Paloma, 10km
out, are *Cortijo Las Piñas* (☎ 956 68 51 36)
and attractive *Cortijo Valdevaqueros* (same
owners as the Hurricane Hotel), almost on the
beach and open from Easter to mid-September.
Both have doubles around 10,000 ptas.

euro currency converter 100pta = €0.60

Places to Eat

Calle Sancho IV El Bravo has plenty of takeaway options, including popular *Ali Baba* with filling, tasty Arabic food. Excellent felafels are 375 ptas, meat kebabs 450 ptas. A few doors away, *Café Central* has good *churros con chocolate* (deep-fried doughnuts with hot chocolate) and a good range of breakfasts from 300 ptas. Main dishes are around 975 ptas.

Delicious options at *Mandrágora (Calle Independencia 3)* include bacalao-stuffed peppers (1300 ptas) and cheese-stuffed chicken breasts (1000 ptas).

The best-value seafood is at *Bar El Sevilla* on Calle Inválidos. There's no name outside – some locals call it El Gallego. Mixed fish-and-seafood fry-ups – excellent with a beer – cost 200 ptas for generous tapas, 950 ptas for a ración (enough for two).

Along the coast, most hotels and hostales (see Places to Stay) have restaurants. The Hurricane Hotel's *Terrace Restaurant* is good for a medium-priced lunch (salads, local fish and seafood).

Entertainment

Bodega de Casa Amarilla on Calle Sancho IV El Bravo is good for an evening drink or lunchtime live flamenco at weekends. On Paseo de la Alameda, *Café Continental* has live music on summer weekend nights. *Tanakas* on Plaza San Hiscio is the biggest discoteca in town, open Friday and Saturday until 5 am.

In July and August the open-air *discoteca* at Balneario Playa Chica, with two dance floors, is fun. Also in summer, a big Moroccan tent called *La Jaima* pops up on Playa de los Lances near the edge of town; from 7 to 10 pm it's a tetería (try a mint tea at sunset), but come midnight it's a popular discoteca.

Getting There & Away

Bus Comes (☎ 956 68 40 38), on Calle Batalla del Salado, 1½ blocks north of Avenida de Andalucía, runs seven or more daily buses to Cádiz and Algeciras; a few to La Línea, Jerez de la Frontera, Sevilla and Málaga; and two on weekdays to Barbate and Zahara de los Atunes.

Boat Services to/from Tangier come and go. At the time of writing, a ferry departed Tarifa at 9 am and Tangier at 5 pm (3 pm Moroccan time), with one-way fares of 3200 ptas for passengers, 9900 ptas for a driver and car. The crossing takes one hour. Additional sailings were planned: check at the harbour or at Marruecotur (☎ 956 68 47 51), Avenida de la Constitución 5/6.

ALGECIRAS
postcode 11280 • pop 102,000

Algeciras, the major port linking Spain with Africa, is an unattractive industrial and fishing town, and a drug-smuggling centre. During summer, the port is hectic with huge numbers of Moroccan workers heading home from Europe for their holidays.

Algeciras was taken by Alfonso XI from the Merenids of Morocco in 1344, but later razed by Mohammed V of Granada. In 1704 it was repopulated by many of those who left Gibraltar after it was taken by the British.

Information

Tourist Office The English-speaking main tourist office (☎ 956 57 26 36), Calle Juan de la Cierva s/n, is open 9 am to 2 pm weekdays.

Money Money-changing touts around the port are a rip-off for pesetas, and you'll get a better deal buying dirham in Morocco. There are banks and ATMs on Avenida Virgen del Carmen and around Plaza Alta, plus ATMs in the port.

Left Luggage In the port, luggage storage is available from 7.30 am to 9.30 pm at 150 to 200 ptas a bag; bags need to be secured. There are also *consigna* (left-luggage office) lockers nearby (400 ptas).

Medical Services & Emergency The Policía Nacional (☎ 956 66 04 00) are at Avenida de las Fuerzas Armadas 6. The Hospital Cruz Roja (☎ 956 60 31 44) is central at Paseo de la Conferencia s/n, on the southern extension of Avenida de la Marina.

Dangers & Annoyances Keep your wits about you in the port, bus station and market,

ANDALUCÍA

and ignore offers from the legions of money-changers, drug-pushers and ticket-hawkers who approach you. (It's worse in Tangier!) Walk purposefully if moving between the Comes and Portillo bus stations in the evening.

Things to See

If you have to spend time in Algeciras, wander up to the palm-fringed main square, **Plaza Alta**, which has a lovely tiled fountain and is flanked by the 18th-century **Iglesia Nuestra Señora de la Palma** and the 17th-century **Santuario Nuestra Señora de Europa**. There's a bustling market in **Plaza Palma** daily except Sunday.

Places to Stay

There's loads of budget accommodation in the streets behind Avenida de la Marina, but night-time market traffic makes sleep difficult. If it's not too hot, try for an interior room. Friendly *Hostal González* (☎ 956 65

28 43, Calle José Santacana 7) has good, clean singles/doubles with bath at 2000/4000 ptas in summer. *Hostal España* (☎ 956 66 82 62, Calle José Santacana 4) has large, clean rooms at 1200 ptas per person but it's right by the market. *Hostal Levante* (☎ 956 65 15 05, Calle Duque de Almodóvar 21) is a little removed from the thick of things; reasonable rooms with shower and 1500/3000 ptas though the corridors are a bit musty.

Hotel Reina Cristina (☎ 956 60 26 22, Paseo de la Conferencia s/n), a brisk five-minute walk south of the port, is an old colonial-style hotel with tropical gardens. Doubles cost 22,000 ptas (16,000 ptas in winter) plus IVA.

Places to Eat

The *mercado* has wonderful fresh produce, and the *Panadería-Café*, at the market end of Calle José Santacana, is excellent for breakfast.

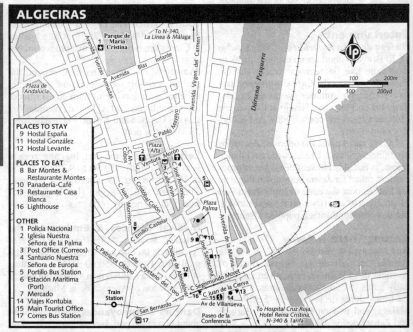

ALGECIRAS

ANDALUCÍA

PLACES TO STAY
9   Hostal España
11 Hostal González
12 Hostal Levante

PLACES TO EAT
8   Bar Montes &
    Restaurante Montes
10 Panadería-Café
13 Restaurante Casa
    Blanca
16 Lighthouse

OTHER
1   Policía Nacional
2   Iglesia Nuestra
    Señora de la Palma
3   Post Office (Correos)
4   Santuario Nuestra
    Señora de Europa
5   Portillo Bus Station
6   Estación Marítima
    (Port)
7   Mercado
14 Viajes Kontubia
15 Main Tourist Office
17 Comes Bus Station

euro currency converter 100pta = €0.60

Restaurante Casa Blanca (Calle Juan de la Cierva 1) is popular for its 900-ptas *menú* of two courses, bread, drink and dessert; other options are moderately priced.

In the evening you can sample tasty tapas at *Bar Montes (Calle Emilio Castelar 36),* with tables out the front. The attached *Restaurante Montes* has a 1100 ptas *menú* with quite a wide choice, and a la carte seafood. English-speaking Christians run the friendly little *Lighthouse,* 200m east of the train station, with decent breakfasts and generally helpful tourist advice.

Getting There & Away
Bus The Comes bus station (☎ 956 65 34 56) is on Calle San Bernardo. To Tarifa there are at least seven buses daily. Buses run to La Línea every 45 minutes from 7 am to 9.15 pm. Other daily services include 10 buses to Cádiz (1260 ptas), five to Sevilla (2100 ptas) and three to Madrid (3375 ptas). There's one bus (except Sunday) to Zahara de los Atunes and Barbate, and a bus to Ronda at 8.30 am weekdays.

Portillo (☎ 956 65 10 55), Avenida Virgen del Carmen 15, operates several buses daily to Málaga (direct, 1¾ hours, 1990 ptas; with stops along the Costa del Sol, three hours, 1390 ptas), and four to Granada (3¾ hours, 2595 ptas).

Bacoma (☎ 956 66 50 67), inside the port, runs up to four services daily to Alicante, Valencia and Barcelona (17 hours, 9915 ptas). Bacoma and Viajes Kontubia on Calle Juan de la Cierva run buses to France, Germany and Holland.

Train From Algeciras station (☎ 956 63 02 02), two direct trains run daily to/from Madrid (six or 11 hours, 9300 or 5200 ptas) and one to/from Granada (four hours, 2665 ptas). All pass through Ronda and Bobadilla, where you can change for Málaga, Córdoba and Sevilla.

Boat Trasmediterránea (☎ 956 65 17 55, 902-45 46 45), EuroFerrys (☎ 956 65 11 78) and other companies operate frequent daily ferries to/from Tangier and Ceuta, the Spanish enclave on the Moroccan coast. Usually at least 20 sailings daily go to Tangier and 40 or more to Ceuta. From late June to September there are ferries almost round the clock to cater for the Moroccan migration, and you may have to queue three hours. Buy your ticket in the port or at agencies on Avenida de la Marina – prices are the same everywhere.

To Tangier, adults pay 3500 ptas one way by ferry (2½ hours), or 4440 ptas by hydrofoil (one hour). A car costs 10,750 ptas, a motorcycle over 500cc costs 3000 ptas.

To Ceuta, it's 1945 ptas by ferry (90 minutes), 3095 ptas by 'fast ferry' (40 minutes). Cars cost 8930 ptas and motorcycles 3000 ptas. Buquebus (☎ 902-41 42 42) crosses to Ceuta in 30 to 35 minutes at least nine times daily (2945/8223 ptas for passengers/cars).

LA LÍNEA DE LA CONCEPCIÓN
postcode 11300 • pop 61,000
La Línea, 20km east of Algeciras, is the unavoidable stepping stone to Gibraltar. A left turn as you exit the bus station will bring you out on Avenida 20 de Abril, which runs the 300m or so from the main square, Plaza de la Constitución, to the Gibraltar border. Facing the border is the slick new municipal tourist office (☎ 956 17 19 98).

Places to Stay
Pensión La Perla (☎ 956 76 95 13, Calle Clavel 10), two blocks north of Plaza de la Constitución, has clean, spacious singles/doubles for 1500/3000 ptas. *Hostal La Campana (☎ 956 17 30 59, Calle Carboneros 3),* off the western side of Plaza de la Constitución, has doubles with bath for 5200 ptas.

Getting There & Away
Bus There are four buses daily to/from Málaga (2½ hours, 1270 ptas), stopping in the Costa del Sol towns; five to/from Tarifa (455 ptas) and Cádiz (2½ hours, 1500 ptas); three to/from Sevilla (four hours, 2640 ptas); two to/from Granada (2475 ptas); and buses about every 30 minutes to/from Algeciras (40 minutes, 235 ptas).

Car & Motorcycle To avoid vehicle queues at the Gibraltar border, many visitors park in La Línea, then walk across. The

ANDALUCÍA

underground Parking Fo Cona just off Avenida 20 de Abril charges 150 ptas an hour or 1000 ptas a day; parking meters cost 165 ptas an hour or 710 ptas for 10 hours (free from 10.30 pm to 9.30 am).

Gibraltar

Looming like some great ship off almost the southernmost tip of Spain, the British colony of Gibraltar is such a compound of curiosities that a visit can hardly fail to stir the interest.

Gibraltar's territory is 5km long and up to 1.6km wide and most of it is one huge lump of limestone, 426m high. To the ancient Greeks and Romans, this was one of the two Pillars of Hércules, set up by the mythical strongman to mark the edge of the known world. (The other pillar was the coastal mountain Jebel Musa in Morocco, 25km south.)

History
In AD 711 Tariq ibn Ziyad, the Muslim governor of Tangier, landed at Gibraltar to launch the Islamic invasion of the Iberian Peninsula. The Rock has carried his name ever since: Jebel Tariq (Tariq's Mountain).

Castile wrested the Rock from the Muslims in 1462. Then in 1704 an Anglo-Dutch fleet captured Gibraltar during the War of the Spanish Succession. Spain ceded the Rock to Britain in 1713, but didn't end military attempts to regain it until the failure of the Great Siege of 1779–83. Britain developed it into an important naval base. During the Franco period Gibraltar was an extremely sore point between Britain and Spain: the border was closed from 1967 to 1985. In 1969, Gibraltarians voted by 12,138 to 44 in favour of British rather than Spanish sovereignty, and a new constitution gave Gibraltar domestic self-government. Today Spain offers Gibraltar autonomous-region status within Spain, but the Gibraltarians continue to reject any compromise over sovereignty, and Britain is constitutionally bound to respect their wishes on the matter. When Spain wants to exert pressure on Gibraltar, it uses such methods as extra-thorough customs and immigration procedures, which cause hours-long delays at the border.

The mainstays of Gibraltar's economy are tourism, the port and financial services (including, Spanish police complain, the laundering of proceeds from organised crime, much of which is invested in property in southern Spain).

Population, People & Language
Of Gibraltar's 29,000 people, about 75% are classed as Gibraltarians, 14% British, and 7% Moroccan. The Gibraltarians are of mixed Genoese, Jewish, Spanish and British ancestry; the Moroccans are mostly temporary workers.

Gibraltarians speak both English and Spanish and, at times, a curious mix of the two. Signs are in English.

Orientation
To reach Gibraltar by land you must pass through the Spanish border town of La Línea de la Concepción (see earlier). Just south of the border, the road crosses Gibraltar airport runway. The town and harbours of Gibraltar lie along the Rock's less steep western side, facing the Bahía de Algeciras (or Bay of Gibraltar).

Information
Tourist Offices Gibraltar has several helpful tourist offices. There's one (☎ 50762) in the customs and immigration building at the border; it's open 9 am to 4.30 pm weekdays. The main office (☎ 45000) is in Duke of Kent House, Cathedral Square; it's open 9 am to 5.30 pm weekdays.

Visas & Documents To enter Gibraltar, you need a passport or EU national identity card. EU, USA, Canada, Australia, New Zealand and South Africa passport-holders are among those who do not need visas for Gibraltar. For further information contact Gibraltar's Immigration Department (☎ 46411).

Those who need visas for Spain should have at least a double-entry Spanish visa so that they can return to Spain from Gibraltar.

Money The currencies are the Gibraltar pound (£) and pound sterling, which are interchangeable. You can spend pesetas (except in pay phones and post offices) but conversion rates aren't in your favour. Change any unspent Gibraltar currency before leaving.

Banks are generally open 9 am to 3.30 pm weekdays. There are several on Main St. *Bureaux de change* have longer hours.

Post & Communications The main post office, at 104 Main St, is open 9 am to 4.30 pm weekdays (in summer to 2.15 pm) and 10 am to 1 pm Saturday.

To phone Gibraltar from Spain, precede the five-digit local number with the code ☎ 9567; from other countries, dial the international access code, then the Gibraltar country code (☎ 350) and the local number.

To phone Spain from Gibraltar, just dial the nine-digit Spanish number.

Bookshops You can stock up on English-language reading material at Bell Books, 11 Bell Lane, and Gibraltar Bookshop, 300 Main St.

Medical Services & Emergency St Bernard's Hospital (☎ 79700) on Hospital Hill has 24-hour emergency facilities. The police (☎ 72500) have a station at 120 Irish Town. In an emergency call ☎ 199 for police or ambulance.

Electricity Electric current is the same as in Britain, 220V or 240V, with plugs of three flat pins.

The Town

Most Spanish and Islamic buildings were destroyed in 18th-century sieges, but British fortifications, gates and gun emplacements are all over the place.

The **Gibraltar Museum** on Bomb House Lane has good historical, architectural and military displays, including a well-preserved Muslim bathhouse and a detailed model of the Rock made in the 1860s. The opening hours are 10 am to 6 pm weekdays and until 2 pm Saturday (£2).

Many of the graves in the **Trafalgar Cemetery** are of British sailors who died at Gibraltar after the Battle of Trafalgar (1805). A short distance south are the **Alameda Botanic Gardens**, open 8 am to sunset daily (free). Just over 1km farther south, **Nelson's Anchorage** on Rosia Rd – open 9.30 am to 5 pm daily except Sunday (free) – contains a 100-ton Victorian super-gun, made in Britain in 1870, and overlooks Rosia Bay, where Nelson's body was brought ashore from HMS *Victory* after the Battle of Trafalgar.

Europa Point

At this southern tip of Gibraltar stand a lighthouse, the Christian Shrine of Our Lady of Europe, and the handsome Mosque of the Custodian of the Two Holy Mosques, opened in 1997 and claimed to be the largest mosque in a non-Islamic country. Phone ☎ 47693 for information on the mosque's opening hours.

Upper Rock Nature Reserve

Most of the upper Rock, starting just above the town, is a nature reserve, with spectacular views and several interesting spots to visit. When the wind is westerly, the Rock is often a fine spot for observing migrations of birds, especially raptors and storks, between Africa and Europe. January to early June is the time for northbound migrations, and late July to early November for southbound. When the wind is calm or easterly, the Tarifa area is usually better. White storks sometimes congregate in flocks of up to 3000 to cross the strait.

The reserve is officially open 9.30 am to 7 pm. Entry by road at £5 an adult, £2.50 a child and £1.50 a vehicle includes all the sights mentioned in this section. These are open to 6.15 or 6.30 pm. Cable-car tickets (see Getting Around) include entry to the reserve, the Apes' Den and St Michael's Cave.

The Rock's most famous inhabitants are its colony of **Barbary macaques**, the only wild primates (apart from *Homo sapiens*) in Europe. Some of these hang around the **Apes' Den** near the middle cable-car station; you'll often see others at the top cable-car station or Great Siege Tunnels. Legend

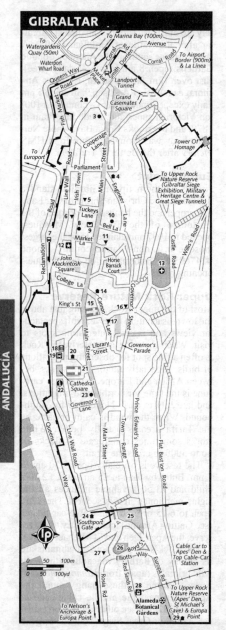

GIBRALTAR

PLACES TO STAY
2 Emile Youth Hostel
4 Continental Hotel
14 Cannon Hotel
20 Bristol Hotel
24 Toc H Hostel
26 Queen's Hotel
29 Rock Hotel

PLACES TO EAT
5 House of Sacarello
6 The Clipper
11 Viceroy of India
16 Three Roses Bar
17 Cannon Bar
27 Piccadilly Gardens

OTHER
1 Bus No 9
3 Tourafrica
7 Bus No 10
8 Bland Travel
9 Post Office (Correos)
10 Bell Books
12 Police
13 St Bernard's Hospital
15 Roman Catholic Cathedral
18 Gibraltar Museum
19 Bus No 3
21 Anglican Cathedral
22 Tourist Office
23 Gibraltar Bookshop
28 Lower Cable-Car Station

has it that when the apes (probably introduced from North Africa in the 18th century) disappear from Gibraltar, so will the British.

From the **top cable-car station**, you can see Morocco in clear weather. Down the precipitous eastern side of the Rock is the biggest of the old water catchments that channelled rain into underground reservoirs. Today these have been replaced by desalination plants.

About 20 minutes' walk south down St Michael's Rd (or 20 minutes up from the Apes' Den), **St Michael's Cave** is a big natural grotto that was once home to Neolithic inhabitants of the Rock. Today, apart from attracting tourists in droves, it's used for concerts, plays, even fashion shows. There's a cafe outside.

Princess Caroline's Battery, about a half-hour walk north (downhill) from the top cable-car station, houses a **Military Heritage Centre**. From here a road leads up to the impressive **Great Siege Tunnels**, hand-hewn by the British during the 1779–83 siege for gun emplacements. They constitute a tiny proportion of the more than 70km of tunnels in the Rock, most of which are off limits.

On Willis's Rd, which leads down to the town from Princess Caroline's Battery, are the **Gibraltar, A City Under Siege** exhibition and the **Tower of Homage**, the last vestige of Gibraltar's Muslim castle built in 1333.

Dolphin-Watching

The Bahía de Algeciras has a sizable population of dolphins, and from about April to September, several boats make two or more daily trips out to see them; at other times of the year there's usually at least one in daily operation. Most go from Watergardens Quay or adjacent Marina Bay. The trips last about 2½ hours and adult prices range from £12 to £15. Tourist offices have full details. You'll be unlucky if you don't get plenty of close-up dolphin contact.

Work

Gibraltar is better than anywhere in Spain, except Palma de Mallorca, for finding an unpaid yacht-crew place. Ask around at Marina Bay harbour.

Places to Stay

The independent *Emile Youth Hostel* (☎ 51106, Montagu Bastion, Line Wall Rd) has 43 places in two- to eight-person rooms for £12, including continental breakfast. The ramshackle old *Toc H Hostel* (☎ 73431), tucked into the city walls at the southern end of Line Wall Rd, has beds at £6 a night and cold showers.

Queen's Hotel (☎ 74000, 1 Boyd St) has a restaurant, bar and singles/doubles at £20/30 (£36/40 with private bath or shower). Reduced rates of £14/20 and £16/24 are offered for students and young travellers. All rates include English breakfast. *Cannon Hotel* (☎/fax 51711, 9 Cannon Lane) also has decent rooms, each sharing a bathroom with one other, for £22.50/34.50, including English breakfast.

Continental Hotel (☎ 76900, 1 Engineer Lane) has cosy rooms at £42/55, including continental breakfast. The rooms at *Bristol Hotel* (☎ 76800, 10 Cathedral Square) are pleasant enough but expensive at £47/61 interior or £51/66 exterior.

The venerable *Rock Hotel* (☎ 73000, 3 Europa Rd) has rooms at £160 or £165, including English breakfast, and a good restaurant and pool.

If Gibraltar prices don't grab you, there are economical options in La Línea.

Places to Eat

Most of the pubs serve British pub meals. *Three Roses Bar (60 Governor's St)* does a big all-day breakfast for £3.50. *Cannon Bar (27 Cannon Lane)* has some of the best fish and chips in town, with big portions for £4.75. At *Piccadilly Gardens* pub on Rosia Rd you can sit in the garden and have a three-course dinner for £9.95. Another pub with good food is *The Clipper (78B Irish Town)*.

For a restaurant meal, the chic *House of Sacarello (57 Irish Town)* is a good bet, with good soups for around £2 and excellent daily specials from £5.50 to £6.10. The Indian food at *Viceroy of India (9/11 Horse Barrack Court)* is usually pretty good; it has a three-course lunch special for £6.75.

There's a line of pleasant waterside eateries at Marina Bay.

Shopping

Gibraltar has lots of British high-street stores, such as Marks & Spencer, Mothercare and The Body Shop (all on Main St) and Safeway (in the Europort development at the northern end of the main harbour). Shops are normally open 9 am to 7.30 pm weekdays, and until 1 pm Saturday.

Getting There & Away

Air GB Airways (☎ 79300) flies daily to/from London. Return fares from London range from around UK£175 to UK£275, depending on the season. Monarch Airlines (☎ 47477) flies daily to/from Luton, with return fares from about UK£100 to UK£250.

ANDALUCIA

Morocco's Regional Air Lines (☎ 79300) flies Gibraltar to Casablanca most days for £104 return.

Airline offices are at the airport, but you can book through travel agencies.

Bus There are no regular buses to Gibraltar, but La Línea bus station is only a five-minute walk from the border.

Car & Motorcycle Vehicle queues at the border (which is open 24 hours) often make it less time-consuming to park in La Línea and walk across the border. To take a car into Gibraltar you need an insurance certificate, registration document, nationality plate and driving licence. You do *not* have to pay any fee, despite what would-be con artists might try to tell you as you queue at the border.

Boat The passenger catamaran *Mons Calpe II* sails daily except Monday and Saturday to/from Tangier (75 minutes) for £18/33 one-way/return. There are also normally two vehicle ferries a week to/from Tangier, taking about two hours for £18/30 one way/return per person and £40/80 per car. You can buy tickets for the catamaran at Bland Travel (☎ 77012), 81 Irish Town, and for the ferry at Tourafrica (☎ 77666), ICC Building, Main St.

Getting Around

The 1.5km walk from border to town centre crosses the airport runway. A left turn off Corral Rd takes you through the pedestrian Landport Tunnel into Grand Casemates Square. Alternatively, several bus lines (40p a ride) run from the border into town about every 15 minutes from 8.30 am to 8.30 pm. No 9 goes to Market Place; No 3 (to 11.30 pm) stops at Cathedral Square and the bottom cable-car station, then goes on to Europa Point; and No 10 runs to Europort (stopping at Safeway), then Reclamation Rd near the centre. Fewer buses go after 2 pm Saturday and none on Sunday.

All of Gibraltar can be covered on foot, and much of it (including the upper Rock) by car or motorcycle. You can also ascend

by the cable car which, weather permitting, leaves Red Sands Rd Monday to Saturday every few minutes between 9.30 am and 5.15 pm. Adult fares are £3.65/4.90 one way/return. For the Apes' Den, hop off at the middle station.

Málaga Province

Málaga province in south central Andalucía is best known for the Costa del Sol, Spain's most densely packed holiday coast. But it's much more than that. The province has a vibrant capital city, some wild, dramatic hill country and fascinating old towns such as Ronda and Antequera. Málaga's international airport is many people's point of entry into Spain.

MÁLAGA

postcode 29080 • pop 528,000

Málaga is ignored by many visitors who slip straight off from its airport to the Costa del Sol resorts. But this lively, very Spanish port city, set against a sparkling blue Mediterranean, has hidden charms – wide, leafy boulevards, good museums, impressive monuments, some charmingly dilapidated streets and great *joie de vivre*. Málaga stays open very late and inspires a fierce devotion among its citizens.

History

Probably founded by Phoenicians, Málaga flourished in the Muslim era, especially under the Granada taifa in the 11th century and later the Emirate of Granada, whose chief port it was. Its fall to the Christians in 1487 was a big nail in the emirate's coffin.

Prosperity arrived in the 19th century with a dynamic middle class, led by the families of Larios and Heredia, who founded varied industries. The popularity of Málaga dessert wine ('mountain sack') in Victorian England was also profitable until the phylloxera bug devastated the vineyards in the late 19th century. Early tourism helped compensate: in the 1920s Málaga became the favourite winter resort of rich *madrileños*.

In the civil war Málaga was initially a Republican stronghold. Hundreds of Nationalist sympathisers were killed before the city fell to the Nationalists in February 1937 after being bombed by Italian planes. Particularly vicious reprisals followed.

Málaga's economy has enjoyed plenty of spin-off from the tourism on the Costa del Sol since the 1960s, but youth unemployment is high.

Orientation

The central axis is Paseo del Parque-Alameda Principal-Avenida de Andalucía. The main streets leading north into the old town are Calle Marqués de Larios, ending at Plaza de la Constitución, and Calle Molina Lario. The city is dominated by the Gibralfaro, the hill rising above the eastern half of Paseo del Parque. The main shopping district is between Calle Marqués de Larios and Calle Puerta del Mar.

Information

The helpful regional tourist office (☎ 95 221 34 45), at Pasaje Chinitas 4, is open 9 am to 7 pm weekdays and 10 am to 2 pm weekends. The main municipal tourist office (☎ 95 260 44 10), Avenida de Cervantes 1, also helpful, is open 8.15 am to 2 pm and 4.30 to 7 pm weekdays, and 9.30 am to 1.30 pm Saturday. Smaller tourist offices are at the airport, bus station and elsewhere.

There are plenty of banks with ATMs on Calle Puerta del Mar and Calle Marqués de Larios. The main post office is at Avenida de Andalucía 1. Public Internet services with plenty of computers include Spider.es on Calle Méndez Núñez and Pasatiempos on Plaza de la Merced. Both charge 100 ptas per 15 minutes and open long hours.

Atlante Mapas, Calle Echegaray 7, is a terrific source of maps and guidebooks.

The Policía Nacional (☎ 95 204 62 00) have an office at Plaza de la Aduana 1. The Policía Local (☎ 95 212 65 00) are at Avenida de la Rosaleda 19. The main general hospital is Hospital Carlos Haya (☎ 95 239 04 00) on Avenida de Carlos Haya.

Take care of your valuables in the dark corners of the centre and at the bus station, where pickpockets and bag-snatchers have been known to operate.

Alcazaba

The Alcazaba, at the lower, western end of the Gibralfaro, was the palace-fortress of Málaga's Muslim governors. Begun in 1057 by the fearsome Granada taifa ruler Badis, it has two rings of walls, lots of defensive towers, and staggered entrance passages. With luck, when you go, several years of renovation work will be over and the whole Alcazaba will be open, with explanatory displays. At the time of writing only half, entered from Plaza de la Aduana, was able to be visited (9.30 am to 7 pm daily except Tuesday; free).

Below the Alcazaba, a **Roman theatre** is being excavated.

Castillo de Gibralfaro

Above the Alcazaba rises the older Castillo de Gibralfaro, built by Abd ar-Rahman I, the 8th-century Cordoban emir, and rebuilt in the 14th and 15th centuries. The views from the castle are great. Open 9 am to 6 pm daily (free), the expansive and impressive fortress includes an interesting little museum.

The Alcazaba and castle are connected by a curtain wall called La Coracha. You can walk up a path beside this to the castle, or take bus No 35 from Avenida de Cervantes (roughly every 45 minutes).

Catedral

Málaga's cathedral, on Calle Molina Lario, was begun in the 16th century on the former site of the main mosque. Building continued for two centuries. It is known locally as La Manquita (the One-Armed) since its southern tower was never completed. The cathedral has an 18th-century baroque facade but the inside is Gothic and Renaissance. Of special interest are the 17th-century wooden choir stalls, finely carved by Pedro de Mena.

The cathedral is open 9 am to 6.45 pm daily except Sunday and holidays (300 ptas). Enter from Calle Císter. Explanatory panels in English, French and Spanish tell you what's what inside.

ANDALUCÍA

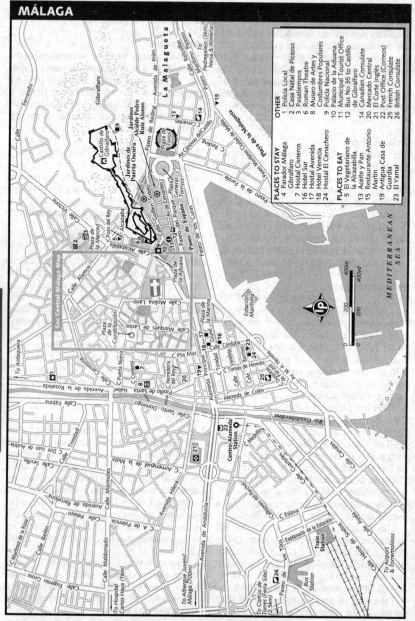

MÁLAGA

PLACES TO STAY
4 Parador Málaga Gibralfaro
7 Hostal Cisneros
16 Hotel Sur
17 Hostal Avenida
18 Hotel Venecia
24 Hostal El Cenachero

PLACES TO EAT
5 El Vegetariano de la Alcazabilla
13 Aceite y Pan
15 Restaurante Antonio Martín
19 Antigua Casa de Guardia
23 El Yamal

OTHER
1 Policía Local
2 Casa Natal de Picasso
3 Pasatiempos
6 Roman Theatre
8 Museo de Artes y Costumbres Populares
9 Policía Nacional
10 Palacio de la Aduana
11 Municipal Tourist Office
12 Bus No 35 to Castillo de Gibralfaro
14 Canadian Consulate
20 Mercado Central
21 El Corte Inglés
22 Post Office (Correos)
25 French Consulate
26 British Consulate

ANDALUCÍA

MEDITERRANEAN SEA

Museo Picasso & Museo de Málaga

The 16th-century Palacio de Buenavista on Calle San Agustín, in Málaga's medieval Judería (Jewish quarter), is being converted into a major new Picasso museum, with 186 Picasso works donated or lent by his daughter-in-law, Christine Ruiz-Picasso, and grandson. The museum is due to open in late 2002.

The Picasso donation means that the Museo de Málaga, the Buenavista palace's previous occupant, with art and archaeology collections, has had to move out. Until a new home is found for it, selections of the art are usually on display in the nearby Palacio de la Aduana – well worth a look.

Casa Natal de Picasso

The house where Picasso was born in 1881, at Plaza de la Merced 15, is a centre of exhibitions and research on Picasso and contemporary art – some good shows are held. It's open 11 am to 2 pm daily, plus 5 to 8 pm Monday to Saturday (free).

Alameda Principal & Paseo del Parque

The Alameda Principal, now a busy thoroughfare, was constructed in the late 18th century as a boulevard over what were then the sands of the Guadalmedina estuary. It's lined with old trees from the Americas.

The palm-lined Paseo del Parque was laid out in the 1890s on land reclaimed from the sea. The 18th-century **Palacio de la Aduana** (Customs House) on its northern side originally had the sea lapping at its doors. **Paseo de España**, along the southern side, is full of tropical plants and is a refuge from the bustle of the city.

Museo de Artes y Costumbres Populares

The Museum of Popular Arts, in an old inn at Pasillo Santa Isabel 10, is a fun place to visit, especially with children. The collection focuses on everyday life and includes items connected with farming and fishing. Note the cabinets containing *barros* (painted clay figures) of the highwayman, the rider from Ronda and other characters from *malagueño* folklore. Barros of this type fascinated early travellers influenced by the Romantic movement. Hours are 10 am to 1 pm Monday to Saturday and 5 to 8 pm (4 to 7 pm, 1 October to 15 June) weekdays; 200 ptas, under-16s free.

Beaches

Sandy city beaches stretch several kilometres in each direction from the port. Playa de la Malagueta is handy to the centre, with several places to eat and drink close by.

Language Courses

Foreigners courses run by the Universidad de Málaga (☎ 95 227 82 11, fax 95 227 97 12) are very popular. Four-week intensive Spanish courses cost 83,000 ptas (plus accommodation). For information, you can write to Universidad de Málaga Cursos de Español para Extranjeros, Inés Carrasco Cantos (Directora), Avenida de Andalucía 24, 29007 Málaga. There are many private language schools too; the main tourist offices can help with information.

Special Events

Semana Santa processions in Málaga are solemn and spectacular. The platforms bearing the holy images, known as *tronos,* are large and heavy, needing up to 150 people to carry them. Each night from Palm Sunday to Good Friday, six or seven tronos are carried through the city, watched by big crowds. A good place to see them is the Alameda Principal, where they pass through between about 7 pm and midnight.

One Saturday night every May, Málaga's port area becomes a massive dance venue for World Dance Costa del Sol, with as many as 200,000 people jumping to top commercial bands and DJs.

The nine-day Feria de Málaga beginning in mid-August is the biggest and most ebullient of Andalucía's summer fairs. From late morning till early evening, especially on the two Saturdays, celebrations take over the city centre, with music and dancing in the packed streets and bars, and horses and riders parading round a circuit of streets. At night the fun switches to large feria grounds at

ANDALUCÍA

Cortijo de Torres 4km south-west of the centre, with fairground rides and lots more music and dancing. Málaga stages its main bullfight season at this time.

Places to Stay – Budget

The Inturjoven youth hostel, *Albergue Juvenil Málaga* (☎ 95 230 85 00, Plaza Pío XII No 6), 1.5km west of the centre and a couple of blocks north of Avenida de Andalucía, has 110 places, most in double rooms. Bus No 18 from the Alameda Principal along Avenida de Andalucía goes most of the way.

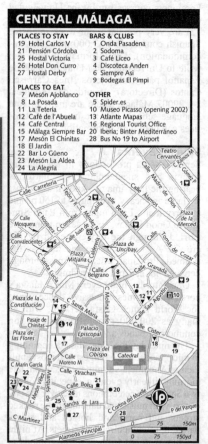

CENTRAL MÁLAGA

PLACES TO STAY	BARS & CLUBS
19 Hotel Carlos V	1 Onda Pasadena
21 Pensión Córdoba	2 Sodoma
25 Hostal Victoria	3 Café Liceo
26 Hotel Don Curro	4 Discoteca Anden
27 Hostal Derby	6 Siempre Asi
	9 Bodegas El Pimpi
PLACES TO EAT	
7 Mesón Ajoblanco	OTHER
8 La Posada	5 Spider.es
11 La Tetería	10 Museo Picasso (opening 2002)
12 Café de l'Abuela	13 Atlante Mapas
14 Café Central	16 Regional Tourist Office
15 Málaga Siempre Bar	20 Iberia; Binter Mediterráneo
17 Mesón El Chinitas	28 Bus No 19 to Airport
18 El Jardín	
22 Bar Lo Güeno	
23 Mesón La Aldea	
24 La Alegría	

The homy *Pensión Córdoba* (☎ 95 221 44 69, Calle Bolsa 9) has singles/doubles with shared bath for 1500/3000 ptas. *Hostal Avenida* (☎ 95 221 77 28, Alameda Principal 5) has clean, basic rooms at 1820/3100 ptas.

Hostal Cisneros (☎ 95 221 26 33, Calle Cisneros 7) is spotless and friendly. Rooms are 2800/4800 ptas, or 5800 ptas for doubles with bath, plus IVA. *Hostal El Cenachero* (☎ 95 222 40 88, Calle Barroso 5) is a fair bet at 3900/5900 ptas for rooms with bath.

Friendly *Hostal Derby* (☎ 95 222 13 01, Calle San Juan de Dios 1) has spacious rooms with bath for 4500/6000 ptas. Find its bell beside the big studded street door.

Places to Stay – Mid-Range & Top End

At these prices, private bath, TV (often cable) and air-con are standard. Just east of the cathedral, *Hotel Carlos V* (☎ 95 221 51 20, Calle Císter 10) has comfortable doubles for 8300 ptas. The popular, recently remodelled *Hostal Victoria* (☎ 95 222 42 24, Calle Sancha de Lara 3) has 16 rooms at 8500 ptas. *Hotel Sur* (☎ 95 222 48 03, Calle Trinidad Grund 13) charges 9100 ptas. The modernised *Hotel Venecia* (☎ 95 221 36 36, Alameda Principal 9) has 40 agreeable rooms at 10,500 ptas.

The large *Hotel Don Curro* (☎ 95 222 72 00, fax 95 221 59 46, Calle Sancha de Lara 7) offers singles/doubles for 9800/13,850 ptas (a bit more in August). The refurbished *Parador Málaga Gibralfaro* (☎ 95 222 19 02, e gibralfaro@parador.es) has an unbeatable location on the Gibralfaro just south of the castle, and a good restaurant. Rooms are 14,000/17,500 ptas plus IVA.

Places to Eat

A Málaga speciality is fish fried quickly in olive oil. *Fritura malagueño* consists of fried fish, anchovies and squid. Cold soups are popular: as well as *gazpacho* and *sopa de ajo* (garlic soup), try *sopa de almendra con uvas* (almond soup with grapes).

Near Plaza de la Constitución *Café Central*, on Plaza de la Constitución itself, is a noisy local favourite: food prices are reasonable, and there's plenty of choice. It closes mid-evening. *Málaga Siempre Bar (Pasaje de Chinitas 7)* serves a good range of tapas (150 ptas including a beer) and coffee. *Mesón El Chinitas (Calle de Moreno Monroy 4)* is a fancy place serving many *andaluz* dishes for 1400 to 2500 ptas, and a *menú* for 2200 ptas.

A short walk north-east from Plaza de la Constitución, the barn-like *La Posada (Calle Granada 33)* is great for tapas and raciones of *carnes a la brasa* (chargrilled meat): 1600 ptas for lamb chops. *Mesón Ajoblanco (Plaza de Uncibay 2)* provides tasty fare from meat-and-potato mini-brochettes (650 ptas) to *tablas* (boards) of cheese, meats or *ahumados* (smoked fish) for 1200 to 1800 ptas.

For a reasonably priced sit-down meal at a pavement table, head for pedestrian Calle Marín García and Calle Esparteros. *La Alegría, Bar Lo Gueno* and *Mesón La Aldea* serve plenty of fish and other dishes under 1000 ptas.

Near the Catedral *Café de l'Abuela*, on Calle San Agustín, offers a coffee-juice-croissant/tostada breakfast for 350/400 ptas. On this same street (leading to the future Museo Picasso), the soothing *La Tetería* serves a huge range of teas, crepes, pastries and sorbets. *El Jardín* on Calle Cañón, with a pleasant terraza behind the cathedral, serves platos combinados from 700 ptas.

Elsewhere The colourful *Mercado Central* on Calle Atarazanas, built in the 19th century, has terrific fresh produce. The atmospheric old bar *Antigua Casa de Guardia (Alameda Principal 18)*, nearby, serves inexpensive Málaga wine from the barrel and good seafood tapas, closing about 10 pm.

Relaxed *El Yamal (Calle Blasco de Garay 3)*, south of the Alameda, cooks up excellent Moroccan food: fish or chicken dishes cost 1225 to 1500 ptas, and a tasty salad with hummus and flat bread is 675 ptas (closed Sunday evening).

In the La Malagueta area, the fairly upmarket *Aceite y Pan (Calle Cervantes 5)* and *Restaurante Antonio Martín*, on Plaza de la Malagueta facing the beach, do good fish and seafood.

El Vegetariano de la Alcazabilla (Calle Pozo del Rey 5) has a good range of dishes between 950 and 1100 ptas, including a very nice Greek salad for two, wholemeal pasta and *empanadillas de espinacas* (spinach pies); closed Sunday.

Entertainment

The weekly *Informaciones de Málaga,* available free from tourist offices, is a useful source of what's-on information.

The narrow old streets north of Plaza de la Constitución heave with people having a good time from about midnight on fine weekend nights. Bars playing great music for a predominantly 20s and late-teens crowd are particularly thick around Plaza Mitjana and Plaza de Uncibay.

Among them are the warren-like *Bodegas El Pimpi (Calle Granada 62),* attracting fun lovers with its sweet wine and thumping music; *Café Liceo (Calle Beatas 21),* an old mansion turned young music bar, buzzing after midnight in the second half of the week; *Siempre Así (Calle Convalecientes 5),* playing flamenco and rumba from 9.30 pm Thursday to Saturday; and *Sodoma (Calle Juan de Padilla 15),* with house music from 11 pm the same nights. *Discoteca Anden,* on Plaza de Uncibay, rages till dawn Thursday to Saturday. *Onda Pasadena (Calle Gómez Pallete 9)* is a good live music bar, usually with jazz on Saturday from 11.30 pm and flamenco or other genres midweek.

Pedregalejo, a beach suburb 4.5km east of the centre, buzzes until late in summer.

The *Teatro Cervantes (Calle Ramos Marín s/n)* has a good program of music, dance and theatre.

Getting There & Away

Air Málaga's busy airport (☎ 95 224 88 04), receiving scheduled and charter flights from many European cities, is 9km south-west of the centre. Typical discount or charter London-Málaga return fares, for instance, range from UK£100 to UK£150 depending on season. The budget airlines easyJet and Go

ANDALUCÍA

can cost less. The cheapest New York–Málaga round-trip fares range between about US$500 and US$900 depending on season. Iberia, Royal Air Maroc (☎ 902-21 00 10) and Morocco's Regional Air Lines fly to Casablanca daily; return fares are around 40,000 ptas on Iberia and start at 33,900 ptas on Royal Air Maroc. Binter Mediterráneo flies to Marrakesh for around 30,000ptas return. For details on international flights and fares, see the Getting There & Away chapter. Most airline offices are at the airport. Iberia and Binter Mediterráneo (☎ 902-400 500) have a city office at Calle Molina Lario 13.

Within Spain, Iberia flies daily nonstop to/from Madrid and Barcelona. To Barcelona, a one-way ticket and the cheapest return both normally cost around 29,000 ptas, but winter deals can cut that to 14,500 ptas. Air Europa (☎ 902-401 501), flying nonstop to/from Madrid and Bilbao, and Spanair (☎ 902-13 14 15), to/from Madrid and Barcelona, have similar fares to Iberia's but they're worth checking for offers.

For a flight out of Spain, check the ads in the free newspaper Sur in English. Agencies such as Servitour (☎ 95 256 60 00) offer occasional one-way flights to London for 6500 ptas (but more often 12,000 to 20,000 ptas). You can always go along to the airport early in the morning and ask around the offices for standby tickets; if you get a flight, it will be cheap.

Bus Málaga's bus station (☎ 95 235 00 61) is on Paseo de los Tilos, 1km west of the centre. Frequent buses run along the coasts and to Sevilla (2½ hours, 1900 ptas) and Granada (1½ to two hours, 1185 ptas). Several buses daily go to inland towns, including Córdoba (2½ hours, 1570 ptas), Antequera and Ronda. At least seven buses daily run to Madrid (six hours, 2650 ptas) and a few to Valencia (10 hours, 6025 ptas) and Barcelona (15 hours, 9035 ptas). There are also buses to Morocco, Germany, England, Portugal, France and the Netherlands.

Train The train station (☎ 95 236 02 02) is on Explanada de la Estación around the corner from the bus station.

Four or more quick daily Talgo 200s run to/from Madrid (four to 4½ hours, 7000 to 8200 ptas). Three other Madrid trains cost 4700 to 5500 ptas, taking up to 13 hours.

Nine or more daily trains go to/from Córdoba (two to 2½ hours, 2100 to 2800 ptas). To Sevilla (2½ hours, 2130 ptas) there are five TRDs daily. For Granada there are no direct trains but you can get there in 2¼ hours for 1800 ptas with a transfer at Bobadilla. For Ronda you must also usually change at Bobadilla.

For Valencia and Barcelona (13 to 14 hours, 6400 to 8400 ptas) there are two or three trains daily, two of them overnight.

Car Rental There are several agencies at the airport, many with cars for under 20,000 ptas a week.

Boat Trasmediterránea (☎ 95 206 12 18), Estación Marítima, Local E1, operates ferries to/from Melilla daily (except Sunday, mid-September to mid-June) taking 7½ hours (4020 ptas in the cheapest seat, 16,125 ptas for a car). Also from the Estación Marítima, the high-speed Buquebus (☎ 95 222 79 05) sails to/from Ceuta (1½ hours) at least twice daily (passenger 4995 ptas, car 8995 ptas).

Getting Around
To/From the Airport The Aeropuerto train station is a five-minute walk from the airport (follow signs from the departures hall). Trains run every half-hour from 7 am to 11.45 pm to Málaga's main station (11 minutes, 135 ptas) and the Centro-Alameda station beside the Río Guadalmedina. Departures from the city to the airport are from 5.45 am to 10.30 pm. Fares are slightly higher on weekends and holidays.

Bus No 19 to the city centre (135 ptas), from outside the airport arrivals hall, goes about every half-hour from 7 am to midnight, stopping at the city bus and train stations en route. Going out to the airport, you can pick it up at the western end of Paseo del Parque and outside the stations, from 6.30 am to 11.30 pm.

A taxi between the airport and city costs around 1300 ptas.

ANDALUCÍA

COSTA DEL SOL

The Costa del Sol, a string of resorts along the coast from Málaga to Gibraltar, might best be described as an international strip stuck on the bottom of Spain. Its recipe for success is sunshine, beaches (though with mostly grey-brown sand, these are not Andalucía's best), warm Mediterranean water, cheap package deals and plenty of nightlife and entertainment. The resorts were once fishing villages, but there's little sign of that now. Launched as a 1950s development drive for impoverished Andalucía, the Costa del Sol is now a series of townscapes from one end to the other – arguably Europe's finest example of how overdevelopment can ruin a spectacular landscape.

Activities

The *costa* is good for sport lovers, with nearly 40 golf clubs, several busy marinas, tennis and squash courts, riding schools, swimming pools and gyms. Many beaches have facilities for sports such as windsurfing, water-skiing and paragliding.

Accommodation

In August and the second half of July, it's a very good idea to ring ahead for a room. Outside these peak months, room rates in many places come down sharply. The costa has about 15 camping grounds.

Getting There & Away

Trains go about every half-hour, 5.45 am to 10.30 pm, from Málaga city and airport stations to Torremolinos and Fuengirola. Buses from Málaga link all the resorts, and services to places such as Ronda, Cádiz, Sevilla and Granada go from the main resorts. Bargain rental cars for 14,000 to 20,000 ptas a week are available from local firms in the main resorts.

Torremolinos

postcode 29620 • pop 32,000

'Torrie', which led the Costa del Sol's mass tourist boom of the 1950s and '60s, is a concrete high-rise jungle designed to squeeze as many paying customers as possible into the smallest possible space. It spruced itself up somewhat in the 1990s.

Costa del Sol Highways

The recently opened A-7 Autopista del Sol, bypassing Fuengirola, Marbella, San Pedro de Alcántara and Estepona, makes driving along the Costa del Sol a lot easier for those willing to pay its tolls (600 ptas Mijas-Marbella, 470 ptas Marbella-Estepona, coming down to 495 and 290 ptas respectively from October to May). The old 'Death Highway' along the costa, the N-340, is now not quite so over-populated. But the N-340 remains a key to orientation on the costa, as many places use Km numbers on it as part of their address. These numbers rise from west to east: Estepona is at Km 155 and central Marbella at Km 181. Km markers aside, undoubtedly the most useful sign on the N-340 is 'Cambio de Sentido', indicating that you can change direction to get back to a turning you have missed. Meanwhile, beware of other motorists and watch out for animals and inebriated pedestrians.

Orientation Torremolinos' main pedestrian artery is Calle San Miguel, running most of the 500m from Plaza Costa del Sol (on the main road through town) down to Playa del Bajondillo. South-west of Playa del Bajondillo is Playa de la Carihuela, once the fishing quarter.

The bus station (☎ 95 238 24 19) is on Calle Hoyo north-east of Plaza Costa del Sol. Buses to Málaga, Benalmádena, Mijas and Fuengirola stop on Avenida Palma de Mallorca, 200m south-west of Plaza Costa del Sol. The train station is on Avenida Jesús Santos Rein, off Calle San Miguel.

Information Torremolinos has tourist offices: on Playa del Bajondillo (☎ 95 237 19 09); on Calle Borbollón Bajo (☎ 95 237 29 56), La Carihuela; on Plaza de la Independencia (☎ 95 237 42 31), a block inland from Plaza Costa del Sol; and in the ayuntamiento (☎ 95 237 95 11) on Plaza de Blas Infante. All open at least 10 am to 1.30 pm weekdays, and from June to September the first two open 10 am to 2 pm and 5 to 8 pm daily.

ANDALUCÍA

Things to See & Do The beaches of Torremolinos' are wider, longer and a paler shade of grey-brown than most on the costa.

In the swish Puerto Deportivo (marina) at Benalmádena Costa, just south-west of Torremolinos, **Sea Life** is a good modernistic aquarium of mainly Mediterranean marine creatures, open 10 am to 6 pm daily (995 ptas). **Tivoli World**, five minutes' walk from Benalmádena–Arroyo de la Miel train station, is the costa's biggest amusement park. In summer it's open daily, late afternoon to after midnight; in other seasons at weekends only (600 ptas plus rides; look into the 'Supertivolino' ticket for children).

Places to Stay & Eat A couple of dozen hostales and hotels are within a few minutes' walk of Torremolinos' train and bus stations. The tourist offices can supply lists. Pleasant *Hostal Micaela (☎ 95 238 33 10, Calle Bajondillo 4),* near Playa del Bajondillo, has doubles with bath for 4650 ptas plus IVA. Just across from Playa del Bajondillo, the small *Hostal Guadalupe (☎ 95 238 19 37, Calle del Peligro 15)* charges 5000/6000 ptas for singles/doubles with bath.

In La Carihuela, 1.5km south-west of the centre, *Hostal Flor Blanco (☎ 95 238 20 71, Pasaje de la Carihuela 4)* is almost on the beach and several of its 12 rooms, with bath, have sea views. Doubles are 5900 ptas plus IVA. *Hotel Miami (☎ 95 238 52 55, Calle Aladino 14),* a few blocks back from the beach, is a quaint 1940s villa turned into a small hotel with nice gardens, and doubles for 7500 ptas.

Besides British breakfasts and British beer, Torremolinos has no shortage of good *seafood places,* many of them lining the Paseo Marítimo in La Carihuela.

Entertainment The weekend nightlife at Benalmádena, Costa's Puerto Deportivo, attracts mainly young people from all along the coast. The bars really start to throb after midnight on Friday and Saturday. Torremolinos itself has a big gay scene; most gay bars are on Calle Nogalera off Avenida Jesús Santos Rein.

Fuengirola
postcode 29640 • pop 43,000

Fuengirola, 18km down the coast from Torremolinos, has more of a family scene but is just as densely packed. The narrow streets between the beach and Avenida Matías Sáenz de Tejada (where the bus station is) constitute what's left of the old town, with Plaza de la Constitución at its centre. The train station is a block farther inland on Avenida Jesús Santos Rein. The tourist office (☎ 95 246 74 57) is at Avenida Jesús Santos Rein 6, near the train station.

The **Castillo de Sohail** at the south-western end of Fuengirola dates from the 10th century; open daily except Monday (200 ptas). The **Hipódromo Costa del Sol**, Andalucía's only horse-race track, was due to open in 2000 at Urbanización El Chaparral, a few kilometres south-west.

Places to Stay & Eat Friendly *Hostal Italia (☎ 95 247 41 93, Calle de la Cruz 1),* in the heart of things a couple of blocks from the beach, has singles/doubles with bath around 6400/8000 ptas. *Hostal Cuevas (☎ 95 246 06 06, Calle Capitán 7),* along the street, is smaller, with doubles for 4950 ptas. *Hostal Marbella (☎/fax 95 266 45 03, Calle Marbella 34),* just south-west of Plaza de la Constitución, is friendly and clean with rooms for 6500/8000 ptas.

Along Calle Moncayo, a block back from the beachfront in the centre, you can choose from a host of British *bars* and Italian, Chinese, Indonesian and even Spanish *restaurants,* many with *menús* for 800 or 900 ptas.

Mijas
A village of Muslim origin in the hills 8km north of Fuengirola, Mijas is surrounded by villas and *urbanizaciones* (housing estates) and full of busloads up from the costa, but remains a pretty place. It has lots of restaurants, cafes and craft shops. Frequent buses run from Fuengirola.

Marbella
postcode 29600 • pop 86,000

Marbella, overlooked by the dramatic Sierra Blanca 28km west of Fuengirola, has always been the Costa del Sol's glossiest resort. It was the building of the exclusive Marbella Club Hotel, just west, in the 1950s by the part-Mexican, part-Austrian Alfonso von Hohenlohe that turned Marbella into a playground of the international jet set. In the 1980s Marbella went into a decline, but Jesús Gil y Gil, mayor since 1991, has restored its position as the Costa del Sol's quality resort, albeit controversially. Heavy-handed police methods helped cleanse the streets of prostitutes and drug addicts, but Gil's critics argue that much serious organised crime goes unchecked. He strongly encouraged property development and by 2000 was facing a growing mountain of lawsuits, including the bizarre *Caso Atlético* in which he was accused of illegally diverting 450 million ptas of Marbella council money to Atlético Madrid football team (of which he was president).

Orientation The N-340 through town takes the names Avenida Ramón y Cajal and Avenida Ricardo Soriano. The old town is centred on Plaza de los Naranjos. The bus station is on the northern side of the Marbella bypass, 1.2km from Plaza de los Naranjos.

Information The helpful tourist offices on Glorieta de la Fontanilla (☎ 95 277 14 42) and at Plaza de los Naranjos 1 (☎ 95 282 35 50) are open 9 am to 8 or 9 pm daily except holidays.

The Policía Nacional (☎ 091) are on Avenida Doctor Viñals in the north of town. The Hospital Europa (☎ 95 277 42 00) is 1km east of the centre on Avenida de Severo Ochoa.

Things to See & Do Pretty **Plaza de los Naranjos**, with its 16th-century ayuntamiento, is the heart of the largely pedestrianised old town. Nearby on Plaza de la Iglesia is the **Iglesia de la Encarnación**, begun in the 16th century. A little farther east, the **Museo del Grabado Español Contemporáneo**, on Calle Hospital Bazán, houses work by Picasso, Miró and Dalí. It's open daily except Saturday (300 ptas). Just to the north, along streets such as Calle Arte

and Calle Portada, are remains of Marbella's old **Muslim walls**.

Down to the east of the old town, in Parque de la Represa, is the charming **Museo Bonsai**, devoted to the Japanese miniature-tree art, open daily (500 ptas).

Playa de la Fontanilla, west of Glorieta de la Fontanilla, and Playa de Casablanca, beyond Playa de la Fontanilla, are longer, broader and less crowded than the central beaches.

Several excursion boats a day usually go from Marbella's Puerto Deportivo (marina) to **Puerto Banús**, the Costa del Sol's flashiest marina, 5km west, for around 700/1100 ptas one way/return. The Banús harbour is surrounded by varied eateries and drinkeries (cheaper as you move east), and the Aquarium de Puerto Banús, similar to Sea Life at Benalmádena Costa, opens daily most of the year.

There are good walks in the **Sierra Blanca** starting from the Refugio de Juanar hotel, a 17km drive from Marbella.

Places to Stay *Camping Marbella 191* (☎ 95 277 83 91, N-340 Km 184.5), on the beach 3km east, charges around 3000 ptas a site in high season and closes in winter. Three bigger, less expensive year-round sites are in the next 10km of the N-340 east.

The modern Inturjoven *Albergue Juvenil Marbella* (☎ 95 277 14 91, Calle Trapiche 2) has room for about 140 in rooms for one to four people.

There are plenty of hostales in the old town. British-run *Hostal del Pilar* (☎ 95 282 99 36, [e] hostal@marbella-scene.com, Calle Mesoncillo 4) is popular with backpackers. Singles, doubles and triples, with shared bathrooms, cost 1500 to 2000 ptas per person depending on the season, and there's a bar. *Hostal El Castillo* (☎ 95 277 17 39, Plaza San Bernabé 2), near the Islamic walls, has plain singles/doubles with bath for 3200/5600 ptas. Recently renovated *Hostal Enriqueta* (☎ 95 282 75 52, Calle Los Caballeros 18) has doubles/triples with bath for 7000/9000 ptas.

Just south-east of the old town, small hostales cluster on greenery-bedecked Calle

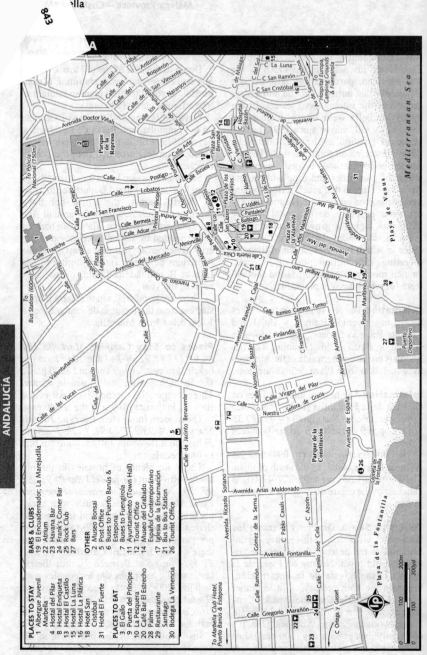

PLACES TO STAY
1 Albergue Juvenil Marbella
4 Hostal del Pilar
8 Hostal Enriqueta
13 Hostal El Castillo
15 Hostal La Luna
16 Hostal La Pilárica
18 Hotel San Cristóbal
31 Hotel El Fuerte

PLACES TO EAT
3 El Gallo
9 Puerta del Príncipe
10 La Pesquera
20 Café Bar El Estrecho
28 Palms
29 Restaurante Santiago
30 Bodega La Venencia

BARS & CLUBS
19 El Encuadernador, La Marejadilla
22 Atrium
23 Havana Bar
24 Frank's Corner Bar
25 Rock Club
27 Bars

OTHER
2 Museo Bonsai
5 Post Office
6 Buses to Puerto Banús & Estepona
7 Buses to Fuengirola
11 Ayuntamiento (Town Hall)
12 Tourist Office
14 Museo del Grabado Español Contemporáneo
17 Iglesia de la Encarnación
21 Bus to Bus Station
26 Tourist Office

euro currency converter 100pta = €0.60

San Cristóbal and nearby streets. Among them, charging 5000 to 6000 ptas for doubles with bath, are *Hostal La Luna* (☎ 95 282 57 78, Calle La Luna 7) and *Hostal La Pilárica* (☎ 95 277 42 52, Calle San Cristóbal 31).

Above the hostal bracket, you'll normally pay 10,000 ptas or more for a double in summer. *Hotel San Cristóbal* (☎ 95 277 12 50, Avenida Ramón y Cajal 3) has doubles at 11,600 ptas plus IVA. The 263-room *Hotel El Fuerte* (☎ 95 286 15 00, Avenida El Fuerte s/n) has doubles at 16,400 ptas plus IVA.

Places to Eat For a local adventure head for *El Gallo* bar (Calle Lobatos 44), which has egg and chips for 300 ptas and the cheapest *langostinos pil pil* (king prawns in chilli garlic sauce) in town at 550 ptas (closed Tuesday). *Café Bar El Estrecho* (Calle San Lázaro 12) is a good spot for varied tapas (175 to 200 ptas) and raciones.

On Calle Huerta Chica, the *Puerta del Príncipe* serves good grilled meat and fish from around 950 to 2000 ptas, and *La Pesquera* next door concentrates on seafood, at similar prices.

On Playa de Venus beside the Puerto Deportivo, *Palms* has interesting salads from 950 ptas. *Restaurante Santiago* (☎ 95 277 00 78, Paseo Marítimo 5) is a seafood specialist overlooking this beach. Two courses cost around 4000 ptas. *Bodega La Venencia* (Avenida Miguel Cano 15), nearby, serves delectable ham tapas and montaditos starting at 175 ptas, plus raciones.

Entertainment On little Calle San Lázaro, the bars *El Encuadernador* and *La Marejadilla* stay lively late, even in the low season when the rest of the old town has gone home. A line of *music bars* and *discotecas* at the Puerto Deportivo throbs till dawn in summer. An older crowd gravitates to Calle Camilo José Cela area, where *Frank's Corner Bar*, *Rock Club*, *Atrium* and *Havana Bar* are among the main hang-outs.

Getting There & Away Buses to Fuengirola, Puerto Banús and Estepona, all about half-hourly, have a stop on Avenida Ricardo

Soriano. Other services use the bus station (☎ 95 276 44 00) in the north of town.

Getting Around From the bus station, bus No 7 (135 ptas) runs to Avenida Ricardo Soriano; returning from the centre to the bus station, take No 2 from Avenida Ramón y Cajal (see map for stops).

Estepona
postcode 29680 • pop 36,000
Estepona, south-west of Marbella, has controlled its development relatively carefully and remains a fairly agreeable seaside town. The oldish centre, around leafy, traffic-free Plaza Las Flores, is quite pleasant.

The tourist office (☎ 95 280 09 13) is at Avenida San Lorenzo 1 in the west of the centre. The bus station (☎ 95 280 02 49) is 400m farther west, on the seafront Avenida de España.

Selwo Costa del Sol (☎ 95 279 21 50), at Las Lomas del Monte, 6km east of Estepona, is a new safari park with 200 animal species from around the globe. Some animals are viewed from 4WD vehicles, others on foot. Hours are 10 am to 6.30 pm daily except Monday in winter (2500/1750 ptas for adults/children). A Selwo bus runs from Málaga, Torremolinos, Fuengirola and Marbella, but from Estepona a taxi is best.

Accommodation in central Estepona is limited. Old-fashioned *Hostal El Pilar* (☎ 95 280 00 18, Plaza Las Flores 22) has doubles with shared/private bath at 4700/5300 ptas. Friendly *Pensión San Antonio* (☎ 95 280 14 76, Calle Adolfo Suárez 9), a block east of the plaza, has basic singles/doubles for 2200/ 3900 ptas. On the seafront, *Hotel Buenavista* (☎ 95 280 01 37, Paseo Marítimo 180) has doubles with bath for 6500 ptas.

You'll find a dozen or two *restaurants* and *tapas bars* on and near Plaza Las Flores. Nightlife focuses on the marina at the western end of town.

Casares
postcode 29690 • pop 3200
Casares, clinging to steep hillsides below a well-preserved Muslim castle, 18km from Estepona (10km inland), offers wonderful

ANDALUCÍA

views, and the Sierra Crestellina to its north-west provides good walking opportunities.

Pensión Plaza *(☎ 95 289 40 88, Plaza de España 6)* has adequate doubles with bath for around 2800 ptas.

Three buses run from/to Estepona daily except Sunday. The last one back leaves Casares at 4 pm.

EL CHORRO & BOBASTRO

Fifty kilometres north-west of Málaga, Río Guadalhorce carves its way through the awe-some **Garganta del Chorro** (El Chorro Gorge), 4km long, up to 400m deep and as little as 10m wide. The gorge is traversed not only by the main railway in and out of Málaga but also by a footpath, the **Camino del Rey** (King's Path), which for long stretches becomes a concrete catwalk cling-ing to the gorge wall 100m above the river. The gorge is a magnet for rock climbers, and there are other good walks in the area.

Swiss-owned Finca La Campana (see Places to Stay & Eat) offers climbing courses, and climbing, caving, walking and mountain-bike trips, and rents out mountain bikes for 1500 ptas per day. Aventur El Chorro in El Chorro village, a tiny settlement around El Chorro train station, above a dam just south of the gorge, also has mountain bikes.

The Camino del Rey is in a dangerously decayed state and unless long-discussed re-pairs are actually made, you should not at-tempt to walk along it. But you *can* view the gorge and camino by walking along the rail-way. From El Chorro village, follow the road to the eastern side of the reservoir for 900m, then walk 2.25km north along the railway, passing through several tunnels numbered from 10 to 7 (there's plenty of space at the side should a train come). The Camino del Rey begins along the cliff face to your left between tunnel Nos 10 and 9, and after a short distance crosses to the western side of the gorge. After tunnel No 7 a narrow concrete footbridge crosses the gorge to the camino – but within a short dis-tance in either direction along the camino from here you reach impassable gaps.

Near El Chorro is **Bobastro**, the hill-top redoubt of the 9th-century rebel Omar ibn

Bandoleros & Guerrilleros

Andalucía's complicated sierras, full of ravines, caves and hidden valleys, have al-ways offered refuge to those who didn't get on with the authorities of the day. As long ago as the 9th century the hill fortress of Bobastro, near El Chorro Gorge, was the epi-centre of prolonged, widespread opposition to Cordoban rule led by Omar ibn Hafsun, a sort of Islamic Robin Hood. Ibn Hafsun came from a landed family of *muwallads* (Christian converts to Islam) but turned to banditry after killing a neighbour. Reputedly a defender of the peasants against taxes and forced labour, he quickly gained followers and popular sup-port, and at one stage controlled territory from Cartagena to the Strait of Gibraltar.

In the 19th century some of the bandits (*bandoleros*) who preyed on the rich also be-came folk heroes. The most famous was El Tempranillo (the Early One), born in 1800 at Jauja, near Lucena in Córdoba province. At the age of 22 he claimed: 'The king may reign in Spain, but in the sierra I do'. Blond and courteous to women, El Tempranillo reputedly demanded an ounce of gold for each vehicle crossing his domain.

It was the activities of these bandits that led the government to set up the Guardia Civil, Spain's rural police force, in 1844. Many ban-doleros were then forced into the service of the *caciques* (local landowners and political bosses), or even of the Guardia Civil itself. El Tempranillo met his end this way, murdered by an old comrade.

The last of the bandolero breed was Pasos Largos (Big Steps), an orphan from the El Burgo area, east of Ronda, who turned to poaching and murdered a game warden who had re-ported him to the police. He was killed in 1934 in a cave shoot-out with the Guardia Civil.

After the civil war the Andalucian sierras became the refuge of a new kind of fugitive: communist *guerrilleros* waging the last resis-tance to Franco. The Sierra Bermeja, north of Estepona, and the mountains of La Axarquía, east of Málaga, were among their hide-outs. This little-known chapter of Spanish history closed in the 1950s.

Hafsun (see the boxed text 'Bandoleros & Guerrilleros'). From El Chorro village, follow the road up the far (west) side of the valley and after 3km take the signposted Bobastro turning. Three kilometres up here an 'Iglesia Mozárabe' sign indicates a path to the remains of a remarkable little Mozarabic church cut from the rock. It's thought that Ibn Hafsun, originally a Muslim, converted to Christianity (thus becoming a Mozarab) before his death in 917, and was buried here. When Bobastro was finally conquered in 927, his remains were taken for posthumous crucifixion outside Córdoba's Mezquita. A farther 2.5km up the road is the top of the hill, with faint traces of Ibn Hafsun's rectangular *alcázar* (fortress) and magnificent views.

Places to Stay & Eat

At El Chorro village, small *Camping El Chorro* (☎ 95 211 26 96) charges 1400 to 1600 ptas for two people with tent and car. *Pensión Estación* (☎ 95 249 50 04), in the train station, has four clean little singles/doubles for 2000/3500 ptas. *Apartamentos La Garganta* (☎ 95 249 51 19, e elchorro@ vnet.es), a few metres south, has apartments for up to five people for 6000 to 10,000 ptas, and a good restaurant. It also runs *Refugio de Escalada La Garganta* with bunks for 600 ptas. *Restaurante Estación* (or Bar Isabel), a popular climbers' gathering spot, serves platos combinados from 375 to 550 ptas. Accommodation at *Finca La Campana* (☎/fax 95 211 20 19), 2km from the station (signposted), ranges from bunks for 1500 ptas to apartments for up to four people at 4000 to 8000 ptas.

Getting There & Away

There's just one train to El Chorro daily from each of Málaga, Ronda and Sevilla. Timetables change from time to time, however. No buses run here.

RONDA

postcode 29400 • pop 34,500

Though just an hour up from the Costa del Sol, Ronda is a world away from the coastal scene. Straddling the awesome, 100m-deep El Tajo Gorge amid the beautiful Serranía de Ronda mountains, it attracts its quota of visitors, but many of them return to the coast in the afternoon.

For most of the Muslim period, Ronda was capital of its independent, or almost independent, statelet. Its near-impregnable position kept it out of Christian hands until 1485.

Orientation

The old Muslim town, known as La Ciudad, stands on the southern side of El Tajo. The newer town to the north has most of the places to stay and eat, and the bus and train stations. Three bridges span the gorge, the main one being the Puente Nuevo. Both parts of town come to an abrupt end on their western side with cliffs plunging away to the valley of the Río Guadalevín.

Information

The regional tourist office (☎ 95 287 12 72), Plaza de España 1, is open 9 am to 7 pm weekdays and 10 am to 2 pm Saturday. A new municipal tourist office on Plaza Teniente Arce should also be open by the time you visit.

Banks and ATMs are mainly on Calle Virgen de la Paz and Plaza Carmen Abela. The Policía Local (☎ 95 287 13 69) are at Plaza Duquesa de Parcent s/n.

Plaza de España & Puente Nuevo

Chapter 10 of Hemingway's *For Whom the Bell Tolls* tells how at the start of the Spanish Civil War the 'fascists' of a small town were rounded up in the town hall, then clubbed and flailed as they ran the gauntlet between two lines of townspeople 'in the plaza on the top of the cliff above the river'. At the end of the line the victims, dead or still alive, were thrown over the cliff. The episode was based on real events in Ronda, though the actual perpetrators were apparently a gang from Málaga. The Parador de Ronda on Plaza de España was once the town hall.

The majestic Puente Nuevo (New Bridge) spanning El Tajo from Plaza de España was completed in 1793. A Ronda tradition claims that its architect, Martín de Aldehuela, fell to his death that year, trying to engrave the date

ANDALUCÍA

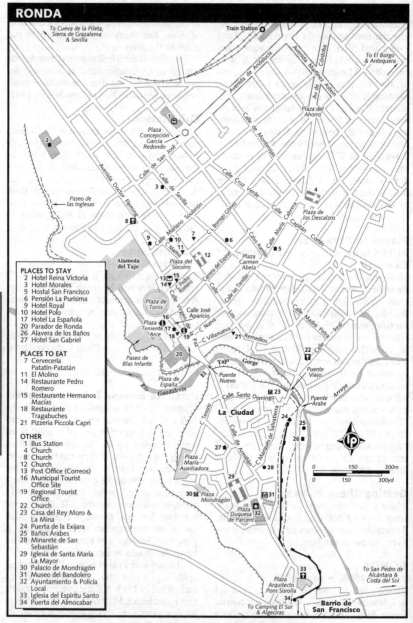

RONDA

To Cueva de la Pileta,
Sierra de Grazalema
& Sevilla

Train Station

To El Burgo
& Antequera

Avenida de Andalucía

Avenida Martínez Astein

Av. de Córdoba

Plaza del
Ahorro

Calle de Monterejas

Plaza
Concepción
García
Redondo

Calle de San José

Calle de Sevilla

Calle Cruz Verde

Calle Cabrera

Avenida Doctor Fleming

Paseo de
las Inglesas

Calle Mariano Soubirón

C. Borrego Gómez

Calvo Asenjo

Calle María Capitán

Cortés

Plaza de
los Descalzos

Plaza
Carmen
Abela

Alameda
del Tajo

Calle María

Plaza del
Socorro

Carrera del Espinel

Calle las Tiendas

Calle Madre Petra

Real

Plaza de
Toros

Calle Virgen de la Paz

Calle José
Aparicio

C. Nueva

C. Villanueva

Los

Remedios

Calle

Plaza
Teniente
Arce

Paseo de
Blas Infante

Plaza de
España

Río Guadalevín

El Tenorio

Tajo Gorge

Puente
Nuevo

El Tajo

Puente
Viejo

Arroyo

Puente
Árabe

Calle Santo
Domingo

La Ciudad

Calle de Armiñán

C. Marqués de Salvatierra

To San Pedro de
Alcántara &
Costa del Sol

Plaza
María
Auxiliadora

Plaza
Mondragón

Plaza
Duquesa
de Parcent

Plaza
Arquitecto
Pons Sorolla

To Camping El Sur
& Algeciras

Barrio de
San Francisco

PLACES TO STAY
2 Hotel Reina Victoria
3 Hotel Morales
5 Hostal San Francisco
6 Pensión La Purísima
9 Hotel Royal
10 Hotel Polo
17 Hotel La Española
20 Parador de Ronda
26 Alavera de los Baños
27 Hotel San Gabriel

PLACES TO EAT
7 Cervecería
   Patatín-Patatán
11 El Molino
14 Restaurante Pedro
   Romero
15 Restaurante Hermanos
   Macías
18 Restaurante
   Tragabuches
21 Pizzería Piccola Capri

OTHER
1 Bus Station
4 Church
8 Church
12 Church
13 Post Office (Correos)
16 Municipal Tourist
   Office Site
19 Regional Tourist
   Office
22 Church
23 Casa del Rey Moro &
   La Mina
24 Puerta de la Exijara
25 Baños Árabes
28 Minarete de San
   Sebastián
29 Iglesia de Santa María
   La Mayor
30 Palacio de Mondragón
31 Museo del Bandolero
32 Ayuntamiento & Policía
   Local
33 Iglesia del Espíritu Santo
34 Puerta del Almocabar

0   150   300m
0   150   300yd

ANDALUCÍA

euro currency converter 100pta = €0.60

on the bridge's side. Historians, however, insist that Aldehuela died in 1802, nine years after the bridge was opened.

La Ciudad

The old Muslim town retains a typical *medina* character of narrow streets twisting between white buildings.

The first street to the left after you cross the Puente Nuevo leads down to the **Casa del Rey Moro**, Calle Santo Domingo 17. This 18th-century house, supposedly built over remains of a Muslim palace, is itself closed, but from 10 am to 7 pm daily, you can visit its cliff-top gardens, and climb down La Mina, a Muslim-era stairway cut inside the rock right down to the bottom of the gorge (600 ptas).

From the Casa del Rey Moro head back up towards **Plaza María Auxiliadora**, which has fine views, then continue to the **Palacio de Mondragón**, probably originally built for Abomelic, ruler of Ronda in 1314. Of its three courtyards, only the Patio Mudéjar preserves an Islamic character. A horseshoe arch leads into a small cliff-top garden. Some rooms house a museum of local prehistoric life. The palace is open 10 am to 6 pm (to 3 pm weekends); 250 ptas.

A minute's walk beyond is Plaza Duquesa de Parcent, where the **Iglesia de Santa María La Mayor** stands on the site of Muslim Ronda's main mosque. The tower betrays clear Islamic origins, and the handsome galleries beside it, built for viewing festivities, also date from Muslim times. Just inside the entrance is an arch, covered with Arabic inscriptions, which was the mosque's mihrab. The church was begun in Gothic style, but as building went on over the centuries, tastes changed and it wound up with an 18th-century baroque northern end. It's open 10 am to 8 pm (to 6 pm in winter) daily (200 ptas).

Nearby at Calle Armiñán 65, the **Museo del Bandolero** is dedicated to the banditry for which central Andalucía was once renowned (see the boxed text 'Bandoleros & Guerrilleros'). It's open 10 am to 8 pm (to 6 pm in winter) daily (350 ptas). Beside the museum, steps lead down to an impressive stretch of La Ciudad's old walls. Follow

them down to the **Puerta de la Exijara**, originally the entrance to Islamic Ronda's Jewish quarter, outside the walls. A path continues down to the beautiful 13th- and 14th-century **Baños Árabes** (Arab Baths), open 9.30 am to 1.30 pm and 4 to 6 pm Tuesday, 9.30 am to 3.30 pm Wednesday to Saturday (free). From the northern side of the nearby **Puente Viejo** (1616) you can make your way back up to Plaza de España via a small park along the gorge's edge.

Plaza de Toros & Around

Ronda's elegant bullring, Plaza de Toros, on Calle Virgen de la Paz, is one of the oldest in Spain – it opened in 1785 – and has seen some of the most important events in bullfighting history (see the boxed text 'Ronda's Fighting Romeros'). Open 10 am to 6 pm daily (400 ptas), it contains a small **Museo Taurino**, which includes photos of famous visitors, including Ernest Hemingway and Orson Welles.

Vertiginous cliff-top views open out from **Paseo de Blas Infante**, behind the Plaza de Toros, and the shady **Alameda del Tajo** park nearby.

Ronda's Fighting Romeros

Ronda can justly claim to be the home of bullfighting. In the 18th and 19th centuries, three generations of the Romero family from Ronda established most of the basics of modern bullfighting on foot (previously it had been done on horseback as a kind of cavalry training-cum-sport for the nobility). Francisco Romero, born in 1698, invented the use of the cape to attract the bull, and the *muleta,* its cloth replacement in the kill. His son Juan introduced the matador's supporting team, the *cuadrilla;* and grandson Pedro (1754–1839) perfected an elegant, classical style, still known as the Escuela Rondeña (Ronda School), in which matadors work very close to the bulls. Pedro's skill was such, it's said, that outlaws from the bandit-ridden mountains around Ronda would risk capture to see him in action. He became director of the country's first bullfighting college (in Sevilla) at the age of 77.

Special Events

Ronda's bullring stages relatively few fights, but in early September it holds some of the most celebrated in Spain, the Corridas Goyescas, in which top matadors fight in 19th-century costumes as portrayed in Goya's Ronda bullfight scenes. These are the culmination of a general fiesta, the Feria de Pedro Romero.

Places to Stay

Camping El Sur (☎ 95 287 59 39), a good small site 2km south-west of town on the A-369 Algeciras road, charges 1860 ptas plus IVA for two adults with a car and tent.

The bright *Pensión La Purísima* (☎ 95 287 10 50, Calle Sevilla 10) has nine singles/doubles at 2000/3000 ptas. *Hostal San Francisco* (☎ 95 287 32 99, Calle María Cabrera 18) charges 2000/4000 ptas with bath.

A bit more money can buy you considerably better accommodation. *Hotel Royal* (☎ 95 287 11 41, Calle Virgen de la Paz 42) has 29 decent rooms with bathroom for 3500/5700 ptas plus IVA. *Hotel Morales* (☎/fax 95 287 15 38, Calle Sevilla 51) has pleasant rooms with bath for 3500/6000 ptas and is full of information for travellers who want to explore the town and nearby parques naturales.

Hotel Polo (☎ 95 287 24 47, Calle Mariano Soubirón 8) has 33 spacious singles/doubles at 6300/9500 ptas plus IVA.

Alavera de los Baños (☎/fax 95 287 91 43, Hoyo San Miguel s/n) is another small, attractive hotel near the Baños Árabes, with an interesting restaurant and rooms costing 7000 ptas a single, 9000 or 10,000 ptas a double, including breakfast.

The only hotel in La Ciudad is the charming *Hotel San Gabriel* (☎ 95 219 03 92, e sangabriel@ronda.net, Calle José M Holgado 19), a converted 18th-century mansion with 16 stylish rooms, all different, for 9000/11,000 ptas plus IVA.

Hotel La Española (☎ 95 287 10 52, Calle José Aparicio 3), just off Plaza de España, charges 12,600 ptas plus IVA for comfortable doubles.

Hotel Reina Victoria (☎ 95 287 12 40, Avenida Doctor Fleming 25), built by a British company in the 1900s, has fine cliff-top gardens and an air of old-fashioned comfort. Rooms start at 9900/15,600 ptas plus IVA. Bright rooms at the cliff-top *Parador de Ronda* (☎ 95 287 75 00, e ronda@ parador .es, Plaza de España s/n) start at 14,800/18,500 ptas plus IVA.

Places to Eat

Typical Ronda food is hearty mountain fare, strong on stews, trout, game such as rabbit, partridge and quail, and, of course, oxtail.

On Plaza del Socorro, *El Molino* is popular for its pizzas, pasta and platos combinados from 550 to 775 ptas and varied breakfasts. Bright *Cervecería Patatín-Patatán* (Calle Lorenzo Borrego Gómez 7), nearby, serves sherry and wine at 125 to 150 ptas a glass, and a range of tasty tapas from 100 ptas (ask for the *carta de tapas*!).

Restaurante Hermanos Macías (Calle Pedro Romero 3) is a friendly, reliable, mid-range eatery with meat and fish main dishes from 800 to 1600 ptas.

Restaurante Pedro Romero (☎ 95 287 11 10, Calle Virgen de la Paz 18) is a celebrated spot dedicated to bullfighting, with classic *rondeño* food and a set lunch for 1650 ptas plus IVA (plus drinks). The recently opened *Restaurante Tragabuches* (☎ 95 219 02 91, Calle José Aparicio 1) has quickly gained a fine reputation. Two courses will cost you between 3000 and 5000 ptas plus IVA (closed Monday).

Pizzeria Piccola Capri (Calle Villanueva 18) has some tables overlooking the gorge and serves reasonable-value tortillas, pizzas and pasta for 500 to 700 ptas.

Entertainment

A modest *zona de movida* (nightlife area) centres around the foot of Avenida Doctor Fleming.

Getting There & Away

Bus The bus station is at Plaza Concepción García Redondo 2. Los Amarillos (☎ 95 218 70 61) goes to Málaga (two hours, 1075 ptas) and Sevilla (2½ hours, 1285 ptas) three to five times daily. Comes (☎ 95 287 19 92) has buses to Arcos de la Frontera, Jerez de la Frontera and Cádiz five times daily, and to Algeciras (1010 ptas) weekdays. Portillo (☎ 95 287 22 62) runs to Marbella and Málaga (1110 ptas) three or four times daily. Further services run to other sierra towns and villages.

Train Ronda station (☎ 95 287 16 73), on Avenida de Andalucía, is on the scenic Bobadilla-Algeciras line. Five or more trains run daily to/from Algeciras (1½ to two hours, 910 to 1500 ptas); two to/from Córdoba and Madrid; and one each to/from Granada (2¼ hours, 1775 ptas) via Antequera and (except Sunday) Málaga (two hours, 1175 ptas). For Sevilla, and further trains to/from most of the above destinations, change at Bobadilla or Antequera.

Getting Around
Occasional buses run to Plaza de España from Avenida Martínez Astein, across the road from the train station.

AROUND RONDA
The beautiful green hill country of the Serranía de Ronda, dotted with white villages, stretches in all directions from Ronda, continuing westward into north-eastern Cádiz province (see Parque Natural Sierra de Grazalema earlier in this chapter).

Parque Natural Sierra de las Nieves
This 180 sq km protected area, south-east of Ronda, offers some good walks. Torrecilla (1918m), the highest peak in the western half of Andalucía, is about a five-hour return walk from Área Recreativa Los Quejigales, which is 10km east by unpaved road from the A-376 Ronda–San Pedro de Alcántara road.

Camping Conejeras (☎ 619-18 00 12), 800m off the A-376 on the Los Quejigales road, charges 350 ptas per person/tent/car. It closes for July, August and September.

A great little hotel within striking distance of the park is the *Posada del Canonigo* (☎ 95 216 01 85, Calle Mesones 24), a restored mansion in the small town of El Burgo. Singles/doubles with bath are 4000/

6000 ptas and there's a moderately priced little restaurant. Management has information on walking routes and can organise horse riding.

Cueva de la Pileta
Palaeolithic paintings of horses, goats, fish and even a seal, dating from 20,000 to 25,000 years ago, are preserved in this large cave 19km south-west of Ronda. You'll be guided by kerosene lamp by one of the knowledgeable Bullón family, from the farm in the valley below, one of whom discovered the paintings in 1905 when searching for bat-dung fertiliser.

Cueva de la Pileta (☎ 95 216 73 43) is 250m (signposted) off the Benaoján–Cortes de la Frontera road, 4km from Benaoján. One-hour tours at 10 and 11 am, noon and 1, 4 and 5 pm daily cost 800 or 900 ptas per person, depending how many turn up. Guides speak at least some English and German. If you come on a busy day you may have to wait, but you can ring ahead to try to book a particular time.

Benaoján is served from Ronda by two Los Amarillos buses (weekdays) and up to four trains daily.

ANTEQUERA
postcode 29200 • pop 40,000
Antequera, set on the edge of a plain 50km north of Málaga, with rugged mountains to the south and east, is one of Andalucía's most attractive towns. Its 'golden age' was the 15th and 16th centuries, when dozens of churches and mansions were built.

Orientation & Information
The old heart of town is below the north-western side of the hill-top Muslim Alcazaba. The main street, Calle Infante Don Fernando, begins here on Plaza de San Sebastián and runs north-west. The tourist office (☎ 95 270 25 05), at Plaza San Sebastián 7, is open from at least 10 am to 1.30 pm and 5 to 7 pm Monday to Saturday, and until 2 pm Sunday.

Things to See
The main approach to the Alcazaba is through the **Arco de los Gigantes** archway,

ANDALUCÍA

built in 1585 incorporating stones with Roman inscriptions. What remains of the **Alcazaba** affords great views. Just below it, the **Colegiata de Santa María la Mayor**, a 16th-century church, boasts a beautiful Renaissance facade (open 10 am to 2 pm except Monday; free).

The pride of the **Museo Municipal** on Plaza Coso Viejo is 'Efebo', a beautiful 1.4m bronze Roman statue of a patrician's teenage 'toy boy', unearthed near Antequera in the 1950s. Museum tours (200 ptas) are given between 10 am and 1.30 pm and 4 and 6 pm Tuesday to Friday, and between 10 or 11 am and 1.30 pm Saturday and Sunday.

The retablo of the **Iglesia del Carmen**, on Plaza del Carmen about 500m south-east of the museum, is one of the high points of churrigueresque sculpture, carved in red pine by *antequerano* Antonio Primo and spangled with statues of angels, saints, popes and bishops. The church is open 11.30 am to 2 pm Monday and 10 am to 2 pm other days, plus 4 to 7 pm Saturday (200 ptas).

Some of Europe's largest megalithic tombs stand on the fringes of Antequera. The **Dólmen de Menga** and **Dólmen de Viera** are 1km from the centre on the road leading north-east out to the N-331. About 2500 or 2000 BC the local folk managed to transport dozens of huge rocks from nearby hills to construct these earth-covered tombs for their chieftains. Menga is 25m long, 4m high and composed of 32 slabs, the largest weighing 180 tonnes. Menga and Viera are open 9 am to 3.30 pm Sunday and Tuesday and until 6 pm Wednesday to Saturday (free). A third big dolmen, the **Dólmen del Romeral** (1800 BC), is a further 3km out of town.

Places to Stay & Eat

Friendly *Camas El Gallo* (☎ 95 284 21 04, *Calle Nueva 2),* just off Plaza de San Sebastián, has clean, small, no-frills singles/doubles for 1400/2400 ptas. Another friendly place, *Pensión Madrona* (☎ 95 284 00 14, *Calle Calzada 25),* 400m north-east, has pleasant rooms with bath at 2750/3850 ptas and a good, economical restaurant. Rambling *Hotel Colón* (☎ 95 284 00 10, *Calle Infante Don Fernando 31)* offers varied

good rooms with bath for 2600/4000 ptas plus IVA (more in August and at Easter and Christmas). *Hotel Castilla* (☎/*fax 95 284 30 90, Calle Infante Don Fernando 40)* has comfy, new rooms with bath for 4500/6500 ptas, and an excellent-value restaurant: ham, eggs and chips for 600 ptas.

Restaurante La Espuela (Calle San Agustín 1), off Calle Infante Don Fernando, offers traditional country fare such as wild boar, venison and oxtail for 1000 to 2400 ptas, as well as pizzas and pasta from 700 to 900 ptas, all plus IVA. It also serves *menús* for 1000 or 2100 ptas plus IVA (closed Monday).

Getting There & Away

The bus station is 1km north of the centre, on Calle Sagrado Corazón de Jesús. Several daily buses run to/from Málaga, and three to five each to/from Osuna, Sevilla (Prado de San Sebastián), Granada and Córdoba.

The train station is about 1.5km north of the centre at the end of Avenida de la Estación. Two to four trains a day travel to/from Granada, Sevilla, Ronda and Almería. For Málaga or Córdoba, change at Bobadilla.

AROUND ANTEQUERA
El Torcal

Nature has sculpted this 1336m mountain 16km south of Antequera into some of the weirdest, most wonderful rock formations you'll see anywhere. Its 12 sq km of gnarled, pillared and deeply fissured limestone began life as sea bed 150 million years ago. A visitor centre (☎ 95 203 13 89) here is open 10 am to 2 pm and 4 to 6 pm (3 to 5 pm in winter) daily.

A 1.4km marked walking trail starts and ends near the visitor centre. To see any more of El Torcal, you're supposed to go with a guide from the visitor centre: recently, two-hour trips (600 ptas) were leaving at 10.30 am Sunday.

Buses from Antequera will get you there, or back, but not in one day. Drivers should leave Antequera on the C-3310 towards Villanueva de la Concepción. The El Torcal turn-off is 12km out.

Laguna de Fuente de Piedra
When not dried up by drought, this shallow lake, close to the A-92 20km north-west of Antequera, is one of Europe's two main breeding grounds for the spectacular greater flamingo (the other is France's Camargue). After a wet winter as many as 16,000 pairs of flamingoes breed at the lake. They arrive in January or February, with the chicks hatching in April and May, and stay till about August.

The Centro de Información Fuente de Piedra (☎ 95 211 10 50) at the lake, on the edge of Fuente de Piedra village, is open 10 am to 2 pm and 4 to 6 pm (6 to 8 pm during daylight saving) Wednesday to Sunday. For viewing the flamingoes, a vehicle and binoculars are advantageous, as you may find the birds cluster towards the far side of the lake, a 6km or 7km drive away, and fly away if you get *too* close.

Hostal La Laguna (☎ 95 273 52 92), just off the A-92 in Fuente de Piedra, has doubles for 5000 ptas.

Buses run between Antequera's bus station and Fuente de Piedra village at least three times daily.

JANE SMITH

Laguna de Fuente de Piedra is Spain's main breeding site for flamingoes.

EAST OF MÁLAGA
The coast east of Málaga, sometimes described as the Costa del Sol Oriental, is less developed than the coast to the west.

Behind the coast, the attractive La Axarquía region, dotted with white villages of Muslim origin linked by snaking mountain roads, climbs to the sierras along the border of Granada province. There's good walking here (best in April and May and from mid-September to late October). Once impoverished and forgotten, La Axarquía has experienced a surge of tourism and an influx of expat residents in recent years. Information on La Axarquía is available at tourist offices in coastal towns such as Nerja, Torre del Mar and Torrox.

Nerja
postcode 29780 • pop 14,000
Nerja, 56km from Málaga, is older, whiter and marginally more charming than the towns to its west, though inundated by tourism. The tourist office (☎ 95 252 15 31) is in the centre at Puerta del Mar 4, near the Balcón de Europa lookout point, which has good coastal views. The best beach is Playa Burriana, on the eastern side of town.

Places to Stay The pleasant *Nerja Camping* (☎ 95 252 97 14), about 4km east on the N-340, charges 2200 ptas for two people with tent and car.

In August, try to arrive early in the day to ensure a room in town. A good, economical choice is *Hostal Mena* (☎ 95 252 05 41, Calle El Barrio 15), a short distance west of the tourist office. Singles/doubles with bath are 2250/4500 ptas (more in August, less from October to June). Prices are similar at *Hostal Atenbeni* (☎ 95 252 13 41, Calle Diputación Provincial 12), one block north of Calle El Barrio, and *Hostal Nerjasol* (☎ 95 252 22 21, Calle Arropieros 4), four blocks north of the tourist office.

The central *Hotel Cala Bella* (☎ 95 252 07 00, Puerta del Mar 10) and *Hotel Portofino* (☎ 95 252 01 50, Puerta del Mar 2) have some doubles with good beach views – respectively 6500 and 9000 ptas plus IVA in high season. *Parador de Nerja*

ANDALUCÍA

(☎ 95 252 00 50, Calle Almuñécar 8), above Playa Burriana charges 19,000 ptas plus IVA.

Places to Eat One of the best feeds is at the open-air *Merendero Ayo* towards the eastern end of Playa Burriana, where a plate of paella, cooked on the spot in great sizzling pans, is 675 ptas.

Havelí (Calle Cristo 44), north off Puerta del Mar, is a good, medium-priced Indian restaurant with a roof terrace in summer. It opens evenings only. *Ostería di Mamma Rosa (Edificio Corona, Calle Chaparil),* about a 10-minute walk west of Puerta del Mar, is another good medium-priced option.

Getting There & Away Alsina Graells (☎ 95 252 15 04), on the N-340 near the top of Calle Pintada, has around 14 daily buses to/from Málaga, eight to/from Almuñécar, several to/from Almería and two to/from Granada.

Around Nerja

The big tourist attraction is the **Cueva de Nerja**, 3km east of town just off the N-340. This enormous cavern remains very impressive despite the crowds traipsing continually through it. It's open 10 am to 2 pm and 4 to 6.30 pm daily (750 ptas). About 14 buses daily run from Málaga and Nerja.

Farther east the coast becomes more rugged and scenic and with your own wheels you can head out to some good **beaches** reached by tracks down from the N-340 around 8km to 10km from Nerja.

Cómpeta & Around

postcode 29754 • pop 2700

A good base for exploring La Axarquía and the mountains is the village of Cómpeta, 17km inland. It produces some of the best of La Axarquía's sweet white wine.

Things to See & Do Perhaps the most exhilarating walk is up the dramatically peaked **El Lucero** (1779m). From its summit, on a clear day, you can see both Granada and Morocco. This is a demanding full day's return walk from Cómpeta, but it's possible to drive as far up as Puerto Blanquillo pass (1200m)

via a slightly hairy mountain track from Canillas de Albaida, 3km north-west of Cómpeta. From Puerto Blanquillo a path climbs 200m to another pass, Puerto de Competa. One kilometre down from this, past a quarry, the summit path (1½ hours) diverges to the right across a stream bed, marked by a green-and-white paint blob on the far bank. The booklet *25 Walks in and Around Cómpeta & Canillas de Albaida* by Albert & Dini Kraaijenzank, available locally, covers a range of other, mostly less strenuous, day walks.

Árchez, a few kilometres down the valley from Cómpeta, has a beautiful Almohad minaret next to its church. From Árchez a road winds 8km south-west to **Arenas**, where a steep but driveable track climbs to the ruined Muslim **Castillo de Bentomiz**, crowning a hill top.

Places to Stay & Eat *Hostal Alberdini (☎ 95 251 62 41),* at La Lomilla, 1km southeast of Cómpeta, with spectacular views, has singles/doubles with bathroom for 3000/5000 ptas (discounts for more than one night), and a reasonably priced restaurant. Beautifully renovated *Casa Azahara (☎/fax 95 251 61 53, Calle Carretería 9),* just off the central Plaza Almijara, does B&B for 3500/6000 ptas, with private bath. Cómpeta has plenty of *restaurants.*

Getting There & Away Two or three buses daily run from Málaga to Cómpeta and Canillas de Albaida, via Torre del Mar.

Córdoba Province

The big draw here is Córdoba city, capital of Al-Andalus when Al-Andalus was at its peak. Its Mezquita (mosque) is one of the most magnificent of all Islamic buildings.

CÓRDOBA

postcode 14080 • pop 310,000

Standing on a sweep of the Río Guadalquivir with countryside stretching far in every direction around, Córdoba is both provincial and sophisticated. The most popular time to visit is from about mid-April to mid-June, when the skies are big and blue but the heat tolerable, and the city's beautiful patios are at their best, dripping with foliage and blooms.

History

The Roman colony of Corduba, founded in 152 BC, became capital of Baetica province, covering most of today's Andalucía. This major Roman cultural centre was the birthplace of the writers Seneca and Lucan. In AD 711 Córdoba fell to the Islamic invaders and soon became the peninsula's Muslim capital. It was here in 756 that Abd ar-Rahman I set himself up as the independent emir of Al-Andalus.

Córdoba's heyday came under Abd ar-Rahman III (912–61), who in 929 named himself Caliph, setting the seal on Al-Andalus' *de facto* independence of the Abbasid caliphs in Baghdad. Córdoba was then the biggest city in Western Europe, with a population somewhere between 100,000 and 500,000. It had dazzling mosques, patios, libraries, observatories, aqueducts, a university and highly skilled artisans in leather, metal, textiles, glazed tiles and more. Abd ar-Rahman III's court was frequented by Jewish, Arab and Christian scholars.

At its peak, the Córdoba caliphate encompassed most of the Iberian Peninsula south of the Río Duero, plus the Balearic Islands and some of North Africa. Córdoba became a place of pilgrimage for Muslims who could not reach Mecca or Jerusalem.

Towards the end of the 10th century, Al-Mansour (Almanzor), a fearsome general, took the reins of power and struck terror into Christian Spain, making over 50 *razzias* (forays), in 20 years. But after the death of Al-Mansour's son in 1008 the caliphate descended into anarchy. Berber troops terrorised Córdoba and in 1031 the caliphate collapsed into dozens of taifas. Córdoba became part of the Sevilla taifa in 1069.

Its intellectual traditions, however, continued. Twelfth-century Córdoba produced two of the most celebrated of all Al-Andalus' scholars: the Muslim Averroës (Ibn Rushd) and the Jewish Maimonides, men of multifarious talents best remembered for their philosophical efforts to harmonise religious faith with reason.

Córdoba was taken in 1236 by Fernando III and became a provincial town of shrinking importance. The decline only began to be reversed with the coming of industry in the late 19th century.

Orientation

The World Heritage-listed medieval city, fascinating to explore, is immediately north of the Río Guadalquivir, a labyrinth of narrow streets focused on the Mezquita. North-west of the Mezquita was the Judería (Jewish quarter). The main square of modern Córdoba is Plaza de las Tendillas, 500m north of the Mezquita.

Librería Luque, Calle Conde de Gondomar 13, sells city and Michelin maps at about half the prices of the tourist shops near the Mezquita.

Information

Tourist Offices The helpful regional tourist office (☎ 957 47 12 35) faces the Mezquita at Calle de Torrijos 10. It's open 10 am to 6, 7 or 8 pm (according to season) Monday to Saturday and until 2 pm Sunday and holidays. The municipal tourist office (☎ 957 20 05 22) on Plaza de Judá Levi, a block farther west, is open 8.30 am to 2.30 pm weekdays, sometimes longer in summer.

Money The main concentration of banks and ATMs is around Plaza de las Tendillas and Avenida del Gran Capitán.

Post & Communications The main post office is at Calle José Cruz Conde 15. El Navegante Café Internet (☎ 957 49 75 36), Llanos del Pretorio 1, is open 9 am to 1 am daily, offers 15/30/60 minutes online for 250/350/600 ptas.

Medical Services & Emergency The main general hospital, Hospital Reina Sofia (☎ 957 21 70 00), is 1.5km south-west of the Mezquita at Avenida de Menéndez Pidal s/n. The Policía Nacional (☎ 957 47 75 00) are at Avenida Doctor Fleming 2.

Business Hours Opening times for Córdoba's sights change frequently – check with

CÓRDOBA

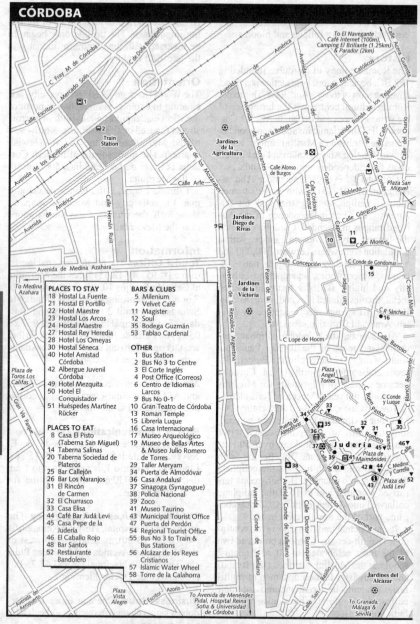

PLACES TO STAY
18 Hostal La Fuente
21 Hostal El Portillo
22 Hotel Maestre
23 Hostal Los Arcos
24 Hostal Maestre
27 Hostal Rey Heredia
28 Hotel Los Omeyas
30 Hostal Séneca
40 Hotel Amistad
   Córdoba
42 Albergue Juvenil
   Córdoba
49 Hotel Mezquita
50 Hotel El
   Conquistador
51 Huéspedes Martínez
   Rücker

PLACES TO EAT
8 Casa El Pisto
   (Taberna San Miguel)
14 Taberna Salinas
20 Taberna Sociedad de
   Plateros
25 Bar Callejón
26 Bar Los Naranjos
31 El Rincón
   de Carmen
32 El Churrasco
33 Casa Elisa
44 Café Bar Judá Levi
45 Casa Pepe de la
   Judería
46 El Caballo Rojo
48 Bar Santos
52 Restaurante
   Bandolero

BARS & CLUBS
5 Milenium
7 Velvet Café
11 Magister
12 Soul
35 Bodega Guzmán
53 Tablao Cardenal

OTHER
1 Bus Station
2 Bus No 3 to Centre
3 El Corte Inglés
4 Post Office (Correos)
6 Centro de Idiomas
   Larcos
9 Bus No 0-1
10 Gran Teatro de Córdoba
13 Roman Temple
15 Librería Luque
16 Casa Internacional
17 Museo Arqueológico
19 Museo de Bellas Artes
   & Museo Julio Romero
   de Torres
29 Taller Meryam
34 Puerta de Almodóvar
36 Casa Andalusí
37 Sinagoga (Synagogue)
38 Policía Nacional
39 Zoco
41 Museo Taurino
47 Municipal Tourist Office
47 Puerta del Perdón
54 Regional Tourist Office
55 Bus No 3 to Train &
   Bus Stations
56 Alcázar de los Reyes
   Cristianos
57 Islamic Water Wheel
58 Torre de la Calahorra

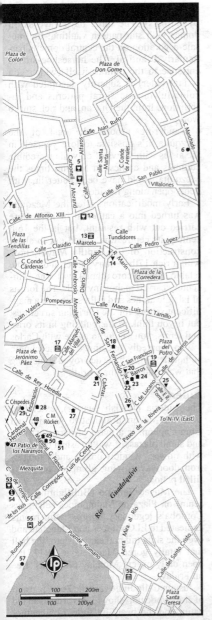

tourist offices for the latest times. Most places except the Mezquita close on Monday, and closing times are generally earlier in winter than summer.

Mezquita

This superb mosque can seem a little bewildering at first. Because of the Christian alterations to the original Islamic structure and the darkness they imposed, you need a bit of imagination to picture the Mezquita as it was, an architectural unity open to and in harmony with its surroundings. It has some truly beautiful features, among them the famous rows of two-tier arches in mesmerising stripes of red brick and white stone, and the more elaborate arches, domes and decoration around the splendid *mihrab* (prayer niche). The outside of the building has thick stone walls punctuated by ornate portals.

History Abd ar-Rahman I founded the Mezquita in 785 on the site of a church that had been partitioned between Muslims and Christians, reputedly purchasing the Christian half from the Christian community. Abd ar-Rahman II (821–52) and Al-Hakim II in the 960s extended the Mezquita southwards to cater for Córdoba's expanding population. Al-Hakim II created the existing mihrab and its surrounds. Under Al-Mansour, eastward extensions were made.

What you see today is the Mezquita's final Islamic form with one big alteration: a 16th-century cathedral right in the middle (hence explaining the often-used description 'Mezquita-Catedral').

Entry The main entrance is Puerta del Perdón, a 14th-century mudéjar gateway on Calle Cardenal Herrero, beside a 16th- and 17th-century tower. From April to September the Mezquita is open 10 am to 7.30 pm Monday to Saturday, 3.30 to 7.30 pm Sunday; in other months, 10 am to 5.30 pm Monday to Saturday, 2 to 5.30 pm Sunday and holidays (800 ptas).

Inside the entrance is the pretty **Patio de los Naranjos** (Courtyard of the Orange Trees), from which a door leads into the Mezquita itself.

ANDALUCÍA

JANE SMITH

These pillars and two-tiered arches of brick and stone are a magnificent feature of the Mezquita.

Inside the Mezquita The mihrab is visible straight ahead from the entrance door, in the far (south) wall. The first 12 east-west aisles inside the entrance, a forest of pillars and arches, comprise the original **8th-century mosque.** This incorporated columns and capitals – of various coloured marbles, granite and alabaster – from the site's previous Visigothic church, from Roman buildings in Córdoba and elsewhere, and even from ancient Carthage. The columns support two tiers of arches, suggestive of aqueducts and/or date palms. The use of bi-coloured materials for the arches was inspired. Subsequent extensions required more columns, most made locally. The final Islamic building had 1300 columns, of which 850 remain.

In the centre of the building is the Christian cathedral, surrounded by Islamic aisles, pillars and arches. Just past its western end begins the approach to the mihrab, marked by heavier, more elaborate arches.

The bay immediately in front of the mihrab and the bay to each side of it form the **maksura**, where the caliphs and their retinues would have prayed (today enclosed by railings). The three bays have skylit domes with star-pattern vaulting: the mosaic decoration on the central dome is particularly beautiful. The horseshoe-arched entrance to the **mihrab** itself (which you cannot enter) is superbly decorated with colourful mosaic floral patterns and inscriptions from the Qur'an, and rich stucco work.

Wandering around the rest of the Mezquita, it's possible to lose yourself in the aisles with views of only the incredible columns and arches. In Muslim times the Mezquita would have been better lit, with doors open along its sides.

Early modifications after the Mezquita was turned into a cathedral in 1236 were carried out with restraint, but in the 16th century its centre was ripped out to allow construction of the **Capilla Mayor**, now with a rich 17th-century jasper and marble retablo, and the **coro** (choir), with fine 18th-century carved mahogany stalls. The forests of Islamic arches and pillars provide a magnificent setting for the Christian structures, but if you think of the building in its original terms, you've got to agree with Carlos I who reputedly exclaimed to the church authorities: 'You have destroyed something that was unique in the world'.

Judería

The Judería (Jewish quarter), extending from the Mezquita almost to Avenida del Gran Capitán, is a maze of narrow streets and small plazas, of whitewashed buildings with flowery window boxes, and wrought-iron doorways giving glimpses of plant-filled patios.

The **Museo Taurino** (Bullfighting Museum) on Plaza de Maimónides celebrates Córdoba's legendary *toreros,* with rooms dedicated to El Cordobés and Manolete and even the skin, tail and ear of Islero, the bull that fatally gored Manolete in 1947. It's open daily except Monday (450 ptas, free on Friday).

Just up Calle Judíos are the **Zoco**, a group of craft workshop/showrooms around an old patio, and the beautiful little 14th-century

ANDALUCÍA

Sinagoga, one of Spain's very few surviving medieval synagogues. It retains its upstairs women's gallery, and Hebrew inscriptions and intricate mudéjar patterns in stucco; open 10 am to 2 pm and 3.30 to 5.30 pm Tuesday to Saturday, 10 am to 1.30 pm Sunday and holidays (free for EU citizens, 50 ptas for others). The **Casa Andalusí**, Calle Judíos 12, is a 12th-century house prettily decked out with exhibits relating to Córdoba's medieval Muslim culture, but also including a Roman mosaic in the cellar – open 10.30 am to 7 or 8 pm daily (300 ptas).

Just west of the top of Calle Judíos is the **Puerta de Almodóvar**, an Islamic gate in the old city walls.

Alcázar de los Reyes Cristianos

Alcázar de los Reyes Cristianos (Castle of the Christian Monarchs), just south of the Mezquita, began as a palace and fort for Alfonso X in the 13th century. From 1490 to 1821 the Inquisition operated from here. The Alcázar's large gardens, full of fish ponds, fountains, orange trees, flowers and topiary, are among the most beautiful in Andalucía. The building houses a royal bathhouse and a museum, with some Roman mosaics of most interest. It's open 10 am to 2 pm and 6 to 8 pm (4.30 to 6.30 pm October to April) Tuesday to Saturday, and 9.30 am to 3 pm Sunday and holidays (300 ptas, free on Friday).

Puente Romano & Around

Just south of the Mezquita, the Guadalquivir is crossed by the much-restored **Puente Romano** (Roman Bridge). Just downstream, near the northern bank, is a restored **Islamic water wheel**.

At the southern end of the bridge is the **Torre de la Calahorra**, a 14th-century tower housing a museum highlighting the intellectual achievements of Islamic Córdoba and focusing rather rose-tintedly on its reputation for religious tolerance. A 55-minute taped commentary, available in several languages, guides you through the displays, which include good models of the Mezquita and Granada's Alhambra. It's open 10 am to 2 pm and 4.30 to 8.30 pm daily (to 6 pm, October to April); 500 ptas.

Museo Arqueológico

Córdoba's Archaeological Museum is in a Renaissance mansion at Plaza de Jerónimo Páez 7. A reclining stone lion takes pride of place in the Iberian section, and the Roman period is well represented with large mosaics, elegant ceramics and tinted glass bowls. The upstairs is devoted to medieval Córdoba, including bronze animals from Medina Azahara. The museum is open 3 to 8 pm Tuesday, 9 am to 8 pm Wednesday to Saturday and 9 am to 3 pm Sunday and holidays (free with EU passport or identity card, 250 ptas otherwise).

Plaza del Potro

This attractive, pedestrianised plaza, 400m north-east of the Mezquita, was a hang-out for traders and adventurers in the 16th and 17th centuries and is mentioned in *Don Quijote*. A former hospital houses the **Museo de Bellas Artes**, with the same hours and prices as the Museo Arqueológico and a collection of paintings by mainly Córdoban artists, and the **Museo Julio Romero de Torres**, devoted to local painter Julio Romero de Torres (1880–1930), who specialised in sensual portraits of Cordoban women. The latter is open daily except Monday (450 ptas, free on Friday).

Roman Temple

A ruined Roman temple has been partly restored, with 11 columns standing, on Calle Claudio Marcelo east of Plaza de las Tendillas.

Language Courses

Centro de Idiomas Larcos (☎ 957 47 11 03), Calle Manchado 9, and Casa Internacional (☎ 957 48 06 42), Calle Rodríguez Sánchez 15, offer Spanish courses. Their Web sites are, respectively, www.larcos.net and www.cybercordoba.es/casa_internacional (click on 'courses', 'enrolment' etc for details). A typical two-week course, including shared apartment accommodation, is around 60,000 ptas. For information on one-month courses at the university, contact the Servicio de Lenguas Modernas y Traducción Técnica (☎ 957 21 81 33, e si3goluj@uco.es),

ANDALUCÍA

Edificio E U Enfermería, Avenida de Menéndez Pidal, 5° planta, 14071 Córdoba.

Special Events
Spring and early summer is the chief festival time for Córdoba. The major events are:

May
Concurso & Festival de Patios Cordobeses See the boxed text 'Córdoba's Patios'; at the same time there's a busy cultural program. Held in the first half of the month.

May/June
Feria de Mayo 10 days of party time for Córdoba. Held in the last week of May/first days of June

June/July
Festival Internacional de Guitarra Two-week celebration of the guitar with live classical, flamenco, rock, blues and more; top names play in the Alcázar gardens at night. Held in late June/first half of July.

Places to Stay
Many of Córdoba's lodgings are built around charming patios. Accommodation is generally plentiful, though single rooms for a decent price are scarce. Try to book ahead during the main festivals. Prices are generally reduced from November to mid-March; some places also cut their rates in hot July and August.

Places to Stay – Budget
Camping *Camping El Brillante* (☎ 957 27 84 81, Avenida del Brillante 50) is about 1.25km north of Plaza de Colón. It costs 2160 to 2280 ptas plus IVA for two adults with a car and tent. Bus Nos 10 and 11 run to/from the train and bus stations.

Youth Hostel The excellent Inturjoven *Albergue Juvenil Córdoba* (☎ 957 29 01 66), perfectly positioned on Plaza de Judá Levi, has room for 167 people in rooms holding two to five.

Hostales The friendly *Hostal Rey Heredia* (☎ 957 47 41 82, Calle Rey Heredia 26) has a plant-filled patio and singles/doubles for 1500/3000 ptas (2000/4000 ptas with bathroom). Nearby, friendly *Huéspedes Martínez*

Córdoba's Patios
Córdoba's patios have two origins: Roman and Muslim. For the Romans, the patios provided a meeting place; during Islamic times, they were used for rest and recreation. Today, both these purposes are maintained – patios provide a haven of peace and quiet, shade during the searing heat of the summer, and a place to entertain.

In the first half of May, you'll notice 'Patio' signs in Córdoba's streets and alleys; this means that you're invited to view what is for the rest of the year closed to the world by heavy wooden doors or partly hidden by wrought-iron gates. At this time of year the patios are at their prettiest as new blooms proliferate. Many patios will have been entered in the annual Concurso de Patios Cordobéses, a competition with prizes for the best patios. The tourist office can provide a map of patios open for viewing. If you don't have a lot of time, those in the vicinity of Calle de San Basilio, about 400m west of the Mezquita, are some of the best.

During the concurso, the patios are generally open 5 pm to midnight weekdays, and noon to midnight weekends. Entry is usually free but sometimes there's a container for donations.

Rücker (☎ 957 47 25 62, e hmrucker@alcavia.net, Calle Martínez Rücker 14), with clean rooms for 2000/3500 ptas, is a stone's throw east of the Mezquita.

There are some good hostales to the east, farther from the tourist masses. Simple, old-fashioned *Hostal El Portillo* (☎ 957 47 20 91, Calle Cabezas 2) has seven rooms at 1500/3000 ptas. *Hostal Los Arcos* (☎ 957 48 56 43, Calle Romero Barros 14), with a pretty patio, has rooms for 2500/4000 ptas, and doubles with bath for 5000 ptas. *Hostal Maestre* (☎ 957 47 24 10, Calle Romero Barros 16) has 20 clean, spacious rooms with bath at 3000/5000 ptas.

Hostal La Fuente (☎ 957 48 78 27, Calle de San Fernando 51) has 40 rooms with bath, TV and air-con. Compact singles are 3500 ptas, doubles 6000 ptas. It has courtyards for sitting out and serves a decent breakfast.

Just north of the Mezquita, *Hostal Séneca* (*☎/fax 957 47 32 34, Calle Conde y Luque 7*) is charming with friendly management and a pleasant patio; rooms are 2550/4700 ptas with shared bath or 4750/ 5900 ptas with private bath, including breakfast. Phone ahead.

Places to Stay – Mid-Range
Hotel Los Omeyas (*☎ 957 49 22 67, fax 957 49 16 59, Calle Encarnación 17*) is modern but in attractive traditional style, with good singles/doubles for 5000/8500 ptas plus IVA. *Hotel Mezquita* (*☎ 957 47 55 85, Plaza Santa Catalina 1*), across the street from the Mezquita, offers 21 good rooms at 5150/9850 ptas plus IVA. *Hotel Maestre* (*☎ 957 47 24 10, Calle Romero Barros 4*) has plain but bright rooms for 3800/6500 ptas plus IVA, and garage parking for 850 ptas a night.

Places to Stay – Top End
Hotel El Conquistador (*☎ 957 48 11 02, Calle Magistral González Francés 15*), facing the Mezquita, has comfortable rooms for 18,000/22,000 ptas plus IVA. In the Judería the attractive *Hotel Amistad Córdoba* (*☎ 957 42 03 35, Plaza de Maimónides 3*) has doubles for 18,000 ptas plus IVA. Córdoba's modern *Parador* (*☎ 957 27 59 00, Avenida de la Arruzafa s/n*) is 3km north of the centre on the site of Abd ar-Rahman I's summer palace. Rooms are 14,000/17,500 ptas plus IVA.

Places to Eat
A couple of dishes common to most Córdoban restaurants are *salmorejo*, a very thick tomato-based gazpacho with bits of hard-boiled egg on top, and *rabo de toro* (oxtail stew). Some top restaurants feature recipes from Al-Andalus such as garlic soup with raisins, honeyed lamb, or meats stuffed with dates and pine nuts. The local tipple is wine from nearby Montilla and Moriles, similar to sherry.

There are lots of places to eat right by the Mezquita, some expensive, some mediocre, some awful. A few better-value places are a short walk west into the Judería. A longer walk east or north will turn up further options.

Around the Mezquita Tiny *Bar Santos* (*Calle Magistral González Francés 3*) is a good stop for bocadillos (200 to 300 ptas), tapas (150 ptas) and raciones (500 ptas). The *tortilla española* is excellent. *El Caballo Rojo* (*Calle Cardenal Herrero 28*) specialises in Mozarabic food from caliphal times. The *menú* is a hefty 2950 ptas plus IVA but here you're guaranteed something different from the usual fare. *Restaurante Bandolero* (*Calle de Torrijos 6*) provides media-raciones from 250 to 1000 ptas; a la carte, expect to pay 3000 to 4000 ptas for three courses with drinks.

Judería *Casa Pepe de la Judería* (*Calle Romero 1*) serves tasty tapas and raciones in its bar and in rooms around its little patio, and has a good restaurant with most main dishes in the 1600 to 2400 ptas zone. *El Rincón de Carmen* (*Calle Romero 4*), has a patio with a *menú* for 1600 ptas and an attached cafe doing good snacks and breakfasts. *El Churrasco* (*☎ 957 29 08 19, Calle Romero 16*) is one of Córdoba's best restaurants, with rich food, generous portions and attentive service. The *menú* is 3500 ptas and mains start at 2000 ptas.

Café Bar Judá Levi, on Plaza Judá Levi, serves platos combinados from 700 ptas. Hole-in-the-wall *Casa Elisa* (*Calle Almanzor 34*) serves excellent take-away hot bocadillos for 150 to 275 ptas.

East of the Mezquita *Taberna Sociedad de Plateros* (*Calle San Francisco 6*) is a popular tavern serving reasonably priced tapas (closed Monday). A coffee and tostada is 200 ptas at *Bar Los Naranjos* on Calle de San Fernando. On pedestrian Calle Enrique Romero de Torres (a nice place to sit at sunset), *Bar Callejón*, with tables outside looking up to Plaza del Potro, serves omelettes, main dishes and platos combinados for 500 to 900 ptas, and a three-course *menú* for 1200 ptas.

The convivial *Taberna Salinas* (*Calle Tundidores 3*), a little farther north, serves good, inexpensive Córdoban fare. Dishes such as *revuelto de ajetes, gambas y jamón* (scrambled eggs with garlic shoots, prawns and ham) and *chuletas de cordero* (lamb chops) cost 675 to 775 ptas; closed Sunday.

City Centre *Casa El Pisto (Plaza San Miguel 1),* officially Taberna San Miguel, is an atmospheric old watering hole with a good range of tapas, media-raciones (500 to 1000 ptas) and raciones, and inexpensive Moriles wine. There are tables behind the bar (closed Sunday).

Entertainment

Most bars in the medieval city close around midnight. *Bodega Guzmán (Calle de los Judíos 7)* is an atmospheric local favourite, with wines from the barrel. There's a fairly good flamenco show most nights at *Tablao Cardenal (Calle de Torrijos 10),* starting at 10.30 pm (2800 ptas, including one drink).

Córdoba's liveliest bars are mostly in the newer parts of town. *Casa El Pisto* (see Places to Eat) is one. More youthful places gather steam around midnight on Friday and Saturday. *Soul (Calle Alfonso XIII 3)* attracts a student/arty crowd and stays open to 3 am nightly. Nearby, *Velvet Café (Calle Alfaros 29)* and *Milenium (Calle Alfaros 33)* may have live bands a couple of nights a week. *Magister,* on Calle Morería, brews its own tasty beer (five varieties at around 250 ptas a glass).

The *Gran Teatro de Córdoba (Avenida del Gran Capitán 3)* has a busy program of concerts, theatre, dance and film. The *Filmoteca de Andalucía (Calle Medina y Corella 5)* regularly shows subtitled foreign films for 150 ptas.

Shopping

Córdoba is known for its *cuero repujado* (embossed leather) goods, silver jewellery (particularly filigree) and attractive pottery. Craft shops congregate around the Mezquita: the best place for embossed leather is Taller Meryam on Calleja de las Flores.

Getting There & Away

Bus The bus station (☎ 957 40 40 40) is on Plaza de las Tres Culturas, behind the train station. Varied companies run at least 10 buses a day to/from Sevilla (1225 ptas),

eight to/from Granada (1515 ptas), six to/from Madrid (1600 ptas) and five or more to/from Málaga (1570 ptas) and Jaén. Other destinations include Carmona, Antequera, Cádiz, Baeza, Úbeda, Valencia, Barcelona and some towns in Extremadura.

Train The station (☎ 957 40 02 02) is on Avenida de América, 1km north-west of Plaza de las Tendillas.

About 20 trains daily run to/from Sevilla (45 minutes to 1¼ hours, 1090 to 2800 ptas). Options to/from Madrid range from several daily AVEs (1¾ hours, 6100 to 7200 ptas) to a middle-of-the-night Estrella (6¼ hours, 3700 ptas).

Several daily trains head to Málaga (two to three hours, 2000 to 2800 ptas), Cádiz and Barcelona, and one to Jaén. For Granada (four hours, 1900 ptas), you must change at Bobadilla.

Getting Around

Bus No 3 (115 ptas) from the street between the train and bus stations runs to Plaza de las Tendillas and down Calle de San Fernando, east of the Mezquita. For the return trip, you can pick it up on Ronda de Isasa, just south of the Mezquita.

Taxis cost around 600 ptas from the stations to the Mezquita.

For drivers, Córdoba's one-way system is nightmarish, but routes to many hotels and hostales are fairly well signposted, with a 'P' if they have parking.

AROUND CÓRDOBA
Medina Azahara

In 936 Abd ar-Rahman III began the building of a magnificent new capital for his new caliphate, 8km west of Córdoba, and by 945 was able to install himself there. The glory of the new city, Medina Azahara (or Madinat al-Zahra), was short-lived, however. Between 1010 and 1013, during the caliphate's collapse, Medina Azahara was wrecked by Berber soldiers.

Though less than one-tenth of the city has been excavated, and what's open to visitors is only about a quarter of that, Medina Azahara is still intriguing, and its country location adds to the appeal. It's open 10 am to 2 pm and 6 to 8.30 pm (4 to 6.30 pm October to April) Tuesday to Saturday, and until 1.30 or 2 pm Sunday (free with an EU passport, 250 ptas otherwise).

The visitor route leads down to the **Dar al-Wuzara** (House of the Viziers), a substantial building with several horseshoe arches, fronted by a square garden. Down to the east from here is the **Portico**, a row of arches similar to those of the Córdoba Mezquita, which fronted a military parade ground. From here you follow the path downhill, with views over a ruined mosque, to the most impressive building, the **Salón de Abd ar-Rahman III**. This was the caliph's throne hall, with beautiful horseshoe arching and carved stone decoration of a lavishness then unprecedented in the Islamic world.

Getting There & Away Córdoba Vision (☎ 957 23 17 34) runs tours to Medina Azahara twice daily, except Sunday afternoon and Monday, for 2500 ptas. You can book at many hotels in town. The nearest you can get by bus is the Cruce de Medina Azahara turn-off on the A-431, a 3km walk from the site. City bus No 0-1 will drop you at the Cruce. At the time of writing this departed Avenida de la República Argentina at 9.40 and 11.20 am and 1, 2, 3.20 and 6 pm daily. A taxi costs 3900 ptas for the return trip, with one hour's waiting.

LA SUBBÉTICA

Córdoba's beautiful, mountainous southeast is known as La Subbética after the Sistema Subbético mountain chain. The village of **Zuheros**, rising above a sea of olive trees south of the N-432, is a beautiful base for exploring the region, with a castle perched before some surreal picturesque crags. A 4km drive up behind the village is the **Cueva de los Murciélagos**, with neolithic rock paintings of goats and people; guided visits (550 ptas) take place several times on Saturday, Sunday and holidays but only at noon and 7 pm in July. Zuheros' good *Hotel Zuhayra* (☎ 957 69 46 93, Calle Mirador 10) has singles/doubles with bath for

4600/6200 ptas plus IVA, and has information on walking routes.

The town of **Priego de Córdoba**, farther south-east, has a series of outstanding baroque churches, built in the 18th century when the town enjoyed a textiles boom. The very helpful tourist office (☎ 957 90 06 25) at Calle del Río 33 is open 9 am to 1 pm Tuesday to Sunday. Priego's churches are normally open 10 am to 1 pm daily; the highlight is the Sagrario chapel of the **Parroquia de la Asunción**, an amazing confection of white stucco and sculpture with a beautiful windowed dome. The **Fuente del Rey** at the end of Calle del Río is a wonderfully elegant 1780s fountain that would be more at home in the gardens of Versailles: water flows from 139 spouts into three curvaceous pools. Priego's central *Hostal Rafi* (☎ 957 54 07 49, Calle Isabel la Católica 4) has good doubles with bath at 4300 ptas plus IVA.

Empresa Carrera runs buses to Zuheros and Priego from Córdoba's bus station.

Granada Province

As well as the world-famous city of Granada, this eastern province includes mainland Spain's highest mountain (Mulhacén in the Sierra Nevada) and the beautiful Las Alpujarras valleys south of the Sierra Nevada.

GRANADA
postcode 18080 • pop 241,000
At first, modern Granada with its traffic fumes and high-rise apartment blocks seems a world away from its Muslim past. However, the famous Alhambra, dominating the skyline from its hill-top perch, and the fascinating Albayzín, the old Islamic quarter also rising above the modern city, are highlights of a visit to Spain.

The city has more to offer. Its setting, with the backdrop of the often snow-clad Sierra Nevada, is magnificent; its greenness is a delight and the climate pleasant especially in spring and autumn. Granada also has some impressive and historic post-Reconquista buildings, and, thanks to its university, a vibrant cultural life and nightlife.

Granada is a wealthy city with an international feel. In tandem with this wealth subsists an underclass: you'll see quite a few beggars.

History

The Romans settled in the vicinity of the Alcazaba (part of the Alhambra) and Albayzín. The Visigoths built city walls and laid the foundations of the Alcazaba. Muslim forces, with the help of the city's Jews, took Granada in 711. It was ruled from Córdoba until 1031, and later from Sevilla. The Islamic city came to be called Karnattah, from which 'Granada' is derived (*granada* also happens to be the Spanish for pomegranate, the fruit on the city's coat of arms).

After the fall of Córdoba (1236) and Sevilla (1248), Muslims sought refuge in Granada, where Mohammed ibn Yousouf ibn Nasr (Mohammed al-Ahmar) had recently founded the Nasrid dynasty and established an independent emirate. Stretching from the Strait of Gibraltar to east of Almería, this became the final remnant of Al-Andalus, ruled from the lavish Alhambra palace for 250 years. The Nasrids paid tribute to Castile until 1476 but also played off Aragón against Castile and at times sought assistance from the Merenid rulers of Morocco.

Nasrid Granada became one of the richest cities in medieval Europe, flourishing with its swelled population of traders and artisans. Two centuries of artistic and scientific splendour peaked under Yousouf I and Mohammed V in the 14th century.

But by the late 15th century the economy had stagnated, the rulers had retreated into a hedonistic existence inside the Alhambra, and violent rivalry had developed over the succession. One faction supported the emir, Abu al-Hasan, and his harem favourite Zoraya. The other faction backed Boabdil, Abu al-Hasan's son by his wife Aixa.

In 1482 Boabdil rebelled, setting off a confused civil war. The Christian armies that invaded the emirate that year took full advantage. They pushed across the emirate, besieging towns and devastating the

countryside, and in 1491 they finally laid siege to Granada. After eight months, Boabdil agreed to surrender the city in return for the Alpujarras valleys and 30,000 gold coins, plus political and religious freedom for his subjects. On 2 January 1492 the Catholic Monarchs, Isabel and Fernando, entered Granada ceremonially in Muslim dress. They set up court in the Alhambra for several years.

Religious persecution soon soured the scene. Jews were expelled from Spain soon after Granada fell. Persecution of Muslims soon led to revolts across the former emirate and eventually to their expulsion from Spain in the 17th century. (See History in Facts about Spain and under Las Alpujarras in this chapter.)

Having lost much of its talented populace, Granada sank into a decline that was only arrested by the interest drummed up by the romantic movement in the 1830s. This set the stage for the restoration of Granada's Islamic heritage and the arrival of tourism.

When the Nationalists took over Granada at the start of the civil war in 1936, an estimated 4000 *granadinos* with left or liberal connections were killed, among them Federico García Lorca, Granada's most famous writer. Granada today still has a reputation for conservatism.

Orientation

The two main streets, Gran Vía de Colón and Calle Reyes Católicos, meet at Plaza Isabel La Católica, with Calle Reyes Católicos continuing north-east to Plaza Nueva then Plaza Santa Ana. Cuesta de Gomérez leads up to the Alhambra, atop the hill north-east of the centre, from Plaza Nueva. Carrera del Darro leads up to the old Islamic district, called the Albayzín, from Plaza Santa Ana. Southward, Calle Reyes Católicos extends to Puerta Real, Granada's main plaza.

Most major sights are within walking distance of the centre, though there are buses if you don't want to walk uphill. The bus station (north-west) and train station (west) are out of the centre but linked to it by plenty of buses.

Information

Tourist Offices The helpful provincial tourist office (☎ 958 22 66 88), on Plaza de Mariana Pineda, east of Puerta Real, and the more central regional tourist office (☎ 958 22 59 90), in the Corral del Carbón on Calle Mariana Pineda, both are open 9.30 am to 7 pm weekdays and 10 am to 2 pm Saturday. Bus and train information is posted in a room adjacent to the regional office.

Money There are several banks with ATMs on Gran Vía de Colón, Plaza Isabel La Católica and Calle Reyes Católicos.

Post & Communications The main post office is at Puerta Real s/n. Net (☎ 958 22 69 19), Calle Santa Escolástica 13, is open daily 9 am to 11 pm (from 4 pm Sunday), is one of many places offering Internet access; 200 ptas per hour.

Bookshops Cartográfica del Sur, Calle Valle Inclán 2, west of the centre, is a good map and guidebook shop.

Laundry Friendly Lavandería Duquesa, Calle Duquesa 24, charges around 1100 ptas to wash and dry a bag of clothes.

Medical Services & Emergency For urgent medical help, the Cruz Roja (☎ 958 22 22 22) is at Cuesta de Escoriaza 8. The Hospital San Juan de Dios (☎ 958 24 17 24) is fairly central at Calle San Juan de Dios 15. The Policía Local (☎ 958 29 35 01) are at Plaza del Carmen 5, and the Policía Nacional (☎ 958 27 83 00) at Calle de la Duquesa 15.

Alhambra & Generalife

Perched on La Sabika, the hill that overlooks Granada, this monument is the stuff of fairy tales. From outside, its simple, unadorned red fortress towers and walls may seem surprisingly plain, though their Sierra Nevada backdrop and the cypresses and elms in which they nestle are undeniably magnificent.

Inside the marvellously decorated Palacio Nazaries (Nasrid Palace) and the Generalife (the Alhambra's gardens), you're in for a treat. Water is an art form in both places, and even around the exterior of the Alhambra the sound of running water and the greenness are a world removed from the bustle of the city and the dryness of much of Spain.

The spell can be shattered by the average 6000 visitors who traipse through this Unesco World Heritage Site each day, so try to visit first thing in the morning, late in the afternoon or – a magical experience – at night. (For night visits, only the major rooms of the Palacio Nazaries are open.)

The Alhambra has two main parts, the Alcazaba (Fortress) and the Palacio Nazaries. Also within it are the Palacio de Carlos V, the Iglesia de Santa María de la Alhambra, two hotels and a few restaurants, souvenir shops and refreshment stalls (see Places to Stay and Places to Eat). The Generalife is a short walk north-east.

History The Alhambra, from the Arabic *al-qala'at al-hamra* (red castle), was a fortress from the 9th century. The Nasrids of the 13th and 14th centuries turned it into a fortress-palace complex adjoined by a small city (medina), of which nothing remains. It was Yousouf I and Mohammed V, in the 14th century, who built the Palacio Nazaries: Mohammed V was responsible for much of the palace's decoration.

In 1492 the Catholic Monarchs moved into the Palacio Nazaries, and in time the palace mosque was replaced with a church, and a convent, the Convento de San Francisco, was built. In the 16th century Carlos I destroyed a wing of the Palacio Nazaries to make space for a huge Renaissance palace, called the Palacio de Carlos V using his title as Holy Roman Emperor.

In the 18th century the Alhambra was abandoned to thieves and beggars, and during the Napoleonic occupation it was used as a barracks and narrowly escaped being blown up. In 1870 it was declared a national monument after the huge interest stirred by romantic writers such as Washington Irving, who had written *Tales of the Alhambra* in the palace during his brief stay in the 1820s. Since then it has been salvaged and heavily restored.

ANDALUCÍA

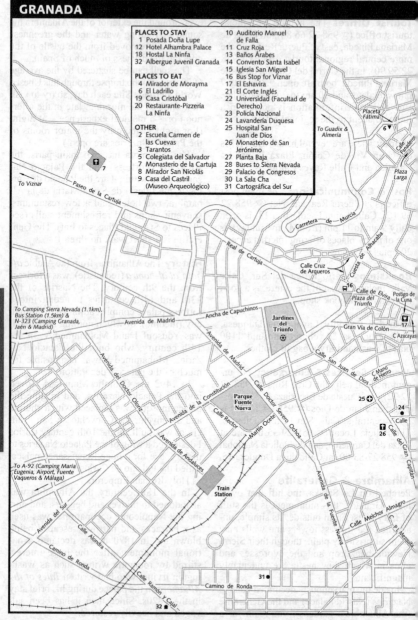

GRANADA

PLACES TO STAY
1 Posada Doña Lupe
12 Hotel Alhambra Palace
18 Hostal La Ninfa
32 Albergue Juvenil Granada

PLACES TO EAT
4 Mirador de Morayma
6 El Ladrillo
19 Casa Cristóbal
20 Restaurante-Pizzería
La Ninfa

OTHER
2 Escuela Carmen de
las Cuevas
3 Tarantos
5 Colegiata del Salvador
7 Monasterio de la Cartuja
8 Mirador San Nicolás
9 Casa del Castril
(Museo Arqueológico)
10 Auditorio Manuel
de Falla
11 Cruz Roja
13 Baños Árabes
14 Convento Santa Isabel
15 Iglesia San Miguel
16 Bus Stop for Viznar
17 El Eshavira
21 El Corte Inglés
22 Universidad (Facultad de
Derecho)
23 Policía Nacional
24 Lavandería Duquesa
25 Hospital San
Juan de Dios
26 Monasterio de San
Jerónimo
27 Planta Baja
28 Buses to Sierra Nevada
29 Palacio de Congresos
30 La Sala Cha
31 Cartográfica del Sur

To Guadix &
Almería

Placeta
Fátima

Plaza
Larga

To Viznar

Paseo de la Cartuja

Real de Cartuja

Carretera de Murcia

Calle Cruz
de Arqueros

Cuesta de Alhacaba

Calle de Elvira
Plaza del
Triunfo

Postigo de
la Cuna

Ancha de Capuchinos

Jardines
del
Triunfo

Gran Vía de Colón

C Azacayas

To Camping Sierra Nevada (1.1km),
Bus Station (1.5km) &
N-323 (Camping Granada,
Jaén & Madrid)

Avenida de Madrid

Avenida de Madrid

Avenida del Doctor Olóriz

Avenida de la Constitución

Calle san Juan de Dios

C Mano
de Hierro

Calle Doctor Severo Ochoa

25

24

Calle

Parque
Fuente
Nueva

Calle Rector

Martín Ocete

26

Calle del Gran Capitán

Avenida de Andaluces

To A-92 (Camping María
Eugenia, Airport, Fuente
Vaqueros & Málaga)

Avenida del Sur

Calle Alondra

Camino de Ronda

Calle Ramón y Cajál

Train
Station

Avenida de la Fuente Nueva

Calle Melchor Almagro

P Mezquita

31

Camino de Ronda

32

euro currency converter 100pta = €0.60

ANDALUCÍA

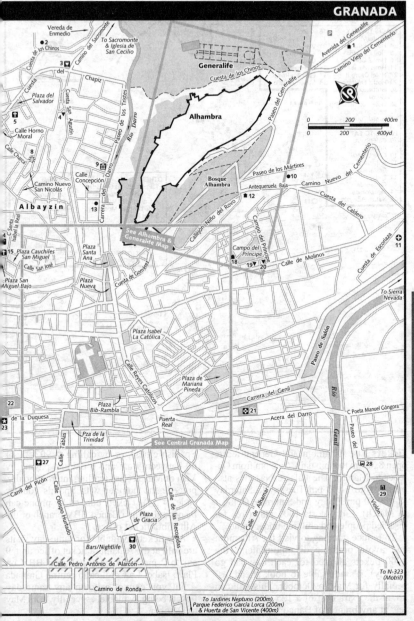

GRANADA

Vereda de Enmedio

● 2

To Sacromonte & Iglesia de San Cecilio

3

Chapiz

Plaza del Salvador

4 ▼

Calle Horno Moral

Calle Charca

8

9 ▥

Calle Concepción

Camino Nuevo San Nicólas

13

Albayzín

C Santa Isabel la Real

4 ●
15 Plaza Cauchiles San Miguel

Calle San José

Plaza San Miguel Bajo

Plaza Santa Ana

Plaza Nueva

Cuesta de Gomérez

See Alhambra & Generalife Map

22

● de la Duquesa
23

Cuesta del Sacromonte

To Sacromonte & Iglesia de San Cecilio

Camino del Sacromonte

Cuesta de los Chinos

Cuesta San Agustín

Paseo de los Tristes

Río Darro

Carrera del Darro

Generalife

Cuesta de los Chinos

Alhambra

Bosque Alhambra

Paseo del Generalife

Avenida del Generalife

P

● 1

Camino Viejo del Cementerio

RP

0   200   400m
0   200   400yd

Paseo de los Mártires

●10

Antequeruela Baja

Camino Nuevo del Cementerio

Cuesta del Caldero

▣ 12

Callejón Niño del Rollo

Campo del Príncipe

18

Campo del Príncipe

19▼ 20

Calle de Molinos

Cuesta de Escoriaza

✚ 11

To Sierra Nevada

Plaza Isabel La Católica

Plaza de Mariana Pineda

Carrera del Genil

Calle Reyes Católicos

Plaza Bib-Rambla

Puerta Real

See Central Granada Map

⚑ 21

Acera del Darro

Paseo de Salón

Río Genil

C Poeta Manuel Góngora

Paseo del

Tablas

Pza de la Trinidad

27

Carril del Picón

Calle Obispo Hurtado

Calle

Plaza de Gracia

Calle de las Recogidas

Bars/Nightlife

30

Calle Pedro Antonio de Alarcón

Camino de Ronda

Calle de Alhamar

⚑ 28

▥ 29

Violón

To N-323 (Motril)

To Jardines Neptuno (200m), Parque Federico García Lorca (200m) & Huerta de San Vicente (400m)

ANDALUCÍA

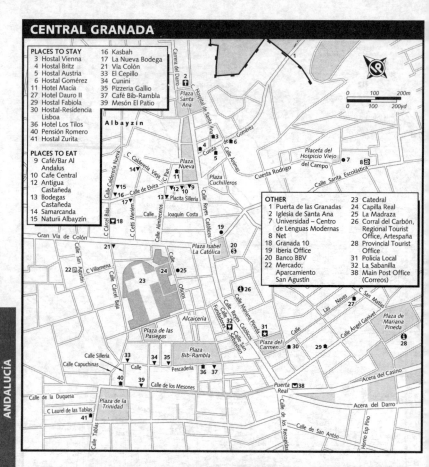

CENTRAL GRANADA

PLACES TO STAY
3 Hostal Vienna
4 Hostal Britz
5 Hostal Austria
6 Hostal Gomérez
11 Hotel Macía
27 Hotel Dauro II
29 Hostal Fabiola
30 Hostal-Residencia Lisboa
36 Hotel Los Tilos
40 Pensión Romero
41 Hostal Zurita

16 Kasbah
17 La Nueva Bodega
21 Vía Colón
33 El Cepillo
34 Cunini
35 Pizzeria Gallio
37 Café Bib-Rambla
39 Mesón El Patio

PLACES TO EAT
9 Café/Bar Al Andalus
10 Cafe Central
12 Antigua Castañeda
13 Bodegas Castañeda
14 Samarcanda
15 Naturii Albayzín

OTHER
1 Puerta de las Granadas
2 Iglesia de Santa Ana
7 Universidad – Centro de Lenguas Modernas
8 Net
18 Granada 10
19 Iberia Office
20 Banco BBV
22 Mercado; Aparcamiento San Agustín
23 Catedral
24 Capilla Real
25 La Madraza
26 Corral del Carbón, Regional Tourist Office, Artespaña
28 Provincial Tourist Office
31 Policía Local
32 La Sabanilla
38 Main Post Office (Correos)

Tickets The Alhambra and Generalife are open 8.30 am to 8 pm daily (to 6 pm from October to March). The Palacio Nazaries also opens 10 to 11.30 pm Tuesday to Saturday (8 to 9.30 pm Friday and Saturday, October to March). Entry costs 1000 ptas (free for disabled people and children under eight).

To reduce queuing to visit the Alhambra and avoid possible disappointment (the 8000 tickets allotted for each day can go quickly), it's advisable to book ahead, especially for May to October. This you can do, at the extra cost of a 125-ptas booking fee, at any branch of Banco BBV (in many Spanish cities), or by calling ☎ 902-22 44 60 between 9 am and 6 pm and paying by Visa or MasterCard (calling internationally, precede the number with Spain's country code, ☎ 34). Tickets booked by phone can be picked up at a Banco BBV branch or the Alhambra ticket office.

Any tickets available for same-day visits are sold at the Alhambra ticket office and, 9 am to 2 pm weekdays, at Banco BBV on Plaza Isabel La Católica in central Granada – but you cannot rely on any same-day tickets being available, especially from May to October.

Tickets are stamped with a half-hour time slot for entering the Palacio Nazaries, though you can stay as long as you like once inside it. If you buy your ticket the day of your visit, the time slot may be several hours after the time of your purchase (though in mid-winter it may be almost immediately).

Ticketing arrangements change from time to time as the authorities strive to cope with the huge number of visitors. You may soon be able to book online.

Getting There & Away The 'Alhambra Bus' runs between Plaza Nueva and the Alhambra ticket office every 10 minutes, 7.45 am to 10 pm (120 ptas). Bus No 32 runs between the ticket office and the Albayzín.

Walking up Cuesta de Gomérez from Plaza Nueva you soon reach the **Puerta de las Granadas** (Gate of the Pomegranates), built by Carlos I. Above this are the Bosque Alhambra woods. If you already have your ticket, you can climb a path to the left up to the austere **Puerta de la Justicia** (Gate of Justice), constructed by Yousouf I in 1348 as the Alhambra's main entrance.

The ticket office is at the far (east) end of the complex, adjacent to the Alhambra car parks, 1km from the Puerta de las Granadas. To reach it, ignore the path to the Puerta de la Justicia and continue ahead outside the Alhambra walls.

Alcazaba What remain of the fortress are the ramparts and several towers. The most important is the **Torre de la Vela** (watchtower), with a winding staircase up to its top terrace, which has splendid views. It was here that the cross and banners of the Reconquista were raised in January 1492. In the past the tower's bell rang to control the irrigation system of the Vega, the fertile plain surrounding Granada.

Palacio Nazaries The Nasrid Palace (also called the Casa Real, Royal House), with its intricately carved stucco walls, fine knotted wooden ceilings, elaborate honeycomb vaulting and beautifully proportioned rooms and courtyards, is in marked contrast to the austere Alcazaba. Arabic inscriptions recur in the stucco work.

Mexuar These rooms, through which you normally enter the palace, date from the 14th century and were used for bureaucratic and judicial purposes. The general public would not have been allowed beyond them. At the far end of the much-altered first room, the council chamber, is a small, lavishly decorated room (originally a prayer room) overlooking the Río Darro. From here you pass into the **Patio del Mexuar**, with a small fountain, and the mudéjar **Cuarto Dorado** (Golden Room) on its left. Opposite the Cuarto Dorado is the entrance to the Serallo, through a beautiful facade of glazed tiles, stucco and carved wood.

Serallo This was the official residence of the emir or sultan. Its rooms surround the **Patio de los Arrayanes** (Patio of the Myrtles), named after the hedges flanking its rectangular pool and fountains. Through the northern portico is the **Sala de la Barca** (Hall of the Boat) with a beautiful inverted-boat-shaped wooden ceiling. This room leads into the impressive **Salón de Embajadores** (Hall of Ambassadors), where the emirs would have conducted their negotiations with Christian emissaries. Its domed cedar ceiling is remarkable, the repeating patterns of the stuccoed and tiled walls mesmerising. The grey walls of the Palacio de Carlos V loom above the southern end of the patio.

Harén The harem, surrounding the famous **Patio de los Leones** with its fountain feeding water through the mouths of 12 stone lions, was built during Mohammed V's reign. The patio's gallery is supported by 124 slender marble columns, producing a delicate oriental effect with a hint of a medieval cloister.

Of the four halls bordering the patio, the **Sala de los Abencerrajes** on the southern side is legendary for the murders of the noble Abencerraj family, whose leader, the story goes, dared to dally with Zoraya, Abu al-Hasan's harem favourite. (Historians say the Abencerrajes also favoured Boabdil in the palace power struggle.) The stalactite

ANDALUCIA

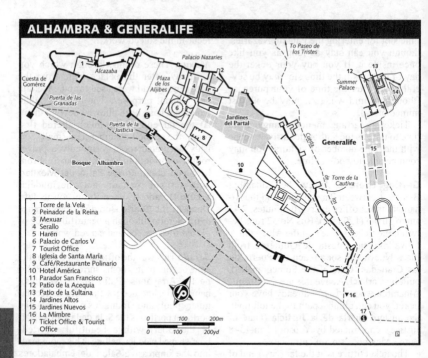

ALHAMBRA & GENERALIFE

1 Torre de la Vela
2 Peinador de la Reina
3 Mexuar
4 Serallo
5 Harén
6 Palacio de Carlos V
7 Tourist Office
8 Iglesia de Santa María
9 Café/Restaurante Polinario
10 Hotel América
11 Parador San Francisco
12 Patio de la Acequia
13 Patio de la Sultana
14 Jardines Altos
15 Jardines Nuevos
16 La Mimbre
17 Ticket Office & Tourist Office

ANDALUCÍA

vaulting on the room's tall, domed ceiling produces a star-like effect.

At the eastern end of the patio is the **Sala de los Reyes** (Hall of the Kings) with a leather-lined ceiling painted by 14th-century Christian artists. Its name comes from the painting on the central part, thought to depict 10 Nasrid emirs.

On the northern side of the patio is the richly decorated **Sala de las Dos Hermanas** (Hall of the Two Sisters), named after the two slabs of white marble beside its fountain. This was the room of the sultan's favourite paramour. At its far end is the enchanting **Sala de los Ajimeces**, the favoured lady's dressing room and bedroom, with low windows through which she could look over the Albayzín while reclining on ottomans and cushions.

Other Sections From the Sala de las Dos Hermanas, a passageway leads through deserted rooms that were used by Washington Irving. The **Peinador de la Reina** (Queen's Dressing Room), the last of these, was a dressing room for Isabel, wife of Carlos I. From here you descend to the **Patio de los Cipreses** (Patio of the Cypresses).

Outside the palace is a group of recent gardens, the **Partal**, bordered by palace towers and ramparts. From here there's an exit to the Palacio de Carlos V, or you can continue to the Generalife.

Palacio de Carlos V This huge Renaissance palace, the dominant Christian building in the Alhambra, was begun in 1527 by Pedro Machuca, a Toledo architect who studied under Michelangelo, and was never completed. The building is square but contains a surprising circular, two-tiered courtyard with 32 columns. Were the palace in a different setting, its merits might be more readily appreciated.

On the ground floor, the **Museo de la Alhambra** has a wonderful collection of

Muslim artefacts from the Alhambra, Granada province and Córdoba – and detailed explanatory texts in English and Spanish. A highlight is the elegant Alhambra Vase, decorated with gazelles. The museum is open 9 am to 2.30 pm Tuesday to Saturday (free).

Upstairs, the **Museo de Bellas Artes** has an impressive collection of paintings and sculptures, including a notable carved wooden relief of the Virgin and Child by Diego de Siloé, and a small enamelled screen from around 1500 that belonged to El Gran Capitán (Gonzalo Fernández de Córdoba), the Catholic Monarchs' military right-hand man. It's open varying hours, daily except Monday (free for EU residents, 250 ptas for others).

Other Christian Buildings The **Iglesia de Santa María** was built between 1581 and 1617 on the site of the former palace mosque. The **Convento de San Francisco**, now the parador, was erected upon an Islamic palace. Isabel and Fernando were buried in a sepulchre in the patio before being transferred to the Capilla Real.

Generalife The name means 'Garden of the Architect'. These palace gardens on the hillside facing the Palacio Nazaries are a beautiful, soothing composition of terraces, patios, fountains, trimmed hedges, tall trees and, in season, flowers of every hue. The Muslim rulers' summer palace is in the farthest corner. Within it, the **Patio de la Acequia** (Court of the Long Pond) has a long pool framed by fountains whose shapes sensuously echo the arched porticoes at each end. Off the Patio de la Acequia is the **Patio de la Sultana**, almost as lovely and with the trunk of a 700-year-old cypress tree where Abu al-Hasan supposedly caught his lover, Zoraya, with the chief of the Abencerraj clan, leading to the murders in the Sala de los Abencerrajes. Above here are the modern **Jardines Altos** (Upper Gardens), and a stairway with cascading waterfalls. Back towards the entry are the **Jardines Nuevos** (New Gardens). A pleasant alternative path back to town is down Cuesta de los Chinos, following a gully between the Generalife and Alhambra.

Capilla Real

The Royal Chapel, on Calle Oficios adjoining the Catedral, is Granada's outstanding Christian building. Built in elaborate Isabelline Gothic style, it was commissioned by the Catholic Monarchs as their mausoleum, but not completed until 1521 – hence their temporary interment in the Convento de San Francisco.

The illustrious monarchs lie in simple lead coffins in the crypt beneath their marble monuments in the chancel, which is enclosed by a stunning gilded wrought-iron screen created in 1520 by Bartolomé de Jaén. The coffins, from left to right, are those of Felipe El Hermoso (Philip the Handsome, husband of the monarchs' daughter Juana la Loca), Fernando, Isabel, Juana la Loca (Joanna the Mad) and Miguel, the eldest grandchild of Isabel and Fernando. The carved effigies of the first four, reclining above the crypt, were a tribute by Carlos I to his parents and grandparents. The representations of Isabel and Fernando are slightly lower than those of Felipe and Juana, apparently because Felipe was the son of the Holy Roman Emperor, Maximilian. The chancel's dense plateresque retablo is by Felipe de Vigarni (1522). Note its kneeling figures of Isabel and Fernando, attributed to Diego de Siloé, and the paintings below depicting the defeat of the Muslims and subsequent conversions to Christianity.

In the sacristy is a museum with an impressive collection, including Isabel's sceptre and silver crown and Fernando's sword. Isabel's personal art collection, mainly Flemish, occupies one room; there's also Botticelli's *Prayer in the Garden of Olives,* and two fine statues of the kneeling monarchs by Vigarni.

The Capilla Real is open 10.30 am (11 am Sunday) to 1 pm and 4 to 7 pm daily (3.30 to 6.30 pm in winter); 300 ptas.

Catedral

Adjoining the Capilla Real, the chunky Gothic/Renaissance cathedral, with its cavernous interior, was begun in 1521, and dir-ected by Diego de Siloé from 1528 to 1563. Work was not completed until the

ANDALUCÍA

18th century. The main facade on Plaza de las Pasiegas, with its four heavy buttresses and arched doorway, was designed by Alonso Cano. The lavish Puerta del Perdón on the north-western facade has statues carved by de Siloé. Much of the interior is also the work of de Siloé, including the gilded and painted Capilla Mayor, where you'll find carvings of the Catholic Monarchs at prayer, by Pedro de Mena – either side of the tabernacle above the lovely carved and painted pulpits – and Cano's busts of Adam and Eve.

The Catedral is open for tourists 10.45 am to 1 pm and 4 to 7 pm Monday to Saturday, and 4 to 7 pm Sunday (300 ptas). Enter from Gran Vía de Colón.

Islamic Buildings near the Capilla Real

La Madraza Opposite the Capilla Real remains part of the old Muslim university, La Madraza – now with a painted baroque facade, but retaining an octagonal domed prayer room with stucco lacework and pretty tiles. The building is now part of the modern university, but you can look inside whenever it's open.

Alcaicería Just south-west of the Capilla Real, the Alcaicería was the Muslim silk exchange, but what you see now is a restoration after a 19th-century fire, filled with tourist shops.

Corral del Carbón Originally a 14th-century *caravanserai* (inn) for merchants, this building has also been an inn for coal dealers (hence its modern name, 'Coal Yard') and a theatre. It retains a lovely Islamic facade with an elaborate horseshoe arch, and houses a tourist office and government-run crafts shop. To find it, cross Calle Reyes Católicos from the Capilla Real and look for the sign pointing down an alley.

Albayzín

A wander around the hilly streets and aged alleys of the Albayzín, Granada's old Muslim quarter on the hillside facing the Alhambra across the Río Darro, is a must. The name of this World Heritage Site derives from 1227 when Muslims from Baeza settled here after their town was conquered by the Christians. For a few decades after the Reconquista the Albayzín survived as Granada's Muslim quarter. Muslim ramparts, cisterns, gates, fountains and houses remain, and many of the Albayzín's churches and *cármenes* (large walled villas with gardens) incorporate parts of Islamic buildings. Bus Nos 31 and 32 from Plaza Nueva go to the upper Albayzín.

Carrera del Darro & Paseo de los Tristes One approach to the Albayzín is up Carrera del Darro from Plaza Nueva. On Plaza Santa Ana is the **Iglesia de Santa Ana**, incorporating a former mosque's minaret in its bell tower, as do several churches in the Albayzín. Stop at Carrera del Darro 31 to see the remains of the 11th-century **Baños Árabes** (Muslim Baths), open 10 am to 2 pm Tuesday to Saturday (free).

Carrera del Darro 41 is the Renaissance Casa del Castril, home to the **Museo Arqueológico**, with finds from Granada province. This was being overhauled at the time of writing. Previously, the Islamic room upstairs displayed some lovely *azulejos,* carved wood and fine ceramics.

Shortly after the museum, Carrera del Darro becomes Paseo de los Tristes (also called Paseo del Padre Manjón), with a number of cafes and restaurants with outdoor tables, and a dramatic view directly up to the Alhambra's fortifications.

Upper Albayzín From the top end of Paseo de los Tristes, Cuesta del Chapiz heads up to Plaza del Salvador, where the **Colegiata del Salvador**, a 16th-century church, still contains the Islamic courtyard of the mosque it replaced. It's open 10.30 am to 1 pm and 4.30 to 6.30 pm daily (100 ptas). From here Calle Panaderos leads to **Plaza Larga**, with an Islamic gateway at the top end of the Albayzín's surviving Muslim ramparts, and lively *bars* offering cheap *menús*. From Calle Panaderos, Calle Horno Moral and Calle Charca lead to the **Mirador San Nicolás**, which has fantastic views of the Alhambra and Sierra Nevada.

Descent from Mirador San Nicolás

Descending from the mirador along Camino Nuevo San Nicolás, which becomes Calle Santa Isabel la Real, you pass the **Convento Santa Isabel**, a former Islamic palace. Its church has a mudéjar ceiling. The **Iglesia San Miguel** on nearby Plaza de San Miguel Bajo occupies the site of a former mosque. To wend your way back to the centre, follow Plaza Cauchiles San Miguel and then Calle San José, which meets the top of picturesque **Calle Calderería Nueva** with its teterías (Arabic-style tea rooms). Alternatively, enjoy getting lost – but not too late at night.

Sacromonte

Camino del Sacromonte leads from Cuesta del Chapiz up Sacromonte hill to the **Iglesia de San Cecilio**, passing caves dug into the hillside that have been occupied by gitanos since the 18th century.

Plaza Bib-Rambla & Around

Just south-west of the Alcaicería is the large, pleasant Plaza Bib-Rambla, with restaurants, flower stalls and a central fountain with statues of giants. This plaza was the scene of Inquisition lashings and burnings, jousting and bullfights. Today buskers, mime artists and street sellers provide more gentle entertainment.

Nearby Calle de los Mesones, pedestrianised and with modern shops, heads north-west to leafy **Plaza de la Trinidad**. From here Calle de la Duquesa leads past the university founded by Carlos I (now the Law Faculty, with the main campus north of the city centre) to the 16th-century **Monasterio de San Jerónimo** on Calle del Gran Capitán. This features more work by the talented Diego de Siloé, including the larger of the monastery's two cloisters and much of the attached church. El Gran Capitán is reputedly buried beneath the church's altar, beside which stand statues of him and his wife María. The monastery is open 10 am to 1 pm and 4 to 7 pm daily (3 to 6.30 pm in winter); 300 ptas.

Monasterio de La Cartuja

The ornate La Cartuja Monastery is a 20-minute walk north of the Monasterio de San Jerónimo, off Paseo de la Cartuja (or take bus No 8 from Gran Vía de Colón). The monastery, with an imposing sand-coloured stone exterior, was built between the 16th and 18th centuries. Its baroque interior oozes wealth, especially the lavish sacristy, decorated in brown and white marble and stucco, and the adjacent sanctuary *(sanctum sanctorum)*, a riot of colour and patterns with twisted marble columns, a beautiful frescoed cupola and loads of statues, paintings and gilt. La Cartuja is open 10 am to 1 pm (to noon on Sunday) and 4 to 8 pm (3.30 to 6 pm in winter) daily; 300 ptas.

Huerta de San Vicente

This house where Federico García Lorca spent summers and wrote some of his best-known works is a 15-minute walk from the centre, on Calle del Arabial. It was once surrounded by orchards and today the new Parque Federico García Lorca separates it from whizzing traffic in an attempt to recreate the tranquil environment that inspired Lorca. The house contains some original furnishings including Lorca's desk and piano, some of his drawings and other memorabilia, and exhibitions connected with his life and work. Head down Calle de las Recogidas from Puerta Real to Calle del Arabial, and the park is just to the right.

Huerta de San Vicente is open 10 am to 1 pm and 5 to 8 pm (4 to 7 pm in winter) Tuesday to Sunday, with guided tours in Spanish on the hour (300 ptas, free on Wednesday).

Courses

With its many attractions and youthful population, Granada makes a good place to study Spanish. The university offers a variety of intensive programs: a four-week, 80-hour course costs 62,000 ptas. Contact Universidad de Granada (☎ 958 22 07 90, fax 958 22 08 44), Centro de Lenguas Modernas, Cursos Para Extranjeros, Placeta del Hospicio Viejo s/n (Realejo), 18071 Granada. Among the many private schools, one good choice is Escuela Carmen de las Cuevas (☎ 958 22 10 62, fax 958 22 04 76), Cuesta de los Chinos 15, 18010 Granada (in the Albayzín). It offers classes in flamenco

ANDALUCÍA

dance, guitar and song, Spanish language at all levels, and history, literature and art. Its Web site is at www.carmencuevas.com.

Organised Tours

Tours by Granavisión (☎ 958 13 58 04) include the Alhambra and Generalife (4250 ptas) and Granada Histórica (4400 ptas). Phone direct or book through any travel agent.

Special Events

Semana Santa and the Corpus Christi feria, nine weeks later, are the big two. Benches are set up in Plaza del Carmen for viewing the Semana Santa processions. At Corpus Christi, fairgrounds, drinking, sevillana dancing and bullfights are the go.

Around 3 May, the Día de la Cruz (Day of the Cross), squares, patios and balconies are adorned with crosses (the 'Cruces de Mayo') made of flowers. Horse riders, polka-dot dresses and sevillana dancing add to the colour. The Festival Internacional de Música y Danza in late June/early July features open-air performances (some free) in historic sites.

Places to Stay

There should be no problem finding a room in Granada, but you should book ahead for Semana Santa.

Places to Stay – Budget

Camping There are several camping grounds within about 5km of Granada, all accessible by bus. All charge 450 to 600 ptas per adult, per tent and per car. Closest and biggest, though closed November to February, is *Camping Sierra Nevada* (☎ 958 15 00 62, Avenida de Madrid 107), 3km north-west of the centre and 200m from the bus station. There are big, clean bathrooms, a pool and a laundry. Bus No 3 runs between here and Gran Vía de Colón in the centre.

Year-round camping grounds include *Camping Granada* (☎ 958 34 05 48, Cerro de la Cruz s/n, Peligros), 4km north of Granada (take exit 123 from the N-323), and *Camping María Eugenia* (☎ 958 20 06 06, Carretera A-92 Km 286), en route to Santa Fé.

Youth Hostels The Inturjoven *Albergue Juvenil Granada* (☎ 958 27 26 38, Calle Ramón y Cajal 2) is 1.7km west of the centre and 600m south-west of the train station. It's a large, modern building with 93 rooms (singles to quadruples) and a pool. From the bus station, take bus No 3 to the cathedral, then change to No 11, whose circular route will drop you at the hostel.

Hostales & Pensiones Cheap hostales bunch in a few separate areas. At peak times rooms tend to fill up before noon, especially on Cuesta de Gomérez.

Plaza Nueva & Around Most of these places offer parking for 1000 ptas per day. *Hostal Gomérez* (☎ 958 22 44 37, Cuesta de Gomérez 10), with a lively, multilingual owner, has nine well-kept singles/doubles/triples at 1600/2700/3700 ptas. Friendly *Hostal Britz* (☎/fax 958 22 36 52, Cuesta de Gomérez 1) has clean singles/doubles for 2340/3900 ptas, or 4000/5400 ptas with bath. Popular *Hostal Vienna* (☎ 958 22 18 59, Calle Hospital de Santa Ana 2), just off Cuesta de Gomérez, charges 3000/4000 ptas for singles/doubles with shared baths. English and German are spoken. The same people run *Hostal Austria* (☎ 958 22 70 75, Cuesta de Gomérez 4), where rooms, all with bath, cost 3500/5500 ptas.

Near Puerta Real Friendly, family-run *Hostal Fabiola* (☎ 958 22 35 72, Calle Ángel Ganivet 5, 3rd floor) has 19 good rooms, some with balcony and all with private bathroom, at 1800/4000/5000 ptas for singles/doubles/triples. Two blocks north, the friendly *Hostal-Residencia Lisboa* (☎ 958 22 14 13, Plaza del Carmen 27) has singles/doubles for 3900/5600 ptas with bath, 2600/3900 ptas without.

Plaza de la Trinidad The good, family-run *Pensión Romero* (☎ 958 26 60 79, Calle Sillería 1) has rooms for 1700/2900 ptas, some with balconies. *Hostal Zurita* (☎ 958 27 50 20, Plaza de la Trinidad 7) has good-value rooms for 2000/4000 ptas, and doubles for 5000 ptas with bathroom.

Near the Alhambra *Posada Doña Lupe* (☎ *958 22 14 73, Avenida del Generalife s/n)* has more than 40 rooms. Management does not like to show you them first but in our experience they're clean. Rates start at 1500 ptas per person for interior rooms with showers and windows onto corridors. Better doubles are from 3950 to 7500 ptas plus IVA. There's a cafe, a small rooftop pool, and a list of house rules. The Alhambra Bus from Plaza Nueva stops nearby.

Places to Stay – Mid-Range

Decent, standard city-centre-type hotels include the good-value *Hotel Macía* (☎ *958 22 75 36, fax 958 22 75 33, Plaza Nueva 4),* with singles/doubles for 6820/10,275 ptas; *Hotel Los Tilos* (☎ *958 26 67 12, fax 958 26 68 01, Plaza Bib-Rambla 4),* at 5350/8130 ptas; and *Hotel Dauro II* (☎ *958 22 15 81, Calle Las Navas 5),* at 9790/12,575 ptas.

Hostal La Ninfa (☎ *958 22 79 85, Campo del Príncipe s/n)* has 12 attractive rooms, with bath, TV, and heating at 7490/8560 ptas. Doubles are 13,375 ptas at the *Hotel América* (☎ *958 22 74 71, fax 958 22 74 70, Calle Real de Alhambra 53),* within the Alhambra grounds but only open March to October. Reserve well in advance as there are only 13 rooms.

Places to Stay – Top End

The distinctive, neo-Islamic *Hotel Alhambra Palace* (☎ *958 22 14 68, Peña Partida 2),* close to the Alhambra, has wonderful views over the city. Rooms are 18,190/24,075 ptas. *Parador San Francisco* (☎ *958 22 14 40,* e *granada@parador.es, Calle Real de Alhambra s/n)* can't be beaten for its location within the Alhambra and its historical connections. Rooms cost 28,250/35,310 ptas. Book well ahead.

Places to Eat

Granadino cuisine uses seafood and tropical fruits from the nearby coast, the meats and sausages of the province's interior and the excellent vegetables from the Vega around the city. A hint of the Muslim past is evident in seasonings and desserts. The famous *tortilla Sacromonte* is an omelette combining ham, prawns or oysters, greens and offal. Barflies will be pleased to find that tapas are often free at night.

Plaza Nueva & Around Popular *Cafe Central* on Calle de Elvira offers everything from good breakfasts to *menús* (from 1100 ptas) to fancy coffees. A few doors away, with tables on Plaza Nueva in good weather, *Café/Bar Al Andalus* has good cheap Arabic food to eat in or take away; tasty felafel in pitta bread costs 300 ptas, and spicy meat main dishes around 1000 ptas.

La Nueva Bodega (Calle Cetti Meriém 3) has reliable and economical food, if a little oily. *Menús* start at 950 ptas. Delicious food in a more *típico* setting can be had at *Bodegas Castañeda* (an institution among locals and tourists alike) and *Antigua Castañeda*, back to back on Calle Almireceros and Calle de Elvira. Try the montaditos (325 ptas) with toppings such as smoked salmon with avocado and caviar. More elaborate dishes cost around 1700 ptas. Both have barrels of potent *costa* wine from the Sierra de la Contraviesa.

Near the Catedral *Vía Colón (Gran Vía de Colón 13)* is a smart, popular cafe-bar serving up fancy bocadillos (from 450 ptas) and typical granadino main dishes (from 1400 ptas). The *menú* is 975 ptas.

For fresh fruit and vegies, the large covered *mercado* is on Calle San Agustín, a block west of the cathedral.

Alhambra & Around Even the kiosks here charge marked-up prices. The *Café/Restaurante Polinario* has bocadillos to go; its buffet lunch is 1350 ptas plus IVA. *Parador San Francisco* has a pricey restaurant and a terrace bar with a lovely view, open 11 am to 11 pm daily, where teas and coffees cost 260 ptas, bocadillos from 825 ptas. *La Mimbre* on the corner of Cuesta de los Chinos, with tables in a leafy garden under the Alhambra walls, serves medium-priced granadino fare.

Albayzín Three blocks north-west of Plaza Nueva, atmospheric Calle Calderería Nueva has restaurants, teterías, health-food shops

ANDALUCÍA

and takeaway food places. *Kasbah*, one of the most popular teterías, makes a relaxed stop: try a pot of one of the numerous teas on offer (300 ptas) or a wine with a slice of fancy cake. *Naturii Albayzín (Calle Calderería Nueva 10)* has interesting vegetarian *menús* with an Arabic twist for 950 or 1250 ptas plus IVA, including hunks of delicious wholemeal bread. No alcohol is served.

Lebanese *Samarcanda* on Calle Calderería Vieja has excellent Arabic food, with hummus and felafel each at 500 ptas and main dishes such as fish tagines for 900 ptas (small portions, though).

Near the top of the Albayzín, Plaza Larga and nearby Calle Panaderos have lively cafes and bars with 850-ptas *menús*. *El Ladrillo* on Placeta Fátima is a fun seafood place spilling into the street in fine weather. Big platters called *barcos* cost 1200 ptas.

For a splash-out, try the highly regarded *Mirador de Morayma* (☎ 958 22 82 90, *Calle Pianista Carrillo 2)*, in a lovely *carmen* off Cuesta San Agustín. Expect to pay around 1500 ptas for a main course (closed Sunday).

On the western edge of the Albayzín, Plaza San Miguel Bajo has a couple of lively bars with meals and tapas, and is popular with students.

Plaza Bib-Rambla & Around *Café Bib-Rambla* is great for breakfast. Coffee and toast with butter and excellent marmalade cost 400 ptas at its tables on the plaza. *Pizzeria Gallio (Plaza Bib-Rambla 10)* serves tasty Italian food. Try *pizza florentina*, with spinach and bechamel sauce (840 ptas plus IVA). Drinks are expensive. *Cunini* on Calle Pescadería is an expensive seafood restaurant with tables outside. The *menú* is 2400 ptas. *El Cepillo*, a few doors west, is a cheaper seafood restaurant, with *menús* at 800 ptas; it's packed at lunchtime, closed Sunday.

Plaza de la Trinidad & Around *Mesón El Patio (Calle de los Mesones 50)* is a mid-priced restaurant with the usual Spanish/granadino mix of food, and a pleasant patio. A breakfast of coffee, juice, bread, eggs and bacon is 500 ptas but you can't have it before 10 am.

Campo del Príncipe This plaza south of the Alhambra buzzes at night. Of its several restaurants, *Casa Cristóbal* has *menús* from 950 ptas and serves wonderful *sangría*. *Restaurante-Pizzería La Ninfa*, at No 14, is an excellent Italian eatery.

Entertainment
Guía de Granada, available at kiosks at the beginning of each month for 100 ptas, has entertainment listings.

Bars, Clubs & Live Music You can as easily dance the night away here as in most places in Spain. The flyer *YOUthING* details many music venues.

Around Plaza Nueva The streets just west of Plaza Nueva are lively on weekend nights. *Bodegas Castañeda* and *Antigua Castañeda* (see Places to Eat), with free tapas if you're standing at the bar after about 8 pm, make a good start to the evening. Nearby, there are popular bars with good music on Placita Sillería and Calle Joaquín Costa. *Granada 10* disco on Calle Cárcel Baja has varied dance music. It opens about midnight and gets going at about 2 am. Don't look too scruffy. Cover is 1000 ptas including one *copa;* subsequent drinks are expensive.

Several of the bars on Carrera del Darro and Paseo de los Tristes get lively with a studeny crowd after midnight.

La Sabanilla (Calle San Sebastían 14), near the Alcaicería, is Granada's oldest bar: though showing its age, it's worth a visit.

Elsewhere Don't miss *El Eshavira (Postigo de la Cuna 2)*, a roomy jazz and flamenco club down a dark alley off Calle Azacayas. The bar is open from 10 pm nightly, with live music some nights.

Planta Baja (Calle Horno de Abad 11), near Plaza de la Trinidad, features dance, tribal, house and deep house music from 1 to 6 am on weekends. It's also a live music venue.

From about 11 pm at weekends, crowds head for Calle Pedro Antonio de Alarcón, 1km or so south-west of town, where a string of *music bars* provide cheap drinks and tapas.

View of Sevilla's Torre del Ore, which was built in 1220 (Andalucía).

Tried and true transport (Andalucía)

Ornate window at the Alhambra (Granada)

Ronda rises above the Río Guadalevín valley (Andalucía).

Procession piece (Andalucía)

Spanish dancer (Andalucía)

Alhambra doorway (Granada)

A colourful Semana Santa street procession in Granada (Andalucía)

Just east of Calle Pedro Antonio de Alarcón, **La Sala Cha** *(Calle Ancha de Gracia 4),* open at least Friday and Saturday nights, has live music and DJ evenings.

Some of the Sacromonte caves turn into lively discotecas during university terms. *El Camborio* is a popular one, open year round on weekends from 11 pm; entry is 600 ptas.

Flamenco It's difficult to see flamenco that's not geared to tourists, but some shows are more authentic than others and attract Spaniards as well as foreigners. Try the Friday or Saturday midnight shows at *Tarantos (☎ 958 22 45 25 day, 958 22 24 92 night, Camino del Sacromonte 9),* in a cave; 3900 ptas. *Jardines Neptuno (☎ 958 52 25 33),* on Calle del Arabial, south-west of the centre, has a tourist-oriented flamenco performance at 10.15 pm nightly (3900 ptas; with dinner 7900 ptas). For these shows, you can pre-book tickets at the venues or through hotels and travel agencies. Some offer free transport. If some of Granada's top professionals are performing, you're in for a good evening. If not, you may be disappointed!

El Eshavira (see Bars, Music & Dancing) has live flamenco some nights. Top flamenco artists sometimes perform in Granada's theatres and concert halls – watch for ads and posters.

Some travellers go to the Sacromonte caves to see flamenco but it's touristy and a bit of a rip-off. Watch your back if you go up there alone at night!

Other Entertainment The notice board in the foyer of La Madraza, on Calle Oficios, has large posters listing forthcoming cultural events. The *Auditorio Manuel de Falla (Paseo de los Mártires s/n),* near the Alhambra, stages weekly orchestral concerts.

Shopping

A distinctive local craft is *taracea* (marquetry), used on boxes, tables, chess sets and more – the best has shell, silver or mother-of-pearl inlays. You can watch experts at work in the shop opposite the Iglesia de Santa María in the Alhambra, and in a shop on Cuesta de Gomérez.

Other granadino crafts include embossed leather, guitars, wrought iron, brass and copperware, basket-weaving, textiles and, of course, pottery. Places to look include the Alcaicería, the Albayzín, Cuesta de Gomérez and Artespaña in the Corral del Carbón.

The Plaza Nueva area is good for ethnic clothes and jewellery. For general shopping, pedestrianised Calle de los Mesones has countless shops.

Getting There & Away

Air Iberia (☎ 958 22 75 92), with an office at Plaza Isabel La Católica 2, flies daily to/from Madrid and Barcelona.

Bus Granada's bus station, on Carretera de Jaen (continuation of Avenida de Madrid), is 3km north-west of the centre. All services operate from here except to a few nearby destinations such as Fuente Vaqueros, Viznar and the Estación de Esquí Sierra Nevada (see those sections). Alsina Graells (☎ 958 18 54 80) runs to Córdoba (three hours, 1515 ptas, eight daily), Málaga (1½ hours, 1185 ptas, 15 daily), Sevilla (three hours, 2400 ptas, nine daily), Las Alpujarras (see the Las Alpujarras section for details), Jaén, Baeza, Úbeda, Cazorla and Almería. At least nine daily buses go to Madrid (five/six hours, 1960 ptas). Bacoma (☎ 958 15 75 57) has daily services to Alicante, Valencia and Barcelona (14 hours, 7915 ptas). Buses to Guadix and Mojácar are by Autedia (☎ 958 15 36 36).

Train The station (☎ 958 27 12 72) is 1.5km west of the centre on Avenida de Andaluces, off Avenida de la Constitución.

Three or four trains run daily to/from Antequera (1¼ hours, 1000 ptas), Sevilla (three hours, 2415 to 2665 ptas), Almería (2¼ hours, 1775 ptas), Guadix and Linares-Baeza. One daily train goes direct to Ronda (2¼ hours, 1775 ptas) and Algeciras. For Málaga (1795 ptas) and Córdoba (2290 ptas) you must change trains at Bobadilla.

To Madrid there's a Talgo at 3.40 pm (4.35 pm on Saturday), taking six hours for 3800 ptas, and a night train (9½ hours, 3600 ptas). One train daily goes to Valencia and Barcelona (12½ hours, 6100 ptas).

ANDALUCÍA

Getting Around

To/From the Airport The airport (☎ 958 24 52 23) is 17km west of the centre on the A-92. At least four airport buses (☎ 958 13 13 09) daily leave the centre, from the Palacio de Congresos, stopping on Gran Vía de Colón just beyond Plaza Isabel La Católica. The fare is 725 ptas. A taxi costs 2700 ptas.

Bus City buses cost 120 ptas. The tourist offices have a handy route booklet. Bus No 3, at intervals of up to 20 minutes, runs from the bus station to the Catedral stop in the centre (you can't see the cathedral itself from the bus). To reach the centre from the train station, walk ahead to Avenida de la Constitución and pick up bus No 3 or 11 going to the right (east).

Car & Motorcycle Access to some of Granada's main central streets is restricted. From the north-west you can drive along Gran Vía de Colón as far as the Aparcamiento San Agustín car park, a block before the cathedral. For other parts of the centre, we suggest you phone your accommodation to ask about access. Alternatively, use the *circunvalacíon* (ring road) to reach the Alhambra car park and leave your vehicle there.

Taxi Taxis line up on Plaza Nueva. Most fares within the city are 400 to 700 ptas.

AROUND GRANADA

Granada is surrounded by a fertile plain called La Vega, planted with poplar groves and crops ranging from melons to tobacco. The Vega was an inspiration to the writer Federico García Lorca, who was born and, as fate had it, killed here.

Fuente Vaqueros

The house where Lorca was born in 1898, in this village 17km west of Granada, is now the **Casa Museo Federico García Lorca**. The place brings the spirit alive, with numerous charming photos, posters and costumes for his plays, and paintings illustrating his poems. A short video captures him in action with the touring Teatro Barraca.

The museum is open for hourly guided tours in Spanish, 10 am to 1 pm and 4 to 6 pm (5 to 7 pm April to June; 6 to 8 pm July to September) daily except Tuesday (300 ptas). To get there take an Ureña bus from outside Granada train station. On summer weekdays this service runs almost hourly 9 am to 9 pm in both directions; on weekends it's every two hours. Fewer buses run in winter.

Viznar

To follow the Lorca trail to the bitter end, you must make your way out to this village 8km north-east of the city. When the Nationalists took over Granada at the start of the civil war in 1936, Lorca was arrested and taken with hundreds of others to Viznar to be shot. Outside the village, on the road to Alfacar, is the **Parque Lorca**, with a granite block marking the spot where he is believed to have been killed. His body has never been found.

A bus to Viznar leaves Plaza del Triunfo at 12.30 pm weekdays, returning from Viznar at 4 pm. You can call the Martín Perez company (☎ 958 15 12 49) to check the schedule.

GUADIX
postcode 18500 • pop 20,000

The A-92 north-east from Granada starts off through forested, hilly country before entering an increasingly arid landscape. Guadix (gwah-**deeks**), 55km from Granada, is famous for its cave dwellings – not prehistoric remnants but the homes of about 3000 modern-day townsfolk. The typical 21st-century cave has a whitewashed wall across the entrance, and a chimney and TV aerial sticking out of the top. Some have many rooms and all the mod cons.

Guadix has a tourist office (☎ 958 66 26 65) at Carretera de Granada s/n, on the Granada road leaving the town centre.

Things to See

At the centre of Guadix is a fine sandstone **catedral**, built in the 16th to 18th centuries in a succession of Gothic, Renaissance and baroque styles. It's open 11 am to 1 pm and 4 to 6 or 7 pm Monday to Saturday.

A short distance south, on Calle Barradas, is the entrance to the 15th-century Muslim castle, the **Alcazaba**. It's open 9 am to 2 pm Monday to Saturday and a few afternoon hours on weekdays).

From the Alcazaba there are views south to the main cave quarter, the Barriada de las Cuevas, where the **Cueva Museo** on Plaza de Padre Poveda recreates typical cave life – open 10 am to 2 pm and 4 to 6 pm weekdays, and until 2 pm Saturday (200 ptas).

Places to Stay
Hotel Mulhacén (☎ 958 66 07 50, Avenida Buenos Aires 41), on the Murcia road 600m from the centre, has doubles with bath for 5775 ptas. Good singles/doubles are 5500/7500 ptas plus IVA in the central *Hotel Comercio (☎ 958 66 05 00, Calle Mira de Amezcua 3)*.

Cuevas Pedro Antonio de Alarcón (☎ 958 66 49 86), in Barrio San Torcuato 3km from the centre off the Murcia road, has comfortable modern cave-apartments at 5000/6900/9900 ptas plus IVA for singles/doubles/quadruples – plus a pool and restaurant.

Getting There & Away
Guadix is about one hour from Granada and 1½ hours from Almería by several daily buses or four daily trains.

SIERRA NEVADA
The Sierra Nevada, which includes mainland Spain's highest peak, Mulhacén (3478m), forms an almost year-round snowy backdrop to Granada. The range stretches about 75km from west to east, extending into Almería province. All its highest peaks (3000m or more) are towards the Granada end. The upper reaches of the range form the 862-sq-km **Parque Nacional Sierra Nevada**, the biggest of Spain's dozen national parks – a rare high-altitude environment that is home to about 2000 of Spain's 7000 plant species, including 66 endemics. Andalucía's largest ibex population (about 5000) is here too.

Surrounding the national park, at lower altitudes, is the 848-sq-km **Parque Natural Sierra Nevada**. The Centro de Visitantes El Dornajo (☎ 958 34 06 25), on the A-395 about 10km before the Estación de Esquí Sierra Nevada, has plenty of information on the Sierra Nevada.

Getting There & Away
Autobús Viajes Bonal (☎ 958 27 31 00) runs three or four daily buses to the ski resort from Bar Ventorrillo on Paseo del Violón near the Palacio de Congresos in Granada. The one-way/return fare costs 425/800 ptas. A taxi from Granada will cost you about 6000 ptas.

The Sierra Nevada road, crossing over the top of the range from the ski station to Capileira in Las Alpujarras, is now closed to unauthorised vehicles some 4km up from Pradollano. For information on transport to/from Las Alpujarras, see the Las Alpujarras section later in this chapter.

Estación de Esquí Sierra Nevada
The ski resort Estación de Esquí Sierra Nevada (☎ 958 24 91 19/11), on the northern flank of the range at **Pradollano**, 33km south-east of Granada, is Europe's most southerly ski resort and one of Spain's biggest and liveliest. It can get very crowded at weekends and holiday times.

The resort has 45 downhill runs (five black, 18 red, 18 blue and four green) totalling 61km, and 19 lifts. Some runs start almost at the top of Veleta, the Sierra Nevada's second-highest peak. The season normally lasts from December to April. A one-day ski pass costs from 3200 to 3900 ptas, depending when you go. Skis, boots and sticks can be rented for 2600 ptas daily; snowboards are available too. The resort has at least three ski schools. Nonskiers can ride cable cars from Pradollano (2100m) to Borreguiles (2645m) for 1075 ptas return.

Places to Stay Room reservations are highly advisable in the ski season. Pradollano's Inturjoven youth hostel, *Albergue Juvenil Sierra Nevada (☎ 958 48 03 05)*, open all year, has 214 places in rooms holding two or four. Its low season, price-wise, is May to November.

ANDALUCÍA

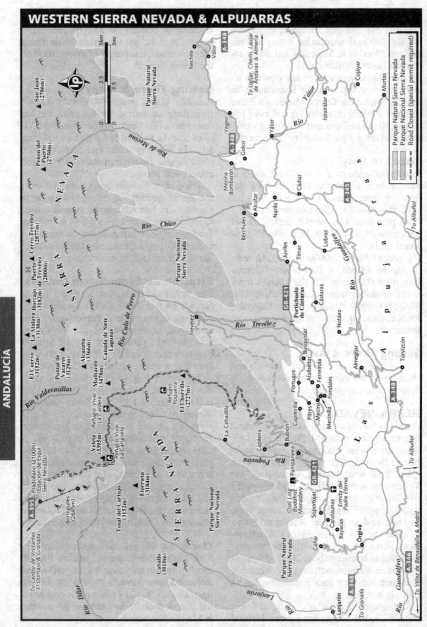

The resort has around 15 hotels and hostales, with doubles between about 8000 and 12,000 ptas at less expensive places such as *Hotel Telecabina* (☎ 958 24 91 20) and *Hostal El Ciervo* (☎ 958 48 04 09). The best deals are ski packages that you should try to book at least two weeks ahead through the resort's central booking service (☎ 958 24 91 11, e agencia@cetursa.es). A two-night half-board hotel package with two days' ski passes costs from 15,000 to 40,000 ptas per person.

Outside the ski season only a few hotels stay open.

Walking

The Sierra Nevada's two highest peaks: Mulhacén (3478m) and Veleta (3395m) rise to the south-east of the ski station and above the head of the Poqueira valley on the southern side of the range.

The best conditions in the high mountains (early July to early September) unfortunately don't coincide with the most comfortable months down in the Alpujarras valleys on the southern side of the Sierra Nevada where most ascents start (April to mid-June and mid-September to early November). In the Sierra Nevada – which are serious mountains – be prepared for cloud, rain or strong cold winds any day, and come well equipped. The temperature on the mountain tops averages 14°C less than in the highest Alpujarras villages.

The best overall maps of the western Sierra Nevada and Alpujarras are Editorial Alpina's *Sierra Nevada, La Alpujarra* (1:40,000) and the CNIG's *Sierra Nevada* (1:50,000). The Alpina is more up-to-date (published 1999) but the CNIG covers a bigger area. You should be able to get one or both at the El Dornajo and Pampaneira information offices or at shops in Trevélez.

Lonely Planet's *Walking in Spain* details eight days of good walking in Las Alpujarras and the high Sierra Nevada.

Veleta From the Pradollano ski station in July and August you can walk up Veleta in three or four hours. From Veleta to the top of Mulhacén is about another five hours'

walk and you would need to sleep in a *refugio* (see the Mulhacén section following).

Mulhacén By virtually any route from the Las Alpujarras region on the southern flank of the Sierra Nevada (see the later section), it's six or more hours' walking (plus halts) to the top of Mulhacén – so it's advisable to sleep in one of three mountain *refugios,* or camping. The modern, 87-bunk *Refugio Poqueira* (☎ 958 34 33 49, 608-55 42 24), towards the top of the Poqueira valley at 2500m, is open all year at 1000 ptas per person, with prepared meals (dinner 1600 ptas), blankets and showers available. Book ahead if possible.

Higher up, just above the Sierra Nevada road, are two free, 12-place *refugios vivac* – stone shelters with boards to sleep on: *Refugio Vivac La Caldera,* below the western flank of Mulhacén, 1½ hours up from Refugio Poqueira, and *Refugio Vivac La Carigüela,* 2½ hours farther west along the road, at the 3200m Collado del Veleta pass below the summit of Veleta.

Camping in the sierra is allowed only with official permission. Check with the Pampaneira visitor centre (see that later section) on how to obtain this: procedures, recently at least, were straightforward and almost instantaneous.

To climb Mulhacén from Trevélez you can climb steeply to the Sierra Nevada road near El Chorrillo (2727m), from which the road, then a branch track, and finally a path take you to the summit (five or six hours from Trevélez, plus halts). A more attractive route heads north-west from Trevélez up to the Cañada de Siete Lagunas, a lake-dotted basin below the eastern side of Mulhacén, then up the rocky Cuesta del Resuello ridge leading to the summit – about seven hours' walking from Trevélez, but you have the option of camping in the *cañada* (glen).

From Capileira, you can walk to the Refugio Poqueira in about five hours, then reach the summit in 2½ hours via the Río Mulhacén valley and the steep western flank of Mulhacén.

The Sierra Nevada road is closed to unauthorised vehicles 8km up from Capileira.

ANDALUCÍA

LAS ALPUJARRAS

Below the southern flank of the Sierra Nevada lies one of the oddest crannies of Andalucía, the 70km-long jumble of valleys known as Las Alpujarras. Arid hillsides split by deep ravines alternate with oasis-like white villages set beside rapid streams and surrounded by gardens, orchards and woodlands. Despite a burst of tourism in the last decade or two, Las Alpujarras remains a world apart, with a rare sense of timelessness and mystery. Its bizarre history saw a flourishing Muslim community replaced en masse by Christian settlers in the 16th century. Reminders of the Muslim past are ubiquitous in the form of Berber-style villages and the terraced and irrigated land.

History

The Alpujarras rose to prominence in the 10th and 11th centuries as a great silkworm farm for the silk workshops of Almería. This activity had arisen hand in hand with a wave of Berber settlers in the area. Together with irrigated agriculture, it supported at least 400 villages and hamlets by the late 15th century.

On his surrender to Fernando and Isabel in 1492, Boabdil, the last Granada emir, was awarded the Alpujarras as a personal fiefdom. He soon left for Africa, however, and as Christian promises of tolerance gave way to forced mass conversions and land expropriations, Muslims rebelled in 1500 across the former Granada emirate, with the Alpujarras in the thick of things. When the revolt failed, Muslims were given the choice of exile or conversion. Most converted, but the change was barely skin-deep. A new repressive decree by Felipe II (Philip II) in 1567, forbidding Arabic names, dress and language, sparked a new Alpujarras revolt in 1568. Two years of vicious guerrilla war ended only when Felipe brought in his half-brother, Don Juan of Austria, to quash the insurrection.

Almost the whole Alpujarras population was deported to Castile and western Andalucía, and most of the villages were re-peopled with settlers from the north. The rest were abandoned. Over the succeeding centuries, the silk industry fell by the wayside and great swaths of the Alpujarras' woodlands were lost to mining and cereal growing.

Books

South From Granada by Gerald Brenan, an Englishman who lived in the Alpujarras village of Yegen in the 1920s and '30s, is a fascinating picture of what was then a very isolated, superstitious corner of Spain. Another Englishman, Chris Stewart, settled here more recently, as a sheep farmer near Órgiva. His entertaining *Driving over Lemons* tells of Las Alpujarras life in the 1990s.

Walking

There's a wealth of good walks linking valley villages (see later under Pampaneira, Bubión & Capileira) or heading up into the Sierra Nevada (see that section earlier).

Accommodation

It's worth booking ahead for rooms during Semana Santa (Easter) and from June to September. In addition to hotels or hostales, many villages have apartments and houses for short-term rental.

Food

Alpujarras food is basically hearty country fare, with good meat and also local trout. Trevélez is famous for its *jamón serrano* (mountain-cured ham), but many other villages produce good hams too. A *plato alpujarreño* consists of fried potatoes, fried eggs, sausage, ham and maybe a black pudding, usually for around 700 ptas.

Getting There & Away

Buses to the Alpujarras are run by Alsina Graells (☎ 958 18 54 80) in Granada. From Granada, they run three times daily to Órgiva (1½ hours), Pampaneira (two hours), Bubión, Capileira and Pitres (2¾ hours), with two continuing to Trevélez (3¼ hours) and Bérchules (3¾ hours). Alsina also operates a twice-daily Granada-Ugíjar bus service via Órgiva, Cádiar and Yegen, and daily Málaga-Órgiva, Almería-Bérchules and Almería-Ugíjar buses except Sunday and holidays.

Órgiva

postcode 18400 • pop 6100

The western Alpujarras' scruffy main town is at its most interesting on Thursday morning, when locals and the Alpujarras' sizable international and New-Age community converges to buy and sell everything from vegetables to hippie jewellery at a colourful market in the upper part of town, the Barrio Alto. There are banks, some with ATMs, on and near the main street, Calle Doctor Fleming.

Among several accommodation options, *Pensión Alma Alpujarreña* (☎ *958 78 40 85, Avenida González Robles 49),* between the bus stop and town centre, has singles/doubles for 2000/4000 ptas (doubles with bath 5000 ptas). It serves reasonably priced food, including vegetarian dishes, indoors and outdoors.

Pampaneira, Bubión & Capileira

Pampaneira: postcode 18411 • pop 350
Bubión: postcode 18412 • pop 370
Capileira: postcode 18413 • pop 580

This trio of villages clinging to the side of the deep Barranco de Poqueira ravine, 14km to 20km north-east of Órgiva, are three of the prettiest, most dramatically sited and most touristed in Las Alpujarras. Their white-washed stone houses seem to clamber over each other in an effort not to slide down into the gorge, while streets decked with flowery balconies climb haphazardly in between.

Capileira, the highest of the three at 1440m, is the best base for walks. Pampaneira and Bubión are 1050m and 1300m, respectively.

Information The Centro de Visitantes de Pampaneira (☎ 958 76 31 27), on Pampaneira's square, Plaza de la Libertad, has plenty of information on the Alpujarras and Sierra Nevada, including maps for sale, and can inform you about walks and mountain refuges. It's open 10 am to 2 pm and 4 to 6 pm (5 to 7 pm from around May to mid-October) Tuesday to Saturday, and until 3 pm Sunday and Monday; English is spoken.

There are ATMs just outside the car park in Pampaneira and at La General bank on Calle Doctor Castilla in Capileira. All three villages have small supermarkets.

Things to See All three villages have solid 16th-century **mudéjar churches** (open only at Mass times), small **weaving workshops**, descendants of a textile tradition that goes back to Muslim times, and plentiful craft shops.

Given the somewhat Himalayan character of the Poqueira landscape, it's not entirely surprising that there's a small Tibetan Buddhist monastery, **Osel Ling** (Place of Clear Light), high on the far side of the valley from Pampaneira. The monastery welcomes visitors at certain times (call ☎ 958 34 31 34 for hours). You can walk to it from any of the three villages, or drive up from the turning marked 'Ruta Pintoresca', opposite the Ermita del Padre Eterno chapel on the GR-421, 5km below Pampaneira.

Walking Eight trails ranging from 4km to 23km (two to eight hours) are marked out in the Barranco de Poqueira ravine with little colour-coded posts, and shown and described on Editorial Alpina's *Sierra Nevada, La Alpujarra* map. Most start from Capileira, though No 1 (6km) is a circuit from Pampaneira, and No 6 (23km) is a circuit from Bubión. Route No 4 from Capileira (8km, 3½ hours) takes you up to the hamlet of La Cebadilla, then down the western side of the valley and back up to Capileira.

You can walk from Capileira to Trevélez in about five hours using a broad track heading to the right 4km up the Sierra Nevada road from Capileira, 200m after the Km 8 marker. This track is driveable too.

Nevadensis (☎ 958 76 31 27, ⓔ nevadensis@ arrakis.es), a group of mountain guides who run the visitor centre at Pampaneira, offers guided walks and treks, with a minimum of five people usually needed. A five-hour outing in the Barranco de Poqueira costs 2300 ptas per person; a combined 4WD and foot ascent of Mulhacén is 4000 ptas per person.

Other Activities Depending on the season, Nevadensis (see Walking) can organise horse riding (around 4000 ptas per person

ANDALUCÍA

for two hours or 8500 ptas per day), ski touring, mountain biking, climbing, paragliding and 4WD trips.

Places to Stay & Eat

Pampaneira Two good hostales face each other across Calle José Antonio at the entrance to the village. *Hostal Pampaneira* (☎ 958 76 30 02) has singles/doubles with bathroom for up to 3000/4000 ptas, and the village's cheapest restaurant (trout or pork chops for 650 ptas). *Hostal Ruta del Mulhacén* (☎ 958 76 30 10) has rooms with bath for 3100/4250 ptas. *Restaurante Casa Diego*, along the street on Plaza de la Libertad, has a pleasant upstairs terrace and serves most main dishes for between 600 and 1200 ptas; trout with ham, and local ham and eggs, are among the cheaper dishes.

Bubión *Hostal Las Terrazas* (☎ 958 76 30 34, Plaza del Sol 7), below the main road, has pleasant singles/doubles with bath for 2750/3900 ptas. *Villa Turística de Bubión* (☎ 958 76 31 11), at the top of the village, has comfortable self-catering apartments for up to six people (12,000 ptas plus IVA for two or three), and a restaurant. *Restaurante Teide*, by the main road, is good, with a three-course *menú* for 1100 ptas plus IVA. Up the street is the convivial, pub-like *Café-Bar Fuenfría*, with a terraza opposite.

Capileira *Hostal Paco López* (☎ 958 76 30 11, Carretera de la Sierra 5) has singles/doubles with bath from 2000/3000 ptas. *Mesón Hostal Poqueira* (☎/fax 958 76 30 48, Calle Doctor Castilla 6), just off the main road, has good rooms with bath for 2400/4000 ptas, and a popular restaurant. Up the street and round a right-hand bend is *Restaurante Ruta de la Nieves* (☎ 958 76 31 06, Carretera de la Sierra s/n), with eight decent rooms at the same prices. *Finca Los Llanos* (☎ 958 76 30 71, fax 958 76 32 06), at the top of the village, has classier apartments at 12,000 ptas plus IVA for two people.

Bar El Tilo on Plaza Calvario, just down from the far end of Calle Doctor Castilla, has good-value raciones. *Casa Íbero*, below the church (follow signs), serves original

international food ranging from couscous or vegetarian croquettes to lamb with ginger sauce (800 to 1300 ptas).

Pitres

postcode 18414 • pop 500 approx
• elev 1250m

Pitres is almost as pretty as the Poqueira Gorge villages but less touristed. The valley below it, with five hamlets – Mecina, Mecinilla, Fondales, Ferreirola and Atalbéitar, all grouped with Pitres in the *municipio* called La Taha – is particularly fascinating to explore, with ancient paths wending their way through lush woodlands to the ubiquitous tinkle of running water.

Camping El Balcón de Pitres (☎ 958 76 61 11), on the western side of Pitres, opens all year, charging 1725 ptas plus IVA for two adults with a car and tent. *Refugio Los Albergues* (☎ 958 34 31 76), two minutes' walk down a path from the GR-421 road on the eastern side of Pitres, is a small German-owned walkers' hostel, with bunks for 1000 ptas and an equipped kitchen (closed 10 January to 15 February). *Fonda Sierra Nevada* (☎ 958 76 60 17), on Pitres' plaza has simple singles/doubles at 1700/3400 ptas.

Trevélez

postcode 18417 • pop 800 • elev 1476m

Trevélez, in a valley almost as impressive as the Poqueira Gorge, claims to be the highest village in Spain (but Valdelinares, Aragón, reaches above 1700m) and produces famous jamón serrano. Hams are trucked in from far and wide for curing in Trevélez's dry mountain air.

Along the main road you're confronted by a welter of jamón and souvenir shops, but a wander into the upper parts reveals a lively Alpujarran village. La General bank just above the main road has an ATM.

Places to Stay & Eat

Camping Trevélez (☎ 958 85 87 35), 1km from Trevélez along the GR-421 towards Busquístar, is open all year, charging 1665 to 2050 ptas plus IVA for two adults with car and tent. It also has cabins at 2500/5500 ptas plus IVA for two/four people.

Alpujarras Houses

If you have been to Morocco you may notice a resemblance between villages in the Alpujarras and those in the Atlas mountains, from where the Alpujarran style was introduced in Muslim times by Berber settlers.

Most houses are of two storeys, with the lower one still often used for storage and animals. The characteristic *terraos* or flat roofs, with their protruding chimney pots, consist of a layer of *launa* (a type of clay) packed on to flat stones laid on wood beams. Nowadays there's often a layer of plastic between the stones and launa, for extra waterproofing.

Whitewash is a fairly modern introduction too: the villages used to be stone-coloured.

Restaurante González (☎ 958 85 85 31, *Plaza de Don Francisco Abellán s/n), by the main road at the foot of the village, has singles/doubles for 2000/3000 ptas and doubles with bath for 4500 ptas, plus a good-value restaurant.

Hostal Fernando (☎ 958 85 85 65, *Pista del Barrio Medio s/n), by the road heading up through the village, has clean rooms with bath from 2000/3500 to 2500/4500 ptas.

A little higher, on Plaza Barrio Medio, signs point to *Hotel La Fragua* (☎ 958 85 86 26, *Calle San Antonio 4), with Trevélez's most comfortable rooms at 2800/5500 ptas with bath. Its good restaurant, *Mesón La Fragua*, a short walk away, offers exotica such as fig ice cream (500 ptas) as well as excellent *solomillo* (sirloin) available several ways for around 950 ptas.

East of Trevélez

East of Trevélez the landscape becomes barer and more arid, yet there are still oases of greenery around the villages. The central and eastern Alpujarras are almost as impressive as the west, and pull in far fewer tourists.

Bérchules, 17km from Trevélez, is in a green valley stretching far back into the hills, with attractive walks. *La Posada* (☎ 958 85 25 41, *Plaza del Ayuntamiento 3) is a sturdy old village house turned into simple lodgings

with walkers in mind. Bed and breakfast is 2000 ptas per person, English is spoken and vegetarian dinners are available.

Cádiar, in the valley bottom 8km south of Bérchules, is one of the bigger Alpujarras villages (2000 people), and more appealing than it looks from afar. Two kilometres south, just off the A-348 towards Órgiva, is the excellent *Alquería de Morayma* (☎/fax 958 34 32 21), an old farmstead marvellously renovated to provide a dozen comfortable and unique rooms and apartments ranging from 7000 to 12,500 ptas plus IVA (the biggest hold four). There's good, moderately priced food, a library of Alpujarras information, and fascinating art and artefacts everywhere.

Gerald Brenan's home in the 1920s, **Yegen**, is 12km east of Bérchules. Brenan's house, just off the main plaza with the fountain, has a plaque. Parts of the valley below Yegen have a particularly moon-like quality. You can pick up a leaflet on local walks at the friendly *Café-Bar Nuevo La Fuente* (☎ 958 85 10 67), on the village plaza, where singles/doubles are 1300/2600 ptas.

Válor, 5km east of Yegen, was the birthplace of Aben Humeya, leader of the 1568 rebellion, and on 14 and 15 September stages celebrated Moros y Cristianos festivities recreating that conflict. *Hostal Las Perdices* (☎ 958 85 18 21, *Calle Torrecilla s/n), in the centre, has doubles with bath for 3500 ptas. *Fonda El Suizo* also has rooms and meals.

Ugíjar, 7km south-east of Válor, has two hostales. Beyond it, the Alpujarras, and the A-348, continue east into Almería province.

THE COAST

Granada's rugged, cliff-lined, 80km coast has a few reasonably attractive beach towns, linked by several daily buses to Granada, Málaga and Almería.

Salobreña

postcode 18680 • pop 10,000

Salobreña's huddle of white houses rises on a crag between the N-340 and the sea. The helpful tourist office (☎ 958 61 03 14) on Plaza de Goya, 200m off the N-340, is open daily except Sunday. Up at the top of the

ANDALUCÍA

town is the impressive 13th-century **Castillo Árabe**, open 10 am to 2 pm and 4 to 8.30 pm daily – the 400-ptas ticket also includes the nearby **Museo Arqueológico**. Below all this is a long, dark-sand **beach**.

Clean, friendly *Pensión Mari Carmen* (☎ *958 61 09 06, Calle Nueva 32)* and *Pensión Arnedo* (☎ *958 61 02 27, Calle Nueva 15)* have reasonable doubles for under 3000 ptas. Little *Restaurante Pesetas* on Calle Bóveda serves up good tapas and meals. *El Peñón*, by the big rock dividing Salobreña's main beach, does good seafood.

Almuñécar
postcode 18690 • pop 21,000
Almuñécar seems from the road an uninviting agglomeration of apartment blocks, but it has a more attractive older heart around the 16th-century **castle**. Popular with Spanish holidaymakers, it's a not-too-expensive resort with pebbly beaches.

The bus station is at Avenida Juan Carlos I No 1, just south of the N-340. The tourist office (☎ 958 63 11 25), open daily, is on Avenida de Europa, just back from Playa de San Cristóbal.

Things to See Just behind Playa de San Cristóbal is a tropical bird aviary, the **Parque Ornitológico Loro-Sexi**, open daily (300 ptas). (*Loro* means parrot and Sexi was possibly the Phoenician name for Almuñécar.) On top of the hill above is the post-Reconquista **Castillo de San Miguel**, with great views – open daily except Monday. The 300-ptas ticket includes the nearby **Museo Arqueológico**, in 1st-century Roman galleries called the Cueva de Siete Palacios. Antiquity lovers should also seek out the **Necrópolis Puente de Noy**, a Phoenician and Roman cemetery with over 200 excavated tombs, about a half-hour walk west of the centre.

Places to Stay Budget hostales are in the streets south of the bus station. Basic but clean *Hostal Victoria* (☎ *958 63 00 22, Plaza de la Victoria 6)* has doubles with bath for 4000 ptas, but usually opens only in July and August. The better *Hotel Victoria II* (☎ *958 63 17 34, Plaza de Damasco 2)* has doubles

for 6000 ptas in high season. Almost on Playa de San Cristóbal, *Hotel Casablanca* (☎ *958 63 55 75, Plaza San Cristóbal 4)* provides comfortable doubles at 9000 ptas plus IVA.

Jaén Province

Relatively little-visited Jaén has a landscape alternating between impressive mountain ranges and rolling country covered with olive trees (it produces about 10% of the world's olive oil). The Parque Natural de Cazorla is perhaps the most beautiful of all Andalucía's mountain regions. The province's urban highlight is the marvellous Renaissance architecture of Andrés de Vandelvira, born in 1509 at Alcaraz in neighbouring Albacete province.

The N-IV from Madrid enters Andalucía through the Desfiladero de Despeñaperros pass in the Sierra Morena. The rout of the Almohad army by Christian forces in 1212 at Las Navas de Tolosa, just south of the pass, was a key event of the Reconquista, opening the doors of Andalucía to the Christians.

The Jaén diet is pretty traditional but richly varied, with plenty of game (partridge, venison, wild boar), especially in the mountains. Many bars still have the endearing habit of serving free tapas with drinks.

JAÉN
postcode 23080 • pop 113,000
The provincial capital is a likeable university city, well worth a bit of your time.

Orientation
Old Jaén huddles beneath the high, castle-topped Cerro de Santa Catalina hill. The focal point of the newer part of town is Plaza de la Constitución, from which Calle Roldán y Marín (becoming Paseo de la Estación) heads north-west to the train station, 1km away. The bus station is on Plaza de Coca de la Piñera, 250m north of Plaza de la Constitución.

Information
A new tourist office, expected to open morning and afternoon every day, was due

to open in 2000 at Calle de la Maestra 13, near the cathedral.

There's no shortage of banks or ATMs on Plaza de la Constitución and Calle Roldán y Marín. Librería Metrópolis, Calle del Cerón 17, is good for maps and Spanish-language guidebooks.

The main general hospital is the Hospital Ciudad de Jaén (☎ 953 22 24 08) on Avenida del Ejército Español. The Policía Municipal (☎ 953 21 91 05) are on Carrera de Jesús, near the cathedral.

Things to See

Jaén's huge **Catedral** was built mainly in the 16th and 17th centuries, and mainly to the designs of Andrés de Vandelvira. Its highlight is the south-western facade on Plaza de Santa María, with an array of 17th-century statuary, much of it by Sevilla's Pedro Roldán. The interior is open 8.30 am to 1 pm and at least 5 to 7 pm daily (free).

The Renaissance **Palacio de Villardompardo**, on Plaza de Santa Luisa de Marillac, houses: the **Museo Internacional de Arte Naif**, with a large international collection of colourful naïf art; the beautiful 11th-century **Baños Árabes** (Arab Baths), one of Spain's biggest Islamic bathhouses; and the **Museo de Artes y Costumbres Populares**, devoted to pre-industrial Jaén province. It's all open 9 am to 8 pm Tuesday to Friday, 9.30 am to 2.30 pm weekends (free with any passport or national identity card).

The **Museo Provincial**, Paseo de la Estación 27, has an excellent archaeological collection; the highlight is the room of 5th-century BC Iberian sculpture from Porcuna. It's open 3 to 8 pm Tuesday, 9 am to 8 pm Wednesday to Saturday and 9 am to 3 pm Sunday (100 ptas, free with an EU passport or national identity card).

Jaén's most exhilarating spot is the top of the Cerro de Santa Catalina, where the **Castillo de Santa Catalina** was surrendered to Fernando III in 1246 by Granada after a six-month siege. The castle is open 10 am to 1.30 pm (to 2 pm in winter) daily except Wednesday (free). It's a circuitous 4km drive up from the city centre (800 ptas by taxi), but you can walk up in an hour using a steep path almost opposite the top of Calle de Buenavista. If you walk, you deserve to treat yourself to a drink in Parador Castillo de Santa Catalina next to the castle!

Places to Stay

Mosquitoes can be a nuisance in the cheaper Jaén hotels.

Hostal Rey Carlos V (☎ 953 22 20 91, Avenida de Madrid 4), near the bus station, provides basic singles/doubles for 2700/3700 ptas. *Hostal La Española* (☎ 953 23 02 54, Calle Bernardo López 9), has sagging beds but more character – rooms are 2000/3800 ptas, or 4250 to 4750 ptas for doubles with bathroom.

Hotel Europa (☎ 953 22 27 00, Plaza de Belén 1) and *Hotel Xauen* (☎ 953 24 07 89, Plaza del Deán Mazas 3) are both good mid-range hotels charging around 5500/8500 ptas.

Parador Castillo de Santa Catalina (☎ 953 23 00 00), atop the Cerro de Santa Catalina, has spacious rooms at 14,000/17,500 ptas plus IVA, and a pool and classy restaurant.

Places to Eat

Atmospheric old bars serving raciones and tapas near the cathedral include *La Barra* (Calle Cerón 7), *El Gorrión* (Calle de Arco del Consuelo 7) and *La Manchega*, with entrances on both Arco del Consuelo and Calle Bernardo López. La Manchega also does good-value platos combinados for 500 ptas and inexpensive breakfasts. *Casa Vicente* on nearby Calle Francisco Martín Mora is much classier, specialising in pork and venison; three courses will be around 3000 ptas.

Short Calle Nueva, off Calle Roldán y Marín, has a string of good places to eat and drink. A top choice is *Mesón Río Chico* (☎ 953 24 08 02, Calle Nueva 2), with both a downstairs *taberna* serving excellent tapas and raciones of meat, revueltos and fish (try the *solomillo al roquefort* ración for 1200 ptas) and a more expensive upstairs restaurant.

You can buy almost any type of fresh foodstuff at the large, modern *Mercado Central San Francisco* on Calle de los Álamos.

ANDALUCÍA

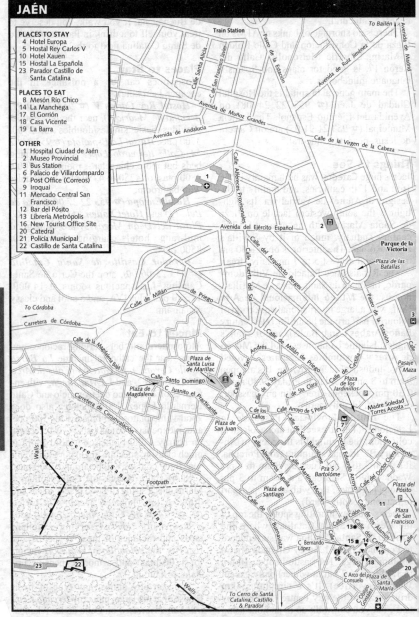

JAÉN

PLACES TO STAY
4 Hotel Europa
5 Hostal Rey Carlos V
10 Hotel Xauen
15 Hostal La Española
23 Parador Castillo de
   Santa Catalina

PLACES TO EAT
8 Mesón Río Chico
14 La Manchega
17 El Gorrión
18 Casa Vicente
19 La Barra

OTHER
1 Hospital Ciudad de Jaén
2 Museo Provincial
3 Bus Station
6 Palacio de Villardompardo
7 Post Office (Correos)
9 Iroquai
11 Mercado Central San
   Francisco
12 Bar del Pósito
13 Librería Metrópolis
16 New Tourist Office Site
20 Catedral
21 Policía Municipal
22 Castillo de Santa Catalina

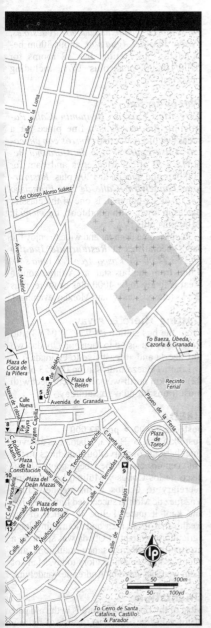

To Baeza, Úbeda,
Cazorla & Granada

Plaza de
Coca de
la Piñera

Plaza de
Belén

Recinto
Ferial

Calle
Nueva

Avenida de Granada

Plaza
de
Toros

Plaza
de la
Constitución

Plaza del
Deán Mazas

Plaza de
San Ildefonso

0   50   100m
0   50   100yd

To Cerro de Santa
Catalina, Castillo
& Parador

Entertainment

Groovy drinking spots include the artsy *Bar del Pósito (Plaza del Pósito 10)* and *Iroquai (Calle de Adarves Bajos 53),* which plays good music (usually with live rock, blues, flamenco or fusion Thursday). For some atmospheric old-town bars, see Places to Eat.

Getting There & Away

Bus From the bus station (☎ 953 25 01 06) seven or more daily buses run to Granada (1½ hours, 930 ptas), Baeza (45 minutes, 465 ptas), Úbeda (1¼ hours, 545 ptas) and Córdoba, two to Cazorla (two hours, 960 ptas), and others to main Andalucian cities, Madrid, Albacete, Valencia, Barcelona and around Jaén province.

Train Most days there are only four departures from Jaén station (☎ 953 27 02 02). One, at 8 am, goes to Córdoba (1½ hours, 1175 ptas), Sevilla and Cádiz. Three go to Madrid.

BAEZA

postcode 23440 • pop 15,000

The heyday of this country town 48km north-east of Jaén was the 16th century, when local nobility ploughed much of their wealth from grain growing and textiles into constructing gorgeous Gothic and Renaissance buildings.

Orientation & Information

The heart of town is the long, wide Paseo de la Constitución. The bus station is about 700m east on Paseo Arco del Agua. The tourist office (☎ 953 74 04 44) on Plaza del Pópulo, just west of Paseo de la Constitución, is open 9 am to 2.30 pm weekdays and 10 am to 1 pm on alternate Saturdays.

Things to See

Opening times of some buildings vary unpredictably from published hours.

In the centre of beautiful **Plaza del Pópulo** is the Fuente de los Leones (Fountain of the Lions), built with carvings from the Iberian and Roman village of Cástulo and topped by a statue traditionally believed to represent Imilce, a Cástulo princess who was married to Hannibal. The southern side of the plaza is lined by the plateresque Casa del Populo from about 1540 (housing Baeza's tourist office), and on the western side stands the Antigua Carnicería (Old Slaughterhouse) of 1548.

Baeza's **Antigua Universidad** (Old University), on Calle del Beato Juan de Ávila, was founded in 1538 and closed in 1824. Today it's a high school, open 10 am to 1 pm and 4 to 6 pm Tuesday to Sunday (free). The main patio has two levels of elegant Renaissance arches. Round the corner on Calle San Felipe Neri stands the early 16th-century **Palacio de Jabalquinto**, a mansion with a flamboyant Isabelline Gothic facade and lovely Renaissance patio – normally open the same hours as the Antigua Universidad (free). Across the square, the 13th-century **Iglesia de la Santa Cruz** may be the only Romanesque church in Andalucía.

The main facade of Baeza's eclectic **Catedral**, nearby on Plaza de Santa María, is in 16th-century Renaissance style, as is the basic design of the interior (by Andrés de Vandelvira and Jerónimo del Prado). But the building also has earlier Gothic features such as the 13th-century Puerta de la Luna (Moon Doorway) at the western end. The interior is open 10.30 am to 1 pm and 5.15 to 7 pm (4.15 to 6 pm in winter) daily; free.

A block north of Paseo de la Constitución at Paseo del Cardenal Benavides 9, the **ayuntamiento** has a marvellous plateresque facade.

Places to Stay

Some prices go up a few hundred pesetas from about June to September.

Friendly *Hostal El Patio* (☎ 953 74 02 00, *Calle Conde Romanones 13)* occupies a 17th-century mansion with a large covered patio. Singles/doubles are 2000/3000 ptas (2500/3500 ptas with shower); doubles with bath are 4000 ptas. Another friendly place, *Hostal Comercio* (☎ 953 74 80 67, *Calle San Pablo 21),* has decent rooms with shower and toilet for 2083/3337 ptas.

Hotel Confortel Baeza (☎ 953 74 81 30, *Calle de la Concepción 3)* has cosy rooms for 700/10,200 ptas plus IVA, with breakfast.

The relaxed *Hospedería Fuentenueva* (☎ 953 74 31 00, e *fuentenueva@mx4.redestb.es, Paseo Arco del Agua s/n),* about 300m beyond the bus station, has 12 rooms for 6700/10,500 ptas plus IVA, including breakfast.

Places to Eat

Cafetería Churrería Benjamín (Calle Patrocinio Biedma 1) is a fine place for a breakfast of good, crisp *churros con chocolate. Casa Pedro (Paseo del Cardenal Benavides 3)* offers fried eggs and ham for 600 ptas and a *menú* at 1200 ptas. *Restaurante Vandelvira (Calle de San Francisco 14),* in an ex-convent, is one of the classier places in town, with good food; the *menú* is 2100 ptas plus IVA.

People come from far and wide to enjoy the Jaén specialities at *Restaurante Juanito* (☎ 953 74 00 40, *Paseo Arco del Agua s/n),* 750m from the bus station. A three-course meal is likely to be 4000 ptas or more, plus drinks (closed Sunday and Monday evenings).

Getting There & Away

From the bus station (☎ 953 74 04 68), up to 15 daily buses go to Jaén and Úbeda, two to Cazorla and at least five to Granada.

Linares-Baeza train station (☎ 953 65 02 02) is 13km north-west. Buses connect with most trains Monday to Saturday.

ÚBEDA

postcode 23400 • pop 32,000

Just 9km east of Baeza, Úbeda has an even finer heritage of marvellous buildings. In the 16th century one of the Úbeda gentry, Francisco de los Cobos y Molina, became first secretary to Carlos I; his nephew Juan Vázquez de Molina succeeded him in the job and kept it under Felipe II. Much of the wealth that these men and flourishing local agriculture brought to Úbeda was spent on a profusion of Renaissance mansions and churches that remain its glory today. Many of them were designed by Andrés de Vandelvira.

Orientation

Most of the fine architecture is in the old part of town in the south-east, a web of narrow streets and expansive plazas. Budget accommodation and the bus station are in the drab new town in the west and north.

Information

The tourist office (☎ 953 75 08 97) is in the 18th-century Palacio Marqués de Contadero, Calle Baja del Marqués 4. It's open 8 am to 3 pm Monday to Saturday.

You'll find the biggest concentration of banks and ATMs on Plaza de Andalucía and nearby Calle Rastro. There's a Centro de Salud (Health Centre; ☎ 953 75 11 03), with an emergency section, on Calle Explanada.

Plaza Vázquez de Molina

This plaza, Úbeda's architectural crown jewel, is almost entirely surrounded by beautiful 15th- and 16th-century stone buildings.

Capilla de El Salvador Facing along the plaza from its eastern end, this 1540s church, founded by Francisco de los Cobos y Molina as his family funerary chapel, was Vandelvira's first commission in Úbeda. The basic concept is by Diego de Siloé but Vandelvira added plenty of his own touches, including the elaborate main facade, which is an outstanding piece of plateresque design.

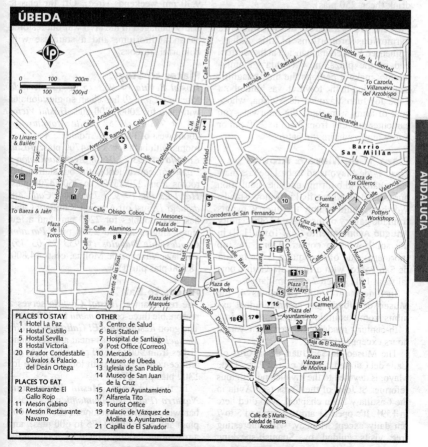

ÚBEDA

PLACES TO STAY
1 Hotel La Paz
4 Hostal Castillo
5 Hostal Sevilla
8 Hostal Victoria
20 Parador Condestable Dávalos & Palacio del Deán Ortega

PLACES TO EAT
2 Restaurante El Gallo Rojo
11 Mesón Gabino
16 Mesón Restaurante Navarro

OTHER
3 Centro de Salud
6 Bus Station
7 Hospital de Santiago
9 Post Office (Correos)
10 Mercado
12 Museo de Úbeda
13 Iglesia de San Pablo
14 Museo de San Juan de la Cruz
15 Antiguo Ayuntamiento
17 Alfarería Tito
18 Tourist Office
19 Palacio de Vázquez de Molina & Ayuntamiento
21 Capilla de El Salvador

ANDALUCÍA

The sacristy, by Vandelvira, has a portrait of Francisco de los Cobos y Molina. The richly decorated chancel is modelled on Siloé's Capilla Mayor in Granada cathedral, with a frescoed dome. The Cobos family crypt is beneath the nave. The church is open 10.30 am to 2 pm and 4.30 to 6 pm daily (350 ptas).

Palacio del Deán Ortega Next to the Capilla de El Salvador stands what was the abode of its chaplains – in fact one of Vandelvira's finest palaces, and now Úbeda's parador. Its courtyard is a fine spot for a drink (beer, 250 ptas).

Palacio de Vázquez de Molina The harmonious proportions of this Italian-influenced Vandelvira mansion at the western end of the plaza, now Úbeda's ayuntamiento, make it perhaps the most magnificent building in the town. It was built about 1562 for Juan Vázquez de Molina, whose coat of arms surmounts the doorway. You can enter any day from 9 am to 2.30 pm or 5 to 9 pm to admire the patio.

Plaza 1° de Mayo & Around

Plaza 1° de Mayo used to be Úbeda's market square and bullring, and the Inquisition burnt heretics where its kiosk now stands. Worthies could watch the merry events from the gallery of the elegant 16th-century **Antiguo Ayuntamiento** (Old Town Hall) in the south-western corner. Along the top (northern) side of the square is the **Iglesia de San Pablo**, with a fine Late-Gothic portal from 1511 (open 7 to 9 pm daily).

Just north at Calle Cervantes 4, the **Museo de Úbeda** has archaeological exhibits from Neolithic to Muslim times in a 14th-century mudéjar house; open varied hours except Monday.

The **Museo de San Juan de la Cruz** on Calle del Carmen, a block east of Plaza 1° de Mayo, is devoted to the mystic and religious reformer St John of the Cross (see Ávila in the Castilla y León chapter), who died here in 1591. It's open 11 am to 1 pm and 5 to 7 ʼm daily except Monday, with interesting ꞓe visits guided by Spanish-speaking

monks. Even if you can't understand them, you'll still get a look at a couple of the saint's fingers and some of his bones, preserved in cabinets, and other memorabilia.

Hospital de Santiago

Andrés de Vandelvira's final building, completed in 1575, and one of his masterpieces, is on Calle Obispo Cobos, in the west of town. This sober, grand-scale, late-Renaissance building (no longer a hospital) has been dubbed the Escorial of Andalucía. It's open 8.30 am to 2 pm and 4 to 10 pm weekdays, and 11 am to 2.30 pm and 6 to 9.30 pm weekends (free). Off the classic Vandelvira two-level patio are a chapel, badly damaged in the civil war but restored as an auditorium, and a staircase with colourful frescoes.

Places to Stay

Hostal Sevilla (☎ 953 75 06 12, Avenida Ramón y Cajal 9) has clean singles/doubles with bath for 2000/3800 ptas. *Hostal Victoria* (☎ 953 75 29 52, Calle Alaminos 5), 200m west of Plaza de Andalucía, has good rooms with bath for 2600/4700 ptas. *Hostal Castillo* (☎ 953 75 04 30, Avenida Ramón y Cajal 16), convenient to the bus station, has rooms from 2200/3500 to 2600/4700 ptas. *Hotel La Paz* (☎ 953 75 21 40, Calle Andalucía 1), just off Avenida Ramón y Cajal, has good doubles for 7200 ptas and a few small singles around 2500 ptas. *Parador Condestable Dávalos* (☎ 953 75 03 45), on Plaza Vázquez de Molina, costs 14,800/18,500 ptas plus IVA.

Places to Eat

The restaurant at *Hostal Castillo* serves a reasonable three-course *menú* for 1100 ptas. The good *Restaurante El Gallo Rojo (Calle Manuel Barraca 3)* has meat and fish main dishes from 900 to 1800 ptas plus IVA, and a three-course *menú* with lots of choice for 1300 ptas plus IVA.

In the old town, *Mesón Restaurante Navarro (Plaza del Ayuntamiento 2)* has a bar with excellent raciones (1200 to 1600 ptas) and bocadillos (175 to 600 ptas), and a restaurant serving typical local fare at the

Hacienda Benazuza (Sevilla)

Two old *amigos* sharing an afternoon coffee (Andalucía).

Las Alpujurras (Andalucía)

Vineyard flowers (Andalucía)

Los Cotos, a rockface in El Chorro Gorge (Andalucía)

Plaza de España (Sevilla)

Olive groves around Baeza (Andalucía)

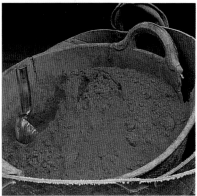

Bittersweet, smoked paprika (Extremadura)

The beautiful town of Trujillo (Extremadura)

A cherry-picker taking a rest (Extremadura)

back. *Mesón Gabino* on Calle Fuente Seca is a cellar restaurant with decent food at middling prices.

Lunch or dinner in the *Parador Condestable Dávalos* costs around 4000 ptas but the food is excellent.

Shopping
The typical green glaze on Úbeda's attractive pottery dates from Muslim times. Several workshops on Cuesta de la Merced and Calle Valencia, north-east of the old town, sell their wares on the spot. Alfarería Tito, Plaza del Ayuntamiento 12, has a large selection too.

Getting There & Away
Bus The bus station (☎ 953 75 21 57) is at Calle San José 6, 1km west of the heart of the old town. Alsina Graells runs to Baeza, Jaén and Granada several times daily, and to Cazorla three or four times. Other buses head to Córdoba, Sevilla, Málaga, Madrid, Albacete, Valencia, Barcelona and around Jaén province.

Train The nearest station is Linares-Baeza, 21km north-west, which you can reach by Linares-bound buses.

CAZORLA
postcode 23470 • pop 8500
Cazorla, a hillside town of narrow old streets 45km east of Úbeda, is the main gateway to the Parque Natural de Cazorla. It can get pretty busy at Spanish holiday times.

Orientation & Information
Plaza de la Constitución is the main square of the northern, newer part of town. Plaza de la Corredera is 150m south along Calle Doctor Muñoz. Plaza de Santa María, 300m farther south-east, is the heart of the oldest part of town.

The Oficina de Turismo Municipal (☎ 953 71 01 12), Paseo del Santo Cristo 17, 200m north of Plaza de la Constitución, only opens in summer. Quercus (☎ 953 72 01 15), Calle Juan Domingo 2 (just off Plaza de la Constitución), provides some tourist information as well as selling maps and excursions.

Things to See
At one end of lovely **Plaza de Santa María** is the large shell of the **Iglesia de Santa María**, built by Andrés de Vandelvira in the 16th century but wrecked by Napoleonic troops. A short walk up from here, the ancient **Castillo de la Yedra** houses the Museo del Alto Guadalquivir, with art and relics of past local life (open varying hours, daily except Monday). The picturesque ruins of a Knights Templar castle top a sheer crag in **La Iruela** village, 1km east of Cazorla (uphill).

Places to Stay
Tiny *Camping Cortijo San Isicio (☎ 953 72 12 80)*, off the Quesada road 4km from central Cazorla, charges 1400 ptas plus IVA for two adults with a tent and car. You should find it open from March to October.

The spick-and-span Inturjoven *Albergue Juvenil Cazorla* youth hostel (☎ 953 72 03 29, Plaza Mauricio Martínez 6), 200m uphill from Plaza de la Corredera, accommodates 120.

The friendly, clean *Hostal Betis (☎ 953 72 05 40, Plaza de la Corredera 19)* has singles/doubles from 1200/2500 to 1500/2800 ptas. *La Cueva de Juan Pedro (☎ 953 72 12 25, Calle La Hoz 2)*, on Plaza de Santa María, has six rooms with bath and kitchen for 2000/4000 ptas.

Hotel Guadalquivir (☎/fax 953 72 02 68, Calle Nueva 6), just off Calle Doctor Muñoz, is a grade better; rooms with bath are 4200/5800 ptas plus IVA. *Hotel Peña de los Halcones (☎ 953 72 02 11, Travesía del Camino de La Iruela 2)*, 400m uphill from Plaza de la Corredera, has good-sized, pleasant rooms for 7500/8200 ptas plus IVA, and a restaurant and pool.

Places to Eat
Mesón Don Chema (Calle Escaleras del Mercado 2), off Calle Doctor Muñoz, does typical local fare from 700 to 1600 ptas. *La Forchetta (Calle de las Escuelas 2)*, down from Plaza de la Constitución, serves pizzas and pasta for 500 to 850 ptas. The fancier *Restaurante La Sarga (Plaza del Mercado s/n)*, nearby, does a 1700-ptas, four-course *menú*, and mains for 1200 to 1800 ptas.

ANDALUCÍA

Down on Plaza de Santa María, ancient, wood-beamed *La Cueva de Juan Pedro* serves up traditional Cazorla fare such as rabbit, trout, *rin-rán* (a mash of bacalao, potato and dried peppers), wild boar and venison as raciones for 800 to 1000 ptas.

Getting There & Away
Alsina Graells runs two daily buses to/from Úbeda, Baeza, Jaén and Granada. The main stop in Cazorla is Plaza de la Constitución. Quercus has timetable information. A couple of other buses run just between Úbeda and Cazorla.

PARQUE NATURAL DE CAZORLA
The 2140-sq-km Parque Natural de las Sierras de Cazorla, Segura y Las Villas (to give it its full title) is the biggest protected area in Spain. It's a crumpled, memorably beautiful region of several rugged mountain ranges, divided by high plains and deep valleys, often thickly forested. You stand a chance of seeing ibex, mouflon (a large wild sheep), red or fallow deer or wild boar here. The ibex lives mainly on rocky heights; the others prefer forests, but you may come across deer or boar on some of the main roads. Some 140 bird species nest in the park;

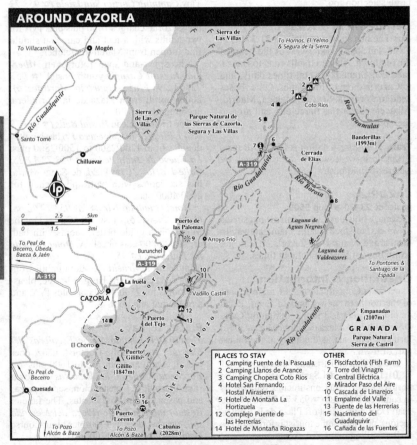

AROUND CAZORLA

PLACES TO STAY
1 Camping Fuente de la Pascuala
2 Camping Llanos de Arance
3 Camping Chopera Coto Rios
4 Hotel San Fernando; Hostal Mirasierra
5 Hotel de Montaña La Hortizuela
12 Complejo Puente de las Herrerías
14 Hotel de Montaña Riogazas

OTHER
6 Piscifactoria (Fish Farm)
7 Torre del Vinagre
8 Central Eléctrica
9 Mirador Paso del Aire
10 Cascada de Linarejos
11 Empalme del Valle
13 Puente de las Herrerías
15 Nacimiento del Guadalquivir
16 Cañada de las Fuentes

euro currency converter 100pta = €0.60

the lammergeier, which disappeared from the park in 1986, is being reintroduced.

The Guadalquivir, Andalucía's longest river, rises in the south of the park and flows north into the Embalse del Tranco de Beas reservoir, then west towards the Atlantic Ocean.

The best times to visit are late April to June, and September and October, when the vegetation is at its most colourful and the weather at its best. In spring, the flowers are magnificent. Of the park's 2300 plant species, 24 are unique, including the beautiful Cazorla violet. Peak visitor periods are Semana Santa, July and August.

Orientation & Information

The A-319 from Cazorla winds over the 1200m Puerto de las Palomas pass and down to the Empalme del Valle junction, where it turns north to follow the Guadalquivir valley.

The main information centre is the Centro de Interpretación Torre del Vinagre, 16km north of Empalme del Valle on the A-319; it's open daily, except Monday in winter, 11 am to 2 pm and for two or three afternoon hours. In an adjoining building is a Museo de Caza (Hunting Museum) with stuffed park wildlife, and just along the road is a botanic garden of the park's flora.

Editorial Alpina's 1:40,000 *Sierra de Cazorla,* covering the south of the park, and *Sierra de Segura*, covering the north, are the best maps. You should be able to get them locally. Lonely Planet's *Walking in Spain* details three-day walks in the park, including an 18km mountain loop from Cazorla.

Getting There & Away

Exploring the park is much easier on your own wheels, but limited bus services exist. Carcesa (☎ 953 72 11 42) runs buses daily except Sunday from Cazorla's Plaza de la Constitución to Coto Ríos (1¼ hours), via Empalme del Valle, Arroyo Frío and Torre del Vinagre. Schedules vary with the season: Quercus in Cazorla has timetables. At last check, buses left Cazorla at 5.45 or 6.30 am and 2.30 pm, and set off back from Coto Ríos at 7 or 8 am and 4.15 pm.

Sierra de Cazorla Drive

This itinerary of about 60km is a good introduction to the parts of the park nearest Cazorla for those with wheels, with a couple of stops to stretch your legs. It's all passable for ordinary cars, if bumpy in places.

Head first up to La Iruela, 1km east of Cazorla, and turn right along Carretera Virgen de la Cabeza (a sign says 'Ermita' and 'Merendero de Riogazas'). About 8km along here, during which the road ceases to be paved, is **El Chorro**, a gorge that is a good spot for watching vultures. Just beyond, where another unpaved road comes up from the south-west, head left to wind around over the **Puerto Lorente** pass and down to a junction after 12km. Fork right here and after 200m a 'Nacimiento del Guadalquivir' sign points down to the official **source of the Guadalquivir** on your left.

The road heads a short distance past the Nacimiento to the **Cañada de las Fuentes** picnic area, a convenient stop. From here head back northward down the beautiful valley of the infant Guadalquivir. At a T-junction after 14km, about 1km beyond the northern end of the Complejo Puente de las Herrerías, go left; after 400m **Sendero de la Cerrada del Utrero** begins on the right. This marked 2km loop walk takes you under imposing cliffs to the Cascada de Linarejos waterfall, then above a narrow reservoir on the Guadalquivir. After another 3.5km along the road you're at Empalme del Valle, from which it's 17km back to Cazorla.

Río Borosa Walk

Though it gets busy at weekends and holiday times, this walk of about seven hours return (plus stops) is the park's most popular for good reason. It follows the exuberantly vegetated course of the Río Borosa upstream to two beautiful mountain lakes; an ascent of 500m in the course of 12km from Torre del Vinagre. Using the bus to Torre del Vinagre, you can do it as a day trip from Cazorla.

A road signed 'Central Eléctrica', opposite Torre del Vinagre, soon crosses the Guadalquivir and, within 1km more, the Borosa. The marked start of the walk is on

ANDALUCÍA

your right beside the Borosa. After 40 minutes, diverge to the right from the main track along a path signed 'Cerrada de Elias' for a beautiful 30-minute section through the gorge of this name. Rejoining the main track, continue for 40 minutes to the Central Eléctrica, a small hydroelectric station. Just past this, a sign points you on up towards the Laguna de Valdeazores. This path will lead you, via some dramatic mountain scenery and two tunnels supplying water to the power station (there's room to stay dry as you go through), to the two lakes – Laguna de Aguas Negras (a reservoir), then the natural Laguna de Valdeazores.

The route is dotted with good, drinkable trackside springs, the last of them at the Central Electrica.

Hornos

Overlooking the northern end of the Embalse del Tranco, Hornos is a small village atop a high rocky outcrop with a small, ruined Islamic castle and panoramic views.

El Yelmo

About 10km north-east of Hornos on the A-317 is the Puerto de Horno de Peguera pass and junction. One kilometre to the north from here, a dirt road turns left to the top of El Yelmo (1809m), one of the most distinctive mountains in the north of the park. It's 5km to the top, an ascent of 360m – driveable, but better as a walk, with superb views and griffon vultures wheeling around the skies. At a fork after 1.75km, go right.

Segura de la Sierra

Easily the most spectacular and interesting village within the park, Segura sits 20km north of Hornos atop an 1100m hill crowned by a castle dominating the countryside around. When taken in 1214 by the Knights of Santiago, Segura was one of the very first Christian conquests in Andalucía.

As you approach the upper, older part of the village, there's a tourist office, open in Semana Santa and summer only, beside the Puerta Nueva arch. In other seasons tourist information is available 8 am to 3 pm weekdays from the ayuntamiento (☎ 953 48 02

80), just through the arch. Segura's major monuments are normally left open all day every day, but you might want to check this before proceeding. The **Baño Moro** (Muslim Bathhouse) from about 1150, on Calle Caballeros Santiaguistas, has three rooms (for cold, tepid and hot baths), a barrel vault with skylights, and horseshoe arches. The **castle**, at the top of the village, has Muslim (or maybe even earlier) origins. From its three-storey keep there are great views across to El Yelmo and far to the west.

Organised Tours

A number of operators offer trips to some of the park's less accessible areas, plus other activities. Hotels and camping grounds in the park can often arrange for them to pick you up.

The highest-profile operator is Quercus (☎ 953 72 01 15), some of whose guides speak English or French. It has offices in Cazorla and at Torre del Vinagre. Quercus offers 4WD trips from these centres to *zonas restringidas* (where vehicles are not normally allowed) for 3000 to 3700 ptas per person a half-day or 5000 to 5500 ptas a full day, as well as guided walks and photographic outings.

Places to Stay

There's plenty of accommodation in the park but little in the budget bracket except about a dozen camping grounds. At peak times it's worth booking ahead. See the Around Cazorla map for locations of the following places, except those in Hornos and Segura de la Sierra.

Complejo Puente de las Herrerías (☎/fax 953 72 70 90) has camping space for about 1000 people at 510 ptas per adult, per tent and per car, plus rooms and cabins costing from 6955 ptas for two people to 21,935 ptas for 10. Facilities include a restaurant and pool, and you can arrange activities such as horse riding and climbing.

Hotel de Montaña Riogazas (☎ 953 12 40 35, e hotelriogazas@cibercentro.es), at Km 4.5 on the road from La Iruela to El Chorro, is an attractive little hotel with singles/doubles for 4000/5800 ptas plus IVA. It opens June to October, plus the Christmas and Semana Santa holiday periods.

Most accommodation is dotted along the A-319 north of Empalme del Valle. At Arroyo Frío village, 6km from Empalme del Valle, the modern *Complejo Turístico Los Enebros* (☎ *953 72 71 10), Hotel Cazorla Valle* (☎ *953 72 71 00)* and *Hotel Montaña* (☎ *953 72 70 11)* all have doubles between 7000 and 9000 ptas.

Two kilometres north of Torre del Vinagre is the turning to the cosy *Hotel de Montaña La Hortizuela* (☎*/fax 953 71 31 50),* in a tranquil setting 1km off the A-319, where rooms with bath are 4500/5500 ptas plus IVA. It has a good restaurant and a pool.

A farther 1km north on the A-319 are *Hotel San Fernando* (☎ *953 71 30 69),* with rooms at 6700/8475 ptas plus IVA, and the older *Hostal Mirasierra* (☎*/fax 953 71 30 44),* charging 4200/5200 ptas plus IVA. Both have pools.

Within the next 4km on (or just off) the A-319 are three medium-sized *camping grounds* beside the Guadalquivir, all charging around 1100 ptas for two adults with a car and tent.

In Hornos, *Bar El Cruce* (☎ *953 49 50 35, Puerta Nueva 27)* has a few decent rooms with bath at 3100/3700 ptas, and good food. Round the corner, *El Mirador* restaurant (☎ *953 49 50 19, Puerta Nueva 11)* has eight rooms with bath for 2700/3900 ptas.

The only accommodation in Segura de la Sierra is *Mesón Jorge Manrique* (☎ *953 48 03 80, Calle de las Ordenanzas del Común 2),* near the ayuntamiento, with just a few rooms at 1800/3500 ptas, or 4000 ptas for a double with bath, and a small restaurant.

Almería Province

Andalucía's easternmost province is the most parched part of Spain, with large expanses of rocky semidesert. Remote and long impoverished, Almería has used its main resource, sunshine, to stage a bit of a comeback in recent decades, through tourism and intensive horticulture in ugly plastic greenhouses.

ALMERÍA
postcode 04080 • pop 168,000

As the chief port of the Córdoba caliphate and, later, capital of an 11th-century taifa, Islamic Almariya grew wealthy weaving silk from the silkworms of the Alpujarras. Devastated by an earthquake in 1522, Almería is today a likeable and lively port city, hub of a mining and horticultural region.

Orientation & Information

The centre lies between the Alcazaba fortress and the Rambla de Belén, a *paseo* created from a dry river bed. Paseo de Almería, cutting north-west from Rambla de Belén to the Puerta de Purchena intersection, is the main artery, with numerous banks.

The helpful provincial tourist office (☎ 950 62 11 17), on Plaza Bendicho, is open 10 am to 2 pm and 5 to 8 pm weekdays. The regional tourist office (☎ 950 27 43 55), at Parque de Nicolás Salmerón s/n, is open 9 am to 7 pm weekdays, and 10 am to 2 pm weekends.

The Policía Local (☎ 950 21 00 19) are at Calle Santos Zárate 11. The main public hospital, Hospital Torrecárdenas (☎ 950 21 21 00), is on Pasaje Torrecárdenas in the north of the city.

Alcazaba

The hefty hill-top Alcazaba on Calle Almanzor, founded in 955 by the Córdoba caliph Abd ar-Rahman III, still dominates Almería and commands great views, though earthquakes and time have spared little of its internal splendour.

The lowest of its three compounds, the Primer Recinto, originally served as a military camp and a refuge in times of siege. The Segundo Recinto was the heart of the Alcazaba. At its eastern end is the **Ermita de San Juan** chapel, converted from a mosque by the Catholic Monarchs, who took Almería in 1489. On the northern side are the remains of the Muslim rulers' palace, the **Palacio de Almotacín**. The **Ventana de la Odalisca** (Concubine's Window) here gets its name from a slave girl who, legend says, jumped to her death from the window after her Christian prisoner lover had been thrown from it. The

ANDALUCÍA

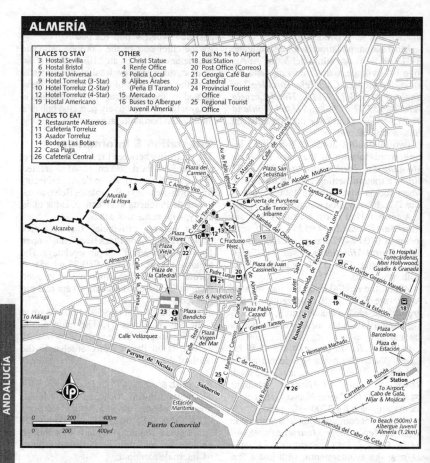

ALMERÍA

PLACES TO STAY
3 Hostal Sevilla
6 Hostal Bristol
7 Hostal Universal
9 Hotel Torreluz (3-Star)
10 Hotel Torreluz (2-Star)
12 Hotel Torreluz (4-Star)
19 Hostal Americano

PLACES TO EAT
2 Restaurante Alfareros
11 Cafetería Torreluz
13 Asador Torreluz
14 Bodega Las Botas
22 Casa Puga
26 Cafetería Central

OTHER
1 Christ Statue
4 Renfe Office
5 Policía Local
8 Aljibes Árabes
   (Peña El Taranto)
15 Mercado
16 Buses to Albergue
   Juvenil Almería

17 Bus No 14 to Airport
18 Bus Station
20 Post Office (Correos)
21 Georgia Café Bar
23 Catedral
24 Provincial Tourist
   Office
25 Regional Tourist
   Office

Tercer Recinto, at the top end of the Alcazaba, is a fortress added by the Catholic Monarchs.

It's open daily except 25 December and 1 January, 10 am to 2 pm and 5 to 8.30 pm from mid-June to September, and 9 am to 6.30 pm at other times (free with EU passport or identity card, 250 ptas otherwise).

Catedral

Almería's weighty cathedral is at the heart of the old part of the city below the Alcazaba. Begun in 1524, its fortress-like appearance, with six towers, was dictated by pirate raids from North Africa.

The spacious interior, open 6 to 8 pm daily (free), has a Gothic ribbed ceiling and uses jasper and local marble in its trimmings. The chapel behind the main altar contains the tomb of Bishop Villalán, the cathedral's founder, whose broken-nosed image is a work of Juan de Orea, who also created the Sacristía Mayor with its fine carved stonework.

Beach

A long, grey-sand beach fronts the palm-lined Paseo Marítimo, east of the city's centre.

Places to Stay

The Inturjoven youth hostel, *Albergue Juvenil Almería* (☎ 950 26 97 88, Calle Isla de Fuerteventura s/n), accommodates 170, nearly all in double rooms. It's 1.5km east of the centre, beside the Estadio de la Juventud stadium, three blocks north of Avenida del Cabo de Gata. Take bus No 1 'Universidad' from the eastern end of Rambla del Obispo Orbera and ask for the albergue or the stadium.

Hostal Americano (☎ 950 28 10 15, Avenida de la Estación 6) is a good choice near the bus and train stations. Well-kept singles/doubles cost from 2850/5540 ptas with washbasin, to 3915/6410 ptas with bathroom.

Hostal Universal (☎ 950 23 55 57, Puerta de Purchena 3) has simple but sizable rooms for 2000/4000 ptas, with shared bathrooms. Nearby, the better *Hostal Sevilla* (☎ 950 23 00 09, Calle de Granada 23) has rooms with TV and bath for 3600/5500 ptas plus IVA. *Hostal Bristol* (☎ 950 23 15 95, Plaza San Sebastián 8) is similar.

Hotel Torreluz (☎ 950 23 43 99), on Plaza de las Flores, is actually three separate hotels: the two-star establishment has good rooms for 5350/8825 ptas; the three-star charges 7385/11,425 ptas; and a double in four-star luxury is 19,260 ptas.

Places to Eat

A bustling local breakfast favourite is *Cafetería Torreluz* on Calle de las Flores. The classy *Asador Torreluz* grill on Calle Fructuoso Pérez offers fish and meat dishes between 1500 and 3000 ptas. *Bodega Las Botas* (Calle Fructuoso Pérez 3) is an atmospheric sherry bar serving varied tapas, mediaraciones (600 to 1100 ptas) and raciones.

Simple *Restaurante Alfareros* (Calle Marcos 6), near Puerta de Purchena, has a good three-course lunch and dinner *menú*, including wine, for 1000 ptas. *Casa Puga* (Calle Jovellanos 7) has few rivals as Almería's best tapas bar. Shelves of ancient wine bottles set the tone, and tasty bites such as swordfish *a la plancha* cost a reasonable 100 to 125 ptas each.

Bright *Cafetería Central* on Avenida de Federico García Lorca serves pasta and salads

for around 700 ptas, and platos combinados and main dishes from 700 to 2000 ptas.

Entertainment

A dozen or two music bars cluster in the streets between the post office and cathedral. Some open from late afternoon. The veteran *Georgia Café Bar* (☎ 950 25 25 70, Calle Padre Luque 17) sometimes stages live jazz.

Live flamenco often happens at weekends at the *Peña El Taranto* (☎ 950 23 50 57), which was recently on the verge of moving into the renovated Aljibes Árabes (Arab Water Cisterns) on Calle Tenor Iribarne.

Getting There & Away

Air Almería airport (☎ 950 21 37 00) receives flights from several European countries (mainly charter) and has daily Iberia scheduled services to/from Barcelona and Madrid. Tarleton Direct (☎ 01604-633633 in the UK) specialises in flights to Almería from Manchester and London. For one-way international fares leaving Almería, try Tarleton Direct locally (☎ 950 33 37 34) or other agencies such as Viajes Cemo (☎ 950 62 70 19).

Bus The bus station is 400m east of Rambla de Belén on Plaza Barcelona. Five or more daily buses run to Granada (2¼ hours, 1300 ptas), eight to Málaga (3¼ hours, 1945 ptas), three to Sevilla (five hours) and 10 or more to Murcia, plus others to Jaén, Úbeda, Córdoba, Madrid, Valencia and Barcelona.

Train The train station (☎ 950 25 11 35) is on Plaza de la Estación, 200m south of the bus station. Four daily trains run to/from Granada (2¼ to three hours, 1610 to 1775 ptas), three to/from Sevilla and two to/from Madrid.

Car & Motorcycle Avis, Europcar, Hertz and local company Atesa (☎ 950 29 31 31) have car rental desks at the airport.

Boat Trasmediterránea (☎ 950 23 61 55), at the Estación Marítima, sails to/from Melilla six days a week, and three times daily from mid-June to late August. The trip takes up to eight hours. The cheapest passenger

ANDALUCÍA

accommodation, a *butaca* (seat), is 4020 ptas one way; a car is 16,125 ptas.

Getting Around
The airport is 9km east of the city; the No 14 'Aeropuerto' bus runs between the city (western end of Calle del Doctor Gregorio Marañón) and airport every 30 to 45 minutes from about 7 am to 9.30 pm.

AROUND ALMERÍA
Mini Hollywood
Beyond Benahadux, to the north of Almería, the landscape becomes a series of canyons and rocky wastes that look straight out of the Arizona badlands, and in the 1960s and '70s Western movie makers shot dozens of films here. Locals played Indians, outlaws and cavalry while Clint Eastwood, Raquel Welch, Charles Bronson and co did the talking bits. The movie industry has left behind three Wild West town sets that are open as tourist attractions. Mini Hollywood (☎ 950 36 52 36), the best known and best kept, is 24km from Almería on the Tabernas road. Parts of more than 100 films, including *The Magnificent Seven* and *The Good, the Bad and the Ugly,* were shot here. At noon and 5 pm a bank hold-up and shoot-out is staged.

Also here is a Reserva Zoológica with 100-odd species of African and Iberian fauna.

Both are normally open 10 am to 9 pm daily from April to October, to 7 pm daily except Monday in other months. Adult/child tickets cost 1200/850 ptas for Mini Hollywood or 2395/1200 ptas for both attractions.

You need your own vehicle to visit from Almería.

Níjar
Attractive and unusual glazed pottery, and colourful striped cotton rugs known as *jarapas,* are made and sold in this small town 31km north-east of Almería. It's well worth a little detour if you're driving this way.

CABO DE GATA
Some of Spain's most beautiful and least crowded beaches are strung between cliffs and capes of awesome grandeur around this arid promontory east of Almería city. Though Cabo de Gata is certainly not undiscovered, it has a wild, elemental feel and is far enough from the beaten track to seem positively deserted compared with most Andalucian beach areas. With a couple of exceptions in July and August, its scattered villages remain very low-key.

You can walk along, or not far from, the coast from Retamar in the north-west to Agua Amarga in the north-east, but there's little shade (see Lonely Planet's *Walking in Spain*).

It's worth calling ahead for accommodation anywhere on Cabo de Gata during Semana Santa and in July and August. Camping is only allowed in the four organised camping grounds.

Getting There & Away
From Almería bus station there are four or more buses daily to El Cabo de Gata village by Autocares Becerra (☎ 950 22 44 03); two daily on weekdays, one or two on Saturday, and one on Sunday from around June to September, to San José by Autocares Bernardo (☎ 950 25 04 22); one daily except Sunday to Las Negras by TM (☎ 950 22 81 78); and two a week to Agua Amarga by Autocares Bergarsan (☎ 950 26 42 92) and to La Isleta del Moro by Autocares Bernardo.

There's no bus service from Mojácar.

Centro de Interpretación Las Amoladeras
About 2.5km west of Ruescas, this is the main information centre (☎ 950 16 04 35) for the **Parque Natural de Cabo de Gata-Níjar**, which covers Cabo de Gata's 60km coast plus a thick strip of hinterland. It should be open 10 am to 2 pm and 5 to 9 pm daily from mid-July to mid-September, and until 3 pm daily except Monday at other times.

El Cabo de Gata Village
Fronted by a long straight beach, this village (officially San Miguel de Cabo de Gata) is composed largely of holiday houses and apartments, but has an old nucleus, with a small fishing fleet, at the southern end. A bank on Calle Iglesia has an ATM.

CABO DE GATA

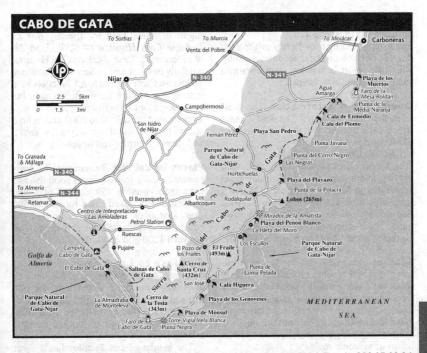

South of the village stretch the **Salinas de Cabo de Gata** salt-extraction lagoons. In spring many greater flamingoes and other birds call in here while migrating to breeding grounds farther north. Some stay on here to breed, then others arrive in summer: by late August there can be 1000 flamingoes here. There's a public viewing hide just off the road 3km south of the village. You should see a good variety of birds any time except winter, when the salinas are drained.

Places to Stay & Eat

Camping Cabo de Gata (☎ 950 16 04 43), near the beach, 2km north of the village, is open all year, charging 2200 ptas plus IVA for two adults with a car and tent.

Restaurante Mediterráneo (☎ 950 37 11 37), towards the southern end of the village seafront, has a few singles/doubles for 4000/6000 ptas, with shared baths. It serves decent seafood and meat for 750 to 1100 ptas. On the left as you enter the village from

Ruescas, *Hostal Chiri-Bus* (☎ 950 37 00 36, Calle La Sardina 2) has five nice, modern rooms with bathroom for 3500/5000 ptas. Nearby, *Pizzeria Pedro* (Calle Islas de Tabarca 2) serves fine pizzas and pasta at middling prices.

Hostal Las Dunas (☎ 950 37 00 72, Calle Barrionuevo 58), at the northern end of the village, has clean rooms with bath for 4500/6500 ptas plus IVA.

Faro de Cabo de Gata & Around

Beyond the Salinas de Cabo de Gata, the road winds 4km round the cliffs to the **Faro de Cabo de Gata** lighthouse at the promontory's tip. A turning by *Bar José y María* (serving seafood), just before the lighthouse, leads up to the **Torre Vigía Vela Blanca**, an 18th-century watchtower atop 200m cliffs, with awesome views. Here the road ends but a walking and cycling track continues down to Playa de Mónsul (one hour on foot).

ANDALUCÍA

San José
postcode 04118 • pop 175

San José, spreading round a bay on the eastern side of Cabo de Gata, becomes a mildly chic little resort in summer, but remains a small, pleasant, low-rise place.

Orientation & Information The road from the north becomes San José's main street, Calle Correo, with the beach a couple of blocks down to the left.

On Calle Correo you'll find a natural park information office (☎ 950 38 02 99), open varying hours daily (except Tuesday from September to May), a bank, an ATM and a small supermarket. A municipal tourist office (same phone and hours) stands on the nearby plaza. These offices can tell you about bicycle rental, horse riding, boat trips and diving.

Beaches San José has a sandy beach but two of the best beaches on Cabo de Gata lie south-west along a dirt road. **Playa de los Genoveses**, a broad strip of sand about 1km long, with shallow waters, is 4.5km away. **Playa de Mónsul**, 2.5km farther on, is a shorter length of grey sand, backed by huge lumps of volcanic rock.

Places to Stay *Camping Tau* (☎ 950 38 01 66), open April to September, has a shady site 400m from San José beach, with room for 185 people at around 500 ptas per person, per tent and per car. Follow the 'Tau' sign pointing left as you approach central San José from the north.

Albergue Juvenil de San José (☎ 950 38 03 53, *Calle Montemar s/n)* is a friendly non-Inturjoven youth hostel that holds 86 people in bunk rooms of up to eight, at 1300 ptas a night. It opens 1 April to 1 October, and for Christmas-New Year and long weekends. Heading towards Camping Tau, turn right after crossing a river bed, then first left.

Hostal Bahía and *Hostal Bahía Plaza* (both ☎ 950 38 03 07), on Calle Correo in the centre, have 34 attractive singles/doubles with bathroom, for 5000/7500 ptas.

Half a dozen other hostales and hotels have similar or higher prices. If you fancy staying a while, consider renting an apartment.

For something slightly different for two nights or more, head for friendly *Bar El Refugio Cala Higuera* (☎ 950 52 56 25, ℮ *albergerar@larural.es)*, on Cala Higuera, a pebbly bay just east of San José. Continue 200m past Camping Tau to a T-junction, then turn right and follow the signs. Ten rustic but cosy rooms for two to five people, some with kitchen, cost from 3000 to 8000 ptas in high season (maybe less if you stay a few days), and there's a terrace restaurant.

Places to Eat *Bar-Restaurante El Emigrante* on Calle Correo serves good fish and meat mains around 850 to 1400 ptas, and omelettes or a mixed salad for 400 to 500 ptas. Just back from the far end of the beach, the popular *El Ancla* has seafood between 1200 and 2100 ptas.

San José to Las Negras

The rugged coast north-east of San José allows only two small settlements, the odd fort and a few beaches before the village of Las Negras, 17km away as the crow flies. The road spends most of its time ducking inland.

The hamlet of **Los Escullos** has a short beach. You can walk here along a track from Cala Higuera (see Places to Stay in the San José section). The large *Camping Los Escullos* (☎ 950 38 98 11), 900m from the beach, is open all year. *Hotel Los Escullos* (☎ 950 38 97 33), by the beach, has about 20 rooms at 8000 or 9000 ptas. *Casa Emilio* (☎ 950 38 97 32), behind it, has eight singles/doubles for 4500/6500 ptas. All three places have restaurants.

La Isleta del Moro, 1km farther north-east, is a tiny pueblo with a beach and a couple of fishing boats. *Casa Café de la Loma* (☎ 950 52 52 11), just above the village, run by a friendly English-speaking German, has six nice rooms starting at 3500/4500 ptas, and in summer a *vegetarian restaurant* with good weekly flamenco nights.

From here the road heads inland past the former gold-mining village of Rodalquilar. About 1km past Rodalquilar is the turning to **Playa del Playazo**, a good beach between two headlands, 2km along a level track. From

ANDALUCÍA

here you can walk near the coast to **Las Negras**, which is on a pebbly beach. *Camping La Caleta (☎ 950 52 52 37)*, open all year in a cove 1km south of Las Negras, has little shade but a nice pool. *Hostal Arrecife (☎ 950 38 81 40, Calle Bahía 6)* has rooms with bathroom for 4000/6000 ptas. Other accommodation is mostly holiday apartments and houses to let.

Las Negras to Agua Amarga

There's no road along this secluded, cliff-lined stretch of coast, but walkers can take an up-and-down path of about 11km giving access to several beaches. At **Playa San Pedro**, one hour from Las Negras, a ruined hamlet houses a small hippie colony. It's 1½ hours on to **Cala del Plomo** beach, with another tiny village, then 1½ hours more to Agua Amarga.

Drivers must head inland from Las Negras through Hortichuelas. A mostly unsealed road heads north-east cross-country from the bus shelter in Fernán Pérez. Keep to the main track at all turnings and after 10km you'll reach a sealed road running down to Agua Amarga from the N-341.

Agua Amarga is a pleasant tourist-cum-fishing village on a straight sandy beach. *Hostal Restaurante La Palmera (☎ 950 13 82 08, Calle Aguada s/n)*, at the eastern end of the beach, has 10 pleasant rooms for 7000 to 11,000 ptas plus IVA (depending on views). On Calle La Lomilla just up from the western end of the beach, *Hotel Family (☎ 950 13 80 14)* has nine lovely rooms from 8000 to 12,000 ptas, including a big breakfast. An excellent four-course *menú*, for 2000 ptas, is served nightly and for weekend lunches.

MOJÁCAR

postcode 04638 • pop 4000

Mojácar, north-east of Cabo de Gata, is two towns: the old Mojácar Pueblo, a jumble of white, cube-shaped houses on a hill top 2km inland, and Mojácar Playa, a modern beach resort strip, 7km long but only a few blocks wide. Though dominated by tourism, the Pueblo is very picturesque, and Mojácar Playa has few high-rise buildings, a long, clean beach, and quite a lively summer scene.

From the 13th to 15th centuries, Mojácar found itself on the Granada emirate's eastern frontier, finally falling to the Catholic Monarchs in 1488. Tucked away in an isolated corner of one of Spain's most backward regions, it was decaying and half-abandoned by the mid-20th century, before its mayor started luring artists and others with giveaway property offers.

Orientation & Information

Pueblo and Playa are joined by a road that heads uphill from a junction by the Parque Comercial shopping centre towards the northern end of Mojácar Playa.

The tourist office (☎ 950 47 51 62) is on Calle Glorieta, just off Mojácar Pueblo's main square Plaza Nueva, in the same building as the post office and Policía Local (☎ 950 47 20 00). It's open 10 am to 2 pm and 5 to 8 pm weekdays (9 am to 4 pm from about November to May), and until 1 pm Saturday.

Things to See & Do

Exploring the Pueblo is mainly a matter of wandering the winding streets with their flower-decked balconies and nosing into craft shops, galleries and boutiques. **El Castillo** at the topmost point is private property (and not a castle), but there are great views from the public terraces around it. The fortress-style **Iglesia de Santa María** dates from 1560 and may have once been a mosque.

The most touching spot is the **Fuente Mora** (Moorish Fountain) in the lower part of the Pueblo. Though remodelled in modern times, it maintains the Muslim tradition of turning water into art. An inscription records the speech made here, according to legend, by Alavez, the last Islamic governor of Mojácar, to the envoy of the Catholic Monarchs in 1488. It translates, in part:

Though my people have lived in Spain more than 700 years, you say to us: 'You are foreigners, go back to the sea.' In Africa an inhospitable coast awaits us, where they will surely tell us, as you do – and certainly with more reason – 'You are foreigners: cross the sea by which you came and go back to your own land'. Treat us like brothers, not enemies, and let us continue working the land of our ancestors.

ANDALUCÍA

Places to Stay

Mojácar Pueblo The small but pleasant *Camping El Quinto* (☎ 950 47 87 04), 2km west on the Turre road, charges 1900 ptas plus IVA for two adults with a car and tent. *Pensión Casa Justa* (☎ 950 47 83 72, Calle Morote 7) is reasonable value with singles/doubles at 2500/5000 ptas (6000 or 7000 ptas for doubles with bath). Nearby, *Hostal La Esquinica* (☎ 950 47 50 09, Calle Cano 1) charges 2500/4500 ptas. The charming *Hostal Mamabel's* (☎ 950 47 24 48, Calle Embajadores 5) has eight big, characterful rooms, with sea views and bath, for 9000 ptas plus IVA a double. *Pensión El Torreón* (☎ 950 47 52 59, Calle Jazmín 4) is another beautiful house with great views, and just five doubles, with shared bath, at 6000 ptas. Apparently Walt Disney was born here!

Mojácar Playa The shady *Camping El Cantal* (☎ 950 47 82 04), 1km south of the Parque Comercial, has room for 800 people at 2300 ptas plus IVA for two adults with car and tent. *Hotel Bahía* (☎ 950 47 80 10), just south, has doubles with bath for 6500 ptas.

Hotel Playa Río Abajo (☎ 950 47 89 28), at the northern end of town, has 18 nice rooms in a pleasant garden fronting the beach for up to 9000 ptas plus IVA. It has a pool, restaurant and bar. From La Rumina bus stop, head towards the beach and you'll find it.

Places to Eat

Mojácar Pueblo *Restaurante El Viento del Desierto*, on Plaza Frontón, is good value, with main courses such as beef bourguignon or rabbit in mustard for 650 to 800 ptas. *Hostal Mamabel's* serves up some of the best food in Mojácar, with a three-course *menú* for 1800 ptas, plus drinks and IVA.

Mojácar Playa There are plenty of places along Paseo del Mediterráneo. *Restaurante Chino La Gran Muralla*, 2km south of the Parque Comercial, has fair-value Chinese set meals from 625 to 1750 ptas. *Antonella*, just above the beach near Cueva del Lobo bus stop, pulls in the customers with its medium-priced pizzas and pasta. In low season it only opens evenings and for Sunday lunch.

Entertainment

Lively bars in Mojácar Pueblo include *La Escalera* on Calle Horno, *Budú Pub* on Calle Estación Nueva and *Siglo XXI* on Calle Enmedio. To burn up some energy after midnight on weekends and holidays from Semana Santa to October, head for one of Mojácar's open-air discotecas: *Master* halfway between Pueblo and Playa, *Pascha* by the beach just north of Camping El Cantal, or *Tuareg* on the Carboneras road 3.5km out of Mojácar Playa. At *Tito's* bar, towards the southern end of Mojácar Playa, you can sit on outdoor steps overlooking the beach, sometimes to the sound of live music.

Getting There & Away

Buses stop at the Parque Comercial and at the Fuente stop at the foot of Mojácar Pueblo. The tourist office has timetables. Two or more daily buses run to/from Almería (1¾ hours), Murcia (two to three hours), Granada (4¼ hours) and Madrid. Buy tickets on the bus except for Madrid, which you need to book at a travel agency. Buses to Alicante, Valencia and Barcelona go from Vera, 16km north.

Getting Around

A local bus service runs a circuit from the southern to northern ends of Mojácar Playa, then back to the Parque Comercial, up to the Pueblo (Calle Glorieta), then back down to the Parque Comercial and Hotel Indalo at the southern end of the Playa. It runs about every half-hour in summer, and every hour in winter.

Extremadura

Extremadura, a large, sparsely populated tableland bordering Portugal, is one of Spain's least-known gems. It's not totally without tourists but is far enough from the beaten track to give you a genuine sense of exploration. The *extremeños* themselves have a flair for this: many epic 16th-century conquistadors of the Americas, including Francisco Pizarro and Hernán Cortés, sprang from this land.

Though much of Extremadura is flat, wooded sierras rise up along its northern, eastern and southern fringes. The north particularly is a sequence of beautiful ranges and green valleys, dotted with old-fashioned villages that make for great exploring.

Extremadura's most interesting towns form a convenient triangle in the centre. Cáceres and Trujillo are full of reminders of the conquistadors and the Reconquista. Mérida was the main city of the Iberian Peninsula in Roman times and today has Spain's finest collection of Roman ruins.

Two of Spain's major rivers, the Tajo and the Guadiana, cross Extremadura from east to west. Those with an interest in wildlife should do their utmost to get to the craggy Parque Natural Monfragüe, straddling the Tajo between Plasencia and Trujillo, which has some of Spain's most spectacular bird life.

The name Extremadura probably means 'beyond the Río Duero'. In the 10th and 11th centuries the name was given to territory held by Christians in what's now southern Castilla y León.

In the 13th century, when most of Extremadura fell to Alfonso IX of León, the name was transferred to the newly acquired lands. Huge tracts of territory, granted to the knightly orders and nobility who had led the Reconquista, were turned over to livestock, especially sheep, leaving scant chance of gain for the rest of the population, a reason why many extremeños were willing to try their luck in the Americas in the 16th century (see the boxed text 'Extremadura & America' later

Highlights

- Charming Trujillo, cradle of conquistadors
- Spain's finest Roman remains at Mérida
- Spectacular birds of prey at Parque Natural Monfragüe
- Exploring the lush valleys, ancient villages and high ranges of the north
- Cáceres' perfectly preserved medieval centre
- Serene Guadalupe, tucked away among the hills

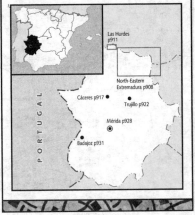

in this chapter). The riches some of these folk brought back turned Extremadura briefly into a prosperous place, but Spain's expulsion of the *moriscos* (Christianised Muslims) in the 17th century contributed to a decline.

In the 1970s a new wave of emigration took many hard-up extremeños to jobs in northern Spain and abroad. There's still minimal industry: sheep and pig farming, and olive, cork and fruit-growing are among the region's most important economic activities.

Extremadura is very hot in high summer and can be bitingly chilly in winter. Climatically, the best times to travel here are the second half of April, May, September and the

EXTREMADURA

EXTREMADURA

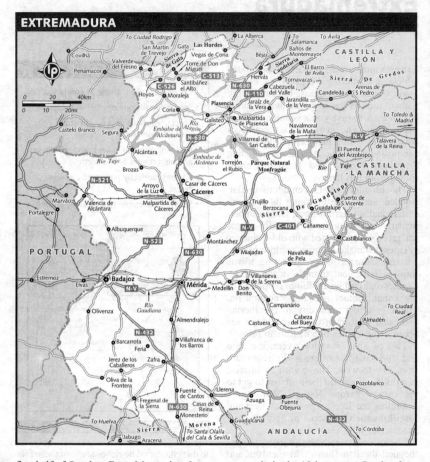

first half of October. From May to late June you could have a ball touring the main towns' major fiestas. Among other diversions, this is when Spain's top matadors head for extremeño bullrings. A good Web site to check before heading for Extremadura is www.turismoextremadura.com.

Extremadura is often said to have two types of food: the fine fare that originated in its wealthy monasteries and convents, and a more rough and ready peasant cuisine. The Convento de San Benito at Alcántara concocted recipes so good that even the French borrowed them when their armies came this

way early in the 19th century. *Perdiz al estilo/modo de Alcántara* is a dish you'll find on many good menus.

From the peasant tradition comes the delicious *caldereta*, a hearty casserole of lamb *(cordero)* or kid *(cabrito)*, and simple roast lamb *(cordero asado)*. But you might think twice about *chanfaina*, an offal stew, or *ancas de rana*, frogs' legs, which usually come deep-fried *(rebozadas)*.

Extremadura is pig country too and the *cerdos ibéricos* that feed on the acorns from its plentiful oak trees end up as some of the choicest *jamón* (cured ham) in Spain. Jamón from the villages of Montánchez and Piornal is among the best.

Basic Extremadura country wine is known as *pitarra*. More unusual and potent is the range of fruit liqueurs and potent *aguardientes* (eaux de vie, 40%-plus alc/vol) from the Valle del Jerte and elsewhere.

Northern Extremadura

In the far north of Extremadura you're in the western reaches of the Cordillera Central, a beautiful jigsaw of uplands and valleys forming an arc around Plasencia from the Sierra de Gredos in the east to the Sierra de Gata in the west. In the north-east, three lush green valleys – La Vera, the Valle del Jerte and the Valle del Ambroz – stretch down towards the old city of Plasencia. Watered by rushing mountain streams called *gargantas*, and dotted with almost medieval villages, these valleys have a good network of places to stay and some excellent walking routes. A useful tool is the Editorial Alpina guide booklet *Sistema Central: Valle del Jerte, Valle del Ambroz, La Vera,* which includes a map showing many walking routes. Try to get it before you arrive: if not, the tourist office in Cabezuela del Valle (see that section later) may have copies.

The remote and mysterious Las Hurdes region in the northernmost tip of Extremadura has a harsher sort of beauty, while the Sierra de Gata in the north-west is almost as isolated, but prettier and more fertile.

LA VERA

La Vera is the northern side of the valley of the Río Tiétar, at the foot of the western Sierra de Gredos and the Sierra de Tormantos. Its many crops include raspberries, tobacco, asparagus and paprika. The C-501 from Plasencia to Arenas de San Pedro in Castilla y León runs along the valley.

Information

There's a helpful tourist office (☎ 927 17 05 87, e turisma@ayto-jaraiz.es), open daily (mornings only on weekends), at Plaza Mayor 18 in Jaraíz de la Vera, and another (☎ 927 56 04 60) at Plaza de la Constitución 1, beside the church in Jarandilla de la Vera. Most sizeable villages in the region have banks and post offices.

Things to See & Do

Cuacos de Yuste, 45km north-east of Plasencia, has its share of typical medieval La Vera streets, with half-timbered houses leaning at odd angles and overhanging upper storeys supported by timber or stone pillars. Look for the Casa de Juan de Austria on Plaza de Juan de Austria, where Carlos I's illegitimate son Don Juan de Austria – later a charismatic general and admiral who won the Battle of Lepanto in 1571 – stayed while visiting his father at the Monasterio de Yuste.

Two kilometres north-west of Cuacos is the **Monasterio de Yuste**, to which the gouty Carlos I, having handed over the world's biggest empire to his legitimate sons, retired in 1557 to spend his dying years. The serenity of the setting makes it easy to understand his choice. The monastery is occupied by a closed order of Hieronymite monks, but the church and the simple royal chambers – with the ailing monarch's bed placed to give him a direct view of the altar – are open 9.30 am to 12.30 pm and 3.30 to 6.30 pm Monday to Saturday, 9.30 to 11.30 am and 3.30 to 6.30 pm Sunday. Entry is by guided tour in Spanish (100 ptas).

The road to the monastery continues 7km to **Garganta la Olla**, another picturesque village from where you can head over the 1269m **Puerto de Piornal** pass to Piornal and the Valle del Jerte.

Jarandilla de la Vera, 10km north-east of Cuacos de Yuste, is a bigger village with a 15th-century fortress-church on the main square (below the main road), and a *parador* occupying the 15th-century castle where Carlos I stayed for a few months while Yuste was being readied for him. A Roman bridge over the Garganta Jaranda below the village makes a focus for short rambles. Of the longer walks, the Ruta de Carlos V (see Valle del Jerte later in this chapter) is one of the most enticing. To start this walk from the

EXTREMADURA

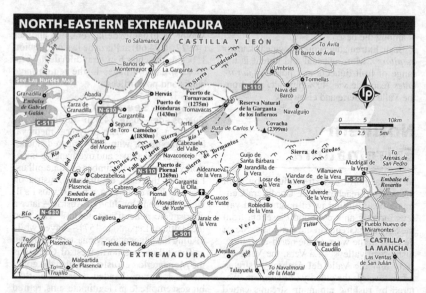

NORTH-EASTERN EXTREMADURA

Jarandilla end, head north-west out of the village along the C-501 for a few minutes. Opposite the 'Camping Jaranda 300m' sign is a curve of disused road on the right, with a track off it that runs up between a hedge and a red-brick building. At the end of the hedge the track bends left, then right. At this second bend look for a faint arrow on the wall pointing you up a path to the left beside a wire fence. This is the Ruta de Carlos V.

Other La Vera villages with particularly fine traditional architecture are **Jaraíz de la Vera**, **Valverde de la Vera** and **Villanueva de la Vera**, which also contains the sparse remains of a 15th-century castle.

Places to Stay & Eat

There are camping grounds – often with good riverside positions – in many villages. Most only open from March/April to September/October, but *Camping Godoy* (☎ 927 57 08 38) at Losar and *Camping La Vera* (☎ 927 56 06 11) at Jarandilla stay open all year. Both charge 450 ptas per car, per tent and per person.

On the main road in Cuacos de Yuste, *Pensión Sol* (☎ 927 17 22 41) has good singles/doubles for 1900/2900 ptas. *Hostal Moregón*

(☎ 927 17 21 81), two doors along, gives you rooms with bath for 3500/6000 ptas plus IVA. Both have restaurants.

In Jarandilla de la Vera, *Hostal Jaranda* (☎ 927 56 02 06, e hoteljaranda@rete mail.es, Avenida Soledad Vega Ortiz 101) on the main road has rooms with bath for 4500/7400 ptas plus IVA, including breakfast, and a *menú del día* (daily set meal) with wine for 1200 ptas plus IVA. *Hostal Marbella* (☎ 927 56 02 18), a few doors along, charges 5000 ptas plus IVA for doubles. *Hostal La Posada de Pizarro* (☎ 927 56 07 27, Calle Cuesta de los Carros 1), in the lower part of the village, has doubles with bath for 6500 ptas plus IVA and is run by a friendly, English-speaking owner. *Parador de Jarandilla* (☎ 927 56 01 17, e jarandilla@parador.es) is suitably splendid, with rooms for 14,000/17,500 ptas plus IVA.

Getting There & Away

Mirat runs a bus on weekdays from Cáceres and Plasencia to Talayuela (Sunday, to Madrigal de la Vera), stopping at the villages on the C-501 in La Vera. There are also one or two Mirat buses on weekdays from

Plasencia to as far as Garganta la Olla and Losar de la Vera. From Madrid's Estación Sur de Autobuses, the Doaldi line runs daily buses to La Vera.

VALLE DEL JERTE

This valley, separated by the Sierra de Tormantos from La Vera, grows half of Spain's cherries and turns into a sea of white blossom in April. The N-110 Plasencia-Ávila road runs up the valley, crossing into Castilla y León by the 1275m Puerto de Tornavacas pass. Tourist information is available from the Asociación de Turismo Rural del Valle del Jerte (☎ 927 47 25 58), Paraje de Peñas Albas s/n, Cabezuela del Valle.

Things to See & Do

The village of Piornal, at a height of 1200m on the south-eastern flank of the valley, is a good base for walks along the Sierra de Tormantos via the PR-19 path, or down to Navaconcejo in the valley via the PR-15. The lower part of the village, below the main road, is the more old-fashioned. Piornal temperatures can be pleasant in August but cold in September and can even snow in early April!

In the valley, Cabezuela del Valle has a particularly medieval main street, Calle El Hondón. A 35km road crosses from just north of Cabezuela over the 1430m Puerto de Honduras to Hervás in the Valle del Ambroz. For walkers, the PR-10 trail to Gargantilla climbs roughly parallel – it's a one-day walk. From Jerte, there are walks in the beautiful Reserva Natural de la Garganta de los Infiernos, focused on a mountain river tumbling down the Sierra de Tormantos.

Tornavacas, with a huddled, medieval centre, is the starting point of the Ruta de Carlos V. This 28km trail (PR-1) is marked by red and white arrows and follows the scenic route by which Carlos I (who was also Charles V of the Holy Roman Empire – hence the path's name) was carried over the mountains to Jarandilla de la Vera on his way to Yuste (see La Vera earlier in this chapter). It's possible to walk it in one day – just as Carlos' bearers did back in the 1550s. To start, from Tornavacas' Plaza de la

Iglesia head down Calle Real de Medio past the *ayuntamiento* (town hall), and keep going down past the post office *(correos)*. Turn left just past the Ermita de los Humilladeros, a little chapel with black railings, cross a small bridge and turn right. The route crosses the Sierra de Tormantos by the 1479m Collado (or Puerto) de las Yeguas.

Places to Stay & Eat

Camping Río Jerte (☎ 927 17 30 06), 1.5km south-west of Navaconcejo, is open all year and charges 475 per person, per tent and per car. *Camping Valle del Jerte* (☎ 927 47 01 27) by the Río Jerte 2km south-west of Jerte village, near the entrance to the Reserva Natural de la Garganta de los Infiernos, is open from mid-March to September, and charges slightly less.

In Piornal, *Pensión Los Piornos* (☎ 927 47 60 55) on Plaza de las Eras near the bus stop charges 2000/4000 ptas for plain singles/doubles. About 1km out of Piornal on the road to Garganta la Olla, *La Serrana Hospedería* (☎ 927 47 60 34, e icb@bme.es) provides high-quality hotel facilities for an affordable 5000/7000 ptas plus IVA.

In Cabezuela del Valle, *Hotel Aljama* (☎ 927 47 22 91, Calle Federico Bajo s/n), almost touching the church across the street, has nice rooms for 3000/4900 ptas plus IVA. There are numerous *eateries* on nearby Calle El Hondón.

Hotel Los Arenales (☎ 927 47 02 50), 2km south-west of Jerte on the N-110, has good rooms with bath for 4000/6000 ptas plus IVA, and a restaurant.

Hostal Puerto de Tornavacas (☎ 927 19 40 97), a couple of kilometres up the N-110 from Tornavacas, is an inn-style place with rooms for 2500/4600 ptas plus IVA, and a *restaurant* specialising in extremeño food.

Top of the range for the area is *Hospedería Valle del Jerte* (☎ 927 47 04 02, e deljertehosp@tpi.informail.es, Calle Ramón Cepeda 18) in the heart of Jerte. Unlike most *hospederías*, it has a modern feel and an out-of-place Japanese garden. It will cost you 10,000/15,000 ptas plus IVA per night.

Good local *trout* is available in almost every eatery in the Valle del Jerte.

Getting There & Away

From Plasencia there's one bus a day, weekdays, to Piornal and four a day, weekdays (one on Saturday and Sunday), up the Valle del Jerte to Tornavacas.

VALLE DEL AMBROZ

This broader valley west of the Valle del Jerte is the route of the N-630 running north from Plasencia to Béjar and Salamanca in Castilla y León.

Hervás

postcode 10700 • pop 3965

The valley's main focus of interest is this pleasant small town with the best surviving 15th-century **barrio judío** (Jewish quarter) in Extremadura, where many Jews took refuge in the hope of avoiding the Inquisition. There's a tourist office (☎ 927 47 36 18) at Calle de Braulio Navas 4, open 10 am to 2 pm and 4 to 6 pm Tuesday to Friday (mornings only on weekends). El Lagar crafts shop on Rincón de Don Benito has displays on old Jewish life. To get your bearings, you can climb up to the **Iglesia de Santa María**, on the site of a ruined Knights Templar castle at the top of the town. The **Museo Pérez Comendador-Leroux** in an 18th-century mansion on the main street, Calle de Asensio Neila, houses works of the interesting Hervás-born sculptor Enrique Pérez Comendador (1900–81) and his wife, the French painter Magdalena Leroux. It's open from Tuesday to Sunday for varying hours (free).

Granadilla

About 22km west of Hervás, Granadilla is a picturesque old fortified village that was abandoned after the creation in the 1960s of the Embalse de Gabriel y Galán reservoir, which almost surrounds it. Since then it has been restored as an educational centre open 10 am to 1 pm and 4 to 6 pm daily except Sunday afternoon and Monday (free).

Places to Stay

Accommodation is unbelievably sparse in the area and your best bet is *Camping El Pinajarro* (☎ 927 48 16 73, e campinpinajarro@teleline.es), 1.5km from Hervás on the more southerly of the two approach roads from the N-630, which is open from mid-March to late September and charges 500 ptas plus IVA per adult, per car and per tent. You may find the odd house with an 'Habitaciones' or 'Camas' sign in Hervás' barrio judío.

Getting There & Away

Los Tres Pilares runs two buses on weekdays between Plasencia and Hervás (440 ptas). Enatcar has a few services daily between Cáceres, Plasencia and Salamanca via the Valle del Ambroz, stopping at the Empalme de Hervás junction on the N-630, 2km from the town.

LAS HURDES

Las Hurdes was long synonymous with grinding poverty, disease and chilling tales of witchcraft, evil spirits and even cannibalism. In the 16th century, a Carmelite monastery was founded in the Valle de Las Batuecas, across the border in Castilla y León, to counteract the demons. In 1922 the miserable existence of the *hurdanos* prompted Alfonso XII to declare during a horseback tour 'I can bear to see no more'. In the 1930s Luis Buñuel made Las Hurdes the subject of his film about rural poverty, *Las Hurdes – Terre Sans Pain* (Land without Bread). Today Las Hurdes has shaken off the worst of its poverty, but the atmosphere in some of its more isolated and inbred villages has that 'there be strangers in town' feel.

The rocky terrain yields only small terraces of cultivable land along the river banks, but has an austere beauty. The huddles of small stone houses look almost as much like slate-roofed sheep pens as human dwellings. Here and there are clusters of beehives that produce high-quality honey. The Casa de la Cultura in Caminomorisco (on the C-512) houses a tourist office (☎ 927 43 51 93).

Things to See & Do

The heart of Las Hurdes is the valley of the Río Hurdano, north-west from Vegas de Coria on the C-512 Coria-Salamanca road.

From Nuñomoral, 7.5km up the valley, a road heads west up a side valley to such

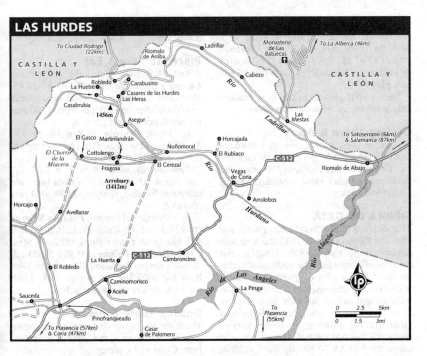

LAS HURDES

isolated and old-fashioned villages as **Fragosa** (turn south at Martinlandrán), **Cottolengo** and **El Gasco**. Various tracks head off into the hills from this valley: there's a good walk from El Gasco to the 70m waterfall **El Chorro de la Miacera**.

Back in the main valley, **Asegur**, 5km north-west of Nuñomoral, has many stone houses that look as though they grew out of the hillside. Four kilometres up, **Casares de las Hurdes** is almost cosmopolitan. Between Asegur and Casares, another side road heads west to **Casabrubia** and **La Huetre**, from where you can head off for more walks into the hills.

Beyond Casares de las Hurdes, the road winds up through Carabusino and Robledo to the border of Salamanca province. Drivers could continue to Ciudad Rodrigo (25km), but a right turn 20m before the border marker will take you winding 9km down through forest to the picturesque, isolated village of **Riomalo de Arriba** with more

stone houses. From Riomalo de Arriba the road continues through Ladrillar and Cabezo to **Las Mestas**. From Las Mestas you can turn north to the Valle de las Batuecas and La Alberca (see Sierra de la Peña de Francia in the Castilla y León chapter), or continue 3.5km down to rejoin the C-512.

Places to Stay & Eat

You'll find the closest camping grounds on the C-512 at Riomalo de Abajo and Pinofranqueado. *Camping Del Pino* (☎ 927 67 41 41) at Pinofranqueado is open from April to November and charges 475 ptas per person, per car and per tent.

Pensión El Abuelo (☎ 927 43 51 14) in Caminomorisco has comfortable singles/doubles with bath for 3000/4000 ptas. *Hostal Riomalo* (☎ 927 43 40 20) in Riomalo de Abajo has rooms with bath for 2500/3500 ptas, and a popular restaurant. Also on the C-512 there are *hostales* in Pinofranqueado and Vegas de Coria.

EXTREMADURA

Pensión Hurdano (☎ *927 43 30 12*) in Nuñomoral has decent rooms, some with bath, for 1700/3000 ptas. *Hostal Montesol* (☎ *927 67 61 93, Calle Lindón 7*) in Casares de las Hurdes has doubles for 3000 to 3500 ptas plus IVA.

Nearly all the places to stay have reasonably priced *restaurants* or *comedores*.

Getting There & Away

Autocares Cleo runs a bus on weekdays from Plasencia to Vegas de Coria, La Huetre, Casares de las Hurdes (830 ptas) and back, and another (also weekdays) to El Gasco and back.

SIERRA DE GATA

The Muslims built several castles here, and after the Reconquista in 1212 the area was controlled by the Knights Templar and Knights of Alcántara. The traditional architecture features a lot of granite stonework with external staircases, and several of the villages huddled in the hills have impressive 16th-century churches. Olives and other fruit are grown in the lower parts of the area's wooded valleys. There's a tourist office (☎ 927 14 70 88) by the C-526 in Moraleja and another in Hoyos (☎ 927 51 45 85), Calle Marialba 12.

The two main roads through the region – the C-526 north from Coria to Ciudad Rodrigo and the C-513 west from the Valle del Ambroz to Penamacor in Portugal – cross near the biggest and one of the most attractive villages, **Hoyos**, which has some impressive *casas señoriales* (mansions) and a ruined 16th-century convent. To the east, **Santibáñez el Alto** has a substantial castle dating back to the 9th century, with fine views; **Torre de Don Miguel** has more casas señoriales and an elm tree in its plaza mayor (main plaza), said to be 500 years old; **Gata** has some of the best traditional architecture and another ruined convent.

In the west, locals speak a unique dialect thought to stem from Asturian and Leonese settlers in the Reconquista. **San Martín de Trevejo** is a pretty place with traditional buildings amid a landscape of oak and chestnut woods. **Valverde del Fresno** is larger but also picturesque (if a little spooky), with a ruined castle and a handsome plaza mayor.

Places to Stay & Eat

About 5km from Gata, the picturesque *Camping Sierra de Gata* (☎ 927 67 21 68, @ entorno@blasfer.com) is open mid-March to mid-October, and charges around 500 ptas per adult, per car and per tent.

In Hoyos, *Pensión El Redoble* (☎ 927 51 40 18, Plaza de la Paz 14) has singles/doubles for 1500/2500 ptas.

Pensión Avenida (☎ 927 67 22 71, Avenida de Almenara 12) in Gata is a little more comfortable, charging 2500/3000 ptas plus IVA.

In Valverde del Fresno, *Pensión Sajeras* (☎ 927 51 02 49, Calle Francisco Pizarro 43) has basic rooms for 1300/2600 ptas, while *Hotel La Palmera* (☎ 927 51 03 23, Avenida Santos Robledo 10) has rooms with bath for 3000/5000 ptas plus IVA. Most places have a *restaurant* attached.

Getting There & Away

There are one or two daily buses into the region from Plasencia and (except Saturday) from Coria and Cáceres.

CORIA & AROUND

South of the Sierra de Gata, the old part of Coria is still surrounded by what are claimed to be Europe's most perfectly preserved **Roman walls**. The most impressive stretch of walls is along Calle Horno. The helpful tourist office (☎ 927 50 13 51), at Avenida de Extremadura 39A, is open daily. Free Internet access is available just south of the cathedral on the 1st floor of the Seminario Mayor building; it's open 10 am to 2 pm and 5 to 9 pm Tuesday to Friday and Saturday mornings.

The impressive **catedral** on Plaza Catedral, open 9.10 am to 1.30 pm and 3.45 to 7 pm daily, was built between the 14th and 17th centuries. Primarily a Gothic construction, it has plateresque decoration around the portals, a tall tower and a very wide nave. A small museum is housed inside with shorter opening hours (200 ptas). Below the cathedral stands a fine old stone bridge, abandoned in the 17th century by the Río Alagón, which now takes a slightly more southerly course.

Galisteo village, 26km east of Coria, is worth popping into for a look at its intact Almohad walls, the remains of a 14th-century fort known as the Palacio, with a curious octagonal cone-shaped tower, and the *mudéjar* brick apse on its old church.

Coria's Fiestas de San Juan around 24 June feature bull running in the streets of the old town.

Places to Stay & Eat
In Coria, *Pensión Piro* (☎ 927 50 00 27, *Plaza del Rollo 6*), just outside the old walls, has singles/doubles for 1500/2000 ptas and decent, inexpensive food. *Hotel Montesol* (☎ 927 50 10 49), by the Río Alagón just off the Cáceres road, has rooms with bath for 3000/4500 ptas plus IVA. The only restaurant inside the walled city is *Restaurante Casa Campana* on Plaza de San Pedro, offering a fine *menú* for 1100 ptas. If you can't decide what to order, let the chef choose.

Getting There & Away
The bus station (☎ 927 50 01 10) is on Calle Chile in the new part of town, about 1km from the old part. There are buses at least once daily to/from Plasencia, Cáceres, Salamanca and Madrid.

PLASENCIA
postcode 10600 • pop 37,299

This bustling and pleasant old town rising above a bend of the Río Jerte, is the natural hub of northern Extremadura. Founded in 1186 by Alfonso VIII of Castilla, Plasencia only lost out to Cáceres as northern Extremadura's most important town in the 19th century. It retains a very attractive old quarter of narrow streets with some stately stone buildings.

Orientation & Information
The heart of town is the lively Plaza Mayor, meeting place of 10 streets and the scene of a Tuesday market since the 12th century. The bus station is at Calle Tornavacas 2, about 1km east, and the train station is off the Cáceres road about 1km south-west.

There are tourist offices at Calle del Rey 8, a few steps east off Plaza Mayor (☎ 927 42 21 59), and on Plaza de la Catedral facing the cathedral (☎ 927 42 38 43, @ turismo@ plasencia.com). You'll find one or both open 10 am to 2 pm and 5 to 7 pm daily. Internet access is available at Bar Arsenal on Museo de la Carne, two minutes' walk from the bus station towards the centre of town.

Things to See
The **catedral** on Plaza de la Catedral, a quick wiggle south-west from Plaza Mayor, is actually two cathedrals: the 13th- and 14th-century Romanesque Catedral Vieja around the side, and the 16th-century Catedral Nueva, a mainly Gothic building with a handsome plateresque facade. Both are open 9 am to 12.30 pm and 4 to 6 pm Monday to Saturday (later in summer) and 9 am to 1 am Sunday. The Catedral Nueva is free, while the Catedral Vieja is 150 ptas and contains the fine Capilla de San Pablo, a lovely cloister and cathedral museum (Spanish and Flemish art dating from the 15th to 17th century). The Catedral Nueva was never finished so seems disproportionately tall for its length. The carvings on its early 16th-century choir stalls alternate between the sacred and the obscene: their carver, Rodrigo Alemán, is said to have been an unwillingly converted Jew who took the chance to mock the Christian church. The choir stalls are behind a locked *reja* (grille), dividing the choir from the rest of the church, but the attendant may be willing to open it for you.

Nearby on Plazuela del Marqués de la Puebla is the **Museo Etnográfico-Textil**, with an interesting display of local crafts and costumes, normally open Wednesday to Sunday but Monday to Saturday in July and August (free).

Among the numerous old churches and mansions in town, some of those most worth a look are the **Casa de las Dos Torres** on Calle Santa Isabel, the **Iglesia de San Nicolás** on Plaza de San Vicente Ferrer, and the **Iglesia de San Martín** on Plazuela de San Martín, all dating from the 13th or 14th century. San Martín, now an exhibition hall,

EXTREMADURA

has a retablo with paintings by the noted 16th-century extremeño artist Luis Morales, known as El Divino Morales. Also look for the much-loved bell-ringer *El Abuelo Mayorga* on top of the ayuntamiento on Plaza Mayor. At the eastern end of town is a series of pleasant **parks** crossed by a 16th-century **aqueduct**.

Special Events
Plasencia stages its lively Feria y Fiestas de Junio over a few days in the first 10 days of June.

Places to Stay & Eat
Camping La Chopera (☎ 927 41 66 60), about 4km north-east on the N-110, has a shady site and a popular restaurant and pool. It charges around 450 ptas per adult, per car and per tent.

There are four places to stay in the centre. *Hostal La Muralla* (☎ 927 41 38 74, Calle de Berrozana 6) charges from 2000/2500 to 3500/4000 ptas plus IVA for singles/doubles. It fills up fast, so book ahead. *Hotel Rincón Extremeño* (☎ 927 41 11 50, Calle Vidrieras 6) has good rooms with shower or bath for 4400/5900 ptas. *Hotel Alfonso VIII* (☎ 927 41 02 50, e hotelalfonsov111@ cl.cajaextremadura.es, Avenida Alfonso VIII 34) charges from 8800/ 15,000 ptas plus IVA in the high season. The highly rated *Parador* (☎ 927 42 58 70, e plasencia@ parador.es) is naturally gorgeous and is situated in an old convent. Doubles cost 18,500 ptas plus IVA.

The *cafes* under the arches on Plaza Mayor are a fine place to watch Plasencia go by. *La Taberna Extremeña* on Calle Vidrieras, just off Plaza Mayor, and *Bar La Muralla*, next to Hostal La Muralla, serve reasonably priced *platos combinados* and *raciones*. Many of the dozens of *bars* in the centre serve free tapas with drinks.

Entertainment
There are plenty of lively *bars* in the streets either side of Calle Talavera, south off Plaza Mayor, and on Callejón de San Martín, north-west off Plaza Mayor. *Café España* on Plaza Mayor is always crowded.

Getting There & Away
From the bus station (☎ 927 41 45 50) there are up to 12 daily buses to Cáceres (690 ptas) and Salamanca, up to six to Mérida and four to Sevilla, and other services – but not always daily – as far afield as Madrid, Badajoz, Valladolid, Bilbao, San Sebastián and Barcelona. Direct buses to Trujillo, via the Parque Natural Monfragüe, only go on Monday and Friday.

From the train station (☎ 927 41 00 49) there are two or three trains daily to/from Madrid (3½ hours), Cáceres (1½ hours), Mérida (2½ hours) and Zafra, and trains six days a week to/from Sevilla (seven hours) and Badajoz.

PARQUE NATURAL MONFRAGÜE
This natural park straddling the Tajo valley is home to some of Spain's most spectacular colonies of birds of prey. Among its 178 feathery species are over 200 pairs of black vultures (the largest concentration of Europe's biggest bird of prey) and important populations of two other rare large birds, the Spanish imperial eagle (about 10 pairs) and the black stork (about 20 pairs). From March to October is the best time to come, as the vultures, storks and others spend winter in Africa.

Orientation & Information
At the hamlet of Villarreal de San Carlos on the C-524/EX-208 Plasencia-Trujillo road is an information centre (☎ 927 19 91 34), open 9 am to 2.30 pm and 5 to 7 pm daily. From Villarreal, several marked walking trails take you to some good lookout points, some of which you can drive to as well. Villarreal is near the confluence of the Tajo and Tiétar Rivers, both of which are dammed not far upstream.

Things to See & Do
One of the best spots to head for is the hilltop **Castillo de Monfragüe**, a ruined 9th-century Muslim fort about 1½ hours walk south from Villarreal (or a few minutes' drive). This is a great spot for watching **birds** in flight from the Peña Falcón crag on

the opposite (west) bank of the Río Tajo. Peña Falcón's residents at the last count included 80 pairs of huge griffon vultures, three pairs of black storks, and one pair each of Egyptian vultures, peregrine falcons, golden eagles and eagle owls – the latter another giant of the bird world with a 1.5m wingspan. You can get a closer look at Peña Falcón from Salto del Gitano, by the road below the Castillo de Monfragüe.

Another walk (2½ hours return) goes west from Villarreal de San Carlos to **Cerro Gimio**, where you may see black vultures nesting. This bird is distinguishable from the griffon vulture by being all black. A further good bird-viewing spot is the **Mirador de la Tajadilla**, about a three hour round-trip walk from Villarreal (you can also drive there), which is noted for griffon vultures

and Egyptian vultures in flight (the griffon is the bigger).

Places to Stay & Eat

The nearest place to stay is ***Camping Monfragüe*** (☎ 927 45 92 33, e luzpilar@ bbvnet.com), open all year, 14km north on the C-524/EX-208. Camping is about 475 ptas plus IVA per adult, per tent and per car, and there are six four-person bungalows for 7000 ptas plus IVA. There's a restaurant and pool, and bikes for rent at 1500 ptas per day.

At Monfragüe train station, 1.5km off the C-524/EX-208 from Camping Monfragüe, ***Residencial Parque Natural Monfragüe*** (☎ 927 40 47 60, ☎ 689 31 45 12) has bunk rooms for two or four people at 2000 ptas per person and meals available. Make sure you ring ahead.

Woolly Wanderers

If you travel the byways of Extremadura, Castilla y León, Castilla-La Mancha or western Andalucía you may find your road crossing or running beside a broad grassy track, which might have signs saying *cañada real* or *vía pecuaria*. What you've stumbled upon is one of Spain's age-old livestock migration routes. The Visigoths are reckoned to have been the first to take their flocks and herds south from Castilla y León to winter on the plains of Extremadura – a practice that not only avoided the cold northern winters but also allowed pastures to regenerate.

This twice-yearly *trashumancia* (migration of herds) grew to epic proportions in the late Middle Ages when sheep became Spain's economic mainstay. Huge clouds of dust raised by the migrating flocks were a characteristic sight in a countryside that was now often emptied of other agriculture and human habitation by the dominance of this single beast. (Don Quijote thought one pair of such dust clouds were armies advancing to do battle with each other and charged into the fray, only to find he was spearing sheep instead of valiant knights.) The powerful sheep owners' guild known as the Mesta established a vast network of drove roads, which is said eventually to have totalled 124,000km.

The biggest drove roads – veritable sheep freeways up to 75m wide – were the *cañadas reales* (royal drove roads). The Cañada Real de la Plata – roughly following the Roman Via Lata from north-west to south-west Spain – passes just west of Salamanca, enters Extremadura by the Valle del Ambroz, crosses the Parque Natural Monfragüe and then follows stretches of the C-524/EX-208 to Trujillo.

Come the easy truck and train transport of modern times, and a decline in the importance of sheep and in the attractions of the shepherd's life, the trashumancia has dwindled to a trickle. Many of the cañadas have been made unusable by new roads, spreading towns, reservoirs, rubbish tips and farms. The nearest most Spaniards come to a migrating sheep today is when Proyecto 2001, a campaign dedicated to keeping the drove roads open, takes a flock of 2000 or so through downtown Madrid each October. Proyecto 2001 has staged full-scale trashumancias of thousands of sheep each year since 1993, aiming to revitalise the trashumancia, arrest the loss of public land, and maintain the drove roads for their environmental value.

EXTREMADURA

The nearest hostales are in the village of Torrejón el Rubio, 16km south of Villarreal de San Carlos. **Pensión Avenida** (☎ 927 45 50 50, Calle San José s/n) and **Pensión Monfragüe** (☎ 927 45 50 26, Paseo de Pizarro 25), on the C-524/EX-208, both have decent rooms with shared bathroom at around 3000 ptas a double. Each also has a restaurant. The modern-style **Hospedería Parque de Monfragüe** (☎ 927 45 52 45, e h-monfrague@alextur.net), located 39km south of Plasencia on the road to Trujillo, charges 10,000/12,400 plus IVA, breakfast included. Delectable smells waft from a couple of **bars** at Villarreal de San Carlos.

Getting There & Away

The only bus service is by the Izquierdo company, which runs buses on weekdays from Trujillo to Plasencia and back, with stops at Torrejón el Rubio and Villarreal de San Carlos, and a bus on Tuesday from Torrejón el Rubio to Plasencia and back. Six or seven hours at Monfragüe can be had before returning the same day.

Monfragüe train station (called Palazuelo-Empalme on some maps; ☎ 927 45 92 32) is 16km north of Villarreal de San Carlos. It's served by two or three trains daily to/from Madrid and Plasencia, and one or two daily to/from Cáceres and Mérida.

Central Extremadura

CÁCERES

postcode 10001 • pop 77,768

At the heart of Cáceres, Extremadura's second biggest city, stands an old town so little changed since the 15th and 16th centuries that it's often used as a film set. Cáceres is a pleasant and lively place that does a good job of combining the old with the new, helped along by a sizeable student population.

A key goal for anyone hoping to control Extremadura, the city was captured from the Muslims by the Christian kingdom of León three times between 1142 and 1184 but was retaken by the Muslims each time.

The fourth conquest, by Alfonso IX of León in 1227, proved permanent. Noble Leonese families started settling here in the late 13th century, and during the 15th and 16th centuries they turned its walled nucleus into one of the most impressive concentrations of medieval stonemasonry in Europe.

Orientation

The heart of Cáceres is the 150m-long Plaza Mayor, with the walled old town, the Ciudad Monumental, rising on its eastern side. Around Plaza Mayor and the Ciudad Monumental extends a tangle of humbler old streets that give way, about 450m to the south-west, to the straight Avenida de España lining the Parque Calvo Sotelo and Paseo de Cánovas. This is the modern half of central Cáceres. From the southern end of Paseo de Cánovas, Avenida de Alemania runs 1km south-west to the train and bus stations.

Information

The tourist office (☎ 927 24 63 47), at Plaza Mayor 3, is open 9.30 am to 2 pm and 4 to 6.30 pm weekdays (5 to 7.30 pm in summer) and 10 am to 2 pm weekends and holidays. Tourist information is also available in the Palacio Carvajal in the Ciudad Monumental, open 8 am to 9 pm weekdays and 10 am to 2 pm weekends and holidays. Or check the official Web site at www.dip-caceres.es. Ciberjust (☎ 927 62 72 74, e ciberjust@ arrakis.es), Calle Diego Maria Crehuet 7, the best Internet cafe in Cáceres, is also the closest to the old town, a couple of blocks south of Plaza de San Juan.

You'll find banks and ATMs along Calle Pintores, off Plaza Mayor. The main post office is at Paseo Primo de Rivera 2 facing Parque Calvo Sotelo.

The Policía Nacional (☎ 091) are at Avenida Virgen de la Montaña 3 off Parque Calvo Sotelo. The Hospital Provincial (☎ 927 25 68 00) is on the western side of Parque Calvo Sotelo.

Ciudad Monumental

The Ciudad Monumental is worth two visits – one by day to look around and visit what you can, and one by night to soak up

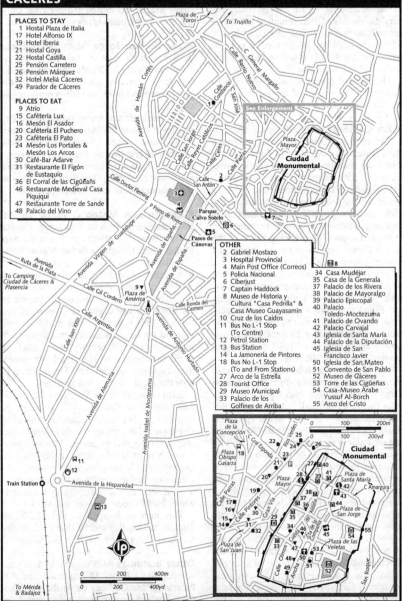

CÁCERES

PLACES TO STAY
1 Hostal Plaza de Italia
17 Hotel Alfonso IX
19 Hotel Iberia
21 Hostal Goya
22 Hostal Castilla
25 Pensión Carretero
26 Pensión Márquez
32 Hotel Meliá Cáceres
49 Parador de Cáceres

PLACES TO EAT
9 Atrio
15 Cafétería Lux
16 Mesón El Asador
20 Cafétería El Puchero
23 Cafétería El Pato
24 Mesón Los Portales &
Mesón Los Arcos
30 Café-Bar Adarve
31 Restaurante El Figón
de Eustaquio
36 El Corral de las Cigüeñas
46 Restaurante Medieval Casa
Piquiqui
47 Restaurante Torre de Sande
48 Palacio del Vino

OTHER
2 Gabriel Mostazo
3 Hospital Provincial
4 Main Post Office (Correos)
5 Policía Nacional
6 Ciberjust
7 Captain Haddock
8 Museo de Historia y
Cultura "Casa Pedrilla" &
Casa Museo Guayasamin
10 Cruz de los Caídos
11 Bus No L-1 Stop
(To Centre)
12 Petrol Station
13 Bus Station
14 La Jamonería de Pintores
18 Bus No L-1 Stop
(To and From Stations)
27 Arco de la Estrella
28 Tourist Office
29 Museo Municipal
33 Palacio de los
Golfines de Arriba
34 Casa Mudéjar
35 Casa de la Generala
37 Palacio de los Rivera
38 Palacio de Mayoralgo
39 Palacio Episcopal
40 Palacio
Toledo-Moctezuma
41 Palacio de Ovando
42 Palacio Carvajal
43 Iglesia de Santa María
44 Palacio de la Diputación
45 Iglesia de San
Francisco Javier
50 Iglesia de San Mateo
51 Convento de San Pablo
52 Museo de Cáceres
53 Torre de las Cigüeñas
54 Casa-Museo Árabe
Yussuf Al-Borch
55 Arco del Cristo

EXTREMADURA

euro currency converter €1 = 166pta

the atmosphere of accumulated ages. Many of its mansions – all carved with the heraldic shields of their founding families – are still in private (often absentee) hands; others are used by the provincial government, the local bishop and sections of the Universidad Extremeña.

The Ciudad Monumental is still almost surrounded by walls and towers rebuilt by the Almohads about 1184.

Plaza de Santa María Entering the Ciudad Monumental from Plaza Mayor through the 18th-century **Arco de la Estrella** arch, you'll see ahead the **Iglesia de Santa María**, Cáceres' 15th-century Gothic cathedral. From February to September, Santa María's tower will be topped by the ungainly nests of the white storks, which make their homes on every worthwhile vertical protuberance in the old town. The clacking beaks of the chicks demanding food are sometimes the loudest sounds you'll hear. On the outside corner of the church is a statue of San Pedro de Alcántara, a 16th-century extremeño ascetic who dedicated himself to reforming the Franciscan order. Inside the church, stick 100 ptas in the slot to the right of the sacristy/museum door to light up the fine carved cedar retablo of 1549–51. Entry to the museum costs 200 ptas.

The cathedral stands on one of the Ciudad Monumental's handsomest plazas, Plaza de Santa María, which is also fronted by such other fine buildings – all in 16th-century Renaissance style – as the **Palacio Episcopal** (Bishop's Palace), the **Palacio de Mayoralgo** and the **Palacio de Ovando**, this last built by Cáceres' leading clan of the 16th and 17th centuries. Just off the north-eastern corner of the plaza is the **Palacio Carvajal**, another old mansion now used to lodge visiting dignitaries and as the offices of the local tourism department. Free guided visits are available daily – ask at the information desk.

Not far away in the north-western corner of the walled city, the **Palacio Toledo-Moctezuma** was once the home of a daughter of the Aztec emperor Moctezuma, brought to Cáceres as the bride of conquistador Juan Cano de Saavedra. Today, it's the Archivo Histórico Provincial and sometimes stages exhibitions; otherwise, only the unexciting patio is open.

Plaza de San Jorge South-east of Plaza de Santa María past the fine Renaissance-style **Palacio de la Diputación**, is Plaza de San Jorge above which rises the **Iglesia de San Francisco Javier**, an 18th-century Jesuit church.

The **Casa-Museo Árabe Yussuf Al-Borch**, nearby at Cuesta del Marqués 4, is a private house decked out by its owner with all sorts of Oriental and Islamic trappings to capture the feel of Muslim times. Its opening hours are erratic (200 ptas). The **Arco del Cristo** at the bottom of this street is a Roman gate.

Plaza de San Mateo & Plaza de las Veletas From Plaza de San Jorge, Cuesta de la Compañía climbs to Plaza de San Mateo where the **Iglesia de San Mateo**, traditionally the church of the landowning nobility, has a plateresque portal and a rococo retablo (it's usually only open for services).

Just to the east on Plaza de las Veletas is the **Torre de las Cigüeñas** (Tower of the Storks). This is the only tower of Cáceres' that did not have its battlements lopped off in the late 15th century, on Isabel la Católica's orders, to stop rivalry between the city's fractious nobility. The building is now the local military headquarters.

Also on Plaza de las Veletas is the excellent **Museo de Cáceres**. This museum is housed in a 16th-century mansion built over an elegant 12th-century cistern *(aljibe)* – the only surviving bit of Cáceres' Muslim castle – which is its prize exhibit. It also has an interesting archaeological section, rooms devoted to traditional crafts and costumes, and a good little fine arts display that includes works by El Greco, Picasso and Miró.

The museum is open 9 am to 2.30 pm Tuesday to Saturday and 10.15 am to 2.30 pm Sunday (200 ptas, free with an EU passport).

Other Buildings Also worth a look as you wander the Ciudad Monumental are the **Palacio de los Golfines de Arriba** on Calle Olmos, which was Franco's headquarters for

EXTREMADURA

a few weeks early in the civil war; the **Casa Mudéjar**, one of few buildings in Cáceres to show Muslim influence, on Cuesta de Aldana; and on Plaza de los Caldereros, the **Casa de la Generala**, now the university law faculty and the **Palacio de los Rivera**, the university's rectorate.

On Plaza de Publio Hurtado just outside the old walls, the **Museo Municipal** is given over to bright, attractive, acrylic paintings of Cáceres and Extremadura by local artist Massa Solís – open from Tuesday to Friday for varying hours; free.

South of Ciudad Monumental by Plaza de San Francisco is **Museo de Historia y Cultura 'Casa Pedrilla'** and **Casa Museo Guayasamin**. The former houses a number of displays on history and culture plus a collection of works by extremeño painters, while the later presents the dark work of painter Oswaldo Guayasamin. Both museums are free and open 11 am to 2 pm and 5 to 8 pm Tuesday to Saturday, and Sunday morning.

Special Events

Every year since 1992, Cáceres has staged the Spanish edition of the WOMAD (World of Music & Dance) festival, with international bands ranging from reggae and Celtic to African, Indian and Australian Aboriginal playing in the old city's squares. If you're heading this way in the first half of May, keep an eye on the papers for information or call ☎ 927 21 56 51 or try the Web site at www.bme.es/womad.

The Ferias de Cáceres, for a week around the end of May and early June, feature bullfights, concerts, fireworks and plenty of fun.

Places to Stay – Budget

Camping Ciudad de Cáceres (☎ 927 23 04 03) is 3km from the centre on the N-630 to Plasencia. It's quite a pleasant camping ground, and open all year at 475 ptas plus IVA per adult, per car and per tent.

There's plenty of choice for rooms around Plaza Mayor, though the area can get noisy on weekend nights. *Pensión Márquez* (☎ 927 24 49 60, Calle Gabriel y Galán 2), just off Plaza Mayor, is a friendly family-run place with clean singles/doubles

for 1500/3000 ptas. *Pensión Carretero* (☎ 927 24 74 82, Plaza Mayor 22) has simple, decent rooms for 2000/3500 ptas. Outside summer it usually closes during the week. *Hostal Castilla* (☎ 927 24 44 04, Calle Ríos Verdes 3), one block from the plaza, has adequate rooms for 2000/4000 ptas.

Away from the hustle and bustle, *Hostal Plaza de Italia* (☎ 927 24 77 60, Calle Constancia 12) has clean, pleasant rooms with shower and TV for 3500/5500 ptas.

Places to Stay – Mid-Range & Top End

Hotel Iberia (☎ 927 24 76 34, Calle Pintores 2), just off Plaza Mayor in a 17th-century building, is a bargain and full of character with rooms with bathroom and TV for 5000/7000 ptas plus IVA.

Hostal Goya (☎ 927 24 99 50, e hotel goya@ inicid.es, Plaza Mayor 31) has pleasant doubles with TV and shower for 6500 ptas, 8500 ptas with bath. *Hotel Alfonso IX* (☎ 927 24 64 00, Calle Moret 20) offers reasonable rooms from 4600/7900 ptas. A good 450 ptas breakfast is available.

Parador de Cáceres (☎ 927 21 17 59, e caceres@parador.es, Calle Ancha 6), in the Ciudad Monumental, occupies a 14th-century mansion with rooms from 14,000/17,500 ptas plus IVA. *Hotel Meliá Cáceres* (☎ 927 21 58 00, Plaza de San Juan 11), in a 15th-century mansion just outside the Ciudad Monumental, has good modern rooms for 16,700/21,000 ptas plus IVA.

Places to Eat

Plaza Mayor & Around *Cafétería El Puchero* (Plaza Mayor 33) is a popular hang-out with a huge variety of eating options, from good *bocadillos* (around 400 ptas) and *raciones*, to a la carte fare. *Cafétería El Pato*, a block down the arcade, has excellent coffee and an upstairs restaurant with good three-course *menús*, including wine, for 1200 to 2000 ptas plus IVA.

Mesón Los Portales and *Mesón Los Arcos* at the bottom of Plaza Mayor and *Cafétería Lux* (Calle Pintores 32) all do platos combinados from 600 to 900 ptas. *Mesón El Asador* (Calle Moret 34), just off

EXTREMADURA

Calle Pintores, is good for roast and grilled meat and has *menús* from 1500 to 2600 ptas. Its bar serves bocadillos from 500 ptas and dozens of raciones and tapas.

Café-Bar Adarve off Calle Pintores is not a bad spot for breakfast – 190 to 225 ptas for coffee and a *tostada* or croissant.

Restaurante El Figón de Eustaquio (Plaza de San Juan 12) is a good bet for a traditional extremeño meal. The three-course *menú de la casa*, with wine, is 1700 ptas plus IVA. A la carte mains are generally between 850 and 2600 ptas plus IVA.

Reputedly the best restaurant in Cáceres, if not Extremadura, is *Atrio (Avenida de España 30, Bloque 4)*. Planted at the base of what looks like a block of flats, you don't expect to find a restaurant serving up the highest quality extremeño food. Of course you pay for the quality with mains around the 5000 ptas mark.

Good shops to inspect local hams, sausages, cheeses and fruit liquor are *La Jamonería de Pintores* on Calle Pintores, and *Gabriel Mostazo* at the corner of Calle San Pedro and Calle San Antón.

Ciudad Monumental The Ciudad Monumental has several medium to expensive restaurants serving mainly traditional food in suitably ancient surroundings. *Menús* are 2200 ptas plus IVA at *Palacio del Vino* on Calle Ancha (also with a bar serving tapas and raciones); 2500 and 3900 ptas at *Restaurante Medieval Casa Piquiqui (Calle Orellana 1)*; and mains are between 1750 and 2800 ptas plus IVA at *Restaurante Torre de Sande*, with tables in a nice courtyard, on Calle de los Condes. The *restaurant* at the Parador de Cáceres at Calle Ancha 6 is pretty good – especially its *caldereta de cordero* (lamb stew). The *menú* is 3700 ptas plus IVA.

For a more economical bite, *El Corral de las Cigüeñas* on Cuesta de Aldana has raciones from 600 ptas. Or visit the *Convento de San Pablo* on Plaza de San Mateo, where the nuns bake and sell tasty snacks such as *pastas con almendra* (almond pastries; 500 ptas) and *yemas de San Pablo* (candied egg yolks; 700 ptas). A revolving dumb waiter enables the nuns, who are members of a closed order, to sell the goodies without seeing or being seen by customers. Hours are 9 am to 1 pm and 4 to 7 pm Monday to Saturday.

Entertainment

The bottom (north) end of Plaza Mayor, and nearby streets such as Calle Gabriel y Galán and Calle General Ezponda, are full of lively *late night bars*, most with recorded music.

El Corral de las Cigüeñas in the Ciudad Monumental is a popular place for a drink on a summer evening, with a couple of palm trees poking out of the old courtyard and occasional live music from flamenco to blues.

Just south of the Ciudad Monumental on Calle Pizarro is a cluster of popular bars, including *Captain Haddock*, playing an eclectic music mix. The new part of the city offers up some good locals around Calle Dr Fleming.

Getting There & Away

Bus Minimum daily services from the bus station (☎ 927 23 25 50) include at least six to Trujillo (450 ptas) and Madrid (3½ hours, 2420 ptas); five each to Mérida (1¼ hours, 675 ptas) and Plasencia; three each to Salamanca (three to four hours, 1705 ptas), Zafra and Sevilla (four hours, 2090 ptas); two or more to Badajoz; and one each to Córdoba and Barcelona. To most places there are more services on weekdays.

Train There are three to five trains a day to/from Madrid (3½ to five hours, from 2385 ptas) and Mérida (one hour); two or three each to/from Plasencia (1¼ hours), Badajoz (two hours) and Barcelona; and one to/from Sevilla (5½ hours, 2245 ptas). The single daily train to Lisbon (six hours, from 4475 ptas) leaves in the middle of the night. The station can be contacted on ☎ 927 23 37 61.

Getting Around

Bus No L-1 from the stop outside the train station – also close to the bus station – will take you into town. The nearest stop to the centre is the fourth, on Plaza Obispo

EXTREMADURA

Galarza. From there, it's a short walk to Plaza Mayor. Returning to the stations, pick up the bus at the same stop.

AROUND CÁCERES

About 3km south of Malpartida de Cáceres (11km west of Cáceres on the N-521) can be found the **Museo Vostell Malpartida**, in what was an old wool washhouse on the edge of a peaceful dammed lake. The museum, set up by Wolf Vostell, contains over 200 weird and wonderful contemporary art works by a number of artists. Some are slightly disturbing and hard to comprehend, but captivating all the same. The site is surrounded by **Los Barruecos**, a natural granite rock park, which is worth the visit alone. Unfortunately, you need your own wheels to get there.

The museum is open 10 am to 1.30 pm and 5 to 7.30 pm Tuesday to Sunday (students half-price, free on Wednesday).

ALCÁNTARA
postcode 10980 • pop 1876

This historic and pleasant small town is 62km north-west of Cáceres on a route to Portugal, the C-523. There's a tourist office (☎ 927 39 08 63) on the way in from Cáceres at Avenida de Mérida 21; it's closed Monday and afternoons on weekends.

Alcántara is Arabic for 'the bridge'. The finest **Roman bridge** in Spain – 204m long, 61m high and built without mortar – spans the Río Tajo west of the town, below a huge modern dam holding back the Embalse de Alcántara reservoir. There's a memorial to the bridge's architect, Caius Julius Lacer, in a small Roman temple on the river bank.

The town itself has old walls, remains of a castle, and many fine old buildings. From 1218 it was the headquarters of Orden de Alcántara, an order of Reconquista knights that ruled much of western Extremadura as a kind of private kingdom. The order built the 16th-century **Convento de San Benito**, famous for its recipes, with Renaissance exterior, Gothic cloister, plateresque church interior and a beautiful three-tier gallery. The 13th-century **Iglesia de Santa María de**

Dehesas

The Spanish word *dehesa* means, simply, pastureland, but in parts of Extremadura and the Sierra Morena, where the pastures are often dotted with evergreen oaks, it takes on a dimension that sends environmentalists into raptures of delight. Dehesas of *encina* (holm oak) or *alcornoque* (cork oak) are a textbook case of sustainable exploitation. The bark of the cork oak can be stripped every nine years for cork (*corcho*) – you'll see the scars on some trees, a bright terracotta colour if they're new. The holm oak can be pruned about every four years and the wood used for charcoal. Meanwhile, livestock can graze the pastures and in autumn, pigs are turned out to gobble up the fallen acorns (*bellotas*) – a diet considered to produce the best ham of all.

Such, at least, is the theory. In practice a growing number of Extremadura's dehesas are used to far less than their full potential. Some belong to absentee landlords who use them only for shooting; others are left untended simply because people are finding easier ways of earning a crust.

Almócovar, a mix of Romanesque and Herreran styles, contains tombs of masters of the Orden de Alcántara and paintings by El Divino Morales.

Your only accommodation option, *Hostal Kantara Al Saif* (☎ 927 39 02 40, *Avenida de Mérida s/n*), has doubles with bath from 4500 to 6500 ptas plus IVA, depending on the season.

Buses run daily except Sunday from Cáceres.

TRUJILLO
postcode 10200 • pop 9315

Trujillo is one of the most perfect little towns in Spain. It can't be much bigger now than it was in 1529 when its most famous son, Francisco Pizarro, set off with his four half-brothers and a few other local buddies for an expedition that culminated in the bloody conquest of the Inca empire (see the boxed text 'Extremadura & America' in this chapter).

EXTREMADURA

Trujillo is blessed with a broad and fine plaza mayor, from which rises its remarkably preserved old town, packed with aged buildings exuding history. If you arrive from the Plasencia direction, you might imagine that you've driven through a time warp into the 16th century.

Information

The tourist office (☎ 927 32 26 77), on Plaza Mayor, is open 10 am to 2 pm and 4.30 to 7 pm daily. The post office is at Calle Encarnación 28, south of the centre. The Policía Local are in an alley off Plaza Mayor.

Things to See

Plaza Mayor A large equestrian **statue of Pizarro**, by American Charles Rumsey, dominates Plaza Mayor. There's a tale that Rumsey originally did the piece as a statue of Hernán Cortés, to present to Mexico, but Mexico (which takes a poor view of Cortés) didn't want it, so it was given to Trujillo as Pizarro instead!

On the plaza's southern side, the corner of the **Palacio de la Conquista** sports the carved images of Pizarro and his lover Inés Yupanqui (sister of the Inca emperor Atahualpa) and, to the right, their daughter

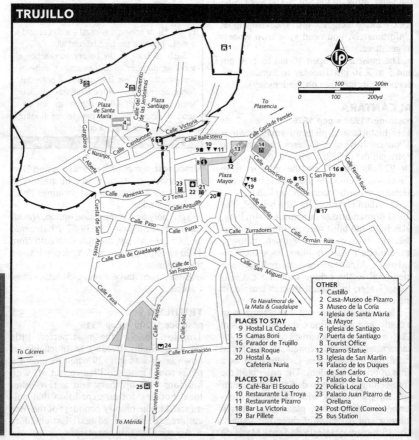

TRUJILLO

OTHER
1 Castillo
2 Casa-Museo de Pizarro
3 Museo de la Coria
4 Iglesia de Santa María la Mayor
6 Iglesia de Santiago
7 Puerta de Santiago
8 Tourist Office
12 Pizarro Statue
13 Iglesia de San Martín
14 Palacio de los Duques de San Carlos
21 Palacio de la Conquista
22 Policía Local
23 Palacio Juan Pizarro de Orellana
24 Post Office (Correos)
25 Bus Station

PLACES TO STAY
9 Hostal La Cadena
15 Camas Boni
16 Parador de Trujillo
17 Casa Roque
20 Hostal & Cafetería Nuria

PLACES TO EAT
5 Café-Bar El Escudo
10 Restaurante La Troya
11 Restaurante Pizarro
18 Bar La Victoria
19 Bar Pillete

Francisca Pizarro Yupanqui with her husband (and uncle) Hernando Pizarro. The mansion was built in the 1560s for Hernando and Francisca after Hernando – the only Pizarro brother not to die a bloody death in Peru – had spent 20 years in jail in Spain for the killing of Diego de Almagro. Above the corner balcony another carving shows the Pizarro family shield – two bears and a pine tree – surrounded by the walls of Cuzco, plus Pizarro's ships at Tumbes, and Atahualpa with his hands in two chests of gold surrounded by seven Inca chiefs. The inside of the palacio is not open to visitors.

Overlooking the Plaza Mayor from the north-eastern corner is the mainly 16th-century **Iglesia de San Martín**, with a number of noble tombs inside (normally only open for services). Its towers, like many in Trujillo, support the precarious nests of storks for much of the year. Across the street from the church is the 16th-century **Palacio de los Duques de San Carlos**, now a convent but open for visits daily (100 ptas). It has a classical-style patio and a very grand staircase.

Through an alley from the south-western corner of Plaza Mayor is the **Palacio Juan Pizarro de Orellana**, originally a miniature fortress converted into a Renaissance mansion by one of the Pizarro cousins who took part in the conquest of Peru and lived to reap the benefits back home. It's now a school and you can visit its patio, decorated with Pizarro and Orellana coats of arms. It's open 10 am to 1 pm and 4 to 6 pm weekdays and 11 am to 2 pm and 4.30 to 7 pm weekends (free).

Upper Town The 900m of walls circling the upper town date from Muslim times. It was here that after the Reconquista the newly settled noble families erected their mansions and churches. All the following are open 10 am to 2 pm and 4.30 to 7 pm and charge 200 ptas each.

The **Iglesia de Santiago** on Plaza Santiago was founded in the 13th century by the Knights of Santiago, and their conchshell emblem is a recurring motif.

The **Iglesia de Santa María la Mayor** on Plaza de Santa María is a hotchpotch of 13th- to 16th-century styles, with a Romanesque

tower. Inside are the tombs of leading Trujillo families of the Middle Ages, plus that of Diego García de Paredes (1466–1530), a Trujillo warrior of legendary strength who according to Cervantes could stop a mill wheel with one finger. The church has a fine retablo with Flemish-style paintings done in about 1485 by Fernando Gallego from Salamanca.

The 15th-century **Casa-Museo de Pizarro** was the ancestral home of the great conquistador family. Restored in the style of the 15th and 16th centuries, the house contains informative displays (in Spanish) on the Inca empire and the Pizarros. Whether Francisco Pizarro ever lived here is doubtful. Though he was the eldest of his father Gonzalo's nine children (by four women), Francisco was illegitimate and not accepted as an heir. However, it was to this house that Francisco was brought in triumph by his siblings on his visit to Trujillo in 1529.

At the top of the hill and affording great views, Trujillo's **castle**, of 10th-century Muslim origin and strengthened later by the Christians, is impressive though empty.

The **Museo de la Coria** has further displays on the conquest of the Americas, in a restored former convent. It's only open 11.30 am to 2 pm weekends and holidays; free.

Special Events
The Ferias y Fiestas de Trujillo, with bullfights, music and partying, last for a few days in early June.

Places to Stay
Camas Boni (☎ 927 32 16 04, *Calle Domingo de Ramos 7*) is good value with small but well-kept singles/doubles from 2000/3000 ptas, and doubles with bathroom for 4500 ptas. *Casa Roque* (☎ 927 32 23 13, *Calle Domingo de Ramos 30*) has singles for 3000 ptas and doubles with bath for 3500 ptas. *Hostal Nuria* (☎ 927 32 09 07, *Plaza Mayor 27*) has nice rooms with bath for 3300/5500 ptas. The friendly *Hostal La Cadena* (☎ 927 32 14 63, *Plaza Mayor 8*) is also good, charging 5500 ptas for doubles with bath.

Parador de Trujillo (☎ 927 32 13 50, e *toledo@parador.es*), on Plaza de Santa

EXTREMADURA

Extremadura & America

Many extremeños jumped at the opportunities opened up by Columbus' discovery of the Americas in 1492.

In 1501 Fray Nicolás de Ovando from Cáceres was named governor of the Indies by the Catholic Monarchs. He set up his capital, Santo Domingo, on the Caribbean island of Hispaniola. With him went 2500 followers, many of them from Extremadura, including Francisco Pizarro, an illegitimate son of a minor noble family from Trujillo. In 1504 Hernán Cortés, from a similar family in Medellín, east of Mérida, arrived in Santo Domingo too.

Both young men prospered in the new world. Cortés took part in the conquest of Cuba in 1511 and settled there to raise livestock and trade the gold mined by the Indians whose labour he had been granted. Pizarro, in 1513, accompanied Vasco Núñez de Balboa (from Jerez de los Caballeros in south-west Extremadura) to Darién (Panama), where they discovered the Pacific Ocean. Pizarro eventually rose to be mayor of the town of Panama.

In 1519 Cortés led a small expedition to what's now Mexico, which was rumoured to be full of gold and silver. By 1524, with a combination of incredible fortitude, cunning, luck and ruthlessness, Cortés and his band had subdued the mighty Aztec empire. Though initially named governor of what he had conquered, Cortés soon found royal officials arriving to usurp his authority. He came back to Spain in 1528 to see King Carlos I, who confirmed him as captain general of Nueva España but not as governor. Cortés returned to Mexico in 1530 but, increasingly discontented, returned again to Spain in 1540, this time to a cool reception. He never went back to Mexico, dying in a village near Sevilla in 1547. There's a monument to him in Medellín.

Pizarro, obsessed by tales of another empire of silver and gold south of Panama, formed in 1524 a partnership with two other colonists, Diego de Almagro and the priest Hernando de Luque, to search for it. In 1526 they reached the Inca town of Tumbes on the coast of Peru. But, unable to gain the support of their governor in Panama for a bigger expedition, in 1529 Pizarro followed Cortés' trail back to Spain to see the king, bringing llamas and other gifts. He met Cortés in Toledo,

---

Clara, is in a beautiful former convent dating from the 16th century. Rooms are 12,000/15,000 ptas plus IVA.

Places to Eat

There are plenty of places to eat, but the best of all is *Restaurante La Troya (Plaza Mayor 10)*. What the 1990 ptas *menú* doesn't tell you is that portions are gigantic and that they also give you a large potato omelette and salad for starters, and an extra main course later on! It's hard to refuse the hearty food and a good walk is required after the meal. *Caldereta* (stew) is a main course speciality. If you're not *that* hungry, there are great tapas here too. Elsewhere on Plaza Mayor, *Hostal La Cadena* and *Restaurante Pizarro* do normal-size meals; *Caféteria Nuria* has salads and egg dishes for 550 to 750 ptas and meat and fish from 800 ptas; *Bar La Victoria* has a range of breakfasts

for 150 to 450 ptas; and *Bar Pillete* is Trujillo's classiest cafe and has the best position.

Café-Bar El Escudo up the hill on Plaza Santiago has moderately priced raciones and platos combinados.

The Parador de Trujillo has an excellent *restaurant*, but you're looking at around 4000 ptas for a full meal.

Getting There & Away

The bus station (☎ 927 32 12 02) is 500m south of Plaza Mayor, on Carretera de Mérida. At least six buses run daily to/from Cáceres (45 minutes, 390 ptas), Badajoz and Madrid (2½ to four hours, 2350 ptas), and four or more to/from Mérida (1¼ hours, 1020 ptas). For buses to/from Villarreal de San Carlos (for Parque Natural Monfragüe) and Plasencia (see the Parque Natural Monfragüe section earlier).

Extremadura & America

won royal backing for his project, and got himself named, in advance, governor of what was to be called Nueva Castilla.

Before returning to Panama Pizarro visited Trujillo where he received a hero's welcome and picked up his four half-brothers – Hernando, Juan and Gonzalo Pizarro and Martín de Alcántara – and other relatives and friends. Their expedition finally set off from Panama in 1531, with just 180 men and 37 horses. With a perhaps even more incredible combination of the factors by which Cortés had succeeded in Mexico, Pizarro crossed the Andes and managed to capture the Inca emperor Atahualpa in Cajamarca despite his having an army of 30,000 on hand. The Inca empire, with its capital in Cuzco, extended from Colombia to Chile. Atahualpa offered to buy his freedom by filling with gold the room where he was held. The conquistadors took the gold but the following year executed Atahualpa.

However, few of their leaders survived to enjoy their spoils for long. By the time the last Inca resistance had been quelled in 1545, Francisco and Juan Pizarro, Martín de Alcántara and Diego de Almagro had all been killed in Inca revolts or in their own quarrels (Francisco is buried in Lima cathedral). In 1548 Gonzalo Pizarro, too, was executed, after rebelling against the new Spanish viceroy.

Other extremeño members of the expedition did survive to make their mark elsewhere. In about 1540 Hernando de Soto, from either Jerez de los Caballeros or nearby Barcarrota (both places claim him), became the first European to discover the Mississippi. Shortly afterwards Francisco de Orellana, from Trujillo, found the Amazon, floating down it by raft for eight months from the Andes to the Atlantic.

Altogether 600 or 700 people from Trujillo made their way to the Americas in the 16th century, so it's hardly surprising that there are at least seven Trujillos in North, Central and South America today. There are even more Guadalupes, for conquistadors and colonists from all over Spain took with them the cult of the Virgen de Guadalupe in eastern Extremadura. The cult of the Virgen de Guadalupe remains widespread in Latin America today.

GUADALUPE
postcode 10140 • pop 2457

Tucked away among the picturesque hills of eastern Extremadura, the attractive old village of Guadalupe is home to an important monastery, housing a statuette of the Virgin, Nuestra Señora de Guadalupe, which for centuries has been one of Spain's most revered. Lovers of remote countryside can drive or walk off from Guadalupe into craggy sierras divided by deep, green valleys with chestnut and oak woodlands as well as olive groves and vineyards.

Orientation & Information

Buses stop opposite the ayuntamiento on Avenida Conde de Barcelona, which is a two-minute walk from the central Plaza de Santa María de Guadalupe (or Plaza Mayor). The monastery rises above the plaza.

The helpful tourist office (☎ 927 15 41 28), on the plaza, is open 10 am to 2.30 pm and 4 to 6 pm Tuesday to Friday (mornings only on weekends). Most banks have ATMs. Around the centre are numerous craft and souvenir shops.

Real Monasterio de Santa María de Guadalupe

The monastery was founded in 1340 by Alfonso XI on a site where a shepherd had not long before found an effigy of the Virgin that had been hidden years earlier by Christians fleeing from the Muslims. The monastery became one of Spain's most important pilgrimage sites and an important centre for the study of medicine.

In the 15th and 16th centuries, the Virgin of Guadalupe was so revered that she was made patron of all the territories conquered by Spain in America. On 29 July 1496,

EXTREMADURA

Columbus' Indian servants were baptised in the fountain in front of the monastery, an event registered in the monastery's first book of baptisms.

The monastery is open 9.30 am to 1 pm and 3.30 to 6.30 pm daily. It costs nothing to enter the church, where you will find the Virgin's image, a 12th-century Romanesque work occupying the place of honour in the retablo, but the one-hour guided tour of other rooms (300 ptas) shouldn't be missed.

At the centre of the monastery is a 15th-century mudéjar cloister, off which are three museums. The **Museo de Bordados** contains wonderfully embroidered altar cloths and vestments, including cloaks that belonged to the Catholic Monarchs; the **Museo de Libros Miniados** has a fine collection of illuminated choral song books from the 15th century on; and the **Museo de Pintura y Escultura** includes paintings by El Greco and Goya and a beautiful little ivory crucifixion attributed to Michelangelo. The superbly decorated baroque **sacristía** is hung with 11 paintings by Zurbarán and a lantern captured from the Turkish flagship at the Battle of Lepanto (1571). The **Relicario-Tesoro** houses a variety of other treasures, including an exquisite baroque chandelier, a 200,000-pearl cape for the Virgin, and the jewel-encrusted crown with which Alfonso XIII crowned her *Reina de las Españas* (Queen of the Hispanic Countries) in 1928. Finally the tour reaches the **camarín**, a room behind the church's retablo where the image of the Virgin is revolved for the faithful to contemplate her at close quarters and kiss a fragment of her mantle.

Walking

The tourist office has printed material on walks in the area, including an informative leaflet in Spanish on the Ruta de Isabel la Católica, a marked cross-country route of about 12km to Cañamero village, southwest of Guadalupe.

Special Events

There are fiestas and processions during Semana Santa and on 8th and 30th of September and 12th of October. At such times it's essential to book accommodation in advance.

Places to Stay

Camping Las Villuercas (☎ 927 36 71 39) has a pretty site in a river valley a short distance off the C-401, 3km below Guadalupe. It's open all year and has a bar, restaurant and swimming pool.

There's no shortage of places to stay in the village, all a short walk from the monastery. The following prices are for singles/doubles with bath or shower: *Pensión Tena* (☎ 927 36 71 04, Calle Ventilla 1), 2000/ 3000 ptas; *Mesón Típico Isabel* (☎ 927 36 71 26, Plaza de Santa María de Guadalupe 13), 3000/ 4000 ptas plus IVA; *Hostal Lujuan* (☎ 927 36 71 70, Calle del Licenciado Gregorio López 19), 3000/4000 ptas plus IVA; and *Hostal Cerezo II* (☎ 927 15 41 77, Plaza de Santa María de Guadalupe 33), 3000/5000 ptas plus IVA.

Parador Zurbarán (☎ 927 36 70 75, ℮ guadalupe@parador.es, Calle Marqués de la Romana 12), a converted 15th-century hospital opposite the monastery, has rooms from 12,000/15,000 ptas plus IVA. Much better value is *Hospedería del Real Monasterio* (☎ 927 36 70 00) on Plaza de Su Majestad El Rey Juan Carlos I, centred on the monastery's beautiful 16th-century Gothic cloister, with rooms for 5350/7900 ptas plus IVA. Book ahead.

Places to Eat

Numerous cafes and restaurants around the centre offer *menús* for 1100 ptas or so. *Hospedería del Real Monasterio* has a *menú* for 2100 ptas plus IVA, and a bar opening on the spectacular Gothic cloister which you should go out of your way to visit.

Parador Zurbarán has a sedate *restaurant* with a *menú* for 3200 ptas plus IVA, but a better time can be had at *Mesón El Cordero (Calle Convento 27)*, near the Hospedería del Real Monasterio. It specialises in *cordero asado en horno de leña* (roast lamb from a wood-fired oven) for 1600 ptas. Alternatively, there's a 1500 ptas *menú*.

Getting There & Away

There are two buses on weekdays (and one on Sunday) to/from Cáceres (960 ptas) and

Trujillo. Travelling to/from Mérida or Badajoz, you need to change buses at Miajadas (bus station ☎ 927 34 77 97), served by two buses a day to/from Guadalupe. Two daily buses (one on Sunday) run to/from Madrid (2100 ptas) via Talavera de la Reina. The tourist office has timetables.

Southern Extremadura

MÉRIDA

postcode 06800 • pop 51,830

Mérida stands on the site of the Roman Augusta Emerita, founded in 25 BC for veterans of Rome's campaigns in Cantabria. With more than 40,000 inhabitants, it became the capital of the Roman province of Lusitania, and the largest Roman city on the Iberian Peninsula and its political and cultural hub. Mérida remained an important city under the Visigoths and held out against the Muslims until 713, after which it fell into decline. This continued after the Reconquista by Alfonso IX in 1230 as the inhabitants moved away, leaving Mérida abandoned until the era of the Catholic Monarchs.

Mérida has more Roman ruins than anywhere else in Spain, around which a lively city has grown up. Since 1983 it has been the seat of the Junta de Extremadura, the Extremadura regional government.

Orientation

The train station on Calle Cardero is a 10-minute walk from the central Plaza de España. Much of the city's accommodation lies between the two.

From the bus station, on Avenida de la Libertad on the southern side of the Río Guadiana, it's a 20-minute walk but you have a spectacular view of the Puente Romano from the modern suspension bridge.

The most important Roman ruins are on the eastern side of town, but all are within walking distance. Pedestrianised Calle Santa Eulalia, heading north from Plaza de España, is the main shopping street.

Information

The helpful tourist office (☎ 924 31 53 53, ⓔ otmerida@bme.es) is right by the gates to the Roman theatre and amphitheatre. It's open 9 am to 1.45 pm daily, plus 5 to 7.15 pm weekdays (4 to 6.15 pm in winter). Another good source of information is the Web site at www.medeas.com/merida. Ware Nostrum (☎ 924 38 86 58) is a funky Internet cafe on Calle del Baños.

Several banks on Plaza de España and the streets north off it have ATMs. The main post office is on Plaza de la Constitución. For an ambulance call ☎ 924 38 10 18. The Hospital General (☎ 924 38 10 00) is on Calle Enrique Sánchez de León, south-west of the bus station.

Roman Remains

For 800 ptas (400 ptas for EU citizens with a student or Euro26 card, free for under-18s and over-65s) you can buy a ticket for the Teatro Romano, Anfiteatro, Casa del Anfiteatro, Casa del Mitreo, Alcazaba, Iglesia de Santa Eulalia and Arqueológica de Morería. All these, except Santa Eulalia, which closes on Sunday, are open daily from 9 am to 1.45 pm and 5 to 7.15 pm (4 to 6.15 pm in winter). Entry to just the Teatro Romano and Anfiteatro is 600 ptas. With either ticket you get a detailed booklet in Spanish on Mérida's monuments.

The **Teatro Romano** was built around 15 BC to seat 6000 spectators. Its two-tier backdrop of stone columns is particularly impressive. The adjoining **Anfiteatro**, opened in 8 BC for gladiatorial contests, had a capacity of 14,000. Nearby, the **Casa del Anfiteatro**, a 3rd-century mansion, has remains of paintings and exceptionally good mosaics. The **Casa del Mitreo**, a 2nd-century Roman suburban house on Calle Oviedo, has mosaics in almost every room and top-quality frescoes.

Other Roman monuments are dotted around the city and can be seen at any time. The **Puente Romano** over the Guadiana, 792m long with 60 granite arches, is one of the longest bridges ever built by the Romans. The 15m high **Arco de Trajano** over Calle Trajano may have served as the entrance to the provincial forum, the

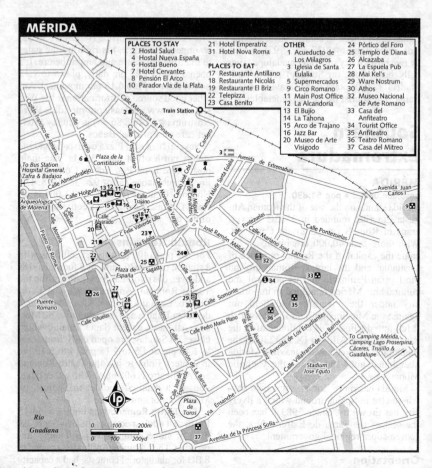

MÉRIDA

PLACES TO STAY
2 Hostal Salud
4 Hostal Nueva España
6 Hostal Bueno
7 Hotel Cervantes
8 Pensión El Arco
10 Parador Vía de la Plata

21 Hotel Emperatriz
31 Hotel Nova Roma

PLACES TO EAT
17 Restaurante Antillano
18 Restaurante Nicolás
19 Restaurante El Briz
22 Telepizza
23 Casa Benito

OTHER
1 Acueducto de Los Milagros
3 Iglesia de Santa Eulalia
5 Supermercados
9 Circo Romano
11 Main Post Office
12 La Alcandoria
13 El Bujío
14 La Tahona
15 Arco de Trajano
16 Jazz Bar
20 Museo de Arte Visigodo

24 Pórtico del Foro
25 Templo de Diana
26 Alcazaba
27 La Espuela Pub
28 Mai Kel's
29 Ware Nostrum
30 Athos
32 Museo Nacional de Arte Romano
33 Casa del Anfiteatro
34 Tourist Office
35 Anfiteatro
36 Teatro Romano
37 Casa del Mitreo

plaza where the government of Lusitania province was conducted. The **Templo de Diana** on Calle Sagasta stood in the municipal forum, where the city government was based, and is well preserved since most of it was incorporated into a mansion in the 16th century. The restored **Pórtico del Foro**, the municipal forum's portico, is nearby on Calle Sagasta.

North-east of the amphitheatre on Avenida Juan Carlos I are the grassed-over remains of the 1st-century **Circo Romano**, the only surviving hippodrome of its kind in Spain. It could accommodate 30,000 spectators and may sometimes have been filled with water for spectacles involving ships.

The remains of the **Acueducto de Los Milagros** off Calle Marquesa de Pinares are highly favoured by nesting storks.

Museo Nacional de Arte Romano

This excellent museum houses a superb collection of statues, mosaics, frescoes, coins and other Roman artefacts. It's open 10 am to 2 pm and 5 to 7 pm Tuesday to Saturday (4 to 6 pm in winter) and 10 am to 2 pm Sunday and holidays (400 ptas but free on

Saturday afternoon and Sunday, students 200 ptas, free for under-18s and over-65s).

Alcazaba

This large Muslim fort on Calle Graciano was built in AD 835 on a site that already had many Roman and Visigothic remains. The 15th-century monastery in its northwestern corner now serves as the Junta de Extremadura's presidential offices.

Iglesia de Santa Eulalia

Originally built in the 5th century in honour of Mérida's patron saint (who was martyred in Roman times and according to tradition buried at this site), this church on Avenida de Extremadura was completely rebuilt in Romanesque style in the 13th century. A museum and open excavated areas enable you to identify Roman houses, a 4th-century Christian cemetery and the original 5th-century basilica. Outside the church, the Hornito de Santa Eulalia Martir shrine was built in 1612 from the remains of a temple of Mars, the Roman war god.

Museo de Arte Visigodo

Many of the Visigothic objects unearthed in Mérida are exhibited in this museum just off Plaza de España, open daily except Monday (free).

Arqueológica de Morería

Nowhere near as spectacular as the Roman remains, this excavated Moorish quarter is still worth a look and contains the remains of a cemetery, walls and houses.

Special Events

The prestigious Festival de Teatro Clásico at the Roman theatre in July and early August features Greek, Roman and more recent drama classics. Mérida lets its hair down a little later than most of Extremadura, in its Feria de Septiembre.

Places to Stay

Camping Mérida (☎ 924 30 34 53) on Carretera de Madrid, 2km east of the edge of town, is open all year and costs 475 ptas plus IVA per person, per tent and per car. A nicer site, a little cheaper but only open from May to mid-September, is *Camping Lago Proserpina* (☎ 924 12 30 55), 5km north of Mérida by a reservoir that is still held back by a Roman dam.

Pensión El Arco (☎ 924 31 83 21, Calle Miguel de Cervantes 16) is great value and deservedly popular with backpackers. Spotless singles/doubles with shared bathroom cost 1800/3500 ptas. *Hostal Bueno* (☎ 924 30 29 77, Calle Calvario 9) is also good value at 2500/4500 ptas. Nearly all rooms have a bathroom; the modernised ones upstairs are the best.

Hostal Salud (☎ 924 31 22 59, Calle Vespasiano 41), a five-minute walk from the train station, has decent rooms with bath for 3000/5500 ptas. *Hostal Nueva España* (☎ 924 31 33 56, Avenida de Extremadura 6) has simple rooms with bath for 3200/5700 ptas.

The more upmarket *Hotel Cervantes* (☎ 924 31 49 61, ℮ informacion@hotelcervantes.com, Calle Camilo José Cela 8) has comfortable rooms for 6000/9000 ptas plus IVA. The international-style *Hotel Nova Roma* (☎ 924 31 12 61, Calle Suárez Somonte 42) charges 8000/11,295 ptas plus IVA. *Hotel Emperatriz*, undergoing refurbishment at the time of writing, is a former palace and in a prime spot on Plaza de España, so it's worth checking out to see if it has reopened. *Parador Vía de la Plata* (☎ 924 31 38 00, ℮ merida@parador.es, Plaza de la Constitución 3) has rooms for 9200/16,500 plus IVA. Originally part of the Roman provincial forum, it has subsequently been a mosque, a convent and an asylum.

Places to Eat

For a cheap bite to eat, *Telepizza* on Plaza de España has fast pizzas from 750 ptas, or head for the two *supermercados* on Calle Camilo José Cela.

Casa Benito on Calle San Francisco is a great old-style wood-panelled bar and restaurant, decked out with bullfight photos and posters. It does local fare at reasonable prices in the form of tapas, raciones or main dishes.

There are three good eateries in a line on Calle Felix Valverde Lillo. The popular *Restaurante El Briz* at No 5 does a great

EXTREMADURA

montado de lomo (pork loin sandwich) for 350 ptas and has a restaurant at the back with a *menú* for 1350 ptas. Next door, the upmarket **Restaurante Nicolás** has a 2000 ptas *menú,* while **Restaurante Antillano** at No 15 has a *menú* for just 1200 ptas.

Parador Vía de la Plata has a *menú* for 3500 ptas plus IVA featuring specialities such as marinated partridge and wild boar stew.

Entertainment

La Alcandoria and **El Bujío** bars on Calle Holguín and **La Tahona** on Calle Alvarado have varied live music some nights – usually Thursday or Friday. Nearby is the classy late-night **Jazz Bar**, just off Plaza de la Constitucíon. Calle John Lennon, southeast of Plaza de España, has a line of late-night music bars, including **La Espuela Pub**, and a large disco, **Mai Kel's**, open 11 pm to 5 am Friday and Saturday. Three blocks away at Calle Baños 29 is the gay bar *Athos*, a little different than your run-of-the-mill late-night bar.

Getting There & Away

Bus From the bus station (☎ 924 37 14 04) at least seven daily buses run to Badajoz (680 ptas), Sevilla (1550 to 1590 ptas) and Madrid (from 2755 ptas) and at least four to Cáceres (675 ptas) and Trujillo (820 ptas). Daily buses also go to Lisbon, Barcelona, Córdoba, Jabugo, Huelva, Ayamonte, Plasencia and Salamanca.

Train There are at least four trains a day to/from Badajoz (one hour, 410 ptas); and two or more to Cáceres (one hour, 515 ptas), Ciudad Real, Madrid (five to six hours, 2945 ptas), Plasencia, Zafra and Barcelona. One daily train runs to/from Sevilla (4½ hours, 1685 ptas). The station can be contacted on ☎ 924 31 81 09.

BADAJOZ

postcode 06001 • pop 122,510

Badajoz, the provincial capital of the southern half of Extremadura, straddles the Río Guadiana just 4km from Portugal. It's an old but now sprawling and industrial city visited by few travellers who are not heading to or from Portugal. The centre was probably once handsome, but now most of it is either modern but uninspired or old and dilapidated. Dilapidation plumbs amazing depths in the streets below the old Muslim Alcazaba (Fort), especially on Plaza Alta. However, you might find Badajoz's unpretentiousness vaguely refreshing. Badajoz's big bash is the Feria de San Juan, for a week around 24 June.

Formerly the capital of a Muslim *taifa* (kingdom), Badajoz was conquered by Alfonso IX of León in 1230 and subsequently became the scene of much military conflict. It was first occupied by Portugal in 1385, and again in 1396, 1542 and 1660. It was besieged during the War of the Spanish Succession, and three times by the French in the Peninsular War. In 1812 the French were driven out by the British in a bloody battle that cost 6000 lives. In the civil war, the Nationalists carried out atrocious massacres when they took Badajoz in 1936.

Orientation

Plaza de España, around the cathedral, is the centre of the old town; west of it are narrow pedestrianised streets, with a number of places to eat and drink. The main commercial centre is to the south, around Avenida Juan Carlos I and Paseo de San Francisco.

The bus station on Calle José Rebollo López is 1km south of the centre. The train station, on Avenida de Carolina Coronado, is 1.5km north-west of the centre, across the river.

Information

The municipal tourist office (☎ 924 22 49 81) on Pasaje de San Juan, just off Plaza de España, is open 9 am to 3 pm and 4 to 8 pm weekdays and 9 am to 1 pm Saturday. For regional information, the Junta de Extremadura tourist office (☎ 924 22 27 63) is at Plaza de la Libertad 3, just south-west of Paseo de San Francisco; it's open 9.30 am to 2 pm and 4 to 6.30 pm weekdays and 9.45 am to 2 pm weekends.

There are plenty of banks, most with ATMs, dotted all over the city and the main post office is on Plaza de la Libertad.

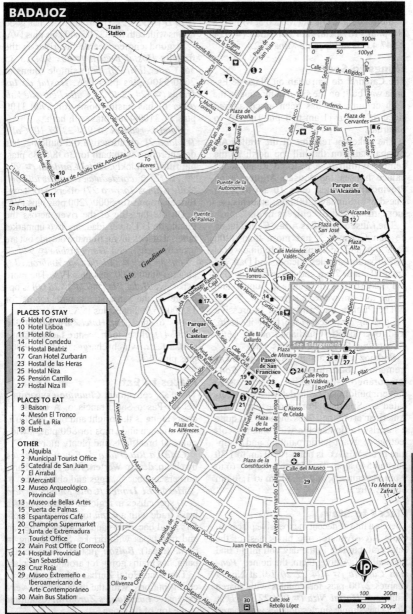

BADAJOZ

Train Station

Puente de la Autonomía

Puente de Palmas

Río Guadiana

Parque de la Alcazaba

Alcazaba

Plaza de San José

Plaza Alta

Calle Meléndez Valdés

Calle Hernán Cortés

Parque de Castelar

Plaza de Minayo

Paseo de San Francisco

Plaza de la Libertad

Plaza de los Alféreces

Plaza de la Constitución

Calle del Museo

To Mérida & Zafra

To Olivenza

Plaza de España

Plaza de Cervantes

See Enlargement

To Cáceres

To Portugal

PLACES TO STAY
- 6 Hotel Cervantes
- 10 Hotel Lisboa
- 11 Hotel Río
- 14 Hotel Condedu
- 16 Hostal Beatriz
- 17 Gran Hotel Zurbarán
- 23 Hostal de las Heras
- 25 Hostal Niza
- 26 Pensión Carrillo
- 27 Hostal Niza II

PLACES TO EAT
- 3 Baison
- 4 Mesón El Tronco
- 8 Café La Ria
- 19 Flash

OTHER
- 1 Alquibla
- 2 Municipal Tourist Office
- 5 Catedral de San Juan
- 7 El Arrabal
- 9 Mercantil
- 12 Museo Arqueológico Provincial
- 13 Museo de Bellas Artes
- 15 Puerta de Palmas
- 18 Espantaperros Café
- 20 Champion Supermarket
- 21 Junta de Extremadura Tourist Office
- 22 Main Post Office (Correos)
- 24 Hospital Provincial San Sebastián
- 28 Cruz Roja
- 29 Museo Extremeño e Iberoamericano de Arte Contemporáneo
- 30 Main Bus Station

EXTREMADURA

euro currency converter €1 = 166pta

The Cruz Roja (☎ 924 22 22 22) is south of the centre at Calle del Museo 5, while the Hospital Provincial San Sebastián (☎ 924 22 47 43) is at Plaza de Minayo 2.

Things to See

The **Catedral de San Juan** on Plaza de España was built on the site of a mosque in the 13th century but has been much altered since. It's open 11 am to 1 pm Tuesday to Saturday.

The unkempt remains of the walled **Alcazaba** stand on the hill top north of the centre. Within it, a restored Renaissance palace houses the **Museo Arqueológico Provincial**, which is open 10 am to 3 pm Tuesday to Sunday (200 ptas; students, senior citizens and EU citizens free).

The **Museo de Bellas Artes**, Calle Duque de San Germán 3, has more than 1200 paintings and sculptures, including works by Zurbarán, Morales, Picasso and Dalí. It's open 10 am to 2 pm and 4 to 6 pm Tuesday to Friday (6 to 8 pm in June to August) and 10 am to 2 pm weekends (free).

The **Puente de Palmas**, an impressive 582m-long granite bridge built in 1596, leads over the Río Guadiana from the 16th-century city **Puerta de Palmas** gate.

Badajoz's pride and joy is the **Museo Extremeño e Iberoamericano de Arte Contemporáneo**, situated in an impressive modern building at Calle del Museo 2, dedicated to Spanish, Portuguese and Latin American art of the 1980s and 90s. It's quite a surprise to find such a wide-ranging collection of avant-garde painting and sculpture here. MEIAC is open 10.30 am to 1.30 pm and 5 to 8 pm Tuesday to Saturday (6 to 9 pm in summer), and 10.30 am to 1.30 pm Sunday (free).

Places to Stay

There's a line of decent inexpensive places on Calle Arco-Agüero, one block east of the cathedral, but late in the day you might find them all full. Among them, the homely **Pensión Carrillo** (☎ 924 22 20 14) at No 39 charges 2700 ptas for doubles with shared bathroom; **Hostal Niza** (☎ 924 22 38 81) at No 34 has simple singles/doubles with shared

bathrooms for 1700/2804 ptas; and **Hostal Niza II** (*☎ 924 22 31 73*) at No 45 has good rooms with bath for 3271/5600 ptas plus IVA.

A good choice nearer the river is the friendly **Hostal Beatriz** (*☎/fax 924 23 35 56, Calle Abril 20*), with simple rooms at 2650/5300 ptas plus IVA. **Hostal de las Heras** (*☎ 924 22 40 14, Calle Pedro de Valdivia 6*) has basic rooms for 2900/3100 ptas, or 3100/4400 ptas with bath.

Hotel Cervantes (*☎ 924 22 37 10, Calle Trinidad 2*), an attractive old building, has decent rooms with bath for 3638/5885 ptas, but fills up quickly. **Hotel Condedu** (*☎ 924 20 72 47, ✉ condedu@cempresarial.com, Calle Muñoz Torrero 27*) offers very comfortable rooms for 5000/7200 ptas plus IVA.

On the far side of the river, across the Puente de la Universidad, are two upmarket hotels that look awful from the outside but are actually pretty good. **Hotel Lisboa** (*☎ 924 27 29 00, Avenida de Adolfo Díaz Ambrona 13*) charges 6000/8000 ptas plus IVA. The more expensive **Hotel Río** (*☎ 924 27 26 00*) is opposite on the same street, with rooms for 12,000/16,000 ptas plus IVA.

Best of all is **Gran Hotel Zurbarán** (*☎ 924 22 37 41*), closer to the centre facing Parque de Castelar, which charges 12,000/19,000 ptas plus IVA.

Places to Eat

There's a convenient **Champion** supermarket on Paseo San Francisco. A couple of doors along is the bright and breezy **Flash**, with chicken and chips for 800 ptas, a wide range of breakfasts and plenty more.

Café La Ria (*Plaza de España 7*) serves up cheap, decent Western food such as hamburgers and bacon, eggs and chips.

Mesón El Tronco (*Calle Muñoz Torrero 16A*) specialises in regional food and does a brisk trade with a *menú* for 1250 ptas. It offers good bocadillos and raciones in the bar, and free tapas with drinks. Specialising in *carne* (meat), **Baison**, just off Plaza de España, has mains going for around 1000 ptas.

The Gran Hotel Zurbarán has a range of eating options, with the excellent but very expensive **Los Monjes Zurbarán** restaurant at the top of its range.

Across the river, Hotel Río has a popular medium-priced *restaurant*.

Entertainment

Late-night bars are scattered around the streets near the cathedral. Among the liveliest are *Espantaperros Café* on Calle Hernán Cortés, *El Arrabal* with garden bar on Calle de San Blas, and the huge *Mercantil* music bar on Calle Zurbarán. The cool *Alquibla* is a friendly chilled-out bar on Calle Virgen de la Soledad and the pick of the crop.

Getting There & Away

Bus From the bus station (☎ 924 25 87 50), at least seven daily buses run to Mérida (665 ptas), Trujillo (1215 to 1515 ptas) and Madrid (3245 to 3795 ptas), five or more to Zafra (750 ptas) and Sevilla (1670 ptas), four to Lisbon (2025 ptas) and at least two each to Cáceres (825 ptas), Plasencia, Salamanca, Córdoba and Barcelona.

Train There are four or more trains a day to Mérida (410 ptas), two or three each to Barcelona, Ciudad Real and Madrid (five to eight hours, 4100 to 4700 ptas); one or two to Cáceres (1¾ hours, 1600 to 1800 ptas); and one (except Saturday) to Plasencia. The 8.15 am train from Badajoz connects at Mérida with a train for Sevilla (six hours). Two trains a day run to Lisbon (five to six hours). The station can be contacted on ☎ 924 27 11 70.

Getting Around

To get into town from the train station, take bus No 1 to Calle Alonso de Celada, just off Paseo de San Francisco. A number of buses run from the bus station into town.

AROUND BADAJOZ
Olivenza

postcode 06100 • pop 10,499

About 24km south of Badajoz on the C-436 lies Olivenza, a town that clings to its strong Portuguese heritage. The whitewashed houses pay testament to the fact that Olivenza has only been Spanish since 1801.

It's a rewarding walk through the town taking in the convents and churches scattered about. Smack bang in the centre is the 14th-

century **castle**, which now houses a small ethnographic museum, open 11 am to 2 pm and 4 to 6 pm Tuesday to Sunday (free). To the south of the city around the 18th-century **Puerta del Calvario** is the largest section of the impressive original defensive **walls**. The tourist office is located at the southern end of Plaza de España (closed Monday).

Accommodation can be found on the C-436 on the way to Badajoz. *Hotel Heredero* (☎ 924 49 08 35) has singles/ doubles for 4500/7300 plus IVA while *Los Amigos* (☎ 924 49 07 25) is the cheaper option charging 2500/3500 plus IVA. There are plenty of places to eat around Plaza de España.

Buses to Badajoz run almost every hour during the week from the bus station, five minutes' walk north of Plaza de España.

ZAFRA

postcode 06300 • pop 14,884

The pretty town of Zafra, 66km south of Mérida, originally a Muslim settlement known as Zafar, is a convenient stop between Badajoz or Mérida and Sevilla. It's also a base for exploring Extremadura's little visited far south.

The tourist office (☎ 924 55 10 36), on the central Plaza de España, is open 11 am to 2 pm and 5 to 7 pm weekdays and 10 am to 2 pm weekends and holidays.

Zafra's 15th-century **castle**, now a parador, was built over the former Muslim *alcázar* (fortress) by order of Lorenzo Suárez de Figueroa, the first Conde de Feria. His descendants commissioned Juan de Herrera to design the Renaissance marble patio. The town's most interesting squares are **Plaza Grande** and the adjoining **Plaza Chica**, both with arcades and cafes.

Places to Stay & Eat

Pensión Carmen (☎ 924 55 14 39, *Avenida de la Estación 9*), about 250m east of Plaza de España, has decent rooms for 3500/7000 ptas, and a moderately priced restaurant.

There's no shortage of mid-range hotels. *Hotel Las Palmeras* (☎ 924 55 22 08, *Plaza Grande 14*) has rooms with bath for 4500/ 9000 ptas plus IVA. *Hotel Don Quijote* (☎ 924 55 47 71, *Calle Huelva 3*), just off

EXTREMADURA

Plaza Grande, has rooms for 5500/8500 ptas plus IVA. Both have restaurants with *menús* for about 1100 ptas.

Hotel Huerta Honda (☎ 924 55 41 00, *Calle Lopéz Asme 30)*, just west of the parador, has good rooms for 8,720/10,900 ptas plus IVA, a nice patio and bar with tapas, and main courses for 2100 to 2600 ptas in its stylish *Restaurante Barbacana.* Set in an old palace, the *Parador Hernán Cortés* (☎ 924 55 45 40, ✉ zafra@para dor.es, Plaza del Corazón de María 7) has rooms for 14,000/17,500 ptas plus IVA and the restaurant in its marble patio does a *menú* for 3500 ptas plus IVA.

Getting There & Away

The bus station (☎ 924 55 39 07) is on Carretera Badajoz-Granada, about 500m northeast of the centre, and the train station (☎ 924 55 02 15) is 1.5km south-east of the centre at the end of Avenida de la Estación. One or two trains per day run to Cáceres, Huelva, Madrid, Mérida, Plasencia and Sevilla.

AROUND ZAFRA

Those with a yearning to get off the beaten track have much scope here. Apart from the main roads to Sevilla and Córdoba, other roads through the rolling Sierra Morena into Andalucía head south-west through Fregenal de la Sierra into northern Huelva province and south-east into the Parque Natural Sierra Norte in Sevilla province. Trains bound for Huelva and Sevilla also go through these regions.

In **Fregenal de la Sierra**, you'll find a castle and adjoining church, both dating from the 13th century, together with a bullring and market square in an unusual grouping. Walled **Jerez de los Caballeros**, 42km west of Zafra, was a cradle of conquistadors (see the boxed text 'Extremadura & America' earlier) and has a Knights Templar castle and several handsome churches, three of them with towers copying the Giralda in Sevilla. There's a tourist office (☎ 924 73 03 72) at Plaza de San Agustín 1.

Feria, 4km off the Badajoz-Zafra road about 20km from Zafra, is dominated by an impressive hill-top 15th-century castle, as is **Burguillos del Cerro**, south-west of Zafra. Just outside **Casas de Reina** on the Guadalcanal road are impressive remains of a Roman theatre and a hill-top Muslim castle.

The tourist offices in Zafra and Jerez de los Caballeros can put you in the picture about other interesting spots to visit. Fregenal de la Sierra, Jerez de los Caballeros and Almendralejo have hostales and hotels.

Language

SPANISH

Spanish nouns are marked for gender (either masculine or feminine) and adjectives will vary according to the gender of the noun they modify. Where necessary, both forms are given for the words and phrases below – the masculine generally ends in 'o', the feminine in 'a'.

Pronunciation

Spanish pronunciation isn't difficult, given that many Spanish sounds are similar to their English counterparts, and there's a clear and consistent relationship between pronunciation and spelling. If you stick to the following rules you should have very few problems making yourself understood.

Vowels

Unlike English, each of the vowels in Spanish has a uniform pronunciation that doesn't vary. For example, the Spanish 'a' has one pronunciation rather than the numerous pronunciations we find in English, such as 'cat', 'cake', 'cart', 'care', 'call'. Many Spanish words have a written accent (as in *días*) generally indicates a stressed syllable and doesn't change the sound of the vowel. Vowels are pronounced clearly even if they are in unstressed positions or at the end of a word.

a	as the 'u' in 'nut', or a shorter sound than the 'a' in 'art'
e	as in 'met'
i	somewhere between the 'i' in 'marine' and the 'i' in 'flip'
o	similar to the 'o' in 'hot'
u	as the 'oo' in 'hoof'

Consonants

Some Spanish consonants are the same as their English counterparts. The pronunciation of other consonants varies according to which vowel follows and also according

to which part of Spain you happen to be in. The Spanish alphabet also contains three consonants that are not found within the English alphabet: **ch**, **ll** and **ñ**.

b	softer than in English; sometimes as in 'be' when initial or preceded by a nasal
c	a hard 'c' as in 'cat' when followed by **a**, **o**, **u** or a consonant; as the 'th' in 'thin' before **e** and **i**
ch	as in 'church'
d	as in 'do' when initial; elsewhere as the 'th' in 'then'
g	as in 'get' when initial and before **a**, **o** and **u**; elsewhere much softer. Before **e** or **i** it's a harsh, breathy sound, similar to the 'h' in 'hit'
h	silent
j	a harsh, guttural sound similar to the 'ch' in Scottish *loch*
ll	as the 'lli' in 'million'; some people pronounce it rather like the 'y' in 'yellow'
ñ	a nasal sound, as the 'ni' in 'onion'
q	as the 'k' in 'kick'; 'q' is always followed by a silent **u** and is combined only with the vowels **e** (as in *que*) and **i** (as in *quien*)
r	a rolled 'r' sound; longer and stronger when initial or doubled
s	as in 'see'
v	the same sound as **b**
x	as the 'ks' sound in 'taxi' when between two vowels; as the 's' in 'see' when preceding a consonant
z	as the 'th' in 'thin'

Semiconsonant

Spanish also has the semiconsonant **y**. When at the end of a word or when standing alone as a conjunction it's pronounced like the Spanish **i**. As a consonant, it's somewhere between the 'y' in 'yonder' and the 'g' in 'beige', depending on the region.

Greetings & Civilities

Hello/Goodbye.	*¡Hola!/¡Adiós!*
Yes/No.	*Sí/No.*
Please.	*Por favor.*
Thank you.	*Gracias.*
That's fine/ You're welcome.	*De nada.*
Excuse me.	*Perdón/Perdoneme.*
I'm sorry. (excuse me, forgive me)	*Lo siento/ Discúlpeme.*
What's your name?	*¿Cómo se llama?*
My name is ...	*Me llamo ...*

Language Difficulties

Do you speak English?	*¿Habla inglés?*
Does anyone speak English?	*¿Hay alguien que hable inglés?*
I understand.	*Entiendo.*
I don't understand.	*No entiendo.*
Please write that down.	*¿Puede escribirlo, por favor?*

Getting Around

What time does the ... leave/arrive?	*¿A qué hora sale/ llega el ...?*
boat	*barco*
bus (city)	*autobús, bus*
bus (intercity)	*autocar*
train	*tren*
tram	*tranvía*
next	*próximo*
first	*primer*
last	*último*
I'd like a ... ticket.	*Quisiera un billete ...*
one-way	*sencillo/de sólo ida*
return	*de ida y vuelta*
1st class	*de primera clase*
2nd class	*de segunda clase*
left-luggage office	*consigna*
timetable	*horario*
bus stop	*parada de autobus*
train station	*estación (de ferrocarril)*
the underground	*el metro*
I'd like to hire a car/bicycle.	*Quisiera alquilar un coche/una bicicleta.*

Signs – Spanish

Entrada	**Entrance**
Salida	**Exit**
Abierto	**Open**
Cerrado	**Closed**
Información	**Information**
Prohibido	**Prohibited**
Habitaciones Libres	**Rooms Available**
Ocupado/Completo	**No Vacancies**
Comisaría	**Police Station**
Servicios/Aseos	**Toilets**
Hombres	**Men**
Mujeres	**Women**

I want to go to ...	*Quiero ir a ...*
Can you show me (on the map)?	*¿Me puede indicar (en el mapa)?*
Where is ...?	*¿Dónde está ...?*
near	*cerca*
far	*lejos*
Go straight ahead.	*Siga/Vaya todo derecho.*
Turn left.	*Gire a la izquierda.*
Turn right.	*Gire a la derecha/ recto.*

Around Town

I'm looking for ...	*Estoy buscando ...*
a bank	*un banco*
the city centre	*el centro de la ciudad*
the ... embassy	*la embajada ...*
my hotel	*mi hotel*
the market	*el mercado*
the police	*la policía*
the post office	*los correos*
public toilets	*los servicios/ aseos públicos*
the telephone centre	*el locutorio*
the tourist office	*la oficina de turismo*
the beach	*la playa*
the bridge	*el puente*
the castle	*el castillo*
the cathedral	*la catedral*
the church	*la iglesia*

the hospital	el hospital
the lake	el lago
the main square	la plaza mayor
the mosque	la mezquita
the old city	la ciudad antigua/ el casco antiguo
the palace	el palacio
the ruins	las ruinas
the sea	el mar
the square	la plaza
the tower	la torre

| What time does it open/close? | ¿A qué hora abren/cierran? |
| How much is it? | ¿Cuánto cuesta?/ ¿Cuánto vale? |

Accommodation

camping ground	camping
guesthouse	pensión/casa de huéspedes
hotel	hotel
youth hostel	albergue juvenil

Where is a cheap hotel?	¿Dónde hay un hotel barato?
What's the address?	¿Cuál es la dirección?
Could you write it down, please?	¿Puede escribirla, por favor?
Do you have any rooms available?	¿Tiene habitaciones libres?

a bed	una cama
a single room	una habitación individual
a double room	una habitación doble
a room with a bathroom	una habitación con baño
to share a dorm	compartir un dormitorio
for/one two nights	para una/dos noches

How much is it ...?	¿Cuánto cuesta ...?
per night	por noche
per person	por persona

Is breakfast included?	¿Incluye el desayuno?
May I see it?	¿Puedo verla?
Where is the bathroom?	¿Dónde está el baño?

Emergencies – Spanish

Help!	¡Socorro!/¡Auxilio!
Call a doctor!	¡Llame a un doctor!
Call the police!	¡Llame a la policía!
Where are the toilets?	¿Dónde están los servicios?
Go away!	¡Váyase!
I'm lost.	Estoy perdido/a.

Food

breakfast	desayuno
lunch	almuerzo/comida
dinner	cena

I'd like the set meal.	Quisiera el menú del día.
Is service included?	¿El servicio está incluido?
I'm a vegetarian.	Soy vegetariano/ vegetariana.

Health

I'm ...	Soy ...
diabetic	diabético/a
epileptic	epiléptico/a
asthmatic	asmático/a

I'm allergic ...	Soy alérgico/a ...
to antibiotics	a los antibióticos
to penicillin	a la penicilina

antiseptic	antiséptico
aspirin	aspirina
condoms	preservativos/ condones
contraceptive	anticonceptivo
diarrhoea	diarrea
medicine	medicamento
nausea	náusea
sunblock cream	crema protectora contra el sol
tampons	tampones

Time, Days & Numbers

What time is it?	¿Qué hora es?
today	hoy
tomorrow	mañana
yesterday	ayer
in the morning	de la mañana

in the afternoon	*de la tarde*
in the evening	*de la noche*
Monday	*lunes*
Tuesday	*martes*
Wednesday	*miércoles*
Thursday	*jueves*
Friday	*viernes*
Saturday	*sábado*
Sunday	*domingo*
January	*enero*
February	*febrero*
March	*marzo*
April	*abril*
May	*mayo*
June	*junio*
July	*julio*
August	*agosto*
September	*setiembre/septiembre*
October	*octubre*
November	*noviembre*
December	*diciembre*

0	*cero*
1	*uno, una*
2	*dos*
3	*tres*
4	*cuatro*
5	*cinco*
6	*seis*
7	*siete*
8	*ocho*
9	*nueve*
10	*diez*
11	*once*
12	*doce*
13	*trece*
14	*catorce*
15	*quince*
16	*dieciséis*
17	*diecisiete*
18	*dieciocho*
19	*diecinueve*
20	*veinte*
21	*veintiuno*
22	*veintidós*
23	*veintitrés*
30	*treinta*
31	*treinta y uno*

40	*cuarenta*
50	*cincuenta*
60	*sesenta*
70	*setenta*
80	*ochenta*
90	*noventa*
100	*cien/ciento*
1000	*mil*

one million	*un millón*

BASQUE

The Basque language is one of the oldest in the world, and a key to primitive Europe. It's the oldest surviving pre-Indo-European language in Europe; Hungarian and Finnish arrived considerably later. In a territory straddling France and Spain, and divided by the Pyrenees, Basque is spoken by 800,000 of the 2.4 million people who live in the territory known in Basque as *Euskadi*.

Pronunciation

An English-speaker shouldn't have many difficulties with Basque pronunciation. There are no written accents, and stress is flexible. Vowels are pronounced as in Castilian. There are two distinct 'r' sounds to be aware of: one, much as the English 'r' when at the beginning or middle of a word; and the other, like a cross between the Scottish 'r' and the growl of a two-stroke motorbike: 'r-r-r-r-r-r'. Consonants are pronounced as in English with the exception of the following:

g	always hard, as in 'goat'
h	silent in Spanish Basque Country; as the 'h' in 'hat' in French Basque Country
rr	the growly 'r'
tx/ts	as the 'ch' in 'chew'
tz	as the 'tz' in 'tzetze'
x	as the 'sh' in 'ship'
z	as the 's' in 'sun'

Basics

Hi!	*Kaixo!*
Good morning.	*Egunon.*
Good night.	*Gabon.*
Goodbye.	*Agur.*

See you later.	*Gero arte.*
Please.	*Mesedez.*
Thank you.	*Eskerrik asko.*
Excuse me.	*Parkatu.*
How do you say	*Nola esaten da*
that in Basque?	*hori euskaraz?*

Finding Your Way

Where's the toilet,	*Non dago komuna,*
please?	*mesedez?*
At the end.	*Azkenean.*
Straight ahead.	*Zuzen-zuzenian.*
On the left.	*Ezkerretara.*
On the right.	*Eskuinetara.*

Small Talk

How are you?	*Zer moduz?*
Very well, thanks.	*Oso ongi, eskerrik asko.*
What's your name?	*Nola duzu izena?*
I'm called Quentin.	*Nire izena Quentin da.*
Where are you from?	*Nongoa zara?*
I'm from ...	*Ni ... naiz.*

Food

Waiter!	*Aizak!/Aizan!* (m/f)
I'd like ...	*... nahi nuke.*
a beer.	*garagardo bat*
a bottle of wine	*botila bat ardo*
beefsteak with chips	*xerra patata frijituekin*
a little bread	*ogi piska bat*
water	*ura*
mineral water	*metalura*
fish	*arraina*
vegetables	*barazkiak*

Numbers

1	*bat*
2	*bi*
3	*hiru*
4	*lau*
5	*bost*
6	*sei*
7	*zazpi*
8	*zortzi*
9	*bederatzi*
10	*hamar*

CATALAN

Catalan is one of the Romance, or neo-Latin, languages such as French, Italian, Portuguese, Romanian and Spanish. It's not a dialect of any other language and its nearest relative is Occitan, spoken colloquially in southern France. It's the mother tongue of up to seven million people, most of whom also speak at least one other language. It has a number of local dialect variations: in Catalunya, most of Valencia, the Balearic Islands, the strip of Aragón that borders Catalunya, Andorra, Roussillon (in France), and in and around L'Alguer (Alghero) in Sardinia.

Pronunciation

Catalan sounds are not hard for an English-speaker to pronounce but you should note that vowels will vary according to whether they occur in stressed or unstressed syllables.

Vowels

a	stressed, as in 'far'; unstressed, as in 'about'
e	stressed, as in 'pet'; unstressed, as the 'e' in 'open'
i	as the 'i' in 'machine'
o	stressed, as in 'pot'; unstressed, as the 'oo' in 'zoo'
u	as the 'u' in 'humid'

Consonants

b	pronounced 'p' at the end of a word
c	as in 'cat' before a, o, and u; as in 'race' before e and i
ç	like 'ss'
d	pronounced 't' at the end of a word
g	as in 'go' before a, o and u; as the 's' in 'measure' before e and i
h	silent
j	as the 's' in 'pleasure'
r	a strongly rolled 'r' when at the beginning of a word; as in 'red' when in the middle of a word; in the east it's often silent at the end of a word
rr	a strongly rolled 'r'
s	as in 'so' at the beginning of a word; as 'z' in the middle of a word
v	in Barcelona it's pronounced as 'b'; as 'v' in other areas

LANGUAGE

x   mostly as in English but sometimes as 'sh'

Other letters are pronounced approximately as in English. There are, however, a few odd combinations:

ll   repeat the 'l'
qu   like 'k'
tx   like 'ch'

Basics
Hi!	*Hola!*
Good morning/ Goodbye.	*Bon dia.*
Good afternoon.	*Bona tarda.*
Good night.	*Bona nit.*
Goodbye.	*Adéu.*
See you later.	*A reveure.*
Please.	*Sisplau/Si us plau.*
Thank you.	*Gràcies.*
Thank you very much.	*Moltes gràcies.*
You're welcome.	*De res, company.*
Excuse me.	*Perdoni.*
How much is it?	*Quant val?*
Do you speak English?	*Parla anglès?*
Could you speak Castilian please?	*Pot parlar castellà sisplau?*
I understand.	*Ho entenc.*
I don't understand.	*No ho entenc.*
How do you say that in Catalan?	*Com es diu això en català?*
today	*avui*
tomorrow	*demà*

Finding Your Way
Where's the toilet, please?	*On és el lavabo, si us plau?*
At the end.	*Al fons.*
On the left.	*A mà esquerra.*
On the right.	*A la dreta.*

Small Talk
I'd like you to meet ...	*Li presento ...*
Pleased to meet you.	*Molt de gust.*
Delighted!	*Encantat/ Encantada.* (m/f)

What's new?	*Què hi ha?*
How are you?	*Com esteu?*
Very well, thanks.	*Molt bé, gràcies.*
Take care.	*Passi-ho bé.*
What's your name?	*Com es diu?*
My name is ...	*Em dic ...*
I like ...	*M'agrada ...*
OK.	*Val/D'acord.*
Where are you from?	*D'on ets?*

I'm from ...	*Sóc de ...*
UK	*Anglaterra*
USA	*América*
New Zealand	*Nova Zelanda*
Australia	*Austràlia*

Food
Catalan food is among the best in Spain. For names and descriptions of typical dishes, see the boxed text 'Catalan Cuisine' in the Catalunya chapter.

breakfast	*esmorzar*
lunch	*dinar*
dinner	*sopar*

Waiter!	*Cambrer!*
May I see the menu please?	*Puc veure el menú, sisplau?*

I'd like ..., please.	*Voldira ... si us plau.*
a beer	*una cervesa*
a bottle	*una ampolla*
a drop of wine (No BYO here!)	*un glop de vi*
a little bread	*una mica de pa*

I'm vegetarian.	*Soc vegetarià.*

Numbers
1	*un/una*
2	*dos/dues*
3	*tres*
4	*quatre*
5	*cinc*
6	*sis*
7	*set*
8	*vuit*
9	*nou*
10	*deu*

GALICIAN

The language of the natives of Galicia tends not to be promoted as vigorously as Basque or Catalan. Although signs in Galician (*galego* to the locals) have popped up all over the region, you'll generally hear Castilian spoken, not Galician. As you get further off the beaten track, your chances of encountering people who prefer not to speak Castilian will grow. A close cousin of Portuguese, Galician is nevertheless distinct from its neighbour.

Useful Words & Phrases

Hello!	*Ola!*
Goodbye.	*Adeus/Até logo.*
See you later.	*Vemos-nos.*
Please.	*Por favor.*
Thank you.	*Gracias/Graciñas.*
That's fine/ You're welcome.	*De nada.*
What's your name?	*Como se chama?*
My name is ...	*Chamo-me ...*
Excuse me/Sorry.	*Perdoa.*
Do you speak English?	*Falas inglés?*
I don't understand.	*Non entendo.*
Please write that down.	*Por favor, pódemo escribir?*
How do I get to ...?	*Como se vai a ...?*

When does the bus/ train arrive/leave?	*A qué hora chega/ sae o autobús/tren?*
Where is a cheap hotel?	*Onda hay un hotel/ unha fonda?*
I'm looking for ...	*Estou buscando ...*
What's the address?	*Cal é o enderezo?*
What time is it?	*Qué hora é?*

open	*aberto*
closed	*pechado*

Numbers

1	*unha/un*
2	*duas/dous*
3	*tres*
4	*catro*
5	*cinco*
6	*seis*
7	*sete*
8	*oito*
9	*nove*
10	*dez*

Glossary

Unless otherwise indicated, these terms are in Castilian Spanish. For help in decoding menus, see the Food Glossary.

abierto – open
abogado de oficio – duty solicitor
acequia – Islamic-era canals
aficionado – enthusiast
agroturismo – another word for *turismo rural*
ajuntament – Catalan for *ayuntamiento*
alameda – tree-lined avenue
albergue – refuge
albergue juvenil – youth hostel; not to be confused with *hostal*
alcalde – mayor
alcázar – Muslim-era fortress
alfiz – rectangular frame about the top of an arch in Islamic architecture
altar mayor – high altar
alud – avalanche
años de hambre – literally 'years of hunger'; a period in the late 1940s when Spain was hit by a UN-sponsored trade boycott
apartado de correos – post office box
área de acampada – see *zona de acampada*
armadura – wooden *mudéjar* ceiling, especially one like an inverted ship's hull
arroyo – stream
artesonado – *mudéjar* wooden ceiling with interlaced beams leaving a pattern of spaces for decoration
auto de fe – elaborate execution ceremony staged by the Inquisition
autonomía – autonomous community or region: Spain's 50 *provincias* are grouped into 17 of these
autopista – tollway
autovía – toll-free dual-carriage highway
AVE – Tren de Alta Velocidad Española; high-speed train
ayuntamiento – city or town hall
azulejo – glazed tile

bakalao – ear-splitting Spanish techno music (not to be confused with *bacalao*, salted cod)

balcón – balcony
baño completo – full bathroom, with a toilet, shower and/or bath, and washbasin
barranco – dry river bed
barrio – district/quarter (of town or city)
biblioteca – library
bici todo terreno – mountain bike
bodega – literally, a cellar (especially a wine cellar); also means a winery, or a traditional wine bar likely to serve wine from the barrel
bomberos – fire brigade
bota – sherry cask or animal-skin wine vessel
botijo – jug, usually an earthenware one
BTT – abbreviation for *bici todo terreno*
buceo – snorkelling (also used to mean diving; see *submarinismo*)
buzón – letter box

cajero automático – automatic teller machine (ATM)
calle – street
callejón – lane
cama – bed
cambio – in general, change; also currency exchange
campings – officially graded camping grounds
caña – a beer in a small glass
cante hondo – literally 'deep song'; song of the *gitanos*
capeas – amateur bullfights
capilla – chapel
capilla mayor – chapel containing the high altar of a church
carmen – walled villa with gardens, in Granada
carnaval – carnival; a period of fancy-dress parades and merrymaking in many places, usually ending on the Tuesday 47 days before Easter Sunday
carretera – highway
carta – menu
casa de huéspedes – guesthouse; also *hospedaje*
casa de labranza – a *casa rural* in Cantabria

942

casa de pagès – a *casa rural* in Catalunya

casa rural – a village or country house or farmstead with rooms to let

casco – literally 'helmet'; often used to refer to the old part of a city (more correctly, *casco antiguo/histórico/viejo*)

castellano – Castilian; a term often used in preference to *'español'* to describe the national language

castellers – Catalan human-castle builders

castillo – castle

castro – Celtic fortified village

català – Catalan language; a native of Catalunya

catedral – cathedral

caudillo – Franco's title; roughly equivalent to the German *Führer*

cava – Spanish equivalent of champagne

caza – hunting

centro de salud – health centre

cercanías – local trains serving big cities' suburbs and nearby towns

cerrado – closed

certificado – certified mail

cervecería – beer bar

chato – glass

churrigueresque – ornate style of baroque architecture named after the brothers Alberto and José Churriguera

cigarrales – country estates

ciudad – city

claustro – cloister

CNIG – Centro Nacional de Información Geográfica; producers of good quality maps

cofradía – same as *hermandad*

colegiata – collegiate church

coll – Catalan for *collado*

collado – mountain pass

comarca – district; grouping of municipios

comedor – dining room

comisaría – National Police station

completo – full

comunidad – fixed charge for maintenance of rental accommodation (sometimes included in the rent)

comunidad autónoma – see *autonomía*

condones – condoms

conquistador – adventurer; pilgrim

consigna – left-luggage office or lockers

converso – Jew who converted to Christianity in medieval Spain

copas – drinks (literally 'glasses'); *ir de copas* is to go out for a few drinks

cordillera – mountain range

coro – choir (part of a church, usually in the middle)

correos – post office

corrida de toros – bullfight

Cortes – national parliament

costa – coast

cruceiro – standing crucifix found at many crossroads in Galicia

cuenta – bill (check)

cuesta – lane (usually on a hill)

custodia – monstrance

DELE – Diploma de Español como Lengua Extranjera; language qualification recognised by the Spanish government

día del espectador – cut-price ticket day at cinemas (literally 'viewer's day')

diapositiva – slide film

dolmen – prehistoric megalithic tomb

ducha – shower

duro – literally 'hard'; also a common name for a 5 ptas coin

embalse – reservoir

embarcadero – pier or landing stage

encierro – running of bulls Pamplona-style (also happens in many other places around Spain)

entrada – entrance

ermita – hermitage or chapel

església – Catalan for *iglesia*

estació – Catalan for *estación*

estación de autobuses – bus station

estación de esquí – ski station or resort

estación de ferrocarril – train station

estación marítima – ferry terminal

estanco – tobacconist shop

extremeño – Extremaduran; a native of Extremadura

farmacia – pharmacy

faro – lighthouse

feria – fair; can refer to trade fairs as well as to city, town or village fairs that are basically several days of merrymaking; can also mean a bullfight or festival stretching over days or weeks

ferrocarril – railway

FEVE – Ferrocarriles de Vía Estrecha; a national train company

fiesta – festival, public holiday or party

fin de semana – weekend

flamenco – means flamingo and Flemish as well as flamenco music and dance

funicular aereo – cable car; also called *teleféric*

fútbol – football (soccer)

gaditano – person from Cádiz

gaita – Galician version of the bagpipes

gallego – Galician; a native of Galicia

garum – a spicy, vitamin-rich sauce made from fish entrails in Roman Andalucía, used as a seasoning or tonic

gatos – literally 'cats'; also a colloquial name for *madrileños*

gitanos – the Roma people (formerly known as the Gypsies)

glorieta – big roundabout

GRs – senderos de Gran Recorrido; extensive network of long-distance paths

guardía civil – police

gusanitos – corn puffs sold at *kioscos*

habitaciones libres – literally 'rooms available'

hermandad – brotherhood, in particular one that takes part in religious processions

hórreo – Galician or Asturian grain store

hospedaje – guesthouse

hostal – establishment providing accommodation in the one- to three-star category; not to be confused with *albergue juvenil*

hostal-residencia – *hostal* without any kind of restaurant

huerta – market garden; orchard

humedal – wetland

iglesia – church

infanta/infante – princess/prince

IVA – *impuesto sobre el valor añadido,* or value-added tax

judería – Jewish *barrio* in medieval Spain

kioscos – kiosk; newspaper stand

la gente guapa – literally 'the beautiful people'

lavabo – washbasin

lavandería – laundrette

librería – bookshop

lidia – the art of bullfighting

lista de correos – poste restante

litera – couchette or sleeping carriage

llegada – arrival

locutorio – private telephone centre

luz – electricity

macarras – Madrid's rough but (usually) likable lads

madrileño – a person from Madrid

madrugada – the 'early hours', from around 3 am to dawn – a pretty lively time in some Spanish cities!

manchego – La Manchan; a person from La Mancha

marcha – action, life, 'the scene'

marisquería – seafood eatery

mas tasas – plus tax

medina – Arabic word for town or city

menú – short form for *menú del día*

menú del día – daily set meal available at lunchtime, sometimes in the evening too; often called just a *menú*

mercadillo – flea market

mercado – market

mercat – Catalan for *mercado*

meseta – the high tableland of central Spain

mihrab – prayer niche in a mosque indicating the direction of Mecca

mirador – lookout point

modernisme – literally 'modernism'; the architectural and artistic style, influenced by Art Nouveau and sometimes known as Catalan modernism, whose leading practitioner was Antoni Gaudí

modernista – an exponent of *modernisme*

mojito – popular Cuban-based rum concoction

monasterio – monastery

morería – former Islamic quarter in a town

morisco – a Muslim converted (often only superficially) to Christianity in medieval Spain

moro – 'Moor' or Muslim (usually in a medieval context)

movida – similar to *marcha;* a *zona de movida* is an area of a town where lively bars and maybe discos are clustered

Mozarab – Christian living under Muslim rule in medieval Spain; those who left for Christian territory often took their Islamic-influenced Mozarabic style of architecture and decoration with them

mozarabic – style of architecture developed by Mozarabs, Christians living under Islamic rule, adopting elements of classic Islamic construction to Christian architecture

mudéjar – see *Mozarab;* also refers to a decorative style of architecture

muelle – wharf or pier

municipio – municipality, Spain's basic local administrative unit

muralla – city wall

museo – museum

museu – Catalan for *museo*

muwallad – descendant of Christians who converted to Islam in medieval Spain

nezakal turismoa – *turismo rural* (Basque)

objetos perdidos – lost and found office

oficina de turismo – tourist office; also *oficina de información turística*

Páginas Amarillas – phone directory (the 'Yellow Pages')

Pantocrator – Christ the All-Ruler or Christ in Majesty, a central emblem of Romanesque art

parador – one of a chain of luxurious state-owned hotels, many of them in historic buildings

parque nacional – national park; strictly controlled protected area

parque natural – natural park; protected environmental area

paseo – promenade or boulevard

pasos – figures carried in *Semana Santa* parades

peña – a club, usually of flamenco *aficionados* or Real Madrid or Barcelona football fans; sometimes a dining club

pensión – small private hotel

pinchadiscos – DJs

pintxos – Basque for *tapas*

piscina – swimming pool

plateresque – early phase of Renaissance architecture noted for its intricately decorated facades

platja – Catalan for *playa*

plato combinado – literally 'combined plate', a largish serve of meat/seafood/omelette with trimmings

playa – beach

plaza de toros – bullring

porrón – jug with a long, thin spout through which you (try to) pour wine into your mouth

port – Catalan for *puerto*

PP – Partido Popular (People's Party)

PRs – *senderos de Pequeño Recorrido;* footpaths for day or weekend walks

presa – dam

preservativos – condoms

prohibido – prohibited

pronunciamiento – pronouncement of military rebellion

provincia – province; Spain is divided into 50 of them

PSOE – Partido Socialista Obrero Español (Spanish Socialist Worker Party)

pueblo – village

puente – bridge; also means the extra day or two off that many people take when a holiday falls close to a weekend

puerta – gate or door

puerto – port or mountain pass; see also *port*

punta – point or promontory

RACE – Real Automóvil Club de España

ración – meal-sized serve of *tapas*

rambla – avenue or river bed

rastro – flea market, car-boot (trunk) sale

REAJ – Red Española de Albergues Juveniles, which is the Spanish HI youth hostel network

real – royal

Reconquista – the Christian reconquest of the Iberian Peninsula from the Muslims (8th to 15th centuries)

refugi – Catalan for *refugio*

refugio – shelter or refuge, especially a mountain refuge with basic accommodation for walkers

reja – grille, especially a wrought-iron one dividing a chapel from the rest of a church

RENFE – Red Nacional de los Ferrocarriles Españoles; the national rail network

reredos – decoration behind an altar

reservas nacional de caza – national hunting reserves, where hunting is permitted but controlled
retablo – altarpiece
Reyes Católicos – Catholic Monarchs; Isabel and Fernando
ría – estuary
río – river
riu – Catalan for *río*
rodalies – Catalan for *cercanías*
romería – festive pilgrimage or procession
ronda – ring road

sacristía – sacristy; the part of a church in which vestments, sacred objects and other valuables are kept
sala capitular – chapter house
salida – exit or departure
santuario – shrine or sanctuary
Semana Santa – Holy Week, the week leading up to Easter Sunday
Sephardic Jews – Jews of Spanish origin
servicios – toilets
sevillana – Andalucian folk dance
SGE – Servicio Geográfico del Ejército (Army Geographic Service); producers of good quality maps
sida – AIDS
sidra – cider
sidrería – cider bar
sierra – mountain range
s/m – on menus, an abbreviation for *según mercado,* meaning 'according to market price'
s/n – sin número (without number), sometimes seen in addresses
submarinismo – scuba diving
supermercado – supermarket

tablao – tourist-oriented flamenco performances
taifa – small Muslim kingdom in medieval Spain
tapas – bar snacks traditionally served on a saucer or lid *(tapa)*
taquilla – ticket window
tarjeta de crédito – credit card
tarjeta de residencia – residence card

tarjeta telefónica – phonecard
techumbre – roof, or specifically a common type of *armadura*
telefèric – cable car; also called *funicular aereo*
temporada alta/media/baja – high/mid/low season
terraza – terrace; often means a cafe's or bar's outdoor tables
tertulia – informal discussion group or other regular social gathering
tetería – teahouse, usually in Middle Eastern style with low seats around low tables
tienda – shop or tent
topoguías – detailed Spanish walking guides
torno – revolving counter in a convent by which nuns can sell cakes, sweets and other products to the public without being seen
torre – tower
transept – the two wings of a cruciform church at right angles to the nave
trascoro – screen behind the *coro*
trono – literally 'throne'; can also mean the platform an image is carried on in a religious procession
turismo – means both tourism and saloon car; *el turismo* can also mean 'tourist office'
turismo rural – rural tourism; usually refers to accommodation in a *casa rural* and associated activities such as walking and horse riding
tympanum – semi-circle above the main entrance of a church

urbanització – Catalan for *urbanización*
urbanización – suburban housing development
urgencia – emergency

vall – Catalan for *valle*
valle – valley
v.o. – abbreviation of *versión original;* a foreign-language film subtitled in Spanish

zona de acampada – country camp site with no facilities, no supervision and no charge; also called *área de acampada*

Food Glossary

Spain has such huge variety in food and food terminology from place to place that you could travel the country for years and still find unfamiliar items on every menu. This is nothing new: Don Quijote visited one inn which had nothing to offer except a type of fish which 'they call *abadejo* in Castilla, *bacalao* in Andalucía, in other parts *curadillo* and in others *truchuela*'. Still, you should be able to decipher a good half of most worthwhile menus with the help of the following lists:

Ways of Cooking & Preparing Food

a la brasa – chargrilled
a la parrilla – grilled
a la plancha – grilled on a hotplate
a la vasca – with parsley, garlic and peas; a Basque green sauce
adobo – a marinade of vinegar, salt, lemon and spices, usually for fish before frying
ahumado/a – smoked
albóndiga – meatball or fishball
aliño – anything in a vinegar and oil dressing
allioli (or alioli) – garlic mayonnaise
asado – roasted
caldereta – stew
caldo – broth, stock, consomme
casero/a – home-made
cazuela – casserole
cocido – cooked; also hotpot/stew
croqueta – croquette
crudo – raw
escabeche – a marinade of oil, vinegar and water for pickling perishables, usually fish or seafood
espeto – spit
estofado – stew
fideuá – a *paella* made with noodles instead of rice
flamenquín – rolled and crumbed veal or ham, deep fried
frito – fried
gratinada – au gratin
guiso – stew

horneado – baked
horno – oven
olla – pot
paella – rice, seafood and meat dish
pavía – battered fish or seafood
pil pil – garlic sauce usually spiked with chilli
potaje – stew
rebozado – battered and fried
relleno – stuffed
salado – salted, salty
seco – dry, dried
tierno/a – tender
zarzuela – fish stew

Basics

aceite (de oliva) – (olive) oil
ajo – garlic
arroz – rice
azúcar – sugar
bollo – bread roll
confitura – jam
espagueti – spaghetti
fideo – vermicelli noodles
harina – flour
macarrones – macaroni
mayonesa – mayonnaise
mermelada – jam
miel – honey
mollete – soft bread roll
pan – bread
panecillo – bread roll
pimienta – pepper
sal – salt
salsa – sauce
soja – soy
tostada – toasted roll
trigo – wheat
vinagre – vinegar

Soups & Snacks

bocadillo – bread roll with filling
ensalada – salad
entremeses – hors d'oeuvres; starters
gazpacho – cold, blended soup of tomatoes, peppers, cucumber, onions, garlic, lemon and breadcrumbs

media-ración – half serve of *tapas;* see *ración*
meriendas – afternoon snacks
montadito – small bread roll with filling, or a small sandwich, or an open sandwich (often toasted)
pincho – a tapa-sized portion of food; *pintxo* in Basque; also a *pinchito* (see Carne & Aves)
pitufo – small filled baguette or roll
ración – meal-sized serving of *tapas*
sopa de ajo – garlic soup
tabla – selection of cold meats and cheeses
tapa – snack on a saucer or lid *(tapa)*

Frutas (Fruit)
aceituna – olive
aguacate – avocado
cereza – cherry
chirimoya – custard apple, a tropical fruit
frambuesa – raspberry
fresa – strawberry
granada – pomegranate
higo – fig
lima – lime
limón – lemon
mandarina – tangerine
manzana – apple
manzanilla – a type of olive (also means camomile and a type of sherry)
melocotón – peach
melón – melon
naranja – orange
pasa – raisin
piña – pineapple
plátano – banana
sandía – watermelon
uva – grape

Vegetales/Verduras/Hortalizas (Vegetables)
alcachofa – artichoke
apio – celery
berenjena – aubergine, eggplant
calabacín – zucchini, courgette
calabaza – pumpkin
cebolla – onion
champiñones – mushrooms
col – cabbage
coliflor – cauliflower
espárragos – asparagus

espinacas – spinach
guindilla – chilli pepper
guisante – pea
hongo – wild mushroom
judías blancas – butter beans
judías verdes – green beans
lechuga – lettuce
maíz – sweet corn
patata – potato
patatas a lo pobre – poor man's potatoes (potato dish with peppers and garlic)
patatas bravas – spicy fried potatoes
patatas fritas – chips, French fries
pimiento – pepper, capsicum
pipirrana – salad of diced tomatoes and red peppers
puerro – leek
seta – wild mushroom
tomate – tomato
verdura – green vegetable
zanahoria – carrot

Legumbres (Pulses) & Nueces (Nuts)
almendra – almond
alubia – dried bean
anacardo – cashew nut
cacahuete – peanut
faba – type of dried bean
garbanzo – chickpea
haba – broad bean
lentejas – lentils
nuez – nut, also walnut
piñón – pine nut
pipa – sunflower seed

Pescados (Fish)
aguja – swordfish
anchoa – tinned anchovy
atún – tuna
bacalao – salted cod (soaked before cooking, it's prepared many different ways and can be succulent)
boquerones – anchovies marinated in vinegar or fried
caballa – mackerel
cazón – dogfish
chanquetes – whitebait (baby fish – illegal but not uncommon)
dorada – sea bass
lenguado – sole

merluza – hake
mero – halibut, grouper, sea bass
mojama – cured tuna
pescadilla – whiting
pescaíto frito – small fried fish
pez espada – swordfish
platija – flounder
rape – monkfish
rosada – ocean catfish, wolf-fish
salmón – salmon
salmonete – red mullet
sardina – sardine
trucha – trout

Mariscos (Seafood)
almejas – clams
bogavante – lobster
búsano – sea snail, whelk
calamares – squid
camarón – small prawn, shrimp
cangrejo – crab
cangrejo de río – crayfish
carabinero – large prawn
chipirón – small squid
choco – cuttlefish
cigala – crayfish
frito variado – a mixture of deep-fried seafood
fritura – same as *frito variado*
gamba – prawn
langosta – spiny lobster
langostino – large prawn
mejillones – mussels
ostra – oyster
peregrina – scallop
pulpo – octopus
puntillita/o – small squid, fried whole
sepia – cuttlefish
venera – scallop
vieira – scallop

Carne (Meat) & Aves (Poultry)
beicon – bacon (usually thinly sliced and pre-packaged; see *tocino*)
bistek – thin beef steak
butifarra – thick sausage (to be cooked)
cabra – goat
cabrito – kid, baby goat
callos – tripe
carne de monte – literally 'mountain meat' such as venison or wild boar

caza – hunt, game
cerdo – pig, pork
chacinas – cured pork meats
charcutería – cured pork meats
chivo – kid, baby goat
chorizo – red sausage
chuleta – chop, cutlet
churrasco – slabs of grilled meat or ribs in a tangy sauce, popular in Galicia
codorniz – quail
conejo – rabbit
cordero – lamb
embutidos – the many varieties of sausage
faisán – pheasant
filete – fillet
hamburguesa – hamburger
hígado – liver
jabalí – wild boar
jamón (serrano) – ham (mountain-cured)
lengua – tongue
lomo – loin (of pork unless specified otherwise), usually the cheapest meat dish on the menu
longaniza – dark pork sausage
morcilla – blood sausage, ie, black pudding
pajarito – small bird
paloma – pigeon
pato – duck
pavo – turkey
pechuga – breast, of poultry
perdiz – partridge
picadillo – minced meat
pierna – leg
pinchito – Moroccan-style kebab
pollo – chicken
rabo (de toro) – (ox) tail
riñón – kidney
salchicha – fresh pork sausage
salchichón – cured sausage
sesos – brains
solomillo – sirloin (usually of pork)
ternera – beef, veal
tocino – bacon (usually thick; see *beicon*)
vaca, carne de – beef
venado – venison

Productos Lácteos (Dairy Products) & Huevos (Eggs)
leche – milk
mantequilla – butter

nata – cream
queso – cheese
revuelto de... – eggs scrambled with...
tortilla – omelette
tortilla española – potato omelette
yogur – yoghurt

Postres (Desserts) & Dulces (Sweet Things)
bizcocho – sponge cake
churro – long, deep-fried doughnut
galleta – biscuit, cookie
helado – ice cream

natillas – custards
pastel – pastry, cake
tarta – cake
torta – round flat bun, cake
turrón – almond nougat or rich chocolatey sweets that appear at Christmas
yema – candied egg yolk

Other
caracol – snail
empanada – pie
hierba buena/menta – mint
migas – fried breadcrumb dish

Acknowledgements

Thanks

Many thanks to the travellers who used the last edition and wrote to us with helpful hints, useful advise and interesting anecdotes. They include:

Jeff Adams, Herbert J Addison, Brian Agnew, Tim Allen, Luis J Alvarez, Joel Amy, Patty Andersen, James Anderson, Seonaid Anderson, Phillip Andre, D Andrew, Cathy Anstey, Emanuela Appetiti, Lynda Appleby, O Arav, Febe Armendariz, Philip Armstrong, Marcos Arzua, Greg Ashforth, Azita Ashragian, Anni Baker, Emma Baker, J Baranowski, G Barnes, Mark Baroni, Carl Bassett, Arto Becker, Jochen Beier, John Berta, Carol Berwick, Bill Birch, Stav Birnbaum, Polly Bishop, Anita Bocquee, Henrik Borckdorff, Audrey & Roy Bradford, Ann-lise Breuning, Aric Bright, Martin Broeuner, Vicki Brooke, Caroline Brugger, Brian G Burke, Ronald Burr, Peter Busby, Helen Byme, Georgina C, Jeffrey L Campbell, Arno Caras, Michele & Pete Card, Eden Carmichael, Robert Carpenter, Rusty Cartmill, Peter Carty, Helen Casey, Steve Castroman Souto, Mike Cavendish, Allen Chao, Marcel Checa, Wong Wai Cheung, Susan Chin, William Chung-How, Damian Clair, Simone Clark, Nick Clifton, Claudia Coebergh, Kathy Collard, Richard Collins, Bernhard Conoplia, Jennifer Coombs, Karen Cooper, Richard Corbett, Jaime Felipe Moreira Cordoro, John Couani, Steven Coverdale, Ed Cowan, Dorie Cox, Camille Crederville, Leo Crofts, Cameron Crowe, Stephen Cummins, Alexander Curiss, CM Cuthbertson, Marlene Dalli, Sonja Damboch, Richard Davie, Michael Davies, John DeGelleke, Frank Devlin, Carol Dieterichs, Lior & Galit Dor, Jairo Dorado-Cadilla, Jean Dorrell, A Drinkwater, Charles DuBois, Shirley Duke, Anusha Edwards, Pierre Elias, Efrat Elron, Guido Ernst, Sara Esdahl, Sheila Eustace, Ruth & Peter Faulkner, Mick Fielden, Minerva Figueroa, Jim Flahaven, Tobias Flaitz, Steven Flanders, Susana Fortini, Michelle Fox, Shawn Francis, Loek Frederiks, Wendy Frew, Robuta Friend, Julia Fueyo Alvarez, Sherry Fynbo, Sebastian Galka, Kevin Galton, Michael Gardocki, John Gee, Yaniv Gelnik, Helen Georghiou, Amy Getchell, M Gething, Kathleen Gibbings, Brendon Gibson, LE Gilbert, Marten Gillfors, Meynardi Giorgio, Planet Glassberg, Tony Goff, Jill Gonzales, Francisco Gonzalez, Tricia Goodlet, Ian D Goodwin, Vander Goten Pascal, Emilio Goyarre, Laura Greaves, Stephen Grech, David Green, Lou & Sue Greenwood, Olav Gressner, Cristina Grillanda, Manuel J Grimaldi, Graham Groome, Michael K Gschwind, Eirikur Gunnsteinsson, Jez Hall, Tom Hall, Gretal Hammond, Mark Hammond, Les P Harasymek, Ghita Harris, Leonie Harris, Michael Hart, W B G Hart, Judith Hayes, Brian Haynes, Thomas Haywood, David Healey, Maartje Heerkens, Hetty Hessels, Joris Hilgers, Richard Hill, Julie Hirsch, Amber Hobson, Ann Hobson, Isabelle Hochstaetter, Harry & Anne Hodgkinson, Paul Holloway, Ulla-Berith Holmgard, Peter Hopley, Kacey Houston, Alistair How, Scott Hudson, Sharon Hurst, Paul Ichilcik, Henry Jablonski, Dag Jenssen, Linda Johnson, Karen Jones, Catherine Joseph, Tomas Dosil Tobio Jr, Saskia Juinen, S Juster, Erik Kabel, P Kaill, Ming-Hua Kao, Andrew Kazin, A Keigher, Charles Kelland, Claire Kennedy, Karen Kepke, Amanda King, Andreas Klahr, Richard Klein, Huub Kloosterman, Kathy Knight, Kathy Kronenberg, Alexandre Lalonde, Suzanne Lampard, Baylor Lancaster, Peter Langdon, Ton Langenhuyzen, Joey Lau, Martine van der Lee, Rachel Lee, Rosanna Lee, Laura Lenardson, Almond Leung, Rebecca Levin, Dodi Levine, Annie Levy, Simon Li, Li-Chin Lin, John Lindsay, Ashley List, Linda Liu, Marc Lobmann, Clive Long, Sam Loose, Kathryn Lovemore, Jim Lowther, Trish Lu, Sabine Ludwig, Jez Lugg, Mark Lydon, KP Lynch, Maril M, Vivian Mackereth, Eric & Mercedes Madsen, Orlaith Mannion, Chris Mantz, Amy & Dan Marcus, Wouter Mareels, Juan Martfnez, Jose-Angel Martinez, Dianna Mason, Jost Maurin, Ronald L Mayfield, Rene Maynez, Sheila McCahey, Thomas McCarthy, Ross McGregor, Jo McLean, Billy McMillan, Gordon McNenney, Michael Mee, Jaap Meijer, Tomas Alonso Millan, Amanda Millar, Dale Mitchell, Donna Mitchell, Ann Mocchi, Joaquin Antonio Moliner, Mauro Moroni, Susan Morris, Hugo Morriss, Gabriele Mross, Marc N, Mark Nettlesheim, Holly E Neumann, L Nicol, E Nicoletates, Wim Niehaus, Jim Nielsen, Marc Norman,

Phil O Brien, Herman Olij, Wallace M Olson, Chris Onisiphorou, Leo Orenstein, Carmelo Orosz, Benj Osborn, Stephanie Oswald, Rob Packer, Nick Parissis, Adam Parker, Gordon S Patton, Natasa Pavselj, Sian Perera, Alex Perry, Lars Peter, Cianne Philadelphia, Cameron Phillips, Peddo Picaop, Tom Pike, Lucy C Porter, Lara Punal Garcia, BM Puplett, Harriet Purves, Gene Quan, Reg Quelch, Patrick Quigley, J Rain, Manuel Ramos, Eric Rasmussen, Javier Remon, Ton Renders, Monica Robinson, Vanessa Rodrigues, Angela Rooney, Sandra Ross, Griff Round, Jose Rovira, James Rowley, E Ruitenberg, C Russo, Catriona Rust, Krzsztof Rybak, Lorenzo Salvioni, Valerie & Alan Samuel, Julian Sanchez-Ballesteros, Alberto Sanz Granda, Tobias Schade, Rene Schneider, Malcolm Scott, Steve Scott, Diane Shaw, Jenny Shaw, David Sheehan, Bryan Sherman, Valerie Shipp, Frank Sierowski, Gary Simpson, Steve Slittler, Peg Smith, Craig Smart, Dick Snyder, Conny Soeters, Philip B Springer, Yvette Stack, Mark Staples, J Starritt, Natalie Stauffer, Jaap Stavenuiter, Bas Steemers, Sigurlaug Stefansdottir, Yvonne Steinmann, Michael Stewart, Volker Stolz, Elin Stuart, Rachel Suddart, Jill Swartz, Tibor Sztaricskai, Oliver Taylor, Chris Terauds, Samuel Thomas, Ilonka Tiemens, John H Timoney, Travelling Tom, Gregory Tuck, Geoff Turner, Heather Tweddle, Amaia Urberuaga, Ida M Valero, Zoltan Vamosi, Tania van Megchelen, Michel van Montfort, Esther van Rein, Jos Van Rijswijk, Frank Van Thillo, Sabrina Vandierendonck, Stephany Veen, Cynthia & Jan Vercruysse, Jenny Versloot, Frans P de Vries, Andy Wagner, Yolande Wahrmann, Ali Wale, Heather Wallace, Sharon Watson, Barbara Webster, Duncan Webster, David Weeks, Deborah & Becca Weinstein, I Wells, Lisa White, Camilla Wikstrom, Ed Wilde, Arthur Wilkinson, Mirianne & Erik Willemse, Amanda Williams, Ann Williams, Dr Cliffard Williams, Neil Williams, Michael Wimpfheimer, John Winkelman, Alfred Wise, Zuzanna Wojcik, Helen & Nat Wood, Jon Wood, Cliff Woolford, Kat Wrobel, Andrew Yale, Geoff Yeates, Melanie Yennadhiou, Peter de Youf, Anson Yu, Justin Zaman

LONELY PLANET

You already know that Lonely Planet produces more than this one guidebook, but you might not be aware of the other products we have on this region. Here is a selection of titles that you may want to check out as well:

Europe on a shoestring
ISBN 1 86450 150 2
US$24.99 • UK£14.99 • 179FF

Walking in Spain
ISBN 0 86442 543 0
US$17.95 • UK£11.99 • 140FF

Spanish phrasebook
ISBN 0 86442 475 2
US$5.95 • UK£3.99 • 40FF

Mediterranean Europe
ISBN 1 86450 154 5
US$27.99 • UK£15.99 • 189FF

Andalucia
ISBN 1 86450 191 X
US$17.99 • UK£10.99 • 139FF

World Food Spain
ISBN 1 86450 025 5
US$12.95 • UK£7.99 • 100FF

Portugal
ISBN 1 86450 193 6
US$19.99 • UK£12.99 • 149FF

Barcelona
ISBN 1 86450 143 X
US$14.99 • UK£8.99 • 109FF

Europe phrasebook
ISBN 1 86450 224 X
US$8.99 • UK£4.99 • 59FF

Morocco
ISBN 0 86442 762 X
US$19.99 • UK£12.99 • 149FF

Barcelona City Map
ISBN 1 86450 174 X
US$5.99 • UK£3.99 • 39FF

Madrid
ISBN 1 86450 095 6
US$17.99 • UK£11.99 • 139FF

Available wherever books are sold

LONELY PLANET

Guides by Region

L onely Planet is known worldwide for publishing practical, reliable and no-nonsense travel information in our guides and on our Web site. The Lonely Planet list covers just about every accessible part of the world. Currently there are 16 series: Travel guides, Shoestring guides, Condensed guides, Phrasebooks, Read This First, Healthy Travel, Walking guides, Cycling guides, Watching Wildlife guides, Pisces Diving & Snorkeling guides, City Maps, Road Atlases, Out to Eat, World Food, Journeys travel literature and Pictorials.

AFRICA Africa on a shoestring • Cairo • Cairo City Map • Cape Town • Cape Town City Map • East Africa • Egypt • Egyptian Arabic phrasebook • Ethiopia, Eritrea & Djibouti • Ethiopian (Amharic) phrasebook • The Gambia & Senegal • Healthy Travel Africa • Kenya • Malawi • Morocco • Moroccan Arabic phrasebook • Mozambique • Read This First: Africa • South Africa, Lesotho & Swaziland • Southern Africa • Southern Africa Road Atlas • Swahili phrasebook • Tanzania, Zanzibar & Pemba • Trekking in East Africa • Tunisia • Watching Wildlife East Africa • Watching Wildlife Southern Africa • West Africa • World Food Morocco • Zimbabwe, Botswana & Namibia
Travel Literature: Mali Blues: Traveling to an African Beat • The Rainbird: A Central African Journey • Songs to an African Sunset: A Zimbabwean Story

AUSTRALIA & THE PACIFIC Auckland • Australia • Australian phrasebook • Australia Road Atlas • Bushwalking in Australia •Cycling New Zealand • Fiji • Fijian phrasebook • Healthy Travel Australia, NZ and the Pacific • Islands of Australia's Great Barrier Reef • Melbourne • Melbourne City Map • Micronesia • New Caledonia • New South Wales & the ACT • New Zealand • Northern Territory • Outback Australia • Out to Eat – Melbourne • Out to Eat – Sydney • Papua New Guinea • Pidgin phrasebook • Queensland • Rarotonga & the Cook Islands • Samoa • Solomon Islands • South Australia • South Pacific • South Pacific phrasebook • Sydney • Sydney City Map • Sydney Condensed • Tahiti & French Polynesia • Tasmania • Tonga • Tramping in New Zealand • Vanuatu • Victoria • Walking in Australia • Watching Wildlife Australia • Western Australia
Travel Literature: Islands in the Clouds: Travels in the Highlands of New Guinea • Kiwi Tracks: A New Zealand Journey • Sean & David's Long Drive

CENTRAL AMERICA & THE CARIBBEAN Bahamas, Turks & Caicos • Baja California • Bermuda • Central America on a shoestring • Costa Rica • Costa Rica Spanish phrasebook • Cuba • Dominican Republic & Haiti • Eastern Caribbean • Guatemala • Guatemala, Belize & Yucatán: La Ruta Maya • Healthy Travel Central & South America • Jamaica • Mexico • Mexico City • Panama • Puerto Rico • Read This First: Central & South America • World Food Mexico • Yucatán
Travel Literature: Green Dreams: Travels in Central America

EUROPE Amsterdam • Amsterdam City Map • Amsterdam Condensed • Andalucía • Austria • Baltic States phrasebook • Barcelona • Barcelona City Map • Berlin • Berlin City Map • Britain • British phrasebook • Brussels, Bruges & Antwerp • Brussels City Map • Budapest • Budapest City Map • Canary Islands • Central Europe • Central Europe phrasebook • Corfu & the Ionians • Corsica • Crete • Crete Condensed • Croatia • Cycling Britain • Cycling France • Cyprus • Czech & Slovak Republics • Denmark • Dublin • Dublin City Map • Eastern Europe • Eastern Europe phrasebook • Edinburgh • Estonia, Latvia & Lithuania • Europe on a shoestring • Finland • Florence • France • Frankfurt Condensed • French phrasebook • Georgia, Armenia & Azerbaijan • Germany • German phrasebook • Greece • Greek Islands • Greek phrasebook • Hungary • Iceland, Greenland & the Faroe Islands • Ireland • Istanbul • Italian phrasebook • Italy • Krakow • Lisbon • The Loire • London • London City Map • London Condensed • Madrid • Malta • Mediterranean Europe • Mediterranean Europe phrasebook • Moscow • Mozambique • Munich • the Netherlands • Norway • Out to Eat – London • Paris • Paris City Map • Paris Condensed • Poland • Portugal • Portuguese phrasebook • Prague • Prague City Map • Provence & the Côte d'Azur • Read This First: Europe • Romania & Moldova • Rome • Rome City Map • Russia, Ukraine & Belarus • Russian phrasebook • Scandinavian & Baltic Europe • Scandinavian Europe phrasebook • Scotland • Sicily • Slovenia • South-West France • Spain • Spanish phrasebook • St Petersburg • St Petersburg City Map • Sweden • Switzerland • Trekking in Spain • Tuscany • Ukrainian phrasebook • Venice • Vienna • Walking in Britain • Walking in France • Walking in Ireland • Walking in Italy • Walking in Spain • Walking in Switzerland • Western Europe • Western Europe phrasebook • World Food France • World Food Italy • World Food Ireland • World Food Spain
Travel Literature: Love and War in the Apennines • The Olive Grove: Travels in Greece • On the Shores of the Mediterranean • Round Ireland in Low Gear • A Small Place in Italy • After Yugoslavia

LONELY PLANET

Mail Order

Lonely Planet products are distributed worldwide. They are also available by mail order from Lonely Planet, so if you have difficulty finding a title please write to us. North and South American residents should write to 150 Linden St, Oakland, CA 94607, USA; European and African residents should write to 10a Spring Place, London NW5 3BH, UK; and residents of other countries to Locked Bag 1, Footscray, Victoria 3011, Australia.

INDIAN SUBCONTINENT Bangladesh • Bengali phrasebook • Bhutan • Delhi • Goa • Healthy Travel Asia & India • Hindi & Urdu phrasebook • India • Indian Himalaya • Karakoram Highway • Kerala • Mumbai (Bombay) • Nepal • Nepali phrasebook • Pakistan • Rajasthan • Read This First: Asia & India • South India • Sri Lanka • Sri Lanka phrasebook • Tibet • Tibetan phrasebook • Trekking in the Indian Himalaya • Trekking in the Karakoram & Hindukush • Trekking in the Nepal Himalaya
Travel Literature: The Age of Kali: Indian Travels and Encounters • Hello Goodnight: A Life of Goa • In Rajasthan • A Season in Heaven: True Tales from the Road to Kathmandu • Shopping for Buddhas • A Short Walk in the Hindu Kush • Slowly Down the Ganges

ISLANDS OF THE INDIAN OCEAN Madagascar & Comoros • Maldives • Mauritius, Réunion & Seychelles

MIDDLE EAST & CENTRAL ASIA Bahrain, Kuwait & Qatar • Central Asia • Central Asia phrasebook • Dubai • Hebrew phrasebook • Iran • Israel & the Palestinian Territories • Istanbul • Istanbul City Map • Istanbul to Cairo on a shoestring • Jerusalem • Jerusalem City Map • Jordan • Lebanon • Middle East • Oman & the United Arab Emirates • Syria • Turkey • Turkish phrasebook • World Food Turkey • Yemen
Travel Literature: Black on Black: Iran Revisited • The Gates of Damascus • Kingdom of the Film Stars: Journey into Jordan

NORTH AMERICA Alaska • Boston • Boston City Map • California & Nevada • California Condensed • Canada • Chicago • Chicago City Map • Deep South • Florida • Great Lakes • Hawaii • Hiking in Alaska • Hiking in the USA • Honolulu • Las Vegas • Los Angeles • Los Angeles City Map • Louisiana & The Deep South • Miami • Miami City Map • New England • New Orleans • New York City • New York City City Map • New York City Condensed • New York, New Jersey & Pennsylvania • Oahu • Out to Eat – San Francisco • Pacific Northwest • Puerto Rico • Rocky Mountains • San Francisco • San Francisco City Map • Seattle • Southwest • Texas • USA • USA phrasebook • Vancouver • Virginia & the Capital Region • Washington DC • Washington, DC City Map • World Food Deep South, USA • World Food New Orleans
Travel Literature: Caught Inside: A Surfer's Year on the California Coast • Drive Thru America

NORTH-EAST ASIA Beijing • Beijing City Map • Cantonese phrasebook • China • Hiking in Japan • Hong Kong • Hong Kong City Map • Hong Kong Condensed • Hong Kong, Macau & Guangzhou • Japan • Japanese phrasebook • Korea • Korean phrasebook • Kyoto • Mandarin phrasebook • Mongolia • Mongolian phrasebook • Seoul • Shanghai • South-West China • Taiwan • Tokyo
Travel Literature: In Xanadu: A Quest • Lost Japan

SOUTH AMERICA Argentina, Uruguay & Paraguay • Bolivia • Brazil • Brazilian phrasebook • Buenos Aires • Chile & Easter Island • Colombia • Ecuador & the Galapagos Islands • Healthy Travel Central & South America • Latin American Spanish phrasebook • Peru • Quechua phrasebook • Read This First: Central & South America • Rio de Janeiro • Rio de Janeiro City Map • Santiago • South America on a shoestring • Santiago • Trekking in the Patagonian Andes • Venezuela
Travel Literature: Full Circle: A South American Journey

SOUTH-EAST ASIA Bali & Lombok • Bangkok • Bangkok City Map • Burmese phrasebook • Cambodia • Hanoi • Healthy Travel Asia & India • Hill Tribes phrasebook • Ho Chi Minh City • Indonesia • Indonesian phrasebook • Indonesia's Eastern Islands • Jakarta • Java • Lao phrasebook • Laos • Malay phrasebook • Malaysia, Singapore & Brunei • Myanmar (Burma) • Philippines • Pilipino (Tagalog) phrasebook • Read This First: Asia & India • Singapore • Singapore City Map • South-East Asia on a shoestring • South-East Asia phrasebook • Thailand • Thailand's Islands & Beaches • Thailand, Vietnam, Laos & Cambodia Road Atlas • Thai phrasebook • Vietnam • Vietnamese phrasebook • World Food Thailand • World Food Vietnam

ALSO AVAILABLE: Antarctica • The Arctic • The Blue Man: Tales of Travel, Love and Coffee • Brief Encounters: Stories of Love, Sex & Travel • Chasing Rickshaws • The Last Grain Race • Lonely Planet Unpacked • Not the Only Planet: Science Fiction Travel Stories • Lonely Planet On the Edge • Sacred India • Travel with Children • Travel Photography: A Guide to Taking Better Pictures

Index

Text

Bold indicates maps.

Bold indicates maps.

Boxed Text

MAP LEGEND

CITY ROUTES

Freeway	Freeway	====	Unsealed Road
Highway	Primary Road	===	One Way Street
Road	Secondary Road		Pedestrian Street
Street	Street	⊏⊐⊏⊐	Stepped Street
Lane	Lane	)===	Tunnel
	On/Off Ramp		Footbridge

REGIONAL ROUTES

	Tollway, Freeway		Minor Road
	Primary Road	- - - -	Unsealed 4WD track
	Secondary Road	==≡≡	Unsealed Road

BOUNDARIES

▬▬▪▬▪▬	International
▬▬▪▪	Autonomous Community
▬▪▬▪▬	Province
▬▬▬	Fortified Wall

HYDROGRAPHY

	River, Creek
	Lake
⊙ ⇥	Spring; Rapids
⑤ ⊣⊢	Waterfalls

TRANSPORT ROUTES & STATIONS

⊶○	Local Railway	⊢⊣⊞⊢	Cable Car, Chairlift
⊦+++)	Underground Rlwy	----⊟	Ferry
⊦+++-	Disused Railway	----⊀	Walking Trail
⊶Ⓜ	Subway, Station	⋯⋯	Walking Tour
▬⊟▬	Lightrail Tram		Path

AREA FEATURES

	Building		Market		Beach
⊛	Park, Gardens		Sports Ground	++++	Cemetery
	Plaza		Swamp		

POPULATION SYMBOLS

⊙ **CAPITAL**	National Capital	● **City**	City	● Village	Village
◉ **CAPITAL**	Provincial Capital	● **Town**	Town		Urban Area

MAP SYMBOLS

■	Place to Stay	▼	Place to Eat	●	Point of Interest
✈	Airport	⚓	Dive Site	🏛	Museum	🏰	Stately Home
❸	Bank	✉	Embassy, Consulate	Ⓟ	Parking	⊠	Shopping Centre
▣	Bus Terminal	♨	Fountain	)(	Pass	▣	Swimming Pool
▣	Cable Car, Funicular	⊕	Hospital	▣	Police Station	☎	Telephone
🏰	Castle	⊚	Internet Cafe	✉	Post Office	▣	Theatre
⛪	Church	☀	Lookout	▣	Pub or Bar	❶	Tourist Information
🎬	Cinema	🗿	Monument	▣	Ruins	🐾	Zoo

LONELY PLANET OFFICES

Australia
Locked Bag 1, Footscray, Victoria 3011
☎ 03 9689 4666 fax 03 9689 6833
email: talk2us@lonelyplanet.com.au

USA
150 Linden St, Oakland, CA 94607
☎ 510 893 8555 TOLL FREE: 800 275 8555
fax 510 893 8572
email: info@lonelyplanet.com

UK
10a Spring Place, London NW5 3BH
☎ 020 7428 4800 fax 020 7428 4828
email: go@lonelyplanet.co.uk

France
1 rue du Dahomey, 75011 Paris
☎ 01 55 25 33 00 fax 01 55 25 33 01
email: bip@lonelyplanet.fr
www.lonelyplanet.fr

World Wide Web: www.lonelyplanet.com *or* AOL keyword: lp
Lonely Planet Images: lpi@lonelyplanet.com.au